Bloodstains

An Epic History of the Politics That Produced and Sustained the American Civil War and the Political Reconstruction that Followed

Volume 4: *Political Reconstruction and The Struggle for Healing*

A Study by Howard Ray White

Herein, in Volume 4, You Live through the Political Times that Followed the American Civil War.

Herein you live, yes live, through those turbulent and amazing times. Why? Because, in Volume 4, much of the pertinent history continues to be told through parallel biographies of the major politicians of the times. Howard Ray White takes you back. He takes you back to those years so that you may *live* them yourself, because he wants you to personally experience those times and draw your own conclusions about the politics that caused the Civil War, about the politics that produced and sustained such horrific fighting, suffering and death, and — in Volume 4 — about the politics of the 20-year Reconstruction Era and the corresponding struggles for healing that followed Confederate surrender.

Have you long wondered what caused the American Civil War? Why were the seceded States **not** allowed to go in peace? Why did 36,000 Federal have to die? Do you doubt the reasons commonly accepted in today's society? Have you found the history of the Republican Party's Political Reconstruction Era baffling? Then you must read White's Volume 4, for he unravels the confusion while spiriting you along on a journey through which you *live* those 20 years of Political Reconstruction, of struggle. If you have the time, Howard Ray White has the means.

The four volumes of *Bloodstains* are White's first books. Unlike the vast majority of historians, he is not a product of American Academia. To the contrary, he is a scientifically trained retired chemical engineer (Vanderbilt University, 1960). Consequently, White is free to present history from a factual, "scientifically correct" perspective, even when doing so is not today considered "politically correct." And White tells the history and relates the biographies with measured feelings of passionate involvement, for his grandfather's farmhouse was a Federal field hospital at the Battle of Murfreesboro (Stones River). He explains: "As a child, the bloodstains on the floors cried out to me to someday tell them 'Why'." The result, the *Bloodstains* series, presents the history as White organized it for his personal study and for your maximum understanding. After reading *Bloodstains*, you will know "Why" with unshakable conviction, for you will have *lived* it. And White's powerful index will facilitate inquiry and reader analysis.

The four volumes in this series are –

- Volume 1: *The Nation Builders* (2002);

- Volume 2: *The Demagogues* (2003);

- Volume 3: *The Bleeding* (2007) and

- Volume 4: *Political Reconstruction and The Struggle for Healing* (2012).

Bloodstains and other works by Howard Ray White are available as print books and as e-books. See www.howardraywhite.com, www.southernhistorians.org or amazon.com for details.

Reaction from past readers is extraordinary. They have been truly moved. Examples:

- "I have learned more from your books about the politics of America than from all other sources. Thank you for taking time to put the mess into a logical format." (Florida reader).

- "The best true histories of America I have studied." (Virginia reader).

- "Your work cries out to be studied! Utilizing parallel biographies of the main political participants is unlike anything I have ever read." (Iowa reader).

Bloodstains

An Epic History of the Politics That Produced and Sustained the American Civil War and the Political Reconstruction that Followed

Volume 4: *Political Reconstruction and The Struggle for Healing*

From May 1865 to March 1885 — With much of the history being told through parallel biographies of Jeff Davis, Thad Stevens, Charles Sumner, Wade Hampton, Lucius Lamar and Grover Cleveland.

A Study by Howard Ray White

The other three volumes in this **series** are:

Volume 1: *The Nation Builders*

From the Ancient British Isles to March 1848 — With much of the history being told through parallel biographies of Andrew Jackson, Sam Houston, Jeff Davis, Stephen Douglas, Thad Stevens, Abe Lincoln and Charles Sumner.

This first became available in August 2002.

Volume 2: *The Demagogues*

From March 1848 to April 1861 — With much of the history being told through parallel biographies of Abe Lincoln, Jeff Davis, Stephen Douglas, Thad Stevens and Charles Sumner.

This first became available in January 2003.

Volume 3: *The Bleeding*

From May 1865 to March 1885 — With much of the history being told through parallel biographies of Abe Lincoln, Jeff Davis, Thad Stevens and Charles Sumner.

This first became available in April 2007.

Overview of the Four Volumes of *Bloodstains*

Bloodstains: An Epic History of the Politics That Produced and Sustained the American Civil War and the Political Reconstruction that Followed is presented in four volumes: *The Nation Builders*, *The Demagogues*, *The Bleeding*, and *Political Reconstruction and the Struggle for Healing*. This is the fourth volume: *Political Reconstruction and the Struggle for Healing*.

Volume 1: *The Nation Builders* establishes the background upon which the subsequent volumes can be more accurately judged. I explain why I was moved to undertake such a vast study as is presented in these pages. A concise history of the British Isles is presented with emphasis on consequential population diversity and the pitiful and futile struggle to find good government within a monarchial system. I also present a brief history of the Native American people of the southeast quarter of North America. Having established these origins, the work moves briskly through the American colonial period and through the American Revolution, because understanding that background is important to understanding the political struggles before, during and after the American Civil War — in other words, the background that gave rise to a Northern States Culture and a Southern States Culture. The westward movement into Tennessee — much of it told through parallel biographies of Andrew Jackson and Sam Houston — portrays the spirit and hardships endured by the nation builders. About 1817 the 5 major biographies in *Bloodstains* become the primary conduits through which the history is presented. The lives of these 5 most significant Civil War era politicians are presented in parallel to enhance understanding of actions and reactions to the same events. One is lawyer Abe Lincoln, the most prominent leader of the Illinois Republican Party. He would become the only Federal President ever elected through a purely sectional political campaign. Another is farmer and military commander Jeff Davis, West Point graduate, Mexican War military hero, and Senator from Mississippi. He would be elected President of the Confederate States of America. A third is lawyer Stephen Douglas, the Illinois Democratic Party leader and for many years the most powerful man in the Federal Senate. His reactionary tactics would destroy the national Democratic Party, thereby facilitating a takeover of the Federal Government by the sectional Republican Party. A fourth is lawyer Charles Sumner of Boston, a literary, somewhat effeminate bachelor. He would become, as Senator from Massachusetts, the idealistic guru of the Republican Party. The fifth is lawyer and ironworks owner Thad Stevens of Pennsylvania, a man eager to lead whatever political combination looked powerful enough to defeat Democratic Party politicians. As Republican Party Whip and Chairman of the House Ways and Means Committee, he would become the most powerful man ever to sit in the Federal House of Representatives. And we follow Sam Houston from Tennessee to Texas and through him witness the struggle to establish the Republic of Texas and to win support for an invitation to merge the Republic of Texas into the United States. The War with Mexico soon follows, but victory is bitter, for it produces the sectional political fight that gives birth to *The Demagogues*.

Volume 2: *The Demagogues* explains the rise of Exclusionism, and how it grew into the powerful political force that gave birth to a victorious sectional Republican Party. Since issues of morality and race relations permeate the politics of this period, I depart briefly from the narrative history to explore the origin of the races of man and the tenants of human morality as presented by Jesus Christ. Then the narrative history resumes where it had concluded in Volume 1. An immense influx of immigrants and tumult in northern States politics gives rise to the Secret Order (Know Nothings) and its American Party, which destroys the already-weakened Whig Party. The organized, northern-States-funded Terrorism in "Bleeding Kansas," and the corresponding hateful propaganda dispensed through the demagoguery of unethical newspapermen and ambitious politicians, is truthfully described in detail. "Bleeding Kansas" provides the Republican Party the propaganda weapon — the politics of Exclusionism — it needs to destroy the Secret Order and its American Party. Through the biographies of idealistic Charles Sumner and scheming Thad Stevens, the rise of the Republican Party in Massachusetts and Pennsylvania is presented. Emphasis is given to the political struggle in Illinois between the Democrats, led by Stephen Douglas, and the Republicans, led by Abe Lincoln. Throughout this volume, Mississippi farmer and past military commander Jeff Davis, from his positions as Secretary of War and as the leading Senator from the southern States, leads the majority of Democrats in their efforts to fight with truth the Exclusionist political demagoguery that is destroying the national character of the Federal Government. Eventually the politics of Exclusionism becomes so powerful, that Stephen Douglas and many northern States Democrats feel compelled to embrace it as well, for Republicans are rapidly capturing State governments throughout the northern States. As Douglas strives to force Exclusionism upon the national Democratic Party, he splits that Party into two sectional parties, thereby leaving no political force capable of stopping a Republican takeover of all the northern States and the Federal Government. So the sectional Republican Party gains an easy victory in the race for President and, equally important, secures the Office of the Governor in every northern State. This is quickly followed by the secession of 7 Democrat States and the election of Jeff Davis as President of the Confederacy. By deceitful manipulations President Lincoln and fellow Republican leaders incite the Confederates to, in a defensive move, fire cannon at Fort Sumter while Federal warships threaten from beyond the breakers. Immediately afterward, although Confederate shelling killed no Federal in Fort Sumter, Lincoln usurps the powers assigned to Congress and the Supreme Court, ignores the limitations in the Federal Constitution, and proclaims a Federal military invasion of the Confederacy.

Volume 3: *The Bleeding* presents the tragic story of the American Civil War — more correctly named the Federal Invasion of the Confederacy. Refusing to participate in Abe Lincoln's invasion of the Confederacy, 4 States — Virginia, North Carolina, Tennessee, and Arkansas — quickly secede and join in defending the Confederacy. Empowered by Republican control of the Governor's Office in every northern State, and having obviously prepared in advance, State militia from those States quickly descend upon Maryland, and Missouri and intimidate Kentucky as Republicans successfully execute the first phase of their invasion plan, which is to subjugate the Democrat governments of Maryland, Kentucky and Missouri. Because it is immensely important, the Federal subjugation of these three States is covered in great detail. Through Stephen Douglas, who dies of illness as the invasion gets underway, I report how many northern States Democrats team up with their Republican adversaries in support of the Federal invasion campaign. Then follows the account of the invasion and defense of the Confederacy— told primarily through the biographies of Abe Lincoln and Jeff Davis. And through the biographies of Thad Stevens and Charles Sumner, I relate the political maneuvering in the Federal House and Senate. This volume gives apt attention to Republican imprisonment of political opponents, to mistreatment of prisoners of war, to media censorship and to other political issues. Furthermore, this study shows how, as the invasion bogs down, Republican policy toward African Americans evolves from plans for deporting them, to making Federal soldiers of them, to making Republican voters of them. Although this is a history of politics, major battles are reported to make the history sufficiently comprehensive, but the emphasis is on the soldiers and sailors, not the generals. The reader witnesses the Federal War against Civilians, particularly the devastation campaign of William Sherman's army in Georgia and South Carolina. I also report the surprising and immensely important elevation to Vice President of Andrew Johnson, an ex-Democrat Senator from Tennessee who had earlier committed treason against his State. When prominent Maryland actor John Wilkes Booth kills Abe Lincoln, Johnson of Tennessee becomes Federal President. Volume 3, *The Bleeding* concludes shortly afterward with the final conquest of the Confederacy and the imprisonment of Jeff Davis at Fortress Monroe.

Volume 4: *Political Reconstruction and the Struggle for Healing* presents the complex history of what the Republicans called "Reconstruction," essentially "Political Reconstruction," meaning creating government political structures unlike those "Constructed" by the Federal Constitution. In practice, Republican "Political Reconstruction" was basically the remaking of conquered State Governments around Republican Political Machines aimed at sustaining Republican Party control of State and Federal governments during and after the re-admittance of the 11 conquered Confederate States, whose European American population would fiercely hate Republican politicians for generations yet unborn, a sentiment that would be shared also by most voters in Maryland, Kentucky and Missouri for several decades. Be assured that the Republican's "Reconstruction" had nothing to do with rebuilding what the Federals had destroyed in their conquest of the Confederacy — "Reconstruction" reconstructed nothing of a physical nature.

In the early pages of Volume 4 we witness how Republican leaders purposely abuse political prisoner Jeff Davis in Fortress Monroe in a prolonged attempt to break his spirit. Fortunately, with help from wife Varina, and surprisingly even from Horace Greeley, whose New York *Tribune* had been the most effective "Bleeding Kansas" propaganda organ, Davis eventually gets released on bond. Finally, realizing that Federal lawyers would lose their case against Davis if they were to bring him to trial, Republicans abandon plans to prosecute him on a charge of treason. Davis' Federal citizenship would never be restored, because he symbolized State Sovereignty: the Constitutional principle upon which the United States Government had been established and the principle that the Republicans had destroyed. Later generations of Americans would permit Confederate military leaders, such as Robert Lee, to be admired, but never Confederate political leaders, especially never the capable Jeff Davis.

Meanwhile, lawyer and House Ways and Means Chairman Thad Stevens, Representative from Pennsylvania, so powerful that he is practically a dictator over the Federal House, schemes to confiscate 85% of the land in the conquered Confederate States — a program that comes very close to being implemented. While Stevens schemes to confiscate land, lawyer and Republican Party idealistic guru Charles Sumner, Senator from Massachusetts, encourages building Republican Political Machines in the conquered Confederate States by limiting voting access by European American men while organizing majority Republican Political Machines comprised of political adventurers and gullible African American men and political adventurers.

This early post-war period of American history climaxes with the Senate's Impeachment trial of President Andrew Johnson, the prosecution team being led by Representative Thad Stevens. But the Senate falls one vote short of convicting Johnson — that vote from a conscientious Senator from — surprise — Kansas. By the vote of a man from Kansas, formerly "Bleeding Kansas," the conquered Confederate States escape the land confiscation and more extreme persecution that would have followed the replacement of Andrew Johnson of Tennessee with Ben Wade of Ohio.

We follow Mary Lincoln's emotional struggles and Robert Lincoln's harassment. Representative Thad Stevens dies in the summer of 1868, soon after Andrew Johnson is acquitted on Impeachment charges. We then continue to follow Federal political activity in Washington through the life of Senator Charles Sumner to his death in early 1874.

Realizing that the story of Political Reconstruction and the Struggle for Healing needed to be told on a State-by-State basis, for each State presented its unique story, I present South Carolina and Wade Hampton for one State story and Mississippi and Lucius Lamar for the other State story. To a lesser extent the Reconstruction of Louisiana is covered, as well. Detailed coverage of the Kuklux resistance movement provides insight and balance. The "Reconstruction" stories from South Carolina, Mississippi and Louisiana give the reader an excellent picture of Republican "Political Reconstruction," which concludes with Democrat "Home Rule" throughout the former Confederate States by early 1877.

In northwestern Mississippi, Lucius Lamar wins election in 1872 to the Federal House, providing an effective southern States Democrat voice in Washington. In 1876, Wade Hampton wins election as Governor of South Carolina, ending corrupt Republican rule over its people. Democrats also win control over the Mississippi and Louisiana State governments. Eventually, by the summer of 1877, the people of all of the former Confederate States have achieved "Home Rule," Federal troops have been withdrawn and their respective Democratic Parties have achieved political control throughout their homelands. This concludes *Political Reconstruction*.

Democrats in the Mississippi Legislature elect Representative Lucius Lamar to the Federal Senate where he is joined by many other former Confederates seated in that body, including Wade Hampton, who leaves the office of Governor to become a Senator from South Carolina. Democrats win control of the Federal House from 1875 to 1881 and from 1983 to 1989. They win control of the Federal Senate from 1879 to 1881.

Meanwhile, in 1881, Jeff Davis, at his beach house in Mississippi, completes his two-volume history, *"The Rise and Fall of the Confederate Government."*

We turn our attention to the Democratic Party's struggle to reform the Federal Government, which, except for the Democratic House, is controlled by Republicans, still drunk with power and corrupt. Grover Cleveland, Democrat of Buffalo, New York, enters our pages as he fights for honest, properly limited and good government. We step back and experience a brief, but complete biography of Cleveland, up to the beginning of his job in January 1882 as Mayor of Buffalo. Then he is launched onto the chronological pages as he rapidly advances from Mayor of Buffalo, to Governor of New York, to President of the United States.

The Struggle for Healing concludes, in 1885, 24 years after the sectional Republican Party had taken control of the Federal Government, with the 1884 election of Democrat Grover Cleveland as Federal President and his inauguration. Cleveland's election reestablishes two-party politics at the Federal level, forcing reform within the Republican Party — burying the "bloody shirt," truncating political corruption, dismantling the graft-ridden spoils system and allowing far fewer gifts of government jobs to party workers.

Following Cleveland's inauguration in early 1885, this four-volume history concludes in an Afterward chapter. Wade Hampton leaves the Senate for a Federal job as Railroad Commissioner, retiring thereafter to enjoy old age and Confederate reunions. Lucius Lamar leaves the Senate to become a Justice on the Federal Supreme Court, holding that post until death. Grover Cleveland loses his re-election bid, but wins a second term as President in the 1892 election. Thereafter, he enjoys old age until his death in 1908. Jeff Davis continues to live at his beach house, while helping to celebrate Confederate reunions and monument dedications. At his death in December 1889, Davis is honored by the most moving funeral ever conducted in the States that once were the Confederate States of America. He is survived by his wife Varina, who lives on to write for Joe Pulitzer's *New York World*. Her death in 1906 concludes my study.

Table of Contents

12

Dedication

This epic history of the politics that produced the American Civil War is dedicated to six little words. Every word consists of only one syllable. It is important that you understand that the sixth word stands out far above the other five as unique to human intelligence, for that word represents God's gift to humankind. It is by diligent and persistent study of issues related to the first five words that we humans acquire sufficient depth of understanding to acquire the wisdom embodied in the sixth word. The first five words are *"what," "who," "where," "how,"* *"when"* and "how." The sixth word is *"why."*

This book presents an epic history that is rich with truthful presentation of "what," "who," "where," "how," and "when." But, throughout this vast study, I shall refrain from presenting a handy, condensed summation of "why." If you were to accept my summation of "why" — just because I told you so — you would be behaving as a child. And this is not a children's book. No, this book insists that you advance to a much higher intellectual plane — a plane perhaps higher than you reached for in seeking a college or post-graduate degree. I seek to draw you up to an invigorating plane upon which you can truly unleash God's gift of wisdom. As you read this book you will slowly, but steadily acquire a clear understanding of "why." And you will understand "why" without me telling you so. You will understand why because you will have "lived" those times with uncanny perception, and thereby — for perhaps the first time in your life — truly understand "what," "who," "where," "how," and "when." You will understand them so clearly and so deeply that you will know "why." In your heart you will know "why." In your bones you will know "why." A thousand times you will know "why." You will know "why" because you will have "lived" the history with all-seeing eyes and all-hearing ears, and through that knowledge, you will have unleashed God's gift of wisdom.

Wisdom

"What" imparts minimal knowledge;

"Who" may put a face on it;

"Where" expands its usefulness, and

"How" can reveal its workings.

Yet, although I have seen

"When" produce the educated man,

I have learned that only

"Why" unleashes God's gift of wisdom.

And this study is also dedicated to a telling of the truth, and that alone. For it is neither dedicated to being fair or to being even-handed; nor is it dedicated to a sympathetic treatment of good intentions gone bad. This study will not omit a bit of meaningful history because its telling is too painful or too embarrassing. It does not view racial history with one eye fixed on present-day political correctness. And it rejects outcome-based judgments, for I abhor the excuse that the end justified the means. No, this study, this work, is none of these, for it is solely dedicated to an incorruptible telling of the truth — dedicated to often telling the ugly truth, for so much of it is simply ugly. But fear not my friends, for truthful knowledge is the engine of success, while misconception is the bondsman of the brain. So, as you read these pages, cast aside old misconceptions and find new understanding. For Jesus Christ constantly honored the truth, whether in the hearts of men or in the word of God:

"Then you will know the truth, and the truth shall set you free." (John 8:32)

The Bloodstains

My grandfather lived on a farm in Middle Tennessee, a few miles outside of Murfreesboro, on Asbury Road. During the War Between the States, the terrible Battle of Murfreesboro was fought on this and surrounding farms as 1862 concluded and 1863 began. Granddad's farm was in the thick of battle, and, while men fought, Federal surgeons used his farmhouse as a field hospital. I really got to know the place when my family lived on Granddad's farm for a year while Dad built our new house in Nashville. That was in 1948, three years after World War II. I was ten years old. Our family occasionally found parts of weapons, bullets, buckles and other military items in the cedar thickets and pastures, and especially while plowing the fields. In the farmhouse I stared at the numerous bloodstains that were visible in the wood of the unpainted stairs and floors. The Federal military graveyard down the road contained row after row of gravestones that seemed to go on and on. It held over 6,000 graves of Federal dead.

The battlefield map identified Granddad's house as the Widow Burrus house because she was the owner of the house and farm back then. I occasionally looked over at the little overgrown Burrus family graveyard that was situated in a cotton field about 100 yards from the house. The tombstones told me that the immigrant father, Lafayette Burrus, had been born in Amherst County, Virginia, in 1799 and had died eight years prior to the battle. His wife Eliza, known as Widow Burrus at the time of the battle, had been born somewhere near Murfreesboro. She lived until 1875. There were gravestones for two daughters and two sons.

Every school day, as my school bus traveled beside the Federal graveyard, I watched rows and rows of gravestones file past the bus window. I recall that, as I looked out the window, I often mourned all those dead men — over 6,000 Federal soldiers. And, as I lamented the untimely deaths of these men, my childhood mind sought the answer to what I considered then a simple question: "*Why*?" Why did men from the northern States come to Tennessee bent on conquest? Had not their grandfathers fought alongside my Tennessee, Carolina and Virginia ancestors for our nation's independence?

It seems like almost everyone chose one side or the other in that war. How had men from the northern States acquired such intense hatred of Tennesseans and other southern States men in such a short time? How had northern States political activists accomplished such a thing? Why had their propaganda been so compelling?

World War II had ended only three years prior to those school-day trips past the thousands of gravestones, so stories of those horrible events were still fresh in my mind. I could not understand how Adolph Hitler had filled the hearts of the German people with such hatred. I could not fathom why Gentile Germans had suddenly perceived the Jewish Germans, who they had lived and worked alongside for generations, to be hated enemies. Gentile Germans had stolen everything from the Jews, hunted them down and crowded them into concentration camps. There they had treated them much worse than African American slaves, as they extracted as much work from them as their shriveled bodies could produce. Then they had stripped them naked and shot them or gassed them to death. Finally, they had cremated the bodies in giant furnaces, or dumped them into huge holes in the ground. That had been 1938 to 1945.

At the time of my daily trips past the gravestones on the way to school, the iron curtain had closed off Eastern Europe. Although Western Europe was regaining sanity, many people in the Soviet sphere were suffering greatly, and I weighed that issue as well as I puzzled over the rows of gravestones from my school bus window — for, at that very time, millions were dying under the hard hand of Communist militants. China was engaged in a civil war that the Communists seemed to be winning. And much blood would flow as Communist militants eliminated China's upper class — that is everyone not lucky enough to escape to Formosa.

The world had witnessed the awesome atomic bomb three years previously. With such conflict in the Communist part of the world, my occasional thoughts of a future atomic war were understandably frightening.

Although I occasionally pondered the horrors chronicled above, mine was a happy and normal childhood; yet I would occasionally think about them. At those times my mind attempted to understand how humanity could be made to suffer Communist persecution, World War II and the War Between the States. Were the political causes in any way similar?

At that time, I had not learned the details of the Battle of Murfreesboro. Oh, I would ask questions that my parents, uncles and grandfather would attempt to answer in a manner fitting an inquisitive boy. But no one could explain why the war had occurred. By the time I reached my teens I understood the battle basics. The terrible battle had occurred between Christmas and New Year's Day 85 years previously, a 11 years before Granddad had been born. A Federal army, made up of soldiers from Ohio, Illinois, Indiana, Michigan, and other northern States, had invaded Tennessee the previous spring and conquered Nashville. The Battle of Murfreesboro had been the start of the Federal drive down the railroad line from Nashville to Chattanooga, to Atlanta and on to the coast at Savannah. The Confederate Army of Tennessee had been defending Murfreesboro and the railroad. It was made up of men from Tennessee, Alabama, Mississippi, Georgia, Arkansas, Texas, and other Confederate States. As the battle had raged in front of and across Granddad's farm, Federal surgeons had used our farmhouse as a field hospital. The bloodstains covering the upstairs floors were from horrible wounds and from amputations performed by Federal surgeons and assistants, who sawed off irreparable arms and legs, tossed them out the window, drew the skin tight against the stump and stitched it closed. The battle had been terribly brutal; about 3,000 men had been killed, and a much higher number had been wounded.

Living in that old battlefield farmhouse, amid the bloodstains, transformed my country's war history into a very personal story — a powerful story of terrible times 85 years back into the past. Yet I readily tucked it away, safely in the back of my mind.

As the years of my life went by, when I occasionally encountered discussion of the war, those bloodstains would come forward and haunt me with their crying: "Someday you must tell us '*Why?*'." Whenever I encountered books, movies or dramas about the War Between the States, my heart would be heavy over the tragedy of it all. Although others would marvel at the generals and military tactics, I would despair of the vicious politics that somehow had caused the bloody conflict. As a teenager, as a college man, as a young father, as a career chemical engineer, as a grandfather — throughout those many happy years, beneath the surface — I hoped to eventually find understanding. Yet it would largely elude me, for my search for the truth remained a casual thing. Perhaps this book will tell me "*Why?*'." Perhaps this movie will help, or this documentary. But none did. Perhaps a deep understanding would forever elude me.

Then one day I finally resolved to undertake a *determined study* of the political history of that era. Passing into my late fifties, I came to realize that the time for truly serious study had come. No longer would I wait for some book or movie to come to me with the answers; I would search them out. Now was the time to launch a determined personal search for the answer to the "*Why?*" that called out from those bloodstains — those bloodstains that ever pleaded to be understood. Mine would be a thorough and critical search, born of perseverance and dogged structure. I resolved to cover a vast time, a huge continent, three great races of mankind, and ugly politics, and more ugly politics, for I would be wrestling with the propaganda laid down by clever and secretive political partisans. I would be sorting fact from fiction, sifting for the truth, probing into the hearts of powerful men long dead. A deep understanding requires such a wrestle.

Perhaps you have read much of "*Who?*", "*What?*", "*Where?*", "*How?*" and "*When?*" Those questions are the easy ones. In this work I have tackled the tough one — that profound little three-letter word that so often defies understanding — that profound little three-letter word that must be mastered to acquire wisdom — the simple yet elusive word, "*Why?*'."

Terminology, Capitalization and Style

Concerning Terminology

A great philosopher lived and taught in China about 2,500 years ago. His name was Confucius. And his teaching has profoundly influenced Chinese thought down through the ages and even through to modern times. Like men before and after, Confucius was struggling to make his mind more efficient at understanding the world around him. That struggle led him to conceive a most useful rule. Confucius concluded:

"To understand an issue you need to call it by the right name."

Such a rule sounds, at first reading, to be so simple and obviously appropriate. It seems unnecessary that we should bother to insist that it be consistently applied. But if you pause to ponder upon the power of words, recalling how we are constantly bombarded with carefully selected, sometimes downright deceitful, words that are intended to persuade us to "vote for that candidate," "buy that product," "embrace that cause," etc., then you will surely recognize the importance of Confucius' rule. Confucius was right. He realized that the study of an issue should be directed at understanding it and thereafter applying the "right name" so that confusion over that particular issue no longer complicates the study of subsequent issues. So Confucius used that rule and found it useful. His students embraced that rule, too, found it useful, and passed it down to succeeding generations. I embrace that rule as well and have applied it throughout this study. As you read this study you will often see where my investigation has prompted me to rename an issue to help me understand our history. You remember that I presented this concept near the beginning of *Bloodstains*, Volume 1, *The Nation Builders*, and that application of the rule was of tremendous importance in understanding Volume 2, *The Demagogues* and Volume 3, *The Bleeding*. Well, Confucius' rule will be equally important to us as we study the Era of *Political Reconstruction and the Struggle for Healing*. If I had not chosen to lighten your load by assigning more meaningful words in the spirit of Confucius, you would be continually confused by a steady stream of propaganda-driven terminology. I hope such renaming helps you better understand our political history. For example, people engaged in agriculture and animal husbandry own and operate "farms," not "plantations." They are "farmers," not "planters."

You will encounter "bonded African Americans" and "independent African Americans" instead of "slaves" and "freedmen." "Anti-slavery" agitators are called "Exclusionists," or "Abolitionists," or "Deportationists," depending on whether they advocated keeping African Americans out of the northern States and the National Territories, or making bonded African Americans independent where they lived, or deporting African Americans to Africa and South America. In fact no issue is named "anti-something," for every issue must be named for what its advocates favor — not what its advocates say they are against. "The American Civil War" must be named the "Federal Invasion of the Confederacy." Two sovereign nations existed when Abe Lincoln became Federal President, and he intentionally conspired to draw Confederate fire at Fort Sumter so he would have a rallying issue when he Proclaimed a Federal Invasion 3 days later. Soldiers are referred to as "Federals" and "Confederates." There are no references to "Yankees" and "Rebels," or to "North" and "South" That Federal program to politically re-make the conquered Confederate State Governments, to ensure their being dominated by Republican Political Machines, does not sound like just "Reconstruction" to me. I remember all too well the Marshall Plan, which helped to reconstruct the European economic infrastructure that had been devastated by World War II. In today's usage "Reconstruction" sounds too much like, well, what construction workers do. So I will call the Republican's post-conquest agenda "Political Reconstruction."

Even when I encounter inappropriate names in material that I am quoting verbatim, I will change the words there as well. You will note that the new name for every renamed word is set off in squared-off brackets to alert you of what I have done. After a while you should find yourself reading through those brackets as if they were transparent.

I will be applying terminology that will help you recalibrate your mind back to the 1870's and 1880's. And I will add balance. I will avoid using present-day terms that infer to modern readers a nation controlled by a strong central government. This will steady your understanding of the era following the conquest of the States that had organized under the Confederate Government, helping you keep in mind what had been the very limited power of the Federal Government, in legal terms, and the greater importance then of the various State Governments before the military conflict and before three coerced Amendments to the Federal Constitution changed the character of governmental relationships.

Concerning Capitalization

You will find my system for capitalizing words rather old fashion. That in itself is good, for I want you to transport yourself back to the times presented in *Bloodstains* so you can "live in the history" as a contemporary, instead of "judge the history" as a present-day critic. I capitalize many words that were commonly capitalized 150 years ago, though not today. This is a book about political events, so words naming an organization are capitalized, even if they are not the official name of that organization. For example, I will capitalize "Confederate Government," "Virginia Government," and "Federal Government." I will capitalize "Federal Senate," "Massachusetts Legislature," "Federal Navy," etc. Capitalization helps these words jump out at you, and it serves as a frequent reminder that these were specific governmental organizations, which were composed of people who had specific jobs. I want you to see the Federal Government as an organization made up of people, not as a function within society. I will capitalize "State" to remind you that each State had been sovereign. I will capitalize words representing single-issue political movements, such as "Abolitionism," "Political Reconstruction," "Deportationism," "Terrorists," "Secessionists," "Republican Political Machines," etc. I will capitalize words representing political jobs such as "Governor," "Federal Senator," "Federal Representative," "Chairman," "Legislator," "State Senator," "Secretary," "President," "Vice President," etc. To distinguish more clearly between the Federal House and the Federal Senate I will say "Representative" instead of "Congressman" and say "House and Senate" instead of "Congress." To me the expanded use of capitalization adds punch to the dialog and continually reminds us of the "power seeking" that is inherent in political activity.

Concerning Style

Bloodstains, presented in 4 volumes, is an epic history covering a vast period of time, and knowledge of the time setting is important to understanding each paragraph, in fact each sentence within each paragraph. The history is presented, as far as is practical, as a narrative in chronological order to ensure that you fully comprehend how different political leaders reacted to the same events. This is crucial in Volume 4, *Political Reconstruction and the Struggle for Healing*. As you read, you will be aware of an imaginary "time line" moving down the page. When I am presenting information consistent with the "time line" it will be expressed as "he wrote." When I am presenting information that occurred significantly before the "time line," it will be expressed as "he had written." And when I am presenting information that occurred significantly beyond the "time line," it will be expressed as "he would write." In writing *Bloodstains* I have attempted to consistently and carefully apply this principle.

I intentionally avoid the use of words that are outside of the normal vocabulary of a person who graduated from high school with good marks. So, although *Bloodstains* has great length, it is not complicated by words beyond common usage. I also intentionally avoid personal descriptions of individuals, their appearance or dress, or whether they were considered handsome or not. I do this in hopes you will focus on what men did without being distracted by what men looked like. I have included no pictures, maps or drawings in this study. I realize that maps can be useful, and suggest you do as I did when greater understanding is sought: consult maps from other sources.

I will present numbers as "figures" instead of as "words," even when quoting from another source. Perhaps it is my training in science and engineering, but when I read 11 instead of eleven, or 200 instead of two hundred, or $15,000,000 instead of fifteen million dollars, I comprehend it faster. Even though using words for numbers two through twelve is considered proper style in today's writing, I will use the figures instead.

You will observe that, due to its narrative and biographical style, much of *Bloodstains* resembles a "soap opera" television series as the reader experiences a continuation of the lives of Jeff Davis, Thad Stevens and Charles Sumner, and is introduced to the lives of Lucius Lamar, Wade Hampton and Grover Cleveland — and, except for introductions of the last three men, all of it presented in a parallel format, with frequent abrupt scene changes. Watching a "soap opera" is surely confusing at first, but after a while, you will understand the overall story well enough to follow the abrupt scene changes. I expect you will handle the frequent scene changes in *Bloodstains* equally well.

I do not use footnotes. Instead, at the end of selected paragraphs, I put, in squared-off brackets, the appropriate reference in a shorthand format. For example "[R118;7-8]" means Reference number 118, pages 7 through 8. At the end of this book all references are listed by number, so this method should serve our needs well.

Although *Bloodstains*, presents an objective political history of our country, my writing is in the classical narrative style, resembling a novel, a gripping story, a tale purposefully focused on politics, but where the characters were all real people with real families. You will experience personal letters, emotional events, orations, and family life struggles. You will identify heroes and villains. You will share Jeff Davis' struggle for survival in a casemate at Fortress Monroe. You will even go bear hunting with Wade Hampton and go fishing with Grover Cleveland. If you become teary-eyed on occasion, that's acceptable — real men are allowed to cry.

More than any other American writer, I am indebted to James Michener for sparking my interest in history and biography. Through historical novels such as *Hawaii*, *Caravans*, *The Source* and *Centennial*, Michener taught me to love learning about history, to love experiencing history through the lives of people, to love living it within his epic tales. And I hope, in *Bloodstains*, you will see evidence of Michener's zest for telling a story, his passion for revealing history through the lives of people, and his belief that experiencing the epic sweep of history is necessary to its understanding. Although Michener presented history mostly through fictional characters, and there are no fictional characters in *Bloodstains*, I hope you will see evidence of his influence as you continue to read my study.

Wade Hampton, III — His Life through May 23, 1865

In *Bloodstains*, Volume 4, *Political Reconstruction and the Struggle for Healing*, you will read much about Wade Hampton III of South Carolina, for he plays an immense role in the political life of the southern States following their conquest by Federal forces. In *Bloodstains*, Volume 1, *The Nation Builders*, you read brief mention of his grandfather, Wade Hampton I, commanding a large force of American soldiers in a failed attempt to invade Canada and conquer Montreal during the War of 1812. In *Bloodstains*, Volume 2, *The Demagogues*, you read brief mention of Samuel Howe, the Massachusetts Abolitionist and Exclusionist leader, and his wife becoming friends with Wade Hampton III's brother Frank and his wife Sally Baxter Hampton, a native of New York State, during a Cuban vacation and you read of the Howe's subsequently visiting South Carolina as guests of the Frank Hampton's and the Wade Hampton's. In *Bloodstains*, Volume 3, *The Bleeding*, you read brief accounts of Wade Hampton III as a senior commander of Confederate cavalry under Robert Lee, and, following Confederate surrenders in Virginia and North Carolina, briefly as an advocate for continuing armed resistance via a massive cavalry retreat westward across the Mississippi River where, from bases in Texas and Mexico, mounted fighters would continue to fight for independence from Federal rule. Wade Hampton III was, by any measure, a heroic man; and through his life we can live much of the history presented in *Bloodstains*, Volume 4, *Political Reconstruction and the Struggle for Healing*. So, at this point I will present a short biography of the man, his grandfather and his father, concluding with the day Jeff Davis was imprisoned in Fortress Monroe, May 22, 1865.

So here is a fascinating and important short biography of Wade Hampton III of South Carolina. If you want to know more about this heroic man, I recommend you read one or more of my five favorite biographies: *Wade Hampton III*, (the best for scholarly political biography) by Robert K. Ackerman (2007); *Giant in Gray*, (the first of the four modern biographies) by Manly Wade Wellman (1949), *Wade Hampton, Confederate Warrior, Conservative Statesman*, (another good political biography, admiring) by Walter Brian Cisco (2004), *Gentleman and Soldier, The Extraordinary Life of General Wade Hampton* (basically a very good military history) by Edward G. Longacre (2003), and *Wade Hampton, Confederate Warrior to Southern Redeemer*, (the newest) by Rod Andrew, Jr. (2008). [R197, R198, R199, R200, R208]

On March 28, 1818, Wade Hampton III was born to Wade Hampton, Jr. and his wife Ann Fitzsimmons Hampton at the Charleston, South Carolina home of the mother's parents (this home still stands in historic Charleston and is worthy of viewing).

The baby's maternal grandfather, Christopher Fitzsimmons, an Irish immigrant, was a wealthy and politically influential cotton factor and "shipping magnate" who had invested profits in farms and in bonded African Americans to work them. The baby's paternal grandfather, Wade Hampton I, descended from Virginia pioneers, was a hero of America's Defense of Independence (Revolutionary War), and a very prosperous farmer with large acreage in South Carolina, Mississippi and Louisiana.

The baby's father, Wade Hampton II, age 28, and his mother, Ann, age 25, had married 12 months previously, receiving two notable wedding presents: from the bride's family a 730 acre farm near Augusta, Georgia and from the groom's family a 3,000 acre farm on the Congaree River near Columbia, South Carolina, complete with a new two-story house, not yet totally complete, which the couple had named "Millwood." The couple put Mauma Nelly, a trusted and devoted bonded African American servant, in charge of caring for baby Wade III. As other children were born to Wade II and Ann, Mauma Nelly would take similar responsibility for them.

Let's step back and discuss the grandfather, Wade Hampton I.

Paternal grandfather Wade Hampton I, on his wedding day being about 27 years old, married the widow Martha Epps Howell, about 30 years old at the time and mother to a young son. Martha's parents had died earlier leaving to her 2,500 acres of South Carolina farmland and two homes. But Martha died after only a year of marriage, without bearing any Hampton children. Then, in 1786, Wade I, at the time about 32 years old, married Harriet Flud, age 18, daughter of a wealthy farmer from Santee, South Carolina. Harriet gave birth to Wade II on April 21, 1791 and Francis, in 1793. But second wife Harriet died of a fever epidemic in 1794, when the brothers were only 3 years and 1 year old. On July

4, 1801 Wade I, then 47 years old, took a third wife, Mary Cantey, age 22 and Harriet's step-sister. Over a span of 15 years, Mary would bear several Hampton children.

At the time of grandfather Wade I's death on February 4, 1835, when young Wade, III was almost 17 years old, the estate, valued at $1,641,065, would be divided equally among wife Mary, married daughters Caroline Hampton Preston, and Susan Hampton Manning, and son Wade II. (Family tradition tells that Wade I's Will had stipulated that the entire estate go to the eldest son, Wade II, but that Wade II tore up the document and made sure the estate was split up among the widow and his siblings.) At the time Wade II owned the Woodlands farm near Columbia, South Carolina, consisting of 2,054 acres of swampland and 4,230 acres of upland. This was his home.

Grandfather Wade I had farmed on a giant scale. The total number of bonded African Americans who lived on and worked on the Hampton farms varied from time to time, but an 1827 estimate was 2,001 people. He had operated several farms in South Carolina, including farms totaling 12,000 acres in Richland District, where Columbia was situated. He had applied crop rotation principles and good farming practices. He had raised corn, indigo, hemp, barley, peas and much cotton and molasses. His largest farm, named Houmas, located in Ascension Parish, Louisiana, contained 148,000 acres and bordered the Mississippi River for 12 miles. Here, on this the most profitable of all the Hampton farms, vast amounts of sugar cane was grown and harvested (1,700 hogsheads of molasses produced in 1834). The Widow Mary Cantey Hampton and daughters Caroline Hampton Preston and Susan Hampton Manning jointly inherited the huge Houmas sugar farm (plantation). The Preston's would live there and manage the vast operation. Wade II was most interested in expanding the family's Mississippi cotton farms. So he decided that he would inherit the Walnut Ridge cotton farm, 2,529 acres, in Issaquena County, Mississippi.

Let's now move forward to young Wade Hampton III

Young Wade Hampton, III learned much from his grandfather during his youth, much about what it meant to be a Nation Builder. Several times Grandfather Wade I, at the time in his seventies, had told the boy, then school age, about the long-ago horrible experience of returning to the devastation around his family's pioneer cabin and trading post in the Upstate South Carolina backcountry on the Middle Tyger River, which was, at the time, only one mile from the boundary with the Cherokee Nation. It was an eyewitness account — grandfather to grandson — of what had occurred on July 1, 1776, during the defense of Independence, a military conflict (The American Revolution) of which South Carolina had played such an important role. The grandson learned how his grandfather, then about 22 years old, had returned to the cabin site to witness devastation everywhere. Dead of a swift raid by Cherokee warriors (at the time aligned militarily with the British military) was the elder Wade's father Anthony Hampton, his mother Elizabeth Preston Hampton, his older brother Preston and his little nephew, the infant child of his sister Elizabeth Hampton Harrison. Nine-year-old nephew John Bynum had been kidnapped and taken away to some Cherokee town. The bodies of the dead had been scalped and the cabin had been burned to the ground. The grandfather told his grandson how his sister Elizabeth Hampton Harrison, while hiding in a cane brake, had watched a Cherokee take her infant son by the ankles and swing him against a tree bashing in his skull.

Brother Preston Hampton's nearby cabin had also been attacked and there Cherokee warriors had killed his two children. Preston's wife Betty had been found, "wandering and out of her mind." Other nearby families suffered similar losses. Militia leader Aaron Smith had been killed along with his wife, their 5 children and their 5 bonded African Americans. Jacob Hite and his wife had been killed and the remainder of his family and his bonded African Americans had been kidnapped.

The Hampton family had been heavily involved in fur trade with the Cherokee towns beyond the Blue Ridge Mountains in present-day western North Carolina, which was then part of the Cherokee Nation. Two years earlier, as part of the British military campaign, brothers Edward and Preston Hampton had been captured while trading in the Cherokee Nation — captured by a mixed force consisting of both Cherokees and some Carolinians who were loyal to the British Government. But before the brothers could be taken to British prisons in Florida they had managed to escape and make their way back to South Carolina. So, on the day of the massacre, the Hampton's had been special and easy targets of the Cherokee warriors who had been persuaded to make more intense war against Carolinians in support of Great Britain's military campaign to conquer the thirteen newly independent States, all of them having driven out their respective British governors, dissolved their colonial legislatures, joined together in a mutual defense compact, and declared themselves to be independent States.

Grandfather Wade told his grandson that, at the time of the massacre, he and brothers Edward, Henry and Richard had been down at the coast, near Charles Town, helping with the successful repulsion of the June 28, 1776 attack by a British fleet of warships. The British fleet, wounded, departed for New York City, having no intention of attacking the lost colonies of Maryland, Virginia, North Carolina, South Carolina or Georgia. The British military would concentrate available forces on retaking the northern colonies from Pennsylvania through Massachusetts, because there the people were congregated around larger seaport towns, and a British base in Canada was nearby. Furthermore, it appeared that a greater part of the people in those colonies could be persuaded to be loyal to the British Government.

Upon receiving news of the Hampton family massacre, the Hampton brothers, Wade, Edward, Henry and Richard, had rushed back to Upstate South Carolina to join in the fight on the western front. Warriors from throughout the Cherokee Nation had attacked settlers near the eastern and southern boundaries of their nation. Determined to retaliate, settlers from the Watauga region of present-day eastern Tennessee, from the western settlements in the vicinity of Asheville, from the settlements of Upstate South Carolina and from the settlements of Upstate Georgia had embarked on counterattacks. The campaign was swift and telling.

And Grandfather Wade Hampton told grandson Wade, III about his memories of those revolutionary days and imprinted on the boy what it meant to be a Nation Builder. Grandfather told grandson about being a Representative in the South Carolina Legislature and about the family's mercantile trade, thriving by 1778, with locations at Charles Town and near what would become Columbia; about being a major supplier of Continental forces. Grandfather explained to grandson how he was absent from Charles Town when British forces captured the city in May 1780, an event that motivated him to take up the fight. He told the boy about subsequently raising a regiment of South Carolina volunteers during early 1781, recruiting even into North Carolina; about his conference with George Washington's second-in-command, Nathanael Greene; about a battle with British forces at Friday's Ferry on the Congaree River; about capturing British forces at Goose Creek; about being Thomas Sumter's cavalry commander, and about the very important and major victory on September 8, 1881 at Eutaw Springs, where Hampton had taken overall command after commander William Henderson had been wounded. The grandfather told about how victory at Yorktown had occurred the following month and how, two years later, the peace agreement had been signed at Paris, declaring that each of the 13 former colonies was separately an independent State and in control of its land going westward to the Mississippi River — free to negotiate for land with the Native American nations. The grandfather explained that the stage was thus set for building a nation comprised of sovereign States, stretching westward to the Mississippi River, without interference from the British Government. And the grandson realized that the biggest losers of all were the people of the Cherokee Nation, who had chosen the wrong side in hopes the British Government would protect them from the advancing settlements to the east of their tribal lands.

Grandfather Wade Hampton I surely amazed his grandson with stories about events following the military victory against Great Britain. He told of business success not only in South Carolina, but also in huge and newly established western farms in the lower Mississippi Valley, especially the Louisiana sugar cane farm named Houmas and the Mississippi cotton farms named Walnut Ridge and Wild Woods. He told his grandson about days at Columbia in the South Carolina House of Representatives, to which he had been elected and reelected. Grandfather told grandson about voting in the 1788 South Carolina State Convention, which had been established to ratify or reject the submitted Federal Constitution, which proposed to unite the 13 States under a new Federal Government, which would be decidedly limited in power but considerably more powerful than the government of the Confederation Congress, which it aimed to replace. Grandfather explained that he and many upstate South Carolinians had voted against putting their State under the proposed Federal Government because of fears that it might exert too much power. Even so, he said, the South Carolina Convention approved the Federal Constitution. But surely Grandfather made sure that Grandson understood his concern about losing State Rights to a Federal Government that might someday violate the limits of the Federal Constitution.

Grandfather told grandson about resuming an active military leadership role in 1808, at the age of 54. He told about his work as a Federal officer in charge of overseeing recruiting in South Carolina and overseeing major improvements in Charleston's harbor defenses, especially the strengthening of Fort Moultrie, which was in very bad disrepair. He told stories about the following year, 1809, when he was ordered to go west to help improve defenses at New Orleans, which was convenient to his vast sugar farm, Houmas.

Then came stories of Grandfather's military leadership in the War of 1812, a renewed conflict with Great Britain that had been especially encouraged by frontier settlers. He told of President James Madison recommending him and three others for promotion to Major General in the Federal Army and of the Federal Senate's quick confirmation. He told of leading 4,000 Federal troops and 1,500 militiamen on an invasion of Canada under the overall direction of James Wilkinson — the capture of Montreal was the military objective — the conquest of Canada was envisioned. Grandfather told grandson that victory in this second war against British imperialism would advance American's dreams of winning control over all of the land of North America. But Hampton's 4,000 Federal troops and 1,500 militiamen camped at Chateaugay, Quebec, near the border with New York State, in no way resembled the fearless and determined Carolinians he had known, who had fought alongside him in the first war against the British Government. His men might have shown some bravery and determination previously when it came to defending their homes against attack, but, for the most part, they were not willing to risk their lives in an invasion of Canada. The attack went miserably. Hampton's army advanced northward down the Chateaugay River and into Canada. His 5,500 men were opposed by only 1,600 British and Canadian troops under Charles de Salaberry, of which only 460 were deployed as a blocking force. Amazingly, these 460 defenders turned back Hampton's much larger force with little loss of life. Reports about defensive strength were exaggerated and deceived the grandfather, who decided to withdraw from Canadian soil after only 5 days of effort. Shortly afterward James Wilkinson's troops were defeated at the battle of Chrysler's Farm, which was the companion invasion thrust Wilkinson had personally led into Canada. Grandfather Hampton, his confidence gone upon realizing that he had failed to inspire his men to risk their lives in conquering Canada, then resigned his military commission. It was years later that the grandfather was describing this personal defeat to his grandson.

But the boy's father, Wade Hampton II and his uncle, Frank Hampton, were also fighting to defeat British forces in the War of 1812. In December, 1814, father Wade had been at the family's vast Louisiana farms when Andrew Jackson was rallying men to defend New Orleans against imminent British attack. Father Wade quickly joined a militia company and on January 7 accepted Andrew Jackson's invitation to become a member of his staff. At dawn on the following day, January 8, 1815, the British advanced against Jackson's well positioned men, who were outnumbered 2 to 1. The slaughter of Redcoats was amazing. The British suffered 700 killed, 1,400 wounded and 500 captured. The Americans suffered 7 killed and 6 wounded. "That brief morning battle remains today 'the most decisive victory ever won by an American army over a foreign foe.'" And father Wade Hampton was there. It was father Wade Hampton who had raced northeastward on horseback with Andrew Jackson's report of the New Orleans victory for delivery to Washington City. "Accompanied by a [bonded African American] leading a spare horse, [Hampton] traveled 750 miles through forests and over swollen streams to Columbia in ten and a half days." He then proceeded by boat to Washington City. President James Madison received news of the amazing feat on the fourth of February, 27 days after the victory. (I am not sure if first news at Washington City was from Hampton or from others). However it did first arrive in Washington City, news of the victory "caused wild rejoicing." Furthermore, the news destroyed plans by secession-minded Commissioners from the Hartford Convention of the New England States, who were, at the time, approaching the outskirts of Washington City with demands for much greater independence for Massachusetts and conspiring States, demands that history would show to have resembled the then future secession of South Carolina in 1860.

So it is easy to see how the grandfather's stories about the Defense of Independence (Revolution) and the father's stories about the Battle of New Orleans had instilled in the grandson a strong passion to carry on the family's tradition of Nation Building.

The father, Wade Hampton II, also played a major role in developing the son's character and the son's opinions about personal relations, business management, society and government:

The Hampton farms were large and they spread from South Carolina to Louisiana. Approximately 2,000 bonded African Americans lived on and worked on those farms. The grandfather and the father "used the most modern methods of planting, and he took considerable interest in acquiring and developing the best breeds of stock: cattle, sheep, swine, and especially horses." And those horses won many races at South Carolina race tracks (you might like to visit lovely Hampton Park a former race track in Charleston, SC. It's situated next to The Citadel). Managing such a vast and dispersed business, the success of which was important to so many individuals, was a great responsibility and the father surely impressed upon the son of that reality.

The father was influential in non-agrarian businesses as well. He was a Director of the Bank of South Carolina. And he had invested heavily in a project to connect Charleston to Cincinnati by railroad.

The father's home, Millwood, was a popular social gathering place. According to historian Robert Ackerman, it was "the social center of South Carolina." Situated on the outskirts of the State capital, political and business leaders often frequented this Hampton home. In addition to numerous notable South Carolinians, on separate occasions the father entertained the Whig Party's two most famous leaders, Henry Clay of Kentucky and Daniel Webster of Massachusetts.

The father surely influenced the son's opinions about government. Although never a Governor of his State, the father was extremely influential in seeing to it that the man he liked was recruited and was victorious at the polls: two examples are the election of brother-in-law James Hammond, Governor, 1842-1844, and the election of brother-in-law John Manning, Governor, 1852-1854. The father's political career was brief: the State Senate from 1826 to 1830.

And the son acquired a love of the outdoors sporting life from his grandfather and from his father, named by one authority on the subject as "the First Sportsman of the land." All Hampton's were expert horsemen. Favorite outdoors sporting activities were hunting and fishing. Bear hunts in Mississippi were exciting. Trout fishing at the family mountain retreat at Cashiers Valley, near the border between North Carolina and South Carolina, were favorite summertime escapes from the oppressive heat of Columbia.

Others helped shape the son's personality and character as well, beginning with Mauma Nelly, the bonded African American and devoted family servant who cared for him as a baby and a little boy. Close daily association with African Americans influenced the character, attitudes and personality of Wade Hampton III much as similar relationships had and would influence millions of European American children born and raised in the southern States. On the typical large farm, bonded African Americans and European Americans played together as children and worked together as adults. The men hunted together. Biographer Robert Ackerman would write:

". . . Wade Hampton II had a reputation of kindness to his [bonded African Americans]. In 1850 this Hampton wrote with obvious pleasure of his distributing Christmas gifts to his [bonded African Americans] at Walnut Ridge on the Mississippi [River]. Each received a blanket, a pair of stockings, a handkerchief, a calico dress and checked apron (to each woman), and a fine bleached shirt and fancy pants (to each man). . . . Hampton II was exceeding indulgent with his [bonded African Americans]. Dr. Robert W. Gibbes, who treated the Hampton [bonded African Americans], stated his belief that this master was indeed kind to his human property. A perusal of the . . . Census of 1850 found an impressive number of very old [bonded African Americans] in the possession of Wade Hampton II, a number [of them] aged 100 and over, surely an indication of less-than-severe treatment."

Wade Hampton III lost his mother at age 3 years. His father remarried a third time when the lad was 10 years old, taking his second wife's younger step-sister Mary Cantey. This union would produce 5 daughters and one son.

Wade Hampton was 40 years old when his father died. His formal education was classical. At Rice Creek Academy he learned Greek and Latin grammar. Then at age 14 he entered South Carolina College, located in Columbia. Since it was considered an entry requirement at the college, it is assumed that, by age 14 Wade had learned Greek and Latin grammar and had read "the whole of Virgil, Cicero's orations, Xenophanes' Cyropedia, one book of Homer, and more." His most distinguished professor was Francis Lieber who had come down from Massachusetts to teach at the college. You will recall that Lieber was a close friend and confidant of Charles Sumner and you will recall the 1863 "Lieber Code" concerning principles of civilized warfare. Hampton graduated from South Carolina College in 1836, at the age of 18 years.

Two years later, at age 20, Wade Hampton III married Margaret Preston of Virginia. The bride was the daughter of Francis Preston, who had been a military leader in the War of 1812 and a member of the Federal House. Furthermore, the bride was the sister of John Preston, who was married to the groom's aunt, Caroline Hampton Preston. Caroline's brother-in-law, William Preston was a Harvard-trained lawyer, with a practice in Columbia, and the occupant of one of South Carolina's two seats in the Federal Senate. Of Wade Hampton III's marriage, biographer Robert Ackerman would write, "Obviously, Wade Hampton's marriage was advantageous."

Although Wade Hampton III helped his father with management of the South Carolina farms, his main interest was the Mississippi cotton farmland. His grandfather had begun Mississippi farming with the Walnut Ridge farm. Wade III expanded the family's holdings, buying 3,250 acres in Washington County, Mississippi, dividing that into two farms — Wild Woods and Bayou Place — and later adding more acreage to Bayou Place. Looking closer to home, his father and his brother Kit together purchased 2,300 acres of mountain land in Cashiers Valley, which became a favorite family retreat for hunting, fishing and getting away from the South Carolina lowlands summer heat. Wild Woods became Wade Hampton III's Mississippi home.

Wade Hampton III loved to go bear hunting in Mississippi, generally not far from the Mississippi River. The hunting parties were rather elaborate, complete with boats and barges, horses and dogs. The boats conveyed the party to the hunting grounds; the dogs went after the bear scent; the men followed on their horses; the dogs cornered the bear, and then the real excitement began. More often than not at that time, Wade Hampton III, host of the hunting adventure, advanced toward the bear with a long knife, made sure the bear was distracted by the barking dogs, and at the opportune time rushed in and killed the surrounded bear with the long knife. Biographer Robert Ackerman would observe that "Theodore Roosevelt in *The Wilderness Hunter* said that Hampton killed 80 bear with the long knife." Obviously Wade Hampton III was swift, strong and fearless.

In 1846, at the age of 28, Wade Hampton III accompanied his Aunt Caroline Hampton Preston and her husband John on a vacation trip to Europe. Wade's wife Margaret, pregnant at the time with their third child, chose to remain behind. This trip, complete with important letters of introduction, provided the young Hampton with important knowledge of British government and society and added to his list of influential personal connections.

Although in the prime of life during the War Against Mexico, Wade Hampton III did not become involved in the American military campaign aimed at taking land from the Mexicans.

Wade Hampton III's wife Margaret Preston Hampton died in 1852. The widower was 34 years old. There were 4 children: Wade IV, 12; Preston, 9; Sally, 7, and Harriet, 4. Since Wade was busy with managing the South Carolina farms and the Mississippi farms, his unmarried sisters took responsibility for raising the children.

The year 1852 was also the start of Wade Hampton III's political career. He took a seat in the South Carolina House of Representatives. Furthermore, in December Aunt Susan Hampton Manning's husband John was elected to the Federal Senate. Wade served on the Committee on Federal Relations and the Committee on Agriculture. In 1856 he was given a seat in the Ways and Means Committee. In 1858 the rising politician was elected to the South Carolina Senate, where he served on the Committee on Federal Relations. He would remain in the South Carolina Senate until his obligations in the military defense of the Confederacy would require his full-time attention.

On January 27, 1858 Wade Hampton III took, as his second wife, Mary McDuffie of South Carolina. He was 40 years old and she was 28. She was the daughter of the late George McDuffie, a former Governor and Federal Senator. Her inheritance was substantial and Wade had assisted Mary in business matters. From that relationship a romance had flowered.

Two weeks after the wedding, on February 9, Wade Hampton III, the groom, lost his father. Wade Hampton II had almost reached the age of 67 years. You will recall that Grandfather Wade Hampton I had lived to be 81 years old. By any measure these two elder Hampton's had led full, productive and historically important lives. Grandson Wade Hampton III would do so as well.

Biographer Robert Ackerman would surmise from "family tradition" that Wade Hampton II had prepared a Last Will and Testament bequeathing his entire Estate to the eldest son, Wade Hampton III, but that Wade III had torn up the Will in secrecy in order to divide up the Estate among his sibling and the widow, Mary Cantey Hampton. That he did as Administrator of the Estate. There was a lot of debt owed on the vast Hampton farms, so inheriting land and bonded African Americans carried with it assumption of huge debts. Perhaps Wade III was uncomfortable with the assumption of all of that debt.

Three years prior to his death, Wade Hampton II had conveyed Walnut Ridge, a 2,529 acre Mississippi cotton farm, along with its bonded African Americans, to sons Wade III and Christopher (Kit), but this conveyance included assumption of a heavy $400,000 mortgage debt. During the family division of the father's Estate, in July 1858, Kit conveyed his half-share in the Walnut Ridge farm to Brother Wade III, giving him full ownership. You will recall that Wade III had previously purchased two other Mississippi cotton farms, Wild Woods and Bayou Place, including assumption of their large mortgages. So by acquiring Walnut Ridge farm as well, Wade III had obligated himself to pay off large debts on those heavily mortgaged Mississippi cotton farms. (In 1860 Wade III would report that he owned 12,000 acres in Mississippi and 1,000 bonded African Americans who lived on the land and worked it.) Kit took the remaining Hampton Mississippi cotton farm, Linden, positioned adjacent to Wild Woods farm. Frank Hampton inherited Woodlands farm and the Machines near Columbia, South Carolina. The four daughters received the Millwood house and 1,079 acres near Columbia. So the vast Hampton business enterprise, first divided up at the death of the grandfather, was further divided up at the death of the father. But, during the 1850's cotton farming was very profitable once the farm became productive, and meeting mortgage dates was normally not difficult for the highly leveraged agriculturalist. Apparently, Wade III and Brother Kit took joint ownership of the mountain retreat at Cashiers Valley, North Carolina.

Although Wade Hampton III remained a Senator in the South Carolina Senate, during 1859 and 1860, he spent most of his time in Mississippi managing his vast cotton farms. During those years, he took little interest in national politics and the Republican Party's intense political sectional agitation that was emanating from the northern States. Republican Party political activists were far away to the north, beyond Kentucky, whereas down in Mississippi, the crops were good and the prices firm. Gross revenue on the order of $1,000,000 was the norm, and considerable profit was retained after paying the mortgage debt and the expenses. He departed South Carolina for Mississippi during October, 1860.

By November 1860 it was apparent that the Republican Party, a purely sectional, northern States political organization, would soon control the office of Federal President and the Governor's office in every northern State. And that Party, which had come to power by inciting hatefulness toward the southern States culture and its political leaders, apparently would be able to exert dangerous control over the southern States in the Federal House and Senate. So Governor Francis Pickens of South Carolina called a Special Session of the State House and Senate to consider calling a State Constitutional Convention to address the issue of State Secession. The South Carolina Senate did convene, but Senator Wade Hampton III remained on his Mississippi cotton farms. He did not travel to South Carolina to attend the Special Session. Perhaps there was too little time to make the long trip, or perhaps he believed he would be unable to stop the State Secession movement. Nevertheless, there is reason to believe that he would have voted against authorizing the Constitutional Convention if he had been present. But, if so, he would have been the only Senator voting "No," for on November 10 every Senator present voted to authorize election of Delegates on December 6 to meet in Convention on December 17. Hampton arrived in South Carolina on November 24, but did not seek to be a Delegate or attend the Secession Convention as a lobbyist. The Secession Convention opened in Columbia, but quickly relocated to Charleston in the face of a smallpox scare. On December 20, it voted unanimously to secede. Six other States did likewise. On February 4, Delegates from 7 independent and sovereign States met at Montgomery, Alabama and united under the new government of the Confederate States of America. Jeff Davis, also a Mississippi cotton farmer, was elected Provisional President.

In mid-March, 1861, Wade Hampton III departed Columbia for his Mississippi cotton farms. He wrote from Mobile, Alabama on March 27 and from his Wild Woods farm on April 9. His farms were along the Mississippi River, south of Memphis and north of Vicksburg. They were vulnerable to Federal attack by gunboats and troop transports. After a few days, while making plans with farm supervisors and laying plans on how to deal with the many issues those supervisors might face, Hampton learned that, in response to Abe Lincoln's warships and troop transports gathered outside of Charleston Harbor, Confederates had evicted the Federal garrison holed up at Fort Sumter. He further learned that Abe Lincoln had used the cannon fight — his coveted "first shot" ploy — as his excuse to proclaim the Federal Invasion of the Confederacy on the following day, April 15.

Upon learning this news, Hampton quickly departed his Mississippi cotton farms and hurried back to Charleston, South Carolina. There he met with the military commander, Pierre Beauregard, and Governor Francis Pickens and offered to personally organize, and to a great extent personally finance, a "legion" of over 1,000 men, consisting of foot soldiers, cavalry and flying artillery. Beauregard and Pickens were supportive and gave letters of introduction to use at meetings with Confederate officials at Montgomery. Hampton rushed to Montgomery and met with Jeff Davis and Cabinet officials. Several meetings took place, the last being with Davis on April 27. The plan was approved and Hampton hurried back to Charleston, arriving on April 30. He quickly arranged for notices to be published in several South Carolina newspapers, describing the "Hampton Legion" and encouraging volunteers to come forward to serve for 1 year enlistments.

Not being trained as a military leader, Hampton focused on recruiting experienced officers. And he was quite successful. The Hampton Legion would be led by an unusually gifted cadre of experienced officers. He also recruited his two sons, Wade IV and Preston, who left South Carolina College to join in the defense of the Confederacy. He recruited his brother Frank who would serve him well. Volunteers came forward rapidly, many coming as whole companies of men. By May 7, five days after the announcement of the Hampton Legion, he wrote War Secretary Leroy Walker that he had "many more troops than I am authorized to accept."

Using his cotton receipts to pay for the arms, Hampton ordered 400 Enfield rifles to be sent from England for his legion foot soldiers and 6 mobile field cannon for his artillery battery. The rifles and cannon were to be shipped soon and delivered by a blockade runner. Cavalrymen were required to furnish their own sabers and pistols as well as their own horses, but were reimbursed for feeding and caring for them. During the last days of May and the first two weeks of June members of the Hampton Legion gathered at a large field on Hampton property near Columbia and began organizing and drilling. On June 10 Hampton wrote Pierre Beauregard — who was in northern Virginia overseeing the defense of Manassas Junction and the surrounding area: "I most earnestly ask to be attached to your command. . . . There is no one under whom I would so willingly and proudly serve as yourself."

On June 28 the Hampton Legion broke camp and set out for the Columbia railroad station. The men without horses were headed for Richmond, Virginia via railroad, but the cavalry would have to continue on toward Virginia on horseback, for no railcars were available for the horses. At the head of the marching column, riding a powerful horse, was Wade Hampton III, a large and very skillful equestrian of exceptional strength. The man looked fearsome. Biographer Edward Longacre would write: "Around his waist hung a brace of Colt pistols and a scabbard holding a long, straight-bladed sword that, at 6 pounds in weight, only a soldier of great strength could have wielded effectively." Two days later the Legion's foot-soldiers arrived at Richmond and established camp in a "spacious field" not far from the railroad. On July 16 Jeff Davis came to the Legion camp and ceremoniously presented the men the Legion's flag. That same day 36,000 Federal soldiers marched south from Washington City to embark on the first major invasion of Virginia.

At midnight, as July 19 ended and July 20 began, the foot-soldiers of the Hampton Legion boarded railcars for a quick trip to reinforce the defenders at Manassas Junction. The cavalry and the artillery were ordered to travel by road because there was no room on the train for the horses. It was about daybreak when they arrived at Manassas Junction. Soon after the train arrived, Hampton instructed his soldiers: "Men of the Legion; I am happy to inform you that the enemy are in sight." And the Legion soon afterward played a major role in repulsing the Federal advance on Manassas Junction. They marched north toward the Stone Bridge where the Warrenton Turnpike crossed Bull Run, but, before reaching that objective, shifted toward the west to reinforce the hard-pressed Confederate left. As they approached the Robinson House near the Turnpike they encountered heavy fire and returned in kind. Seeing that Federals were advancing past them down the Turnpike, Hampton ordered his Legion to retreat in parallel up the hill behind them. Fighting was intense. One survivor wrote, "Never have I conceived of such a continuous, rushing hailstorm of shot, shell, and musketry as fell around and among us for hours altogether." Hampton's horse was shot and killed. Then he grabbed a rifle and shouted, "Watch me, boys; do as I do." Taking careful aim he carefully shot distant Federal officers. The legion retreated further up the hill, arriving at the Henry House. Thomas Jackson's Virginians were putting up stiff resistance to the left. From their vantage points they continued to systematically deliver well-aimed shot to the advancing Federals. Barnard Bee was the senior Confederate commander in the vicinity of Henry House Hill. Observing the determined, brave and effective officers and soldiers under Wade Hampton and Thomas Jackson, Bee reportedly admonished other troops under his command, "Look! There stands Jackson like a stone wall. Let us determine to die here, and we will conquer!"

Hampton ordered his men to charge a Federal battery that had been most troublesome. At the start of the charge, "Hampton was struck in the temple over his left eye by a shell fragment or buckshot." The wound looked bad but would prove to be minor. The Federal battery was overtaken. The Federal attack was stopped. Federals began retreating in panic northward toward Washington City. The Hampton Legion pursued the fleeing soldiers. The Federal panic became awesome as men threw down their weapons and other encumbrances to hasten their flight. The Legion pursued them for two miles beyond Bull Run.

The following day Confederates gathered much abandoned weaponry from the battlefield and from the ground across which the Federals had fled. And that day Jeff Davis and Pierre Beauregard visited Hampton and his men, praising him and them for their major contribution to the impressive victory. Concerning Jackson, as you know, the name would stick. Thomas Jackson would become known as "Stonewall Jackson." After a few days a surgeon removed "the piece of canister" from above Hampton's eye and he eventually fully recovered without any loss of eyesight.

During the fall of 1861 and the winter of 1861 and 1862 Wade Hampton's Legion maintained defensive positions in northern Virginia along the Potomac and the Occoquan rivers. In early March 1862 the Hampton Legion and the other Confederate defenders withdrew southward about 50 miles to establish a more defensible line just below the Rappahannock River. The Legion took a position just west of Fredericksburg.

But, instead of advancing toward Richmond from the north, the Federals chose to advance from the east. By April they were spreading out from their toehold at Fortress Monroe. Hampton's men responded by moving south to block their advance. They were in the thick of battle during the Confederates counterattack at Fair Oaks and Seven Pines on May 31, 1862. During that battle, Hampton's foot was struck by a Minié ball, shattering some bone. Bleeding considerably, Hampton remained in the saddle while a surgeon "carved out the slug." But there would be some infection and he would be incapacitated. He would go home to South Carolina to recover, not returning until late June.

By this time the men of the Hampton Legion had been assimilated into the Confederate Army in the customary manner, leaving the Legion organizational concept to history. Hampton, now a brigadier general, was given a brigade under Stonewall Jackson, taking command on June 27 near Gaines Mill. On June 30, with White Oak Bridge destroyed, Jackson's advance seemed to be halted across White Oak Swamp. But Hampton found another way around, which promised to allow Confederates to sneak behind the Federal lines and, hopefully, inflict great damage, perhaps destroying much of the Federal army. But Jackson refused to try the tactic, and the opportunity was lost. The following day the Confederates attempted a frontal assault at Malvern Hill, suffering huge losses, but driving the Federals back to Fortress Monroe. Hampton would always regret what, many believe, had been an opportunity to avoid the subsequent great loss of life at Malvern Hill.

With the Federals driven back from Richmond, Robert Lee reorganized the cavalry under the overall command of J. E. B. (Jeb) Stuart. And, on July 26, 1862, Wade Hampton was chosen to command one of Stuart's cavalry brigades. He would remain a cavalry commander thereafter. Included in his command was the flying artillery he had organized and personally equipped for the Hampton Legion.

Expanded in armaments, his flying artillery consisted of 6 howitzers, 2 six-pounders and 4 twelve-pounders. Hampton's cavalrymen saw action in the counter-invasion into Maryland during September 1862, but did not encounter the worst fighting at Sharpsburg. They did an effective job of covering the Confederate retreat back to Virginia, demonstrating at Williamsport to draw away the enemy.

The next month Jeb Stuart and Wade Hampton, with 1,800 selected cavalrymen, returned north on a second counterattack and raid, occupied Mercersburg, Pennsylvania, then turned east and captured Chambersburg, Pennsylvania, occupying it for about 24 hours during October 10 and 11. There, Stuart named Hampton to be the "Military Governor" of Chambersburg. The Confederate raiders continued to ride around the Federal army, going east to near Gettysburg before turning south to reenter Maryland and pass through New Market before crossing the Potomac River into Virginia at White's Ford. During the long raid across Federal territory, the Confederate cavalrymen destroyed military supplies and railroad equipment and acquired horses and foodstuffs. It is generally believed that the above-mentioned raid played prominently in Abe Lincoln's decision to replace George McClellan with Ambrose Burnside as head commander over the Federal forces charged with capturing Richmond.

Wade Hampton proved to be a brilliant leader of cavalry raiders. On November 27, while Federals approached Fredericksburg, Virginia, Hampton led 174 cavalrymen on a raid in which they captured 5 Federal officers, 87 Federal troops and 100 horses without the loss of a single man. On December 10 Hampton led 520 cavalrymen from Brandy Station on another raid, reaching Federal stores at Dumfries on the twelfth. There the raiders captured 50 Federals and 24 sutler's wagons. Without losing one man, they returned with the captives and wagonloads of goods on the fourteenth. On December 17 Hampton led 315 cavalrymen on a raid of Federal stores at Occoquan. His men overpowered 20 Federal pickets and took possession of warehouses containing Federal goods plus a large Federal wagon train. Approaching Federals prevented taking all of the goods back to Confederate lines, but Hampton's men did return safely with about one fifth of the goods that had been captured. They returned to their lines on the twentieth with 150 prisoners, 20 well-stocked wagons and 30 stands of rifles. Several disloyal Virginia civilians, accused of helping the Federal invaders, were also captured and taken behind Confederate lines; among them was John Underwood, "whom Hampton described as 'a noted Abolitionist and traitor'." (Underwood, originally of New York State, but residing in Virginia since the 1850's, had been appointed in 1861 by the Lincoln Administration to the office of Virginia District Judge, his Court to be in Alexandria to ensure Federal protection.) Writing home on Christmas Day, Hampton informed his sister Mary Fisher Hampton: "We have stirred up the [Federals] greatly of late and they swear that my raids shall be stopped. But I shall teach them that it is hard to catch me on the ground I know so well."

Yet, the Confederates were slowly losing their advantage over Federal cavalry, which was methodically gaining in experienced riders and, more importantly, in the numbers of and the health of their horses. But Hampton's men and their mounts got some relief when, in early March 1863, they were ordered to retreat to Southside Virginia to graze the animals. Leaving his men there, Hampton traveled on to South Carolina in search of horses for 150 of his dismounted cavalrymen. By mid-May he was back in Virginia with the fresh horses. Joined again with his entire command, he set up headquarters at Culpeper Court House.

By late that month Robert Lee had decided on another counter-invasion of Maryland and Pennsylvania. The cavalry's job, over 9,000 strong, under the overall command of J. E. B. Stuart, would be to shield the massive Confederate army from probing Federal cavalrymen, who would be in search of Lee's army. Lee wanted to keep his army's position secret. The first clash with Federal cavalry occurred on June 9 at Brandy Station, located on the Orange & Alexandria Railroad, 7 miles east of Culpeper. It developed into a huge cavalry fight involving thousands of cavalrymen. The Confederates were taken by surprise and the fight lasted from dawn to late afternoon, when the Federals withdrew. But the result was not the customary Confederate cavalry victory, for the Federal cavalry fought well and inflicted considerable damage. In the words of biographer Edward Longacre, the Confederates, "had been taken by surprise and placed on the defensive for much of the fight, and they had held the field by a razor-thin margin."

The cavalry battle at Brandy Station was an especially severe blow to Wade Hampton, for during the fighting, his brother Frank, finding himself behind the enemy's lines with only 30 men and in desperate need of reinforcements, had been mortally wounded trying to stop more than 1,000 retreating Federals. When notified shortly afterward, Wade rushed to be with Frank. Of Frank's courage, biographer Edward Longacre would write, "It had been an exercise in futility, but one that illustrated the courage and daring that had defined Frank since boyhood. Wade Hampton remained by his brother's side, clutching his hand, until, at about 8:00 pm, Frank died of his wounds." Wade's son Preston accompanied the body to Columbia, South Carolina, where the casket lay in state in the Capitol. There Mary Chesnut, among the mourners, penned in her diary, "How I wish I had not looked! I remember him so well, in all the pride of his magnificent manhood."

On June 17 Hampton's cavalry, numbering about 1,400 men, headed on northward bringing along the cavalry's supply wagon train. Four day later there was another battle at Rector's Cross Roads and Upperville. A strategy meeting between Robert Lee and Jeb Stuart followed in which it was agree that some cavalry would lead Lee's army into Maryland and Pennsylvania while the greater part, about 4,500 men, under Stuart, would move northward far to the east as a blocking force. Lee and Stuart agreed to come together near the Susquehanna River (Harrisburg Pennsylvania would be the major town in the vicinity). Hampton's 1,400 men would go with Stuart. On June 25 Stuart's men headed for the gap in the Bull Run Mountains. They made uninterrupted progress to Fairfax Station, bypassed Washington about 20 miles to the west, forded the Potomac River near Rushville on June 28, and there captured and paroled several hundred Federals and destroyed their transport boats. Staying clear of the Federal capital and Baltimore, they headed north, only stopping at Sykesville to capture 125 Federal supply wagons and their mules and to destroy considerable track on the Baltimore & Ohio Railroad. It would prove to be a mistake, but Stuart insisted on bringing along the 125 captured supply wagons. He put Hampton in charge of bringing them along.

Stuart and Hampton's cavalry force did not encounter meaningful opposition until it reached Hanover, Pennsylvania, about 7 miles north of Maryland. There, on June 30, it was attacked by 3,500 Federals. Hampton's men were at the rear with the wagon train. The fighting lasted all day, but the Federals eventually withdrew. At this critical point in time Stuart was unaware of Robert Lee's arrival at Gettysburg, only 15 miles west of his position at Hanover. Unfortunately for the Confederate cause, Stuart led his men on a forced drive north by north-west toward Carlisle, Pennsylvania instead of due west towards Gettysburg. On July 1 Stuart's lead cavalrymen attacked garrisoned Carlisle while Hampton's cavalry and wagon train halted 10 miles to the southeast at Dillsburg. But before Carlisle could be forced to surrender, scouts rushed to Stuart's side to inform him of the great battle raging at Gettysburg. Stuart immediately ordered his men to abandon the attack on Carlisle and head south toward Gettysburg, which was 30 miles away. Hampton's cavalry likewise headed for Gettysburg with their wagon train.

About 5 miles northeast of Gettysburg, near Hunterstown, Hampton became engaged in what ought to have been a minor attack by what appeared to be a single Federal soldier. Preoccupied with searching out his attacker, Hampton foolishly paid no attention to his rear. At that moment a Federal cavalryman galloped out of the woods and struck Hampton across the back of his head with the flat side of his saber. Apparently Hampton's hair and felt hat cushioned the blow, preventing a fatal injury. A surgeon treated the 4-inch cut with a court plaster and Hampton struggled to continue in command, but with a serious headache. He and his command continued on toward Gettysburg, along the way thankfully delivering the burdensome 125 captured wagons to Robert Lee's quartermasters. Hampton's cavalry reached the Gettysburg battlefield that day, taking their assigned position at Cress' Ridge.

Confusion in orders created a poorly conceived cavalry charge from Cress' Ridge with Hampton at the head. Once underway the charge could not be called off. Hampton spurred his men on: "Charge them, my brave boys, charge them!" Biographer Edward Longacre would write, "Coolly maintaining his seat, Hampton confronted a succession of [Federals], dispatching each with a deadly swipe of polished steel. For several minutes, as troopers shouted, horses heighed, pistols cracked, and sabers clanged, [Hampton] hewed a path through the [Federal] ranks. . . . Numerous would-be opponents, intimidated by the sweep of his broadsword, gave him a wide berth as he bulled his way forward." But Federal reinforcements arrived, turning the fight against the Confederates. While sword-fighting against a Federal at his front, from Hampton's blind side another "struck him twice about the skull, reopening the previous day's wound and inflicting new, more serious ones." The Confederates began a retreat back to Cress' Ridge. Hampton, still atop his mount, received yet another wound as his horse leaped a fence: "a piece of red-hot shrapnel slammed into his right hip. This, his fourth wound in two days, left him almost helpless, barely able to remain in the saddle." These four wounds forced Hampton to relinquish his command and submit to the care of a surgeon. His trip home was by ambulance. The following day, defeated at Gettysburg, Robert Lee ordered all to retreat back to Virginia. The ambulance wagon train was the first to go.

The ambulance wagon train reached the Potomac late on July 5, but had to remain on the north bank for a week until a bridge was constructed. At Staunton, Hampton was transferred to a railroad car bound for the military hospitals at Charlottesville. Soon it was determined that he should be taken home to Columbia, South Carolina for an extended recovery. Under the care of his family Hampton did recover in due time and was back at headquarters near Culpeper Court House, Virginia, on November 5, 1863.

Two days later, on November 7, Federals under George Meade began crossing the Rappahannock River toward Robert Lee's Federals. This was a major Federal attempt to advance toward Richmond before winter weather set in. Lee quickly ordered a strategic retreat back to the Rapidan River, which was successful. For the next three week's Hampton's cavalrymen proved very effective in scouting Federal maneuvers and blocking Federal attempts to break through to attack the Confederate rear. After failing to launch an effective attack at Mine Run, which Federal's initiated on November 26, Meade, 5 days later, ordered a retreat north to establish winter headquarters north of the Rapidan River.

Hampton's cavalrymen established their winter quarters on the Richmond-Fredericksburg & Potomac Railroad, south of the main Confederate lines. In a December letter home, he wrote, "we are miles away from the enemy, but if he makes a raid, we will be in the right place to catch him." True enough, but what Hampton's men most sorely needed was good forage for their horses. His men hailed from the Carolinas and Georgia, too far away for furloughs home to nourish and/or trade horses. So Hampton spent considerable effort seeking ways to build up the health of their essential horseflesh. Poorly prepared as they were, his cavalrymen where severely challenged when asked to stop a daring raid on Richmond from the northeast by 3,500 Federal cavalrymen under Judson Kilpatrick. Other Confederates were chasing another Federal raiding party, made up of 500 Federal Cavalrymen under Ulric Dahlgren, the group rapidly swinging around the region on the west to get in position to enter the city from the southwest. Severely depleted of strong horses, Hampton gathered a force of 305 mounted men and headed toward Richmond in pursuit of Kilpatrick's 3,500. Kilpatrick's Federals reached the outlying defenses of the capital first, that being the morning of March 1, but, surprisingly, a makeshift collection of defenders succeeded in repulsing the attack. Following the line of the Federal's retreat, Hampton's men caught up with them during the night as they were camping. His men, only 305 strong and outnumbered 10 to 1, launched a swift night-time attack against the nearest campsites and this bold move sent the Federals fleeing back to the safety of their lines. To the west other Confederates captured many of Dahlgren's 500 cavalrymen and killed their leader. You will recall that the papers found on Dahlgren's body revealed his men had planned to kill Jeff Davis and every other Confederate Government leader they could find. Two weeks later Hampton and what remained of the two South Carolina cavalry regiments headed home by railroad to visit family and to restore the strength and health of their horses.

Wade Hampton returned from Columbia during late April 1864 and reported to his headquarters on May 2. His South Carolina cavalrymen returned as well, but some required additional furlough to make ready. Two days later, on May 4, the entire eastern Federal army of 122,000 men crossed the Rapidan River, beginning a new and massive attack on Richmond. This time Ulysses Grant was in charge. Confederate defenders were outnumbered 2 to 1. This would be called the Wilderness Campaign. Hampton and his men were supporting Confederate infantry at Spotsylvania when the overall Confederate cavalry commander, Jeb Stuart, decided to leave half of his force, including Hampton's, and ride off with the other half in an attempt to turn back what he perceived to be a Federal cavalry raid on Richmond by 10,000 riders led by Philip Sheridan. Sheridan's men were eventually forced to withdraw, but not before they had mortally wounded Jeb Stuart on May 11 at Yellow Tavern. Stuart died the following day.

At Jeb Stuart's death, Wade Hampton became senior commander over Robert Lee's cavalry.

But Robert Lee was not comfortable giving Wade Hampton authority over either of the other two major cavalry commanders unless they were fighting in the same engagement. When separated, Lee wanted son Rooney Lee and/or nephew Fitz Lee to report directly to him when separated from Hampton. The first test of Hampton's leadership occurred on May 28 in fighting between cavalry forces at Haw's Shop. Both sides fought dismounted and intensely. Hampton would always consider that battle, "the severest the Cavalry had ever been engaged in." And it illustrated a new style of fighting for cavalrymen defending Virginia. Unlike past days under Jeb Stuart, who relied so often on fighting mounted using fast charges with sabers and pistols, Hampton preferred to use horses for scouting enemy movements and for speedy arrival to and withdrawal from battle.

Another cavalry fight occurred at Haw's Shop, within earshot of the Cold Harbor massacre of Federals on June 1, 2 and 3. Following that, Hampton's cavalrymen continued to press Philip Sheridan's Federal cavalry. A major engagement occurred at Trevilian Station on the Virginia Central Railroad on June 11 and 12. Sheridan's force of about 8,000 men faced Hampton's force of about 5,000. Fighting was fierce and for a time it looked like George Custer's Federals, who had successfully maneuvered into the Confederate rear, would make off with hundreds of horses that the dismounted fighting Confederates were relying on for their escape. But Hampton personally intervened, rallying those able to reach mounts, and leading a reinforcing charge against Custer's men, forcing the Federal commander to suffer major losses among his men. Overall, both sides suffered major losses in the two days of fighting at Trevilian Station. Federals lost 102 killed, 470 wounded and 435 missing. Confederate losses were proportional. Sheridan ordered a retreat. A South Carolinian engaged in the fighting, wrote of what he saw the next day: "We found the field in our front covered with their dead." Hampton's men continued to press Sheridan, including harassment of the 900 wagons of supplies he was escorting southward to support what would become the siege of Petersburg. But Hampton's men were unable to inflict major damage and Sheridan successfully reached the Federal lines east of Petersburg on June 26.

On June 20 Ulysses Grant had ordered the start of a project to dig a tunnel to a spot beneath a section of the Petersburg defensive earthworks for the placement of explosives. The next day he had dispatched a major cavalry force to get behind (south of and west of) the Confederate Petersburg defensive lines and destroy the Weldon and Petersburg Railroad. Cavalry under Rooney Lee and a brigade of Petersburg defenders fought these Federal cavalry raiders daily but could not drive them away. But on June 26 help from Hampton's cavalry was promised since they were unable to any longer confront Sheridan's cavalry, which had reached Grant's base east of Petersburg. So Hampton's cavalry headed south to give Rooney Lee support. They arrived on June 28 and encountered 3,300 Federals returning from destroying track on the Southside Railroad and noted that Rooney Lee's men were pressing them from the west. Hampton's men engaged them from the east and heavy fighting ensued. The Federals were forced to fight to their front and to their rear. Fighting continued the next day as the Federals maneuvered to Reams Station. Confederates managed to surround the Federals. But instead of surrendering, the Federal commander, James Wilson, ordered his men to abandon everything and "run for their lives, every man for himself." In one incident Hampton and a few staffers and helpers managed to capture 100 Federals, but many managed to escape the Confederate net and reach safety behind the Petersburg siege line. They had abandoned all of their artillery. This ended Federal attempts to circumvent Petersburg. Grant decided to rely instead on successfully breaching the eastern defensive earthworks with explosives that would be placed at the end of the tunnel that his troops were digging. The successful escape of so many fleeing Federals illustrated that Hampton's men were exhausted and that their mounts sorely needed rest and nourishment. Accordingly, Robert Lee ordered Hampton and his men to retire, make camp south of Petersburg, and only perform picket duty to protect themselves. And Federals would not challenge Hampton for 6 weeks.

But, on August 1 Ulysses Grant sent Philip Sheridan and some of the Petersburg siege cavalry to the Shenandoah Valley with new orders to oversee the elimination of Jubal Early's Confederates and to destroy civilian property and food supplies. This was a major escalation of the Federal's war against civilians. Robert Lee responded by transferring Fitz Lee and his cavalrymen from the defense of Petersburg to the support of Jubal Early in the Shenandoah Valley. Very soon afterward, on August 11, Robert Lee promoted Wade Hampton, giving him full authority over Rooney Lee and his command. Hampton named Calbraith Butler to his old job. They remained in the defense of Petersburg and Richmond.

Hampton's command saw more action immediately, upon being called to defend Richmond against a combined attack from the southeast by soldiers and cavalrymen. Again Hampton's cavalrymen did most of their fighting dismounted. Hampton's men fought from August 16 to August 18, eventually forcing the Federals to withdraw. Of his "riding infantry," Hampton wrote home, "they charge infantry and take breast-works, and they are as steady in a fight as our best troops." Hampton's cavalrymen were tested again on August 25, south of Petersburg, when they mostly fought dismounted in their successful efforts to drive off Federal infantrymen and cavalrymen who had been tearing up the tracks of the Petersburg and Weldon Railroad. The total force of Confederates engaged in this effort succeeded in killing or wounding 600 Federals and capturing 2,100 Federals, 9 cannon and 3,000 stands of arms. Hampton's efforts received high praise for him and his men, but he wrote home that persistent fighting dismounted and charging of fortifications "is not the work for cavalry." He added, "We have been fighting infantry too much of late." But Robert Lee was impressed and realized that Confederate cavalry under Hampton was consistently reliable; he wrote, "The cavalry always fight well now." Lee rewarded Hampton's men with rest and grass for their mounts. They moved to good water 10 miles south of Petersburg to regain strength.

Two weeks later, Hampton's scouts, including the clever George Shadburne, operating behind enemy lines in disguise, found that a huge herd of Federal beef cattle was lightly guarded and vulnerable to capture even though they were very far from the Confederate lines. Hampton proposed a cattle rustling raid and Lee heartily agreed. By September 14, preparations were complete for a diversionary strike to distract Federals during the cattle raid. All set out to play their roles. Hampton would lead the raiders. Upon reaching Sycamore Church, which was on the route toward the beef cattle, Hampton's raiders surprised 250 Federals, killing, wounding or capturing 219, and taking their high-technology 16-shot Henry rifles — prized weapons. Thereafter, a Henry rifle was always among Hampton's personal firearms. Further on, Hampton's men reached Coggin's Point where 70 Federal civilians were guarding and managing the 3,000 head of cattle. Unsuccessful were the guardians' efforts at stampeding the herd to make capture more difficult. Also unsuccessful were subsequent Federal cavalry efforts to recapture the herd from Hampton's men. Hampton cleverly divided up his cattle and his teams of drovers, making following them more difficult. Furthermore, Confederate cavalrymen had advanced to forward positions, ready to give battle when the beeves approached Confederate lines. While covering cavalry fought off recapture efforts, Hampton's men drove the herd across a reconstructed bridge spanning the Blackwater River, then across the Nottoway River at Freeman's Ford, then across Rowanty Creek on Wilkinson's Bridge. Biographer Edward Longacre would write, "Thus ended the most unusual operation of Hampton's military career, and one of the most satisfying. During the three-day excursion into the enemy's rear, he and his men had marched more than 100 miles, and had captured, in addition to the cattle, more than 300 Federals, all at the cost of only 61 Confederate casualties. These facts were highly pleasing to all involved in the effort to relieve the chronic hunger pangs of the defenders of Petersburg." The count of cattle taken and delivered to Confederate lines was 2,486 head. Robert Lee praised Hampton's leadership for its "skill and boldness" and added, "You will please convey to the officers and men of your command my thanks for the courage and energy with which they executed your orders." The beef cattle were turned over to the management of Lee's commissary officers.

Hampton's major assignment was to offer cavalry support in protecting the South Side Railroad from Federal destruction, for that railroad was the last remaining route connecting the Petersburg and Richmond area to secure Confederate country, where food and other supplies could be brought in. It went southwestward to Danville, Virginia and central North Carolina. If the South Side Railroad was destroyed, Confederates would be forced to abandon Petersburg and Richmond to the Federals. Hampton's men guarded defensive works along Vaughan Road. Federal attacks on September 29 and 30 were repulsed, as were attacks on October 1. Then the attacks stopped and Hampton's men were undisturbed for almost a month.

Then, on October 27, Ulysses Grant launched a more massive and more determined attack on the railroad defenders in heavy rain. The situation looked almost impossible when the Federal Second Corp infantry managed to make its way to Hampton's rear. Hampton galloped off at a furious speed, determined to lead his cavalrymen to a blocking position at Burgess' Mill, on White Oak Road. His men followed, quickly erected defensive works and held off the Federal advance, giving reinforcements time to arrive.

When the advance of the Federal Second Corp infantry was arrested, Hampton's cavalrymen, under Calbraith Butler, mounted a charge in support of the Confederate infantry thrust. Hampton's son

Preston, assigned to Hampton's staff and not obligated to risk his life in cavalry charges, threw caution to the wind and raced off with the chargers near the head of the column. The result was a family tragedy involving sons Preston and Wade IV, both of whom were assigned to their father's staff. The following is the account as told by biographer Edward Longacre:

"Preston Hampton, unable to resist the temptation to join in the charge, placed himself near the head of Butler's column and put spurs to his mount. His son's impetuosity troubled Hampton, who appears to have been seized by a foreboding. He sent Preston's brother to stop him, then galloped after his older son, followed by his other aides. They reached Butler's column a minute or so too late. As Zimmerman Davis of the Fifth South Carolina Cavalry recounted, "I saw a staff officer, who appeared to be riding to meet me, fall from his horse. I galloped up to see who he was and to render assistance when General Hampton and his staff rode up. We all dismounted and General Hampton stooped over the prostrate form, gently raised his head and kissed him saying: 'My son, my son'.""

Preston had taken a gunshot wound to the groin. By the time his father reached him, the young man's eyes had rolled up in his head and he was drifting into unconsciousness. While the general and his subordinates bent over Preston, as if to shield him from the rain, a Minié ball thudded into the back of Wade IV, who toppled over almost onto his brother. [Zimmerman] Davis dragged the older boy from the line of fire, then went looking for Dr. [Walter] Taylor. By the time he returned with Hampton's surgeon and a wagon in which to convey the brothers to a field hospital, Preston had breathed his last. 'Too late, doctor,' his father murmured. The general then remounted and rode off to direct Hart's battery as it shelled Hancock's now wavering ranks. [Zimmerman] Davis marveled at the accuracy of the battery's fire, which he attributed to Hampton's supervision. Years later, he remembered what 'an ennobling and inspiring sight [it was] to see this grand hero, with the kiss from the lips of his dead son still warm upon his own, while the other son was being borne from the field severely wounded, thus subordinating parental affection to duty to his country'."

A few hours later Hampton, was notified that son Wade IV was not in danger and would recover. Preston's body was taken to Columbia by a fellow cavalryman, a family friend. After the burial, wife Mary McDuffie Hampton rode the railroad up to her husband's quarters to "share his grief." But trouble persisted: while Mary was away from their Columbia home it was thoroughly burglarized by people never identified. In addition to stealing every portable thing of value, the thieves "scrawled [political] epithets on the walls." This violation of his home, coupled with the death of Preston hardened Hampton's heart toward his adversary, the Federal invaders. From that point forward he eagerly killed at every opportunity. This was no longer a gentleman's war. Even so, his home, the grand Millwood mansion, would soon be burned to the ground by William Sherman's Federal devastators.

Hampton and his cavalrymen continued to defend the South Side Railroad during November, December and early January.

As 1864 drew to a close, that portion of his cavalrymen under Galbraith Butler received orders to relocate to South Carolina in an attempt to stop William Sherman's Devastators. Hampton was notified that he could go with them to South Carolina as well. On January 19, 1865, Hampton and his staff departed on the South Side Railroad for South Carolina. On February 4 President Jeff Davis requested that Hampton be promoted to Lieutenant General; on February 20 the Senate approved. Among Confederate cavalry commanders, only Nathan Bedford Forest would receive a similar rank, but that would be dated after Hampton's promotion. Therefore, for a time, Hampton would be the Confederate's highest ranking cavalry commander.

Biographer Edward Longacre would write, "Hampton, Butler and their men arrived in Columbia to the huzzahs of an embattled people, who viewed them as deliverers. With [William Sherman's Devastators] already in their State and heading toward them, the local residents were grasping at any sign that their families and homes would be defended." After parading through the city, the cavalrymen made camp and Hampton went to his late father's home, Millwood, to spend a little time with wife Mary and the children, who were staying there. On February 10 Pierre Beauregard gave Hampton command of all troops in or near Columbia, including Joe Wheeler's cavalry and some infantry, a total of about 6,000 effective fighting men. Defending Columbia from Sherman's Devastators seemed hopeless, but Hampton seemed determined to make the best of it. He ordered warehoused cotton placed in streets at key locations to give cover for defensive efforts. That was a bad idea, for it invited lighting fires too near buildings. On the morning of February 16 Sherman's Devastators arrived at the south bank of the Congaree River and began shelling Columbia. Hampton's cavalry under Galbraith Butler put up a significant fight during that day through about 9 AM the following morning, but his cavalry under Joe Wheeler engaged in little fighting. Anyway, stopping 60,000 Devastators with 6,000 Confederates was hopeless. During his week of command over the situation in Columbia Hampton made poor decisions. He failed to make the best of the hopeless situation. The cotton was not removed to a fire-safe location and burned. The town's ample liquor stores were not destroyed. The military supplies were not removed or destroyed. The bank vaults were not emptied and removed.

On the night of February 17 Sherman's Devastators ransacked Columbia and burned down much of the city, using the bales of cotton as handy fire-starters. The rape and pillage was awful. It was the most despicable time in William Sherman's career. Among the many buildings destroyed were Hampton's home and Millwood Mansion, the grand home of his late father. Hampton's extended family and the loyal servants had fled earlier and were all safe. That same day William Hardee led his troops out of Charleston, the "other city," which Sherman had decided to skip over.

On February 22, Hampton's command moved from Pierre Beauregard to Joe Johnston, for Jeff Davis had agreed to place Joe Johnston in charge of all Confederate forces in the western theater. On the other side, William Sherman's Devastators moved on towards Goldsboro, North Carolina to there join forces with John Schofield's troops, which were at the time occupying abandoned Wilmington (February 22). This juncture of Federals would increase total troop strength to 100,000 fighting men and outnumber Johnston's force 5 to 1. So Johnston's immediate objective was to concentrate his forces and seek an opportunity to, separately, fight one wing of Sherman's Devastators, then the other wing, then Schofield's troops. This was a last-ditch campaign to prevent Sherman's Devastators from uniting with Ulysses Grant in the siege of Petersburg and Richmond. First Johnston had to stop Sherman's Devastators before they reached Goldsboro, North Carolina. To do this he needed lot of luck and the best efforts of Hampton's cavalry. Hampton and his men scouted the terrain and harassed the advancing Devastators, paying special attention to Judson Kilpatrick's Federal cavalry, a long-time adversary. Kilpatrick cavalry was especially dangerous: their mounts were quality horseflesh and their firearms were advanced repeating rifles. But Hampton's men did catch Kilpatrick in camp on March 9 at Monroe's Crossroads asleep in a house with young and beautiful Mary Boozer of a family of South Carolinians who supported the Federal invasion campaign. Hampton's men took 500 prisoners, but overlooked Kilpatrick, who raced out of the house he was in, dressed only in long underwear and a shirt. Seems the Confederate who encountered the fleeing man in underwear asked him where was Kilpatrick. The answer: "There he goes on that black horse!" The Confederate went chasing the black horse, allowing Kilpatrick to escape. This episode was known as "Kilpatrick's Shirttail Skedaddle." Amusing, but this attack on Kilpatrick's camp did little harm to the Devastator's advance towards Goldsboro.

The big fight would occur on March 19 at Bentonville, North Carolina. Joe Johnston and Hampton decided to launch a massive attack on Sherman's west wing, expecting to defeat it before the east wing could reinforce. The plan was Hampton's creation. But Hampton's March 19 attack plan was not executed rapidly enough: Hardee's infantry was late taking its position and the east wing of Devastators was able to reinforce more quickly than anticipated. Desperate fighting raged all day. But, badly outnumbered and without hope that they had any real chance to stop the Federal conquest of their nation, Confederates were not fighting as fiercely as they had in the past. Federal reinforcements from the east wing began arriving and by noon on March 20 stood united as a formidable fighting force. There was skirmishing and maneuvering on March 21. That afternoon Johnston received reports that John Schofield's troops had occupied Goldsboro. That evening Johnston ordered a retreat. He moved his headquarters to Smithfield. On March 23 Sherman's men reached Goldsboro, creating a Federal force 90,000 to 100,000 strong. There was nothing Johnston's Confederates could do to prevent such a massive army from reinforcing Ulysses Grant at Richmond.

But it was not necessary for Ulysses Grant to wait for those reinforcements to arrive. His troops broke defensive positions at Five Forks, which fell on April 1. The fall of the South Side Railroad was eminent. Confederates evacuated Richmond on April 2. Jeff Davis and the Confederate Government rode the South Side Railroad to Danville, Virginia. Confederate fighting men tried to make their way southwest toward North Carolina. They were chased and forced to follow the course of the Appomattox River. There was heavy fighting at Sayler's creek on April 6. The next day Ulysses Grant demanded that Lee surrender his army. Robert Lee complied and surrendered to Ulysses Grant on April 9 at Appomattox Court House.

On April 12 Joe Johnston and Perrier Beauregard met with Jeff Davis and the Confederate Government in Greensboro, North Carolina. Although Davis believed negotiations with William Sherman would be fruitless and waste valuable time needed for the western retreat he believed possible, relenting to pressure from most of his Cabinet, he agreed to authorize Johnston to negotiate with Sherman. The railroad could be used no longer, for George Stoneman's Federal cavalry took possession of Salisbury that day. On April 15 Jeff Davis and the Confederate Government mounted horses and took the back roads southwestward toward Charlotte. The next day, from his headquarters near Durham, Johnston, through Hampton's cavalry command, sent a message to Judson Kilpatrick directed to William Sherman seeking to negotiate terms of surrender. Hampton and son Wade IV were in the vicinity of the Bennett house during these negotiations, but did participate.

On April 19, Hampton, seeking a way to avoid surrender of a remnant of the Confederate forces, wrote a letter to Jeff Davis.

"My Dear Sir:

"Having seen the terms upon which it is proposed to negotiate, I trust that I may be pardoned for writing to you in relation to them. . . . There are now not less than 40,000 to 50,000 men in arms on this side of the Mississippi [River]. On the other are as many more. . . . If we keep any organization, however small, in the field we give Europe the opportunity of aiding us. The main reason urged for negotiation is to spare the infliction of any further suffering on the people. Nothing can be more fallacious than this reasoning. No suffering which can be inflicted by the passage over [the Confederacy] of the [Federal] armies can equal what would fall on us if we return to [Federal control]. We shall have to pay the debt incurred by the [Federal Government] in this [invasion], and we shall live under a base and vulgar tyranny. No sacrifice would be too great to escape this train of horrors, and I think it far better for us to fight to the extreme limit of [the Confederacy], rather than to reconstruct the [southern States] upon any terms. If we cannot use our infantry here let it disband, calling upon them for volunteers for the Cavalry — collect all our mounted force and move towards the Mississippi. When we cross that river we can get large accessions to the cavalry and we can hold Texas. As soon as forces can be organized and equipped, send this cavalry force into the country of the [Federal States] and they will soon show that we are not conquered. If I had 20,000 mounted men here I could force Sherman to retreat in 20 days. Give me a good force of cavalry and I will take them safely across the Mississippi [River] — and if you desire to go in that direction it will give me great pleasure to escort you. My mind is made up. As to my course I shall fight as long as my government remains in existence, when that ceases to live I shall seek some other country, for I shall never take the 'oath of allegiance.' I am sorry that we paused to negotiate, for to my apprehension, no evil can equal that of a return to [Federal control]. I write to you, my dear Sir, that you may know the feelings which actuate many of the officers of my command. They are not subdued, nor do they despair. For myself I beg to express my heartfelt sympathy with you and to give you the assurance that my confidence in your patriotism has never been shaken. If you will allow me to do so, I can bring to your support many strong arms and brave hearts — Men who will fight to Texas, and will seek refuge in Mexico, rather than in the [conquered States].

"With best wishes I am,

"Very Respectfully Yours,

"Wade Hampton"

Hampton wrote a second letter to Jeff Davis on April 22, making the same plea, and adding, "Wish to see you as soon as convenient." Davis agreed to meet. He and the Confederate Government were still in Charlotte. On April 26 Hampton and Joe Wheeler traveled to Charlotte by train. Biographer Edward Longacre would describe the meeting:

"The President and his generals thrashed out the details of the plan Hampton had proposed, which Wheeler supported and which the President viewed as the only way to keep alive the dream of Southern [States] independence. Late in the afternoon, when Hampton and Wheeler left to rejoin their commands, they carried authorization from Davis to form an escort not only by recruiting volunteers, but by impressing horses, weapons, and other needed resources."

But when Hampton and Wheeler arrived in Greensboro they learned that Joe Johnston had surrendered their commands.

Hampton then looked for an excuse to consider himself, personally, not surrendered. He argued that he was away on civilian business when the surrender took place. He sought a ruling from Joe Johnston on the legality of that argument. Eventually, he determined that his command, including officers was surrendered, but he was not. Catching up at Hillsboro with a large group of his more determined cavalrymen, then in retreat to be available to further resistance, he arrayed them in column and addressed them. He would later report, "I adjured them to prove themselves now, as they had always done, good soldiers, by obeying the command of General Johnston, by whom his army had been surrendered; that I knew they were willing to share my fate, whatever it might be, but they would go as outlaws if they went with me." The men relented. Hampton and his staff continued on to Charlotte, arriving late on April 28, too late to join Jeff Davis and the Confederate Government, for it had departed earlier and was then at Yorkville, South Carolina. Firmly instructing the more reluctant warriors in his command that they could no longer fight, Hampton dismissed his staff and set out for Yorkville the next morning, forded the swollen Catawba River, and rode on persistently, not arriving until the early morning hours of April 30.

Although Jeff Davis and the Confederate Government had departed several hours earlier toward the southwest by an undisclosed route, Hampton's wife and children were at Yorkville, for that was where they had fled to escape William Sherman's Devastators. Extremely weary after the very difficult ride from Charlotte, Hampton fell "into the arms of his loving wife," and went to bed. He was not recovered for several days. By that time Joe Wheeler was in Yorkville. Together, wife Mary McDuffie Hampton and cavalry commander Joe Wheeler helped Hampton sort through his options and decide what he should do. Mary urged her husband that she, the children, and his extended family desperately needed his help to survive the recent destruction and the trying times ahead under Republican domination. All of their farms in South Carolina were devastated and their burden of debt was great. All of the investment in Confederate bonds was worthless. If the lenders did not foreclose on their lands the Republicans might confiscate them. Wheeler agreed that Hampton was more needed in South Carolina than at the head of a retreating cavalry. Wheeler would ride on after Jeff Davis and the Confederate Government and explain the situation. A letter was drafted and Wheeler departed Yorkville in pursuit of Jeff Davis and the Government. Wade Hampton III had made his decision to stay in South Carolina, regain his health and fight for his family and his State by non-military means.

Lucius Lamar of Mississippi — His Life through May 23, 1865

In *Bloodstains*, Volume 4, *The Struggle for Healing*, you will read much about Lucius Q. C. Lamar, Jr. of Mississippi, for, like Wade Hampton of South Carolina, Lamar would play an immense role in the political life of the southern States following their conquest by Federal forces. In *Bloodstains*, Volume 1, *The Nation Builders*, you read brief mention of his uncle, Mirabeau Lamar — gallant fighter under Sam Houston for Texas Independence at the decisive Battle of San Jacinto. This uncle became Texas Secretary of War, Texas Vice President and then President of the Republic of Texas (1838-1841). Although Lucius Lamar was in the Federal House as a Representative of Mississippi from December 1857 until the secession of that State in early 1861, his contributions did not merit coverage in Volume 2, *The Demagogues*. Neither was Lamar mentioned in *Bloodstains*, Volume 3, *The Bleeding*. His worthy efforts helping raise a regiment of Mississippi volunteers was not mentioned because he soon thereafter suffered repeated illness and was forced to withdraw from active command. Soon afterward, his diplomatic mission to Russia, initiated by the Jeff Davis Administration in November 1862, was also not noteworthy, for it was called off in the summer of 1863, before he reached Russia. But, as you will see, the life of Lucius Lamar will be important to our understanding of Mississippi and the history as covered in *Bloodstains*, Volume 4, *Political Reconstruction and the Struggle for Healing*. So, it is now appropriate to catch you up with a brief biography of Lucius Lamar's life up to May 23, 1865, the day Jeff Davis is imprisoned at Fortress Monroe.

Lucius Quintus Cincinnatus Lamar II was born on September 17, 1825 at his grandfather's house near Eatonton, Putnam County, Georgia (on the stagecoach road almost midway between Atlanta and Augusta). The father was Lucius Quintus Cincinnatus Lamar I and the mother was Sarah Bird Lamar, both parents being natives of the State of Georgia. The baby's paternal grandfather was John Lamar, also of Georgia.

An early pioneer family, Lamar ancestors had emigrated from France to Maryland, probably in the 1660's, and their descendants had relocated to South Carolina and Georgia in 1755. John Lamar, the baby's grandfather, was a successful Georgia farmer, living to the age of 64 years. John Lamar's oldest son was named Lucius I. He would become Lucius II's father.

The life of Lucius I is noteworthy. Removing for some time to Connecticut to study law, Lucius I returned to Georgia with recognized legal skills. He opened his new law office at Milledgeville, Georgia, but seemed to be too principled to be a particularly successful trial lawyer. So he took on the tedious job of compiling the State's statutes from 1810 to 1820 for publication as Volume III of the "*Georgia Statutes*." In 1821 he had the good fortune to partnership with Joel Crawford, a former Judge and prominent attorney. After this union his law practice was notably successful. In 1830 he was appointed to the office of Judge of the Ocmulgee Circuit Court, made vacant by the death of Thomas Cobb — a notable lawyer, judge and former Federal Representative and Federal Senator.

At the bench, Judge Lamar was successful and respected. However, great difficulties developed, the total nature of which remains unclear. But the consequence is certain. Death took him on July 4, 1834. Murder seemed not to have been suspected. The death was ruled a suicide. There was no economic difficulty; the family had ample money and would be reasonably well off afterward. Biographer Edward Mayes, preferring to say "a withering bolt fell," circumvented the word suicide. But biographer James Murphy went straight to the point. Yet what drove Judge Lamar to take his own life remains a mystery. One report alleges, "Judge Lamar had suffered severe dyspepsia with high fever, from which he never completely recovered, and that he had killed himself in a moment of delirium." Another report alleges, " 'insanity, resulting from accidental derangement of the cerebral organism,' was 'probably the true and only cause'." The death left son Lucius II fatherless at age 8 years. Furthermore, the lad's grandfather, John Lamar, had died one year earlier, so there was no grandfather to fill the void. Judge Lamar left 5 children who attained maturity. The Lamar family had sufficient monetary assets to continue in reasonable comfort without benefit of the father, but the rearing of young Lucius II fell heavily on his mother. History shows she would be up to the task.

Lucius Lamar II's mother, Sarah Bird Lamar, was also of an "historic" Georgia family, going back to 1768 when her grandfather Micajah Williamson and his wife Sarah Gilliam Williamson settled in Georgia on a large farm. Times were terrifying during the war in Defense of Independence

(Revolutionary War). Husband Micajah, a colonel in the Georgia forces, left for the field while wife Sarah attempted to manage the large farm with its bonded African American workers. The war story is gripping:

> While Micajah was away fighting with his command Sarah was at home managing the farm in support of their large family of sons and daughters. Near the end of the war a force of British soldiers, Tories and Indians descended on the farm and burned the main house, the outbuildings and most of the contents. They forced Sarah to watch as they hanged her 12-year-old son and they posted a large reward for Micajah's head. But Micajah, remaining with his command, managed to survive. Sarah and the children survived by fleeing to the mountains of North Carolina.

Micajah Williamson died in 1795 at the age of about 60 years, leaving 5 sons and 6 daughters. Mention of several of these siblings is appropriate. Daughter Nancy married John Clarke one of Georgia's governors. Daughter Sarah was twice married, first to a judge and, second, to Charles Tait, a Federal Senator. Daughter Mary was the mother of John A. Campbell, a Justice of the Federal Supreme Court, who is mention several times in *Bloodstains*, Volumes 2 and 3.

Another daughter was Susan, who would become Lucius Lamar II's grandmother. Susan married Thompson Bird, a physician, of Maryland stock, who was trained in Virginia at William and Mary College and in Philadelphia at its "celebrated" medical college. Dr. Bird practiced in Georgia, first in Milledgeville, then in Macon. A daughter, Sarah Bird, married Lucius Lamar I, this couple being the parents of baby Lucius II.

So we see by baby Lucius Lamar II's genealogy that his was a most impressive heritage and much could be expected of his life.

After the death of her husband Sarah Bird Lamar would remain a widow for 17 years, from 1834 to 1851, at which time she would marry Hiram Troutman, spending the remainder of her life in his home near Macon, Georgia. By the time of this second marriage, her son Lucius II would be grown, almost 26 years old. Sarah would die in 1879 at the ripe old age of 77 years.

Shortly after her first husband's death, Sarah moved with young Lucius II and the children to Covington, Georgia to enable them to be educated at the Georgia Conference Manual Labor School, a Methodist school for boys that stressed manual farm labor alongside book studies. Lucius attended this school while 10 through 13 years of age. At that point (1838) the Methodists transformed their Manual Labor School into Emory College and relocated facilities a distance of three miles to Oxford, Georgia, about 25 miles east of Atlanta. Sarah relocated her family to Oxford as well, built a new house and thereby continued her children's education. By August 1841 Lucius was ready to enter Emory College as a freshman. Excelling in the classics and oratory, but struggling somewhat in math, Lucius graduated in July 1845 at the age of 19 years.

The President of Emory College was Dr. August Longstreet, "eminent as a lawyer, judge, polemic, educator and divine." Dr. Longstreet, also an ordained Methodist minister, was at the center of efforts to defend the right of members and leaders of the Methodist Church to own bonded African Americans if desired, an issue then being intensely challenged by many northern States Methodist leaders as evil behavior that should result in banishment of such individuals from participation in the life of the church. This agitation from the northern States became intense during Lucius Lamar's college years of 1841 to 1845. The Wesleyan Methodist Church, established in 1842 in some northern States, made non-slaveholding a condition of membership, intensifying agitation from the north. At the General Conference of American Methodists, held in New York City in 1844, many northern States delegates demanded the resignation of Bishop James O. Andrew of Georgia. To this demand, Dr. Longstreet offered a "Declaration of the Southern Delegates" — in essence a "Plan of Separation" — which quickly went into effect, splitting Methodists into a Northern States Conference and a Southern States Conference. This intolerant agitation and expression of hatred toward southern States Methodists, intensely felt at Emory College, did much to shape Lucius Lamar's fundamental belief that individual liberty and State Rights were "sacred," and that oppressive religious dogma was "evil".

Lucius Lamar graduated from Emory College in 1845 and began studying law at Macon, Georgia under the direction of Absalom Chappell, a relative by marriage. Two years later he was admitted to the Georgia bar. Soon afterward, in July 1847, Lucius married Virginia Lafayette Longstreet, the daughter of Dr. Longstreet, the esteemed President of Emory College. According to biographer Edward Mayes, "The Longstreet family, into which Mr. Lamar married, became in the fullest sense his own family." Therefore, a brief history of the Longstreet family is appropriate.

Lucius' father-in-law, Dr. Longstreet, was of Dutch descent, his emigrant ancestor having arrived in 1657 at Long Island in the colony of New Netherlands (now New York State). Moving forward in time a few generations, we find that Dr. Longstreet's parents, natives of New Jersey, migrated to Georgia, where Dr. Longstreet was born in 1790. He attended Yale College, graduated in 1813 and was trained in law in Connecticut. Returning to his home State of Georgia, he was admitted to the bar in 1815. In 1817 he married Frances Eliza Parke, a native of Georgia, who had just finished her education at Warrenton. The newly-weds settled in Greensboro, Georgia. As a young lawyer Longstreet found success in his trade and as an elected member of the Georgia Legislature. After only 5 years in law practice, in 1822, he was named Judge of the Ocmulgee Circuit, an honor for so young a man. He became known as Judge Longstreet. But interests outside of law attracted the talented Judge Longstreet and wife Virginia — they became more interested in serving the Methodist Church. In the words of biographer Edward Mayes, "He and his wife became earnest seekers and professors of religion." The couple had two daughters to survive infancy — the second child, Virginia, already mentioned, would become the wife of Lucius Lamar, and the first child, Fannie would marry Dr. H. R. Branham and become a close life-long companion to the Lamar's, who would call her "sister Fanny". The sister-in-law was called "Sister Fanny" because Virginia and Lucius Lamar had a daughter on July 20, 1848, whom they named Frances Eliza (Fannie) Lamar.

In September 1849 Dr. Longstreet moved to Oxford, Mississippi to be President of the University of Mississippi, which had been established the previous year. Both Lamar and Branham soon afterward followed with their wives, arriving in 1850. Of the trip biographer Edward Mayes would write: "Mr. Lamar's trip was made overland in a rockaway and two wagons, carrying his wife, infant daughter, and servants." Lucius was admitted to the Mississippi bar during that year and was elected adjunct professor of mathematics.

1850 was the year of the struggle between the northern States and the southern States over access for bonded African Americans to the vast western territories, recently taken from Mexico. Political agitation over Exclusionism was intense. Admission of California as a new State was central to the struggle. Mississippi was to elect its Governor the following year, 1851, and Federal Senator Henry Foote of Mississippi, who had angered many in his State by voting for California statehood, with bonded African Americans excluded, was seeking the office. Foote was the candidate of a newly organized Mississippi Union Party. You will recall from reading *Bloodstains*, Volume 2, *The Demagogues*, that at this time Federal Senator Jeff Davis of Mississippi resigned his seat to be the gubernatorial candidate of the Mississippi State Rights Party in a desperate attempt to defeat Foote. During this campaign season, Davis was greatly handicapped by illness, so others had to step in to help. In September 1851, during Davis' illness, Foote came to Oxford to speak. State Rights supporters appealed to young Lucius Lamar to oppose Foote in addressing the crowd. Young Lamar, as a "Sampson" went upon the stump against Foote, the "Goliath," of his day, "whose adroitness and pugnacity were unmatched in the State." No record of Lamar's speech survives, save a portion of the notes he had prepared beforehand. History tells us that Lamar was the victor. Biographer Edward Mayes would later write, "His success was considered phenomenal. The college students, especially, were wild with excitement and pride, and bore him away from the hustings upon their shoulders" and reports were heard in the capital of the State about "the powers of the young orator." Of the results of the vote that November, you will recall that Foote won the race for Governor over Davis by a small margin. This political campaign was the beginning of Lucius Lamar's political career, but, at the time, he had little interest in a Mississippi political career.

During the summer of 1852 Lucius Lamar left the University of Mississippi to again practice law in Georgia, first in Covington, then in Macon. His wife and young daughter remained in Oxford with the Longstreet's. She would give birth to the couple's second child in 1853, a son named Lucius Quintus Cincinnatus Lamar. Although away from his family and the children, Lamar's law practice was good and he was elected to the Georgia Legislature in 1853. However, his success in law and politics was not matched with success in managing approximately 15 bonded African Americans that he and his wife owned, mostly through inheritance it is believed. They must have been a drain on the family's resources in Georgia. So in 1854, the couple arranged to relocate them from Georgia to Mississippi, placing them on farms outside of Oxford that needed more workers. Dr. Longstreet, still President of the University, agreed to manage the arrangements. But new plans soon surfaced. A year later, at age 30, Lamar left Georgia for good, returning to Oxford, Mississippi to a newly purchased farm he called "Solitude".

This farm consisted of 1,100 acres, 12 miles from Oxford, along the Tallahatchie River. A sound four-room farmhouse was already there, as were several cabins for the bonded African Americans, who were reunited with the Lamar family, but little of the land had been cleared for cultivation. Main crops were corn and cotton. Hogs were raised for their meat. Of the Lamar family's farm life, biographer Edward Mayes would write: "It was the life of the [southern States] farmer of the highest type. [He was] surrounded by his [bonded African Americans], to whom he was at once master, guardian, and friend, loved and petted by his women folk and his children, visited by cultivated and attractive friends for days and even weeks, and visiting them in turn." Even "Sister Fannie" and her husband Dr. Branham were at the farm most of the time. Although a peaceful and romantic setting, the Lamar farm was not destined to be much of a money maker. There was a large debt on the land. Even with 27 bonded African Americans on hand in 1857, only 200 acres would be cleared for cultivation by 1860 and records for that year would show production of only 1,000 bushels of Indian corn and 43 bales of cotton. War would soon follow.

Lamar continued to practice law, partnering with Christopher Mott and James Autrey, with an office at Holly Springs. Mott was an esteemed lawyer and a veteran of the War Against Mexico, serving in the famous First Mississippi Regiment, which, you will recall, had been commanded by Jeff Davis. Autrey, a Democrat and successful at politics, was in the Mississippi Legislature.

Two years after Lamar settled in at "Solitude," his father-in-law, Dr. Longstreet, resigned as President of the University of Mississippi. The following year, 1857, he accepted the office of President of South Carolina College, located at Columbia. He would hold that post until 1861, the year almost all of the students left to join the Confederate army. So, in 1857, son-in-law and father-in-law became separated by great distance, one in Mississippi and the other in South Carolina. But this year of 1857 represented the dawning of Lamar's political career, which was destined to be most noteworthy.

In July 1857 Lucius Lamar accepted the Mississippi Democratic Party nomination for the Federal House seat serving his district. His opponent was James Alcorn, candidate of a party composed of former Whigs and American Party adherents (known in history as "No-Nothings" or members of the "Secret Order"). You will recall that, in the northern States during the preceding year of 1856, all political opposition to the Democratic Party had coalesced in the new Republican Party. And you will recall that this Republican Party only operated in the northern States because is message was aggressively sectional, aggressively hateful toward southern States people and their political leaders. So, these developments in the northern States had greatly weakened opponents of the Democratic Party in the southern States and in Mississippi. Lamar won the election and proceeded with Virginia to Washington City, planning to be on hand in early December. They took a room at Brown's Hotel, along with Representatives Orr and Chesnut of South Carolina, Clay of Alabama, and other Democrats.

Lamar delivered his first speech before the Federal House on January 13, 1858. The speech was of great length and scholarly structure — a ringing testimony to the sanctity of State Rights and to a limited Federal Government. Lamar's extensive comments on Kansas Territory are important to our understanding of the man and the times. Kansas had just applied for Statehood, in full compliance with territorial law, submitting a State Constitution that permitted bonded African Americans to live therein. But as you recall, at this time the Kansas Statehood application was being denied in the House and Senate. Yet Kansas was at this time organized as a State within, although not recognized as a State without. President Buchanan was pressing members of the House and Senate for approval of Kansas Statehood based on the Kansas State Constitution, and Exclusionists were struggling to defeat progress toward approval. Lamar strongly advocated approval in the House and delivered clear legal arguments to support his advocacy:

> Applying thoughtful legal arguments, he said, in part, "I hold that [the Kansas State Constitution was created at] a Convention of the people called by the regularly constituted authority, and with the previous assent of Congress. I hold that [our] Kansas Bill was an enabling act, vesting the

Territorial Legislature with power to call such a Convention." Furthermore, our Kansas Bill, "pledges the faith of [the Federal Government] that [Kansas] shall be received into the Union 'with or without [African American bonding], as its Constitution may prescribe at the time of such admission.' It also declares the 'intent and meaning of this act' to be, 'not to legislate [African American bonding] into any Territory or State, nor to exclude it therefrom; but to leave the people thereof perfectly free to form and regulate their institutions in their own way, subject only to the Constitution of the United States and the provisions of this act." Following the first election of members of the Territorial Legislature, "the qualifications of voters and of holding office, at all subsequent elections, shall be such as shall be prescribed by the Territorial Legislature."

Lamar contrasted the clear legality of, 1), admitting Kansas on the basis of its current application, and 2), the past illegalities surrounding the admission of California in 1850. In reference to the California shenanigans, he said, "It is rather late in the day for this gentleman to begin to rectify such irregularities. We need go no further back than California. She was begotten by a military general, and forced into the family of States by the Caesarean operation of an Executive *accoucheur*. Yes, sir, without any previous assent of Congress, without even the authority of a Territorial Legislature, without any census, a band of roaming adventurers was lugged into the Union over all law and precedent, as the coequal of the oldest State of this Union, because it happened to be a [State that excluded bonded African Americans]."

Moving later in his message toward his close, Lamar continued: "The convention of Kansas having declared in their fundamental law that the right of property in [bonded African Americans], already existing, shall not be interfered with, has only given a constitutional sanction to a principle as old as the foundations of free government; and, sir, Congress is bound by the most solemn obligation that honor can impose to admit her with this very clause in her Constitution. Sir, we of the [southern States] demand the redemption of your pledge. The issue is boldly tendered, and we are ready to go before the great Areopagus of the American people upon it; and when the enemies of Kansas shall attempt to justify their opposition to her by invoking a principle which has deluged Europe in blood, only to sink her into more degraded deposition, we will justify her admission upon the principles which lie at the foundation of our Republic. We will call upon the people to stand true to the traditions of our ancestors and the practice of the [Federal Government] when Washington was President and the men of the Revolution ministered at the altars of liberty.

"Congress has no more right to call a [second] convention of the people of Kansas than it has the right to call such a convention in New York. . . . [Kansas] is no longer a Territory of these United States; she has, by your own authority and permission, thrown off the habiliments of territorial dependence, and stands now a State, clothed with all the attributes and powers of a State, and asks permission as an equal in this noble confederation of sovereignties. You may reject her application if you will, but it will be at your own peril."

As you know, the Federal House and Senate did ignore the legalities concerning Kansas Statehood, just as it had for California. Kansas would be forced to hold a new election for a constitutional convention. By that time, so many settlers from the southern States would have been driven out of Kansas Territory by Exclusion Terrorists, led by men like Jim Lane, James Montgomery and John Brown, that northern States Exclusionists would have the upper hand, and win political control of the Kansas Government. Kansas would be admitted to Statehood in March 1861, following the secession of 7 southern States. Perhaps Lucius Lamar was seeing the future on January 13, 1858. By January 1861, Republican sectionalism would have become so intense that southern States people would feel driven to withdraw their States from the Federal Government — to secede. The northern States afterward would expend 360,000 Federal lives on the battlefields of the southern States in a four-year military campaign to force those States back under the Federal Government. Did Lucius Lamar foresee such death and destruction when he said, "You may reject her application if you will, but it will be at your own peril"? Perhaps he did.

In June 1859 Mississippi Democrats renominated Lucius Lamar for a second term in the Federal House. He was reelected in November without opposition, and returned to Washington City in late November. During the Federal House session beginning in December, Lamar stood his ground for State Rights, while assuring his adversaries, "For one, I am no Disunionist *per se*. I am devoted to the Constitution of this Union, and as long as this republic is a great <u>tolerant</u> republic, throwing its loving arms around both sections of this country, I, for one, will bestow every talent which God had given me for its promotion and its glory." But sectional agitation intensified with the approaching 1860 elections.

Lucius Lamar was a Mississippi Delegate to the Democratic National Convention in Charleston, South Carolina, which convened on April 23, 1860. He walked out with the other Mississippi Delegates, leaving the Convention broken over the right of bonded African Americans to live in the National Territories. Thus split into two sectional parties, Delegates later reconvened separately to create a Northern Democratic Party and a Southern Democratic Party. Lamar was despondent of success in politics and felt incapable of making progress. The fight was leaving him.

In June 1860 Lucius Lamar accepted a position at the University of Mississippi as the Ethics and Metaphysics chair. His plan was to return to Washington City in December to complete his two-year term in the Federal House, but to withdraw from politics afterward. But many people called for him to carry their torch. The editor of the *Vicksburg Whig*, an opposition newspaper, wrote, "In our judgment Mr. Lamar is the ablest man in either branch of Congress from this State, and far ahead of the generality of Congressmen from the [old] Southwest."

Shortly after the November 1860 Republican Party landside in the northern States, including the election of Abe Lincoln to the office of Federal President, it was clear to most southern States leaders, Lucius Lamar among them, that the sovereignty of the southern States was in grave jeopardy. He expressed his concern to his father-in-law Dr. Longstreet in a letter to Columbia, South Carolina dated November 13, 1860. Here Lamar advocated State Secession, with South Carolina taking the leading role.

"If South Carolina will only have the courage to go out [of the Union] all will be well. We will have a Southern Republic, or an amended Federal Constitution that will place our institutions beyond all attack in the future."

Lamar's obvious optimism over the success of State secession reflected his lack of military experience and his limited experience with Republican political leaders and the powerful industrial, banking, railroad and commercial tycoons behind them.

Concurrently, Mississippi made progress toward secession herself. Senator Jeff Davis and 5 of the 6 Mississippi Federal Representatives met with Governor John Pettus at Jackson on November 22. The Mississippi Legislature had been scheduled to convene in a special session 4 days later. Representative Reuben Davis submitted a resolution, "that the Governor insert in his message to the Legislature a recommendation that they call a Convention for the purpose of seceding the State of Mississippi by separate State action." This resolution meant: do not coordinate secession with other States, for that takes too long; simply proceed toward secession independent of other States — then get together with them to form a new Confederate Government. A vote was taken. Representatives William Barksdale and O. R. Singleton joined Reuben Davis in the affirmative. Senator Jeff Davis and Representatives Lucius Lamar and Albert Brown voted against it. Governor Pettus, voting in favor, broke the tie. The recommendation to move rapidly toward secession was adopted. A telegram was sent to the Governor of South Carolina the next day advocating rapid secession proceedings at that State. Historians believe both Jeff Davis and Lucius Lamar were close to advocating secession, but felt a less rapid, more coordinated process was advisable. We do know that Jeff Davis, based on his extensive experience as an important leader in the War Against Mexico, as a Federal Senator and as Secretary of War, was rightfully most fearful that a massive and difficult-to-defend Federal invasion would follow State secession.

As scheduled, the Mississippi Legislature convened and received the Governor's annual message, which said, in part:

"Can the lives, liberty, and property of the people of Mississippi be safely entrusted to the keeping of that [northern States] sectional majority which must hereafter administer the Federal Government?

"I think they **cannot**, for the following reasons:

"They have exhibited a low selfishness in seizing all the [National] Territories, which are the common property of all the States. They have deliberately attempted to, and have succeeded in educating a generation to hate the [southern States people]. They have sworn to support the Federal Constitution, [but] deliberately passed laws with the palpable intent to violate one of the plainest provisions of that compact. They have sent large sums of money to Congress, for the purpose of bribing the members of that body to pass laws to advance their private interests. They have attempted to degrade us in the estimation of other nations, by denouncing us as barbarians, pirates and robbers — unfit associates for Christian or civilized men. They have excited our slaves to insurrection [example: Nat Turner], advised them to burn our property and murder our people, and [example: Bleeding Kansas] have furnished them with arms and ammunition to aid them in their bloody work. They have murdered [men from southern States] in the lawful pursuit of [runaway bonded African Americans], and failed to punish their citizens for these flagrant violations of [Federal law]. They have furnished money and arms for the invasion of a slaveholding State [example: John Brown's gang in Virginia], and when the punishment awarded to treason and murder by all civilized nations overtook the invaders [example: the capture of John Brown], they threatened the dastardly revenge of midnight incendiaries, tolled bells in honor of traitors and murderers, and rewarded the family of the chief traitor [John Brown's family] as never was rewarded that of any soldier who fell in defense of the country, and held him up as an example of [what they falsely alleged to be a] heroic devotion to a just and glorious cause. Their press, pulpit, lecture room, and forum teem daily and nightly with exhortations to their people to press forward this war on our institutions, even to the drenching of [southern States] fields with the blood of [northern States] citizens. In view of all this long catalogue of insults and injuries, in view of the fact that [these hostile northern States] must continue to increase in power [within the Federal Government], I feel that I am warranted in saying that the [northern States] people have forfeited the confidence of the people of Mississippi; and that the lives, liberty, and property of ourselves — and our children after us — ought not to be entrusted to rulers elected by such a people."

The Mississippi Legislature concurred with the Governor and called for a Mississippi Convention to meet on January 7, 1861.

Meanwhile, Lucius Lamar, having arrived, was present in his seat when the Federal House convened in Washington City on December 3, 1860. He remained only a few days. Quickly discouraged by the hostility of northern States Republicans, Lamar left Washington on December 12, returning to Mississippi to campaign as a Delegate to the upcoming Mississippi Convention. He would resign his seat in the Federal House on January 12, 1861, a formality.

Two days following Lamar's departure from the city, 30 southern States Representatives and Senators, including Jeff Davis, signed a resolution advocating State secession. The resolution stated:

"To Our Constituents:

"The argument is exhausted. All hope of relief in the [existing Federation] is extinguished, and we trust the [southern States] will not be deceived by appearances or the pretense of guarantees. . . . In our judgment, the Republicans are resolute in the purpose to grant nothing that will or ought to satisfy the [southern States]. We are satisfied the honor, safety, and independence of the [southern States] people require the organization of a [Confederacy of Southern States] — a result to be obtained only by separate State secession." [R17:368-369]

The Mississippi Convention met at Jackson on January 7, 1861. By this time South Carolina had already seceded. Two-thirds of the Delegates were considered to be unconditional secessionists. The remainder were against secession or they established conditions, such as only acting in conjunction with other States. Lucius Lamar, a recognized leader among the advocates of unconditional State secession, presented a resolution that a Committee of Fifteen be appointed by the President of the Convention, William Barry, to quickly draft and ordinance of secession to move the State toward inclusion under a new Confederate Government made up of South Carolina and other seceded States.

Lamar's motion to establish the Committee of Fifteen passed; he was named Chairman and 14 others were named to the Committee. Not inclined to quibble over language, the Committee met, encouraged

Lamar to draft an Ordinance, reconvened and approved his language. During the morning, just two days after the Committee had been proposed, Lamar reported its Ordinance of Mississippi Secession to the Convention Delegates. The language of the Ordinance follows:

"An ordinance to dissolve the union between the State of Mississippi and other States united with her under the compact entitled, 'The Constitution of the United States of America.'

"The people of Mississippi, in Convention assembled, do ordain and declare, and it is hereby ordained and declared, as follows, to wit:

"Section 1. That all the laws and ordinances by which the said State of Mississippi became a member of the Federal Union of the United States of America be, and the same are hereby, repealed, and that all obligations on the part of said State, or the people thereof, be withdrawn, and that the said State doth hereby resume all the rights, functions, and powers which, by any of said laws and ordinances, were conveyed to the Government of the said United States, and is absolved from all the obligations, restraints, and duties incurred to the said Federal Union, and shall henceforth be a free, sovereign, and independent State.

"Section 2. That so much of the first section of the Seventh Article of the Constitution of this State as requires members of the Legislature and all officers, both legislative and judicial, to take an oath to support the Constitution of the United States be, and the same is hereby, abrogated and annulled.

"Section 3. That all rights acquired and vested under the Constitution of the United States, or under any act of Congress passed in pursuance thereof, or under any law of this State, and not incompatible with this ordinance, shall remain in force and have the same effect as if this ordinance had not been passed.

"Section 4. That the people of the State of Mississippi hereby consent to form a federal union with such of the States as have seceded or may secede from the Union of the United States of America, upon the basis of the present Constitution of the United States, except such parts thereof as embrace other portions than such seceding States."

That afternoon, the yeas and nays were called for. Of this moment biographer Edward Mayes would write:

"The galleries and the floor of the Hall were crowded with spectators of the solemn scene. . . . As each member responded in tones vibrant with intense feeling suppressed. . . . A stillness as of death held the great assembly. . . . When the call was completed, and the President [of the Convention], rising, announced the result — ayes 84, nays 15 — a profound silence for some time prevailed. . . . [Then] members and spectators arose, and with bowed heads united in the prayer [by Rev. Whitfield Harrington] . . . for God's blessing on the momentous step just taken. . . . A fire bell, from an engine house in the capitol yard, first announced the tidings. Then there was a booming of cannon and a ringing of rejoicing bells . . ."

Lamar was not named to go to Montgomery, Alabama, to establish the Provisional Confederate Government and elect a Confederate President. But afterward he was in active attendance as a Delegate when the Mississippi Convention met in March to vote on ratifying the Provisional Confederate Constitution and placing Mississippi under the Confederacy. Ratification passed by a vote of 78 to 7.

Anticipating a Federal invasion, Christopher Mott, a veteran of Jeff Davis' regiment in the War Against Mexico and one of Lamar's two law partners, moved quickly to raise and command a regiment of Mississippi volunteers to help defend the newly seceded States. Lamar gave Mott all possible recruiting help and, although without any personal military experience, he was named second in command. This regiment, the first raised in Mississippi, was designated as the 19th Mississippi.

By June 1 the 19th Mississippi was in Richmond, Virginia, allowing Lamar an occasion to join with President Jeff Davis in addressing a crown of well-wishers from a balcony of the Spotswood Hotel. Davis addressed the crowd first, then Virginia Governor Henry Wise, followed by Lamar's closing remarks. Lamar reminded the crowd that, from the beginning, Confederate State political leaders only sought peaceful, open and non-competitive co-existence with the Federal States, but, so far, their sincere offer was rejected by northern States political leaders, whose lies and demagoguery had encouraged hatred and misunderstanding within their people. Then Lamar explained the consequences, sad as they were:

> "If [the northern States people] had not been blinded by passion, maddened by fanaticism, and excited by the loss of power; had they consented to a peaceful separation of these two sections, it would have afforded the strongest evidence of the capacity of man for self-government ever presented to the world. But they did not do it. They proclaimed war and subjugation. They have called upon you to abandon your right of self-government, to surrender your civil liberty."

But a time of war was at hand. Notably strong as a legal and political leader, Lamar proved to be weak as a soldier and military leader. A recurring illness would prevent significant contributions in the field of battle. The first attack of illness struck on or about July 1, 1861, and prevented him from advancing to the front with his regiment. Biographer Edward Mayes would characterize this recurring illness as follows:

> "Before the regiment left Richmond, [Lucius] Lamar suffered the first attack of a physical infirmity, which pursued him during the whole of his [remaining] life, which hung over him always, a veritable sword of Damocles. It was a violent vertigo, something like an apoplexy, accompanied by unconsciousness more or less prolonged, and followed by more or less of paralysis of one side. Sometimes even his speech was affected."

Characterizing this illness in modern medical terms is difficult. The symptoms are not unlike a stroke or brain bleed. Yet they would return on occasion. Lamar went home to Mississippi in July, recovered somewhat and returned to Richmond in November.

Lamar spent most of the winter in Richmond, helping Jeff Davis on occasion, and hoping for a more complete recovery of his strength. During this time Lamar recommended to Davis that he make Burton Harrison his personal secretary. Like Lamar, Harrison had been a professor at the University of Mississippi. You will remember that Harrison would be most helpful to Jeff and Varina Davis, especially during the 1865 retreat from Richmond. During February Lamar traveled south in hopes of improving his health. He returned in March, went to the lines and joined his 19th Mississippi Regiment, which had wintered over near Yorktown. A few days later, on May 5, the regiment was in a hard fight in the Battle of Williamsburg. This engagement was Lamar's first real fight. In this battle the regiment suffered about 25 percent killed, wounded or captured, and the regimental commander, and Lamar's former law partner Christopher Mott, was killed in action — "shot through the breast with a Minié ball." Lamar, second in command, took charge. For a few days Lamar shouldered that immense responsibility. But ten days after the loss of Mott, Lamar, was again struck down by recurring illness. Of this moment biographer Edward Mayes would write:

> "About the 15th of May, as [Lamar] was reviewing his regiment, his vertigo returned suddenly, and in a most violent form. He fell as if he had been shot. The soldiers raised him upon a litter, covered him with the regimental flag, and carried him to his tent. From thence an ambulance conveyed him to friends in Richmond. His connection with the line was over."

At this point in your reading you may ask yourself why I have made the life of Lucius Lamar an important window into the history presented in *Bloodstains*. I know his life seems a poor choice at this point, for his military career was a miserable failure. But by the close of Volume 4 I expect you will be satisfied that my choice was wise. Remember, the history in *Bloodstains* is focused on the people and their political leaders, not on battles and military leaders. This study of Lamar, of Mississippi, like Hampton of South Carolina, will help us understand the "Politics that Produced the American Civil War."

In late 1862, Dr. Longstreet, having return to Oxford, Mississippi from Columbia, South Carolina, wrote son-in-law Lucius Lamar of the anticipated devastation to be inflicted upon that part of the State. In a letter dated November 13, Longstreet wrote: "Your [farm] will soon be a battle-field. We shall be whipped on it, and the [Federals] will make a desert of it. . . . It matters but little whether it be made the camping-ground of our forces during the winter, or fall into the hands of the enemy. . . . The prospect before us is awful." He went on to report that Lamar's wife and children were relocating to Georgia. The destruction of the holdings of the Longstreet and Lamar families was soon to come.

Six days after Dr. Longstreet penned that letter, the Jeff Davis Administration appointed Lucius Lamar "Special Commissioner of the Confederate States to the Empire of Russia." His main instruction was to persuade the Russian Government to extend official recognition to the Confederate States of America, for which some hope remained at the time. His instructions further advised him to, upon arriving in Europe, confer with the two primary Confederate Commissioners, James Mason in London and John Slidell in Paris, prior to striking out for St. Petersburg, "in order to inform yourself fully of the condition of affairs in Europe at the time of your arrival, and if any important change shall have occurred rendering your compliance with any part of your present instructions impolitic or unadvisable, you may exercise your own discretion, after conference with one or both of these gentlemen, in postponing the execution of them until further instructions from Richmond."

Lamar was in Mississippi at the time of his appointment. To reach Europe, he had to run the Federal blockade of the Confederate coastline. The trip was difficult and consumed much time. He planned to leave North America from Matamoras, Mexico, near where the Rio Grande flows into the Gulf, just south of Texas. In mid-December 1862, he began his journey, starting on a riverboat that took him up the Red River to Alexandria, in the middle of Louisiana. He switched to a hack, riding overland for 4 days to the Sabine River (the Louisiana-Texas border). A riverboat took him down the Sabine and he went overland on to Houston. Then he rode overland to San Antonio, arriving on January 3, 1863. By various means he made his way to Matamoras and there boarded a French vessel, "Malabar," which took him to Havana, Cuba. He reached Havana on February 3. From there he took vessels to the Virgin Islands and on to England, reaching London on March 1, 1863. Although able to travel, he was still partially disabled by difficulty with his left leg. It had taken Lamar over 3 months to reach Europe, and two major Federal military victories would be only 4 months away: the conquest of Vicksburg, which would open the full length of the Mississippi River, and the repulsion of the Confederate counter-offensive at Gettysburg. These two Federal victories and other military advances would greatly discourage those European leaders who supported recognition of the Confederacy.

Lamar spent considerable time with James Mason in London, getting to know the difficulties in securing British recognition and military help. He also went to France, seeking the same information and connections. Opportunities to gain support from the French Emperor seemed promising, but only if the British cooperated. Although the months were passing by, Lamar had not yet believed the time was right to travel to St. Petersburg. The situation needed to improve there first. Why would leaders of the Russian Empire want to support State Secession in North America while it was struggling "to put down the Polish insurrection in her own domain?" And perhaps Lamar was awaiting official Confederate Senate confirmation of his appointment as Commissioner to Russia. Then, on June 11, with the Mississippi River and Vicksburg on the verge of falling entirely into Federal control, the Confederate Senate decided against confirmation. Lamar received notice of the vote in mid July. On July 22 he confirmed receipt of the report, but did not immediately make arrangements to travel back to the Confederacy. He hoped he might be able to use to advantage the important personal connections he had made in Great Britain and France. But no important gains were achieved. Around November 1 he sailed from Liverpool for Halifax, to Bermuda, and from there on a blockade runner, *Ceres*, to Wilmington, North Carolina. The *Ceres* arrived off the North Carolina coast in early December, but the "run" into Wilmington did not go well:

> "As the *Ceres* was nearing the Carolina coast she was sighted and pursued by a Federal ship, and in her flight was stranded. The vessel had to be abandoned, and recourse had to boats. Mr. Lamar was enabled to save but little of his luggage . . . however, he got in safely."

By this time Federals had overrun Oxford, Mississippi and Lamar's farm, Solitude. They had also burned Dr. Longstreet's home and his papers. Lamar's family was safe in Georgia, and he went to see them, staying for three weeks before departing for Richmond.

Lamar arrived in Richmond about January 1, 1864. He first reported to Jeff Davis and Judah Benjamin, explaining the diplomatic situation in Europe. Then he helped out a bit in the War Department. By late February Davis asked him to travel back to Georgia to encourage support from officials in the State Government, many of whom were very angry about the recent Confederate Government's suspension of the *writ of habeas corpus*. The Georgia Legislature convened on March 10 and Lamar was on hand, talking with political leaders and delivering speeches, including at the State House, at Milledgeville,

Columbus and Atlanta. The speech in Atlanta, called the "State of the Country" speech, was most helpful. The Georgia Legislature did pass resolutions critical of the suspension of the *writ of habeas corpus*, but moderated their anger by expressing confidence in President Davis. Lamar remained in Georgia, encouraging support for the war effort and loyalty to the Confederate Government in Richmond.

The family was living in Georgia, at Oxford and Macon. Lamar's wife and children had fled to Oxford, Georgia from Oxford, Mississippi along with Dr. Longstreet. Lamar's mother, who you will recall had remarried, still lived in Macon in her second husband's home. Like so many Confederate families, Lamar's was mourning deaths. His sister died in May and his brother Thomas was killed in battle near Petersburg in June.

Following Abe Lincoln's reelection in November, Lamar was forced to flee the Federal destruction inflicted by William Sherman's huge army of Federal Devastators, which burned and pillaged a 60-mile-wide swath across Georgia from Atlanta to Savannah. Lamar was in Richmond by December 1. There he helped with legal issues before a military court. He fled Richmond with Robert Lee's army, acting as an aide to General James Longstreet, and was surrendered at Appomattox Court House on April 9.

Following the surrender, a group of officers were discussing where each would go next. Some talked of leaving the country for South American or elsewhere. Lamar was not among those. He told these officers:

> "I shall stay with my people, and share their fate. I feel it to be my duty to devote my life to the alleviation, so far as in my power lies, of the sufferings this day's disaster will entail upon them."

Lamar returned to Richmond for a few weeks. Then on or about May 20, he departed Virginia for Georgia, planning to continue on with his family to Mississippi. He was only in the early stages of this travel on May 22 — the day that Mary Todd Lincoln and her sons departed the President's Residence in Washington City — and the day that Jeff Davis was imprisoned at Fortress Monroe.

In subsequent pages, which resume our history as of May 23, 1865, you will follow the life of Lucius Lamar, but hereafter you will see him within the sweep of events unfolding chronologically in this story of a torn nation's "struggle for healing."

Forward to Volume 4, *Political Reconstruction and The Struggle for Healing*

In *Bloodstains*, Volume 1, *The Nation Builders*, you came to understand that two cultures had evolved in those United States.

First there was the southern States culture, typified by Virginians, who had been most influential in settling North America and expanding westward all the way to the Pacific Ocean. The southern culture treasured individual liberty and confident individual self-reliance. The southern culture wanted government to be "limited in power" to only that given it "by the consent of the governed." The southern culture was insistent that the Federal Government honor State rights as guaranteed in the Federal Constitution. For the most part *The Nation Builders* were of the southern culture. The southern culture was dominant among the populations from Maryland and Delaware southward to Florida; across the southern halves of Ohio, Indiana and Illinois and down through Kentucky and Tennessee to the Gulf Coast, and from Missouri through Arkansas and Louisiana and westward through Texas. Far more than half of the settled land east of the Rocky Mountains belonged to people of the southern culture. The vast majority of African Americans lived among people of the southern culture, including all bonded African Americans and more than half of all independent African Americans. The southern States had not experienced heavy immigration from Europe during the 1840's and the 1850's, so its population was, culturally speaking, rather uniform.

Second, there was the northern States culture, typified by the people of Massachusetts; who had been often reluctant to support westward territorial expansion; who had consistently argued for high import taxes to artificially inflate prices of domestic goods, and who had generally advocated expanding the power of the Federal Government beyond that allowed in the Federal Constitution. The northern culture had origins in the restrictive church-state society of colonial Massachusetts and its neighboring colonies. This culture had spread westward from Massachusetts across the Great Lakes regions to Minnesota. The northern culture exhibited a "holier than thou" attitude toward others and an aggressive personality — traits that people of the southern culture often found irritating and unmannerly. Religious infatuations with Transcendentalism and Rationalism had confused the northern culture and led it away from the core, Biblical Christian values held by many of the southern culture.

During the 1840's and 1850's heavy immigration from Europe into the Northern States — from Massachusetts and surrounding States, westward along the Great Lakes — especially from Ireland and the Germanic States — had created a cultural mix in the northern States that was not present in the southern States.

In *Bloodstains*, Volume 2, *The Demagogues*, during the 1850's, you learned about the various ways politicians exploited this new cultural mix of native born and immigrant, giving rise to many political parties and political strategies. But, in spite of the rapid immigration and population expansion, the old-family northern culture had remained politically dominant, consolidating power in the amazing eruption of the Republican Party during the 1856 elections.

Excerpting further from *Bloodstains*, Volume 2, *The Demagogues*, I now present a summary of how the Republican Party and the Abe Lincoln Administration initiated the war I am calling the "Federal Invasion of the Confederacy":

Abe Lincoln had proclaimed the Federal Invasion of the Confederacy on April 15, 1861. The first day of *Bloodstains*, Volume 3, *The Bleeding*, is 5 days later, April 20, 1861. I will give you a little background; then we will resume the *Bloodstains* narrative history at April 20.

Lincoln's war was the culmination of the political Sectionalism that had divided those United States into two antagonistic sections. One section, the northern States, had recently become politically dominated by the Republican Party, a new organization which had come to power in those States by agitating over Terrorism in "Bleeding Kansas," by agitating for exclusion of bonded African Americans from the National Territories and all future States, and by inciting hatred toward southern States politicians by tricks such as "Bleeding Sumner." The Republican Party did not exist in the southern States. Republicans wanted it that way.

By late 1856 the Republican Party had become very powerful in the northern States and was rapidly gaining control of State Governments in that section, eventually winning control of every northern State government by early 1861. Although Abe Lincoln, a lawyer in Springfield, Illinois, had been of little political significance in the early 1850's, he had been the most influential politician during the founding of the Illinois Republican Party in 1856.

The Republican Party, in its 1860 Northern States Convention at Chicago, had nominated Abe Lincoln for President. At that time Democrats were mortally divided. Why?

> Firstly, because of political agitation in the northern States over excluding bonded African Americans from the National Territories and all future States.

> Secondly, because of Illinoisan Stephen Douglas' demand that Democrats nominate him for President without compromise.

These political strains had produced a devastating split in the Democratic Party at its 1860 National Convention at Charleston, South Carolina. Therefore, Republicans easily won the election for President by carrying all of the northern States in a four-way race.

The Republican Party's reliance on Sectionalism and its intentions to diminish State rights and expand Federal power had persuaded 7 coastal States to secede from the Federal Government before Democrat James Buchanan's term as President had expired — these States were South Carolina, Georgia, Florida, Alabama, Mississippi, Louisiana and Texas.

By the way, you should know that, in 1860, the Federal Constitution disallowed any method for preventing State secession. State secession was not rebellion. It was only undoing the political process by which a seceding State had empowered the Federal Government at the latter's birth. This political principle is an essential historical fact that the student of true American history cannot ignore or corrupt.

Well, those seceded States had joined together to form the Confederate States of America and had elected Jeff Davis to be Provisional President. And Davis had dispatched Confederate Commissioners to Washington City to meet with the upcoming Lincoln Administration and, hopefully, seek political accommodations between the two nations.

But, from the first day in power, the Lincoln Administration had refused to recognize State secession or the Confederacy and had alleged that people in seceded States were in rebellion against their respective State Governments. Abe Lincoln refused to communicate with the Confederate Commissioners even once. He was the foremost advocate of conquering the Confederacy by military force and subjugating her States. From the outset, well before coming to Washington City, Lincoln had decided on war instead of compromise and peaceful coexistence.

Seeking a pretext for his war, Lincoln had embraced a Federal Navy scheme to, from a staging area in the New York Naval Yard, simultaneously dispatch Federal fleets of warships and transports to Fort Sumter at Charleston and to Fort Pickens in Florida. These were the only forts in the Confederate States that were manned by Federal soldiers. Lincoln had persuaded his Cabinet to agree to the Navy mission — intended to incite the Confederates to fire the "first shot" — which he believed would help him win support among the people of the northern States for his war of invasion.

It would take the Lincoln Administration 16 days to carry out the military scheme aimed at gaining its pretext for war. Abe Lincoln's fleet of Charleston-bound warships began arriving offshore, outside of Charleston Harbor, on April 11. The next day, April 12, under orders from President Jeff Davis, Confederates fired artillery at Fort Sumter for many hours, intending to drive off the Federal garrison before the warships entered the harbor. For a while Federals answered with artillery fire from the fort. The Federal garrison surrendered on April 13 and agreed to leave on April 14. The Federal warships never entered the entrance to the harbor and never fired any guns. They left, too. No one was killed on either side by the artillery shells, but that did not deter Lincoln. He had his "first shot" excuse for proclaiming his invasion campaign.

The next day, April 15, Abe Lincoln Proclaimed the Federal Invasion of the Confederacy and the Federal War Department sent telegrams to every State capital demanding that each State immediately provide militiamen in the amount specified. A total of 75,000 State militiamen were thus demanded.

Every northern State was controlled by a Republican Governor, and they had been preparing their State militia for a quick response to the anticipated call for troops. Regiments of Massachusetts militiamen would be quickly boarding railroad cars for the trip south and be passing through Baltimore, Maryland 4 days later. There, the first war deaths occurred.

The Governors of Delaware, Maryland, Kentucky, Missouri, Virginia, North Carolina, Tennessee and Arkansas — States where the Republican Party was without any political influence — refused to send the militiamen Lincoln had requested. The Virginia Constitutional Convention, still in session in Richmond awaiting developments, voted to secede on April 17, two days after Lincoln's Proclamation. North Carolina, Tennessee and Arkansas would successfully secede and join the Confederacy.

The first military objective of the Lincoln Administration was to subjugate the State Governments of Delaware, Maryland, Kentucky and Missouri, all of which were mostly controlled by Democrats and all of which were essentially devoid of Republicans.

It is instructive to view the "War Between the States" as having been the "War Between the Republican Party and the Democratic Party." It is even more instructive to view it as the "Republican Party Military Campaign to Conquer the Democratic Party," whose people just wanted to be left alone and govern themselves.

From this point forward Exclusionism, the major political passion that had empowered the Republican Party throughout the Federal States, is firm government policy and no long a political issue. Without question bonded African Americans would be excluded from all National Territories and all future States. The only remaining political issue involving African Americans is the choice between Deportationism and Abolitionism. Deportationists want African Americans made independent and immediately deported to Africa, Central America and, or South America. Abolitionists want bonded African Americans made independent in the Federal States of Delaware, Maryland, Kentucky, and Missouri and in the States of the Confederacy. If they are pure of heart, they are willing to let them remain in those States and perhaps even migrate into the northern States and live there. But the more militant Republican faction wants to delay this, to keep them bonded in Delaware, Maryland, Kentucky and Missouri throughout the military invasion campaign — but, as a military measure, immediately make them independent in the States of the Confederacy, expecting the resulting turmoil to facilitate their conquest. But Exclusionism still remains a guttural passion of European Americans living in the northern States. That passion is not dead. It will resurface as a political force that attempts to impede African American migration into the northern States, for their migration northward will be a major fear following the conquest of the Confederacy.

From reading *Bloodstains*, Volume 3, *The Bleeding*, you will recall that Abe Lincoln had called for a special session of the Federal House and Senate on July 4, 1861. We realize that he was delaying that gathering until he hopefully had subjugated Maryland, Kentucky and Missouri and prepared the Federal military for a successful launch of his invasion of the Confederacy. Then, in July, Abe Lincoln would justify before the Federal House and Senate his invasion of the Confederacy by alleging that he had been "trapped by events beyond his control." He would pretend that his naval missions to land Federal reinforcements and supplies at Fort Sumter and at Fort Pickens in no way constituted acts of aggression. He would pretend the Confederate States of America did not exist as he spun tales about insurrection against State governments. He would pretend that Federal defensive forces were under attack by aggressive soldiers of the Confederate Government who were seeking to destroy the Federal Government — not the other way around — thereby alleging that his call for troops was merely a defensive response to that alleged threat of aggression. He would allege to the Federal House and Senate that "no choice was left but to call out the war power of the Government; and so to resist force, employed for its destruction, by force, for its preservation." [R6;294]

Between April 20, and June 3, 1861 events moved at rapid speed as additional States seceded and joined the Confederacy. The people of Maryland, Kentucky and Missouri struggled against tyranny but failed to avoid Federal subjugation. The Confederate Government relocated to Richmond, and Federals began the invasion of the Confederacy with successful attacks upon vulnerable northwestern Virginia.

It was early in the Federal Invasion campaign, on June 3, 1861, the event that Joseph Smith had prophesied came to pass, and Stephen Douglas did "feel the weight of the hand of the Almighty upon" his body as he drew his last breath at the age of 48 years. And it was late in that invasion campaign, on April 14, 1865, that John Wilkes Booth killed Abe Lincoln at Ford's Theater. So, of the five major political leaders whose lives have helped us understand so much of the era covered in Bloodstains, only Jeff Davis, Charles Sumner and Thad Stevens remain.

Condensed Histories of Political Control of Subjugated and Conquered States as Viewed from May 23, 1865

This chapter presents the story of the Republican Party's program of Political Reconstruction on a State-by-State basis. *Bloodstains* presents the detailed State history only for South Carolina and Mississippi and considerable, but limited history of Louisiana, recognizing that far too little room exists in this book series to treat in detail every one of the 15 effected States. So, it is in this chapter that the history is presented for the remaining States, such as Kentucky and Arkansas. In reviewing this history, be reminded that the American Civil War was a political struggle between Republicans and Democrats, which escalated into State Secession followed by military conquest. In the States of the northern culture, Republicans, through their sectional Party, had risen to power, from beginnings in 1854, with an agenda to expand Federal power far beyond the limits imposed by the Federal Constitution — being completely successful in that campaign and winning control of all northern State governments. Democrats, not sectional but national in scope, having held power for many decades, favored firmly retaining the limits on Federal power as stipulated in the Federal Constitution — in their campaigns winning overwhelming support among southern culture voters, but suffering stark defeat in the States dominated by the northern culture. So in reading the State political histories presented below, keep in mind that the swings from Democrat control to Republican control to military control to Republican control to Democrat control reveal the rise and fall of Republican Political Reconstruction. Yet, we observe that the final result or Political Reconstruction all across the country, both north and south, was the destruction of the Constitution's limits to Federal power, opening the floodgates for that power to grow and grow into the enormous being it is today, reducing the power of each State to little more than a super-sized county.

Delaware

Democrats remained relevant in Delaware with minimal difficulty. Democrat William Burton had held the office of Governor of Delaware from January 1859 to January 1863. He was a physician and a long-time Democrat from the southern part of the little, three-county State. Burton was replaced by Democrat-turned-Republican William Cannon, who held the office of Governor beginning in January 1863. Cannon was a wealthy merchant from southern Delaware. A former Democrat, he had obediently switched to the Republican Party in 1862, a process perhaps considered temporary. Upon Cannon's death in March 1865, the Speaker of the Delaware Senate, Gove Saulsbury, Democrat, rose to the office of Governor. Saulsbury was a physician from Dover, located in the center of the State. The Delaware Governor's office would be in firm Democrat control for the next 6 years under Saulsbury's leadership, until January 1871. And it would be 30 years into the future, 1901, before the Delaware Republican Party would become powerful enough to hold the office of Governor. Thereafter, Delaware would be a two-party State.

Maryland

Surrounding the Federal Capital of Washington, the Maryland State Government had been the most vulnerable to Republican subjugation, much of it reported in Volume 3, *The Bleeding*. Augustus Bradford of Baltimore, supported by the Maryland Union Party, had held the office of Governor since January 1862. His term would end in January 1966, when he would be replaced by Thomas Swann, of Baltimore and also of the Maryland Union Party. Swann would hold the office until January 1869. While in office he would switch to the Maryland Democrat Party. The Maryland Democratic Party would retain the office of Governor, uninterrupted, for 27 more years, through 1896.

Kentucky

Among the four Democrat States of the southern culture that had been subjugated by Republican forces in the first months of the conflict, Kentucky is most suitable for an extended historical presentation. Delaware was too small to matter; Maryland was too close to the capital to have a chance to preserve State Rights, and Missouri was too politically divided internally to be representative — St. Louis was a large city and the gateway to the West with a large German population and land along the Missouri River and north of it was easy to reach and due west of Illinois. For this reason, the history for Kentucky is expanded.

You will recall that the Whig Party had been very influential in Kentucky prior to its demise following the Zachary Taylor/Millard Fillmore Administration of 1849 to 1853. Influential Kentucky Whigs had included Henry Clay and John Crittenden. The Kentucky Whig Party had controlled the office of Governor from 1836 to 1851, finally giving it up to Democrat Lazarus Powell, who held the office from 1851 to 1855 (Afterward, Democrat Powell had represented Kentucky in the Federal Senate from March 1859 to March 1865). A former Whig turned Know Nothing, Charles Morehead, had succeeded Powell as Governor, giving the Whig Party one last gasp, from September 1855 to August 1859. Thereafter politicians opposed to the Democratic Party had organized around other names, reflecting more or less friendly attitudes toward the ambitions of the sectional Republican Party north of the Ohio River.

Democrat Beriah Magoffin had been Governor of Kentucky since August 1859 and was in office when Abe Lincoln called for troops to invade the Confederacy (and, although unsaid, to quickly subjugate other Democrat States, including Kentucky). Magoffin had refused to provide troops and stood firmly for a neutral status for his State. But, as you know, Federals had proceeded to subjugate Kentucky anyway, arming militants with the State and intimidating the Legislature and those inclined to support letting Confederate States secede in peace. By summer of 1862 the Kentucky Legislature had pressured Magoffin to resign the office of Governor, which he agreed to do if allowed to pick his successor, because Lieutenant Governor Democrat Lynn Boyd had died. A deal had been struck — Speaker of the Kentucky Senate John Fisk, a "Union Democrat," to whom Magoffin was opposed, stepped down, the Senate elected Magoffin's man James Robinson, a "moderate conservative," to the Speaker's Chair, Magoffin resigned, Robinson rose to the office of Governor, and the Senate re-elected Fisk as Speaker. By that method Democrat James Robinson became Governor. A Kentucky lawyer, Robinson had been a Whig when elected to the Kentucky Senate in 1851, but had switched to the Democratic Party. He completed Magoffin's term as a Democrat in September 1863.

The 1863 contest to elect a new Governor to replace James Robinson had been spirited to say the least. Kentuckians favoring negotiating an end to the military invasion campaign had called themselves Peace Democrats and nominated Charles Wickliffe for Governor. By the way, as a Whig Lieutenant Governor, Wickliffe had once before risen to be Governor of Kentucky, from 1839 to 1840, finishing the term of fellow Whig James Clark, so he was familiar to older voters. Kentuckians favoring the Federal agenda had organized as the Union Democratic Party and nominated Thomas Bramlette for Governor. Born in Kentucky, a lawyer and a Judge beginning in 1856, Bramlette had resigned from the bench in August 1861 to join the Federal Army. Then in July 1862, he had resigned from the Army to accept Abe Lincoln's appointment as U. S. District Attorney for Kentucky. In that capacity he had vigorously enforced war-time laws against Confederate sympathizers. To ensure a Bramlette victory, the Federal authority over Kentucky had thrown Wickliffe in jail to intimidate voters and prevent his election. The vote tally showed that Union Democrat Bramlette defeated imprisoned Peace Democrat Charles Wickliffe by 68,000 versus 18,000. Federal intimidation (striking names off ballots, martial law, arrests, disfranchisement, loyalty oath demands, etc.) and the absence of Kentucky voters who were away fighting in the Confederate Army had reduced the vote total to approximately half of that cast in 1860. Union Democrats had also won almost all of the Kentucky House and Senate contests. Although, following the election the Union Democrats had consistently denounced the Lincoln Administration when campaigning, they had supported the invasion campaign from Bramlette's taking office in September 1863 forward to May 23, 1865. Bramlette would also be supporting the Republican program of Political Reconstruction as it would apply to his State, so we ought to consider Bramlette to actually be a Republican.

In August 1864, Abe Lincoln, to influence the election for President, had again proclaimed martial law in Kentucky and suspended the writ of *habeas corpus* and the Federal commander over Kentucky had used it liberally, angering many in the State. Nevertheless, in November 1864 the Democrat Party carried Kentucky for George McClellan, defeating native son Lincoln in the State by a wide margin. Not counting the soldier vote, McClellan received 61,478 votes versus 26,592 for Lincoln. The votes totaled less that two thirds of those cast in 1860.

In February 1865, as the conquest of the Confederacy neared its climax, Senator Lazarus Powell of Kentucky had won approval of a Federal law prohibiting interference in elections by the Federal military, but the State remained under martial law. Although Kentuckians hoped for less Federal interference in future elections, Federal interference would continue.

On another subject, during early 1865, African Americans were reported to be "almost valueless as laborers" as many drifted about the State and congregated in the larger towns and cities. You will recall that Abe Lincoln's Proclamation declaring Confederate bonded African Americans to be independent had excluded those living in Kentucky. During February the Kentucky Legislature had rejected the Federal Amendment to make Bonded African Americans Independent (13th) — in the House by a vote of 57 versus 28 and in the Senate and by a 21 to 12 vote. A Federal tabulation estimated the 1860 population of Kentucky bonded African Americans at 230,000. Of those, 28,818 of the men had been enticed into the Federal Army, making them and an estimated 72,000 wives and children legally independent by virtue of military service. Approximately half of the remaining 129,000 were estimated to have been made legally independent by virtue of their owners having joined the Confederate Army. Therefore, only about 65,000 were assumed to still be legally bonded as of mid-1865.

Following the Legislature's rejection of the Federal Amendment to make Bonded African Americans Independent (13th), the commander of Federal troops in Kentucky, John Palmer of Illinois, began a broad and persistent campaign to make these remaining 65,000 bonded African Americans independent anyway. First, he demobilized European American soldiers first, retaining his African American troops until last. Even after the surrender of the Confederate Army in Virginia, Palmer had African American soldiers going about the state recruiting African American men who were found wandering or without work and this was continuing into June. By mid-May his soldiers were handing out freedom-to-travel passes to any African American willing to take one, and a steady stream of them were crossing the Ohio River into Ohio, Indiana and Illinois. By the end of May 5,000 would have crossed the Ohio River from Louisville alone.

Overall, the political attitudes of European American Kentuckians had not changed over the war years. They still believed in State Rights and were overwhelmingly opposed to the Republican Party of the northern States. Many Kentucky men were returning from fighting in the Confederate Army, generally to heroes' welcomes, and there was much talk about men of their beliefs regaining control of the Kentucky State Government. But, as of May 23, 1865, Union Democrats firmly controlled the State Government and the Federal Government still had the people of Kentucky under martial law.

By 1867, with Republican energies focused on Political Reconstruction of the conquered Confederate States, control over Kentucky would be relaxed and that year's election would give men a chance to vote with their hearts for a Kentucky State Government controlled by the Democratic Party. That they would do, electing Democrats John Helm as Governor and John Stevenson as Lieutenant Governor. But Helm would die in office, after serving only 5 days. Therefore, Democrat Stevenson almost immediately would rise to the office of Governor to complete the term in February 1871.

Thereafter, the Kentucky Democratic Party, led mostly by returning Confederate veterans, would control the office of Governor until 1895, a span of 27 years. From that point onward Kentucky would experience a two-Party system, with both Democrats and Republicans holding office at times.

Missouri

Since 1861, Missouri had been engaged in a State Civil War, raging within a War Between the States, making political control a series of conflicts. After Federals had secured their subjugation of the Missouri State Government, Republicans controlled the office of Governor. In that context, Willard Hall had held the office of Governor from January 1864 to January 1865. A Missourian and former Democrat representing Missouri in the Federal House, Hall had supported the Republican Party in the struggle within his State in reaction to the Federal subjugation campaign, and had commanded a national guard unit supportive of the Federal cause. In January 1865, Hall had been replaced by Thomas Fletcher, who would be Governor until January 1869. Fletcher had been a Republican since 1856 and had commanded Missouri and Federal troops in many Civil War battles. Gratz Brown, a Republican in the Federal Senate since 1864, would resign and replace Fletcher, running the office of Governor until January 1873. As noted in *Bloodstains*, Volume 2, *The Demagogues*, Brown had been a key founder of the Missouri Republican Party, organized to support the campaign for Abe Lincoln. Brown would be replaced in 1873 by Democrat Silas Woodson, who would hold the job until January

1875. Thereafter, Democrats would hold the office of Governor, uninterrupted, until 1909, a span of 36 years.

Virginia

Virginia was the State which Federals had divided into two governments in the second year of the Invasion Campaign, creating the so-called State of West Virginia. Francis Pierpont had been a leader in setting up an 1862 secession movement among western Virginia counties, which had become occupied by Federal forces and isolated from fellow Virginians by repeating north-south mountain ridges that oriented residents toward the Ohio River while isolating them from central and eastern Virginia. Thus was created West Virginia.

Abe Lincoln had rewarded Pierpont by appointing him to lead a so-called shadow Virginia Government set up just south of Washington City. So, when Richmond fell to Federal forces in the Spring of 1865 and the Confederate Government retreated into North Carolina, Abe Lincoln appointed Francis Pierpont to be the Provisional Governor of the conquered State of Virginia. Pierpont would hold that job from May 1865 to April 1868, a point when the More Militant Republicans in the Federal House and Senate would take control of governing the conquered States and established their program of Political Reconstruction. This would establish John Schofield as Military Ruler over Virginia, who in turn would name Henry Wells as Governor. Wells was a Federal army commander and political opportunist from Michigan.

After military rule was relaxed, Democrat Gilbert Walker would win election to the office of Governor, assuming the job in September 1869 and holding it until January 1874. Democrats would hold the office of Governor thereafter until 1970, that is except for a brief episode when the Democratic Party would split into factions contesting how Virginia and West Virginia were to share in paying off past bond debt (Readjuster debate) — a period of Democrat rule which would last 101 years.

By the way, the last Democrat to hold the office of Governor prior to 1970 would be Mills Godwin, Jr. In 1969 the Virginia Republican Party would offer candidate Lynwood Holton, who would win the office of Governor. As a young man, politically active and living in Virginia at the time, I would attend the Virginia State Convention, support Holton and work to win his election. I recall it being an historic event, but do not recall realizing at the time that the Republican Party had been shut out of the office of Governor for 101 years. Virginians had been slow to see merit in the Republican Party. Their ancestors had suffered so much 100-odd years earlier. Although, by 1969, Republicans and Democrats would have swapped political philosophies concerning what constituted good government, the majority of Virginia voters would have remained true to their ancestor's political beliefs. So, in that year, the majority would simply leave the Democratic Party, embrace Republicans and elect their candidate for Governor.

West Virginia

As you recall, in violation of the Federal Constitution and the Virginia State Constitution, the so-called State of West Virginia had been created by the Federal Government on June 20, 1863, with Republican Arthur Boreman holding the office of Governor until February 1869. Republican William Stevenson, also of the western counties, would hold the office from March 1869 until March 1871. He would be followed by John Jacob, who would occupy the office in March 1871, briefly as an Independent, then as a Democrat. The Democratic Party would control the office of Governor from that point until 1897.

As a requirement for becoming a new State, Abe Lincoln had demanded that the West Virginia State Constitution make immediately independent the few bonded African Americans who lived in those former Virginia counties, a demand encouraged by the occupying Federal troops and agreed to by the leaders who supported secession from Virginia. Francis Pierpont, of western Virginia, had been an active leader of the western county secession movement from its beginning and was rewarded with the position of Provisional Governor of the Republican Party's so-called shadow government of Virginia, situated just across the Potomac River from the Federal capital.

North Carolina

Zebulon Vance had been the Governor of Confederate North Carolina since September 1862 and would leave the office on May 29, 1865 in response to the Federal conquest of his State. For the office of

Provisional Governor, Andrew Johnson would quickly appoint William Holden, a Raleigh newspaperman who had become comfortable calling himself a Republican. Johnson had been impressed by Holden's outspoken criticism of the Confederate Government during the 4-year defensive effort. Conservative Jonathan Worth, also of North Carolina, would be elected to replace Holden and hold the office from December 1865 to July 1868. While out of office, Holden had worked to organize the North Carolina Republican Party and its Political Machine, which would permit him to win election and hold the office of Governor from July 1868 to December 1870. Two other North Carolina Republicans would follow Holden in the office — Tod Caldwell (December 1870 to July 1874) and Curtis Brogden (July 1874 to January 1877). Republican rule would be terminated by the 1876 election of Zebulon Vance, who would hold the office from January 1877 to February 1879. Except for a 4-year period (1897 to 1901), Democrats would hold the office of Governor of North Carolina until 1973, for by that time Democrat politics would be too liberal to consistently win elections.

Tennessee

Only 10 weeks prior to May 23, 1865, Andrew Johnson had been the Military Governor of conquered Tennessee, based in the capital at Nashville (the Federal's first major conquest), having been appointed to that post in October 1862 and having given it up on March 4, 1865 to enable his rise to the Office of Federal Vice President. In fact, in earlier years (October 1853 to November 1857), Johnson had been the elected Democrat Governor of Tennessee, that being prior to his election to the Federal Senate, also as a Democrat. Johnson, formerly a tailor from eastern Tennessee, had been a prominent Democrat in the State's politics for many years. Edward East, a Tennessee lawyer who had opposed secession and become a Republican, had risen to the office of Governor when Johnson left to become Vice President. East's days in the Governor's office had been short, however, for, with Federals overseeing the election process, Republican William Brownlow had been elected to the office and assumed it on April 5, 1865.

Tennessee would escape the Military Rule era of Republican Political Reconstruction, the only conquered State to be so spared.

William Brownlow, who would hold the office of Governor until February 1869, had been and would be a notable figure in Tennessee politics. Originally a circuit-riding preacher in Virginia and North Carolina, Brownlow had settled in eastern Tennessee and become an outspoken newspaperman. He had opposed Tennessee secession and her defense against Federal invasion forces. Opposition from Tennessee Confederates had forced him to flee north during the thick of fighting, where he had toured northern States, agitating in favor of the Federal campaign of conquest. Brownlow would be replaced by Republican Speaker of the Tennessee Senate, Dewitt Senter, in February 1869, in response to the former's election to the Federal Senate.

Dewitt Senter, also of Tennessee, would be replaced by Democrat John Brown on October 10, 1871. Brown would hold the office of Governor until January 1875. Formerly a lawyer in middle Tennessee and a supporter of secession, Brown had joined the Tennessee militia in 1861 as a private and risen steadily in rank, eventually rising to the rank of Major General. He had participated in numerous battles, including the horrific Battle of Franklin where 6 of his fellow Confederate Generals had been killed. He and his men had been surrendered with Joe Johnston's forces in 1865. With the exception of 8 years, Democrats would hold the office of Tennessee Governor until 1971, a span of 100 years of almost unbroken Democrat rule.

Arkansas

After Federals had gained control over Arkansas, Abe Lincoln arranged a special election for the office of Governor, which replaced Democrat Governor Harris Flanagin with Republican Isaac Murphy, the latter taking office on April 18, 1864. Although born in Pennsylvania, Murphy was of Arkansas. Democrat Harris Flanagin had held the office of Governor since November 1862.

When Arkansas became subject to Military Rule, a special election elevated a Federal commander, Powell Clayton, to the office of Governor, effective July 1868. Of Pennsylvania and Kansas, Clayton had fought with Federals in Missouri and Arkansas, rising to the rank of brigadier general of volunteers in August 1864. Clayton would be elected to the Federal Senate and take his seat in March 1871. This would elevate Republican Ozra Hadley to the office of Acting Governor. Hadley was of New York and

Minnesota. Republican Elisha Baxter would follow Hadley, holding the office of Governor to November 1874. Baxter would the last Republican Governor of the era.

Democrat Augustus Garland would be elected Governor of Arkansas, ending the era of Political Reconstruction, and holding the office from November 1874 to January 1877. Born in Tennessee and of Arkansas, Garland had been a lawyer and politician in his State as well as a member of the Confederate Congress in Richmond. When Republicans moved in Congress to prevent former Confederates from practicing law, he challenged the act and won the argument in the Federal Supreme Court, greatly helping former Confederates to navigate the legal pitfalls in various Political Reconstruction laws (*Ex parte Garland*, January 14, 1867, a 5 versus 4 decision). He would be elected to the Federal Senate, holding his seat from 1877 to 1885. Grover Cleveland would appoint him U. S. Attorney General; he would be confirmed and he would hold that job from March 1885 to March 1889.

Thereafter, Democrats would consistently hold the office of Arkansas Governor — that is except for the unusually well-financed campaign by the grandson of John D. Rockefeller, Winthrop, who would briefly parlay his family's huge wealth into political success in his adopted State. As a Republican, Winthrop Rockefeller would hold the office of Governor from 1867 to 1971. As a practical matter, it would not be until the 1980 election of Republican Frank White that a normal Republican candidate would win the office of Arkansas Governor, thereby ending 108 years of Democrat control of the State. Democrat Bill Clinton would succeed Republican White as Governor (1983-1992). Soon afterward Republican Mike Huckabee would win the office (1996 to 2007). Therefore, it would not be until 108 years after the end of the Political Reconstruction Era that Arkansas would become a two-party State.

South Carolina

Columbia, lay prostrate, severely destroyed by William Sherman's Devastators — 60,000 strong — having begun their hateful work by leaving Atlanta in flames on November 15, 1864, a few days after Abe Lincoln's reelection, and concluding with the burning of South Carolina's capital city on February 18, 1865. You will recall from reading of the destruction in *Bloodstains*, Volume 3, *The Bleeding*:

> "They burned Columbia and stole or destroyed everything of value. The citizens were terrorized and rapists roamed the streets, falling upon confused African American girls and women more often than the more wary European American females. Sherman's Federals destroyed all the public buildings, all the factories, 1,300 homes, and even the Ursuline Convent. A minister wrote, 'Hell was empty, and all its devils were in this devoted city, learning new deviltry from [Federal] teachers. A perfect reign of terror existed'." [V3, page 492]

Among the many buildings destroyed in and around Columbia were Wade Hampton's home and his late father's grand residence, Millwood Mansion, where brother Kit and the sisters had been living. So Wade and Kit would be making plans to replace the loss with two new, but modest, homes. Governor Andrew Magrath, having earlier retreated upstate to Greenville with the Government, returned on May 3, seeing ashes where the once-beautiful Capitol building had stood. Yet, State Government officials, in accordance with Governor Magrath's executive order of May 12, were making a best effort attempt to carry out their job functions, within the framework of a conquered State. But their submissive attitude would not satisfy Federal troops, which would soon arrive, on May 25, and arrest Governor Magrath and imprison him in Fort Pulaski, near Savannah. Wade Hampton was in Columbia by mid-May, having left the family in safety in Yorkville. He had probably already submitted to Federal authority and signed military personal surrender/parole papers.

The remainder of the South Carolina story will be told in great detail in future pages as we follow Wade Hampton.

Georgia

Democrat Joseph Brown was Governor of Georgia as of May 23, 1865, having held that office since November 1857. Three weeks later, on June 17, Andrew Johnson would replace Brown with Democrat James Johnson (no relation), a Georgia lawyer who had opposed secession and avoided supporting the Confederate defensive effort. Governor Johnson would hold the office only briefly, being replaced by Democrat Charles Jenkins on December 14, 1865. Born in South Carolina and at the time of his election as Governor a Justice of the State Supreme Court, Jenkins would hold the office of Governor until Military Rule was imposed on the State.

Thomas Ruger, as Military Ruler, would occupy the office of Governor from January 1868 to July 1868. Born in New York and trained at West Point, Ruger had been practicing law in Wisconsin when Abe Lincoln called for troops. You will recall Ruger as a prominent commander of Federal troops during the resulting military campaign. A few months later the newly-organized Republican Political Machine would elect Republican Rufus Bullock over Democrat John Gordon (a prominent former Confederate commander), the winner holding the office of Governor from July 1868 to October 1871. Born in New York, Bullock had moved to Atlanta in 1857 for a job with a telegraph company. When Bullock would be forced to resign near the end of his term, Republican Benjamin Conley, President of the Georgia Senate, would be elevated to the office of Governor. Although born in New Jersey Conley had arrived in Georgia in his youth. He would hold the office for only 2 months before ending the era of Republican Political Reconstruction in Georgia. Conley would be turning the office over to Democrat James Smith on January 12, 1872.

Democrat James Smith would begin an era of 131 years of unbroken Democrat rule. Born in Georgia, a successful lawyer, a member of the Confederate Congress and a former commander in the Confederate Army, Smith had been severely wounded at the Battle of Cold Harbor (1864). He would be unopposed in the election that elevated him to the office of Governor. By the way, former Democrat Governor, Joseph Brown (1857 to 1865), would be elected to the Federal Senate and hold his seat from 1880 to 1891. Many decades later, in 2003, Republican George Perdue would hold the office of Georgia Governor, becoming the first of his Party to hold that position in a span of 131 years.

Florida

Democrat John Milton held the office of Governor of Florida from October 1861 to May 1, 1865. Born in Georgia, a lawyer and early advocate of secession and State Rights, Milton had committed suicide on May 1, 1865 rather than submit to Republican rule. The President of the Florida Senate, Democrat Abraham Allison, had stepped up to the office of Governor from that point to May 19, 1865, when the Federal conquest made the office irrelevant. Andrew Johnson would appoint, William Marvin to be Provisional Governor, and he would take office on July 13, 1865. Marvin had been born in New York and had come to Florida when Andrew Johnson had appointed him U. S. Attorney of Florida Territory at Key West. Andrew Johnson appointed Democrat David Walker to replace Marvin, and Walker would hold the office of Governor from December 1865 to July 1868. Born in New York, but having moved to Florida in 1837, Walker had been a Whig long ago and had opposed secession, but he had loyally supported the military defense of his State.

Republican Harrison Reed would hold the office of Governor from July 1868 to January 1873. Born in Massachusetts and later of Wisconsin, Reed had come to Florida in 1863 when Abe Lincoln had appointed him Tax Commissioner charged with handling seized property. Although elected Governor by the force of Florida's Republican Political Machine, Reed's four and a half years in that office would be at times rocky. In November 1868 Reed would suffer Impeachment charges when Lieutenant Governor William Gleason would proclaim himself Governor. Again, in February 1872 Reed would be forced to contend with Impeachment charges leveled by Lieutenant Governor Samuel Day. But Reed would carry on and hold the office until January 1873.

Republican Ossian Hart, a Florida lawyer who had opposed secession, would hold the office of Governor from January 1873 to his death from pneumonia in March 1874. Republican Marcellus Stearns, the Lieutenant Governor, would replace Hart and hold the office until January 1877. Born in Maine, Stearns had joined the Federal army, lost his arm and been sent to Florida, where he had remained. Stearns would be the last Republican Governor of Florida during the era of Political Reconstruction.

Democrat and businessman George Drew would hold the office of Governor from January 1877 to January 1881. Born in New Hampshire, Drew had moved to Georgia in 1847 and set up a machine shop, then moved into Florida where he had set up a saw mill and entered into the lumber business. The Republican Party would be excluded from the office of Florida Governor for the next 90 years, not winning an election to that office until 1967.

Alabama

Democrat Thomas Watts had held the office of Governor of Alabama from December 1863 to May 1, 1865, leaving in response to the Federal conquest of his State. Born in Alabama Territory, Watts was a lawyer and a farmer. Soon afterward Andrew Johnson appointed Democrat Lewis Parsons to the office of Governor. Born in New York, Parsons had moved to Alabama in 1840, practiced law and had fought in defense of the Confederacy as a Lieutenant. Democrat Robert Patton would be elected to the office of Governor, holding the office from December 1865 to July 1868. Born in Virginia, Patton had moved to Alabama in 1818 become a farmer (did not practice law), joined the Whig Party, opposed secession but supported the military defense of his State. After March 1867 Patton's authority would be severely limited as Wagner Swayne would assume a superior position as Military Governor, holding it for the remainder of Patton's term. Born in Ohio and graduated from Yale, Swayne had risen to the rank of Major General in the Federal Army, losing a leg in the course of the fighting.

Republican William Smith would hold the office of Governor from July 1868 to November 1870. Of Alabama and a lawyer, Smith had opposed secession, left his State and joined the Federal Cavalry. Although the Alabama Republican Political Machine was well organized, the next election would be won by a Democrat, an unusual event at that time among the conquered States.

Democrat Robert Lindsay would hold the office of Governor from November 1870 to November 1872. Of Scotland, Lindsay had opposed secession but fought in defense of his State in the cavalry. As the candidate of both the Alabama Democratic Party and the Alabama Conservative Party, Lindsay narrowly won out over the incumbent Republican Governor, William Smith.

But Republicans regained the office of Governor with candidate David Lewis. Of Alabama, a lawyer and a former Democrat, Lewis would be a recent convert to the Republican Party. Lewis would hold the office of Governor from November 1872 to November 1874. It would be 93 years before another Republican would hold the office.

After defeating incumbent David Lewis, Democrat George Houston would hold the office of Governor of Alabama from November 1874 to November 1878. Born in Tennessee, Houston was a lawyer and cotton farmer. A Democrat in the Federal House when Mississippi had seceded and being 50 years old at the time, Houston had decided to return home to his farm and law practice.

Mississippi

Democrat Charles Clark was the Governor of Mississippi from November 1863 to May 22, 1865, leaving the office in response to the Federal conquest of his State. Born in Ohio and moving to Mississippi where he practiced law, Clark, before being elected Governor, had been a commander over State troops, been captured, held as a prisoner of war and released. Andrew Johnson would appoint former Whig William Sharkey to the office of Provisional Governor, a term that would run from July 1865 to October 1865. Born in Tennessee, a lawyer and Justice in the Mississippi Supreme Court, Sharkey had been a Whig before that Party's decline, had opposed secession and had withheld his support of the defense of his State. Democrat Benjamin Humphreys would be elected Governor and hold the office from October 1865 to June 1868. Born in Mississippi, Humphreys was a former Brigadier General in the Confederate Army.

After Republicans imposed Military Rule, Adelbert Ames would be appointed Military Governor of Mississippi, an office he would control from June 1868 to March 1870. Ames was also Military Ruler over Mississippi and Arkansas. Born in Maine and graduated from West Point, Ames would be engaged in command of Federal troops throughout the invasion campaign (by the way, he had married the daughter of Ben "Beast" Butler of Massachusetts). Ames would be a major figure in Mississippi Republican politics during the era of Political Reconstruction. Getting himself elected as a Republican to the Federal Senate, Ames would smoothly transition from the office of Governor to the Senate, holding that position from March 1870 to 1874.

Republican James Alcorn would hold the office of Governor from March 1870 to November 1871. Born in Illinois, then living in Kentucky, then Mississippi, Alcorn was a lawyer, wealthy land holder and cotton farmer. In earlier years he had been a Whig. Alcorn had fought in defense of the Confederacy, risen to Brigadier General and for a while had been held as a prisoner of war. Getting himself elected to the Federal Senate, Alcorn would resign the office of Governor in November 1871 to relocate to Washington City. Republican Lieutenant Governor Ridgley Powers would finish Alcorn's term as Governor (November 1871 to January 1874). Adelbert Ames would resign his seat in the Federal Senate and again hold the office of Governor of Mississippi, this time from January 1874 to March 1876. And this would be the last Republican to hold that office until 1992, 116 years into the future.

Democrat John Stone would hold the office of Governor from March 1876 to January 1882. Initially Stone had risen to the office of Governor from the position of President of the Mississippi Senate at the time that Adelbert Ames resigned to avoid an Impeachment trial. Afterward, Stone would win re-election to the office, holding it until January 1882. Born in Tennessee and relocating to Mississippi, Stone had fought in the Confederate Army. He had been captured in early 1865 and imprisoned at Johnson's Island, from which he was eventually released.

The history of Mississippi Political Reconstruction will be presented in great detail in later pages.

Louisiana

Of the 11 conquered States, Louisiana suffered the most protracted, contentious struggle over Political Reconstruction. It was two regions — 1), the city of New Orleans, its seaport and areas easily controlled from there and 2), the rural farming region of the State. The first fell to Federal Control early; the second did not fall until the conquest of the Confederacy was being consummated. Ben "Beast" Butler of Massachusetts had been the first Republican to rule over occupied New Orleans, early establishing a harsh military policy. From the start, New Orleans and the conquered portion of Louisiana had been a Republican experiment in Political Reconstruction.

Democrat Thomas Moore, a farmer by occupation, had held the office of Governor of Louisiana from January 1860 to January 1864, followed by Democrat Henry Allen, who would delay until June 2, 1865 giving up on maintaining what would become no more than a government in exile. Earlier, Allen, a lawyer and farmer by occupation, had been a general in the Confederate Army. Allen was loath to give up. Federals were out to kill him when he fled to Mexico and wrote a book, "*Travels of a Sugar Planter*." Yet his life would be cut short, for he would die in Mexico in April 1866 at the age of 46.

Soon after the Federal conquest of New Orleans, Andrew Johnson had appointed George Shepley as Military Governor, a job he held from July 1862 to March 1864. A Maine lawyer and Brigadier General, Shepley had exercised control over the regions of the State controlled by Federal forces, ceding the rest to Democrat Governor Thomas Moore. Exploring initial experiments in Political Reconstruction, Republicans, empowered by Federal occupation forces, had established an election process within the region of their control, resulting in the election of Michael Hahn as civilian Governor. Born in Germany, then moving to Texas, then New Orleans in 1840, Hahn was a former Democrat who had decided to support the occupiers. Hahn resigned in March 1865 to take a seat in the Federal Senate, to which he had arranged to be elected, but Republicans refused to seat him. Hahn's resignation elevated Lieutenant Governor James Wells to the office of Governor. Having inherited several sizable Louisiana farms and experienced northern States schools, Wells was comfortable in supporting the occupiers. Upon being forced out of office by General Philip Sheridan in June 1867, Wells would become Chairman of the Returning Board (responsible for certifying election results), holding that job from 1873 to 1877 and playing a significant roll in stealing for Republicans elections won by Democrats — example:

> Stealing the election for Republican Rutherford Hayes, which had been won by Democrat Samuel Tilden.

As Military Ruler over Louisiana and Texas, Philip Sheridan would appoint Republican Benjamin Flanders to the office of Governor of Louisiana, to be held from June 1867 to January 1868. Born in New Hampshire and married to a native of that State, Flanders had moved to New Orleans in 1843 to be a newspaperman. He readily supported the occupiers. Winfield Hancock would replace Sheridan as Military Ruler, dislike Flanders and replace him with Joshua Baker, a graduate of West Point and a wealthy Louisiana farmer. Although graduating from West Point, Baker had only served two years in the Federal Army (1819-1821). He would be labeled as a Democrat turned Republican. When

Hancock would depart as Military Ruler, Baker would be out as well, holding the office of Governor only from January 1868 to June 1868.

With Republican Political Reconstruction in full force, Henry Warmoth would be elected Governor and hold the job from June 1868 to December 1872. Born in Illinois, then relocating to Missouri, Warmoth was a lawyer who had fought in the Missouri infantry and then been named Judge of the Provost Court in New Orleans, where he had remained. Only 24 years old at the time of his election Warmoth would win the 1868 contest by only a small margin over the Democrat candidate. Eventually facing Impeachment charges, Warmoth would resign in December 1872, allowing Lieutenant Governor Pinckney Pinchback to rise to the office of Governor. Born in Georgia of very slight African ancestry (one eighth or less), Pinchback had moved to Ohio as a teenager, then come to New Orleans after the arrival of the Federals, helped recruit African Americans for the military and become engaged in politics. He would hold the job of Governor until January 1873.

Two men would be elected to the office of Governor to replace Pinckney Pinchback and both would attempt to form governments. Jointly supported by the Democrats and the Liberal Republican Faction, John McEnery, the apparent vote winner, would claim the office and not give up until May 1873. Supported by the "Customshouse Faction" of the Republican Party, William Kellogg, the apparent vote loser, would eventually receive military support from Ulysses Grant, force Democrat McEnery out of contention and instill himself in the office, which he would not give up until January 1877. Born in Vermont, Kellogg had moved to Illinois where he practiced law, had fought with Federals in Missouri and then received Abe Lincoln's appointment as Collector of Federal Customs in the Port of New Orleans. He was a leader of the "Customshouse Faction" of the Louisiana Republican Party.

In 1876 two men would be elected to the office of Governor to replace Republican William Kellogg, seemingly a rerun of the contested election of 1872. Both would claim the office as of January 1877. Democrat Francis Nicholls, the apparent winner by 8,000 votes, was a native of Louisiana and a brigadier general in the Confederate Army, losing a foot and an arm on separate occasions. Another leader of the "Customshouse Faction" of the State Republican Party was Stephen Packard — born in Maine, an officer in the Federal Army, and appointed by Ulysses Grant to be U. S. Marshall at New Orleans. Packard, the apparent vote loser, would claim the office of Governor briefly, fail to win military support from Rutherford Hayes and give up in April 1877, thereby ending the era of Political Reconstruction in Louisiana. It would be 103 years before a Republican would again hold the office of Governor of Louisiana, that being David Treen (1980 to 1984).

A Louisiana lawyer and farmer, Democrat Francis Nicholls would hold the office of Governor until January 1880. Later he would be elected again to the office of Governor, holding it from 1888 to 1892. He would then become Chief Justice of the Louisiana Supreme Court.

Texas

Huge in size and at the far western end of the Confederacy, Texas had proven difficult to conquer. Democrat Pendleton Murrah had been Governor since November 1863. Born in South Carolina, and a lawyer by trade, Murrah would turn over his office in June 1865 and flee to Mexico with other Confederate leaders in hopes of preserving a government in exile, I suppose. But he would soon die there of TB in August of 1865. As Lieutenant Governor, Fletcher Stockdale would rise to the office of Texas Governor, holding it until August 1865, but under the thumb of Federal occupiers. Stockdale had been a Kentuckian, moved to Texas and practiced law.

The next Governor, Andrew Hamilton, had been born in Alabama moved to Texas in 1846, practiced law and become an outspoken critic of Confederate Texas, in fact leaving his State for the Federal States midway through his home State's military defense to speak against the Confederacy. When Abe Lincoln noticed Hamilton's activism, he had named him "Governor of Texas" and sent him to New Orleans to represent a government in waiting. After the conquest was completed, Andrew Johnson, knowing of this background, would appoint Hamilton to the office of Governor of Texas, an office he would hold from June 1865 to August 1866. With Republican Hamilton in office, one would presume that Democrat Fletcher Stockdale would be irrelevant, but Texas is big country. Anyway, Stockdale would be out of the picture by August 1865.

Democrat James Throckmorton would be elected by a huge margin over the Republican candidate and take the office of Governor in August 1866. Born in Tennessee, a physician, then a lawyer, Throckmorton had fought with Confederates. As the more harsh version of Political Reconstruction arrived in Texas he would understandably refuse to comply with certain demands, resulting in his dismissal by the Military authority. As Military Ruler, Philip Sheridan would appoint Elisha Pease to replace Throckmorton as civilian Governor, to take the office in June 1867. Born in Connecticut, Pease had moved to Mexican Texas in 1835 at the age of 24 and had been elected Governor of the State of Texas at the age of 41, holding the office from 1853 to 1857. So Pease was an experienced Texan in tune with his people, so one would think. But, to the contrary, perhaps due to former ties to Connecticut, Pease was supporting the Federals and was a key leader in establishing a Texas Republican Party. However, he would fail to gain significant support from Texas Republicans or Democrats and would resign in September 1869.

Republican Edmund Davis would replace Republican Pease as Governor. Born in Florida and arriving in newly-independent Texas in 1848, Davis had opposed secession so earnestly in 1861 that he had fled the State for New Orleans, where he expressed support for the Federal occupying force. He had then traveled to the Federal capital where Abe Lincoln asked him to raise a regiment from fellow Texans who had fled to Louisiana. Davis had returned to New Orleans, raised a regiment and fought for the Federals. In the 1869 race for Governor, Davis would narrowly defeat the Democrat candidate and hold the office from January 1870 to January 1874. Davis would be the last Republican Governor of Texas for the next 100 years.

Democrat Richard Coke would hold the office of Governor in January 1874. Born in Virginia, educated at William and Mary College, and entering into a career in law, Coke had arrived in Texas in 1852. He had supported secession and enlisted as a private in defense of the Confederacy. He was wounded, then raised a company of men for which he served as Captain. After the defeat of the Confederacy he would be elected to the Texas Supreme Court, but would be removed from the bench by Philip Sheridan. He would be elected to the Federal Senate and would step down as Governor in December 1876, transferring the office to Lieutenant Governor Richard Hubbard. Coke would hold his Senate seat until 1895.

Democrat Richard Hubbard would hold the office of Governor until January 1879. Born in Georgia and trained as a lawyer, Hubbard had also fought with Confederates. Grover Cleveland would appoint Hubbard to the office of Minister to Japan, where he would be engaged in important diplomacy while Japan would be emerging from a feudal society and entering onto the world stage.

Revisiting the Final Three Days of *Bloodstains*, Volume 3, *The Bleeding*

I am repeating the last three days covered in *Bloodstains*, Volume 3, *The Bleeding* as introduction to the start of Volume 4, *Political Reconstruction and The Struggle for Healing*.

May 19, 1865

The *William P. Clyde*, with Jeff, Varina and the other captives, arrived in the Chesapeake Bay on May 19 and weighed anchor off Fortress Monroe to await orders. Although Jeff Davis did not yet know it, Edwin Stanton had decided to imprison both him and Clement Clay in Fortress Monroe; masons were already busy at work converting two gun rooms into prison cells while the captives were being held aboard the Federal boat. At the same time Stanton was arranging to replace the commander at Fortress Monroe with a man he could trust to carry out his plans to break Davis' notably tough spirit. Stanton and like-minded Republicans were eager to convict Davis of treason and complicity in arranging to have Abe Lincoln killed. Since the current commander at Fortress Monroe was a West Point graduate, Stanton feared he might become sympathetic to Davis' plight. Stanton refused to consider any West Point graduate or any officer in the Federal Army. There was too much residual admiration of Davis' service as Secretary of War in the Franklin Pierce Administration. Furthermore, Stanton wanted a man from the heartland of the Republican Party. He found in the Massachusetts volunteer forces a young man who he figured would do his bidding without questions — a high-ranking State Militia commander named Nelson Miles. Ulysses Grant had recommended Miles to Stanton and his reasoning was revealed in a telegram he sent to Henry Halleck in which he said, "the object being to put an officer at Fortress Monroe who will by no possibility permit the escape of the prisoners to be confined there."

May 20

Jefferson Davis Howell was the first Confederate captive to be taken away. He was being sent to prison because he was Jeff Davis' brother-in-law. Throwing his arms around his sister, Howell assured Varina as he was led away, "They have come for me; goodbye, do not be uneasy." Varina would write in her *Memoir*, "The cheery smile of the boy, as he went over the side of the vessel to an unknown fate, haunts me yet." Varina would explain, "He and the other gentlemen of our traveling party were taken off together to their carefully concealed destination." But the major Confederate leaders in the party remained on board to await their fate.

Next, Federals prepared to transfer Alexander Stephens and John Reagan to another Federal warship, the *Tuscarora*, to transport them to be imprisoned at Fort Warren in Boston Harbor. Stephens weakly shook Jeff Davis' hand before being led away, but John Reagan, who would later write, "I loved him as I never loved any other man," found parting with Jeff ever so difficult. Reagan opened his *Bible* and read with Jeff the Sixteenth Psalm, which is attributed to King David:

"Preserve me, O God: for in thee do I put my trust.
O my soul, thou hast said unto the Lord, Thou art my Lord: my goodness extendeth not to Thee;
But to the saints that are in the earth, and to the excellent, in whom is all my delight.
Their sorrows shall be multiplied that hasten after another god: their drink offerings of blood will I not offer, nor take up their names into my lips.
The Lord is the portion of mine inheritance and of my cup: Thou maintainest my lot.
The lines are fallen unto me in pleasant places; yea, I have a goodly heritage.
I will bless the Lord, who hath given me counsel: my reins also instruct me in the night seasons.
I have set the Lord always before me: because He is at my right hand, I shall not be moved.
Therefore my heart is glad, and my glory rejoiceth: my flesh also shall rest in hope.
For Thou wilt not leave my soul in Hell; neither wilt Thou suffer Thine Holy One to see corruption.
Thou wilt shew me the path of life: in Thy presence is fullness of joy; at Thy right hand there are pleasures for evermore."

Federals put Joseph "Fighting Joe" Wheeler, Preston Johnston and F. R. Lubbock and Burton Harrison on another tugboat to be transported to their fate. Wheeler, Johnston and Lubbock would be transported to Fort Delaware. Burton Harrison would be sent to be imprisoned in Washington City. Edwin Stanton wanted Harrison close by in Washington City, figuring that, after his spirit was broken, he would be readily accessible to the team of Federal lawyers that Stanton planned to assemble to prosecute Jeff Davis and the others. Biographer Hudson Strode would write:

> "For Davis the parting with Harrison was the saddest of all. They had become deeply attached to each other. Harrison had not fought on the battlefields, because [Jeff Davis] had found him too valuable in Richmond; but nevertheless he was an outstanding hero of the Confederacy. He had often risked his life for [Davis], and had served him with an efficiency, devotion, and indefatigable cheerfulness that perhaps no other private secretary in history ever surpassed."

It was about this time, sometime in May, that William Lloyd Garrison announced that he was resigning from the American Exclusion and Abolition Society (American Antislavery Society). Apparently, Garrison figured the Society's work was finished. He said as much when he explained that he was resigning because the organization had no purpose now that African American bonding was ended. Yes, African American bonding was being outlawed everywhere, so Garrison spoke the truth when he explained Abolitionism was no longer a political issue. But the Exclusionism issue was at a crisis stage, for newly independent African Americans were awakening to new opportunities to leave the devastated southern States and migrate into the northern States, where the economy was still booming and jobs were available. The conquered States were bankrupt, as were former Confederate farmers and businessmen. Only an insignificant few had any money with which they could pay wages, even though the fields and shops cried out for workers. The meteoric rise of the Republican Party in the northern States had been enabled by Republican Exclusionism propaganda. But, ironically, the Republican conquest of the Confederacy had broken down the Pennsylvania-to-Kansas barricade — which had been so diligently strengthened over the preceding 30 years by politicians opposed to the Democratic Party — and African Americans were already moving north across that broken barricade in increasing numbers. Charles Sumner would plead with Garrison to lead the American Exclusion and Abolition Society in a new cause — that being advocating legal and voting rights for newly independent African Americans — but Garrison would have none of that. Sumner could not even inspire Garrison to join the fight against "this miserable and cruel experiment of [Andrew Johnson's]". Perhaps Garrison wanted to see Johnson succeed with his policy of retaining a remnant of State Rights while he remade the former Confederate State Governments, for preserving a remnant of State Rights would facilitate rebuilding the Pennsylvania-to-Kansas barricade against northern migration by African Americans. So, it's rather obvious that Garrison loved Exclusionism more than he loved Abolitionism. Perhaps he never loved Abolitionism, and only used Abolition rhetoric to inoculate Exclusion propaganda with a shield of self-righteousness.

Garrison would close down his propaganda organ, the *Liberator,* and ride off into the sunset. But he would not entirely succeed in shutting down the American Exclusion and Abolition Society, for Wendell Phillips would persuade a majority of Society members to keep the organization alive under his leadership. Under Phillips the Society would take on a new mission of advocating legal and voting rights for African Americans. But the disruption of the Society by Garrison's withdrawal would leave "some of Sumner's most staunch backers divided and confused."

May 22

Mary Lincoln, Tad and Robert left the President's Residence (The White House) for Chicago on this the final day chronicled in *Bloodstains,* Volume 3. For many reasons, this day, May 22, 1865, is the fitting transition between Volume 3, *The Bleeding* and Volume 4, *Political Reconstruction and The Struggle for Healing.* Elizabeth Keckley would later write about her 5 weeks with Mary, secluded in the President's Residence, the packing to return to Illinois and the agreement to go along on the trip to Chicago. During the long funeral train tour, through the northern States and out to Springfield, and through Mary's extended mourning, Andrew Johnson had patiently worked in outside offices until she decided, in her own good time, to turn over the President's Residence to him and his family. Elizabeth Keckley recalled that:

> "For five weeks [Mary] was confined to her room. Packing afforded quite a relief, as it so closely occupied us that we had not much time for lamentation. Letters of condolence were received from all parts of the country, and even from foreign potentates, but Mr. Andrew Johnson never called on the widow, or even so much as wrote a line expressing sympathy for her grief and the loss of her husband. Robert called on him one day to tell him that his mother would turn the [President's

Residence] over to him in a few days, and he never even so much as inquired after their welfare. [Mary] firmly believes that Mr. Johnson was [involved] in the assassination plot.

"In packing, [Mary] gave away everything intimately connected with [Abe], as she said that she could not bear to be reminded of the past. The articles were given to those who were regarded as the warmest of [Abe's] admirers. All of the presents passed through my hands. There was much surmise, when [Mary] left the [Residence], what her 50 or 60 boxes, not to count her score of trunks, could contain. Had the [Federal] Government not been so liberal in furnishing the boxes, it is possible that there would have been less demand for so much transportation. The boxes were loosely packed, many of them with articles not worth carrying away. [Mary] had a passion for hoarding old things, believing, with Toodles, that they were 'handy to have about the house.' The bonnets that she brought with her from Springfield, in addition to every one purchased during her residence in Washington [City], were packed in the boxes [for transport] to Chicago. She remarked that she might find use for the material some day, and it was prudent to look to the future. I am sorry to say that [Mary's] foresight in regard to the future was only confined to cast-off clothing, as she owed, at the time of [Abe's] death, different store bills amounting to $70,000. [Her husband] knew nothing of these bills, and the only happy feature of his [having been killed] was that he died in ignorance of them. Had he known to what extent his wife was involved, the fact would have embittered the only pleasant moments of his life.

"Robert was frequently in the room where the boxes were being packed, and he tried without avail to influence his mother to set fire to her vast stores of old goods. 'What are you going to do with that old dress, mother?' he would ask. 'Never mind, Robert, I will find use for it. You do not understand this business.' [To which Robert replied], 'and what is more, I hope I never may understand it. I wish to Heaven the car would take fire in which you place these boxes for transportation to Chicago, and burn all of your old plunder up;' and then, with an impatient gesture, he would turn on his heel and leave the room. . . .

"At last everything was packed, and the day for departure for [Illinois] came. I can never forget that day; it was so unlike the day when the body of the President was borne from the hall in grand and solemn state. Then thousands gathered to bow the head in reverence as the plumed hearse drove down the line. There was all the pomp of military display — drooping flags, battalions with reversed arms, and bands playing dirge-like airs. Now, the wife of the [late] President was leaving the White House, and there was scarcely a friend to tell her good-by. She passed down the public stairway, entered her carriage, and quietly drove to the depot where we took the cars. The silence was almost painful.

"It had been arranged that I should go to Chicago. When [Mary had] first suggested her plan, I strongly objected; but I had been with her so long, that she had acquired great power over me. 'I cannot go [to Chicago] with you, Mrs. Lincoln,' I [had] said, when the idea was first advanced. 'But you must go to Chicago with me, Elizabeth; I cannot do without you.' 'You forget my business, Mrs. Lincoln. I cannot leave it. Just now I have the spring trousseau to make for Mrs. Douglas, and I have promised to have it done in less than a week.' 'Never mind.' [Adele] Douglas can get some one else to make her trousseau. You may find it to your interest to go. I am very poor now, but if [the Federal House and Senate] makes an appropriation for my benefit, you shall be well rewarded. . . .'"

"When Mrs. Douglas learned that [Mary] wished me to accompany her [to Chicago], she sent me word: 'Never mind me. Do all you can for Mrs. Lincoln. My heart's sympathy is with her.' Finding that no excuse would be accepted, I made preparations to go to Chicago with [Mary]. The green [rail] car had specially been chartered for us, and in this we were conveyed to [Illinois]. Dr. [Anson] Henry accompanied us, and he [would be] remarkably attentive and kind. The first night out, [Mary] had a severe headache; and while I was bathing her temples, she said to me: 'Elizabeth, you are my best and kindest friend, and I love you as my best friend. I wish it were in my power to make you comfortable for the balance of your days. If [the Federal House and Senate] provides for me, depend upon it, I will provide for you'."

Meanwhile, on the morning of May 22, Little Jeff, then 8 years old, came running to Varina, "pale with horror," crying, "They say they have come for Father; beg them to let us go with him!" While German-speaking immigrant soldiers waited for Jeff to be handed over to them, a Federal officer brought Jeff to Varina for some brief parting words. "It is true," Jeff told Varina. "I must go at once." Then Jeff whispered into Varina's ear, "Try not to cry. They will gloat over your grief." Varina mustered enough control to comply, later writing: "The desire to lessen his anguish enabled me to bid farewell quietly." Then Jeff quickly kissed Varina and the children and walked down the gangplank to the waiting tugboat. Clement Clay was also taken down to the waiting tugboat while his wife Virginia looked on. As Varina watched Jeff ride off toward Fortress Monroe, she made a striking observation about the nature of the Federal invasion of the Confederacy. Much later she would record that observation in her *Memoir*:

"We parted in silence. As the tug bore [Jeff] away from the ship, he stood with bared head between the files of undersized German and other foreign soldiers on either side of him, and as we looked, as we thought, our last upon his stately form and knightly bearing, he seemed a man of another and higher race, upon whom 'shame would not dare to sit'."

Shortly after Jeff Davis and Clement Clay were taken off to be incarcerated in Fortress Monroe, the Federals aboard the *William P. Clyde* stole most of the items in the Clay and Davis trunks. In her *Memoir* Varina would write:

"We were now visited by a raiding party, headed by Captain Hudson. They opened our trunks and abstracted everything they desired to have. Among these articles were nearly all my children's clothes. My boy Jeff seized his little uniform of Confederate gray, and ran up to me with it, and thus prevented its being taken as a trophy. . . . Then Captain Hudson valiantly came with a file of men to insist upon having my shawl. . . . We were anchored out a mile or two in the harbor, and little tugs full of mockers, male and female, came out. They steamed around the ship, offering, when one of us met their view, such insults as were transmissible at a short distance. Some [Federal] officers visited the ship [and] . . . two or three of them looked into my sisters' stateroom, with whom [Virginia] Clay was sitting. She said, 'Gentlemen, do not look in here, it is a ladies' stateroom.' One of them threw the door open and said, 'There are no ladies here;' to which [Virginia] Clay responded, 'There certainly are no gentlemen there'."

Meanwhile, Charles Dana, an assistant to Edwin Stanton, was carefully watching Jeff Davis for signs of a weakness that could be exploited in the upcoming interrogation and trial. In his report to Stanton late that day, Dana would write, "In leaving his wife and children, Davis exhibited no great emotion, though he was violently affected." When the tugboat landed, the Federals paraded Jeff Davis and Clement Clay around the grounds at Fortress Monroe as if gloating over the display of their new prisoners. Then they locked Jeff Davis in casemate number 2, and they locked Clement Clay in casemate number 4. Casemates numbers 1, 3 and 5 were designated for the guards. And there would be plenty of guards. The new commander of Fortress Monroe, Nelson Miles, had assigned about 70 soldiers to guard the two prisoners in spite of the fact that they were being locked in very secure casemates. And Charles Dana wanted to begin moderate torture immediately. He handed Miles an official order directing him to engage a blacksmith to fasten iron manacles and fetters on Davis' hands and feet:

"[Nelson] Miles is hereby authorized and directed to place manacles and fetters upon the hands and feet of Jefferson Davis and Clement C. Clay whenever he may think it advisable in order to render their imprisonment more secure. By order of [Edwin Stanton]."

And Miles would eagerly comply the next morning. Stanton had picked a good man to oversee his program to break the spirit of the two captives.

We now begin Volume 4, *Political Reconstruction and The Struggle for Healing*, on May 23, 1865, the day after the last day covered in *Bloodstains*, Volume 3, *The Bleeding*.

May 23, 1865 through March 1866 — Transition to Political Reconstruction During the First Year of the Andrew Johnson Administration

May 23, 1865

Monroe was the most formidable of all Federal fortresses. Called the Gibraltar of the Chesapeake, the interior of the fortress was protected by 30-foot granite walls, which measured up to 90 feet thick in the more solid sections. A 1.25 mile moat, measuring from 60 to 150 feet wide by 8 feet deep, surrounded the outer walls. How could Jeff Davis' jailers possibly dream up an attack plan by which a rescue squad of former Confederates might assault Fortress Monroe and make off with Jeff Davis? Why he was perhaps the most securely jailed captive in American history, from the nation's beginning to the present day. Anyway, Jeff Davis did not want to get away. He wanted to stand trial on a Federal Government charge of treason. Davis was confident that he and his defense team would surely win such a court battle against the Federal Government, and by that victory, heap great honor on all Confederate defenders — living, maimed and dead. If Republican Party leaders, through the Federal Government they controlled, wanted to take on Davis in a court fight, the defendant would be eager and ready to go at it. But Davis already feared the Republican leaders would come to realize the grave weakness of their legal position and eventually shrink away from a court confrontation. As the night of May 22 approached, Davis sat upon his hard iron cot, picked up his Bible, which was the only possession allowed, and read the Sixteenth Psalm.

Jeff Davis awoke to schemes of torture. On May 23 Nelson Miles ordered one of his officers, Jerome Titlow, to have a blacksmith attach heavy leg irons on Davis' ankles. At first Titlow was astonished, for he recognized the virtual impossibility of any rescue or escape. But, since Miles intended to apply torture, not improve security, he firmly ordered the bewildered Titlow to comply. Just before sundown, blacksmith H. C. Arnold and a helper entered the captive's cell under Titlow's oversight. "I have an unpleasant duty to perform, sir," Titlow announced as they entered. "My God," Davis exclaimed in disbelief, "you don't intend to iron me!" "Those are my orders, sir," Titlow replied. "But the [invasion of our States] is over; the [Confederacy] is conquered. For the honor of America you cannot commit this degradation. No such outrage as you threaten me with is on record in the history of nations. The world will ring with this disgrace." But Titlow repeated, "Those are my orders, sir." "I shall never submit to such an indignity. It is too monstrous. I demand that you let me see [Nelson Miles]." Titlow explained that Miles had left the fort for a while. "Then postpone the execution of the order until someone telegraphs to [Andrew] Johnson. There is some terrible mistake." Firming his resolve, Titlow announced, "The orders are from Washington, sir. And my orders are peremptory. [Jeff] Davis, you are an old soldier and know what orders are; it is needless to say that an officer is bound to execute an order given him." Persisting, Davis scolded, "It is obvious there could be no necessity for such an order to make my imprisonment secure." Titlow repeated, "My duty is to execute this order. It is folly for you to resist." Enraged, Davis shouted, "Let your men shoot me at once." Biographer Hudson Strode would describe the struggle that developed after Titlow terminated the argument with a final and firm order: "Smith do your work!"

> "As the blacksmith stooped to place the clasp of the shackle round [the] ankle, Davis seized him with frenzied strength and threw the brawny fellow across the room. Recovering himself, the furious blacksmith made for the prisoner with lifted hammer. He would have struck him down if Titlow had not caught his arm. Simultaneously, one of the sentinels lowered and cocked his musket and advanced on Davis. Titlow quickly interposed, and in a loud voice ordered the men not to fire. The next moment Titlow saw Davis and a sentinel struggling, both having hold of the musket. Titlow called to the officer in the outer room to bring four of his best men at once, unarmed. As the sentinel finally wrenched the musket from [Davis'] grasp, four stalwart soldiers made their appearance. "Men," Titlow said, "I wish you to take [Jeff] Davis, with as little force as possible. All four instantly closed on him. The contest was brief. [Davis] was thrown on his cot and held down by the four men. Though he could not see the blacksmith approach with the irons, as he felt him grasp for a leg, with a last supreme effort, Davis kicked him off. "[Jeff Davis]," Titlow noted in a written report, "showed unnatural strength." It was all the four men could do to hold him while the blacksmith riveted the clasp round one ankle, his helper holding the sledge

hammer. The other clasp was locked on with a heavy brass lock, 'the same as is in use on freight cars,' Titlow wrote."

As Titlow turned to leave the cell Davis sat up on the cot and, with unnatural effort, put his shackled feet on the floor. Then Titlow looked back and later recorded his own emotion: "It was anything but a pleasant sight to see a man like Jefferson Davis shedding tears, but not one word did he say." The following day, May 24, Nelson Miles telegraphed Charles Dana: "Yesterday I directed that irons be put on Davis' ankles, which he violently resisted, but he became more quiet afterwards. His hands are unencumbered." The he closed with notification that "the females" were shipped to Savannah earlier that day.

Miles' "females" were in fact Varina Davis and Virginia Clay. Varina had been stripped and searched, and her luggage had been ransacked by Federals looking for evidence that could be used to prosecute Jeff, and for anything that they wanted for themselves. For example, the Federals took almost all of the children's clothes. Varina and the children were shipped to Savannah where she was allowed to locate a hotel room. But she was forced to remain in Savannah and subjected to close surveillance by Federal detectives who noted all visitors and constantly looked for circumstances that might be used to help prosecute Jeff.

But of equal importance was the appointment of Dr. John Craven as chief surgeon in charge of the health of Jeff Davis and Clement Clay. John Craven would become Davis' good and faithful friend and provide life-saving care in spite of Republican political efforts to ruin his health. Hudson Strode would describe John Craven in his Davis biography:

"Craven, a kindly man in his early forties, with sandy hair and beard and light blue eyes, had practiced medicine in Newark, New Jersey, before the [invasion of the Confederacy]. He had two hobbies: natural history and his diary. The latter was to prove fortunate for [Davis], as its publication in book form in 1866 [would] help secure his release. Craven was alarmed at [the captive's] appearance. After his first visit he wrote: '[Jeff] Davis presented a very miserable and affecting aspect, his eyes restless and fevered, his head shifting from side to side for a cool spot on the pillow. His pulse was full and at ninety, tongue thickly coated, his extremities cold and his head troubled with a long-established neuralgic disorder.' He was 'so emaciated that his skin chafed easily against the slats of the iron cot, which was covered with only a thin mattress. His hard pillow was stuffed with hair. Craven ordered an additional hospital mattress and a softer pillow, for which Davis thanked him courteously."

Jeff Davis was hardly able to stand with the heavy leg-irons, for they cut into his skin, especially when he struggled to walk. Apparently, the effective immobility produced by the leg irons was equivalent to being chained down onto the bed. But Davis suffered additional purposeful tormenting treatment. Soldiers walked back and forth inside his cell, right beside his bed day and night, constantly, with heavy boots to keep up a constant clomp, clomp, clomp. A light was always burning in his room, for Davis' long-suffering eye illness was well known and Stanton was aware that complete darkness was the relief and continuous light was the irritation. But it seems that Edwin Stanton, Charles Dana and Nelson Miles were unable to keep the Davis torture program secret from curious newspapermen for very long. Three or four days after Davis was locked in the cell at Fortress Monroe, newspapermen with the Philadelphia *Inquirer* and the Philadelphia *Telegraph* published the details of Davis' torment. By the fifth day, the New York *Daily Tribune* was printing the story. Although citizens of the Federal States had, during the previous four years, been taught to hate Jeff Davis, now that the invasion was consummated, and the last dead were buried, rather few were persuaded to see any justice in leg-iron torture, and other intentional torments. Some Democrats reminded readers that Jeff Davis had been an outstanding Secretary of War in the Franklin Pierce Administration, but was presently being tortured in irons by the current Secretary of War, Edwin Stanton. Even some Republicans criticized Stanton's methods. On May 29 Thurlow Weed, the powerful New York Republican leader, wrote Stanton:

"I could not believe the accounts of Ironing Davis, but they seem authentic. If true, it is a great error and a great calamity. . . . I hope that this dreadful cloud may not obscure the glory of other achievements. . . . The world is with us. But this wholly unnecessary severity with a [Federal] prisoner will lose us a great advantage." [R19;229-238]

Meanwhile, on May 29 Andrew Johnson issued an Amnesty Proclamation that would enable selected men to participate in elections planned for remaking State governments in the former Confederacy. The text of this Amnesty Proclamation is worthy of a careful read, for it was fundamental to the Federal program for remaking the governments in the former Confederate States. Johnson's Amnesty Proclamation, dated May 29, 1865 follows:

"Whereas, [President Abraham Lincoln], on the 8th day of December 1863, and on the 26th day of March 1864, with the object to suppress the [then] existing [secession of several States], to induce all persons to return to their [Federal] loyalty and to restore the authority of the United States [over seceded States], did issue proclamations offering amnesty and pardon to certain persons who had, directly or by implication, participated in the said [secession and defense thereof]; and, whereas, many persons who had so engaged in said [secession and defense thereof] have, since the issuance of said Proclamation, failed or neglected to take the benefits offered hereby; and whereas many persons who have been justly deprived of all claim to amnesty and pardon thereunder by reason of their participation, directly or by implication, in [defense of secession] since the date of said Proclamation, now desire to apply for and obtain amnesty and pardon:

"To the end, therefore, that the authority of [the Federal Government] may be restored, and that peace, order and freedom may be established, I, Andrew Johnson, President of the United States, do proclaim and declare that I hereby grant to all persons who have directly or indirectly participated in the [defense of said secession], except as hereinafter excepted, amnesty and pardon, with restoration of all rights of property, except as to [bonded African Americans], and except in cases where legal proceedings, under [Federal laws], providing for confiscation of property of persons engaged in [defense of secession] have been instituted, but on the condition, nevertheless, that every such person shall take and subscribe the following oath or affirmation, and thenceforward keep and maintain said oath inviolate, and which oath shall be registered for permanent preservation and shall be of the tenor and effect following, to wit:

"I, _____, do solemnly swear (or affirm), in the presence of Almighty God, that I will henceforth faithfully support and defend the [Federal] Constitution and the union of the States thereunder, and that I will in like manner abide by and faithfully support all laws and proclamations which have been made during [the period of State secession] with reference to [making bonded African Americans independent]. So help me God."

African American men in the Confederate States, at this time essentially independent, were assumed "loyal" and not required to take the above oath. African American men who had fought in the Confederate military or the home guards or had provided logistical support to Confederate military forces were automatically granted amnesty without appearing before an official to take the oath. Even the few African American men who had previously owned bonded workers were not required to take the oath. Only European American men were required to take it, if permitted. Women and children were not required to take the oath.

Johnson's Amnesty Proclamation excluded 14 classes of men. I have condensed the description of those 14 classes of men for a more rapid read:

1   Confederate civil or diplomatic officers or foreign agents.

2   Judges and others who "left judicial stations" held prior to secession to aid in its defense.

3   Military officers above colonel in Confederate army or lieutenant in Confederate navy.

4   Former members of the Federal House or Senate who resigned to aid in defense of secession.

5   Former officers in the Federal army or navy who resigned to aid in defense of secession.

6   Men alleged to have mistreated imprisoned Federals held in Confederate POW camps.

7   Men who left the Confederate States or the United States to aid in defense of secession.

8   Confederate officers who were educated at United States military academies.

9   Former and recent Confederate Governors who held that office in any seceded State.

10 Men who left a Federal State, especially Delaware, Maryland, Kentucky and Missouri, to aid in defense of secession.

11 Men who attacked the commerce of the Federal States at sea, on lakes, on rivers or from Canada in efforts to defend secession.

12 Men presently in military, naval or civil confinement as prisoners of war or for offenses of any kind.

13 Men who presently own property valued on the tax rolls at or above $20,000 who cannot prove to oath takers that they never gave aid to the defense of secession.

14 Men who took an oath under the Lincoln program who subsequently gave aid in the defense of secession.

Andrew Johnson's Amnesty Proclamation then concluded with the following directive:

"Provided, that special application may be made to the President for pardon by any person belonging to the [excluded] classes, and such clemency will be liberally extended as may be consistent with the facts of the case and the peace [within our land] and [the] dignity of the [Federal Government]."

"The Secretary of State will establish rules and regulations for administering and recording the said amnesty oath, so as to insure its benefit to the people and [to] guard the [Federal Government] against fraud."

That same day, May 29, Andrew Johnson issued a Proclamation announcing his appointment of William Holden as Military Governor of North Carolina, and issued instructions for the election of Delegates to a Constitutional Convention to rewrite the North Carolina State Constitution. [R201;9-11]

Meanwhile, on June 1 in Boston, Charles Sumner, while delivering his planned eulogy of Abe Lincoln, responded to Andrew Johnson's Proclamation, warning that only by forcing the remade governments of the conquered States to allow African American men to vote could "the [military campaign] waged by [Abe] Lincoln be brought to an end, so as to assure peace, tranquility, and reconciliation." Obviously, Sumner believed that only continued Republican Party domination of Federal and State Governments could deliver "peace, tranquility, and reconciliation." Yet, Sumner remained hopeful that Andrew Johnson would take whatever steps were necessary to force the conquered States to make African American men eligible to vote. Their votes were essential to continued Republican political control, especially since the vast majority of European American men were being denied their right to vote. Sumner received a letter from Thad Stevens urging that the more militant Republican faction join together and defeat Johnson's program — "Could we collect bold men enough to lay the foundation of a party to take the helm of this [Federal] Government, and keep it off the rocks?" Sumner would remain a little hopeful that Johnson might yet change his mind, cautioning political friends that Johnson's announcement was "inconsistent with what he said to me, and to others." But as similar plans to remake ex-Confederate State Governments would emerge from the Johnson Administration, Sumner would become resigned to accept them as Johnson's policy. Yet Sumner would struggle to explain Johnson's "change, which seemed like a somersault or an apostasy." Perhaps Johnson suffered from some "strange hallucination," he would speculate. Biographer David Donald concluded that Sumner's amazement was not just political posturing, for it appeared that Sumner "could not conceive that Johnson quite literally believed in the constitutional guarantee of [State Rights], including [a State's right] to regulate [who is qualified to vote]". [R73;223-226, R96;211]

Meanwhile, upon hearing the news of Jeff's leg-irons and other mistreatment, Varina wrote John Craven from her confinement at Savannah:

"Shocked by the most terrible newspaper extras issued every afternoon, which represent my husband to be in a dying condition, I have taken the liberty of writing you. . . . Would it trouble you too much to tell me how he sleeps — how his eyes look — are they inflamed? — does he eat anything? — It seems to me that no possible harm could accrue to your government from my knowing my sorrow. . . . If you are only permitted to say he is well, or he is better, it will be a great comfort to me, who has no other left."

And Varina enclosed a prayer that nine-year-old Maggie had composed and had taught the younger children to say as grace before meals:

"Dear Lord, give our father something he can eat, and keep him strong, and bring him to us with eyes that can see and in his good senses to his little children, for Jesus' sake, Amen."

Expressing concern over the torture of Jeff Davis, an editorial in the London *Times* cautioned: "We urge the impolicy of shedding the blood of a man" who came so close to succeeding at defending the independence of the Confederacy, and we advise the victorious Federals to "be content with success."

Edwin Stanton must have been shocked at how the initial newspaper reports of Jeff Davis' torment, especially the application of heavy leg-irons, had produced such intense public criticism, even from prominent Republican leaders. And the criticism was growing every day. So Stanton reacted quickly to order the leg irons removed. On May 28, after only five days of leg-iron torment, the blacksmith entered Davis' cell and removed the painful immobilizers. Unaware of the public condemnation that had been heaped on Stanton because of the newspaper reports, Davis thanked John Craven for his supportive influence when he came by later in the afternoon. Davis would look more and more to Craven for support, and, eventually Craven would be credited with saving Davis' life.

And men of action were persuaded to get directly involved. On May 31, Charles O'Conor of New York, who was considered the most capable lawyer in the northern States, wrote a letter to Jeff Davis which he forwarded through the Federal War Department. O'Conor was moved to offer his services in the defense of Jeff Davis and wanted to announce that desire through proper legal channels. There would be slight delays but, because of O'Conor's prominence, his letter would be handed to Davis on June 7, just a week after it had been written. In the letter O'Conor said:

"Gentlemen who have no personal acquaintance with yourself, and who never had a connection by birth, residence or otherwise with any of the Southern States, have requested me to volunteer as counsel for the defense, in case you should be arraigned upon an indictment which has been announced in the newspapers. . . . I beg leave to tender my services accordingly. I will be happy to attend, at any time and place that you may indicated, in order to confer with yourself or others in relation to the defense. . . "

A few days later, on June 7, acting on the decision by Edwin Stanton and Attorney General James Speed, Nelson Miles allowed Davis to read John O'Conor's letter. After reading the letter, Jeff Davis asked for paper and pen so that he could respond. Hoping to be directed to deny the request, Nelson Miles sent a dispatch to a superior in Washington asking if he should comply or refuse. In response, the superior instructed Miles to supply paper for only that "specific purpose." It then appeared that this one reply to the lawyer's offer would be the only exception to Stanton's policy of completely isolating Davis from contact with the outside world. So Davis received a pen and one sheet of writing paper, upon which he carefully composed a reply to Charles O'Conor. In the brief response Davis accepted O'Conor's offer, but confessed that he had been kept in such isolation that he was personally ignorant of any charges. Therefore, Davis urged: "Though reluctant to tax you with the labor of coming here, I must request you to obtain the requisite authority to visit me for the purpose of a full conference."

Nelson Miles inspected Davis' written response and forwarded it superiors in Washington. Both Edwin Stanton and James Speed carefully read the response and, after, wrestling with legal options, decided to return the letter to Davis complaining that it was "an improper communication." So Jeff Davis tried his hand again at composing a reply to John O'Conor's offer to serve as legal counsel. Davis dropped any expression of thanks for the offer, while still accepting the thing, and handed the new letter to Miles for another Republican review. Stanton and Speed apparently decided to burn the second letter or otherwise prevent it getting back to O'Conor. But O'Conor was not a man to let Edwin Stanton merely pocket veto his offer to be of service. On the tenth day without receiving a reply to his May 31 letter, O'Conor told Edwin Stanton that such delay was unacceptable and requested that he be permitted to hold "a personal interview with the accused," Jeff Davis. Stanton flatly refused while applying the legal excuse that, since Davis was confined in a military prison cell, he was "not in civil custody." It seems that O'Conor gave up on his direct maneuver to hold a meeting with Davis, but he would study pertinent information as it became known and wait for events to mature, always at the ready to be of service. Another outstanding lawyer, George Shea, also offered to defend Davis. And the Governor of

Mississippi, not yet been purged by the Federal Government, wrote O'Conor that his State would pay a fee of $20,000 toward Jeff Davis' legal defense fund. But O'Conor replied that he could not accept monetary payment for defending Jeff Davis, for he only desired "to serve America by furthering prompt justice." [R19;239-242]

Meanwhile on June 14, from the Caledonia ironworks at South Mountain, Pennsylvania, Thad Stevens, ironworks owner and powerful Republican leader, again wrote Charles Sumner pleading with him to gather political forces in Massachusetts to oppose Andrew Johnson's program for remaking the former Confederate State governments. Stevens was incensed over Johnson's moves to remake State governments in Mississippi, Louisiana and Arkansas, all before the Federal House and Senate reconvened. Stevens wrote: "get up a movement" in Massachusetts while I do the same in Pennsylvania. "If something is not done [Andrew Johnson] will be crowned king before Congress meets. How absurd his interfering with the internal regulations" of the conquered States, while pretending that they had never seceded. But, in spite of pleadings from Thad Stevens and other like-minded militants, Charles Sumner, during June, continued to urge members of his political faction to delay any plans to threaten Andrew Johnson with Congressional force. He wrote Salmon Chase, explaining that Andrew Johnson was trying to support their demand that African American men vote in the conquered States, and, advising against a break in relations, he admonished that "we must keep him ours unless he makes it impossible to go with him." Sumner did not yet feel it was "impossible to go with him." But Sumner reminded everyone, that Congress held veto power over any remade State Governments that emerged from the work of Andrew Johnson and his appointed Military Governors. Congress, when it would convene in December, would only have to refuse to admit the Representatives and Senators sent from those remade State Governments. They could just deny the submitted credentials, and Johnson could do nothing to stop them. Yet Sumner urged like-minded Republicans to speak out against remade State Governments that did not include voting by African American men. He wrote Ben Wade, "I wish you would make a speech soon or write a letter," and he quizzed Carl Schurz, "When shall you speak? We must all speak." [R73;225-226, R96;211]

Meanwhile, during the first few weeks of Jeff Davis' imprisonment at Fortress Monroe the guards that were in constant oversight were dutifully carrying out orders from Nelson Miles and higher-ups to unrelentingly torment Davis by walking back and forth, inside his cell room, right beside his bed. One of these guards, Elisha Kisner wrote about one of his turns at harassing Davis with constant bedside walking:

"Davis was lying on his bed, apparently trying to get a nap, and our orders were to pace his room constantly, but under no consideration to speak or enter into any conversation with him. My shoes, which were then new, screeched as I passed his bed and this seemed to annoy him. Once as I passed him, he turned to me and growled, 'I wish you'd make less noise.' I replied, 'I wish you'd keep quiet.' The he turned over with his face to the wall, and I kept walking back and forward past his bed. In a minute or two he growled again, 'Can't you keep quiet?' To this I replied, 'Can't you hold your jaw?' Then he got up and commenced to walk the floor, mad as a caged lion. I passed him and turned to go back, when I met him about the middle of the room. Just as I was about to re-pass him he suddenly sprang at me, and with his left hand caught me by the throat. I struggled to get loose, but he held me as though I had been in a vise. I could not use my gun, as he held me close to him. I struggled for breath, but he had shut off my wind. The scuffle drew the attention of the other guard and also the officer outside, when he rattled his sword against the iron-gated door, and then [Jeff Davis] let loose of me and went back to his bed."

John Craven had often complained to Nelson Miles that the incessant pacing beside Jeff Davis' bed was counteracting his efforts to quiet Davis' nerves. But Miles had not, up to that point, softened his orders. But perhaps Miles was influenced on or just before June 23, by Varina's new letter, which had arrived at Fortress Monroe, and was handed to the addressee, John Craven that day. In her letter to Craven, Varina told of receiving horrid newspaper reports depicting "chains and starvation":

Will you not, my dear sir, tell me the worst? Is he dying? Taken from me with only ten minutes warning. I could see that he was quite ill; indeed suffering from fever at the hour of our separation. . . With a blaze of light pouring upon the dilated pupils of eyes always sensitive to it, chains fettering his emaciated limbs, coarse food served, as the newspapers describe it, in the most repulsive manner - hope seems denied to me. . . . Please try to cheer him about us, for we are kindly cared for by [ex-Confederate] friends who love him here. Will you not trouble to write me, only this once?"

Nelson Miles strictly forbade Craven from writing back to Varina, but Craven was able to quietly tell Jeff some news of Varina and the children. Perhaps Varina's letter influenced Miles, for the same day that John Craven was given Varina's letter, Miles ordered that the pacing activity be relocated to just outside the bars of Davis' cell. Even there the pacing noise could still reach Davis' ears and the guards could still constantly watch Davis through the two cell doors made of spaced iron bars. However, Miles was encouraged to find the next morning that the relocation of the pacing guards had permitted Davis to get the first good night's sleep of his imprisonment at Fortress Monroe.

On June 13, by a Proclamation, Andrew Johnson appointed Benjamin Perry to the office of South Carolina Provisional Governor. Wade Hampton had been pleased with the appointment of fellow South Carolinian Perry, who was from Upstate, near Greenville. To Perry he wrote, "It was with the greatest satisfaction that I saw your appointment as Governor, and I hail it as the only gleam of sunshine which has fallen on the State since this black cloud has spread over our horizon."

This Proclamation instructed Perry, "at the earliest practicable period,

"to proscribe such rules and regulations as may be necessary and proper for convening a Convention to be composed of Delegates to be chosen by that portion of the people of the said State who are loyal to the United States, and no others, for the purpose of altering or amending the [State] Constitution thereof, and with authority to exercise within the limits of said State, all the powers necessary and proper to enable such loyal people of the State of South Carolina to restore said State to its constitutional relations to the Federal Government, and to present such a republican form of State Government as will entitle the State to the guaranty of the United States therefore, and its people to protection by the United States against invasion, insurrection and domestic violence; provided, that in any election which may hereafter be held for choosing Delegates to any State Convention as aforesaid no person shall be qualified as an Elector, or shall be eligible as a member of such Convention, unless he shall have previously taken and subscribed the Oath of Amnesty, as set forth in the President's Proclamation of May 29, 1865, and is a voter qualified as prescribed by the Constitution and laws of the State of South Carolina in force before the 20th day of December, 1860, the date of the so-called Ordinance of Secession; and the said Convention when convened, or the Legislature that may be there-after assembled, will prescribe the qualifications of [permitted future voters] and the eligibility of persons to hold office under the Constitution and laws of the State — a power which the people of the several States composing the Federal Union have rightfully exercised from the origin of the [Federal] Government to the present time." [R201;13-14]

So in this groundbreaking Federal directive, voter participation was limited to European American men who had not been civil, economic or military leaders in South Carolina, but had been registered voters therein at the time of the fall elections of 1860. However, a door was left open for civil, economic and military leaders to individually seek a grant of amnesty from President Johnson, which would enable future voter and civil participation, and Wade Hampton was exploring that avenue. By the way, as of 1856, no State restricted voting to owners of property — North Carolina had been the last to do so, and had eliminated that requirement four years previously.

Wade Hampton had many pressing concerns during this summer of 1865. His farms in South Carolina and Mississippi were heavily mortgaged and of questionable future profitability. He stood to lose everything to creditors if not to Federal confiscation. Would his former bonded African Americans be happy working for wages and sufficiently productive to make economic sense of a farming business, especially with regard to his Mississippi farms? But first the damage wrought by Federal destruction had to be repaired. Little could be expected from the 1865 growing season, which was too far gone for planting. Could he get two good crops, one in 1866 and another in 1867? Would he be blessed or cursed by weather those years? There was no financial cushion for enduring bad weather or unproductive workers. Meanwhile, numerous South Carolina farmers were exploring the alternative of relocating to another country, such as Brazil, and some actually made the move. But Hampton would reject the idea and would encourage those who asked his opinion with these words: "The very fact that our State is passing through so terrible an ordeal as the present, should cause her sons to cling the more closely to her. . . . I recommend that all who can do so should take the oath of allegiance to the United States Government. . . . War, after four years of heroic but unsuccessful struggle, has failed to secure for us our rights for which we engaged in it. To save any of our rights — to rescue anything more from the general ruin — will require all the statesmanship and all the patriotism of our citizens. . . . [should we then fail], we can then seek a home in another country."

There was one event of mid-summer that surely cheered the Hampton family spirit. On June 24 Wade's 20-year-old daughter, Sarah Hampton, wed John Haskell, age 22, who had lost his right arm fighting to defend the Confederacy. Called Sally, Sarah had been the first child born to Wade and his first wife Margaret. Wed in Columbia's Trinity Episcopal Church, located just beyond the zone of Federal destruction, the couple would head to Mississippi to make their life there. [R199;166-169, R200;91-96]

(3Q65)

Meanwhile, in Mississippi, on July 1, William Sharkey, whom people called Judge Sharkey, notified the citizens of the State that he had been appointed Governor of Mississippi by President Andrew Johnson, and, as part of the announcement, "expressed a desire to carry out the President's wishes to restore civil government as speedily as possible." (Sharkey's appointment had been communicated on June 18 from the Johnson Administration through William Seward's office.) By his July 1 Proclamation, Sharkey reappointed all government officials who had been holding offices at the time Federal forces took control of the State, insisting that each must take the Federal Oath of Amnesty and encouraging citizens to bring to his attention disagreeable conduct of any official who was found not faithful in his duties, for, as Governor, he reserved the right to remove any reappointed official whose performance was not satisfactory. "The proclamation directed sheriffs to hold an election in each county on August 7 for delegates to a State Convention to be held in Jackson on August 14." Trustees were directed to reopen the State University in Oxford. (This would allow Lucius Lamar to resume teaching there.) The new Governor encouraged law and order and directed that "crime must be suppressed and guilty persons must be punished." Although only Federal military courts were in operation in Mississippi, Sharkey refrained from reactivating the civil and criminal courts in the State. However, he would, on July 12, authorize a new State Court of Equity to "sit in Jackson with jurisdiction in all contracts for cotton or other personal property, and with power to proceed in a summary manner, on petition, to enforce specific performance or annual contracts, upon due notice to parties concerned." With the election of Delegates being only 3 weeks off, Sharkey's proclamation spurred increased activity by Federal troops to complete administering the Oath of Amnesty to European American men who were not in the 14 classes which were excluded from participation. Of this, historian James Garner would write: "During June and July, the military authorities were busy administering the Oath, and those who were entitled to its benefits came up almost without exception, and took it, although to most of them it was gall and wormwood."

Historian James Garner would consider William Sharkey a very good choice for Provisional Governor:

"It is doubtful if a better selection could have been made. Judge Sharkey was born to Irish parents on the river Holston in Tennessee, near the close of the 18th century. He was in [Andrew] Jackson's army at the age of 15, and was present at the Battle of New Orleans. He attended the common schools of Greenville, Tennessee, read law at Lebanon, emigrated to Mississippi, served in the legislature, and in 1833 went upon the bench as Chief Justice of the High Court of Errors and Appeals, where he presided with distinction for more than 20 years." He had been a Whig in politics, had opposed State secession and had not enlisted in the Confederate military, thereby retaining eligibility for the new office of Governor. [R204;75-81]

Meanwhile, as the summer drew on, Wade Hampton would worry that he would not be permitted to participate in the political life of his State, even as a voter, until he received a grant of amnesty. So in August he would submit to Andrew Johnson his application for a grant of amnesty, which Provisional Governor Benjamin Perry would endorse. Hampton's letter to Johnson would say, in part, "I have only to add that I make this application from a sense of duty and that it is my purpose, if it is acceded to, to devote myself honestly and zealously to the restoration of law and order in my State and to the interests of my country." Perry's letter of endorsement would report, in part, that Hampton was encouraging fellow South Carolinians to "become loyal citizens and remain in their country" and his decision to do likewise "will have good influence in determining the course of others." Furthermore, Perry would assure Johnson, Hampton had been "no agitator" for State secession.

During August Wade Hampton, in spite of his own political limitations, would be talking with friends and past leaders in Columbia regarding how all could best deal with the upcoming South Carolina Constitutional Convention demanded by Andrew Johnson. How should those South Carolina voters who were not in one of more of Andrew Johnson's 14 classes of excluded military, civil and economic leaders be involved in submitting to Federal demands for a remade State Government? Our best insight into Hampton's thinking on this matter would be drawn from a letter he would write to Columbia Mayor James Gibbes on August 20. In this letter Hampton would ask of himself the question: "Is it desirable that the people of the State should take any action looking to a restoration of civil government at present?" He then would answer the question: "I think not." He would reason, if South Carolina is by Federal law deemed to presently be a "State," then "she has the right to administer her government under such a constitution and by such laws as she chooses" with full voter participation allowed and without submitting to Federal demands. On the other hand, if South Carolina is by Federal law deemed to be a conquered Federal territory or province, then Federal political leaders were responsible for providing her "a proper government." Given that the Federals were grossly interfering with the political life of the State, Hampton would reason that she was a conquered Federal territory or province and, therefore, the voters who were not excluded by Federal authority should refuse to participate in the election of Delegates, but "remain passive" until, by Federal decree, "a government is given to her, or is forced upon her." He would assure that Federals "will, doubtless in good time provide a government" for our State. If the permitted voters remain passive, as he would be recommending, then, "The people, though conquered, will not have the additional humiliation and reproach which they would bring on themselves, if they consent to destroy their own constitution which was bequeathed to them by their fathers."

In a way Wade Hampton would follow his own advice and, in latter August, would leave Columbia with his family for the solitude and cool air of the Hampton mountain retreat in Cashiers Valley, where he could rest, enjoy his family and hunt. [R199;166-169, R200;91-96]

Meanwhile on July 6, Thad Stevens, while working at his lawyer business in Philadelphia, wrote to Andrew Johnson, saying that he had not found even one leading Republican Representative or Senator who approved of the Executive policy for remaking conquered State Governments, or for granting Executive pardons to former Confederate leaders who asked for them. Stevens warned that such pardons would make it difficult for Congress to enact planned legislation needed to enable Federal confiscation of property belonging to former Confederates and selling those properties to pay off the Federal bonds issued to finance the invasion of the Confederacy. Stevens asked: "Can you not hold your hand and wait the action of Congress, and in the meantime govern [the conquered States] by Military rulers?" [R96;212]

On July 11, John Craven noted his concern over the intense pain that Jeff Davis had been suffering in his eyes. Upon entering the cell that morning, Craven found Davis "very desponding, the failure of his sight troubling him, and his nights almost without sleep." But Craven had already made considerable progress in eliminating some intentional torments. Edwin Stanton, who claimed to be an Episcopalian, as was Davis, had been persuaded to let Jeff have a Prayer Book in addition to the personal Bible that had originally been his only permitted reading material. Starting on or just before July 1, guards had been permitted to bring Davis histories from the fort's library as well as some selected magazines. And occasionally, he was even permitted to read newspapers. The most common newspaper made available to him was the New York *Herald*. But newspapers and magazines made available to Davis were carefully checked and selected "with a view to their [political loyalty] principles, lest his mind be corrupted by any hint of [secessionist] doctrines." As Craven and Davis talked on the morning of July 11, Davis mentioned a New York *Herald* article which had mentioned that, in addition to Charles O'Conor, Reverdy Johnson of Maryland had announced he was willing to help with his defense when the case came before Federal Court. Davis told Craven that he was grateful that another prominent northern States lawyer had announced his willingness to help. But Jeff wanted Craven to understand that the most important issue was not the defense of Jefferson Davis; the most important issue was the defense of the a State's Constitutional right to secession. Craven recorded Jeff's appeal as follows:

"My own fate is of no importance in this matter, save to the Government on which history will devolve the responsibility for my treatment. My people attempted what your people denounced as a revolution which must prove disastrous to their liberties unless promptly remedied by legal decision. State Sovereignty, the cornerstone of the [Federal] Constitution, has become a name. There is no longer power or will in any State that would dare refuse compliance with any tinkle of [William] Seward's little bell."

Before Craven left, Davis appealed again for some dark-time and some privacy:

"I confess, Doctor, this torture of being watched begins to prey on my reason. The lamp burning in my room all night would seem a torment devised by someone who had intimate knowledge of my habits, my custom having been through life never to sleep except in total darkness."

And Davis again urged Craven to push Nelson Miles and his superiors harder for an order that would permit two-way communication with Varina. Davis admonished, "Even criminals condemned to death for heinous crimes are allowed not only correspondence with their wives, but interviews at which no jailer stands within earshot."

As the summer of 1865 progressed Stanton's Federal agents continued their search for evidence with which they could charge Jeff Davis with involvement with John Wilkes Booth and the shooting of Abe Lincoln. Federals had discovered the personal Davis trunk that M. C. Clark had taken to Florida and given to Senator Yulee's wife to be hidden for safekeeping. Stanton's agents took the trunk to Washington and poured over every family letter and every confidential note dealing with Confederate business matters. But they found nothing that could be remotely useful in charging Davis with helping Booth. And attempts to set up stooges to frame Davis with false sworn testimony were not succeeding. One such attempt had been exposed and killed by L. C. Turner, a member of Stanton's investigation team who was apparently an honorable man. In this particular con, a fellow named Charles Dunham, using the alias Sanford Conover, had offered to bring "witnesses" to Joseph Holt, a man from a Southern State who figured it was his "special duty to accomplish the ruin of [Jeff] Davis. Receiving Holt's agreement to pay for such incriminating "witnesses," Dunham recruited fakers from the criminal community in Manhattan. Then one-by-one he brought them to Washington, put them through intensive rehearsals, and then brought them before Stanton's investigators to tell their story. But Turner became suspicious and, with the help of a Congressional Committee got one of the "witnesses," a fellow named Campbell, to confess to the con. Dunham, alias Conover, fled, but was eventually captured and jailed.

By mid-July, Johnson's Cabinet was becoming rather desperate about what crime, if any, they could successfully accuse Jeff Davis of committing. Although his many agents had been digging for three months, Edwin Stanton could not produce any evidence that linked Jeff Davis to John Wilkes Booth. And Salmon Chase, as Chief Justice of the Federal Supreme Court firmly warned Johnson's Cabinet:

"If you bring these [Confederate] leaders to trial, it will condemn the [leaders of the Federal States], for, by the [Federal] Constitution, [State] secession is not rebellion." And Chase added: "Lincoln wanted Jefferson Davis to escape; and he was right. His capture was a mistake. His trial will be a greater one. We cannot convict him of treason. Secession is settled. Let it stay settled."

Varina, still confided by house arrest to remain in Savannah, Georgia, continued her campaign to bring help to her husband, who she suspected might still be in chains. During June she had written a letter to Horace Greeley and enclosed an article from the Savannah *Republican*.

"How can the honest men and gentlemen of your [Federal States] stand idly by to see a gentleman maligned, insulted, tortured and denied the right of trial by the usual forms of law? Is his cause so strong that he must be done to death by starvation, confined air, and manacles? With all the archives of our [Confederate] Government in the hands of your [Federal] Government, do [Federal agents] despair of proving [Jeff Davis] a rogue, falsifier, assassin and traitor — then [Federals] must in addition guard him like a wild beast, and chain him for fear his unarmed hands will in a casemated cell subvert the government? Shame, shame. . . Is no one among you bold enough to defend him? . . . "

Greeley answered Varina's letter, but took care to boldly address the envelope to "Mrs. Varina Davis, wife of Jefferson Davis, from Horace Greeley." And then he sent it to Varina by way of Edwin Stanton. Varina's letter to Horace Greeley must have been helpful, for he subsequently urged George Shea to press for an early trial. Shea determined to personally check into the matter. He traveled to Montreal and examined the Confederate Government archives that had been stored there for safekeeping. After reading hundreds of Confederate documents, Shea became convinced that Jeff Davis was in no way guilty of helping John Wilkes Booth kill Abe Lincoln or of contributing to mistreatment of Federal prisoners at the large Confederate Prisoner-of-War camp near Andersonville, Georgia. At this point, then, George Shea and Horace Greeley joined with Charles O'Conor in pushing for a speedy trial.

Varina wrote George Shea on July 14, to present her thinking on legal issues and to appeal personally for his legal help. First, she informed him, "I am accused of no wrong, yet I am confined here without redress." Turning to the defeated people of the conquered States, she wrote, "For our downtrodden people I crave 'amnesty' — whatever that may be — permission to breathe God's air and gain their bread by the sweat of their brows. But for me and mine, we crave no amnesty. We have been robbed of everything except our memories." Of the Republican Party's four-year propaganda campaign to sell their invasion as an effort to unite Confederates and Federals, Varina minced no words: "There is no bond uniting us to the [people who live in the Federal States]. A great gulf of blood rolls between us. My spirit shrinks appalled from attempting to cross it." Then she advised Shea that Jeff's only "offence" derived from his belief that the United States Constitution meant what it clearly said — that the States were sovereign — and could therefore be characterized as "an inexpedient assertion of an undeniable right." Varina advised Shea that Stanton's agents, who were "mousing among the archives," were clearly desperate for any shred of evidence that might be used to frame Jeff. And of invasions upon her personal privacy, she complained of Stanton's agents "polluting with their unhallowed gaze the precious records of my few happy hours, and selling garbled extracts to those papers whose readers need a gentle excitement." Then Varina closed with a poignant lament: "I am unhinged by sorrow, and forget that you have not lived in an invaded country and that your ire has not been lighted at the funeral pyre of friends and homes forever lost."

George Shea must have taken Varina's letter to heart, for he "immediately made renewed efforts to secure [Varina's] complete freedom from military surveillance."

By July 20, John Craven was very disturbed about how Jeff Davis' confinement in the prison cell was destroying his fragile health. In fact Davis himself was genuinely worried that he might be dying. "If death without trial is the object of the Washington people," he told Craven, "I wish they would take quicker means of dispatching me." And he explained to Craven that their desire for him to die in prison was understandable because a trial would "surely develop many things unpleasant to those in power." But Davis assured Craven that he wanted to live long enough to participate in a trial, for he was confident and most eager to prove in a courtroom setting that State secession was allowed in the United States Constitution. Jeff stressed, "This is the last remaining labor which life can impose on me as a public duty." Looking at Davis and listening to his arguments, Craven realized how silly were the Federal's notions that Davis might escape from Fortress Monroe. That night Craven wrote in his diary, "If all the doors and gates of the fort were thrown open [Davis] would not leave. The only duty left to him — his only remaining object — was to vindicate the action of his people, and his own action as their representative, by a fair and public trial."

Jeff Davis had not been allowed to set foot out of his prison cell since he had been locked up two months previously. And the confinement was destroying his health. So, John Craven must have convinced Nelson Miles, for health reasons, to grant Davis a little time outside of his prison cell. It was only four days later, on July 24, that Miles appeared at the barred door of the cell and announced that, in the afternoon, Davis would be allowed one hour of outside exercise. At the appointed time, Miles and the Officer of the Day led Davis from his cell, each steadying him by holding onto one arm. They walked slowly outside and up along the ramparts, from which he could view the Chesapeake and breath in the saltwater breeze. John Craven, who watched from a distance, observed that "While [the prisoner's] carriage was as proud and erect as ever, not losing a hairs breadth of his height from any stoop, his step had lost its elasticity, and he had frequently to press his chest, panting in the pauses of exertion." During the walk, Jeff observed that a crowd of curious onlookers had gathered outside the walls to gape at him as he walked upon the ramparts. This scene, perhaps, brought back memories of the gratitude that Black Hawk had expressed in his autobiography, which had been written while he likewise had been imprisoned at Fortress Monroe many years previously. Black Hawk had reported:

> "We started . . . in a steamboat under the charge of a young war chief who treated us all with much kindness. He is a good and brave young chief with whose conduct I was very much pleased. . . . People crowded to the boat to see us, but the war chief would not permit them . . . knowing from what his feelings would have been if he had been placed in a similar situation, that we did not wish a gaping crowd around us."

Of that first day's exercise, Craven wrote in his diary: "The hour allowed proved twice too much;" and Davis was returned to his cell after only thirty minutes outside. But he would strengthen, and draw great benefit from the outside exercise. That night Davis told Craven, "the sense of breathing air not drawn through iron bars was a glorious blessing, only to be fully appreciated by prisoners." And after a few days of outside exercise, Craven would notice a decline in debilitating nervous tension. And Davis would take a genuine interest in studying Macaulay's *History of England.* [R19;246-254]

On or shortly before July 24, R. J. Haldeman, acting in support of Clement Clay, who was also imprisoned at Fortress Monroe, personally appealed to Thad Stevens in Lancaster for help in gaining Clay's release. Haldeman assured Stevens that neither Clay nor Jeff Davis had any knowledge of John Wilkes Booth's gang — that the killing of Abe Lincoln was the act of Maryland men who merely hated Lincoln's invasion of the Confederacy. Haldeman was probably surprised when Thad Stevens totally agreed with that assessment, agreeing there was no evidence that Clay and Davis had any knowledge of Booth's team. Stevens assured Haldeman that neither Clay nor Davis would ever be convicted of treason in a court of law because, although Abe Lincoln had often alleged that Federal military forces were fighting to put down a rebellious faction of citizens, the behavior of Federal officials during the invasion proved that the Federal Government recognized the belligerent character of the Confederate States. Stevens even offered to serve as a defense lawyer for Clement Clay, when the proper time arrived. However, Stevens refused to make any move to support Clay's release from prison on bail. In fact he demanded that Haldeman keep their conversation a secret. Obviously, Stevens wanted Clay and Davis to remain in jail, as political prisoners, stripped of their rights to a timely trial, until Congress completed derailing Andrew Johnson's program for re-making governments in the conquered States and instituting its own program — complete with Republican Political Machines empowered by the votes of African American men and confiscation of vast farmlands. He might have wished that the two prisoners die of disease, but he did want them formally executed, believing execution might weaken the resolve —held by the more militant Republican faction — to confiscate vast farmlands in the conquered States. Executing two top Confederate leaders would gain the Federal Treasury nothing. Massive confiscation of the farms of thousands of former Confederate citizens would gain much for the Federal Treasury. After the meeting, Haldeman wrote Clement Clay's wife in Alabama, informing her that the imprisonment and eventual trial involved "profound questions of statesmanship and party." In other words, Clement Clay was purely a political prisoner. [R96;212]

Sometime during the last few days of July, Varina decided to send the three oldest children to Canada to attend school away from the annoyance of Stanton's agents. Her mother, Margaret K. Howell, who was not under Federal house-arrest, would take the Children on an ocean steamer to safety in Canada. Robert Brown, the loyal African American servant, who had been urging Varina to get the children out of the States, would accompany them and offer male protection. An African American nursemaid that was serving the family would also go. Varina would remain in Savannah to comply with Federal confinement orders. Just prior to departing for Canada, Varina suggested to her daughter, Maggie, that she write a letter to her father, trying hard to say nothing that Federal censors might think objectionable. Perhaps Edwin Stanton and Nelson Miles would allow Jeff to see such a letter from his daughter. Maggie agreed and wrote with feeling, concentration and determination. One sentence stood out: "My Darling Father, the Lord is Your Shepherd, you shall not want." Showing the letter to her mother Maggie asked hopefully, "This letter will not make the [Federals] mad, will it? They won't object to the Bible, will they?" The letter was mailed, but the Federals would object to even the Bible, for they would not let Jeff see his daughter's letter. Varina kissed the children — Jeff, Maggie and William — goodbye as her mother, Robert Brown and the nursemaid departed. Little Winnie, who was about 13 months old, remained with her mother.

At some point on the ocean trip, Robert Brown would be confronted by a rather hateful man who had supported the Federal invasion. This man would harass little Jeff and taunt him with hateful slurs about his imprisoned father. After a while Brown would figure that little Jeff had endured enough of this torment. So Brown would approach the tormentor, a European American, and would ask the man, in a legal sense, "Do you consider me, an African American, your equal?" Unaware of Brown's intentions, the man would reply with the politically correct answer: "Certainly." "Then take this from your equal," Robert would say, as he "knocked the fellow flat on the deck." Being knocked down by an African American man would immediately reset the tormentor's mind. Rejecting any idea of equality, he would get up and ask the ship's captain to have Brown punished. But the captain would understand the situation and would refuse to do so. So, by their wits, and with Robert Brown's help, Margaret K. Howell would keep her grandchildren out of harm's way as, together, they would conveyed them to safety in Canada. [R19;257]

Meanwhile, the Kentucky State elections, held on August 7, resulted in broad defeat of the Union Democrat candidates (also called Radicals) and victory for most Conservative Democrat candidates. Conservative Democrats held between 58 and 60 of the 100 Kentucky House seats. The Kentucky Senate was close, perhaps 20 to 18 in favor of the Conservatives. Five of the nine Representatives elected to the Federal House were Conservatives, but the vote across the State was close: 57,502 versus 54,008. Turnout was estimated at approximately 50 percent. A major issue during the campaign had been how to deal with the not-yet-ratified Amendment to make bonded African Americans independent. Another major issue concerned whether or not returning Confederates should be given the right to vote and, or hold office.

John Palmer, commander over Federal troops in Kentucky, had openly used his soldiers in many attempts to help Union Democrats win elections. He had threatened to arrest and hold for military trial any man who attempted to vote in violation of rules against voting by men who had supported the Confederacy, including, "Those who displayed Confederate flags or assisted; or who cheered for a Confederate leader; or rejoiced at Confederate victories; or voluntarily sent food to Confederates, . . . and so forth." Historian Merton Coulter would write, "Soldiers were stationed around the polls, and at many places there were [African Americans], holding lists of names of people whom some Radicals thought should not vote. If such a proscribed person attempted to approach the polls, he was pointed out to a soldier and jostled off to prison." Scores of men were thusly excluded, but few of those "jostled off" had been Confederate soldiers. Palmer's use of his Federal soldiers to control voting clearly violated the Federal law of February 25, 1865, "forbidding military interference with elections." Soldiers and commanders would not be prosecuted for violating Federal and State law but Conservative Democrats would use their new majority power to make adjustments. They would declare vacant 8 House seats and 4 Senate seats, and order new elections, eventually giving their party almost all of those contested seats.

Since Confederate soldiers had returned to Kentucky "in large numbers," the stage was being set for the vanquished in war to become the victors in peace. But not yet! The Kentucky Expatriation Act, passed in October 1861, still made felons of Kentuckians who returned to the State after enlisting in the Confederate Army. And martial law was still in effect. Future elections were expected to be more solidly Conservative Democrat. [R180;272-286]

In early August Edwin Stanton gave in to pressure from George Shea and Charles O'Conor and permitted Varina Davis to leave Savannah. The Federal agents who had kept Varina under surveillance since her arrival in Savannah had not turned up any incriminating evidence, and, as Stanton became more despondent over prospects for convicting Jeff of some crime, he was relaxing his grip over both Varina and Jeff. In a letter to Varina dated August 3, Shea intoned "Come to New York!" He assured her that Horace Greeley was "a good and firm friend of those who need a friend." But Varina was did not think the time was right to travel to New York. So she accepted an invitation to stay with George Schley and his wife at Mill View, Georgia. Mill View was about five miles from Augusta. Biographer Hudson Strode would write:

"[Varina] moved to their guesthouse with her baby Winnie and the new nurse, Mary Ahern, a sweet-tempered, kind [person],' who had been born in Ireland and brought to Georgia when three years old. [Mary's] father had cultivated a little place near Savannah, which had been devastated by [William Sherman's Federals]. Mary was a Catholic, and she had been recommended by convent nuns. The baby and Mary Ahern adored each other at sight, and Mary was to remain with the Davises for more than a dozen years." [R19;259]

Meanwhile on August 14, at Jackson, Mississippi, in compliance with the previously mentioned proclamation of Governor William Sharkey, 100 Delegates, elected a week earlier to the Constitutional Convention, gathered to draft a new Constitution for the State government. This was the first convention to be held in the former Confederate States — others would soon follow. All but 2 of the 100 Delegates managed to qualify. Governor Sharkey opened the proceeding by reading a dispatch from President Andrew Johnson:

"I am gratified to see that you have organized your Convention without difficulty. I hope that without delay your Convention will amend your State Constitution abolishing [African American bonding] and denying to all future legislatures the power to legislated that there is property in man; also that they will adopt the Amendment to the [Federal Constitution likewise abolishing African American bonding]. If you could extend [voting rights to men of full or partial African descent] who can read the [Federal] Constitution in English, and write their names, and to [men of full or partial African descent] who own real estate valued at not less than $250, and pay taxes thereon, you would completely disarm the adversary and set an example the other States will follow. This you can do with perfect safety, and you thus place the Southern States, in reference to [men of full or partial African descent], upon the same basis with the [northern States]. I hope and trust your Convention will do this, and, as a consequence, the [More Militant Republicans, termed "Radicals"], who are wild upon [giving voting rights to all men of full or partial African descent], will be completely foiled in their attempt to keep the [conquered] States from renewing their relations to the [Federal Government] by not accepting their Senators and Representatives."

President Johnson's advice to give voting rights to literate and tax-paying African American men was a wise and serious instruction, which Mississippians should have agreed to do, for the vote of such men would have been small in number, not influencing many elections. And it would have blunted to some extent the aggressive ambitions of the More Militant Republicans. However, many European Americans in Mississippi could not read and many did not own real estate valued at $250 or more. So, the whole idea of associating voting rights with education and wealth in land was an emotional problem for men of both races.

Committees were organized to address various issues and deliberation began. Mississippi's Ordinance of State Secession was declared "null and void" by a vote of 81 to 14, and other ordinances passed by the previous Convention of 1861 were "repealed," thereby retrenching the document back to before secession. By a vote of 87 to 11 the revised Constitution read: the institution of African American bonding, "having been destroyed in the State of Mississippi" shall not hereafter exist in the State. The revised Constitution "accorded to the [African American] certain civil rights, such as the privilege of bringing suit in the courts and of acquiring and holding real estate," but, importantly, it did not allow African Americans to testify in court with regard to matters concerning European Americans, only with regard to matters concerning other African Americans. However, sadly, Delegates had not the political courage to follow Andrew Johnson's advice of giving voting rights to African American men who could read English and write their names, or who paid modest or higher real estate taxes, which would have made Mississippi rights similar to those granted in some northern States. The Convention set the first Monday in October for elections to State and county offices, including members of the Legislature, and for election of Representatives to the Federal House. [R204;82-94]

Meanwhile, Lucius Lamar was winding down his visit at Oxford, Mississippi, with the family of his father-in-law, Augustus Longstreet. He had left Richmond, Virginia on May 20, realizing with sadness four personal losses from the fighting — two brothers and two former law partners, James Autrey and Christopher Mott. So Lucius knew that, to practice law in a partnership, he would need to find someone new. Fortunately, for part of the journey he traveled with Edward Walthall, a Mississippi lawyer and a high-ranking officer in the former Confederate army. Born in Virginia and brought to Mississippi by his parents as a child, Walthall had a home and former law practice in Coffeeville, Mississippi, a village located about 30 miles south of Oxford. As it turned, out time spent traveling with Walthall had begun the process that was leading to a law practice partnership agreement that Lamar and Walthall would sign on or about September 1. The office would be in Coffeeville, on the Mississippi Central Railroad line. Both men figured leadership positions in government were out of the question, both being former Confederate officers. So, together they would return to the practice of law. The practice would thrive until the summer of the following year, 1866, when Lamar's health would "give way" and the partnership would be dissolved. Of this time working with Walthall, biographer James Murphy would write:

> "In their practice the two veterans did fairly well by the standards of the day. Undoubtedly, Lamar benefited from Walthall's reputation as a foremost lawyer and former district attorney in Coffeeville. . . . With this assistance Lamar made some headway in meeting his financial obligations and slowly paid off bills dating back to [before 1861]. So numerous were the collectors that he had begun to think, 'I never paid for anything in my life.' By March 1866, he felt heartened enough to make light of his situation. [Varina] Davis [would write] that 'in Lamar's woeful account of his difficulties I forgot for a time my griefs, and laughed heartily.'" [R206;85-88, R205;119-120]

Meanwhile, from his Caledonia Ironworks Thad Stevens wrote Charles Sumner on August 17, to inform him of a recent trip to Washington City. There Stevens had called on Navy Secretary Gideon Welles, who was supportive of Andrew Johnson's program for remaking governments in the conquered States. Stevens must have been prying for a sense of how much Cabinet support Johnson was enjoying, for he and Welles were from different factions of the Republican Party. Of that meeting, Welles had recorded in his diary: "Thad Stevens called on me on business, and took occasion to express [the views held by the Party's More Militant Faction], and had a sarcastic hit or two but without much sting."

> "I was called away from Washington before I had an opportunity to talk with [Andrew Johnson] on [remaking the governments in the conquered States] as I [had] intended. In other things he seemed nearly right. But I presume I could have done no good [if I had met with him]. Johnson has the reins [and Edwin] Stanton and [Salmon] Chase desire to be the architects, and fear Congress [will kill their program when it reconvenes]. Stanton has started [remaking the] Virginia [State Government]. How ridiculous [that one is]. But perhaps a very low farce was thought necessary amidst so many bloody tragedies. I have written very plainly to [Andrew Johnson] urging delay. But I fear he will pursue his wrong course [by establishing] illegal courts and [by] usurping [power belonging to Congress]. [I] know not where you and I shall [stand on these issues when Congress reconvenes]. While we can hardly approve of all the acts of the [Executive Branch of the Federal Government], we must try to keep out of the ranks of the [Democrats]. The danger is that so much success [in eliminating resistance to Federal rule in the conquered States] will reconcile the people [of the northern States] to almost any [Federal program for re-making those governments]."

The same day that he wrote Sumner, Stevens was involved in opening-day political maneuvering at the Republican State Convention meeting in Harrisburg. His Faction outvoted Simon Cameron's Faction to elect the Chairman of the Pennsylvania Republican State Committee. And Stevens' Faction seemed in control of the resolutions committee and the floor vote. Resolutions endorsed Andrew Johnson's presidency (to avoid aligning with Democrats), high import taxes, vigilance against European influence on the American continents, and Federal confiscation of farms in ex-Confederate States. But there was no Pennsylvania resolution that advocated allowing African American men to vote. Fearing an influx of more African Americans from Maryland and nearby Virginia, Republicans appeared to be anxious to avoid doing anything that might limit their future ability to constrain African American migration into their respective States. They were worried about the consequences to their communities that might devolve from elevating the citizenship status of African American men. Yet, in his letter to Stevens on August 20, Sumner refrained from chastising Pennsylvania Republicans for failure to support his plan to empower Republican Political Machines in the conquered States thorough the votes of African American men. Sumner only praised, as "excellent" the Pennsylvania resolution calling for Federal confiscation of farms in the conquered States. Sumner added, "Such a voice from Pennsylvania has salvation in it." [R96;213]

Meanwhile, Edwin Stanton relaxed his grip a bit over Jeff Davis. On August 21, acting on orders from Washington, Nelson Miles told Jeff that he could write his wife, but his letters would have to pass Federal censors. Delighted, Jeff wrote his first letter to Varina:

"My Dear Wife,

"I am now permitted to write to you under two conditions, viz., that I confine myself to family matters, and that my letter shall be examined by [Attorney-General James Speed] before it is sent to you.

"Tomorrow it will be three months since we were suddenly and unexpectantly separated, and many causes, prominent among which has been my anxiety for you and our children, have made that [quarter-year] in seeming duration long, very long. I sought permission to write to you that I might make some suggestions as to your movements and as to domestic arrangements.

"This will sufficiently explain to you the omission of subjects on which you would desire me to write. I presume it is, however, permissible for me to relieve your disappointment in regard to my silence on the subject of future action toward me, by stating that of the purpose of the authorities I know nothing. . . .

"The confidence in the shield of innocence with which I tried to quiet your apprehensions and to dry your tears at our parting, sustains me still. If your fears have proved more prophetic than my hopes, yet do not despond. 'Tarry thou the Lord's leisure, be strong, and He will comfort thy heart.' Every day, twice or oftener, I repeat the prayer of St. Chrysostom.

"To the surgeon and regimental chaplain I am under many obligations; the officers of the guard and of the day have shown me increased consideration, such as their orders would permit. The unjust accusations which have been made against me in the newspapers of the day might well have created prejudices against me. I have had no opportunity to refute them by proof, and can, therefore, only attribute the perceptible change to those good influences which are always at work to confound evil designs.

"Be not alarmed by speculative reports concerning my condition. You can rely on my fortitude, and God has given me much of resignation to his blessed will. . . .

"Remember how good the Lord has always been to me, how often He has wonderfully preserved me, and put your trust in Him.

"Farewell. May He, whose most glorious attribute is mercy, guide and protect and provide for my distressed family.

"Once more, farewell. Ever affectionately,

"Your Husband,

"Jeff'n. Davis." [R30;168-170]

Meanwhile, writing on August 26, Thad Stevens replied to Charles Sumner's letter of August 20th:

"I am glad you are laboring to arrest [Andrew Johnson's] fatal policy. I wish the prospect of [our] success were better. I have twice written him urging him to delay his hand until Congress meets. Of course he pays no attention to it. Our editors are generally cowards and sycophants. I would make a speech as you suggest if a fair occasion offered. Our [plans for remaking governments in the conquered States and there initiating Federal confiscation of farms] were embodied in [the Pennsylvania State Republican Party] resolutions at Harrisburg. Amidst much chaff, [empowering African American men with the vote] was passed over as heavy and premature. [Let us] get the [conquered States] into a territorial condition [under the rule of Congress], and [enabling the votes of African American men living in those territories] can be easily dealt with [without obligating the Federal States in the north to do likewise].

"I think [remaking the conquered States into Federal territories] should be our great aim. Then Congress can manage [the desired legislation to confiscate farms and to eventually remake those State Governments under Republican Party rule]. We need a good Committee on Elections. [But] I fear [the attitude of the Committee Chairman, H. L.] Dawes. Can [his support] be brought right? [We must] exclude [Representatives and Senators from] all [remade governments in the conquered States] until [we have established remade governments in all those] States. I wish you would sound [out Dawes' level of support] and let me know [what you learn]. It may be proper to 'reconstruct' that Committee." [R96;213]

Meanwhile at Fortress Monroe, as the sun rose on September 1, Jerome Titlow, already mentioned as one of Nelson Miles' officers, thought Jeff Davis appeared to be so sick that death might come soon. So Titlow rushed to waken John Craven. Upon initial examination, Craven thought the pulse indicated "extreme prostration of the vital forces," and concluded that Davis "seemed to be sinking rapidly." But Davis rallied and the crisis passed. However, the close call gave Craven the evidence he needed to sell Nelson Miles and his superiors in Washington on the urgent need for healthier quarters in which to confine Davis, particularly with winter approaching. Work would soon begin on preparing secure quarters in Carroll Hall, a conventional building within Fortress Monroe. [R19;262]

That same day in London, Judah Benjamin penned a letter to Varina Davis. As mentioned in Volume 3, Judah had left Jeff Davis on May 3, as both had agreed, on the outskirts of Washington, Georgia. After, a few weeks, news reports that Federals had captured Davis and other signs of irrecoverable defeat had convinced Benjamin that no Confederate Government in exile could be established in Texas or Mexico. So he had traveled on to London to help from there with legal defenses. In fact, in an interview with a newspaperman for the London *Times*, Benjamin so confidently praised Jeff Davis' conduct during his Presidency that the resulting newspaper article would convince many that the Johnson Administration had no basis for any trial whatsoever. Benjamin well knew that rallied international pressure would weigh heavily on Charles Sumner, Andrew Johnson, Edwin Stanton and other Federal leaders. The main purpose of the letter to Varina was to notify her that her husband's salary through June 30, worth $12,500 in Federal dollars, was on deposit at a London bank for him and would be transferred to her as soon as she advised the most secure method of handling the transaction. And Benjamin urged Varina to use the money for family needs, for more was on hand to cover legal fees:

"The money now placed at your disposal, my dear [Varina] Davis, is your husband's; it is the money of the [Confederate Government] paid to you in his behalf; you are indebted for it to no individual and are under no obligations to any one for it. You can therefore use without any scruple of delicacy. I beg however that you will not apply any of it toward the personal use of [Jeff] Davis or any expenses of his trial or defense; for I know, I am absolutely certain, that a very large sum, five times as much as will probably be wanted, is already placed in perfectly safe hands to be used solely for his service, and for the expenses of his defense and that of the other prisoners, until his release from captivity." [R30;171]

Before closing the letter, Benjamin, in one extraordinary sentence, described the hardships and perils he had managed to overcome between Washington, Georgia and London:

"After weeks spent in solitary travel on horseback through the forests and marshes of Florida in constant peril of capture: after passing 23 days in an open boat at sea, and crossing the Gulf Stream in a yawl: after being forced to put back to St Thomas in the Steamer on which I had taken passage for [Britain] in consequence of the ship's taking fire at night at sea; after every imaginable contretemps and danger, I reached London on the night of [August 30] nearly four months after I parted from [Jeff Davis], charged by him to perform certain public duties in Nassau and Havana, and then to rejoin him in Texas." [R30;172]

Benjamin closed with a personal statement of devotion and admiration:

"Good bye, my dear [Varina] Davis. God bless you and your little ones. I dare not trust myself with the expression of my feelings for your noble husband, for my unhappy friend.

"Every yours devotedly

"J. P. Benjamin." [R30;170-172]

Meanwhile in Pennsylvania, perhaps Thad Stevens was carrying out Charles Sumner's suggestion when he delivered a major speech in Lancaster on September 6, where he advocated his program for confiscating 85 percent of the land in the conquered States and relegating the region to the status of Federal Territories under the rule of Congress. The speech was read far and wide, being published word-for-word in the September 11th issue of the New York *Tribune*. Readers of this work should remember that a "republican form of government" does not necessarily equate to a government dominated by the "Republican Party." Readers should also understand that 200 acres is not an unusually large farm. In fact part of the 200 acres might well be a swamp, very rocky or a steep mountain slope. Remember that, at this time in history, the Federal Government was giving away, free of charge, 160 acre homesteads to whoever went to the western plains, settled there and toughed it out for a few years. Owning 200 acres, of itself, did not make a man wealthy. Readers should see Stevens' extremely harsh criticism of the Blair's as a warning to Andrew Johnson that he will be next if he persists in his policies. Readers need to also remember that the selling prices for land in the conquered States, even good cleared, productive land, was severely depressed. In part, Stevens said the following:

"The armies of the Confederate States having been conquered and subdued, and their territory possessed by the [Federal Government], it becomes necessary to establish [remade State] Governments therein, which shall be republican in form and principles. . . . It is desirable that such a course should be pursued as to exclude from those Governments every vestige of [African American] bondage; and render the same forever impossible in this nation; and to take care that no principles of [State secession] shall be incorporated therein. . . . We hold it to be the duty of the [Federal] Government to inflict [deserved] punishment on [past defenders of State secession], and so weaken their [political power] that they can never again endanger the [sovereignty of the Federal Government]; and so [remake] their municipal institutions as to make them republican in spirit as well as in name.

"We especially insist that the property of [leading former Confederates] should be seized and appropriated to the [Federal Treasury in partial] payment of the [Federal] debt, caused by the unjust and wicked [defense of the Confederacy] which they [undertook in response to our Federal invasion forces].

"How can such punishments be inflicted and such [confiscations enacted] without doing violence to established [governmental] principles? Two positions have been suggested. First: to treat those States as never having [seceded from] the [rule of the Federal Government]. . . . Second: To accept the position in which they [seceded from the rule of the Federal Government, became] an independent government *de facto*, and an alien enemy to be dealt with according to the laws of war. . . .

"In [remaking the Governments in the conquered States] . . . no remaking can be effected in [those] States if they have never left the [rule of the Federal Government]. But remaking those [State Governments] must be effected; the foundation of their institutions, both political, municipal, and social, must be broken up and re-laid, or all our blood and treasure have been spent in vain. This can only be done by treating and holding them as a conquered people. Then all things which we can desire to do, follow with logical and legitimate [governmental] authority. . . . Whether those [African American men] who have [help fight] our battles should be allowed to vote, or only those with a [noticeable percentage of European American ancestry], I leave to be discussed in the future, when Congress can take legitimate cognizance of it.

"There are some 6,000,000 [European Americans living] in the [southern States]. The number of acres of land is 465,000,000. Of this, those who own above 200 acres each number about 70,000 persons, holding in aggregate, (together with State-owned land), about 394,000,000 acres, leaving for all the others, [holding below 200 acres each,] about 71,000,000 acres. By thus [seizing] the [farms] of the [people owning over 200 acres, who we can suppose represent the leading Confederates], the [Federal] Government would [take to itself] 394,000,000 acres, [and would control land owned by cities and towns as well], and yet nine-tenths of the people [living in the conquered States] would remain untouched [by this Federal land confiscation program]. Divide this [confiscated] land into convenient farms. Give, if you please, 40 acres to each adult [African American man]. Suppose there are 1,000,000 of them. That would require 40,000,000 acres, which, deducted from 394,000,000, leaves 354,000,000 acres for [the Federal Government to] sell. Divide [these 354,000,000 confiscated acres] into suitable farms and sell it to the highest bidders. I think it, including town property, would average [selling for] at least $10 per acre. That [sale] would produce [for the Federal Treasury] $3,540,000,000.

"Let that be applied as follows, to wit:

1. Invest $300,000,000 in 6% [Federal] bonds, and add the interest semi-annually to the pensions of those who have become entitled by this villainous [defense of the Confederacy].

2. [Give out] $200,000,000 to [reimburse] the damage done to [Federal owners of naval ships, farms, businesses and other properties and likewise to those few Confederate owners who can prove that they supported the conquest of their Nation.]

3. Pay the residue, being $3,040,000,000, toward [paying holders of Federal Government bonds and other debt documents].

"If the [land within the conquered States] is ever to be made a safe Republic, let [that land] be cultivated by the toil of the [new] owners, or the [wage-earning] labor of intelligent citizens. This must be done even though it drives [the owners of 200 or more acres of land] into exile. . . .

"It is far easier and more beneficial to [deport] 70,000 proud, bloated, and defiant [owners of 200 or more acres of land] than to [deport] 4,000,000 [African Americans from that region, who are [already acclimated to working Southern farmland] and [presumed to be] loyal to the [Federal] Government. This latter scheme ('colonization' of [newly independent African Americans]) was a favorite plan of [Marylanders, Montgomery and Frank Blair and their father, Frank, Sr.], with which they had for a while inoculated our late sainted President, [Abe Lincoln]. But a single experiment made him discard it and its advisers. Since I have mentioned the Blair's, I may say a word more of these persistent apologists of the [conquered States, plus Maryland, Kentucky and Missouri]. . . . They are a family of considerable power, some merit, of admirable audacity and [abominable] selfishness. With impetuous alacrity they seize the White House, and hold possession of it, as in the [past Lincoln Administration], until shaken off by the overpowering force of public indignation. Their pernicious counsel had well nigh defeated the reelection of Abraham Lincoln; and if it should prevail with the [Johnson] Administration, pure and patriotic as [Andrew] Johnson is admitted to be, it will render him the most unpopular Executive - save one James Buchanan, of course - that ever occupied the Presidential chair. But there is no fear of that. He will soon say, as [Abe] Lincoln said, "Your time has come!"

"Is this great conquest [of the Confederate States] to be in vain? That will depend upon . . . the next [Federal] Congress. To Congress alone belongs the power of [remaking the conquered State Governments], of [imposing] law [upon] the vanquished. . . . Under [Andrew Johnson's program for remaking the conquered State Governments] every [conquered] State will send [past defenders of the Confederacy] to [the Federal] Congress, and they, with [the Democrats] in the [northern States], will control Congress, and will occupy the White House. . . .

"Young men, this duty devolves on you. Would to God, it only for that, I were still in the prime of my life, that I might aid you to fight through this last, greatest battle [to overturn society in the conquered States]."

Upon reading Stevens' speech we need to remember that the "highest bidders" that he envisioned would be wealthy speculators from the northern States (and maybe a few from Maryland, Kentucky and Missouri, and maybe a few foreigners) because everyone living in the conquered States was bankrupt. Horace Greeley printed Stevens' speech in full, word-for-word, in the September 11, 1865 issue of the widely read New York *Tribune*, but he offered critical editorial comment elsewhere in his paper. Greeley complained that Stevens "seems not to care for giving" African American men access to the polls. And Greeley submitted: "We protest against any warfare on [property in the conquered States] . . . because the wealthier [people there], being more enlightened and humane that the ignorant and vulgar, are less [hostile toward the African Americans]." Greeley even warned that, as a practical matter, Stevens' confiscation plan would not work out the way he theorized it would. [R96;214-217]

Eight days later, Charles Sumner presided over the Massachusetts State Republican Convention held at Worcester. And he used that forum to attack Andrew Johnson's program for remaking the ex-Confederate State Governments. Sumner, who dared not personally investigate conditions in the ex-Confederate States, used letters from correspondents to allege that violence persisted in that region and that "the [secessionist] spirit still prevails" there. He charged that Congress, not Andrew Johnson, held "plenary powers over the whole subject" of remaking ex-Confederate State Governments. And he admonished Johnson to force remade ex-Confederate State Governments to include African American men among eligible voters. Johnson had the power to do that, Sumner reasoned. If he could require those remade State Governments to outlaw African American bonding and to repudiate all Confederate debt, then he could force them to accept the votes of African American men. And Congress could certainly force the same result, he argued, again going through his Constitutional theories on "state suicide" and "guarantee a republican form of government." Struggling as always, to twist the meaning of the Federal Constitution to somehow legally prove it authorized Federal subjugation of the ex-Confederate States, Sumner alleged that the words meant something "which was not fully revealed to [the men who wrote the document]; but which we must now declare [to be its meaning] in the light of our institutions." Of this twisted reinterpretation, Biographer David Donald wrote:

> "Perhaps it ought to be said simply that the whole problem of [remaking ex-Confederate State Governments] was extra-constitutional and that every theory of [that remaking] required the twisting of the words in the Constitution to purposes never envisaged by the framers of that venerable document."

Yet, David Donald would conclude that Sumner's listeners "found his appeals strongly persuasive." And Sumner's appeal to Massachusetts pride helped to further persuade the Delegates and those reading newspaper accounts of the Convention proceedings. "Massachusetts means always to keep on the right road, and by unerring instinct knows the way," he intoned. Follow Massachusetts, he urged other States. The voting power of Massachusetts African American men, who were perhaps more European than African in their ancestry, and whose vote total was too small to be very important, enabled Massachusetts Republicans to loudly crow throughout the northern States that they were "holier than thou." And Sumner cried that the vote of African American men in the conquered States was essential because that region was "full of spirits who have sworn undying hatred, not only of the [Federal Government], but to reason itself." If such men were allowed a seat in Congress, not one "would vote to pay the interest on the national debt." Then, to scare bondholders more pointedly, Sumner held a Federal bond up over his head so all could see, and alleged that such Federal bonds would have no value if the Federal Government continued to embrace Andrew Johnson's program for remaking the Governments in the conquered States. Then Sumner concluded: "This is not the first time that I have battled with the barbarism of [African American bonding]. I battle still, as the bloody monster retreats to its last citadel; and, God willing, I mean to hold on, if it takes what remains to me of life." Perhaps I should comment that those were mighty tough words from a man who had displayed such lack of physical courage after receiving a caning at the hands of Preston Brooks. After the convention concluded, Sumner would arrange for 20,000 copies of his Worcester speech to be circulated. [R73;226-228]

Meanwhile at Fortress Monroe on September 25, Jeff Davis was permitted to see the letter Varina had written 11 days earlier. It had been written with alarm, for Varina had seen newspaper reports that Jeff was very sick. Although Varina and the children had written many previous letters, orders from Edwin Stanton had prevented Nelson Miles from showing any of those letters to Jeff, although John Craven had been permitted to see some letters from Varina.

> "My darling Husband,

> ". . . My dear, dear Husband, tell me precisely how you are. Do not let my inevitable sorrow be swelled by uncertainties. You do not save me anything. I see in the papers accounts of every pang. Why not tell your poor helpless wife in your own sweet kind way the worst, and thus enable me to defy the penny-a-liners who for an item would wring the last drop of blood out of a broken heart. If your health has failed to the extent represented, am I not the one most deeply interested?"

Continuing her letter, Varina had written that she had sent appeals to Nelson Miles, Andrew Johnson and James Speed "making request if by any means now at length I might have a prospect by the will of God to come unto you." She thought little Jeff, Maggie and William were safe and well with her mother and Robert Brown in Canada, but apologized for not having recent news from them. Varina explained that she planned to remain at the Schley home near Augusta until she received more definite news. Then Varina reported her fond satisfaction over Robert Brown's devotion to her and the children:

"As to Robert Brown I could not tell you what he has been to me. I gave him 75 dollars, which was the sum he specified as necessary to replace a part of the clothes taken from him by the Federals at our capture, but very soon found that he paid bills for which he had received no money . . . . He seemed much hurt when I told him that I did not desire to take his money. . . . He explained that so long as the children wanted an education and his hands could make it for them, they could not want."

". . . The only use he has made of his newly acquired [independence] was to knock a [European American] man down who made use of some abusive remarks before the children, when he was going to New York on the ship, and he was borne out in his course by the Captain, who examined into the case and pronounced the assault justifiable." [R19;174-175]

Varina then presented some news about Jeff's brother, Joe and some other family members before closing with these words:

"May God bless you and keep you, dearest honored husband. The all absorbing love of my whole life seems so poor a tribute to your worth. I can never hope to be worthy of you, only count all my love to one for rightness and pray that I may soon see you — the prayers of the righteous avail much.

"Devotedly,

"Your Wife." [R30;173-175]

Meanwhile on September 27, the South Carolina Constitutional Convention, meeting in Columbia, concluded the work of creating a new State Constitution, having convened two weeks earlier. The Convention had been made up of 117 men elected as Delegates in a September 4 election. Wade Hampton had been among the elected, but being in remote mountains at Cashiers Valley with family, he had not received word in time to return to Columbia to participate. Many had received their pardons from Andrew Johnson barely in time to qualify to be seated as Delegates. In all, throughout South Carolina, Johnson would pardon 845 men, 650 of those needing it because they owned $20,000 or more in property.

Recognizing reality of life in their State, the new South Carolina Constitution stipulated "the [bonded African Americans] in South Carolina having been [made independent] by the action of [Federal] authorities, neither [bonding of persons] nor involuntary servitude, except as a punishment for crime whereof the party shall have been duly convicted, shall ever be reestablished in this State." This ratified the fact that all formerly bonded African Americans were independent, and it was understood that the same were individually responsible for rearing their families and earning their livings. But very few Delegates saw any reasonable way of giving newly independent adult African American men the right to vote, especially since essentially none yet owned taxable property and their numbers, if voting, would permit them to take over State and local governments with anticipated dire consequences. There was a little talk of giving a few the right to vote based on ability to read and write or ownership of taxable property. And history would suggest a little of that thinking would have been helpful to progress in South Carolina. But the Delegates chose to limit as follows the qualifications necessary to be a voter or to hold office. Note that Federal military men would not be allowed to vote.

"He shall be [an independent European American man] who has attained the age of 21 years, and is not a pauper, nor a commissioned officer or private soldier of the army nor a seaman or marine of the navy of the United States. He shall, for two years next preceding the day of election, have been a citizen of this State; or for the same period an emigrant from Europe, who had declared his intention to become a citizen of the United States, according to the [Federal] Constitution and [Federal] laws. He shall have resided in this State for a least 2 years next preceding the day of election, and for the last 6 months of that time in the district in which he offers to vote."

Anticipating a need to greatly expand the court system in response to the sudden remaking of the State's social structure, many Delegates felt it was also prudent to lay the groundwork for establishing a network of new courts, to be known as District Courts, to handle cases involving African Americans, stipulating that these new courts "shall have jurisdiction of all civil causes wherein one or both of the parties are persons of [noticeable African ancestry], and of all criminal cases wherein the accused is a person of [noticeable African ancestry]."

Delegates made some other major changes to modernize the State Constitution. The Federal President and Vice President would be elected directly by voters via the Electoral College, not by the Legislature. As before, the Legislature was to elect Senators for the State's two seats in the Federal Senate. Delegates apportioned the counties into 4 Districts for representation in the Federal House. The Governor and Lieutenant Governor were to be elected by voters directly to 4-year terms, no longer by the Legislature. The Governor was made more powerful, in the future holding the power to veto legislation. And the Lieutenant Governor was made President of the State Senate. The State Senate was made up of one Senator from each election District, except Charleston would get two because of its high population. The State House would "consist of 124 members, to be apportioned among the several election districts of the State, according to the number of [European American] inhabitants contained in each, and the amount of all taxes raised by the General Assembly, whether direct or indirect, or of whatever species, paid in each." This redistribution of power across the State — taking seats from Charleston and the older low country region and giving seats to the upstate region — was a revolution in the distribution of political power. Governor Benjamin Perry had encouraged this redistribution in his opening remarks, calling the old apportionment of seats "unequal and unjust." He used an extreme example to drive home his point: "Twenty or 30 voters in one of the parishes, whose population and taxation combined entitle it to only one member of the House of Representatives, have the same representation in the Senate that 3,000 voters have in Edgefield District, whose population and taxation entitle it to 6 members in the House. This is contrary to all republican principles of political justice and equality."

Apparently, to get the new government up and running as quickly as possible, voter ratification across the State was to be omitted. Instead they were told to go to the polls in 3 weeks, on October 18, to elect State officers and members of the State House and State Senate. Immediate election of Representatives to the Federal House could wait, so November 22 was set for their election. Again to speed the process of enacting new laws to meet the pressing needs of the State's new social structure, the Convention approved the creation of a two-man commission to draft laws to be recommended to the new Legislature when it was to convene on October 25. Governor Benjamin Perry would quickly name Judge David Wardlaw and Abbeville lawyer Armistead Burt to the two-man commission, and they would set to work on their assignment, which was "to prepare and report to the Legislature what laws will be necessary and proper in consequence of the alterations made in the [State Constitution], and especially to prepare and submit a code for the regulation of labor and the protection [of] and government of the [African American] population of the State." Certainly, with the economy in shambles, hardly anyone with any money to pay workers, and the winter season approaching, there was an urgent need to help find living work for newly independent African Americans and to protect them from abuse. [R201;14-20]

(4Q65)

Meanwhile in Mississippi on October 2, voters elected officials for the State Government, in accordance with the Constitution as it had revised in August. The primary issue during the campaign had been whether or not to allow African Americans to testify in court over issues involving European Americans — many voters fearing that this court-room right, if granted, would lead to voting rights for men of full or partial African ancestry. A majority of those elected to the Legislature were opposed to allowing African American testimony, but the "ablest leaders" among those elected favored African American testimony. Benjamin Humphreys, a former Mississippi Whig and high ranking Confederate officer, was elected Governor over a candidate who viewed allowing African American testimony more favorably. Concerning the Federal House, those elected "were all old-line Whigs except one," a Democrat who had opposed State secession. Of the Mississippi election, historian James Garner would write:

"The result of the election was unfavorably regarded [in the northern States], and was cited as an illustration of the popular preference for ex-Confederates as against [men who had opposed State secession]. Although the President was disappointed at the defeat of [Humphreys' opponent], upon the recommendation of Governor Sharkey, he sent Humphreys a pardon in the first week of October."

At about this time Federal officials released from prison Charles Clarke, Governor of Mississippi during the Confederate years. Also, President Johnson "restored the privilege of the writ of *habeas corpus*, which had been suspended since December 1863." Governor Humphreys would be inaugurated on October 16, although for some time he would not be recognized by the Federal Government as the real executive of the State, Johnson deciding instead to have his appointee, Provisional Governor Starkey, continue to represent Mississippi concerning many matters, such as distribution of pardons — this arrangement would persist for considerable time. [R204;94-96]

Meanwhile, at Fortress Monroe, on October 2, Nelson Miles finally ordered Jeff Davis to be moved from the walled-up casemate in which he had been imprisoned since May 22, to a newly-fortified, but comfortable and heated room in Carroll Hall. It was none too soon, as winter was approaching, and for the previous few weeks, at night and during the early daylight hours, foggy air from the bay had often immersed the open-air casemate in a penetrating dampness. Hudson Strode describes the move:

"Later that very morning [Jeff Davis] was moved to a second-story room in the northwest bastion of the fort. Davis' good-sized corner room in Carroll Hall had a fireplace in the center of the end wall. The opposite wall opened into the room occupied by the officer of the guard and was divided by an iron-grating door. The two doors on the side walls opened into a corridor and a veranda respectively. They, too, had iron bars, and one had in addition a panel shutter in which were inserted two panes of glass. Sentinels paced just outside [the prisoner's] room; one along the gallery; one along the passageway; and still another in the guardroom. Davis might be watched from three directions.

"The furnishings were Spartan. A basin and pitcher stood on a chair with a broken-off back that served as a washstand. In a chimney recess were an empty bookshelf and pegs on which to hang clothes, but [Davis] [would not be] allowed to have any garments except those he wore. He [would still change] his linen according to General Miles' whims. A pleasing refinement, however, was a folding screen which [would enable] him to wash unobserved. For four and a half months heretofore he had had the eyes of sentries on him not only when he bathed, but when he used the portable commode."

Jeff would write Varina nine days later "The dry air, good water and a fire when requisite have already improved my physical condition. . . ." And just as important was the reduction in intentional torment. Instead of constantly pacing alongside his bed within the prison cell, Miles' guards constantly paced, still within hearing, but outside the room. Yet Miles, who well knew how light hurt Davis' sensitive eyes, continued ordering his guards to burn a lamp all night long within Davis' room. Yet, John Craven had succeeded in persuading Miles to have the guards turn the wick a little lower. [R19;263]

Let us looking at the general political activity across all of the conquered States:

By October people living in the conquered States were busily implementing Andrew Johnson's program for remaking their State Governments. As in almost all northern States, qualified voters in the former Confederate States would continue to be limited to adult men of essentially pure European ancestry (in fact, at this time no northern State permitted voting by African American men in any politically-significant number). Voters qualified by this method were electing Delegates to State Conventions and, abiding by Federal demands, these Delegates were drawing up new State Constitutions that repudiated past State debt, repudiated their rights to State Sovereignty, and confirmed that all bonded African Americans were immediately independent. And these qualified voters were, in turn, ratifying these new State Constitutions. Democratic leaders in each conquered State were reforming their respective Party, anticipating that voters qualified in this manner would vote for Democratic Party candidates over Republican Party candidates by enormous margins. Qualified voters were electing Democrats as Legislators, Governors and Federal Representatives. The newly-organized State Legislatures, packed with Democrats, were electing Federal Senators and ratifying the Amendment to the Federal Constitution that, when ratified by sufficient States, would reaffirm that all bonded African Americans were independent.

And these new Representatives and Senators were preparing to travel to Washington City to attend the opening session of the Congress on December 4. [R96;217-218]

Ratification by the States of the Federal Amendment confirming that all bonded African Americans were independent had begun on February 1, 1865. On December 18th it would reach the requisite 27 States. During February the Amendment had been approved by 12 States in which no bonded African Americans lived (Illinois, Rhode Island, Michigan, New York, Maine, Kansas, Massachusetts, Pennsylvania, Missouri, Ohio, Indiana, Nevada, and Minnesota); and by 5 States in which bonded African Americans did live (Maryland, puppet West Virginia, conquered Virginia, subjugated Missouri, and conquered Louisiana). During that same month Legislatures of 2 States in which bonded African Americans lived (Delaware and Kentucky) voted to reject the Amendment. During March, April and May the Amendment had been approved by 3 States in which no bonded African Americans lived (Wisconsin, Vermont, and Connecticut) and in 2 conquered States where they did live (Tennessee and Arkansas). During those 3 months, it had been rejected by the Legislature representing conquered Mississippi. During the summer (July 1) it was approved by New Hampshire. During November and December it would be approved by the new legislatures of 4 conquered States containing large populations of African Americans: South Carolina (November 13) Alabama (December 2), North Carolina (December 4), and Georgia (December 5). At this point, with only one more State ratification needed to give the Amendment the force of Federal law, the Legislature in far-off Oregon State would become involved. Since gaining Statehood, the people of Oregon had prohibited independent people of noticeable African descent from even living in their State — there's was the ultimate act of Exclusionism. In fact, the African American prohibition was in the Oregon State Constitution. Apparently many Oregonians, worried that a few independent African Americans might move way out to their fair State, had put off voting for the Amendment as long as its ratification was in doubt. But with only one more State needed to complete the ratification process, the Oregon Legislature would decide in mid-December that holding out any longer was politically foolish. So, on December 11, those Legislators would vote to ratify the Amendment. One week later, upon receipt of the formal documents from Oregon, William Seward, speaking for the Federal Government, would declare the Amendment ratified. From that day forward owning a bonded African American would violate the Federal Constitution. So it was during October, 1865 that it became apparent to Republican politicians, including Thad Stevens and Charles Sumner, that the conquered people of the former Confederacy, acting in accordance with Andrew Johnson's policies, were agreeing to the principle that all bonded African Americans were independent, even though paying jobs were essentially non-existent where they lived. [R78;1103,1865]

In early October Thad Stevens lambasted Andrew Johnson in a speech at Gettysburg for giving out pardons to former Confederates so freely, alleging that Johnson was using the Executive patronage power and the pardoning power to "build up a throne." The Gettysburg *Star* reported him saying, "I was lately in Philadelphia, and heard of a case (a sample of many others) which stirred my blood, cold as it is," because Andrew Johnson had pardoned a former Confederate and ordered that Federal Agents return to him the $100,000 worth of Philadelphia City Bonds previously confiscated. "[Andrew Johnson] is too much of a [low-class commoner]," Stevens submitted, "to indulge in such absolute ideas" regarding legal rights to property ownership. "At the same time Stevens was striving to better clarify his proposals for confiscating 85% of the land within the conquered States. He wrote Charles Sumner hoping he might know where to find information about Alexander II's Russian land redistribution program. Not long before Abe Lincoln had proclaimed the invasion of the Confederacy, Alexander II had begun a program to give mobility to people who were bound by serfdom laws to work on specific farms. And Alexander II had ordered that some acreage from large farms be redistributed to newly-mobile farm workers. Inquiring of this Russian program, Stevens wrote: "Where can I find in English a correct history of the condition of Russian serfs and the terms of their [recent mobility] - I know not where to look for it." In late October he again wrote Sumner:

"I have just returned [home] and got [your letter]. [Delegates to] our [Republican] State Convention [were] nearly all [in agreement with us] when [our plan] was explained to them. So have I found everybody when properly informed, except [for] office holders. I am sure our Members of Congress would all be [in agreement with us] if we had no villainous newspapers [to contend with]. How far [newspapermen] may intimidate [Members of Congress] I know not.

"[William] Seward and others are making great efforts to sustain [Andrew] Johnson's [policy].

"I am trying to get up a [Federal] Soldier's Convention to denounce his policy. How it will succeed I know not, but should find no trouble if I had a little more time — the [Executive] patronage is hard to fight against. I wish New York [State] might be lost [to Democrats], but fear it will not."

At this point Stevens is apparently so angry over Andrew Johnson's support among New York State Republican leaders that he is hoping the New York State Democratic Party might defeat them in upcoming elections, thereby giving New York State's more militant Republican Faction a better chance to gain control of their Party. [R96;217-218]

Meanwhile on October 17, Margaret Howell and Jeff's nephew, Joe Davis arrived in Montreal, Canada. They immediately deposited in the vault of the Bank of Montreal, the valuable Confederate Letter Books, which they had secreted in the false bottom of one of their luggage trunks. These valuable documents would be useful in documenting the history of the Confederate Government, and Jeff Davis' role therein. [R19;266]

Meanwhile, the Mississippi Legislature gathered on October 16, the same day as Governor Benjamin Humphreys was inaugurated, the inaugural address serving as his message to the Legislators. Concerning the status of newly independent African Americans, the incoming Governor said:

"The highest degree of elevation in the scale of civilization to which they are capable morally and intellectually must be secured to them by education and religious training; but they cannot be admitted to political or social equality with the [European American] race. It is due to ourselves and to the [European] immigrants invited to our shores, and it should never be forgotten to maintain the fact, that ours is and it shall ever be, a government of [European American] men."

He further urged that State and local governments deal justly with African Americans and encourage them to choose employment capable of sustaining them and their families, but that labor contracts, once agreed to, must be fulfilled.

In Humphreys' logic concerning race and "political or social equality," we see a critical flaw, which needs to be explained here:

A group whose racial ancestry ranges from pure African to almost pure European does not represent a "race" nearly to the extent that a group of Americans of essentially pure European ancestry does. So Humphreys' argument that "race" limited the potential attainment of "all" African Americans ignored the obvious fact that thousands upon thousands were far more European than African in their ancestry, that many, many African Americans (approaching a majority) were, genetically speaking, a mix of two races. We see today that the African American exhibiting absolutely no evidence of European blood is an unusual and small minority of the population. In 1865 the unusually wide distribution of intellectual and moral ability within the pure-to-mixed-race population of African Americans, which ranged from quite limited to admirable, was far broader than was the corresponding distribution characterizing the population of European Americans. On the other hand, with regard to physical ability, African Americans, as a group, were equal or superior to European Americans as a group.

With regard to African Americans giving testimony in courts, Governor Humphreys advised that the Constitution and justice required the African American be protected in his person and property, which could only be assured through an "independent and enlightened judiciary." Mississippi "courts, therefore, should be opened to the [African American], and he be permitted to testify and introduce such testimony as he or his attorney may deem essential to establish the truth of the case. It is an injustice to our courts and juries to say that they will not protect innocent [European American] or [African American] men from false testimony and the perjury of [African American] witnesses." But the crucial issue was allowing an African American to testify in court for or against a European American, and Humphreys did not specifically urge adoption of that measure. With regard to ratifying the Amendment to the Federal Constitution making bonded African Americans independent in all States, Humphreys gave no guidance. The Mississippi Legislature would engage in protracted debate and law-writing for the next 6 weeks. [R204;111-112]

Meanwhile in South Carolina, elections were held on October 18 in accordance with the new State Constitution finalized on September 27. For the office of Governor James Orr barely edged out Wade Hampton by a vote of 9,928 to 9,185. Other State officers and the members of the State Senate and State House were also elected. (The election of Representatives to the Federal House was scheduled for three weeks later, on November 22.) If the truth were told, Hampton probably would have won the election if ballots had not been discarded to prevent election of such a former high-ranking Confederate officer. Hampton knew the score and discouraged voting for him. But Andrew Johnson had prepared for the possibility of Hampton's election by asking Attorney General James Speed to hasten to the executive desk the South Carolinian's application for pardon (Hampton's request for pardon had not yet been signed.) Hampton and his friends had even run newspaper notices to discourage votes, such as the notice published in the Columbia *Daily Phoenix* on October 13:

> "Several nominations of Wade Hampton, for the office of Governor, having been made in the Charleston and other papers of the State, we are authorized to state that, for various reasons, he cannot consent to be a candidate for the office. Highly appreciating the confidence of his fellow citizens throughout the State, it is proper to make this announcement, to prevent embarrassment to his friends and those who are disposed to vote for him for Governor."

A month after the election of James Orr, Wade Hampton would publish a letter to his supporters in the *Daily Phoenix* issue of November 15 offering encouragement and expressing deep appreciation for their confidence in him. Some excerpts are noteworthy:

> Of unity in purpose, he wrote: "Every association of the past, every duty of the present, every hope of the future, bid us still to stand 'shoulder to shoulder.' The work before us demands all the patriotism, all the courage, all the endurance of our whole people. Let no party strife, no minor issues, no petty politics, divert us from the great and pressing work of the hour. That of reanimating, as far as possible, our prostrate and bleeding State."

> Of brotherhood in suffering, he wrote: "Here we have worshipped the God of our father's; here amid charred and blackened ruins, are the spots we once fondly called our homes; and here we buried the ashes of our kindred. All these sacred ties bind us."

> Of their confidence in him, he wrote, "This I shall cherish as one of the proudest recollections of my life, for it assures me of your belief that I have tried to do my duty. It only remains for me, in bidding you farewell, to say that whenever the State needs my services she has only to command and I shall obey." [R201;20, R199;173-174]

Meanwhile, political pressure to release Jeff Davis was mounting from within the Federal States and from Europe. During October, a Delegation of Baltimore ladies presented to Andrew Johnson a petition, containing thousands of signatures, which requested that Jeff Davis be set free. And, during late October, a Delegation of Italian Americans from New York presented Johnson a petition from Milan, Italy, which also begged for his release. [R19;267]

On the other hand, Edwin Stanton and his agents were planning to execute Henry Wirz on November 10, based on the rigged military court finding that he had committed war crimes while in charge of the large Confederate military prison camp near Andersonville, Georgia. Stanton, his top leaders and the Lincoln Administration needed such a conviction to distract voters and future historians from their own cruelty toward their own men. Suffering among Federals imprisoned at Andersonville and elsewhere was the result of the Lincoln Administration's refusal to exchange prisoners and the destruction of vast stores of Georgia foodstuffs by William Sherman's Federal horde of devastators. Suffering among imprisoned Federals was not the fault of Henry Wirz. Although hanging Wirz would offer useful distraction, it would do little to justify the Federal invasion of the Confederacy in the minds of future historians. Only by prosecuting Jeff Davis, could Stanton accomplish that goal. But none of his agents had turned up even a shred of evidence that could be used to manipulate a case against Davis. And Stanton had to overcome the considerable public support that had been shown for their celebrity prisoner.

So, in desperation, Stanton sought to make Wirz give false testimony against Davis to save his own skin. Would Wirz do that? Would he help Stanton send Jeff Davis to the gallows to save his own skin? R. B. Winder, a former Confederate officer imprisoned across from Wirz's cell door, observed

Stanton's agents encourage Wirz to save his own life by helping them hang Davis. Winder later wrote down the following account in a letter to Varina:

"The door of the room which I occupied while in confinement at the Old Capitol Prison was immediately opposite Wirz's door, both of which were occasionally open. About two days before his execution I saw three or four men pass into the room, and upon their coming out, Wirz told me that they had given him assurances that his life would be spared and his liberty given him if he could give any testimony that would reflect upon [Jeff] Davis, or implicate him directly or indirectly, with the treatment of prisoners of war, as charged by the [Federal] authorities — that he indignantly spurned these propositions and assured them that he had never been connected with Davis, either officially, personally, or socially . . . that the offer of his life could not purchase [from] him [and act of] treason and treachery [against the people of the conquered States]."

And Wirz's lawyer and his minister, Father Boyle, were also present when Stanton's agents again assured Wirz that "a high Cabinet officer" — obviously, that would be Stanton himself — would see to it that he was released unharmed if he would only accuse Jeff Davis of war crimes at the Confederate prisoner of war camp near Andersonville. Courageously, as the clock counted down to the time of his hanging, Wirz told these friends, "I would not become a traitor to him or anyone else to save my life."

Of Wirz's self-sacrificing stance, which meant so much to the honor of the Confederacy, and obstructed so meaningfully Republican schemes to glorify the history of their conquest, Jeff Davis would later write:

"Arrested while under protection of a parole, tried in time of peace by a Military Commission of officers, in a service to which he did not belong, denied the favorable testimony of those who came, and subpoenas for other witnesses of like character — without these ordinary means, granted to the accused in all civilized countries, he died a martyr to conscientious adherence to truth." [R19;267-268]

Meanwhile, Charles Sumner continued his campaign to build Republican Parties in the conquered States by making voters of all the African American men living therein. He compiled a collection of his "resolutions, articles, and Senate speeches" on remaking those State Governments and had the work published in a 32-page pamphlet which he titled *Security and Reconciliation for the Future*. And, in a letter published in Theodore Tilton's weekly, *The Independent*, he appealed to fortune-seekers in the northern States who aspired to make money in the conquered States: "I would say to the merchant, who wishes to open trade with this region — to the capitalist, who would send his money there — to the emigrant, who seeks to find a home there — begin by assuring [also, legal and voting rights for African American] men. And Sumner encouraged continued punishment of former Confederates in a "long, learned" article published in the *Atlantic Monthly*. Apparently to dramatize the alleged dangers that Carl Schurz would be facing during his upcoming tour of the conquered States, Sumner talked some friends into paying a well-publicized "hazardous duty premium" on Schurz's life insurance policy. Sumner also arranged for a talented writer to accompany Schurz to ensure maximum propaganda value. Sumner also corresponded often with other Federal Representatives and Senators, attempting always to warn them of the impending loss of political power that would result from Andrew Johnson's willingness to honor some degree of State Rights in the remaking Governments in the conquered States. To E. D. Morgan, Senator from New York, Sumner warned "the [former Confederates] are springing into their old life and the [Democrats in the Federal States] also." Although his thinking was contradicted by the racial polices of sister States to the north, Sumner alleged that Andrew Johnson's policy for remaking State Governments was "flagrantly unconstitutional, because it sets up a discrimination of [race]," and "also against common sense, common humanity, and openly against Almighty God."

Yet, except for a few northeastern States, where the African American population was both small and of substantial mixed race ancestry, the northern States had not permitted African American men to vote. And most people seemed concerned that, if the Federal Government was permitted to force South Carolina to admit the votes of African American men, why not Illinois? Why not my state, my county, my town? The Republican Party had been founded on advocating Exclusionism, not Abolitionism, and those two appeals conveyed directly opposite meanings. Exclusion keeps African Americans far, far away. Abolition invites them to become a neighbor. Yet, the Republican Party desperately needed to build majority Republican Parties in the conquered States, and the only way to do that was to create a majority African American electorate in each of them. Even so, the Republican State Convention in Wisconsin soundly endorsed Andrew Johnson's policies toward the conquered States, and Wisconsin voters rejected a proposal to give voting rights to the African American men who lived in their State — few as they were. Although neighboring Massachusetts had, for many years, permitted its few African American men to vote, voters in neighboring Connecticut rejected a proposal to permit their African American men to do so. Governor, O. P. Morton, campaigned mightily against giving voting rights to African American men who lived in Indiana, alleging that such a move would "result in a war of races." And at a Convention of New York Republicans, Delegates resolved to applaud Andrew Johnson's "eminently wise and just" policies. So, for these reasons, Charles Sumner and like-minded Party-builders were rather discouraged as the opening of Congress loomed on the horizon.

Winter Davis wrote Charles Sumner that the only way to build majority Republican parties in the conquered States was to — before admitting their Federal Representative and Senators – pass a Federal law or a Federal Constitutional Amendment that compelled those States to permit African American men to vote. Such a move would be impossible after those States were admitted, Winter Davis feared. And Thad Stevens, ever worried about losing his powerful position, wrote Sumner asking for advice: "Is it possible to devise any plan to arrest the [Federal] Government in its ruinous course? Is there no way to arrest the insane course of the [Johnson Administration]?" Stevens, who had reluctantly resigned himself to support voting by African American men as the only way to retain power, had failed during October to convince a majority of the Pennsylvania Republican Delegates to back a resolution calling for making African American men eligible to vote. Ben Wade was despondent as well: "The [African Americans] of the [conquered States] will be compelled to hew out their own way to [equal legal and voting rights] by the power of their own right arm . . . if by an insurrection they could contrive to slay one half of their oppressors, the other half would hold them in the highest respect and no doubt treat them with [equal legal and voting rights]." After slaying 360,000 Federals and 260,000 Confederates, in the Federal Invasion of the Confederacy, Wade apparently hoped to resume the killing — to add 3,000,000 to the carnage. [R73;230-231]

Sumner also sought support among individual members of Andrew Johnson's Cabinet. Attorney General James Speed was supportive of making African American men voters in the conquered States, but complained he could not influence his boss. Interior Secretary James Harlan disapproved of Johnson's policy but cautioned Sumner against fighting Johnson too vigorously, for extreme hatefulness would drive him away and into the arms of the Democratic Party. Of all Cabinet members, Edwin Stanton was most willing to cooperate with Sumner. When Stanton had visited Boston in September, both men had professed to be in agreement on the objective to build Republican Party Machines in the conquered States, empowered by the votes of African American men. In response to Sumner's advocacy before the Massachusetts Republican Convention for long-term military occupation of the conquered States, Stanton agreed that Sumner had "asked him to do only what he wanted to do." But Sumner did not even approach William Seward about forcing conquered States to accept the votes of African American men, because Sumner sensed that Seward was firmly opposed to overriding that aspect of State Rights. Sumner was rebuked in his attempt to win over Gideon Welles. Welles insisted that the less affluent European American men in the conquered States could be won over to vote Republican, so the votes of African American men would not be necessary. And Treasury Secretary Hugh McCulloch labeled as demagoguery Sumner's public warning that commercial prosperity in the northern States and the ability of the Federal Government to pay its huge debt was dependent upon making voters of all African American men in the conquered States. McCulloch countered, "Nothing can be more damaging to our credit than the openly expressed opinion by leading men, that there may arise contingencies in which the [Federal] debt will be repudiated."

And Sumner and Treasury Secretary Hugh McCulloch were at odds over how the latter was handling his problem of finding, in the conquered States, banking men who had never supported in any way their State or the Confederate Governments after 1860. McCulloch needed to establish a network of Federal Treasury agents in the conquered States, but Congress had prohibited the hiring of any Federal employee who had ever supported State of National governments in the former Confederate States. Biographer David Donald described McCulloch's dilemma: "Since there were not enough qualified [men in the conquered States] who had never borne arms against the [Federals] or in any other way assisted the Confederacy, McCulloch, after consulting with [Andrew Johnson] decided that the law had not been intended to apply to the present circumstances and went ahead making provisional appointments throughout the [conquered States]." Sumner complained that such a move was an "open disregard of an Act of Congress," but failed to persuade McCulloch to change his policy. Sumner probably favored hiring Treasury Agents from the northern States and sending them into the conquered States, for men such as that could help build Republican Party Political Machines. However, such a move would surely increase in that region a more intense hatred toward the Federal Government. So, on balance, Sumner figured he had little support for forcing Governments in the conquered States to make voters of their African American men. Angry, he complained that the men in the Cabinet were "all courtiers, unhappily, as if they were the counselors of a king."

Among Boston intellectuals, only Sumner's old friend, Wadsworth Longfellow, seemed supportive of his campaign to force conquered States to accept the votes of African American men. Biographer David Donald observed that, after suffering through the four-year invasion, the younger intellectuals in the northeastern States thought differently than their father's generation:

"This new breed of intellectuals thought of themselves as rigorously and scientifically trained in the empirical school, and they veered away from Sumner's grand generalizations about human nature and progress. Considering Great Britain the nearly perfect society, they wanted, as did British reformers, minimal government and a civil service [employees] chosen by merit — and therefore from the ranks of educated men like themselves; and they objected to Sumner's dropping of the civil service reform question after one trial, to his indifference to the tariff question, to his sweeping advocacy of increased [Federal Government] power, and to his frequent invocation of French and Roman law. But more than anything else, the new generation distrusted Sumner's unabashed zeal for [alleged] good causes. Many of them had fought in the [invasion] and had been touched with fire; their emotions and their rhetoric had been singed. They were distrustful of the high-sounding phrase, suspicious of the [alleged] glorious cause. In particular, they were growing disillusioned about the [African American]. Without for a moment regretting the end of [African American bonding] or doubting the necessity of [an invasion] to end it, they did not romanticize the [African American] man as God's image in ebony. Now [an independent] man, he must make his own way. Why Sumner should insist upon special protection for the [African American] was incomprehensible." [R73;228-235]

Meanwhile on November 13 in South Carolina, the State Legislature concluded a Special Session aimed at organizing itself, electing two Federal Senators and ratifying the Amendment to the Federal Constitution that confirmed that African American bonding was unlawful. Elected Federal Senators were former Governor Benjamin Perry and John Manning. The Federal Amendment was ratified. However, many doubted that ratification would persuade Republican leaders to seat South Carolinians in the Federal House and Senate. The South Carolina Legislature would reconvene in regular session soon afterward, on November 27. [R201;20-24]

Meanwhile, two days later, Ben "Beast" Butler wrote Thad Stevens from Lowell, Massachusetts: "I should be glad to see you if possible upon matters presented by the present political crisis." (You will recall that Jeff Davis had given Butler the name, "The Beast," because of the military terrorism he had inflicted on the residents of New Orleans during her subjugation under Federal occupying forces.) Aiming to be a political ally to both Butler and Sumner, Stevens welcomed a visit from Butler, writing back, "I expect to be in Washington about the middle of next week. I should be glad to see you at my rooms at 279 S. B. Street, Capitol Hill." Biographer Richard Current would observed that Stevens' "brick house behind the Capitol [would become] the headquarters of men plotting to undo" Andrew Johnson's program for remaking the Governments in the conquered States. When Butler arrived at Stevens' house he presented a draft of a bill, which would send Federal Agents throughout the conquered States to build Republican Political Machines empowered by the votes of African American men and to elevate their social, economic and political power above that of the European American men of the region. Butler told Stevens that by such a bill they would "commence the fight" in the conquered States against [European American] injustice to [African Americans], enabling the latter to keep "the weak-kneed brethren of the Republican Party" under their control. Stevens was probably enthusiastic about Butler's bill, but he recognized that legislative planning had to be briefly set aside to make room for the most urgent issue of the next two weeks — for Stevens was intently focused on denying seats to any Federal Representatives or Senators arriving from any of the Governments of the conquered States. He probably reminded Butler of his earlier letter to him, written in Lancaster, in which Stevens had advised, "we must put the [conquered] States under Territorial Governments at once, or they will [gain seats in] Congress one by one through [the Johnson Administration's] influence." Stevens was most concerned about Federal Representative H. L. Dawes of Massachusetts, who was Chairman of the House Standing Committee on Elections. Stevens feared that Dawes would feel compassionate toward the region's newly elected Federal Representatives and Senators, and favor approval of their credentials. Since both he and Dawes were from Massachusetts, Stevens was hopeful that Butler might persuade Dawes to favor denying seats to those men. However, Butler confessed that neither he nor Charles Sumner could persuade Dawes to do that. [R96;219-220]

Two days later in Mississippi, on November 17, Provisional Governor William Sharkey received a telegram from Andrew Johnson instructing him to remain in that appointed office in spite of the Inauguration of the newly-elected Governor, Benjamin Humphreys, and that he should "report [to Washington] from time to time when progress was being made by the Legislature. Johnson also "admonished him" to see to it that the Legislature ratify the Amendment that confirmed that bonded African Americans were independent, and enact suitable laws "for the protection of [African Americans] in person and property as justice demanded." And he urged Sharkey to "use his influence with the Legislature to secure the admission of [African American] testimony in [Mississippi] courts." Johnson added, "I do hope that the [people of Mississippi] will see the position they now occupy, and will avail themselves of the favorable opportunity of once more restoring civil governments." But the Mississippi Legislature would be slow in accommodating the wishes of the Republicans in Washington. [R204;96]

The following day, at Fortress Monroe, Nelson Miles ordered John Craven to discontinue all conversation with Jeff Davis except that which was medically necessary. In Miles' words: "In future, your conversation with [Jeff Davis] will be confined strictly to professional matters." As a result, John Craven's diary concerning "the world's most famous prisoner" came to a sudden end. Craven had been a sympathetic listener and an intelligent conversationalist. And those conversations, on wide ranging topics, had contributed greatly to the preservation of Davis' mental health during those endless days of intensive torment. And Craven thought himself fortunate to have such an opportunity to talk frequently with "a superbly informed and fascinating conversationalist." Craven thought Miles order "cruel and unnecessary," as it most certainly was. But Miles wanted to be cruel, and Edwin Stanton probably urged him on in the matter. [R19;268-269]

Meanwhile on November 22 in South Carolina, Wade Hampton delivered an address to a mixed crowd of African Americans and European Americans at Richland Fork, near Columbia. He explained that "our fields must be tilled," but "unless this is done speedily, famine will destroy what little has escaped fire and the sword." He encouraged African Americans to contract as farm laborers and encouraged the farm owners to offer jobs. To owners of farms, he encouraged offering up reasonable labor contracts, advising them to deal "with [the African American worker] fairly, frankly and equitably. Let him see that [we farmers] not only recognize his newly acquired rights, but that we will protect him in the enjoyment of those rights." Turning to the African Americans present, he explained to them the importance of hard work, learning new skills and acquiring education. "You must not think, because you are [independent like European Americans], that you are their equal, because you are not. You will have to do a great many things you cannot do [presently] before you begin to be as great as they are. You will have to be able to write a book, build a railroad, a steam engine, a steamboat, and thousands of other things you know nothing of." So look to your friends in South Carolina, he advised, because "the [northern States people] don't care for you, and they would be perfectly willing to see you die off, so that room can be made for their poor people." To African Americans hoping for Federal doles of free land, he warned, "President Johnson thinks as I do." He explained that they had been made independence at the cost to former owners of $800 to $1,000 per person — farmers cannot give away their land, too. Perhaps his most important advice was this:

"You are [independent] — free to seek you own happiness — free to do the best you can for yourselves — free to work, and free to starve if you do not work. Freedom has its duties as well as its pleasures. And the first duty of every free man is to support himself and his family."

Wade Hampton would be heading to his large farms in Mississippi to see what could be made of them at this point. He was trying to make a go of it as were most of his former bonded African Americans. A newspaper item stated, "We see it stated that every able-bodied [African American], who was once [a bonded worker of Wade Hampton's], is now hired by him; men at $10 per month and women at $8.00, without board. He expects to raise 300 bales of cotton this season — and means to give [independent African American] labor a fair trial." But there would be problems with sluggish productivity. [R199;174-175, R200;103]

We now turn our attention to Massachusetts and Lewis Parsons, the man Andrew Johnson had appointed as Military Governor of Alabama. During November Parsons arrived in Boston to promote the sale of Alabama State bonds. The Federal conquest had left the Alabama State Government bankrupt, and Parsons was in search of capital to begin anew. He arrived in Boston with a letter of encouragement from Edwin Stanton. And Massachusetts Governor John Andrew and Reverend Henry Beecher were inclined to offer a courteous reception before Boston's Union Club, whose membership included many very wealthy and influential men. But Charles Sumner had no intention of giving Parsons a civil reception in Boston. He attended the Union Club meeting so as to harass the man. Sumner hated Parsons because he was an appointee of Andrew Johnson and because Parsons publicly opposed making voters of African American men living in Alabama. To Sumner, Parson's policies meant sure defeat for the Republican Party. So, as soon as Parson had concluded his appeal to the members of the Boston Union Club, Sumner rose and blasted the man unmercifully. Sumner charged "that Alabama was a very bogus State, not more than half converted from disloyalty [to Federal authority], and, though perhaps not intending to take up arms again [in defense of State Rights, was] yet fully intending to reestablish institutions, as nearly as possible, on the old basis of injustice [to] and [bondage of] the [African American] race." Scolding Sumner for such discourtesy, John Andrew admonished that, "Until this moment, he had hoped [Lewis] Parsons would be treated by gentlemen as a gentleman." And he continued to rebuff Sumner "in a very personal and offensive strain," before "concluding with an appeal for cooperation with, rather than antagonism to, the [conquered States]." This confrontation at the Boston Union Club further strained relations between John Andrew and Charles Sumner and further split the Massachusetts Republican Party into two Factions: one intent on long-term political domination of the conquered States, the other willing to allow them to retain a remnant of State Rights. [R73;235-236]

Meanwhile in Jackson, Mississippi, the Legislature wound up its heated session, publishing many laws in the last days of November, typically from November 21 to 29. These laws demonstrated the crisis atmosphere in the State as two sides tugged for political support. On the one hand, leaders of the Mississippi Republican Party and of the Newly Independent African American Men's Bureau sustained hope among African Americans that large farms would be confiscated, broken into 40-acre parcels and distributed among their families. On the other hand, owners of those farms desperately needed workers to agree to labor contracts for the upcoming 1866 farming season. The result had been idleness among African Americans — not unlike a strike by unionized workers in later years — which in turn had encouraged Legislators to enact new tough laws designed to regulate the African American population. Packages of such laws, like those adopted in late 1865 in Mississippi — to become known, collectively, as the "African American Code of 1865" — were being adopted throughout the former Confederate States, some in less stringent forms than in Mississippi, others very similar. The bulk of these laws, nicknamed "Jim Crow" laws, are itemized below in abbreviated form. They generally went into effect in Mississippi on the second Monday of January 1866, and regulated racial mixing, care of orphans and the poor, work and labor contracts, morality, marriage, parenting, habitat, status in courts, right to assemble, right to bear arms, and so forth:

Racial Transportation Rules. "It shall be unlawful for . . . any [African American] to ride in any first class passenger cars set apart, or used by, and for [European Americans]" . . . with the exception of females "traveling with their mistress, in the capacity of maids." The fine ranged from $50 to $500.

Care and Education of Orphans (Apprentice). "It shall be the duty of . . . [the county] Probate Courts . . . to apprentice . . . [African Americans] under the age of 18 . . . who are orphans, or whose parent or parents have not the means or who refuse to provide for and support said minors, ... to some competent and suitable person, on such terms as the Court may direct, having a particular care to the interest of said minor: Provided, that the former owner of said minors shall have the preference when, in the opinion of the Court, he or she shall be a suitable person for the purpose. . . . The said master or mistress . . . shall furnish said minor with sufficient food and clothing, treat said minor humanely, furnish medical attention in case of sickness [and] teach, or cause to be taught, him or her to read and write, if under 15 years of age. . . Said master or mistress shall have the power to inflict such moderate corporal chastisement as a father or guardian is allowed to inflict on his or her child or ward at common law. . . . If any apprentice shall leave the employment of his or her master, without his or her consent, said master or mistress may pursue and recapture said apprentice, and bring him or her before any Justice of the Peace of the county, whose duty it shall be to remand said apprentice to the service of his or her master or mistress, [except that], if the Court shall believe that said apprentice had good cause to quit his said master or mistress, the Court shall discharge said apprentice from said indenture, and also enter a judgment against the master or mistress for not more than $100, for the use and benefit of said apprentice. . . . If any person entice away any apprentice from his or her master or mistress . . . said person . . . shall be deemed guilty of a high misdemeanor . . . ." Apprentice arrangements concluded when a female became 18 years old, when a male became 21.

Unlawful Assembly or Racial Mixing. "All [African Americans] in this State, over the age of 18 years, found on the second Monday of January 1866, or thereafter, with no lawful employment or business, or found unlawfully assembling themselves together, either in the day or night time, and all [European American men] so assembling themselves with [African Americans], on terms of equality, or living in adultery or fornication with a [female African American], shall be deemed vagrants, and on conviction thereof," if an African American, shall be fined $50 and may be imprisoned up to 10 days, if a European American man, he shall be fined $200 and may be imprisoned up to 6 months. . . . If an African American fails to pay a fine within 5 days, "it shall be the duty of the Sheriff of the proper county to hire out said [African American] to any person who will, for the shortest period of service, pay said fine and forfeiture and all costs: Provided, a preference shall be given to the employer, if there be one . . . . The same duties and liabilities existing among [European Americans] of this State shall attach to [African Americans] to support their indigent families and all [African American] paupers . . . . [And] a poll or capitation tax [shall be levied] on each and every [African American] between the ages of 18 and 60 years, not to exceed the sum of $1 annually, [to be used] for the maintenance of the poor [African Americans] of this State. . . . [Refusal to pay said $1 tax] shall be *prima facie* evidence of vagrancy, and it shall be the duty of the Sheriff . . . to hire for the shortest time such delinquent tax payer to anyone who will pay the said tax [and costs]."

Right to Sue in Court. "All [African Americans] may sue and be sued, implead and be impleaded, in all the courts of law and equity of this State, and may acquire [and dispose of] personal property . . . in the same manner that [European Americans] may, [but they shall not] rent or lease any lands or tenements except in incorporated cities or towns . . . ."

African American Marriages. "All [African Americans] may intermarry with each other, in the same manner and under the same regulations that are provided by law for [European Americans]: Provided, that the Clerk of Probate shall keep separate records of the same."

Past African American Cohabitation Legitimized. "All [African Americans] who do now and have herebefore lived and cohabitated together as husband and wife shall be taken and held in law as legally married, and the issue shall be taken and held as legitimate for all persons . . ."

Interracial Marriage Prohibited. "It shall not be lawful for any [African American] to intermarry with any [European American] . . . and any person who shall so intermarry shall be deemed guilty of a felony, and upon conviction thereof shall be confined in the State penitentiary for life, and [by law] those shall be deemed [African Americans] who are of pure [African] blood, and [those of mixed race, including persons who are of nearly pure European blood, but are] descended from a [person of predominantly African blood going back] to the third generation, inclusive — though one ancestor in each generation may have been a [European American]."

Testifying in Courts. "[African Americans] shall be competent [witnesses] in civil cases when a party or parties to the suit . . . . They shall also be competent witnesses in all criminal prosecutions where the crime charged is alleged to have been committed by a [European American] upon or against the person or property of [an African American. . . . [and] shall in all cases be subject to the rules and tests of the common law as to competency and credibility."

Written Record of Domicile and Employment. "Every [adult African American] shall, on the second Monday of January, 1866 and annually thereafter, have a lawful home or employment, and shall have written evidence thereof . . . ."

Contracts for Labor. "All contracts for labor made with [African Americans] for longer period than one month shall be in writing, and in duplicate, attested and read to said [African American], . . . of which each party shall have one [copy of said written contract]; . . . and if the laborer shall quit the service of the employer before the expiration of his term of service, without good cause, he shall forfeit his wages for that year up to the time of quitting."

Return of Laborer Prematurely Quitting Contract. "Every civil officer shall, and every person may, arrest and carry back to his or her legal employer any [African American working under contract] who shall have quit the service of his or her employer before the expiration of his or her term of service without good cause; and said officer and person shall be entitled to receive for arresting and carrying back every deserting employee aforesaid the sum of 5 dollars, and 10 cents per mile from the place of arrest to the place of delivery . . . [to be paid by the employer and deducted from deserting employee's wages]: Provided, that said arrested party, after being so returned, may appeal . . . and the decision of the county court shall be final."

Persuading Laborer to Prematurely Quit Contract. "If any person shall persuade or attempt to persuade, entice, or cause any [African American] to desert from the legal employment of any person before the expiration of his or her term of service . . . he or she shall be guilty of a misdemeanor, and, upon conviction, shall be fined not less than $25 and not more than $200 and costs . . ."

Legal Right to Charge by Affidavit. "It shall be lawful for any [African American] to charge any [European American or African American] by affidavit, with any criminal offense against his or her person or property, and upon such affidavit the proper process shall be issued and executed as if said affidavit was made by a [European American] . . ."

General Penal Laws Likewise Apply. "The penal laws of this State, in all cases not otherwise specially provided for, shall apply and extend to all [African Americans]."

Disarmament. "No [African American], not in the [Federal] military service . . . and not licensed to do so by the Board of Police of his or her county, shall keep or carry firearms of any kind, or any ammunition, dirk or bowie knife, and on conviction, [shall be fined up to $10 plus costs], and all such arms or ammunition shall be forfeited to the informer; and it shall be the duty of every civil and military officer to arrest any [African American] found with any such arms or ammunition . . ."

Disturbing the Peace, etc. "Any [African American] committing riots, routs, affrays, trespasses, malicious mischief, cruel treatment to animals, seditious speeches, insulting gestures, language, or acts, or assaults on any person, disturbance of the peace, exercising the function of a minister of the Gospel without a license from some regularly organized church, vending spirituous or intoxicating liquors, or committing any other misdemeanor, the punishment of which is not specifically provided for by law, shall, upon conviction, . . . be fined not less than $10 and not more than $100, and may be imprisoned, . . . not exceeding 30 days."

Fire-arms Sells. "If any [European American] shall sell, lend, or give to any [African American] any fire-arm, dirk or bowie knife, or ammunition, or any spirituous or intoxicating liquors, such person or persons so offending, upon conviction . . . shall be fined not exceeding $50 and may be imprisoned, . . . not exceeding 30 days."

Paying Fines by Laboring (Garnishee). "If any [African American] convicted of any of the misdemeanors provided against in this act, shall fail or refuse for the space of 5 days, after conviction, to pay the fine and costs imposed, such person shall be hired out by the Sheriff or other officer, at public outcry, to any [European American] who will pay said fine and all costs, and take said convict for the shortest time." [R207;281-290, R204;113-115]

Reaction to these laws, in Mississippi and elsewhere, drew a storm of protest across the northern States, where the passions inflamed by the horrific war, concluded only 7 to 8 months earlier, encouraged most to suspect that former owners of bonded African Americans were engaged in evil schemes designed to take away the newly-granted independence of the African Americans they had formerly owned, re-subjugating them by other means. Such suspicions were easily encouraged given ignorance in the northern States of the chaotic social, legal and economic conditions that existed across the defeated southern States during the summer and fall months of 1865. Historian James Garner would write:

"This legislation created a storm of opposition in the [northern States]. The various acts were printed entire in many newspapers, and severely commented upon by editors. It was said that their enforcement would mean reestablishment of [African American bonding] in another form. The reenactment of [laws resembling the old code regulating African American bonding], they said, was a return to [African American bonding] pure and simple. The vagrant act applied only to [African Americans]. Only the [African American] was required to have a home within a certain time. It deprived him of the ancient right of trial by jury. Offences that had no relation to idleness, such as the non-payment of taxes, for example, were denominated vagrancy, and punished as such."

Some of the regulations concerning African Americans seem to have served little useful purpose and perhaps made matters worse. For example, did preventing African Americans from renting land outside of the boundaries of towns contribute to an orderly and peaceful society, or did it actually make matters worse? Historian James Garner would observe: "the movement of [African Americans] to the towns and cities was one of the special complaints of the [European Americans] at this time, and yet, strangely enough, their legislation, instead of encouraging the African American men to rent land in the country, tended to drive them to the towns, where they must suffer from idleness, vice and disease." Furthermore, preventing African Americans from testifying in court on cases only involving European Americans, probably of little benefit to Mississippi society, was an easy target for northern States political agitators looking for clear examples to rally voters against the new southern States governments. [R204;116-117]

But we people of the twenty-first century need to understand the conditions in America in 1865, both in the southern States and in the northern States. Historian James Garner's observations a few years later are helpful in that regard:

"The sudden [independence of bonded African Americans] and the too generous course of the [Federal Government] in furnishing them with the means of subsistence during their idleness, not only deranged the labor system of the [southern States], but demoralized the [African American] laborers to such a degree that to the planters of the State in 1865 the outlook was disheartening. The [newly independent African American] man was made to believe that liberty meant license, that as he had been [made independent] by a powerful government, he would also be clothed and fed by it whether he chose to labor or not. He was told by unscrupulous [African American men's] Bureau agents and [African American] soldiers that he ought not to work for his former [owner] for any promise of compensation, that his [independence] was not secure so long as he remained on the old [farm], and that the [Federal Government] in due time expected to confiscate the land of the [former owners] and divide it up among the [former bonded African Americans]. As a result, the [newly independent African American men] left the [farms] and moved to the towns or military camps, refusing to make contracts or to fulfill them when made. The amount of robbery and larceny was alarming. The farmer's swine were stolen for pork, his cows were penned in the woods and milked, and his barns and cotton houses were broken open. If [the farmer] was fortunate enough to procure laborers to plant his fields, he had no assurance that they would remain with him until the crop was harvested. In fact, it was almost certain that they would not. The legislature was made up for the most part of small [farmers], none of the able members of the [Constitutional Convention] having been chosen to seats in it. . . . Laws were passed, most of which, when impartially enforced, as they generally were, did not work injustice to the [African American]. Their purpose was to force him to cease his roving and become a producer."

It is furthermore important that we understand that the 1865 law in Mississippi "against vagrants was not more severe than those of many northern States." Six examples are worthy of mention. Note that, of the 6 examples below, all but Indiana were populated entirely by people of the northern culture, causing readers of this history to question the frequently-stated allegation that, concerning European Americans during the 1800's, those of the northern culture were morally superior to those of the southern culture.

Wisconsin Vagrants — defined "as all idle persons who had no visible means of support, and all persons wandering abroad and not giving a good account of themselves, or who begged bread from door to door. Vagrancy was punishable by imprisonment not exceeding 90 days." (Statutes of 1878, page 465.)

Massachusetts Vagrants — here, vagrancy laws were almost identical to Wisconsin and, where different, were more severe. (Supplement to General Statutes, Volume 1, 1860-1872, Chapter 235, page 260.)

New York State Tramps — defined persons as described in the Wisconsin statue as "tramps." "Upon conviction they were to be imprisoned at hard labor in the nearest penitentiary for a period not exceeding 6 months." (Statute of 1881, Volume 3, page 1898.)

Maine Vagabonds and Persons Refusing to Work — "all persons who refused to work, or who had no ordinary calling or lawful business, were required to be sent to the workhouse. All vagabonds or idle persons going about begging in town or country, or neglecting their calling or employment, or misspending what they earned and not providing support for themselves and families, were imprisoned not exceeding 6 months." (Statutes of 1871, page 260.)

Connecticut Idle Persons — "all persons who had no means of supporting themselves, all beggars who wandered abroad from place to place without lawful business, and all who misspent what they earned, were subject to imprisonment at hard labor not exceeding 60 days." (Revised Statutes of 1866, Chapter 4, page 642.)

Indiana Vagrants and Persons Refusing to Work — "any person, male or female, over 14 years of age, who had made no reasonable effort to procure employment, or who had refused to labor and was found begging from door to door, was subject to a fine of $30. Going about begging and asking subsistence was vagrancy." (Revised Statutes of 1881.) [R204;118-119]

Meanwhile, from his Washington home, Thad Stevens and fellow conspirators planned the *coup d'etat* by which the more militant Faction of the Republican Party would seize control of the Federal House and Senate by barring the admission of Representatives and Senators from the Governments of the conquered States. Biographer Richard Current would describe the plan:

"The first move of the [more militant Faction], according to Stevens' plan, would be to shut and bar the doors of [House Chambers to prevent entry by Representatives] from the [remade Governments of the conquered States]. Through his friend Edward McPherson, whom he had made Chief Clerk of the [Federal] House in 1863, [Thad] was able to prevent the names of the [these Representatives] from being entered on the roll. He had to confess, though, that if their credentials should be referred to the Standing Committee on Elections, whose Chairman was [H. L.] Dawes, he and the [more militant Faction] would be 'gone.' He planned therefore to pass a resolution at the outset declaring that there were no 'States' in the [conquered region] to be represented, and then to secure the appointment of a Special Committee which would deal with the question of the admission of [their Representatives], and which would take charge of the whole business of devising a program for [revising the rules for remaking the Governments of the conquered States]. But suppose the [Federal] Senate should admit the Senators elected by [the State Legislatures that had gathered in accordance with Andrew Johnson's policies for remaking the Governments in those conquered States]? But suppose [Andrew] Johnson should veto the scheme [that Thad was devising]? [Thad] and the [Faction members] who consulted with him [had] thought of everything. To bind the [Federal] Senate and House together, [the conspirators] decided to make their Special Committee a joint one and to provide that neither [the House nor Senate] should admit members from a State which the other refused to recognize. To avoid the possibility of a veto, they would accomplish all of this by means of a Concurrent Resolution, which differed technically from a Joint Resolution, [thereby allowing the rule to take] effect without [Andrew Johnson's] approval."

It seems that political observers knew about Stevens' plans for denying seats to Representatives and Senators from the remade Governments of the conquered States. Editors at the New York *World* summed up the fight among Republicans this way: "The whole question as to the action of Congress, then, is, does Andrew Johnson represent the views and policies of the Republican members, or is Thad Stevens, with his [militant], extreme ideas, the true exponent of the Party?" A White House meeting between Stevens and Johnson, held on November 29, produced no agreement, not even a softening of the differences in the two Republican Factions. The test would come in the first December Republican Party Caucus: could Andrew Johnson's men convince enough Republicans to embrace the old wartime "Union" slogan and accept the Representatives and Senators elected by the qualified voters of the conquered States? [R96;220-221]

Meanwhile, from Montreal, Maggie Davis, age 10, sat down on November 30 and wrote again to her father — hoping again that the Federals would allow this letter to get through. Perhaps, she had been encouraged to believe that today's letter, which she was writing at the Sacred Heart Convent near Montreal would be the first one to get through. Well, it turns out that this was the time that Edwin Stanton and, or, his agents decided to discontinue their practice of forbidding Jeff Davis from seeing his children's letters. The following letter from Maggie was allowed to reach the father:

"It gave me great pleasure when I found out that I could write to you for I have written to you before but my letters have been intercepted, but that does not prevent me from writing to you now.

"Darling Father, I will now tell you about the children — dear little Billie is so changed that you would not know him for he is so good and looking so well and Jeff is the same way and so is dear Grandma and Aunty, and Jeff and Billie send much love to you and many kisses, dear Father. All I want in this convent is you and sweet Mother and sweet little Pie Cake, for I am treated so kind, precious Father.

"The Arch Bishop of Halifax came to the convent and was very kind to me and in remembrance of you gave me some beautiful presents which consisted of a prayer book, which was beautifully bound with Ivory, and the clasp is pure Silver, and he also gave ma a pretty little gold Cross; it is set with rubies and in the center is a emerald. Precious Father I send you these little pictures with more affection than I can express. Precious Father, please write to me soon. I went home the other day for a congé and while I was there it snowed and Grandma let Billie go out to play in it and when he came in he wanted to know why God made the snow and Grandma told him to make the earth moist so the when Fruit came it would be good and also [so] the people could skate. Precious Father, if you are allowed, please send us your picture and some of your hair. I have the ribbon for good behavior, and my Mistress said that she was very much pleased with me for she said that I was very good and that I was trying very hard to speak French. My Precious Father, I must now stop, but I will continue to write to you. All send both love and kisses. Good bye. I remain your most affectionate little Pollie.

"Maggie H. Davis"

The other two Davis children were doing well in Canada, too. Young Jeff's schoolmistress had written Varina from Lennoxville reporting that he was "very truthful and loveable," and the Archbishop of Halifax had urged Varina to let him help educate Jeff at a college of her choice in Canada or Great Britain. Little Billie was doing well with his grandmother in a village midway between Montreal and Lennoxville. [R19;270, R30;210]

Meanwhile in early December, the Kentucky Legislature began its regular Session. It was now controlled by Conservative Democrats. Top priority was given to removing political and social impediments to returned Confederates. Governor Bramlette set the tone in his opening message, asking, "Are they to be crushed — humiliated — debased by continued punishment? Or shall they be forgiven — trusted — restored?" Within days, the Legislature repealed and removed all political disabilities from the statutes, most importantly the Expatriation Act of 1861, which was cast out by votes of 62 to 32 in the House and 22 to 12 in the Senate. Federals had withdrawn martial law in October and the writ of *habeas corpus* would eventually be restored to Kentucky, at the time the only State outside the former Confederacy remaining under that punishment. Soon Kentucky would be "in the hands of the Confederates." In other words, former Confederates and their friends would be dominating Kentucky political life for decades to come. [R180;287-292]

Meanwhile in Washington City, Charles Sumner arrived back in town on December 2, ready for opening day at the Federal Senate. It appears he arrived in a despondent mood, in spite of expectations of success with the Republican conspiracy schemed up by Thad Stevens — aimed at denying seats to the Representatives and Senators from the remade Governments of the conquered States. About a month earlier, Sumner had written John Bright, lamenting, "It is doubtful how Congress will stand. Those who are associated with [Andrew Johnson] in his policy think it will unite with them. Others . . . feel sure that it will be firm the other way. . . . I know many who I am sure will not yield. I shall not. . . . If [Johnson] perseveres the [coalition of Republicans and militant Democrats that had joined together to elect Abe Lincoln] is broken up." Fully expecting such a break-up, Sumner called on Andrew Johnson at the White House later in the day of his arrival to engage in debate. He told Francis Lieber that his intent in confronting Johnson was to make sure "that [Andrew Johnson] shall break with us and not we with him." But Johnson was a skillful politician and warily approached his visitor with the aim of provoking Sumner to fire the first shot. Biographer David Donald wrote: "For two and one-half hours the men circled each other warily, looking for openings." Finally Sumner became angry and charged that Johnson "had thrown away the fruits of the victories of the [Federal] Army." When Johnson asked for specific examples, Sumner recounted stories from letters he had received which described violence where "the poor [newly independent African American men] in Georgia and Alabama were frequently insulted by [former Confederates]." Sumner also recounted stories of fist-fights and even murder. To that Johnson inquired:

"Mr. Sumner, do murders ever occur in Massachusetts?
    "Unhappily yes, Mr. President."
"Do people ever knock each other down in Boston?"
    "Unhappily yes, Mr. President."
"Would you consent that Massachusetts should be excluded from [seats in the Federal House and
        Senate] on this account?"
    "No, Mr. President, surely not."

By the end of their confrontation, Johnson figured it likely that "arrogant and dictatorial" Charles Sumner would be among the leaders who would seek his destruction upon the opening of Congress. And Sumner figured that Andrew Johnson was "ignorant, pig-headed and perverse" in pursuing a policy for remaking the Governments in the conquered States that would surely ruin the Republican Party. And, based on Sumner's belief that only his Party could save the Federal Government from ruination, he had deceived himself into believing that the ruin of the Republican Party was tantamount to the ruination of the Federal Government. After describing his visit to like-minded Republicans the next day, Sumner would exclaim: "But thank God Congress will do its duty." [R73;237-238]

A few hours after Sumner's meeting with Andrew Johnson, Republican Representatives from the northern States gathered for their first Caucus. Congressman Rutherford Hayes, who would one day become Federal President, observed that, "Thad Stevens made the important motions." A Faction, seeking to weaken Stevens' immense political power, did succeed in getting enough votes to break his House Ways and Means Committee into three separate Committee segments. But Stevens remained Chairman of the segment that controlled monetary appropriations, and seemed determined to weld as much power as he could muster. Biographer Richard Current would write, "[Stevens] stormed and threatened to break up the Caucus if the members did not adopt his [scheme to ensure that the Republican Party would control political life in the conquered States]." And Stevens won his fight to bind Republican Representatives to a pledge to support his Reconstruction Program, the first step toward that goal being to deny seats to Representatives from the conquered States. A New York *Times* Newspaperman would write that Republican Representatives "made a formal surrender of the Republican Party to the guidance of Thad Stevens." [R96;221]

Two days later, on December 4, the House and Senate assembled. Andrew Johnson was hoping that Republicans would agree to seat Horace Maynard of Tennessee, because Maynard, like he himself, had remained in Congress during the Federal Invasion of the Confederacy. Maybe Maynard's admittance would break down resistance to the acceptance of others from the former Confederate States. Who was Horace Maynard?

Born and educated in Massachusetts, Horace Maynard relocated to Knoxville, in East Tennessee, at the age of 25, where he taught at what is now the University of Tennessee, and later established a Knoxville law practice. Politically, he always opposed the Democratic Party, first as a Whig and later as a "No Nothing" and then a "Unionist." When Tennessee seceded four years after taking his seat, Maynard remained in the Federal House, a Representative without a State. In this regard I-am-not-a-Democrat Maynard followed the same path as I-am-a-Democrat Andrew Johnson, also of East Tennessee, a Senator without a State. Both politicians had remained in Congress following the secession of their State.

But Thad Stevens was ready to spring a trap that would effectively destroy Andrew Johnson's remade Governments. Biographer Richard Current would later describe the action:

"When at last Congress assembled on December 4, the stage was well set for the dramatic and momentous events that were to follow. On Capitol Hill the air was as balmy as on a May day. Inside the scene was resplendent. The Chief Clerk, while helping spin the plot, had seen to the redecoration of the Hall of Representatives, where it was to be played. On the main floor 'a new Brussels carpet of a tasteful pattern and in cheerful colors' had been laid, and the diplomats' and ladies' galleries had also been 'handsomely refurnished.' Soon after the doors were opened on the spring like December morning, a 'brilliant and fashionable' crowd thronged the corridors and galleries. At their desks on the floor of the House the actors were prepared for the parts assigned them. On one side sat the leader of the Democrats, James Brooks, a wily and well-experienced politician from New York. On the other sat 'Thad Stevens, grim looking, cool, with a ready wit, perfect courage and the sort of independence which long experience, assured position and 70 years of age gives an able man.'

"McPherson, [the Chief Clerk], began to call the roll. When he passed over [Horace] Maynard's name, Maynard rose and, shaking his credentials in his hand, demanded recognition from the clerk. McPherson refused to recognize him and offered to state his reasons but Stevens spoke up: 'It is not necessary. We know all.' When Brooks attempted to protest, Stevens rose to a point of order and (in the Pennsylvania Legislature [decades earlier] on December 4, 1838) announced that nothing except the election of a Speaker might be discussed until the House should have been organized. 'Why, this is not parliamentary propriety, if it is even decency,' expostulated Brooks. When Maynard appealed to Stevens to grant the floor to him, [Thad] replied: 'I cannot yield to any gentleman who does not belong to this body — who is an outsider.' To the repeated appeals of Brooks and Maynard [Thad] responded with remarks which, 'jerked out with the peculiar acerbity of the great [more militant Faction leader],' created a laugh at their expense while he dismissed them with 'a Podsnappian wave of the hand.' Finally, they gave up. After the election of officers he was ready for 'springing the drop.' Introducing the resolution for a Joint Committee of Fifteen on [Reconstructing the Governments of the Conquered States], he staved off motions to adjourn, stifled debate, and, under a suspension of the rules, saw the measure pass by a vote of 139 to 35. He then moved that the House adjourn, the motion was carried, and 'the old war horse leaned back squarely and gloriously triumphant.'

"By this *coup d'etat* Stevens had completely overturned [President] Johnson's well-laid plans. 'The new members, and others weak in their understanding,' [Gideon] Welles [would write] in his diary, 'were taken off their legs as was designed, before they were aware of it.'" [R96;222-223]

While Thad Stevens was directing efforts in the House to establish a Joint House-Senate Committee that would be responsible for all legislation reconstructing the Governments of the conquered States, Charles Sumner was — simultaneously — busy in the Senate introducing a series of bills designed to carry out his own plans for reconstructing those Governments. David Donald would describe this package of legislation Sumner was introducing on the floor of the Senate:

"The program Sumner announced called for broad changes throughout the [conquered States]. Because Congress had the constitutional duty to guarantee to each State a republican form of government, it should sweep away the regimes Johnson had set up and insist that throughout the former Confederacy there must be 'no denial of rights, civil or political, on account of race,' so that 'all persons shall be equal before the law, whether in the court-room or at the ballot-box.' To secure this goal, a Provisional Governor in each [conquered] State should register all male citizens and allow them an opportunity to swear an oath repudiating secession, upholding the [Federal Government] debt, and pledging always to 'discountenance and resist any laws making, any distinction of race.' Whenever a majority adhered to this oath, the State should hold a Constitutional Convention, but no soldier or officer of the [former Confederate military force] could vote in the election or be chosen as a Delegate. The Convention must then frame a new State Constitution that would disavow secession, [continue to] prohibit [African American bonding], permanently disqualify all high-ranking [former Confederate military and government officials] from holding [future] office, and pledge that henceforth there would be 'no distinction among inhabitants . . . founded on race, [or former social or economic condition].' Only when this document was approved by a majority of eligible voters — a term which under Sumner's plan would include [African American men] but exclude most former Confederate [men] — could a State be readmitted to representation in [the Federal] Congress."

"Sumner's plan further provided that, until all his stipulations were accepted, the [conquered] States should remain under [Federal-appointed Governors who would be] directed to preserve [African American's] rights. . . . Under his plan civilian appointees would succeed military officer [appointees], whom he distrusted, as the Governors of the [conquered States]; all the principal [past] Confederate leaders and, indeed, most [European Americans living in the conquered States] would be excluded from any share in political life, whether in the State [Government] or the [Federal Government]; and, for perhaps a generation, the [African Americans] would have an opportunity, under Federal protection, to grow in independence, in knowledge, and in political wisdom."

It seems that observers in the gallery rather easily sensed that few Senators appeared willing to support Sumner's legislative package. Sumner and Stevens were advocating similar Reconstruction programs, but Sumner was not effectively leading the Party. Why? David Donald would explain that "Stevens was an organization man, who worked through Committees and exerted influence through his control of the machinery of the [Federal] House; when he could not get a majority of his Party to support his favored positions, he accepted whatever compromises were necessary." On the other hand, Sumner was, "despite his seniority, a political outsider; he disliked Committees, except when he was Chairman, was ineffectual in caucus, and proved inept at drafting legislation. He announced principles, as from on Mount Sinai, and deplored the compromises needed to transform ideals into legislative reality." Before the day was over the Senate, like the House, had refused to seat the Senators elected from the conquered States. Stevens' *coup d'etat* had been executed with perfect precision. [R73;238-240]

On the following day, the Clerk read Andrew Johnson's message to Congress. In recognition of the *coup d'etat*, Johnson had meekly struck out language that praised the "restoration of the Union," a slogan for which so many dying Federal soldiers had figured they had been fighting to achieve. Understanding his defeat, Johnson "had to take a negative and defensive tone. The theory that the [conquered] States could be extinguished, he declared would be fatal to the Federal Constitution." He could only warn of damage to the Constitution. Poet Theodore Tilton, of New York, happily wrote Thad Stevens, saying, "The way in which you have opened Congress and thrown down the gauntlet to [Andrew Johnson's policies] has pleased our [more militant Faction] friends hereabouts so thoroughly that we are all hearty, merry, and tumultuous with gratitude!" [R96;223-224]

Nevertheless Charles Sumner reacted angrily to Andrew Johnson's message, calling it a "whitewashing message." Sumner alleged that Johnson's cover-up of alleged violence in the conquered States was as bad as Franklin Pierce's so-called cover-up of the violence that Sumner alleged Kansas settlers from southern States had committed against so-called "peace-loving" Kansas settlers from the northern States during the mid-1850's. Sumner's comparison to "Bleeding Kansas" was totally up-side down, for in "Bleeding Kansas," history shows that it was the settlers from the northern States who were committing the vast majority of the atrocities. But Sumner never sought the truth. He would never risk exposure to facts, would never investigate controversy with an aim for getting to the bottom of things. He firmly understood what he wanted to achieve and collected only supportive stories, always fearing that the facts, if uncovered, might invalidate his arguments. Better to bury the facts. [R73;240]

The Federation's powerful industrialists and financiers, most of whom lived in the arc of northeastern States anchored by Pennsylvania, New York and Massachusetts recognized that, of all the politicians in Washington City, Thad Stevens was the most skillful at achieving their goal, which was "to convert the votes of the many into the policies of the few." Many were meeting and corresponding with Stevens to facilitate attaining their goals. They recognized that, to build further upon their war-time financial gains, the Republican Party had to retain control of the Federal Government and the ruling Faction within that Party had to be supportive of their interest. But, collectively, they had only a few votes, even when counting the votes of their employees. To retain a dominant influence they had to facilitate converting "the votes of the many into the policies of the few." And they shared Stevens' fear that, after the 1870 census, Democrats would again control the Federal House by winning all of the seats in the former Confederate States, most of the seats in Delaware, Maryland, Kentucky and southern Missouri, New Mexico and California, a few of the New Jersey and New York seats, and most of the seats in States west of Pennsylvania. Republicans could not control the Federal Congress by the strength of the seats they could count on within the arc that ran from Pennsylvania to Massachusetts. Thad Stevens explained that, converting the African American population in Delaware, Maryland, Kentucky, Missouri and the conquered States from three-fifths of a person to a full person would cause those States to gain a much larger share of Federal House seats. And, if all European American men were allowed to vote in the conquered States, Democrats would get almost all of those Congressional seats. [R96;226-229]

After hours, Stevens was effective in using Washington's political lobby to further his goals — goals for Reconstruction — for sustaining high taxes on imports — and even a new tax on <u>exports of cotton</u>, about which you will soon read more. The owner of Reading Iron Works, fearing that a deflationary Federal monetary policy would produce a drop in iron prices, wrote Stevens: "it is a fallacy that we have too much money in circulation." The owner of the Barree Forge, first expressed his agreement that "the major part of the [European American population living in the conquered States] should undergo Purgation," and then revealed that the desired political favor was high Federal import taxes to keep iron prices artificially high. Stevens maintained ties with Josiah Perham, a lobbyist for the Northern Pacific Railroad, and Tom Scott, a leading official of the Pennsylvania Railroad. Scott wanted favorable Federal legislation concerning the Kansas Route of the Eastern Division of the Union Pacific Railroad. Stevens was more likely to meet with lobbyist and like-minded Representatives and Senators around the poker table at his home that at parties elsewhere in town. Actually, I find it hard to imagine a wealthy lobbyist leaving Stevens' poker table without having artfully lost a bundle of money. During such poker games, "Lydia Smith would bustle about, setting up the table for the players, adjusting the lamps, bringing in refreshments, and attending to other details in wifely fashion." Though most insiders recognized Lydia, an African American of mostly European American ancestry, as merely a devoted servant of many years, some misunderstood the nature of her influence over Stevens. One frequent visitor that winter would write, "The influence of this [African-European American] mistress was largely the cause of Stevens' bitter animosity [toward European Americans who lived in the southern States]." Biographer Richard Current would later explain: "That was a belief widespread among men who little understood the politics of iron and railroads."

Rutherford Hayes, a freshman Representative from Ohio, was just getting to know how Thad Stevens exerted dominant power over the Federal House. Of his early observations and deductions, Hayes included this observation in a letter home to his wife, dated December 7:

"He is witty, cool, full of and fond of 'sarcasms,' and thoroughly informed and accurate. He has a knack of saying things which turn the laugh on his opponent. When he rises everyone expects something worth hearing, and he has the attention of all. You remember his speech on confiscation [of 85 percent of the land in the conquered States]. He is [more militant] throughout, except, I am told, he [does not] believe in hanging [former Confederate officers and government officials]. He is a leader." [R96;226-229]

Meanwhile at Fortress Monroe, Jeff Davis was allowed to see his first visitor on December 11. Charles Minnegerode, Rector of St. Paul's in Richmond, and Jeff's pastor, had repeatedly sought permission from Washington City authorities to visit Davis. Until this last attempt he had been turned down. Hudson Strode described this momentous event in Jeff's life:

"In these 6 wearing months Davis had not been allowed a visitor. At his rector's unexpected appearance before the grated door it was difficult for him to control his emotion. Minnegerode had considerable difficulty in controlling his own. [Minnegerode would later write:]

> "The noble man showed the effect of the confinement, but his spirit could not be subdued, and no indignity — angry as it made him at the time — could humiliate him. . . . I was his pastor, and of course our conversation was influenced by that and there could be no holding back between us. I could come to sympathize and comfort and pray for him. At last the question of Holy Communion came up. He was very anxious to take it. He was a purely pious man, and felt the need and value of the means of grace. But there was one difficulty. Could he take it in the proper spirit — in the frame of a forgiving mind, after all the ill treatment he had been subjected to? He was too upright and conscientious a Christian man 'to eat and drink unworthily' — i.e., not in the proper spirit, and, as far as lay in him in peace with God and man."

"The clergyman left [Jeff Davis] alone to meditate on the matter, while he inspected the fort. He had spoken about the Communion service to [Nelson] Miles, who had agreed to make preparations. A couple of hours later, he was again escorted by [Miles] to the prison door. Minnegerode was gratified to find Davis ready to commune, "to pray 'Father, forgive them.'"

"It was a most solemn hour. A goods box covered with a white cloth served as an altar. Night had fallen, and the fortress was shrouded in silence. [Nelson] Miles ordered the three sentinels to stop their pacing. They stood like statues. It was the first utter quiet Davis' frayed nerves had known in more than half a year. Though Miles himself declined to leave, he had the grace to turn his back on the scene and lean against the mantelpiece in the anteroom as Jefferson Davis knelt and the minister spoke softly: 'Take, eat, this is my body which is given for you.'

"After his rector's visit Davis was better prepared to endure the dark December days in which prison rigors continued unabated." [R19;271-272]

Meanwhile in Washington City, Republican Senators caucused on December 11, give or take a day, to vote on Thad Steven's resolution to empower the Joint House-Senate Committee to decide if and when to seat Representatives and Senators from the conquered States. Stevens figured that such a Joint Committee would present a unified front that Andrew Johnson would be powerless to circumvent. And Charles Sumner agreed with Stevens on the proposed strategy to thus empower the Joint Committee, but Sumner was unable to persuade enough fellow Republican Senators to concur. The Senators voted to include an amendment that canceled the stipulation that neither body should act independently in admitting members. Then they approved the resolution. It seemed like double talk, but when it arrived back at the House Thad Stevens successfully moved to adopt it with little debate. Stevens figured there was sufficient Party commitment to deny seats to all Representatives and Senators from the remade Governments in the conquered States. Better to avoid an open floor fight over details of language. Perhaps the language dispute was simply senatorial pride: many Senators abhorred letting Representatives participate in deciding if and when to seat new Senators. There was a working understanding: No one would be admitted from the conquered States, if at all, prior to the final report from the 15-man Joint House-Senate Committee. And all papers bearing on the subject would be referred to that Committee without debate.

Thad Stevens was named to the 15-man Joint House-Senate Committee on Reconstructing the Remade Governments of the Conquered States. In fact Stevens was the Co-Chairman, representing the House side of the Committee. But, in spite of his top seniority and his intense interest in the issue, Charles Sumner was denied even a seat on the Committee. Senate Republicans named William Fessenden as Co-Chairman of the Senate side. Fessenden would later write: "[Charles] Sumner was very anxious for the place, but, standing as he does before the country, and committed to the most [militant] views, even his friends declined to support him, and almost to a man fixed upon me." And Fessenden hoped at the outset to find some middle ground where he could cooperate with the Johnson [Administration], for he wrote, "If Sumner and Stevens and a few other such men do not embroil us with [Andrew Johnson], matters can be satisfactorily arranged." But Fessenden realized that the "yelping of the dogs" of men like Charles Sumner were capable of driving Johnson back into the Democratic Party.

Even without clear authority to decide if and when to seat Representatives and Senators from the conquered States, the Joint Committee was very powerful. Of its activity David Donald would write:

"There [would be] no evidence that the Joint Committee ever considered any of Sumner's numerous Reconstruction proposals. Just as Trumbull, another of Sumner's Republican foes, [had taken] complete charge of the [Newly Independent African American Men's Bureau] Bill, broadening, and continuing the work of the [Federal] agency that Sumner had helped create, and also of the Civil Rights Bill, giving to [newly independent African American men] the [Federal Government's] legal guarantees that Sumner so long had advocated, so Fessenden was in command of the Constitutional Amendment which would provide a long-range solution to the [Republican Party's political problems that required reconstructing the remade Governments of the conquered States]. Once more Sumner was [being] shut out." [R73;240-241, R96;223-224]

On December 18, William Seward proclaimed fully ratified and a part of Federal law the Amendment to the Federal Constitution that confirmed that bonded African Americans were immediately independent — the Thirteenth Amendment. Georgia had ratified on December 6, giving a total of 27 ratifications, three quarters of the sum of the Federal States and the conquered States (36). You will recall that Mississippi was not among the States ratifying this Amendment, although all African Americans living in that State were independent and none were bonded to another person. Why did Mississippi refuse to ratify an Amendment that required its people to do what they had already done through their new Mississippi Constitution? Historian James Garner would explain the reasoning of the Mississippi legislators, which had persuaded them to vote against ratification of the proposed Amendment:

"On December 4, [in the Mississippi Legislature], the Joint Standing Committee on State and Federal Relations . . . declared that the first and main article of the [proposed] Amendment had already been adopted by the State of Mississippi in so far as her own territory was concerned, and was a part of her [State] Constitution in almost the same language as the proposed Amendment; that it was not possible for the State by any act or in any manner to change that [fact]; that [African American bonding] had been abolished in good faith; the State would abide by it, and consequently the adoption of the proposed Amendment could have no practical effect in Mississippi.

"The chief objection was the second section [of the proposed Amendment], which empowered [the Federal House and Senate] to enact the appropriate legislation to carry the first section into effect. [African American bonding] having been totally abolished . . . except in Kentucky and Delaware, [which had never seceded], the [proposed] Amendment was not necessary to coerce the people of [any but those two States] to abolish it. Moreover . . . the second section contained a dangerous grant of power by the States at a time most unpropitious for enlarging the powers of the Federal Government. Besides, it was unwise and inexpedient to reopen a subject which would afford a theme for radicals and demagogues to use against the best interests of the country, . . . the question of [African American bonding] being settled in all the States except [Kentucky and Delaware] . . . .

"The Joint Standing Committee report concluded: 'Connected as the [two sections of the proposed Amendment] are, a ratification of the first [section] and a rejection of the second [section] would be inoperative and of no effect — therefore, the rejection of both [sections] is recommended.'" [R204;120]

Ironically, it was the votes of remade State Legislatures in the conquered States, elected in accordance with the policies of Andrew Johnson, which had made possible the ratification of the Amendment in accordance the legal theory that the conquered region was made up of 11 Federal States. Andrew Johnson and Salmon Chase were operating under the dubious legal principle that the remade Governments in the conquered States had never left and had always been under the Federal Government, meaning they therefore had to be counted as part of the 27 States required to make the Amendment Federal law. Obediently, the South Carolina Legislature had ratified the Amendment on November 13, as had the Legislatures of Alabama on December 2, and North Carolina on December 4, and Georgia on December 5.

It was on the same day as William Seward's announcement of the Ratification — December 18, 1865 — that Thad Stevens launched his program to reduce the conquered States to the status of Federal

Territories to be ruled by the Federal Military and appointed militant Governors under the direction of the Federal House and Senate. With the Amendment now "in the bag," and being satisfied over the trick played upon the never-seated Representatives and Senators from the conquered States, Stevens reasoned it was time to reduce the conquered States to Military Rule as Federal Territories — even the Carolinas and Georgia, even the mother of all States, Virginia, even the former Republic of Texas. Having moved from colonies to Independent States these five had never been Federal Territories. Now they were to be! Stevens rose up in the House and thundered:

> "A candid examination of the power and proper principles of Reconstruction can be offensive to no one, and may possibly be profitable by exciting inquiry. . . . The President assumes . . . that the late [Confederate] States have lost their Constitutional relations with the Union and are incapable of representation in Congress, except by permission of the [Federal] Government. It matters but little . . . whether you call them *States out of the Union, and now conquered Territories*, or assert that because the [Federal] Constitution forbids them to do what they did do, that they are therefore *Only Dead . . . until the [Federal] Government shall . . . permit them to occupy their former position*. . . .

> "Whether conquered Territories or Dead States, they "cannot restore their own existence 'as it was,' Whose especial duty is it to do it? In whom does the [Federal] Constitution place the power? Not in the Judicial Branch of the Government, for it only adjudicates and does not prescribe laws. Not in the Executive, for he only executes and cannot make laws. Not in the Commander-in-Chief of the [Federal Army], for he can only hold them under Military Rule until the sovereign Legislative power of the conquerer shall give them law. . . .

> "The fourth article [of the Federal Constitution] says: 'New States may be admitted by the Congress into this Union.'

> "In my judgment this is the controlling provision in this case. Unless the law of nations is a dead letter, the late war between two acknowledged belligerents severed their original compacts, and broke all the ties that bound them together. The future condition of the conquered power depends on the will of the conqueror. They must come in as new States or remain as conquered provinces. Congress — the Senate and House of Representatives, with the concurrence of the President — is the only power that can act in the matter."

At this point Thad Stevens entered into a legal proof to support his argument that the conquered States must be reverted to conquered Territories, even South Carolina. He cited legal opinions, including, evidence "when the conclusive opinion of the [Federal] Supreme Court is at hand," whereby it ruled:

> "Hence, in organizing this [State secession], they have acted as States claiming to be sovereign over all persons and property within their respective limits, and asserting a right to absolve their citizens from their allegiance to the Federal Government. Several of these States have combined to form a Confederacy, claiming to be acknowledged by the world as a sovereign [group of States]. Their right to do so is now being decided by wager of battle. The ports and territories of each of the States are held in hostility to the [Federal] Government. . . . The Proclamation of Blockade is itself official and conclusive evidence to the Court that a state of war existed."

Stevens even cited South Carolina law, submitting — "One of the first resolutions passed by seceded South Carolina in January, 1861, is as follows:

> "'Resolved, unanimously, That the separation of South Carolina from the Federal Union is final, and she has no further interest in the Constitution of the United States; and that the only appropriate negotiations between her and the Federal Government are as to their mutual relations as foreign States.'"

At this point in his speech before the House, Stevens was legally and historically correct in his conclusion, but in error in parts of his argument. Yes, since their respective secession votes, the former States of the Confederacy had always been out of the Union and holding the status of foreign States. No, an argument based on the idea, "because the [Federal] Constitution forbids them to do what they did do," is an invalid argument. The [Federal] Constitution, although not describing a procedure for secession, clearly presents no road-blocks to State Secession, a principle widely accepted before 1861.

His legal premise concluded, Stevens entered upon his plan for Reconstruction, anchored in the principle that, "Congress must create States and declare when they are entitled to be represented."

"It is obvious from all this that the first duty of Congress is to pass a law declaring the condition of these [to be] outside or defunct States, and providing proper civil governments for them. Since the conquest, they have been governed by martial law. Military Rule is necessarily despotic, and ought not to exist longer than is absolutely necessary. As there are no symptoms that the people of these provinces will be prepared to participate in constitutional government for some years, I know of no arrangement so proper for them as Territorial Governments. There they can learn the principles of freedom and eat the fruit of foul rebellion. Under such governments, while electing members to the Territorial Legislatures, they will necessarily mingle with those to whom Congress shall extend the [voting] right of suffrage. In Territories, Congress fixes the qualifications of Electors; and I know of no better place, nor better occasion, for the conquered [Secessionists] and the conqueror to practice justice to all men, and to accustom themselves to make and obey equal laws. . . .

"According to my judgment, they ought never to be reorganized as capable of acting in the Union, or of being counted as valid States, until the [Federal] Constitution shall have been so amended . . . so as to secure perpetual ascendancy to the Party of the Union; and so as to render our [Federal] Government firm and stable forever.

"The first of those Amendments [to the Federal Constitution will be] to change the basis of representation among the States, from [the] Federal [census of total population] to [a count of] actual voters [registered]. Now [the Federal Constitution states that] all the [independent African Americans] . . . and three-fifths of the [bonded African Americans] are represented, though [by State laws, with minor exceptions,] none of them have votes. [Before the bonded were made independent] the [southern] States [had] 19 [Federal] Representatives [resulting from the population census of bonded African Americans]. [Now that they] are now [independent, these States] can add, for the other two-fifths, 13 more [Federal Representatives], making the representation 32. I suppose the [African Americans who had long been independent] in [the southern] States will give at least 5 more, making the representation of [African Americans not allowed to vote] about 37. The whole number of Representatives in the House [prior to secession had been] 70. Add the other two-fifths and it will be 83 [once all are re-admitted].

"If the Amendment [I propose] prevails, and those States [deny the vote to African American men] it will deduct about 37 [from their allocation of Representatives], leaving them but 45, which would render them powerless for ever. [On the other hand, if the Amendment were to fail,] the 83 southern [States Representatives], with the Democrats that will in the best time be elected from the [northern States,] will always give [Democrats] a majority in Congress and in the Electoral College. They will at the very first election take possession of the [office of President] and the halls of Congress — I need not depict the ruin that would follow. Assumption of the [Confederate] debt or repudiation of the Federal debt would be sure to follow. The oppression of the [newly independent African American]; the re-amendment of their State Constitutions, and the re-establishment of [African American bonding] would be the inevitable result.

"If the Amendment [I propose] prevails, and those States should, [on the other hand], grant the right [to vote] to [African American men], I think there would always be [Republican-voting European American men] enough in the [southern States], aided by the [African American vote,] to divide the representation, and thus continue the Republican [Party] ascendancy."

In essence, Thad Stevens argued that, either way the southern States reacted to his proposed Amendment, the Republican Party would continue to control the Federal Government. Stevens then turned to his favorite subject, taxes on foreign trade, but this time he was not talking taxes on imports. He was talking about <u>taxes on exports</u> — taxes on exported cotton. Stevens proposed an Amendment to the Federal Constitution that would empower the Federal Government to tax exports leaving the States for ports in foreign nations.

The importance [of] "the proposed Amendment to allow Congress to lay a duty on exports . . . cannot well be overstated. It is very obvious that for many years the [southern States] will not pay much under our internal revenue laws. The only article on which we can raise any considerable amount is cotton. It will be grown largely at once. With <u>ten cents a pound export duty</u> it would be furnished cheaper to foreign markets than they could obtain it from any other parts of the world. The late war has shown that. Two million bales exported, at 500 pounds to the bale, would yield $100,000,000. This seems to be the chief revenue we shall ever derive from the [southern States]. Besides, it would be a protection [worth $100,000,000] to our domestic manufacturers [of cotton textiles]."

Let us briefly depart from Stevens' speech and look into the actual math of his proposed 10-cent per pound export duty?

History would show that the price of domestic cotton would average 30 cents per pound during the 1866-1870 period, and would drop drastically afterward to an average of 15 cents per pound during the decade of 1871 to 1880. A 10-cent export duty, would, in theory, reduce the price earned by the farmer to 20 cents, then drop it down to only a nickel — effectively destroying the overseas market for American cotton and severely damaging the economy of the southern States and opportunities for African Americans to earn a living. Of course, I suppose cotton mills in Massachusetts would love it. What about the Federal Government getting $100,000,000 per year? Forget that — ten cents times zero exports equals zero revenue. [R210;11-12]

Returning to Stevens' speech, we see that he next turned his attention to regulations directly impacting African Americans in the southern States:

"But this is not all that we ought to do before these inveterate [Secessionists] are invited to participate in our Legislation. We have turned . . . loose 4,000,000 [bonded African Americans] without a hut to shelter them or a cent in their pockets. The infernal laws [formerly regulating African American bonding] have prevented them from acquiring an education, understanding the commonest laws of contract, or of managing the ordinary business of life. This Congress is bound to provide for them until they can take care of themselves. If we do not furnish them with homesteads [on property seized from Secessionists], and hedge them around with protective laws; if we leave them to the Legislation of their [former owners], we had better [have] left them in bondage, [because, in that event] their condition would be worse than that of our [Federals imprisoned] at [the Confederate prisoner-of-war camp near] Andersonville, [Georgia]. . . ."

Regarding the Ratification of the Amendment to the Federal Constitution confirming that African American Bonding was outlawed, Stevens made the following observation:

"So as to establish the principle that none of the [conquered] States shall be counted in [the Ratification process, records show that, since the eighteenth State, Connecticut, ratified on May 4] the Amendment [confirming that African American bonding was outlawed] has been Ratified by the Legislatures of three-fourths of the [24] States [that had never seceded]. . . . I take no account [of West Virginia] or the aggregation of white-washed [Secessionists], who without any legal authority have assembled in the capitals of the [11 other conquered] States and simulated Legislative bodies."

Stevens — although not a believing Jew or a Christian himself — next turned to a religious argument:

"It should now be solemnly decided what power can revive, recreate, and reinstate these [conquered] provinces into the family of States, and invest them with the rights of American citizens. It is time that Congress should assert its sovereignty and assume something of the dignity of a Roman Senate. . . . If we have not yet been sufficiently scourged for our national sin to teach us to do justice to all God's creatures, without distinction of race, we must expect the still more heavy vengeance of an offended Father, still increasing His infliction as He increases the severity of the plagues of Egypt until the Tyrant consented to do justice. And when that Tyrant repented of his reluctant consent, and attempted to re-enslave the [Jewish] people, as our [southern States] Tyrants are attempting to do now, he filled the Red Sea with broken chariots and drowned horses, and strewed the shores with dead men's carcasses."

Stevens moved toward his close:

"This is not a 'white man's Government' in the exclusive sense in which it is used . . . for it violates the fundamental principles of our gospel of liberty. This is man's Government; the

Government of all men alike . . . . [However], if equal privileges were granted to all, I should not expect any but [European American] men to be elected to office for long ages to come. The prejudice engendered by [African American bonding] would not soon permit merit to be preferred to [race]. But it would still be beneficial to the weaker race. In a country where political divisions will always exist, their power, joined with just [European American] men, would greatly modify, if it did not entirely prevent, the injustice of majorities. Without the right [of African Americans to cast votes] in the [southern States] — [and here I am not talking about the northern States] — I believe the [newly independent African Americans] had far better been left in bondage. . . .

"Sir, this doctrine of a "white man's Government" is as atrocious as the infamous sentiment that damned the late Chief Justice, [Roger Taney] to everlasting fame; and, I fear, to everlasting fire [in the agony of Hell]."

Stevens, himself an Atheist, apparently needed to close with more religious pander, this time punching a jab at the late Chief Justice of the Federal Supreme Court, Roger Taney, a Democrat appointed to that office by Andrew Jackson in 1836. You will recall that Republicans had assailed Taney unmercifully over the Court's decision in the 1857 case involving an African American named Dred Scott, that case coinciding in time with "Bleeding Kansas," "Bleeding Sumner," and the rise of the Republican Party in the northern States.

At this point Thad Stevens had concluded his transformational speech, which perhaps more significantly than any other during the remaking, and then the Reconstruction, of the conquered States, defined the ordeal through which the southern States people were about to be forced to submit to and endure as they dealt with the "Struggle for Healing" — an era that would demand all of their powers of patience, cooperation, restraint, compliance and endurance, while always seeking a route by which they could eventually achieve the great goal of "Home Rule." [R96;229]

Although Andrew Johnson was nearly overwhelmed by the challenges presented during this month by the more militant Faction of the Republican Party, he was striving to drive Charles Sumner and Thad Stevens from the mainstream Faction which he was struggling to lead. And he remained defiant to some extent. On December 14 his Administration notified William Sharkey, Provisional Governor of Mississippi, that he should relinquish his office to Benjamin Humphreys, the elected Governor, for "the time had come when, in the judgment of the President, the care and conduct of affairs in Mississippi might be remitted to the properly constituted authorities, chosen by the people thereof, without danger to the peace and safety of the United States. [Sharkey] was [accordingly] instructed to transfer the papers and property of the State, then in his custody, to Governor Humphreys. . . . This completed the [remaking of the Mississippi State Government] according to the presidential policy." But Johnson was about to lose control over his presidential policy. [R204;121, R73;255]

On December 21 Provisional South Carolina Governor Benjamin Perry followed through with orders from Andrew Johnson to turn over the records of the Governor's Office to the new and elected Governor, James Orr, who had been sworn into office over 3 weeks earlier. A lifelong South Carolinian, Orr was from Anderson in the northwest part of the State. A graduate of the University of Virginia, he became a lawyer and newspaperman and a member of the State Legislature (1844-1857). Terms in the Federal House followed (1849-1859), being elected Speaker in 1857. He had been reluctant to embrace secession, but supported his State when it came, raising a regiment of riflemen in 1861, commanding it in the field, then leaving to take a seat in the Confederate House in 1862. One of his first acts was to advise the people of South Carolina of the relative powers of his civilian government verse the power of occupying Federal troops:

"The order suspending the *writ of habeas corpus*, issued by the [Federal] President, has not been modified or revoked in this State, and the military authority is therefore paramount in all such matters as they are instructed to take jurisdiction of, and as such will be respected by all orderly and law-abiding people.

"The military claim jurisdiction in all cases of disloyalty to the [Federal] Government and infractions of its laws; to preserve order and discipline in and near their garrisons; to adjudge and determine all controversies in which [African Americans] and [European Americans] are engaged, including violations of State laws by [African Americans]; in all cases of wrong or injury done to its officers and soldiers; and is an auxiliary in aiding treasury agents to recover [Federal] property, and the Newly Independent African American Men Bureau in supervising contracts with [African Americans]. Whenever, therefore, a person is arrested by military authority on either of the above grounds, they have jurisdiction of the case, and are instructed not to obey any *writ of habeas corpus* for the release of such person.

"In all controversies between citizens, arising out of wrongs or injuries done to person or property, and in all violations of the penal code by citizens, the laws are in full force, and the courts will be opened henceforth on every circuit to administer law and punish crime." [R201;26-27]

A major task of the South Carolina State Legislature during the December session was the enactment of new laws intended to establish the relations of newly independent African Americans to the State Government and to European Americans. This package of laws originated with the October and November work of Judge David Wardlaw and Armistead Burt of the two-man Code Commission created by the Constitutional Convention. These laws were developed as four acts: "1) an act preliminary to the legislation induced by [making bonded African Americans independent; 2) an act to amend the criminal law; 3) an act to establish District Courts; 4) an act to establish and regulate the domestic relations of [African Americans] and to amend the law in relation to paupers and vagrancy." Critics of laws of this nature called them, collectively, the "Black Code." In understanding the need for laws on this subject, we must take our mind back in time to the environment of that time and place. A summary of these laws, as established for South Carolina, now follows:

1. Because African Americans were of mixed race ranging from pure African ancestry to almost pure European ancestry, with occasional ancestry also from Native Americans, the laws defined a "person of color" as being anyone whose European ancestry was less than seven-eighths, or appeared to be such. I will continue to call these "persons of color" by the term "African Americans". A European American, called a "white person," was anyone whose European ancestry was seven-eighths or more European. Obviously a person's appearance was often a determining factor in classifying him or her. I will continue to call these people "European Americans".

2. African Americans were not entitled to social or political equality with European Americans, but the law did protect their right "to acquire, own and dispose of property, to make contracts, to enjoy the fruits of their labor, to sue and be sued, and to receive protection under the law in their persons and property.

3. The penalty for an African American convicted of murder or the rape of a European American female was death.

4. The penalty for an African American convicted of assaulting a European American employer, family member of employer, or assigned supervisor was whipping or imprisonment.

5. To help control theft of food for trade, an African American convicted of selling farm products without written permission from the farmer was charged with a misdemeanor.

6. African Americans were allowed to keep shotguns and hunting rifles but not pistols or army-style muskets or rifles.

7. An African American convicted of making liquor or selling it was charged with a misdemeanor.

8. An African American from outside of South Carolina could not move into the State seeking residency unless he or she entered into a bond of $1,000 to ensure good behavior and a self supporting job.

9. A new District Court was authorized to adjudicate all civil cases involving an African American and all criminal cases where the accused was an African American.

10. An African American had the right to trial by jury except for summary judgments of "small and mean causes."

11. The new District Court was also authorized to adjudicate cases involving a European American accused of murdering an African American.

12. An African American as plaintiff or defendant in a civil case was entitled to access to African American witnesses as was an African American charged with a criminal offense.

13. An African American had the same legal rights as a European American in cases involving wills, estates, probate, inheritance, etc.

14. An African American couple living together at the time the law began were automatically declared to have been married retroactively as husband and wife, without need of special ceremonies.

15. Bigamy was disallowed, requiring African Americans in such cases to choose one mate.

16. Therefore, every African American baby was the legitimate child of his or her mother and the father who claimed him or her, if any.

17. The rights to marriage ceremony and a marriage license were available to all.

18. Marriage between a European American and an African American was disallowed. Marriage between homosexuals was not allowed.

19. Procedures for establishing labor employment contracts were defined, including setting the working from sunrise to sunset except on Sunday with reasonable interval for breakfast and dinner; and including responsibility on the part of the employee for property losses resulting from his or her negligence, dishonesty or bad faith.

20. Lost working time not caused by the employer shall be deducted from wages and if the employee receives during lost work time some food, nursing and other necessaries, those are deductible from wages.

21. Night work and outdoor work in inclement weather shall not be requested of employees except in case of necessity.

22. Employees are free to leave the farm at will on Sundays, to return by sunset.

23. Recognizing that employees have differing productivities, an employment contract should rate the productivity of that person as full, three-fourths, half or one-forth and the expected workload, productivity and wages should be in agreement.

24. Persons visiting employees on farms or other work premises must have the permission of the owner of the property.

25. When an employee needs to leave the farm or other work place, except for Sundays, he or she needs to get permission from the employer.

26. If an employer breaks the employment contract and wrongfully discharges the employee, the employee has recourse to recover lost wages.

27. A household servant should work under a contract similar to a farm worker and be governed by similar rules.

28. Limited welfare relief was to be provided to African American paupers, but those convicted by a jury of three in magistrate's court should be punished for vagrancy.

Such were the laws concerning African Americans living in South Carolina. These differed from the laws in Mississippi, but followed a similar pattern to effect control over behavior. [R201;27-31]

On Christmas Eve, in the small town of Pulaski, Tennessee, some young men started a social club "to cheer the monotony of their penniless positions." In the tradition of men's fraternities, the fellows first called their club "Kuklio" from the Greek word meaning "band." A bit later they would add the Scottish word "clan;" and eventually the name would expand into "Ku Klux Klan." The club's first activity was to serenade their sweethearts at night while carrying torches and concealing their identities by draping white sheets over their bodies with only eye-holes cut out for visibility. They sometimes draped their horses with white sheets, too. After a few such night rides from sweetheart to sweetheart, the men began observing less criminal activity among African American men, a problem that had worsened considerably since the conquest of the State. It seems that ancient African traditions of voodoo and related ghostly superstitions still influenced African American thought. The night riders in white sheets must have spooked a significant number into behaving themselves. Hudson Strode would write: "When it was discovered that the young men's masquerade, which had begun as a lark, had helped intimidate the [African Americans], the movement spread to other communities." Within 17 months, the Ku Klux Klan movement would be popular throughout the conquered Confederate States, and Nathan Forrest would be elected its first Chief. At that meeting the purpose of the organization would be as defined as "the protection of women and property and civilization itself." By this resistance tactic, many European American men in the conquered States would transform their political activity into an underground movement, as they wrestled with the "Struggle for Healing." And when asked by authorities for any information about the Ku Klux Klan they would take their clue from the 1850's "Secret Order" of the northeastern States. They would be "Know Nothings." [R19;359]

Wade Hampton and his wife Mary were not together for Christmas. Wade had arranged earlier for a core group of African American employees to travel from South Carolina to his Mississippi farms, especially to his beloved Wild Woods farm, paying all travel expenses, of course. Then Wade had left for the farms in early December. He had stopped briefly in Montgomery, Alabama on December 11 to address the State Legislature. A week later, while on a riverboat steaming up the Mississippi River, he had written of progress to his sister Mary Fisher. He had found the Wild Woods house intact, unlike Jeff Davis' farmhouse Brierfield, which Federal troops had destroyed. By Christmas he was probably at his Wild Woods farm where the African Americans who had preceded him were already at work. He would later report home with this news of his arrival: "The [African Americans] all seemed delighted to see me. There are a good many here, who have relations in South Carolina, and they are very anxious that they should come out [as well]." In a January 31 letter to sister Mary Fisher, he would ask her to help encourage more farm workers to join him, suggesting he needed 100 additional employees, and his son Wade needed 50 more as well. He would suggest she get Mr. Taylor, a neighbor farmer, to help with the hiring of these additional employees. [R199;174-175, R200;104]

Christmas day was especially sad for Jeff Davis. He remained in prison, still not formally charged with any crime, and still denied access to a court trial. He was simply a political prisoner, in a military fort, beyond the reach of defense lawyers in State or Federal Courts. He was unable to receive any visitors — not even his wife. It was lonely, indeed. But the day was even more disheartening than would have been expected, because Christmas was the day that Nelson Miles ordered John Craven removed as Davis' physician. Craven had to leave Fortress Monroe immediately. When John stopped by Jeff's prison room to say goodbye, Jeff, as a token of his immense gratitude, gave John his last valuable possession: his meerschaum pipe.

But John Craven's helpfulness toward Jeff Davis would not end with his departure from Fortress Monroe, for he would take with him his memories and a diary of notes on conversations with Davis. And in Great Britain, Craven would write and publish a book that would add greatly to public pressure to let Jeff Davis go free. Craven's book would be titled: *The Prison Life of Jefferson Davis*.

Nelson Miles immediately brought in a new military physician, George Cooper, to attend to Jeff Davis' medical needs. Miles was replacing Craven with a military doctor who shared the most militant Republican attitudes of punishment toward imprisoned Confederates, someone who agreed politically with, say, Thad Stevens. And he figured he had such a man in Cooper. But Miles had not researched Cooper quite thoroughly enough. For example, Miles must not have realized that, although Cooper was of the northern States, his wife had been born and raised in Virginia, and had been opposed to Abe Lincoln's order to send invasion forces into the Confederacy. Biographer Hudson Strode observed that, "like his predecessor, in spite of himself, [Cooper] was soon to become impressed by [Jeff] Davis' qualities and the charm of is conversation." [R19;272-273]

The Year of 1866

(1Q66)

We now move into 1866, visiting first Charles Sumner's activities.

As mentioned before, Sumner's knowledge of conditions in the conquered States was limited to what others told him by word or by letter. And it seems that, to a great extent, his attitude was shaped by the stories of abuse that arrived in frequent letters written by Republicans who were in the region as Federal soldiers, Bureau agents or as self-employed opportunity seekers. In his letter to Elizabeth Argyll, Sumner wrote that one of the letters he had received had reported that, "In most places the [newly independent African American men] are worse off than when [bonded], being exposed to the brutality and vindictiveness of their old [owners], without the old check of self-interest." Certainly, the devastation and bankruptcy produced by the Federal invasion made life hard for everyone in that region, and the problems facing African American men surely did exceed the problems facing European American men. African American men were jobless and homeless. Many, deluded into expecting a soon-to-arrive gift of 40 acres, had been loitering about during the summer and fall of 1865, simply waiting for their gift. Those were deluded into equating independence to a life of leisure, for they did not realize that a successful farm, if it provided more than a subsistence living, required agri-tech-management, financial management, risk management, employee management and market savvy. The vast majority only knew the life of the farm worker, where others handled all management issues.

Only African American men such as Ben Montgomery of Brierfield Farm understood the essential work of the farm owner and/or his hired farm supervisor. And Ben Montgomery had learned farm management from Joseph Davis and Jeff Davis during a time of economic prosperity, when money was available to pay bills and farm produce, such as cotton, sold at attractive prices, typically 12 cents per pound. Although well-prepared and unusually intelligent, Ben Montgomery was facing almost insurmountable problems making a go of farming on Davis Bend. During the first months following the conquest of the Confederacy, farm owners had no money to pay African Americans who sought farm work, so deals were struck to share-crop or to provide rent-free housing, pig pens, chicken runs, and garden plots with a promise to pay back-wages after the farm's produce was sold at market. Certainly, the writer of the previously mentioned letter to Charles Sumner was right when he wrote, "in most places the [newly independent African American men] are worse off that when [they had been bonded]." But perhaps the writer failed to understand the farmer's need to negotiate wage-payment arrangements necessitated by his abject bankruptcy when he alleged that the newly independent African American men were "being exposed to the brutality and vindictiveness of their old [owners]." And Charles Sumner, having never run a successful business, and having scant understanding of agriculture in the former Confederate States, was eager to view all hardship stories in political and racial terms. Therefore, Sumner quoted from such letters to justify his opinion that Andrew Johnson's program for remaking conquered State Governments meant surrendering "our [potential Republican Party voters], [European American and African American alike], the true [supporters of the Republican-led Federal Government] to a terrible fate." And Sumner told Gideon Welles that, "while he could not denounce [Johnson's program] as the greatest crime ever committed by a responsible ruler, he did proclaim . . . it the greatest mistake which history has ever recorded."

Biographer David Donald would further explain how, during January, the frustrated Charles Sumner — excluded from membership in the powerful House-Senate Joint Committee on Reconstruction — raged violently upon the Senate floor:

> "Day after day in the Senate, Sumner denounced [Andrew] Johnson in language so intemperate as to astonish even those who had known him for years. [Gideon] Welles could hardly credit the 'impetuous violence' of his speeches, and [William] Stanton, whom Sumner thought a wholehearted supporter, dismissed his views as 'absurd and heretical.' Senator [E. D.] Morgan thought he was acting 'as if demented.' Observing the hostility that Sumner and other [like-minded Republicans] exhibited toward [former Confederates of European descent], former Attorney General [Edward] Bates, [writing in his diary,] tried a bit of amateur psychoanalysis: 'They feel that they deserved to be hated by the [former Confederate] people for [the Republican's] cruel conspiracy to degrade and ruin the [conquered] States, and, naturally enough, they conclude that their bad passions are imitated, and their malicious hatred reciprocated [by those conquered] people." [R73;241-242]

My study persuades me to embrace Edward Bates' analysis of Sumner's behavior. And the same psychology applies to interpreting the earlier terrorism in "Bleeding Kansas." Republican propagandists assumed that Kansas settlers from the Southern States were attacking fellow settlers from the northeastern States with the same violence and hatred displayed by the latter. They refused to check out a story lead if it suggested that a fight constituted settlers from a southern State defending against an attack by settlers from a northeastern State. But attacks by settlers from the southern States, when discovered, were greatly exaggerated by Republican propagandists to justify attacks by Jim Lane, James Montgomery, John Brown and other terrorists who had come in from the northern States.

Not all Massachusetts Republican leaders were supportive of Sumner's program for Reconstruction. The most serious opposition within the State was from Massachusetts Governor John Andrew, who thought his proposals too militant. Furthermore, Andrew remained antagonistic towards Sumner for his part in blocking a potential Secretary job in Abe Lincoln's Cabinet. Andrew had been eager to exploit sectional propaganda to build the emerging Republican Party in its first few years. In fact, he had given the terrorist John Brown notable support. But, by 1866, Andrew was more interested in reaping benefits to Massachusetts businessmen and investors – benefits that would suffer from the social upheaval advocated by Sumner and Thad Stevens. For that reason, John Andrew was supportive of Andrew Johnson's program for remaking the Governments in the conquered States. To Andrew, "A [Secessionist] vote is the best of all if it is only cast in the right way." And, it seems that Andrew did not embrace the theory that making voters of African American men in the conquered States was essential to the continued domination of the Republican Party. So Andrew Johnson's supporters struck a deal with the Governor of Massachusetts: if the Governor supported the Johnson Administration program for the conquered States, then it would let him select the men for all Federal jobs in the State — Charles Sumner would have no say in the matter. And, the Johnson Administration pledged to cooperate with Andrew in "organizing a new [political] Party or manipulating the [existing combination that had re-elected Abe Lincoln in 1864] in just such way as might seem fit." Biographer David Donald further would explain the attitudes of the many Republicans in Massachusetts who thought like John Andrew:

> "[Sumner] lacked the popularity of [Andrew], the war Governor, whether among the local politicians, the returning veterans, or the Boston businessmen. In addition, Sumner's Reconstruction plans opened him to serious challenge. Republicans in Massachusetts, proud that their State had the first public school system in America and distrustful of the Irish and other unlettered immigrants, found it hard to accept Sumner's view that all the [newly independent African American men] of the [conquered States] ought to be [allowed to vote], regardless of ability or even literacy. Andrew spoke for a majority when, declaring himself a 'radical believer in [giving voting rights to] all men of competent capacity, irrespective of [race] or national origins,' he deplored 'the raising of the general question of [giving voting rights to] [African American men] of the [conquered States], as yet.' Certainly the [African Americans] must be guaranteed equal civil rights [before the law], Andrew argued, but [the right to vote] was a privilege, to be distributed 'according to capacity and desert,' and before receiving it the [newly independent African American men] needed to demonstrated their ability to grow 'in knowledge and in admitted capacity for exercising the political functions of citizenship'."

And John Andrew strongly opposed the Amendment Sumner had re-introduced in the Senate in early December 1866, which would apportion Representatives to the Federal House based on the population of men who were qualified to vote (Sumner had originally introduced the Amendment in February 1865). Andrew was concerned that Massachusetts would loose seats in the House because his State had a large population of new immigrants who had not yet achieved citizenship. So counting only male citizens hurt Massachusetts. Furthermore, Andrew was concerned that, since women significantly outnumbered men in Massachusetts, counting men instead of men, women and children would hurt Massachusetts. In a widely publicized address delivered on January 5, Andrew called Sumner's apportion plan "a delusion and a snare." Sidestepping politically-explosive voter issues involving women and immigrants, Andrew appealed instead to principle: "By diminishing the Representative power of the [southern States, including Maryland, Kentucky and Missouri,] in favor of other States, you will not increase [those people's] love for the [Federal Government]. Nor, while Connecticut and Wisconsin refuse [to allow African American men to vote], will you be able to convince [the citizens of those southern States] that your Amendment was dictated by political principles, and not by political cupidity." But ingenious politicians in Congress would soon invent a fix to Massachusetts' dilemma. In a few days Sumner's bill would be replaced by another which cleverly based a State's allocation of

Representatives on the total population — men, women, children, citizens and aliens — but excluded all African Americans from the count if that State refused to let African American men vote. Allocated that way, Massachusetts would receive a generous number of seats in the Federal House. Feeling trapped by such political criticism, Charles Sumner was planning to oppose the Amendment when it came to the Senate floor for debate.

In early January 1866 Thad Stevens proposed an Amendment to the Federal Constitution as he had advocated in his December speech. This Amendment was similar to Charles Sumner's February, 1865 Amendment, re-introduced in December 1865, which would have also drastically changed the formula for allocating seats in Congress to the individual States based on the population of men who were qualified to vote. Sumner's Amendment had presented an opportunity to "trade:" if a State refused to let African American men vote, then it would lose seats in the Federal House in proportion to the percent of men denied the right to vote. Stevens Amendment proposed a similar opportunity for "trade." It would allocate seats based on a census of each State's population of adult men who had been legally certified as qualified voters. This Amendment offered continued Republican Party control of the Federal Government without making voters of African American men — a political position Stevens probably wanted to avoid since his own State of Pennsylvania denied African American men access to its polls. Like Charles Sumner's Amendment bill of February, 1865, Stevens' proposed Amendment permitted a State Constitutional Convention or Legislature to exclude African American men from the polls by accepting loss of part of their Federal House seat apportionment.

During January, "almost every morning between ten o'clock and noon," Stevens, as Co-Chairman, worked with members of the Joint House-Senate Committee on Reconstruction to gather reports from the conquered States that purported to show that, in that region, newcomers from the northern States and African Americans were not safe. Stevens wanted these reports to support Republican allegations that further expansion of Federal military control over the former Confederate people was necessary. And Stevens was pushing his Constitutional Amendment proposal through the Committee as well.

The House was simultaneously involved with a bill to make voters of African American men living in the District of Columbia. During mid-January a caucus of House Republicans, in defiance of Thad Stevens' directive, voted to support an amendment the District of Columbia bill to requiring potential voters to pass a literacy test to prove he possessed a minimum level of education. Republicans figured most African American men would fail the test, but the vast majority of European American men would pass. Stevens opposed the amendment to the bill because he feared a literacy test policy in the District of Columbia would become a precedent which Democrat politicians in the conquered States could emulate to defeat the anticipated Republican Political Machines empowered by the votes of African American men. So Stevens persuaded the leader of the Democrats in the House, Representative Fernando Wood, to convince fellow Democrats to vote against the literacy-test amendment, suggesting that the African American voting bill would fail to pass if not amended. Stevens' trick worked. The Democrats voted to kill the education-test amendment to the bill. But Stevens had meanwhile gathered enough Republican votes to pass the unamended bill, and he did win its passage. By such tactics Stevens was enabling voting by African American men who lived outside the southern States, where their vote was not likely to swing many elections, so that he could establish precedent for their voting in southern States, where their vote alone would be the basis for Republican Political Machine rule.

By the end of January, having completed deliberations in the Joint Committee on Reconstruction, Thad Stevens moved to force through the House passage of his Constitutional Amendment to apportion Federal House based on the population of men who were qualified to vote. Stevens sped the bill through with limited debate, giving himself most of the last hour. Stevens' speech "was unusually sarcastic and bitter, even for him." He accused Andrew Johnson "of usurpations greater than those that had cost Charles I his head." The many Republican Representatives who supported his bill laughed when Stevens derided Andrew Johnson and the few Republican Representatives, such as Henry Raymond of New York, who had supported Johnson's policies. Stevens had the votes: the Constitutional Amendment to apportion Representatives according to the population of qualified voters passed the House by a vote of 120 to 46. The proposed Amendment to the Federal Constitution advanced to the Senate. [R73;241-245, R96;231-232, R98;262-264]

When the proposed Amendment advanced from the House to the Senate, Charles Sumner was afraid to be supportive in spite of the fact that, he had introduced a similar Amendment in the Senate. The problem he faced was the rather recent realization that the Amendment would reduce the number of seats allocated to Massachusetts, because Massachusetts had an unusually large population of aliens and an unusually high population of women — categories that would no longer be tabulated toward appropriation of Federal Representatives, whether as a result of Stevens' Amendment or his own Amendment. So, when Stevens' Amendment arrived at the Senate, Massachusetts politicians rose up in opposition — not because of its intent to punish ex-Confederate States, but because of the just-mentioned demographics trap that was peculiar to Massachusetts.

On February 5, Charles Sumner rose in the Senate and delivered a five-hour oration, titled "The Equal Rights of All," which would occupy 67 pages in a future publication of Sumner's *Works*. Although he admitted that the definitions of "republic" by ancient philosophers and other historical figures were "absolutely fallacious and inapplicable," Sumner dragged his colleagues through a long presentation of "everything on the subject from Plato to the last French pamphlet." Undoubtedly, Sumner was stuffing his oration with loosely connected history and literature to cover up the fact that his speech intentionally "contained almost no arguments against specific provisions of [the Amendment being debated]." Henry Dawes, likely one of the few to pay much attention to Sumner's oration, wrote his wife that the speech was "a wonderful production full of splendid platitudes, crammed with book learning, but utterly void of any practical adaptation of the present exigency." Biographer David Donald surmised that Sumner "disguised the irrelevance of his argument by the vigor of his language." Although not a Christian himself, Sumner's closing appeal was stuffed full with references to his notion of a God:

> "Show me a creature, with lifted countenance looking to Heaven, made in the image of God, and I show you a Man who, of whatever country or race, whether browned by equatorial sun or blanched by northern cold, is with you a child of the Heavenly Father, and equal with you in all the rights of human nature. You cannot deny these rights without impiety. . . . It is not enough that you have [made bonded African Americans independent]. By the same title we claim [making them independent] do we claim equality [before the law] also? . . . One is the complement of the other. . . . The Roman Cato, after declaring his belief in the immortality of the soul, added, that, if this were an error, it was an error he loved. And now, declaring my belief in [making bonded African Americans independent] and [making them equal before the law] as the God-given birthright of all men, let me say, in the same spirit, if this be an error, it is an error I love — if this be a fault, it is a fault I shall be slow to renounce — if this be an illusion, it is an illusion which I pray may wrap the world in its angelic forms."

Sumner's emotional appeal against the Constitutional Amendment was surprisingly effective in consolidating his supporters in Massachusetts. Newspaper accounts seemed to convince his old following of Abolitionists and Exclusionists that he was continuing the emotional appeals of past victorious campaigns. The fact that Sumner himself had submitted a similar Constitutional Amendment, only 12 months previously, was apparently judged to be insignificant. Although the opposite was more true, voters were persuaded that former Governor John Andrew was following Sumner's lead in opposing the Amendment. And Sumner himself was extremely pleased with the impact his oration produced in Massachusetts. He wrote a friend that he considered the speech "the best thing of my life," and added "I am glad to know that [John] Andrew agrees with me in opposing the Amendment." Charles Sumner was setting the stage to strike down, throughout the Federation, a State's right to establish for itself the requirements for its citizens to become qualified to vote. If the Federal Government seized the power to require all States to permit African American men to vote, then the apportioning formula in Stevens' Amendment, now being considered by the Senate, would be irrelevant. Sumner had decided to discard the apportionment penalty he himself had previously advocated so that he could move further toward subjugating all States — North, South and West — beneath an all-powerful Federal Government.

On the other hand many Republicans in the Senate and House, who had little knowledge of Sumner's competitive maneuvering against John Andrew, were furious at Sumner for his inconceivable political about-face. William Fessenden publicly denounce Sumner's oration as a "very violent — I had almost said virulent — attack" upon the proposed Amendment. And to colleagues he confided: "[Charles] Sumner, with his impracticable notions, his vanity, his hatred of [Andrew Johnson] . . . is doing infinite harm." Salmon Chase urged Sumner to vote for the Amendment in spite of his attack so that it "may not be defeated and especially that it may not be defeated by your vote." And Thad Stevens admonished Sumner to vote for the Amendment so that, if it was "to be slain it will not be by our friends."

Not all of the Republican Senators who in the Party's more militant faction agreed with Sumner in opposing the Amendment. Ben Wade, who's State of Ohio refused to let African American men vote, said of Sumner's oration: "It's all very well, Sumner, but it has no bones in it." And Zachariah Chandler complained humorously, "Sumner is one of them literary fellows." But 7 other Republicans agreed with Sumner's goal of moving beyond the Amendment to outright subvert a State's constitutional right to legislate voter qualifications. All Democratic Senators opposed the Amendment, but for the opposite reason – they wanted to preserve a State's right to regulate, without penalty, the basis for qualifying African American men as voters. So 8 Republicans, Sumner among them, joined with all the Democratic Senators in voting against the Amendment. Since a two-thirds vote was needed for approval, those votes were just enough to defeat the measure and prevent it being submitted to the State Legislatures for Ratification. Thad Stevens was furious that the Amendment had been killed by "the united forces of self-righteous Republicans and unrighteous [Democrats]," denouncing his "puerile and pedantic criticism." Lyman Trumbull thought Sumner devious and unscrupulous. James Grimes called him "a cold-blooded, selfish, dangerous man." William Fessenden called him a "malignant fool." [R73;244-247, R19;273-274]

Meanwhile at Fortress Monroe, Charles Minnegerode was permitted to visit Jeff Davis again in February, and there he again administered a Communion service in Jeff's jail room. Sensing a cautious admiration of Davis while talking with some of the officers of the guard detail, Minnegerode decided he should attempt to confront Edwin Stanton himself. A few days later he went to Washington City and gained access to Stanton's office. There Stanton "received the Rector of St. Paul's coldly and spoke not a word in reply to anything he said." Toward the end of this one-way conversation, Minnegerode pleaded that "without the least danger of any kind as to [Jeff] Davis' safe imprisonment, he might enjoy some privilege, especially the liberty of the fort, or there would be danger of his health failing completely." Finally Stanton spoke: "It makes no difference what the state of the health of Jeff Davis is. His trial will soon come on, no doubt. Time enough till that settles it." But Stanton was actually bluffing, for the prospects for putting Davis on trial were growing more unlikely by the month. Charles O'Conor and William Reed were bombarding Stanton with legal arguments designed to force him to charge Davis with some crime and try that issue in court, or, as he should, let the poor man go. Imprisoning a man for political reasons without due process of law was a violent violation of the Federal Constitution. In a February 12 missile, O'Conor accused Stanton of attempting "to slay without form or ceremony." And there is good reason to figure that Stanton would like to receive news that Jeff Davis was dead, that is, if he himself were not implicated. But George Cooper's medical attention was helping Davis to hold on. After a few days of getting acquainted, Cooper had apparently become determined to in no way help Nelson Miles torment Jeff Davis. Cooper observed that the noise of Federal guards incessantly tramping just outside his room still pressed through the bared doors, constantly jarring Davis' nerves, and he observed the damage inflicted by Miles insistence that the lamp burn all night. And Cooper succeeded in persuading Miles to let Jeff tie Varina's black-fabric eyeshade over his eyes, and that offered great compensating comfort. Varina had made the eyeshade in January and had sent it to Fortress Monroe. In his next letter, Jeff described the immense relief he had received from the eyeshade. Perhaps it was the success of Varina's eyeshade that convinced Nelson Miles to give up on his night-light torment and also agree to let George Cooper turn down the lamp some more. [R19;273-274]

Meanwhile, Charles Sumner was becoming more irrelevant. Finding himself more and more isolated from the give and take of political negotiations, Sumner became more and more a loner who carefully wrote out literary orations that denounced bills as they came before the Senate, reading them with feeling before his colleagues from printer's proof sheets. He avoided the human interaction that Stevens, Fessenden and Trumbull seemed rather good at. Biographer David Donald concluded: "Since his childhood, when [Sumner] discovered that nothing he could do would ever satisfy his father or endear him to his mother, he had found that his triumphs turned into ashes, and he needed to move constantly onward, from one achievement to the next." And Sumner was only comfortable dealing with former Confederates as a stereotypical class of people. For example, in May of the previous year, Sumner had been tricked into attending a dinner party to which William Aiken of South Carolina was also invited. Before secession Aiken had been a very wealthy farmer and a Federal Representative. But Federal devastation of his State had made him destitute. When Sumner attempted conversation by asking Aiken about South Carolinians he had known from before secession, the replies were "he is dead," or "he is in hiding" from the Federals, or "he has nothing left" after the devastation inflicted by William Sherman's hoard of Devastators. Finally Aiken told his own story, using a rather humorous and joking tone to reduce the gravity of his words. And Aiken added that the torment had driven his wife mad. Biographer David Donald would describe Sumner's reaction:

> "Embarrassed 'to find himself so triumphant before his human ruin,' Sumner fled [his host's] house as soon as dinner was over. As though afraid to show pity, he kept saying: 'But this man is a [South Carolina State secessionist, a] traitor [to the Federal Government], he was involved in [Confederate efforts to circumvent the Federal blockade], his case is terribly bad.' Thereafter he took greater care to avoid any such encounters; he preferred to deal with categories rather than with men." And even more he hid behind his notions of principle as illustrated in a portion of one Senate debate: "It is not I who speak. I am nothing. It is the cause, whose voice I am, that addresses you."

Sumner held up business in the Senate for weeks to block the organization of Montana Territory and Colorado Territory because the bills excluded African Americans from voting in Territory Legislature elections. Proponents of this exclusion argued that, because there are so few African Americans in those territories, their vote is of no consequence. But Sumner replied, "If there but one, that would be enough to justify my opposition." But when faced with advocates of Federal legislation that would require the established northern States, such as Connecticut and Illinois, to allow resident African American men to vote, Sumner replied that the loss of African American votes in such States was "on so small a scale that it is not perilous to the [Federal Government]." And when confronted by the just-emerging movement to permit women to vote, Sumner told advocates that their movement was not timely because their campaign might derail his efforts to force States to permit African American men to vote. So Sumner refused to help the women.

Perhaps Sumner encountered the greatest friction with William Fessenden, the powerful and effective Senator from neighboring Maine. As mentioned earlier, Fessenden had accepted the post of Co-Chairman of the Joint House-Senate Committee on Reconstruction because he had thought that to be the only way to keep Sumner out of the group. A practical politician, Fessenden often criticized Sumner for delaying legislation by fussing over details he disliked. Fessenden delighted in pointing out the "inconsistencies and irrelevancies" in Sumner's literary and long-winded orations. When Sumner based his argument on broad and abstract "principles," Fessenden would counter, "My constituents did not send me here to philosophize." Eventually, Sumner became so furious at Fessenden, that he refused to have any further personal relationship with the man — from that point on Sumner would neither recognize nor speak to Fessenden. Such was his capacity to harbor hatred. [R73;251-254]

The history now turns toward an interrogation of Robert Lee by Jacob Howard's Sub-Committee. Unlike Charles Sumner, Jacob Howard of Michigan was a practical and pragmatic Republican, not relegated to the sidelines, but made Chair of one of the four Sub-Committees of the Joint House-Senate Committee on Reconstruction. William Fessenden, Co-Chairman of Committee had charged Howard's Sub-Committee with investigating political conditions in Virginia, North Carolina and South Carolina. The other three Sub-Committees were responsible for investigating political conditions in the other conquered States. Like Stevens and Fessenden, Howard sided with the more militant Faction of the Republican Party. Born in Vermont and educated there and in Massachusetts, he had migrated west to Detroit to practice law and engage in politics as a Whig. A leader in establishing the Michigan Republican Party in 1854, he had risen to power with it, entering the Federal Senate in 1861. As a Virginian, Robert Lee was among the former Confederates required to testify before Howard's Sub-Committee, which was taking testimony from January 23 through April 19.

On February 17 Robert Lee was sworn in and questioned by Howard and his Sub-Committee for two hours. Lee begin the engagement "determined to say no more than was demanded of him." Straight-on he apologized that he rarely discussed matters with politicians and lived a "very retired" life. Wisely he gave answers that were general and free of any hint of conjecture. He only spoke of himself, not for others. Space here only affords a few samples of the exchanges:

> Although there were no rumors of war, Howard asked Lee if former Confederates would fight to defend the United States in the event of a war with a foreign power. Lee replied, "I cannot speak with any certainty on that point," thereby submitting a factual answer free of any conjecture. Howard asked Lee if at any time he had sworn any "oath of fidelity or allegiance to the Confederate Government?" (Did Howard ever realize that he had asked the wrong question; that Lee's allegiance was to his native State, Virginia, which had been the sovereign and the basis of his citizenship?) Truthfully, Lee answered, "I do not recollect having done so . . ."

> A Sub-Committee member, Henry Blow, Republican of Missouri, was more inclined toward sympathetic interchange. Henry was born in Virginia and spent his youth on an Alabama farm before moving to St. Louis, where he received some college education and then entered into the paint and lead mining business, which eventually made him wealthy. You will recall the Blow family with regard to the bonded African American Dred Scott, who had been owned by Henry's father, the late Peter Blow, a former officer in the Federal Army. You will recall that the Federal Supreme Court had adjudicated a case by which advocates for Dred Scott had sought to have him declared independent on the basis of his having accompanied Peter Blow as a body servant, for long periods, during Army assignments in northern States and Territories. The Court heard arguments and then ruled that accompanying Peter Blow as a body servant in northern States did not constitute a basis for Scott's independence. Although Henry Blow supported the Republicans in the 1861 subjugation of the Missouri State Government, he was of the Southern Culture and not a supporter of the more militant Faction of the Republican Party. Henry Blow asked Robert Lee:

>> "You do not feel down there that, while you accept the result, we are as generous as we ought to be under the circumstances?"

>> Lee quickly answered, "They think that the North can afford to be generous."

>> Blow continued, "That is the feeling down there?"

>> Lee assured, "Yes, and they think it is the best policy — those who reflect upon the subject and are able to judge."

>> Blow elaborated, "I understand it to be your opinion that generosity and liberality toward the entire [southern States region] would be the surest means of regaining their good opinion?"

>> Lee then confirmed, "Yes, and the speediest!"

Howard then took another turn as he resumed his questioning, now with a focus on the possible conviction of Jeff Davis on the alleged crime of treason against the United States.

>> Howard insisted, "They do not generally suppose that it was treason against the United States, do they?

>> Lee replied, "I do not think that they so consider it."

>> Howard continued, "In what light would they view it? What would be their excuse or justification? How would they escape in their own mind? I refer to the past."

>> Lee explained, "I am referring to the past and as to the feelings they would have. So far as I know, they look upon the action of the State, in withdrawing itself from the Government of the United States, as carrying the individuals of the State along with it; that the State was responsible for the act, not the individual."

>> Howard pressed on, "And that the Ordinance of Secession, so-called, or those acts of the State which recognized a condition of war between the State and the [Federal] Government, stood as their justification for their bearing arms against the Government of the United States?"

>> Lee affirmed, "Yes, sir. I think they considered the act of the State as legitimate; that they were merely using the reserved right which they had a right to do."

Howard reframed the question as a personal one, while giving legal permission to refuse to testify against one's-self. Howard continued, "State, if you please — and if you are disinclined to answer the question you need not do so — what your own personal views on that question were."

Lee again affirmed, "That was my view; that the act of Virginia in withdrawing herself from the United States carried me along as a citizen of Virginia, and that her laws and her acts were binding on me."

In Lee's answer we grasp the legal dilemma confronting the Republican lawyers who were charged with convicting Jeff Davis of treason. Davis was a citizen of Mississippi and "her laws and her acts were binding on" him as well.

Shortly afterward the Sub-Committee asked Lee to give his opinion of how people of the former Confederate States viewed the possibility of allowing African American men the right to vote. Recognizing that African American men, as voters, would be pawns in the hands of demagogues, Lee answered, "My own opinion is that, at this time, they cannot vote intelligently, and that giving them the right of suffrage would open the door to a great deal of demagoguism, and lead to embarrassments in various ways. What the future may prove, how intelligent they may become, with what eyes they may look upon the interests of the State in which they may reside, I cannot say more than you can."

Next, upon being quizzed about "cruelties practiced towards [Federal] prisoners," Lee submitted a detailed answer:

"I suppose they suffered from the want of ability on the part of the Confederate States to supply their wants. At the beginning of the war I knew there were sufferings of prisoners on both sides, but, as far as I could, I did everything in my power to relieve them, and urged the establishment of the cartel, which was established. . .

"I made several efforts to exchange the prisoners after the cartel was suspended; I do not know why it was suspended; I do not know to this day which side took the initiative; I know that there were constant complaints made on both sides . . .

Referring to the Christian Association, which had come south to Petersburg, seeking access to Confederate Prisons, Lee reported, "I offered then to send to City Point all the prisoners in Virginia and North Carolina, over which my command extended, provided they returned an equal number of mine, man for man. I reported this to the War Department, and received an answer that they would place at my command all the prisoners [held by Confederates], if the proposition was accepted. I heard nothing more on the subject."

The question concluded, the Sub-Committee got nothing they sought. This questioning reinforced Lee's determination to avoid political engagement. Shortly afterward he wrote Varina Davis:

"I have thought from the time of the cessation of hostilities that silence and patience on the part of the South was the true course; and I think so still. Controversies of all kinds will, in my opinion, only serve to continue excitement and passion, and will prevent the pubic mind from acknowledgment and acceptance of the truth."

The next month he would write to Jubal Early:

"We shall have to be patient, and suffer for a while at least; and all controversy, I think, will only serve to prolong angry and bitter feelings, and postpone the period when reason and charity may resume their sway. At present the pubic mind is not prepared to receive the truth." [R151;526-527]

Meanwhile, in early February in Washington City, the House received a bill from the Senate that enlarged the powers of the Newly Independent African American Men's Bureau. Thad Stevens submitted an amendment to the bill that would confiscate land in the conquered States and, using that land, give each adult African American man a small farm of 40 acres, apparently free of charge. But Stevens only persuaded 37 Republicans to support his amendment! He failed to get it incorporated into the bill to expand the Bureau. His passion for confiscating 85% of the land in the conquered States would have to wait for another opportunity. Editors of the New *York Herald* noted: "That wrathful voice had lost its mastery, that severe satire its power, and that extended forefinger its omnipotence." On February 19, Andrew Johnson vetoed the bill to expand the Bureau. That in itself was not unusual, for Johnson had vetoed dozens of bills, only to have them overridden by two-thirds votes in both houses of Congress. But an attempt to achieve two-thirds override votes the next day, February 20 failed by two votes. Thad Stevens was so infuriated that he terminated further consideration — by the Joint House-Senate Committee on Reconstruction — on allowing Andrew Johnson's home State of Tennessee to send Representatives and Senators to Congress. Gideon Welles recorded in his diary that Andrew Johnson believed, "The unmistakable design of Thad Stevens and his associates was to take the [Federal] Government into their own hands and to [disqualify Johnson] by declaring" that his home State was not within the United States. The failure to override infuriated Charles Sumner who was being observed at the time by the British Minister, Frederick Bruce, who happened to be in the Senate gallery as the votes were tabulated. In Sumner, Bruce saw similarities to Robespierre, the notorious and guillotine-happy leader of the French Revolution: "Sumner's face was a picture of venom and defeat. He is a dangerous man. His vanity is unbounded; he has no human sympathies, and is remorseless in carrying out his doctrines. I should judge him to be very like Robespierre." [R73;256, R96;232-233]

Meanwhile, Thad Stevens, Charles Sumner and other like minded political leaders from the northeastern States were feeling the wrath of the States to the west, from Ohio to Iowa, where farmers had immediate concerns that transcended the agitation over Reconstruction of the conquered State Governments. To a significant degree, the more militant Republicans of the north-eastern States were exploiting political agitation over Reconstruction policy to divert attention away from issues of immediate concern in the western States (now called the Mid-West), where farmers were clamoring for reduced import taxes and Federal help in transporting and exporting their farm products. No Republican politician was more eager for high import taxes, and more clever at building alliances to sustain them, than was Thad Stevens. And Sumner was unsurpassed at playing the role of militant moral leader. Therefore, these two and like-minded Republicans were being opposed by men in the western States from Ohio to Iowa, who were organizing public meetings to demand reduced import taxes and to advocate Federal agreement to a Canadian offer to let American shippers use Canadian canals. American farmers realized that Federal officials could negotiate with European nations to lower import taxes on both sides of the Atlantic, if allowed by Congress to do so. And American farmers realized that opportunities existed for the Federal Government to aid transportation of western farm goods to east-coast markets and seaports, if allowed to do so by northeastern States politicians, who had for generations opposed measures that would help western farmers compete in the eastern States with the local farmers of the region. On February 15 an angry western State farmer wrote House Ways and Means Committee Chairman Justin Morrill with this warning: "What we want and are determined to have is access to the markets of the world. It is evident that the Committee had no conception of the feeling which exists here on this subject. I tell you now in sober earnest what will be the result of the smothering policy. The [conquered States] cannot be kept out of [the Federal] Congress forever. When [that region] does come back the [politicians of the southern States and the western States] will join hands and rule this country. Despairing of any hope of justice from the [politicians of the northeastern States] we shall form alliances to secure justice for ourselves."

Meanwhile, less militant Republicans held a mass meeting at Grover's Theater on February 21 in recognition of George Washington's birthday. After the speeches were concluded, many of those in attendance paraded to the White House to cheer the leader of their faction, Andrew Johnson, who returned their enthusiasm by presenting them an impromptu speech from the north portico of the White House. Of Johnson's mood, biographer Richard Current would write: "He could not forego an extemporaneous harangue against the 'irresponsible central directory' that had usurped the powers of government." But what concerned Johnson most about a realignment of the "powers of government?" I am persuaded that Johnson was more concerned about Federal usurpation of State Government powers than about the Federal House and Senate usurping powers normally within the jurisdiction of the Federal Executive and Judicial. Johnson was fighting to retain a remnant of State Sovereignty as he battled fellow Republicans who sought to complete the reordering of the Federal Government into an all-powerful authority. Johnson told supporter gathered below the portico:

"I fought traitors and treason in the [southern States]; I opposed [Davis, Toombs, Slidell . . . . Now when I turn around, and at the other end of the line find men — I care not by what name you call them — who will stand opposed to the restoration of the Union of these States, I am free to say to you that I am still in the field."

"Give us the names at the other end. Name them! Who are they?" echoed other voices.

"I say [Thad] Stevens of Pennsylvania is one; I say Mr. Sumner of the Senate is another, and Wendell Phillips is another."

After much applause, another voice called out, "Give it to Forney!"

"I will simply say that I do not waste my time upon dead ducks." Then Johnson mentioned the threats in Congress to impeach him, and letters he had received threatening to kill him. To those challenges he answered, "Are those who want to destroy our institutions and change the character of the [State Governments and the Federal Government] not satisfied with the blood that has been shed? Are they not satisfied with one martyr? Does not the blood of Lincoln appease the vengeance and wrath of the opponents of this government? Is their thirst still unslaked? Do they want more blood?"

Immediately, Charles Sumner alleged that Andrew Johnson's speech from the portico constituted proof that he was as heartless and as unwise as he (Sumner) had for months been alleging. At three o'clock the next day Thad Stevens walked into the Federal Senate Chamber, sat down beside Charles Sumner and "began an animated conversation with him about [Andrew Johnson's] remarks." Stevens and fellow Republican Representatives, meeting in caucus on the evening of the following day, agreed to raise a more militant Faction election campaign fund that would be a competitor to the Republican National Committee fund, which was controlled by pro-Johnson political leaders. This was one more step toward isolating Andrew Johnson from the Republican Party organization. Sumner supporters, especially in Massachusetts increased their attacks on Andrew Johnson with particular focus on the impromptu speech from the portico. Many sent letters to Sumner praising his attacks upon Johnson. The Boston Board of Aldermen immediately passed resolutions that praised Sumner's "eminent loyalty, patriotism and statesmanship," and condemned as false "any accusation, no matter by whom made," which likens Sumner to former political leaders. The State Legislature passed resolutions which denounced Andrew Johnson's portico speech as "unbecoming the elevated station occupied by him, and unjust reflection upon Massachusetts, and without the shadow of justification or defense founded upon the private or public record of our eminent [Charles Sumner]." In fact, the endorsement of Charles Sumner by Massachusetts politicians and newspapermen was so fervent and so widespread that John Andrew decided to give up his behind-the-scenes campaign to get Sumner's Federal Senate job — Andrew announced his retirement from politics.

Andrew Johnson's public attack, by name, on Thad Stevens, Charles Sumner and Wendell Phillips served to unite the Republican Party. Republican Representatives and Senators closed ranks to ensure no more vetoes would be sustained. Furthermore, to present a united front against Johnson's requests to seat Representatives and Senators from remade Governments in the conquered States, the Senate reconsidered it's December vote and — over Charles Sumner's protests — agreed with Thad Stevens that no Representative or Senator from a conquered States would be seated until both the House and the Senate voted its approval. A reporter for the New York *Herald* noted: "All [Republican politicians] will soon be forced to choose between the alternatives — accept [Andrew] Johnson or Thad Stevens as their leader. There will soon be no [middle] ground upon which [Republican politicians] can stand." And biographer Richard Current would explain that Stevens' strategy was just that: "to narrow the middle ground." Thad Stevens, Charles Sumner and like-minded Republicans realized that their opposition to Andrew Johnson might well force their target to leave the Republican Party and return to the Democratic Party, which he had abandoned after the secession of Tennessee. In short, the more militant Republican Faction was risking losing the Office of President for the last 3 years of the Johnson Administration. Of the reaction to Johnson's impromptu portico speech, Attorney General Ed Bates wrote, "His enemies charge him with letting down his dignity by that speech, [but] what a burlesque it is for such men as [Ben] Wade and [Thad] Stevens to whine about dignity."

Republicans also searched for infractions with which they might expel sitting Democrats from the Federal Senate. Charles Sumner pounced on a report of alleged voting irregularities that he received from some New Jersey Republican politicians. He presented the charges to the Senate and sparked a Republican movement to oust, by a simple majority vote, New Jersey's Senator, John Stockton. Republicans felt assured that Stockton's replacement would be a Republican, so that would be one less vote to sustain Andrew Johnson's vetoes. And every vote was most important. But a snag developed when it became evident that the Senate would probably fail by only one vote to oust Stockton. But there might be a way, for Lot Morrill had promised to abstain from voting "to oust" so that a sick Democratic Senator would not have to leave his sick-bed and appear to vote to "not oust." But honor among thieves and Republican Senators was a fleeting thing, for Charles Sumner and William Fessenden told Morrill — in a voice easily heard by others — to break the pairing and vote "to oust." And Morrill, whose word was far from his bond, voted "to oust." At that point John Stockton, who — as a point of honor had refrained from voting for himself — demanded that he be allowed to vote, too. So Stockton voted to "not oust." At that, Sumner seized the floor and appealed passionately for "those principles of justice which will be a benefit to our [Federal Government] for all time." And Sumner called Stockton's decision to cast a vote further evidence that he must be ousted — in spite of the fact that Stockton was merely canceling Morrill's deceitful vote. After Sumner's appeal other Republicans switched their votes, and gave their Party a sufficient number to oust Stockton. Senator John Stockton, Democrat of New Jersey, was kicked out of the Federal Senate without cause — a political travesty. But not all Republicans voted to oust. Some, like Lyman Trumbull, could not bring themselves to do such a dishonorable and unconstitutional thing. But a sufficient number did. [R73;25-259, R96;232-235]

March 1866 Through February 1867 — Republican Domination During the Second Year of the Andrew Johnson Administration

Varina set out from Georgia toward Mississippi in early March. Edwin Stanton had agreed to let her leave Georgia based on a recommendation by James Steedman, the Federal commander over the area. Steedman, of Ohio, a former Democrat leader and supporter of Stephen Douglas, whom Varina had known in Washington City, "had shown some sympathy and a desire to help her in her troubles." But the Federal military had ordered Varina to stay away from Fortress Monroe. Burton Harrison accompanied her on the trip to Mississippi, for he had been released from a "miserable incarceration" in a Federal prison in Washington City. As mentioned earlier, Stanton had selected Harrison for the Washington City prison because he had hoped Davis' personal secretary would give his agents their best opportunity for gathering incriminating evidence against Jeff Davis. But Harrison, who had never observed any incriminating activity, persistently rebuffed attempts by Stanton's agents to make him fabricate such evidence. By January, Stanton had given up hope of getting anything useful from Harrison. So Harrison had been set free on January 25. Also accompanying Varina and Burton to Mississippi were the Davis' baby girl, Winnie, the baby's nurse, Mary Ahern, and a servant, Frederick Maginnis. Maginnis was an African American whose ancestry was at least half European. A past servant to Pierre Beauregard, Maginnis had admired Jeff Davis during his presidency in Richmond. So, looking for work after the defeat of the Confederacy, Maginnis had approached Varina in Savannah and obtained a job as her servant. Varina intended to visit numerous relatives in different parts of Mississippi and Louisiana, and Burton hoped to visit his mother in Oxford, whom he had not seen in almost 4 years. Varina explained in a February 23 letter to Jeff that Burton, "had decided that he cannot settle down until I am safe in Canada."

> "So he goes South with me the morning of the 27th, and then I shall go to Canada. Everywhere on the railways we have free passage — so that it costs but little to travel. I do not despair of seeing you — after I have seen the children. May the Lord have you in his holy keeping until then."

Just before leaving for Atlanta, the first leg of their journey, Varina wrote the following loving letter to her imprisoned husband. The day being their wedding anniversary, she was marking the beginning of their 22nd year of marriage:

> "This, my only love, is our wedding day — the saddest and gladdest day of my life contrasted does not leave me so full of cheering thoughts to send you in your deprivaties and restraints. But I can at least thank you for all the high and honorable lustre which you have shed upon me — all the support and love showered upon my family, and how shall I characterize the shield of loving, generous, manly devotion, which had prevented me from feeling the bitter blasts of this hard, stormy world, 'commixed and contending.' May the church unite our souls in Heaven, if man has put us asunder on earth. I thank you every hour of my life for your love — for your bright example, as the source of all temporal happiness to me. In looking back over these last 22 years of my life it seems that they absorb the whole brightness and sweetness of my existence. With love unspeakable, dear, beloved Husband, with prayers immeasurable your wife's throbs, and thanks God that it is her privilege to suffer and love you.

> "Devotedly and gratefully,

> "Your wife"

Varina wrote Jeff again from Canton, Mississippi in early March. The exact date is uncertain, for the first page of the letter is missing. She was at the home of Jeff's nephew, Joseph R. Davis, who had been an officer in the Confederate Army.

Before leaving Macon, Varina and Burton had attended a party given by the Whittle's. There were many guests, but most touching was Varina's account of meeting the host's brother:

> "At dinner I sat near Colonel Whittle's brother, whose empty sleeve was buttoned to his coat — a grave quiet young man of 30 I suppose, whose other strong arm and brawny shoulders and determined eyes seemed to say all which might have been possible to him had not his youth been

blighted — and he tread so softly and reverently over the grave of our cause. Tears arose in his eyes, and his hand and lips trembled when a silent toast was drunk . . ."

Arriving in Atlanta, Varina reported that, "Mr. Mackey met me again, profuse in hospitality." From there the train steamed to Chattanooga. On the next leg to Grand Junction, Varina reported that "many people came and spoke lovingly of you and kissed the baby." Then she added, "The feeling is bitter about your imprisonment." After the next leg to Holley Springs, Burton proceeded on to Oxford to reach his mother sooner; he would rejoin Varina's party later. Varina reported that Holley Springs "is nearly destroyed but pretty still. A number of ladies and gentlemen met me at the cars." When Varina's train arrived at Oxford, she reported that "the students came to the cars, as did Mrs. Harrison and her daughter, but I barely got time to speak to them, and then left [Burton] there. When the train reached Coffeeville, Varina reported that "Lucius Lamar came down to see me — and urged my going to them, and after a few minutes stay he decided to go on to Canton with me." Varina enjoyed Lamar's company for a couple of days, for she added, "in Lamar's woeful account of his difficulties I forgot for a time my griefs, and laughed heartily." Of the situation on Joseph Davis' farm, Varina reported that the newly independent African Americans "are working very well on Joe's place and he has no difficulties with them at all." [R19;274-275, R30;234-237, R90;266-267]

Lucius Lamar received a letter from Clement Clay, posted from Huntsville, Alabama and dated March 15. Clay had been recently paroled from imprisonment at Fortress Monroe, not far from the cell that held Jeff Davis (Andrew Johnson would formally release Clay on April 18). Excerpts from Clay's letter describe the suffering inflicted on both prisoners:

"Your fraternal letter only reached me on yesterday. . . . I assure you it gave me great pleasure to hear from you and to read the generous sentiments of love and sympathy you felt. . . .

"I was treated as the vilest felon; crucified in body and soul; subjected to indignities and outrages more disgraceful to the United States Government than humiliating to me; and would have been murdered by the slow tortures, conceived in devilish malignity and Yankee ingenuity, but for the grace of God. It is too long and painful a tale of horrors to write to you. If we live, you will hear it or see it in print some day, I think. . . .

"I left our friend and chief, [Jeff Davis], in delicate, not bad, health. His beard is snowy white, his step not as firm and elastic as formerly, and his voice is stridulous. Guarded and goaded as he is, he cannot long survive. I trust that the guard will be removed from his prison before long; it is kept there, not for his security, but, I fear, to torture him. There is scarcely an officer in the Fortress besides the commandant (a Massachusetts militant Republican . . .) who does not regard his treatment as cruel and unmagnanimous and mean." [R205;122]

Meanwhile, in Washington City, turning to another issue, the political fight between advocates of tight money and the advocates of easy money continued. For the most part, farmers and industrialists wanted easy money (paper money that was nothing but paper money), but bankers and wealthy investors wanted tight money (paper money in limited supply that many hoped would be made exchangeable for gold and silver coin). The debate split the Republican Party, many Republican politicians being on each side of the money issue. Treasury Secretary Hugh McCulloch, a fighter of runaway inflation, was an advocate of tight money, but Thad Stevens, an iron industrialist and opportunistic politician, was an advocate of easy money. About mid-March, Justin Morrill, Chairman of one of committees that had been carved out of Stevens' former Ways and Means Committee, submitted to the House floor McCulloch's tight money bill, which permitted the Federal Treasury to remove considerable paper money from circulation. Thad Stevens severely weakened the bill by successfully attaching an amendment that prohibited the Treasury Secretary from withdrawing from national circulation more than $10,000,000 of Federal paper money over the subsequent 6 months or more than $4,000,000 per month thereafter. A reporter for *Harper's Weekly* wrote: "Contraction [of the currency] at this rate may fairly be considered no contraction at all." During the same days of March, Stevens attacked Andrew Johnson in speeches on the House floor and in contrived legal maneuvers. During debate in the Joint Committee, Stevens attached a resolution that declared that the State of Tennessee had earlier left the Federal Government and thereby had no right to Statehood status until invited back by the Federal House and Senate. This was a clever trap. If Andrew Johnson vetoed the bill, then he might be impeached for lack of United States citizenship, for his home State was Tennessee. If Andrew Johnson signed the bill, then he was agreeing that only the Federal House and Senate could rule over the conquered States and Reconstruct their governments. On another occasion during March, Stevens took the House floor and attacked Johnson unmercifully, sarcastically beginning with, "I must apologize to the House for the tameness of the remarks I am about to make." Then Stevens lambasted Johnson and accused him of drunkenness during his February 21 impromptu speech on the White House portico. [R96;238-239]

Meanwhile, the issue of Colorado Statehood, delayed for weeks by Charles Sumner's opposition, was arriving toward a vote. In spite of the certainty that admission of Colorado as a new State would give Republicans two more crucial Senate votes, by which they could more certainly override Andrew Johnson's vetoes, Sumner was fervently opposed to granting Statehood. He wanted the two additional Republican votes, but he would not compromise in his determination that Colorado submit to his demand that it allow African American men to vote. Many settlers from Kansas had moved further westward into Colorado Territory, and their submitted Colorado Constitutional stated that, like Kansas, Colorado would exclude African American men from the polls. Five years earlier, during the first weeks of the Lincoln Administration, Sumner had joined with other Republicans in voting to grant Statehood to Kansas with full knowledge that African American men would be denied the vote. In fact, Federal Senators and Representatives had to fight hard to make Kansas Republicans even allow African Americans who were independent to live in their State, because Exclusionist prejudice was stronger-felt in Kansas than perhaps anywhere else in North America. But Republican politics had totally changed since 1863. Sumner and like-minded Republicans now realized that continued Republican Party domination of the Federal Government required that they subjugate the conquered States through Republican Political Machines empowered by the votes of African American men — and forcing all States (not just those with large African American populations) to permit African American men to vote somehow made the Republican scheme seem more in keeping with the Federal Constitution. But there were only about 90 African Americans in Colorado Territory, advocates of Colorado Statehood argued, and many northern States that then denied the vote to African American men had many times more such men than Colorado. Such inconsistency was preposterous, they charged. But Charles Sumner had a rationale for such inconsistency, as biographer David Donald would write:

> "We are not called to sit in judgment of those [State] Constitutions; we have no power to revise them; we are not to vote upon them. . . . The main point was to establish, as both a principle and a precedent: 'No more States with [any established legal rights denied to African Americans]! . . . 'Tell me not that it is expedient to create two more [Republican] votes in this Chamber,' he scolded his colleagues, 'Nothing can be expedient that is not right.' Though [the House and Senate would] finally vote to [grant Statehood to Colorado], Sumner, along with [William] Fessenden and [James] Grimes, [would warn that] they would help sustain [Andrew Johnson's expected] veto, so as to establish authoritatively 'that, from this time forward, no State shall be [granted Statehood] with a [State] Constitution [that denied any established legal rights to African Americans]'." [R73;259]

Colorado Statehood would not be granted for many years — not until 1876.

Meanwhile, from New Orleans, Varina posted a letter to her husband dated March 18:

> "It is impossible to tell you the love which has been expressed here for you — the tenderness of feeling for you. People sit and cry until I am almost choked with effort to be quiet. But it is a great consolation to know that a nation is mourning your suffering with me and to be told hourly how far above reproach you are — how fair is your fame. The [former Confederate leaders] are nearly all here. [James] Longstreet is in a commission business, as is [Joseph] Wheeler — so, I may say, are all the ex-generals. I have seen [Samuel] Ferguson, [Joseph] Wheeler, and [Dabney] Maury. This last night, Maury sent you a message full of love and respect. All sent you grateful messages of kindness, but none so warmly as he — [Wade] Hampton, [John] Preston, Robinson, and the Owens, both, Tom Byrnes, [J. U.] Payne, [Pierre] Soul´e in very warm terms of which I will tell you. It seems to me that I never saw so many old friends in one place before. Dick Taylor looks well, has leased the canal here at a large sum, and expects to make a large amount by it. He is a warm hearted man." [R30;240-241]

The next day, from New Orleans, Wade Hampton wrote home to sister Mary Fisher to report that he had come down to the city to meet wife Mary and son McDuffie and accompany them up river to Wild

Woods farm. And he too reported seeing Varina Davis and other Confederate friends. They would soon be at the farm. Son McDuffie, 7, was quite active about the farm. He reported, "I scarcely ever seen him here, as he is on the rampage all the time." But the lad did join his father in some hunts. He would report, "In my last 3 hunts we have killed 5 bears, one panther and one wild turkey; McDuffie goes hunting with me sometimes. But all was not fun for Wade Hampton. He knew it would take hard work, good weather and luck to return his farm to profitability, pay off the debts and avoid bankruptcy. [R199;179, R200;104]

(2Q66)

Meanwhile in Washington City, shortly before April, on March 27, Andrew Johnson had vetoed the Civil Rights bill, another of his many vetoes. Immediately upon receiving news of it, Charles Sumner had "rushed from one hotel to another" to warn of the necessity to rally forces to override it. Republicans had recently ousted from the Senate, Democrat John Stockton of New Jersey, but his replacement, Republican Alexander Cattell, would not arrive until September 19. Yet, as April dawned, one more vote was needed to override, and Senator Edwin Morgan, Republican of New York, appeared to be the best prospect for conversion to their viewpoint. On April 7 Sumner and like-minded Senate Republicans would finally reach their vote goal and override the veto. Thad Stevens would lead the House to override on April 9. So, on that date, the Civil Rights bill became Federal law. If Republicans had not ousted Stockton from the Senate and converted wayward Morgan, Johnson's veto would have been sustained. But the slim margin of that vote was a warning to Republican Senators of the necessity of agreeing more fully on a program for Reconstructing the Governments of the conquered States, with particular focus on building Republican Political Machines empowered by the votes of African American men. In a public display of unity, Sumner reluctantly decided to shake hands with Senator William Fessenden, of Maine, to display a return to speaking terms. But their relations would remain strained.

As the time of Fall elections approached, Republicans in the House and Senate became concerned over the lack of progress in their Reconstruction program. The new Civil Rights bill, passed over a veto, gave Federal Agents authority over African American legal issues in the conquered States, but Congress had failed to override Andrew Johnson's veto of its bill to continue the Newly Independent African American Men's Bureau, and it had failed to submit to State Legislatures two Amendments to the Federal Constitution — one to Nationalize Citizenship (14th), another to Enable Voting by African American Men (15th). If disagreements on Capitol Hill were not overcome, Johnson would be able to trumpet to voters how he was making progress in remaking Governments in the conquered States while Republicans in Congress were stalemated by internal squabbles and indecision. Alarmed over the prospect of giving Johnson the political advantage, Republicans strove harder to agree on a plan.

The Joint House-Senate Committee on Reconstruction had, in early March, submitted to the Senate an Amendment to the Federal Constitution that would force States to permit African American men to vote after the passage of 10 years time — to 1877 and beyond. In the intervening 10-year period, if a State denied voting by African American men, it would lose proportional representation in the Federal Congress. The Amendment would force all States to give African Americans all of the established legal rights right away, except for the right to vote, which a State could choose to hold back for up to 10 years. This was not an unreasonable concept, since so many African American men had just become independent and had never before even had to make their way as independent men, earning wages in the working world, much less ponder the best men for elected government jobs. But this Amendment would not enable the Republican Party to subjugate the conquered States under Republican Political Machines. Long before the ten-year waiting period would be concluded, the Democratic Party would be solidly entrenched in the conquered Confederate States and, when augmented by the anticipated recovery of the Democratic Party in the northern States, Democrats would again be capable of winning control of the Federal Government. Reacting to that fear, Charles Sumner and like-minded Republican Senators fought the bill with all the influence they could muster. Of course, the Amendment permitted northern States, such as Illinois, a 10-year delay before they would be forced to permit voting by their African American men. In fact, northern States Republicans feared they would fail to get three-quarters of the State Legislatures as required to ratify the Amendment, unless the 10-year implementation delay was offered, because so few northern States allowed African American men the vote. Sumner objected to the concept, "that the [former owners of bonded African Americans] have a right to withhold [the right to vote] from the [newly independent African American men] for 10 years longer." To arguments that the 10-year delay was necessary for acceptance by enough northern States Legislatures, Sumner replied, "I must do my duty, without looking to the consequences." And, since blocking an Amendment to the Constitution in the Senate only took one-third of the votes, Sumner and like-minded Republicans joined with Democrats to block passage. The Joint House-Senate Committee on Reconstruction was forced to devise another plan to force the conquered States to permit voting by African American men. [R73;260-262, R96;240-241]

Meanwhile, Varina Davis wrote of her efforts to free her husband. After a 15-day stay in New Orleans, Varina's party, including Burton Harrison took a riverboat up to Vicksburg. She reported that "On the boat were a large number of [African Americans who appeared to be discharged Federal soldiers] "going to Davis Bend" with pistols, trinkets and calico to sell there. We passed our home [on Davis Bend] in the night," she wrote. While in Vicksburg, Varina intentionally avoided going out to her and Jeff's Brierfield farm out on Davis Bend, because the Federal Army had, many months earlier, installed unfriendly African Americans in their house for spite, and Federal Agents of the Newly Independent African American Men's Bureau were keeping a close eye on the place, looking for any opportunity to agitate the situation. In an April 12 letter posted by Varina in New York City, she tells more of her stay in Vicksburg, her journey on to New York City and her first days in New York.

"When I arrived at Vicksburg it was just as day broke. I put [Winnie] and Mary [Ahern] in a room in the Prentiss House still kept by McMakin, and walked up to see Brother Joe [Davis]. No one was up, but the birds were 'singing blithe and gay' in the garden, where the lilacs, yellow jasmine, hyacinths, and violets were in full blossom — and sweet as if a civil rights bill had been passed for their protection. Lize [Mitchell] — her spirits are good and she seemed overflowing with love for you, her 'dear good gentle Uncle.' Then came in Brother Joe [Davis] — changed in that his hair has grown whiter — but otherwise about as well as any old gentleman of his age that I ever saw and as bright. He does not even lie down in the day now. He has a rockaway and two mules in which Jack drives him to and fro — he likes the excitement of being in a little town, and goes around a good deal. He would have long since received back his property, but he refused to pay the blackmail which [Thomas, a former Federal officer and now a Bureau Agent,] offered to levy upon him. He said he would not be accessory to a bribe, so he can not get [his farm property] until a court is assembled upon his charges against [Thomas] — which he hopes will be soon. He tells me that [the African Americans that he had once owned] are doing very well [on his farm property]. I sent [the very capable African American and our past farm supervisor,] Ben Montgomery, $20 to [help him provide for our 100-year-old formerly bonded African American,] Uncle Bob. [Of other African Americans we once owned], I saw William C, Tom, Grandisen and Jack A, also George Green — they were very glad to see me — but talked like proprietors of the land. William told me [all of them] are getting along very well [out on our Brierfield farm] — 'but 'twas n't like old times.' But they have all changed.

"You have every reason to feel happy about Brother Joe's health. I begged him to come to me in Canada in the summer, and stay with me, which he promised to do — when I trust in God you may see him. He was quite out of money and I gave him $400 — and your Griffith dressing gown as he had none. He was very affectionate and begged me to stay with him longer. I read the largest part of your letters to him, and he seemed delighted and comforted and very grateful — full of love for you. . . .

"We got on the 'Virginia' and came up safely, without expense, to St. Louis. We reached Louisville to find Preston Johnston and his wife awaiting us at his house — and we staid with them two days. [William] Preston came down to see me, delighted, begged as if for life to get [little] Jeff to educate, and offered everything but was kindly refused — he is a noble man. Johnston's account of our children was in the main satisfactory. We got on the mail boat and went to Cincinnati very safely — still perforce guests. The Superintendent of the line sent us on by the new English railway, and the Erie broad gauge road. We had sleeping cars, and every comfort until finally we arrived [in New York City] safely — were very kindly received. Malie Brodhead joined me yesterday and we have had a nice cozy time. I have seen Dr. [John] Craven and Anne and his dear wife. God bless and keep them, for all they have done for you in your hour of extreme agony. I have seen [Attorney Charles] O'Conor and am well satisfied with his course [in defense of your legal rights]. Dick Taylor has also been affectionate as a brother and son.

"I am kept in the parlor until 12 at night from 10 in the morning — so that it is now late. Make yourself easy, my dearest, about the permission [for me] to go to you. I have no fears, because I will have from [Andrew Johnson], or from the considerate and kind [Attorney General James Speed], an exact permit as to what I may, or may not do. Keep heart, dear love — look forward. We will be happy yet, so very happy.

"It is one o'clock, yet I cannot bear to stop but must do so — as I have a few notes to write of civility. [Burton] Harrison is all in the world to me that a grown son could be, and is very thoughtful and affectionate — full of love and care for you. May the Lord bless and keep you safe is the prayer of devotedly, you poor old Wife."

Varina had remained in New York for about a week because Charles O'Conor remained so hopeful that Andrew Johnson would, any day, telegraph that he had decided to permit her to visit her husband at Fortress Monroe. But, on or about the tenth day of waiting, Varina proceeded on to Canada to spend time with her mother and the children and cope with any family problems she feared she might discover. She knew she could quickly return if O'Conor telegraphed any news from Andrew Johnson. Remaining protective, Burton Harrison accompanied her. Varina's first letter to Jeff from Canada, written in Montreal, was begun on April 14. She reported that their son, Billy was "immensely grown" and "sweet and loving," and that little Maggie was plump, "but not rosy" — talking "often of you, and always sweetly." But she wrote that her mother was sick in bed "with a severe attack of bronchitis," and that her sister, Margaret was "out of health" — a conditioned diagnosed as "some nervous shock." She "has no appetite, and cries if she hears a loud noise." Two days later, Varina's brother, Jeffy D. Howell, brought little Jeff to Montreal from his boarding school to see his mother. Varina found little Jeff to be "a little boisterous, but otherwise unchanged, except that he is very healthy, and much grown." She advised that Burton Harrison planned to return to New York in a few days — "He is a dear, warmhearted [man], full of generosity and love for you." Then she closed: "With warmest love and brightest hopes, my beloved Husband, I am devotedly, your Wife." [R30;243-247, R19;278]

On April 18, Clement Clay, the only remaining former Confederate political prisoner, save Jeff Davis, was formally released from his parole from Fortress Monroe, by an order signed by Andrew Johnson. No imprisoned Confederate had been charged and prosecuted for any crimes except for Henry Wirz, who had been condemned by a Military Court on false charges related to his oversight of the Confederate prisoner-of-war camp near Andersonville, Georgia. You will recall that Wirz had been executed to divert attention from the reality that suffering in Confederate prisoner-of-war camps had resulted from Federal refusal to exchange prisoners and from the intentional Federal Army campaign to destroy food stores and transportation facilities throughout the Confederacy. And killing Wirz helped divert attention from the unnecessary and hateful cruelty that had been imposed upon prisoners in Federal prisoner-of-war camps. But Republican leaders had grown more and more fearful of any court trial that might give former Confederates a forum where they could prove that a State was sovereign and, based on the wording and intent of the Federal Constitution, that a State legally possessed a right to secede from the Federal Government. The Republican program to politically Reconstruct the conquered States could easily be thwarted by such a trial. Yet Republican leaders were determined that Jeff Davis must remain imprisoned at Fortress Monroe, at least until after the Fall elections. Imprisoned, Davis would be unable to help Democrats in the northern States as they appealed to voters to let the conquered States retain a remnant of State Rights. And imprisoned, Republican candidates could better appeal for votes by inciting hatred toward Jeff Davis and southern States people. But Republicans were realizing more than ever that it would not serve their best interests to let Davis die in prison. So on April 20, Nelson Miles extended Davis' allowed time outdoors from one hour to two hours. Hudson Strode would write, "two hours away from the maddening tramp of army boots was a boon of no small significance." And, to explain how much he benefited, Davis wrote, "You cannot imagine how one shut out from all direct communication with his friends dwells upon every shadow and longs for light." Thad Stevens certainly favored continued imprisonment. The day after Clay's formal release, Stevens told a New York *Times* reporter that the Federal Government ought to, at the least, confiscate Clay's property.

A little earlier, Congress had appointed an Investigation Committee to report to the whole body on the so-called "evidence" that Edwin Stanton's agents had accumulated against Jeff Davis — the anticipated outcome being a recommendation that Davis be tried by a Commission of the Court. Charles Sumner's political and personal friend, the lawyer and jurist Francis Lieber, had been invited a few weeks earlier to study all of the so-called "evidence" that Edwin Stanton's agents had gathered in search of a basis for prosecuting Davis. Studious by nature, Lieber had examined thousands of records. Then he had contemplated upon their legal meaning. Lieber had discovered nothing significant that could be used to implicate Davis in Abe Lincoln's death at the hands of John Wilkes Booth, and he found nothing that could be used to convict Davis for the suffering in any Confederate prisoner-of-war camp, not even the huge camp near Andersonville, Georgia. So, about this time, Francis Lieber felt compelled to report to both Stanton and the Investigation Committee, the following conclusion: "Davis will not be found guilty and we shall stand there completely beaten." If a trial were held, Edwin Stanton and Republicans would have to argue over the meaning of the Federal Constitution. Prosecutors could charge Davis with treason on the assumption that State Secession violated the Federal Constitution. But Davis' lawyers would argue that a State was Sovereign, and that the nation's founders and the Federal Constitution clearly said so. If Republicans allowed themselves to be formally forced to confront that defense argument in a court setting, Davis and his lawyers might be successful in stopping or even rolling back the Republican program to politically Reconstruct the conquered States and evolve toward an all-powerful Federal Government. And control of the Federal Government was essential to continuing Republican domination of State and local governments. But Edwin Stanton was not yet ready to release Davis from prison, certainly not before the Fall elections. In fact he would begin a process leading to an indictment on a charge of treason, realizing that he could abandon the case whenever he chose. In the meantime, the process leading to indictment would supply stories for Republican propagandists. With that in mind, Stanton, late in April, for the first time since his imprisonment 11 months previously, permitted Davis to talk to a lawyer. Charles O'Conor expressed confidence that he and Davis could win against any charge the Federals were contemplating. [R19;278-279, R96;242]

Meanwhile in later April, the Joint House-Senate Committee on Reconstruction submitted to the Senate a revised Amendment to the Federal Constitution that would force States to enable voting by African American men. This Amendment was similar to the March 10-year-waiting-period version, which had been defeated by Democrats in combination with Charles Sumner and a few other like-minded Republicans. However, this April version did have some language revisions that irritated Sumner a bit less. Like the March version, the April version reduced a State's apportionment in the Federal Congress if it did not permit voting by African American men. Of the March version, Sumner had complained that such racial language "actually grafted into the text of the [Federal] Constitution inequality and caste on account of [skin] color, and tied the hands of Congress against any exercise of power to remove it." But reading through the rather similar newer April version, Sumner found "nothing in it positively offensive." Sumner also liked the stronger civil rights language in the April version, and the addition of language repudiating the debt of the Confederate Government. Of course, including the bit about repudiating Confederate debt in the Federal Constitution was totally unnecessary, but it facilitated helpful newspaper editorials.

At first Sumner fought the April version, calling it "grossly inadequate to the occasion," because it failed to present "those principles which are essential to the peace and stability of the [country]." Sumner was yet fearful that the Amendment would not ensure success in establishing Republican Political Machines in the conquered States. He sought a delay in debate and in voting "in order that all just influences may come to Congress from the [people of the northern States], and that Congress itself may be inspired by the fullest and amplest consideration of the whole question." In short, Sumner wanted more time for newspapermen and local politicians to agitate the people and encourage letters and resolutions. And Sumner apparently got his delay, for debate would not resume on the Amendment until late May. [R73;262]

Meanwhile on April 27, Thad Stevens pushed a bill to give an enormous amount of Federal land to the Northern Pacific Company, while Democrats argued against such an unnecessary giveaway of the peoples' assets. A Representative from Indiana "protested against giving to a private corporation lands aggregating more than the entire area of Indiana." An Illinois Representative, speaking of the bill's sponsor, Stevens, complained: "Men engaged in the iron interest are anxious, of course, to make railroad iron. . . . This road is to be built of American iron, cost what it may." But Stevens retorted by explaining his grand view for westward expansion. Biographer Richard Current would condense it as follows:

> "[Stevens] went on to tell his dubious hearers how the [railroad] company planned to bring laborers from the [northern nations] of Europe, pay them in land, and colonize them along the right of way — "men who will always be on the side of [Republican Party principles], who will always be ready to aid [Federal officials], in any [regional movements against Federal authority]. . . . "God grant that we may soon fill up that country with such a population that, with the people of the great [States of the northern region], may be a counterpoise to the [people of the southern States], whose Representatives when they [are eventually seated] will never permit us to do anything which may interfere with their projects." [R96;243]

Meanwhile, on April 28, the Joint House-Senate Committee on Reconstruction submitted to the House and Senate its Amendment (proposed 14th Amendment) to the Federal Constitution that was intended to nationalize citizenship. Thad Stevens, Co-Chairman of the Joint Committee, and Robert Owen had become engaged in discussion on these matters weeks earlier. Robert Owen, son of the famous English socialist, had suggested to Stevens a plan for Reconstruction that the latter had, in turn, submitted to his Joint Committee for consideration. Owen's plan had called for allocating seats in the Federal House based on each State's census of eligible male voters. It would make ineligible for Federal House or Senate seats all former Confederates with past leadership experience until after July 4, 1876. His plan would restrict voting to European American men until that same date. After voting by African American men, the conquered States would receive their full apportionment of 66 House seats. But before that time, they would only receive 42 House seats. "Surely you can manage that number," Owens submitted. "Perhaps," replied Stevens, then adding: "But you forget the Senate. The 11 [conquered States] would be entitled to their 22 Senators," regardless of who was allowed to vote. The Joint House-Senate Committee on Reconstruction had earlier made Owen's plan the core of its draft Constitutional Amendment.

But the Amendment, when submitted to the House and Senate, would not focus on voting by African American men. Instead it would focus on nationalizing citizenship, because the Committee had deleted the section that made African American men eligible to vote after July 4, 1876, and had expanded the Amendment by adding three more sections. With that language Stevens would report it out of the Joint Committee on April 28. Infuriated over the Joint Committee's revamping of his plan, Owen had complained to Thad Stevens and received this reply: "Don't imagine that I sanction the shilly-shally, bungling thing that I shall have to report to the House tomorrow."

While the House debated the Amendment that had evolved in to a plan to nationalize citizenship, politically involved people around the nation expressed their widely ranging views. Wendell Phillips told Stevens the Amendment was a "fatal and total surrender" to the combination of Democrats and less militant Republicans. A former Confederate from Virginian wrote Stevens: "While we of [Robert Lee's army] were passing the [Caledonia] Iron Works . . . and seeing them in flames, I thought it wrong to destroy so much valuable property. But since the [conquest of the Confederate States] and having seen so many of your vile measures, . . . I only wish you had been in your works and had been subjected to a little fire yourself." After a week of debate, Stevens feared that less militant Republicans might succeed in striking the third section of the Amendment, which would deny House and Senate seats to former Confederate leaders prior to July 4, 1876. So Stevens took the floor to derail that movement and to make a closing appeal for passage of the measure without change. "Give us the third section or give us nothing," Stevens challenged. "Do not balk us with the pretense of an Amendment which throws the [Federal Government] into the hands of the [former Confederate leaders] before [Reconstruction of the Governments of those States has been completed]. . . . Gentlemen tell us it is too strong . . . It is too lenient for my hard heart. Not only to 1870, but to 18070, every [former Confederate] who shed the blood of [Federal] men should be prevented from exercising any power in [the Federal Government]." Stevens carried the day. He stopped the movement to strike out the section denying seats to former Confederate leaders and pushed through the House its passage of the Amendment to Nationalize Citizenship. The Amendment, to become the Fourteenth, was forwarded to the Senate.

Meanwhile, Thad Stevens had financial problems at his iron works. The restrictions that Thad Stevens had imposed on Treasury Secretary Hugh McCulloch, concerning limits on reducing the supply of paper money, had not been sufficient to prevent difficulties in financing the reconstruction of Caledonia Ironworks. Stevens', John Sweeney, and the construction contractor "were frantically in search of funds with which to pay off the [construction] debt," because money was exceptionally scarce in and around Hagerstown, Shippensburg and Chambersburg. The Federal banking system was severely limiting money available in the conquered States, and, to a lesser extent, limiting money available to States west of the Appalachian Mountains. Even rural Pennsylvania counties were suffering from lack of banking funds. Those suffering from banking contraction resented the fact that banks in the coastal region from Philadelphia to Boston were receiving a much more generous money supply from the Federal banking system. But the worst was yet to come, for the Federal Government was intentionally driving State-chartered banks out of business. On July 1, all State-issued paper money would be subjected to a 10 percent Federal Tax. The Federal Government was moving to a National banking system where all paper money was of National Bank issue. A businessman from Newville Pennsylvania wrote Stevens:

> "I am sorry indeed to say our credit is strained. . . . The Farmers and Mechanics Bank of Shippensburg has thus far kept us afloat, but . . . this bank [is] conducted under State Charter. . . . I do hope and pray that you will see the Committee on Banks and have them to report a bill favorable to the extension of the time of redeeming their [paper money] at least one year, and within that time give those few banks who are conducted under the State Charter the privilege to come in under the National [Banking] System; and . . . exonerate them from the payment of the 10% tax maturing on July 1." [R96;245-247]

Meanwhile in Virginia in early May, Edwin Stanton and like-minded Republicans began their indictment process by blessing the convening of a Grand Jury in Richmond — that city having been chosen because the Confederate capital had been located there. Judge John Underwood presided over that region's Federal District Circuit Court, and he was obviously thrilled at the opportunity to punish Jeff Davis. As mentioned earlier, Underwood, originally of New York State, had moved to Virginia during the 1850's, but had left the State after the Federal Invasion began. Appointed District Judge in 1861 by the Lincoln Administration, Underwood had operated from a Federal Court in Alexandria during the military defense of Virginia. The Grand Jury was made up of ordinary men, including many illiterate African American and European American men. Republicans hoped that, by using a Jury filled with illiterates, they stood a much better chance of winning the upcoming legal and intellectual debate over the meaning of words in the Federal Constitution. But even illiterate men, graduates of the school of hard knocks, often displayed sound common sense and wariness toward pompous intellectuals. So, in his opening charge to this Grand Jury, Underwood, perhaps already feeling he was the underdog, blasted away from he start, making every effort to cloud reason with passion, emotion and hatred:

> "Jefferson Davis, yeoman, not having fear of God before his eyes, nor weighing the duty of his said allegiance, but being moved and seduced by the institution of the devil, and wickedly devising against the peace and tranquility of the [States under the Federal Government], to subvert, and to stir, move, and incite insurrection, rebellion and war . . ."

Perhaps Underwood had lifted his extremely hateful language from an account of one of those early Salem, Massachusetts witchcraft trials, inspired by the Puritan Church. Reading the charge soon thereafter, Robert Lee's wife wrote in disgust to her friend, Mrs. Chilton:

> "Have you read Underwood's charge to his grand jury, five of whom are [African Americans]? It is the most remarkable piece of composition I ever read, the most false and vindictive — that such a creature should be allowed to dispense justice is a perfect farce. I think this meanness and wickedness have affected his brain."

In spite of his Inquisition-inspired ugliness, Underwood succeeded in persuading his gullible Grand Jury to vote to indict Jeff Davis. So, Davis was finally charged with a crime, that being treason against the Federal Government.

Varina frantically telegraphed Andrew Johnson, on or shortly before May 9, pleading with him to let her visit Jeff at Fortress Monroe, for she had received word that her husband was dying. In her *Memoir* Varina would describe what would be a truly momentous event:

"A few days after our arrival, a rumor came to Montreal that [Jeff] Davis was dying. Upon hearing this, I telegraphed [Andrew Johnson]: 'Is it possible that you will keep me from my dying husband?' He responded by a permission to go, subject to conditions to be stated at the Fort, and sent a telegram from [Nelson] Miles saying that Davis was in his usual health.

"I left Montreal that night, and with my infant, her nurse, and Frederick [Maginnis] went to Fortress Monroe, arriving there at four o'clock AM, a cold, raw morning, on May 10, just a year from the surrender of the Confederacy. There was no hotel there then, and we sat in the little open waiting-room until half-past 10. . .

". . . An officer came and walked with me to Carroll Hall, on the opposite side of the Fort. There were three lines of sentries, which each required a pass-word of the officer, and at last we ascended a stairway, turned to the right, and entered the guard-room, where three young officers were sitting. Through the bars of the inner room I saw [my husband's] shrunken form and glassy eyes; his cheek bones stood out like those of a skeleton. Merely crossing the room made his breath come in short gasps, and his voice was scarcely audible.

"His room had a rough screen in one corner, a horse-bucket for water, a basin and pitcher that stood on a chair with the back sawn off for a washstand, and a hospital towel, a little iron bedstead with a hard mattress, one pillow, and a square wooden table, a wooden-seated chair that had one short leg and rocked from side to side unexpectedly, and a Boston rocker, which had been sent in a few weeks before. His table-cloth was a copy of the New York *Herald* spread on the little table. I was locked in with him and sent the baby, [with Frederick, back to a casemate Nelson Miles had provided us].

"The bed was so infested with insects as to give a perceptible odor to the room. [My husband] knew so little of such things that he could not imagine what annoyed him so at night, and insisted it was some cutaneous affection. His dinner was brought after a while by one of the men, and was good enough, had it not been slopped from one dish to another in the carriage and covered by a gray hospital towel. To a fastidious taste, rendered much more so by illness, this was very offensive. [Dr. George Cooper's wife] had, however, added oysters to the menu that day, and he ate one and nothing else, but his vitality was so low that even this small amount gave him intense gastric pain. The passing of the three sentinels by the doors and window rendered me, though in strong health, so nervous I could scarcely keep my eyes still.

"He was bitter at no earthly creature, but expressed supreme contempt for the petty insults inflicted hourly upon him by [Nelson] Miles, who, he said, had exhausted his ingenuity to find something more afflicting to visit upon him. Among other things, he told me that [Nelson] Miles never walked with him without saying something so offensive and irritating as to render the exercise a painful effort."

A member of Nelson Miles' staff apparently persuaded him to let Varina have a casemate room so she and her baby would be able to remain at Fortress Monroe in reasonable comfort for a while in hopes that her presence would improve her husband's health. At first Miles restricted her visits with Jeff to a few specific hours during the day, but after a while, she would persuade him to let her spend evening with him, until bedtime. However, Varina would not be allowed to walk outdoors on the ramparts with Jeff. Biographer Hudson Strode would write: "Miles reserved that privilege for himself; it afforded him a daily opportunity to needle [the prisoner] with mocking remarks about the [former Confederate States] or make offensive attacks on his admired friends.

Before long, Varina's influence was readily evident at Fortress Monroe. Dr. George Cooper soon wrote to Andrew Johnson urging a reduction in the purposeful torment, "Unless the [Federal] Government desires the captive to die under his sufferings." And apparently in response, an order came a bit later from Washington instructing the three-guard detail to discontinue its constant tramping. And Nelson Miles found that he could not easily intimidate Varina Davis, either. Apparently, Miles had found it necessary to constantly reprimand subordinates for sympathetic behavior toward Jeff Davis. For example, he often fussed at Dr. George Cooper's wife for occasionally putting oysters on the prisoner's dinner plate. Then one day, Miles confronted Varina over a package she had received, which he understood contained a dressing gown for Jeff Davis that some ladies from St. Louis. Miles shouted at Varina, "This fort shall not be made a depot for luxuries and such delicacies as oysters for Jeff Davis. I shall have to open your packages and see that this is not done." But Varina knew how to fight fire with fire. She stood up, looked him square in the eye and insisted "I am not your prisoner. You would not find yourself justified by the laws in infringing on my private right." Shocked at Varina's veracity, Miles backed off muttering, "I guess I couldn't."

A few days later, Andrew Johnson dispatched his Treasury Secretary, Hugh McCulloch, to Fortress Monroe to ascertain first-hand, the condition of the prisoner's health. McCulloch visited privately with Jeff and then visited with Varina in Nelson Miles' presence. Not at all intimidated by the officer, Varina seized the opportunity to disclose Miles' practices of intentional tormenting his prisoner. Varina knew that, as a Member of Andrew Johnson's Cabinet, McCulloch was by far the more powerful, and Miles knew it, too. Varina was undoubtedly effective in her denunciations. For example, when she mentioned Miles' petty fussing over Jeff's being given occasional oysters, McCulloch turned to Miles and deplored "General, oysters on the seacoast are hardly to be classed as luxuries, are they?" [R13;757-760, R19;279-282]

Meanwhile, Charles Sumner seemed to intensify his book-work as his health deteriorated during May. Perhaps this immersion was a reaction to his mother's serious illness, for that worried him. His mother was his last surviving relative, save a married sister in California with whom he had lost meaningful contact. That sister, Julia Hastings, lived in San Francisco and had been back East only once during the past 10 years. She rarely wrote to either their mother or Charles. Charles knew that his mother was being attended by an excellent doctor, and had a paid companion living with her, but he still wished he could be in Boston more often. But Charles was sick himself. The illness seemed to be the result of worry and lack of exercise. His angina pectoris pains returned. Sleep was difficult without benefit of medicine. He sought out Doctor Brown-Sequard for an examination, and, sure enough, the quack declared that Charles was suffering from the "original injuries 10 years ago," that had been inflicted by the caning administered by Representative Preston Brooks, of South Carolina. How convenient that the French quack was traveling in the northeastern States when Sumner needed him! [R73;266]

Meanwhile, on May 24 in Memphis, Tennessee, Representative E. B. Washburne, reported back to Thad Stevens concerning his investigation there of an earlier violent episode in the city. "The [African Americans] had nothing to do with it but to be butchered," Washburne wrote. Based on such experience Washburne concluded that African American Tennesseans and newly arrived European American Republicans were in great danger of violent harm. And Washburne reported that sometimes, "instead of [former Confederate men] being Reconstructed as [Republicans], I find some of the [newly arrived Republican] men Reconstructed as very good [ex-Confederates]." [R96;254]

Meanwhile, Dr. George Cooper, although he was able to converse face-to-face with Varina at Fortress Monroe, for some reason decided to answer in writing a written plea he had received from her. Cooper's letter, dated May 23, would be more important than its reading would reveal:

"Madam,

"I am in receipt of your communication of date in which you ask of me 'how the health of your husband can be recruited, as you see him growing weaker and sinking daily.'

"I have done all in my power to keep his health up, but I must own I see him becoming more and more weak day by day. He has been well cared for in the matter of food; the tramp of the sentinels he no longer hears. He has exercise one hour in the morning and as much as he wishes for after 4 in the afternoon.

"Notwithstanding, he fails and the only thing left is to give him mental and bodily rest and exercise at will.

"This can be only by having the Parole of the Fort with permission to remain with his family now residing there.

"He will then probably recuperate."

"Your Obedient Servant

"George E. Cooper

"Surgeon, U. S. A."

Varina quickly passed Cooper's letter to a friend, who in turn quickly passed it on to a newspaperman at the New York *World*, or she sent it to the newspaperman herself. However that newspaper received the letter, knowledge of the letter prompted an immediate and strong editorial:

> "[Dr. George Cooper's report on Jefferson Davis' health problems] cannot be read by any honorable and right-minded [citizen], no matter what his sectional feelings or his political opinions may be, without a sickening sensation of shame for [our country] and burning flush of indignation against the persons who have prostituted their official position to inflict upon [our country's] name an ineffaceable brand of disgrace by the wanton torture of an invalid, lying a prisoner in the strongest fortress of the [land]. . . .
>
> "The [people] will have a serious account to settle with the functionaries who could thus represent them in the eyes of Christendom and of history."

And several other widely-read newspapers picked up on the story and printed similar editorials. Nelson Miles must have received news of the New York *World* editorial the same day it was published, for on May 26 — only three days after George Cooper had written his letter — Miles complained to a superior in Washington City, Adjutant General E. D. Townsend, "that newspapermen were doing him great injustice, for he had only been obeying orders from superiors in the Federal War Department. Miles followed up that complaint with another letter to Townsend, marked "confidential," in which he blamed Dr. George Cooper for the newspaper criticisms:

> "I regret to say that I think [Dr. George] Cooper is entirely under the influence of [Jeff and Varina] Davis, the former of whom has the happy faculty that a strong mind has over a weaker to mould it to agree with its views and opinions. [George] Cooper's wife is a Secessionist. . . . Yesterday [Cooper] had a private interview with Davis and [his lawyers, Charles] O'Conor and George Shea."

Unrelentingly, Varina kept pouring on the pressure. Her next move was to go to Washington City and seek an audience with Andrew Johnson. And it appears that she had cleverly advised several friends in Washington City of her upcoming agenda, for, when she arrived on Saturday, May 27, and the next day she was honored by visits from many old Washington friends. Two visitors were especially important: Senator Willard Saulsbury of Delaware and Senator Reverdy Johnson of Maryland. A newspaperman wrote for the Sunday edition of the New York *Tribune* that such immediate attention toward Varina Davis represented "unseemly haste." In the Monday edition the shocked newspaperman added:

> "The great sensation of the [Federal] Capital today has been the appearance of Senator Saulsbury at the Church of the Ascension 'clothed and in his right mind' as an escort for [Varina] Davis. After church a noted [Secessionist] procured an open buggy, and took a Sunday evening drive with [Varina] Davis about the principal streets of the city."

No question about it: Varina wanted everyone in Washington City, and the northern States as well, to know that *Varina Davis was back in town*. She figured the publicity would further pressure Andrew Johnson to accede to her intended requests.

Andrew Johnson rejected Varina's first written request for an appointment, but after Senators Reverdy Johnson, Willard Saulsbury and Representative Daniel Voorhies of Indiana "went to him and remonstrated rather sharply," Varina reported, "he appointed an hour to see me." This was Varina's first opportunity to ever talk with Andrew Johnson, for, traveling in difference social circles during Varina and Jeff's Washington days, they had never met. Varina would later write in her *Memoir*:

> "[Andrew Johnson] was civil, even friendly, and said 'We must wait, our hope is to mollify the public toward him.' I told him that the public would not have required to be mollified but for his Proclamation that [Jeff] Davis was accessory to [John Wilkes Booth's killing of Abe Lincoln], and added, 'I am sure that, whatever others believed, you did not credit it.' He said he did not, but was in the hands of wildly excited people, and must take such measures as would show he was willing to sift the facts. I then responded that there was never the least intercourse between [Jeff] Davis

and Booth, or an effort to establish it, and remarked that, 'if Booth had left a card for [Jeff] Davis as he did for you, [Andrew Johnson], before [Booth shot Lincoln], I fear my husband's life would have paid the forfeit;' to which [Johnson] bowed assent, and after a moment of silence remarked, now this was all over, and time was the only element lacking to [Jeff] Davis' release.

"I remarked that, having made a Proclamation predicated upon the perjury of base men suborned for that purpose, I thought he owed [Jeff] Davis a retraction as public as his mistake. To my astonishment, he said that he was laboring under the enmity of many in both houses of Congress, and if they could find anything upon which to hinge an Impeachment they would degrade him; and with apparent feeling he reiterated, 'I would if I could, but I cannot.'

"While we were speaking, a Senator well-known now, but of whom I had never heard, insisted upon an audience and was admitted. He was a lop-sided man who stood on one leg by preference. He declined to sit, but stood quite near me, with one leg twisted around his stick, and threatened [Andrew Johnson] in such a manner as would have been thought inadmissible to one of our servants. [After her White House meeting, Varina would be told by friends that she had described Thad Stevens.] [Andrew Johnson] met [the Senator's] threats with rising color but a solid calm which was not defiance, nor was it indignation. It was a very painful sight to me, and I tried not to hear. At last the Senator left, and [Johnson] said, 'I am glad you saw a little of the difficulty under which I labor; trust me, everything I can do will be done to help [Jeff] Davis — has he thought of asking for a pardon?' I answered 'No, and I suppose you did not expect this.' He said he did not, and added 'just now I cannot withdraw the Proclamation' in which I accused Jeff Davis of encouraging John Wilkes Booth. He kindly hoped the pardon granted to [Jeff's older brother, Joseph] Davis had covered our [Mississippi farm] property also. I could not press him further. It was a new phase of humanity to me, I felt sorry for a man whose code of morals I could not understand. And so we parted, with kind words and courteous manner on his part, and much sympathy for his miserable state on mine."

Thad Stevens' biographer, Richard Current, would provide the following analysis of Stevens' intent toward Jeff Davis:

"What Stevens really desired was to have [Jeff] Davis brought to trial on a charge of treason, to defend him and win his acquittal, and thereby prove [in a court of law] that, as President of the Confederacy, [Davis] had been no mere rioter or rebel, but the leader of a belligerent, subsequently defeated in war. Kept indefinitely in prison or simply turned loose, Davis would serve as a sort of [one-person] scapegoat for all the [alleged] sins of [all the former Confederates]. There must be no [one-person] scapegoat, however, [according to Stevens' plans], if [he] was to be unrestrained in dealing with the [conquered] States as conquered Provinces and [to be unrestrained in] making the victory of [northern States] capitalists complete."

When Varina returned to Fortress Monroe, she told Jeff all about her trip to Washington City and her meeting with Andrew Johnson. She mentioned the suggestion that he ask for a pardon. But Jeff told Varina he flatly refused to ask for a pardon, as Andrew Johnson and Varina both knew he would, for asking for a pardon was tantamount to admitting that you were guilty of some sort of crime. To the contrary, Jeff's determination to persevere, in the face of Nelson Mile's months of intentional torment, had been intensified by his eagerness to have his day in court, for there he expected to justify before the world that each State had been Sovereign. [R19;284-285]

Charles O'Conor and George Shea were almost as intent on helping Jeff as was Varina. While she was in Washington pressuring Andrew Johnson, O'Conor and Shea had been in Fortress Monroe planning their line of defense with Jeff. Of particular importance were matters of procedure to be followed in a court trial on the indictment delivered by John Underwood's Grand Jury. When the Federal District Court opened in Richmond on June 5, four lawyers for Jeff Davis were on hand to press for a speedy trial date and for setting bond. William Reed, one of the four lawyers, opened with a demand to know what was to be done with the indictment against Jeff Davis. Then Reed insisted that he desired a speedy trial for his client whatever the charges might be and whatever civil court might be chosen in any State Federal's chose. Reed further appealed for honest sympathy:

"We may be now here representing, may it please the Court, a dying man. For 13 months he has been in prison. The [Federal] Constitution guarantees to him not only an impartial trial, but a speedy trial."

For two days Davis' lawyers and prosecutors argued before the Court. The issue was legally a can of worms, because the various prosecutors had not yet fully agreed on which organization owned the prisoner, Jeff Davis. Did the conquered State of Virginia own Davis? Did the Federal Judiciary own Davis? Or, did the Federal Military own Davis? If the Military owned him, as all appearances indicated, why was he not being scheduled for trial in a military court? Finally, the tangle among prosecutors was settled by the Assistant Federal District Attorney: he ruled that Jeff Davis was a prisoner of conquered Virginia, "under order of [Andrew Johnson], signed by [Edwin Stanton]." Following that logic, the Federal District Attorney reasoned that Davis should be tried in the Federal District Court that covered Virginia. After the prosecutors sorted out that mess, Reed formally moved that Jeff Davis be released on bail until the time of his trial. The request was denied. And no trial date was set. It appeared that Edwin Stanton and his agents and collaborators were willing to confine Jeff Davis in Fortress Monroe until Hell froze over, or at least until after the fall elections — meaning at least 4 more months of imprisonment. [R19;283-285, R30;248-249, R13;769-771, R96;247-248]

On May 23 the Senate had again taken up the Constitutional Amendment to Nationalize Citizenship. Sumner had opposed similar language earlier in hopes voters would petition for more aggressive language. But when the amendment came again to the Senate floor, Sumner made only token opposition, apparently only intending to provide propaganda to Massachusetts newspapermen. In response William Fessenden admonished: "If we adopted the advice of [Charles Sumner] to wait until we got every particle that by any possibility might throw light on the subject, we should wait until the next century." Backing down quickly, Sumner apologized, saying, "I hope I was not understood to make any formal opposition to proceeding with this measure. Most probably I am in error; but I have performed my duty, and in a humble way satisfy myself by making this declaration."

When the Amendment came to a vote in the Senate on June 8, Sumner was among those voting his approval. So were three other like-minded Republicans who had earlier joined him in opposition to March's version. The vote to approve was 32 to 10. Democrats ridiculed Sumner for his about-face on the Amendment, for his "no" vote in March and his "yes" vote in May was over such similar language. But politicians understood what wind had picked up Sumner and turned him around. Sumner was scared of the progress Andrew Johnson was making in building a new political party in the northern States. Would Johnson's National Union Party Convention and his planned country-wide speaking tour cripple the Republican Party? Anyway, there was a lot of pressure to vote "yes" from his supporters in Massachusetts. William Claflin, a high-ranking Republican leader in the Party, had warned that "people desire to have some position on which they can stand in opposition to [Democratic Party] policy." And after the vote, a Boston newspaper received the news "with considerable favor as the only measure we are likely to get passed this session." Even the usually hostile Springfield *Republican* thought Sumner displayed "noble manner" in acting "for the sake of harmony and the [Federation]." The Senate had changed the Amendment language, most particularly by precisely defining National Citizenship: "all persons born or naturalized in the United States and subject to the jurisdiction thereof, are citizens of the United States and of the States wherein they reside." So, the Amendment, as modified was returned to the House for its approval of the changes. National citizenship was to trump State citizenship, greatly facilitating Federal subjugation of the State Sovereignty defined in the original Constitution. [R73;263-265]

On June 11 the House of Representatives of conquered Virginia, by a vote of 105 yeas to 19 nays, resolved that [Jeff] Davis "should be held in custody as a prisoner and subjected to a trial according to the laws of the land." Even the Virginia Legislature was urging the Federal Government to get on with the trial. Many people wanted a public trial to afford Jeff Davis the opportunity to defend the right of State Secession under the Federal Constitution.

Since there was no trial date and no hope for bail, many more months of imprisonment were expected, and thoughts of that made Edwin Stanton more anxious than ever to keep Jeff Davis alive at Fortress Monroe. Further torment to break the prisoner's spirit was out of the question. So Stanton made another concession to lift Davis' spirits. He permitted friends to write and to visit him. One of the first allowed letters from friends was penned by Mary Lee, Robert Lee's wife. Mary had written the letter long ago, a few days after Davis had been imprisoned. In spite of the painful arthritis she suffered in her hands, Mary had also copied all 6 verses of her favorite hymn to accompany the letter. But she had not mailed it, anticipating that prison authorities would not permit its delivery, or perhaps it had been returned with notice that delivery was refused and she was resending. In any event, she had kept the letter, and mailing it on June 6, she hoped to see it delivered. Mary Lee boldly addressed the envelope to "Ex-President Jefferson Davis:"

"My heart has prompted me, my dear friend, ever since I knew of the failure of our glorious cause to write to you and express my deep sympathy — how much more since I learned [of] your captivity, your separation from your beloved family and your incarceration in a solitary dungeon. If you knew how many prayers and tears had been sent to Heaven for you and yours, you could realize that you were not forgotten. We did so long to hear that you could reach in safety some foreign clime where you could enjoy the repose and consideration which seems to be denied you in your own country. Oh why did you delay and fall into the hands of those whose only desire is to humiliate and destroy you? The only consolation I can now offer you, besides our deep attachment and remembrance of you, is contained in the words of my favorite hymn which I have transcribed for you. As a Christian I feel confident that you have fortitude 'to bear the cross and despise the shame' and even to pray for your persecutors.

"As I know not if this letter will be allowed to reach you I will not say more — you can imagine all we would say and feel and know that one sentiment animates the hearts of your true friends and among them, believe, there is no one truer than

"Yours,

"Mary C. Lee." [R30;249-250]

Meanwhile, Thad Stevens introduced a railroad subsidy bill in the House and succeeded in keeping it out of the Special House Committee on the Pacific Railroad, for he feared that his bill would die if it was referred to that Committee. Stevens' bill would grant a large amount of Federal land along a new route being planned by the Eastern Division of the Union Pacific Railroad. The bill also extended the time limit within which the Kansas Pacific and the Northern Pacific had to finish railroad construction in order to qualify for their respective grants of Federal land. And Stevens found himself trying to devise a bill to give further Federal Government help to the St. Croix and Lake Superior Railroad without conflicting with the Federal assistance program sought by Josiah Perham and the other investors in the Northern Pacific Railroad. Biographer Richard Current would observe:

"Already the capitalists were quarreling, as they had on the money issue, over the spoils of Republican success, and even the railroad builders could not agree among themselves. It was up to Stevens, as their broker, to satisfy as many as possible and still keep peace among them." [R96;248]

Meanwhile, the Constitutional Amendment to Nationalize Citizenship (the 14th), having passed the Senate with modifications, returned to the House. After permitted debate neared completion, Thad Stevens rose to deliver the closing speech. Stevens' words indicated he did not like the revisions inserted by the Senate, but he apparently felt that his goals would be best served by giving the revisions his lukewarm support: "I do not pretend to be satisfied with it. And yet I am anxious for its speedy adoption, for I dread delay." On June 13 the Fourteenth Amendment passed the House by a vote of 120 to 32.

On June 16 Secretary of State William Seward submitted the Amendment to the States for Ratification. Among notable people opposed the Amendment to Nationalize Citizenship was President Andrew Johnson, who made his opposition known. But he had no say in the matter. It would take ratification by three-quarters of the State legislatures to make the Amendment part of the Federal Constitution.

The final wording broke the Fourteenth Amendment into five sections:

Section One ensured that African Americans would be considered citizens of the United States and of respective States in which they lived. As a result of the deceptive second sentence, which had been cleverly inserted by John Bingham, this section reserved regulation of corporations to the

Federal Government by making it much more difficult for State Governments to regulate them. In reading the language, remember that lawyers apply law to a corporation as if it is a "citizen" and a "person." To clarify its influence on laws concerning corporations, I have added them to the language. Section One:

"All persons born or naturalized in the United States, and subject to the jurisdiction thereof, are citizens of the United States and of the State wherein they reside. No State shall make or enforce any law which shall abridge the privileges or immunities of citizens of the United States [or of corporate citizens of the United States]; nor shall any State deprive any person [or corporation] of life, liberty, or property, without due process of law; nor deny to any person [or corporation] within its jurisdiction the equal protection of the laws."

Section Two reads like its intent was to punish with reduced representation any State who's Legislature refused to admit African American men to the polls. However, the Republican Party was determined to make sure that no Legislature or Constitutional Convention in a conquered State would actually get the power to deny voting by African American men, because the Republican Party intended for Section two to facilitate is developing plans to there set up Republican Political Machines. Notice how citizenship is nationalized here as well. By the way, the language had been twisted around and worded obliquely to keep representation high in States, like Massachusetts, where male citizens of voting age were an unusually low fraction of the total population (as mentioned earlier, Massachusetts had an unusually high percentage of women and aliens). Section Two:

"Representatives shall be apportioned among the several States according to their respective [total population] numbers, counting the whole number of persons in each State, excluding [Native Americans] not taxed. But when the right to vote in any election for the choice of electors for President and Vice President of the United States, Representatives in Congress, the Executive and Judicial officers of a State, or the members of the [State] Legislature thereof, is denied to any of the male inhabitants of such State, being 21 years of age, and citizens of the United States, or in any way abridged, except for [persons who helped defend the former Confederate States, or persons convicted of a crime], the basis of representation therein shall be reduced in the proportion which the number of such male citizens shall bear to the whole number of male citizens 21 years of age in such State."

Section Three prevented all former Confederates from holding any local, State or Federal office-level job, civil or military, including all elected positions, if they had previously held a local, State or Federal office-level job, civil or military, including all elected positions, prior to their support of the defense of the Confederacy. Basically all former Confederates with past political or military leadership experience were prohibited from holding political or military office. Of most importance to Thad Stevens and Charles Sumner was the restriction that prevented voters in the conquered States from electing former Confederate leaders to the Federal Congress and Senate. One is reminded of the Russian Revolution of 1917, where all past leaders — the educated, successful, experienced and capable men — were subjugated, and the novices — the easily manipulated puppets of the clever elite — were suddenly thrust into leadership positions. With experienced leaders prohibited from interfering, the Republican Party would have no trouble establishing effective Republican Political Machines empowered by the votes of newly independent African American men. This denial of offices to former Confederates was to remain in effect as long as one-third of the House and one-third of the Senate wished. Section Three:

"No person shall be a Senator or Representative in Congress, or elector of President and Vice President, or hold any office, civil or military, under the United States, or under any State, who, having previously taken an oath, as a member of Congress, or as an officer of the United States, or as a member of any State Legislature, or as an executive or judicial officer of any State, to support the Constitution of the United States, shall have engaged in [helping defend against the invasion of the Confederacy, even including those who only gave aid or comfort to Confederate defenders]. But Congress may by a vote of two-thirds of [the House and two-thirds of the Senate], remove such disability."

Section Four required that the Federal Government fully honor all the debt it incurred in the invasion of the Confederacy, including future debt that would be required to fund pensions for Federal military personnel, and bounties that were due to owners of independent ocean raiding vessels, referred to as "privateers." Although making it part of the Federal Constitution served no useful purpose, Section four also made it unconstitutional for any Federal or State office to pay out any money to cover any debt related to the defense of the Confederacy or to compensate any owner for the loss of the service of a bonded African American. Section Four:

> "The validity of the public debt of the [Federal Government], authorized by law, including debts incurred for payment of pensions and bounties for services in [support of the Federal invasion of the Confederacy], shall not be questioned [by any Federal or State office]. But neither the [Federal Government] nor any State [Government] shall assume or pay any debt or obligation incurred in [efforts to defend the Confederacy against the Federal invasion], or any claim for the loss or [forced immediate independence] of any [bonded African American]; but all such debts, obligations and claims shall be held illegal and void."

Section Five ensured that, upon ratification, State Legislatures further relinquished their State's individual sovereignty — a status which the Federal Constitution had originally guaranteed to each. Similar enforcement language had been inserted in the Constitutional Amendment to Make African Americans Immediately Independent (13th). Of course, little remained of State Sovereignty after the Federal Government invaded the Confederacy on the pretense that 11 States, had not seceded, but remained under the Federal Government — a pretense Federals were very afraid to expose to litigation in a treason trial of Jeff Davis. Since March, 1861 the Federal Government had become all-powerful, but Republicans wanted to add language to the Federal Constitution which would help the Supreme Court expand and solidify the dominance of the Federal Government. Furthermore, the Republicans in the House and Senate wanted to ensure that they, not Andrew Johnson or his successor, held the power to enforce laws designed to punish former Confederates and to control Governments in the conquered States through Republican Political Machines. Section Five:

> "The [Federal] Congress shall have power to enforce, by appropriate legislation, the provisions of this article."

Republicans needed three-fourths of the State Legislatures to give the Amendment the force of Constitutional Law, and they wanted to include the 11 conquered States and the Democrat States of Delaware, Maryland, Kentucky and Missouri in the tally leading to the three-fourths margin. In June 1866 the United States was composed of 25 accepted States plus the 11 conquered States. And Nebraska was nearing a population that would enable it to receive Statehood. That totals to 37 potential States, including Nebraska. Three-fourths of that sum would be 28 States, and that was the number from which a ratification vote was required. That math meant that compliant Governments, empowered by Republican Political Machines, needed to be established in approximately half of the conquered States to provide the margin Republicans needed — a scheme of coercion that would forever cause many Americans to question the legality of the 14th Amendment. How could its ratification have been legitimate if obtained by coercion?

> 16 States were certain to approve (CN,IL,IN,IA,KS,ME,MA,MI,MN,NH,OH,OR,PA,RI,VT,WI).
> 4 States were probable (NV,NJ,NY,WV).
> 1 Territory would be granted Statehood soon, and be probable (NE).
> This totals 21 States likely to ratify.
> 1 States was far from certain (CA)
> 4 States were doubtful (DE, KY,MD,MO).
> 11 States required subjugation under Republican Political Machines.
> Three-fourths would be 28 States (Therefore, 28 minus 21 means 7 more States needed)

The coercion began immediately! The Joint House-Senate Committee on Reconstruction issued its long-awaited report in mid-June. It was a lengthy document, full of selected testimony, which purported to prove that former Confederates could not be trusted with voting and governmental responsibility. The report alleged that the Federal Army would need to rule over the people of the conquered States for the foreseeable future. Delighted, Thad Stevens had 1,000 copies printed, which he prepared to use in the Fall Republican political campaign to reelect men to State and Federal offices. [R96;249]

Meanwhile, Charles Sumner's mother died in mid-June. He had arrived in Boston four days before her death, for he had been alerted that the end was probably only days away. Upon returning from the funeral, Charles entered his mother's house, where, while not away in Washington City, he had been living for so many years as a bachelor, and cried, "I have now no home!" Perhaps without his mother, he considered the place a house instead of a home, or perhaps he figured the place would be sold to split the revenue with his sister out in California. As he mourned his loss, he wrote Elizabeth Argyll: "She was an excellent and remarkable person, whose death leaves me more than ever alone." [R73;267]

(3Q66)

At the time of the death of Charles Sumner's mother, he was suffering from poor health, and with the death of his mother weighing on his mind, his thoughts strangely turned to finding himself a wife. Now, Sumner was exceptionally late in grasping such thoughts, for he was 55 years old and counting. But, within a few days after the funeral, Sumner was dreaming of marriage when he found himself on a carriage ride with a friend, E. L. Pierce. Pierce was a young lawyer from Milton, Massachusetts, "who was becoming his most trusted political confidant." As they rode in the carriage, Sumner asked Pierce his thoughts on "the conditions which inclined people to marriage." Then Sumner explained, "that for the first time in his life he had now the means to support a family, and if he should meet someone who inspired him, he felt at liberty to marry." Actually, Sumner had met a widow in Washington that interested him, though that was still just his secret. In a letter to Wadsworth Longfellow a few days later, Sumner enthused, "When we meet again, I may have something to tell you; and certainly I shall have much on which to seek your communion. I have come to an epoch in life. My mother is dead. I have a moderate competency. What next?"

Sumner's romantic interest was toward Mrs. Alice Mason Hooper, the wealthy widow of William Hooper, who had died in 1863 while an aide to General Banks during the Federal invasion of Louisiana. Since her husband's death, Alice and her daughter had been living with her father, Jonathan Mason, in the family home in Boston's wealthy Beacon Hill neighborhood. Her father was a wealthy man. Alice's father-in-law, Representative Samuel Hooper, who represented the Boston-area District in the Federal House, was "one of the richest men in Boston." Alice had received about $75,000 from her deceased husband's estate, and her deceased husband's maternal grandfather, William Sturgis, had given her and her 7-year-old daughter a lot of money as well. Alice's Boston heritage went back a long way. She was the granddaughter of a past Federalist Senator who had made his fortune in developing the wealthy Beacon Hill residential area of Boston. And her sister was the wife of the wealthy Charles Appleton. [R73;269-273]

During the past winter, Alice, along with her daughter, had spent the winter social season in Washington City as a guest of her father-in-law, Representative Samuel Hooper. Both being from Boston, Sumner had long been a good friend of Samuel Hooper, and, over the years, he had often visited in Hooper's Washington home. So it had been natural that Charles and Alice had found themselves together rather often during the past winter. But, for much of the time spent together, Charles was the sick patient and Alice was the nurse. Alice had come down to Washington City and volunteered for nursing duty during the Federal invasion of the Confederacy, and, more recently, seemed to take pleasure in performing that service for sickly Charles. So Alice was attractive to Charles in several ways. She was beautiful; she was wealthy; and she was comfortable nursing his numerous neuroses. When he became sick from too much book-work and too little exercise, and mental flashbacks to his caning at the hands of Preston Brook's exacerbated his neurosis, Alice would be there to nurse him back to health. And, surprisingly, Alice was interested in Charles. She was very fascinated by Sumner's intellectual, literary and political mind, and by his statue as a glorious leader of the most militant Republicans, for, mentally, she shared his political enthusiasms. [R73;269-273]

Biographer David Donald would write of Sumner: "Though he had carried on mild flirtations in his youth, he had never, so far as can be determined, been in love with a woman. The story that, in his early manhood, he 'had failed in a suit in which his whole heart was enlisted,' was probably a myth, perhaps started by Sumner himself to explain his unwed state." Biographer David Donald made an exhaustive study of Sumner historical materials. At first he was perhaps suspicious that Sumner might have been homosexual, so he was alert to any evidence that might indicate such behavior. But he found none. Of suspected homosexual activity, Donald concluded, "I have found not the slightest evidence in Sumner's entire career." Yet he had never become romantically involved in younger years. Julia Ward, who had known Sumner socially when he was a young man, had long ago written in her diary that he had "no heart." I find it fitting to characterize Sumner as simply "an incomplete man." [R73;271]

In dramatic contrast to Alice, Charles Sumner was not a wealthy man. His father, although well-to-do in later life as the Sheriff of the Boston area, had never been wealthy by the Beacon Hill standard familiar to Bostonians. So he had received no family money in his younger days. Nevertheless, Charles had never been willing to put in the long working hours necessary to become a successful lawyer. Instead he had preferred to travel, spend time with friends, pursue literary projects, or engage in political activity. He had no lodging expenses while in Boston, for he simply stayed with his mother. But as a bachelor, with only his pay as a Federal Senator, amounting to $3,000 plus travel expenses, he had experienced no difficulty paying for comfortable lodging and meal service in Washington City, buying handsome clothes, or paying for vacations, books or an occasional rare collectible that caught his fancy. He had always arranged for others to pay the bulk of his campaign debts. So, by 1866 he had saved $5,000, which he had invested conservatively in Federal Government bonds. But Sumner would need that money for living expenses if he failed to win his next Senatorial election, for he had no job to which he could return. But with his mother's death, he stood to inherit enough money to buy a suitable house in Washington City. Now he felt he could marry without suffering any financial embarrassment. Why was Sumner not wealthy like so many Republican Senators? First, he had never had a good-paying steady job. Second, he had not inherited wealth. Third, he had never invested wisely. But the fourth and main reason was this: Sumner, an exception for the times, had always refused to accept bribes, gifts or subsidized investment offerings, like discounted railroad stock or real estate. The reading of his mother's will would reveal that Charles was to receive the 13-room, three-story house in Boston, while he and his sister, Julia, would split equally about $66,000 in cash and securities. [R73;271-272]

Meanwhile the Jefferson Davis saga continued. Dr. John Craven's notes and recollections of his days with Jeff Davis at Fortress Monroe were made available to the public through a book that was published in mid-summer. Biographer Hudson Strode would write: "The book created a stir and immediately became a best seller." And he observed that the book created much sympathy for Jeff Davis' plight among Americans, as well as much criticism for the "sadistic" treatment he had suffered at the hands of Nelson Miles. Without question, Craven's book was very helpful to Davis' cause, and constricted the realistic options available to Edwin Stanton and like-minded Republicans. Written before Varina had managed to get Dr. Cooper's May appeal into major newspapers, beginning with the New York *World*, Craven's introduction at the front of his book opened with: "It must be remembered that during the past year Davis has lain a silent prisoner in our strongest fort, unable to reply by so much as a word to the myriad assaults which have been made both on his private character and public course." Therefore, Craven submitted: "The case against [Davis] must indeed be weak which cannot bear allowance of a single voice to be raised in his defense." Aside from telling much about the torment Davis had been forced to endure, much was made of Craven's perception of the prisoner's character: "His self-control was the feature of his character, knowing that his temper had been high and proud, which most struck me during my attendance." And Craven predicted that, "the character of [Jeff] Davis, we believe, will receive justice in history." But Craven attracted criticism upon himself, as well. Dripping with intended sarcasm, Harper's Weekly called Craven, "a physician who apparently sat at [Davis'] feet to catch the drops of wisdom which fell from his mouth; a physician who has prepared a book about [this prisoner] whom he calls 'ex-President' and 'distinguished captive'." [R19;287-288]

Returning to Wade Hampton, we find him in Mississippi and in South Carolina. Hampton was apparently pleased with the progress of the crops growing on his Mississippi farms — writing sister Mary Fisher that the weather was good and the African American employees were working the crops as had been hoped, and suggesting a good crop was expected, he reported: "They give no trouble and behave well." In July, his daily attention not needed during midseason, he left the farms and returned east to Columbia on business, leaving the family behind. He had contracted for a modest new house to be built near the ruins of the more grand home that had been destroyed by William Sherman's Devastators, which had been named "Diamond Hill." Looking forward to completion, he named the new home, "Southern Cross." During past communication with Robert Lee and had promised to help accumulate documents for a history, so there were some papers to gather up as well. [R200;105-106]

But Wade Hampton was perhaps a better manager of his Mississippi farm that the typical farmer of the State. Mississippi had suffered immensely from acts of deliberate destruction by Federal forces, given uncontested access up and down the Mississippi River for the last half of the invasion campaign. Of the situation in the first months following the surrender, Mississippi historian James Garner would write:

> "The people were generally impoverished; the farms had gone to waste, the fences having been destroyed by the armies or having decayed from neglect; the fields were covered with weeds and bushes; farm implements and tools were gone; live stock had disappeared so that there were barely enough farm animals to meet the demands of agriculture; business was at a standstill; banks and commercial agencies had either suspended or closed on account of insolvency; the currency was in a wretched condition; the disbanded Confederate soldiers returned to their homes to find desolation and starvation staring them in the face . . . . About one-third of the [European American] breadwinners of the State had either been sacrificed in the contest or were disabled for life . . . . The number of dependent orphans alone was estimated to be 10,000. . . . There was hardly a home in the State in which there was not mourning for some member of the family who had been killed [defending the Confederacy]. . . . To supply [amputees] with artificial limbs, one fifth of the State revenues were appropriated in 1866."

An example is given of one Mississippi family, prior to State Secession, consisting of "a happy home of 5 sons and 2 daughters." Then tragedy struck! All five sons and the husbands of the two daughters had died defending the Confederacy, and the "mother, heartbroken with grief, had died a raving maniac." Only the elderly father remained.

A Mississippi census taken in 1966 revealed that the European American population had declined by 10,499 — from 353,899 to 343,400 — but suffering was far greater among the African American population, which had declined by 56,146 — from 437,404 to 381,258. Some of the African American loss was probably resettlement in northern States, but much of it was believed to have been from untimely death from hardships resulting from fighting. In fact, Governor Benjamin Humphreys would later report that he had owned 59 juvenile African Americans at the time of surrender in 1865, but only 20 survived "hardships" due to the invasion, followed by struggles caused by immediate independence.

In 1860 normal Mississippi personal property had been valued at $135,000,000, plus $218,000,000 in bonded African Americans held. In mid-1866, there was no personal property in bonded African Americans, and normal personal property had plummeted. It would slowly rise to only $59,000,000 by 1870.

The value of real estate had plummeted in a frantic sell-off. "Newspapers contained whole columns of advertisements of [large farms] for sale at a 'sacrifice.' One of these consisted of 2,690 acres, of which 1,100 were in cultivation, priced at $26,900 — little more than it had cost to build the farm house alone in 1959. A [large farm] 3 miles from Corinth was sold for 35 cents per acre. "A correspondent of a northern [States] journal informed its readers that the cheapness of the lands 'amazed' those who knew something of their value in former years; and to him the productiveness of the half-cultivated fields was even more amazing." During 1865 and 1866 many from the northern States, such as Ohio, came to Mississippi, bought farms and set out to make a fortune cultivating cotton. Of those efforts historian James Garner would write:

> "The remorseless energy and thrift of the northern [States farmer] and the exacting nature of the service which he demanded, did not appeal to the slow-going [African American] who was accustomed to the patience and forbearance of the Southerner." A majority of the farmers from the northern States would be unsuccessful, and by 1867 they would virtually abandon the farming business and become office holders."

The 1860 Mississippi cotton crop had been 1,202,507 bales, but the 1866 crop would be far less. It would rise to only 565,559 bales by 1870. In 1866 and 1867 farmers would be struggling against floods, droughts and insects, resulting in yields of cotton that could not even pay for the food and clothing of the laborers, based on the 50 percent share-crop arrangement prevalent in those years, when there was no cash to pay laborers except in a share of the year-end crop proceeds. "The failure, however, would not be due solely to floods, droughts and insects, but more substantially to the "unreliable character of [African American] labor." People of the State had made impressive progress in taming the land along the Mississippi River. In 1861, 310 miles of continuous levees stretched from the base of the hills near the Tennessee line to Brunswick Landing in Warren County protecting from overflows the Yazoo basin comprising 4,000,000 acres of as fertile land as there is on the globe, and constituting the heart of the cotton zone of the United States. Although sparsely settled, this region in 1860 produced 220,000 bales of cotton and 2,500,000 bushels of corn." But during the fighting, farms had been severely damaged and the levees had been cut in many places, allowing the floods of 1867 to "complete the destruction." [R204;122-126]

Meanwhile in Washington City, throughout July, Thad Stevens seemed determined to extend the House and Senate session as long as possible, even though most Republican Representatives were desperate to escape the capital's heat and return home to campaign for re-election. Many of the more militant Republicans feared being out-maneuvered back home by the less militant Faction that supported Andrew Johnson, or, if they survived that, perhaps suffering defeat at the hands of a Democratic Party challenger. But, with personal re-election considered a certainty, Stevens figured keeping Representatives in their seats as long as possible prevented Johnson from campaigning to soften the more militant Republican Faction's program for Reconstruction, and being in session blocked the Executive from firing appointed Federal officeholders and replacing them with Johnson supporters. On July 8, Senator William Fessenden wrote his wife, Francis: "Some are in favor of not adjourning at all, but I see nothing to be gained by staying, and the majority of the Senators agree with me. . . . Stevens is determined to stay as long as possible, and his position in the House enables him to obstruct and delay us." Referring to fears of defeats at the polls, Fessenden added: "Members are terribly afraid of their constituents." Of concerns about Federal officeholders being fired, Fessenden explained: "the [incumbent] officeholders are frightened out of their wits." In this atmosphere, some were out of town frequently, missing much of the debate and some of the voting, making it difficult for Stevens get the remainder to vote as he wished, as in the case of Tennessee Statehood. Many Representatives and Senators seemed ready to grant Statehood to Tennessee to show that some progress was being made in readmitting conquered States and to legitimize Andrew Johnson's citizenship, but Stevens opposed the plan. And they refused to give in to pressure by Stevens to proceed with Republican Reconstruction legislation, daring not to alarm voters back home with notions that African American men might soon be voting in their precincts as well. But Tennesseans knew the score and took action. On July 19 the Tennessee Legislature ratified the Federal Amendment to Nationalize Citizenship (14th). Although Stevens protested, the House and Senate completed the bargain, voting 5 days later, on July 24, to admit the re-made State of Tennessee. Andrew Johnson's Tennessee would escape the worse of Republican Reconstruction. Since Nashville had been conquered during the first year of the Federal invasion, four years had been available for the Republican Party to build its Tennessee Republican Political Machine, giving northern States Republicans confidence that the Party could control the Tennessee State Government. Furthermore, that would be one of the conquered States from which Ratification of the 14th Amendment was essential. [R96;252-253]

Meanwhile, election propaganda considerations, tempered by fears of facing Jeff Davis and his talented lawyers in court, ruled scheduling over the alleged trial date. Although Judge John Underwood had persuaded his Grand Jury to indict Jeff Davis in early May, Edwin Stanton and other Republican leaders were extremely fearful of, prior to the Fall elections, giving Davis and his lawyers a chance to defend the former Confederate President and the right of State Secession. So during mid-summer, Republican leaders carefully scheduled the treason trial for the first Tuesday in October. That would make it start on or about the day that the October wave of voters went to the polls. Republican newspapermen could disseminate the most effective propaganda if the trial was opening when the first wave of votes went to the polls, recognizing that the trial could be quickly recessed until after the November wave of voters went to the polls whenever it appeared the defense was scoring too many points. [R19;289]

Meanwhile in Kentucky, voters went to the polls in early August to demonstrate that former Confederates were moving toward control of their State Government. On May 1, in Louisville, former Confederates had resurrected the Old Kentucky Democratic Party. Their Convention, announced earlier in the Louisville *Courier*, had been well attended by Delegates from 85 counties, although the only State office of importance was Clerk of the Court of Appeals. For that office old Kentucky

Democrats had selected Alvin DuVall, who had returned to Kentucky after being forced off the ballot in 1863 and forced to flee the State to escape Federal arrest. "Resolutions were adopted condemning the Federal Government for its usurpations, sympathizing with the southern States in their troubles, recognizing the abolition of slavery, but demanding the right to regulate the political status of [African American men]." The established Conservative Democrat Party had convened in Louisville on May 30 and selected R. R. Bolling to oppose DuVall. But Bolling had withdrawn, allowing a fragile fusion of Conservative Democrats and Union Democrats (basically Republicans) to oppose the Old Kentucky Democrat Party. This fusion of parties selected E. H. Hobson to oppose DuVall. The contrast was stark, for Hobson had led the Federal cavalry that had captured Kentuckian John Hunt Morgan, the legendary Confederate cavalry commander. Numerous former Conservative Democrats switched to support the Confederate-led old Kentucky Democratic Party. The Andrew Johnson Administration did not allow Federal soldiers to interfere at the polls and former Confederates voted in large numbers. As a result Old Kentucky Democrat DuVall won by a large majority: 95,979 versus 58,035. The contest was quite spirited as well, reminiscent of the former war years. Historian Merton Coulter would report, "In many places there was violence at the polls and no fewer than 20 deaths were reported." Turnout was high, exceeding the previous year by almost 70,000 votes. Historian Merton Colter would conclude, "The [Old] Democratic Party was now definitely launched, composed of the majority of Kentuckians, and unquestionably in the complete control of the [former] Confederates." The Kentucky Legislature would not Ratify the Federal Amendment to Nationalize Citizenship (14th) until March 18, 1976, 110 years after it had been submitted, and, obviously, long, long after its vote really mattered. [R180;303-311]

Meanwhile, support for releasing Jeff Davis surged. Notable Republicans, on August 24, issued a joint letter to Andrew Johnson strongly urging him to release Davis from prison. Perhaps the most surprising signer of that letter was Gerrit Smith, the extremely wealthy long-time patron of Abolitionists and Exclusionists, including the notorious John Brown. Smith amended the letter with a personal note beside his signature: "I deem very long confinement in prison without a trial an insult to the [former Confederate States] . . . and a no less deep dishonor to the [Federal] Government and the [northern States]. Smith reaffirm his position a little later when he stated: "We have neither moral nor legal right to put on trial under the [Federal] Constitution, those whom we have recognized as belligerents and under the protection of the law of war. . . . The [former Confederate States, in their Secession], reached the dignity and rights of a party to a civil war."

By August, Edwin Stanton had totally shut down Nelson Miles' efforts to break Jeff Davis' spirit by incessant torment and isolation. No further attempt would be made. Davis' determination to persevere — against every torment that Miles devised — had convinced Stanton and like-minded Republicans that, even after the Fall elections, no effort should be made to restart the torment. In fact, their greatest fear had become that Davis might die in prison and that his death might rally opposition to the Republican Reconstruction program. Keeping Davis alive, but muzzled, was the new objective. To that end, Andrew Johnson ordered Nelson Miles, only 27 years old, to be mustered out of the Federal volunteer army. Miles, who had directed Davis' imprisonment for 15 months, protested the order, and accused Johnson of kicking him out because of "the base slanders and foulest accusation which [Democratic Party newspapermen have] heaped upon me." Johnson ignored Miles' plea, and, when September 1 dawned, Nelson Miles was making ready to say his goodbyes. Biographer Hudson Strode wrote that Miles' "departure marked the happiest day [Jeff and Varina] had known since the capture in May, 1865." Strode added: "For the rest of his long life Nelson Miles would be explaining, apologizing for, or blaming on others his base treatment of [Jeff Davis]." Before long, Miles would re-enlist into the regular Federal Army at a lower rank and go west to fight Native Americans, whom, Strode would note, "he [would slaughter] with remarkable dexterity." One would think that being a self-taught military man (not schooled at West Point) would limit advancement, but the youthful Miles would take a different path. He would marry the niece of William Sherman and rise in the Federal Army. Up and up, he would go until, in 1895, he would reach the pinnacle: Commanding General of the United States Army (later renamed the Army Chief of Staff). Miles' 15-month torment of Jefferson Davis certainly would not get in the way of frequent promotions. Perhaps promoting Nelson Miles was the Republican Party's way of demoting Jeff Davis.

Edwin Stanton installed a humane and civil officer to replace Nelson Miles. The mission was different, and that called for a different sort of officer — his name was Henry Burton. Within the limits of his orders, Burton would "be most considerate of the feelings" of Jeff and Varina Davis. Before long, Burton would allow Jeff "the freedom of the fort," and permit Varina to accompany him on his walks on the ramparts. And Varina would come to enjoy the company of Henry Burton's wife, "a warm-hearted, sympathetic, talented Mexican" of substantial Spanish heritage, who had come from California. Since Burton's wife still hated the Federal Army for taking so much Mexican territory during the War Against Mexico, the two ladies "would often sit together and secretly 'abuse the [Federals]'."

It was about this time that Dick Taylor managed to get into Fortress Monroe to visit Jeff and Varina. It had been a difficult struggle to get permission in Washington City, but upon his arrival at the Fort, Henry Burton honored Taylor by receiving him at the boat landing and escorting him to his quarters for a morning breakfast. Burton probably thought it proper, since Dick Taylor was the son of former President Zachary Taylor. Burton's wife would have been, perhaps, cooler toward Dick Taylor, if she dwelt much on his father Zachary's military leadership in the War Against Mexico.

The difficult part had been getting permission make the visit. Taylor had twice obtained a meeting with Andrew Johnson where he had begged permission to visit his brother-in-law, Jeff Davis. (You will recall that Jeff's first wife, Sara Knox, who had died soon after their marriage, had been Zachary Taylor's daughter). Although Johnson had shown outward courtesy, Taylor thought he displayed "an obstinate, suspicious temper," which required that "like a badger, one had to dig him out of his hole." And Johnson had refused to answer "yes" or "no." Instead, he had recommended that Taylor separately visit Thad Stevens and Charles Sumner and seek their permission to visit Jeff Davis.

Less determined men would have given up. But not Dick Taylor! He had sought out Thad Stevens and to get his permission as Johnson had required. Stevens had warmed up by telling Taylor that he wanted "no restoration of the [conquered States] under the [Federal] Constitution," which he called "a worthless bit of old parchment." Stevens had then warned Taylor that the European American people of the conquered States would never be trusted with political power, because they would eventually join forces with Democratic politicians from the northern States. And Stevens had next forewarned Taylor that Congress would soon be legislating to empower the Federal Army to seize the farms and homes of former Confederates and give them to African American men. Stevens had been apparently frank about his plans for the Republican Reconstruction program. But Stevens had shown little interest in Jeff Davis, for he had told Taylor that he was convinced that Republicans could do nothing with him. If Andrew Johnson had promptly ordered the execution of Confederate leaders, Stevens had reasoned, that would have been well and good, but he considered the time for hanging past. He had lamented that "Johnson had only pluck enough to hang those two poor devils, [Henry] Wirz and [Mrs.] Surratt." Toward the end of the meeting Stevens had submitted that he thought Johnson's refusal to grant the visit was silly, but then he had closed with the explanation he would not support the visit either, because he wanted to be able to blame the granting of permission squarely on Johnson.

Taylor had doggedly proceeded on to seek Charles Sumner's permission. Of that encounter, biographer Hudson Strode would write, "[Charles] Sumner, in high-flown language, put Taylor off with quotations from the classics, modern poets, and [Harriet Beecher] Stowe." Persistently, Taylor had proceeded on in hopes of at least getting William Seward's permission. Strode would describe that meeting: "[William] Seward, who entertained him at dinner with 'fatted calf' for the prodigal, seemed to favor the object of his mission. At least as far as Taylor could 'gather his meaning under the cloud of words with which he is accustomed to cover his slightest thought'." So, empty handed, Dick Taylor had returned to the White House to beg again of Andrew Johnson. Strode figured that Taylor had "finally worried Johnson into giving him permission to visit his brother-in-law Jefferson Davis."

Strode would describe the meeting at Fortress Monroe between brother-in-laws Dick Taylor and Jeff Davis:

> "It was with considerable emotion that Dick Taylor reached the barred room in which [Jeff Davis] was confined. The two men had been devoted friends since 1831 in the wilds of Wisconsin when Taylor was just a boy and young Lieutenant Davis was courting his sister, Sarah Knox. Now they met in silence and merely clasped hands. Taylor could not speak. Finally [Jeff] said, 'This is kind, but no more than I expected.'

" 'Pallid, worn, gray, bent, feeble, suffering from inflammation of the eyes,' Taylor wrote, 'he was a painful sight for a friend.'

"When they sat down, Davis 'uttered no plaint,' but confessed the light kept burning all night in his room had 'hurt his eyes a little' and that the noise made every two hours by relieving the sentry 'prevented much sleep.' 'However,' he said, 'everything has changed for the better since [the arrival of Henry] Burton, who strains his orders from Washington to the utmost in my behalf.'

"Taylor related details of his visit to Washington, of his reception by Johnson and half a dozen other strategic persons. Optimistically, he declared that if he could not secure [Jeff's] immediate release on bail, he felt certain that he could obtain permission for [Varina] to live with him.

" 'You may solicit favors for me,' Davis said, 'but I decline to solicit any for myself.' At the hope of having [Varina] with him, however, [Jeff's] countenance brightened. He asked numerous questions about the condition and prospects of the [former Confederate States] which Taylor answered in as favorable a light as he could, without absolutely lying."

Then Taylor took a few moments to "abuse the Federals." He told Jeff how he had witnessed in Washington City, "the martial tread of hundreds of volunteer [high-ranking officers], just disbanded." He said they were "gorged with loot," and that "they spent it as lavishly as Morgan's buccaneers after the sack of Panama. Their women sat at meat, resplendent in jewels, the spoil of [former Confederate] matrons. The camp followers of the [Federal] army were there in high carnival and, in character and numbers, they rivaled those attendants of Xerxes."

Through the efforts of Dick Taylor, Davis' lawyers and others, Andrew Johnson and Edwin Stanton soon thereafter ordered that a suite of rooms be prepared at Fortress Monroe for Jeff, Varina and the baby. Accordingly, Henry Burton would assign them a four-room apartment in Carroll Hall. Acceptance of furniture sent in by friends in Baltimore and Norfolk would be permitted, and Varina would soon make the four-room apartment look like home. Jeff and Varina would even be permitted to have servants in the apartment as well. Ellen, the African American nurse who had been forced to leave Varina about the time Jeff was taken into Fortress Monroe, would return as housemaid. And Frederick Maginnis was permitted to work there as Jeff's personal servant. Frederick would help nurse Jeff back to health much as James Pemberton had done in the terrible winter of 1832 in the wilds of Wisconsin, when Jeff had almost died of pneumonia. And Frederick, "a courteous, refined gentleman in his instincts," attempted to return some sense of honor to the prison apartment. For example, one time a woman rang the bell asking to see "Jeff." "I know no one by that name," Frederick replied. "Aren't you his servant?" ""You are entirely mistaken, madam. I happen to serve the ex-President of the Confederacy." Of course Varina helped nurse Jeff, too. She would read to him all night long, for the sound of her reading seemed to produce a sounder sleep. But as she read she kept a finger on his pulse, least it become alarmingly weak. And when it did, she awoke him and gave him a sip of wine or a bite to eat before resuming his sleep. [R19;291-294]

Meanwhile, Wade Hampton had composed a detailed and thoughtful letter to Andrew Johnson, encouraging support in the northern States for the policies of his Administration and presenting to the people of the northern States a clear view of the true situation in the conquered States. History does not know Johnson's thoughts upon receiving Hampton's letter. But it was published in the *Metropolitan Record and New York Vindicator*, a Democrat newspaper of New York City, whose editor, John Mullaly, was sympathetic to the cause of the southern States. This letter was also published as a broadside. The letter expressed support for Johnson's policies toward remaking the governments of the conquered States, adding, "But for you the [conquered States section] would have found in peace far greater horrors that she encountered during war." You are not to blame, he wrote, for that destructive agenda emanating from the Federal House and Senate, which he characterized as, "that malignant spirit of fanaticism, which demands as the price of reunion, the complete degradation and the absolute ruin of the [conquered States]." He denounced "brutal [African American] troops under their no less brutal and more degraded [Federal] officers. Then calling it "that Hydra-headed Monster, he accused the Newly Independent African American Men's Bureau of "swindling the [African American man], plundering the [European American] man and defrauding the government." Concerning the welfare of the typical African American, Hampton wrote, "whilst he was [bonded], [he] was happy, useful, honest and industrious. But his unfortunate association with men from the northeastern States has corrupted him." Consequently, we "turn him over willingly to those who imported him from Africa, sold him to us, and then stole him to make him [independent]." The concluding remarks of Hampton's letter to Andrew Johnson are worth reading:

"The [conquered States section] unequivocally 'accepts the situation' in which she is placed. Everything that she has done, has been done in perfect good faith, and in the true and highest sense of the word, she is loyal. By this I mean, that she intends to abide by the laws of the land honestly; to fulfill all her obligations faithfully and to keep her word sacredly. And I assert that the [northern States region] has no right to demand more of her. You have no right to ask, or to expect that she will at once profess unbounded love to the [Federal Government], from which for four years she tried to escape, at the cost of her best blood and all her treasure. Nor can you believe her to be so unutterably hypocritical, so base as to declare that the 'Flag of the [United States]' has already usurped in her heart the place which has so long been sacred to the 'Southern Cross.' The men [of our section] who make such professions are renegades, or traitors and they will surely betray you if you trust them. But the brave men who fought to the last in a cause which they believed and still believe to have been a just one, who clung to their colors as long as they waved and who, when their cause was lost, acknowledged their defeat and accepted the terms offered to them — as they were true to their convictions in the one case, they will prove to their obligations in the other. Many sacrifices have been demanded of the [conquered States], as the price of [being accepted back into the Union]. These she has made; but she will abase herself for no earthly consideration. She will not return to the Union an unequal partner. She will accept no left-handed alliance. She regards herself as fully the peer in honor, in reputation, in character, and in glory of any other portion of the Republic, and she will never consent to tarnish her name, by inscribing on her escutcheon with her own hand, that she has been guilty." [R199;180-181]

Meanwhile in Oxford, Mississippi, Lucius Lamar began a new job as a professor at the University of Mississippi, initially taking on a huge teaching load, including courses in Mathematics, Metaphysics and Law. He was rather adept in all of these fields, but, even though travel was not required as it had been in the law practice, the work load was heavy — not the reduced work load that he had sought when he and Edward Walthall had dissolved their law partnership during the summer, and the University, in June, had elected Lamar "to the Chair of Ethics and Metaphysics." Although the law partnership with senior partner Edward Walthall had been financially rewarding, and had enabled Lamar to pay off accumulated debts, with interest, going back to before 1861, the law work and required travel had been hard and his less-than-robust health had consequentially suffered. Having left Coffeeville a few weeks earlier, Lamar and his family now lived in Oxford, near the University. In January of 1867 Lamar's work load at the University would be reduced as he would be elected to fill the Chair of the School of Law, which would, from that point forward, be his exclusive responsibility. While at the University of Mississippi, Lamar would remain in contact with former Confederate leaders, such as Clement Clay, Burton Harrison and Jeff Davis. [R205;124-125, R206;89]

During August 14, 15 and 16, supporters of Andrew Johnson, approximately 7,000 strong, staged a large Convention in Philadelphia aimed at rallying support for his policies for remaking the Governments in the conquered States, and demonstrating opposition to the Reconstruction programs of Thad Stevens and like-minded more Militant Republicans. Supporters from all sections were in attendance — northern States, southern States, conquered States, Delaware, Maryland, Kentucky and Missouri. No section was omitted. Pitched as a "National Union Convention," supporters had a variety of previous political allegiances, including the less Militant Faction of the Republican Party, the Democratic Party, and the parties that had operated during the days of the Confederate Government. In a remarkable display of conciliation, the Massachusetts Delegation and the South Carolina Delegation paraded into the convention hall with their arms linked. The more Militant Republicans accused the less Militant Republicans of being traitors.

Two weeks later, on September 3, the more Militant Republican Faction held its Convention, also in Philadelphia. This group was led by the many Republican Representatives and Senators who opposed Andrew Johnson's policies and more or less supported Thad Stevens' Reconstruction Program. However, Stevens had chosen to vacation at Bedford Springs, Pennsylvania instead, feeling the need to rest and recuperate from a summer illness. A significant number of African Americans attended and their leader Frederick Douglass was among the Delegates from Rochester, New York. In a display of social equality, which received prominent newspaper coverage, Douglass was seen arm-in-arm with the well-known New York Abolitionist and associate of Henry Ward Beecher, Theodore Tilton (for titillating reading about adultery, explore the Beecher-Tilton Affair and its 1875 court trial). Douglass delivered a political address at the Convention as well. The Convention's primary advocacy was for empowering African American men with the right to vote.

The day following the opening of the more Militant Faction Convention, Thad Stevens addressed a political rally near Bedford Springs, a "fashionable resort" in Pennsylvania where he was vacationing. He had written out the speech and previously telegraphed it to the New York *Tribune*, so the audience at Bedford was of minor concern to Stevens — He was speaking to voters throughout the northern States: "We shall hear repeated, ten thousand times, [by Democratic Party politicians and supporters of Andrew Johnson,] the cry of '[African American] equality!' . . . [They will suggest that our more Militant Republican Faction] would thrust [the African American man] into your parlors, your bedrooms, and the bosom of your wives and daughters [and] even make your reluctant daughters marry [African American] men." Stevens told the crowd that he had refused to sign the revised 1837-38 Pennsylvania State Constitution, because it took the right to vote away from Pennsylvania's African American men. However, Stevens announced he now had a change of heart. At this point forward, he would be advocating revising the Pennsylvania Constitution to again permit voting by the State's African American men. Why? Because voting by African American men was necessary to empower Republican Political Machines in the conquered States and the country's voting laws needed to be national, not sectional. Stevens knew that the African American vote would not hurt Republicans in his State, and it was only through the votes of African American men that Republicans could ever control the Governments of the conquered States. Stevens explained it this way: "I care not what you may say of [African American] equality — I care not what you may say of [the policies of our more Militant Republican Faction], these are my principles, and with the help of God I shall die with them."

From an attendee at the more Militant Faction Convention, Thad Stevens read: "A good many people here are disturbed by the practical exhibition of social equality in the arm-in-arm performance of [Frederick] Douglass and [Theodore] Tilton. It does not become [our Faction] to particularly object. But it was certainly unfortunate at this time. The old prejudice, now revived, will lose us some votes. Why it was done I cannot see except as a foolish bravado." Stevens also had reason to fear lost of votes over patronage vote buying. In another letter he read: "I learned that [Andrew Johnson's men do not intend] to make the [political] appointments for Pennsylvania until after the October election so that the votes of the bought may be secured first. I also learned that the same office is offered to half a dozen or more hungry expectants. I had supposed that one office should buy only one traitor [to our Faction], but by this plan, one office may buy several."

During his September political campaigning Thad Stevens developed a plan for crippling Andrew Johnson's power of political appointment. The centerpiece was a new back-dated Federal law which he rough-drafted and mailed to William Fessenden, seeking his thoughts on the matter:

> "Section 1: No person who has been nominated by the President for office and to which nomination the Senate refused its advice and consent shall hold any office under the United States [Government] until the expiration of four years from his such rejection provided that the Senate may at any time remove said disability by a vote of two thirds of the members present.

> "Section 2: Whenever any person is nominated by the President for any office which requires the advice and consent of the Senate and the same office had been filled by another person previously to such appointment; the person thus appointed shall not enter upon the duties of his office until confirmed by the Senate. Whenever such nomination shall not be confirmed by the Senate his predecessor shall retain the office. This section shall take effect from and after the 4th of March, 1866."

History would prove Stevens' rough-draft to be of immense importance, for it would become the basis for entrapping and impeaching Andrew Johnson. [R96;254-259]

Meanwhile at Fortress Monroe, during September additional prominent friends were permitted to visit Jeff and Varina. Franklin Pierce, who Hudson Strode would insist "had never swerved from his personal devotion," came from New Hampshire to visit and encourage his friend. Wade Hampton came up from South Carolina for a "long visit." Others visited as well. [R19;295]

Meanwhile, on October 1 in South Carolina, Federal military officials stopped blocking the State's civil and criminal judicial cases concerning the comprehensive set of African American regulations that had been established by the Legislature in its December 1865 acts. You will recall reading that long list of regulations (in my presentation there were 28 items). They concerned the courts, employment, living procedures, etc. And you will recall, I would expect, thinking to yourself as you read those regulations that those rules were rather reasonable considering the difficult times and conditions of South Carolinians at that point in history. Although rather reasonable for the times, the Legislature had become determined to repeal those regulations in hopes the Federal military would then give back to the State its normal authority for operating its judicial system of courts. So it had convened in Special Session on September 4 to legislate "such modifications of existing laws with reference to [African Americans] as will entitle the tribunals of this State to exercise jurisdiction over them in all cases, and such a reorganization of these tribunals as may be best adapted to this end." Basically, the revised law struck out every reference to bonded African Americans by name, so it put both races on an equal footing in the regulated categories. The key race-leveling paragraph of the revised code read:

> "All persons hitherto known in law in this State as [bonded African Americans] or as [independent African Americans] shall have the right to make and enforce contracts, to sue, to be sued, to be affiants and give evidence, to inherit, purchase, lease, sell, hold, convey and assign real and personal property, make wills and testaments, and to have full and equal benefits of the rights of personal security, personal liberty and private property, and of all remedies and proceedings for the enforcement and protection of the same, as [European Americans] now have, and shall not be subjected to any other or different punishment, pain or penalty for the commission of any act or offense than such as are prescribed for [European Americans] committing like acts or offenses."

You will recall that political agitation in the northern States over the issue of equal rights in the conquered States was an enabling activity aimed at enhancing the power of the Republican Party. We would suppose the relaxation of the law in South Carolina was designed to take this issue away from Republicans. Furthermore, we should find it telling to observe that the ability of South Carolina leaders to give African Americans equal rights without undue alarm is evidence of the remarkable progress that both races had made during the previous 16 months. Notably, when the Legislature would adjourn in a few weeks, on December 21, at the end of its last regular session, there would be no further legislation enacted under the 1865 Constitution, which had informally retained for the natural leaders of the State the political influence their families had exercised over several generations. [R201;31-32]

In early October Wade Hampton spoke to a gathering of Confederate veterans at Walhalla, South Carolina, located in the Upstate region. He said he hoped Andrew Johnson would be reelected in 1868 and that his supporters, represented by those who had gathered in Philadelphia in August, would gain seats in the Federal House and Senate during the Fall elections. Then he expressed anger at Federals for forcing the State to approve the Amendment making Bonded African Americans Independent (13th) and then denying her seats in the Federal House and Senate. Of the typical African American, he said:

> "He came to us a heathen, we made him a Christian. Idle, vicious, savage in his own country; in ours he became industrious, gentle, civilized. . . . A great responsibility is lifted from our shoulders by his [being made independent]. . . . As a [bonded man] he was faithful to us; as an [independent] man, let us treat him as a friend. Deal with him gently, kindly, and, my word for it, he will reciprocate your kindness. . . . If you wish to see him contented, industrious, useful, aid him in his effort to elevate himself in the scale of civilization, and thus fit him, not only to enjoy the blessings of freedom, but to appreciate its duties." [R199;183-184]

Seeking support for his plan for remaking the Governments of the conquered States, Andrew Johnson had engaged in a widely publicized northern States campaign tour, starting northward to New York on August 27, then westward to Chicago, then southward to St. Louis and eastward back to Washington City, returning on September 15. The more Militant Republican newspapers had made great jest of the effort, accusing Johnson, who spoke with a southern States accent, of being a drunkard, and worse. Joining in the hateful chorus, Thad Stevens delivered a final campaign diatribe in Lancaster in early October:

"I come not to make a speech, but for the want of one. When I left Washington [City] I was somewhat worn by labors and disease, and I was directed by my physician neither to think, to speak, nor to read until the next session of Congress, or I should not regain my strength. I have followed the first injunction most religiously, for I believe I have not let an idea pass through my mind to trouble me since Congress adjourned. The second one — not to speak — I was seduced from keeping; and I made a speech at Bedford — the only one I have made. The one — not to read — I have followed almost literally. It is true; I have amused myself with a little light, frivolous reading. For instance, there was a serial account from day to day of a very remarkable circus that traveled through the country, from Washington [City] to Chicago and St. Louis, and from Louisville back to Washington [City]. I read that with some interest . . . I expect great wit from the celebrated character of its clowns. . . . I shall not describe to you how sometimes they cut outside the circle, and entered into street brawls with common blackguards; how they fought at Cleveland and Indianapolis. But, coming round, they told you, or one of them did, that he had been everything but one. He had been a tailor — I think he did not say drunken tailor. He had been a constable. He had been city alderman. He had been in the Legislature. God help that Legislature! He had been in Congress; and now he was President. He had been everything but one — he had never been a hangman, and he asked leave to hang Thad Stevens."

Pennsylvania voters cast their ballots on October 10. The more Militant Republican Faction was generally victorious over Democrats and less Militant Republicans. And Republican John Geary won the race for Governor. The New York *Times* and the New York *Herald* both concluded that in early November, when the remaining States would hold their elections, the more Militant Republican Faction would control a majority in the Federal House. The *Times* submitted that, "The question [how to remake or Reconstruct the Governments of the conquered States] may have been more or less modified in particular localities, as in that represented by [Thad] Stevens, but as a rule this has been its shape — the [policies of Andrew Johnson] or [the policies of Congress]? And the answer leaves room neither for equivocation nor doubt. It is overwhelmingly against [Andrew Johnson]." [R96;259-260]

Shortly before the start of voting in October, Republican leaders had arranged to postpone Jeff Davis' scheduled treason trial to the Spring of the following year — 1867. The postponement had probably been planned all along, for the October schedule date was merely set to provide story material, during August and September, with which Republican propagandists might persuade voters to better hate former Confederates and therefore reelect Republican candidates. It was early in October when Charles O'Conor sent for Burton Harrison to ask him to go to Fortress Monroe and tell Jeff and Varina of the postponement. Harrison had just arrived in New York City the previous day from a recuperative stay in Europe, but he agreed to go immediately to Fortress Monroe to deliver the sad news. Harrison stayed at Fortress Monroe for two days, telling stories about his stay in Europe to help Jeff and Varina rebound from the initial disappointment. He told of seeing Dudley Mann, the Slidell's, Robert Toombs, and others in Paris. And Jeff thought Harrison well recovered from the scurvy and other ailments suffered during his harsh imprisonment in Washington City. But gloom would settle upon Jeff and Varina soon after Harrison's departure. On October, 18, Varina would write her mother in Montreal, Canada, who was there with the older children:

"Jeff grows hourly weaker, more exhausted. He has now to cling to the banister, and to use his stick in descending the steps, and staggers much in walking. This decision of [Andrew Johnson] that he must be left to the Republicans, that he [himself] can do nothing for him, seems to promise that [Jeff's remaining] life will be spent in prison. It is in the power of the judge to postpone [Jeff's] trial from one time to another and this they have done — I am too grieved, too agonized to talk of this. God knows what we shall do — what can we do." [R19;296]

Meanwhile, wedding bells rang in Boston. Charles Sumner married Alice Mason Hooper on October 17. As previously described, Alice was the widow of the deceased son of the Federal Representative from Boston, and the daughter of wealthy Bostonians who lived in posh Beacon Hill. Alice had considerably more money than did Charles and had always been accustomed to a luxurious life style. But Charles had just received inheritance from his mother's estate, and that would help. Charles and Alice were married by the Episcopal Bishop of Boston in the home of her brother-in-law, William Appleton. The wedding had taken place in spite of discouragement from Alice's relatives, who had taken "no pains to conceal how distasteful the whole affair was to them." They were surely concerned about Charles being 55 years old and sickly; whereas the bride was young and vivacious. The newly-weds left Boston for a three-week honeymoon at Newport, Rhode Island. [R73;274]

(4Q66)

Meanwhile, Varina continued to write Horace Greeley encouraging him to help persuade Republican leaders to set Jeff Davis free. And Greeley remained sympathetic. The November 9 issue of Horace Greeley's New York *Tribune* contained his editorial strongly advocating Davis' immediate release. The editorial reviewed the history of allegations; it lamented purposeful delay in bringing forth charges and in postponing scheduled trial dates. Greeley added that "Congress, [Andrew Johnson] and [Salmon Chase] were in a complete muddle on the subject." And Greeley flatly criticized Johnson for not publicly retracting his 18-month old Proclamation that Jeff Davis had helped John Wilkes Booth kill Abe Lincoln. But most of all, Jeff Davis was pleased at this segment of the editorial:

> "It is neither just nor wise to send forth a prisoner of state with the brand of murder on his brow; and a naked failure to prosecute is but equivalent to the Scotch verdict, 'Not proved.' . . . A great government may deal sternly with the offenders, but not meanly; it cannot afford to seem unwilling to repair an obvious wrong."

And Jeff and Varina's hopes were also lifted by a letter received from Dick Taylor in which he reported on a recent three-hour meeting with Andrew Johnson at the White House. Taylor reported great confidence that Jeff would be granted bail until the Federal Government summoned him to a trial. [R19;297]

During November, Charles Sumner and his new family left Boston and moved into a furnished house at 322 I Street in Washington City. The new occupants consisted of Charles and Alice, Alice's daughter, Bell, Bell's nurse, and Bell's little dog. Plus there were the servants that were hired within days of their arrival. As he looked forward to married life in Washington, Charles wrote Mrs. John Lodge: "I hope to be very happy. Tardily I begin." Charles was busy during the first weeks in Washington City, ordering crystal and china, finding a French tutor for Bell, and so forth. And he had to rent a pew at the Church of the Epiphany for Alice, who — in stark contrast to the rather atheistic Charles — was a devout Episcopal. Some were amused that the coach and horses that Sumner acquired had once belonged to Confederate supporter and British minister, Richard Lyons; and that the dining room servant Charles hired had been Roger Taney's favorite employee. Excited that he finally had a home at which he could entertain, Charles would soon began inviting friends over. Early guests would include Wadsworth Longfellow and Francis Lieber. Charles and Alice would have guests for dinner almost every night, as they looked forward to their abode becoming a meeting place for "men of ideas and women of the highest culture, . . . all imbued with great national sentiments." In that spirit, Charles and Alice would invite Thad Stevens, Baron Gerolt, and Sir Frederick Bruce; on another night they would invite Edwin Stanton and Senator Lot Morrill; on another it would be the new French minister, M. Jules Berthémy; and there would be the night when they hosted the new French attaché, the Marquis de Chambrun so they could introduce him to Henry Dawes and Schuyler Colfax. And Charles and Alice enjoyed the reciprocal hospitality of other homes. But they steadfastly refused invitations to dine with Andrew Johnson at the White House. Marriage to a rich widow and inheritance from his late mother was indeed transforming Charles Sumner. [R73;275-277]

Meanwhile, Thad Stevens was returning to the capital, arriving after mid-November to his residence, which Lydia Smith had been keeping up for him since he had departed in early August to vacation and campaign. Compared to Charles and Alice Sumner, Thad's house featured a different sort of social entertainment, but was perhaps a place where greater influence was peddled. Newspapermen often came by Stevens' home seeking insight into the country's political future. And questions about the relationship between Thad and Lydia were infrequent. On some days Stevens seemed too ill "to talk on political topics." But on other days, when he appeared healthier, they found him "freely predicting an immediate Impeachment" of Andrew Johnson.

While Stevens was struggling to regain his health at home, under Lydia Smith's kind attention, Edwin Stanton was at his office in the War Department scheming to circumvent the provision in the Federal Constitution that placed the Federal Military under the direction of Andrew Johnson, who was, according to the Federal Constitution, "Commander in Chief" of the Army and Navy as well as

"President." Toward effecting his scheme, Stanton dictated to one of the members of the Joint House-Senate Committee on Reconstruction, George Boutwell of Massachusetts, his draft of a law designed to prohibit Andrew Johnson from assigning Ulysses Grant to any post other than Washington City without the consent of the Senate. Grant was the Commanding General of the Army, and Stanton and others had persuaded him to support the Federal House and Senate during the more Militant Faction's planned Impeachment of Andrew Johnson. So, Stanton wanted Grant in Washington City, to defy with Federal troops any retaliatory order that Johnson might issue against him in his capacity as Secretary of War or against leaders of the House or Senate. Boutwell showed Stanton's draft law to Thad Stevens, "who readily agreed to include it in the next Army Appropriation bill."

At the same time Stevens was drafting his own bills designed to deprive Andrew Johnson of the normal powers to appoint people to Federal offices, and to deprive Johnson of his power to direct the affairs of the Federal Army and Navy as stipulated in the Federal Constitution. Stevens was also supporting more Militant Faction Senators who were planning to review all Federal appointments that Andrew Johnson had made while the House and Senate were in recess and to reject all appointees who had no history of supporting the more Militant Faction's political aims, while returning those jobs to the previous occupants. [R96;262-263]

Meanwhile, in Fortress Monroe, Mary Stamps came to visit Jeff and Varina in late November. Mary was the widow of Jeff's nephew, Isaac Stamps. She had been with Jeff and Varina in Richmond while her husband had moved north with Robert Lee's army to counter-attack in Pennsylvania. And it was at Gettysburg that Isaac Stamps had been killed. Mary and Jeff were close, and perhaps that was useful considering the sensitive question she brought with her to Fortress Monroe. Mary had been at Jackson with her father, Mississippi Governor Benjamin Humphreys, when Jeff's brother Joseph had called to ask a favor of her. Joseph was apparently tormented over the likelihood that his and Jeff's farms on Davis Bend would be confiscated by the actions of Thad Stevens and like-minded Republicans, perhaps soon after the Federal Congress resumed its session in December. Timing was good, for there was an interlude in Federal subjugation of the Mississippi State Government, and Governor Benjamin Humphreys was a family friend. And, with he himself being in his eighties, and Jeff being in prison with no certainty of release, Joseph felt it imperative that some arrangement be made while communications were permitted. Joseph's legally-trained mind had seized upon a method by which confiscation could be circumvented. Joseph was certainly thankful that all 3,000 acres — including Jeff and Varina's farmland and farmhouse — were solely in his name. He figured it a certainty that Federals would have already confiscated some or all of the farmland if a portion had been deeded in Jeff's name. Joseph's plan was to sell all 3,000 acres to Ben Montgomery for $300,000, to be fully financed by the seller at 6% interest. Ben Montgomery, who was of mixed African and European ancestry, had been the most capable bonded African American on either brother's farm. He had been a supervisor for many years. He was literate and confident in business dealings. Every since Ben's childhood, Jeff and Joseph had both encouraged and helped him develop those abilities. Joseph had figured it was time to see what Ben could make of his talents. But most importantly, if Ben Montgomery owned the farms, it was not likely that Federal Agents would confiscate them, and therefore Joseph's interest-bearing loan would remain valid. Furthermore, if in a few years, Ben failed to keep up the payments, Joseph might have the right to foreclose on the land and thereby get the farm back in some future year. Joseph had confidence in Ben, and his very capable sons, Thornton and Isaiah, but farming was not the profitable business it had been before the Federal invasion. That four-year invasion had forced European textile companies to encourage cotton production elsewhere, and by 1866, India was a formidable competitor. The former Confederate States' share of the European market had plunged, and 1867 and beyond looked quite soft. Ben Montgomery would have a tough time making the 6% interest payment in spite of his admirable capabilities. But Joseph would not sell to Ben Montgomery without Jeff's permission. Even though he held the deed to all the land, Joseph considered part of the land Jeff's. Mailing a letter to Jeff explaining the idea was out of the question, for Joseph knew that Federal agents checked Jeff and Varina's mail, and they might well swoop down upon Davis Bend and seize the land if they ever learned of Joseph's plan. So Joseph wanted Mary Stamps to go to Fortress Monroe and talk confidentially with Jeff about the proposal. Hopefully she would receive Jeff's permission and return to Mississippi to report back to Joseph. [R19;298-299]

Jeff Davis seemed surprised when Mary Stamps disclosed Joseph's farm-sale proposal, for he had hoped to return to his farm and work it in his old age. He had hoped his children could finish growing up there. Yet he well realized that, if he delayed in his reply, and the upcoming session of the Federal House and Senate expanded the Federal confiscation program, he and Joseph might receive nothing for their 3,000 acres. And Jeff shared Joseph's confidence in Ben Montgomery and his two sons, Thornton and Isaiah. Seeing the wisdom in Joseph's plan, Jeff told Mary Stamps to tell Joseph that he gave his blessing to the deal. [R19;298-299]

Meanwhile in Washington City on December 3 the House and Senate convened on December 3 to start the last session of its term, which was to end on March 4, 1867. But, before the session began, Thad Stevens, Charles Sumner and like-minded leaders of the more Militant Faction had decided to convene the next House and Senate 9 months prior to the date prescribed in the Federal Constitution. The Federal Constitution says: "The Congress shall assemble at least once in every year, and such meeting shall be on the first Monday in December, unless they shall by law appoint a different day." Stevens, Sumner and others wanted a different day — March 5 or soon thereafter, 1867. Why? Because the recently elected Representatives and Senators to be seated in that Congress would be more supportive of the Republican Reconstruction Program and more willing to convict Andrew Johnson on a charge of Impeachment. And schemers intended to trap Andrew Johnson with their Tenure of Office bill.

In the Senate Charles Sumner enthusiastically supported the Tenure of Office bill, which George Williams of Iowa introduced during the first day of the new session. In fact Sumner wished for Congress to usurp even more power from the Executive. He alleged before fellow Senators that "the power of [both] appointing and removing members of the [President's] Cabinet more properly belonged to the Senate as a permanent body than to the President." Sumner did not even want an incoming President to select his own advisers. Why? In Charles Sumner's opinion, it was because "the Senate was less liable to become depraved and bad than the President." And Sumner wanted the Senate involved in removal proposals covering more categories of Federal employees than stipulated in the bill then on the floor. Sumner wanted Senate control over dismissing any Federal employee making over $1,000 per year. To challenges that his plan would severely "lumber up and encumber the business" of the Senate, Sumner replied, "I am willing to act on an inspector or a night watchman; and if I could, I would save him from [Andrew Johnson's] tyranny." At another point Sumner explained that, in past years, Senators had not considered such tight control over individual Federal employees because "there was no such duty of our fathers" to constrain a President "who had become the enemy of his country." [R73;277-279]

Meanwhile, in the House, Thad Stevens eagerly moved ahead with the Republican Reconstruction program, as he introduced on December 13 a bill to revise the basis of the Government of conquered North Carolina. A milder version of Reconstruction, the bill was designed to replace the remade North Carolina State Government with a new State Constitution and State Government that was based on the votes of all men living in the State, of all racial backgrounds, who could demonstrate a basic ability to read and write. The Governor of the remade North Carolina State Government and other North Carolina political leaders had met earlier with Stevens in Washington and volunteered to support a plan where voting was restricted to men of all races who could read and write. The bill made sense in that some African American men would become immediately involved in political affairs, and through schooling, the vast majority of African American men would eventually become qualified voters. The North Carolinians recognized that good government was dependent on a responsible electorate. Although an ability to read and write did not mean a man would be a responsible voter, it was the only practical method of choosing a responsible electorate that included African American men. Although he introduced the bill, Stevens disliked it because it would not create a dominant North Carolina Republican Political Machine. Stevens only introduced the bill because he thought it would "gain time, and allow public sentiment to develop itself in the direction he desired." A reporter for the Philadelphia *Press* would write, on December 18: "The bill reported by [Thad] Stevens, on Thursday last, is the beginning of the inevitable end." By that he meant "the inevitable end" of State Governments empowered exclusively by the votes of European American men. [R97;462-463]

Meanwhile, over in the Senate, Charles Sumner was not through blasting away at Andrew Johnson. Applying obtuse abuse, Sumner continued: "I do not dwell upon his open exposure of himself in a condition of intoxication, while taking the oath of office — nor do I dwell upon the maudlin speeches by which he has degraded the [country] as it was never degraded before — nor do I hearken to any reports of pardons sold, or of personal corruption. He went on, calling Andrew Johnson, "the successor of Jefferson Davis . . . the minister of discord . . . an enormous and malignant usurper, through whom the [country] is imperiled." And Sumner fired a few cannonballs at William Seward as well, who he accused of cooperating with Johnson in the removal of some of his favorite diplomats. In that spirit, Charles Sumner, as Chairman of the Senate Foreign Relations Committee, would consistently reject Andrew Johnson's diplomatic nominees.

Sumner was also in the thick of efforts to contrive a basis for impeaching Andrew Johnson. On December 16 he wrote W. W. Story that, even if Republicans in Congress implemented a Reconstruction program that ensured Republican control of the Governments in the conquered States, we would still "encounter the appointing power of [Andrew Johnson], which would put in office men who sympathize with him. It is this consideration which makes ardent representatives say that he must be removed." Yet Sumner, at this point, avoided taking a public stand favoring Impeachment.

During this time Sumner did his best to promote legislation that would make voters of the African American men living in the capital. Their votes would have little impact on local or national politics, but such legislation would be a start toward building Republican Political Machines in conquered States — "a policy not only strictly for the District of Columbia, but in some sense for the country at large." But Sumner would not be distracted by talk of giving women access to the polls. Voting was only for men. When Democrats sought to confound the voting issue for the District of Columbia by amending the bill to also give women access to the polls, Sumner refused to be distracted from his party-building goal. He responded that giving women access to the polls was "obviously the great question of the future," but he was opposed to letting the bill become "clogged, burdened, or embarrassed" by the inclusion of voting rights for women who lived in the capital.

The Senate was also debating Nebraska Statehood. Here, Sumner fully supported Statehood for Nebraska, but only if the Nebraska Constitutional Convention contributed in spirit to the Republican program for building Republican Political Machines in the conquered States far to the south. There were so few African American men in Nebraska Territory that whether they voted or not was rather unimportant. But the Convention had submitted to Congress a State Constitution which excluded African American men from voting. Sumner resolved to fight the measure every way he could, in spite of the fact that Republicans desperately needed the State of Nebraska for one more vote to Ratify the Federal Amendment to Nationalize Citizenship (14th) and maybe also for Impeachment. During Senate floor debate Ben Wade attempted to push aside Sumner's concern, calling the voting prohibition "a little miserable technicality." But Sumner replied, "Sir, can a question of human rights be a technicality?" Basically Sumner had drawn a firm line across which he refused to step: "No more States with the word '[European race]' in their Constitution." However, Sumner failed to persuade the Senate to reject Statehood for Nebraska, for too many wanted Nebraska voting for the Amendment to Nationalize Citizenship. But he did shore up his principle by winning acceptance of a Proviso offered by George Edmunds, which required Nebraska voters to later amend their State Constitution to make voters of African American men. The Proviso violated the Federal Constitution, but Republican politicians had not felt constrained by that document since 1861. [R73;279-283]

At this point in Thad Stevens' political career, he apparently aspired to be elected to the Federal Senate, in spite of his age, his declining health and the great power he held in the House. A Stevens for Senate campaign was being discussed and, in mid-December Philadelphia newspaperman John Forney, who had withdrawn his name from consideration, endorsed Stevens for the Federal Senate. Encouraged by that new support Stevens traveled back to Chambersburg during the Christmas recess to build support for his election to that august body. Stevens was apparently driven by an insatiable ambition and his next dream was to be known as "Senator Stevens of Pennsylvania." Perhaps Stevens was drawn to Chambersburg because Confederates had burned the town to the ground, and evidence of that action was still abundant. Alexander McClure visited Stevens in his Chambersburg hotel to talk politics. McClure looked at the old and sickly man and wondered how Stevens could live out a 6-year term as Senator. But Stevens "begged McClure to help elect him." McClure countered, "To leave [the House] for the Senate would be to give up the fullest powers, the highest honors, that the country could bestow." Stevens was not convinced; he still desperately wanted to become a Federal Senator before he died. And Forney was pushing Stevens for the Senate job through his newspaper. [R96;263-264]

Meanwhile in South Carolina, Legislature adjourned on December 21, concluding law-making under the 1865 State Constitution, which had retained power for traditional leaders of the State. One of its final deliberations was to vote up or down on the Federal Amendment to Nationalize Citizenship (14th). Governor James Orr had strongly denounced the proposed Amendment. Regarding citizenship issues in sections 1 and 4, he said, in part, it would confer upon the Federal House and Senate "the absolute right of determining who shall be citizens of the respective States." As would be expected he voiced strong opposition to the provision in section 3 that excluded former Confederate officials from holding office. If this Amendment is ratified by sufficient States, "we not only have no guaranties that our people would be admitted" into the House and Senate, "but there are unmistakable indications that they would still be excluded." Better to reject the Amendment, he advised, and preserve our own self-respect and the respect of our posterity by refusing to be the mean instruments of our own shame." Legislators united around that argument: every State Senator voted "no" as did all but one Representative in the State House. [R201;33-34]

As Christmas approached Charles Sumner began grumbling about home life. Until his recent marriage he had been a confirmed bachelor. It was hard for him to adjust at the age of 55. His first complaint dealt with money. Biographer David Donald would conclude: "Used to renting furnished rooms in Washington, he was appalled by the cost of running a household, complete with coachman and nursemaid." Sumner grumbled that his living expenses were "now very different from what they were in other days. On Christmas Eve he complained, "I can for the present pay my debts," but he lamented that there seemed to be no end to the financial drain. What was he to do? His answer to cutting expenses was to stop renting and buy a house instead. That's right, Charles and Alice decided to get out from under their $575 per quarter rent obligation on their furnished house and, instead, buy a brand-new $30,000 dream-house that was under construction. The dream-house faced across Lafayette Square toward the White House. The cost of the dream-house was 10 times Sumner's annual salary as a Senator, but, at least he had the inheritance to pay the purchase price. Anyway, Charles expected to earn additional money by delivering an extensive lecture series during the summer months. It would be the first moonlighting work that Sumner would undertake since he first became a Senator. [R73;289]

It is now Christmas, 1866. Jeff, Varina and the baby spent Christmas in their four-room apartment in Fortress Monroe. Biographer Hudson Strode would write: "On this Christmas of 1866 when he looked out of door or window it was not through iron bars. No lamp burned at night. He was not waked every two hours by the changing of the guards. But he was still a prisoner whom his accusers would not bring to trial." I do not know if Wade Hampton spent Christmas in Columbia or with his family at his Mississippi farm, but, whichever, the season was saddened by the death 13 days earlier of his devoted sister Mary Fisher Hampton, age 33 years. You will recall that Mary Fisher had never married and had been very devoted to Wade. "According to family tradition she came down with fever while nursing the aged Mauma Nelly, who had been a devoted and beloved African American servant to the Hampton family." [R19;302, R199;184]

The Year of 1867

(1Q67)

Notable events were also taking place in Canada. Early in 1867, Great Britain consolidated the British colonies in North America into the Dominion of Canada. The new Canadian Federal Government would come into being on July 1 of the same year. In part, this was a defensive move, for Britain had every reason to fear a Federal invasion of her British colonies. So, as a defensive measure, she lumped the colonies, including French-speaking Quebec, into one Commonwealth. This consolidation to the north of the United States boundary American infuriated politicians from the northeastern States, such as those in Massachusetts, including politicians across the Great Lakes region and out to the Pacific Northwest region. Many of these politicians had long held bold ambitions to invade the vast land to the north and organize it into new States under the Federal Government. Potential incidents, contrived if necessary, useful to inciting an invasion included — a claim against Great Britain for compensation for vessels and cargoes lost to Confederate raiders, such as the highly successful C. S. S. Alabama — a dispute over the ownership of San Juan Island in the Pacific Northwest — an excuse involving the Fenian raids into Canada — and there was related violence from others who were traveling back to Ireland to attack British rule there — a dispute over tariffs and enforcement of tariffs over the long boundary. Then there would be the ever-handy struggle over fishing rights off the lucrative Canadian North Atlantic coastline. Certainly war was something to be feared. [R73;361]

Meanwhile in Kentucky, the State Legislature convened, eager to voice its concerns about the Federal Amendment to Nationalize Citizenship (14th). The Legislature "promptly rejected the Amendment," and almost unanimously approved a resolution asserting that Kentuckians were "unalterably opposed to [African American] suffrage, whether unlimited or special, general or qualified." Then the Legislature turned to electing a Federal Senator to fill the seat being held by Garret Davis, who had been elected in 1861 to fill the remaining term of John Breckinridge, who, you will recall, had resigned to give his all to the defense of the Confederacy. Garret Davis — formerly a Whig, then, in 1860, a supporter in the Constitutional Union Party and John Bell — had begun his Senate career as firmly opposed to Kentucky secession, but had moderated considerably to become very critical of the Republican Party. At this time in our history, January 1867, Kentucky Democrats and Conservatives joined forces to reelect Garret Davis to the Federal Senate by a vote of 78 to 41, giving further evidence that Kentucky would be ruled by former Confederates and their friends for the foreseeable future. [R180;316-317]

On January 3, Thad Stevens introduced his personal substitute bill to Reconstruct the Governments of the conquered States. The Joint House-Senate Committee on Reconstruction had submitted its bill to the House floor earlier, but not liking the Committee's wording, Stevens was submitting his substitute bill, which would regulate 10 conquered States, Tennessee being excluded. In those States, Stevens' bill stipulated that most European American men would be excluded from voting — any man who had been at least 21 years old when Abe Lincoln became President was excluded if he had held a Confederate local, State or Federal governmental office, served in the Confederate Army or Navy, or had for any other reason sworn allegiance to the Confederate Government. African Americans living in the conquered States were to be considered as having never supported the Confederacy, although many had. Therefore, Stevens' bill would facilitate Republican Political Machines empowered by the votes of African American men and he persuaded the House to accept his substitute over the bill submitted by the Committee, of which he was Co-Chairman.

Meanwhile, Charles Sumner and like-minded Republicans were intensifying their propaganda campaign against Andrew Johnson's program for remaking the Governments in the conquered States. They denounced news from the conquered States reporting that several remade Legislatures had voted against Ratifying the Federal Constitutional Amendment to Nationalize Citizenship (14th). Sumner charged that refusal to Ratify the Amendment was proof that Andrew Johnson had failed in his program for remaking those State Governments. Sumner and like-minded Republicans strongly denounced the Supreme Court ruling in the Milligan case. They trumpeted reports of violence, claiming them to be proof that stronger Federal military control was needed to prevent former Confederates from terrorizing or attacking people who came down from the northern States. These and similar events were moving Republicans like William Fessenden and James Grimes to align with Sumner in opposition to Andrew Johnson's programs. Gideon Welles said, "At a deadlock, unable to go forward and not manly enough to retreat," Republicans like Fessenden and Grimes have "no alternative . . . but to follow Sumner."

Meanwhile in January 7, Thad Stevens left Washington City with newspaperman John Forney and traveled to Harrisburg to campaign for Federal Senator from Pennsylvania. Republicans in the State Legislature would soon meet in caucus and select their candidate. Soon after arriving, Stevens discovered that Forney's support was inadequate. Of the many politicians who owed Stevens reciprocal political favors, most seemed inclined to dodge the obligation. F. S. Stambaugh is a good example. Through the votes of employees at Caledonia Ironworks, Stevens had gotten Stambaugh elected to the State Legislature, but he was refusing to, in turn, support Stevens for Federal Senator. "You must be a bastard!" Stevens cursed at Stambaugh upon learning of his defection. "I knew your father, and he was a gentleman and an honest man." Stevens denounced the Republican Legislators from his own Lancaster County who were refusing support him. The top candidates for the upcoming Senate job were Simon Cameron, Andrew Curtin and Thad Stevens. Stevens attempted to persuaded Curtin to join him in rebuffing the Legislators and going "to the people" with an appeal for support, but Curtin declined. Nevertheless, Stevens publicly announced that he refused to become obligated to politicians who became involved in the "hidden intrigues" that prevailed in a "secret caucus." But the people did not rally to an independent bid. Republican Legislators proceeded to hold their caucus. The caucus vote was taken: Cameron, 46; Curtin, 23 votes, and Stevens only 7 votes. Stevens was badly beating!

He was an unwell and old man, obviously poorly suited for a new 6-year job. Furthermore, from his powerful position in the Federal House, State Republicans were depending on Stevens existing political power to ensure that their Party would dominate the Federal Government for generations yet unborn. That was clearly Thad Stevens' job, and he had best stick to it.

On January 16 the House debated with intensity Thad Stevens' substitute bill to Reconstruct the Governments in the conquered States. Some amendments were attacked by less Militant Republicans and they succeeded in referring the bill back to the Joint House-Senate Committee on Reconstruction. Stevens would be back at his job as Co-Chairman attempting to persuade fellow members of the Joint Committee that his was the best Reconstruction program.

By mid-January Charles Sumner was taking pride in the changed position of many of the Republicans who had previously rejected his demand that the Federal Government force northern States to permit voting by African American men. Many were in agreement that, as new States, both Nebraska and Colorado must permit voting by African American men. So he was becoming more confident that Republicans in the Senate and the House would move forward with legislation designed to overthrow the remade "sham" Governments in the conquered States, "so that we can begin again and build on the [people who will be loyal to the Republican Party]. . . . "Congress is doing pretty well," Sumner enthused. "Every step is forward."

While the members of the Joint House-Senate Committee on Reconstruction deliberated on the mechanics for destroying the existing remade Governments in the conquered States, Charles Sumner was waging a propaganda war. Although he had not been invited to be a member of this Committee, he was the funnel through which the fledgling Republican Political Machines — now emerging in the conquered States — delivered their propaganda to the Senate and sympathetic newspapermen. He passed on to fellow Senators stories that African Americans in the conquered States were constant victims of "terrorism and extortion," that rebellion against Federal control was "fiercer and more intolerant than it was at the middle of 1861." At the same time, Sumner was launching direct attacks against the remade State Governments and individuals in those States. He attempted to put through legislation that would have directly destroyed the existing remade State Governments, but he failed to get enough votes. On another occasion he urged exclusion of all former Confederates from the new protections against creditors that were being established in the bankruptcy bill being debated on the Senate floor. Another day he was demanding that all court cases in the conquered States that involved any African American, whether civil or criminal, be moved from the State court to the Federal court.

On the other hand, Charles Sumner seemed to be arriving at his Senate seat looking rather tired. With Washington in the midst of its social season, Alice did not want to turn down any invitations to party. Alice was rather "high-strung and quick-tempered," and prone to tease Charles rather harshly in an apparent effort to break through his serious temperament, to evoke a bit of humor. But on occasion Alice could be downright cruel — like the time she "lashed out in the carriage as they left for their honeymoon." About the time of their wedding, one of Alice's long-time friends had been heard to say, "I should like to see Sumner the first time Alice says to him — 'Go to hell; God damn you – it is none of your business'." But Charles seemed to be too idealistic in his interaction with his wife to realize how seriously his marriage was troubled, even during its first few weeks. Another example: Alice apparently rather detested the father of her deceased first husband, Representative Samuel Hooper, but Charles insisted on having his friend Hooper over for dinner once a week. Trying to get through Charles' insensitivity, Alice ranted on about how she "would not have [Hooper] near her, that he was stupid and a nuisance." [R73;283-285,290-291, R96;266-267, R97;464]

On February 6 Thad Stevens reported to the floor of the House his revised bill from the Joint House-Senate Committee on Reconstruction — he had succeeded in persuading a majority of the Committee to adopt his program for subjugating the conquered States through Military Rule. Only Tennessee was exempted. The House "entered, without delay, upon a debate on this bill, which lasted for several days." Thad Stevens' new Military Rule bill would divide the conquered region into 5 Military Districts, each of which was to be ruled by a Federal Army General through designated subordinates. Federal Military Rule would be the supreme law, superior to local and State law in all situations. The existing remade State Governments would be declared invalid and without power. By declaring invalid all remade Governments in the conquered States, Stevens' Military Rule bill was consistent with a separate bill to Reconstruct the State Government in Louisiana, which was proceeding through the House on a parallel course.

The following day, Thad Stevens delivered an emotional speech advocating his bill, saying in part:

"For two years [supporters of the Republican Party living in] those 10 [conquered] States have endured all the horrors of the worst anarchy of any country. Persecution, exile, and murder have been the order of the day within all these [States] so far as the [men there who support the Republican Party] were concerned, whether [European American] or [African American], and more especially if they happened to be [African American]. We have seen the best men — those who stood by the [Federal flag], driven from their homes and compelled to live on the cold charity of a cold [northern States people]. We have seen [former Confederates] flitting about everywhere, through your cities, around your doors, melancholy, depressed, haggard, like the ghosts of the unburied dead on this side of the river Styx, and yet we have borne it with exemplary patience. We have been enjoying our 'ease in our inns;' and while we were praising the [the people of the conquered States] and asking in piteous terms for mercy for [them]; we have been deaf to the groans, the agony, the dying groans from dying and murdered victims, which have been borne to us by every [informer from that region]."

Stevens then announced that floor debate was nearing a conclusion, warning, "Tomorrow, God willing, I will demand a vote." The next day, however, Stevens failed to win a vote to close debate. After a further week of debate an amendment would be submitted to Stevens' bill, which would Reconstruct State Governments in the conquered States while allowing most former Confederates to be qualified voters. Stevens would fight with all his resources to defeat this amendment. He was losing ground.

The Federal House briefly turned its attention to Reconstructing the Government of conquered Louisiana, in response to a bill introduced to the floor by Thomas Eliot of Massachusetts. After Republican politicians had incited the July 30, 1866 riot in New Orleans, Eliot had moved to establish a House Investigating Committee to gather information on the political situation in Louisiana. That Committee had completed the desired job of gathering incriminating allegations against the European American population in that State, and Eliot had used those allegations to justify the voting scheme dictated by his bill: the bill would deny voting rights to about 95% of the European American men living in Louisiana. With only 5% of the European American men eligible to vote and 100% of African American men eligible to vote, Republicans figured their Republican Political Machine would control the Louisiana State Government and its Federal Representatives and Senators for generations yet unborn. Eliot's bill to Reconstruct the Louisiana State Government was introduced into the House on February 11 and it passed the following day.

That same day an amendment to Thad Stevens' Military Rule Bill was introduced in the House, drafted by Representative John Bingham and Senator James Blaine, stating that Federal Military Rule over a conquered State, as proposed by Stevens' bill, would end and its Government would be recognized as legitimate, once the people of that State, 1), voted to give voting rights to all adult men, with only a few exceptions, 2), adopted a new State Constitution giving all adult men the right to vote, and, 3), Ratified the Federal Amendment to Nationalize Citizenship. Thad Stevens strongly objected to this amendment because, until three-fourths of the States Ratified the Amendment to Nationalize Citizenship, many leading former Confederates would be permitted to participate in political activities.

Recognizing that Republicans would have difficulty winning elections in the conquered States if most of the European American men were permitted to vote, Stevens mounted an intense attack upon the amendment to his Reconstruction bill. On February 13 he reminded fellow Representatives that amending the bill would encourage "universal [acceptance of citizenship for former Confederate leaders] and universal Andrew Johnsonism [and] it lets [into the polls] a vast number of [former Confederates] and shuts out [of the polls] nobody." He accused Republicans who favored the amendment of "hugging and caressing" former Confederates, whose hands and clothes were dripping "with the blood of [dead and wounded Federal soldiers and sailors] and [dead Confederate soldiers and sailors, not killed in battle, but <u>murdered</u> by the actions of their leaders]." Stevens argued that no proposal should pass if it did not ensure, without a doubt, that Republican Political Machines would thrive and be totally dominant in the conquered region. So he demanded that his bill be voted upon prior to considering the Bingham-Blaine amendment. His demand was sustained. A vote was taken.

Stevens' Reconstruction bill was approved, without amendment, by a vote of 109 to 55. The vote was not even close. After the Speaker announced the tally, Stevens crowed this somewhat religious but certainly not Christian flourish: "I wish to enquire, Mr. Speaker, if it is in order for me now to say that we endorse the language of good old Laertes that Heaven rules as yet and there are gods above?" That day Thad Stevens' bill to Subjugate the Conquered States through Military Rule proceeded to the Senate. [R96;271-272, R97;464-465]

The Republican movement to Subjugate the Conquered States through Military Rule greatly distressed Jeff Davis, Varina and their friends and relatives. Mary Brodhead, Jeff's niece, who had married a Federal Representative from Pennsylvania and settled in his state, wrote Jeff on February 10, telling how Thad Stevens had been trying to get through Congress "a monstrous bill to bring more disaster on the [conquered States]." Mary added that she had appealed to Governor Bigler and Simon Cameron to help defeat the measures. "Every one I met of our friends seems very desponding, fear every kind of trouble — businesses of all kinds seem prostrate and then this mad Congress, no one can tell what will be the result." Seven days later, Varina wrote Mary Stamps, lamenting that, "The newspapers turn me sick with terror." And she added:

> "We suppose from all we can gather that the [conquered] States were last night, Saturday, under martial law, restored to the condition of [Federal] Territories and civil law abrogated. . . . The night will be long and dark for this generation, and for how many others? Plunder will destroy the land, and life sighed out in military prisons by more suffering, for by the provisions of this new bill the [Federal] Military commanders over the Districts have the power to condemn and execute by Court Martials." [R19;303]

Shortly after winning passage in the House of his Military Rule Bill, Thad Stevens received lucrative news from a political supporter in the Pennsylvania Legislature — life was good. That legislative body had voted to route a new railroad near Stevens' Caledonia Ironworks property. "I think the bill quite liberal, indeed, so much so, that we can almost [route the railroad wherever] we wish. D. V. Ahl will doubtless see you [before] this [letter] reaches you and will ask you whether we need any [legislative] supplements or anything further [of a legislative nature] . . . It is a great pleasure for me to do anything that may directly or indirectly interest or serve you." [R96;272-273]

During February France withdrew the last French troops from Mexico, and Maximilian's control of the Mexican Government began to crumble. The diplomatic efforts of Charles Sumner and William Seward had contributed to Maximilian's demise. Sumner had been opposed to sending Federal troops to Mexico to topple the French-backed puppet Government headed up by Maximilian, because he believed time and diplomacy could achieve the same result, and he wanted to focus the power of the Federal Government on Reconstructing society in the conquered States. Biographer David Donald would write: "Any foreign embroilment, Sumner recognized, might turn the Republican Party 'away from guarding the poor [newly independent African American man],' and lead to the immediate readmission of the [conquered States]." Sumner had figured, correctly it was turning out, "that Maximilian's throne will fall without any thing from us." But, applying the bluff, Sumner had purposefully deceived the French Minister on several occasions into believing that the House of Representatives might lose patience any day and authorize an invasion of Mexico to oust Maximilian. During September, 1866, Sumner realized that he was succeeding with his combination of behind-the-scenes diplomatic threats and restraint within his Senate Foreign Relations Committee. It was because of Sumner's efforts that the French Minister assured him there would be "substantial withdrawal of French troops from Mexico before next winter." And, during February of that winter, the last French troops did leave. All were gone. Sumner need no longer be concerned that Reconstruction of the Governments in the conquered States might be slowed by a military crisis in Mexico. [R73;354-358]

But, with Sumner, success seemed to be often entangled with failure. By mid-February, Charles and Alice were having serious marital difficulties. And members of Washington's social set were gossiping about how Alice was seeing so much of Friedrich von Holstein, a titled attaché of the Prussian Embassy. Soon after arriving in Washington in December, von Holstein had called on Charles Sumner in his capacity as head of the Senate Foreign Relations Committee. And Alice had taken a liking to the Prussian soon thereafter. When Alice wanted to spend time with the diplomatic set and other society people her age, more and more she would ask Friedrich to accompany her. [R73;291]

Two bills designed to Reconstruct the Governments of the conquered States arrived at the Senate on the same day, February 13. Thad Stevens' bill to Subjugate the Conquered States through Military Rule delighted Charles Sumner. However, Thomas Eliot's bill to Reconstruct the existing Louisiana State Government — qualifying as voters only about 5% of the men of European ancestry, while establishing a Republican Political Machine to control the votes of all African American men — delighted him even more. Sumner thought Stevens' bill faulty because it did not condemn the existing Governments in the conquered States, which he called "sham governments." Such laxity in the application of suitable language convinced Sumner that Stevens' bill was "thoroughly vicious in every line and in every word from the first to the last." On the other hand, many Senate Republicans preferred Stevens' military rule approach, and voted to set aside for a while Eliot's Reconstruction of the Government of Louisiana. But Stevens' bill encountered immediate opposition from Sumner and like-minded Republicans who wanted to skip Military Rule and proceed immediately with establishing Governments for the conquered States that would be, with certainty, dominated by Republican Political Machines. These men wanted Louisiana to set the legal pattern for establishing a dominant Republican Political Machines in each conquered State. So Sumner fought for delay, hoping to prevent any measure from passing until the next Senate session. He hoped to then push through legislation that would disallow voting by almost all European American men, thereby guaranteeing successful Republican Party Political Machines empowered by the votes of African American men.

During a February 17 caucus of Republicans, Charles Sumner was selected as one of the 7 members of a Caucus Study Committee to recommend amendments to Thad Stevens' Military Rule bill. John Sherman, of Ohio was the Chairman of the Study Committee. John was also the brother of William Sherman, who, you will recall, had commanded the Federal Horde of Devastators that had burned Atlanta and then laid waste to so much of Georgia and South Carolina during the latter days of the Federal Invasion of the Confederacy. Of his attitude at this time John Sherman would later write:

> "I heartily joined with my political associates in the measures adopted to secure a [Republican dominated] reorganization of the [conquered States]. I was largely influenced by the [allegedly] harsh treatment of [African American men] in [those States] under acts adopted by the [remade State] Legislatures. The [alleged] outrages of the Ku-Klux Klans seemed to me to be so atrocious and wicked that the men who committed them were not only unworthy to govern, but unfit to live."

During the Caucus Study Committee's subsequent meeting later in the day, Sumner persuaded the other 6 to accept his position that there had to be an amendment to Stevens' Military Rule bill that declared the existing remade State Governments invalid. But he was having great difficulty moving a majority of the Committee away from the notion that, if each of those invalid Governments, or their respective successors, only approved the Federal Amendment to Nationalize Citizenship (14th), then each should be declared valid. That Amendment, most members of the Committee believed, would be sufficient to empower dominant Republican Political Machines. But Sumner warned that the Amendment would not become law until three-fourths of the States Ratified it, and Republicans wanted to count among the States asked to Ratify, those that were now conquered and subjugated political entities, making the math difficult and the legality of the political process questionable. In the meantime, prior to the Amendment becoming law, Sumner feared that former Confederates would exercise too much political power. Sumner sought a new, expansive rewriting of the remade State Constitutions, and the accompanying delay such procedures would invariably cause. He insisted that after the remade Governments in the conquered States approved the Amendment to Nationalize Citizenship they would have to give the vote to all adult African American men, elect Delegates to a new Constitutional Convention, and there write a new State Constitution. Only then could, the people elect a Governor and a Legislature and be approved by Congress as valid Reconstructed State Governments.

John Sherman presented his Study Committee's majority report to the reconvened Republican Caucus that evening, and afterward, Charles Sumner presented his opposing views in a minority report. Sherman's report was not an amendment to Thad Stevens' Military Rule bill; it was a substitute for it, for, although it also established Federal Military Rule, it emphasized Reconstructing Governments in the conquered States in such a way that Republican Political Machines would be certain to dominate. Oversight of Federal Military Rule would be given to Andrew Johnson, and conditions for terminating Military subjugation were written into the bill — both concepts that Sumner passionately disliked. In his minority report Sumner demanded that each conquered State had to give the vote to all African

American men, elect new Delegates to a State Constitutional Convention, rewrite its Constitution, and then elect its Legislature and Governor. Sumner figured that process would give the Republican Party the additional time it needed to strengthen and test its vital Political Machines to ensure they would be dominant. Sumner assured fellow Republican Senators that, "It was in our power to decide this question and to supersede its discussion in the [conquered States]." The Republican Senators apparently listened carefully to Sumner's political logic. They recognized that the drawn-out process he wanted was vastly more suitable for building solid Republican Political Machines. Why? Because it would take time to organize African American men and set up those Machines. The election of Delegates to the State Constitutional Conventions would test the Machines' effectiveness; and the election of Republican Governors and Legislators would be the big payoff. Soon after Sumner finished presenting his argument, the Caucus took two stand-up votes. By a majority of two votes, the Republican Caucus endorsed Sumner's plan for Reconstructing the Governments in the conquered States. Elated, Sumner called that vote "a prodigious triumph" — a statement no future historian would question.

Anticipating ample time would be available to build Republican Political Machines, Charles Sumner turned to facilitating the process by increasing Republican interaction with African American men in the conquered States. He wanted more "machinery" in John Sherman's bill to facilitate the Reconstruction of the Governments. He wanted Federals to establish schools for African American men and he wanted much of the land in the conquered States to be confiscated and handed over to African American men. With such interaction and gift-giving, he figured that the Republican Political Machines would dominate the region for generations. He complained that Sherman's bill was yet "horribly defective" for it was "[Reconstructing Governments in the conquered States] without machinery or motive power." Sumner wasn't stupid. He knew that a Republican Political Machine needed "machinery and motive power."

About three o'clock on February 17 Charles Sumner awakened Thad Stevens, asleep at his home, in a state of great anger and excitement. Sumner had just come from the Senate, where John Sherman had introduced the above-mentioned substitute to Stevens' Military Rule bill without sufficient "machinery." And he urged Stevens to contrive a plan for defeating the Sherman substitute bill if it passed the Senate and returned to the House. That day Stevens prepared his plans to filibuster the Sherman substitute bill for the next two weeks to push the legislation into the next session of the House and Senate, for the expected the new membership would be more in favor of what he and Sumner wanted to do.

The Senate debated John Sherman's substitute for Thad Stevens' Military Rule bill all day and on into the night. Charles Sumner did not doze in his Senate seat until 6:22 the next morning (February 18), to be present when the final vote was taken. He left the Senate early because he was disappointed that the bill did not contain more "machinery" and "motive power." Anyway there were ample votes for passage of the substitute bill, so he thought it unnecessary to "remain till morning to swell the large and ascertained majority." The substitute bill passed the Senate by a vote of 29 to 10. But Sumner's real reason for skipping the vote was more defiance than need of sleep. At the next Senate session he would defiantly declare: "I did not vote for the Act as it passed the Senate."

Two weeks remained in the current session when John Sherman's substitute for Thad Stevens' Military Rule bill arrived back at the House. Having agreed with Charles Sumner, Stevens set out immediately, on February 18, to lead a filibuster of the Sherman substitute with the aim of postponing a vote until the next session of the House and Senate, both of which would contain many new members. Seeking support for delay among Democrat Representatives, Stevens alleged that, in the next session, he would obtain passage of a bill they would find preferable to the Sherman substitute. Urging delay on the House floor, Stevens explained that, unlike Sherman's bill, his bill had only proposed a "police regulation" of the conquered States because of the "anarchy and oppression" that was allegedly prevalent in the region. Stevens explained that establishing the rules for Reconstructing the Governments of the conquered States had to wait until after the Federal Government had instituted a program of confiscation of the farms, homes and businesses of former Confederates:

> "As far as I can ascertain, more than $2,000,000,000 of property belonging to the [Federal Government], confiscated not as [secessionist's property] but as enemy's property, has been given

back to enrich [former Confederates]. [The people in the Confederate States who, during the fighting, sided with the Federals, and] whose houses have been laid in ashes, whose farms have been robbed, whose cattle have been taken from them, are to suffer poverty and persecution, while Wade Hampton and his black horse cavalry are to revel in their wealth and [former Confederates] along the Mississippi Valley are to enjoy their [large homes]. Sir, God helping me and I live, there shall be a question propounded to this House and to this [country] whether a portion of the debt [issued to finance the Federal invasion of the Confederacy] shall not be paid [to the Federal Government] by [the sell of] confiscated property [belonging to former Confederates]."

Stevens' filibuster did not consume the two weeks remaining in the session. By the second day he obtained a vote in the House to refuse to concur with the Sherman substitute bill. So the bill was returned to the Senate with a demand that the Senate rework the bill.

Charles Sumner was rather pleased to learn that the House had refused to concur with the Sherman substitute bill. After short debate, the Senate voted to make no changes to the Sherman substitute. Again the Senate leadership refused to name a House-Senate Conference Committee to negotiate differences in the two bills, which disappointed Sumner, who was hoping that, in Conference, the House bill would prevail.

At this point Thad Stevens apparently decided against another filibuster. Instead, two important amendments were added by the House to the Sherman substitute bill. One amendment stipulated that until each Government in a conquered State was accepted by the Federal House and Senate, its State and local governments were to be purely provisional. The other amendment stipulated that no man excluded from office by the Amendment to Nationalize Citizenship "shall be permitted to take part in the [Reconstruction] of the [conquered] States." With these important amendments added to the Sherman substitute, "Stevens gave up the struggle and let it go through." Accordingly, the House voted to accept the amended Sherman substitute bill, sending it back to the Senate. Stevens hoped "he could undo [the bill] in the next Congress."

When the House-amended bill was brought to the Senate floor, Sumner voted in favor, as did all other Republican Senators and one Democrat. The tally was overwhelming: 35 yeas versus 7 nays.

Andrew Johnson vetoed the bill.

On March 2 Thad Stevens and the House voted to override the veto. The same day the Senate voted to also override, with Charles Sumner voting with the majority. So on March 2, 1866, the Federal Act to Reconstruct the conquered States through Military Rule became law.

In its final form the Act began with the following preamble. The word "loyal" in the following sentence was to be interpreted by Federal officials as "supportive of the Republican Party."

"Whereas, no legal State Governments or adequate protection for life or property now exists in the [conquered] States of Virginia, North Carolina, South Carolina, Georgia, Mississippi, Alabama, Louisiana, Florida, Texas and Arkansas; and whereas it is necessary that peace and good order should be enforced in said States until loyal and republican State Governments can be legally established:"

The first four sections of the bill were primarily drafted by Thad Stevens. They dealt with the subjugation under Federal Military Rule of all conquered States except Tennessee.

The fifth section was primarily drafted by John Sherman of the Senate and eventually amended by the House. It required that any valid Government in a conquered State must be established by the votes of only men who did not support the defense of the Confederacy against the Federal Invasion. Thus the law excluded all former Confederate soldiers, sailors, government employees, munitions plant workers, taxpayers, and so forth. In electing Delegates to the Reconstructed State Constitutional Convention, the Act disallowed voting by almost every European American man living in the State and encouraged voting by all African American men, who, although many had helped defend the Confederacy, would not be challenged by Republican voter registration workers. Every subjugated Government had to submit its new State Constitution to the Federal House and Senate for approval or disapproval. To be approved, a Reconstructed State Government had to ratify the Amendment to Nationalize Citizenship (14th). The Act specifically prohibited a State from escaping Military Rule before the Amendment was

Ratified by three-fourths of the States (including those in the conquered region). Furthermore, no man who had supported the Confederacy could hold any office in any provisional State or local Government.

The sixth section made absolutely clear that the Federal Government would be in complete control, through Military Rule, of even the least local governmental issue:

> "And be it further enacted, that, until the people of [conquered States] shall be by [Federal] law admitted to representation in the [Federal] Congress, any civil Governments which may exist therein shall be deemed provisional only, and in all respects subject to the paramount authority of the [Federal Government] at any time to abolish, modify, control, or supersede the same; and in all elections to any Office under such provisional Governments [the right to vote and acquisition of any government office shall be restricted to only men who did not support any Confederate State or local government or the Confederate military defensive effort]."

As it finally passed, a hard-to-please, Charles Sumner was not happy with the Act to Reconstruct the Conquered States through Military Rule. He worried that the "law was a very hasty and crude act of legislation," and thought it came "short of what a patriotic Congress ought to supply for the safety of the [country]." There was good reason for Sumner and Stevens to be disappointed: Republicans had not yet confiscated 85% of the farms, homes and enterprises in the conquered States — and that was where the big money was to be made. [R73;286-291, R93;315-317, R96;273-274, R97;467]

Just before adjournment, on March 3, the House overrode Andrew Johnson's veto, making the Tenure of Office Act Federal law. This Act was a trap intended to facilitate the Impeachment of the President. The Act restricted the powers normally held by the President by requiring that certain men could not be removed from office without the approval of the Senate. The intent was to use the Act to prevent Andrew Johnson from removing Edwin Stanton as Secretary of War, or, if he attempted to do so, to use that event as legal grounds for Impeachment.

March 1867 Through February 1868 — Political Reconstruction During the Third Year of the Andrew Johnson Administration

(1Q67)

Declining to wait until the first Monday in December to begin, the newly-elected House and Senate assembled 9 months earlier, on March 4, 1867 to open their first session at the earliest possible moment. Republican Representatives and Senators were obviously determined to immediately convene the new House and Senate to ensure that they — not Andrew Johnson — controlled the Reconstruction of the Governments of the conquered States through Federal Military Rule. This was a dramatic departure from tradition, because the two houses of Congress had previously always deferred assembling until early December. The first order of business was to expand the just-enacted law to Subjugate the Conquered States through Military Rule. To that end Republican leaders drafted a supplemental bill that directed the 5 Military Dictators to create and oversee new voter registration organizations charged with evaluating and registering as voters all men whom they judged to be qualified. All previous voter rolls were to be voided, as everyone would have to register anew through the new military-controlled voter registration organizations. The supplemental bill contained other organization directives as well, all aimed at ensuring that Republican Political Machines were rapidly and efficiently constructed in the ten conquered States (Andrew Johnson's Tennessee omitted). Both the House and the Senate would pass the supplemental bill. Andrew Johnson would veto the bill. Then both the House and the Senate would vote to override the veto. It would become law on March 23, 1867.

A few days before the House passed the supplemental bill, Thad Stevens had attempted to deliver a speech he had written some weeks earlier in which he again advocated Federal confiscation of the vast majority of farms, homes and enterprises in the conquered States. He had previously arranged for the entire speech to be set in type at the Washington *Chronicle*. But Stevens was too ill to read his speech for very long. After reading only the beginning he handed the speech to the House Clerk, Edward McPherson, who read the remainder in its entirety. Stevens and many other Republicans were eager to get on with the big-money business of confiscating farmland.

Andrew Johnson obediently proceeded to carry out the new law to Subjugate the Conquered States through Federal Military Rule.

To the First Military District, which contained the State of Virginia, he appointed General John Schofield (born in New York; trained at West Point; commanded under Nathaniel Lyon in Missouri; then under William Sherman at Atlanta, then under George Thomas in Tennessee).

To the Second Military District, which contained the States of North Carolina and South Carolina, he appointed General Daniel Sickles (born in New York; worked as lawyer and politician in New York; commanded troops in conquest of Virginia).

To the Third Military District, which contained the States of Alabama, Florida and Georgia, he appointed General John Pope (born in Kentucky; raised in Illinois; trained at West Point; fought in Mexico under Zachary Taylor; commanded under John Fremont in Missouri and under Henry Halleck in Mississippi, then defeated by Robert Lee at Second Battle of Manassas).

To the Fourth Military District, which contained the States of Arkansas and Mississippi, he appointed General Edward Ord (born in western Maryland; trained at West Point; fought in Florida against Seminole Nation; served in California and Pacific Northwest, then commanded under Ulysses Grant in the Mississippi Valley, at Vicksburg and finally in Virginia).

To the Fifth Military District, which contained the States of Louisiana and Texas, he appointed General Philip Sheridan (born in New York; raised in Ohio; trained at West Point; served in California and Pacific Northwest; commanded troops under Henry Halleck in Missouri and Mississippi Valley; moved to cavalry; commanded cavalry in Tennessee and Virginia).

Before long these military dictators would be removing Governors, judges and other officials of State and local governments wherever they found it expedient. Under Republican Military Rule, 4 of the 10 Governors would be removed: Governor James Throckmorton would be removed in Texas, Governor

James Wells would be removed in Louisiana, Governor Charles Jenkins would be removed in Georgia, and Governor Benjamin Humphreys would be removed in Mississippi.

Meanwhile, Charles Sumner, obviously embarrassed over Alice's public display of their marital fight, projected an even more autocratic, "I told you so," patronizing image, particularly toward newer members of the Senate. He repeated bragged that he had always been ahead of others in advocating new policies concerning the Confederates, in both war and in Reconstruction. He claimed to have been: right in enforcing Abolition in occupied regions within the Confederacy to speed the completion of her conquest; right in charging Andrew Johnson of collaborating with the Confederate Government; right in denouncing the notion that the Republican Party could remain dominant by merely passing a Constitutional Amendment that forced States to accept the votes of African American men, and right in calling totally inadequate the most recent Congressional plan for Reconstructing the Governments of the conquered States.

However, William Fessenden, John Sherman, and Lyman Trumbull saw to it that "I-told-you-so" Sumner was excluded from committee work on drafting legislation concerning Reconstruction. So Sumner would have to wait for drafted bills to be submitted to the Senate floor. Then he would blast forth charging, "We shall regret hereafter that we have not done more." But being excluded from the Senate Committees did not prevent Sumner from drafting his own bill and an accompanying set of resolutions for Reconstructing the Governments of the conquered States and confiscating most of the farmland. And Sumner introduced his bill to accomplish that on March 6, just two days after the Special Session had begun. In each conquered State, Sumner's bill required:

> The appointment of a new Military Governor; the appointment of a Legislative Council that consisted of "13 of the most fit and discreet persons of the state," each having proved he had been completely loyal to the Federal Government throughout the period beginning with secession and ending in conquest, and each pledging to "resist all laws making any distinction of [racial origin];" establishment of taxpayer-funded public schools which "were open to all;" establishment of political machinery to individually qualify as voters all male citizens of voting age and individually disqualify all male citizens who had supported the Confederacy as military leaders, as politicians, as authors, as publishers, as editors, as tax-payers, as speakers, or as preachers; provide Federal oversight of the election of Delegates to each new State Constitutional Convention by the newly registered voter groups; provide Federal oversight to the drafting of each new State Constitution, ensuring that each included language declaring that "all persons shall be equal before the law;" and provide Federal oversight of the Ratification of each State Constitution by the new voter bases.

After Sumner's proposed program was consummated in a conquered State, and after Congress voted that the citizens of that State "are loyal and well disposed toward the [Federal Government]," then Congress would be right in admitting their seating the Representatives and Senators. Of course, what Sumner meant by "loyal and well disposed toward the [Federal Government]," was "loyal and well disposed toward the Republican Party." Republicans had, for years, applied the word "loyal" to identify only the people who supported their Party — those opposing the Republican Party were "disloyal" and spoken of as "traitors" and "copperhead snakes."

Sumner attached a series of resolutions to his bill, for he also wanted a social revolution in those conquered States, which would elevate the African American man to an equal or higher economic level than his European American neighbors. One resolution demanded that the Federal Government see to it that homesteads "be secured to the [newly independent African American man], so that at least every head of a family may have a piece of land." Sumner's resolution regretted that already "the [larger farms] of the [conquered States had not] been [confiscated and] divided and subdivided among the [African American] population." To launch his wealth-redistribution program, Sumner resolved to confiscate most of the property from "every [owner of land] who had [supported the defense of the Confederacy]." That confiscated land, the Federal Government "should convey to the [newly independent African American men]" who had lived and worked on that land before confiscation. Like Thad Stevens, Sumner was convinced that the Republican Party could not successfully Reconstruct the conquered States "unless in some way we secured to the [newly independent African American man] a piece of land." But Sumner did not talk openly about the main reason he and like-minded Republicans wanted to confiscate enough farmland for hundreds of thousands of 40-acre subsistence farms and settle an African American family on each little farm. Each family thus settled was one family that did not migrate north to farms and to cities like Boston, Philadelphia, Buffalo and Chicago. Republican Exclusion passions, the passion that had primarily created and built the Party in 1854 through 1860, required that their political leaders make every effort to keep African Americans down on the farm — by that they meant "way down South on the farm."

Charles Sumner received little support for his personal bill for Reconstructing the conquered States. First, he was opposing the Republican leadership. Second, many Senators opposed such revolutionary Federal interference in State Governments, and feared the momentum might later effect their own States. Those less determined to ensure the success of Republican Political Machines in the conquered States were opposed to denying the vote to so many citizens of those states. Some worried about Sumner's language: "all persons shall be equal before the law." Would that mean that States like Illinois and New York would have to remove their African American legal exclusions. What about the restrictions California placed on Chinese? What about the restrictions placed nearly everywhere on Native Americans? Concerned that teachers might be forced to educate European American and African American children in the same classrooms, a Senator asked Sumner if his bill meant "that each and every school shall be open to children of both races?" Based on Sumner's acquaintance with Massachusetts schools, where the ancestry of African American children was about half African and half European, and where they represented a small minority in most classes, Sumner had long advocated integrated classes. But in answering the question, he hedged his thinking: "If I should have my way, according to the true principle, it would be that the schools, precisely like the ballot-box or the rail cars, should be open to all. But the proposition is necessarily general in its character; it does not go into details . . . ." It would appear that Sumner hoped to sell his program for requiring schools for all without requiring integrate classes. He apparently figured he could convince Congress to force integrated classrooms later, during the final State admission process. [R73;295-299, R96;275, R97;471-472]

Meanwhile, Jeff Davis remained imprisoned at Fortress Monroe while Varina went to Baltimore in mid-March to confer with lawyers and to appeal to John Garrett for help. Varina had learned that Garrett was sympathetic and that he had as much or more personal influence over Edwin Stanton than any man in the Federation. Garrett was President of the Baltimore and Ohio Railroad. He had made an effort to support the Federal invasion with his important railroad, and Stanton should be appreciative of that, Varina reasoned. And Garrett had paid Stanton handsome legal fees for his services as a lawyer for the Baltimore and Ohio. But most importantly, people in the know had convinced Varina that John Garrett was probably one of Stanton's real friends, and Stanton had very few real friends. Hudson Strode summarized the account of this important mission:

"In secrecy, wearing a thick black veil, Varina was taken to Garrett's Baltimore home by an attorney friend. Would he not use his influence with Stanton to effect her husband's release, she begged; for he was 'slowly dying in prison.' She assured him that Secretary of the Treasury [Hugh] McCulloch, the only Cabinet minister who had seen [Jeff], would support his aid. She presented [Jeff's] case so well that she made a profound impression on Garrett. He decided to go to Washington the following Saturday.

"Garrett first called on the sympathetic McCulloch, who was somewhat astounded at 'the fool's errand,' and then on the Attorney General, Henry Stanbery. The latter told him Stanton was sick and would see absolutely no one. But Garrett drove straight to his house, and was ushered into the sickroom, where Stanton lay inert on a lounge.

"As Garrett informed [Varina] next day, he immediately and frankly stated the purpose of his surprise visit. Stanton became very angry and 'exhibited much displeasure.' But Garrett was one man Stanton could not back down. He told him that Davis' death in confinement at Fortress Monroe would be most inconvenient to the authorities of the [Federal Government]. He said that at least two Cabinet ministers favored his release and that [Andrew] Johnson was only waiting for Stanton's approval. Finally, after a heated discussion, Garrett's logic and humanity won. In his weakened condition, Stanton said he would not object to the Attorney General's arranging for [her husband's] release [on bail, awaiting trial]. Garrett thanked him and drove back to the amazed Stanbery's office, where preliminary papers were drawn up. On his return to Baltimore, Garrett dispatched a man to New York to invite Horace Greeley to come to see him at once to discuss bondsmen, of whom Greeley had offered to be one.

"When Garrett told [Varina] all that had happened so quickly, she was overcome with tears of gratitude and relief. While Stanbery could give no specific promise as to time, he thought Davis might be released in a fortnight. Charles O'Conor went to Washington to arrange the terms of the release. Among [wealthy men from the northern States] who were willing to put up $25,000 each for bail, besides Horace Greeley, were Gerrit Smith and Cornelius Vanderbilt." [R19;304-305]

Meanwhile, on March 18, events progressed in South Carolina. Wade Hampton was among headlined speakers at a large political gathering of the State's African Americans at an outdoor Columbia rally. Sponsored by the African M. E. Church, chief speakers were Beverly Nash, an African American entrepreneur and Reverend D. Picket, an A. M. E. minister. Hampton was one of the five European American men who had been invited to "say a few words." The event was covered extensively by newspapers in South Carolina, New York and elsewhere, with particular attention given to Hampton's remarks. Newspapermen were intrigued by the fact that the Hampton family had owned several, perhaps many, of the attending African Americans. How would those in the political gathering perceive his remarks, considering the emotional aspect of past bondage and of their anticipated new right to vote? Excerpts of Hampton's brief remarks follow:

"No personal motives can possibly sway me for I am no longer a citizen of the United States or of the Confederate States. . . . The bill which gives the right [to vote] to you disfranchises me." . . .

"From many of you I have met not only kindness, but affection. I cannot forget how faithfully some of your people clung to me through all the perils and privations of the war. I cannot forget that it was one of you, [Kit Goodwyn], who was always the first at my side when I was wounded, and the last to leave me. Such affection is not often met with, nor is it easily forgotten, and while I have a crust of bread it shall be shared with this well-tried, this true, this trusty friend. . . .

"Why should we not be friends? Are you not Southern men, as we are? Is this not your home as well as ours? Does not that glorious Southern sun above us shine alike for both of us? Did not this soil give birth to all of us? And will we not all alike, when our troubles and trials are over, sleep in that same soil?"

He advised them to all work toward building up the former Confederate States, for if they can be made to prosper, he promised that all will prosper alike. Beverly Nash, the prominent African American entrepreneur, told the audience that he hoped all African American men would be allowed to vote and advised them all to responsibly use that right by selecting each candidate purely on his merit for office. But the Reverend Picket said he hoped that the right to vote would be restricted to men who qualify by education and property ownership. The political rally concluded with a torchlight parade though the streets of Columbia, where the "strictest order prevailed."

Of this political rally in Columbia, the New York *Times* said, "the whole spirit of the meeting is represented to have been of the most cordial good feeling," and the newspaper saw as most noteworthy, "that, in the heart of South Carolina — a State in which [African Americans] are largely in the majority — one of the foremost of the [former] Confederate Generals, and himself, once the largest [owner of bonded African Americans] in the country, should meet [those he had formerly owned] in this frank and manly style, and so unreservedly accept the situation, is a fact to out-weigh volumes of hostile invective and misrepresentation." But the New York *Tribune* called the political gathering a "farce" and called Nash and Picket, "black copperheads."

Notwithstanding the rhetoric, Hampton was convinced that African American men would soon exercise a controlling majority of the votes in South Carolina elections, save the upstate counties — that was reality. So, he reasoned, the best strategy for the State's European Americans was to campaign straight-out for their votes in hopes they could be persuaded to choose responsible candidates. [R199;185-187, R200;110]

Meanwhile Military Rule arrived for Mississippi when, on March 26, Edward Ord, a high-ranking Federal officer, took command over the Federal Military District consisting of the conquered States of Mississippi and Arkansas, with headquarters in Vicksburg. As mentioned earlier, Ord had been appointed by President Andrew Johnson in accordance with the Act to Reconstruct the Governments of the Conquered States through Military Rule. A native of Cumberland, Maryland, Ord had graduated from West Point, showing remarkable ability in mathematics. Following the War Against Mexico, he had worked in California on Corps of Engineers projects. Although a Marylander and of the southern culture, he did not resign his commission. During the Federal's Mississippi campaign, "he had commanded [William] Sherman's right wing at Corinth, his left wing at Jackson, and was present at the surrender of Vicksburg." So, in every way, Mississippi was now under the rule of the man who had conquered her people. A week after notifying the people of Mississippi and Arkansas of his appointment, Ord visited Jackson and won considerable praise for what was anticipated to be his even-handed treatment of the people over which he was to rule — his background as a Marylander probably working to his advantage. Of Ord's Jackson visit, historian James Garner would observe:

> "The Jackson *Clarion* assured [Ord] that all the people, both officers and private citizens, would 'strive conscientiously to promote the public peace and avoid collisions with the military power.' This seems to have been the general feeling."

> The editor added, "He is an educated officer of the old United States Army, who, in fighting the battles of his Government during the late war, obeyed orders and did what he doubtless believed to be his duty. The war having closed, he has no spirit of revenge or partisan malice to gratify, and will strive to execute the law, under which he is acting, to the letter. Our people will ask no exemptions which are not accorded to their brethren of the other excluded States."

Although Ord was in supreme command over the people of Mississippi and Arkansas, he soon issued orders directing the existing local and State governments to continue to operate, with existing personnel remaining on the job, performing customary duties, including collecting taxes — at the same time proclaiming all such governmental offices to be only "provisional." Ord had grossly insufficient manpower of adequate experience and skills to take over governmental functions except at the highest levels. So he demanded that local and State governments in both States continue operating, but under his oversight. Ord proclaimed that he would personally appoint men to all of the civil offices that were vacant or that would become vacant, and demanded a listing of all such offices. Ord only removed a few Mississippi men from office during his first weeks, removals being "for failure to do impartial justice to persons accused of crime." Early on he launched an extensive program to get men registered to vote who were not disqualified by Federal law, focusing of course on getting all African American men registered, none of whom were disqualified. This was job one for Ord's command. Federals assumed without question that all men showing physical evidence of acceptable age and of African ancestry were qualified to vote. [R204;161-168]

Meanwhile on March 26 in Washington City, Charles Sumner introduced a bill "to enforce the several provisions of the Constitution abolishing [African American bonding], declaring the immunities of citizens, and guaranteeing a republican form of government [in the States] by [forcing them to give the vote to African American men]." In advocating passage of his bill, Sumner told his colleagues there was no need to wait for "the slow process of [a Federal] Constitutional Amendment." Why, if Congress can require the conquered States to give voting rights to African American men, then Congress can require the States to the north to do the same. And, with the Fall elections looming on the horizon, Sumner explained how the added votes of African American men would help the Republican Party win more elections: "Every [State north of the conquered States] will move into line with the [added votes of African American men] to strengthen the Republican [Party] cause. Maryland and Delaware will be [remade into Republican Party States] — to say nothing of Kentucky. . . . One vote in Congress [to force all States to permit voting by African American men] and the allowance would never be taken away. [Our vote on this measure] will be immortal."

Fellow Republican Senators were far too aware that Exclusion passions in the Northern States would lose the Party far more votes in the upcoming election than the Party could recoup with the new votes of African American men. So they quietly voted to kill Sumner's voting rights bill in Committee. But Democrats and newspapermen were not so willing to let Sumner's plea die. They had witnessed over the years how what Sumner advocated one year, although denounced by his Party at the time, seemed to consistently become embraced the following year and written into Federal law. Would Federal control over citizenship and voting rights be next? James Dixon warned about "the propositions which

[Charles Sumner] makes one year, and which are criticized by his colleagues as extreme, . . . those colleagues [will] support with greater zeal and vehemence, if possible, than he, the year following." And those Republican politicians who supported Andrew Johnson rather freely warned voters that Sumner's proposals might soon become law. In fact, Sumner was becoming a liability to Republicans, who were seeking election in November, and many moved to distance themselves from him. [R73;299-300]

Three days later, William Seward invited Charles Sumner to his house in the evening. Congress was scheduled to adjourn the next day. Sumner certainly viewed the invitation as strange, for he and Seward were hardly on speaking terms — and they were in no way social friends. Seward's note made clear the invitation was not social in nature: "Can you come to my house this evening? I have a matter of public business in regard to which it is desirable that I should confer with you at once." But when Sumner arrived at Seward's house, he found him mysteriously absent. Why would a fellow invite you over to his house and then disappear? Apparently Seward had disappeared on purpose — for he figured his son Frederick and the Russian Minister, Edward de Stoeckl, could best influence Sumner if the father was absent. And Seward's son, Frederick, was well connected and well informed. As Frederick began explaining why Sumner had been summoned to the Seward home, he appeared to be shocked. And he had every reason to be shocked, for he had no idea that Russia and the Federal Government were working on a deal to transfer rights to Alaska from Russia to the American Federal Government. The deal was being pushed by Russia, who at the time was desperate for hard money. Anyway, Russian Government had figured that any deal was better than waiting for the militant, expansionist Federals to invade Alaska and seize Russian America without compensation. It correctly recognized that long-term ownership of Alaska was impossible. Their efforts to establish settlements in North America had been too little and too late. As previously mention, Canada would be lucky to escape conquest by the Federals. Russia's problem was hopeless — the Russian settlements in vast and isolated Alaska had no chance whatsoever. As Frederick showed Sumner a map of Alaska, it was obvious that Alaska blocked Canadian access to much of the Pacific Ocean. The Vancouver region of Canada would be pinched — like a salmon's tail in a bear's jaw — between Federal Alaska and the Territory that would become the State of Washington. Ownership of Alaska would be another Federal move toward eventual domination or subjugation of Canada. Sumner listened until midnight as Frederic and the Russian Minister described the benefits of the deal. Yet, Sumner did not commit himself to support the proposed treaty of sale. The Russian Government was offering to sell its rights to Alaska for $7,200,000 in hard currency. The map defined what the Russian Government considered to be the boundaries of its ownership. We should not assume that the Canadian Government ever agreed to those boundary lines, but Canadians were powerless to defend a more westward or a more northward boundary. At about midnight, Frederick Seward and Edward de Stoeckl bid Sumner goodnight. They had to go over to the White House for a treaty signing ceremony with Andrew Johnson. William Seward and Andrew Johnson were going to sign the Alaska Purchase Treaty that night. Shortly thereafter, the Senate would be reconvened in a Special Session to consider Ratification of the Treaty. The Russians needed money fast, and Seward wanted to strike while the iron was hot.

Biographer David Donald would write of Sumner's previous support for plans aimed at eventual seizure of the provinces of Canada, for that would expand the political power of the northern States:

> "The acquisition of Russian America posed a real dilemma for Sumner. An Expansionist, he was not 'so cold or philosophical as to regard with insensibility a widening of the bounds of [his] country.' In the past he had helped to block schemes to seize Mexico and Cuba because [those schemes] would extend [the political power of States in the south, which then permitted African American bonding], but for many years he had hoped for [seizure of Canadian land]. Russian America he had never seriously thought of, but at least since 1849 he had longed for that day when 'natural law' would sweep Canada 'into the wide orbit of her neighbor' and, during the secession crisis, he had briefly considered the [seizure] of Canada as a counterweight to the [loss of seceded States]. Now Seward's treaty revived his hopes, for he promptly saw that the purchase of Russian America would put the United States 'face to face to England alone' in North America and that then the United States could begin to 'squeeze England out of the continent'."

Although Sumner embraced territorial expansion to the north, he was mad at his political enemy, William Seward, for excluding him from all negotiation activity with the Russian Minister. Already mad that Senate Republicans had been excluding him from Committees that were writing Reconstruction legislation, he now discovered that he had also been excluded from negotiations with Russia, even though he was Chairman of the Senate Foreign Relations Committee — the very Committee that would consider Ratification of the Treaty. No wonder Sumner felt personally hurt. But he was much to blame himself for the personal feud between Senate Foreign Relations Committee Chairman and Secretary of State. David Donald would write: "Sumner felt that Seward should have notified him of these negotiations in advance, and he was unhappily aware that approval of the Treaty would imply endorsement of Seward's foreign policy, and perhaps [the] Andrew Johnson Administration as a whole."

The next morning William Seward came to the Senate chamber to personally appeal for quick approval before the scheduled adjournment, seeking an immediate floor vote. However, Sumner opposed such hasty action and appealed to fellow Senators to instead refer the Treaty to his Senate Foreign Relations Committee for review. Sumner probably moved for referral to make sure his name was associated with Alaska, but the Russian Minister would later write, "If it had been immediately submitted to a vote, it would have been rejected." To avoid a delay on the Treaty until the next scheduled Senate session, Andrew Johnson summoned the Senate into a Special Session to begin April 1.

When the Senate reconvened on April 1, Charles Sumner immediately called a meeting of the Senate Foreign Relations Committee to begin a review of the Treaty. Everyone was in attendance except for Oliver Morton of Indiana. Referring to Russian America as "Seward's Farm," William Fessenden asked, "What have we been buying?" After Sumner reported what he knew of the negotiations with Russia, comments within the Committee indicated the Treaty would be rejected. At this point Sumner had not announced his support for the Treaty, but he must have felt it necessary to introduce more persuasive arguments in favor of purchase. So he suggested that, by purchasing Alaska, the Federal Government "would be in a better position, subsequently, to oust Great Britain from the North American continent" and take Canada. But Reverdy Johnson warned of, "no squeeze without a war," to which Sumner argued, the "[Federal Government] control [over Canada]" would be accomplished "better without pressure than with pressure." In other words, Sumner thought the Expansionist threat implied by the purchase of Russian American would better facilitate the taking of Canada than an accomplished "squeeze tactic." Sumner explained, that if Seward had allowed him to be involved, he "would have kept [the Alaska purchase negotiations secretly] in hand, but delayed [its consummation]." Unable to recommend approval, but unwilling to recommend squashing the Treaty, the Committee voted to delay action until newspapermen had more time to report on the Treaty and politicians had gathered a sense of the public sentiment.

Charles Sumner told William Seward that his Committee was delaying further action on Russian America. Then Sumner warned the Russian minister, Edward de Stoeckl, that it was firmly against approval, and recommended that Russia withdraw the Treaty. Sumner was manipulating the situation toward what he felt he would have done had Seward involved him in the negotiations. But Seward did not back off. Instead, he began a campaign to individually persuade each member of Sumner's Committee. Biographer David Donald would write: "Night after night [Seward] invited the Senate luminaries, usually including Sumner, to dine at his 'elegant establishment,' where, according to the newspapers, over brandy and cigars he conducted a 'diplomatic symposium'."

Seward's "brandy and cigar symposiums," coupled with positive responses from the simultaneous newspaper stories, made substantial progress persuading members of Sumner's Committee to consider embracing the treaty. Yet most committeemen still did not want hasty Ratification. Commercial and mercantile businessmen in the northeastern States strongly favored the purchase. Smithsonian Institution scientists praised Alaska's "valuable minerals, furs, and other natural resources." Louis Agassiz, who had expressed a concern about taking land without asking the people who lived there, was placated by reports "that there is, as yet, hardly any population" living there. Furthermore, the purchase was popular in the western States. So, within a few days, Sumner was secretly persuaded that, "A bargain once made must be kept."

Yet, there was still a lot of opposition to immediate Ratification when Sumner's Committee reconvened on April 3. William Fessenden advocated a postponement or a vote against the Treaty. Simon Cameron declared that he would vote for Ratification if he must, but preferred to postpone action until

December. Reverdy Johnson termed his position as "not prepared to vote against" Ratification. But only one member, probably Oliver Morton, said he was eager to vote for immediate Ratification. Then Fessenden joked that he would go along with Morton if William Seward would "be compelled to live there." With laughter, Reverdy Johnson added, "That will be carried unanimously; I'll go for it and lead off" for the Democrats.

At this point Charles Sumner began his campaign to persuade his Committee to recommend Ratification. He opened by complaining that he was not especially enthusiastic about the purchase, that he knew very little about Russian America's resources, that Seward was at fault for negotiating without conferring earlier with him and his Committee, that the deal involved a lot of money, and that the money might better be used to fund Republican programs in the conquered States. Even so, Sumner told committeemen that he could not personally oppose Ratification. "I wish there were not so many [northeastern States] men on the Committee," he openly lamented. Then he explained: "If [this Committee] should go against [Ratification], it would be put down against [those States], and I don't want to deal [them] such a heavy blow." With those reservations, Sumner assured his Committee that he favored immediate Ratification. Yet, he could not stop blubbering his reservations: "I regret very much to go for this Treaty. I've a heavy load to carry." And the clerk that was writing down what everybody was saying added his own personal comment in the margin: "Yes and it's harder when you don't want to carry it." And, in spite of such a wavering endorsement by Chairman Sumner, four other Committeemen joined him in voting to recommend ratification. Perhaps Sumner had learned that being too forceful and domineering can fuel reactionary emotions. I any event, his strategy worked. Only William Fessenden of Maine and James Patterson of New Hampshire voted to oppose Ratification. The Committee advocated no amendments. Sumner was ready to present the Treaty to the Senate floor.

On April 8 Charles Sumner stood before the Senate and, for two and one half hours, advocated Ratification of the Treaty without amendment. The Senate was in secret session, so no public record of his speech exists, but it is known that, throughout, he spoke extemporaneously before his colleagues. And, for him that was a most uncharacteristic style. The next day William Fessenden delivered the minority report and moved to delay further consideration of the Treaty. However, this crucial motion to delay was voted down, 12 to 29. Immediately thereafter, a motion was made to Ratify the Treaty. The vote to Ratify was overwhelming: 37 versus 2 — one of those negative votes belonging to Fessenden. The American Federal Government had agreed to purchase Russian America. All that remained was to get the Federal House to appropriate the money.

Charles Sumner proudly wrote Wordsworth Longfellow: "My course had a decisive influence." Sumner never spoke truer words. Sumner was being excluded from the group of Senators directing Republican Reconstruction, but he was still very influential on foreign policy issues. Of Sumner's respected foreign policy leadership ability, Senator Henry Anthony of Rhode Island agreed, saying Sumner "ought to control those of us who have not given very particular attention to it ourselves." But the triumphant Sumner was upset over the secrecy that prevented the public from recognizing his crucial role in the purchase of Russian America. So he would take it upon himself to research Russian America further and to publish complementary information about the vast region. During his time of study, he would explain to a friend, "I am living with seals, and walruses, and black foxes and martins in Russian America." [R73;303-309]

Meanwhile in the conquered States, former Confederates, who cherished democratic ideals and constitutionally-limited government, were sickened by the political destruction they were witnessing. In the words of contemporary historian Alexander Harris: "Political manipulation in the [conquered States] became a sort of mutual admiration school for corrupt office-seekers and [uninformed African Americans]." It was in April that former Confederate leaders began legal cases in Georgia and Mississippi that were designed to, after successive appeals, enable the Federal Supreme Court to declare unconstitutional the Act to Reconstruct the Governments of the Conquered States through Military Rule. A majority of the Supreme Court Justices believed the bill unconstitutional and hoped that a suitable test case would be brought before their body. But having been so often intimidated by the more Militant Republicans in the House and Senate, the not-so-courageous Justices needed help and encouragement. [R97;473-474]

Meanwhile, as Alice Sumner spent more and more time with the Prussian diplomat, Friedrich von Holstein, Charles became more and more reclusive. David Donald would explain how she intimidated him:

> "Soon the two were frequently seen together in public, and Holstein accompanied Alice to 'matinees and soirees,' and in other public places, and occasionally escorted her from the Senate, where both had been to hear [Charles] speak." Sure that she had no guilt to hide, Alice made no secret of their meetings. Once in the late spring, [Charles], returning home unexpectedly, found her about to get into a carriage with Holstein and another young couple from the diplomatic set.

> "Where are you going Alice?" he asked.

> " 'I am going to enjoy myself, she replied defiantly.

> " 'But where are you going?'

> " 'That does not concern you,' she snapped, and off they drove.

> "Humiliated, [Charles] thereafter pretended not to see the two when they appeared in public, conspicuously turning his back to avoid them." [R73;292]

On another occasion, when Charles asked Alice where she was going, she snarled: "God damn you, 'tis none of your business, I will go where I please, with whom I please." Lacking the manly traits that would have moved him to administer the spanking Alice deserved, Charles said no more as Alice headed off to party with Holstein or another of her young friends. There are indications that, after the newness of marriage wore off — and that took only a few weeks, it seems — Alice found Charles exceedingly boring. Holstein was "very possibly sexually impotent, and simply a handy and safe companion with which Alice could socialize with the diplomatic set and other fun-loving people her own age. Washington rumors of a love affair were most probably false."

The friendship, or whatever it was, came to an end. On April 16 the Bismarck Government in Berlin issued orders instructing Holstein to return to Prussia "as soon as circumstances permit." Charles Sumner later swore he had nothing to do with Holstein's recall and, most likely, the head of the Prussian embassy in Washington, Baron Gerolt, realized on his own that he had to get Holstein away from the wife of the powerful Chairman of the Senate Foreign Relations Committee. [R73;293-294]

Meanwhile during April, we find that Thad Stevens, far from well, had spent most of his time at home or attending Committee meetings. He continued to advocate confiscation of the vast majority of farmland in the conquered States and sought to delay — until after approval of a Federal confiscation programme — the creation of Reconstructed Confederate State Governments by Republican Political Machines. But Stevens' confiscation programme was not attracting enough supporters, and the majority in the House and Senate were moving to begin Reconstruction with a Federal Confiscation Act. Some Republican Representatives in the House were advising newspapermen that the Governments in the conquered States would be Reconstructed without Federal Confiscation of most of the farmland. At one point in April, an angry Thad Stevens threatened: "Much is to be done by the people and Congress before any Representative or Senator or States can be recognized. Who authorized any orators to say there would be no confiscation [of farmland in the conquered States]?" [R96;277]

Meanwhile, Varina returned to Fortress Monroe before the end of April. After ensuring that the momentum that she had created though John Garrett was not going to abate, Varina had traveled on to Montreal, Canada to spend time with the children. Varina had been anticipating, as the closing days of April approached, that Jeff's release would be imminent, and she wanted to be present to help his lawyers defeat any snares that Edwin Stanton might lay. Biographer Hudson Strode would write that Varina's "persistence and courage had seemingly proved effective. By winning the support of [John] Garrett she had accomplished more than [Jeff's] coterie of able [lawyers] had been able to do. But [Jeff] could not give himself over to unrestrained joy. He had fed on promises too long. Varina, however, prepared to pack."

Soon after her return, Franklin Pierce again visited Jeff at Fortress Monroe. Pierce assured him that the Federal Government would never carry out a trial on a charge of Treason because Republicans knew that a trial on that charge would likely end up vindicating State Secession. Franklin asked Jeff what he planned to do after his release on bail. Jeff replied that going to Canada to visit the children would be the immediate plan; beyond that he had none. He expected to remain in eastern North America to be readily available to appear in court if summoned by the Federals. Jeff so hoped that he would have an opportunity to vindicate State Secession in a high-powered courtroom setting. [R19;306]

On May 6, Charles O'Conor notified Burton Harrison that he needed him in New York City. The time to carry out release procedures on Jeff Davis' behalf was at hand. When Harrison arrived, O'Conor handed him the precious writ of *habeas corpus* — the legal paper by which the Federal Military and the Federal Court would be compelled to release Davis on bail. Harrison took the writ to Richmond and compelled the Clerk of the District Federal Court to sign it. Then Harrison, accompanied by a Federal Marshall, took a boat down the James River to Fortress Monroe to fetch Jeff Davis. It was Friday, May 10, 1867 — by chance the second anniversary of Jeff and Varina's capture in southern Georgia by Federal cavalrymen. At Fortress Monroe, Harrison presented the writ to Henry Burton. The writ commanded Burton, "to present the body of Jefferson Davis" in the Federal District Court at Richmond on May 13. Burton understood his order and was apparently quite comfortable with it. Burton spent the evening in Jeff and Varina's four-room apartment talking amid the packed luggage. Then he retired to a room provided for him elsewhere in the Fortress. Of the next three days biographer Hudson Strode would write:

> "On Saturday, [Jeff and Varina], accompanied by [Henry] Burton, Dr. [Charles] Cooper, and [Burton] Harrison, took the boat *John Sylvester* for Richmond. [Henry] Burton, who had always been as kind as regulations permitted, had not dispensed with guards altogether. Though still the jailer, he asked for no parole, and on the river acted like a member of a pleasant party on an outing. At the little landings on the James clusters of people gathered to pay their respects to their former President. At the [farm] called Brandon, the ladies of the house, relatives of Burton Harrison, came aboard bearing bouquets. They embraced [Varina], wept over the ravages prison life had made in his appearance, and shed tears of joy at his expected release.

> "At Richmond, among the concourse on the wharf were many [African Americans] whom [Republican political organizers] had instructed to show insolence. But the presence of [Federal] soldiers kept them in order — 'or perhaps it was the dignity of [Jeff Davis],' who descended to the wharf on Burton Harrison's arm. At the sight of [Jeff] Davis, the men in the crowd silently took of their hats. [Varina] was seated in the carriage of James Lyons, her husband's old friend and [at the time] one of his [lawyers]. [Henry] Burton, Dr. [Charles] Cooper, and Harrison entered an open carriage with [Jeff] Davis. All along the streets men stood with hats in hands, while women waved handkerchiefs from the windows.

> "A reporter on the Richmond *Enquirer* carefully noted [Jeff] Davis' appearance after his two years in prison:

>> " 'He wears a full beard and mustache, which in a measure conceals the ravages made by sorrow and suffering upon his face, but his countenance, although haggard and care-worn, still preserves the proud expression and the mingled look of sweetness and dignity for which it was ever remarkable. His hair is considerably silvered, but his eye still beams with all the fire that characterized it in the old time, and he seems every inch a king.'

> "When his carriage reached the entrance of the Spotswood Hotel, [Davis saw that the sidewalks were banked thick with bareheaded men with grave faces. In the hotel he was given the very rooms he had occupied 6 years before when he had arrived from Montgomery as President of a new nation, which the [former Confederates had then] expected to be everlasting. In his private parlor scores of old friends called, bringing flowers. The ordeal proved trying, and it was a great relief when at last the family was left to rest.

> "The next morning, Sunday, [May 12], [Jeff and Varina] remained in their rooms except for a secret trip to the cemetery to lay flowers on the grave of their boy Joseph, who had been killed in a fall in 1864. After church and during the afternoon [Jeff] Davis received friends and kissed all the pretty girls. Harrison noted that 'he kissed the prettiest again on their departure.' He wrote to Connie in Europe: 'No stranger would suppose for an instant that the quiet gentleman who receives

his visitors with such graceful elegance and dignity is the State prisoner . . . whose trial for Treason against a mighty [Federal] Government today attracts the interest of all mankind.'

"After the respite of Sunday, tension again gripped the city on Monday, [May 13], the day set for the [bail hearing]. Few citizens felt really assured. There was no telling what tricks the abominable Judge [John] Underwood had up his sleeve. Some feared that as soon as the [Federal] Military relinquished [control of] Davis, Underwood would throw him into the local jail [as a prisoner of the Federal Court]. During the morning hours, in all parts of [Richmond], women knelt in prayer, while the men on the streets 'wore the most anxious faces.' The citizens' nervous excitement was kept under control, however, because they were warned that any public outburst might [hurt Davis' chances for bail].

"Varina was not going to the courtroom; she would stay in her room and pray in private. When her husband left her, she thought he looked very well in his black suit with the flecks of gray. To avoid the crowd in front of the hotel Burton Harrison slipped [Jeff] out the back door to a carriage waiting in the courtyard with a small [Federal] Military escort.

"Before the legal proceedings began, privileged persons, including some ladies and [newspapermen], had been allowed into the courtroom, which was in the old Customs House. Eager crowds packed the stairways and passages. A few minutes before 11:00, [Jeff] Davis' [team of 6 lawyers] entered and took their seats. All were men of distinction. Charles O'Conor and [George] Shea were the New Yorkers. Philadelphia's William Reed, a prominent Democrat of Pennsylvania, was the third [man from the northern States]. Virginia was represented by her best legal minds: Robert Ould, [John] Tucker, and James Lyons.

"Just before the clock struck 11:00, the double doors were opened and the public rushed in to take every available seat. While the clock was still striking, the famous Horace Greeley entered, and was greeted with warm handshakes by gentlemen on both sides behind the bar. The crowd buzzed with pleasure because the papers said definitely that Greeley had come to sign [Jeff] Davis' bail bond.

"At last Jefferson Davis, somewhat flushed with nervous excitement, appeared, following [Henry] Burton in full uniform, and trailed by the Court Marshall. He was conducted to a comfortable chair, used as the prisoner's dock, by [Henry] Burton with 'more of the manner of a sympathizing friend than of his keeper.' Though [Davis] showed marks of extreme weakness, he seemed cheerful and bowed to several friends. As George Davis, last Attorney General of the Confederacy, wrote his son:

> " '[Jeff] Davis is only the shadow of his former self, but with all his dignity and high, unquenchable manhood. As he entered the densely crowded courtroom, with his proud step and lofty look, every head reverently bowed to him and a stranger would have sworn that he was the judge and Underwood the culprit'."

"After a few moments, the Marshal crossed the room and asked Burton Harrison to take a chair beside [Davis]. Harrison wrote that in taking his seat next to [Davis] he felt 'as exalted as if he were enthroned beside a king.' Shortly, to everyone's surprise, further courtesy was offered: [Jeff] Davis was invited to leave the prisoner's dock and sit within the bar, close to his [lawyers]. Throughout the proceedings Harrison was beside [Davis].

"Everything went smoothly, as the Attorney General has assured [Davis' lawyers], though Underwood in his preliminary remarks managed to get in some unnecessary jabs at Davis' sensibilities. Then [Underwood] declared that [Davis] had [at that time] passed from the control of [Federal] martial law and was 'under the protection of American Republican law and was in the custody of the Marshal.' People held their breaths in apprehension. Davis wondered what species of law 'American Republican law' could be. But O'Conor announced the readiness of the defense and said he desired immediate trial. William Evarts, [prosecuting lawyer] for the [Federal Government], replied that the case could not be heard at the present [Federal Court] term. Again the crowd was breathless, until, as by prearrangement, [John] Underwood declared the case bailable. Motion for bail was then made; the prosecution [lawyers] consented. After a stump speech by Underwood praising the magnanimity of the [Federal] Government, the bail was fixed at

$100,000. [Charles] O'Conor announced there were at least 10 gentlemen in court who were willing to go surety.

"The several [gentlemen from the northern States] went up to sign the [bail] bond, beginning with Horace Greeley, followed by Gerrit Smith and August Shell, who signed for Cornelius Vanderbilt. Seven others signed. Then the Marshal was directed to release [Jeff Davis].

"The crowd in the courtroom burst into unrestrained shouts of joy. The first to congratulate [Jeff] Davis was [Henry] Burton, followed by Dr. [Charles] Cooper. Someone rushed to a Maine Street window of the Customs House and yelled at the top of his lungs, '[Jefferson Davis] is bailed!' A mighty roar rose from the people below. The cry of delight was taken up from street to street and re-echoed from hill to hill.

"As people surged around Davis, he whispered to Burton Harrison to get him out as quickly as possible. With O'Conor on one side and Ould on the other, [Jeff Davis] came out of the Bank Square door. He was greeted not with hurrahs, but with the [Confederate Battle] Yell, ear-splitting, triumphant.

"[Reverend Charles] Minnegerode and Burton Harrison rode in the open vehicle with Jefferson Davis. 'Our carriage passed with difficulty through the crowd,' [Minnegerode] wrote. 'The rejoicing [African Americans], with their tended affection, climbed upon the carriage, shaking and kissing his hand, and calling out, 'God bless [Jeff] Davis'.'"

"All along the way to the Spotswood Hotel, [Jeff Davis] was saluted by that [Confederate Battle] Yell. But when his carriage reached the hotel entrance, a grave silence fell upon the throng. The men seemed too moved to shout. As Jefferson Davis rose to step down, one deep voice commanded, 'Hats off, Virginians!' 'Five thousand uncovered men,' wrote Harrison, 'did homage to him who had suffered for them.' In a tribute of emotional silence, [Jeff] Davis descended and entered the hotel.

"The people on the stairs and in the upper hall pressed back in respect. [Varina] received [Jeff] in their suite. After embracing [Varina], [Jeff] turned to [Charles] Minnegerode and said: 'In my sufferings you have comforted and strengthened me with your prayers. Should we not now kneel together and return thanks?' [Varina] led the way into the adjoining room. Harrison locked the door. Around the center table the three persons who had meant most to Jefferson Davis in his tribulations dropped to their knees with him. Each silently in his own way expressed his gratitude. And then, overcome by emotion, each of them realized that the others were crying. In the words of [Charles] Minnegerode: 'There, in deep-felt prayer and thanksgiving, closed the story of Jefferson Davis' prison life.'

"When Burton Harrison at last opened the door, joyful friends rushed in and enfolded [Jeff Davis] with loving embraces.

"Because the excitement was so wearing to him, [Varina] and [Burton] Harrison thought it best to get [Jeff] out of Richmond as quickly as possible. Harrison got the family aboard a steamer for New York that night.

"At the dock Davis bade an affectionate farewell to his jailer, [Henry] Burton, and sailed away while Richmond celebrated. The animosities of war were at least momentarily forgotten. Burton and Dr. [Charles] Cooper were invited to a series of feasts. For the first time since [the Federals completed their conquest of the Confederacy], the best houses of Richmond entertained [people from the northern States who were in town].

"Throughout the [conquered States, Tennessee and Kentucky] there was jubilant rejoicing at the announcement that 'the caged eagle' was once more free. But the rejoicing was mingled with regret that Jefferson Davis had not been allowed his coveted opportunity to vindicate [State Sovereignty,] the cause of the Confederacy, in the Federal Courts 'and in the hearing of the world.'

"Because of his long imprisonment, the scandal of his shackling, and the nobility with which he bore indignity and suffering, the popularity of Jefferson Davis [among former Confederates] was marvelously revived. During the last agonizing year of [desperate fighting], when the

[Confederacy's] resources wore to shreds, he had known a sharp diminution in popular acclaim. But [at the time of his release from Federal prison] he found himself hailed with all the pride and devotion that were first accorded him as [the newly-elected] President of the Confederate States of America." [R19;306-311]

Down at the University of Mississippi in Oxford, Lucius Lamar, professor of law, upon hearing the wonderful news about Jeff Davis' freedom, suggested to his students that they contribute to a gift of appreciation for the former President of the Confederate States and fellow Mississippian. A total of $500 was collected, $40 from Lamar himself, and temporarily deposited in a local bank. Unfortunately, the bank failed 3 days later. Lamar responded by contributing a new $500 of his own money. That money did reach Jeff Davis. He would later tell this story to a friend: "I got the money for Jeff and sent it to him. Poor fellow, he doesn't know what the $500 cost."

Meanwhile, on May 15 in Washington City, Charles Sumner took the Senate floor to present a learned dissertation on the natural resources and strategic value of Russian America. Sumner detailed the region's coastal waters, geography, timber, wildlife, suspected minerals, and people. And he emphasized its strategic value in accomplishing the long-range goal of expanding the reach of the Federal Government to include the entire North American continent. He called the purchase "another step to the occupation of [all of] North America." He pointed out that the purchase "diminishes from North America one of the monarchical powers." All understood that the only remaining monarchical power was Great Britain, which controlled Canada. Biographer David Donald would write:

> "The speech was a remarkably accurate and well-informed conspectus of the history and natural resources of the new territory, and it was influential both in shaping public opinion at large and in persuading members of the [Federal] House to appropriate the purchase price specified in the Treaty. Of more lasting influence was Sumner's concluding injunction that the newly acquired land must not bear 'any name borrowed from classical antiquity or from individual invention;' instead its name must be 'indigenous, aboriginal, one of the [original and primitive inhabitants] of the soil' — namely, 'Alaska'."

Sumner had received help from Louis Agassiz, who was concerned about the people living in Russian America. And he had tapped the knowledge and resources of J. E. Hilgard of the Coast Survey and Spencer Baird of the Smithsonian. Furthermore, Sumner and his helpers had scoured the Washington libraries for information. The work was well-researched and thorough. Sumner's speech would occupy 163 pages when his *Works* would be latter printed. The New York *Herald*, which detested Sumner's literary political style, found the speech "unquestionably the most encyclopedic of all encyclopedic works ever elaborated by the learned Senator and his private secretaries." A proponent of the purchase, Henry Halleck would write that Sumner had "completely exhausted the subject, as well as his readers."

Sumner's campaign to build support for purchasing Alaska worked. The Federal House would soon vote to appropriate the required $7,200,000. Furthermore, that would be $7,200,000 that it would not have available to finance the Republican Reconstruction Programme in the conquered States. Many, especially men Massachusetts and neighboring States, would call Alaska, "Seward's Folly" and, "Seward's Ice-box." But to a great degree, the peaceful acquisition of Russian America less Seward's than Sumner's accomplishment.

Yes, "Alaska" was Charles Sumner's finest hour. [R73;309-310]

Meanwhile, under Federal Military oversight, Republican-dominated voter registration organizations in the conquered States were registering African American men, while evaluating others and registering those they deemed qualified. The Five Military Rulers had appointed Boards of Registration in their respective Military Districts, which had set up organizations to carry out the registrations and evaluations. They were also proclaiming dates for election of Delegates to Constitutional Conventions and for voter Ratification of State Constitutions to be drafted by those Conventions. The detailed field work was being carried out by Auxiliary Boards of Registration, which were also appointed by each Military Ruler's organization. Alexander Harris would write: "The registration of voters, which [took place in the 10 conquered States], was purely a work of political partisanship, engineered in the interests of that Party which [had] secured the passage of the laws, under which the proceedings were held." A European American man seeking to register, who did not display the characteristics desired by agents of the Republican Political Machine "were subjected to an ordeal of scrutiny that was sufficient to deter all save the boldest from the undertaking." [R97;475]

Meanwhile, Jeff Davis progressed toward Canada. Burton Harrison arranged for Jeff and Varina to stay in a New York hotel when they disembarked from the steamer that they had boarded in Richmond. But Jeff seemed quite weary, and crowds of well-wishers seemed to make matters worse. In a letter to his mother, Burton wrote that Jeff "is looking very thin and haggard, and has very little muscular strength. But his spirits are good." So, before long Burton drove Jeff and Varina out to Charles O'Conor's home at Fort Washington on the Hudson River where he could more easily build up his strength before boarding the train for Montreal. And after a few days at O'Conor's house, Jeff so longed to see his children that, although still weak, he was eager to board the train for Montreal. However, Burton, Jeff and Varina were somewhat concerned about being harassed during the train trip through New York State on the route to Montreal. So they decided that Burton and Jeff should go up on one day, and Varina should follow on the next day. In fact, Varina made a public display of attending the theater with friends the evening that Jeff and Burton left, perhaps to trick newspapermen into thinking that Jeff was still in town. But Jeff and Burton made the trip across New York State without major problems, although "he was hooted in the New York [State] stations along the route." [R19;312]

Jeff's reunion with his children in Montreal was surely filled with emotion, thanksgiving and joy, but he had difficulty being with his children for very long periods. Edwin Stanton and Nelson Miles had subjected Davis to tormenting treatment for so long that his nerves were terribly raw. Although the two youngest children, not yet in school, were eager to play and spend time in the room with their recovering father every day, Jeff found prolonged interaction too painful. Varina would write: "Great was the joy of our reunion, but the motion and life about us drove [Jeff] wild with nervousness; he said the voices of people sounded like trumpets in his ears." [R19;313,R13;797]

While Jeff and Varina were thrilled over their freedom to spend time together, Charles and Alice were far from pleasant toward each other as, together, they rode the train from Washington to Boston after the Senate session concluded. And Alice's rage toward Charles increased as the train steamed along, for he had handed her a novel which featured "an immoral woman who had betrayed her husband." Believing Charles was admonishing her through that novel — and he probably was — she disembarked from the train in Boston in a livid rage. Biographer David Donald would write: "As [Charles] unlocked the [door to his inherited Boston home], she spat a 'God damn you' at him, swept ahead to their bedroom, and slammed the door in his face. From [that] time, she [would insist] upon separate sleeping quarters." A few days after the Sumner's June 9 dinner with Wadsworth Longfellow, Alice and her daughter, Bell left Charles' already-sold house and moved to Lenox, "where for a time she kept up the fiction that he would join her later." But Charles would never speak to his wife again. That seemed to be his method of dealing with people he disliked: he would consistently shun the person, even to the extreme of never speaking to him or her ever again. There, Charles sat, alone in the empty house he had inherited from his mother, the house he had sold to raise money to pay for the still unfinished dream-house in Washington. The death of his mother had moved him to propose marriage to Alice. During the fast-paced turmoil of that marriage, Alice had persuaded him to sell the Boston home where he had lived for so many years with his mother and use that money to purchase a large new dream-house in Washington City. Applying poetic language to the sad state of affairs, Longfellow wrote of Charles, sitting in his already-sold Boston home, "gloomily like Marius on the ruins of Carthage." [R73;294-295]

Meanwhile, as Jeff Davis settled into a routine in Montreal, he began to receive letters from many friends. In one letter Franklin Pierce offered Jeff, Varina and the children full use of his vacation cottage:

> "My cottage at Little Boon's Head will be ready to receive all your family by the middle of August. The latter part of that month and the whole of September is usually delightful there. The place will be as quiet as could be desired — and I need not express how much pleasure I should find in trying to make everything agreeable to you."

In another letter Robert Lee wrote:

"Your release has lifted a load from my heart which I have not words to tell, and my daily prayer to the great Ruler of the World is that he may shield you from all future harm, guard you from all evil and give you that peace which the world cannot take away. That the rest of your days may be triumphantly happy, is the sincere and earnest wish of your most obedient faithful friend and servant."

Although Franklin Pierce's cottage sounded delightful, Varina persuaded Jeff to accept James Mason's invitation to visit him in the village of Niagara near Toronto, where he had established a residence away from the reach of Federal harassment. A former Confederate officer, George Denison, described the reception given Davis as he disembarked from the river boat at Toronto:

"I heard a couple of hours before the steamer arrived that [Jeff] Davis was coming on her. I went around and started a number of friends to pass the word through the city for as many as possible to come down to the wharf and give him a reception. By the time the vessel arrived a crowd of several thousand people filled the landing place. I got on a pile of coal with a number of friends to give the signal and start the crowd to cheer. As [Jeff] Davis appeared on the gangway with [James] Mason and [Charles] Helm, I was so astonished at the emaciation and weakness of [Jeff] Davis, who looked like a dying man, that I said to a friend near me, 'They have killed him.' Then I called for cheers, and nothing could have been more cordial and kingly than the welcome he got."

With lifted spirits and amid deep breaths from the breeze coming in off the lake, Davis exclaimed to his companions "I feel that I am once more breathing free air." And at Niagara wharf, Davis was buoyed by greetings from Jubal Early, Beverly Tucker and other former Confederates.

On an evening soon after his arrival in Niagara, Jeff Davis gave a crowd of serenaders a little impromptu speech:

"Gentlemen, I thank you sincerely for the honor you have this evening shown to me. It shows that true British manhood to which misfortune is always attractive. May peace and prosperity be forever the blessing of Canada, for she has been the asylum for many of my friends, as she is now an asylum to myself. I hope that Canada may forever remain a part of the British Empire, and may God bless you all, and may the British flag never cease to wave over you."

And, about four days later, Davis attended an agricultural fair with James Mason and Mason's grandchildren. The trip to Niagara was definitely helping him regain his strength and his spirit. And Davis thought the trip was perhaps even a life-saving event. Biographer Hudson Strode would write that Davis said later that "he felt the loving hospitality in Niagara among devoted [former Confederate] friends may have saved his life." [R19;313-317]

Meanwhile, on June 12 in Mississippi, Edward Ord, Military Ruler over the Federal District composed of Mississippi and Arkansas, reacting to intense pressure to "stay" several legal proceedings that threatened widespread bankruptcy and economic collapse — "issued an order staying and suspending, until the 30th of December, all proceedings for the sale of land under cultivation, or of the crops, stock, implements, or other material used in tilling such land, in pursuance of any execution or writ, where the debt was contracted prior to January 1, 1866." Ord deserves credit for recognizing this threat and acting to moderate it. On the other hand, Ord held no sympathy for helping men who were converting their corn to untaxed whiskey, as he issued orders "to seize all distilleries that did not pay the legal taxes assessed on them, and sell their property for the benefit of the poor." Ord was apparently angry with men who had rather make black market whiskey of their corn than supply it to the poor for corn bread.

On the other hand Ord encouraged the poor African Americans to work, admonishing them to "not neglect their [work] to engage in political discussion, but to continue to comply with their [work] contracts, and thus avoid the threatened famine, [because] at the proper time for them to have their names registered as voters they [would] be informed through the proper channels." To police such work contracts, Ord insisted that "the removal of all crops [from the fields] was forbidden until the shares of laborers were ascertained and assigned to them."

Ord paid special attention to two classes of thievery by citizens — stealing seed cotton and stealing horses — and he engaged his Military Courts in trying cases of these sorts (as we all know, trying civilians in military court was at the time unconstitutional in every northern State, as it now is in every

State). Horse and mule stealing was the worst crime. I have found it helps my understanding of what life was like in those days when I compare my knowledge of present-day criminal activity to the criminal activity in Mississippi during Ord's 9 months of Military Rule. You decide, but it seems to me folks were rather well behaved in Mississippi during 1867:

> During Ord's 9-month rule, 41 Mississippi men — all civilians, none in the military — would be tried in Military Court on criminal charges, and 33 would be convicted. On the charge of stealing one or more horses and/or mules, 25 would be convicted. Other convictions would be: 3 for assault upon an African American; 1 for murder of an African American; 1 for rape; 1 for disloyalty; 1 for selling a pistol to a soldier, and 1 for robbery. The punishment for the murder of the African American would be 10 years in prison. Sentencing of the 3 men convicted of assault on an African American would range from 2 to 3 years. Horse thieves would be required to serve, typically, 2 years in prison, but often 5 years. The man convicted of robbery would be sentenced to 7 years at the maximum-security Federal prison at Dry Tortugas.

It is helpful to compare this 9-month 1867 record for the whole State of Mississippi to the 12-month 2006 record for the capital city, Jackson. Records for that year, collected within the boundaries of the capital city, show 40 murders, 160 rapes, 1,022 violent robberies and 514 aggravated assaults. And that was just the "violent crimes." The non-violent crimes totaled 13,208. The city population that year was 184,256 people, 79 percent of them African American. A comparison like this puts in perspective the statistics collected during the Reconstruction Era, which Republicans used to justify the destruction of State Sovereignty and the implementation of their political Reconstruction programme.

The Mississippi and Arkansas legislatures were in session during Ord's command. He forced the Arkansas Legislators to disband, but permitted the Mississippi Legislators to remain. But he would block enforcement of any Mississippi laws he disliked. Ord's dictatorial stance would prompt the Chief Justice of the Mississippi Supreme Court to resign, and the other Justices would also resign shortly thereafter.

Edward Ord would be replaced in December. Of his 9 months of Military Rule over Mississippi and Arkansas, historian James Garner would conclude:

> "There were local charges that [Ord] abused his powers and was an irresponsible despot, but it does not appear that he violated the spirit of the [Federal acts designed to Reconstruct the Governments of the conquered States], although it will be admitted that he might have administered them with less rigor and severity." [R204;168-171]

Meanwhile in Washington City, the Republican leadership of the House and Senate gave notice of a July Special Session, prompted by evidence that Andrew Johnson was not forcing his five Military Rulers to make sure that their Boards of Registration were excluding sufficient former Confederate men to ensure Republican Party victories at the polls. Andrew Johnson had sought a ruling from Attorney General Henry Stanbery, or Ohio, on "certain doubtful points" in the Act that had established Military Rule. Stanbery's opinion, issued on June 12, gave more Militant Republicans reason to worry that, "Altogether too small a number of [former Confederate men] would be denied the right to vote," if it was not overturned.

Just before Congress reconvened for July's Special Session, a reporter from the New York *Herald* interviewed Thad Stevens. Asked if he still advocated confiscation of the farms of former Confederates, Stevens replied that he could only hope to win legislative approval for "mild confiscation" because "philanthropists" like Horace Greeley and Gerrit Smith were confessing that Federals had been equally responsible for causing the Federal Invasion of the Confederacy. Asked why he favored Impeachment of Andrew Johnson, Stevens replied that the Pennsylvania Republican Party needed an Impeachment trial to excite its voter base. He quipped: "This corruption [in the Pennsylvania Republican Party] will certainly beat us here next election, unless we draw out the Republican strength by getting up a furor and excitement on impeachment." [R96;282, R97;476]

(3Q67)

Two days after Congress reconvened, on July 5, Republicans caucused to close political ranks in response to the upcoming Fall campaigns. One of the chief objectives was to muzzle Charles Sumner, but he did not fully appreciate their intent until the caucus began. A "gag-rule" resolution was proposed to limit legislative business "to removing the obstructions which have been or are likely to be placed in the way of the fair execution of the [Reconstruction] Acts." Sumner objected as strongly as possible, but the majority voted to adopt the "gag rule." "I will not be bound by any such proposition," Sumner threatened. But William Fessenden replied: "Then you should not have voted on the subject, if you did not mean to be bound by the decision of the majority." Sumner continued to fume and fuss. And he did refuse to be gagged. Criticizing Sumner's repeated attempts to introduce bills on the Senate floor, Fessenden accused him of resorting to his usual personal code: "Heads I win; tails you lose." But Fessenden retained the support of enough Republican Senators to kill every significant amendment that Sumner introduced during that summer session — even though, at one point, Ben Wade "stepped down from his Chair as Presiding Officer to support [Sumner]."

A second supplemental bill was drafted to expand upon the Act to Reconstruct the Governments of the Conquered States through Military Rule. This bill made more clear the supremacy of the Military Ruler. Its supplemental language enunciated the entire and complete supremacy of the Federal Military power throughout the 10 conquered States. It enlarged the power of the five Military Rulers. And it decreed that the Boards of Registration had the "fullest latitude of investigation, and the power of rejecting whomsoever they deemed proper." This second supplemental Reconstruction bill was finally passed over Andrew Johnson's veto on July 19. Charles Sumner had only succeeded in amending the bill in one small way. He had added language stating that the act "shall be construed liberally, to the end that all the intents thereof may be fully and perfectly carried out."

Thad Stevens had been infuriated by Andrew Johnson's veto and figured he might increase public denunciation of Johnson and Johnson supporters if he could accuse them of being members of Masonic Lodges. The idea must have come to him upon reading that Johnson had traveled to Boston earlier in the summer to dedicate a new Masonic Temple. So Stevens asked Edward McPherson, the House Clerk, to gather the names of all Masons who held seats in the House and Senate. When presented McPherson's preliminary list, Stevens realized that he would lose more than he would gain by resurrecting the long-ago political agitation against members of Masonic Lodges, because many Masons were among the more Militant Faction of the Republican Party, including Schuyler Colfax and Ben "Beast" Butler. [R73;300-301, R96;286, R97;476]

Meanwhile in Canada, soon after Jeff's return to Montreal, in late June or early July, he and Varina were given a furnished house at 1181 Mountain Street. Anonymous former Confederates had paid the rent through September. After the family settled into these pleasant quarters, Varina encouraged Jeff to take on a project of writing his history of the Confederacy. Biographer Hudson Strode would explain:

"As soon as the family was settled, to rouse [Jeff] from his lassitude, [Varina] suggested that he begin writing his history of the [Confederate effort to defend against the Federal invasion]. So [Jeff] sent for the Confederate letter-and-message books that Margaret Howell had brought in a false bottom of her trunk and deposited in the Bank of Montreal. [Varina] was prepared to copy all the passages he would mark as significant and to arrange them by dates. For the first days, [Jeff] merely read desultorily. Before long be came upon the telegram he had sent [Robert] Lee from Danville on April 9, 1865, the day of Appomattox. It began: 'You will realize the reluctance I feel to leave the soil of Virginia and appreciate my anxiety to win success north of the Roanoke.'

"With a stricken expression on his face [Jeff] pushed the book away from him. Recalling the shock of surrender and all the anguish of the terrible struggle, [Jeff] rose and began pacing the room. Then he said to [Varina] in a low, strained voice, 'Let us put them by for a while. I cannot speak of my dead so soon.' It was to be a full decade before he could bring himself to face the task again." [R19;318]

Meanwhile, Thad Stevens began preparations for his death. On July 13, fearing that he probably had only a few months to live, drew up and signed his Last Will and Testament. He bequeathed to Peacham, Vermont $1,000 for the town library and $500 for graveyard upkeep. He bequeathed small legacies to two relatives: Thaddeus M. Stevens and a son of Simon Stevens. Then he bequeathed to "Lydia Smith, my housekeeper, $500 a year during her natural life, to be paid semi-annually, or at her option she may receive $5,000" as a one-time payment. (Four months later he would pen a codicil bequeathing $1,000 toward the upkeep of Stevens Hall at Pennsylvania College and — "out of respect for the memory of my mother" — $1,000 toward building a Baptist church in Lancaster.) The remainder of his estate, Stevens bequeathed to his nephew, Thaddeus Stevens, Jr. But Stevens sought to manage the young man's future life in the process and create a competition for the remaining money as well. Stevens required 5 years to pass before his nephew would receive one quarter of the remaining money. Three quarters of the remaining money would be given to the nephew or "to erect, establish and endow a house of refuge for the relief of the homeless and indigent orphans" in Lancaster. The nephew would receive the bequest if he was able, after the 10 years had passed, to prove that he had not taken even one drink of beer, wine or whiskey over that time span. If people in Lancaster who wanted the money for an orphanage were able to prove that the nephew had taken one or more drinks, then they got the money. So, Thad Stevens, who never knew married life and the give and take of raising children, was yet determined to, even from the grave, domineer over this nephew. Ten years later the independent-minded nephew would explain to his friends that he had simply not wished to deprive Lancaster orphans of his uncle's bequest. [R96;284-285,292]

Meanwhile, in Mississippi, on July 29, the Military Ruler, Edward Ord, notified State and local Government officials in the Federal Military District comprising Mississippi and Arkansas, which he commanded, that, in accordance with the July 19 act of the Federal House and Senate, all such officials showing evidence of being disloyal were to be immediately removed from office and replaced with new men whom he would appoint. He further announced that State and local governments were to be remade, or reconstructed, based on the votes of qualified men without regard to the color of their skin, and warned State and local officials that any obstruction or speech-making in opposition to this Federal policy would result in removal from office. Historian James Garner would observe:

> "This announcement was shortly followed by the removal of most of the municipal officers of Vicksburg, in order to 'secure an equal and just administration of the laws upon all alike, and to secure the best interests of the citizens thereof.' Several local officers were also removed in Choctaw, Kemper, Holmes, Neshoba and Washington counties."

In all, Ord removed about 25 men, and appointed about 75 men, the people of Mississippi accepting his dismissals and appointments without significant resistance. By the way, one of Ord's appointees was Isaiah Montgomery, a son of Benjamin Montgomery, both formerly bonded African Americans held by Jefferson Davis (Readers of *Bloodstains* will recall occasional coverage in previous volumes of Benjamin Montgomery and his two sons). Isaiah "was made a Justice of the Peace, and was probably the first [African American] in the State to hold public office." He would be the only African American Delegate in the Mississippi Constitutional Convention of 1890 and would, for many years, hold office as Mayor of Bayou, Mississippi. [R204;168-169]

Meanwhile on July 18 in Canada, Jeff Davis made an appearance at the Theatre Royal where the play, "The Rivals," was being presented as a fund-raising effort for a charity called the [Former Confederate] Relief Association. Montreal papers noted that the theater was crowded with "the elite of the city." And the audience made a fuss over cheering Jeff Davis' attendance. At one point a British voice cried out from the audience, "We shall live to see the [former Confederacy] a nation yet!" And others called to the orchestra to play "Dixie," which the musicians managed to do amid prolonged applause. But such shows of enthusiasm for Jeff Davis by Canadians were beginning to anger Federal newspapermen, including those working for Horace Greeley's New York *Tribune*. In response to the Theatre Royal display of affection, the *Tribune* warned:

> "The fuss made over the arch [Confederate] on this occasion proves that the Canadians are in a very bad condition of mind. They won't recover their equanimity until they are formally [conquered and made subservient to our Federal Government]."

Jeff and Varina decided to leave the house in Montreal in September and board at a hotel in Lennoxville, a village in the eastern part of Quebec Province. The school situation there was quite good and little Jeff had done well in his school at Lennoxville the previous year. [R19;319-320]

Meanwhile in the conquered States, during and around August, Republican leaders ordered the various Boards of Registration to carefully review their lists of the men who had been allowed to register to vote. Projected counts of expected Democrat and Republican votes were made. Where Republicans were projected to have less than an absolute, unquestioned majority, the Boards were instructed to strike off some suspected Democrat voters, alleging that those men were deemed not qualified. By these straw vote edits, the Republican Political Machines gained assurance that their men would win in the future State Constitution elections. Such political editing would elicit sarcasm from contemporary historian Alexander Harris. He would write: "This was an admirable safety valve, in the control of expert politicians."

Meanwhile sparks were flying between Andrew Johnson and Edwin Stanton. By August, Johnson had become thoroughly incensed at Stanton's refusal to voluntarily resign his job as Secretary of War. Stanton knew that Johnson wanted his resignation, but he was too stubborn to supply it. So, on August 5, Johnson wrote Stanton this terse message:

"Sir: — Public considerations of a high character, constrain me to say that your resignation, as Secretary of War, will be accepted."

Unmoved, Stanton replied in the following mocking manner:

"Sir: — . . . In reply, I have the honor to say, that public considerations of a high character, which alone have induced me to continue at the head of this Department, constrain me not to resign the office of Secretary of War, before the next meeting of Congress."

Shortly afterward, on August 12, Andrew Johnson informed Edwin Stanton that he was suspended as War Department head and he, Johnson named Ulysses Grant as acting Secretary of War. Since the Senate was not in secession, Johnson did not have to immediately notify that political body of the personnel change in the War Department. He could wait until the Senate convened in early December. [R97;478,488]

With the special summer session of Congress concluded, Thad Stevens left Washington City for Lancaster during early August. And he must have regretted being too infirm to attend the cornerstone laying ceremony for "Stevens Hall" at Pennsylvania College. But he was not too infirm to worry that the Democratic Party might succeed at teaming up with Andrew Johnson and retaking control of the Federal Government. In an August 16 letter to Edward McPherson, Stevens wrote:

"What may turn up next session [of Congress] is hard to say. The [members of the less Militant Republican Faction] are a base set — Trumbull, Fessenden, Sherman, [and] Wilson will ruin us. [So] we [of the more Militant Faction] must establish the doctrine of [Federal Government Supremacy] over all the States in [decreeing who is permitted to vote], or [the Republican Party] shall finally be ruined. We must thus bridle [State Rights advocates in] Pennsylvania, Ohio, Indiana et cetera, or the [conquered States], being [permitted representation in Congress], [will force the nation to] drift into [Democratic Party control]." [R96;288]

Being frightened over the possibility of a Democratic Party resurgence, Thad Stevens was determined to further subjugate the Democrat States, such as Tennessee and Kentucky, under an all-powerful, Republican-dominated Federal Government. This would be the final step in destroying the last vestiges of State Sovereignty as defined in the Federal Constitution. Let us review the history:

Determined to preserve State Sovereignty, 7 southern States had seceded a few weeks prior to the day the sectional Republican Party took control of the Federal Government back in March, 1861. And the people of 4 more southern States had followed in voting for secession rather than participate in a Federal Invasion of the Confederacy. Three other States — Delaware, Maryland, Kentucky — had taken various, eventually-futile, neutrality stands and Missouri had broken out into a full-fledged in-State Civil War, which the Federal-backed Faction had eventually won. Having subjugated Delaware, Maryland, Kentucky and Missouri, and afterward having conquered and subjugated the 11 States of the Confederacy, Stevens was finally turning to final subjugation of Delaware, Maryland, Kentucky and Missouri, and — the final step — subjugation of the northern States to prevent a Democrat resurgence and to ensure continued national political domination by the Republican Party.

In short, Stevens planned to admit African American men to the polls in Delaware, Maryland, Kentucky, Missouri and all States to the north "as an ultimate means of saving the Republican Party." At one point in late October Stevens would even advocate the conquest of Cuba, making bonded African Cubans immediately independent, building a Republican Political Machine there and making that island a State within the United States. Certainly, Stevens was expanding his enthusiasm for buttressing the Republican Party with the votes of Machine-led African American men. [R96;288,291]

Republicans were furious at Charles Sumner for the criticism he hurled against Party leaders during a newspaper interview with James Redpath (you will recall Redpath as one of the most effective Republican propagandists during the worst years of Bleeding Kansas terrorism). Redpath's account of the Sumner interview would be published as a supplement to the Boston *Advertiser* on September 4, and many other newspapers would also carry the story. The timing was terrible. With elections just two months off, Republican politicians were making every effort to present united opposition toward Andrew Johnson and toward Democratic politicians. Perhaps Sumner's anger toward the Republican leadership was hardened by his marital problems. He had not communicated in any way with Alice for three months. She had totally avoided him while spending the summer in the Berkshires. His Boston house was sold, but the Washington dream-house was not yet finished. He was surely depressed over those disappointments. But most of all, Sumner was mad at the Republican leadership for excluding him from the powerful committees shaping the Party's Reconstruction programme. So, when Redpath arrived for the interview, he had found the Senator easy to anger. Sumner criticized less senior Republican Congressmen and Senators for being indifferent to what he considered the suffering of Republicans in the conquered States. He called George Edmunds, "a prodigy of obstructiveness and technicality," and blamed Roscoe Conkling for similar behavior. But Sumner reserved his strongest acid for William Fessenden, whose actions he thought "akin to insanity," and representative of a lawyer "of the *nisi prius* order." Sumner claimed Fessenden's "drag on [Reconstruction]" resembled the actions of "perverse, pig-headed and brutal" Andrew Johnson. Of course calling Andrew Johnson "perverse, pig-headed and brutal" was acceptable Republican propaganda. The furor that Sumner was precipitating resulted from him saying that Fessenden's behavior resembled Johnson's, and saying so just two months before Election Day. As would be expected, Sumner's denunciations of fellow Republicans in the Redpath interview would worsen his future political exclusion from important Senate committees. Typical of criticism leveled at Sumner would be that of the New York *Times*, which warned readers that Sumner "is prepared to disregard the [Federal] Constitution, deprive the States of powers expressly vested in them, and remodel everything [political] according to his philanthropic inclinations."

The September issue of the *Atlantic Monthly* carried Charles Sumner's extensive article on Alaska and on how its purchase was another step toward eventual Federal control over the whole North American Continent. The magazine's editor apologized for the great length of Sumner's article, but explained that the message in the article was of vital importance to Americans because of "its bearing on Canada and especially on Mexico." While readers across the States were reading the *Atlantic Monthly* article, Sumner was completing preparations for a 22-site, 6-week speaking tour where he would publicly advocate an agenda for expanding the boundaries of the country, especially to the north.

It was about this time that Alice Sumner concluded her summer vacationing in the Berkshires and, taking Bell with her, boarded a ship for Paris, where she intended to live with her sister. Relatives had arranged for the steamship tickets to bear an alias in an attempt to prevent Boston society from learning about the trip. Charles would probably know nothing of the trip for some time, for Alice had not corresponded with her husband even once during her summer vacation in the Berkshires. [R73;301-302,310-312]

On September 14 Thad Stevens sat down and wrote a letter to W. B. Mellius, a Republican politician who was concerned about allegations by Democratic Party politicians to the effect that he, Thad Stevens, had fathered one or more mixed-race, African-European children. Stevens explains, in this letter, how he had employed many African American live-in servants over a period of 40 years, but "so far as I know . . . none of them became pregnant during that time." Stevens chose language that appeared to testify that none of his female servants had become pregnant under his roof, even those married at the time. Of course a married servant becoming pregnant by her husband would have reflected no dishonor upon Stevens and he was surely not making an effort to deny such a thing. He was simply using that story line to testify that, within the walls of his house, he had not impregnated any of his servants, not even Lydia Smith. Stevens' cleverly contrived defense follows:

"From the time I began business (40 odd years ago) I have kept house through the agency of hired servants. . . . Those servants were of various [skin] colors; some white, some black and others of all intermediate colors. . . . They have resided with me for various periods from one month to 15 years. . . . I believe I can say that no child was ever raised or, so far as I know, begotten under my roof. Sometimes husband and wife have worked the one for me and the other for another, generally at the same time, cohabiting together on Saturday nights. But I believe none of them became pregnant during the time." [R96;288]

Meanwhile in Mississippi, the process of registering qualified voters was nearing completion by early September. The totals of qualified registered men, by race, as of this time, were as follows:

European American men deemed qualified and registered:	46,636.
African American men registered:	60,167.
Total registered men:	106,808.

The count showed that, of the 61 counties, 33 had African American voting majorities, and, overall, 56 percent of voters were African American men. By the time of the election of Delegates to the Mississippi Constitutional Convention, to be held in November, the voter registration rolls would total 139,327, and of that number a solid majority would be African American men (I do not have a racial breakdown of the 139,327).

Mississippi historian James Garner would describe how Edward Ord had set up the organization and procedures for the registration campaign — for Mississippi voter registration had been a carefully controlled Federal Military operation, with no connection to the State or local governments. During the registration campaign in Mississippi, Ord had in place 1,817 Federal troops, stationed in 13 locations, including 269 at Vicksburg, 242 at Jackson and 256 at Grenada.

"The chief political duty" of Edward Ord, commander of the Military District comprised of Arkansas and Mississippi, "was to make a careful registration of the new electorate, as defined by the [Federal Reconstruction Acts]. To protect the registration officers from interference while in the discharge of their duties, he made liberal requisitions upon the [Federal] War Department for troops, and organized a large number of parties of mounted men to assist in the work of the registration [campaign]. On the 15th of April, he appointed by special order a [Federal] Board of 4 military officers, who were charged with the duty of dividing the State into a convenient number of Election Districts for the purpose of facilitating the work of registration. It was also made the duty of this Board to examine and recommend applicants for the positions of Registrar [in each county], and in order to procure suitable persons, the Board was directed to correspond with the 'most prominent and reliable [men living in the State who had never supported State secession or the Confederacy].' [To ensure that only men who had never supported State secession or the Confederacy were] appointed [to be Registrars], the Board was directed to make a record in each case, giving fully the reasons for recommending the applicant. A [County Elections] Board of 3 Registrars was appointed for each county. Each appointee was required to subscribe to and file in [Ord's office] an oath that he had never voluntarily given aid, countenance, counsel, or encouragement to persons engaged in [armed defense against Federal invasion forces]; and that he had never sought, accepted, or attempted to exercise the functions of any office whatever under the authority [of a seceded State or the Confederate Government], nor yielded a voluntary support to any such authority. Of course, few of the native [European American men of Mississippi] could take such an oath. As a consequence, [the appointed County] Registrars were for the most part [African American men, Federal] military officers, and [former Federal] soldiers who had settled in the State since the [conquest of the Confederacy]"

Between April 24 and May 30, Edward Ord had appointed the Board of Registrars for each county. "Registrars were [instructed] to give the strictest interpretation of the law, and exclude every person whose qualification there might be any doubt. . . . [Furthermore], no person should be entitled to vote by reason of any . . . pardon or amnesty," which might be handed down by the Federal House, Senate or President.

By early June, with Edward Ord's registration organization and procedures established, the campaign to register qualified Mississippi voters had begun in earnest. Mississippi historian James Garner would describe the Federal-controlled registration process:

> "The work of registration began early in June. The Registrars, accompanied by soldiers, clerks, and assistants proceeded from precinct to precinct. Only males 21 years of age, who had resided in the State one year, and who could take an oath of which the following was the substance, were entitled to be registered as legal voters. [The oath:]

The applicant was made to swear:

- That he "had never been a **member** of any legislature, nor held any executive or judicial **office** — and afterward engaged in [defense against Federal invasion forces], or had given aid or comfort to [Confederates];

- "That he had never taken an **oath** — as a member of the [Federal House or Senate] or as an officer of the [Federal Government or military], or as a member of any State legislature, or as an executive or judicial officer of any State — **to support the [Federal Constitution]**, and afterward engaged in [support of State Secession] or gave aid or comfort to [Confederates]." [R204;171-174]

This oath was more exclusive than one would suspect, as historian James Garner would explain:

> "These stringent requirements in effect disqualified most of the prominent and influential [European American] citizens, for there were few of that class who had not at some time held a petty office. They had all served the cause of the Confederacy."

The situation in South Carolina was similar. The books listing registered voters were closed on September 30, revealing that the Union League's voter registration program had built a powerful Republican Political Machine capable of dominating politics across most of the State for generations to come. Only 10 upstate counties would be politically competitive. Statewide the books listed as voters 78,982 African American men and 46,346 European American men. The Union League, which had expanded to totally dominate the political affairs of the State's African American men, was led by Francis Cardozo, a Charleston preacher of partial African American ancestry who had never been bonded. In the words of Hampton biographer Walter Brian Cisco, "The league was almost entirely [African American], and virtually every [African American] voter was a member." By this time, Wade Hampton realized that it would not be possible for European American men and African American men to forge sufficient political bonds to give South Carolina honest government in the near term. It was apparent that the Union League and Republican operatives from the northern States held the immediate power. Yet Hampton was still advocating efforts to forge bonds of political friendship where possible.

A vote to enable a State Constitutional Convention was schedule for November 19 and 20 and most European American voters were advocating staying away from the polls, in hopes their absence would reduce the total vote below a majority of registered voters, thereby invalidating the election. But Wade Hampton remained insistent that all registered European American men encourage political friendships with African Americans and go to the polls and vote against the proposed Convention. He had come to accept the reality that African American men would be allowed to vote, but advocated that limits be placed on voter qualifications, equally for both races, that would require "a slight educational and property qualification of all classes" of voters. He further advised in a letter published in newspapers throughout the State on and about August 29:

> "Let our people remember that the [African Americans] have, as a general rule, behaved admirably, and that they are in no manner responsible for the present condition of affairs. Should they, in the future, be misled by wicked or designing men, let us consider how ignorant they necessarily are, and let us, only the more, try to convince them that we are their best friends." [R199;190-191]

Meanwhile, Charles Sumner was working a real job as he set out on his extensive lecture tour in early October, headlined: "Are We a Nation?" He had scheduled the speaking tour primarily to raise money, for his living expenses had skyrocketed since his marriage. The marriage was a lost cause, but the financial obligations remained. Although Sumner had toured Europe several times, he rarely traveled west of the Appalachians or south of the Potomac. The speaking tour was his first trip west of the

Appalachians since 1855 — the formative days of the then-budding Republican Party. Sumner rather detested men who lived west of Pennsylvania, telling members of Boston's Saturday Club that "he never met a well-educated man from the west." He much preferred to associate with literary men from Massachusetts and surrounding States or with European intellectuals. Sumner suffered from a persistent cold during the tour. Biographer David Donald would write of Sumner's speaking tour: "Many listeners detected an irritating tone of condescension in [Sumner's] voice, for he was too tired and too unwell to conceal his conviction that he was bringing light to the heathen." Although he was not a Christian man, Sumner was convinced that, if there was a God, that God surely supported his political thinking, and it was from that political-religious view that Sumner presumed he was "bringing light to the heathen."

While Charles was delivering lectures in the mid-western States, Boston society was gossiping about his marital problems. By mid-October Charles Adams had heard that Alice planned to sue "for a divorce on the ground of impotence." But, for many years, Alice would continue to insist that her husband had been impotent and his political enemies would often expound upon the alleged deficiency. Although there seems to be no earlier record of the thing, college classmates would recall that Sumner was known to be impotent at Harvard, and had thereby acquired the nickname: "The Stag." Biographer David Donald was unable to draw a clear conclusion on the validity of the impotence charge. Doctor Charles Brown-Sequard and another physician would examine Sumner's body after his death and pronounce his genitals perfectly normal. Furthermore, Sumner's deep voice and masculine appearance suggested ample male hormone levels. But, for years into the future, Sumner's political enemies would call him "The Great Impotent." By the way, I inserted the "impotence" story in *Bloodstains* to provide a brief moment of levity, for so much of this history is such a sad tale.

Sumner's speaking itinerary included Milwaukee, Dubuque, Toledo, and many other cities in today's Mid-west. Returning to the northeastern States, he lectured at Boston on November 12, and followed with deliveries at Providence and Portland. The final audience gathered at New York City's Cooper Institute on November 19 to hear a tired and still-hoarse delivery. Newspaper accounts of Sumner's "Are We a Nation?" speaking tour were as polarized as his rhetoric. The Boston *Post* called the thing "unmistakable tedious" and "decidedly soporific." The New York *World* thought it "prolix . . . puerile and ostentatious." But those were Democratic newspapers. A pro-Sumner newspaper, the *Independent* praised Sumner's "high and holy passion for the American nation" and thought such passion gave the oration "the harmony of an ode, the unity and rhythm of a poem, whose soul is patriotism." Julia Ward Howe wrote in her diary that her friend's lecture was "on the whole . . . valuable and instructive." Sumner's closest political adviser, Ed Pierce, praised his "tone, thought, sweep, general principle and aspiration," but Pierce was more timid about Sumner's advocacy of military conquests into Canada and Mexico. On that account, Pierce advised, "It perhaps declares a somewhat higher Caesarism than some minds would assent to." And Sumner's advocacy of Federal control over a complete continent did have roots in the ancient Roman Empire. R73;311-312]

Meanwhile in the conquered States, from September through February of the following year, 1868, Republican-dominated Boards of Registration were staging elections for Delegates to State Constitutional Conventions in the 10 States subjugated under Federal Military Rule. Republican Party leaders had completed their careful pruning of the voter registration lists to ensure victory for their Political Machines. A voter could cast his vote for a Delegate to represent his District at a Convention which would rewrite the State Constitution, or he could vote for continuing the existing State Constitution without modification. Alexander Harris would observe how completely subjugated the European Americans in those conquered States must have felt: "In most of the [conquered] States, few voted at these elections except [African American men], and also a small number of [European American men], chiefly [recent] emigrants from the [northern States]." Republican Machine candidates were, for the most part, a mix of African American and European American men of no recognized past accomplishment. Harris would write: "Neither character nor intellectual worth were considered in the selection of the individuals who were to re-frame the prostrated fabric of the [country]." And he would add: "corrupt personages were chosen to fill the seats that had [previously] been honored by the ablest and purest patriots to whom America had given birth." Only in Virginia would opponents of re-writing the State Constitution muster a significant minority vote — there 36 percent of voters would favor no change to their State Constitution. In the other 9 States undergoing Reconstruction, a much smaller percentage would be voting to retain their Constitutions. A correspondent from Montgomery, Alabama would describe Republican Machine tactics in the New York *World*:

> "The [African American men] were everywhere driven to the polls by the chiefs of the [Republican Party Machine]. The day before the election, [Republican] agents traveled through Montgomery County, and summoned the [African American men] to come to the city and vote, telling them that General Swain had ordered them to do so, and would punish them if they did not. On the afternoon before the day of the election, thousands of [African American men] marched into Montgomery in regularly organized regiments, each man bearing arms; and at night they camped around the city as a besieging army. The danger of a disturbance was so great that the Military authorities ordered them to be disarmed."

Voters in the States that held their national elections in October delivered "an overwhelming endorsement" of the State Rights policies of Andrew Johnson. Upon hearing the returns, powerful financier Jay Cooke wrote his brother Henry: "What bad news, sad news tonight. Pennsylvania and Ohio gone Democratic and the sad lessons of the [struggles to conquer the Confederacy] all forgotten." But Henry's letter in reply showed little disappointment, for he seemed to be looking forward to reducing the power of the more Militant Faction in the Party. He blamed the Republican defeats on "ultra infidelic radicals" like Thad Stevens, because he had been "dragging the Republican Party into all sorts of isms and extremes" — and on Ben Wade, because he had been "uttering agrarian doctrines" and "trying to array labor against capital" — and on Ben "Beast" Butler because he had been advocating "wholesale repudiation" of the Federal debt — and on Thad Stevens because he had been "advocating the idea of a flood of irredeemable paper money sufficient in volume to drown the whole country." [R96;290, R97;479]

(4Q67)

Delegates to the Alabama Constitutional Convention gathered in Montgomery on November 5. This was the first State Constitutional Convention to be held in the 10 States undergoing Reconstruction. Many of the Delegates were African American men, only half of whom could even write their name, and most of the European American Delegates were ill-prepared for the job. Such were the men who — in violation of what would appear to be the intent of the Federal Constitution — were empowered to "subvert their State Sovereignties." This overview should be helpful:

> Former Confederates, defeated in battle and in politics, were twice-embittered toward the Republican Party, for the northern States had repeatedly excluded African American men from participating in their political affairs, even though such men were a small and inconsequential minority. New York State had allowed African American men to vote if they owned property and thereby paid taxes, but that State's voters had repeatedly refused to permit other African American men to vote (by a 63% vote in 1860 and by a 72% vote in 1864). In 1862, by a majority of 71%, Illinois State voters had enacted a law which excluded any African American from entering their State with intent to live there, and at the same time they had voted (by a majority of 86%) to exclude from voting or holding political office the African American men who already lived in their State. In 1865 voters in Connecticut had defeated a proposition to begin admitting African American men to their polls. In 1867, by a large majority, voters in Ohio voted to continue to exclude African American men from their polls. At about the same time, voters in Kansas and Minnesota likewise voted to continue to exclude African American men from voting (of course, such behavior was totally in character for the people of Kansas). In the spring of 1868 voters in Michigan would reject a revised State Constitution because it contained a provision that would have allowed African American men to vote. So former Confederates, embittered by military defeat and destruction of their homeland, were also embittered by the hypocrisy of Republican voters in the northern States, who refused to permit African American men to participate in their society as political equals, while elevating to positions of superior political power the pliant African American men in the conquered States. Subjugation of former Confederates under Federal Military Rule did, to a greater extent than the forced independence of former bonded servants, intensify in that region European American "rage" and "bitter hostility" towards the Republican Party and the compliant African American race. Since they had previously worked together to defend the Confederacy against the Federal Invasion, African Americans and European Americans

had maintained friendly relations. But that was in the past. Under Military Rule the Republican Party was succeeding in embittering the African American against the European American and vice versa. What could have been a mutual effort to rebuild the region's invasion-shattered economy was degraded, by Republican Political manipulation, into a destructive societal struggle. Yet, in less time than one generation, the Republican Political Machines would disappear, and remnant friendships between the two races would survive and others would be rekindled. Societal destruction would not be complete, not everlasting. [R97;481-482]

Meanwhile in Mississippi, in the latter part of November, qualified voters cast ballots for or against authorizing a Mississippi State Constitutional Convention and for Delegates, who would gather at Jackson to write the new Constitution, should said Convention be authorized. I do not have the exact date of the election, which may have taken place over several days, as election officials perhaps moved about gathering votes. It was generally believed that authorizing the Convention would lead to a new State Government, which would be subservient to the votes of African American men, almost none of them being tax payers and essentially all of them being organized into a massive voting block by Republicans from the northern States who also paid little or no taxes. Rejection would mean that Mississippi would continue to be ruled by the Federal Military and remain subservient to the political prejudices of northern States politicians. The Federal law controlling the rules of the election stipulated that, for the Convention to be legally authorized, a majority of qualified, registered voters had to cast ballots in favor of the measure — meaning that the political organizers controlling the votes of the African American men had to be diligent in getting the vast majority of those men to the polls with proper instructions, even if most European American men boycotted the vote. A turnout below 50% would void the election. Edward Ord's military organization selected 3 men to run the election at each precinct: a Registrar, a Judge and a Clerk, all paid $6 per day from Federal funds. These had to swear by oath that they had never supported State secession or the Confederacy. I have no evidence that poll watchers were allowed. No former Confederate officer was allowed to run for Delegate, but former Federal officers and recent residents of the State, were allowed to do so. During the fall political campaign the qualified voters of Mississippi had chosen from among three political strategies:

> A Republican State Convention, held in Jackson on September 10, had established an official Mississippi Republican Party. It had been well attended and energized. "About one-third of the Delegates were [African American men]," and the others were election Registrars, agents of the Newly Independent African American Men's Bureau, and "men from the northern States who had recently taken up their abode in the State." A newspaper reporter in attendance wrote, "Two things are clear: first, the [African American] vote is in the majority; second, it will be controlled by a few [European American] men."

> A "Constitutional Union Convention," held in Jackson on October 15, poorly attended but influential, advocated boycotting the election in hopes that Republicans would fail to get a majority of qualified, registered voters to the polls.

> A "respectable minority of the leading politicians and editors," of the State, confident that the Convention would be approved, encouraged qualified European American voters to go to the polls and vote for Delegates who, although they would be a small minority, might provide helpful influence at the Convention. An editorial in the Jackson *Clarion* advocated that the European American people of Mississippi needed to "make the most of the situation and form an alliance with the [African Americans] politically by a full recognition of their rights to vote and hold office, acquire ascendancy over them, and become their teachers and controllers instead of allowing the Republicans to do so."

By the time of the election, in the latter part of November, there were 139,327 qualified, registered voters, according to the official records, which was considerably more than the 106,803 men recorded as registered in the aforementioned early September report. A majority of those 139,327 voters would consist of any vote total above 69,664. Election officials — the vast majority of them being in favor of the proposed State Constitutional Convention and free from oversight by the opposition (no poll watchers as far as I can tell) — reported that the required hurdle of 69,664 votes, that being a "majority of registered voters," was barely cleared by the end of the vote tally process — cleared by only 75 votes! How convenient! I do not have evidence of fraud, but I know of no reason not to be suspicious.

Approval for a Mississippi Constitutional Convention won by 50.05 percent of the registered voter rolls has to be suspect. Few men opposed to the Convention bothered to vote. Opposition votes only totaled 6,277, thereby making the boycott the primary sentiment of European Americans, and thereby placing very, very few native Mississippi European American Delegates in attendance.

Approximately two weeks following the election, on December 10, Edward Ord, commander over the Military District consisting of Mississippi and Arkansas, would issue an order "declaring that inasmuch as a majority of the votes cast were for a [Mississippi Constitutional] Convention, it would assemble" in one month, on January 7, 1878. Two weeks following that order, another would arrive from Washington on December 28, directing Alvan Gillem, another high ranking Federal officer, to take over command of the Military District consisting of Mississippi and Arkansas. Ord would receive orders to move west and take command of the Department of California. Ord had commanded over Mississippi and Arkansas for about 9 months. Federal policy called for frequently moving commanders to new assignments for political reasons. [R204;176-181]

Meanwhile in Richmond, Jeff Davis and Robert Lee appeared in the Federal District Court on November 26 to answer questions before a Jury on the Treason charge leveled against both Davis and Lee. The air in Richmond was tense, for Virginia subjugated under Federal Military District Number One, and Federal troops were garrisoned in the city to ensure complete Federal control. Jeff and Robert's meeting at lawyer Robert Ould's house the previous day was the first time Davis and Lee had been together since the retreat from Richmond in March of 1865. Of the previous day's meeting Robert Lee had written his wife: "[Jeff] Davis looks astonishingly well and is quite cheerful. He enquired particularly after you all." But shortly thereafter Jeff had received a telegram reporting that Varina's mother, Margaret Howell, had died. Certainly the timing had been horrible, for Jeff had felt compelled to leave Montreal several days previously, so he could confer with his New York lawyers and then his Virginia lawyers. Yet, although very sick, Varina's mother had not seemed in danger of dying when Jeff was leaving, and Varina was there to see that she received the best care. The funeral would be the next day, November 27, at Christ Church Cathedral in Montreal, and there was no way for Jeff be at Varina's side.

Robert Lee was called into the courtroom first, leaving Jeff Davis sitting on the bench outside. The Jury was a mixture of European Americans and African Americans. John Underwood was presiding. During two hours of questioning, Federal Prosecutors made Robert Lee tell the Jury of many past Confederate troop movements all of which were common public knowledge. And, apparently too scared of the former President's skills before a Jury, the Federal Prosecutors dared not call Jeff Davis into the courtroom. Davis remained sitting on the bench outside. Somehow the Federal prosecutors, the Judge and the Jury concluded that Lee's account of Confederate troop movements constituted "proof of armed insurrection against the [Federal Government]." It seems that the Federals had decided that this November judicial exercise would be recast as only a preliminary hearing. That way they could put off again the day when Federal Prosecutors would have to face Jeff Davis and his able lawyers in a courtroom setting. To complete the arrangement, one of the Federal Prosecutors, William Evarts of New York, proposed that the formal trial be held on the third Wednesday of March, 1868. That was five months off — giving more time for Republican propagandists to advocate political subjugation and land confiscation without exposing themselves to Jeff Davis' courtroom defense of State Sovereignty. [R19;324-325]

Meanwhile, Thad Stevens arrived in Washington City on November 13 feeling stronger, though not well. Lydia Smith either accompanied him to Washington City or had stayed there keeping house during his absence. Four days before leaving his Lancaster home, Stevens had issued a letter to Lydia's son Isaac, now an adult, commanding him to leave the Lancaster house and never return. Although he held the young man's mother in high regard, Stevens was obviously determined to rid himself of the services and burdens of the son:

> "Sir: Take notice that before Tuesday night next you have all your things away from my house and that you do not yourself enter my house during my absence to sleep or for any other purpose, under the penalty of being considered a housebreaker."

Four days after his arrival in Washington City, Stevens obtained more pills with instructions from his doctor, Henry Carpenter:

"If the action of the liver should be suspended, as indicated by the grey or ash colored stools, a blue pill may be taken at bedtime and repeated next morning or evening as may be necessary.

"If the effusion into the pericardium, or the dropsical affection of the heart, should increase — as you will know by the usual oppression, as experienced before — take one of the diuretic pills at bedtime, and repeat every 6 or 8 hours if necessary until relieved. Take as much nourishing food as your stomach will comfortably receive and digest — with as much of the punch wine, brandy, whiskey or beer as may be necessary and agreeable."

Stevens spent his first week in Washington City directing, from his home, the more Militant Faction's unfolding plans for the upcoming session of the Federal House. One plan aimed to increase the Republican Party voter base by expanding into the Federal States voting rights for African American men. Another aimed at Impeachment of Andrew Johnson. And Stevens drafted legislation which would force Andrew Johnson to give the Office of President to Ben Wade after the House voted for Impeachment, to regain it only if he was acquitted by the Senate. The House being scheduled to convene on the morning of November 21, Stevens made the short trip to the Capital building in a closed carriage, and then lay on a sofa in his Committee room to conserve energy while others gathered. When it was time to go to his seat in the House Chamber, Stevens brushed off offers of assistance with: "I can go alone; I am not so dead as some of my newspaper friends have reported me." And when Charles Sumner appeared in the House to commiserate, Stevens made no attempt to sit down while he and Sumner talked. But, in the words of biographer Richard Current: "he could not hide for long the effects of his rheumatism and jaundice and dropsy, symptoms of his failing legs and liver and heart."

During the organization the House and Senate the leadership did not resurrect the Joint House-Senate Committee on Reconstructing the Governments of the Conquered States — the group of 15 men also known as, "The Directory." In its place the House leadership established a House Committee on Reconstructing State Governments in the Conquered States, and named Thad Stevens its Chairman.

Andrew Johnson thought he had a pledge from Ulysses Grant that he, Grant, would refrain from yielding the office of Secretary of War back to Edwin Stanton in the event the Senate voted to not concur with the personnel change. Johnson wanted Grant to hold the office, as Acting Secretary, until replaced by another Johnson appointee or until the Federal Judiciary became involved, because he, Johnson, wanted to place the anticipated dispute over the constitutionality of the Tenure of Office Act before the Federal Supreme Court. The Grant-replaces-Stanton personnel change was to be Johnson's test case. If Grant freely gave the office back to Stanton, Johnson figured he had little in the way of a test case. So he had sought Grant's pledge to respect the Office of the President, to which he reported. And Grant seemed to have agreed, in so far as the wording of his letter to Johnson implied:

"I shall, in that event, either hand you my resignation as acting Secretary of War, or let a mandamus be issued against me to surrender the office."

So, when the Senate rejected the appointment of Grant to the office of Acting Secretary, Grant was going to turn the office back to Johnson for another appointment, or he was going to force the Judicial Branch of the Federal Government to become involved, thereby setting up a test case for Johnson.

The Republican Party program to Impeach Andrew Johnson for politically opposing the majorities in the House and Senate would threaten to destroy the checks and balances by which the Federal Constitution distributed political power among the Executive, Legislative and Judicial branches. It would threaten to reduce the Federal President, at the time Andrew Johnson, to a subservient role not unlike the King of Great Britain. And it was threatening to elevate the leader in the Federal House, at the time Thad Stevens, to the most powerful role in the Federal Government — a role similar to the Prime Minister of Great Britain. To Impeach for acts of treason or for criminal actions was permitted under the Federal Constitution, but it did not permit impeaching a president because he took opposing political views to those of the majority in the Legislative branch or because he spoke out in opposition to those views, or because he vetoed a lot of bill sent to his desk. But Thad Stevens aimed to violate that provision of the Federal Constitution.

The first vote on Impeachment took place in the House on December 7. It was a vote on an Impeachment bill submitted, with Thad Stevens' guidance, by James Ashley. Apparently the leading Representatives were yet quite afraid that Impeachment would backfire and hurt their political stature.

So they tapped Ashley, a junior Representative from Ohio, to officially sponsor their Impeachment bill. As would be summarized by contemporary historian, Alexander Harris: "The Impeachment bill charged Andrew Johnson with 'high crimes and misdemeanors;' with usurpation of power and violation of law; and also, that he had made a corrupt use of the appointing, the pardoning and the veto power; and had corruptly interfered in elections."

Too ill to spend much time on the House floor, Stevens barely arrived at his seat in time to vote:

> "He went to the capitol in a closed carriage; two men carried him up the steps in a chair, and from his Committee room he totteringly made his way with the aid of the benches and his cane to his seat. He arrived there just in time to cast the last vote in favor of the resolution. His vote was not enough. For the time being Impeachment was lost."

The vote was 56 for impeachment, versus 108 against. Impeachment would have to wait.

Shortly after the Impeachment vote was taken, Thad Stevens held a conference in his home to instruct a Delegation of Republican Machine men from the conquered States, who had traveled up to Washington City. The Delegation was made up of both African American men and European American men. Stevens explained to the Delegation that English law required that a British official had to be charged with treason or criminal activity to be Impeached, but he alleged that the Federal Constitution also permitted a Federal official to be Impeached for taking political views in opposition to the majority of members of the House. Then Stevens related his hopes for new legislation. Biographer Richard Current would write:

> "Turning to the [African American] Delegates, he told them he was about to introduce a bill to give them a special and separate representation in Congress, the [African American men] in each State to elect their own congressman at large. He promised them further that [Federal] confiscation [of farmland] would yet have its day, asked them about the [larger tracts of farmland and larger homes] in their respective neighborhoods, and disposed of the opponents of [Federal] confiscation as tender-hearted fellows whose tenderness was really a softening of the brain." [R96;294-296, R97;487-489]

Meanwhile, around the first of December, Charles Sumner finally moved into his new dream-house in Washington City. But he moved in alone without any hope that Alice would ever return and complete the "dream." A letter received by Charles on Thanksgiving Day from the father of Alice's first husband and a close friend of Sumner's, Representative Samuel Hooper, of Boston, explained Alice's position. Based on that letter, biographer David Donald would write: "Only when Hooper reassured him that Alice would prefer 'to brave anything rather than continue to live with you,' did he finally take up residence in his still unfurnished house where he hoped to find more privacy than rented rooms would afford." But Sumner moved in harboring hatred toward Alice. He studied the literature on female villains and concluded that "No picture can adequately show the completeness of her vileness." He began a rumor that Alice had gone to Europe to abort a baby she had conceived with Friedrich Holstein.

Charles Sumner had not seen his wife, Alice or his step-daughter, Bell since they had left him around the end of April, 1867. Sadly, he would never see them ever again. Alice and Bell would soon return to Europe and, except for a few trips back to The States to visit relatives, Alice would remain there forevermore. She would die in Europe in 1913. Alice would divorce Charles in 1873 "by mutual agreement." She would never remarry. And Charles would never remarry. In fact, Charles would never mention his wife, later to become his ex-wife, by name. When forced to speak of her, he would use the term "that woman."

Biographer David Donald would study the marriage in considerable detail and draw some interesting conclusions. Donald would observe that Alice "complained not so much of [Charles'] total impotence as of his inability 'fully' to satisfy 'what every matured woman considers a just desire'." That would lead Donald to conclude that "sexual incompatibility was at the base of the Sumner's difficulties." Donald would conclude that Alice desired a more manly husband. The more the hot-tempered Alice nagged Charles for not meeting her needs, the more "she despised him for breaking into tears." And Donald would expand on that line of thinking:

"Sumner could not play the domineering husband. There had always been a passive, essentially feminine element in his composition; even in his courtship it was Alice who had been the pursuer and he the pursued. She had the experience of a former marriage; though he had read Michelet's *L'Amour* and knew all the literature about sex, he was probably a virgin. Doubtless he proved an awkward and often ineffectual lover."

Donald would explain Charles' reluctance to talk through his marital problems with Alice and seek advice from others:

"Sumner had become increasingly unwilling to believe that he could learn from anyone. During his sufferings after [he was caned by Preston Brooks] he had come to rank himself among the holy company of the martyrs, and thereafter he craved admiration more than instruction or even solace." A friend of both, writer William Bryant, explained: "A woman is not content with a husband who is exclusively occupied with himself and his own greatness." The treatment that Charles had chosen to apply to a departed Alice was consistent with his behavior toward others during past personal disputes. In the early days of their marital problems, Charles "avoided doing or saying anything." When their marital problems rose toward a climax, Charles "resorted to the silent treatment." After Alice left, Charles "refused to write to her during the long summer." When he needed to forward mail to Alice, Charles "mailed it to her without any covering comment."

Finally, Donald would add the following conclusion:

"In domestic as in political warfare [Charles] had no thought of compromise, and he was determined to regard the break with [Alice] as final and irreparable. In his eyes Alice had been wicked, and he adopted toward her the strategy he always used when dealing with evil: the moral blockade. Since neither silence nor forbearance could change her course, he would preserve his own purity by cutting her totally out of his life." [R73;316-320]

I need only add the following comment to David Donald's excellent assessment of Charles Sumner, the man:

Charles Sumner — the most important leader and hero of the intellectuals and literary activists within the Republican Party, the Chairman of the Senate Foreign Relations Committee, the Senate's most militant proponent of destroying the Confederate States economically and socially, and the Senate's most militant proponent of dominating the politics of the conquered States through Republican Political Machines empowered by the votes of African American men — was an *incomplete man.*

Meanwhile on December 12, Andrew Johnson formally informed the Senate that he had suspended Edwin Stanton as Secretary of War and had named Ulysses Grant as acting Secretary of War. And Johnson listed for the Senators the reasons for his change in personnel. Republican leaders in the Senate would ponder this for a while, for they needed time to develop a plan of attack. [R97;488]

During December, William Seward and the Russian Minister, Edward de Stoeckl, repeatedly pressured Thad Stevens to push through the Federal House a bill authorizing Federal funds for the purchase of Alaska. The Purchase Treaty had been signed months earlier, but, during its special summer session, the House had failed to pass a bill authorizing the payment of $7,200,000. The big holdup seemed to be a claim by B. W. Perkins, a dealer in military arms, who asserted that the Russian Government owed him a lot of money for military supplies that he had delivered but for which he not been paid. Perkins wanted the Federal Congress to deduct what he was owed from the Federal payment to the Russian Government and hand that money directly over to him. And many Representatives, including Thad Stevens, thought that the House ought to do just that. But, during December de Stoeckl seems to have won Simon Stevens' support. Simon (not a relative) wrote Thad on December 19:

"In the Russian matter, I find [Edward de] Stoeckl very, very anxious. So much so that he has asked one or two friends in Washington [City] whether or not Congress is really delaying his appropriation on account of the Perkins' claim. When he asked me about that question last Monday I told him I could not tell about it. . . . [de Stoeckl] said he should try and see you and see if the Perkins claim could not be settled outside of Congress."

As Christmas recess neared, Thad Stevens saw defeated his bill which would have admitted into the Federal House, from each conquered State, one Representative at Large who would be of partial or complete African American descent. But he did see passed the remainder of his bill to revise the Federal programme for Reconstruction of the Governments of the conquered States, including the item to revise the prior requirement that, to ratify a State Constitution in a conquered State, the affirmative vote had to exceed one half of the number of voters registered by that State's Republican-dominated Board of Registration. Stevens' revision only required affirmation to exceed one half of the men voting, designed to eliminate the opposition's "boycott" strategy. And Stevens must have been looking forward to Christmas. His workmen at the Caledonia Ironworks were striving to make an 1867 goal of 600 tons of iron. Working in two feet of snow, they had made 31 tons during the first week of December, and, if able to maintain that pace, expected to reach the 1867 goal of 600 tons by the end of the month. And his nephew, Thaddeus, Junior had written him from Caledonia with a promise of pork and turkey:

> "We are going to butcher tomorrow so you can inform [Lydia] Smith that she may look for her hogs soon. We are going to kill eight and I think [John] Sweeney proposes to send you two. He has a turkey for you also." [R96;297-298]

Jeff and Varina spent the Christmas season in Mississippi. It was Jeff's first trip back to his home county since he had been summoned to Montgomery, Alabama in February 1861. They had left the children in Canada — the older at boarding schools, the younger with relatives or friends — and taken the train to Baltimore. There, they had stayed with friends for a few days before boarding a ship for Havana, Cuba. Jeff had withdrawn some of his last Confederate paycheck in Havana, which Judah Benjamin had deposited in a Cuban bank, for Jeff and Varina needed money for school tuition and living expenses. After a few days layover in Havana, they arrived in New Orleans on December 24. Varina would explain in her *Memoir*: "The Canadian winter proved too severe for [Jeff's] enfeebled frame, and he was advised to spend it in the South." At New Orleans, "The lobby of the St. Charles Hotel was jammed with well-wishers, and some men strove to embrace him with unabashed tears pouring down their cheeks." Five years of torment, robbery and subjugation by Federals had troubled most everyone, and New Orleans had suffered worst during all five of those years, including suffering the ravages of Ben "Beast" Butler. Varina reported that one old Methodist minister was so distraught that he was clinging to the hope that God would yet use Jeff Davis to somehow drive the Federals from the conquered States. The old minister had sought out Davis and, while looking upon him hopefully, declared: " 'Now, Lord, let Thy servant depart in peace, since I have seen His salvation'." [R19;327,R13;804]

The Year of 1868

(1Q68)

Meanwhile after Christmas, Thad Stevens prepared a speech advocating that Federal funds be authorized to fund the Alaska Purchase Treaty. And when William Seward called on him after Christmas pressing for the appropriation bill, Stevens must have told him that he was working on it. Anyway Edward de Stoeckl was please, for he wrote to the Russian Government in St. Petersburg: "I am counting on the influence of [Thad] Stevens, who at first supported that [claim by B. W. Perkins] but who now is working earnestly on our side." But funding the purchase of Alaska was not Stevens' priority; it would wait while he advanced legislation more important to the survival of the Republican Party. [R96;298]

After a short stay in New Orleans, Jeff and Varina traveled to Vicksburg. During one day Jeff traveled over to his and his brother's farms to survey the damage. Varina would later write:

> "We found our property all destroyed, our friends impoverished, and our old brother[, Joseph,] very feeble, but cheery. As many of our [previously owned African Americans] as could, came to see us, and [Jeff] paid a few hours' visit to the rest at [our now-sold farm,] Brierfield and [Joseph's now-sold farm,] Hurricane, [and] witnessed the destruction the [Federals] had worked, which had blotted out the labors of his life . . . ." [R13;804]

Ben Montgomery, to whom Joseph had sold the farms with personal financing, explained to Jeff how he had failed to turn a profit on the farms during the past season. The cotton crop had suffered terribly because of Mississippi River flooding and insect damage from army worms and boll worms. (This was a wide-spread problem in Mississippi. Historian James Garner would write, "The cotton crop had been almost a total failure in 1867, employers being unable to meet their obligations either to laborers or merchants from whom they obtained their supplies.") Joseph had given Ben Montgomery a loan to cover the full purchase price of the farms, but Montgomery had no money to pay the already past-due interest. Not even a portion. But neither Joseph nor Jeff dared seek foreclosure for failure to pay the interest due them, because it remained their hope that, with official ownership in Ben Montgomery's hands, the farms would escape confiscation at the hands of Federals such as Thad Stevens. In fact, Jeff took some of his meager financial reserve and gave it to the African Americans at Brierfield farm to help them survive the coming months. This Jeff did even though he no longer had any responsibility to care for them, as compared to former times. The visit to Brierfield and Hurricane must have been extremely sad for Jeff. Those farms had been his and Joseph's love and life's work. He found Joseph's large farmhouse burned to the ground. The Federals had even burned up the books in Joseph's separate library building where Jeff had "studied constitutional law and read world literature." Although he visited some of his fields, Jeff probably avoided going up to his farmhouse, Brierfield, for Federals had situated a family of hostile African Americans there. [R19;327, R204;182]

Meanwhile, Delegates to the Mississippi Constitutional Convention gathered on January 7 in Jackson. Two days later, Alvan Gillem would arrive to take command over the Military District ruling over Mississippi and Arkansas. Gillem had been in command of the sub-district of Mississippi since the creation in March 1867 of the Department of Mississippi and Arkansas under Edward Ord, so he was taking a promotion to also command over Arkansas. Of Gillem, historian James Garner would write that he "was a native of Tennessee, a personal friend of President Johnson, had distinguished himself for gallantry in the [Federal] army, and had taken a leading part in the reorganization of [the Tennessee State Government]."

Historian James Garner would conclude that the 100 Delegates at Jackson constituted "the most remarkable political assemblage ever convened in Mississippi." Among the 61 counties in Mississippi, the 32 with African American majorities were given 70 Delegates, while the 29 with European American majorities were given 30 Delegates. Of the Delegates in attendance, 17 were African American; 20-odd were from northern States, nearly all former Federal soldiers; 29 were native Mississippi European Americans who supported the Republican agenda, and 19 were Mississippi European Americans holding conservative political philosophies. There were some contested seats, holding the body below the planned 100 Delegates, 83 having answered the roll call on opening day.

First order of business in Jackson was fixing daily pay and mileage allowances for Delegates and hiring 30 Convention employees and fixing their pay, which ranged from $15 per day for a reporter and a secretary, to $10 per day for several others, to $5 per day for many lesser jobs, down to a wood chopper at $2.50 per day. Every employee hired was either an African American or a European American from a northern State. Delegates fixed their compensation at $10 per day and 40 cents per mile. Mileage payouts to Delegates would average about $160 per man, and range up to $240. Mississippi tax payers were to pay for the cost of the Convention, an irony, considering that hardly any Delegate or employee had ever paid meaningful taxes in the State — a rare example of the seldom found "free lunch." But there was a compensating factor: payments would be made in State warrants, which would prove to be worth only 65 or 70 cents on the dollar.

Rather ignoring the purpose to which they were sent to Jackson, Delegates set aside the job of writing a State Constitution in order to first engage in political legislating about which they had no authority, gleefully earning $10 per day, plus mileage, while playing around as if they were Legislators. Typically each Convention day lasted 3 hours. Examples of such playing around follow. After a substantial political fight, an attempt to declare vacant all civil offices in Mississippi failed. A scheme to raise taxes for a State welfare relief program for African Americans was approved, but Alvin Gillem refused to issue the military order needed to enforce the program, stating that the Newly Independent African American Men's Bureau was capable of caring for those truly in need and that ample opportunities for wage-earning work existed throughout the State. The Convention pressed for other "relief" measures, but, in every case Gillem refused to authorize any of them. An attempt was made to provide transportation money to those African Americans who had been brought to Mississippi as bonded persons and now wished to return to their former home outside the State — this, too, Gillem refused to endorse. A scheme to give land to many African Americans was hatched, which alleged that, while bonded persons, they had somehow earned rights to own certain portions of the lands they had worked. Again, Gillem declined to endorse the scheme. While all of this was going on, the Convention "was instituting an inquisitorial investigation into the affairs of Benjamin Humphreys, the provisional Civil Governor. The inquisition accused Humphreys of wrongdoing in warning of a feared African American insurrection and in handling charity sent down by ladies in Baltimore. Finding no legitimate violation, Gillem declined to support the inquisition.

Now, the Mississippi Constitutional Convention was authorized by Federal law to levy a property tax to generate revenue sufficient to pay the cost of holding the Convention. Elaborate taxation schemes were approved. One tax scheme, passed on February 12 with 36 sections — aiming to collect 3 or more times the revenue needed — was authorized by the Convention, but Alvin Gillem only ordered enforcement of section 27. On February 27, the Convention passed another taxation ordinance, levying a general tax equal to 50 percent of the State's 1867 real property tax; a special tax of 1.5 percent on merchant inventories and all personal property, except for cotton, which was taxed at 50 cents per bale. Gillem agreed with this substantial taxation scheme and issued an order directing the Sheriffs of each county to proceed with the collections. Historian James Garner would write, "The taxes were paid reluctantly, of course, and the Convention seems to have had ample funds to meet its enormous expenses."

The sole legitimate mission of the Convention, as you know, was to write a Mississippi State Constitution. Well, finally, after a month of procrastination, a Committee of Fifteen was selected to draft a proposed Constitution. A resolution to only modify the existing Constitution where necessary was rejected outright, the majority desiring to make the new version as different from the existing version as possible. Of most importance to Delegates were issues involving qualifications required to hold office and qualifications required to vote. Concerning the issue of who would be allowed to vote, a minority worked diligently to exclude African American men who could not read or write, matching existing provisions in several northern States. This would lead to an "acrimonious debate" followed by, on the 86th day of the Convention, an overwhelming vote to ignore the ability to read or write. After that vote, 14 of the 19 European American Delegates would resign, walk out and returned to their homes. In all the Convention would take 115 days, yielding $1,150 pay to each Delegate, and concluding on May 18. The final results of the Convention will be presented a few pages later, at the proper chronological time. [R204;186-203]

Meanwhile in Washington City, in a public letter issued during January, Thad Stevens worked at persuading fellow Republican politicians to embrace a movement to enable African American men to vote in the northern States. Voting African American men were becoming the majority in most conquered States, but few were allowed to the polls in the Federal States. Believing that essentially every African American man would vote for the candidates of the Republican Party, and fearing a resurgence by the Democratic Party, Stevens was becoming desperate to add to Republican voter strength in the northern States. Finally, after two years of disagreement with Charles Sumner on this issue, Stevens had come around to advocating that access to the polls by all adult male citizens "is an inalienable right." And he planned to explain his new political position in the following words: "True, I deemed the hastening of [voting by African American men in the Federal States] as very essential to the welfare of the nation, because without it I believe the [Federal] Government will pass into the hands of the [Democratic Party]." But, on reflection, he decided to reword the last part so it read: "will pass into the hands of the [former Confederates] and their friends." [R96;299]

During this time Thad Stevens took measures to muzzle the Federal Supreme Court, because he and fellow Republicans feared a majority of the Justices might vote to declare in violation of the Federal Constitution the Reconstruction Act and Military Rule over the conquered States. The Supreme Court would soon be hearing a case concerning a Mississippi newspaperman, William McCardle, who had been arrested, charged with publishing "incendiary" articles, and tried by the military organization commanded by Edward Ord, Andrew Johnson's appointed Military Ruler over the District overseeing Mississippi and Arkansas. The McCardle case had been appealed directly from the United States District Court of Mississippi to the Federal Supreme Court in Washington City, because no intermediate Federal appeals court existed. Charles Sumner, Thad Stevens and other Republicans feared the Supreme Court Justices might vote to declare Federal Military Rule over conquered Mississippi in violation of the Federal Constitution. Here is the math: 8 Justices comprised the Federal Supreme Court, and 5 were known to be looking for a test case by which they could revoke Military Rule over the 10 conquered States. The Senate had made the first move to strangle the Supreme Court, in early December passing a law stipulating that, with all Justices voting, a two thirds Supreme Court vote would be, in the future, required to declare unconstitutional a law passed by Congress. Well, 5 of 8 Justices is a vote of 62 percent, but two-thirds is a vote of 67 percent. It was obvious to everyone that the Senate was attempting to strangle the Supreme Court by playing with numbers: the two-thirds hurdle would require a vote of 6 of the 8 Justices, which is 75 percent. In early January the House debated intently the Senate's bill to strangle the Supreme Court. At one point, proposing to stop playing a numbers game, Thad Stevens offered a substitute to the Senate bill, which prohibited the Supreme Court from declaring unconstitutional any Act of Congress pertaining to Federal oversight of the conquered States. Of Stevens' amendment Biographer Richard Current would write: "he would, by law, deprive the [Supreme] Court of appellate jurisdiction over all cases arising from Federal administration [over the conquered States], and for good measure he would forbid that these cases be 'reviewed in any other tribunal in any manner whatever'." But Stevens' direct, in-your-face approach to strangling the Supreme Court was surpassed by a more clever proposal — namely to prohibit the Supreme Court from hearing any appeal from a District Court or a Circuit Court. Since the McCardle case could not be routed to the Supreme Court through an intermediate Appeals Court, it would be excluded from being heard in the Supreme Court. Thus amended, the bill was passed by the House and agreed to by the Senate. Andrew Johnson vetoed the bill. But both the House and the Senate voted to overrule his veto. The Supreme Court was thereby unable to render a decision in the McCardle case or scrutinize any legislation involving Federal Military Rule or making State Governments subservient to Republican Political Machines. [R97;483-484, R96;299]

Meanwhile, after a few days at and around Vicksburg, Jeff and Varina traveled to Locust Grove farm at St. Francisville, Louisiana to visit Jeff's older sister, Anna, and to Rosemont farm at Woodville, Mississippi to visit his sister Lucinda Stamps. I have already mentioned that Lucinda's son, Isaac had been killed near Gettysburg during the 1863 Confederate counter-invasion thrust into Pennsylvania. After that Jeff and Varina traveled to Canton, Mississippi to see Susannah Davis, widow of Jeff's brother Isaac, and mother to Joseph R. Davis, who had been a high-ranking Confederate officer. [R19;327]

But, concerning the Republican political family, there had been no feeling loyalty back in Washington City, even though — on January 11 Andrew Johnson, in the presence of the members of his Cabinet had sought Ulysses Grant's pledge to either turn his office back to the President of hold it until the Judiciary became involve, and once more Grant pledged to do as asked. And, as Johnson had anticipated, two days later the Federal Senate had voted to reject his suspension of Edwin Stanton from the job of Secretary of War. Concluding that action on January 13, the Senate had passed the following resolution:

> "Resolved, That having considered the evidence and reasons given by [Andrew Johnson] in his report of December 12, 1867 for the suspension from the office of Secretary of War of Edwin Stanton, the Senate do not concur in such suspension."

However, Ulysses Grant now violated his pledged to Johnson without hesitation. As soon as Ulysses Grant was informed of the Senate vote, he vacated the office of Acting Secretary of War, and permitted Edwin Stanton to immediately repossess it. By this act of betrayal and deliberate deceit, Johnson became aware that Grant had been in collusion with the more Militant Faction all along. Johnson was beginning to understand that, by helping the Faction's Impeachment schemes, Grant was to receive the Office of President for himself. [R97;489]

On February 10 Thad Stevens began an intensive personal witch hunt in search of "evidence" useful to prosecuting an Impeachment case. The House Judiciary Committee had gathered allegedly incriminating evidence against European Americans living in the conquered States, seeking justification for Federal Military Rule and Republican Political Machines empowered through the votes of African American men. Somewhere in that huge stack of what was alleged to be evidence Stevens' hoped to find bits of alleged criminal activity about which he could argue that Andrew Johnson was culpable. And the editor of the New York *Times* expected he would succeed where others had failed:

"Thad Stevens' eyes are sharper in his old age than those of the Chairman of the Judiciary Committee, and if he can't find some startling offence hidden away somewhere between the covers of 1,300 octavo pages it will be very strange indeed." [R96;300]

You will recall that no evidence exists that Thad Stevens was a Christian man. About this time the Reverend Jonathan Blanchard, an old acquaintance, decided to strive once again to win Thad Stevens' soul to Christ. Blanchard, had called on Stevens many years earlier, when he was a very powerful man in the Pennsylvania State Legislature, but Blanchard's appeal had then fallen on deaf ears. Now, time was running out. So, on February 15, he wrote Stevens, issuing this warning: "You are five years beyond the allotted time of man. . . At present, in every part of the [country] people believe that your personal life has been one prolonged sin; that your lips are defiled with blasphemy! And your body with women!!" He acknowledged that Stevens had done immense good public works, but warned good public works were not the road to Heaven: "The good you have done the [country] (and none has done more if so much) is no offset for vices such as I have named above." Recognizing that Stevens' only tie to Christianity was through memories of his mother's religious convictions, Blanchard beseeched him to embrace his "mother's God." In this letter, Blanchard preached on:

> "I have, after all, a strange hope that you are not to be lost. Though I will not insult your intelligence by arguing that 'whore-mongers and adulterers' are necessarily left outside of Heaven with 'dogs, sorcerers and murderers;' or that if you die in these sins, where Christ is, you cannot come. . . . But, if even now you will go to Christ, He has all the power in Heaven and earth and can make your Scarlet Sins white! I have loved and followed you with a strange fascination!! And now I bid you farewell."

But Thad Stevens was not moved to engage in a correspondence with Blanchard. Perhaps biographer Richard Current was right when he would later speculate that Stevens might have been "obliquely proud" of his reputation for sinful behavior. Current would recall, "Time and again in the past he had sneered at his political enemies as eunuchs, lady's male waiting-maids, old women in pantaloons, effeminate men." These observations would prompt Current to ask: "Was there some quirk of his personality, related somehow to his deep and abiding affection for his mother, that made him glad to be damned for the vices of a manly man?" But, did the Reverend Blanchard understand the principles of Biblical teaching better than he understood the principles of the Federal Constitution and its assurance of State Sovereignty? Within the letter was this nugget of wisdom: "***What makes bad government is bad sinful men***." Those 8 words should had headlined Current's biography. [R96;300-301,R86;364]

Meanwhile in Mississippi, it was February by the time Jeff and Varina arrived at their next stop, Jackson. There Jeff visited with Provisional Governor Benjamin Humphreys, who had somehow, up to that point, managed to avoid being deposed by, Congress or Military Rule. A few pages back, I mentioned that Humphreys' daughter, Mary Stamps, was the widow of Jeff's nephew Isaac Stamps, and one of Jeff's favorite nieces, although through marriage. You will recall that, during the fall of 1866, Jeff's brother Joseph had asked Mary Stamps to travel to Fortress Monroe to secretly obtain Jeff's permission to let Joseph sell Brierfield farm to Ben Montgomery with personal financing. Since Jackson was patrolled by Federal soldiers, Humphreys made sure that no crowd gathered to cheer Jeff and Varina's arrival. Concerning her husband's health that this point, Varina observed that the winter's journey had "not worked the expected improvement in [his] health, and his emaciation did not decrease" during the trip. But that should have been expected, given the destruction, suffering and hopelessness that Jeff saw in Louisiana and Mississippi — and he being powerless to help. But the time was approaching when he needed to start planning for his defense on Treason charges in the Federal District Court trial set for the third Wednesday in March. Would Jeff Davis get his day in court to defend State Sovereignty and prove his actions had not been Treason, as alleged, or would Republican leaders again be too terrified of losing the case to risk facing Davis and his legal team in a courtroom setting? Jeff and Varina left Jackson on February 25, bound for Richmond. [R19;327-328]

Meanwhile, the pending Impeachment agenda was advancing. On February 21 Andrew Johnson finally made his move: he fired Edwin Stanton. To the job of Acting Secretary of War he appointed Lorenzo Thomas. Thomas was Army Adjutant-General, so Johnson had turned again to it for a temporary replacement for Stanton. Ulysses Grant had circumvented Johnson's suspension tactic, so outright dismissal of Stanton had remained the only option. Johnson, knew this would give Thad Stevens the provocation he sought, and Impeachment would likely result. But Johnson was not short on courage. If he was destined to defend the Office of the President against a legislative take-over, to defend the key principle within the Federal Constitution — division of powers among the Legislative, Executive and Judicial branches of the Federal Government — then, from that defense, he intended not to shirk. And Johnson found an error in the wording of the more Militant Faction's Tenure of Office Act.

The first section of the Tenure of Office Act, by the way it was worded, could be argued legally to exclude Cabinet members who had been appointed by Abe Lincoln. And that would be helpful in defending the Office of the President in an Impeachment Trial before the Senate. The first section of the Act read as follows, the italics being mine:

> "Be it enacted by the [Federal Senate and House], that every person holding any civil office, to which he has been appointed by, and with the advice and consent of the Senate; and every person who may hereafter be appointed to any such office, and shall become duly qualified to act therein, is and shall be entitled to hold such office until a successor shall have been in like manner appointed; Provided that the Secretaries of State, of the Treasury, of War, of the Navy, and of the Interior, the Postmaster-General and the Attorney-General, *shall hold their offices respectively for and during the term of the President, by whom they have been appointed*, and for one month thereafter, subject to removal, by and with the advice and consent of the Senate."

So, when Johnson read "*by whom they have been appointed*," he must have smiled and said to himself something like this: "I did not appoint Stanton - Lincoln did! Therefore, I can fire Stanton and defend it with that legal argument — Stanton was Lincoln's man."

When news reached the Senate that Andrew Johnson had ordered Edwin Stanton's dismissal, "Charles Sumner rushed up to the desk of the presiding officer to make sure of the good news." Within minutes, Ben Wade was surrounded by many of the enthusiastic members of the Senate's more Militant Faction. And many of these dashed off memos to Edwin Stanton insisting that he not cooperate in any way with Andrew Johnson. Sumner's memo to Stanton contained only one word. The word was "Stick!"

Since February 1867, Charles Sumner had been "heartily in favor of the Impeachment of Andrew Johnson," when he had figured that Johnson's "foul-mouthed utterances, which are a disgrace to human nature," would serve as sufficient grounds for Impeachment. He had written John Bright that Andrew Johnson "is now a full-blown rebel," and he added "in spirit he is as bad as Jefferson Davis." Yet he had pretended that he would be an impartial juror if and when the Impeachment trial reached the Senate floor. Toward that fiction, Sumner had written Elizabeth Argyll in September 1867, "I have never doubted that [Andrew Johnson] would be impeached," but "I do not say what judgment I should pronounce as a Senator if he were before us." Many Republicans had argued that the gains made by the Democratic Party during the Fall 1867 elections indicated that Republicans should lessen talk of Impeachment; but Sumner steadfastly countered, "Those elections only show more imperatively the necessity for impeachment."

In the Senate Henry Wilson of Massachusetts quickly obtained passage of a resolution that declared the removal of Edwin Stanton to be a violation of Federal Law:

> "Resolved, By the [Federal Senate], that under the [Federal] Constitution and [Federal Laws], the President has no power to remove the Secretary of War and designate any other officer to perform the duties of that office, [even on an interim basis]."

Thad Stevens learned of the Stanton's removal in a note from J. W. Forney, Secretary of the Senate:

> "[Andrew Johnson] removed [Edwin] Stanton and appointed Lorenzo Thomas, but gives no reasons, except that he does so under power vested in him by the [Federal] Constitution. Senate is still in session, but will adjourn before passing needed resolution of disapproval. Stanton has sent a letter to [Johnson] denying report in the evening paper that he had been ousted, and that Thomas was issuing orders; that he would hold on in defiance of threat, (unless evicted by force) until the Senate had pronounced upon the conduct of [Andrew Johnson in this matter]."

Thad Stevens took action immediately. The next morning he called together his Committee on Restructuring the Government of the Conquered States and got the majority to concede that Andrew Johnson had clearly violated the Tenure of Office Act, created to entrap the man. After lunch, at two o'clock the same afternoon, Stevens entered the House Chamber eager to press for an Impeachment vote. He rose and told fellow Representatives that the dismissal of Edwin Stanton was a "high crime and misdemeanor" that was sufficiently grave to justify a vote to Impeach Andrew Johnson. He presented the Committee's report to support that allegation and then submitted the following resolution:

"Resolved, That Andrew Johnson, [Federal President], be impeached of high crimes and misdemeanors."

This launched the House into a heated debate that would last two days.

On February 23 Stevens moved to close the Impeachment debate with a speech from the floor of the Federal House. But his voice failed him at the outset and the Clerk stepped in to read the speech, which I summarize as follows:

Impeachment was a "purely political proceeding." Unlike English Law, a law-abiding man could be Impeached because he merely differed politically from the majority in control of the Legislative branch of government. It might prove impossible to be certain whether Andrew Johnson or Ulysses Grant was telling the truth in their argument over the meaning of a previous agreement. Perhaps neither man was telling the truth. It did not much matter. What mattered was the charge that Andrew Johnson had conspired to violate a law enacted by the Federal Congress. That conspiracy placed Andrew Johnson clearly in the wrong. Then followed the wording of Stevens' indictment.

The next morning Stevens called for a vote. The Impeachment resolution passed overwhelmingly — **by a vote of 126 to 47!**

Later in the day Thad Stevens and John Bingham, of Ohio, went to the Senate Chamber to proudly announce that the House had voted to Impeach Andrew Johnson. In the words of biographer Richard Current: "Pale, emaciated, deathlike, but with a voice surprisingly vigorous and a manner stern and lofty as usual, [Stevens] made the formal announcement to the Senate:"

"In obedience to the order of the [Federal House], we have appeared before you. In the name of the [Federal House] and of all the people of the [Federation of States], we do Impeach Andrew Johnson, [Federal President], of high crimes and misdemeanors in office; and we further inform the Senate that [Representatives in the House] will, in due time, exhibit particular Articles of Impeachment against him, to make good the same; and in their name we demand that the Senate take due order for the appearance of the said Andrew Johnson to answer to the said Impeachment."

The House needed time to contrive the alleged violations, to build its case. Stevens and Bingham assured the Senate that those charges would be delivered soon. The next day a supporter in Lancaster wrote Stevens: "I congratulate you on having got the dogs fairly on the track of the greatest rascal in Christendom." And the Governor of Pennsylvania, John Geary telegraphed Simon Cameron: "The news to-day created a profound sensation in Pennsylvania. The spirit of 1861 seems again to pervade [the people of our State]. Troops are rapidly tendering their services to sustain the [alleged] laws. Let [the House and Senate] stand firm [in their resolve to convict Andrew Johnson]."

Under Thad Stevens' leadership the House established a Special Impeachment Committee to draw up the Articles of Impeachment and present them to the floor for a vote by all members. The Committee consisted of Thad Stevens, John Bingham of northern Ohio, George Boutwell of Massachusetts, James Wilson of Iowa, John Logan of southern Illinois, George Julian of central Indiana, and Hamilton Ward of New York. And House Republicans caucused on February 29 to organize their Impeachment program. [R19;328, R73;332, R96;300-303, R97;490-492]

For many months mail from Republican Political Machine activists in the conquered States had poured into Charles Sumner's office, inciting him to heightened hatred toward European Americans who live among them and against Andrew Johnson. After news of the House Impeachment vote, the volume and intensity of the mail increased. And Sumner blamed Johnson for every alleged evil he found in his mail. In his personal assessment, Sumner believed passionately that Andrew Johnson:

1. Had lived a career that was "compounded of falsehood and usurpation."

2.   Had begun "with promises to make [a legacy of secession] odious," but had "soon installed it in authority."

3.   Had declared "sympathy with [Republican supporters in the conquered States, [both European American and African American]," but had "changed to become their persecutor."

4.   Had himself "continued the worst elements of [African American bonding], an insensibility to right and a passion for power."

5.   Had "patronized massacre and bloodshed, and given a license to the Ku-Klux-Klan."

6.   Had so fully "triumphed in his wickedness that in [the conquered States] no [Republican] man is safe and no murderer of a [Republican] man can be punished."

Thereby worked into an emotional frenzy, Sumner was as certain as tomorrow's sunrise that he saw his "path as clear as day. Never in history was there a great case more free from all just doubt." Such certainty of opinion was readily facilitated by Sumner's fear of personally traveling into the conquered States to witness conditions first-hand. Instead of gathering facts, Charles Sumner would dine in his Washington "dream house" and pontificate.

But much was happening in Charles Sumner's personal life. He was living in the "dream house," which he and Alice had purchased, and, by March 1, was adjusting to living alone in the place. Construction had taken a long time, considering that it stood mid-way through construction when Charles and Alice had signed the purchase agreement around Christmas of 1866. But the "dream house" fell short of cheering him up. He remained lonely and still sought pity from his friends. He had written Wadsworth Longfellow in December that, "I have no heart about it or anything else," but he would still be seeking pity as he would write him again in late March that, "Life is a burden hard to bear in such a desolation as mine." Sumner had written Samuel Howe in January: "Once relieved I shall not be easily tempted into any such cruel bonds" as another marriage. And Sumner withdrew perhaps a bit more into the emotional protection he found in his holier-than-thou shell. Roscoe Conkling, still smarting from the James Redpath article, ridiculed Sumner for pretending to be a "fountain of light." He warned Sumner that fellow Senators were tired of hearing "these stately phases which [Sumner] employs with a view to convincing the Senate that he knows more about this matter than anybody else." Referring to him as "the great orb of the State Department," Conkling advised fellow Senators that he would no longer pay any attention to the Chairman of the Senate Foreign Relations Committee, "who rises periodically in his effulgence and sends his rays down the steep places here to cast a good many dollars into the sea."

The final cost of Sumner's "dream house" came to $28,060, and his father-in-law, Samuel Hooper, figured Sumner would need to spend between $7,000 and $8,000 each year to run the house in appropriate style. David Donald would describe the house:

> "The house, as Edmund Quincy reported, was not very large but well contrived. A compact brick building, it had an air of expensive elegance as it stood behind its green-painted iron fence and looked out over Lafayette Square. Aside from the kitchen and pantries in the basement and small bedrooms for the servants and for Sumner's secretary under the mansard roof, it consisted of 6 large rooms, 3 on each floor. Beyond the entranceway on the ground floor, where Sumner placed a bust of Minerva, there were the parlor, the dining room, and a library, which, however, did not have enough wall space for Sumner's books. Sumner's study, with three large windows, occupied most of the second floor, with his own bedroom and a guest room opening into it from opposite sides."

But, through his biographical research, David Donald would observe that the "dream house" would help Sumner renew his brand of bachelor life-style happiness: "As the furniture began to arrive and the domestic servants began to learn their duties," Sumner would come to "take delight in his new home." He would write Samuel Howe, "I confess the pleasure of space and cleanliness in a beautiful situation with the independence of a house that is my own." Sumner made a fuss of ensuring that his new personal secretary, Moorfield Storey, was comfortable in his bedroom. Storey, 23, of Massachusetts and fresh out of Harvard Law School, would, many years later, write of being grandly shown through the house that first day: "As he did it, he told me that Chancellor Kent had rendered him the same service and had told him that Alexander Hamilton had done it for him, so I became a link in a curious chain." Moorfield Story, Sumner's personal secretary from 1867 to 1869, was at the time passionate about his boss and the more Militant Republican agenda, but that passion would fade — perhaps he would be too close to Sumner and his political friends who came by the house. Perhaps he came to know two much about their character. Perhaps he, like the preacher who had written Thad Stevens, would come to understand that, "**What makes bad government is bad sinful men**." Disillusioned, Storey would leave Sumner in 1869, drift away from the Republican Party, and give his active support to Grover Cleveland in 1884. [R73;321-326,333]

March 1868 Through February 1869 — Political Reconstruction During the Fourth Year of The Andrew Johnson Administration

(2Q68)

As mentioned previously, the House Committee charged with drafting Articles of Impeachment was Chaired by Thad Stevens. On or about March 1, the Committee presented numerous allegedly Impeachable offenses during its presentation on the floor of the House. These were augmented by other suggested Articles submitted by the floor. After some debate, on March 2, 11 allegedly Impeachable offenses were approved for prosecution before the Senate, which would sit as a Jury. The first 8 Articles dealt with alleged offenses related to Andrew Johnson's suspension, and later dismissal, of Edwin Stanton from the job of Secretary of War, to which he had been appointed by the late Abe Lincoln. The 9th Article alleged an offense when, on February 22, Andrew Johnson instructed William Emory, military commander of the Department of Washington, to supposedly disobey a Federal law. The 10th Article alleged that, during the President's Fall 1866 campaign trip out to Chicago, St. Louis and back, Andrew Johnson's denunciation of the House and Senate was in violation of Federal law. The 11th Article, which Thad Stevens had personally crafted, incorporated much of the allegations of the other articles into one item. This article alleged that, during his speech of August 18, 1866, Andrew Johnson had committed an unlawful offense when he had allegedly declared the Federal House and Senate an illegal body; and was also in violation of Federal law when he unilaterally discharged Edwin Stanton from the Secretary of War job on February 21.

After approving the 11 Articles of Impeachment, the House "selected 7 Managers to prepare the case and conduct the [Senate] Trial on the part of the House." Among the 7 was, of course, Thad Stevens. But he was not the official head of the group because he was too sick to stand before the Senate as chief prosecutor. The Managers were John Bingham of Ohio, Chairman, George Boutwell of Massachusetts, John Logan of Illinois, Benjamin "Beast" Butler of Massachusetts, James Wilson of Iowa, Thomas Williams of Pennsylvania, and Thad Stevens. Representatives from Stevens' Pennsylvania and from Charles Sumner's Massachusetts, by comprising 4 of the 7 Managers, were the controlling majority. Although Bingham officially performed the duties of Chairman, everyone knew that Stevens was the most powerful man on the team.

On March 4 the membership of the House, led by the Managers, filed into the Senate for the presentation of the 11 Articles of Impeachment, which detailed the alleged legal offenses on which Andrew Johnson was being indicted. John Bingham, speaking for the Managers, prefaced his reading of the 11 charges with the following words:

> "The Managers of the [Federal House], by order of the [House], are ready at the bar of the [Federal] Senate, if it please the Senate to hear them, to present Articles of Impeachment, in maintenance of the Impeachment prepared against Andrew Johnson, President of the [Federal Government], by the [Federal House]."

The leadership of the Senate had already taken steps to establish rules for the Impeachment Trial and to arrange for the proceedings to be overseen by Salmon Chase, Chief Justice of the Federal Supreme Court. On March 5, Chase arrived at the Senate Chambers and announced:

> "Senators, I am here in obedience to your notice, for the purpose of proceeding with you in forming a Court of Impeachment for the Trial of Andrew Johnson, President of the [Federal Government]. I am now ready to take the oath."

One of Chase's fellow Supreme Court Justices then proceeded to administer to Chase the following oath:

> "That in all things appertaining to the Trial of Andrew Johnson, President of the [Federal Government], now pending, I will do impartial justice according to the [Federal Constitution], so help me God."

The same oath was then administered to each of the Senators, including, of course, Charles Sumner. But objection was raised to the swearing in of Ben Wade because he stood to become President of the Federal Government if Andrew Johnson was convicted. In the words of contemporary historian,

Alexander Harris: "It was argued that one in his position was too much interested to be a competent Judge to try the President, as the rules of equity demanded." But Wade, having no notion of judicial honor, refused to disqualify himself due to conflict of interest. And other more Militant Senators, including Charles Sumner, defended Wade's stand on the issue. After the last Senator was sworn in, Chase declared the body a "High Court of Impeachment." The newly formed "Court" then ordered that a summons be drawn up and delivered to Andrew Johnson, which demanded that he appear before them on March 13 to hear the charges.

Because Charles Sumner refused to associate Impeachment with violating Federal law, he criticized fellow Senators for attempting to treat Impeachment like a criminal court case: "Give me a lawyer to betray a great cause. He can always find an excuse. Technicality and quibble cannot fail." Sumner decried talk of violating the Tenure of Office Act, "without connection with transgressions of the past. . . . There is nothing of usurpation [Johnson] has not attempted," Sumner fumed. On the other hand, the attitude of several Republican Senators toward Impeachment seemed to be influenced by concerns about what Ben Wade would do if given the power of the President. Fessenden "shuddered at the prospect of having Ben Wade in the White House." Former Confederates surely also shuddered at the prospect of increased suffering under a President Ben Wade, for they considered Wade "one of the [their] most malicious foes." The fact that Wade's son had led a Federal regiment of African Americans during the conquest of Tennessee prompted former Confederates to more keenly fear that Wade in the White House would mean confiscation of their homes and their farmland. Also, there was an expectation that, if made President, Wade would appoint Charles Sumner to the Secretary of State job. Sumner had written Elizabeth Argyll that Wade "would have relied upon me and wished me to leave the Senate." But he had written Frances Lieber that Wade "assures me that he had not spoken with a human being about appointments." However, Sumner had added, "he has spoken with me on some possibilities of the future, telling me that I was the only person he had spoken with on the matter." Amusingly, such convoluted reporting indicated that, although Charles Sumner was not a "human being," he was likely to become "Secretary of State."

Looking into the future toward new political horizons, as was his practice, Charles Sumner introduced legislation to ensure that an Impeached Andrew Johnson would be unable to seek future political office. That resolution stipulated that, after Johnson was Impeached, the Senate reserved the right to impose "further judgment" upon him. Sumner's intent was to embroil Johnson in a legal net which would prevent the Democratic Party from nominating him for future elected office. Apparently Sumner feared that Johnson might rally enough public support after Impeachment to be a threat in a future campaign for President.

Meanwhile, Andrew Johnson had assembled his legal defense team, whose members were busy planning defense strategy. The team of 5 lawyers consisted of Henry Stanbery of southern Ohio, Benjamin Curtis of Massachusetts, Thomas Nelson of Tennessee, William Evarts of New York and William Groesbeck of southern Ohio. On March 13, this legal team appeared before the Senate to hear the charges for their client and to ask for 40 days to prepare his defense. The Senate refused to grant 40 days. But the Senate leadership did grant 10 days, demanding that Johnson's lawyers return on March 23, with a summation of its defense against the 11 Articles of Impeachment. [R73;335-336, R19;331, R97;492-495]

Meanwhile, while Republicans in the Federal Senate were scheming to convict Andrew Johnson of "high crimes and misdemeanors," Federal lawyers in Richmond were trying to move forward with convicting Jeff Davis of Treason and other charges. Both Robert Lee and Jeff Davis appeared in the Federal District Court in Richmond on the third Wednesday in March to stand trial on a shorter list of offences. Apparently, at this time Prosecutors formally dismissed their charge that Jeff Davis had helped John Wilkes Booth kill Abe Lincoln. And they also formally dismissed their charge that he had been responsible for alleged war crimes at the huge Confederate prisoner-of-war camp near Andersonville, Georgia. As just reported, the Federal's Chief Prosecutor, William Evarts, was away in Washington City helping defend Andrew Johnson on Impeachment charges. So lesser lawyers were left with the Jeff Davis hot potato, and perhaps happily agreed to postpone the case until after a victor arose from the Impeachment battle. But the Federals did manage to tidy up their charges against Jeff Davis by formally issuing a clearly worded indictment on many charges of Treason against the Federal Government. And amid the charges was one that named as co-conspirators Robert Lee, Judah

Benjamin, John Breckinridge and 17 other named officials. Prosecutors alleged that the evidence to support their package of Treason indictments was derived from the testimony of Robert Lee and 7 others. But, history shows that Republican leaders remained terrified of facing Jeff Davis and his legal team in a courtroom setting. Again, Prosecutors had avoided even calling Davis into the courtroom. So, in recognition of their apprehensions, the Prosecutors and Judge John Underwood postponed the trial date again. The new trial date was set for May 1868. Upon leaving the courtroom Robert Lee had filled Davis in on the testimony he had given. It seems that the Federals had tried to trick him into hiding behind Davis' authority by asking him if he had not been in fact simply acting under Jeff Davis' instructions. But, aware of the Prosecutors' intent, Lee had answered that he, "always consulted with [Davis] when it was practicable to do so," and he added that "they always finally reached the same conclusions." But Lee had insisted before the Court that he, himself must bear the responsibility for his own actions. Federals were not going to divide and conquer. Joking with Davis afterward, Lee mused that his testimony before the Federals must not have been exceptionally compelling because, while he was testifying he had noticed a large African American man in the Jury with his head fallen back, his mouth wide open and obviously fast asleep. [R19;329]

Johnson's team of lawyers returned to the Senate on March 23 and stated its defense argument for each of the 11 Articles of Impeachment. The team argued that Andrew Johnson was innocent of violating the Tenure of Office Act because that law, itself, violated the Federal Constitutional principles of separation of powers, and was therefore an invalid law. The Constitution itself was the substantiating evidence. The Constitution says: "The president shall have power to fill up all vacancies that may happen during the recess of the Senate." It says: "He shall nominate, and by and with the advice and consent of the Senate, shall appoint ambassadors, other public ministers and consuls, judges of the Supreme Court, and all other officers of the United States . . ." And it says: "The Congress may by law vest the appointment of such inferior officers, as they think proper, in the President alone . . ." The Constitution clearly permitted the President freedom to change personnel during a recess of the Senate, and it implied that he could dismiss any officer he chose, fill the job with an acting appointee, and submit to the Senate, when it reconvened, a nominee to permanently fill the temporarily staffed job. Furthermore, the team argued that, since Edwin Stanton had been appointed by Abraham Lincoln, his job was thereby excluded from protection under the Tenure of Office Act. So, even if that Act would have been in agreement with the Federal Constitution, Johnson would have not been guilty of violating it. The team argued that Andrew Johnson could not be found guilty of high crimes and misdemeanors on the basis of public or private speech, because he was a citizen of Tennessee and the United States, and by the Federal Constitution, was guaranteed freedom of speech on matters political. The Constitution says: "Congress shall make no law respecting an establishment of religion, or prohibiting the free exercise thereof; or abridging the freedom of speech, or of the press . . ." This defense was accepted by the Senate and the House as Andrew Johnson's legitimate defense plea, and the Impeachment Trial was ordered to began on March 30. [R97;495]

On the opening day of the trial, Benjamin "Beast" Butler began presenting alleged evidence for the Prosecution team. Of "Beast" Butler, contemporary historian, Alexander Harris would write: "The presentation of the [alleged] evidence was managed mainly by [Butler], who displayed great adroitness and legal ability in this particular. His dexterity, as a criminal lawyer, shone conspicuous on this occasion." During presentation of alleged "evidence," Thad Stevens sat at the Impeachment Managers' table and conferred frequently with Ben Wade, for both were pushing the Senate to move quickly toward a conviction vote. And Charles Sumner agitated in a like manner in and out of the Senate Chamber. Sumner had argued against organizing the Impeachment Trial like a court trial, for he argued that Impeachment — as described in the Federal Constitution — was purely "a political proceeding before a political body with a political purpose." Sumner reasoned that a President's conduct in regard to abiding by or violating law was immaterial to the Senate's judgment on an Impeachment charge. Sumner also urged the quick seating of two Republican, Machine-elected Senators from Reconstructed Arkansas to increase the vote in favor of conviction. And he would repeatedly urge bringing in the two Arkansas men as the Impeachment Trial progressed. The Prosecutorial arguments of the Managers were concluded on April 4th. [R73;334]

Benjamin Curtis led off for the defense lawyers on April 9th "in a logical, learned and argumentative speech, presenting [Andrew Johnson's] defense in the manner he believed the evidence and the law would sustain him." The defense lawyers called in witnesses for interrogation, including Lorenzo Thomas and William Sherman. Presentation of so-called evidence, for both sides, concluded on April 20. The Senate would resume the Trial on April 22. Of this phase of the Trial, historian Alexander Harris would write: "[Thad] Stevens was too prostrated during the whole proceeding, to take any but a subordinate part. In his younger years, on such a trial, he would have shone as a star of the first magnitude." [R97;496]

Meanwhile, Jeff Davis needed to respond to the job offer from the Trustees of Randolph-Macon College at Ashland, Virginia, who had voted on March 30 to offer him the Presidency of their college. Certainly, Davis needed a job, one consistent with his marginal health. But could he accept employment in any leadership position as long as the Federals kept harassing him with Treason indictments and Trial postponements. It had been three years since Andrew Johnson had begun the criminal harassment with a charge that Jeff Davis had helped John Wilkes Booth kill Abe Lincoln. And Davis had not yet had an opportunity to say one word in a courtroom in his defense. Without question, Republican political leaders were terrified of Davis in a courtroom setting. But how was he to get on with his life? Robert Lee had written his son, Rooney on that same day:

"[Jeff] Davis said that he did not know what he should do or what he could turn to for [a job with which he could] support [his family]. As long as his trial is hanging over him, of course, he can do nothing. He can apply his mind to nothing, nor could he acquire the confidence of the business community in anything he might undertake, from the apprehension of his being interrupted in the midst of it."

Representatives of the trustees of Randolph-Macon College met with Jeff in Baltimore where he had briefly stopped on his journey back to Lennoxville, Canada. He expressed a deep appreciation for their job offer, but felt he had to turn it down: "Gentlemen, I am a prisoner of [the Federal Government], released on bail. I feel that I cannot risk the fortunes of any institution by becoming connected with it until the odium cast upon me is removed. If I were free [from criminal prosecution] I would cheerfully consider your proposition."

Charles O'Conor feared that Republicans would arrange to have Jeff Davis killed — with or without a court trial — if they succeeded in making Ben Wade the President and putting men like Ben "Beast" Butler in the Cabinet. O'Conor warned Davis to stay in Canada during the Impeachment Trial, and, if Ben Wade became President, to immediately flee to Europe. It was too easy for Republicans to send kidnappers into Canada. With Davis safe in Europe, O'Conor felt he could better handle circumstances as they developed.

Jeff Davis would share his frustrations with James Mason in a letter dated April 16:

"In Virginia they now have [African American] Jurors, and nearly all the intelligence and respectability of the community have been excluded from the Jury lists by acts bearing on their political opinions. The prospect of a fair trial is certainly bad. . . If [Andrew Johnson] is removed by the pending Impeachment, it cannot be worse for me. May God grant that it be not worse for the [country]."

In a prompt reply, James Mason would present his thoughts:

"Those ignorant brutes who now govern affairs act so strangely to delude the mob at their heels, that it is impossible to know the object of their movements. In one thing they are inconsistent — pertinacity in malice. [Salmon Chase] stands committed to hold the [Federal] Court before [the Federation]. . . . With the world looking on, he cannot rule that to be law which he knows is not law. Bad as it all is, I am yet encouraged in the double aspect, first that there will be no trial — or if there be, that [Salmon Chase] dare not pronounce it treason." [R19;329-331]

Meanwhile in South Carolina, during the first days of the trial of Andrew Johnson, on April 2, Delegates from the various South Carolina Democrat clubs gathered in Columbia to organize a political campaign, focusing on its opposition to Ratification of the proposed State Constitution, as demanded by the Federal Act to Reconstruct the Governments of the Conquered States. In fact the Convention decided to forgo nominating candidates for Governor, etc., realizing that, if they succeeded in defeating the proposed Constitution, the office of Governor would not be created anyway. Wade Hampton was elected to the Democrat State Central Executive Committee in spite of the fact he was, at the time, in Mississippi tending to his farms. All realized political success required pulling many African American men away from the influence of the Republican Union Leagues. Accordingly, the Convention, through its Executive Committee soon published "an address to the [African Americans] of South Carolina" that encouraged them to embrace the friendship of established South Carolina European Americans and to reject the appeals of agitators from the northern States. Excerpts from that "address" follow:

"Your present power must surely and soon pass from you. Nothing that it builds will stand and nothing will remain of it but the prejudices it may create. It is therefore a most dangerous tool that you are handling. Your [political] leaders, both [of European and African ancestry], are using your votes for nothing but their individual gain. Many of them you have only known heretofore to despise and distrust, until commanded by your [Union] Leagues to vote for them. Offices and salaries for themselves are the heights of their ambition, and so that they make hay while the sun shines they care not who is caught in the storm that follows. Already they have driven away all capital and credit from the [southern States]; and, while they draw $11 a day, thousands among you are thrown out of employment and starve simply for lack of work. . . .

We [Democrats] are not in any condition to make you any promises or to propose to you any compromises. We can do nothing but await the course of events — but this we do without the slightest apprehension or misgiving for ourselves. We shall not give up our country, and time will soon restore our control of it. . . . [So] remember that your race has nothing to gain and everything to lose if you invoke that prejudice of race which, since the world was made, has ever driven the weaker tribe to the wall. Forsake, then, the wicked and stupid men who would involve you in this folly, and make to yourselves friends and not enemies of the [European American] citizens of South Carolina. . . ."

When voting days arrived, April 14, 15 and 16, men who had been qualified went to the polls to vote for or against Ratification of the Reconstructed State Constitution. And most also voted to elect a Governor and Federal Representatives, who might be seated in the Federal House if the Republican Party would allow it. South Carolina Democrats were overwhelmingly defeated. The Republican Political Machine swept the election. The new State Constitution was ratified. The vote for Ratification was 70,758 for, 27,288 against and 35,551 not voting, a majority of 62% of registered voters, thereby satisfying the Reconstruction Act. All elected Representatives to the Federal House were Republicans. Republicans would hold large majorities in the State House (124 versus 14) and the State Senate (31 versus 6). Robert Scott of Ohio, a former Federal army officer was elected Governor.

But would this powerful political combination of newly independent African American men and European American adventurers from the northern States be good for the long-term welfare of the former? Wade Hampton — having been responsible for the welfare of over 1,000 African Americans only a few years earlier — thought not. He would return from Mississippi and on May 6 would be speaking in Columbia — to the Democratic Club of Richland. In part he would advise fellow South Carolina Democrats: "Let the [African American] man be told God's truth, that if he expects to escape the fate of the [Native American], he should go in with the Democratic or Conservative party." [R199;192, R201;90-93]

Meanwhile in Washington City, the Senate resumed the Impeachment Trial on April 22, moving on to presentation of legal arguments. Leading off for the Prosecution, George Boutwell spoke for almost two days. Then A. R. Nelson and William Groesbeck followed for the Defense. Thad Stevens read his speech on April 27. On the crucial issue of the applicability of the Tenure of Office Act to Edwin Stanton's job, Stevens argued that "Stanton was appointed Secretary of War by [Abe] Lincoln in 1862 and continued to hold office under [Andrew] Johnson, which by all usage is considered a reappointment." Of Stevens' failing health biographer Richard Current would write:

"Shortly after noon, standing weakly before the bench at which [Salmon] Chase presided, he began to read from a sheaf of printed slips. In a few minutes he asked permission to sit down and continue; after half an hour his voice became inaudible and he handed his script to [Benjamin "Beast" Butler], who read the remaining two-thirds of the address. James Garfield would complain to his diary that the Impeachment Managers were "wading knee deep in words, words, words," and that Stevens appeared to be "reeling in the shadow of death, struggling to read what could not be heard 20 feet off."

Another Manager, Thomas Williams, followed Stevens. Then William Evarts spoke for 4 days straight in support of the Defense. He was followed by Henry Stanbery, who spoke for the Defense on May 1 and May 2. John Bingham presented the closing speech for the Managers, occupying May 4, 5 and 6. In all, the legal discussion by lawyers for the Prosecution and Defense occupied two weeks.

At one point during Senate deliberations, Edmund Ross, one of the two Senators representing Kansas, stopped by Charles Sumner's desk to discuss the Impeachment issue. Ross told Sumner that he had some concerns about Impeachment without solid evidence of legal violations. Sumner had probably assumed from the beginning that the two Senators from Kansas would vote for Impeachment. Had not political agitation over Bleeding Kansas propelled the Republican Party into a position of dominance in the northern States? How could men who had so adroitly combined terrorism and propaganda allow themselves to be restricted by Constitutional barriers when gaining political power was in the offering? Did not all Kansas men think like James Lane? Sumner, who "could not understand [Ross'] misgivings," declined to discuss the technicalities that concerned Ross. "It was a very clear case, especially for a Kansas man," Sumner admonished. He warned Ross that it was inconceivable "that a Kansas man could quibble against his country."

On May 11 each Senator took his turn presenting his opinion on the Impeachment process and on Andrew Johnson's guilt or innocence, each being permitted 15 minutes to speak from the floor. During their presentations, all 12 Democrat Senators stated their opposition to conviction, as Thad Stevens, Charles Sumner and others of the more Militant Faction had expected. But, 4 Republican Senators, when they spoke, said they were opposed to convicting Andrew Johnson of high crimes and misdemeanors. Since a two-thirds vote would be needed to convict, any breakdown in Party discipline greatly alarmed the Impeachment leadership. Now, to oppose the Party leadership in such a critical political battle took great courage and a willingness to abandon future political ambition. The 4 Senators, all seasoned Republicans, were James Grimes of Iowa, William Fessenden of Maine, Lyman Trumbull of Illinois, and John Henderson of Missouri. Contemporary historian Alexander Harris would write: "This was a frightful bomb in the [more Militant] camp. The Impeachers became alarmed. The victory which the [more Militants], on account of partisan subserviency, had scarcely doubted, was already in extreme danger. . . Despair drove them to an adjournment until the 16th of May, in order to see if, in the meantime, the power of Party tyranny would not be able to compel a sufficient number of unwilling Senators to obey those who claimed to be their political masters." Thad Stevens elevated the crises to maximum intensity by alleging that the survival of the Republican Party was at stake. Stevens warned that the "failure of Impeachment, would be the death of the Republican Party." Of the possibility that a Republican Senator would vote to acquit, Stevens sternly warned: "Point me out one who dares to do it, and you show me one who dares to be regarded as infamous by posterity."

And pressure now mounted to, prior to calling for a vote, pack the Senate with Puppet Senators elected by Republican Political Machines in the conquered States. For example, the editor of the Philadelphia *Press*, in the May 13 issue of that paper, urged packing into the Federal Senate as many as 14 new Machine Puppets:

"Now, if the [Federation] in this hour of her extremity, needs [conviction] votes in the Senate, let the [Republican majority] admit at once the Senators from the [Reconstructed State Government] of Arkansas. They are standing, waiting at the door. It is superfluous caution that keeps them out. Bring in [Puppet Senators from additional conquered States], if there is need of them, . . . from Florida, Georgia, Louisiana and the Carolinas."

Horace Greeley, editor of the New York *Tribune*, wrote Thad Stevens that he was "anxious that the *Tribune* should keep up a steady fire on the Impeachment question until the issue is decided. If, therefore, any fact or suggestion should occur to you meantime that seems calculated to aid us in the work, I will trouble you to have it telegraphed at our expense to the *Tribune*." [R73;336, R96;305, R97;497]

Although *Bloodstains* is presenting in detail the history of Reconstruction in South Carolina and Mississippi, space limitations limit detailed reporting on Reconstruction in Virginia, North Carolina,

Georgia, Florida, Alabama, Louisiana, Arkansas and Texas? From which of them could Puppet Senators be drawn to ensure Impeachment? Here is an overview by Contemporary historian Alexander Harris:

> The primary goal of Machine-elected Delegates to the State Constitutional Conventions "was to frame Constitutions which would exclude from the polls as large a number as possible of the [European American] people of the [conquered States], so as to ensure the success of the [Republican Party] by means of the [African American] votes." One method of ensuring exclusion of large numbers of European American men was to exclude leading men who had supported the Confederacy. Another was to demand that, before his voting credentials could be examined, a former Confederate soldier had to stand before hypocritical Republican Machine politicians and recite an humiliating public oath, fully realizing that every effort was being made to deny him the very "political equality" of which he was required to pledge his allegiance. The oath required of voters in Alabama is an example:

>> "I _____ do solemnly swear that I accept the civil and political equality of all men, and agree not to attempt to deprive any person, or persons, on account of race, color or previous condition, of any political or civil right, privilege or immunity, enjoyed by any other class of man."

> Although the oath sounds agreeable to readers today, in 1868 it was a calculated insult to a defeated former Confederate of European American ancestry, and both the hypocritical Republican Machine man and the former Confederate man knew full well that the Machine man held the power to strip the voter rolls of enough European Americans to deliver the vote they were seeking. So, many defeated former Confederates, knowing the futility of political assertiveness, simply refused to be mocked before a Voter Registration Board. The effort was coordinated from the Republican seat of power in Congress. For example, the Chairman of the Florida Republican Machine wrote to Stevens to assure him that, "The [African American] people here have been led to look upon you with the highest respect and the most unshaken confidence." And he explained how the Machine was using African American churches because, "The [African American] preachers are the great power in controlling and uniting the [African American] vote."

> The Federal Reconstruction Act required that a Reconstructed State Constitution had to be Ratified by a majority of the registered voters, not a majority of the voters who showed up at the polls on election day. Well organized Republican Machine workers delivered majority votes — primarily African American votes — in Ratification voting in Arkansas, North Carolina, South Carolina, Louisiana, Georgia and Florida. So in those States the goal of a majority of registered voters was achieved. However, in Alabama, the Machine turned out too few voters to gain a majority those registered. Nevertheless, the Reconstructed Alabama State Government prepared to submit its Reconstructed State Constitution to the Federal Government for approval. [R96; 307, R97;484]

Accordingly, Thad Stevens — being very worried that there were too few Senators willing to vote to convict Andrew Johnson — initiated, in early May, legislative procedures in the House to admit Representatives and Senators from several conquered States to ensure that Johnson was convicted, hoping to delay the Impeachment vote until after he had packed the Senate with the new Machine men. But he had to get quick acceptance in the House of the Reconstructed Governments in several conquered States, and then persuade the Senate to do likewise. First, Stevens submitted an enabling bill for the Reconstructed Arkansas Government, and expedited approval under the previous question. Then he submitted a similar enabling bill to facilitate the approval of the Reconstructed Governments in 5 additional States, such as North Carolina, South Carolina, Georgia, Florida and Louisiana. Democratic Representatives in the House argued that it was inappropriate to so hastily bring new Representatives and Senators into the Federal Government, half-way through the Impeachment Trial. Stevens argued otherwise. At one point, Stevens even countered frankly, making no attempt to hide his political objective, saying: "And I trust [God] will never again permit this [country] to [allow African American bonding]; or in other words that He will never permit the Democratic Party again to gain the ascendancy." Stevens expedited approval in the House under the previous question, winning House approval to accept the Representatives and Senators from Machine-controlled Reconstructed Governments in 6 conquered States. To ensure an Impeachment conviction vote, Senate leaders only had to push through a vote of acceptance for the same 6 State Governments. Stevens had begun the process and the Senate only had to follow through and finish the job! But too many refused to participate in a political move to pack their body with new Machine Senators while in the midst of an Impeachment Trial. So these Reconstructed State Governments would not be approved until sometime after the Impeachment Trial was concluded. [R96;308]

On May 12 Robert Schenck, Chairman of the Committee on Impeachment sent copies of the following telegram to Republican leaders and newspapermen in doubtful States:

"Great danger to the peace of the [country] and the Republican [Party's] cause if Impeachment fails. Send to your Senators public opinion by resolution letters, and delegations."

And Republican newspapermen raged against the 5 Republican Senators who had announced that they would vote against Impeachment: William Fessenden of Maine, Lyman Trumbull of Illinois, James Grimes of Iowa, John Henderson of Missouri, and Joseph Fowler of Tennessee. The strain of the public attacks upon Grimes apparently caused him to become stricken with paralysis. Then there was Senator Edmund Ross of Kansas, who was keeping his intentions secret. And Ross was clearly a target. Ben "Beast" Butler was attempting to bribe Ross with a large sum of money if he agreed to vote for Impeachment; and Republicans in Kansas — the most militant, terrorist-minded politicians in the northern States — were threatening Ross with vast devastation if he voted against Impeachment. Some of the more vicious Republicans fabricated totally-untrue moral scandal in an attempt to crush the man. But Edmund Ross — a remnant of honesty that had somehow survived Bleeding Kansas — seemed determine to vote for what he thought was right "even if the Heavens fell."

Ben Wade, hopeful of rising to the Office of President, moved to get the backing of Ulysses Grant, and presumably the Federal Army as he confided in the Commander in Chief over his choices for Cabinet positions. At the top of the list was the only Federal politician that Jeff Davis ever pronounced a war criminal: Ben "The Beast" Butler.

Jeff Davis followed the Impeachment proceedings mostly from the Canadian newspapers, and most of those were predicting that Senate Republicans would get enough votes to convict. And he and his lawyers knew that his life may well hang in the balance — for a President Ben Wade would likely have had Davis executed or shot in a manner reminiscent of the killing of John Brown.

Finally, voting time had arrived. The Senate convened again as an Impeachment Court on May 16. Thad Stevens arrived early and, prior to the start of business, spent considerable time talking with Charles Sumner. Both men probably figured sufficient Republican Senators would vote to convict Andrew Johnson, but both knew a conviction vote was no certainty. Realizing that this would be the most important day for the Republican Party since the election of Abe Lincoln, both men took their places as the Senate was called to order. Impeachment leaders nervously called for a vote on Impeachment Article 11, the article Thad Stevens had personally drafted to combine into one Article the most destructive allegations. A two-thirds vote was required for conviction. As the roll was called Stevens scowled, "with one unvarying look of contempt" at every Senator who voted to acquit. "The voting went precisely as expected, until [Salmon Chase] came to the name of [Edmund] Ross, who sat idly tearing foolscap into slim strips, as was often his custom."

"Mr. Senator Ross," asked Chase, "How say you? Is the respondent, Andrew Johnson, President of the United States, guilty or not guilty of a high crime and misdemeanor?"

In the words of biographer Hudson Strode, "The personal life of Jefferson Davis as well as the political fate of Andrew Johnson hung on Ross' answer. The people in the gallery held their breaths. Senators on the floor sat stiffly at their desks like 'petrified men.' The little Kansan rose slowly to his feet. Then, clear as a bell, came his answer: 'Not guilty.' Johnson had the bare 19 votes necessary to save him."

"Before adjournment [Salmon Chase] announced that he was ordering an entry in the journal that [Andrew Johnson] had been acquitted. In Lennoxville, Jefferson Davis could take a freer breath. A man named Ross whom he had never met had made a mighty difference in his life." [R19;332]

Of Edmund Ross, Hudson Strode would footnote:

"In Kansas, Ross [would be] burned in effigy, and when his term in the Senate [would expire], he [would retire] poverty-stricken from political life. Though warned never to return to his home State, he [would open] a little printing shop in Coffeyville. Shortly after he was established, a prominent [Militant] named D. R. Anthony from Leavenworth, a gigantic bully, [would attack] him in his shop and beat him with a stick so unmercifully that he [would never regain] his health. Ross [would live] in penury until Grover Cleveland became President and [appoint] him Governor of the Territory of New Mexico. Just before [Ross'] death, Congress [would finally grant] him a pension as a [Federal veteran of the Invasion of the Confederacy]."

All 12 Democrat Senators had voted for acquittal, as had 7 of the 42 Republican Senators. The 7 courageous Republicans were William Fessenden of Maine, Lyman Trumbull of Illinois, James Grimes of Iowa, John Henderson of Missouri, Edmund Ross of Kansas, Peter Van Winkle of the unconstitutional State of West Virginia, and Joseph Fowler of the remade Government of conquered Tennessee. The vote was 35 to convict versus 19 to acquit. If one vote had switched, making the tally 36 to 18, conviction would have passed by the required two-thirds majority. But 10 more Articles of Impeachment remained on the Manager's list. When would they be voted on? Not until after the Republican National Convention to open in Chicago.

Biographer Richard Current would write:

"After the [Impeachment] Court had adjourned [for the day], [Stevens'] servants carried [him] out of the Senate chamber and, riding high above the heads of the crowd in the corridor, he appeared pale, silent, grim. But, as if to indicate that he was not yet done, he summoned his physical resources before reaching the Committee room and insisted on being put down to walk, on his own." [R19;331-333, R96;308, R97;499]

We now turn our attention to the details of Reconstruction in Mississippi, whose Reconstructed Constitutional Convention adjourned two days later, on May 18. The Convention, had lasted 115 days and cost taxpayers almost $300,000, including per diem to Delegates at $116,150; pay to employees and "hanger's-on" of around $150,000, paying 4 new Republican newspapers $28,500 for printing the proceedings, and more payment to printers for printing 20,000 copies of the proposed Constitution (one printing bill was $30,337). For comparison the Constitutional Convention of 1861 had lasted 23 days and the Convention of 1865 had lasted 11 days and cost $14,000.

The Convention had stipulated the procedure for Ratification of the Mississippi Constitution by qualified voters, and specified June 22 for the start of voting and authorized it to continue through such period as commander Alvan Gillem "might direct, in order that every voter should have an opportunity to express his preference." Gillem issued the appropriate order on the following day — qualified voters were to vote "For the Convention" or "Against the Convention" and, on the same ballots "for State officers [and legislators] and Representatives to the [Federal House]." Concerning further details:

Fourteen days before June 22, Registrars were to meet, give notice and, over the course of 5 days, revise the qualified voter lists, sending all records of revisions to Gillem's office. "Each county was to be divided into 3 sections, to [each of] which was assigned a Registrar, who with a Judge and Clerk of his own appointments, was to be held responsible for the conduct of the election." All Registrars were required to swear to the iron-clad oath of July 2, 1862. None but qualified and registered voters were permitted to challenge a vote. "All [Federal] army officers and [Newly Independent African American Men's] Bureau agents were prohibited from electioneering, speaking, or endeavoring to influence voters, although they might instruct [African American men] in regard to their rights as [voters]." This limitation did not apply to Federal soldiers below the grade of officer. Gillem intended to place Federal inspectors at the polls and closely oversee the proceedings. A circular was issued on May 28, defining the boundaries of the Federal House Districts, the State House Districts and the State Senate Districts. Five companies of Federal Troops were brought in from Tennessee to expand the Federal military presence in Mississippi to 32 companies assigned to 63 sites. Observers reasoned that nothing else could be done to prevent fraud against the Republican agenda.

The first political convention of the year had been a gathering of conservative European Americans, held on January 16, very soon after the Constitutional Convention had begun. In honest defiance of the unquestioned reality that Mississippi Republicans were empowered solely by the votes of African American men, the conservative European Americans had set aside polite talk and called themselves the "Democratic White Man's Party of Mississippi." Their platform statement had been equally blunt and to the point:

> The "nefarious design of the Republican Party to place [European American] men of the southern States under governmental control of their late [bonded African Americans], and degrade the [European] race as the [political] inferiors of the African race, is a crime against the civilization of the age, which needs only to be mentioned to be scorned by all intelligent minds, and we, therefore, call upon the [European Americans] of Mississippi to vindicate alike the superiority of their race over the African American, and their [historic] political power to maintain [their] constitutional liberty."

The Mississippi Republican Party had also made an early start at rallying its voters and selecting its candidates, having convened on February 5. It had nominated Beroth Eggleston, a native of Saratoga County, New York, and high ranking Federal army officer who claimed the distinction of having received the surrender of Atlanta. The other nominees had also been European American men from the northern States. Many African Americans, who constituted 99 percent of the Republican vote, had been, and continued to be, outraged over being excluded from office, including the Reverend Mr. Fitzhugh, a well-educated [African American] from a northern State, and a Delegate to the Constitutional Convention, who had published a letter in the Woodville *Republican*, warning of dire consequences for Republican leaders who refused to allow African Americans to hold office. Of those men, he had written, "garbed in the disguise of friends to us, [they] are imposters, and will cause more blood to be spilt than the [Federal acceptance of a Mississippi Government] is worth." Fitzhugh furthermore announced his resignation from the Party, "believing it to be ruinous to [Federal acceptance of Mississippi], and an enemy to the [African] race."

Finally, on February 19, a largely attended, 3-day Mississippi Democratic Party Convention had been held in Jackson. Delegates had endorsed the action of the "Democratic White Man's Party of Mississippi," mentioned above, and encouraged political unity among all opposed to the Republican Party and its Reconstruction agenda. A Committee of Five had been appointed, which had issued an address to the people on April 27, advocating "renewed activity to defeat the [Reconstruction] Constitution. . . . It appealed to all lovers of liberty to assemble and organize, and prepare for the great contest before them. There was a registered majority of 17,000 [African American] men to be overcome, but with eternal vigilance and activity it could be done," the writers had assured. Should Mississippi Democrats adjust their strategy because of the revised Federal Reconstruction law stipulating that a majority of votes cast, not a majority of registered voters, was all that was needed to win Ratification and elect government officials? Mississippi Democratic Party reconvened in Jackson on May 12 to debate and reconsider its tactics. Delegates voted to nominate a State ticket and "advised that an effort be made to defeat the Constitution by outvoting the Republicans." Focusing solely on State politics, the Democrats ignored the upcoming election of the next Federal President. European Americans in the State were especially alarmed that their Constitution, if ratified, would bar from office, "every man who had given counsel or encouragement to a Confederate soldier." Few European Americans who lived in Mississippi at the time of State Secession would escape this exclusion.

The Reconstructed State Constitution required the future State Legislature to Ratify the Amendment to the Federal Constitution to Nationalize Citizenship (14th) before any Representative or Senator received any pay or any legislation became valid. The Convention named a Committee of Five to oversee the Ratification election, to carry out all powers during the adjournment of the Convention, "to appoint three Commissioners for each county to attend the election, be present at the counting of the votes, and forward the result to the Chairman." If Ratification failed, the Committee of 5 was directed to reconvene the Convention.

The State Constitution stipulated that "applicants for voter registration were required to take and subscribe to the "test oath prescribed by the Reconstruction Acts", and swear further that they acknowledged the civil and political equality of all men. No person was eligible to office who, as a member of the Legislature, had voted for the call of the Secession Convention; or who, as a Delegate to [said] Convention, had voted for or signed the Ordinance of Secession; or who had given voluntary aid, countenance, counsel, or encouragement to persons engaged in [armed defense against Federal forces]; or who had accepted or attempted to exercise the functions of any office, civil or military, under a seceded State or the Confederacy, except all persons who had voted for the recently adjourned Convention or who had openly advocated for said Convention. The acts of the Constitutional Convention of 1865 were declared null and void. Davis County was renamed Jones County and its county seat, Leesburg, was renamed Jonesboro. Lee County was renamed Lincoln County. Property ownership and ability to read and write could never be a requirement for voting. Any future attempt at State Secession would violate the State Constitution. It "forbade the making of any distinction among the citizens in reference to the possession, enjoyment, or descent of property." All citizens had the right to travel on public conveyances. The Convention sent a memorial to the Federal House and Senate, naming 130 men for whom political disabilities should be removed. An enthusiast advocate of this memorial explained in a letter to Speaker Schuyler Colfax:

> "We need these [130] men to fill certain positions in the [Mississippi Republican] Party, and to labor for its success, and it is of great importance to us that their disabilities be removed so that the reward of [Party] loyalty may be seen and felt. They have all done us great service, and are still at work fighting valiantly side by side with the best and truest [Reconstructionists] of the Party. We want them for office." [R204;205-213]

Meanwhile, in Washington City Thad Stevens was receiving letters from Pennsylvania Republicans urging bolder, even violent, efforts to subvert the political power held by President Andrew Johnson. They argued the destruction was justified because, "Treason is triumphant," and "Scoundrelism is in the ascendant." One man wrote, "I fear we must all become rascals in self defense" to retain Republican Party control of the Federal Government. Some urged Stevens to keep the Impeachment Trial active through February 1869 to prevent Johnson from helping the Democratic Party in its efforts to elect their candidates to Federal, State and local offices. He was urged to continue the Impeachment Trial through the remainder of Johnson's term in office, voting on only one Article of Impeachment per month while simultaneously arranging to pack the House and Senate with newly admitted Machine Republicans from the Reconstructed Governments of the conquered States. "I shall try," Stevens replied, but he feared that he could not persuade enough Senators to prolong the Impeachment Trial through the election season. But Stevens quickly alleged that some of the Senators who had voted "Not Guilty" had surely been bribed, because "Money is irresistibly powerful." So Stevens set out immediately to draft new Articles of Impeachment, which alleged that Andrew Johnson had committed "high crimes and misdemeanors" by participating in a scheme to bribe the 7 Republican Senators who had voted to acquit. But Stevens was severely limited by his incapacitating illness. He wrote a note to Edwin Stanton on May 20 in which he complained, "I have been confined to bed ever since I saw you. This accounts for my having made no movement. I hope to be up today."

Charles Sumner could not believe the tally that showed that Republicans had failed to Impeach Andrew Johnson by one vote. He figured that Ross had been bribed to vote "Not Guilty." For what other reason would a man from Bleeding Kansas vote to sustain Andrew Johnson, whose heritage was in the Democratic Party, and whose political career had originated in a southern State? And when The Beast would allege numerous frauds had taken place during the Impeachment proceedings, Sumner would embrace those charges as indisputable fact, and support those charges with personal testimony before "the House [Impeachment] Committee himself." But worse of all, in Sumner's view, was the "traitorous" vote of William Fessenden. How could Fessenden vote to sustain Johnson? Surely, it was not because he held legal concerns. Fessenden must have been driven to such madness by his "vindictive hate of [Benjamin] Wade." Why did the Senate rules not permit everyone to vote on the full set of charges in one grand tally? Sumner had so wanted to shout, "Guilty of all, and infinitely more."

Furthermore, Sumner was extremely disappointed in Salmon Chase's behavior during the Impeachment Trial. Sumner and Chase had been the first Republicans to be elected to the Senate. As the Chief Justice presiding over the Senate hearings, Chase had been far too meticulous about ensuring proper legal decorum. If he had acted like a loyal Republican, that alone would have been sufficient to shift the Senate's mood toward a solid vote to Impeach. Not many months earlier, Sumner had been advocating Chase for President. But not now! Biographer David Donald would observe that, ever since Chase had lost hope of being nominated for President, "the Chief Justice [had been drifting] toward the Democrats. . . . With sad bewilderment, Sumner watched his old friend prove during the Impeachment Trial that he was now lost to the Republican Party." [R73;337, R96;309]

The Senate recessed until May 26, so Republicans could attend the Republican National Convention in Chicago. As usual, Charles Sumner declined to attend the Convention. The more Militant Faction hoped that, in the atmosphere of a National Convention, it could force one or more of those 7 Republican Senators to submit to Party discipline and, on or more of the remaining Articles, vote to Impeach. Most figured that, by placing Ulysses Grant at the head of the Party ticket, they would rekindle an intensely militant political discipline. So Ulysses Grant was nominated as the Republican candidate for President on May 21. As usual Sumner expressed his dissatisfaction with the Convention's nomination of Grant, a military man. Sumner had "maintained amicable, if rather distant, personal relations" with Grant, but "temperamentally and intellectually they had almost nothing in common." And Sumner disliked Grant for the same reason he hated Johnson: Grant had ties to the southern States — Grant was married to a Missourian who had grown up around bonded African Americans, and he had voted for James Buchanan for President. Had Grant for a time not sided with Andrew Johnson by agreeing to take Edwin Stanton's job in an attempt to defuse the fight between the President and Congress? As Sumner worried about future strength of Republican Political Machines in the conquered States, he asked, "Who can say that, as President, he would give to the [newly independent African American men] . . . that kindly and sympathetic support which they need?" Back in December, Sumner had told a New York *Herald* newspaperman that Grant, "was a good soldier, and nothing more," since there "was no record of his ever having expressed a political axiom or an idea which could afford the people an insight [into] his capacity for statesmanship." Yet, while having dinner with Grant and Stanton not long before the Chicago Convention, Sumner had rather forced himself to be mildly impressed with the man. And practically every Republican politician believed that only Grant was capable of keeping the White House in Republican control. So, Sumner felt obligated to at least pretend to be supportive of Grant.

The Impeachment Managers met on May 25, the day before the Impeachment Trial was to resume. Thad Stevens and Ben "Beast" Butler urged the group to endorse new Articles of Impeachment that indicted Andrew Johnson for bribery. But they failed to persuade the others. The other Impeachment Managers had apparently become convinced that it was futile and counterproductive to push the proceedings beyond counting votes on the remaining 10 Articles. Sensing very little hope of getting a guilty vote, and being incapacitated by illness, Stevens would decide to stay home the next day.

The Senate reconvened on May 26 to vote on the other 10 Impeachment Articles. The more Militant Faction was hopeful that Party discipline had been successfully instilled among the Republican Senators, but only an official vote tally would reveal the true intentions of each man. A vote was taken on the second Article. The result was the same as before. All Democrats voted not guilty, as did the 7 independent-minded Republicans: Fessenden, Trumbull, Grimes, Ross, Van Winkle, Henderson and Fowler. Desperately, the Republican leadership took another vote — this time on the third Article. Again all Senators voted as they had previously. The Impeachers had failed to convict Andrew Johnson. They knew it and decided to forego asking for a vote on the remaining 8 Articles of Impeachment. [R73;339-340, R96;310, R97;499]

Meanwhile, two days after the final historic "Not Guilty" Impeachment votes, Andrew Johnson's lawyer, William Evarts, turned his attention back to the prosecution of Jeff Davis. But Evarts and other Republicans had no intention of rushing into a Treason Trial anytime soon. That very day Evarts told Charles O'Conor that Jeff Davis' trial would not take place on June 3, as scheduled. Obviously still terrified of confronting, in a courtroom setting, Jeff Davis, Charles O'Conor and the other defense lawyers, Prosecutor Evarts assured O'Conor that the earliest the trial could be rescheduled would be sometime in October. Republicans wanted to propagandize the indictment without facing the truth of State Sovereignty in a courtroom setting. Delay! Delay! Would Jeff Davis ever get his day in court, or would he forever stand accused of the alleged charge of Treason to serve the needs of Republican political agitators? In any event he could do as he pleased until October. If Republicans had succeeded in dumping Andrew Johnson and elevating Ben Wade to the Office of President, it is probable that they would have arranged for Jeff Davis to be killed if he ever returned to The States. [R19;331]

On June 22 the Federal House and Senate, over Andrew Johnson's veto, accepted the Reconstructed State Government in Arkansas and approved the seating of its Representatives and Senators. The Arkansas Legislature had Ratified the Federal Amendment Nationalizing Citizenship (14th) on April 6.

Three days later, on June 25, the Federal House and Senate passed an Act — over Andrew Johnson's veto — assuring that "each of the States of North Carolina, South Carolina, Georgia, Florida, Alabama and Florida, shall be entitled and admitted to representation in [the Federal House and Senate] as a State [under the Federal Government] when the Legislature of such State shall have duly Ratified the [Federal Amendment Nationalizing Citizenship (14th)]," and met other conditions of this Act. (The States of Mississippi, Virginia and Texas were omitted from this Act because they had not yet Ratified Reconstructed State Constitutions.) Soon afterward the House and Senate begin the process of individually admitting, under the Federal Government, 5 of the 6 named Reconstructed State Governments, while setting aside the admission of the Georgia Reconstructed Government until later. The 5 Reconstructed State Governments are listed below, along with the dates when Representatives and Senators were seated and when Ratification was acknowledged:

- Florida (seated on June 25, had Ratified on June 9)
- North Carolina (seated on July 4, Ratification accepted the same day, July 4).
- South Carolina (seated on July 9, Ratification accepted the same day, July 9). .
- Louisiana (seated on July 9, Ratification accepted the same day, July 9).
- Alabama (seated on July 13, Ratification accepted the same day, July 13).

Of course, all of these Reconstructed State Governments were dominated by Republican Political Machines, so the Republican-dominated Federal House and Senate were merely admitting fellow Machine Republicans into their political bodies. And it was a bit ironic that they admitted the Alabama State Government, since its Reconstructed State Constitution had not been ratified by the required majority of registered voters, but Republican Senators must have rationalized away that shortcoming. So, by mid-July, with only Georgia, Virginia, Texas and Mississippi not yet sufficiently organized by their respective State Republican Political Machines, the more Militant Faction was expanding into an overwhelming majority. Andrew Johnson and the Federal Supreme Court would be powerless to oppose any foreseeable future legislation that the House and Senate would enact. By this Reconstruction process Republicans were ensuring that State Citizenship was subordinate to National Citizenship, thereby subjugating the Libertarian principle of State Sovereignty beneath the Nationalist principle of supremacy of National Rule. [R97;484-485, R201;96, R207;476-477]

During June Andrew Johnson appointed Reverdy Johnson to be the new Minister to Great Britain, replacing Charles Adams, of Massachusetts, who had resigned after holding the job since 1861. Johnson, Democrat of Maryland, had been a Federal Senator since 1863 and a member of Charles Sumner's Senate Foreign Relations Committee. Politically, he had been a Whig before becoming a Douglas Democrat. [R73;365]

Thad Stevens had not so absorbed in convicting Andrew Johnson on Impeachment charges that he neglected his interests in the Pennsylvania Railroad and the Eastern Division of the Union Pacific Railroad. He still strived to do political favors for the railroad, and, in return received subsidized stocks and bonds. On June 24 a Union Pacific Railroad lobbyist by the name of John Perry left Stevens a note explaining a profitable bonds-for-stock swap:

"In reply to yours of the [19th of June]: I will state that in the event [the House and Senate] shall provide for the extension of the railroad of the Union Pacific Railroad Company to the Pacific [Ocean], and shall grant the necessary [financial subsidy] in land and bonds, I will give you Government or first mortgage bonds of the [Union Pacific], [in exchange] for the $29,000 of full paid [Union Pacific] stock held by you, [this being] an acceptance of your proposition." [R96;312]

Meanwhile, in Mississippi — one of the 4 conquered States not on an immediate path to acceptance under the Federal Government — her qualified voters cast ballots over a 6-day period beginning on June 22. They were voting "For the Constitution" or "Against the Constitution" and for State officials and Legislators, and Representatives to the Federal House. There was no boycott by qualified European Americans; in fact their participation was very large. It would take a few days to compile the vote, deliberate the significance, and publish the official results. Republicans would be shocked at their amazing loss, all in spite of their careful control over the election process and diligence in denying men deemed not qualified to register. Alvan Gillem, the Federal Military Ruler over Mississippi and Arkansas, surely humiliated, would announce the results on July 10:

Votes for the Constitution	56,231
Votes against the Constitution	63,860
Total Votes	120,091

We can compare this vote to the original record of qualified registered voters as of early September of the previous year:

Registered African American Voters	60,167
Qualified and Registered European American Voters	46,636
Total Voters at that time	106,803

We can also compare this vote to the votes cast for the Constitutional Convention in November of that year:

Total Registered Voters	139,327
Minimum Vote Required to Authorize Convention (50%+1 vote)	69,664
Votes Cast to Authorize Convention (50.05%)	69,739
Votes Cast Against a Convention	6,277

The results for election of State officials and Legislators, and Representatives to the Federal House revealed another heavy Democrat victory. Benjamin Humphreys, the sitting Civil Governor, running as a Democrat, defeated Republican candidate Beroth Eggleston, a former Federal military commander from New York State. Democrats had secured 66 of the 138 members of the State Legislature, only about 12 Legislators being African Americans (11 in the House and 1 in the Senate). Of the 5 Representatives to the Federal House, 4 of those elected were Democrats. Of course, the Constitution being rejected meant that no State Government was formed and none of the elected would take office. Of course, Republicans would not allow this rejection of the Constitution to stand, or recognize those elected to office. A move began immediately to disparage the results, claim voter fraud, and encourage the Federal House and Senate to demand a new election based on a completely new ballot.

Examining the tables above, we observe that votes for the Mississippi Constitution (56,231) were only 81 percent of the votes that had been cast for the Convention (69,739). Furthermore, we observe that votes against the Constitution (63,860) were 37% more that the preliminary record of 46,636 European American qualified registered voters as of September of the previous year. Clearly, European Americans had been energized and Republicans had experienced difficulties in getting their huge block of Africa American men to the polls. Some scare tactics might have been employed to discourage some African Americans, but some were probably incensed that Republican leaders, almost all European American men from the northern States, were taking them for granite, disrespectfully using them only to achieve their own personal ambitions. We are reminded of the objections of the Reverend Mr. Fitzhugh, an educated and influential African American Republican who, as previously mentioned, had, a few months previously, encouraged African American men to join him in turning away from the Republican leaders from the northern States and look for areas of political agreement with native Democrats. Perhaps that had become a strong sentiment working against the Mississippi Republican Party. But, Republicans had friends in Washington City who would overturn the election results. I would surmise that a prejudicial bias among northern States people had worked against their understanding of the mind and temperament of African Americans living in the southern States. In Volume 2, *The Demagogues*, I had discussed that prejudicial bias while presenting an analysis of Harriet Beecher Stowe's popular novel, *"Uncle Tom's Cabin."* Thinking African Americans in the southern States to be ignorant and easily strung along by clever deception, northern States people were only fooling themselves. In fact African Americans in the southern States, giving sufficient time and evidence, were fully capable of talking issues over and reasoning who was on their side and who was just disingenuously using them as pawns. In other words, although very few had been taught to read or write or do arithmetic, most had ample "common sense," what we today call "street smarts."

For some reason, President Andrew Johnson had moved Alvan Gillem out as Military Ruler over Mississippi and Arkansas near the beginning June and replaced him with Irvin McDowell, a very high ranking officer in the Federal army, well known to students of the Federal Invasion of the Confederacy, even though Mississippi election was then scheduled to begin on June 22. McDowell had taken command on June 4, but he was moved out about the time the election results were being finalized and Gillem reinstated, resuming his command on July 4. During McDowell's month in command, he had alleged that the sitting Civil Governor, Benjamin Humphreys — also then, as previously mentioned, the candidate for Governor on the Democratic Party ticket — had violated some rule of conduct by encouraging men to vote against Ratification of the Reconstructed State Constitution. It is hard to make sense of this politically.

Did Republicans bring in McDowell to embarrass Humphreys, in hopes that would lead to his defeat in the June election? Did that action, instead, actually rally voters to Humphreys' side? McDowell named Adelbert Ames, a mid-level Federal commander, to the job of Provisional Governor of Mississippi. But the Civil Governor was not about to acquiesce to this insult without a fight. Humphries refused to leave the Governor's residence and had a telegram from Andrew Johnson backing him up. To Ames, Humphreys replied, "in view of my duty to the constitutional rights of the people of Mississippi, and the disapproval of the President, [I do] refuse to vacate the office of Governor, or surrender the archives and public property until a legally qualified successor under the Constitution of Mississippi is appointed." To no avail: On July 13 Federal soldiers would evict Humphreys and his family from the Residence "at the point of the bayonet." The Mississippi Attorney General was likewise evicted and replaced with a Federal army officer. As mentioned earlier, the Mississippi voters had meanwhile elected Humphreys Governor, but had rejected the Constitution that would have created the office to which they had elected him. [R204;213-217]

Meanwhile in Oxford, Lucius Lamar was supplementing, with legal work, his salary as Chair of the School of Law at the University of Mississippi. His first case had been taken in the spring of the year, and had gone well. During the summer he had agreed to set up a formal law partnership in Oxford with a young lawyer, Edward Clarke, who had worked in Coffeeville under Lamar's former law partner, Edward Walthall, and who would later marry Walthall's niece. Of this new arrangement, biographer James Murphy would write:

> "The two men became fast friends and their practice developed auspiciously. . . . [In a September 21 letter, Edward] Walthall could remark: 'I understand you are getting some good cases. I have never had any doubt about your getting a hand in all the good cases in your region, when you get fairly to work.'"

But sadness would soon visit upon the Lamar and Longstreet families. Lamar's mother-in-law, Frances Eliza Parke Longstreet, an "accomplished and angelic" lady, would die in November. Her husband, Augustus Longstreet, age 78 years, surviving, would remain in the Longstreet home at Oxford. [R205;126, R206;92]

(3Q68)

On July 4 Andrew Johnson issued his third Proclamation of Amnesty, this one reducing the men excluded only Jeff Davis, John Breckinridge, Robert Lee and handful of other former high-ranking Confederates who were then "under presentment or indictment in any court of the United States having competent jurisdiction upon a charge of treason or other felony." Wade Hampton was included in the amnesty, but remained unable to take political office because of the restrictions in the Federal Amendment to Nationalize Citizenship (14th).

Meanwhile, the Democratic Party began its National Convention on July 4 in New York City in Tammany Hall. Among the Delegates was Wade Hampton, who was named to the important Platform Committee. The Platform was submitted three days later and approved by acclamation. It said:

> " . . . [The National Democratic Party demands:

> "First — Immediate restoration of all the States to their rights in the Union under the [Federal] Constitution, and of civil government to the American people.

> "Second — Amnesty for all past political offenses, and the regulation of the elective franchise in the States by their citizens. . .

"In demanding these measures and reforms, we arraign the Radical [Republican] Party for its disregard of right, and the unparalleled expression of tyranny which have marked its career. . . . Instead of restoring the Union, [as pledged at the outset of the Federal Invasion of the Confederacy,] it has, so far as in its power, dissolved it, and subjected 10 States, in time of profound peace, to military despotism and [African American] supremacy. It has nullified there the right of trial by jury; it has abolished the *habeas corpus*, . . . it has overthrown the freedom of speech and the press; it has substituted arbitrary seizures and arrests, and military trials and secret star-chamber inquisitions for the constitutional tribunals; it has disregarded in time of peace the rights of the people to be free from searches and seizures; it has entered the post and telegraph offices, and even the private rooms of individuals, and seized their private papers and letters without any specific charge or notice of affidavit, as required by the organic law; it has converted the American Capitol into a Bastille; it has established a system of spies and official espionage . . . ; it has abolished the right of appeal on important constitutional questions to the supreme judicial tribunals, and threatens to curtail or destroy [said tribunals'] original jurisdiction, which is irrevocably vested by the [Federal] Constitution. . . .

"And we do declare and resolve that ever since the people of [those original 13 States] threw off all subjection to the British [Government] the privilege and trust of [the right to vote] have belonged to the several States, and . . . any attempt by [the Federal House and Senate], on any pretext whatever, to deprive any State of this right, or to interfere with its exercise, is a flagrant usurpation of power which can find no warrant in the [Federal] Constitution, and, if sanctioned by the people, will subvert our form of government, and can only end in a centralized and consolidated government, in which the separate existence of the States will be entirely absorbed, and an unqualified despotism be established in place of a Federal Union of co-equal States. . . ."

On the third day, July 7, by acclamation, the above Democrat platform was adopted by the Delegates.

The Democratic Convention continued. After three days of voting and 23 ballots, Horatio Seymour, former Democratic Governor of New York State, was nominated for President. Then Delegates began nominations for Vice President. Frank Blair of Missouri was among the names offered to the Convention. You will recall that Frank Blair was the son of Francis Blair of Maryland and brother of Montgomery Blair, of Abe Lincoln's first Cabinet. You will also recall that Frank Blair had been a major commander of Federal troops under William Sherman's horde of Devastators. But, in spite of Blair's war record against southern States civilians — most notably against the people of Wade Hampton's beloved home city, Columbia, South Carolina — Delegate Hampton rose and spoke in favor of the man's nomination and seconded the motion that he be nominated (amazing forgiveness). Many Delegates from other southern States also indicated their approval, prompting withdrawal of other names and resulting in the nomination of Blair on the first ballot taken. Before arriving back in South Carolina, Hampton would speak to crowds in New York City and Baltimore. He would arrive in Charleston on July 24 to the cheers of an enthusiastic Democratic Party rally and speak to a large outdoor gathering in front of the Charleston Hotel on Meeting Street. At one point he would tell about his work in writing the Democratic Party Platform at the National Convention, especially the plank that held that Democrats believe the Federal Reconstruction Acts are "unconstitutional, revolutionary and void." Hampton went on to say, that was "my plank in the Platform." The gathering was not all European Americans. It was reported that "400 [African American] conservatives . . . behaved with the greatest propriety throughout the meeting, and, at the close, marched off in a column of fours, cheering for Hampton." Hampton would be the main attraction at a similar Democratic Party rally held in Columbia on July 28. As would be expected, Republican newspapers in the northern States alleged that Hampton's claim of "my plank in the Platform" proved that former Confederate leaders were again seizing control of the Democratic Party. Charles Sumner would adopt a similar argument as he would return to supporting the Republican ticket. Although he would hardly perform any campaign work for Grant, Sumner would campaign for the Republican Party in general. In that spirit he would warn that the success of the "[Confederate] Party, which is the true name for our present [Democratic Party]," would be "terrible for the [country] — as bad as the worst defeat in battle." [R73;340, R199;193-195, R207;481-482]

Meanwhile, back in Washington City, Thad Stevens' efforts to resurrect the Impeachment of Andrew Johnson were finally killed by a House vote taken on July 7. In his latest scheme, he had attempted to divide Texas into three States, each dominated by a Republican Political Machine. With those 6 new Machine Senators, Stevens had argued, there would be ample votes to impeach. And he had drafted new Articles of Impeachment and was pushing for their adoption. But, on July 7, the House voted down Stevens' new Articles. So, unlike Virginia, Texas would escape being carved up to satisfy the ambitions of Republican Machine politicians. [R96;310]

Meanwhile, on July 6 in Columbia, South Carolina, the Republican-controlled State House and Senate convened to begin its domination over the lives of the State's citizens. Here the world was turned up-side-down. The racial makeup of the State Senate was 21 men of European ancestry and 10 of full or partial African ancestry. The racial makeup of the State House was 46 men of European ancestry and 78 of full or partial African ancestry. The 155 men in these two legislative bodies had paid in the past year a total of $635 in taxes to the State Government. The 20 Democrats had paid an average of $10. Of the 135 Republicans, 91 had paid no tax at all and the remaining 44 had paid an average of $10. Each Senator and each Representative earned $6 per day, so, by the second day of the session, on average they had drawn more from the State Treasury than they had paid the previous year in taxes. Although there was no work on Sunday, pay was figured on a 7-day week basis ($42 per week). Furthermore, expenses for travel was allowed at 20 cents per mile, which was used liberally to go home on weekends (example: to Charleston and back: earned $45). This first session of the Legislature would consume 72 working days and Legislative pay, travel and expenses would total $130,000 — an amount equal to $839 for only one member, which is more than the total of $635 paid into the State Treasury the previous year by all 155 members. So being a member of the Legislature was very lucrative in outright pay, not even considering the money earned from graft and fraudulent schemes. Of course the people paying the taxes were the property owners of the State, almost all of them prohibited from seeking a Legislative office by Federal authorities. And those tax rates were about to skyrocket, notwithstanding the general bankruptcy of the population.

The South Carolina House elected Franklin J. Moses, Jr., originally of Sumter, lately of Charleston, to be Speaker and the Senate elected David T. Corbin of Charleston as President Pro Tem. The combined House and Senate immediately Ratified the Federal Amendment to Nationalize Citizenship (14th), as mentioned earlier — almost all, or all, 135 the Republicans voting for the Amendment and all 20 Democrats voting against it. As mentioned earlier, this Ratification fulfilled the requirement for admission of the State's 6 Representatives to the Federal House and admission of two Federal Senators. The Representatives had been previously elected by the voters, but the Federal Senators were now to be elected by a Joint Session of the Legislature. To the short Federal Senate Session (to end March 4, 1871) was elected, on the first ballot by a large majority, Thomas Robertson of Columbia — a 1843 graduate of South Carolina College, a farmer and former owner of some bonded African Americans. To the long Senate session (to end March 3, 1873) was elected, in a heated political fight, Frederick A. Sawyer of Charleston — a Massachusetts teacher who had moved to Charleston a few years before State Secession. Historian John Reynold would complement Sawyer, writing, "Sawyer had no part in corrupting the State Legislature, deported himself with dignity and courtesy, and seemed inclined throughout to be conservative." To the State Supreme Court was elected Franklin J. Moses, Sr. as Chief Justice, and A. J. Willard and Solomon Hoge as Associate Justices. Of these men, historian John Reynold would write:

> Franklin Moses, Sr., a Sumter, South Carolina lawyer and father to the Speaker of the State House, Franklin Moses, Jr., "was recognized throughout the State as a man of decided ability and of much learning in his profession. . . . Willard was a New York lawyer [who had come] to South Carolina as lieutenant-colonel of a [Federal African American] regiment. . . . Hodge had come from Ohio as a captain of a Federal company of infantry, and was practically without experience as a lawyer . . ."

On July 9 Robert Scott was sworn into the office of Governor, taking over from Governor James Orr. Scott had been elected in April under the new Constitution, and was directed by E. R. S. Canby, the Military Ruler over North Carolina and South Carolina, to take over from Orr immediately after the Legislature ratified the Federal Amendment to Nationalize Citizenship (14th). Scott, of Ohio, had been the Federal's chief official over the Newly Independent African American Men's Bureau for South Carolina. So Scott was well connected with the African American voters of the State. Former Governor James Orr was elected as Judge of the Eighth Judicial Circuit, allowing him to continue to contribute his skills in service of the State. J. W. Denney was elected "printer to the State." Year after year, the printing contract let by Republicans for legislative printing work would become a major source of graft, corruption and theft. [R201;106-114]

Meanwhile, back in Washington City, Charles Sumner, by mid-summer, had become rather content living in his dream house. Edmund Quincy, who had visited him several times, had written in May that Sumner was not sorry to be rid of Alice "and restored to his bachelor estate." Sumner would write Mrs. John Lodge in October, "as for that bad woman, do not believe that I have any sorrow, except from the sense of my solitude and disappointment. It is an infinite solace that she is outside of my house never more to disturb me by her presence or to degrade the house." And Sumner would have guests over for dinner more and more frequently. Guests would include Caleb Cushing, who fit in nicely as a widower, members of the diplomatic corps, and many foreign diplomats and visiting foreigners with letter of introduction. Carl Schurz would jokingly tell others that Sumner's standard invitation form was: "Come and dine with me today, and I will show you another Englishman." When Charles Dickens came to visit The States, Sumner's was the only diner invitation he accepted. Apparently occupying his cook and servants with frequent dinner guests was Sumner's way of passing the evening hours in what would otherwise be lonely surroundings. David Donald would write: "Sumner had always been a great talker, but now he talked with a kind of desperation so as to keep his guests on and on, to stave off the inevitable hour when he would be left alone in the great house with his thoughts." Men being shown Sumner's growing collection of things displayed in the rooms of his house would go away impressed by "the ever-present evidences of care and tidiness in his rooms," and by how the place seemed so "neat, clean and sweet." However, a woman with perhaps greater insight would write of the place: "It is full of books and pictures, and many rare old engravings, but it looks like the home of a lonely man."

Charles Sumner campaigned very little for Ulysses Grant, was biographer David Donald would report:

> "[Sumner] could not muster real enthusiasm for his Party's nominee, and no doubt he welcomed his physician's order to stay out of the Presidential canvass lest he further strain his overtaxed vocal cords. Except for very brief remarks at a flag-raising ceremony at the Grant and Colfax Club in his own Boston ward, Sumner delivered but one speech during the campaign, a speech chiefly distinguished by the fact that he made only three passing references to [Ulysses Grant] and spent most of his time defending his own record as Senator." [R73;326-329, 340-341]

Meanwhile, during the first two weeks of July, on several occasions, Thad Stevens urged fellow Representatives to approve a bill to fund the purchase of Alaska — "His voice clearer and louder than it had been for months." At one point he even appealed to Republicans to support Russia because the Czar was himself a Republican — because the Czar had decreed that bonded serfs be made independent. The Russian Minister, Edward de Stoeckl, had been worried for many months that the Federal House might never fund the purchase of Russian Alaska, although the Treaty defining that purchase had been approved by the Federal Senate many months previously. He had been particularly worried about the preamble attached to the bill to fund the purchase, as it had come out of Committee in May, which inferred that the House shared with the Senate the power to approve treaties with foreign nations. Charles Sumner would object to language such as that, de Stoeckl worried, and for good reason, for everyone in Washington City knew how an inappropriate choice of language could anger the man. So de Stoeckl had dispatched his American agent, R. J. Walker, to Stevens' home in May to urge him to modify the preamble so Sumner would not seize upon that as an excuse for delay. And Walker had apparently succeeded in persuading Stevens to help push the funding bill through the House, as was confirmed by the enthusiasm of his advocacy during July. And the House did finally vote to approve funds for the purchase of Alaska.

But, as Thad Stevens' health worsened, he became less and less able to persuade Republican Representatives to vote as he directed. Apparently everyone knew that his remaining days were few, and he would be unable to punish disobedient Representatives from the grave. He became particularly angry when on July 17 he reiterated his demand that the House permit the Federal Treasury to reimburse with paper money — not gold and silver coin — the holders of "five-twenty" Federal bonds. Stevens lashed out, "If I knew that any Party in this country would go for paying in [gold and silver] coin that which is payable in [paper] money, I would vote for the other [Party], Frank Blair and all." Hearing Stevens' threat to switch parties, a Democrat jumped up and shouted, "The Democratic [Party] doors are open, and we will take the gentleman in." But Stevens had no intention of switching parties, as everyone knew.

During these last days of the House session, on July 24, in response to the rejection in late June of the Reconstructed Mississippi Constitution by 53 percent of the votes cast by qualified Mississippi voters, as mentioned earlier, the House passed a bill instructing the Mississippi Constitutional Convention to reassemble and frame a new Reconstructed State Constitution, making no mention of the extensive and punitive restrictions on European American men's right to vote. However, the Senate rejected the bill, leaving Mississippi without guidance. Agitated by persistent political conflict in Mississippi and in Washington, it would take the Federal Government 7 addition months to define for Mississippi an acceptable procedure for securing a new Reconstructed State Constitution.

Shortly afterward, near the end of July, the House adjourned. Soon after that, Edward de Stoeckl, the Russian Minister, began to quietly give out money to those Representatives who had made possible the funding of the purchase of Russian Alaska, most of it going to men who had first obstructed funding by "exposing the Perkins claim." Apparently Thad Stevens was slated to receive $10,000 — for that was what William Seward would tell Andrew Johnson — but Stevens' death would come too soon for him to receive his share of the bribery money. [R96;313-315, 204;219]

Meanwhile, on August 4, Jeff, Varina and the children disembarked from the *Austria* at Liverpool, England amid cheers of welcoming. Biographer Hudson Strode would write: "A hundred friends were there to receive him. Davis' spirits lifted. He came down the gangplank as if he were a completely free man and still the head of a great people." Jeff and Varina had been accompanied on the sea voyage by their British friends, the Rawson's. Jeff's doctor had prescribed a sea voyage, and Jeff hoped to establish business connections in Britain that might evolve into a new career. He had written Howell Cobb on July 6, "I have decided to go to Liverpool to see what may be done in establishing a commission house, especially in cotton and tobacco." By the way, before leaving Lennoxville, Canada, Jeff had there given a friend, Jennie Cummins, the Bible he had used during his imprisonment at Fortress Monroe, complete with many penciled remarks and underlined passages. Jennie would later give the Bible to the Confederate Museum in Richmond, "as a precious relic of the good and great man whom I was fortunate to know in my youth."

Jeff and Varina would place the boys in a good school at Waterloo, which was just outside Liverpool. After visiting at Liverpool with many cordial Britishers and a few former Confederate leaders, including Judah Benjamin, Jeff, Varina and the girls would go to stay with the Norman Walkers at their summer home at Llandudno, which lay amid beautiful surroundings between the sea and the Welsh mountains. Being of Welsh descent on his father's side, Jeff would enjoy meeting a great many people named Davis and going down into the coal mines to observe mining processes, for Jeff had always been interested in mining. But his trips to London in search of business connections would not bear useful fruit. [R19;333-336]

Meanwhile, Thad Stevens was dying. During early August an attack of diarrhea left him "extremely weak," but on August 6 he was able to sit up and handle "his ordinary business." On August 8 Lydia Smith, who remained at his side in the house, wrote Thad's nephew, Thaddeus, Junior, "Your uncle has been quite low. I had almost given up, but he is better. He had diarrhea, which would sit hard on him. He was so weak. I will write to you every day and let you know how he is." Loretta and Genevieve, two Catholic nuns who were of partial African ancestry, assisted Lydia, who was Catholic as well. The two nuns worked as nurses at Providence Hospital, which was located a few blocks from the house. Providence was a hospital for African Americans, which Stevens had helped finance with Federal funds. Many "personal and political friends" visited Stevens on August 11, and after they had left, family and close friends gathered around the bed. Present were his nephew, Thaddeus, Junior, the powerful railroad lawyer Simon Stevens (not a blood relative), Lydia, the two nurses Loretta and Genevieve, and Thad's male African American servant, Lewis West. At one point Simon reported that William Rosecrans had "spoken highly" of nephew Alanson Stevens, who had been killed by Confederates during the fighting at Chickamauga. Thad replied, "He was a brave boy." He dozed off, then awakened to advise: "Simon, the great questions of the day are [further Reconstruction of the Governments in the conquered States], the finances, and the railway system of this country." Later he awoke again to say, "I believe [Ulysses] Grant will be elected, and he will carry out the [laws designed to further Reconstruct the Governments in the conquered States]." Sometime later he roused sufficiently to reassure Thaddeus, Junior: "We'll have a nice trip home; I'll visit the foundry with you, perhaps." Later in the evening two ministers of partial African ancestry came to visit. When asked if he felt like seeing them, Thad replied "Certainly, certainly." The ministers went in. Stevens turned on his side and reached out his hand to them. The ministers sang a few hymns and prayed. Then they left.

It was about nine o'clock when Thad's Washington City physician, N. Young came in again to examine the patient. Young thought it advisable to tell Stevens that he was dying and had little more time left, for Stevens might yet find the heart to accept Jesus Christ as his Savior. But Thad "only nodded." Biographer Richard Current would describe the last hours:

> "An hour later Loretta and Genevieve, two of the [nuns of partial African ancestry], entered the sickroom and prayed. One of them held the old man's wasted hand. After a while the entire household gathered again around the bed. The nuns asked [Thad] if they might baptize him. He made no objection. One of the [nuns] took a glass of water, poured some of it on his head, and pronounced him baptized. . . . After the baptism he opened his eyes, once, twice, then closed them for good. It was now nearly midnight. The only sound came from the hooded dusky nuns, chanting their prayers for the dead."

Thad Stevens never accepted Jesus Christ as his Savior.

The Washington City funeral for Thad Stevens was the biggest display of public grief since the mourning over Abe Lincoln. Former President James Buchanan had died two months previously totally "unhonored and unwept." But the body of Thad Stevens "lay in state in the rotunda of the Capitol" while African American Zouaves soldiers from Massachusetts "proudly kept watch by day and night." Thousands filed by the casket. But not everyone within earshot was consumed by grief. As Republican leader James Blaine and a companion walked through the rotunda, Blaine was undoubtedly relieved to see Stevens pass on to his reward. Blaine complained: "He kept the Party under his heel. . . The death of Stevens is an emancipation for the Republican Party." Biographer Richard Current would write: "Many Republicans were glad enough to be rid of the parliamentary despot whose monetary views had become a source of embarrassment to them." Yet, "His soul, like John Brown's, was to "go marching on" alongside many Republican politicians, not the least of whom was Blaine, as they [would wave the bloody shirt and encourage intense hatred toward Democrats and former Confederates] in one election after another during the next two decades."

Thad Stevens' body was transported to Lancaster, Pennsylvania for a simple final funeral service in the Stevens house, followed by burial in a simple graveyard. Hundreds of townspeople and thousands of visitors from out of town stood outside the house while 8 Protestant ministers performed a general service. And Lydia was probably upset that there was no Catholic priest present. From the house the funeral procession moved to the graveyard, which Stevens had chosen because it was not particularly fashionable and the owners permitted burial of people with noticeable African ancestry. The casket was lowered into a solitary grave. There would be no family buried nearby — just an old bachelor buried alone. [R86;336, R96;318-320]

Meanwhile, as summer closed and fall approached, Charles Sumner and his backers increased their efforts to ensure that the new Massachusetts State Legislature, which would be elected in November, would be pledged to re-elect him to another 6-year term. Month's earlier Sumner men had worried about reports that Ben "Beast" Butler "aims at your seat," considered a serious challenge because Butler was "a military hero to many Massachusetts voters, he "had a strong following among the Irish, and his opposition to specie resumption allowed him to stand as the spokesman for the workingman against the mercantile and banking interests." But Sumner and his supporters had by this summer derailed enthusiasm for Butler by patronage maneuvers, such as allowing Butler to block the nomination of George Gordon — a military commander educated at Harvard and West-Point — to head up the Boston Customs House; by choosing to "utter not word or support" for his old political friend, Richard Dana, who had sought the Republican nomination for Butler's seat in the Federal House, and by diverting Federal jobs, including the Salem Postmaster job, to Sumner men. Eventually, Butler had given up on mounting a campaign.

But Ben "Beast" Butler had not been Sumner's only challenger from within the Massachusetts Republican Party. Sumner had once again been forced to counter a renewed threat from supporters of the late John Andrew, the former Governor, for those politicians had wanted to wrestle away Sumner's Senate job. Andrew had remained a serious threat, even after he had rather shot himself in the foot by opposing the campaign to outlaw alcoholic beverages in Massachusetts, thereby suffering brutal allegations that he himself was an alcoholic. But Sumner supporters had managed to weaken support for Andrew through systematic attacks in their newspaper, the *Commonwealth*. But Andrew had died on October 30, 1867. So who would Andrew men turn too? Their talking list included Adams', Cabot's, Eliot's, Ritchie's, Lee's, Parkman's, and other wealthy Bostonians from long-established prominent families. And they had sought help from William Fessenden, of Maine in helping them select a new man with whom they might defeat Sumner. It had sorted itself out; by the summer of 1868, these politicians had agreed to promote Charles Adams (Charles Francis Adams, Jr.) as their replacement for Charles Sumner.

Charles Adams was descended from two United States Presidents and had been Minister to Great Britain during the past 6 years — safely away from Massachusetts State politics. And Charles Adams had been very effective at discouraging British support for the Confederacy. His son Henry Adams was well-known and active in Republican politics. But another son, John Quincy Adams, Jr. had shunned the Republican Party to join up with the rather feeble Massachusetts Democrats. In fact the Massachusetts Democrats had unsuccessfully run that son for Governor in 1867. Unquestionably, Charles Adams had the potential to garner enough votes in the new legislature to take Sumner's Senate seat away from him. Of that danger, Sumner had written Wadsworth Longfellow on August 4, "If the people of Massachusetts turn from me, I shall not complain. I have done my duty." And Sumner's focus on Senate legislation had abruptly changed after the Impeachment of Andrew Johnson had failed. Instead of denouncing Andrew Johnson and pushing for greater Republican domination over the Governments of the conquered States, Sumner had turned his attention to passing helpful legislation for his supporters back home. Biographer David Donald would write: "he began giving close attention to bills wanted by Massachusetts merchants and shippers, among whom, as Pierce warned, he was 'not so very strong'." For instance, he had worked hard to reduce Federal excise taxes on the rum that Boston shippers exported to Africa, in an effort to preserve a pattern of trade dating back to the colonial era." Playing up to textile manufacturers, such as Edward Atkinson, Sumner had voted against a bill establishing an 8-hour day for laborers in Government facilities such as arsenals and shipyards. Then, on July 11, Sumner had surprised fellow Senators by delivering a long oration on something besides dealing with the conquered States or foreign nations. Sumner titled his unusual speech: "Financial Reconstruction through Public Faith and Specie Payments." Not well-versed in economics himself, Sumner pushed poetic imagery as he urged that, "Every greenback is red with the blood of fellow-citizens" — appearing especially eager to oppose Ben "Beast" Butler's opposition to resumption of specie payments. Sumner wanted Boston industrialists, bankers and merchants to know that, like Edward Atkinson, that "ingenious merchant," he favored backing paper money with gold and silver coin. That speech helped Sumner rebuild support among Boston industrialists, bankers and merchants. For example, William Amory, who had always opposed Sumner's domestic policies, wrote: "The [country] is largely indebted to you for such outspoken truth, so forcible, plainly, and irresistibly set forth, by one whose influence is so great, if not always exerted in the right direction."

This was the background political situation when Edward Pierce praised Charles Sumner before the Massachusetts Republican State Convention on September 9. Hoping to rally Delegates to obligate Republican legislative candidates to pledge their support for the re-election of Sumner, Pierce heaped on the praise. He praised Sumner's "eloquent, fearless and persistent devotion to the sacred cause of human rights." He praised his "diligence and success as Chairman of the Senate Committee on Foreign Affairs." Then he demanded that everyone support Sumner's re-election because of "his fidelity, experience and honorable identification with our [country's] history." Delegates listened devotedly. Perhaps they even swallowed the notion that a man incapable of bouncing back from being whipped with a walking cane could somehow be "fearless." In any event, the reality was that none had a candidate strong enough to sidetrack Sumner. The Bird Machine, Pierce and other supporters had successfully eroded earlier support for Ben "Beast" Butler and Charles Adams — and John Andrew was dead. Consequently, the Delegates rose and endorsed Pierce's praise with "three rousing cheers."

Eight days later, a pleased and now "fearless" Charles Sumner wrote Wadsworth Longfellow: "So at last I have conquered; after a life of struggle."

As election season heated up in Massachusetts Charles Sumner, very concerned that his supporters might fail to be elected to the Massachusetts House and Senate, decided to forgo staying in Washington City in his new dream house, or vacationing in Europe, as he like to do when the Senate was not in session. So, not owning a house in his State (begging the question of how he qualified to be elected Massachusetts Senator), he took a room in Boston's Coolidge House where his senses suffered "constantly the tread of horses and the hiss of steam," for his rooms looked out over a livery stable and a machine shop. Since he would have to stand for election in January in the State Legislature, Sumner was careful to support Grant only mildly, for he feared that Massachusetts voters might find fault in Grant as a man, in spite of how gloriously they still viewed his leadership over the conquest of the Confederate States. Even so, he contributed only a token campaign effort for the Republican Party. [R73;341-348]

Meanwhile in October, Jeff Davis learned that his good friend, Howell Cobb, had "dropped dead in a New York hotel." Besides the feeling of loss over the passing of a dear friend, Jeff was troubled over the loss of his planned business partner. Cobb was to work States-side as the buyer of the cotton and tobacco for the commission house Davis was attempting to establish in Great Britain. Yet, Davis was continuing to have trouble setting up the commission house. Businessmen visiting London from the northern States, wanting the market share that Davis was seeking, were warning Britishers against making deals with Davis because he was "only a prisoner on bail." But Jeff and Varina knew that former Confederate leaders could succeed in the British business climate. Judah Benjamin was proof of that. Already he was "gaining remarkable prestige in his law practice." [R19;338]

Meanwhile, Wade Hampton continued providing leadership to the South Carolina Democratic Campaign. John Quincy Adams II, son of Charles Frances Adams and grandson and great-grandson of the two former President Adams', accepted an invitation to travel down from Massachusetts and speak to South Carolina voters. Because of the Federal Invasion of the Confederacy and the political aftermath, Adams had left the Republican Party and become a Democrat. Speaking in Columbia on October 12, Adams told voters that he had voted for Abe Lincoln, had hated African American bonding and had been opposed to the right of State Secession. But he also hated the Republican Party's current programme of political Reconstruction, whereby South Carolina Democrats were denounced as: "alien enemies; your country conquered; yourselves prisoners of war and your rights of every kind forfeited." Even under such a burden, Adams advised his listeners to, "possess your souls in patience. Call to your aid that grandest of human qualities, self-control, and all will yet be well." Urged on by the crowd, Hampton rose and spoke, too, again defending his role in writing part of the Democratic Party Platform. Publicly, he explained to Adams that South Carolina Democrats did not support voting rights for all men, but would support the same voting rules concerning African Americans that were present policy in Massachusetts. Adams and Hampton appeared later in Charleston, and, near the end of that event, Adams told the audience, "If [Hampton] is a rebel, he is just such a rebel as I am and no more." But, on October 15, any faint hope Democrats had of stopping the election of Ulysses Grant evaporated, for, that day, Republicans won big in the early elections held in Pennsylvania, Ohio and Indiana.

Mostly organized through community Union League groups, the Republican Reconstruction Programme — aimed at ensuring that South Carolina's African Americans and their European American leaders controlled State and local governments — was not without incidents of violence. Many European Americans in South Carolina were greatly angered by the loss of their civil rights, and a few resorted to violent reprisals during the election season. Killed in reprisal were European American S. G. W. Dill of Kershaw and African Americans B. F. Randolph, of Orangeburg, James Martin of Abbeville, Wade Perrin of Laurens and a few others. Several European American men suspected of murder were arrested and imprisoned for a time in Columbia, but, although under Republican rule, none were found guilty and all were eventually freed. The killings would have been more widespread but for the determined non-violent strategy pursued by the vast majority of South Carolina Democrat leaders and their followers. Wade Hampton biographer Walter Cisco would surmise that, "it was the assassination of Randolph that seemed to galvanize the State and conjure up the specter of a race war." Randolph was a State Senator. The killings prompted a meeting between the South Carolina Democratic Party leadership and Governor Robert Scott, called by Scott to seek cooperation in calming nerves. A follow-up meeting was held on October 27 at Scott's home. At this meeting Scott agreed to four conditions for gaining support from the Democratic leadership:

1. Since Ulysses Grant was sure to win election, Scott would use his influence to advocate South Carolina Republicans cross over and vote for Democrat candidate Seymour as a symbol of friendship.

2. Scott would encourage some African American Republicans in the legislature to resign and be replaced by European Americans as a symbol of friendship and to "calm racial feelings."

3. Scott would appoint at least 2 Democrats to the Executive Office.

4. Scott would publicly advocate peace and commend Democrats for advocating likewise.

Scott agreed to all four points and issued a Proclamation on October 30, as promised in item 4 above. But he would never honor his promises to fulfill items 1, 2 or 3. [R199;195-198, R201;103-105]

(4Q68)

On Election Day, the vote in South Carolina for Ulysses Grant was 62,300 versus 45,137 for Seymour. Democrat voters did succeed in electing two men to the Federal House, J. P. Reed of Anderson and William D. Simpson of Laurens, but Republicans in Washington would vote to unseat these two men. It was becoming apparent to Wade Hampton and others that fighting the iron-clad grip that the Union League held over the State's African American men would be a long and difficult battle of wills. Hampton would soon turn his attention to his large farms in Mississippi and their mortgage debts, which threatened to drive him into bankruptcy.

Meanwhile, Reverdy Johnson, Minister to Great Britain, made exceptional progress in negotiations with the British over disputes with the Federal Government. Heightened concern about the increasing power of Bismarck's Prussia, and its threat to the balance of power in Europe, was motivating the British to increased accommodation toward Federal Government demands. Reverdy Johnson was pleased to obtain British agreement to honor the citizenship of ex-Britishers who had become American citizens. The British agreement was patterned after the North Germany agreement, previously mentioned. The British also agreed to participate in a Special Commission to be set up to negotiate the San Juan boundary dispute. Then, on November, 10 Reverdy Johnson and British leader Edward Stanley "signed a Convention which provided for the settlement of all outstanding claims between" the British and the Federals. And Stanley's replacement, George Clarendon, would follow through by also signing the Convention on January 14, 1869. [R73;365]

Meanwhile in Richmond, the Federal Court convened on November 30 to consider the indictment against Jeff Davis on the charge of Treason. This time the charges were not presented to a Jury under the thumb of Federal Circuit Judge John Underwood. They were presented to a Panel of Judges headed up by Chief Justice Salmon Chase. John Underwood was on the panel, but Chase held top power. Robert Ould, one of Davis' defense lawyers, asked the Panel of Judges to quash the indictment. Then on December 3, Charles O'Conor, Davis' leading defense lawyer, demanded that the indictment be squashed because of the recent passage of the Federal Amendment Nationalizing Citizenship (14th), which prohibited former Confederate officers from holding future office in Federal or State governments. O'Conor argued that "disqualification from future office" was "punishment enough" for any charge against Jeff Davis, and O'Conor submitted proof's to validate that position. The Panel of Judges weighed the arguments, but could not agree. Firmly aware that the Federals would lose a full-scale trial, if ever allowed, Chase wanted the Davis thing squashed. On the other hand Underwood was still eager to keep the case alive. On December 5, Chase announced to the public that the Panel of Judges had failed to agree on a decision. However, Chase instructed the Court Reporter to record that he, as Chief Justice, favored quashing the indictment and barring all further legal proceedings because of the punitive effect of the Fourteenth Amendment. Charles O'Conor notified Davis, who had remained in London, that he would have no more trouble from the Federal Courts. And, within four weeks, Jeff Davis would no longer be classified as a prisoner on bail, for he would be considered covered by the General Amnesty Proclamation that Andrew Johnson would issue on Christmas Day, 1868. Jeff and Varina's imprisonment and courtroom battles with the Federals were finally over. [R19;339]

Meanwhile in Mississippi, Wade Hampton filed for bankruptcy in Jackson on December 24, listing mortgage debt at $645,103 and unsecured debt at $367,225 for a total debt of $1,012,328 and listing assets of $235,500 in land and $7,905 in personal property. At the time of State Secession, Hampton had estimated that he held 12,000 acres of land and 900 bonded African Americans. Although Wade Hampton III had struggled mightily for 8 years against huge financial odds, he had not evaded bankruptcy, until now. Biographer Walter Cisco would write:

> "Invading Federals had destroyed his Columbia home and emancipation had swept away his work force. Labor problems, high taxes, and the vagaries of weather had plagued him and all others who farmed during the postwar years. He had a family to support and a wife who required "special care." The political struggle consumed Hampton's time and energy. Faced with these demands and liabilities, perhaps even an entrepreneur of extraordinary shrewdness — a businessman such as the first Wade Hampton — would have failed. Wade Hampton III, like his father, possessed no such gifts."

Yes, wife Mary was suffering from difficulties during childbirth the year before. The baby girl died soon after delivery and continuing debilitating problems from an "enlarged, swollen uterus" would prevent the mother from ever getting completely well.

A year and a half later, bankruptcy Judge R. A. Hill, on July 13, 1870, would free Hampton "from all debts and claims" prior to the filing date. Yet all would not be lost. Hampton would retain his modest home outside of Columbia and his smallest Mississippi farm, called Wild Woods, consisting of 835 acres, not far from the Mississippi River. Wild Woods had been his favorite farm. It appears that potential bidders would avoid taking those properties because of threatened added creditor liabilities. He would rent the Wild Woods farm to share croppers. [R199;198-200, R200;125-126]

The Year of 1869

(1Q69)

On January 19, 1869, the Massachusetts House of Representatives and the Massachusetts Senate voted overwhelmingly to re-elect Charles Sumner to another 6-year term. The House vote had been 216 for Sumner, 14 for Democrat Josiah Abbott and 1 for Nathaniel Banks. The Senate vote had been 37 for Sumner and 2 for Abbott. The new term would be Sumner's fourth and entitle him to be called "Dean of the Senate," for no other Senator would be able to claim that he had worked the job for four consecutive terms. Yes, Charles Sumner could look forward to another 6 years in Washington, where he would host dinner gatherings of intellectual men, collect stuff for his Washington City dream house (no need of a pesky residence in Massachusetts, it appears), Chair his Foreign Relations Committee, and attend to Senate business. Otherwise he could be off on vacation doing whatever interested him. Sumner was 58 years old. He would take great joy in the many congratulatory letters that would arrive from old Abolitionists and Exclusionists — heaped with praise. For example, a January 20 letter from William Garrison would proclaim, "This is no human, but a divine triumph; this is not the wisdom of man, but the power of God." As we read Garrison's words, we should recognize that the "God" he refers to is not the Lord whose Son is Jesus Christ. Sumner was not a Christian man, and it appears that few Exclusionists had been either.

It was about the beginning of 1869 that Charles Sumner began a new project to edit and publish new volumes of his speeches and writings. It would be the first publication of Sumner's works since 1856, so he had 13 years of material from which he could select. Sumner had struck a deal with Lee and Shepard of Boston to handle publication. The books would be sold by subscription and his friends had pledged to purchase enough subscriptions to finance the first two volumes; expectations were that, once deliveries began, subsequent subscription sales would finance the remaining volumes. With publication arrangements in place, Sumner turned to the massive job of studious editing. Biographer David Donald would write, "Day after day Sumner amended and pruned his speeches until he sometimes thought it would have been as easy to rewrite as to revise." On occasion he would become so tired of the editing effort that he would lament, "If I could throw them into the fire, I would, and have an end of them." But more often he would stubbornly declare, as he did to Samuel Howe: "These speeches are my life. As a connected series, they will illustrate the progress of the great battle [against African American bonding], and what I have done in it. I hope it is not unpardonable in me to desire to see them together, especially as I have nothing else." Sumner was confessing that "nothing else" in his life was meaningful. David Donald would write, "For the rest of Sumner's life his spare hours [would be] occupied with this reliving of the past — with careful insertion of newspaper comments on his addresses, of extracts from his correspondence, and of footnotes to document quotations and with some slight deletion of literary or factual excrescences which he [had become to find] embarrassing — and the set ultimately [would] grow to 15 volumes." Whenever he would find someone willing to listen, Sumner would talk about his "book" incessantly. Of Sumner and his "book" James Fields would remark, "I think he loves the author of it."

On February 26, the Federal Senate passed an Amendment to the Federal Constitution, which, if Ratified by the States, would force all State and local governments to allow voting by African American men. It had already passed the House and was ready to be submitted to the State Legislatures. It would become known as the Amendment to Nationalize Voting by African American Men (15th). In spite of his past history of crusading for new African American legislation, Charles Sumner had not been among the Senate leaders involved in advocating passage of the Amendment. Representative George Boutwell of Massachusetts had sponsored the Amendment in the House and William Stewart of Nevada had sponsored it in the Senate. Anyway, Sumner had not even been very supportive of the Amendment. Biographer David Donald would explain: "Unwilling to see the need for an Amendment but unwilling openly to oppose it, [Sumner] was absent on all the crucial roll calls. Sumner had rarely participated in debate on the measure, and when he did become involved, it was because he was seeking, though unsuccessfully, to amend it in ways that sponsors found objectionable. Such behavior prompted fellow Republican Senators to rather shun Sumner as "an impracticable egoist." To be sure, Sumner wanted African American men to vote throughout the States — that was not in dispute. Sumner's major disagreement with proponents of the Amendment was his insistence that the Federal Constitution did not require Amendment. All that was needed, in Sumner's view, was for the House, Senate and President to force all States to allow African American men at their polls by passing and signing a new Federal law commanding it. Furthermore, Sumner feared that the Amendment route would produce "all the poisoned ingredients of prejudice and hate" that he expected to arise during State-by-State Legislative debate over its Ratification. Better to force the thing directly from Washington, Sumner reasoned. Biographer David Donald would further describe Sumner' attitude:

> "Furthermore, to propose an Amendment implied that under the [Federal] Constitution as it now stood 'a Caste and an Oligarchy of the [Race] may be set up by a State without any check from Congress'." To critics who argued that the [Federal] Constitution gave the individual States the right to regulate elections, Sumner replied that the alleged power to regulate was nowhere to be found in that document, which simply declared that the States could set up 'the Qualifications requisite for Elections' in Federal elections. A qualification, he insisted, could not be an unchangeable condition but 'something that can be acquired.' Consequently, unlike 'residence, property, education, or character, each of which is within the possible reach of well-directed effort,' [race] could not be a qualification. 'Are we not reminded that the leopard cannot change his spots, or the Ethiopian his skin?' No Amendment, therefore, was needed. Congress had ample power to act, both under the original [Federal] Constitution and under the recently adopted Thirteenth and Fourteenth Amendments. Senators should leave off footling debate and pass a sweeping act to outlaw caste discrimination in voting [throughout the States]. They should remember that 'beyond all question' the true rule [for interpreting the Federal Constitution] was 'that anything for Human Rights is constitutional'."

Charles Sumner's non-involvement in the Amendment was symptomatic of further retreat from any leadership role. David Donald would explain:

> "Fessenden and Trumbull were estranged from the Party they had helped found. Control of the Republican Party in Congress was falling to a new breed of politicians, whom Sumner did not understand and for most of whom he had little liking. In the Senate the powerful men were not Conkling, who was publicly contemptuous of Sumner, Simon Cameron, as unprincipled and as corruptible as when he had been Secretary of War, and Morton, the efficient Indiana war Governor who considered Sumner an impractical idealist. In the House the new Speaker was James G. Blaine, a political technician committed to no ideology, and two of the principal Republican spokesmen were former [military commanders], John A. Logan, of Illinois, and Ben ["Beast"]

Butler, neither of whom hid their conviction that they were men of action while Sumner was a pompous windbag."

"Sumner and [Ben] Wade were as outspoken in their desire to keep the Republican Party in power as were Conkling and Butler, and all four men were advocates of [allowing African American men to vote]. But to Republican leaders of Sumner's generation, the hegemony of their Party was necessary to preserve the rights of the [newly independent African American men]; to their successors, the protection of the [African Americans] was required in order to assure the success of the Republican Party. There was also a significant difference in rhetoric. Republican veterans of the [Exclusion-Abolition] conflict freely invoked ideals of liberty, justice, and equality — sometimes to cloak selfish purposes; the [new Republicans], considering themselves practical men, eschewed high-flown oratory and appealed to expediency — even to justify disinterested causes.

Elitist, literary, idealistic, and egotistical, Charles Sumner simply did not fit in. On the very first day of the Senate session he had introduced a bill "to provide for the resumption of specie payments on the 4th of July, 1969." But, finding very little support for a return to gold and silver coin, he allowed the issue to die. In general, Sumner took little part in the day-to-day debate and bill-writing activities of the Senate. Because of his awkwardness at negotiating vote-trading deals among fellow Senators, this legislation, which he wanted for his supporters back home, met with defeat. Also, he failed to obtain passage of a bill to lower import taxes on dyes used in Massachusetts textile mills. Likewise, he failed in his effort to obtain, for hopeful New England shipping companies, the subsidy from the Federal Government that they wanted. He failed to obtain Federal money for Massachusetts by his argument that it should be reimbursed for monies paid during the War of 1812. Although the Massachusetts politicians seeking that money planned to use it to finance a "questionable railroad scheme," Sumner fussed and fumed that "a claim presented from Massachusetts hardly receives the favor that a claim form another State might expect and actually receives." Always taking the high road on an issue, he ignored complaints over the intended misuse of the money and complained that "Senators are disposed to attack Massachusetts, to vote against her claims."

Although Charles Sumner exerted little influence on domestic legislation and African American legislation, he still loomed powerful over foreign policy legislation. John Conness, who often criticized bills that Sumner and his Foreign Relations Committee had written, thought Sumner so dominated his Committee that it was appropriate to claim that, "the honorable Senator was the Committee." Through that domination, Sumner succeeded in blocking William Seward's plan to purchase islands in the Caribbean, such as the proposal that Seward had presented in December, 1867, to purchase the Danish West Indies (including today's Virgin Islands). Sumner was killing that one by "silence." Sumner's hostility to the measure infuriated the Danish Minister, Waldemar Rassloff, who had won the support of almost everyone of influence in Washington. While the Danish-American Treaty lay submerged in Sumner's Committee, St. Thomas suffered devastation by a hurricane, an earthquake, and a tidal wave. Yet, Sumner himself was unmoved. Sumner would also block Seward's plan to purchase Samaná bay in the Dominican Republic for a planned American naval base. Andrew Johnson attempted to bypass Sumner's Committee when he asked the Senate to approve the Samaná bay project in advance of his submission of the papers to the Senate. But Sumner's Committee would not be bypassed. Charles Sumner had fought national expansion to the south and the southwest far to long to now give in. He, and like-minded Massachusetts politicians, still viewed national expansion in that direction as a further erosion of their political power in the Federal Government and in America's commerce and industry. Leaders in Massachusetts, because their State was located in the far northeastern corner of the country, had always feared the consequences of being positioned further and further from the central hub of the United States. They had opposed America's merger with the Republic of Texas, opposed taking land from Mexico out to California, opposed taking Cuba, and to some extent even Alaska, and Sumner remained opposed to taking Caribbean islands. On the other hand, during the invasion of the Confederacy, Massachusetts leaders had advocated a simultaneous invasion into nearby Canada.

Since the conquest of the Seceded States, Sumner had attempted to encourage Great Britain to open negotiations on how much she would agree to pay northeastern States marine shippers for past damage they has suffered at the hands of Confederate naval raiders. Sumner had originally believed that, if the British had agreed to pay some money in the first few months following the conquest of the Confederacy, then that would settle the matter. But, since the British had stalled and refused to negotiate, Sumner figured the amount of money required to satisfy the shipping companies and their political allies had grown and grown. On the other hand, the British Minister, Lord Lyons, who thought, "We have no more bitter enemy than Sumner," believed "if we were to yield on this point, there would be no limit to the concessions demanded." Lyons had predicted it would be impossible to maintain peace along the Canadian border if Sumner ever became Secretary of State — an outcome many had predicted during Andrew Johnson's Impeachment Trial.

Of other Federal Government leaders, David Donald would write:

> "Influential Republicans like Chandler and Stanton talked freely about [taking] Canada as compensation for damages done to the [Federals] by British-built naval raiders during the [Invasion of the Confederacy]. Others, like Butler and Banks, hoped there would not be a prompt settlement, so that when Great Britain was next at war the [Federal Government] could follow her precedent and construct warships for her enemies. In August 1865 Sumner passed along to the British Government, through John Bright, Grant's ominous view of the diplomatic situation: 'he cared little whether England paid 'our little bill' or not; — upon the whole he would rather she should not as that would leave the precedent of her conduct in full force for us to follow, and . . . he thought that we should make more out of 'the precedent' than out of 'the bill'."

In view of these "Sumner" problems, William Seward had withheld from Chairman of the Senate Foreign Relations Committee information about negotiations and agreements being arranged by Reverdy Johnson in London. When the British Minister in Washington inquired about the opinions of Sumner and his Committee regarding the agreements being hammered out, Seward had "snorted contemptuously 'that he knew their opinions and what they could sanction better than they did themselves'." It seems that Seward thought he could control Sumner better if he suddenly sprung the Treaty on his Committee as he had done on the deal to purchase Russian America. And Seward probably wanted the political credit from a British Treaty to benefit the Grant Administration instead of Andrew Johnson's. As would be expected, Sumner "was predisposed to question the merits of Reverdy Johnson's treaties" for several reasons. First, he hated Seward and the way Seward excluded him from negotiations with foreign governments. Second, he distrusted Reverdy Johnson, because Johnson had come from a State that had so recently permitted African American bonding. Then there was the news that Reverdy Johnson had shown friendship toward British leaders who had previously befriended the Confederacy. Sumner had fumed upon hearing that Reverdy Johnson had shaken hands with the owner of the Laird shipbuilding enterprise. He had fumed again upon learning that Reverdy Johnson had greeted John Roebuck as a friend, for Roebuck had vigorously defended the Confederacy before the British Parliament during the Federal invasion. So, when Seward finally presented the Johnson-Clarendon Convention to the Senate for Ratification, Sumner prepared to fight it. He warned in a letter to John Bright, now a member of the British Parliament, that, "Our Minister has made it impossible to adopt anything that has been done." It was "not [Reverdy Johnson's] fault," Sumner continued, he "had acted according to his instructions." Then, pointing a finger at William Seward, he reported to Bright that "The feeling toward [Seward] will not help the treaties." And Sumner, who purposely avoided discussing the issue with Ulysses Grant, meekly told Edward Thornton, "that he was not acquainted with Grant's views on the subject," and "that he believed no one knew his views." Why would Sumner think that? Because Sumner, a supreme elitist, thought that "Grant was not capable himself of forming an opinion upon such a subject." But soon after making those statements to Thornton, Sumner did discuss the Treaty with Grant, who asked Sumner if "he did not think it better that it should wait until the new [Grant Administration] is installed." Sumner figured that Grant's advice was perfect ammunition with which he could delay action for a few weeks at least. So he told Thornton several times that Grant wanted the deal set aside until he was sworn in as President.

But what Sumner did not realize was that Grant was perfectly "capable himself of forming an opinion on the subject." In fact Grant firmly believed that, Sumner must be deposed as Chairman of the Senate Foreign Relations Committee. In fact, Grant and his top supporters within the Republican Party were perhaps already laying plans to do just that. A purge of old-school Republican Exclusion/Abolition elitists was in the formative stages, and Charles Sumner was at the top of their hit list. There is an interesting story that describes Grant's opinion of Sumner, who had a reputation for an over-inflated self-esteem that approached godly self-glorification. According to the story, when someone had mentioned to Grant in conversation that Sumner, a non-Christian, had no faith in the Bible, Grant had replied: "Well, he didn't write it." It seems that Sumner was unaware of the scheming afoot to reduce his power. Perhaps his ears were too finely tuned for picking up occasional praise, such as William Seward's comment that only three men were capable of being Secretary of State: himself, Charles Adams and Charles Sumner. And Sumner had surely dreamed of becoming a key member of the Grant Administration Cabinet. He had written Francis Lieber the day after Grant's election that he considered himself "equal in position to anything in our Government under the President." But Sumner added: "I admit, however, that my country has a right to determine where I can work best." Grant had made it a point to play up to Sumner during a December visit to Boston, for he had met with Sumner at that time. But he had also met with Charles Adams. Despite such meetings, Grant was at the same time ensuring that "the country," as represented by the Republican Party leadership, had determined that Sumner would someday "work best" Senate loner stripped of power. And Sumner seemed to be playing his hand rather clumsily. During January and February he had made himself a bit obnoxious, perhaps figuring that such display of power demonstrated his potential at international politics. When the Republican Committee charged with planning the Inaugural activities had asked to use the Capitol building for the gala Inaugural Ball, Sumner had fiercely opposed the request and had succeeded in killing the thing. When friends of Grant had attempted to repeal the Tenure of Office Act to give Grant historically-normal authority to name Federal appointees, Sumner had strongly opposed repeal both in the Republican Caucus and on the Senate floor. The Tenure of Office Act had only been passed, over Andrew Johnson's veto, to either entrap a defiant Johnson or make a compliant Johnson subservient to Congress. As reported earlier, Johnson had chosen the defiant route and had only escaped the Republican Impeachment trap because of Salmon Chase's fair-minded conduct and Edmund Ross' patriotic vote. The Republican leadership believed that, with Johnson's term completed, the Tenure of Office Act was no longer useful or appropriate. But Charles Sumner was defiantly insistent that Congress retain maximum power over the Executive by keeping the Act in force. Sumner's dreams of a Cabinet appointment would be finally destroyed on March 5, when Grant would announce his Cabinet selections. Charles Sumner's name would not be on the list. [R73;329-330,348-368]

Meanwhile, in South Carolina, the State House and Senate concluded its 1868-69 Session on March 14, an expensive ordeal for the tax-paying citizens of the State but a lucrative bonanza for the Legislators themselves. The most significant results of the 1868-1869 Legislative Session are provided below:

A State police force, commonly called the State Constabulary, was established and led by Chief Constable John Hubbard of New York State, a disreputable man alleged to have helped generate some of the false evidence that was used to convict and hang Mary Surratt, the innocent keeper of the house where John Wilkes Booth had boarded. Considerable money went to the Constabulary, which exceeded its 1869 budget of $30,000 by 83%, instead spending $55,000.

"An Act to Suppress Insurrection and Rebellion" empowered the Governor, at his discretion, to establish an armed force of 100 men and to call up the militia and take possession of railroads and telegraph services."

"An act to authorize a State loan to pay interest on the pubic debt" authorized $1,000,000 of South Carolina coupon bonds. Of this historian John Reynold would write, "By this act was inaugurated the series of irregular, unlawful and fraudulent acts committed in connection with the public debt of the State. The board thus created — Scott, Chamberlain and Parker — selected as the "financial agent" one Hiram Kimpton of Boston . . . From the time of his appointment to the end of his career he was the active agent, the constant helper of the Scott-Parker-Chamberlain ring that operated under the name and style of the 'Financial Board'."

"An act to organize townships and to define their powers and privileges" instituted a new and elaborate layer of government under the guise of townships, complete with the lucrative offices of town clerk, three selectmen, one or more surveyors and one constable. Historian John Reynold would explain: "The selectmen were made overseers of the poor, registers in town elections, general supervisors of the affairs of the town and auditors of its accounts. . . . The manifest object of the measure was to create a multitude of offices to be filled by African American men," they being the majority in almost all town meetings.

"An Act to authorize additional aid to the Blue Ridge Railroad Company" pledged the State to guarantee railroad bonds up to $1,000,000 plus guaranteed payments on construction contracts up to a total of $3,000,000. Historian John Reynold would explain, "Out of this act grew the issue of the famous 'Revenue Bond Scrip' — the transactions under this act and in the circulation of the so-called scrip constituting one of the schemes of plunder instituted by the Republican ring in South Carolina." A quick history of the Blue Ridge Railroad is appropriate:

> Originally chartered in 1852 as the Blue Ridge Railroad of South Carolina, the company had planned to build a very challenging, 195-mile, mountain-penetrating railroad from Anderson, South Carolina to Knoxville, Tennessee going through the mountains with as many as 13 tunnels, an enormous engineering project to be sure. After completion, the railroad would connect the coast at Charleston, South Carolina to Knoxville, Tennessee, and by other railroads, to the Ohio River. But the intervening mountains were a huge barrier to be overcome. By early 1861, when all resources had to be diverted to defensive efforts, 44 miles of track had been laid across the less rugged South Carolina region, from Anderson to West Union, and work had begun on several tunnels through the mountains, including a start at digging a planned 1-mile-long tunnel through Stumphouse Mountain.

The Legislature "requested the Governor to take such action as may be necessary to have the more important towns in the State garrisoned by [Federal] troops, that peace and order may be preserved and the rights of the people may be protected." The main purpose, of course, was to use Federal troops as needed to ensure Republican victories during election seasons.

The General Assembly appointed all members of the Board of the University of South Carolina and placed the Governor at the head. Professor's salaries were raised from $1,000 to $2,000, the goal of creating a preparatory school was established and both it and the University were to accept all students without consideration of "race, color or creed."

A State orphan asylum was created, but because it was required to be open to both races, with equal treatment, few if any European American children would enter.

A three-member Statute Revision Commission was created for "the revision and consolidation of the statute laws of the State." David Corbin did almost all of the legal work, using the New York code of Procedure "almost literally." Each Commissioner was paid $3,500, but later accounting would indicate $50,000 had been spent, against the allegation that competent lawyers could have done it for only $5,000 — further indication of abuse of power.

An "Act to Reorganize and Govern the Militia" banned all citizen military forces other than the official "National Guard of South Carolina," which was made up almost entirely of African American militiamen. Historian John Reynold would determine that this Guard "cost in all certainty $200,000, beside a considerable sum fraudulently misapplied in procuring and altering certain arms given by the Federal Government."

An "Act to Provide for the Enumeration of the Inhabitants of this State" consumed expenditures of $76,000 but produced "altogether useless" census tabulations due to the incompetence of the census chiefs ($5 per day) and the census workers ($4 per day).

A "Land Commission" was established, headed by a Commissioner at a salary of $2,000. Historian John Reynold would describe the workings of this experiment:

> "The sum of $200,000 — to be raised by the issue of 6% bonds of the State, running 20 years — was provided for the purchase of improved or unimproved lands, these to be divided into parcels of not less than 25 and not more than 100 acres and sold to actual settlers who should pay therefore in 5 annual installments, commencing at the end of the third year of possession, with annual interest of 6%, reckoning from the date of purchase. Thus was inaugurated a scheme which throughout its workings constituted one of the great frauds that helped to fix the character of Republican rule in South Carolina."

The legislature authorized the Governor to purchase "2,000 stand of arms of the most improved pattern, with the usual complement of ammunition." Winchester rifles were purchased.

The Fifteenth Amendment to the Federal Constitution, Nationalizing Voting by African American Men, was ratified by the Legislature on March 15, 1869, with Republicans voting yes and the few

Democrats voting no (sufficient State Ratifications would exist to make the Amendment law on March 30, 1870).

The Legislature set a tax rate on property at 5 mils and the corresponding county tax rates on property ranged from 3 mils to 7 mils.

The Legislature set lucrative salaries for State officers, including $3,500 for the Governor; $3,000 for the Secretary of State and his clerk; $2,500 for the Adjutant-General; $3,000 for the Comptroller-General; $2,500 for the Treasurer; $3,000 for the Attorney-General, and $2,500 for the Superintendent of Education. Legislators took for themselves the pay rate stated in the Constitution, expanding that for all they could get, including $6 per day including Sundays plus 20 cents per mile for travel, which totaled $130,000 for the 72 working days of the Special Session and even more for the 89 working days of the Regular Session, the latter concluding on March 14, 1869. [R201;114-120]

Meanwhile, Jeff Davis had spent the first three months of 1869 vacationing in France and Switzerland; and there his health improved. He and Varina had left London for Paris just after Christmas. Dudley Mann was their primary host. You will recall that, along with fellow Confederate Commissioners, James Mason and John Slidell, Mann had worked hard during the days of the Defense of the Confederacy — but without success — at encouraging the French Government to recognize the Confederate States of America. Following the conquest of the seceded States, Mann had remained in France. A widower, Mann had a comfortable residence in Paris and a modest country retreat near Chantilly. Thus situated, he was adamant about not returning to The States as long as the Republican Party ruled. Jeff and Varina had spent New Year's Day with John Slidell and his wife, who were also well off financially, and whose daughter Mathilde had married a wealthy Frenchman. Napoleon III had invited Davis to a meeting, but he had declined because he believed it would be inappropriate for him to associate in that way with a man who could have — and Jeff thought should have — acted to help the Confederacy defend against the Federal invasion (Davis had, instead, agreed to accept the honor of a military review). After a few weeks, Varina had returned to London and their children while Jeff stayed on with Dudley Mann. Biographer Hudson Strode would write: "Sitting before Mann's fire, enjoying his pipe, Davis could relax as he had not relaxed in 7 long years. Although the two often dined out, Davis was more pleased when they stayed quietly at home. Tionette, Mann's Belgian cook, took overt joy in preparing favorite dishes for [the guest]." But Davis was shaken back to reality by a letter from his brother Joseph that had been forwarded to Paris, revealing that Ben Montgomery's harvests had again been too small to permit him to make any payment on the mortgage he and Jeff held on the 3,000 acres of farmland they had sold to Montgomery to circumvent Federal confiscation. The Davis brothers were still successfully avoiding confiscation, and they were providing a home and jobs for many of the African Americans they had once owned, but there was no money coming in from their investment in the farms. Jeff was 61 years old and he had four children to educate. He needed to find a suitable job. After spending two weeks in the dry Swiss mountain air — which did cure his nagging cough — Jeff would prepare to return to England. By May, he and Varina would be lamenting that their money was about to be depleted. Davis would thank his primary host, Dudley Mann, with a note that included the sentence: "The quiet days passed with you remain to me the one happy appreciation of recent years." [R19;340-342]

Meanwhile, in Washington City, the Federal House continued to withhold instructions to Mississippi on how it should proceed in securing an acceptable State Constitution. That job was deferred to the newly elected Federal House and Senate, which would convene later in March. Political conflict on this crucial question was continuing, both in Mississippi and in Washington City. [R204;225]

March 1869 Through February, 1873 – Political Reconstruction During the First Ulysses Grant Administration

It is now time to review a summary of the 1868 Federal elections in the summarized format that has begun each 4-year segment of this study. After this review, the narrative history will resume.

Hiram Ulysses Grant was his given name, but he acquired the moniker "Ulysses S. Grant" as a cadet at West Point. Embarrassed that his initials were H. U. G., Grant arranged to reverse the order to U. H. G. However, the enrollment papers submitted by his Congressman, in the appointment of Grant, mistakenly recorded his name as Ulysses Simpson Grant (his mother's maiden name was Simpson). Fellow cadets started calling him Uncle Sam Grant or Sam for short and thereafter his friends called him Sam. Grant eventually adopted the name "Ulysses S. Grant." His fierce, no-peace-talks, prosecution of the Federal Invasion of the Confederacy caused Confederates to call him "Unconditional Surrender" Grant.

Grant was of English and Scotch heritage. His great-great-great-great-great-grandfather, Matthew Grant, emigrated from England in 1630. He settled in Windsor, Connecticut. In 1756, his great-grandfather, Captain Noah Grant, was killed in a French and Indian War battle. His grandfather, also Captain Noah Grant, fought at Bunker Hill and remained in service throughout the Revolutionary War. Afterward, he moved to Pennsylvania and later settled in southern Ohio. Noah Grant established a successful tanning business. His father, Jesse Root Grant, expanded Noah's tanning business into a large and profitable operation. He eventually owned tanneries and leather goods stores in Ohio, Kentucky, Illinois and Wisconsin. Jesse was an avid Abolitionist, which sharply clashed with the attitudes of the vast majority to his southern Ohio neighbors. Although he voted for Andrew Jackson, Jesse supported the Whig Party. In 1821, Jesse married Hannah Simpson, a native of Pennsylvania. An active Methodist, Hannah was a very religious woman. Ulysses was born in 1822 about 25 miles upstream of Cincinnati near the Ohio River. While an infant his parents moved a little further east to Georgetown, Ohio, where Ulysses was raised. Both of Grant's parents lived to old age and were alive when he became President. Ulysses was the oldest of 6 children. His three brothers worked in the family leather-goods business. Two of his three sisters married. One married the Reverend Michael Cramer, who became Minister to Denmark under President Hayes. The other married Abel Corbin who would purposely deceive his brother-in-law, President Grant, to help two scandalous, big-money gold speculators briefly corner the gold market, embarrass the Federal Treasury and ruin some honest businessmen — on Black Friday, September 24, 1869.

In his youth Ulysses Grant enjoyed handling horses and detested working in his father's tannery. He learned the fundamentals of reading, writing and arithmetic at subscription schools in Georgetown, Ohio. As a teenager he worked on farms plowing and harvesting and his ambition at that time was to go into farming or river-boat work. At age 15, he attended Maysville Academy across the river in Kentucky. The next year he attended Presbyterian Academy in Ripley, Ohio. Ulysses was an above average student with a recognized gift for mathematics. In 1838, his father persuaded their Congressman to appoint Ulysses to West Point Academy. Ulysses had not been consulted and the appointment came to him as a surprise. Ulysses had just turned 17 when he entered West Point. He excelled at math and horsemanship, setting a high-jump record on horseback, but finished his West Point training in 1843 ranked in the middle of his graduating class.

Grant was assigned to the United States Army as a brevet second lieutenant. His army career began in Missouri. When the Mexican war began three years later, Grant was sent to Mexico where he fought in General Zachary Taylor's army and later in General Winfield Scott's army. He fought at Palo Alto, Resaca de la Palma, Monterrey, Vera Cruz, Cerro Gordo, Churubusco and Molino del Rey. During the occupation of Mexico City he was promoted to first lieutenant. Grant was apparently a loyal soldier, but he privately opposed the war, for he firmly believed the United States was the aggressor. Much later he wrote, "I do not think there was ever a more wicked war than that waged by the United States on Mexico. I thought so at the time when I was a youngster, only I had not moral courage enough to resign."

Grant married Julia Dent, in 1848 at the bride's home in St. Louis. Julia's father was Colonel Frederick Dent, a successful merchant and operator of a large farm outside of town on which several bonded

African Americans lived and worked. Julia was well educated. The couple had met through her brother who was a West Point classmate. Neither of their fathers approved of the marriage. Grant's father, an outspoken Abolitionist, detested any family connections to a person who operated a farm on which bonded African Americans worked and lived. Julia's father wished for his daughter a more prosperous and happy life than he expected her to have if she was married to an army lieutenant. Grant's parents refused to attend the wedding, but eventually came to accept Julia. Julia remained in St. Louis when Grant was away on military assignments. The couple had two boys, Frederick and Buck, while Ulysses was away on military duty.

After the Mexican War Grant was assigned to posts in New York and Detroit (1848-1851). Then he was moved to the West Coast where he was based in northern California and Oregon Territory (1851-1854). He was promoted to captain in 1853, but resigned the next year to return to his wife and two boys in St. Louis.

Grant either purchased a farm or worked part of the farming property belonging to Julia's parents. He may or may not have used bonded African American help during this period. Grant struggled in the farming business from 1854 to 1858, raising crops and livestock and supplementing that by selling wood in town. Politically, he voted for James Buchanan for President in 1856. Then in 1858 he fell seriously ill with "fever and ague" and decided to quit the farming business and sell his farming assets. That winter he teamed up with Julia's cousin, Harry Boggs, and formed a real estate agency in town, but they failed to make a success of the venture. Looking to the public sector for his livelihood, Grant ran for County Engineer, but lost the election. He took a job at the Court House for a couple of months to make ends meet. Discouraged at his prospects of making a living in St. Louis and perhaps concerned over the possibility of war, Grant moved his family to Galena, Illinois in 1860 where his father had located one of the leather goods stores in the chain of stores he had established. Grant took a job as clerk at the Galena store.

Soon after Lincoln Proclaimed the Invasion of the Confederacy, Grant requested recommission in the United States Army, but never received a reply. So he worked in Galena helping muster Illinois State militia volunteers. In June he was appointed colonel of an Illinois militia infantry unit which was stationed in Missouri. In August he was promoted to brigadier general of United States forces over the southeast Missouri Federal Military District. He commanded the invasion forces that captured Fort Henry, Fort Donelson and Nashville, Tennessee. Lincoln promoted him to major general. Grant oversaw the Federal invasion in the western Confederacy until Lincoln brought him to Washington in March, 1864 to oversee the final assault on Richmond, Virginia. Lee finally surrendered to Grant at Appomattox, Virginia on April 9, 1865. Grant won battles by throwing troops at the Confederate defenders in massive numbers without flinching over the terrible casualties suffered by his men, for example at Cold Harbor, thereby contributing to the final battle statistics showing 360,000 Federal dead versus 260,000 Confederate dead.

President Johnson appointed Grant to be Secretary of War ad interim during 1867 and 1868.

Grant had no serious opposition for the 1868 nomination for President. DeGregorio tells of the Republican National Convention:

> "As Republicans convened in Chicago in May 1868, Grant had no serious opposition for the nomination; he was nominated unanimously on the first ballot. House Speaker Schuyler Colfax of Indiana was nominated for Vice President on the sixth ballot, beating out the early favorite, Senator Benjamin F. Wade of Ohio. The Republican Platform supported [voting rights for all African American men living in the conquered States] but agreed to let [the other States decide their policies regarding that issue], opposed using greenbacks to redeem U. S. bonds, encouraged immigration and endorsed full rights for naturalized citizens, and favored [more harsh treatment of the conquered States] as distinct from the [less harsh treatment sought by] of President Andrew Johnson."

The Democratic Party was only a force outside the conquered States because the Republican Political Machines controlled the Governments in the conquered States, Tennessee excepted. Disadvantaged by Republican domination of the 10 conquered States, Democrats gathered for their 1868 National

Convention as substantial underdogs. DeGregorio tells of their Convention and their candidate for President, Horatio Seymour of New York, lawyer who had lived in that State all his life.

"[Seymour] settled in Utica and was elected its Mayor in 1842. As a New York State assemblyman, 1842 and 1844-1845, he promoted canal development. Elected Governor of New York in 1852, he undertook reforms in education and prisons but was defeated for reelection in 1854, largely because he vetoed a State [alcoholic beverage] prohibition bill, invoking the wrath of the powerful [alcoholic beverage exclusion] forces. With the [Invasion of the Confederacy], he loyally supported [Federals] and the war effort of President Lincoln, whose election he had opposed. However, he denounced the suspension of *habeas corpus* and other emergency measures undertaken by the [Lincoln] Administration. Returned to the [Governor's Office] in 1862, he put down the New York City draft riots of 1863, but many believed that his outspoken opposition to [the draft] had touched off the disturbance in the first place. He also opposed [Federal war measures aimed at making bonded African Americans immediately independent] and called for a negotiated settlement of the war. He was defeated for reelection in 1864. At the Democratic National Convention in New York City in July 1868, Seymour was a Delegate, keynote speaker, and Convention Chairman. He supported Chief Justice Salmon P. Chase for the nomination and genuinely discouraged his own candidacy. The front-runner in early balloting was George H. Pendleton of Ohio, who led on the first 15 tallies, followed in varying order by Sanford E. Church of New York, Asa Packer of Pennsylvania, Joel Parker of New Jersey, James E. English of Connecticut, James R. Doolittle of Wisconsin, and Thomas A. Hendricks of Indiana. The unpopular Johnson, having narrowly survived Impeachment, reached his peak strength of 65 votes on the first ballot, less than one-third of the total necessary for nomination, thus losing his bid for election as President in his own right. Meanwhile, Seymour made it on the board only once, garnering just 9 votes on the fourth ballot. On the sixteenth ballot, Hancock took the lead and held it through the twenty-first tally. On the next vote Hendricks surged ahead, and Seymour picked up 21 Ohio Delegates. Seymour continued to insist that he was not a candidate, but before the results of the twenty-second ballot could be announced, the Convention stampeded to nominate him unanimously. He reluctantly answered the call. Frank Blair of Missouri was nominated for Vice President. The Democratic Platform called for amnesty for all former [Confederates], vowed to leave it to the southern States to decide whether to [continue or rescind African American voting], endorsed the use of greenbacks to redeem bonds, favored dismantling the Freedmen's Bureau and other vestiges of [Republican Political Machines in the conquered States], and supported full rights for naturalized citizens."

Waging a mud-slinging, Confederate-whipping, campaign Republicans won the election with room to spare. DeGregorio tells of the campaign:

"Grant took no part in the campaign and made no promises. A line in his letter of acceptance of the nomination became the Republican campaign theme — "Let us have peace." After four years of [a war of conquest], three years of wrangling over [Political Reconstruction], and the attempted Impeachment of a President, the [people] craved the peace Grant pledged to achieve. Francis Blair, the Democratic nominee for Vice President, was the most active of the candidates. But his pro-Southern speeches alienated many [northern States voters], and Seymour took to the stump to try to undo the damage. Seymour ignored the Democrats' soft-money plank, which advocated the use of greenbacks to redeem [Federal] Government bonds, and thus the issue was not a factor in the campaign. The main issue was [treatment of the conquered States]: Republicans pledged to continue the [harsh] programs enacted over President Andrew Johnson's vetoes. Seymour promised a [less harsh] policy designed to reintegrate the [conquered] States into the [Federal system with less] recrimination. On the low road, Republicans alleged that insanity ran through the Seymour family, citing as evidence the suicide of his father. Republicans waged a "bloody shirt" campaign, tagging the opposition as the Party of Secession and Treason — an allegation that was to haunt Democrats for many years to come. Seymour enjoyed the support of [European Americans in the southern States, but Republican Political Machines in the conquered States ensured that African American men] voted overwhelmingly for Grant and the Party of Lincoln. But Grant's greatest asset was his enormous popularity as a war hero. Although Seymour gave him a good race in the popular voting, he was buried in the Electoral College."

Grant won the presidency with 53% of the popular vote. Seymour received 47%. The Electoral College vote went overwhelmingly to the Republican candidate, Grant receiving 82%. Grant won the electoral votes in 26 States. From north to south they were: Maine, Vermont, New Hampshire, Massachusetts, Connecticut, Rhode Island, Pennsylvania, Ohio, Indiana, Illinois, Michigan, Wisconsin, Minnesota, Iowa, Nebraska, Kansas, California, West Virginia, Missouri, North Carolina, Tennessee, South Carolina, Alabama, Arkansas, Nevada, California and Florida. Seymour won the electoral vote of 8 States. From north to south they were: New York, New Jersey, Oregon, Delaware, Maryland, Kentucky, Georgia and Louisiana. Three States were still under Military Rule and not yet organized under Republican Puppet State Governments. These were Virginia — the cradle of the nation's founding; Mississippi — the home of Jefferson Davis; and Texas — the former Republic agreement to merge with the United States had been so strongly opposed by political leaders in Massachusetts and the other northeastern States.

Northern States voters and Republican Political Machines in the conquered States continued the Republican Party's overpowering majorities in the Federal House and Senate. Republicans held 70% of the new House seats and 84% of the new Senate seats. Democrats controlled the rest. The mid-term election produced substantial gains for the Democratic Party in both chambers, but they remained a certain minority. The Senate Republican majority dropped to 70% and the House Republican majority dropped to 55%. Five (5) seats in the Senate and 5 in the House were occupied by independent Legislators.

Grant appointed Elihu Washburne, of Illinois, to be Secretary of State, but he only served 11 days before he resigned to become Minister to France. Hamilton Fish, of New York, replaced Washburne. Grant appointed George Boutwell, of Massachusetts, to be Secretary of the Treasury. Grant appointed his military friend, John Rawlings, of Galena, Illinois, to be his Secretary of War, but Rawlings died in office in September, 1869. Grant then turned to William Sherman, of Ohio, but Sherman only served one month. Next Grant appointed William Belknap, of Iowa, and he stayed for the duration. Ebenezer Hoar, of Massachusetts was appointed Attorney General. Angering Senate Republicans by ignoring political patronage in his Federal judicial appointments, Hoar failed to win Senate endorsement of his appointment by Grant to the Supreme Court. Grant then appointed Hoar to head the Alabama Claims effort and turned to Amos Akerman, of Georgia, to take the Attorney General job. Having angered railroad tycoons, whose plans he opposed, Grant replaced Akerman with George Williams, of Oregon. Grant appointed Adolph Borie, of Pennsylvania, Secretary of the Navy. After Borie resigned three months later due to his lack of interest in the job, Grant appointed George Robeson, of New Jersey. John Creswell, of Maryland, was appointed Postmaster General. Rewarding merit and resisting patronage, a policy dispute with Grant resulted in Creswell's resignation. Jacob Cox, of Ohio, was appointed Secretary of the Interior. Grant replaced him with Columbus Delano, of Ohio.

The Fifteenth Amendment, Nationalizing Voting by African American Men, was added to the Constitution in 1870.

Having completed the summation of the 1868 Federal elections and the organization of the First Ulysses Grant Administration, the narrative history resumes. [R2;259-275]

(1Q69)

On March 4, the first day of the Ulysses Grant Administration, Andrew Johnson having left office a few hours before, Alvan Gillem, commander of the Military District over Mississippi and Arkansas, was dismissed and replaced by Adelbert Ames, who had been Acting Civil Governor of the State since the forced removal of Benjamin Humphreys and his family from the Governor's Residence, which had been ordered by Irvin McDowell on July 15, 1868, during his brief, one-month, temporary replacement of Gillem.

As mentioned previously, Avan Gillem "was a native of Tennessee, a personal friend of President Johnson, had distinguished himself for gallantry in the [Federal] Army, and had taken a leading part in [remaking the Tennessee State Government]." With Johnson gone, Gillem was "toast," because Mississippi Republicans had persuaded Grant to dismiss the hated commander, in spite of what would objectively be considered an excellent record of achievements since he had taken over on January 9, 1868. You will recall that the 1867 Mississippi cotton crop had been a disaster because of bad weather, insects and unproductive laborers. Well, the 1868 crop had been a major success, the best crop in 8 years. This was partly because Gillem had "urged the farmers to plant extensively, and the [African Americans] to enter into contracts for [1868], assuring both races that each would be held to a strict compliance with their agreements. [African Americans, realizing] that they would receive no aid from the Government, all went to work, and an abundant crop was made, the first [abundant crop] since 1860." As a result, European Americans became convinced that contracted African American labor could be made profitable and African Americans became convinced that no one intended to deprive them of their rightful earnings. It appears that Gillem's even-handed rule over Mississippi was a positive contribution to racial and political peace and the start of sorely needed economic recovery. Perhaps we can credit that achievement to Gillem's background within the Southern Culture.

During Gillem's 14 months of Military Rule, when compared to his predecessor, fewer criminal cases were tried in Mississippi by his Military Commissions — in all 17 cases were tried and 9 of those tried were found not guilty. Three were tried for stealing one or more horses or mules, resulting in one found not guilty and 2 sentenced to 5 years in prison. Four were tried for murder, resulting in 3 being acquitted and one sentenced to 5 years in prison. Four were tried for assault, resulting in 2 being acquitted, one sentenced to 3 years and one to 10 years. Three were tried for robbery, resulting in two being acquitted and one sentenced to 2 years. The other 3 cases were not noteworthy. We observe that in Gillem's 14 months, the Military Commissions were far less involved in trying civilian criminal cases than had been his predecessor, Edward Ord. On the other hand, pressure from the Federal House and Senate forced Gillem to remove more men from State and local offices than had Ord. In all Gillem appointed about 230 men to Mississippi State and local government jobs. In one example, the Mayor of Jackson was removed "for failure to enforce law and maintain order," and an army officer was moved into that job.

Of Gillem's time as Military Ruler over Mississippi and Arkansas, historian James Garner would write, "His theory was to interfere as little as possible with the civil authorities, and to restrict the sphere of the military power to its legitimate function, that of preserving the peace." [R204;182-186]

We now turn our attention to Adelbert Ames. A high ranking Federal army officer, Ames was a native of Maine and a graduate of the Military Academy at West Point. Unlike Gillem, Ames was of the Northern Culture. However, his behavior while Provisional Civil Governor, since his appointment by Irvin McDowell "seems to have been characterized by moderation and tact," encouraging favorable reception of his elevation to Commander of the full Military District comprising Mississippi and Arkansas. Yes, Ames retained his job as Provisional Civil Governor and continued to occupy the Mississippi Governor's Residence in Jackson, moving the District Commander's office from Vicksburg to Jackson for his convenience. But that so-called "moderation and tact" had been a behavior forced upon Ames by Gillem. Now, with Gillem and Andrew Johnson out of the way, Ames showed his true character, in complete agreement with his upbringing in the Northern Culture.

The lobbying effort by Mississippi Republicans in Washington, through members of the Mississippi Constitutional Convention, styled as the Committee of Sixteen, had persuaded the Federal House and Senate to empower the Grant Administration to, for the most part, evict the native Mississippi civil employees from State and local government jobs. A joint resolution of the House and Senate had become effective on February 16, and, as Provisional Civil Governor, Ames, on February 26, began the process of removing civil servants and installing his political friends. The Federal House and Senate had resolved that every civil officer and employee had to swear to the oath of July 2, 1862, or be discharged. Historian James Garner would report, "This practically vacated all the civil offices in the State, for not one in a hundred of the incumbents could take the oath required" — almost to the man, each had in some way been connected to government or military activity during the years of Mississippi's secession. One exception was allowed: a man whose disabilities had been removed by Congress was exempt from removal from office. Historian James Garner would describe the final consequences of this action:

> "[Ames] removed nearly all the State officers, and hundreds of county and local officers. At the same time he appointed 60 sheriffs, 72 circuit and probate judges, 8 judges of the criminal court, 16 prosecuting attorneys, 70 county treasurers, 120 circuit and probate justices of the peace, 165 constables, 370 members of the board of police, 40 coroners, 20 surveyors, 25 city marshals, more

that 300 election registrars, and a large number of minor officials, such a school commissioners, city collectors, superintendents of the poor, county attorneys, trustees of State institutions, etc. . . . No man unaccustomed to civil pursuits, and unacquainted in the State, could have selected 2,000 honest and competent officials out of a body of citizens from which the more intelligent and influential were excluded. . . . The action of [the Federal House and Senate] in handing the local governments over to the former [bonded African Americans], together with a few strangers from other parts of the country . . . certainly complicated the problem by increasing the animosities and passions of the time, inflicting corrupt and expensive government upon the inhabitants, and producing other causes which resulted in persecution, fraudulent elections, and finally revolution."

Without a State Constitution and State Legislature, Ames was empowered to rule Mississippi as a dictator. In another move, Ames would issue an April 29 order declaring African American men to be competent Jurors. He would levy taxes and order collection procedures. Preferring civil courts run by his appointees over military commissions, records show Ames would rely less on military commissions for trying criminal cases, when compared to the previous commander over Mississippi and Arkansas. Only 10 cases would be tried in that manner, 6 of them resulting in "not guilty" verdicts — the only case with stiff penalties would be that of two African Americans who would be sentenced to 10 years in prison for robbery and assault. I suppose Ames preferred his civil legal political appointees over his military commissions. Adelbert Ames would get himself elected to the Federal Senate and resign his job as Provisional Governor on March 4, 1870, after having ruled over Mississippi as a dictator for 12 months. [R204;228;236]

Ulysses Grant first appointed E. B. Washburne to the Secretary of State job. Washburne was a Republican Congressman from Galena, Illinois, Grant's home district. Washburne would bring no international experience to the State Department and, when the Washburne appointment ran into problems, Grant withdrew that name and sought to appoint Senator George Williams, of Oregon, to the job. Like Washburne, Williams had no international experience and he must have recognized those limitations, too, for he declined to accept the job. That prompted Grant to offer the job to Hamilton Fish of New York State. Although Fish considered himself retired, he agreed to take the job. Charles Sumner was furious that Grant had bypassed him for the job, particularly since he had offered up such incompetent men as Washburne and Williams. Perhaps Fish was better qualified than those two, Sumner must have reasoned, but no one was better qualified that he himself. Sumner knew Hamilton Fish well. They had served together in the Senate during the 1850's and there Fish had shared Sumner's passion for Exclusionism and Abolitionism. Biographer David Donald would write that "Sumner had always been assured of a hearty welcome at the Fish's Washington residence, and he had often visited them at their Fishkill, New York, [home] as well." It must have soothed Sumner's hurt feelings a bit when Fish humbly wrote him on March 13: "I hoped that I could rely upon your friendship and your experience and ability, for your support and aid to supply my manifold deficiencies." But Sumner would have great difficulty in persuading the Grant Administration to appoint his favorites for diplomatic appointments. Early Republican leaders had favored men from the northeastern States for diplomatic posts, and Sumner had always believed that policy altogether necessary. In fact he thought men who hailed from west of the Appalachian Mountains were incompetent to deal with European governments. Sumner managed to get John Motley, of Massachusetts appointed to the British Minister's job, but beyond that he suffered the diplomatic appointments of many men from west of the mountains. After two months of the Grant Administration, Sumner would lament in a letter to Francis Lieber, "Our foreign list is poor enough to fill the patriot with despair." [R73;371-373]

Turning attention to the lack of instructions to Mississippi on how to obtain an acceptable Reconstructed State Constitution, Representative Ben "Beast" Butler, of Massachusetts, Chairman of the House Committee on Reconstruction, on March 19, introduced a new bill designed to instruct Mississippi on how to obtain an acceptable State Constitution. The bill stated, the new Mississippi Constitutional Convention "should be authorized to forthwith assemble" and "to have power to appoint a Provisional Governor, and to remove and appoint registrars and judges of election." It then directed the Convention to draft a new State Constitution and submit it to qualified voters for Ratification.

Soon after Butler introduce his bill, Ulysses Grant became involved in debate over procedures to obtain an acceptable Reconstructed State Constitution for that conquered State. Grant's brother-in-law,

Frederick Dent, arranged two meetings between the Constitutional Convention lobbying group from Mississippi (a group of Republicans called The Committee of Sixteen), a Democrat lobbying group from Mississippi (including former Democrat Governor Albert Brown and Judge Horatio Simrall) and the President. Grant heard out both sides. Simrall, actively involved in the room, reported what happened next:

> Then Grant "took from a table a printed copy of the [draft Mississippi] Constitution and referred to the several clauses relating to the [voting restrictions on European Americans] and said, in substance, that these [restrictive] clauses should not be there, that they would be a continual source of discord and disorder, provocative of riots and bloodshed, perhaps, between the races."

> Judge Simrall recorded what happened next: "Addressing himself to [former] Governor Brown and myself, he asked how it would do to submit the Constitution to another vote, first striking out the objectionable clauses. Governor Brown and I consulted, and replied that to us that seemed the shortest way out of the trouble, and we believed it would be satisfactory to our people"

Back in the House, on March 31, Representative John Farnsworth, of Illinois offered a substitute to Ben "Beast" Butler's bill, "providing that the [commander over the Military District including Mississippi] should be empowered to submit the Constitution again to the qualified voters, and that the objectionable clauses should be submitted separately, and if defeated, they should be stricken out of the Constitution." A few days later, Butler brought a revised bill out of his Committee on Reconstruction that resembled the concept advocated by Representative Farnsworth and President Grant. This new bill addressed procedures for obtaining acceptable Reconstructed State Constitutions, not only in Mississippi, but also in Virginia and in Texas. So it covered the three remaining unreconstructed conquered States. This bill "authorized President Grant . . . to submit the Constitutions of Mississippi, Virginia, and Texas to a vote of the people, and at the same time submit to a separate vote such provisions as he might choose. Representative Halbert Paine of Wisconsin objected, and offered a substitute, which authorized Grant "to submit the Constitution, in the first place, as a whole, and then submit it with the objectionable provisions stricken out." The substitute was adopted on April 8 and, by a vote of 125 to 25, the House passed the revised bill and forwarded it to the Senate.

2Q69

The next day, April 9, the Senate debated the bill designed to instruct Mississippi, Virginia and Texas on how each could obtain an acceptable Reconstructed Constitution. Senator Oliver Morton of Indiana submitted an additional requirement that, before a Reconstructed Constitution would be acceptable, each State Legislature would have to meet and ratify the Federal Amendment Nationalizing Voting by African American Men (15th). Only then could its Representatives and Senators be seated. Senator Lyman Trumbull, of Illinois, countered, saying: by "imposing this new condition, the [Federal] Government was breaking faith with those States, inasmuch as [the Federal House and Senate] had already given its solemn pledge that they should be readmitted upon the performance of certain conditions." Other Senators urged Morton not to press his additional demand, for it might delay the adjournment scheduled for the following day. Morton refused to withdraw the additional demand. This forced a vote. The Senate approved the additional demand by a vote of 30 to 20. Then the expanded bill came to a vote. It passed the Senate by a vote of 49 to 9. Seems to me the Senators were most eager to leave town. So were the Representatives over in the House. They concurred with the expanded Senate version, under a suspension of the rules. Then the House and Senate adjourned. This bill empowered President Grant to direct Mississippi, Virginia and Texas on how to configure several versions of their respective draft Reconstructed State Constitutions to allow qualified voters to choose between versions, with or without so-called objectionable sections. Readers should recognize that the bill just passed brings into question the legality of Ratifications of this Constitutional Amendment by Mississippi, Virginia and Texas — obviously, again each State was being forced, coerced to Ratify the Federal Amendment, and to do so during a time when the organic, legal basis for the existence of each, respective State Government was doubtful. [R204;222-228]

On April 13 Charles Sumner presented to the full Senate, his Foreign Relations Committee's report on the Johnson-Clarendon Convention Treaty. The Committee report recommended that the Senate vote against Ratification of the Treaty. The Committee's vote against had been unanimous, so there was no minority report. This was certainly a powerful blow to the future of the Treaty that Reverdy Johnson of

Maryland had so skillfully negotiated as Minister to Great Britain. After delivering the Committee report, Sumner presented an hour-long speech which he titled, "Claims on England — Individual and National." Biographer David Donald would conclude, "It was one of the most influential addresses Sumner ever made, for it [would have] profound consequences both upon his own career and upon [Federal Government] foreign policy."

Sumner's "Claims on England" speech would particularly appeal to the Republican Party leadership, for the big Democratic popular vote in November 1868 (47% for Seymour versus 53% for Grant) gave reason to fear difficulty in re-electing Grant to a future second term. So, Republican leaders were looking for a new issue by which they could deceive a large block of men into voting Republican. The Party's Political Machines in the former Confederate States, would likely be weakening, and would be totally wrecked in a heartbeat if the Democratic Party ever regained control of the Federal Government. The Republican leadership still planned to attract voters in the northern States by inciting war-glorified hatred toward former Confederates (wave the bloody shirt) and by alleging that the Democratic Party in the northern States was a mere tool of former Confederate politicians. But how long could the Republican Party leadership orchestrate their domination over the Federal Government on nothing but hatred of and subjugation of former Confederates? One lost election and the whole power base would collapse like a house of cards. Republican leaders, looking back through the nation's history prior to the formation of the Confederacy, recalled the temporary — yet proven — political power achievable through inciting hatred toward members of Masonic lodges; toward recent immigrants; toward Catholics; and toward African Americans within their States and within the National Territories people of their States hoped to settle. So leaders, like Ulysses Grant, Ben "Beast" Butler, Zachariah Chandler, and Andrew Curtin had concluded over the winter months that the continued dominance of the Republican Party could best be assured by inciting hatred toward Great Britain and the Provinces in Canada. The Irish were already full of hatred toward the London-based British Government. And Canada would be so much easier to conquer than the Confederacy had been, particularly if the Federals timed their invasion to coincide with a point in time when the British were struggling with a European war. Since wars in Europe had been popping up rather often, the wait might be only a few years. So Zachariah Chandler would endorse the position taken by Sumner's Committee, claiming he had held the same position for many years. Ben "Beast" Butler, who was eager to escalate hostilities, would advocate an immediate band on trade with the British. Even Andrew Curtin, former Governor of Pennsylvania, and known as a non-militant, would advocate inciting hatred toward the English as a Party-building measure. Charles Adams would see the unfolding political intrigue as a struggle between factions within the Republican Party. Adams would soon predict that the following groups of people would favor pressing on with a political policy of hatred toward the English: Federal army and navy veterans; Irishmen; disappointed seekers of government jobs; Republican Political Machine men, who he termed "southern adventurers;" and even many Democrats in the northern States. Adams would figure that only "the respectable classes of the Republicans" would oppose a political policy of hatred toward the English. And the new Minister to Great Britain, John Motley of Massachusetts — having replaced Reverdy Johnson of Maryland four months earlier in December 1868 — was Charles Sumner's hand-pick appointee and political confident. Motley had carefully studied issues of international law that might be applied to Federal political attacks on the British and he had read, at least 6 times, the "Claims on England" speech that Sumner was beginning to present to the Senate, and he had "accepted its arguments absolutely."

At the beginning of the "Claims on England" speech, Sumner warned fellow Senators that, as if the Johnson-Clarendon negotiators were "huddling something out of sight," they had failed to remove "the massive grievance under which [the Federal Government] suffered for years." Sumner insisted that the Government's present claim for compensation was grounded in the fact that, "when Civilization was fighting a last battle with [those who permitted African American bonding], England gave her name, her influence, her material resources to the wicked cause, and flung a sword into the scale with [the Confederacy]." Simply ignoring the fact that Abe Lincoln had insisted during the first months of the Invasion Campaign that his military action was not intended to make bonded African Americans independent, Sumner alleged that Britain's original offense was the Queen's Proclamation of May 13, 1861 — recognizing that a state of war existed in North America between the Federals and the Confederates — recognizing the Confederates to be belligerents."

Sumner charged that, like the Lincoln Administration, Great Britain should have pretended that the Confederates were engaged in Treason, not State Secession, in order that "no [Confederate] ship could have been [legally] built in England . . . nor could any munitions of war have been furnished" to the Confederates — because "any Englishman aiding [the Confederates] by fitting out a privateer against the Federal Government would be guilty of piracy." Sumner then alleged that the worst offense was permitting the construction of the *Alabama* and similar Confederate raiders. Those warships, Sumner alleged were "not only British in origin, but British in equipment, British in armament, and British in crews." The British Government had even permitted Confederate warships to be serviced in her ports, Sumner cried. Despite such wrongful action against shippers who were supporting the Federal military campaign, Sumner said he found in the proposed Johnson-Clarendon Treaty not "one soothing word for a friendly power deeply aggrieved." There was nothing but an unsatisfactory arbitration procedure for settling the claims of American businessmen who had lost merchant ships and cargoes.

Then Sumner insisted that the claims of those businessmen had to be restated as part of the claims of the Federal Government, for the Federal Government had to act on their behalf to collect compensation for all claims and then reimburse those businessmen. In Sumner's words, the claims of businessmen had to be "national in contradistinction to individual." And those individual claims had to include losses attributed to "the rise of insurance on all [vessels belonging to American businessmen]" and the loss in their marine shipping market share — "the diminution of our tonnage, with the corresponding increase of British tonnage." Then he added loss of potential profits due to "the falling off in our exports and imports." Finally, Sumner submitted a guess that adding all of those economic shortfalls to the direct economic loss from lost ships and cargoes would increase the compensation demand for businessmen to about $110,000,000. You will probably agree with me that dividing that amount of money among American businessmen, most of whom lived in the northeastern States, would further enrich those already made wealthy by past wartime business profits. But Sumner was in step with his Party, for the Republican Party was the Party of big business and wealth, which was centered in the northeastern States.

After presenting the claims of loses suffered by businessmen, Sumner proceeded to present Federal Government demands as well, for he declared that the claims of lost business profits was "only an item in our bill:" there was "that other damage, immense and infinite, caused by the prolongation of the [military campaign]. Sumner charged that, "through British intervention, the [invasion] was doubled in duration," from 2 years to 4 years. Therefore, Sumner argued, the British were liable for $2,000,000,000 in Federal war expenses, because they owed the Federal Government half of the total invasion cost of $4,000,000,000. This list of claims, Sumner argued was the true claim of the Federal Government and American businessmen; a claim that was "mountain-high, with a base broad as the [North American States], and a mass stupendous as the [State Secession] itself."

Then Sumner threatened the British with the possibility that the Federal Government might just let its claim "rest without settlement, so as to furnish a precedent for retaliation in kind, should [Britain] find herself at war." But, leaving that idea hanging in the background, Sumner went on to advocate denouncing the Johnson-Clarendon Convention Treaty and starting afresh with new negotiations based on his new list of "mountain-high" claims. Sumner demanded that the British admit that they had been wrong to permit some British industrial leaders to trade with the Confederacy, that they were truly sorry for such bad behavior, and that they sincerely apologized for it. He submitted that the Federal claims had to be appraised and the British had to pay compensation according to both common law and Roman law. Sumner then closed by alleging that, "It is not I who say this, it is the Law." By "the Law," Sumner must have been speaking of the emerging international law of the day. Of course, Sumner failed to admit before the Senate that the Confederacy had been itself an independent Federation of Sovereign States, and that the British Government had permitted British industrialists to ship more war materials to the Federals that to the Confederates. If the Confederate Government had existed at the time of Sumner's speech, one would have to reason that the Confederates had as much or more claim for reimbursement for damages as Sumner was claiming for the Federals. But Sumner never gave that notion a thought.

Sumner had apparently received Ulysses Grant's blessings for his "Claims on England" speech. Biographer David Donald would conclude that Grant, "shared [Sumner's] resentment at the conduct of the British" during the Invasion campaign. And, with so much of the massive Federal military power rather easily reactivated, Grant was tempted by his realization "of how easy it would be to conquer Canada in a single campaign." Sumner would soon tell a confidant that he had "conversed with" Grant before delivering his "Claims on England" speech, "and found his views to be in strict conformity with mine." And Sumner would soon tell the same confidant, "Since the speech, [Grant] had thanked and congratulated me." So, it is rather apparent that Grant himself was pleased with Sumner's attack on the British and perhaps hopeful that it might lead to an excuse to launch his massive military might against the almost defenseless Canadians. And Secretary of State Hamilton Fish would soon back Sumner with the power of the State Department, for he would soon convince Sumner that the Federal Government had unassailable claims against the British. He estimated that British behavior had extended the invasion by one year and the British therefore owed the Federal Government not less than $1,000,000,000. Fish did not expect that much money from Britain, but was hopeful the Federals could use that claim to force the British to withdraw from Canada, thereby permitting a take-over of those Provinces.

Biographer David Donald would describe how fellow Senators responded to Sumner's speech:

"No speech Sumner had ever made met with such immediate, almost unanimous approval. Even as he finished speaking, Senator [Henry] Anthony of Rhode Island, who was in the Chair, sent him a note: "That was a great speech." When he sat down, Republicans and Democrats, [Militant and non-Militant], gathered around his chair to congratulate him. Even [William] Fessenden praised Sumner's 'temperate and instructive views,' and Democratic leader [Allen] Thurman [of Ohio] said 'that his words honored the Senate as well as the statesman who uttered them.' Promptly the Senate, with only one dissenting vote, rejected the Johnson-Clarendon Convention, and [Zachariah] Chandler, who often in the past had complained of Sumner's pro-English bias, moved to lift the injunction of secrecy so that his '[Claims on England]' speech could be published."

Upon publication, the "Claims on England" speech drew immense praise from individuals, many of whom surely salivated over the prospect of getting a lot of claims money for themselves. Letters poured into his office full of compliments such as: you exposed with "force eloquence and truth" the Britisher's "perfidy, offensive arrogance, and grasping selfishness" — "no abler speech has ever been uttered in the [Federal] Senate" — you have expounded "justice, wisdom, research, and eloquence" — "God bless you" — "The speech cannot fail to do great good." Presenting praise typical of northeastern States intellectuals, James Russell Lowell declared, "I think you have struck exactly the true note — expressing the [country's] feeling with [good] temper and dignity."

And newspapermen joined the chorus with more praise. Caleb Cushing wrote in the Washington *Chronicle*, "Great Britain receives a distinct impression of the nature and consequences of her hostile intervention in the affairs of the [Federal Government]." Editors at the New York *Herald* thought the "firm and masterly speech" so "manly, outspoken and dignified" that they recommended that Ulysses Grant name Sumner to the Secretary of State job. Revealing that Sumner had expanded his base of political support, *The Nation* admitted that his speech received "the approval of a great majority of the people of the northern States, including many who have no sympathy with his favorite ideas."

Owners of shipping and exporting companies in the northeastern States were uniformly hopeful that the "Claims on England" speech would eventually reward them personally with settlement money from Great Britain. Looking around at the favorable reaction from Boston businessmen who had customarily opposed Sumner, Charles Adams admitted that Sumner had "certainly gained might . . . among those who hate him." And he further predicted "that the end of it all was to be [Federal subjugation] of Canada by way of full indemnity." Agreeing, Senator Zachariah Chandler complained that Sumner had stolen his favorite project: taking Canada. And another confirmed that, "the whole business community are congratulating themselves upon the great speech." Massachusetts Governor William Claflin assured, "No speech of yours ever gave such universal and heartfelt satisfaction." Biographer David Donald would agree that the object was the taking of the Provinces of Canada, as he would write: "Sumner was not, of course, averse to this solution of the difficulty; he had for years looked to the day when [the Providences of] Canada would become [States under the Federal Government], and he had justified the purchase of Alaska as a step toward that end." A few days before Sumner had delivered his speech, he had discussed his aims with the French Minister, Jules Berthémy. After that meeting Berthémy had reported to British officials: I "think that the British possessions on the continent of

America might be accepted" as the price for peaceful settlement of Sumner's claims against Great Britain. And for two years Sumner would hold fast to his designs upon the Canadian people, for in 1871 he would insist that the claims could be settled by permitting the Federal Government to take control of the Provinces of Canada.

But the reaction in Great Britain was quite the opposite, as Irish politician and writer, Justin McCarthy, predicted during his visit to New York City soon after the speech was published there — but before the details arrived in England. When the editor of the New York *Tribune* asked him, "What will the English people think of this speech?" McCarthy immediately answered, "They will regard it as a Declaration of War." And it truly was! There was no way that the British people would stand for paying about $3,000,000,000 in blackmail money to the Federal Government and owners of Federal shipping companies. Sumner's speech was, on the face of it, a call for a Declaration of War. And Sumner knew exactly what kind of war for which he desired his speech to become the pretext: the long-awaited Federal Conquest of Canada.

British newspaper response included statements such as: "Was anything so monstrous ever proposed on this earth before by any man taking the rank of a statesman?" — "childish" — "a womanish speech, mixing up matters of feeling with matters of law" — "wholly actuated by a spirit of revenge — "If it were [Charles] Sumner's object to precipitate a war, he could not be more bitter or more unjust." And the London *Times* issued a series of editorial rebuttals including the following abstract:

"[Charles] Sumner had the questionable honor of contributing more than any other man to [State secession and the subsequent Federal Invasion of the Confederacy] . . . and to the differences which keep the breach open" today. . . . "Nothing human nature was capable of would have satisfied" Charles Sumner during the Federal Invasion campaign. "What he demanded of the Confederate States was, in fact, moral and political self-annihilation." And today, his claims against Great Britain are likewise "of that intuitive sort which has been common in all the tribunals of despotism." The issue is "not one of feeling," and "it remains to be shown that the British Government can be held answerable for any infraction of [international] law."

Biographer David Donald would conclude:

"The fact that it was Sumner who led in rejecting the Johnson-Clarendon Convention gave special virulence to British criticisms. To many in the British Isles, Sumner in the past had seemed the nearest thing to an English statesman the [Federal Government] could produce. Some still remembered him as a young visitor to Britain, eager, admiring, and flushed with social success; others had first met him when, as an [alleged] invalid-martyr after the Brooks [caning], he went abroad to [allegedly] recover his health. Sumner's often expressed love for Great Britain, his broad knowledge of English law and history, and his wide acquaintance among the British governing classes should have made him the [Federal] who best understood the British position on the [claims on England issue]. Had the speech come from a Chandler of a Banks, it would hardly have been noticed, but it seemed an enormous perversity that it should have been pronounced by the one [Federal] politician who most loudly professed to be Britain's friend. " 'How could he make that speech!' exclaimed [Elizabeth] Argyll."

Elizabeth Argyll correctly recognized that her pen-pal, Charles Sumner was "a fanatic" who "never did see more than one side" of an issue. She thought such behavior, "well enough when he had to fight the deviltry of [African American bonding]," but totally inappropriate when he directed his war-mongering tirade against the British and Canadian peoples. [R73;374-407]

Meanwhile, we transport our thoughts to London and Jeff and Varina Davis. Lady Eardley offered them her London house for the spring season, and they accepted graciously. Surprised to find his portrait hanging on the wall, Jeff asked his host about it. She explained that her father, once British Consul at Mobile, Alabama, had greatly admired the Confederate cause. In London during May, June and much of July, Jeff and Varina would enjoy invitations from prominent Britishers who had supported the Confederacy, among them Lord Lothian (William Schomberg Robert Kerr), who had published in 1863 a book, *"The Confederate Secession,"* which he had hoped would influence the British Parliament to recognize the Confederacy. Lord Campbell (William Campbell) was another faithful friend. One day he visited Jeff accompanied by Charles Mackay, a Scottish poet and once editor of the London *Illustrated News*. Mackay and Davis would enjoy each others company. [R19;343]

Meanwhile, the Cabinet of British Prime William Gladstone met on May 1 to discuss the proper British response to Charles Sumner's "Claims on England" speech and the intense, war-mongering hostility that it had produced among Americans who lived within 300 miles of the Canadian border. George Clarendon told fellow Cabinet members that he had made numerous concessions to Reverdy Johnson in an effort to draft a Treaty that would be acceptable to the Federal Senate. No British official would have considered any further concessions beyond those granted. In view of that history, Clarendon said that he was personally outraged at Sumner's "atrocious speech" and the Senate's almost unanimous vote to reject the accord. The Cabinet's report to the Queen included the appraisal that Sumner's speech and the reaction in the Federal Senate "breathes the most extravagant hostility to England." Every day further reports of Federal war-mongering and inflammatory posturing reached London, and indicated further escalation toward war. On May 9 Clarendon wrote: "The news from the United States is very bad, and I believe that [Ulysses] Grant and [Charles] Sumner mean war; or rather that amount of insult and humiliation that must lead to it." But Clarendon dug in and prepared to make a stand, for he thought further concessions to Federal demands would be impossible, for "we should sink into utter contempt if we allowed ourselves to be humiliated, which is clearly the object of [Motley, Sumner and Grant]." But the Federal threat of war was not the only crisis threatening the welfare of the British people, for Germany, under Bismarck's rule, was threatening aggressive moves as well. And, realizing that Sumner fully intended to use the German threat to his advantage in negotiations across the Atlantic, Clarendon warned the Queen: "There is not the smallest doubt that if we were engaged in a continental quarrel we should immediately find ourselves at war with [Ulysses Grant's Federals]. But by May 15, reports from Federal observers had boosted Clarendon's confidence that he would succeed with a firm resistance to further concessions to Federal demands. That day he wrote Edward Thornton: "[Charles] Sumner's speech and the general approval with which it has been received in [America's northern States] have awakened here the spirit with which such insolence should be received; and if [John] Motley, instructed by [Charles] Sumner, thinks he can bully us or, as we are told he expects to do, set the working classes of England against the [wealthy and prominent class which had supported the Confederate cause] in the recent [sectional military and political conflicts in America] he will find himself miserably and deservedly mistaken. . . ."

The other prominent leaders in the British Government and the Opposition Party followed Clarendon's lead and prepared to dig in and resist any further concessions to Federal demands. Henry Bulwer, who knew the political situation in Washington rather well, advised British leaders to stand firm and wait for the hateful rhetoric to die down, because Charles Sumner did not have sufficient influence to speak "as the organ of the [Federal] Government or of the [Federal] Senate." Agreeing, William Gladstone, the Prime Minister, asked members of Parliament to help calm excitement by refusing to debate the alleged claims presented by Charles Sumner, for he was "a man of huge and distempered vanity," and "our arch-enemy." Gladstone actually suggested that Sumner's speech would eventually help the British Government present "our cause before the great tribunal of the civilized world." Then he advised that the resulting pressure from other nations would help Britain settle with the Federal Government on more favorable terms than those offered in the Johnson-Clarendon Convention.

And Charles Adams, America's former Minister to Great Britain, now retired in Massachusetts, had been agreeing with Gladstone when, after reading Sumner's speech, he had written in his diary that the result would be "to raise the scale of our demands of reparation so very high that there is no chance of negotiation left unless the [British] have lost all their spirit and character." Senator James Grimes, of Iowa, who was vacationing in London at the time agreed as well, as he wrote: "Sumner has greatly injured our cause by presenting so many perfectly absurd arguments, and urging them with so much bitterness." Attempting to take advantage of the widespread hatred that Sumner's speech had released in the northern States, Ben "Beast" Butler proposed, on May 24, that the Federal Government order the termination of all commercial trade between Great Britain and the United States. Sumner was a man of ideas, but "The Beast" was a man of action. Charles Sumner himself remained hopeful of huge British concessions. He wrote Francis Lieber on May 30, "How the case shall be settled — whether by money, more or less — by territorial compensation — by apologies — or by an amendment of the Law of

Nations, is still an open question." But biographer David Donald would conclude that Sumner was hopeful that the crisis he launched would elevate him to greater prominence on the international stage:

> "[Sumner] envisioned a memorable and protracted negotiation, comparable perhaps to that leading to the Treaty of Westphalia, in which he might play a shaping role in establishing new rules of international law. To commemorate such a historic peaceful settlement Sumner might just possibly have found room on his crowded study walls for another set of engravings, from which his own likeness would not have been absent."

Although Charles Sumner, Ulysses Grant and Hamilton Fish all agreed that Federal claims against Great Britain should be manipulated to result in the conquest of Canada, there was some disagreement over the language of the claims. Sumner had based his claims against the British primarily on their recognition that the Confederacy was a "belligerent." But Grant wanted to violate the Sumner's alleged rule of international relations himself, rather soon — he wanted to recognize as "belligerents" the patriots who were fighting to overthrow Spanish rule in Cuba. How could Grant help the Cuban patriots defeat the Spanish at the same time that he called a former, but similar, act by the British a violation of the Law of Nations? So Grant wanted to base Federal claims against Britain on something besides the "belligerent" issue. Hamilton Fish agreed — both to please Grant and because he truly believed that any nation had the right to recognize a state of belligerency. Fish's reluctance to place great importance on the belligerency claim derived from his belief that there were "two strong sides to this point of the question." So Fish prepared a set of instructions for John Motley, the man who Sumner had successfully arranged to become the new Federal Minister to Great Britain:

> "[Ulysses Grant] wishes it understood that he does not complain of the fact of the accordance by Great Britain . . . of belligerent rights to the [Confederacy] during the late [invasion]. . . . He recognizes the right of Every Power, when a civil conflict has arisen within another State, and has attained a sufficient complexity, magnitude, and completeness to define its own relations . . . toward . . . the conflict. . . . He does not rest the claims of this nation against Great Britain upon the time of issuing the proclamation of neutrality by the later Government."

As soon as Charles Sumner found out about Fish's instructions to Motley, he was furious with Grant and Fish for moving to set aside his cherished "belligerency" charge as the main basis for Federal claims against Great Britain. He angrily cried to a State Department subordinate, "Is it the purpose of [the Grant Administration] to sacrifice me, — me, a Senator from Massachusetts?" Then Sumner located Fish and insisted on rewriting the instructions. Fish refused to give Sumner full power over that policy issue, but suggested that he, instead, submit a proposed set of instructions for consideration by the State Department. At one point in the heated argument with Fish, Sumner yelled: "Motley shall resign." And he probably figured he could arranged it, if necessary, since he had been the one to get Motley the Minister job in the first place. But Fish replied coolly, "Very Well. Let him. We'll get a better man in an hour."

Charles Sumner enlisted Caleb Cushing's help, and proceeded to draft up alternate instructions for Motley. Fish was rather happy with Sumner's draft, for it permitted Ulysses Grant to help Cuban patriots overthrow the Spanish, while it kept the claims against Great Britain intact. Fish was flexible on language and who got credit for writing it up. If he could keep Sumner's support, their common objective of Federal subjugation of the Provinces of Canada would unquestionably benefit. Pleased that Fish recognized his power, Sumner dispatched Caleb Cushing over to the State Department to work out final language. Then Sumner blessed the language and the instructions were dispatched to Motley. Charles Sumner had satisfied himself that he held considerable power in the Federal execution of his "Claims on England." In the words of David Donald: "So long as he did not insist upon wording that would prevent [Ulysses] Grant from recognizing Cuban Belligerency, he could make [Hamilton] Fish do his bidding." And Sumner took satisfaction in his belief that he had gotten John Motley the Minister job and was directing the instructions. Sumner was surely pleased that, finally, the Federal subjugation of the Provinces in Canada might be near at hand.

Charles Sumner would frequently dine with Ulysses Grant during May and June. While together on May 26, Sumner told Grant that he hoped that he had no problem with the fervor of his, "Claims on England" arguments. Grant replied "not in the least — let it go on." Then Grant assured Sumner that Great Britain was an enemy of the Federal Government, and that her conduct during the Invasion of the

Confederacy "could not be overstated in its mischief." On another occasion Grant told Sumner he was now "entirely satisfied that England made the concession of belligerency 'to injure us'."

On June 7 Ulysses Grant again endorsed Sumner's agitation against Great Britain and assured him that John Motley was "the best man" for the Minister job. Promptly thereafter Sumner cornered Edward Thornton, the British Minister, to warn him that Grant "had expressed his approval of all his arguments." Observing Sumner's wildly militant attitude, Thornton reported back to London that Sumner had become "so carried away by his illusions and his vanity that any reasonable discussion is out of the question." And Sumner enthused to Edward Pierce, "England must listen, and at last yield," and two cherished goals would be eventually attained: firstly, "the withdrawal of [The British] from this hemisphere," (which both men understood would open Canada to Federal conquest); and, secondly, the "remodeling [of] maritime international law." Sumner grandly predicted: "Such a consummation would place our republic at the head of the civilized world." Of Charles Sumner's militancy, Alexander the Great, Julius Caesar, and Genghis Khan would all have been proud. Sumner even persuaded Hamilton Fish issue a statement to newspapermen which included the following blessing:

> "In fact, at no time has [Charles] Sumner been in closer accord or in more direct sympathy with the policy of [Ulysses] Grant than at present, and rumors of disagreement are entirely unfounded."

Biographer David Donald would write: "Satisfied that he was in complete control, Sumner left Washington in the latter part of June, and his Massachusetts friends found him happier than he had been since [before] the breakup of his marriage, full of self-importance and grandly loquacious."

But three days after Ulysses Grant and Charles Sumner had concurred on instructions, John Motley was in London warning George Clarendon, in their first meeting, that "the contingencies of war and peace" were dependent of satisfactory settlement of Federal claims arising from past British involvement with the Confederacy. Motley added that past British recognition of a state of "belligerency" was "the fountain head of the disasters which had been caused to the [people of the northern States], both individually and collectively." Grant thought Motley had been too aggressive in that first meeting for effective diplomacy, and even considered pulling him out of London, but Fish persuaded Grant to let Motley stay on the job. [R73;384-405]

(3Q69)

"On July 13 Ulysses Grant, acting under the authority of the Supplemental Reconstruction Act, concerning conquered Virginia, Mississippi and Texas, passed by the House and Senate on April 9, as previously reported, "issued a Proclamation designating Tuesday, November 30, as the day on which the [draft Reconstructed Mississippi State] Constitution should be resubmitted to [qualified voters]," using two ballots. The first ballot was to allow a voter to vote "for" or "against" the complete Constitution as drafted. The second ballot was to allow a voter to vote "for" or "against" each of 4 controversial sections within the draft Constitution — 3 sections imposing controversial restrictions on the voting rights of European Americans — one section forbidding the loaning of the State's credit. A voter who wanted to see a Mississippi State Government established that was acceptable to the Federal Government, with voting rights and office holding rights for many of the State's European Americans, would be voting "for" the Constitution and "against" the controversial provisions. Grant allowed lots of time for Republicans to organize their voters and for Adelbert Ames, Provisional Governor and commander over the District made up of Mississippi and Arkansas, to replace most of the existing office holders. Both sides had 4.5 additional months for their political organizing. And political campaigning began in earnest, both among Republicans and among the opposition:

> The National Union Republican Party of Mississippi had organized in June. Designed to attract Republicans of a more conservative persuasion, this Party favored a vote for the Constitution and against the controversial provisions, especially the 3 sections that restricted the voting rights of European American men more than demanded by the Federal Government. No State ticket of candidates was nominated.

> Already organized, of course was the regular Mississippi Republican Party, having held their Convention on July 2. It favored a vote for the draft Constitution and, I suspect, against removing the 3 sections restricting voting rights for European American men. A State ticket of candidates was not nominated at this time.

The third group, Historical Democrats, was engaged in strategic deliberations as members sought a Mississippi Government that was acceptable to Federal authority but with no more limitations on the voting rights of European American men than was demanded at the time by Federal laws. Prevalent was advocacy for a fusion of Democrats and the more conservative Republicans, which might be organized as the National Union Republican Party. [R204;237-239]

Meanwhile, Jeff Davis' health was improving. Near the end of July, Charles Mackay sailed with Jeff for Edinburgh Scotland, beginning a wonderful vacation trip, for Mackay would be a wonderful and well informed guide and host. Jeff's travelogue — well documented in letters and newspaper clippings — would include Holyrood Palace, John Knox's home, Melrose Abbey and Dryburg Monastery, the Heart of Bruce, John Blackwood's "Strathtyrum," Loch Lomond, Stirling Castle, Rob Roy's grave and the head of Loch Earn, Robert Burns' home, towns along the Clyde, Inverlochy Castle, the Island of Mull where he visited Fingal's Cave and the ruins of Iona, Inverness, Edinburgh, and Stratford-on-Avon. When Jeff arrived at Yarmouth, Varina thought he looked in better health than at anytime before his capture. Thanking Charles MacKay for devoting so much time and effort on their month-long trip, Jeff wrote: "I would fain spend the balance of my days in Scotland." But summer was over and Jeff and Varina both knew he had to do something appropriate to bring in some money. Jeff was 61 years old, an age when most men were thinking of retirement. But Jeff needed to find a way to make an income capable of sending his four children through school and to provide for old age. Some former Confederate leaders were arranging to start an insurance company in Memphis, Tennessee, and they had written Davis inviting him to be President of the new company. Although a career in insurance did not particularly appeal to him, Jeff would have to give that offer serious consideration. [R19;345-352]

Meanwhile on September 8, the Mississippi National Union Republican Party, the more conservative Republican faction in the State, convened to nominate candidates for State offices, who, if elected and if qualified voters Ratified the draft Reconstructed State Constitution on November 30th, would be taking office in 1870. The election of State officials was scheduled for November 30 as well. Preliminary arrangements had been made to accept Mississippi Democrats under the National Union Republican banner if it nominated Judge Louis Dent for Governor. You will recall that Louis Dent was the brother-in-law of Ulysses Grant. In fact, Dent's primary qualification for the Governor job, was the expectation that he could influence his brother-in-law, Grant, to rule favorably toward Mississippi with Dent elected. Important Mississippi Democrats had already greased the wheels for a Dent nomination and won his acceptance if he were chosen. The National Union Republican Convention was well attended by 320 Delegates from 40 counties. But cooperation between Grant and Dent might have been wishful thinking for, at this point, Grant had given his support to the regular Republican Party. Nevertheless, Dent was nominated for Governor of Mississippi. African Americans had been encouraged to attend the Convention and one, Thomas Sinclair, won the nomination for Secretary of State. Nominations for Lieutenant Governor, Auditor and Treasurer went to former Federal soldiers. Nominations for Attorney General, and Superintendent of Education went to native Democrats.

Three weeks later, on September 30, the regular Mississippi Republican Party held its Convention to likewise nominate candidates for State offices. Beroth Eggleston, formerly of New York State, having made too many enemies, would be set aside in favor of James Alcorn, a native Republican. Ridgley Powers, a former Federal soldier from Ohio, was nominated for Lieutenant Governor. This time some African Americans were also nominated, the most notable being James Lynch, an eloquent preacher from Indiana with slight African ancestry, who was nominated for Secretary of State. Former Federal soldiers were nominated for Auditor and for Superintendent of Education. Native European Americans were nominated for Attorney General and Treasurer. [R204;237-240]

Meanwhile in Oxford, Lucius Lamar was successful with his two jobs: Chair of the School of Law at the University of Mississippi and Senior Partner in the law firm he shared with the young lawyer, Edward Clarke. During the past month of May, Lamar's oldest child, daughter Frances Eliza, known as "Fannie," age 21 years, had married Edward Mayes, who would become Lamar's definitive biographer (see *Lucius Q.C. Lamar: His Life, Times, and Speeches*, AMS Press, New York, 1896). The other children of Lucius were Lucius, III, 16, Sarah Augusta (Gussie), 9, and Virginia (Jennie), 3. Improving financial conditions permitted Lamar to purchase 30 acres "in the northern part of Oxford, and on this premises began the erection of a residence, which [would be] completed in the following April. This home, the first of his own since he had left 'Solitude' in 1857, was the slowly earned fruit of hard labor at his profession." [R205;126]

Meanwhile in Worcester, Charles Sumner was Chairman of the Massachusetts State Republican Convention, held there on September 22. The Convention Hall, full of Delegates, was a great platform from which Sumner could incite hatred toward the English and build Republican support, and he intended to make the most of it. He had titled his speech: "National Affairs at Home and Abroad." Before such an agreeable audience, Sumner lambasted the English for their "great transgression" during the Federal Invasion of the Confederacy. He charged that the Confederate defense of the homeland "obtained its enduring vitality by means of the resources it drew from Great Britain." Let us step aside a moment and conjecture on the emotions in the Convention Hall while Sumner was speaking:

(It was hard for Sumner and others who had never confronted Confederate foot soldiers and cavalry in battle to realize that it was primarily the Southerner's ability and courage in battle that had created the embarrassing battled statistic: 360,000 Federal dead versus 260,000 Confederate dead. It was hard for the self-righteous Massachusetts man to admit that the Confederates were that good in battle. So they were desperately looking for an alternate explanation for the embarrassing kill ratio to prevent Confederates from appearing to have been superior in battle. The explanation for the kill ratio had to lie at the foot of England, so they were supposing. Yes, it was English assistance that had expanded what should have been a straightforward 2-year conquest into a bloody 4-year conflict. No, Confederates could not have been that good at war, not that good! How could they have been tough? They were not hardened in field work and factory work. They owned slaves who did that hard work for them, while they had taken it easy. They were evil. God was on our side, not their's. We must have also been fighting England far more that we had realized at the time.)

(On the other hand, had not the many Massachusetts veterans who had actually faced Confederates in battle witnessed the courage and skill of the Confederate foot soldier and cavalryman? Did they not know the truth of the matter? Yes, they had, and many did. But the kill ratio was embarrassing and it would help veterans save face if the blame fell on England, not on their inferior ability. This line of reasoning would help enhance the Federal veteran's ego among his wife, his mother and father and his sisters, and also among the elders in the community — the older men who were leaders in politics, commerce and industry and who stayed at home to keep the war effort supplied. When little Johnny would ask his father, the veteran, why 3 Federals had to die to kill 2 Confederates, the veteran would answer: "Well, sonny, it was 2 against 1 — we were fighting them and the English, too.")

(And, why was Charles Sumner agitating over "Claims on England," instead of "Claims on Great Britain?" After all, Scotland was in many ways the industrial might of the British Isles. The answer lies in the history of how the United Kingdom arose and in the remaining hatred toward the English felt by the Welsh, the Scots and especially the Irish — and Sumner was certainly playing up to political hatred in Massachusetts of American Irishmen toward the English in Great Britain.)

(I hope this conjecturing sheds light on the demagoguery and political agitation related to the issue being presented at the Massachusetts Republican Convention. Sumner's "Claims on England" was more that a ploy to take over the Provinces in Canada. It was also an exercise in political psychology aimed at enhancing the power of the Republican Party in Massachusetts and other northern States. The conjecturing concluded, we return to the history.)

Sumner further alleged that "Great Britain alone . . . founded on that recognition [of a state of belligerency] a systematic maritime war against the [Federals]; and this to effect the [survival] of a [Government that permitted African American bonding]!" A few days later John Motley would present the text of Sumner's speech to George Clarendon, the British leader. Clarendon would conclude that Sumner was arguing his claims "in a most malignant spirit," and would further lament that Sumner "evidently directs the foreign policy of his Government."

Two days after Sumner's speech before Massachusetts Republicans, Ulysses Grant's Cabinet approved new instructions to John Motley, which Sumner had arranged to have drafted by Caleb Cushing and Hamilton Fish. But those instructions were too vague to allow diplomats to begin negotiations — an indecisiveness which Sumner, Fish and Grant wanted for the moment — because the issue was only useful to incite an invasion of Canada, and the opportune time for that invasion had not yet arrived on the international stage. When the British Minister asked Hamilton Fish for clarification of Federal demands, Fish could only reply that he was waiting from more definite direction from Charles Sumner. When Fish asked Sumner for more definite direction, Sumner replied, "I do not think that at the moment any body here can formularize any proposal to England. Time must intervene, in order to ascertain what the people will require." Then Sumner added, as if by way of warning of dire events to transpire: "This will be seen in the probable debates in Congress." And Sumner was at work preparing the related language that Ulysses Grant would be asked to insert into his upcoming Message for the opening of Congress in early December.

In early October Grant and Fish would notify Sumner and Motley that future negotiations with the British Government, over Federal Claims arising from the Invasion of the Confederacy, would be conducted in Washington, not London. [R73;410-413]

(4Q69)

Meanwhile, Jeff Davis anticipated beginning his job as President of the Carolina Insurance Company on November 23. His office would be in the headquarters at Memphis, Tennessee. Departing England on September 25, Jeff had planned to leave Varina and the Children there until he felt secure in his new job. By the way, Varina and the children would not return to The States until 12 months into the future, November 1870. Jeff had hoped that he would find an offer to work in an administrative capacity for the newly formed Southern Pacific Railroad, but upon his arrival in Baltimore, he found that potential opportunity closed to him. Jeff would certainly have preferred something besides insurance. Dudley Mann had tried his best to motivate Jeff to instead write a history of the Confederacy:

"I cannot refrain from the utterance of my ardent wish that you will at your earliest convenience prepare your Book. This is a requisition which the world of enlightened man makes upon you. And, if you will permit me, I will add that it is due to the truthful history of our times, and to a more enlarged understanding of your own honest, virtuous fame. . .

"I had fondly indulged in the hope of a different pursuit for you. I wished to see you so situated that you would benefit humankind by your rare wisdom and your general knowledge. Strange, strange indeed are the ways of earth when such 'a Light' as yours is concealed under a 'bushel.'

Jeff's brother, Joseph and his great-niece, Lise were in Baltimore when Jeff disembarked. They traveled together by ship, via Cuba to New Orleans, providing Jeff meaningful quality time with these dear family members.

On the way up from New Orleans, Jeff visited with his niece, Mary Stamps, and her father, Benjamin Humphreys, during a stop in Vicksburg. You will recall that Humphreys had been the Governor of Mississippi, until deposed on June 15, 1868 by the Republican Reconstruction Programme. Humphreys told Davis how Adelbert Ames had come to Mississippi to exercise full power as her appointed Federal Military Governor. Humphreys considered Ames one of "the scavengers seeking profit from the prostrate [conquered States]." Ames was well connected to Republican power-brokers, for his wife, Blanche Butler Ames, was the only daughter of Ben "Beast" Butler of Massachusetts. As readers have learned, Blanche's father had earned the title "Beast" during his war-time reign of terror and thievery in and about New Orleans. Humphreys told Davis how Ames had deployed Federal troops to force him and his family out of the Executive Mansion in Jackson.

On November 23 Jeff Davis assumed the job of President of the Carolina Insurance Company, based in Memphis Tennessee. The former President had resigned and the Board of Directors had elected Davis, who had accepted. His annual salary would be $12,000. Very soon afterward, Davis would meet with Wade Hampton, who had served on the Board of the Southern Life Insurance Company, and would get him to agree to oversee the Baltimore, Maryland office with a title of Vice President. By the way, Braxton Bragg would accept the job of overseeing the New Orleans office. Tennessee, unlike the other 10 former Confederate States, was avoiding harsh Military Rule and full Political Reconstruction and this benefited Davis and his company. But former Confederates in Tennessee still suffered humiliating painful discrimination, as Davis knew — at an afternoon party at the Meriwether's house, the hostess informed him that the only man at the party who was permitted by the Federals to vote was the African

American man hired to help pass out the lemonade. Hampton would spend a lot of time in Baltimore working his new job. Yet, in the words of biographer Robert Ackerman, Hampton would still go "to Mississippi from time to time, trying to salvage those plantations." [R19;352-353,359-360,363, R199-200-201]

Meanwhile, in Mississippi, on November 30 and December 1, qualified voters cast ballots "for" or "against" the draft Mississippi Constitution, "for" or "against" 4 controversial sections of that Constitution and "for" preferences for 7 State offices, including Governor. According the Adelbert Ames' official tabulation, the vote to ratify the Constitution as drafted was almost unanimous: 113,735 "for" versus 955 "against". The vote to delete from the Constitution the 3 sections that restricted the voting rights of European Americans more than required by Federal law was overwhelmingly approved by votes of 87,874 versus 2,206; 87,253 versus 2,390, and 88,444 versus 2,170. The vote upheld the section forbidding the loan of the State's credit. So Mississippi would not be restricting the voting rights of European Americans more that dictated by Federal law, a major victory for the future political health of the State.

On the other hand, the ticket of the regular Republican Party won an overwhelming victory over the fusion ticket of the more conservative Republicans and the Democrats, organized as the Republican Union Party of Mississippi. Republican James Alcorn, a native of Mississippi who had aligned with the Republicans, defeated Ulysses Grant's brother-in-law, Louis Dent, by a vote of 76,143 versus 38,133. Alcorn carried all counties with African American majorities and 15 with European American majorities. The other 6 State offices went to Republicans. Republicans elected all 5 of their candidates for the Federal House: 2 were natives of Tennessee, 2 were natives of New York, formerly in the Federal Army, and 1 was native of Illinois, formerly in the Federal Army. All were European Americans. Results showed that the Mississippi House would be made up of 82 Republicans and 25 Democrats. The Mississippi Senate would be made up of 36 Republicans and 7 Democrats. County and local offices had not been up for election, so the political appointees of Adelbert Ames could remain in office for two more years, until challenged in the elections of the fall of 1871. Therefore, it was obvious that Mississippi would be descending into the worst years of Republican rule, empowered by the votes of African American men, but primarily under the control of European American men from the northern States, many of whom had arrived as conquerors.

The election had been peaceful, and, under the rules laid down by Federal authority, was apparently free of major vote fraud. Adelbert Ames, as Military Ruler over Mississippi and Arkansas, had made extensive preparation to oversee the election. He had arranged for the lists of qualified registered voters to be updated. He had appointed Registrars on November 5 and, the next day, had ordered 49 army officers to serve as election inspectors. He had even, "ordered that two European Americans and two African Americans of different political Parties be selected by the Board of Registry in each Precinct to challenge the right of any person to be registered" who was thought to be disqualified. There seems to be no evidence that election fraud defeated the fusion ticket of the more conservative Republicans and the Democrats. Apparently, with all State, county and local offices in the hands of Republicans and under the control of Ames, the political power of incumbent office simply overwhelmed the opposition — all of them on the outside, looking in. The Mississippi Legislature was ordered to convene on January 11. Ames informed Governor-elect James Alcorn that he would remain on the job and in the Governor's Residence until March. Ames was planning to get himself elected to the Federal Senate, and did not want to lose influence before the Legislature elected Mississippi's two Senators. [R204;245-247]

When the Federal House and Senate opened a new Session on December 6, Senators observed that Charles Sumner "was in a buoyant mood." Of opening day, biographer David Donald would write: "For once [Sumner] was in a position to exercise power commensurate with his authority. The death of [William] Fessenden had removed his major rival from the Senate. His summer skirmishes with [Hamilton] Fish had reduced the State Department to following his orders. Most of all, widespread praise for his 'Claims on England' address gave him the right to speak for a broader following than ever before."

But, on that very first day, Simon Cameron presented a Petition, complete with 30,000 signatures, which asked Ulysses Grant to recognize a state of belligerency in Spanish-controlled Cuba. Hamilton

Fish had already warned Charles Sumner of Cameron's plans, so Sumner was all set to direct the Petition to his Senate Foreign Relations Committee. Sumner, like most northeastern States men, hated the thought of Cuba becoming a State under the Federal Government. Their political opposition to helping Cuba was consistent with their long-standing opposition to expansion toward the Caribbean and Mexico. The expansion they sought was to the north, into Canada. Anyway, Cuba contained far too many people of African descent to suit Sumner. And he complained that, "Cubans don't speak our language" and that "the mass of them know very little about our customs or our institutions. They would not be an intelligent acquisition, and I cannot see that they would be valuable in any respect." So Sumner wanted "to avoid involving ourselves in any way." Sumner succeeded in burying in his Committee the Petition to help Cuban patriots. Newspaper denunciations of Sumner's refusal to give the Cubans a hearing on the Senate floor failed to move him — even when a Massachusetts newspaperman referred to Sumner as, "that Old Man of the Sea, who has mercilessly endeavored to crush the Cuban patriots." Sumner did not blink when Senator Matthew Carpenter of Wisconsin rose on the Senate floor on December 15 to passionately plea for the Federal Government to prevent the delivery of 18 coastal warships, called gunboats, which were being built in New York yards for the Spanish Government. Sumner simply rose, following Carpenter's plea, and announced that the 18 coastal warships had already been turned over to the Spanish Navy, and Spanish crews were aboard flying the Spanish flag. [R73;417]

Opening Day for the House and Senate also involved controversies in seating Representatives and Senators from Reconstructed Georgia and Reconstructed Virginia.

You will recall that Georgia had been accepted as a State under the Federal Government to an extent sufficient to permit qualified voters to cast ballots in the 1868 election contest between Republican Ulysses Grant and Democrat Horatio Seymour. And you will recall that Seymour had won the State's Delegates to the Electoral College. Well, although the Georgia Republican Machine controlled the Office of Governor and the State Senate, it had lost control of the State House by 3 seats in the election of April 1868, and was struggling to exercise power in the State as it contended with a House controlled by defiant Democrats and the potential of Impeachment of the Governor. Appealing to Republicans in the Federal House and Senate for help in restoring complete power to Georgia's Republican Machine, Georgia Governor Rufus Bullock, appeared before the Federal Senate on opening day and urged Congress to refuse to seat Representatives and Senators from his State and to return Georgia to Federal Military Rule. Brief background on the political situation in Georgia is appropriate.

In November 1865, in accordance with the remade Georgia State Constitution, voters had elected men to its new Legislature, and for its Governor, Charles Jenkins, of Georgia, "an old-line Whig who had originally opposed Secession." In December, the new Legislature had Ratified the Federal Amendment Making African Americans Independent (13th). But in November 1866, it had voted against Ratification of the Federal Amendment to Nationalize Citizenship (14th) — doing so in accordance with a legal opinion that, "if Georgia was not a State, its Legislature had no role in Ratifying Amendments, and that, if Georgia was a State, the Amendment had not been placed before it Constitutionally." In March 1867 Congress had subjugated Georgia, Alabama and Florida under Federal Military Rule, organized as the Third Federal Military District, commanded first by John Pope, then by George Meade. Meade had deposed Governor Jenkins and put the State under a Military Governor, Thomas Ruger of Wisconsin. In accordance with the Federal Reconstruction Acts, a new Reconstructed Georgia State Constitution had been created in March 1868, obediently giving the right to vote to African American men. The election of the following month had produced the following results — Republican Rufus Bullock (of New York, but had relocated to Georgia in 1857 to work with a telegraph company) defeated Democrat John Gordon (of Georgia, a former Confederate commander) by a vote of 83,527 versus 76,356 — Republicans won control of the State Senate (27 seats versus 17 seats) — but Democrats won control of the State House (88 seats versus 84 seats). The General Assembly in Joint Session, the majority being Republicans, had Ratified the Federal Amendment Nationalizing Citizenship (14th). But Democrats, from their power base in the State House, were blocking much of the Republican agenda. Consequently, Governor Bullock, in March 1869, during voting on Ratification of the Federal Amendment to Nationalize Voting by African American Men (15th), arranged for sufficient negative Republican votes to defeat the measure, apparently in an effort to delay Federal acceptance of Georgia as a

Reconstructed State, in hopes of giving the State's Republican Political Machine another shot at winning control of the State House. And Governor Bullock was in Washington City arguing for that agenda.

With Charles Sumner in the lead, the Senate would agree with Governor Bullock and vote to deny seats to Georgia's two Senators, all Republicans voting to deny seats, except for Republican Joseph Fowler of Tennessee, and all Democrats voting to seat. In the House, Georgia's Representatives would likewise be denied seats.

Charles Sumner also took the lead in delaying Senate action on seating Senators from Reconstructed Virginia — they would not be seated in December. Fanning the fires of hatred to the necessary intensity, he called the Governor of Reconstructed Virginia, Gilbert Walker, a "traitor" and alleged that the Virginia Legislature was "composed of recent [Confederates] still filled and seething with that old [Confederate] fire." He demanded that Virginia must do more to ensure that both African Americans and European Americans "were equally eligible to hold" political office and to ensure that it maintained a "uniform system of public schools," meaning integrated schools. For a few weeks, Sumner's arguments would act to delay acceptance of Reconstructed Virginia, but, as you will soon discover, Virginia would win Federal acceptance a few weeks later, on January 26.

Meanwhile, although the Federal Senate would follow John Sherman's leadership when it would consider financial legislation, Sumner would exercise powerful leadership through to the close of the Senate session in July of 1870. Biographer David Donald would summarize Sumner's active political life during the session:

> "He made a speech on every important measure that came before the Senate, usually a carefully prepared address which he read to his colleagues from printed slips or galley proofs. Active as always on measures involving [Reconstructing governments in the conquered States] and foreign policy affairs, he also spoke 41 times on funding the [Federal] debt and 36 times on the Post Office Appropriation bill. More than any previous session, he was willing to engage in close parliamentary infighting; his persistent, indeed almost pertinacious, battle to secure a pension for Mary Lincoln, in the face of powerful opposition from the Senate Pension Committee, was simply one of his many successes, both small and large, in a session which he dominated."

At the proper point in his session-opening message to Congress, Ulysses Grant repeated Charles Sumner's line of argument in presenting Federal claims against Great Britain for alleged losses from Confederate military defensive efforts. Grant endorsed as "wisely taken," the Senate's rejection of the claims settlement proposed by the Johnson-Clarendon Convention. Then he followed Sumner's reasoning in alleging the "grave wrongs" that had resulted from British trade with the Confederacy. Grant mentioned "the increased rates of insurance; the diminution of exports and imports; the effect upon the foreign commerce of the country; the decrease and transfer to Great Britain of our commercial marine; the prolongation of the [Federal invasion campaign], and the increased cost (both in treasure and lives) of its [consummation]." [R73;413-424]

The Year of 1870

(1Q70)

On the Sunday evening of January 2, 1870, Ulysses Grant strolled over to visit with Charles Sumner, who lived across the street from the White House. Sumner, who was not expecting Grant, was eating with two newspapermen he had invited to dinner when Grant knocked on the door. Grant wanted to personally encourage Sumner to support a Treaty that provided for the Federal Government to take over the Dominican Republic. Actually Orville Babcock had negotiated two treaties, which we might call "Plan A" and "Plan B." "Plan A," Grant's favorite, arranged for the Federal Government to take over the Dominican Republic. "Plan B," existed as a fall-back position, to be submitted if "Plan A" failed to win Senate confirmation. That plan provided for the Federal Government to lease the Dominican Republic's Samaná Bay for a Federal Navy port. Grant outlined the overall concepts within the Treaty and closed with, "I will send the papers over to you in the morning by [Orville] Babcock." Sumner was opposed to taking over any Caribbean island, firstly, because it would be populated mostly by people of African ancestry and, secondly, because it would be too far from the northeastern States. But he assured Grant: "I am [a Grant] Administration man, and whatever you do will always find in me the most careful and candid consideration." John Forney, one of the newspapermen who was dining with Sumner, seemed anxious to quiz Grant about a Sumner political friend, James Ashley. It seems that the Grant Administration was taking action to remove Ashley as Governor of Montana Territory and replace him with a Grant devotee. Sumner had just received a letter from Ashley appealing for help with retaining his job. After Sumner read the letter aloud, Grant scoffed that Ashley was just "a mischief-maker and a worthless fellow." Grant left the house rather pleased with himself for having obtained Sumner's commitment to look at the Treaty without bias. Forney left the house convinced that Sumner would support Ratification of the Treaty, and Forney would muddle matters in future newspaper reports where he claimed that Sumner had committed himself to support Ratification if Grant helped his friend Ashley keep his job out in Montana. Sumner went to bed rather pleased that he had been honored by a visit by Ulysses Grant and that he had shown correct courtesy by his choice of words — there would be plenty of time to kill the Treaty. The Dominican Republic was the last place he wanted the Federal Government to take control over. Orville Babcock came over the next day and presented Sumner a draft of the Treaty. Sumner made a few insignificant language edits, without revealing his opposition to the object of the Treaty, and sent Babcock back to complete the signing ceremony. The signed Treaty would arrive at the Senate on January 10 and be referred to Sumner's Senate Foreign Relations Committee. [R73;434-438]

Meanwhile, on January 26, the Reconstructed Virginia State Government won Federal acceptance when Ulysses Grant signed the bill admitting Virginia, which had just been passed by the House and Senate. The delay for which Charles Sumner had fought so earnestly in December and the first three weeks of January, although successful by some measures, had not had a lasting impact on the progress of events. It had been a hard fight in the Senate, as would be reported by biographer David Donald:

> Between December 9, 1869 and January 21, 1870, 7 roll call votes were taken in the Federal Senate on the seating of Senators from the Reconstructed State Governments of Georgia and Virginia. A study of those votes by David Donald would persuade him that a minority of about 15 Republican Senators had opposed Sumner's agenda for expanding Federal power over public education, voting rights and requirements for holding State and local offices. Lyman Trumbull, Senate Judiciary Committee Chairman, was most often the leader of the group opposing Sumner — others in the group were Matthew Carpenter, George Williams, John Sherman and Roscoe Conkling. About 22 Republican Senators had backed Sumner's agenda for expanding Federal power, including most of the Senators elected by Republican Political Machines in those Reconstructed States that had already been admitted. Sumner also received support from George Edmunds, Justin Morrill and Jacob Howard. But, in the words of Matthew Carpenter, Sumner was "the biggest ox in the herd." A smaller group of Republicans refused to join either group, and were therefore the target of appeals from the two opposing larger groups. Of course, the Democrat Senators were opposed to Sumner's schemes for two reasons — 1), the schemes were obviously designed to perpetuate the Republican Political Machines in the Reconstructed States, and 2), to varying degrees, these Democrats still believed that citizens benefited from State Rights and a Federal Government limited in power by the words of the Federal Constitution. [R73;425-426]

As was his usual practice, Sumner accused opposing Senators of participating in "plots" with "rebels," and of speaking with "the voice of [African American bonding]." (Democrats, long accustomed to being called "Copperhead [snakes]," were perhaps amused that Republicans were applying similarly hateful language while fighting among themselves.) But Lyman Trumbull, revealing his anger toward Sumner, replied sarcastically: "Everything that does not suit [Charles Sumner] is in the interest of [African American bonding]!" And, on January 13, Trumbull attacked Sumner with the question before the Senate: "Who inaugurated him as the leader of the [people who had supported the Federal invasion campaign]? . . . Has he any higher claims to patriotism or to loyalty or to devotion to the [Federal Government] than anybody else?" Then Trumbull warned that Sumner's bill was "impracticable, unreasonable, unconstitutional, and ineffectual." On the day of the final vote on the bill, Trumbull attacked again, scoffing at Sumner's attitude of "infallibility and superiority," reminding the Senate that Sumner had absented himself from crucial votes intended to empower African American men at the ballot box — that Sumner had absented himself when the Senate had voted to force Reconstructed Governments to allow voting by African

American men and when Senators had approved the Federal Amendment to Nationalize Voting by African American Men (15th). Trumbull summed up his analysis of Sumner with these words:

> "The future historian will search the records in vain for the vote of [Charles Sumner] in favor of any of the great measures which have [enabled African American men to vote]."

Biographer David Donald would later add to Trumbull's list of Sumner's failures:

> "Not merely had Sumner failed to support the 15th Amendment and the 1867 Reconstruction Act; he had earlier opposed the 14th Amendment and even the 1866 Civil Rights Act. Of Senate legislation involving African Americans, William Stewart agreed, saying: "I never knew [Sumner] to be for it when there was any chance to make it law." Stewart further explained: "[Sumner] is a theorist, a grand, gorgeous, extensive theorist, but he is not a practical man, and my experience is that he had failed utterly to help [Republicans] to get practical measures."

During this time Ulysses Grant made no criticisms of Sumner, apparently willing to further expand Federal power. Two of his Cabinet members, George Boutwell and Rockwood Hoar, were Sumner men, and, while Republicans were fighting in the Senate, Grant was in the process of pushing Hoar for an appointment to the Federal Supreme Court.

On the other hand, biographer David Donald would conclude that Sumner's personal leadership in the Senate during the 7 weeks of debated over Reconstructed Virginia would prove to be the most commanding and complete of any period in his life.

> Sumner "persuaded a majority of his Republican colleagues, and a majority of the entire Senate as well, to support his views" on further Federal demands for Reconstructing the Governments in the former Confederate States. Sumner's group — strengthened by the recently admitted Republican Machine Senators — had outvoted, by a small margin, the opposing Republican Senators and the Democratic Senators. Sumner's bill ordered the Reconstructed Virginia State Government to pass additional laws that ensured that both European Americans and African Americans were "equally eligible to hold government office." But the biggest directive dealt with the Federal demands in Sumner's bill proscribing how the Reconstructed Virginia State Government would be required to establish public schools — requiring that Virginia copy "the New England system of common schools." Why? Apparently, Sumner thought the Massachusetts system of public schools was "part of the republican form of government as understood by the framers of the [Federal] Constitution. Of such justification for Federal control over local schools, Henry Adams would complain: "that would have seemed to the last generation [of Americans] as strange as though it had been announced that the electric telegraph was an essential article of faith in the early Christian Church." Sumner indicated that his agenda would not be complete until "the powers that the Federal Constitution" originally gave to the State Governments "are in the future to be held by [those State Governments] only on good behavior and at the sufferance of Congress." Ah! Finally! Charles Sumner was making his final moves to make the Federal Congress supreme over all government within the borders of the United States. Sumner envisioned that even Salmon Chase and the Supreme Court would be powerless to enforce a Constitutional restriction to Federal power. Of Sumner's vision for sweeping expansion of Federal power Henry Adams would lament: "the first, decisive, irrevocable step toward substituting a new form of government in the place of that on which American liberties have heretofore rested had been taken, and by it the American people must stand."

Although Sumner passed his bill to impose more Federal restrictions on Virginia, he actually weakened his prospects for long-term Senate leadership. William Stewart had spoken for many Republican Senators with this analysis — Sumner was "a theorist, a grand, gorgeous, extensive theorist," who was in almost every situation unable to "help us get practical" bills passed.

Some background on Virginia politics over the previous two and a half years is helpful. We step back in time to 1867:

During the year 1867 the Virginia Republican Political Machine had been well organized and very effective in getting African American men to the polls to elect Delegates to the new State Convention, which was charged with drafting a new Reconstruction Constitution. The voter registration effort, under the direction of John Schofield, Military Ruler over the Federal District comprising Virginia, had resulted in the registration of 225,933 voters, of whom 120,101 were European Americans and 105,832 were African Americans, a minority of the registration. But gerrymandering had given a boost to the Republican Machine. Voting on October 18 through 21 resulted in a poor turnout by registered European Americans and victory for the Republicans (76,084 votes versus 93,145). Accordingly, when the new Virginia Constitutional Convention assembled in Richmond on December 3, 1867, it consisted of 105 Delegates, 72 being Republicans and 33 being Conservatives. Of the Republicans, 25 were African Americans and 33 were European Americans who had arrived recently from outside the State.

> For President of the Convention, Delegates elected Judge John Underwood, who, you will recall, was also presiding during that year over the prosecution of Jeff Davis on Treason charges. Then Delegates settled down to a long and profitable debate. They were still at it on April 4, 1868, when John Schofield ordered that Provisional Governor Francis Pierpont be replaced by Henry Wells, of New York and Michigan, a high ranking Federal army officer. Wells would replace many of the 5,446 incumbent government officials across the State, generally installing men from the northern States because the vast majority of capable Virginians were politically disqualified due to prior support of their State following its secession. After much debate and many votes, the Convention adopted a Reconstructed Virginia Constitution on April 17, 1868 by a vote of 51 to 36. To be known as the "Underwood Constitution," it allowed for segregated schools (integrated schools had lost out in a hard fight) and unrestricted voting rights for African American men, while disqualifying for office or voting many who had supported their State after its secession (but it did allow the Legislature to remove a man's political disability by a three-fifths vote). But, to become effective, the Underwood Constitution had to be ratified by voters, a process that would be delayed for over a year while "Republican leaders paused in uncertainty, studying the political conditions in hopes of a favorable chance of acceptance."

The summer and fall months of 1868 witnessed "no great political events in Virginia," following the May "not guilty" verdict on the Senate Impeachment Trial of Andrew Johnson. But, when the Federal House convened in December, it passed a bill directing qualified Virginians to vote to ratify or reject the "Underwood Constitution" on "the fourth Thursday in May, 1869." The bill was forwarded to the Senate where considerable debate would occur. Meanwhile, a "Committee of Nine" arose in Virginia to advocate for removing political disabilities from the Virginia Reconstruction Constitution "in the hope that union and harmony may be restored on the basis of universal suffrage and universal amnesty." The Chairman of the "Committee of Nine" was Alexander Stuart, 61, of Staunton, who was well versed in political affairs in both Virginia and Washington City, having been Secretary of The Interior as a Whig in the Millard Fillmore Administration (1850-1853). During January 1869 the Committee worked hard in Washington City for Federal approval of a movement to reconvene the Virginia Constitutional Convention. Important support for the movement was indicated by the New York *Tribune*, by George Stoneman, who had replaced John Schofield as Military Ruler, and by several leading Republican Federal Senators (Charles Sumner not being among them). From the Republican power base in Washington City, the Committee of Nine's advocacy of a new Virginia Constitutional Convention facilitated a splintering within the leadership of the Virginia Republican Political Machine. And from within Virginia, William Mahone, a former Confederate military leader and now President of the Virginia and Tennessee Railroad, was very effective at influencing moderate Republicans and at gathering support for a new Convention. The loser was Provisional Governor Henry Wells, who aspired to be elected Governor of Reconstructed Virginia. Wells lost important influence when the Virginia Republican Party Executive Committee called for a new State Party Convention.

At the Virginia Republican State Convention, which met on March 9, 1869, Provisional Governor Henry Wells succeeded in winning control of the more radical Delegates and the nomination of himself for Governor. But Wells and his supporters had good reason to worry when a Faction of more moderate Republicans managed to nominate Dr. Harris, an African American, for Lieutenant Governor — a strategy by moderates designed to weaken the Republican Party and facilitate the creation of an alternate more moderate Republican Faction, to be called the "True Republican Party." This Faction gathered immediately after the close of the Republican State Convention and nominated Gilbert Walker for Governor and announced that their ticket "strongly opposed the proscriptive features of the Underwood Constitution."

Ulysses Grant, in his Message to Congress, which was read on April 7, "recommended that the Underwood Constitution should be submitted to a popular vote for ratification or rejection, and that a separate vote should be taken upon the adoption or rejection of such sections of the Constitution as might seem expedient." Congress concurred and, on May 14, Grant announced that the election on the Reconstructed Virginia Constitution was to take place on July 6 and that separate votes should be cast for or against the sections restricting voting rights for former Confederates and for or against restricting the rights of former Confederates to hold public office. In the meantime, on April 20, the Grant Administration had replaced the Military Ruler over Virginia, George Stoneman with Edward Canby, who had been born in Kentucky and trained at West Point.

Eight days later the political conservatives in Virginia, under the leadership of William Mahone, gathered as a State Convention so that their nominees for State offices could resign from the contest, thereby paving the way for a Fusion with the "True Republican Party," previously mentioned. "There were now but two State tickets in the field — those of Wells and Walker — and between these two it was easy for conservative voters to choose." The "True Republican Party" accepted the Fusion program and the tickets were merged to include candidates for the Legislature in many conservative Districts. Pressure was applied to African American men in a struggle to tear them away from allegiance to the secret Union Leagues operated by the Virginia Republican Machine. Historian Hamilton Eckenrode would write:

> "The Union Leagues had gone to pieces in many places from threats of the farmers not to employ laborers who were members; the strongest pressure was brought to bear upon the [African American men] in the endeavor to detach them from the Radical Party. . . . Furthermore, in order to gain [African American] votes, the Conservatives nominated several [African American men for the Legislature, a device which worked well."

The July 6 election resulted in victory for the Conservative/True Republican Fusion candidate, Gilbert Walker, over the Radical Republican candidate, incumbent Provisional Governor Henry Wells, the count being 119,535 versus 101,204. The Reconstructed Virginia Constitution was Ratified and voting on the two separate sections resulted in their defeats — the section restricting voting by former Confederates being defeated by a vote of 124,360 versus 84,410 — and the section restricting former Confederates from holding public office being defeated by a vote of 124,715 versus 83,458.

Provisional Governor Henry Wells resigned and Gilbert Walker was inaugurated as Governor of Reconstructed Virginia on September 21 in a peaceful transition. The Reconstructed Virginia Legislature convened on October 5 and Ratified the Federal Amendment to Nationalize Citizenship (14th) and the Amendment to Nationalize Voting by African American Men (15th) by margins ranging from overwhelming to unanimous.

As previously mentioned, it was on January 26, 1870 that Ulysses Grant signed the bill admitting the Reconstructed Virginia Government. The following day, the Military Ruler, Edward Canby, issued an order that "resigned the government of the State to the civil authorities." Finally, "the Reconstruction of Virginia had come to an end after well-nigh 5 years of weary waiting." The Conservatives of the State would assume effective control of the workings of State and local government. William Mahone would exert considerable leadership and found the "Readjuster Movement." The Virginia Democratic Party would eventually come to power and, for 90 years, the best the Republican Party would be able to accomplish would be the election of an occasional Congressman. [R73;419-434, R216]

Two weeks earlier on January 11, the Mississippi State Legislature had met in Jackson to ratify two Amendments to the Federal Constitution and to elect two Federal Senators, in accordance with the message it received from Provisional Governor Adelbert Ames. As previously reported, Republicans were in complete control of the State House and Senate. There were 31 African Americans in the State House and 5 in the State Senate, all Republicans. About 12 in the House and 3 in the Senate were educated ministers; the remaining men were illiterate. European Americans from the northern States and native European Americans from Mississippi would control the House and Senate and largely control the votes of the African Americans, thereby giving Republicans complete domination over the Mississippi Democrats, who represented the tax payers and the economy of the State. The House elected a man from New York for its Speaker. As demanded by the Federal Government, the Legislature immediately Ratified the Amendment to Nationalize Citizenship (14th) by a vote of 23 versus 2 in the Senate and 87 versus 6 in the House. It then Ratified the Amendment to Nationalize Voting by African American Men (15th) by a unanimous vote the Senate and by all but one vote in the House. As I have already mentioned, Ratification under such coercion can be argued to be not legally binding. But that is another story.

The Mississippi Legislature then turned to the election of Federal Senators. A man needed to be selected to fill the unfinished term of Jefferson Davis. Another man was needed to fill the unfinished term of the other former Mississippi Senator. Finally, the plum job among the three: a Senator needed to be selected to serve a new 6-year term beginning March 1, 1871. Governor-elect James Alcorn, basking in the admiration of his fellow Republicans, won the plum, the 6-year term, almost unanimously. You will recall that Alcorn was a native European American of Mississippi. Adelbert Ames, former Military Ruler over Mississippi and Arkansas, won the longer of the short term seats by a large margin over a Democrat. Ames, you will recall, was a Federal military commander and native of Maine. Hiram Revels, in voting that surprised some, won the short-term seat concluding on March 4, 1871, defeating Beroth Eggleston of New York. Hiram Revels was an African American whose background needs to be presented:

> Hiram Revels was born in North Carolina and moved to Indiana in early life, where he attended a Quaker seminary and became a Methodist minister and a teacher. In pastoral work in Baltimore when Abe Lincoln called for invasion forces, he at once entered the Federal army and assisted in raising two African American regiments. He was moved to Jackson, Mississippi while in the army and then moved over to the Federal African American Men's Bureau. After the conquest of the Confederacy he settled at Natchez and later was elected to a seat in the State Senate where he resided at the time of his election to the Federal Senate. A graduate of Knox College, Revels was well-educated, and would prove to be adequately skilled to represent Mississippi in the Senate.

Back in Washington City, on February 3, Ben "Beast" Butler, of Massachusetts and the House Committee on Reconstructing Governments in the Conquered States, introduced a "Mississippi Bill," which provided the rules for accepting the Mississippi State Government and its Reconstructed Constitution, and for seating its Representatives and Senators. Not satisfied with all that Mississippi had done to comply with ever-stringent Federal demands on what the State had to do to satisfy the Federals, Butler aimed to insist on more, to keep the pot stirred. He now demanded that every officer and legislator in Mississippi must swear to the following oath, unless his disability had been previously removed by Federal resolution:

> "I do solemnly swear that I have never taken an oath as a member of Congress or as an officer of the United States, or as a member of any State legislature, or as an executive or judicial officer of any State to support the Constitution of the United States, and afterward engaged in rebellion against the same, or given aid or comfort to the enemies thereof, so help me, God."

But Republicans were freely granting disabilities to their political friends. "Most of the prominent Republicans of the State had already secured the removal of their disabilities," and "by a concurrent resolution of January 15, the disabilities of 139 persons had been removed. Most of them were officers-elect, and the resolution was passed to enable them to qualify."

Ben "Beast" Butler had other demands. His bill placed further limitations on the sovereignty of Mississippi and her people. These added limitations were:

- The Mississippi Constitution shall never be amended so as to deprive any citizen of the right to vote.

- It shall never be lawful for Mississippi to deprive any citizen of the United States, on account of race, color, or previous condition of servitude, of the right to hold office under the Constitution and laws of the State.

- The Mississippi Constitution shall never be amended so as to deprive any citizen of the United States of the benefits and privileges of the public schools.

The Mississippi Bill, as presented by Ben "Beast" Butler, passed the House by a vote of 136 to 56.

The Federal Senate next took up the Mississippi Bill, where it was referred to the Senate Judiciary Committee, Lyman Trumbull of Illinois, Chairman. Trumbull's Committee advocated a substitute that removed the added restrictions imposed by the House, for his Committee wanted to admit Mississippi without imposing further limitations, perhaps fearing the consequential additional erosion of State Rights, for so much had been lost since the Federal Invasion of the Confederacy. But Oliver Morton, of Indiana, and Charles Sumner led the Senate fight against Trumbull's substitute:

Charles Sumner argued that the same directives imposed on Reconstructed Virginia had to also be imposed on Reconstructed Mississippi. In glorious language, Sumner charged that, "the equal rights of all must be placed under the safeguard of one uniform law which shall be the same in all parts of the nation." Sumner was continuing to dismantle the restrictions on Federal power as detailed in the Federal Constitution. Sumner's argument meant that Reconstructed Mississippi would be forced to revise its public school system to conform to "the New England system of common schools," because "that is a part of the republican form of government as understood by the framers of the Constitution." Then, and only then, he argued, could Mississippi's Reconstructed State Government reapply to have its Senators and Representatives seated.

Oliver Morton and Charles Sumner prevailed in the Senate, just as Ben "Beast" Butler had prevailed in the House. On February 17 the Senate voted to reject Trumbull's substitute by a vote of 32 to 27, then voted to pass the Mississippi Bill without amendment by a vote of 50 to 11.

Then, on February 23, Ulysses Grant signed the Mississippi Bill. Back in Jackson, the Reconstructed Mississippi State Government rather quickly passed laws to permit it to conform to the requirements forced upon it by the Mississippi Bill.

Soon after Grant signed the Mississippi Bill, Henry Wilson, of Massachusetts, presented the credentials of Senator-elect Hiram Revels to the Senate, requesting that they be read and that he be sworn in. Some expressed concerns. Was Adelbert Ames, the man who signed Revels' credentials, qualified to do so, as Provisional Governor, since another man had been elected as Mississippi Governor? Had Revels been a citizen of the United States for 9 years as required of a Federal Senator? But these concerns bothered few, and on February 25, by a vote of 48 to 8, Revels' credentials were accepted and he "was escorted to the desk by Wilson and sworn in. As you know, Revels had been elected to the exact Senate seat that had been vacant since Jeff Davis had resigned in response to his State's vote to secede 9 years previously. Well, Charles Sumner was ecstatic over Revels' arrival. He would throw a dinner party in Revels' honor which would be attended by many prominent African Americans as well as Sumner's European American political friends. Sumner would rise up in the Senate and praise Revels' arrival as "an historic event marking the triumph of a great cause." The obvious fact that Revels was mostly of European descent did not seem to dampen the glorious words that came from Sumner's mouth as he enthused: "All men are created equal! . . . Doors will open, exclusions will give way, intolerance will cease, and the great truth will be manifest in a thousand examples. . . . Liberty and Equality are the two express promises of our fathers. Both are now assured." John Whittier wrote Sumner soon afterward: "That swearing in of [Hiram] Revels must have been a sight compensating for much of the labor, trial and obloquy which thee and other pioneers in the march [to make African Americans independent] have endured." An African American from Massachusetts wrote Sumner: "the Great Battle is over — victory has been proclaimed. . . . The mantle of honor must rest upon your shoulders as the greatest champion of liberty." Senator-elect Adelbert Ames would have more trouble with his credentials. His were referred to the Senate Judiciary Committee, which would not report back for a month.

Of Reconstructed Mississippi's acceptance, historian James Garner would write:

"And thus, after having been excluded, to all intents and purposes, [from statehood under the Federal Government] for a period of 5 years, during 3 of which it was treated as conquered territory, and held under military government, the State was restored [to statehood under the Federal Government], but with conditions annexed which very materially impaired its sovereignty, and left it far from being on an equality with the original States [under the Federal Government]." [R204;269-274, R19;360, R73;426-427]

Meanwhile, on March 20, back at Jackson, the now-validated Mississippi Legislature reconvened and James Alcorn was sworn in as Governor. Unlike many top leaders of the Mississippi Republican Party, Alcorn was a native of the State and, for a Republican, considered rather moderate in his political philosophy. But restraining runaway government spending and corruption would be a bigger challenge that he would be able to master. Anyway, 20 months later, on November 30, 1871 he would be resigning his office as Governor and moving to Washington City to take the Federal Senate seat that would be vacated by Hiram Revels, a 6-year seat to which he had already gotten himself elected. Alcorn could take comfort in the realization that he would be moving on to a more splendid life. [204;277-281]

Meanwhile, three weeks earlier, on March 1, the South Carolina Legislature had concluded its session of 83 working days. As with the previous session ended 12 months earlier, it is appropriate to now review the most important legislation promulgated:

The Legislature incorporated the African American school, Claflin University, located in Orangeburg, but required that students be accepted without regard to race or color, thereby opening the school for European American students, should any apply.

The rules for the State's system of free common schools were upgraded from temporary to permanent.

An "act to regulate the publication of all legal and public notices" enabled the Attorney-General, Comptroller General and Secretary of State to jointly select the Republican newspaper in Columbia, *The State*, which charged 25 cents per line ($2.50 per column inch) versus the 10 cents per line previously charged by others in the State.

An "act to alter and amend the charter and extend the limits of the city of Columbia," ignoring the wishes of city residents, extended the municipal boundaries to take in a large number of African Americans, thereby making African American men a firm majority in city elections. Within 4 years the city debt would expand from $360,000 to $850,000, while benefiting residents with permanent improvements in the amount of only $75,000.

Timothy Hurley of Charleston, having come down from a northern State, bribed Legislators with $25,000 to secure passage of "an act to grant certain persons therein named and their associates the right to dig and mine in the beds of the navigable streams and waters of the State of South Carolina for phosphate rocks and phosphatic deposits." The right ran for 21 years. The State was to receive a royalty of one dollar per ton of phosphate rock obtained.

The Land Commission was authorized to issue an additional $500,000 in bonds, increasing the total to $700.000.

An act "to revise, simplify and abridge the rules, practice, pleadings and forms of courts of this State" adopted what was fundamentally a copy of the New York State code, the writer "forgetting in some cases to alter the language to suit existing laws not affected." The previous session had established the Code Commission to draft the State's legal code, normally just called the "code," and D. T. Corbin had done most of the work himself. Historian John Reynold, in would write the following about this "code":

"The adoption of this code gave well-nigh universal dissatisfaction to the lawyers. But after 35 years' use, with immaterial changes suggested by experience, it has come to be regarded an admirable system — the product of legal minds of extraordinary power, worthy of close study by every man aspiring to be an educated lawyer, and of great merit as a specimen of terse, technical and yet scholarly English."

262

So we see evidence in this subject of admiral work from D. T. Corbin and the Republican controlled government of South Carolina. Sadly, this was the exception.

Trial justices were provided for each county, to be appointed by the Governor. This encouraged widespread incompetence and political graft as historian John Reynold would later note:

> "In the selection of trial justices Governor Scott had little or no regard to qualifications of any kind. Many of these officers were grossly incompetent for lack of even elementary education, and some of them were vicious partisans who sought to stir up strife by encouraging [African Americans] to controversies with [European Americans]. Many of the constables were ignorant, some even illiterate, and there were frequent instances of misconduct on their part."

In further example of graft, the Governor's contingent fund for the year, authorized at $25,000, expended over $49,000. Contingent funds for other State officers, authorized in total for $9,300, expended almost $42,000.

An "act to enforce the provisions of the [Federal Civil Rights Act] and to secure to the people the benefits of a republican government in this State" detailed prohibitions directed at "some brutal, ill-disposed and lawless persons in the State who persist in denying and trampling upon the sacred rights of certain of the people." The following is a summation of this act prohibiting discrimination "between persons on account of race, color or previous condition":

> The act prohibited discrimination by common carriers, chartered or licensed businesses and operators of theaters and places of entertainment, including customer seating or accommodations assignments. A person convicted of violating this act was to be fined $1,000 and suffer imprisonment for 5 years at hard labor. The manager of an organization found guilty was to be fined $1,000 and suffer imprisonment for 3 years at hard labor. Any person who shall "aid and abet" the convicted, including supervisors, was to suffer imprisonment for 3 years at hard labor. Any corporation found in violation shall loose its charter or license.

> If the person who alleges he or she has been discriminated against is an African American, "the burden shall be on the defendant party, or parties, so having refused or denied such admission or accommodation, to show that the same was not done in violation of this act." In other words, when an African American pressed the charge, the accused was deemed guilty unless he or she could prove innocence. This violated the Federal Constitution, which requires that the accused be assumed to be innocent until proved guilty.

> If any law enforcement officer of the State fails to "promptly and rigorously enforce" the act, he shall "forfeit his office and pay a fine of $500."

This civil rights act, was perhaps too extreme to be effective. Historian John Reynold would later write:

> "Occasional attempts were made to enforce this act in the courts, but it seems that no case resulted in the conviction of the offender. The [African Americans], as a class, were little affected, and the few who undertook to assert their social rights in the courts were so plainly actuated by the desire for notoriety or political advantage that they gained nothing by their performances. The law [would] soon become a dead letter. It [would be repealed] in 1889."

Just prior to adjournment on March 1, the Legislature appropriated $125,000 for expenses incurred during this session, in which 110 acts were passed.

This concluded the first two years of Republican Machine rule within South Carolina, by African American men and their European American collaborators, many of the latter recently from the northern States. A tabulation of the consequences follows:

State debt increased from $5,407,000 to $14,833,000. A few months later, at the close of December, the debt would be $18,575,000. By that time all counties except Anderson and Fairfield would be in debt. Pay to public school teachers was $57,000 in arrears. The tax revenue for State and counties combined was $1,764,000 (period ending October 1869), and this compared to less that $550,000 per year prior to State secession.

Less than $100,000 was provided each year for free public schools, this going only to African American children. That was only a little more than school spending prior to State secession, which had been $74,400, that going only to help with education of indigent European American children. Of the public school for African Americans, historian John Reynold would later write:

> "Under the Republican Administration the public school system, for the first two years at least, was the merest pretense. Few schools were wholly free — the plan chiefly in vogue being the payment of money to a private school, thus reducing the tuition fees. The [African American] schools received considerable aid from churches or benevolent societies in the northern States and thus managed to keep up a semblance of school work. The collection of the poll tax was so loosely conducted that only those who had some taxable property were required to pay. The [African American people] were thus almost exempted from making the only contribution to the support of government to which, under the [State] Constitution and laws, they were subject."

Fraudulent behavior at the Land Commission was worse, yet. Historian John Reynold would write:

> "The Land Commission, to which the Legislature has allowed $700,000 for the purchase of 'homes for the homeless, lands for the landless,' had accomplished little but the acquisition of quantities of land, much of it at prices far beyond its real value, accompanied with many scandalous transactions. False entries in deeds of conveyance were made, so that the price paid for the property might appear more than the sum received by the seller. In one of these 'deals' the Land Commission divided $90,000 as their profits. The doings of the Commission were tainted throughout with fraud, and there were, besides, irregularities involving loss to the State." [R201;125-135]

Meanwhile, Ulysses Grant, for 9 months, had led an effort to "annex" the Dominican Republic to the United States. The draft of a Treaty of Annexation had been signed and submitted to the Senate Foreign Relations Committee on January 10, where Charles Sumner was preventing its progress. The draft Treaty was an annexation agreement between the Grant Administration and the Dominican Government led by President Buenaventura Báez. The United States Navy and the French Navy were competing for control of the splendid Dominican harbor at Samaná Bay. Sumner biographer David Donald would provide some background:

> "The Báez regime was about to collapse. Chronically bankrupt, [Báez] was currently operating on funds supplied, at an exorbitant rate of interest, by the English firm of Hartmont and on money from the United States Secret Service funds. Meanwhile, a powerful insurrection against his [government] had been started [by a group of Dominicans] and it was receiving assistance from the new President of Haiti, Nissage Saget. Since midsummer of 1869 the Báez regime had been propped up not merely by American money, but by United States naval power. The Secretary of the Navy had ordered the *U. S. S. Tuscarora* into Dominican waters [and informed Haiti that] 'an act of hostility to the Flag of the United States' . . . would 'provoke hostility in return'."

By burying the draft Treaty of Annexation in his Foreign Relations Committee, Charles Sumner had been trying to kill it. Given a few more weeks, he hoped, the Treaty would die because its sponsors in the Dominican Republic would be defeated in the civil war that was raging over the island at the time. This was on Hamilton Fish's mind when, one early March evening, he stopped by Sumner's house to talk. Fish immediately observed that Sumner was in "a morbid and disturbed condition of mind and temper." Attempting to show sympathy, Fish asked Sumner what was making him so sad. Sumner bellowed: "You can't understand my situation. Your family relations are all pleasant. Why, many and many a night when I go to bed I almost wish that I may never awake." Fast of mind, Fish immediately saw an opportunity to remove Sumner from the Senate Foreign Relations Committee at the same time that he helped the poor lonely man seek some happiness. Fish suggested that Sumner simply go to Europe and study and write in a more leisurely atmosphere. Then he offered the job of Minister to Great Britain: "There is the English mission. Take it. It is yours." But Sumner replied: "No, I would not like to interfere with Motley, who is my friend." But Fish quickly tossed out that concern: "You are right; you should go without any official cares or duties." But Sumner would not budge. But Motley was in trouble of losing his job anyway, for Grant was making plans to replace Motley with Frederick Frelinghuysen, of New Jersey.

Then, on March 14, Ulysses Grant, concerned that the Báez government might soon be turned out of office by a political coup or through Haitian aggression, sent an urgent special message to the Senate in an attempt to force Charles Sumner to present a Treaty Ratification recommendation to be debated on the Senate floor. Sumner complied and reported the Ratification question out of Committee. Under Sumner's leadership, the Committee majority report, by a 5-to-2 vote, recommended that the Treaty be refused. During secrete Senate debate Sumner warned that taking the Dominican Republic raised "great financial, political, and moral questions." He expressed concern that Dominican government debt might be too big a burden, prompting military action by nations holding the debt. And most importantly, taking the Dominican Republic would thrust Federal armed forces into the longstanding struggle between Dominicans and Haitians — with the revolutionary Haiti government occupying the western half of the island of Hispaniola, Sumner reasoned that it would be a "very expensive business to maintain peace in the island." Sumner warned that taking the Dominican Republic would start a Federal campaign to acquire many, or all, of the islands in the Caribbean — and Haiti would be next. That the vast majority of people living in the Caribbean were of partial or full African ancestry disturbed Sumner the most. Apparently ignoring Scots, Irish, Germans, French, and Africans, Sumner pleaded that the United States was "an Anglo-Saxon Republic, and would ever remain so by the preponderance of that race." On the other hand, Sumner cautioned, the West Indies were "[mixed African-European] communities" where the "[African] race was predominant." Therefore, Sumner reasoned, those islands "should not be absorbed by the United States, but should remain as independent powers, and should try for themselves to make the experiment of self-government." The Federal Government must limit its involvement in the Dominican Republic to "giving them moral support and counsel, as well as aid them in establishing a firm and energetic republican government of their own." This policy would ensure that the Dominican Republic and other Caribbean nations would emerge as "a free confederacy, in which the [African] race should predominate. . . . To the African belongs the equatorial belt, Sumner effused, "and he should enjoy it undisturbed." He did not say so, but Sumner was also probably working toward establishing the Caribbean as a destination to which African Americans would be encouraged to emigrate. There were so many African Americans living in the former Confederate States, and the more adventurous had already begun a migration wave into the northern States, changing the racial makeup of their populations.

Ulysses Grant came over to the Capitol Building "for several days" and "called some 14 Senators" into the President's room to encourage them to vote to Ratify the Treaty. Grant explained that the faith of the Federal Government had already been pledged and that, in a plebiscite on the question, Dominicans had voted 15,169 to 11 to be annexed to the United States. He described the islands resources as "boundless" and touted Samaná Bay's utility as a base of operations for the American Navy. And Grant explained that, if the Federal Government refused to take the Dominican Republic, the French probably would, for they wanted Samaná Bay for the French Navy. If the French moved in, then the Monroe Doctrine would force the Federal Government to oppose France. After a week of secret debate, Grant realized that Sumner's support among Senate Democrats and a small group of Senate Republicans had the votes to refuse the Treaty, for a two-thirds vote was required for Ratification. So, a vote was deferred for two months while the Senate moved on to other issues. [R73;435-447]

On March 30, the Federal Government validated the Reconstructed State of Texas. Only Georgia remained under Military Rule.

(2Q70)

On April 1, in the Federal Senate, Senator-elect Adelbert Ames of Mississippi was sworn in, after waiting 5 weeks for a decision regarding his credentials. The main problem had been satisfying the constitutional residence requirement. In the words of historian James Garner, Ames "owned no real property in [Mississippi], paid little or no taxes for the support of the government, knew little of the State and its needs; in fact, was a stranger to the people, and had little respect for their tastes, habits, and prejudices. . . . [Regarding that concern, Ames] had been summoned before the Senate Judiciary Committee and asked as to his intention of making Mississippi his permanent residence at the time he [had become] a candidate." Unable to give a satisfactory answer, the Committee reported "that he was not an inhabitant of the State at the time of his election, and was not, therefore, eligible to a seat in the Senate." However, for political reasons, the main body of the Federal Senate summarily rejected that reasoning, by a vote of 40 to 12 and Senator Justin Morrill of Vermont immediately escorted Ames to the desk and he was sworn in. [R204;275-277]

Meanwhile, in Memphis, Tennessee, Jeff Davis was hearing a lot about the deplorable situation in Arkansas, which lay across the Mississippi River. A Federal soldier named Powell Clayton had remained in Arkansas after the completion of the Federal conquest with intent to amass a fortune. Of Powell's despotic rule over Arkansas, Hudson Strode would write:

> "Daring, dominating, shrewd, and unscrupulous, he got the [African American men] and incoming [Federal opportunists] to back him for Governor, and then despotically began plundering everything he could lay hands on. Soon his supporters filled all the important offices. With [approval by the Grant Administration,] he armed [African American men] to enforce his extortion policies. He created his own punitive militia to carry out his will. And according to T. S. Staples, in *Reconstruction in Arkansas*, his militia cost the taxpayers over $300,000. Clayton passed out lists of men opposing his will with the reputed remark that many of them might well be executed. The Federal Government was said to ignore his depredations; for was he not helping to insure Grant's re-election? The Republican Congressional Executive Committee assured him that Federal troops would be at his service if he proclaimed martial law, and the editor of *The Daily Republican*, Clayton's official organ, frankly stated: 'We'll make Arkansas Republican or a waste-howling wilderness'."

Of Arkansas under Powell Clayton's rule, historian Claude Bowers would later write, "soon 2,000 undisciplined [African American men] were preying on the people of 10 counties, stealing, arresting, imprisoning, executing, looting houses, and occasionally violating women." [R19;361]

Jeff Davis was powerless to help his fellow former Confederates, because any move he personally made would surely rally Republican politicians in the northern States to impose even more harsh rule. He could only sadly reflect upon the transformation that the Federals had wrought within the African American population of the former Confederate States. Biographer Hudson Strode would write:

> "Davis reflected that during the [Federal invasion], while most of the able-bodied [European American] men were absent from their homes fighting the invaders, the [African Americans] had behaved commendably. Though many [Federals] had eagerly expected [an African American] insurrection, cases of outrage committed by any of the 4,000,000 [southern States African Americans] were rare indeed. But [by 1869], with hate, rudeness, and vengeance instilled in them by agents of the [Republican Political Machines,] who advocated social equality for the South, the bemused [African Americans] had undergone a drastic change." [R19;361-362]

A University of Minnesota historian would conclude that "Thousands of [northern States] adventurers, drawn by the scent of plunder, had thronged thither to exploit the ignorant [African American male] vote and to organize it as the Republican Party." And Woodrow Wilson would headline the Republican political Reconstruction Program as "A carnival of public crime under the forms of law." [R19;362]

Meanwhile, from Georgia, Governor Rufus Bullock, in an attempt to preserve Machine control, appealed to the Federal Congress to block the State elections scheduled for November, 1870, in spite of the fact that Congress had blessed that election earlier in the Federal bill establishing the basis for seating Georgia's Representatives and Senators. If the election was allowed to take place as scheduled, Bullock simply did not have the votes to keep the Georgia Republican Machine in power. He figured the Democratic Party would win the election, as scheduled, and only Federal intervention could prevent it. A motion to delay the Georgia election until 1872 was presented to the Senate in April and Charles Sumner rose to assume leadership over the faction favoring the two-year delay:

> Sumner damned the scheduled Georgia election as "only an engine of [former Confederate] power," alleging that Senators who urged non-interference were using that old argument for State Rights that has historically been presented by owners of bonded African Americans. State Rights are dead: "a State is not a turtle which can shut itself within its shell, and enjoy its own separate animal existence; but it is a component part of this great Republic." Congress has ample power to regulate affairs in Georgia, and anyone disagreeing might "as well question that the sun shines or the river flows." [R73;448-449]

Wisconsin's Matthew Carpenter again challenged Sumner's repudiation of what little remained of State Rights. Carpenter demanded that Sumner, "emerge from his oracular and profane mysteries" and tell the Senate "precisely where in the [Federal] Constitution Congress was authorized to regulate the election of State officials." Then he condemned Sumner and like-minded Republicans for twisting the truth so blatantly in an attempt to infer that such interference was blessed in some obscure way in the Federal Constitution — that such twisted thinking shows, "how high the tides of intellectual license can rise." Sumner replied to Carpenter on April 18 in a formal speech before a packed Senate chamber:

> Sumner descended into the depths of name-calling as he accused Carpenter of "assuming the antiquated, well-worn, and now blood-bespattered garments of John Calhoun." Employing familiar twisted thinking, Sumner alleged that the limits on Federal power were defined by both the Federal Constitution and the earlier Declaration of Independence, which revolutionary colonial leaders had written to rally defiance against the British Throne. Pretending that both documents somehow jointly defined the powers given to the Federal Government, Sumner lumped the Declaration and the Constitution together as the "two great title deeds which our country holds" — whatever that means. Then Sumner bragged: "The [State Rights] idea that [Senator Carpenter] champions was buried under the apple tree of Appomattox."

At this point Sumner's view was supported by about half of the Republicans in the Senate, and slightly over half of those supporters were Republican Machine men from Reconstructed State Governments. The other Republican Senators would be voting with the Democrats to form a majority opposed to Sumner's ideas. Sumner had lost a lot of Republican following since his power-days of January, including the loss of powerful leaders such as Harlan, Edmunds and Morrill. By close votes Sumner failed to win passage of the Senate bill to postpone State elections in Georgia: (24 vs. 25, 30 vs. 31, and 29 vs. 30). Survival of a remnant of States Rights was dependent on the integrity of such weak threads. Biographer David Donald would write: "it was Sumner's first significant defeat in his attempt to lead the Senate during Grant's Administration." And, in the House, Ben "Beast" Butler would soon abandon his advocacy of a Federally-enforced two-year delay in holding Georgia State elections. By June he would be aligned with Ulysses Grant in favoring no Federal interference in those elections. Of this changed attitude, Butler would explain, "I have the good of my Party to my heart." [R73;449-451]

Charles Sumner did not involve himself much in May's Senate debate over new Federal laws aimed at crushing underground Democrat organizations, such as the secret Kuklux groups, which sought to weaken the overwhelming power of Republican Machines in the former Confederate States and also greatly depended on secrecy and intimidation. Instead, Sumner drafted his own bill to impose more Federal policing in those States, which proposed to involve Federal authorities whenever an African American alleged personal discrimination by providers of public transportation, by innkeepers, by church groups, by cemetery associations, or by school system authorities. Furthermore his bill outlawed segregated schools in those States. Sumner figured, with that much restructuring of southern States society, Republican policing authorities would find ample opportunities to put down underground resistance organizations. But Sumner's bill would lay buried in Lyman Trumbull's Senate Judiciary Committee until the last days of the session, when Trumbull would report the bill to the floor with a recommendation that it be defeated, and it would be. [R73;450]

However, the Republican leadership's bill would not be defeated. On May 30, Ulysses Grant would sign, "An Act to enforce the right of citizens of the United States to vote in the several States of this Union, and for other purposes." Popularly called the "Enforcement Act," its purpose was to "harry and oppress" the European American people and to "perpetuate [African American] rule" in the former Confederate States. Major commands within this Act are presented below:

> "All citizens of the United States who are or shall be otherwise qualified by law to vote at any election by the people in any State, territory, district, county, city, parish, township, school district, municipality, or other territorial subdivision shall be entitled and allowed to vote at all such elections, without distinction of race, color, or previous condition of servitude; any constitution, law, custom, usage, or regulation of any State or territory, or by or under its authority, to the contrary notwithstanding. . . ."

> "If any person by force, bribery, threats, intimidation, or other unlawful means, shall hinder, delay, prevent, or obstruct, or shall combine or confederate with others to hinder, delay, prevent or

obstruct, any citizen from doing any act required to be done to qualify him to vote or from voting at any election as aforesaid, such person shall . . . for every such offense be guilty of a misdemeanor, and shall, on conviction thereof, be fined not less than $500, or be imprisoned not less than one month and not more than one year, or both, at the discretion of the court . . . ."

"If two or more persons shall band or conspire together, or go in disguise upon the public highway, or upon the premises of another with intent to violate any provision of this act, or to injure, oppress, threaten or intimidate any citizen with intent to prevent or hinder his free exercise and enjoyment of any right or privilege granted or secured to him by the Constitution or laws of the United States . . . [each] shall be held guilty of a felony, and, on conviction thereof, and shall be fined or imprisoned or both, at the discretion of the court — the fine not to exceed $5,000, and the imprisonment not to exceed 10 years — and shall, moreover, be thereafter ineligible to and disabled from holding any office or place of honor, profit or trust created by the laws of the United States."

This law, written to apply throughout the United States — north, south and west alike — but, we must assume, not intended for uniform enforcement in all regions — placed the Federal Government and its military and policing powers in a condition of absolute supremacy over all matters related to the election process, including voter registration, campaign events, voter solicitation, balloting and ballot counting. However, it did not demand a secret ballot — I repeat, Did Not Demand a Secret Ballot — thereby permitting Republican Machines to continue to 1) round up African American men, 2) hand each a marked Republican ballot and 3) watch to ensure that each stuffed the ballot in the box. [R201;191-192]

Meanwhile, on May 31 in a renewed effort to win Senate Ratification of his draft Treaty for the Annexation of the Dominican Republic, Ulysses Grant rushed a message to Capitol Hill warning that "a European Power" had offered the Dominican Republic $2,000,000 for Samaná Bay. Obviously that "Power" wanted a military base for its western Atlantic and Caribbean navy. In response, as Chairman of the Senate Foreign Relations Committee, Charles Sumner submitted to the Grant Administration a laundry list demanding more information, including — the name of the "European Power" — a new investigation into previous Treaty negotiations — a new assessment of Dominican foreign debt — copies of all communications from Washington to Federal naval officers in the area — and an explanation of why Dominican authorities had imprisoned Connecticut businessman David Hatch. Ulysses Grant was furious at Sumner. Grant needed the support of two-thirds of the Senate to win Treaty Ratification. Instead, the June 30 vote would be spilt evenly at 28 to 28. The 28 opposing votes were cast by Republicans opposed to taking the Dominican Republic as a Federal Territory and Democrats, who felt obligated to oppose Grant. But this strange alignment of Sumner Republicans and Democrats foretold of Sumner's upcoming downfall. Biographer David Donald would reminds us that, "Back in December 1869, Sumner had called Republicans who cooperated with Democrats traitors to their Party; by June 1870 he was not merely voting with those same Republicans but was an ally of the Democrats himself."

Sumner's behavior in opposing the Dominican Treaty infuriated Grant, and made him determined to have Sumner removed as Chairman of the Senate Foreign Relations Committee. And Grant also resolved to reduce the political influence of the Republican Senators who had followed Sumner's lead, for the Dominican Treaty was a major goal of the Grant Administration. To reduce the influence of Charles Sumner and his supporters, Ulysses Grant would improve his ties to Ben "Beast" Butler, giving him more influence over political appointments concerning men in Massachusetts and neighboring States. He would improve his ties to Roscoe Conklin, and give Conklin's man, Thomas Murphy, the New York City Custom House collector job. Attorney General Rockwood Hoar was a Sumner man, so Grant would dismiss him and replace him with Amos Akerman, a Republican Machine man from Georgia. All of these shuffles were taking place quietly, and only careful observers were noticing the pattern. By July Grant's power realignments would be complete. About that time, New York Senator Ira Harris would write Sumner in alarm: "It seems to me that the present Administration is drifting away from us as its predecessor did." [R73;447-453]

On a related Caribbean issue, the House of Representatives had earlier passed, by an overwhelming majority, a Resolution calling for Ulysses Grant to issue a "Proclamation of Neutrality" in the conflict between Spain and Cuban Patriots, who were fighting for Cuban Independence. However, the House

Resolution was making no further progress, for when it arrived in the Senate, Charles Sumner had made sure it was referred to his Senate Foreign Relations Committee, where he and fellow Committeemen twisted the resolution into meaningless complexity. As presented to the Senate on June 23, Sumner's rewrite called the conflict a "barbarous outrage," condemned the bonding of African Cubans, condemned the "extraordinary efforts of the Spanish Government by violence and blood, to maintain unnatural jurisdiction of Cuba," and expressed sympathy for the cause of the Cuban Patriots. Although his rewrite sounded high and mighty, it did not call for any Federal effort that would be helpful to the Cuban Patriots in their fight for independence from Spain. The House bill was dead and America would not recognize the legitimacy of the cause of the Cuban Patriots. Before long the Spanish Government would complete the re-subjugation of Cuba, and Cubans would have to wait many more years before the Federal Government would take action to drive the Spanish out of Cuba. [R73;419]

Meanwhile, at Oxford, Lucius Lamar resigned his job as Chair of the Law School at the University of Mississippi. He was disgusted with what he perceived to be Republican plans to transform the University into a political propaganda organ, complete with numerous and unqualified African American teachers and students. While many professors seemed willing to stick it out for a while, Lamar was determined to not work in such an environment — he resigned effective at the end of the school year in June. He delivered the June 27 commencement address, essentially his goodbye message, which biographer James Murphy would summarize:

> "He cloaked himself in martyrdom and took leave of the University for the third and final time. With characteristic eloquence and sentimentality he closed his academic career in a commencement address as pertinent to the speaker as to the audience: 'And now, young gentlemen,' he said, 'as you go home I pray that you may have prosperity and happiness through life, with just enough of sorrow to remind you that this earth is not your home'." [R205;127, R206;98]

Lamar's father-in-law, Augustus Longstreet, would die the next month, July, at the age of 80 years. Lamar biographer and son-in-law Edward Mayes would much later describe the scene, based on memories of those present.

> "He died surrounded by the members of his family circle, [Lucius] Lamar and his wife being present. 'The death scene was almost a demonstration of immortality. His mind was clear and his soul was calm, in the assurance of Christian hope. Placing his finger upon his wrist, he marked the beating of his failing pulse [continuing to] his last heart beats, growing fainter and fainter.' —

> "'Look, Jennie, look!' exclaimed [Lucius] to his wife, as, amongst the awe-struck by-standers, 'he beheld a sudden illumination overspread the pale face of the dying man, [his beloved father-in-law], with a look of wonder and joy in his eyes, and every feature expressing unearthly rapture. That was the end'."

Augustus Longstreet had been a prominent leader in Georgia, Mississippi and South Carolina — a native of Augusta, Georgia; an 1813 graduate of Yale College; a prominent Georgia lawyer and judge; a minister in the Methodist Church and President of Emory College in Atlanta from 1839 until 1848; President of the University of Mississippi from 1849 to 1856, and, finally, President of the University of South Carolina from 1857 to 1861, when the school closed to allow students to fight to defend the Confederacy, at which point in time he had reached the age of 71 years. The Longstreet estate would be valued "at about $50,000 in real estate and cash," a portion of which would be inherited by wife Jennie, giving Lucius and the family improved financial resources with which to endure the Republican political assault upon the people of Mississippi.

In late July Lamar would enter into a new law partnership with his brother-in-law, H. R. Branham. Branham's wife Frances (Fannie) and Lamar's wife Virginia (Jennie) were Longstreet sisters. Branham was both a physician and a lawyer, being known as "Dr. Branham." The Longstreet's, the Branham's and the Lamar's had come to Oxford, Mississippi from Georgia, separately, around the years 1849-1850 — an apparent extended-family migration. Lamar's former law partnership with the young lawyer, Edward Clarke, had apparently been dissolved sometime earlier. [R205;38,128, R206,99]

Meanwhile, the stockholders of the Carolina Insurance Company re-elected Jeff Davis as President at their annual meeting, which was held on June 28. Traveling the sales territory considerably since starting his new job in November, Davis had discovered that, wherever he traveled, his presence boosted business. He had particularly worked to improve business in the Atlantic States, hoping to eventually move the company to the large financial center of Baltimore, Maryland. His Memphis friend, Mrs. Minor Meriwether, was pleased with Jeff's improving health, at the time writing:

> "He had endured that which might well bow any man's shoulders, but not even a dungeon and chains had been able to subdue that great man's lofty spirit. He still held himself as erect as [a Native American], his head set well and firmly on his shoulders, his eyes still held their native fire and force. He was tall and slender; his step was firm and steady. [Jeff] Davis' features were finely chiseled; his face, his glance, his general aspect denoted benevolence and impulses were pure and good." [R19;364]

(3Q70)

Immediately following the annual meeting of the Carolina Insurance Company, Jeff Davis left for Virginia and Maryland on business. After working in Richmond he took a few days off and traveled to The Greenbrier, a resort in White Sulphur Springs, West Virginia, where he was pleased to find many old friends. He particularly enjoyed seeing James Murray and Mary Chestnut. Conversation often turned to worry over Federal political oppression, and few had much reason to hope for better times. But Murray was hopeful enough to predict that, "The [Republican-led Federal] Government must fall to pieces of its own rottenness." The Grant Administration was surely proving to be rotten to the core, but Robert Lee had thought no better of the Republican Congress during the Johnson Administration. When Lee had been at The Greenbrier in late August of 1868, he had conversed with William Rosecrans, who, you will recall, had commanded the Federal Army in the battle at Murfreesboro, Tennessee, (Battle of Stones River) where my Grandfather would later live, and where, upon the floors of the farmhouse, the "Bloodstains" would remain. At this encounter Lee had told Rosecrans that, had he foreseen the abuse the Republicans would heap upon the conquered States, he would have somehow led his Confederate Army out of the encircling Federals at Appomattox and headed for the mountains to reorganize the men into underground guerrilla bands — explaining that, at the time of his surrender, he believed Abe Lincoln's political influence could overcome the hatred of men like Charles Sumner and Thad Stevens — a goal Andrew Johnson would prove powerless to accomplish. [R19;366-367]

Meanwhile on July 15, the Federal House and Senate accepted the Reconstructed State of Georgia in spite of the fact that Democrats seemed likely to expand their control over the Georgia House and Senate in the upcoming December election. (The elected would not take their seats until November 1871.) Rufus Bullock's effort to retain power through Federal military intervention was fading away. He had moved to Georgia from his native New York State in 1857 and aligned with the Republican Party following the Federal conquest. Shortly before the new State House and Senate would convene, in late October of 1871, Bullock would flee Georgia to escape Impeachment, and, in a special election two months later, Democrat James Smith, a former Confederate officer, would be elected to complete Bullock's term. "By January 1872, the Georgia State Government would be fully under the control of the 'Redeemers,' as the State's resurgent [European American] conservative Democrats [would come] to be known."

Meanwhile on July 14, Ulysses Grant submitted to the Senate the nomination of Frederick Frelinghuysen to replace Charles Sumner's trusted colleague, John Motley as Minister to Great Britain. Grant's decision to oust Motley appeared to be a direct result of the rejection of the Treaty to annex the Dominican Republic (the Senate had finally rejected the Treaty on June 30 and Grant called for Motley's resignation on July 1). During Senate debate on Frelinghuysen's appointment, Sumner praised Motley "as a generous American, an ultra-American, whose Americanism shone in all his writings and even in the selection of the subject of his history." The dismissal of Motley was, without question, the first of several moves by Grant to maneuver Charles Sumner out of the Chairmanship of the Senate Foreign Relations Committee. And Henry Wilson warned that dismissing Motley would be interpreted by Massachusetts voters as an attempt to punish Sumner for opposing the Treaty to annex the Dominican Republic. But Roscoe Conkling tried to dispense a cover for Grant by spreading the story that Motley was being asked to resign because he had failed to present the Grant Administration's views on its "Claims on England," but that the request had been "postponed out of kindness and consideration" until July. And there was the rumor that Motley's dismissal was prompted by the death of George Clarendon and the subsequent appoint of George Granville as British Foreign Minister.

Sumner and other Massachusetts men had far too little muscle to save Motley's job. When the vote to confirm Frelinghuysen was tallied, only three Senators voted "no." Sumner abstained. But he would not abstain from denouncing Grant when he returned to Boston in late July. At both the Bird Political Club and at the Saturday Political Club, Sumner blasted away at Grant and Secretary of State Hamilton Fish and presented arguments intended to prove that Motley had been obedient to the wishes of the Grant Administration on its "Claims on England" policy. [R73;458-461]

Meanwhile, Jeff Davis sailed on the *Russia* for Liverpool on August 10. He planned to bring Varina and the children home to Memphis. Biographer Hudson Strode would write:

> "In England Davis found his four children flourishing. The little girl [Winnie] talked like a child twice her age. Independent-minded, but winning, she knew how to please when she wanted to. Maggie was quite lovely at 15, almost a young lady. The boys had grown quite enormously. Their mother said she could find no ready-made English suits to fit them and had to have their newest jackets made by a tailor. Thirteen-year-old Jeff took a man's size in the chest, and Billie at 9 required a 13-year-old's clothes."

Although Varina was surely glad to see Jeff, Strode would report that she "dreaded to return to the deplorable condition" of the Reconstructed States, and "she had a disturbing foreboding about Memphis." [R19;368]

Jeff Davis sailed back to Baltimore alone. Varina and the children would follow a few days later. Perhaps Jeff had been spurred to leave more promptly by news that his brother, Joseph had died on September 18. Joseph had been like a father to Jeff, and the loss was deeply felt. But additional sadness awaited Jeff in Baltimore.

Robert E. Lee had died at his home in Lexington, Virginia on October 12, succumbing to a debilitating blood circulation impairment (thrombosis), which had stricken him on September 28. Biographer Douglas Southall Freeman would tell of his last moments:

> "At last, on October 12, daylight came. The watchers stirred and made ready to give place to those who had obtained a little sleep. Out of the windows, across the campus, the students began to move about, and after a while they straggled down to the chapel to pray for him. Now it was 9 o'clock and a quarter past. His old opponent, Grant, was sitting down comfortably to breakfast in the White House. With axe or saw or plough or pen, the veterans of Lee's army were in the swing of another day's work. For him it was ended, the life of discipline, or sorrow, and of service. The clock was striking his last half-hour. In some corner of his mind, not wrecked by his malady, he must have heard his marching order. Was the enemy ahead? Had that bayoneted host of his been called up once again to march through Thoroughfare Gap or around Hooker's flank or over the Potomac into Maryland . . . moving . . . moving forward? Or was it that the war was over and that peace had come?

" 'Strike the tent,' he said, and spoke no more." [R151;581-582]

So it was upon Jeff's arrival from Liverpool that he encountered a reception committee which was waiting patiently to ask him to deliver the memorial address at Robert Lee's funeral. Since Robert Lee had died during Jeff's voyage, the first news he received was from the committee. The service had been scheduled for November 3. Biographer Hudson Strode would write, "The Lee family begged his acceptance, which he heartily gave." [R19;369]

The ceremony was a moving event held at the First Presbyterian Church in Richmond, complete with Confederate Soldiers and Sailors. And the Lee Monument Association was already at work raising funds. This eulogy was Davis' first speech before citizens of a former Confederate State since conquest had been consummated. The Richmond *Dispatch* of the following day described the ovation:

> "As [Jeff] Davis rose to walk to the stand every person in the house rose to his feet, and there followed such a storm of applause as seemed to shake the very foundations of the building, while cheer upon cheer was echoed from the throats of veterans saluting one whom they delighted to honor."

Jeff Davis delivered an appropriately extensive eulogy of which 1,600 words were printed in the next day's edition of the newspaper. Of their close personal relationship, Davis said:

"Robert E. Lee was my associate and friend in the Military Academy, and we were friends until the hour of his death. We were associates and friends when he was a soldier and I a Congressman; and associates and friends when he led the armies of the Confederacy and I presided in its Cabinet. We passed through many sad scenes together, but I cannot remember that there was aught but perfect harmony between us. If ever there was a difference of opinion it was dissipated by discussion, and harmony was the result. I repeat, we never disagreed."

Elsewhere in the address, Davis said, "I never knew Lee to falter to attempt anything ever man could dare." At another spot: "I never in my life saw in him the slightest tendency to self-seeking." And at another: "His moral qualities rose to the height of genius." It is interesting to note that Davis revealed Lee's willingness to consider a desperate guerrilla defense of the occupied Confederacy:

"When in the last campaign he was beleaguered at Petersburg, and painfully aware of the straits to which we were reduced, he said, 'With my army in the mountains of Virginia I could carry on this [defense] for 20 years longer."

Then, referring to the 5 years political Reconstruction, Davis explained, "In surrender [Lee] anticipated conditions that have not been fulfilled."

At the close of his thorough and fitting oration, Jeff Davis said of Robert E. Lee:

"Here he now sleeps in the land he loved so well, and that land is not Virginia only, for they do injustice to Lee who believed he fought for Virginia alone. He was ready to go anywhere on any service for the good of his country. . . . Here the living are assembled to honor his memory and there the skeleton sentinels watch over his grave. This day we write our words of sorrow with those of the good and great throughout Christendom, for his fame is gone over the water." [R19;369-370]

Meanwhile in South Carolina, some violence was afoot leading up to the fall 1870 election. We must remember that, at this time, the State Government presented a real and serious threat to the welfare of the European American residents — a threat to their ability to retain title to their family land, their homes and barns, even worry over getting enough food to properly feed their children. So elections were serious business for European American residents of South Carolina. And the hatreds of war still burned in many men's hearts, even though most men's heads had sorted out that it was important to be non-violent and cooperative. So the hearts and the heads were in a struggle. Breaking points were being occasionally reached. There were two sources of extreme agitation. First was European American men's struggle over submitting to rule by men who had come down from the northern States to grab political power. Second was European American men's struggle with being ruled at the ballot box by the votes of African American men, who were so gullible and unprepared for that important responsibility.

Historian John Reynold would explain how the behavior of the African American men had driven many European American men to prepare to defend their families and their property, with armed force if necessary:

"During the canvass preceding the State election of 1870 the [African American] militia constantly drilled and frequently moved about the country districts, to the disgust of the [European American] citizens and the terror of their wives and children. There were as yet not many acts of actual violence by [African American] militia, but their insolence was naturally a source of much irritation. For self-protection the [European Americans] armed themselves, but they were without actual organization. . . .

"The conduct of the [African American] militia became everywhere worse after the October election. Armed and equipped, they went about in groups or in regular formation, as if seeking a conflict. They incited their fellows to violence and incendiarism. They insulted ladies on the public highways. They moved about in the nighttime, firing their guns and in some instances shooting at dwelling houses. Behind these lawbreakers was the hostile local government sustained by the Federal authority. The apparent helplessness of the [European Americans] . . . seemed to give the idea that the power of the militia was sufficient to insure them immunity, whatever the extent of their crimes against peace and order."

European American fears and feelings of intolerable transgressions — so graphically illustrated to husband, wife and children alike by the behavior of militia companies — coupled with feelings of helplessness — so hard to suppress in the hearts of former battle-hardened Confederate soldiers — gave rise in South Carolina to an organization named the Kuklux Klan, normally referred to as the "Kuklux". The word, "Kuklux" appears to have been derived from the Greek word for "circle" as if in a fraternity of brothers. And all members of the Kuklux were men, for women and children were excluded. The Greek word was "kuklos," but the more scary sounding variation, "Kuklux," seemed to quickly gain favor, perhaps because the clicking sound made when a man shouted "Klux" resembled the sound of a rifle's hammer striking its bullet. Then the one word was broken into two words, "Ku Klux". To denote a group of men, the word "clan," was adopted, as in a Scottish clan, but the spelling was changed to "Klan". The letters, "K. K. K.", certainly spooky enough, became famous signs left behind by members as they attempted to deal with the interests of and the protection of the European American residents of South Carolina and elsewhere in the Reconstructed States. In this book I will use the simple "Kuklux" to describe the group, as did historian John Reynold, who lived during those times, to encourage us toward an objective examination of the history with less of the prejudicial hatred all American's share today toward any small gang that might call itself the "K. K. K." Any little gang today that pretends to be the "K. K. K." is not related to the Kuklux underground groups that organized for self protection during the years of Republican Machine Rule. The Kuklux groups about which I will be reporting disbanded themselves 130 years ago. So do not equate the Reconstruction-era Kuklux to any group of men styled by that or a similar name who alleged to have been active since then.

Because the Kuklux was an underground political organization, its dealings was kept secret from the public, the military and government authorities. Resistance to Republican rule in South Carolina needed to be underground to have any reasonable chance at being effective. Strict discipline was required to maintain secrecy, considering that membership grew into the thousands. So something resembling a blood oath to secrecy was needed to gain membership. This also evolved into, in some cases, a carefully hidden written constitution. One of these constitutions would be found and turned over to Federal prosecutors who would use it in a trial in South Carolina in 1871 and 1872. I will show parts of this Kuklux constitution and the oath each member was required to make upon acceptance.

The oath was a blood oath, to the death. Here is the complete wording of the oath:

"I, _____, before the immaculate Judge of Heaven and Earth, and upon the holy evangelists of Almighty God, do of my own free will and accord, subscribe to the following sacredly binding obligation:

1. "We are on the side of justice, humanity and constitutional liberty, as bequeathed to us in its purity by our forefathers.

2. "We oppose and reject the principle of the Radical [Republican] Party.

3. "We pledge mutual aid to each other in sickness, distress, and especially pecuniary embarrassment.

4. "Female friends, widows and their households shall ever be special objects of our regard and protection."

"Any member divulging or causing to be divulged any of the fore-going obligation shall meet the fearful penalty and traitor's doom, which is death! Death! Death!"

Excerpts from the Constitution follow:

Article 1. "This organization shall be known as the _____ Order, No. _____, of the Kuklux Klan of the State of South Carolina."

Article 2. "The officers shall consist of a Cyclops and Scribe, both of whom shall be elected by a majority vote of the order and hold their office during good behavior."

Article 3. "It shall be the duty of the Cyclops to preside in the order . . . . The Scribe shall keep a record of the proceedings of the order . . ."

Article 4. Every person initiated into this order had to be 18 years or age or older, not a person of color, known to be of "good moral character," in no way incapacitated and had to be proposed as a candidate by the membership search committee.

Article 5. Fines were prescribed for violations of the rules.

Article 6. "Any member who shall betray or divulge any of the matters of the order shall suffer death."

Excerpts from the By-Laws follow:

Article 5. "Each member must provide himself with a pistol, Kuklux gown and signal instrument."

Article 6. Here, disciplining procedures were defined, including trials and appeals, including the threat of the death penalty and including the final appeal to the "Great Grand Cyclops of Nashville, Tennessee," who was empowered to grant a pardon to save the life of one charged.

We today may be squeamish about blood oaths and death penalties for revealing secrets or for squealing on another person, even though we frequently hear of such behavior among militant Muslim leaders today. But, looking back to the 1860's and 1870's, we must remember that those were hard times in South Carolina and the men I write about were former Confederate soldiers and officers who had faced death and seen 260,000 of their fellows die in the defense of their country. They were tough and battle-hardened men. To them death was the proper punishment for revealing secrets that might endanger the lives of dozens or scores of fellow members, just as death by firing squad was considered the fitting punishment for a cowardly soldier who fled from a battlefield. And you will later see that history shows that the discipline within the Kuklux must have been absolute and amazingly effective, for, hard as Federal and State authorities tried, they would be unable to successfully prosecute Kuklux members on charges of voter interference, intimidation or even murder, although many men would spend many days in jail awaiting trial.

Only one incident of Kuklux activity had been alleged in South Carolina, two years previously, during the elections of 1868. Of that incident, it was alleged that members of the Kuklux had "crowded the polls at Rock Hill to prevent [African American men] from voting the Republican ticket. For this alleged conduct nobody was ever arrested or tried." However, the election of 1870 produced considerable Kuklux activity in the State, which will be described shortly, after setting the stage for the 1870 State election campaign, complete with voting results.

On Monday, October 10, voters in South Carolina elected a Governor and other representatives and officials. Republicans remained in total control, the Democratic Party not offering any candidates. The election was between Factions of the Republican Party. The regular South Carolina Republican Party won by a heavy majority over the opposition Faction, Republicans in name, organized as the "Union Reform Party of South Carolina." The regular Republican candidate, the incumbent Governor, Robert Scott, won his second term over Reform candidate Robert Carpenter, by a vote of 85,071 to 51,537. You will recall that Governor Scott had come down from Ohio and had previously headed the Newly Independent African American Men's Bureau in South Carolina. Carpenter, formerly of Kentucky, was the Judge of the First Circuit. Regular Republican candidates for the Federal House defeated their opponents from the Reform Party in all 4 Federal House Districts:

Joseph Rainey, an African American of Georgetown, won in the First District.

Robert DeLarge, an African American of Charleston, won in the Second District, but the Federal House would vote to refuse him a seat because "the election had been so tainted throughout with fraud that nobody was lawfully elected."

R. B. Elliot, an African American of Edgefield, won in the Third District.

A. S. Wallace, a European American of York, took the Fourth District in a contested result. His opponent, I. G. McKissick, would challenge the election result before the Federal House, but fail to win his argument.

The Reform Party had been the first to organize for the election. The movement had begun during a conference of newspaper editors held in Columbia on March 16. The editors had resolved: "In the judgment of this conference a Convention of the people of the State, opposed to Radicalism and in favor of good and honest government, should be held in the city of Columbia at some convenient time, for the purpose of nominating a State ticket, which, while assuring equal and exact justice to all, will afford some degree of security, prosperity and good government."

This Convention, held on June 15 as proposed, had been widely attended by Delegates from across South Carolina. It's Platform, duly approved, asserted that the Convention was "assembled to organize the good people of the State in an effort to reform the present incompetent, extravagant, prejudiced and corrupt administration of the State Government and to establish instead thereof just and equal laws, order and harmony, economy in public expenditures, a strict accountability of office-holders, and the election to office of men of known honesty and integrity." Calling itself, the "Union Reform Party of South Carolina," it had nominated as its candidate for Governor, the First Circuit Judge, Robert Carpenter of Charleston, and as its candidate for Lieutenant Governor, Matthew Butler, who had been the most important cavalry officer in Hampton's Legion, rising to the rank of Major General. A candidate was nominated for each Federal House District. A full ticket was nominated as well for each county, typically nominating an African American for one of the county commissioner seats.

The following month, on July 26 in Columbia, the regular South Carolina Republican Party, referred to as the "Radicals," had held its convention. There, Delegates nominated Robert Scott for a second term as Governor, and a full slate of candidates throughout the State. Within its Platform was the land confiscation and redistribution plank, number 6, which promised to issue:

"An appeal to [the Federal House and Senate] to open to settlement and preemption the 48,000,000 acres of public lands in the southern States — to be sold to the landless under the provisions of the Homestead laws of the United States."

To assure election victories, Governor Scott and the Republicans encouraged considerable racial agitation and intimidation, using the State police, also known as the State Constabulary, to spearhead these efforts, with help from [African American] militiamen, who were duly armed. Historian John Reynold would say of the Constabulary:

"The Constables were in most instances rough characters — it being impossible (even if it had been desired) to get reputable citizens to undertake the work required. [African Americans] were put on the force almost equally with [European Americans] — and the [African Americans] selected were chiefly those whose own conduct was thought likely to bring on a disturbance. The efforts of the Constabulary were directed towards the accomplishment of these objects — to embolden the [African Americans] and inflame them against the [European Americans] to exasperate the [latter], and, by a combination of the two results, to bring about race conflicts which might be used to help the Republican Party of South Carolina."

"The [African American] militia were offensively active during the entire campaign. They drilled frequently — on nearly every occasion marching through some street or public road with bayonets fixed and drums beating. . . . They were especially fond of moving about in independent squads, carrying their guns and firing them off . . ."

Governor Scott had signaled this militant approach to the then-upcoming campaign season during the early months of the year at a speech delivered in Washington City. Of this event, historian John Reynold would write:

"In the early part of 1870 [Scott] made a speech in Washington [City], in which he pretended to depict the rebellious and bloodthirsty doings of the [European Americans] in South Carolina, and declared that the only law for those people was the Winchester rifle. Upon his return to the State he put his theory into practice by arming the [African American] militia and supplying them with an abundance of ball cartridges."

Accordingly, before the start of the campaign season, the Scott Administration issued 7,000 guns to [African American] militia companies, most of which operated in Charleston, Beaufort and the Upstate region, such as Laurens (8 companies armed with 670 rifles and 11,000 rounds of ammo), Union (3 companies with 10,000 rounds of ammo), York (3 companies), Fairfield (3), Chester (3), Spartanburg (3) and in other counties in the region (2 or 3 each). The companies were composed of African American men and led by African American men. Of these [African American] militia, historian John Reynold would write:

> "The captains of the different companies were invariably [African American men] all of them ignorant and some of them so poorly educated that they made their crossmarks in receipting for guns and cartridges. Each company operated in its own neighborhood, without any apparent recognition of superior authority."

Apparently, the State Militia companies were rather free to act as they chose, with the expectation in Columbia that, given a free reign, they were sure to cause trouble and incite pockets of violent retribution. On the other hand, the Scott Administration maintained firm control over its second armed wing, the State police force, called the Constabulary, commanded by John Hubbard and composed of about 500 Constables and assistants, each armed with a Winchester rifle and one or two pistols. Hubbard took orders from Governor Scott and successfully exercised control over his Constables and their assistants. Any group of European Americans caught organizing as community protective militia was disarmed. This forced most European American men to keep their private arms out of sight, but at the ready, if needed, as a last resort, to protect family and home from suffering violence.

The arming of African American militia drew a response from the secret organization known as the Kuklux. Of this, historian John Reynold would write:

> "Whatever the purposes of the organization, as indicated in its constitution and rules, the Klan was quiet until the latter part of 1870. Whatever the hostility of the [European Americans] to the [African American-empowered] government, whatever the acts which made the government at once a disgrace to its agents and a menace to the [European American] race of South Carolina, it is safe to say that the Kuklux would have remained inactive but for the arming of the [African American men] and the conduct of the State militia into which they were enrolled. . . . Threats against [European Americans] — against their persons and property — were not infrequent, yet if matters had rested at talk, the bloody doings of the Kuklux might never have been enacted. But the [African American men] followed the counsels of their leaders with frequent acts of house burning and, in one conspicuous case at least, with murder."

Yet, during this election season, the response of the European American men was tame, focused on self defense. Generally speaking, "for self-protection the [European Americans] armed themselves, but they were without actual organization." They tolerated the frequent practice of armed African American militia marching through town "'company front' so as to occupy the entire street." They tolerated the more violent agitators, such as June Mobley, a member of the State House of Representatives who was of partial African American ancestry, when Mobley "declared that for every Republican killed at the polls, 10 [European American] men should die." Militia activity in Laurens and Camden was particularly noteworthy, but physical violence was avoided during this election season. But tempers would soon reach a boiling point and Kuklux violence would erupt during the coming winter months.

In spite of the militant atmosphere encouraged by the Scott campaign, Scott's opponent, Judge Robert Carpenter of Charleston, the Reform candidate, along with the candidate for Lieutenant-Governor, Matthew Butler, managed to deliver speeches to the people in every county in the State. Of their speaking tour, historian John Reynold would write:

> "[Carpenter and Butler] addressed meetings in every county — sometimes under circumstances requiring coolness, courage and consummate tact to prevent a breach of the peace, possibly attended with bloodshed, such as the [Scott campaign] managers plainly desired."

On Election Day, violence was less frequent than was probably expected, being suppressed by the substantial increase in Federal troops during the time. Historian John Reynold would write:

"There were incipient riots at several polling places, but the coolness of the [European Americans] prevented serious results. In most instances the trouble was caused by the misconduct of the State Constables in interfering where they had no authority. Advised that in the event of bloodshed they would surely be among the sufferers, they very soon changed their procedure. At several county seats there were [Federal] troops, but their officers strictly obeyed orders — their instructions being not to interfere except to preserve the peace"

African American supporters of the Scott campaign not infrequently intimidated and even physically attacked the few and generally more intelligent African Americans who were inclined to support the Reformers — bravely and without protection by today's "secret ballot" laws. Of one incident near Charleston, historian John Reynold would report:

Not far from Charleston, "a number of the more intelligent [African American men] voted the Union Reform ticket, and for this they were pursued by [supporters of the Scott campaign], some of these armed with guns, and in several cases were beaten almost to death. Similar conduct marked the course of [African American men] elsewhere on the coast — [African American men] being cruelly beaten for having voted with the Reformers."

There was bloodshed in Laurens the day following the election, the trouble growing out of a fight between a European American man and a State Constable, to which some State militiamen responded, followed by a retreat into their armory. A group of European American men then proceeded to attack the armory. That fight left 3 militiamen injured, one fatally. After night fell violence continued, resulting in the death of 5 African Americans of the regular Republican Party, including a just-elected Representative to the State House and a candidate for probate judge. Some prominent European American men were arrested and accused of the murders, but none ever went to trial and those arrested were most likely the wrong men.

This completes the account of the 1870 election in South Carolina. Similar stories would persist for 1872, 1874 and 1976. [R201;135-153,182-183]

(4Q70)

Jeff Davis arrived back in Memphis on November 8. He was named as first of 4 Executors of brother Joseph's will. The will bequeathed $20,000 to each of Jeff's 4 children, but there was not cash on hand from which any significant sums could be dispersed, because Ben Montgomery had not paid any interest on the 3,000 acres of farmland along the Mississippi River, which had once been Joseph's and Jeff's farms. The purchase price of $300,000 was due in 1876, but prospects of Montgomery raising that kind of money were slim. Joseph's estate held the deed to the farms as collateral on the loan, but the language of the deed still listed Joseph as owner of both farms, for Joseph had never deeded Jeff's farmland to him. Before the Federal invasion, Joseph's reluctance to deed over the farmland was thought to have resulted from his determination to make sure that Varina or her parents never got the land. But after the Federal invasion into Mississippi, Joseph's reluctance was surely a clever ploy to discourage the Federals from confiscating his brother's land.

Ben Montgomery had understandable problems turning a profit from the two farms. He and his sons had spent considerable money on the construction of levees to contain the Mississippi during floods, for flooding was becoming more of a problem each year as farming activity up-river (particularly in the northern States) destroyed the natural water-holding capacity of prairies and forests. But the Montgomery's levees were less effective than intended because neighboring farmers had not built connecting levees on their sections. Every flood was taking away more valuable top-soil. The Montgomery's demanded greater effort from the African American's they hired as farm workers than had Jeff and Joseph, causing many to quit and seek easier jobs elsewhere (building levees is hard work). Furthermore, African American preachers had come through stirring up discontent. "Tenants moved away; and then back again." It seems that Ben Montgomery, although personally a hard-working and industrious man, was finding out that the typical post-conquest African American laborer refused to believe that being newly independent did not mean getting paid for doing little or nothing. [R19;371-372]

Meanwhile during a 38-day speaking tour booked through James Redpath's "highly organized, professional Lyceum Bureau," Charles Sumner vigorously attacked Ulysses Grant and defended John

Motley's career as Minister to Great Britain. By delivering a total of 38 speeches in the northeastern States and in the States of New York, New Jersey, Pennsylvania, Michigan, and Illinois, Sumner earned $7,000, money he sorely "needed to maintain his expensive Washington household and to subsidize the publication of his *Works*." But the speaking tour had been physically difficult for Sumner, who grew more exhausted, more irritable and more careless the further west he traveled. Sumner won few converts among his audiences, who were generally unreceptive to his legalistic arguments. For example at his speech before students at the University of Michigan, the audience cheered loudly when, after sitting through two and one-half hours of lecture, Sumner said: "In conclusion." Those cheers made Sumner so mad that he refused to accept his speaking fee. And he had been careless about who heard his frequent tirades against the Grant Administration. The most important example of such carelessness took place at the Chicago home of former Congressman Isaac Arnold, where Sumner had stopped to visit after delivering a speech. Sumner blasted away at Grant's "act of sheer brutality" toward Motley, and alleged that underlings such as Orville Babcock, Hamilton Fish, and George Boutwell, were responsible for Administration foreign policy failures. He also criticized Senator Timothy Howe for supporting Grant's foreign policy. But a reporter for the Chicago *Republican* was in the room, heard everything and issued a comprehensive newspaper report that was widely reprinted in major newspapers. Such indiscretion was strengthening Grant's campaign to oust Sumner from his powerful post as Chairman of the Senate Foreign Relations Committee.

To proud to resign, John Motley had decided to force Ulysses Grant to officially fire him — upon receiving Secretary Hamilton Fish's original request for a resignation, Motley had "[sworn] at [Ulysses Grant], damned his countrymen as vulgar and brutal, and wished the damned [Ulysses Grant Administration] might be destroyed." In December, Motley would explain to his most important supporter, Charles Sumner: "I refused to resign because it would be to confess that I had done something which would not bear examination — and I know I have been as faithful, loyal and diligent . . . as [Ulysses Grant] and [Hamilton Fish]."

During this time Ulysses Grant and Hamilton Fish had been experiencing great difficulty in finding a man to replace John Motley as Minister to Great Britain. After the Senate had confirmed Grant's first appointment, the successful appointee, Frederick Frelinghuysen had announced he would not accept it. Thereafter, in succession, Grant and Fish had offered the normally-prized and normally-sought-after Minister job to the following Senators and Congressmen: Lyman Trumbull, Lot Morrill, George Edmunds, Oliver Morton, Timothy Howe, George Williams, and James Blaine. Failing to get a Senator or Congressman, they offered the job to Andrew White, who was President of Cornell University. White refused to take the job. They even offered the job to newspaperman Wendell Phillips, the fellow who had written such powerful Republican propaganda during the days of Bleeding Kansas. Surely Wendell Phillips would relish doing battle against Great Britain; but he refused the job, too. Apparently no one wanted to be hurled into the battle over the Federal Government's "Claims On Britain" and related Federal threats to subjugate Canada. That is, not until the job would be offered to Robert Schenck, a former Congressman from Ohio. Schenck would accept the offer. His appointment to the job would be submitted to the Senate in late January. [R73;461-464,479]

Meanwhile, Varina arrived in Memphis late in November or early in December, a few weeks after Jeff had arrived. In accordance with Jeff's arrangement, Varina had put the two boys in Mr. Brand's church school in Baltimore. The older daughter, Maggie had stayed behind in England under the guardianship of Varina's sister Margaret. So Varina arrived in Memphis with the youngest child Winnie and Mary Ahern, who served as a nanny. For the time being, Jeff, Varina and Winnie lived in a Memphis hotel, for Varina remained hopeful that Jeff might soon relocate.

Friends still encouraged Jeff Davis to launch the long-awaited writing of a major history of the Confederacy. But he believed that too little time remained in the day after fulfilling his duties for the Carolina Insurance Company. One who encouraged Davis to write was William Preston Johnson, who on December 11 urged him by letter, a portion of which is presented below:

"When I see how steady is the trust and affection reposed in you by the great mass of the [former Confederate] people, I feel that you owe it to yourself not to die without vindicating the truth of history. It has rarely been the lot of a man who has acted great deeds to be able by education and circumstances to tell the story of them. I do not believe any man ever lived who could dare to tell in the light more fully what was done in the dark, than you can. It seems to be a friendly duty to warn you not to forget your design." [R19;370-373]

Finally, some good agriculture news: the 1870 United States cotton crop, almost all of it from the southern States, had been far larger than the poor crop of 1869, totaling 3,122,551 bales, of which 2,206,480 were being exported. The 1869 crop had only been 2,366,467 bales, substantially lower than production during the 1851-1860 decade, which had ranged between 2,454,442 and 4,861,292 bales, annually. But the 1870 cotton price was depressed, partly because of increased supply and partly because of a war between France and Germany. The 1870 average cotton price per pound quoted in New York was 23.98 cents, much lower than the 29.01 cents average of 1869, but still far higher than during the 1851-1860 decade, where prices had ranged from 9.50 to 13.51 cents. But production costs had risen substantially following the conquest of the Confederacy, meaning that Mississippi farmers were suffering financial stress in spite of the large 1870 cotton crop. In an autumn address to the Agricultural and Mechanical Association of Carroll and Choctaw Counties (Mississippi), Lucius Lamar offered his advice regarding how farmers ought to adapt to the changing times.

Lamar recommended that Mississippi farmers diversify and rotate crops, use more labor-saving machinery, and pursue higher culture of fewer acres. He warned that, by focusing almost exclusively on the cotton cash crop, farmers were suffering financial loss by spending too much on labor and supplies and, by not rotating, they were also damaging the fertility of their soil. The answer was to diversify crops by also raising meat (hogs, cattle and poultry) and planting food crops (corn, potatoes, etc.). "Those who raise cotton exclusively grow poor; those who raise cotton, corn, meat, potatoes, etc. grow in wealth, and work no harder."

Then Lamar turned his attention to greater mechanization and to an understanding of the proper role of government in the lives of farmers and other citizens. He observed that, in the northern States, ambitious men "were using government as an instrument for [their] own enrichment," whereas, in the southern States, in prior years, men had been insistent on "enforcing the principles of constitutional government." Then Lamar closed his address, advocating that his audience embrace the attitude toward government that had been held by their fathers:

"Choose you then.

"Will you have honor? Then adhere to the practices and principles of our fathers; stand for the rights of the people and for honest government economically administered.

"Will you have [personal] profit? Then cast in your lot with those who administer the government for [personal] profit, who oppress the poor and the laborer . . . .

"I want no response to these questions. I read it in our eyes. The pure spirit of patriotism illuminates your countenance. In vain will the harpies who prey upon our stricken land beckon to you to sell your birthright for a mess of pottage." [R205;129-130, R210;10-11]

Meanwhile in Washington City, Ulysses Grant, as he prepared his Message to Congress, was most concerned about the "Claims on England" issue, which was also most dear to Charles Sumner. Grant was furious at the "semi-independent, but irresponsible" colonial authority that called itself the "Dominion of Canada." But Great Britain steadfastly continued to refuse to pay the Federal Government any money in response to its so-called claims arising from Federal and private losses that had been inflicted by Confederate defenders. The Grant Administration was no closer to forcing money out of Great Britain than it had been during British diplomat John Rose's visit to Washington in July 1869. So Grant decided to raise the stakes in the game. He decided to recommend that the Federal Government borrow money and pay the claims alleged by private individuals and companies, such as higher insurance premiums and losses inflicted by Confederate warships such as the "C. S. S. Alabama." That way, Grant reasoned, the Federal Government would have both "ownership of" and "responsible control of" all American demands against Great Britain.

Furthermore, Ulysses Grant had reason to believe that Great Britain might succumb to increased threats of a Federal invasion into Canada. Why? Because the security of the British Empire was being threatened by a war between France and Prussia, which had been raging for 5 months. Furthermore, the Russians had disobeyed Treaty restrictions and were setting up a fleet of warships in the Black Sea and constructing fortifications in the region. If the Ottoman Empire were to fall to the Russians, then the British colony of India might be next. With war raging in Europe, the British Government had become suddenly anxious to avoid a Federal invasion of Canada which would obviously be accompanied by powerful Federal attacks on the British merchant marine fleet. The British could not fight a war in Europe, India and North America at the same time!

Secretary Hamilton Fish had notified the British Foreign office back on September 26 that the Federal Government would relax two of its previous demands. It would no longer refuse to submit Federal claims to international arbitration, and it would no longer demand that Great Britain make Canada a wholly independent nation by severing all of its "Commonwealth" ties to Canadians. Of course, Fish was not making any pledge to honor the sovereignty of a Canadian National Government, and Great Britain knew that the threat of a Federal invasion would remain a concern. But Fish's relaxation on the arbitration and "Commonwealth" issues encouraged the British Government to plan to send their Diplomat, John Rose, back to the United States to assess the political situation first-hand.

Furthermore, New England fishermen who wanted to fish the rich waters off the Canadian coast were angry that their fishing boats were being seized when they entered fishing grounds claimed by Canada. And "Fenian" Irish Terrorists were raiding into Canada as well. Biographer David Donald would write:

> "In a dispute over the rights of United States fishing vessels operating within what were claimed to be Canadian waters, the [Canadian] Government seized ships without warning and sometimes sold them. Fierce animosity also existed in Canada over damages wrought by the Fenian [Irish] raiders, who in the summer of 1870 [had] again struck from bases in the United States. Canadians suspected that the United States had been behind the brief rebellion led by Louis Riel in the Red River settlement of Manitoba, while in faraway British Columbia settlers were angry over the still unsettled San Juan boundary dispute."

As the Senate convened for business in early December, Charles Sumner, the highest-seniority Republican Senator, was in grave danger of losing his powerful position a Chairman of the Senate Foreign Relations Committee. The Party leadership, Ulysses Grant included, had no further use for the intellectual and dogmatic idealist who had been so useful to the Party during its crucial formative years, when Abolitionism and Exclusionism was central to winning political control over the northern States. The key Republican leader was Zachariah Chandler, who headed up the Republican Senate Caucus Committee, which was responsible for making Committee assignments. Would Chandler's Caucus Committee kick the most senior Republican off the Committee he had chaired since 1861? What about Sumner's most loyal supporters on the Committee: James Patterson and Carl Schurz? Would they be kicked off the Committee as well?

During the Caucus Committee meeting, Chandler moved to suspend the traditional seniority rules to enable his Committee to look at the best men to name to each Chairman position without regard to seniority. That motion went nowhere. Then Chandler moved to replace Carl Schurz on Sumner's Committee, but was rebuffed by others on the Caucus Committee who were too afraid of angering Americans of recent German descent. Finally Chandler moved to replace James Patterson with Roscoe Conkling, but Sumner successfully complained that would be doing "something extraordinary" and Patterson refused to resign the assignment. After several days, on December 8, Henry Wilson succeeded in passing a motion that the Caucus Committee leave the membership of the Senate Foreign Relations Committee untouched and proceed to draw up assignments for all the other Senate Committees. Charles Sumner had survived the immediate crisis, but he unwisely proceeded to overplay his hand the very next day as he renewed his attack on Ulysses Grant's efforts to annex the Dominican Republic and turn it into a Federal Territory.

> On December 9 Charles Sumner put forward a motion demanding that the Grant Administration submit to the Senate all papers and correspondence concerning negotiations over a Treaty to annex the Dominican Republic. Now it appeared that Sumner was beating a dead horse, because it was evident that Grant had insufficient votes in the Senate to win passage of his proposed annexation Treaty, and passage was necessary to authorize the taking of the Dominican Republic. In an attempt to defuse Sumner, Oliver Morton then moved to establish a three-man Committee to travel to the Dominican Republic, study the situation, and report back to the Senate on its findings. Morton's motion was reasonable and offered a way for Grant to save face, for study Committees

could invariable be relied upon to consume several months. Sumner tried to convince the Senate that Morton's motion could not be acted on until after the Senate acted on his Motion, for his information-gathering motion had been offered first. But the Senate ignored Sumner's argument and voted to first consider Morton's Study Committee. Then Sumner attempted to get the issue of Morton's Study Committee referred to his Senate Foreign Relations Committee for evaluation. It would be a few more days before this drama would reach its climax.

On December 21, Charles Sumner rose upon the Senate floor to deliver a long oration against Oliver Morton's motion to send a Study Committee to the Dominican Republic. Seeing a parallel with a Bible story about King Ahab, Sumner would publish the oration in a pamphlet titled "Naboth's Vineyard." Sumner, reliving his past Exclusionism passions, was greatly agitated as the day of his grand oration approached. Biographer David Donald would later conclude why Sumner was so excited:

"He believed that history was repeating itself. The proposal to annex the Dominican Republic was much like the Kansas-Nebraska bill and the [original Kansas State Constitution] — "by which it was sought to subjugate a distant Territory to [politicians who accepted African American bonding]." To make the parallel complete, Sumner expected that he would be the object of physical assault, as he had been in 1856. . . Reliving in his mind the trauma of the [caning administered by Preston Brooks], Sumner rose in the Senate on December 21 in the mood of a martyr prepared to make a final protestation of faith before burning at the stake."

The day for expounding upon "Naboth's Vineyard" arrived:

Rather ignoring the fact that all Morton sought in his resolution was to dispatch a Study Committee, Sumner alleged that the resolution would eventually entangle the Senate in "a dance of blood" from which it could not disengage itself before it would be forced to take control over the Dominican Republic. Sumner denounced Dominican leader Buenaventura Báez as a man detested by the people and only "sustained in power by the [Federal Government] that he may betray his country." He championed the nation of Haiti, which shared the large Caribbean island, Hispanola, with the Dominican Republic. Sumner claimed it was fitting that bonded Haitians of African ancestry had revolted against the French farmers on the western half of Hispanola, beginning in 1791 and, over the span of 13 years, had established a nation populated only by people of pure or partial African ancestry. So it was with intense emotion that Sumner accused Ulysses Grant of planning to take Haiti after he had taken the Dominican Republic. Americans have no business in either Haiti or the Dominican Republic, Sumner argued, for "the ordinance of Nature" had established the whole island as the domain of people of African descent. "It is their's by right of possession, by their sweat and blood mingling with the soil, by tropical position, by its burning sun, and by the unalterable laws of climate."

After Sumner concluded his "Naboth's Vineyard" speech, he was attacked by Republican leaders and found himself supported only by Senators in the minority Democratic Party. The debate went long into the night hours. Many Republicans thought his oration full of "wild expressions upon this simple question of a reference to a Committee," and sending off that Committee was "committing no man to anything:" when it returns, it would be "simply to report the facts and we are to pass upon them." As the hour passed midnight, Roscoe Conkling charged, "No sane man, no man of common sense, not maddened by passion or blinded by bigotry or hate" could have so defamed Ulysses Grant. Sumner's support dwindled further to only the Democrats. Biographer David Donald would conclude: "By the morning hours the new Republican leaders had painted their verbal portrait of Sumner: he was not sane; he was not loyal; and he was not even a Republican."

Then the vote tally struck Sumner about the head as if he was being caned by the ghost of Preston Brooks — the Senate defeated Sumner's motion to refer the question to the Senate Foreign Relations Committee and adopted Morton's resolution for a Study Committee by a whopping vote of 32 to 9. But 30 Senators abstained or were absent (probably in bed asleep). Immediately thereafter, the Senate adjourned. It was 6:37 in the morning.

Ulysses Grant **did** want to annex the Dominican Republic and, probably after that Haiti. This scenario was not a fantasy or a dream; it was Grant's secret objective. He had two reasons. The publicly admitted reason was national expansion and to establish a naval base in the Caribbean. The hidden reason was to facilitate deportation of African Americans from the established States, in both the northern States and in the southern States. He apparently hoped to lure many African Americans to the island of Hispanola once Federal control was in place:

Historian George Henry's study led him to conclude that voluntary Deportation was actually Grant's main motive. The idea was by no means new — Abe Lincoln, in April 1863, had sponsored the deportation of 430 African Americans (men, women and children) to Ile 'Vache, Haiti in a Federal colonization experiment, the first shipment in a planned program for 5,000 Deportees — the project was a sad failure; many died and those found alive were returned to the States 11 months later. In fact Grant would confess his desire for a Deportation Program in his *Personal Memoirs*, where he would state that he had hoped African Americans would emigrate to the island of Hispanola "in great numbers, so as to have independent states governed by their own race." Toward that objective two of the three men Grant selected for the Senate-authorized Study Committee had been prominent Abolitionism and Exclusionism activists and none were navy men. First, Grant selected Senator Benjamin Wade of Ohio, a long-time Exclusionists whose recent Senate re-election bid had failed. Second, he selected Samuel Howe, Sumner's old friend and early cohort in political activism. You will recall that Howe had known the Terrorist John Brown and that his wife Julia Ward Howe had written the John-Brown-inspired poem, "The Battle Hymn of the Republic," in late 1861, which soon afterward was set to the music of William Steffe, a South Carolina Methodist preacher, who had composed it as his religious song of invitation, "Say, Brothers." And, third, he selected Andrew White, President of Cornell, to appeal to the intellectual community. Furthermore, Grant named as Committee Secretary a fourth man, the famous Abolitionist and John Brown supporter, Frederick Douglass. As you will recall, Douglass was descended from a European American father and a mixed heritage European/African American mother. Before the Committee's departure, Sumner would encourage Douglass to oppose taking the Dominican Republic, even though doing so would facilitate the creation of a future hopefully prosperous state governed by men of African American descent. Sumner would explain to Douglass: "It is my nature to stand by the down-trodden . . . it was my duty to expose an act of wrong, one of the greatest in our annals, kindred to the outrage [settlers from the southern States had allegedly committed in Kansas Territory], and, if possible, of more historical importance. But Sumner's attempts to similarly influence his old friend, Samuel Howe would come to naught. Howe would conclude that Sumner had become "morally insane."

Leading Republicans became more determined to dethrone Charles Sumner after enduring his "Naboth's Vineyard" tirade. Roscoe Conkling declared: "The time has come when the Republican majority here owes to itself to see that the Committee on Foreign Relations is reorganized and no longer led by a Senator who has launched against the [Grant] Administration an assault more bitter than had proceeded from any Democratic member of this body." And Hamilton Fish was convinced that Sumner was "crazy – a monomaniac upon all matters relating to his own importance and his relations toward [Ulysses Grant]." Fish decided to find a means to "goad" Sumner into such irrational and verbally violent behavior that the Senate Republican leadership would be compelled to remove him as Committee Chairman. With that motive in mind, during the first days of January, Fish prepared a reply to stubborn John Motley's "End of Mission" dispatch just received from London — and he obtained Ulysses Grant's blessing upon each and every word of the reply. Motley's "End of Mission" dispatch alleged that he had been fired because he was a friend of Charles Sumner and likewise opposed to taking the Dominican Republic. Fish's reply assured Motley that he was "utterly mistaken" in his suspicion that Sumner was to blame for his being fired, adding that "many Senators opposed" taking the Dominican Republic, "openly, generously and with as much efficiency," as did Charles Sumner. Yet, Fish said, that those Senators "have continued to enjoy the undiminished confidence and the friendship" of Ulysses Grant. But Fish sternly warned Motley that Grant was, by his character, "sensitive of betrayed confidence" and prone to look with "scorn and loathing upon one who uses the words and the assurances of friendship to cover a secret and determined purpose of hostility." The dispatch was intended to infuriate Charles Sumner, and Oliver Morton made sure it received wide exposure by calling for its publication during the Senate session of January 5. Three days afterward, Fish wrote in his diary the opinion that Sumner was "partially crazy," with regard to "a certain class of questions, and wherever his own importance, or influence are concerned, or anything relating to himself, or his views, past or present, or his ambition, he loses the power of logical reasoning and becomes contradictory, and violent, and unreasoning, and that is mental derangement."

Meanwhile, British diplomat John Rose arrived in Washington to measure the intensity of the Grant Administration's demands that Great Britain pay enormous sums of money to the Federal Government and to shipping companies in response to "Claims on England" threats. But Rose was not on an official diplomatic mission, for his cover was to "discuss a new United States bond issue to be floated by his banking firm." During an informal meeting, Fish assured Rose that the Federals would not object to the Canadian-British "Commonwealth" arrangement. Furthermore, Fish said that the Grant Administration was abandoning Charles Sumner's "extravagant ideas in reference to England's responsibility for the prolongation of the [invasion] by her premature recognition of belligerency." So Rose interpreted that information as an encouraging change in posture, for Sumner's rhetoric was designed to position Great Britain as having been almost a full-fledged military ally of the defeated Confederacy. Pleased with Fish's offer to reduce the scope of the "Claims on England" charges, Rose suggest that the British Government might agree to pay Federal shippers for the losses they suffered at the hands of Rafael Semmes' crew on the *C. S. S. Alabama*. But Rose said he doubted that the British Government would pay for losses suffered at the hands of any other Confederate warships. So Fish and Rose rather agreed to whittle the list of grievances under the "Claims on England" threat down to just one issue: payment for losses suffered at the hands of Rafael Semmes' crew on the *C. S. S. Alabama*. Of course, Fish realized he could never succeed with stripping Charles Sumner's long list of "Claims on England" grievances down to just the shipping damages suffered at the hands of Rafael Semmes' crew on the *C. S. S. Alabama* until — after Sumner was deposed as Chairman of the Senate Foreign Relations Committee. Biographer David Donald would write of how, "[Fish and Rose] agreed upon an elaborate formula to evade Charles Sumner's wrath and to provide a face-saving avenue for both sides:"

> "Great Britain would first propose the creation of a Joint Commission to settle all the problems connected with Canada — fisheries, San Juan boundary, and the like; the [Federal Government], in accepting, would suggest the inclusion of the [losses suffered at the hands of Rafael Semmes' crew on the *C. S. S. Alabama*] as well; and the British would then agree." [R73;465-483]

The Year of 1871

(1Q71)

Meanwhile in Union County, South Carolina, seeds of violent conflicts, sown by months of African American militant behavior, had germinated and grown and were bearing their fruit — ugly fruit that represented perhaps the saddest tale from the era of Republican "Reconstruction" Rule. This event began on or near the first day of January 1871. Historian John Reynold would describe the trouble:

> "In [early] January, Matt Stevens, an inoffensive [European American] man who had lost an arm in the Confederate service, was going from Union [County] Court House, driving his wagon in which were some barrels of whiskey whence he was transporting in the pursuit of his business as a wagoner. On the public highway he met a company of [South Carolina African American] militia, numbering about 40, some of whom demanded that he should give them whiskey. He complied to the extent of giving them all that he had in a bottle, but refused to let them interfere with the barrels. Thereupon he was seized, abused, beaten and finally shot to death.

> "Among the [European Americans] this murder by the militiamen naturally aroused indignation and alarm. It was assassination pure and simple — assassination by soldiers organized under the law and bearing arms supplied by the State Government. The demeanor of the [African Americans] in Union County showed that as a body they were in sympathy with the slayers of Stevens and would do all in their power to shield them from arrest and punishment."

The European Americans of Union County decided to act with force to prevent a recurrence. They formed "a committee of safety" which moved in and disarmed the militia. Then, acting as a sheriff's posse, they overwhelmed and arrested 13 of the suspects, badly wounding two during the fight, and proceeded to lock them up in the Union County jail. Before long, members of the Kuklux became involved, as historian John Reynold would explain:

> "On January 4, a party of Kuklux, all mounted and each disguised by means of a cap and mask that concealed the head and face, with some sort of gown or wrapper that enveloped the whole body, went to Union jail and seized 5 of the [African American] militiamen charged with participation in the murder of Stevens. Of these, 2 were shot to death and 3 escaped — the impression prevailing

that the Kuklux allowed them to get away because they were thought not to have been actual participants in the crime."

Six days later, the circuit judge, whose district included Union County, ordered that the 8 remaining prisoners be moved out of Union County and jailed in Columbia. This move, easily interpreted as a humane effort to ensure due process of law, was instead seen by many Kuklux as a scheme to circumvent prosecution by relocating the militiamen to the State capital where Republicans and Governor Robert Scott more firmly ruled over all legal matters. The Kuklux then proceeded to dramatically escalate the violence, as historian John Reynold would tell:

> "On Sunday night, January 12, the Kuklux visited Union again — this time in a body, all mounted and disguised, numbering, according to different estimates, from 1,000 to 1,500. They went to the jail, took out the 8 militiamen above mentioned and shot them to death. This bloody work was done quietly. There was no uproar. Sentinels detailed from the ranks of the Kuklux body were posted, and these ordered back any of the town people who came out of their houses. The mounted men retired as quietly as they had come, their ranks well kept and their movements marked by a precision which was well-nigh military."

The retiring Kuklux left behind a note, which said in part, "Once again we have been forced by force to use force. Justice was lame, and she had to lean upon us. . . . 'Let not thy right hand know what thy left hand doeth' is our motto. We want peace, but this cannot be till Justice returns. We want and will have Justice, but this cannot be till a bleeding fight for freedom is fought. . . ."

Historian John Reynold would add, "This latter occurrence made a profound impression not only in South Carolina but in [Washington] and in other parts of the country." The State Legislature, in session at the time, would respond by "calling on President Grant for protection. Very soon Federal troops were sent to the disturbed counties — a company to each of the county seats of York, Union and Spartanburg." Meanwhile, 2 of the 3 at-large [African American] militiamen, who had escaped when the Kuklux first visited the Union jail, would be recaptured and imprisoned. These two would be "tried for murder, sentenced and executed."

So the ratio of men killed in reprisal, would far exceed an "eye for an eye, and a tooth for a tooth," even exceed the threat — "10 would be killed to avenge the murder of one" — mentioned earlier as having been pronounced by an African American leader of State militia. The murder of Matt Stevens would be countered by the execution of 12 — 10 by vigilante execution and 2 by lawful execution. [R201;184-186]

Meanwhile in Washington City, Charles Sumner, who knew nothing of the meeting between Hamilton Fish and British agent John Rose, was stewing over how to punish Fish for being mean to him. Well, Sumner decided to rebuke Secretary Fish by applying the "silent treatment." The "silent treatment" had often characterized Sumner's past behavior, for, over the years, he had inflicted his "silent treatment" upon many political friends as perceived punishment for political disagreements. And you will recall that he had even applied the "silent treatment" to his wife after she had begun taking more interest in the social whirl of Washington's diplomatic set than in staying home to bolster his vanity. So Sumner decided to treat Fish respectfully in business situations but shun him in social situations. A "business situation" soon arose. On January 15 Fish, consulted Sumner on an official basis — for he was still Chairman of the Senate Foreign Relations Committee. What should the Federals say to British agent John Rose regarding the "Claims on England" issue, Fish inquired. Sumner refused to answer, responding that the question required much reflection. But before departing, Fish insisted that he needed Sumner's reply within a day or two. Two days later, on January 17, Fish received Sumner's reply. As expected Sumner objected to the settlement outlined by Fish and Rose. Any suggestion that British payments be limited to losses suffered at the hand of Rafael Semmes' crew on the C. S. S. Alabama would "dishonor the claims arising from the [losses] of other ships, which the [Federal] Government cannot afford to do." Pointing out the threat to peace along the American-Canadian border from "Fenian" Irish terrorists, Sumner demanded "the withdrawal of the British flag" in Canada as a prelude to negotiations. Sumner added that eventually the British should be forced to withdraw totally "from this hemisphere, including Provinces, and Islands." Obviously, Sumner was still insisting that the British withdraw from North America, probably to facilitate an eventual Federal conquest of Canada. Sumner was firm as he closed his response to Fish:

"No proposition for a Joint Commission [to arbitrate the dispute] can be accepted unless the terms" of the arbitration "are such as to leave no reasonable doubt of a favorable result. There must not be another failure."

We need to understand that Charles Sumner's aggressive attitude toward Canada was shared by many other leaders. Biographer David Donald would write of this point in history:

"Consistently, [Ulysses] Grant had favored the independence, if not the outright [conquest], of Canada. Fish, too, had repeatedly pressed this point as an essential condition for a genuine settlement with Great Britain. His instructions to [John] Motley on January 4, 1870, had directed [that he] press the issue of Canadian Independence upon the British ministry."

Although Charles Sumner "was prompt to disavow any intent" to militarily conquer Canada, he had been consistent in facilitating such a conquest as he had steadfastly insisted that "Our object — at least my object — is the withdrawal of the British flag from this hemisphere." But Sumner's eagerness to set the stage for a conquest of Canada seemed to discourage Ulysses Grant for pressing forward toward the same goal. According to biographer David Donald: "Though [Ulysses Grant] in the past had longed for Canada, the mere fact that Sumner insisted upon Canadian independence was enough to make him turn against his previous policy. Grant was apparently so intent on deposing Sumner that he told Fish to push forward toward the settlement he and Rose had outlined. Grant pledged to do "his utmost to carry through the Senate any settlement which it may be possible to make with England."

While Hamilton Fish and John Rose were engaged in unofficial high-level negotiations on "Claims on England," Sumner was still inflicting upon Fish the "silent treatment" — at least in social situations. Well, there was a social situation on January 20 when Robert Schenck hosted a dinner party to which Fish was also invited. Now this party could be construed to be business as well as social, for Schenck was the nominee to become Minister to Great Britain, Fish was the Secretary of State and Sumner was the Chairman of the Senate Foreign Relations Committee. But Sumner, within his mind, classified the party as social and therefore "exhibited marked coldness toward Fish, declining to speak or even to bow to him." Coolly, Fish "at first endeavored not to notice the discourtesy; and addressed Sumner as if nothing had taken place, but this produced no change in his demeanor." Afterward, Sumner explained to John Rose that he had intentionally shunned Fish. The following day Fish wrote in his diary that Sumner had been "cold and distant, evidently not wishing to converse with . . . me." And Sumner's "silent treatment" did not evade the notice of a concerned Roscoe Conkling, who concluded: "Personal terms with [Ulysses Grant], and with [Hamilton Fish], were quite broken off, and a pointed refusal to speak to [Fish] occurred, and was declared as intentional, to Senators and other persons. Business, of course, ceased to be conducted, in the ordinary and suitable modes."

During a meeting on January 24, Hamilton Fish showed British agent John Rose the memorandum he had received from Charles Sumner 7 days previously. Although Rose was not surprised at this evidence of Sumner's continued demand for complete British withdrawal from North America, he feared that Sumner might gain a following for such ideas if the British showed any reluctance to proceed toward an negotiated arrangement to pay the Federals for the losses suffered at the hand of Rafael Semmes' crew on the C. S. S. Alabama. Fish, accordingly, assured Rose that, if the British sent diplomats immediately, no Grant Administration effort would be "spared to secure a favorable result, even if it involved a conflict with the Chairman of the [Senate] Committee on Foreign Relations." Rose then sent an immediate dispatch to London via the trans-Atlantic telegraph cable. The British Government responded just as quickly. An agreement was reached on February 3 to hold a meeting in Washington as soon as possible to settle all claims, British and American, arising out of the Federal Invasion of the Confederacy.

During these weeks, Charles Sumner's mental and physical health had been suffering from the political pressure he was feeling. Biographer David Donald would describe the ordeal within Sumner's body and mind during February 1871:

"By the end of January, Sumner was visibly affected by the prolonged mental excitement under which he had been operating, and his nervousness was intensified by fear of physical assault from [Ulysses] Grant or one of his aides. He began to experience symptoms of the angina pectoris which had periodically affected him in the past. On the night of February 15 the pain in his chest and in his left arm was so great that he could not sleep, but, driven by a sense of duty, he insisted upon going to the Capitol the next day, where he remained for 3 hours. The following day he also attended the Senate session, but he was soon obliged to go home. That evening he suffered paroxysms in the chest and acute pain in his left extremities, and his physician could relieve him only by an injection of bromide. Under doctor's orders, Sumner was obliged to remain at home and rest for the next two weeks. . . Significantly, Sumner himself in speaking of the attack ignored the several bouts of angina he had had in recent years and stressed that his suffering was a direct result of Preston Brook's assault [with a cane, 15 years previously] in 1856." [R73;479-490]

Meanwhile in Columbia, South Carolina, even Republicans in the General Assembly were becoming very concerned over evidence of fraud and unsustainable skyrocketing State debt. Accordingly, a substantial number of House and Senate Republicans, with support of the few Democrats there, voted to set up an Investigating Committee. Called the "Joint Special Financial Investigating Committee," and composed of 2 Republican Senators, 3 Republican Representatives and no Democrats, this 5-man Committee set out to "make a complete and thorough examination of all the accounts of the State Treasurer, Comptroller-General, and Financial Agent since their induction into office, with power to send for persons and papers," with "power to appoint a clerk and an expert if necessary" and with power "to submit any part of the results of their examination to the Attorney-General for his official action." So, we observe that the South Carolina Republican Party was undertaking an in-house financial investigation of the behavior of its key leaders. Would this lead to impeachment proceedings? Time would tell. [R201;176]

Concerning another issue within the State, in the towns beyond Columbia, the Kuklux had been especially active:

> In Union County, in follow-up to the murder of Matt Stevens and the execution of 12 African American militiamen, the Kuklux obtained the resignation of county Republican officials by making extreme threats of bodily harm.

> In Spartanburg County, Dr. John Winsmith, "a citizen of high standing, who had given offense by declaring his purpose to support the Scott ticket in the campaign of 1870," was visited by armed men in disguise. Winsmith fired at the visitors, who fired back inflicting 7 wounds. Winsmith would not press charges and no one would ever be arrested.

> In York County, "there were many raids charged to the Kuklux." Retribution against African Americans was primarily in response to "offensive" behavior by militia marching about, "frequently carrying their guns and always wearing their bayonets and cartridge boxes." After altercations during militia marches up and down the roads threatened to erupt into bloodshed at Yorkville, a European American commander, dispatched from Columbia, investigated and decided to completely disarm that town's militia, sending all arms back to the capital. Over time the toll of African Americans killed in that county would allegedly rise to 5 in number, including African Americans Tom Roundtree and Jim Williams, killed in separate incidences:

>> On December 3, 1870, Tom Roundtree had been taken from his house by a party of men alleged to be Kuklux and shot to death. Three European American men were later arrested and charged in the murder of Roundtree, but their innocence was clearly proven and they were all acquitted by a jury.

>> Jim Williams' militia was especially dangerous, being armed with 96 breech-loading rifles complete with plentiful ammunition. They persisted in marching around, firing guns, making threats and setting fires. On March 7, 1871, in the nighttime, a party of mounted men, numbering about 60, went to the house of Jim Williams, took him into the woods near by and hung him to a tree. Soon thereafter Williams' militiamen turned in their arms and disbanded.

Although I pay primary attention to men being killed or executed, it is appropriate to sample some of the Kuklux activity that was far less violent. Historian John Reynold would provide samples of such activities in the following paragraph:

> "In the course of their operations, more particularly in York and Spartanburg, the Kuklux, or [groups] of men alleged to be such, committed numerous acts against law and order. Irresponsible

men, alarmed by the conduct of the [African American] militia, went far beyond the scope of the organization, considered either as a means of self-protection or as a counterpoise to the Union League. Raids were made with no apparent purpose but to punish the immediate victims for previous threats, sometimes for previous impertinence only. In many cases, according to the testimony of victims, the raiders exacted the promise that these should never again vote the Republican ticket. In some instances the conduct of raiders had no relation either to politics, to race troubles, or to the misconduct of the [African American] militia. A [European American] man was visited and whipped because, against repeated remonstrances, he continued in the illicit sale of whiskey near a church, to the disgust of the community. A [European American] lad was visited and whipped because of continued disobedience to his widowed mother, coupled with conduct otherwise distressing to her. A [European American] man who had long refused or neglected to pay a bill due to [an African American] blacksmith was visited and informed that he must pay the debt or get a whipping." [R201;186-190]

As in South Carolina, the Republican Party in Mississippi had enrolled African American men into "Loyal Leagues" which, in secrecy, bound members to swear to an oath to always vote for Republicans for every office, without question — ensuring a well-oiled and efficient political machine designed to ensure Republican domination over government fro the lowest to the highest offices. It was difficult for an African American man to evade being caught up in the secret Loyal Leagues movement. Historian James Garner would describe the workings of this political machine in Mississippi:

The Loyal Leagues "were secret political organizations among the [African American men], and were generally organized and presided over by their [European American Republican] allies. Meetings were usually held at night in some out-of-the-way place, and were harangued by [European American] Republican speakers. These organizations solidified the [vote of the African American men], for there was a League in every community, and every [African American] man was a member."

All African American men understood that only the candidates selected by the Mississippi Republican Party were, by rigid definition, "true and reliable Union men and supporters of the government." The following is a typical oath to which African American men were required to swear to uphold:

"I will do all in my power to elect true and reliable Union men and supporters of the government to all offices of profit or trust, from the lowest to the highest, in ward, town, county, and general government."

The Mississippi Kuklux, also operating in secrecy, was organized to coordinate opposition to the secret Union Leagues, which were designed to ensure Republican political domination over government from the lowest to the highest offices. In fact, "the Jackson Clarion, on March 21, said, if the Kuklux Klan really existed, it would not recommend its disbandment during the existence of the Loyal Leagues, whose 'conspiracies the Kuklux was intended to circumvent'."

Before engaging with some of the most important incidents allegedly involving the Mississippi Kuklux, let us look at a description of the organization during the 1868-72 time, as would be later reported by historian James Garner. You may observe some similarities to the mystical character of African Voo Doo, which still influences society in Haiti to this day:

"The mysterious organization, gruesome rites, and the strange language of the Klan were well calculated to strike terror into the minds of a superstitious race emasculated by centuries of [being held in bondage]. Its sphere of operations was styled the Invisible Empire; the chief functionary was the Grand Wizard; each State was a Realm ruled over by a Grand Dragon; each [Federal House] District was Dominion, at the head of which was the Grand Titan; each county was a Province under the rule of a Grand Giant; each county was subdivided into Camps or Dens, each governed by a Grand Cyclops. The members of a Den were called Ghouls.

"The mysterious Constitution of the organization was no less terrifying than the manner in which the members disguised themselves when in active service. The prevailing costume was a long white robe reaching to the knees, and slashed up the sides for convenience in running. The covering for the face was a white mask containing holes for the eyes. The headgear was sometimes a high cardboard hat, but more frequently a sort of cap with long ears or horns attached. The front part of the dress was often disfigured with skulls and crossbones or other hideous designs. The horses ridden by the Kuklux were disguised quite as effectively as the riders.

"Meetings were presided over by the Captain, and admission was by password only. Motions for 'waiting upon' certain individuals could be made by any member and were put by the Captain. It was alleged that sometimes the Klan in one community would call upon the Klan in a neighboring community to execute its Decree. This was said to have been a common practice in the counties of Mississippi lying along the Alabama line.

"The most exaggerated tales were circulated among the [African American men] in regard to the character and strength of the Kuklux. The mere rumor that they were 'riding' in the neighborhood was sufficient to cause every [African American] to retire to his cabin. It was common among them to magnify a band of a dozen into a hundred. They were never visited by less than 50, and the number was usually reported to be 200 or 300. The idea was widespread among the [African Americans] during the early days of [Republican rule] that the Kuklux were spirits of dead Confederate soldiers, and were possessed of supernatural powers, such as the ability to take themselves to pieces at will, rattle their bones, and drink whole pailfuls of water. The Kuklux practice of conversing in mysterious and unintelligible language, the [African Americans] called 'mummicking.' They told of a horrible monster who lived in the Yazoo swamps, and went about the land with a flesh bag in the shape of a heart 'hollering for fried nigger meat,' a delicacy for which it had an insatiable appetite.

"The 'Decree' of the Camp [or Den] was usually delivered to the person for whom it was intended by a Captain, in a pompous manner, and was pronounced as an Order of the Grand Cyclops registered in some corner of Hades. If the 'Decree' was simply a warning, the offender was informed that it was the practice of the Klan never to give its warnings but once. The notice was usually posted in some conspicuous place about the premises of the person for whom it was intended."

Perhaps the bloodiest event allegedly involving the Mississippi Kuklux occurred in Meridian on March 6:

Trouble had begun a few days earlier when a Deputy Sheriff was assaulted by some local African Americans, led by a European American school teacher who had come to Meridian from a northern State. The Deputy had come over from Alabama to make some arrests. Meridian officials arrested the school teacher but he soon thereafter "forfeited his recognizance and left for parts unknown." But that did not settle the matter. It seems that the school teacher had political friends and they were upset. They arranged a mass meeting for March 3, which was predominantly attended by African Americans. The leaders of the meeting were three African Americans — William Dennis (deemed a notorious person), Warren Tyler (school teacher), and a Baptist preacher named Moore. European Americans in Meridian believed the three leaders encouraged their African American audience to "take things into their own hands." About an hour after the meeting broke up, the store owned by the Meridian Mayor was found to be on fire. It spread to other buildings, all of them destroyed. European Americans were doubly disturbed because African Americans refused to help fight the fire, calling the inferno "a white man's fire." The three African American leaders — Dennis, Tyler and Moore — were arrested and charged with "creating disorder," a rather minor offense. A trial on that charge was to take place as soon as possible, on Monday, March 6.

Prior to the trial, European Americans gathered at their own mass meeting, adopting resolutions condemning the speeches of the three leaders. Then the trial of Dennis, Tyler and Moore, on the "creating disorder" charge, began before a Magistrate, a Republican. Historian James Garner would describe the ensuing gunfight:

A few moments into the proceedings "a tremendous firing began in the courtroom. The Magistrate fell at the first shot. Twenty or 30 shots rang out almost simultaneously. When the smoke cleared away several dead bodies were found. Dennis, badly wounded, was carried to the Sheriff's office and left on the floor. During the night he was killed. Tyler was found concealed in a barber shop and was quickly dispatched. During the firing Moore feigned death by falling to the floor. He afterward escaped and made his way to Jackson, pursued by a body of armed citizens. He never returned to Meridian."

"In the meantime 3 other [African Americans] had been arrested, carried to the courthouse, and put in charge of a Deputy Sheriff for safe keeping. During the night, they were taken out and killed. The riot ended by the burning of Moore's dwelling house and the [African American] Baptist Church near his residence. In the meantime the Mayor was informed that it was the desire of the [European Americans of Meridian] that he should leave the town. He was accordingly escorted to the train by 300 to 400 men, and left for [a northern State]."

I do not know the number killed from the gunfire in the courtroom, or the racial identity of the "several dead bodies" found. Whatever the situation, it is a sad story — when political stress reaches a boiling point — about how easily deadly racial violence can escalate from merely an attempt to prevent an arrest by a Deputy Sheriff. The European Americans involved in the conflict were presumed to be members of a local Kuklux group, and the incident would be investigated on that basis. [R204;338;351]

Near this time, the 1870-1871 Mississippi school year, a period of 4 months duration, drew to a close. Considerable progress had been made in providing rudimentary education for African American children, teenagers and young men, almost all of whom were starting out by learning first grade basics, regardless of age. Although integration of the races was anticipated according to Mississippi law, integration was not forced and, in practice, all schoolhouses were either for African Americans or for European Americans. The task, obviously huge, of overseeing the creation of a new school system for educating African Americans, the vast majority being first graders, fell upon the State Superintendent of Mississippi Schools, Henry Pease, who had come from a northern State as a Federal soldier and as an agent of the Newly Independent African American Men's Bureau. He had been Superintendent of Education for Louisiana before taking the Superintendent job in Mississippi — valuable experience. Historian James Garner would observe, "His competency was never questioned." Garner would summarize the accomplishments of the first 4-month school year:

"The results of the first year of free education in Mississippi were encouraging. . . . More than 3,000 free schools had been opened, with an attendance of 66,257 pupils. Of the 3,600 teachers employed, all but 399 were [European Americans]. . . . The total expenditures, on account of public education for the year, were $869,766, an amount which exceeded the government expenditures for all other purposes."

Furthermore, charitable donations had resulted in the donation of 500 parcels of land suitable for schools and the construction of 200 schoolhouses.

By way of comparison, public education in Mississippi for 1860 involved 1,116 school houses attended by 30,970 pupils, all of these being European Americans. (Most of these school systems had been funded by the lease or selling of sixteenth section lands, which had been granted to the State by the Federal Government in the early 1800's).

But the high cost of public education in 1870 was alarming, considering the impoverishment of the State at that time. Of mismanagement of schooling expenditures, the Jackson *Clarion* would complain:

"The present system of common schools is a humbug. One million dollars was spent last year, with very little advancement in learning. The *modus operandi* is a very few hours of instruction each day — school closed 8 months of the year: a greedy swarm of useless drones in the shape of school officers doing nothing and living high on extravagant salaries, squandering the vast school funds in thieving combinations and contracts for fine furniture and useless books, and for building fine schoolhouses."

Visions come to mind of eager book sellers pushing books beyond the ability of students and builders pushing expensive construction projects. So, the hurdles were numerous. A schoolhouse was required wherever the names of 25 potential students could be listed. Mississippians of the European American race, based on ample evidence, feared that their children would be forced to sit in mixed-race school houses occupied mostly by African Americans ranging from 6 to 21 years of age — bored, intimidated and restless — while idealistic and unsympathetic teachers, most of them recently arriving from the northern States, devoted all their time with the African Americans in the room, almost all of them restricted in ability to first-grade-level reading instruction — the A B C's, simple addition and subtraction, basic words.

These fears had resulted in serious reactionary responses. Teachers from the northern States had been customarily shunned and they often found no lodging except with African American families — therefore, very high monthly salaries, averaging $60 per month, were needed to attract and retain them once they realized they would suffer emotional hardship and the annual cost of travel from and to their home State. Kuklux intimidation was not uncommon, including setting fire to some schoolhouses and threats that caused some teachers to leave the State. Teachers who openly encouraged Republican political activism were mistreated the most severely.

But the initial fears of Mississippi European Americans were already subsiding, for, under Superintendent Pease's accommodating leadership, it was becoming more evident that segregated schoolhouses would be the norm. Of this observation, historian James Garner would write: "When it became evident, however, that there was no intention of establishing mixed [race] schools, much of the opposition wore away, so that Superintendent Pease was able to report in 1871 that 'a most marvelous revolution in sentiment' in regard to [African American] education had already taken place."

The University of Mississippi at Oxford was likewise allowed to focus entirely on the education of European American students while plans were being laid for advanced African American institutions that would be commensurate with the ability of the more gifted of those students. [R204;354-366]

Meanwhile in Washington City, the new Federal House and Senate assembled on March 4, with the first order of business being to organize its leadership and its Committees. And Charles Sumner was in perilous danger of losing his powerful position as Chairman of the Senate Foreign Relations Committee — not because voters had made the Democrats the majority Party in the Senate — but because Sumner was so out-off-step with the Republican leadership and the Grant Administration that leaders of his Party were willing to violate long-standing seniority rules in order to depose the very man whose "ideology" had played such a major role in leading them to political domination. The power to nominate Republicans to the individual Committees rested with the Republican Caucus Nomination Committee, which consisted of 5 men: John Sherman, of Ohio, Justin Morrill of Vermont, John Pool, of the remade North Carolina State Government, James Nye of Nevada, and Timothy Howe of Wisconsin. The power to confirm Republican Committee appointments rested with the whole Republican Caucus.

Republicans caucused on March 9 to receive the report of the Nominations Committee and to proceed with voting on accepting or rejecting the Committee's assignment and the Chairman recommendations. The Nominations Committee recommended to the Caucus that Charles Sumner be removed as Chairman of the Foreign Relations Committee and be reassigned as Chairman of a new Committee that would be called the "Committee on Privileges and Elections." The actual mission intended for this new Committee remains unclear, but it was clear to everyone in the Caucus, that the new assignment was a means of relegating the grand old Republican ideological leader to the sidelines. The vote in the Nominations Committee had been 3 to 2. Pool, Nye and Howe had voted to depose Sumner. Upon hearing the recommendations, Sumner rose up in protest and challenged past members of his Foreign Relations Committee to tell fellow Republicans, in what way he had "ever failed in any duty of labor or patriotism." Then Sumner stormed out of the room.

John Sherman and Schuyler Colfax attempted to offer an alternate that would, instead, pack Sumner's Committee with two more supporters of the foreign policy advocated by Ulysses Grant and Hamilton Fish. But that attempt to reduce Sumner's influence, while preserving seniority rules, failed. Then, by a vote of 26 to 21, the Republican Caucus voted to depose its long-standing ideological leader, Charles Sumner of Boston, Massachusetts. Caucus members who voted to depose Sumner were primarily the Republicans who had opposed taking the Dominican Republic and the Republicans who represented the Reconstructed State Governments, for the latter felt dependent upon Ulysses Grant for the military support necessary for them to retain their powerful jobs. The vote to depose Sumner was reconsidered the next day. Again the Caucus voted to depose Sumner, although the winning vote margin did drop from 5 votes to 2 votes.

After that second vote, the Republicans moved from the privacy of their Caucus room to join with Democrats in the Senate Chamber. There, Timothy Howe presented the slate of Committee assignments for a formal vote of acceptance. Charles Sumner then rose and pleaded for honoring the long-standing Party seniority rules: "I feel . . . that after 20 years in this [job] I have a right to expect that my associates in this Chamber will not impose upon me a new class of duties when I expressly say that they are not welcome to me." Carl Schurz then challenged: "What are the reasons for this change?" After some squirming in seats, Timothy Howe rose and answered that Ulysses Grant had not instigated the change. However, Howe admitted that the "silent treatment" punishment that Sumner had imposed upon Hamilton Fish (as mentioned a few pages back) had figured into the recommendation that he be deposed. Howe explained that, when Sumner was with Hamilton Fish at a dinner hosted at minister-appointee Robert Schenck's home, Sumner had "not only felt authorized to refuse to answer questions addressed to him by [Hamilton Fish], but . . . told of it after [leaving Fish's presence]. And we know that he even told British diplomat John Rose of it. But that was a social occasion, Sumner's supporters alleged; Fish never "addressed a question to [Sumner] upon official business which [he] refused to answer." Some Party-founding Republicans, such as Lyman Trumbull, of Illinois, bucked the leadership by supporting Sumner. Urging others to support Sumner, Trumbull attested: "I stood by him when he was [caned about the head at] his seat by [Preston Brooks], by the powers of [southern-States politicians]. I stand by him today when the blow [to his head] comes from those who have been brought into power as much through the instrumentality of [Charles Sumner] as of any other individual in the [Federal Government]." Fellow Massachusetts Senator Henry Wilson also spoke in support of Sumner. Aaron Cragin, of New Hampshire, was terribly torn between his sworn pledge to abide by the Republican Caucus vote and his duty, as he saw it, to vote against deposing Sumner. Cragin thought deposing the veteran Party Founding Father "impolitic and dangerous." Yet Cragin would confess, "I yield my judgment to the will of the majority of [the Republican Senators]." The debate lasted 4 hours. I suppose that the Democrat Senators had little to say, for they were such a small minority, they had no hope of making a difference in the outcome. Finally, the vote was called for. The Republican majority voted to accept the proposed Committee assignment, although some opposed to deposing Sumner chose to abstain. Nine Democrat Senators voted against the assignments. For the first time in 10 years Charles Sumner had no control over the foreign policy of the Federal Government.

Contrary to what Timothy Howe had told fellow Senators, Grant was more involved in arranging to depose Charles Sumner than alleged. Later that day Grant would be telling some Senators who called on him at the White House that it had been "necessary to make an example of Sumner in order to teach these men that they cannot assail an Administration with impunity." British diplomat Edward Thornton was not so sure that the Grant Administration had to depose Sumner to move forward with negotiations on the "Claims on England" allegations. In fact, Thornton would later suggest that Sumner was "certainly now the vainest of [the Federals]," and he could therefore be won over by "judicious flattery." But Sumner had many important supporters, evidenced by the letters pouring into his office and influential supporters who rose up in support of their fallen hero. On March 13, Massachusetts Governor William Claflin pledged from Boston: "This attempted disgrace of you and [Massachusetts] . . . has served . . . to show you and the world, the unreserved confidence and esteem reposed in your statesmanship and spotless integrity." Newspapermen were of a divided opinion, but a majority of editors denounced Sumner's removal. Representative James Garfield of Ohio, who would one day be elected President, charged that "no act of either branch of Congress, since I have been a member, equals this in folly." Charles Adams even predicted that "the doom of the Republican Party was sealed" by the Senate vote to depose Sumner. Yet the vote would stick. Sumner's supporters would not succeed in reversing the decision. And Ulysses Grant would strengthen his ties with Representative Ben "Beast" Butler, of Massachusetts, in an attempt to further elevate Butler's supporters in the Massachusetts Republican Party. [R73;490-501]

By this time, mid-March, the South Carolina Legislature was wrapping up its annual session, which had begun on November 22 the previous year. So it is appropriate now to report on what had taken place in that State since the overwhelming fall election victories of the regular South Carolina Republican Party, led by Governor Robert Scott, who, you will recall, had come to the State from Ohio and had headed up the Newly Independent African American Men's Bureau prior to being elected to his first term as Governor two years previously. Republicans held a huge majority over Democrats in the State Senate (25 versus 5) and in the House (104 versus 20), Democrats being almost entirely from Upstate counties.

When the House and Senate were combined, African Americans enjoyed a majority of 16. The State debt at the October 31, 1870 fiscal close, stood at $7,665,908, a little of that perhaps offset by assets that might be later sold.

Early in the session the South Carolina House and Senate combined in joint session to elect a man to fill the expiring Federal Senate seat being held by Republican Thomas Robertson. Robertson actively sought re-election and won handily, getting 87 votes versus 30 for Democrat Matthew Butler and 31 spread out among other Republicans. So Robertson would return to Washington City in March to begin a full 6-year term. Bribery was apparently rampant. Of the bribery preceding the vote, the correspondent for the Charleston *News* reported: "It is understood that $25,000 have been used by Robertson's friends since last night." Following the vote, in a subsequent dispatch, the correspondent added, "We hear, in the knowing circles, that $40,000 was used by Robertson in securing his election. The price of votes was $500 apiece for the rank and file, and for some of the more influential as high as $2,000 was paid. Everyone is 'flush' today, and money can be borrowed easily. Mr. Robertson, with the aid of Governor Scott, has inaugurated this year the reign of bribery." Robertson — an 1843 graduate of South Carolina College in Columbia, a farmer and former owner of bonded African Americans, and more recently a securities trader — had aligned himself with the ruling Republican Party. Although without experience in governmental affairs, he apparently had accumulated sufficient money to pay lucrative bribes.

The South Carolina House re-elected Franklin J. Moses, Jr. of Charleston to the Speaker's chair. Notable legislation during the 1870-71 term of the General Assembly includes the following items:

> A new "act to promote consolidation of the Greenville and Columbia Railroad Company and the Blue Ridge Railroad Company," expanded the previous Assembly's financing "act" on behalf of the Blue Ridge Railroad, thereby setting the stage for even greater graft. You will later learn the extent of this graft and "schemes of robbery formulated by John J. Patterson and his associates, when fully uncovered following the 1876 elections.

> The contract for public printing was awarded to the so-called Republican Printing Company, which was in essence merely Josephus Woodruff, Clerk of the Senate, and A. O. Jones, Clerk of the House. The fixed prices for printing work, as listed in the Act, were "more than double the highest prices that would be paid during the two decades that would follow the overthrow of the South Carolina Republican Party. You will observe that persistent graft centered on the Legislature's printing bills.

> To ensure the continued support of Federal troops during election season, "by a concurrent resolution, President Ulysses Grant was requested to send [to South Carolina, Federal] troops sufficient to protect the people from domestic violence."

During this session, the General Assembly dramatically increased taxes on South Carolina's property owners. The State tax was increased to 9 mils for the fiscal year 1870, an increase of 4 mils. The county tax rate was set at 3 mils minimum, with many counties adding 1 or 2 mils to that burden. At these rates, the total revenue due the State and counties for the 1870 fiscal year came to $2,265,000. But, by advancing the tax due date, legislators were requiring the 1871 tax be also paid within the same year, it being set at 7 mils for the State and about the same for the counties. In total, during this twice-taxed year, the tax burden on South Carolinians totaled $4,085,000, a rate of about 2.5 percent on property with a total assessment of $183,000,000. Comparing the twice-taxed year's burden to that of the once-taxed year of 1860 helps us understand the financial struggle South Carolina property owner's were suffering under Republican rule. In 1860, on a property tax base of $489,000,000, the State Government, under Democrat rule, took in a little over $400,000 in property taxes, less than 0.1 percent (the counties being omitted here). Furthermore, under Democrat rule, the State was solvent and paid its bills on time. [R201;154-161, R199;203]

A Convention of South Carolina tax payers would soon be organized. It would meet from May 9 through May 12. These men would be serious and would win some consideration. This event will be covered a few pages later.

Meanwhile, in Washington City, Charles Sumner, no longer Chairman of the Senate Foreign Relations Committee, was determined to nevertheless fight with everything he had to prevent the Federal

Government from taking by annexation the Dominican Republic and perhaps after that, Haiti. Sumner was fighting with his remaining weapon — his profound ability to deliver grand and elaborate orations on the floor of the Senate. For many weeks he was working hard on his next major speech, to be called, "Violations of International Law and Usurpations of War Powers." He was even committing the three hour and fifteen minute speech to memory — a feat which had been his common practice before suffering the "caning" administered by Preston Brooks, but quite rare afterward. As was his usual practice, he had arranged for copies of the speech to be printed and distributed to newspapermen in advance of his March 27 time slot in the Senate calendar.

Speaking of "War Powers," it seems that Charles Sumner and Ulysses Grant were at "War" with each other. Sumner had told a New York *Herald* reporter earlier in the month that Grant "doesn't know anything, sir. I do not accuse him of any knowledge whatever. He is not a man capable of understanding principles or of grasping anything in a comprehensive view." Biographer David Donald would explain: "Night after night [Sumner] regaled his [dinner] guests with tales of the swindles Grant's aides were perpetuating in [the Dominican Republic] and, escorting his visitors to the door, he [would] stand on the steps, looking out over Lafayette Square toward the White House, and denounce [Grant] in ever louder tones until it seemed that 'all Washington, including [Grant's wife Julia], must hear and the police would have to interfere'." Seemingly in response, Grant would denounce Sumner at every opportunity, even writing to Zachariah Chandler about how, when passing Sumner's house, he would shake his clenched fist at it and tell others in his party: "That man who lives up there has abused me in a way which I never suffered from any other man living." Of course, in this "War" with Sumner, Grant was including among his lesser abusers men like Robert Lee and Jeff Davis.

When the March 27 date arrived, the Senate gallery was filled with spectators as Sumner began his highly publicized oration: "Violations of International Law, and Usurpations of War Powers." He was set to deliver the oration from his desk. The printed text was on his left and his pile of reference books was on his right. German-American leader and fellow Senator Carl Schurz was immediately behind him, ready to pass up additional materials when prompted.

Sumner began by delivering his "proof" that "the usurper [Buenaventura] Báez was maintained in power by our Navy to enable him to carry out the sale of his country, and, secondly, that further to assure this sale, the neighboring Republic of Haiti was violently menaced." Sumner regaled Báez as an "adventurer, conspirator, and trickster, uncertain in opinions, without character, without patriotism, without truth." He denounced Ulysses Grant's chief negotiator, Orville Babcock, as that "young officer, inexperienced in life, ignorant of the world, untaught in the Spanish language, unversed in International Law, . . . and unconscious of the Constitution of his country." Then Sumner assured his listeners that ultimate blame for Federal involvement in the turbulent island of Hispaniola rested on Ulysses Grant — for it was Grant who had "seized the war powers carefully guarded by the [Federal] Constitution, and without the authority of Congress . . . employed them to trample on the independence of and equal rights of two nationals, coequal with ours."

Sumner championed the concept that people living on the island of Hispanola who were of partial and full African ancestry should control the government of Haiti and the government of the Dominican Republic. Although Buenaventura Báez's mother was of African ancestry, Sumner portrayed Dominican politics in racial terms and labeled Grant's support of Báez as "immoral." By alleged analogy, Sumner associated the underground Kuklux resistance movement in America's Reconstructed States to the Báez government's political oppression of Dominicans of little or no European ancestry:

"Pray, Sir, with what face can we insist upon obedience to Law and respect for the African race, while we are openly engaged in lawlessness on the coasts of [the Dominican Republic] and outrage upon [people of African ancestry] represented by [the neighboring nation of Haiti]? . . . It is difficult to see how we can condemn, with proper, whole-hearted reprobation, our own domestic Kuklux, with its fearful outrages, while [Ulysses Grant] puts himself at the head of a powerful and costly proceeding operating abroad in defiance of International Law and the [Federal] Constitution."

Had Ulysses Grant tried "to bestow upon the protection of [Republicans of both races in the Reconstructed American States], one half, nay, Sir, one quarter of the time, money, zeal, will, personal attention, personal effort, and personal intercession, which he has bestowed upon his attempt to obtain half an island in the Caribbean Sea, [the Kuklux] would have existed in name only, while tranquility reigned everywhere within [our country]."

Do not dispossess people of African ancestry from their "natural home in this hemisphere."

Like Grant, Sumner apparently hoped to encourage African Americans to voluntarily accept future deportation to the island of Hispaniola. Perhaps the only difference was that Grant wanted Federal control of the island to ensure it became more attractive for large scale voluntary deportation, whereas Sumner, also hopeful of voluntary deportation, wanted to ensure that no part of Hispaniola would ever become a State under the Federal Government. Sumner abhorred the notion that more people of African descent should become citizens of the United States.

At the conclusion of Charles Sumner's three-hour-plus oration, Oliver Morton rose and accused him of attempting "to fix a crime upon [Ulysses Grant]," since he was expending so much energy toward denouncing an already-rejected Treaty proposal. Timothy Howe labeled the fallen Sumner: a "great man wrecked by his own misguided zeal or his misguided passions." And he, too, accused him of merely attempting to wreck the Grant Administration. Howe taunted Sumner to "take off [the Republican Party] colors, take his position in line with the [Democrats], and strike like a man." But William Garrison praised what he called Sumner's "masterly words for the cause of Justice." Garrison called the oration, "a judicial decision rather than a speech — dispassionate, grave, dignified, exhaustive, admitting of no appeal."

Two days later, on March 29, Charles Sumner submitted a resolution denouncing the Federal Navy's patrol around Hispaniola, for only Congress was authorized to declare war. But the resolution was killed by a 39 to 16 vote to table it. Ulysses Grant soon thereafter withdrew the American Navy patrol from the waters of Hispaniola and advised Congress that "no action be taken at the present session beyond the printing and general dissemination of" the report that had been prepared by the Committee which had studied the annexation proposal. Grant effectively retreated to a position of neutrality and handed "over the whole matter to the judgment of the American people and of their representatives in Congress." The annexation of the Dominican Republic would never again be seriously considered, much to the credit of Charles Sumner's fierce and effective opposition. Would annexation have been useful to the United States? It is hard to say. [R73;510-515]

The island of Hispaniola, discovered by Christopher Columbus in 1492 had suffered a turbulent political history during the 379 years prior to 1871 and would suffer more turbulence over subsequent decades. The focus of political control was at Santo Domingo, established in 1496, with its fine harbor and access to the interior. As decade followed decade, the Spanish had enslaved native Tainos, most of whom died off, and then replaced them with other people imported from Africa. The population thereby evolved into a racial mixture of European, Taino and African. Major commercial products became sugar, beef, hides, tobacco and mahogany. After 200 years of Spanish rule, Spain, in 1697, ceded the western half of Hispaniola to France by the Treaty of Ryswick, a division facilitated by the almost impassable mountain range separating the east from the west. The resulting French colony, Saint-Dominque, soon became the wealthiest colony in the New World with 500,000 people. However, that mountain range was a secure refuge for revolutionaries bent on overthrowing political and economic authority, to the east or to the west, the most dramatic being the overthrow of the western side, Saint-Dominque, by residents of African ancestry, who organized in the mountains, slaughtered many Europeans, drove out the survivors and proclaimed an independent nation for people of African ancestry, named Haiti. Under the leadership of Toussaint Louverture and other Haitians who, prior to the revolution, had learned much from association with European civilization, Haiti made notable progress without a significant European population, including fighting off Spanish invaders and taking control of the eastern half of the island, including Santo Domingo. During 14 years of Haitian rule, from 1795 to 1809, and again for 23 years, from 1821 to 1844, Dominicans of European ancestry suffered much, including confiscation of all the land they owned and expulsion of the Catholic church. Dominicans finally drove out the Haitians in 1844 through a resistance movement, La Trinitaria, giving birth to the Dominican Republic, an independent nation. But retaining independence was difficult, for Dominicans had to repulse five Haitian invasions: 1844, 1845, 1849, 1853 and 1855-56. The frequent need to defend Dominican independence prompted Buenaventura Báez, a successful mahogany exporter and former deputy in the Haitian National Assembly, to engage in negotiations with foreign nations over protective annexation arrangements — making separate appeals to Great Britain, France, Spain, and the United States. But internal fighting between political factions and economic instability made Dominican life difficult — the Dominican Republic was far from a peaceful. By 1861 the nation was bankrupt and once more a colony of Spain. A second revolution resulted in Dominican independence in 1865 and a second Dominican Republic. Although Buenaventura Báez, of partial African ancestry, was President off and on, he continued to seek annexation by a foreign power — a goal never achieved. Báez was the 3rd, 6th, 10th, 13th and 16th President of the Dominican Republic (1849-53, 1856-58, 1865-66, 1868-74 and 1876-78). A political coup cut short his last term as President. He fled to Puerto Rico, at the time under Spanish occupation, where he would remain until his death in 1884. The Dominican Republic would be bankrupt again by 1914, causing Woodrow Wilson to send in American military forces, which would occupy the nation from 1916 to 1924. Neighboring Haiti, populated only by people of African ancestry, digressed into the abject poverty that is typical of African nations, because, following the deaths of the revolutionary generation, no leaders remained who had acquired necessary experience with European civilization. This was the island with which Ulysses Grant wanted to entangle Americans, to which he hoped to attract African Americans from the conquered Confederate States. This was the island with which Charles Sumner wanted no entanglement, two nations on one island for people of African ancestry ruled by people of African ancestry, attractive for settlement by African Americans from the conquered Confederate States. Would annexation have been useful to the United States? It is hard to say.

(2Q71)

By this time the Joint High Commission was nearing the end of its negotiations to reach a settlement of the "Claims on England" issue. Apparently, during occasional social contact during March and early April the British had not found Sumner quite as "insane" as Hamilton Fish had warned. Biographer David Donald would write:

> "Rather to their surprise, the British Commissioners found Sumner himself charming. Expecting to deal with a crazy man, Stafford Northcote was delighted to discover that [Sumner] has 'a negligent ease in his manner which is rather taking,' and even that reserved Scot, John Macdonald, reported that he had a good deal of pleasant talk with Sumner." [R73;504]

Later in April, the British members of the Joint High Commission, along with their wives, were dinner guests at Charles Sumner's home. Of this, biographer David Donald would write:

> "[The British guests] genuinely admired [Sumner's] china and crystal and enjoyed the special mandarin tea, which his friend Anna Lodge regularly supplied him. So successful was the evening that the Commissioners returned for another dinner — this time without their wives — on the following evening. When they left Washington, Sumner showered them with affectionate farewells, with advice to go west and see a prairie, and with *cartes de visite* bearing his latest photograph." [R73;504]

Yet, no one would dare predict how Sumner would react when, a few weeks later, the draft Treaty would be submitted to the floor of the Senate by the Foreign Relations Committee, from which he had been deposed. Stafford Northcote figured that Sumner was "very anxious to stand well with England; but, on the other hand, he would dearly like to have a slap at [Ulysses] Grant." [R73;505]

Meanwhile, on April 20, Ulysses Grant signed "An Act to **Enforce** the Provisions of the [Amendment to the Federal Constitution Nationalizing Citizenship (the Fourteenth)], and for Other Purposes," which would be popularly known as the "Second **Enforcement** Act." This Act removed conflicts of that sort from the jurisdiction of courts in the Reconstructed States and placed them in Federal courts. Historian John Reynolds would describe this law, also called the "Kuklux Act:"

> The "Act imposed penalties upon 'any two or more persons in any State or Territory' who should 'conspire or go in disguise on the highway or on the premises of another for the purpose of depriving, either directly or indirectly, any person or class of persons of the equal protection of the laws, or of equal privileges or immunities under the laws, or for the purpose of preventing or hindering the constituted authorities of any State or Territory from giving or securing to all persons within such State or Territory the equal protection of the laws.' It declared unlawful any

'combination' or 'conspiracy' against the rights declared in the [Amendment Nationalizing Citizenship]."

Violations of the Act carried stiff penalties and threatened imprisonment without due process of law. It warned, "Such combinations shall be deemed a rebellion against" the Federal Government, thereby permitting the President "to suspend the privileges of the writ of *habeas corpus*." No person could serve as a juror in a court if the court suspected he had in the past been associated with any such "combination." Swearing oaths found to be false would result in stiff criminal penalties. It was a tough law, one that could enable imprisonment based on false accusations by Republicans, one to make it easy to imprison Democrats.

In voting for the "Second Enforcement Act," Charles Sumner and had joined with all the Republicans who had voted to depose him from the Foreign Relations Committee. Senator Thurman, a Democrat, while reflecting on Sumner's "War Powers" speech, had told his colleagues how amusing it was to observe him voting to give Ulysses Grant "the power to make 'war' upon the [country's European American] people." But Sumner had truthfully answered that he had always been eager to expand the use of "national power" when required to enforce "national unity and the equal rights of all." He had called it "just centralism" and "generous imperialism," and thought it "for the equal good of all." However, some influential Republicans were coming to realize that "Reconstruction" was too-severely degrading the Federal Government into an immoral beast, bent on monstrous graft and cruelty. The tide would be changing. The "Kuklux Act," also called the "Second Enforcement Act," would be the more Militant Republican Faction's last Federal law aimed at further political subjugation of the conquered States. [R201;193-194, R73;516-517]

Meanwhile on May 8, in Columbia, South Carolina, a Convention of Tax Payers began a 4-day meeting designed to both protest the enormous tax burden the Republican Government had laid upon their properties and to expose the fraudulent behavior of the ruling Party in the State. The call for a State-wide Convention had originated during a March 24 meeting of the Charleston Chamber of Commerce, soon thereafter endorsed by the Charleston Board of Trade. In preparation, meetings had been held in most counties and, in each, two Delegates were selected to attend. The Convention was well organized and conducted as lawfully and intelligently as if Delegates were charged with writing a new constitution for their State. The names of Delegates showed attendance of many men who had been prominent leaders in the State prior to 1865, including Matthew Butler, James Chesnut and Armistead Burt. However, Wade Hampton did not attend, probably being too busy with his farms in Mississippi.

A determined taxpayer revolt was evolving — a serious challenge to Republican rule. The Tax-payer Convention approved the following:

> "Resolved, That this Convention of the property-holders and taxpayers of the State of South Carolina do hereby deem it our duty to declare that the bonds heretofore issued, without legal sanction, and the so-called sterling loan, or any other bonds or obligations hereafter issued purporting to be under and by virtue of the authority of the State as at present constituted, will not be held binding on us; and that we recommend to the people of the State, in every manner and at all times, to resist the payment thereof, or the enforcement of any tax to pay the same, by all legitimate means within their power."

> "Resolved, That we deem it our duty to warn all persons not to receive, by way of purchase, loan or otherwise, any bonds or obligations hereafter issued, purporting to bind the property or pledge the credit of the State; and that all such bonds or obligations will be held to be null and void as having been issued corruptly and improvidently."

A Tax-payer Committee was named to meet with Governor Scott to impress upon him the Convention's concerns and determination, in hopes of mitigating the problem. Fundamental changes in the racial makeup of the governing bodies within the State were conceived, including the proposal that the Legislature fundamentally reform election law such that "the 60,000 taxpaying voters will have a proportionate representation in the Legislature with the 90,000 non-taxpaying voters." It also recommended terminating all wasteful and, or, fraudulent government activities throughout the State.

A Finance Committee had been organized prior to the Convention opening, and it reported that the State debt, in the report of the last fiscal year, stood at $8,865,908. In response, demonstrating the willingness of taxpayers to honor and pay off old debt, if new debt was avoided, the Convention adopted a generous resolution verifying that the $8,865,908 was "a valid debt and that the honor and the funds of the State are lawfully pledged for the redemption thereof." But the message was clear: stop adding to the debt!

Governor Scott recognized the seriousness of this challenge by an organized tax revolt. He declared that the deadline for paying the 1871 tax bill would be extended to March 1, 1872, thereby eliminating the obligation of paying two year's taxes in one year. The Convention adjourned on May 12. [R201;162-170]

Meanwhile, sometime in May Varina and Winnie left Memphis to spend the summer in Maryland, where she had numerous friends. Maggie had returned from England and was attending Mrs. Cary's select boarding school in Baltimore. The two boys had been attending Brand's school in Maryland as well.

Meanwhile in South Carolina, Governor Robert Scott decided to defuse the militant agitation that had given rise to the Kuklux movement, that is for a while, until the next election cycle, perhaps. Historian John Reynold would explain:

> "Governor Scott offered to cooperate with the [European American] people in restoring quiet and preserving order. All the militia companies in the disturbed counties were finally disbanded. In several instances the Governor removed incompetent officials and appointed worthy [European American] men in their places. The Kuklux ceased their operations, so that after the middle of May, there was nowhere any complaint of them. The great cause of trouble — the [African American] militia — no longer existing, the task of restoring peace and order was not difficult. . . . [But] later on, the Federal Government [would use] its power — principally the power of the bayonet — to "suppress" a "conspiracy" which no longer existed and to protect rights which were nowise threatened." [R201;190-191]

Meanwhile in Washington City, progress was being made in settling the "Claims on England" dispute. Although Secretary of State Hamilton Fish had for some time believed that Charles Sumner was going insane, he attempt to keep him informed of progress in the negotiations being held in the city between Federal and British members of the Joint High Commission. Finally, in early May, the Joint High Commissioners completed negotiations and signed the draft "Treaty of Washington." Of course it would be submitted to the Federal Senate and the British Government for ratification before it would take effect. But the signing of the draft Treaty was a major accomplishment. As it turned out, Sumner had not attempted to derail the work of the Joint High Commission as Hamilton Fish and Ulysses Grant had feared. [R73;503]

The Federal Senate began debate over the draft "Treaty of Washington" on May 19. Charles Sumner actually found much in its language to his liking, and thought it mirrored much of the key demands he had made two years previously in his "Claims on England" Senate oration. In his own words, Sumner thought the draft Treaty "was not such a document as he desired, yet he was not disappointed in it." He liked the first article, which admitted "the regret felt by [the British Government]" for allowing British companies to construct the *C. S. S. Alabama* and other Confederacy-bound warships, and "for the depredations committed" by the Confederates who crewed those vessels. He liked the section that stipulated that a 5-man Tribunal would be empowered to decide all issues. He liked the three new rules of international law which would prohibit governments from claiming to be "neutral" while companies within their territory delivered warships, guns and war supplies to a nation at war. He especially liked the fact that the draft treaty "covered all the claims for indirect and national damages mentioned in his [Claims on England]" speech, for the total of all that stuff could amount to an enormous sum of money. And he was pleased that the draft Treaty retained his legal argument that the "indirect" claims of individuals, corporations, and companies were distinctly different from the national claims of the Federal Government. At some time during the debate Sumner delivered a four-hour oration from the Senate floor in advocacy of the draft Treaty (Since debate on treaties is secret and not recorded, we know not exactly what Sumner said). But, as biographer David Donald would point out, "The [draft Treaty] did not, of course, fulfill Sumner's long cherished dream that Canada would become part of the United States." After all debate was concluded, Charles Sumner joined his fellow Republicans in voting, as a block, to ratify the "Treaty of Washington." All Democrats voted against it, considering it in violation of international law. The final vote was therefore 50 for and 12 against. The British would apparently be willing to reduce their military presence along the United States border after the Treaty of Washington would be ratified by both governments and the arbitration would be concluded. After all, the Treaty pledged Ulysses Grant and the Federal Government to respect the sovereignty of the Canadian Nation. A surprise invasion of Canada thereafter would be highly unlikely. [R73;505-506]

(3Q71)

Meanwhile, in South Carolina, a Subcommittee from Washington City arrived to take testimony during most of July, concerning alleged acts of violence by the Kuklux. The Federal House and Senate, before passing the Second Enforcement Act, had set up a Joint Kuklux Investigating Committee, made up of 7 Senators and 14 Representatives. This Committee had taken testimony in Washington City from June 2 through June 29 and then split up into Sub-committees to go out into the Reconstructed States to investigate in the field. The Investigating Sub-committee for South Carolina was made up of Senator John Scott, Republican of Pennsylvania, Chairman, Representative Job Stevenson, Republican of Ohio, and Philadelph Van Trump, Democrat of Ohio. The Investigating Sub-committee would take testimony "from July 10 to July 29 — examining witnesses in Columbia, Union, Spartanburg and Yorkville." The two Republicans focused on testimony that justified the necessity of the Second Enforcement Act and a future need of widespread arrests of suspects without benefit of the writ of *habeas corpus*. On the other hand the lone Democrat on the Sub-committee focused on testimony, when possible, that illuminated the past threatening behavior of the African American militia companies. The majority report, written by the two Republicans, was a complete indictment of the Kuklux in South Carolina, meant to encourage a broad military police action by President Grant's Federal troops — a difficult argument to construct since there had been no complaint of Kuklux violence since mid-May, but the Republicans were up to the job. [R201;194]

Meanwhile, on July 12 in Sewanee, Tennessee, Jeff Davis was present at the commencement exercises at the University of the South. The cool air of the Cumberland Plateau presented an attractive environment, and he was sorely tempted to accept the Trustees' offer to become the University's Vice-Chancellor, or President. Davis was very fond of Bishop William Green, the school's founder and Chancellor. But Davis declined because of two disadvantages. The annual salary of $2,000 would not meet his needs, and he figured Varina would become too bored so far away for city life. But it would have been a wonderful setting for Davis to write his history of the Confederacy — absolutely wonderful. So Davis would continue as President of the Carolina Insurance Company. Two weeks earlier, the Board of Directors had elected him to serve another year. [R19;375]

Back home in Memphis, Jeff, Varina and all four children were at last together in a rented house at 129 Court Street. Except for three months in Montreal, they had not been together in a house since the flight from Richmond 6 years previously. So the Christmas season of 1871 would be especially enjoyable for all. Jeff did not particularly like the house, because "the rooms were small and the plan cranky." But Varina had made the place rather nice. She had purchased some furniture at good prices. But, more importantly, she had gone to Richmond and there "recovered a large part of the furniture she had sold [before fleeing from advancing Federals], and also quantities of ornaments, books, and pictures that had been kept for her by friendly convent nuns." With the help of three servants, the Davis "family lived comfortably." The boys, Jeff and Billie, were in a Memphis public school, and there was talk of sending 14-year-old Jeff to Virginia Military Institute when he became of age. But Jeff was not a very good student, not nearly as good a student as his younger brother, Billie. Billie was bright and outgoing, and showed signs of natural leadership. [R19;376-277]

Meanwhile, on September 26 in Worcester, Massachusetts, Charles Sumner was barely able to defeat Ben "Beast" Butler's bid for the Republican Party nomination for Governor. During the State Republican Convention, Butler supporters were barely outvoted by supporters of Sumner's candidate, William Washburn. It had been a difficult political maneuver. Sumner had pressured all other aspirants for the nomination to withdraw and pledge their supporters to Washburn. Prior to the opening of the Convention, Federal Senators Sumner and Henry Wilson had issued a joint public statement, saying we "deeply regret and deplore the extraordinary canvass which [Ben "Beast"] Butler has precipitated upon [Massachusetts]" and, in our opinion "his name as Governor would be hostile to the best interests of [Massachusetts] and the Republican Party." Butler fired back: "This all comes of your hostility to

[Ulysses] Grant; I am for him, and you are against him." The political bond between Grant and Butler had been rather powerful for many months and Grant had considerable support among the other Massachusetts Representatives in the Federal House. [R73;522-523]

(4Q71)

Meanwhile, in response to formal report of the previously-mentioned Investigating Sub-Committee, Ulysses Grant, on October 12, intent upon demonizing former Confederates and the Kuklux, "issued his Proclamation setting forth the existence of 'unlawful combinations and conspiracies in the State of South Carolina' against 'certain classes of the people' in the counties of Spartanburg, York, Marion, Chester, Laurens, Newberry, Fairfield, Lancaster and Chesterfield, and commanding 'all persons composing the unlawful combinations and conspiracies to disperse and to retire peaceably to their homes within 5 days of the date hereof, and to deliver to [Federal Marshals, deputies or Troops] all arms, ammunition, uniforms, disguises and other means and implements used, kept, possessed or controlled by them, for carrying out the unlawful purposes for which the said combinations and conspiracies are organized." Of course, Grant had never expected South Carolinians to rush home and deliver all their firearms to Federal authorities. So, as planned, 5 days later on October 17, he amended his Proclamation, adding, "The public safety especially requires that the privileges of the writ of *habeas corpus* be suspended to the end that said rebellion may be overthrown." Grant was using the Kuklux Investigating Sub-committee's majority report to justify this Military Police action against the civil rights of the European American people of South Carolina. Military arrests would soon follow. Some newspapermen from the northern States suspected that Grant was grossly over-blowing the threat — waving the bloody shirt, for political effect.

For example, a New York *Herald* reporter would file a report from Spartanburg two weeks later in which he would explain that peace had prevailed in that county for 4 months, "which the Federal officials admit," and that "the Kuklux organization was originally formed for the self-protection of its members, and not for political purposes." The reporter further claimed, "There was not any necessity for the suspension of the writ of *habeas corpus*" because no one was inclined to resist any arrest warrant. After checking out Union County the same reporter filed two days later a report in which he stated, "the Kuklux troubles ended there 7 months ago." But Grant was intent on effecting military arrests in South Carolina and jailing large numbers of European American men for political benefit. Governor Robert Scott was encouraging arrests, too, for he had "issued a proclamation offering a reward of $200 for each person arrested with proof to convict under the Enforcement Act." Large-scale arrests of suspected Kuklux were now underway. [R201; 195-196,216]

Meanwhile on November 28, upon reconvening, the South Carolina Legislature received a bleak annual message from Governor Robert Scott, the last of his second and final term in office. Back on February 13, near the close of the previous session, many Republicans had expressed grave concerns over fraud and unsustainable, skyrocketing State debt when, in the House and Senate, they had voted to name a 5-man joint Republican Investigating Committee. That Committee, made up of 5 Republicans and no Democrats, had much more work yet to do, taking testimony and auditing money flows and checking collateral. This activity was in the background when Scott delivered his message to the Legislature, highlights of which follow:

> The State debt had grown to $11,994,909, an increase of $3,129,000 in only 6 months.

> Annual appropriations, excluding expenses, but including interest paid on debt, had been $817,968 in 1868, $1,191,805 in 1869 and $1,604,053 in 1870 (note that, although annual appropriations were rapidly growing, these general appropriations were not the major cause of skyrocketing debt).

> Taxes collected had been $2,555,053 with $947,881 listed as overdue and outstanding of which a 20 percent penalty was being charged.

> It was claimed that the $700,000 in bonds issued by the Land Commission was covered by "ample equivalent in the lands purchased."

> Scott accused Democrats and angry taxpayers with damaging the State's credit-worthy image, resulting in increased rates of interest charged by holders of State debt. (This was a legitimate accusation, though the threatened tax-payer revolt seems to have been justified.)

The legislative expenses for the previous session totaled $583,651, including $91,500 for furniture, that extravagance being "without warrant of law."

Reduction in spending was advocated in many areas, including — replacing Legislator per diem pay with salaries; abolishing the Codifying Commission; abolishing the Office of Land Commissioner (assigning its work to the Secretary of State); cutting aggregate pay to School Commissioners from $31,500 to $10,000; cutting salaries of all officers except judges by one-third; eliminating the Assistant Adjutant-General's job; eliminating the State Auditor's job (assign work to Comptroller-General); abolishing in each and every county the Auditor's job (assigning there work to Treasurers); cut the pay of the Clerk of the House and the Clerk of the Senate; abolish the exclusive arrangement with the so-called Republican Printing Company, which was "without legal existence," and which was "a flagrant fraud upon the public treasury."

Funds allocated for public schools for the fiscal year just ended was $240,000, of which $150,000 had been appropriated by the legislature and $50,000 was estimated to be coming in from poll taxes, leaving a deficiency of $50,000. Scott reported that "about 67,000" pupils were attending those schools. You will observe that survival of the schools was quite dependent on charity, particularly from northern States contributors (charitable people in South Carolina were struggling to pay the tax burden and avoid foreclosure).

The lunatic asylum was in debt by $21,300 and was continuing services with the greatest of difficulties.

At one point in the message Governor Scott expounded at length about dangers presented by the Kuklux and insisted the threat thus presented "justified the intervention of the Federal Government for its suppression and for the punishment of its members." [R201;170-171]

Meanwhile, on November 30, in Mississippi, as Governor James Alcorn "resigned the office of Governor so he could move to the Federal Senate to occupy the seat being vacated by Hiram Revels, the famous African American. Revels would become President of the new Mississippi University for African Americans. Alcorn had held the job of Governor since March 10, 1870, a period of 20 months. He would be succeeded by R. C. Powers, Lieutenant Governor. Since the successes and failures of Mississippi government have not yet been reported for the years 1870 and 1871, it is appropriate to now take time to do so:

- The system of courts was totally transformed during this time, creating a different judicial system, with new names, and new methods of appointing people to jobs, but not necessarily better of worse than before. Basically, the Legislature discarded the old judicial system and instituted a new system.

  - The old county Probate Courts were replaced by 20 Chancery Courts, each with a Chancellor, appointed by the Governor and approved by the Senate for terms of 4 years. The people were to elect the supporting Chancery Clerk for terms of 4 years.

  - Circuit Courts, 15 in number, were established each with a Judge appointed by the Governor and approved by the Senate for terms of 6 years.

  - The old High Court of Errors and Appeals was replaced by a Supreme Court consisting of 3 Justices appointed by the Governor and approved by the Senate for terms of 9 years.

  - Historian James Garner would conclude, "The judges appointed by Governor Alcorn were, for the most part, [men of the southern States], who, like himself, had affiliated with the Republican Party since its organization in Mississippi in 1867." For Supreme Court Justices, Alcorn appointed H. F. Simrall and E. G. Peyton, both old citizens of Mississippi, and Jonathan Tarbell, a former Federal soldier from New York, considered of the "better class" of northern States men.

- Some large counties were broken up, making way for 6 or 8 new ones, which were named for Republican political heroes, such as Lincoln, Sumner, Colfax, Union, etc. Legislative District lines were redrawn to favor Republican rule — such as combining 10 northwestern counties into Federal House District 1, which had majority European American populations — giving the remainder majority African American populations, thereby diluting the political influence of the Democrats. You will learn that this would permit Lucius Lamar to win election to the Federal House from District 1.

- Memorials were sent to the Federal House and Senate, one asking for the removal of disabilities of all Mississippi citizens not yet so relieved, and another seeking a grant of $2,000,000 and 5,000,000 acres of land to aid in the restoration of the levees.

- Discrimination on account of race was forbidden when seeking juries and in seating travelers in railroad cars, steamboats or stage-coaches.

- For the most part, the character of the African American population was seen as improving. Marriages by ministers were rising in number, understandable insofar as many African Americans who had lived together for decades had never been officially married. During the 5 years of 1866 through 1870, there would be 71 African American couples marry per 1,000 population, exactly matching the European American marriage rate. Church-building by African Americans was advancing. Records from 25 counties showed the number of African American churches rose from 105 in 1865 to 283 in 1870, and the number of ministers rose from 73 to 262. African American businesses were rising in number. Records from 17 counties showed an increase in shoemaking shops from 105 in 1865 to 283 in 1870, and an increase in blacksmith shops from 40 to 112.

- On the other hand, concerns about African American crime were growing. Governor Alcorn, in a letter to the New York *Tribune*, reported 124 murders had been committed across the State from April, 1869 to March 1871, calling that a **"degree of barbarism truly shocking."** This amounted to 5.2 murders per month in an African American population of 455,000, or 1.14 murders per 100,000 African Americans per month. By the way, for comparison, in 2010 Mississippi would experience 208 murders, a rate of 17.3 murders per month in a population of 1,100,000 African Americans, or 1.57 murders per 100,000 African Americans per month. A peak of 409 murders would occur in 1994, a rate of 34.1 murders per month.

- Overall, this analysis indicates that, in the 1970's, African American men were succeeding at taking responsibility for their livelihoods, their families and living as free and independent persons.

On May 13, 1871, the Mississippi Legislature had adjourned, having logged a total of 10-1/2 months of work for the years 1870 and 1871. [R204;281-289]

Meanwhile, Charles Sumner was intent on harassing Ulysses Grant and his Administration from the very first day of the new Senate session, which opened in early December. He would be working closely with Lyman Trumbull, Carl Schurz, former Congressman George Julian and other Senators who were advocating Civil Service Reform to purge the Federal Government of the enormous corruption that seemed to be present within almost all Executive departments. In September, Schurz had encouraged Sumner to join him in a movement to build "a new [political] organization," which he called "the truly national [political] Party of the future." The Republican Party had remained a sectional Party, for it held power in the Reconstructed States only through Republican Political Machines empowered by the votes of African American men, but that remained a minority effort in Maryland, Kentucky and Missouri. Schurz hoped to attract a majority vote from former Confederates his new "National Party." Although most politicians, by the fall of 1871, had come to believe that Grant held an unbreakable lock on the 1872 Republican Party nomination for a second term, Sumner was continuing to attack the President as he had in correspondence all year. Biographer David Donald would write that Sumner "wrote letters, day after day, exposing the limitations and failings of the [Grant] Administration." In those letters Sumner alleged that Grant "quarreled more than all other Presidents;" that he was "the lowest President, whether intellectually or morally, we have ever had;" that he was "the richest since [George] Washington, although he was very poor at the beginning of the [Federal Invasion of the Confederacy];" that, instead of fighting underground opposition such as the Kuklux, he spent time "at entertainments, excursions, [and] horse-races;" so that, consequently, "on him is that innocent blood;" that he "is an incubus and mill-stone upon us;" and that we must tell him "plainly that he cannot expect a re-nomination." Dreamily, Sumner mused, "I wish [for] a President with a little common sense, common justice, and common liberality, who is not always brutal or vindictive."

During December, Sumner and Trumbull attacked the Grant Administration with harassing legislation. In one attack, Sumner moved to abolish by September, 1872, all taxes and duties except for import taxes, import duties and postage stamps — a measure obviously designed to dry up the internal revenue engine that was feeding much of the graft within the Federal Government (taxes on imports represented external revenue). In another attack, Sumner submitted an Amendment to the Federal Constitution to limit Presidents to one 4-year term. But, of greatest importance was Lyman Trumbull's bill, which threatened real harm to greedy politicians. This bill would establish a Joint Congressional Committee on Retrenchment, "with power not merely to investigate recent reports of frauds in the New York customs house but to ferret out malfeasance in all branches of [government]."

Granting amnesty to leading former Confederates would be the most important effort undertaken by Lyman Trumbull, Carl Schurz and other proponents of a "National Republican Party." You will recall that Andrew Johnson had extended full pardon to former Confederates on December 25, 1868, but that the Federal Amendment Nationalizing Citizenship (14th) still prohibited voting by a few thousand former Confederate civil and military leaders, unless they be individually pardoned by a two-thirds vote of both the Federal House and the Federal Senate. So, soon after the House session began in early December, leaders of the anticipated "National Republican Party" submitted an "Amnesty Bill" to grant amnesty to those former Confederate leaders who were still excluded from voting and citizenship — a bill which Charles Sumner firmly opposed. By mid-December the Amnesty Bill passed the House and advanced to the Senate. Because the Amendment Nationalizing Citizenship stipulated that a two-thirds vote was required to give amnesty, the Senate would need a two-thirds vote to pass the "Amnesty Bill."

At this point, Charles Sumner decided to fight the Amnesty Bill obliquely — by attaching an amendment to it that gave the Federal Government vast policing powers over day-to-day societal activities throughout the former Confederate States. All violations to his bill would be dealt with in Federal Courts, thereby excluding State Courts from any say in adjudicating alleged violations. Surely, Sumner thought, the Amnesty Bill would fail to muster a two-thirds Senate vote if his society-shattering amendment were successfully attached, for his amendment required that all persons, regardless of racial origin, be given "equal and impartial enjoyment of any accommodation, advantage, facility, or privilege furnished by common carriers, whether on land or water; by inn-keepers; by licensed owners . . . of theatres or other places of public amusements; by trustees . . . , teachers, or other officers of common schools and other public institutions of learning . . . ; [and] by officers of church organizations, [and] cemetery associations." Sumner's bill also prohibited racial origin from being considered in selecting jurors. His bill also required the repeal of "every law, statue, ordinance, regulation, or custom" that made "any discrimination against any person on account of [racial origin]." It seems that Sumner's amendment was a rehash of unsuccessful bills he had previously submitted in May of 1870 and in January and March of 1871. During debate on his amendment Senator Lot Morrill asked where in the Federal Constitution, the Federal Government was given control over State "matters of education, worship, amusement, recreation, entertainment, all of which enter so essentially into the private life of the people?" In reply, Sumner alleged that Jesus Christ's "Sermon on the Mount" and the American Colonies' "Declaration of Independence" from Great Britain represented a power higher than the Federal Constitution because they were "earlier in time, loftier, more majestic, more sublime in character and principle." (I would hope readers of *Bloodstains* realize Sumner's reply was nonsense.)

Ulysses Grant and his supporters, who represented the mainstream majority of the Republican Party, were opposed to amnesty. These politicians desperately needed political support from the remaining Republican Political Machines in the former Confederate States. And they needed societal strife in those States to help camouflage their political graft and to provide a basis for Army policing and political demagoguery at election time. So the Grant men decided to support Sumner's amendment — politics can surely make unlikely bedfellows. But, when the votes were taken on whether or not to adopt the amendment it failed to pass. But Sumner was not through, for he had the powerful Grant Faction with him because they knew that his amendment was designed to discourage enactment of the "Amnesty Bill." Defiantly, Sumner warned: "There will be another vote on my amendment." The Senate then adjourned for Christmas. [R73;525-535]

Meanwhile, the "Claims on England" controversy was moving toward arbitration in Geneva, Switzerland. Secretary of State Hamilton Fish had assigned to Bancroft Davis the job of compiling legal documents for submission to the Arbitration Board, which listed and justified all government and private "Claims on England." And it had become a long list, indeed. You will recall how pleased Charles Sumner had been to find within the draft Treaty his cherished separate and distinct claims for indirect and national damages. Well, in his compilation, Bancroft Davis had "followed Sumner's argument almost completely." As expected, he sought payment for damages that Confederate crews on British-built warships had inflicted upon those marine shipping companies that operated in support of the United States. But he did not stop there — not by a long shot. He also sought reimbursement for expensed incurred while the Federal Navy pursued those Confederates aboard those warships. Then — and this was the biggie — he sought reimbursement for the full Federal military campaign — Army and Navy combined — for those additional months that he figured British-built warships had enabled the Confederates to stave off defeat. Finally, Bancroft Davis alleged in his report — by some mysterious figuring — that all Confederate defenders would have surrendered after Robert Lee's successful retreat from his Gettysburg counter-invasion campaign, had the Confederates not been supplied with some British-built warships! Fancy that. So obviously, Bancroft Davis was after an enormous sum of money. His "Case of the United States" was carefully edited, printed up as a book and, in December, 1871, was presented to the Geneva Arbitration Tribunal.

Well, when British Diplomats read the long list of damages alleged in Bancroft Davis' "*Case of the United States,*" they were understandably outraged. They refused to proceed with the whole arbitration process and mounted a public campaign to force the Federals to withdraw all claims for damages not directly suffered at the hands of Confederate crewmen who were operating the previously-designated group of British-built warships, such as the *C. S. S. Alabama.* The British commissioners who had participated in the Washington Treaty-writing negotiations protested that Ulysses Grant, Hamilton Fish and Bancroft Davis "were breaking their word," by expanding American claims by such an enormous amount. British newspapermen "raged against [submission to an] arbitration which might impose upon their country a stiffer indemnity than Germany had exacted of France after the Franco-Prussian War." A British cabinet member warned that it would be "wholly incompatible with [British] national honor to admit or to plead" a British defense of such enormous and unfounded claims "before a Tribunal of Arbitration."

Hamilton Fish blinked. He had previously endorsed every word that his hand-picked lawyer, Bancroft Davis, had compiled into the "*Case of the United States.*" But he retreated when faced with the British refusal to continue to arbitration. Fish rather meekly explained that the Treaty's reference to indirect claims — like forcing the British to pay for the most expensive year of the Federal invasion of the Confederacy — had merely been included to prevent "an outcry from the people of the [northern States] and from the majority of the Senators and Representatives." A little later he added that inclusion of the massive indirect claims had also been necessitated by Charles Sumner's "Claims on England" speech and the great outcry of public support it had sparked. Fish assured the British Diplomats that, although demand for such a massive British payment was in the submitted Federal book of claims, neither he nor Ulysses Grant would authorize Federal lawyers to argue for massive indirect claims payments before the Tribunal of Arbitration. Let me paraphrase:

> Fear not, Fish was saying; go ahead and sit down with our lawyers before the Arbitrators. Let your lawyers open your book and we will let our lawyers open our book. Then the lawyers will argue the respective positions before the Tribunal of Arbitration. Relax, my friends, and be assured that our lawyers will skip over all that big-ticket stuff in our book.

But British leaders knew from experience that honor and honesty was sorely lacking in Republican Party leaders. Therefore, the British weren't buying! The Tribunal of Arbitration disbanded until further notice. [R73;506-508]

The Year of 1872

(1Q72)

Charles Sumner resubmitted his amendment to the Amnesty Bill when debate resumed after the Christmas recess. He alleged that the amendment was germane and not out of order because: "A measure that seeks to benefit only [former Confederate leaders] and neglects [African Americans] does not deserve success; it is an unworthy measure, it cannot be sustained by a righteous public sentiment." Then, on January 15, Sumner delivered a major speech advocating his amendment:

> He declared that the "barbarous tyranny" of African American bonding "stalks into this Chamber, denying to a whole race the equal rights promised by a just citizenship." Deforming history for his purposes, Sumner alleged that a primary reason for the Federal Invasion of the Confederacy had been equal rights for that nation's African American population. And he added: "The victory of the [invasion campaign] is vain without the grander victory through which the [Federal Government] is dedicated to the axiomatic, self-evident truth declared by our fathers [when the Thirteen Colonies declared their independence from Great Britain], and reasserted by Abe Lincoln [during his speech dedicating the Federal military cemetery] at Gettysburg." He argued that his amendment would not compel the mixing of races because, "This is no question of society, no question of social life, no question of social equality." He denounced the choice of segregated but equal facilities as "invariably an inferior article." Sumner concluded, "Let the record be made at last, which shall be the cap-stone of the Reconstructed Republic."

Debate over Sumner's amendment to the Amnesty Bill raged for three more weeks. Sumner often rose to deliver extensive defenses of his amendment, as if to personally filibuster the measure. As the days wore on almost all Senators vacated the Chamber whenever Sumner rose to deliver a speech. Spectators quit coming to the galleries to observe, save a hard-core group of African Americans, who attended faithfully to cheer him on. Democrats charged that Sumner's amendment was "palpably unconstitutional," and a "plain usurpation of power that does not belong to Congress at all." They were obviously right. Sumner sat unmoved while Carl Schurz and Lyman Trumbull presented lucid arguments against the amendment.

At this time Frederick Sawyer sat as a Senator representing Reconstructed South Carolina. Born in Massachusetts and elected to the Senate by the South Carolina Republican Political Machine and hoping to win more support from European American voters in his adopted State, he favored the Amnesty Bill and figured Sumner's amendment would prevent it becoming law. In response, Sumner charged Sawyer of being unfaithful to his voter base. Sawyer rebuked the charge. At that point Sumner declared: "Why seeks he now to liberate his soul against me? Is it to gratify the [African American] people of South Carolina? Does he think to win favor among them by striking at me while I am laboring to serve them?" "Striking at me?" — Perhaps Sumner was suffering anew from recollections of the long-ago caning administered by Preston Brooks, who had then also represented South Carolina.

Finally, on February 9, it was time to vote. A simple majority vote would attach the amendment to the Amnesty Bill. Well, the vote was a tie. Democrats and the Republican Faction that supported the Amnesty Bill delivered exactly as many votes as Republicans who opposed the Amnesty Bill. So Sumner had succeeded in swinging some Senators away from the Amnesty Bill. Vice President Schuyler Colfax, holding the tie-breaking vote, chose to kill the Amnesty Bill by voting to attach Sumner's amendment. When the Amnesty Bill came up for a vote afterward, sufficient Senators abstained from voting to prevent attainment of the two-thirds majority required for granting amnesty to former Confederate leaders. [R73;536-539]

Meanwhile in South Carolina, the first wave of Kuklux trials were wrapping up in the Federal Circuit Court in Columbia. All prisoners were European American men and all alleged victims were African American men. The charges were based on the Federal Enforcement Act, whereby it was a crime to interfere with the voting rights of African American men. The limited nature of the law presented problems for the prosecution because the issues before the court, with few exceptions, concerned maltreatment or, in some cases, murder of African Americans who had participated in the State militia, whose conduct and threats had caused European American men to worry about the safety of their families and the security of their property. The Columbia trials had begun in late November, 1871, with Hugh Bond of Baltimore and George Bryan of Charleston sitting together at the bench. Two prominent and well known lawyers had led the defense team: Reverdy Johnson of Maryland, a Democrat who had served as Attorney General in the Zachary Taylor Administration, and Henry Stanbery of Ohio, who had been the Attorney General under Andrew Johnson and who had resigned that post to successfully defend the President in the Federal Senate's Impeachment trial. No former Confederates of the

European American race were allowed to be jurors by Federal law, so the Grand Jury consisted of 21 African Americans and 6 European Americans who had not been Confederates. The panel of Petit Jurors consisted of 39 African Americans and 10 European Americans who had not been Confederates, 6 of them active Republican Party leaders.

Federal troops had been instrumental in encouraging "informers" to come forward and give names of men suspected of being Kuklux. Prisoners had no rights, for the writ of *Habeas Corpus*, had been withdrawn, so we can suspect that Federal troops were engaged in harsh methods to force prisoners to "talk" and "name names," but I have seen no records of that. Fear of arrest by Federal military troops was greatest in York County, where Major Lewis Merrill commanded. There "arrests were made by squads of cavalry, almost always in the nighttime. There were no warrants. The prisoners were taken to jail, there to remain at the pleasure of the Government, without the right to have inquiry made into the cause of their detention." In that county, "every [European American] man, (except, of course, the very few who called themselves Republicans), felt that he was at the mercy of any so-called "informer" who might give his name to Major Merrill as being a Kuklux. The official list of arrested and jailed York County men totaled 195. Several other counties suffered similarly. In Union County, "probably 200" European American men were arrested and jailed. In Spartanburg County, "arrests numbered some hundreds." About 35 were arrested in Newberry. There were several arrests in Chester. The first wave of Kuklux trials, mentioned above, drew from these prisoners, but trying them all in a formal court setting would prove to be a legal impossibility, especially since the Federal Enforcement Act concerned denying voting rights, not physical abuse.

There were 5 Kuklux trials in Columbia during the winter session of Federal Court:

1. Robert Mitchell of York was sentenced to 18 months in prison and fined $100 for conspiring to injure Jim Williams because, according to the Court, Williams had cast a vote in the October 1870 election. Of course the casting of that vote had nothing to do with the harm that had befallen Williams. You will recall that Williams had commanded the African American militia in lower York County, which was very well armed with 96 breech-loading rifles. And you will recall that those men had terrorized the region, firing their guns and causing great worry among the European American men and their families. Especially worrisome had been Williams' public declaration that his men would "kill from the cradle to the grave" if confronted. He never acted on that threat. Williams was found dead, hung to a tree on March 7, 1871, reportedly the work of about 60 men, supposedly Kuklux. A short time afterward that militia "turned in their arms and disbanded."

2. Captain John Mitchell and Dr. Thomas Whitesides, "both men of high character and equally high standing in York County," were sentenced, respectively, to 5 years in prison and fined $1,000 and 1 year in prison and fined $100. These two were being severely punished for whipping Charles Leach, because, as stated by the District Attorney, "he was a [Republican] and voted the [Republican] ticket, heretofore, and to prevent his voting it hereafter."

3. John Millar, although proven not to be a Kuklux, was sentenced to 3 months in jail and fined $20 for conspiring to prevent some African American men from voting in a future election.

4. Dr. Edward Avery of York, was charged with interfering with the voting rights of three African American men, but fled from the State during the trial proceedings, forfeiting his $3,000 bail. "Some months later," he would receive a pardon from the President and return home.

5. Samuel Brown, "a highly respected citizen of York, well advanced in years" pleaded guilty of being a Kuklux but refused to testify against anyone despite extreme pressure from prosecutors. The Court retaliated by sentencing him to 5 years in prison and fined him $1,000.

During this same Court session 50 other European American men, mostly young, pleaded guilty of being Kuklux in exchange for light sentences of not much more than time served (3 months) to as much as 18 months, plus small fines. We recognize that the Kuklux trials were to punish for interfering with the voting rights of Republicans, not convicting people for murder. [R201;189-190,197-211]

Before presenting an account of the lavish corruption in the South Carolina State Government, let us move to Mississippi and examine the results of its Kuklux trials. Many suspected Kuklux had been arrested going back many months. For example, the Federal Attorney for the Northern District of

Mississippi, had testified in November of 1870 before a Joint House and Senate Committee, that "he had under indictment between 200 and 300 persons charged with violation of the Federal Enforcement Law." And the first trial in America under the Enforcement Act would take place in Oxford, Mississippi, in mid May, 1871. Twenty-eight (28) European Americans, jailed for the March 29 killing of an African American in Monroe County, were seeking release on bond prior to their trials. The 8-day trial, involving several very able lawyers and 40 witnesses, "was attended with great interest and excitement. A company of [Federal] infantry and one of cavalry were on hand to maintain order." Of primary concern was by what authority did the Federal Court take control of a murder involving only people of Mississippi, that being a case normally tried in State Court? The Court heard the State rights jurisdiction argument and rendered its decision: Because of authority granted in the Federal Amendment to Nationalize Citizenship (14th), the Federal Enforcement Act — designed to protect African Americans and people who had opposed State Secession — did not violate the Federal Constitution. But would the 28 European Americans be released on bond or be forced to remain in jail until their trials? The Judge released 24 of the 28 from jail to await trial "on their own recognizance" — 16 on bonds of $500 each and 8 on bonds of $5,000 each. When these 28 would appear for their trial all would plead guilty. No individual murder would be identified within the group. All would be convicted. But the sentence would never be carried out. I suppose that society could not accept the execution of 28 men for the murder of 1 man. And this legal technique of unshakable loyalty within indicted groups would do much to protect all. Many would be indicted and tried. An April 20, 1872 report for Mississippi's Northern District would show 490 indicted, 172 arrested, 28 pleading guilty (the same group of 28 previously mentioned), and 14 confessing and agreeing to cooperate with authorities. A subsequent report would list 678 cases of persons indicted, 325 of those cases disposed of, 262 resulting in convictions. The report for the year ending June 20, 1873, would show 268 cases disposed of, 184 resulting in convictions.

Careful analysis of the events involving the Union Leagues and the Kuklux reveals a political struggle that was pursued "regardless of race, color or nativity." More specifically, historian James Garner would write that the Federal program to Reconstruct the Governments of the conquered States, empowered by the votes of African American men, "did not take the form of armed and organized resistance, but of secret retaliation upon the [Republican Party's] agents, and especially favored beneficiaries, regardless of race, color or nativity." [R204;351-353]

Returning to South Carolina, we find that, as the Kuklux trials wound down in Columbia, the "Joint Special Financial Investigating Committee," composed of 2 Republican Senators and 3 Republican Representatives, having completed gathering as much financial and behavioral evidence as time had allowed, was proceeding to report its findings. The picture the Committee painted in that report was both grave and astounding, almost unbelievable. Here are some highlights:

> State Government spending for all purposes, from September, 1868, to October 31, 1870, was $4,184,783. The cost of enrolling and arming the militia was $421,159, and the Committee report charged that "a glaring robbery of the treasury, for personal ambition and gain, had been perpetrate," resulting in a loss "nearly enough to pay the interest on the State debt for one year."

> The total spending by the Land Commission "as far as known" was $746,724, which exceeded by $326,723 the amount realized from the sale of Land Commission bonds. This activity was deemed a "gigantic folly" of which "a more outrageous and enormous swindle could not have been perpetrated and a more subtle manner of concealment perfected." The report accused the Land Commission of paying the exorbitant price, on average, of $7 per acre for what amounted to "the improved and unimproved, eligible or ineligible, the 104,078 acres, sandhill, swamp and otherwise." Members of the Land Commission Advisory Board — made up of Governor Scott, Comptroller Neagle, Treasurer Parke, Attorney General Chamberlain and Secretary Cardozo — were charged with "neglect of duty and unwarrantable violations of law." The report said the members of the Board, not the State, were personally responsible for any loss or damage to the State treasury by reason of the acts of H. H. Kimpton, the Financial Agent the Board had used, recognizing that the Land bonds were only backed by the "personal bond of H. H. Kimpton."

> The State debt, as of October 1871, was $22,371,306 plus $6,887,608 of "contingent liabilities in the shape of endorsements of railroad bonds." Of these amounts, the report concluded that "bonds

in the sum of $6,314,000 had been fraudulently and unlawfully issued." Historian John Reynold would observe, "The figures thus given, compared with those given the Committee of the Taxpayers' Convention in May, 1871, led to the general belief that, in the statements made by the State officials to that Committee, the figures [had been] 'doctored' so as to give out a false report of the debt."

A special 5-man Committee of the South Carolina House, including C. C. Bowen, then explored possible legal responses to the fraud revealed by the work of the "Joint Special Financial Investigating Committee." This resulted in a decision to launch Impeachment proceeding in the House. C. C. Bowen then introduced two Bills of Impeachment before the House on the charge of "high crimes and misdemeanors" — one bill against Governor Robert Scott and the other against Treasurer Niles Parker. Historian John Reynold would describe Bowen as being "late of Georgia, recently arrived here and a resident of Charleston — a tough character all through." These Bills of Impeachment were taken quite seriously, causing Governor Scott to scramble for money to pay the necessary bribes. The fund for maintaining the State militia had been rather idle, it not being an election year, so he took from that account, drawing out $25,545 payable to a "John Mooney," $10,600 payable to a "David Leggett" and $13,500 payable to a "David H. Wilson." These three fellows did not exist; the names were fictitious. Scott took the money and started paying bribes: starting with $15,000 to the Speaker of the House, Franklin Moses, and then with between $5,000 and $200, he went down the line, paying Legislators for their "no" vote. Testimony would later suggest that Scott had offered the sponsor of the Bills of Impeachment, C. C. Bowen, a bribe of $15,000, but that Bowen had held out for $25,000, to no avail. The bill to impeach Scott failed to win House approval by a vote of 65 to 32 and the bill to impeach Parker failed by a vote of 63 to 27. So State Republicans in the House, 75 of them African Americans (compared to 97 votes cast), covered up the horrific fraud revealed to exist within their mostly European American leadership while they took bribe money and kept quiet.

Not long afterward, on March 13, the South Carolina General Assembly concluded its session, having spent 106 days hard at work (?), or so one would hope. Here are the sad numbers of an extravagant spending spree that, although a true account, is hard to believe. The Legislature had spent $1,175,493 on pay and expenses, money that did not go more than a few city blocks beyond the capital building in Columbia. Here is where the money went:

Wine, liquor, cigars, sundries:	$282,514
Printing:	$173,000
Pay for 212 messengers:	$158,738
Furniture:	$116,578
Pay for 155 members:	$102,900
Pay for 23 porters:	$98,640
Legislative accounts and claims:	$73,127
Stationary:	$72,815
Pay for 475 clerks:	$39,316
Fuel:	$11,708
Money for 27 solicitors:	$10,449
Pay for 74 pages:	$8,167
Newspapers:	$5,238
Pay for 16 door keepers:	$3,864
Other Expenses:	$18,439
Total of Above:	**$1,175,493**

As you have come to fully understand, fraudulent behavior was rampant. Noteworthy legislation included:

The act authorizing the Governor to keep an armed force was repealed.

State taxes on property, for the fiscal year commencing November 1, 1871 was set at 8 mils (2 mils for public schools). County taxes were 3 mils generally and a little higher in several counties.

State financial involvement escalated in support of the huge, mountain-tunneling Blue Ridge Railroad Company project, complete with more bribery and fraud in the Legislature. During this session a bill was promulgated that financed State payments to the Railroad through a scheme styled "Revenue Bond Scrip." Governor Scott had originally vetoed the measure, but bribery had been sufficient to override his veto, winning passage by a final Senate vote of 22 to 6 and a final House vote of 84 to 18.

> The Blue Ridge Railroad Company was in financial trouble. Boring long tunnels through 13 mountains, towards the destination of Knoxville, Tennessee, was far more work than the Blue Ridge schemers were capable of pulling off. The company had paid no interest or principle against the $4,000,000 in State-guaranteed bonds that had been issued in 1866 — the company was insolvent and the South Carolina Legislature needed a new scheme. The new scheme involved exchanging $1,800,000 worth of new State-backed railroad bonds, called "Revenue Bond Script," for the earlier State-guaranteed $4,000,000 in railroad bonds. Furthermore, the script was to be used for "payment of taxes and all other dues to the State, except the special tax levied to pay interest on the public debt." A large tax increase of 3 mils, "in addition to all other taxes," was levied as part of the scheme. To put script money in circulation, all "county treasurers were required to receive it in payment of the taxes mentioned." The scheme anticipated paying off the entire Blue Ridge obligation in 4 years. I suppose the Script bonds were printed in conveniently small denominations to be used like State-issued and State guaranteed paper money. Each piece of script paper said, "Due by the State of South Carolina to the bearer thereof."

> John J. Patterson, President of the Blue Ridge Railroad Company, was in the middle of the scheme, and coordinator of the bribes and payoffs needed to win its passage — a considerable hurdle considering Scotts' veto. To finance bribes, Patterson gave State Treasurer Niles Parker an order "to deliver to H. H. Kimpton an amount of Revenue Bond Script due the Blue Ridge Railroad Company equaling $114,250." Further instruction called for $42,857 worth of that script, at par, be used to pay bribery in the House and $71,414 at 70 cents on the dollar be used to pay bribery in the Senate.

Of this scheme, historian John Reynold would write:

> "These [railroad] acts, with the act for the issuance of the Blue Ridge Scrip, constituted one scheme for the benefit of John J. Patterson, H. H. Kimpton and the members of the Financial Board — Governor Scott, Attorney-General Chamberlain, Treasurer Parker and Comptroller-General Neagle."

But the scheme would fail. Historian John Reynold would add a postscript:

> "The Blue Ridge Script [would be declared] void by the State Supreme Court in 1873, and a judgment to the same effect [would be] rendered by the Supreme Court of the United States in 1904."

So we see that, by this time — 7 years after the conquest of the Confederacy, in early 1872 — the Republican controlled South Carolina State Government was an amazing, criminal, unsustainable fraud. Yet several more years would transpire before the honest people of the State, the patient taxpayers, would succeed at throwing the rascals out and instituting a government that would honestly serve all of the people of the State. [R201;172-178]

Meanwhile in Mississippi, the State House organized under an African American Speaker, John Lynch, beginning a trend of elevating a significant number of his race to leadership positions. Several African

Americans would follow Lynch to the Speaker's chair, but only Lynch would merit praise for a job well done. Around 1890, historian James Garner would write this analysis of Lynch's career:

> "He presided over the deliberations of the [Mississippi] House with dignity and impartiality, a fact to which his political opponents bore testimony upon his retirement. He was a slave [prior to 1865], became a Justice of the Peace by appointment from Adelbert Ames in 1869, and, in 1873, was elected to [the Federal House], where he served two terms. He presided over the Republican National Convention in 1884, and is at present a paymaster in the [Federal] Army. He is one of the most intelligent men of his race [and] is conservative in his views . . ." [R204;295-296]

(2Q72)

A Faction of Republican politicians, which called itself the "Liberal Republican Party," held a Faction Convention in Cincinnati on May 1. Prominent Faction leaders included Lyman Trumbull, of Illinois, Carl Schurz, and Gratz Brown. Noteworthy supporting Newspapermen, included Horace Greeley, of the New York *Tribune*, and Bowles of the Springfield, Massachusetts *Republican*. Long-time Boston political machine leader and Sumner supporter Francis Bird supported the Faction, and that troubled Sumner greatly, especially since he did not join the Faction for reasons of his own. It seems that Sumner was not in attendance for several reasons. The Faction's main objective was to rid the Federal Government of graft and corruption. But Sumner's main objective was to maintain power through Republican Political Machines in the Reconstructed States, in spite of the political corruption they inspired. Although Sumner shared not personally in the spoils of corruption, he accepted corrupt practices within government if corrupt people supported his idealistic political goals — especially when involving African American policy. Close Sumner political friends in Massachusetts, who joined him in shunning the Faction, included Samuel Hooper and Edward Pierce. And William Garrison, who you will recall as the publisher of the former *Liberator*, must have agreed with Sumner's judgment on the relative merits of fighting government corruption versus sustaining Republican Political Machines, justifying his support for Ulysses Grant as being the best way to keep the Democrats out of power.

Furthermore, Sumner had been opposed to the potential nominees for President being talked about among Faction members. He thought Lyman Trumbull too weak and had staunchly distrusted Horace Greeley ever since he had helped win the release of Jeff Davis from Fortress Monroe. But Charles Adams was the potential candidate whom Sumner had opposed the most, for, being a fellow Bostonian, an Adams candidacy would severely undermine Sumner's political support in his home State.

But, many believed that Sumner's support of the Faction would be crucial to its viability. August Belmont, who headed up the Democratic Party's financial efforts, had warned that many Republican voters would continue to support Ulysses Grant unless Sumner came forth with a statement which displayed a "most unequivocal attitude" on the issue. David Wells, an opponent of import tax corruption, thought he had won over Sumner during a mid-April visit in Washington. But Howard University Vice-President John Langston had quickly convinced Sumner to renege on his pledge to Wells. Of partial African descent himself, Langston convinced Sumner that the third-party movement being pursued by the Faction would only help the Democratic Party gain control of the Federal Government. And Sumner was aware that Frederick Douglass, also of partial African descent, believed that it was necessary to support Grant to keep the Republican Party in Power. Both Langston and Douglass equated keeping the Republican Party in power with progress for African Americans, even though they knew that would mean continuing unprecedented political graft and corruption.

Francis Bird had made many attempts to get Charles Sumner to join the Faction. Bird had pleaded with Sumner from Boston in a letter dated April 15: "Without your cordial cooperation and vigorous leadership, the movement will be a failure, here and elsewhere." And in a letter dated April 28, he wrote, "You are shorn of power without us. I pray you, be prepared for that." Realizing that he had gained his Senate job through the political efforts of Bird's powerful Boston political organization, and that Bird organization support had saved him from defeat in re-election bids, Sumner was worried that Bird was threatening him with political oblivion if he refused the invitation to join him on the train trip to Cincinnati. Yet he asked Bird to submit a resolution before the Convention which would commit the Faction to support laws which ensured "all citizens" access to the polls, regardless racial origin, so that "all shall be equal before the law." But when Bird asked Sumner if he would support the Faction if the Convention adopted his resolution, Sumner warned that he might not, even then. On the day the

Convention opened, Bird wrote: "Urged by you to the perilous ridge, we are left to fight the battle alone." Yes, Sumner had often urged Republicans "to the perilous ridge," where the political infighting would be horrific, and many political careers would die upon that ridge. But what Bird was learning too late was that Sumner was not a fighting man. He was a just a pompous intellectual who had even been incapable of shaking off a brief caning administered by Preston Brooks. [R73;543-544]

The Faction Convention in Cincinnati nominated Horace Greeley of New York for President and Gratz Brown of Missouri for Vice President. The Faction Party Platform contained a pledge to ensure that citizens of African ancestry held the same legal rights as other citizens. The Platform also pledged to grant amnesty to all former Confederates who were still being denied the same legal rights as American citizens. [R73;539-544]

A few days after the "Liberal Republican Party" Convention concluded in Cincinnati, Charles Sumner resumed his fight for a bill to expand the societal rights of African Americans, especially with regard to forcing integrated school class rooms. Sumner's bill would more clearly force providers of transportation, lodging, entertainment and food to give equal access to African Americans. It would more clearly force courts to include African Americans on juries. It would more clearly take enforcement out of the hands of State Courts and put it in Federal Courts. But most importantly, Sumner's bill would close "separate but equal" schools where they were being provided and force their replacement by "integrated" schools. Even though the vast majority of the country's African Americans had coped as independent people for only 7 years, Sumner was seeking a Federal mandate that all schools in all States, cities, counties (and perhaps even at church-run schools) have integrated class rooms. Sumner ignored the fact that, for a few more decades, children of newly independent African Americans would learn and progress faster in a homogeneous classroom of children of similar age and learning ability than in an extremely diverse classroom in which the teacher would be forced to ignore most students while teaching down to the lowest ability in attendance. There would eventually be a proper time to move to integrated classrooms in States where about half of the students in each class would be of African ancestry. But that time was not 1872. In 1872, family life in almost all States — those living in Sumner's Massachusetts being closest to being an exception — would have been disrupted by Sumner's bill. Although Oregon prohibited families of African ancestry to settle in that State, Massachusetts had a small African American population — of an average ancestry that was between 25% and 40% European. Furthermore, most of that population had been independent for a long time — about two generations.

Sumner demanded abolishment of "the relics of generations of [African American bondage]." Speaking to the majority of Senators from outside New England, Sumner alleged that "separate but equal" schools were "a system of caste, which so long as it endures will render your school system a nursery of wrong and injustice." Seeing a parallel between attending school together as children and voting together as adults, Sumner asked those Senators, "How can you expect the [African American] child or the [European American] child to grow up to those relations which they are to have together at the ballot-box if you begin by degrading the [African American] child at school and by exalting the [European American] child at school?" Of course, several Senators insisted the obvious: the Federal Constitution prohibited the Federal Government from mandating how States operated their public school systems. The language in the Constitution was clear and simple. The typical third-graded student could clearly understand its meaning. And Sumner did not deny that his bill violated the Federal Constitution. He only replied in double-talk: "I have . . . sworn to support the Constitution, and it binds me to vote for anything for human rights." He had no choice, for if he admitted officially that he was intentionally advocating violating the Federal Constitution — in violation of his oath of office — fellow Senators would be empowered to rise up and expel him from the Senate.

Lyman Trumbull insisted that Sumner's African American legislation was unnecessary because, except for forcing school integration, existing Federal Laws already gave African Americans the legal rights listed in the bill: "the same right to travel, the same right to be entertained at a hotel, the same rights . . . exactly as a [European American] person, and . . . the same remedies for their enforcement." Sumner's substitute bill, Trumbull warned, was more than a redundant legal equality bill. It was in fact "a social equality bill." Relishing the fight, the Republican leadership gave Sumner free reign to expound upon his bill — President pro tempore Henry Anthony always allowed Sumner, at any time, to jump up and interrupt whoever had the floor. Why? Perhaps because Republican leaders figured Sumner's demonstrations before the Senate would discourage African American leaders from joining the Liberal Republican Party movement.

Despite his passionate rhetoric, Sumner had no chance of actually winning adoption of his bill. When votes were tallied, only 13 Senators gave support. Some of these Senators represented New England States, where integrated schools were often necessitated by the fact that many towns could not afford to pay for separate teachers for tiny classes of a few African American students. The other Senators voting for the bill had been sent to Washington by Republican Political Machines in the Reconstructed States. Senators fresh from the Liberal Republican Party Convention in Cincinnati generally absented themselves rather than recording a vote against Sumner's bill. The vote assured that each State would retain its authority to choose separate but equal or integrated school systems to best suit its respective needs.

Well, on May 21, Charles Sumner left his Senate seat to go home to bed. It was going to be a long night devoted to intensified Federal suppression of the Kuklux underground political organization. Sumner must have already used his turn to speak on the issue, and, being tired and still suffering from angina, he had decided to go home. He would be been right about it being a long night, but he would be wrong about it being devoted entirely to debate over intensified Federal suppression of the Kuklux. After Sumner had been gone for a while, Matthew Carpenter of Wisconsin decided to seize the opportunity and switch the agenda to a bill that was a winnable and practical alternative to Sumner's failed African American bill. Carpenter's bill did not mandate African American access to juries, did not mandate universal school integration, and did not transfer relevant litigation from State courts to Federal courts. And Republican leaders figured that this bill, while doing little damage to society, could be used to discourage African American voters from switching their support to the Liberal Republican Party and its candidate for President, Horace Greeley. Quite soon after Carpenter moved his African American bill to the front of the agenda, a Sumner associate sent a messenger to rouse Sumner from his bed and get him to come over for debate and voting. Alarmed, Sumner rose up and made his way to the Capitol, which was about a mile from his house. But he arrived too late. The vote had been tallied and Carpenter's rather tame African American bill had passed. Upon his arrival Sumner cried out, "without any notice . . . from any quarter, the Senate have adopted an emasculated [African American] bill." His plea to reconsider the vote got nowhere. In defeat, Sumner warned: "Sir, I sound the cry. The rights of the [African] race have been sacrificed in this Chamber where the Republican Party has a large majority. . . . Let it go forth that the sacrifice has been perpetuated." Perpetuated by whom? Well, Sumner thought it had been perpetuated by Ulysses Grant himself. [R73;545-547]

Meanwhile, in Charleston, South Carolina, a second Federal Court trial of alleged Kuklux members was winding down, having begun at the April term. Historian John Reynold would explain: "The Government's tactics in Columbia (3 months earlier) were repeated in Charleston," and the same two Federal Judges presided. Again, all alleged victims were African American men and all defendants were European American men, none of the latter supportive of the Republican Party. There were 6 Kuklux trials, resulting in the following convictions:

1. William Lowery of York was sentenced to 2 years in prison and fined $10 for offenses against Dick Wilson.

2. Leander Spencer and William Smith of York were tried on the charge of conspiracy to interfere with voting rights and the murder of Tom Roundtree. The Jury could not agree, resulting in a mistrial. These men were never tried again.

3. Elijah Ross Sepaugh of York was also tried on the charge of conspiracy to interfere with voting rights and the murder of Tom Roundtree. Here the jury found the defendant guilty on both charges, but, because many legal experts believed the Federal Enforcement Act violated the Federal Constitution, the Judges suspended sentencing until the Supreme Court heard that question.

4. John Rogers of Union was tried on the charge of conspiracy to interfere with voting rights, the attack on the Union County Jail, and subsequent murders. As in a previous case, the Jury could not agree, resulting in a mistrial. The accused was never tried again.

5. Thomas Zimmerman of Spartanburg was acquitted of the charge of interfering with voting rights and the murder of Wallie Fowler.

6. Robert Higgings of York was tried on the charge of conspiracy to interfere with voting rights and participation in the Kuklux raid in which militia leader Jim Williams was murdered. The defendant was acquitted of murder, but sentenced to 3 years in prison and fined $100 for the conspiracy charge.

As in Columbia, many men pleaded guilty, and many accepted sentences ranging from 3 months to 10 years and fines ranging from $10 to $1,000. In this manner 26 were sentenced without benefit of a trial of their cases. [R201;213-214]

Meanwhile on May 31, Charles Sumner maneuvered himself into position to deliver a long speech he called "Republicanism versus Grantism." Few Senators were on hand that day, and the nature of Sumner's oration had not been previously disclosed. But, soon after word spread through the Capitol that Sumner was delivering a major oration, Senators returned to their seats, and the House adjourned so Representatives could listen from the galleries. The Republican National Convention was scheduled to open in Philadelphia in just 5 days, so this could be a politically important speech. Sumner certainly hoped so. It was by this desperate attack that he hoped to spark a last-minute dump-Grant movement at the Philadelphia Convention. Sumner accused Grant of being "rich in houses, lands, and stock, above his salary, being probably the richest President since George Washington" — "radically unfit for the Presidential office" — as President, "an enormous failure" — and in a mocking parody of the famous praise bestowed upon George Washington: "first in nepotism, first in gift-taking and repaying by official patronage, first in Presidential pretensions, and first in quarrel with his countrymen." Sumner revealed how Edwin Stanton, shortly before his death, had told him in private his opinion of Grant: "I know [Ulysses] Grant better than any other person in the country can know him . . . now I tell you what I know: he cannot govern this country."

Democratic and Liberal Republican newspapers praised Sumner's speech and gave it broad exposure. Horace Greeley's New York *Tribune* enthused that, "Our greatest Senator" has delivered "the greatest speech of his life!" Letters poured into Sumner's office praising his effort as, "the greatest oration . . . in our political history" — "wonderfully able and statesmanlike" — "so unambiguous, so cogent, so complete, . . . so true." But Republican newspapers denounced the vicious attack on Ulysses Grant. The Washington *Republican* warned, "The peerless one is peerless no more. He crawls, bedaubed and bedraggled in the slime of our curbstone politics, retailing the curbstone slanders and scandals of the hour." The New York *Evening Post* concluded that Sumner had "consulted rather his resentments and prejudices than his judgment," that he had failed to "assail the Administration in its most vulnerable places," and consequently the speech would hurt Sumner more that it would hurt Grant. Because they thought the attack was "overdone, and hence a failure," the Springfield (Massachusetts) *Republican* predicted "the people will reject it as a truthful representation of Grant's character." Robert Winthrop, the long-time Massachusetts politician, wrote a friend: "[Sumner] has a wonderful vein of vituperation, and really seems unconscious that he has described himself, when describing [Grant]. His career has been one long Philippic against everybody who did not agree with him, and he has cultivated invectives until he has become callous to the violence and offensiveness." Biographer David Donald would write: "Indeed, the speech was one of Sumner's poorest efforts, clearly reflecting the prolonged mental and emotional stain to which he had been subjected."

John Logan, of Illinois rebuked Sumner's attack of Grant by simply reminding all voters and politicians of how Grant had led the Federal Invasion of the Confederacy to a successful, although tragically bloody, victory. Who would answer Sumner's attack upon Ulysses Grant? Logan submitted that people would "find an answer to that malignant speech of [Sumner's] in every crutch that helps and aids the wounded [Federal] soldier to wend his was along in this land . . . in every wooden arm . . . in the bereaved heart of every widowed mother." He predicted "the weeds of mourning" in the northern States "for the lost son and the lost brother will speak in . . . tones of thunder in defense of one of the most gallant soldiers that ever led a gallant band for the [conquest of seceded States]." [R73;547-551]

Meanwhile, Hamilton Fish and Ulysses Grant gave in to British demands and submitted to the Senate an amendment to the Treaty concerning arbitrating the "Claims on England" issue. The amendment expressly excluded from arbitration all claims for losses suffered as an indirect consequence of the damages inflicted to marine commerce in support of the northern States by Confederate crews aboard British-built warships such as the *C. S. S. Alabama*. Charles Sumner was surely angry that the heart might be cut from the "Claims on England" movement he had founded and nurtured. And he planned to fight that his demands be sustained. Perhaps he was privately yet hopeful for a Federal invasion of Canada. In fact, the New York *Times* had reported that, while among political friends, Sumner had warned that "Great Britain should have been promptly notified, when she proposed to break up the [Arbitration] Tribunal, that the result would be war." But, publicly Sumner declined to threaten war, instead rising in the Senate to expressly deny the New York *Times* report as "absurd and ridiculous." He only attempted to place the blame squarely on Hamilton Fish and Ulysses Grant for retreating from demanding payment for indirect losses. To that end he submitted a motion, "that, without declaring any conclusion on the proposed withdrawal of certain claims, the Senate express the further opinion that the determination of this question belongs properly to the discretion of [Ulysses Grant] in the conduct of the case before the Tribunal of Arbitration. However, fellow Senators defeated Sumner's motion. And shortly thereafter, the Senate approved the amendment to the Treaty by the required two-thirds majority. In protest, Charles Sumner had declined to cast his vote. But the British Government would refuse to accept the amended Treaty as sufficient proof that the Federal Government would not attempt to seek claims from the Tribunal of Arbitration for indirect losses. Instead, the British would obtain the needed assurance by arranging "an informal procedure for excluding indirect claims." Charles Adams would be the principal lawyer representing the Federal side of the case before the Tribunal, and it would be with Adams that the British would achieve the required assurances. [R73;507-508]

Meanwhile, as the Republican Party National Convention opened on June 5 in Philadelphia, it was apparent that Charles Sumner's May 31 speech, "Republicanism versus Grantism," had not significantly discouraged Delegates from nominating him for a second term. But Sumner's vindictive speech had encouraged re-nomination campaign leaders to counterattack by recommending Massachusetts Senator Henry Wilson for Vice President. And Delegates dutifully voted to concur. Apparently, by blasting Grant so intensely, Sumner had succeeded in elevating Henry Wilson to the titular leadership of the Massachusetts Republican Party. And Sumner would find that — with Grant's nomination secured and the "Liberal Republican" Faction weakened — his ability to disrupt orderly proceedings in the Senate was coming to an abrupt end as well.

The day after the Republican National Convention, Sumner set at his desk on the Senate floor through the night looking for a chance to introduce a motion attaching his African American bill as an amendment to the appropriations bill then being debated. Finally, at 7 o'clock, about the time morning broke, Sumner saw his chance. He offered his amendment. But President pro tempore Henry Anthony ruled the motion out of order! What? Had Grant's man, Anthony, not permitted Sumner to attach his African American amendment to other legislation without questioning its being germane? Yes. But that had occurred before Grant secured the nomination for a second term, and now it was obvious that the Liberal Republican movement was losing momentum. The Republican leadership had no more use of Sumner. And Sumner had no more use for the Party that he had been so effective at building. Biographer David Donald would write:

"Sadly, taking up hat and cane, Sumner left the Chamber and the Republican Party."

At the Democratic National Convention at Baltimore, Delegates voted to nominate Horace Greeley for President. Therefore, Greeley would be listed on ballots as being the candidate of both the Democratic Party and the Liberal Republican Party. Democratic Delegates approved a Platform measure that pledged the Party to ensure that African Americans had access to the same legal protection provided European Americans. [R73;551-552]

(3Q72)

On July 13 Charles Sumner wrote Wadsworth Longfellow to explain why he had just decided to support Greeley over Grant: "I have not taken this step without anxious reflection, and I know the differences it wall cause, but I cannot help it. I felt it my duty, which I could not avoid." He predicted that the upcoming election would be "the most remarkable in our political history" because "the Democrats have accepted a [Liberal Republican Party] Platform with a life-time Abolitionist [and Exclusionist] as a candidate." This revolutionary change in the Democratic Party should foreshadow "the final settlement of all the issues [arising out of the Federal Invasion of the Confederacy]." Supporting Greeley over Grant also meant that Sumner's re-election to the Senate would be endangered as well. Sumner was well aware of the political dangers of embracing a third party movement and of bedding down with the Democrats, but emotionally he could not help himself. Amazing! For a generation Sumner had trained Massachusetts voters to regard Democrats as an evil species of humanity. How could he retain their support if he suddenly bedded down with that "evil species of humanity?" Greeley had even helped pay the bail bond for President Jeff Davis!

Sixteen days later, on July 29, Charles Sumner finally made public his support for Horace Greeley. The election in North Carolina, scheduled unusually early, was just a few days away, and any further delay would have prevented him from influencing that election. In an open letter to African American men, Sumner announced that he supported Greeley over Grant and especially encouraged all African American men to also support Greeley over Grant. Greeley happily wrote a friend: "You see that Sumner has spoken! 'Was that not thunder?' I believe no utterance was ever more resonant and effective."

But not all of the well-known northeastern States leaders of the former Abolition/Exclusion political movement were switching their allegiance to Horace Greeley and the awkward coalition of Democrats and Liberal Republicans. Many obviously thought Greeley would lose to Grant no matter what they did, and they did not want to be caught backing a loser. Wendell Phillips charged that Greeley was "wholly untrustworthy," and "surrounded by [political] friends more objectionable that Grant's" political friends. Gerrit Smith published a broadside denouncing Sumner for being "born in affluence and bred in elegance," and praising Grant for being "a poor boy and a laboring man" and for his "patriotism, integrity, and general administration" of the Federal Government.

Massachusetts Republican newspapers universally denounced Sumner for endorsing Horace Greeley. After all, Grant's election would propel a Massachusetts man, Henry Wilson, to the office of Vice President. The glory days of John Adams and Quincy Adams might be in the State's future. No Massachusetts politician could turn his back on that, so they uniformly reasoned. Boston's *Commonwealth*, the most loyal of Sumner newspapers, denounced Sumner for joining forces with the "vindictive, merciless, arrogant, rebellious" Democrats and alleged that southern States Democrats were "carrying terror by night in reckless and secret bands."

J. G. Frisbie, an African American living in New York, scolded Sumner in an August 3 letter, saying, "The alliance you have made with the haters and persecutors of our race has struck the [African American] population of this city with astonishment. The Democrats here hate us as bad as ever, and it is only through the Republican Party that we are safe." Letters like this remind us how, in the northern States, racial hatred and aversion to mixed-race and mixed-ethnicity communities was traditionally more prevalent and potentially more violent than in the southern States.

Charles Sumner returned to Boston in late August. Politically he was almost entirely an outcast. As you know, Francis Bird had joined the Liberal Republicans and was surely pleased to finally have Sumner aboard, even at so late an hour. Few of the former Bird organization men had switched, and only those supported Sumner when he arrived back in Boston. In fact, Francis Bird's political machine held only a tiny fraction of its former influence. Just prior to Sumner's return to Boston, Republicans had held a political rally in Faneuil Hall, and at one point, upon the mention of Sumner's name, the crowd booed and hissed as they spat rejection at their past hero. But Sumner was apparently resigned to his political fate. He had written Wadsworth Longfellow on August 2: "The storm beats, but I could not have done otherwise. My present effort is the most important of my life. Besides bringing an original Abolitionist [and Exclusionist] into the White House, I hope to obtain for [African American men] full recognition of their [political and social independence] throughout the [southern States]." But Longfellow rebuked Sumner for believing in a remade Democratic Party, for he thought it was "a Party that has always shown itself to be corrupt and dangerous." Ebenezer Hoar simply thought Sumner "manifestly insane" for believing in a remade Democratic Party. Francis Lieber predicted that Sumner would lose what little political power he still possessed, whether Grant or Greeley won the election. Of Sumner, Lieber sadly wrote: "He stands on a bridge, and has set fire to both ends."

Sumner made one feeble attempt to break the bonds of military pride that existed between army veterans in Massachusetts and their former senior commander, hoping to thereby persuade voters to support the National Republican Party. Of course, Sumner poorly understood the bonding between military men who had together survived the fighting and lived to celebrate the final victories. He had no military experience, and his personality was rather feminine. Biographer David Donald would explain it this way: "Having always had a low opinion of soldiers and feeling that the real victories of the [invasion] had been won in the Senate Chamber, he failed to recognize the powerful bonds of loyalty which joined the hundreds of thousands of [Federal] veterans in proud memory of their hard-fought battles." Yet Sumner tried. He told the people of Massachusetts that, "The time for the soldier has passed, especially when his renewed power would once more remind [former Confederates] of their defeat. Victory over [former Confederates] should be known only in the [independence the Federal Government has been able to bestow upon the African American]." It should not "be flaunted in the face of the vanquished. . . . It should not be inscribed on regimental colors, or portrayed in pictures at the National Capitol." At this point Sumner had arrived at the point of his argument, for he was going to equate pride among Federal veterans — which should be cast aside for the good of the country — to political support for their past leader, Ulysses Grant — who should be cast aside for the good of the country. Sumner put the argument this way: "But [Ulysses Grant] is a regimental color with the forbidden inscription. . . . It is doubtful if such a presence can promote true reconciliation."

But other than making a feeble argument about regimental colors, what was Sumner to do? If he stayed in Massachusetts and really campaigned for Horace Greeley and Henry Wilson, he would fall even deeper into political oblivion. Well, Sumner decided to skip town and vacation in Europe. It was somewhat a replay of the charade he had conducted in the three-year period following the caning administered by Preston Brooks. The main difference was that, this time, the man was truly falling apart physically. This time, he was not faking it. As usual, he got a doctor's excuse. Something like: if he remained in Massachusetts and "tried to campaign for Greeley, he might simply break down, bodily and mentally, and drag on for years of maimed life." At the appointed time, his small cadre of remaining political friends conveyed him out of Boston harbor aboard a tugboat and put him aboard the steamship, *Malta* as it entered the open sea. They boarded him under the disguise of an assumed name. Sumner probably sneaked about the deck in an effort to avoid recognition during the voyage, too. But he was eventually spotted and news of his sneaking off to Europe eventually coursed through American newspapers. After hearing the news, Ulysses Grant, on August 26, wrote down his thoughts: "Poor old Sumner is sick from neglect and the consciousness that he is not all of the Republican Party. I very much doubt whether he will ever get to Washington again. If he is not crazy his mind is at least so affected as to disqualify him for the proper discharge of his duties as Senator." [R73;552-555, 563-564]

Meanwhile, on August 21, in Tupelo, Mississippi, a Democratic Party Convention nominated Lucius Lamar as their candidate for the Federal House seat designated for northeastern Mississippi, District 1. A few months earlier the Republican-dominated Mississippi Legislature had drawn the 1872 boundaries of the State's 6 Federal House districts to ensure 5 districts would elect Republicans while the other, District 1, was conceded to a Democrat. Biographer James Murphy would explain:

> In the 1871 Mississippi elections "Republicans won control of the Legislature again, but their majority was a small one; and many [African American minority] counties went over to Democratic control. The startled [Republican-controlled] Legislature hastened to consolidate its domination of the State's [seats in the Federal House]. Republican candidates had carried all Districts in 1869, but, in several, their small majorities appeared vulnerable. The Legislature therefore reapportioned the State in 1872 so that 5 of the 6 Districts were rendered absolutely secure while one was conceded to the Democrats. This was achieved by grouping the heavily [European American] counties of northeast Mississippi into a single House District, thereby assuring [African American] majorities in all the other districts."

And Lucius Lamar was emerging as the Democrat whose election was "conceded." Supporters had hoped he would enter into political action upon recognition of this opportunity, even though, before being allowed to take his seat, he would need a pardon from the Federal House and Senate to remove the disability imposed upon him by the Federal Amendment Nationalizing Citizenship (14th), which excluded former Confederate officers from government office. In July, Lamar cautioned supporters of his candidacy with messages such as, "I am not a candidate, but I am so convinced of the impropriety of nominating a man under disabilities, that I cannot see how it should be tendered." At the time Lamar was a member of the State Executive Committee for the Mississippi Democratic-Conservative Party, and he participated in an early August meeting when the Committee decided to seek a fusion with the Mississippi Liberal Republican Party to enable both to campaign for electors pledged to Horace Greeley — that being a joint effort to defeat Ulysses Grant in his bid for a second term. Shortly after that

Executive Committee meeting Lamar decided "to actively solicit support for nomination" to the Federal House. Professing now to believe that his political disability could be removed, Lamar sought to convey that conviction to others." Biographer James Murphy would describe the nomination at Tupelo:

"Lamar apparently succeeded in rallying support, but neither this nor his rather enviable credentials assured an easy victory at the Tupelo meeting of Democrats on August 21. The fear expressed by the Memphis *Appeal* that the weaker candidates might combine to defeat him did not materialize, but 15 ballots passed before he secured the nomination. Since nomination, in this case, was considered tantamount to election, Lamar emerged as an important political figure after 8 years of almost complete retirement."

Lamar would be opposed by Republican Robert Flournoy — a native Mississippian, a European American, an "outspoken" Republican and supportive of harsh Reconstruction. Lamar would campaign across the District during September and early October, often speaking jointly with Flournoy to gathered audiences. But he would become sick in mid-October and retire from the canvas. He would feel better after two independent candidates would drop out and endorse him and when Flournoy would pledge to refuse the House seat should Lamar be elected, but obtain removal of his disabilities. A few days prior to the election, Lamar would feel so fully recovered and so confident of victory that he would travel to Saint Louis and campaign for Horace Greeley. Voting was scheduled for November 5. [R205;172-174, R206;104-109]

By September Wade Hampton's wife Mary was in Baltimore with her husband. Still suffering from childbirth complications arising from the 1867 pregnancy, she was in declining health. Biographer Robert Akerman would write, "She had by now become almost an invalid." Their family consisted of George, 13, Mary Singleton, known as Daisy, 11, and Alfred, 10. Like so many insurance companies across the nation, and most particularly in the southern States, the Carolina Insurance Company was experiencing staggering financial difficulties because of premature deaths. Hampton biographer Walter Cisco would present a brief picture of those troubles:

"The entire life insurance industry in the United States suffered in the decades after the war, due in no small part to the unanticipated long-term effects of wounds and disease on surviving veterans. Davis attributed his own company's problems to the higher-than-expected mortality rate of policy holders. From 1868 to 1870, twenty-three American life insurance companies went out of business. During the next 7 years, 81 more would go under."

During this same month of September, Jeff Davis was working at the Maryland branch of the Carolina Insurance Company. Since Baltimore was a much stronger financial center than Memphis, Davis was there seeking financial help. On September 18 Jeff wrote Varina, "We have many troubles here for the Carolina and I am ill at ease." In a September 29 letter to Varina he further intimated how sloppy accounting and timid management was threatening insolvency:

"My dear Wife,

"Though I have been here longer than anticipated, my work is not done. Whatever has been done or commenced by others was much worse than nothing. There is a fatal weakness in most men, that of conceding too much for the sake of avoiding controversy or offense. Thence comes my present difficulties and will flow drafts on the Company, the question being how far I may diminish them.

"Mrs. Hampton is confined to her room. In the mean time it cripples her Husband as an Agent.

"With love to the Children and a double portion to yourself, I am, as ever your affectionate

"Husband,

"Jefferson Davis." [R199;200, R200;127, R19;379, R30;357]

Meanwhile, Charles Sumner was horrified to learn, upon his September 11 arrival in Great Britain, that Francis Bird had arranged for the Massachusetts Liberal Republican Party to nominate him as their candidate for Governor — Sumner had failed to escape political danger by sneaking off to Europe. The Massachusetts Liberal Republican Party had no chance of electing the next Governor and whoever they put on the ticket would have no potential to return to the regular Republican Party. The nomination was a political death-sentence, blocking Sumner's future re-election to the Senate two years later, which would require strong support from regular Republicans in the State Legislature. Of this, biographer David Donald would write: "The news of the nomination made Sumner indignant, almost frantic, and it cost him what progress he had made, despite seasickness, toward recovery while on shipboard." He immediately cabled Bird, demanding that his name be withdrawn: "I could not and would not serve as Governor . . . Few things in my political life have troubled me more. Nothing has placed me in a position which . . . was so painful." At first Bird pretended to dismiss Sumner's refusal to accept the nomination. But, after more cables, Bird finally relented and permitted the Party to strike "Charles Sumner" from the ballot and substitute "Francis Bird." Bird would be the fall-guy. [R73;556-557]

(4Q72)

On October 10, tragedy struck the Davis family again. Jeff and Varina's son, Billy, was dead, a victim of diphtheria, Jeff having just returned home from his business trip to Maryland. The parents had previously lost two sons, and, with Billy gone, only 15-year-old Jeff, Jr. remained. There were two daughters, Margaret and Winnie. But Billy had been such a bright boy and had already shown so much potential. The loss was most difficult. Biographer Hudson Strode would write, "The father endured his inexpressible grief stoically, as the city and the South grieved with the parents." Varina would suffer emotional illness during her grieving and often complain of numbness in her arms and legs and of mental depression. Memphis Doctors would find nothing wrong organically. They would only be able to prescribe that she seek "cheerfulness." As anyone who had lost a child will tell you, it often takes years to find "cheerfulness."

A few weeks later, Mary Lee would write to "express my deep sympathy:"

". . . That gracious God 'who doth not willingly grieve or afflict the children of men' can alone give you true consolation and on Him can we lean with trust and confidence. I, too lost a lovely little grandchild last Christmas, but He has sent me another, born, too, in my house the past summer. . . . You must all come and make us a visit as I shall never be able to visit you. I am much better since my tour to the Hot Springs this summer but never expect to walk again. You have no doubt heard that Robbie lost his sweet young wife about 9 months after their marriage and before the house, preparing for their reception, could be completed. It is a sad cloud upon his life, but youth is elastic and is rarely crushed save for a time by any sorrow. I pray that God may preserve us and all dear to us both now and forever."

Mary Lee's arthritis remained crippling, but she was carrying on "cheerfully." In those years, death struck down the young with much greater frequency than today. Such losses were a major component of life's rhythm. It is difficult for today's Americans to understand how commonplace was the grieving over the loss of children and young adults. Yet we must attempt to understand that aspect of life if we are to succeed in understanding the history of those times.

Jeff Davis was perhaps too busy with work at Carolina Insurance Company and too busy answering personal correspondence to permit himself to become incapacitated by grief. Biographer Hudson Strode would write of how the Federal invasion had damaged the health of southern States men and the still-crippled the economies of the region:

"The insurance company business was going badly. Yellow fever, malaria, typhoid, effects of old wounds, and various diseases had taken the southern [States] men off at far earlier ages than actuarial calculations anticipated. Many citizens were too poor to pay their premiums, and some solicitors were anything but aggressive. On the whole, Davis had put good men in charge of various agencies: men popular, [of prominent families], honest. As John S. Preston, his General State agent for Virginia, wrote, he himself was 'running down — remorselessly — the impoverished Virginians,' but it was hard to get his subordinates to work at selling policies. Some were too proud to seek and ask." [R30;357-358, R19;380]

Meanwhile, in Louisiana, two Republican factions were fighting over political control of the State Government and possession of the riches attendant to success. The history involves several political leaders whose background I will first present:

The Customshouse Faction

William Kellogg, Republican (Customs House Faction) candidate for Governor.

Born in Vermont, educated in Illinois where he practiced law, an officer in the Federal Cavalry, by appointment Collector of the New Orleans Port (1865-1868), he was appointed a Federal Senator (1868-1872). At this point in the history, Kellogg is running for Governor for the Customs House Faction of the Republican Party.

James Casey, Collector of the New Orleans Port and Ulysses Grant's brother-in-law.

The husband of Julia Dent Grant's youngest sister, Emily Dent Casey, James Casey is from western Kentucky. He fought in the Federal Army. At this point in the history Casey is using his political influence to ensure Kellogg's election.

Stephen Packard, Federal Marshall.

A native of Maine and an officer in the Federal Army, appointed by Ulysses Grant to the office of Federal Marshall in New Orleans in 1871, Packard is now directing William Kellogg's 1872 campaign for Governor.

Pinckney Pinchback, Republican, Incumbent Lieutenant Governor, of very, very slight African American ancestry.

Born in 1837 in Macon, Georgia to father William Pinchback (of mixed Scots-Irish, Welsh and German ancestry) and mother Eliza Stewart (of German, Welsh, Cherokee and African ancestry). Eliza had been William's former bonded servant, based on her slight African heritage, but he had made her independent and they had been living together and having children as common law man and wife. The father William was a successful large-scale farmer, affording an affluent home life — including education for young Pinckney at a private boarding school in Cincinnati, Ohio — until the boy reached the age of 11, at which time the father died. Pinchback relatives inherited the land and mother, son and siblings, now poor, relocated to Cincinnati. Soon thereafter Pinckney left school to work various jobs. At the age of 23, he married Nina Hawthorne of Memphis, Tennessee. Two years later, in 1862, he made his way to New Orleans, recently captured by Federal forces, and helped raise several companies for an all African American Federal regiment. Within a year Pinckney became upset when denied promotion by the bigoted Federal officer corps, who recognized him as being of very slight African heritage. He resigned from the Federal Army in 1863. After the conquest of the Confederate States, Pinckney became active in the Republican Party, was elected a State Senator and rose to President *pro tempore* of the Legislature. From there he advanced to Lieutenant Governor upon the death in 1871 of the incumbent Lieutenant Governor, Oscar Dunn.

The State Officials Faction

Henry Warmoth, Incumbent Governor, Republican, but of the southern culture.

Born in southern Illinois to parents of Dutch ancestry and educated in Illinois public schools, Henry moved west to Missouri as an adult where he practiced law and worked as a District Attorney. When Federals came to subjugate Missouri, he joined the Federal Army (Missouri 32nd Infantry). In 1864 he was appointed Judge of the Gulf Provost Court by Nathaniel Banks. He resigned the following year to run for the Federal House and was elected, but House Republicans refused to let him take his seat. In the April 1868 special election Warmoth ran for Governor, narrowly defeated the Democrat candidate and assumed the office at the age of 27 years. But his office was subservient to Federal occupying forces. Oscar Dunn was elected Lieutenant Governor, but, as mentioned previously, Dunn died in office allowing Pinckney Pinchback, as President pro tempore, to rise to that post. At this time in our history Warmoth is leading many State Officials in a Fusion with Democrats, seeking to win the elections of 1872.

The Democratic Party (Conservatives)

John McEnery, Democrat candidate for Governor.

Was born in Virginia and moved to Monroe, Louisiana, where he practiced law. He was an officer in the Confederate Army. He was elected to the Louisiana legislature in 1866, but Federals prevented his being seated. At this point in the history, McEnery is running for Governor as a Democrat.

Now we move to the history of which these political leaders play major roles. Edward Mayes, also expert on the history of Louisiana politics during those times, would describe the situation as follows:

"Perhaps in no State did the evils attendant upon [Republican Political Reconstruction] assume a form so aggravated and malignant as in Louisiana. The great staples of that commonwealth (cotton, sugar, and rice) poured immense annual wealth into her places of business and her treasury. The city of New Orleans was a great commercial emporium, drawing its clientage from three or four States. There was the carcass, and thither did the vultures flock. All forms of perfidy, all phases of corruption, all aspects of crime, reveled in that high carnival. The body politic was rotten in every branch and through its pettiest ramifications.

"So firm was the hold the [Republicans] had upon the State that they could afford to quarrel amongst themselves — and they did. State Officials constituted one Faction, and Federal Officials (especially the Customhouse people) the other:"

The State Officials Faction was led by the Governor, Henry Warmoth, who was friendly toward Louisiana Democrats.

The Customhouse Faction was jointly led by James Casey, the Collector of the New Orleans Port, who happened to be Ulysses Grant's brother-in-law, with support from Stephen Packard, the Federal Marshall. As might be expected, Grant "gave his personal favor and substantial aid to" this Faction.

"Between those [two] Factions, in the years 1871 and [through October] 1872, there [had been] violent struggles:

"Over the control of the Republican State Convention, in which the Customhouse [Faction] succeeded by a liberal use of [Federal] troops and Deputy [Federal] Marshals.

"Over the Presidency of the State Senate, the State Officials Faction winning in this instance.

"Over the Speakership of the House, in which the [Customhouse Faction] dared to arrest the Governor, the Lieutenant Governor, 4 Senators, and 18 Members of the House by writs from the [Federal] Court, charging conspiracy to resist the execution of [Federal laws], thus securing an advantage, which, however, was soon lost."

So, at the time of the election campaign of 1872, the State Officials Faction was in control. In an attempt to retain this control, the State Officials Faction joined with Conservatives and Democrats, presenting a "Fusion Ticket," nominating John McEnery for Governor. The Customhouse Faction nominated William Kellogg. But the State Officials Faction and its "Fusion Ticket" lost key influence with African American voters when the incumbent Lieutenant Governor, Pinckney Pinchback, of very slight African American descent, switched his support to the Customhouse Faction.

Although the "Fusion Ticket" was the apparent winner, the election results were highly contested. Three organizations (the DeFeriet Returning Board, the State Senate's Forman Board and a Special Committee of Republicans from the Federal Senate) "canvassed" the returns and pronounced their findings, which ended in substantially the same result:

"The Fusion State officers had been elected by majorities ranging from 9,000 to 15,000 [votes], with Conservative or Fusion majorities of 39 members in the House and of 11 members in the Senate."

This, of course, did not satisfy the Customhouse Faction, which canvassed the returns through its own "Lynch Board," a body without legal authority, which manipulated the returns to favor the election of its candidate for Governor, William Kellogg, and purporting to give it majorities in the State House and State Senate, and prepared to use those bogus numbers to seize power over the Louisiana State

Government, with the essential help of "brother-in-law" Ulysses Grant and his Federal troops. This story will continue when the State Legislature convenes in December. [R205;195-196]

Meanwhile, in South Carolina, the State Republican Party was overwhelmingly victorious in fall elections. Republican Franklin Moses of Charleston defeated "Bolting" Republican Reuben Tomlinson of Charleston by a vote of 69,838 to 36,533. The "Bolting" Republicans had left the August 21 South Carolina Republican State Convention over disgust with Moses' nomination, formed a breakaway movement and nominated Tomlinson and a few other candidates. Leaders of the South Carolina Democratic Party had decided to not field a candidate for Governor. The State legislature would be overwhelmingly Republican as well. On joint ballot, Republicans held a 130 to 27 advantage over Democrats and African Americans held a 106 to 51 advantage over European Americans. Ulysses Grant carried the State by 50,000 votes. Vote tallies indicated that about 40,000 European Americans did not bother to vote. Representatives to the Federal House, numbering 5, were all Republicans, and 4 of those were African Americans. Of this time in the political life of South Carolina, historian John Reynold would write, "after 4 years of Republican rule, the [European American] people of South Carolina were in a state of actual subjugation."

The new South Carolina State Legislature would convene on December 10 and elect John J. Patterson to the Federal Senate. You remember Patterson as the President of the fraudulent Blue Ridge Railroad Company, and formerly of Pennsylvania. Vote buying at high prices made Patterson's election possible. Patterson liked to call himself, "Honest John" Patterson. A political associated would later explain this nickname by saying: "Patterson will do what he says. If he promises to pay you he'll do it; if he promises to vote for you he'll do it; if he promises to work for you he'll do it; and if he promises to steal for you he'll do it." Asked during this era if he favored reform within the State Government, Patterson replied: "Why, there are still 5 years of good stealing in South Carolina." You may recall that, like Patterson, Abe Lincoln's nickname, "Honest Abe," was deceptive as well. Lincoln came about that nickname in the following manner:

> As a lawyer in Springfield Lincoln had customarily refused to take any case where he felt his client was on the wrong side of the law, prompting the even-handed lawyers in town to ridicule their associate with the moniker, "Honest Abe," a name that had nothing to do with honesty in personal or legal endeavors.

Regarding Patterson, a written appeal would be sent to the Federal Senate, asking that he not be seated due to his involvement in open bribery. But Patterson would be promptly sworn in. [R201;222-226]

Moving on to the election results in Mississippi, we find that voters in the northeastern part of the State, in Federal House District 1, did, as expected, elect Democrat Lucius Lamar over Republican Robert Flournoy — and by a wide margin. The tally favored Lamar by almost 5,000 votes, a near 2 to 1 ratio. The only pocket of Republican strength was in Lafayette County, where Oxford was located — its 42 percent African American minority and concentration of European American Republicans swinging the tally in Flournoy's favor. Lamar's victory was the result of the Legislature's redistricting plan, previously mentioned, which sacrificed District 1 to Democratic control in exchange for making the other 5 Mississippi Districts "safe" for Republicans. If the boundaries of District 1 had not been gerrymandered by the Republican-controlled Legislature, Lamar would have lost 7,443 to 11,953. Furthermore — being a well qualified and not-too-disagreeable a candidate — Lamar had received pre-election support from several notable Republicans who were, perhaps, seeking future influence with the anticipated winner — suggesting that he would be successful when seeking removal of his political disability and presenting his credentials in the Federal House. Of the 129,163 Mississippi votes cast for President, Ulysses Grant won with a majority of 34,887. [R205;174, R206;109]

Meanwhile in Great Britain, Charles Sumner boarded a ship for Boston in mid-November. He had enjoyed about 9 weeks of vacationing in Britain, France and The Netherlands. It had been expensive, for he had spent more than he could logically afford, in excess of $6,000. Sumner's first weeks in London had rather lacked the social whirl which had enveloped him in younger years. Biographer David Donald would observe that friends who saw him were "struck by the fact that Sumner was a very sick man, with a thin, wrinkled face and watery eyes." One acquaintance had observed that Sumner "spoke with a loudness of tone and vehemence of manner which [indicated] that he had been drifting toward alienation of mind." And John Bigelow had reported that Sumner had "a certain difficulty in giving expression to his ideas, a want of fluency, in fact an absence of clear ideas which usually follow very great fatigue or an apoplectic attack. . . . He is more than ever the center of the system in which he lives. He did not ask a question that indicated the least interest in any mortal but himself."

After a week in London, Sumner had traveled to Boulogne to briefly vacation with George Smalley, a newspaperman with the New York *Tribune*. Then the two had traveled on to Paris where he settled down for several weeks. Sumner had occupied himself rummaging through book stores, freely buying those that caught his fancy. Along the way Sumner had remarked to Smalley, "I dare say you thought from my books at home that I cared nothing for books as books; or for bindings. But you will see." But Smalley had thought Sumner rather a sucker for overpriced merchandise, as he observed that the books "were not so fine as they ought to have been." Biographer David Donald would write, "He spent too much money also on prints and bronzes of indifferent quality, for dealers in antiques found it easy to take him in." William Story, who knew Sumner well, would observe that "The world of art, as art, purely, was to him a locked world. He longed to enter into it, and feel it as an artist does; but the keys were never given to him." After a few days, word had spread that Sumner was in Paris, and invitations to dine had begun to arrive. De Corcelle, father-in-law of the Marquis de Chambrun, had hosted a dinner in his honor. On another occasion, he had dined with President Thiers at the Champs d'Elysée palace. Another time, while visiting with Leon Gambetta, the two had discussed in detail the future of republican government in France.

Sumner had visited Brussels, Antwerp, and The Hague during October. At The Hague he had visited John Motley. Although he had a few more vacation days in Great Britain, Sumner had never felt well enough to make the difficult journey to Inverary to see Elizabeth and George Argyll. But, before leaving for the States, he had visited John Bright, staying overnight with him in Rochdale. [R73;558-561]

Meanwhile, Jeff Davis was feeling pressure to begin work on his history of the Confederacy. Although business worries remained acute, many friends continued to urge that the work begin. Already, many prominent former Confederates had been sending manuscripts of important aspects of Confederate history, as well as important letters and papers. He had received historical information from Dabney Maury, Stephen Lee and Isaac St John, the Confederacy's last Commissary General. Many reminded Davis that Robert Lee had planned to write a history, but death had overtaken him before he could do that. Please, they pleaded, do not wait too long to began your valuable work. And William Reed of Philadelphia wrote to volunteer his help in editing the work. Reed was one of Davis' defense lawyers during the fight to win his release from prison. A letter from Reed's New York City home said:

> "Let me ask you as I have perhaps impatiently in every letter I have written. Is your record and the record of the Confederacy never to be written? . . . . I cannot tell you how much pleasure it would give me to assist in such a work." [R19;380-381]

Before looking into the reconvening of the Federal House and Senate, let us look in on the political shenanigans in New Orleans, Louisiana, where the tug continued between two Republican Factions. As previously mentioned, the "Fusion Ticket" of the State Officeholders Faction had won the election for Governor and won majorities in the State House and Senate. But the Customhouse Faction, led by Ulysses Grant's brother-in-law, armed with a fraudulent manipulation of the returns by the "Lynch Board" and with access to Federal troops, intended to seize the State Government, putting its failed candidate, William Kellogg, in the Governor's office and rigging majorities in the State House and Senate. Setting the stage for Federal support of an anticipated Customhouse Faction coup, the Grant Administration, on December 3, instructed by telegram that the Federal Marshal was to enforce the decrees and mandates of the Federal Courts, no matter who resisted. Two days later Federal Judge Edward Durell, "at midnight, [while] closeted with the [Federal] Marshal and [Kellogg's attorneys], himself drew up or dictated an order directing the Marshal to take possession of the Statehouse and to permit no one to enter it except certain persons described in the order" — whose names constituted the "Judge's list." Of course the "Judge's list" excluded enough successful Fusion Ticket candidates to drop that Faction into the minority in the State House and Senate. Who was Judge Edward Durell?

> It is important to know that Edward Durell was born in New Hampshire, graduated from Harvard College before moving in 1835 to Mississippi, then New Orleans, where he practiced law. Being 40 years old when Louisiana seceded, and since his city was captured early in the resulting conflict,

he did not fight for the Confederacy or for the Federals. So, although from the northeastern States, Durell had lived most of his adult life in Mississippi and New Orleans, thereby absorbing a sound understanding of both cultures.

Acting immediately, before 2 am, the Federal Marshal positioned Federal troops around the Louisiana Statehouse, placed artillery batteries at key points and seized control of the building. The members of the Legislature who had been elected on the Fusion Ticket gathered at City Hall and petitioned Ulysses Grant to remove the Federal troops, but Grant refused. Meanwhile the members of the Legislature who had been elected on the Customhouse Ticket, being on the "Judge's list," entered the Statehouse on December 9 and proceeded to implement the coup. Pinckney Pinchback, the Lieutenant Governor, of slight African American descent and still holding that office, who had, as previously mentioned, switched parties during the past summer and joined the Customhouse Faction, assumed the role of President of the Senate. Across the hall Charles Lowell, the Federal Postmaster, presided as Speaker of the House. Who was Charles Lowell?

> Born in Maine where he was a prominent lawyer, he had been commander over African American Federal troops in Louisiana, which were organized in 1863. After the defeat of the Confederacy, he was both Postmaster of New Orleans and a Republican member of the Louisiana House, where he served as Speaker.

With only 35 days remaining in Henry Warmoth's term as Governor, Republicans in the House immediately approved a Bill of Impeachment against him for alleged "high crimes and misdemeanors," intending to punish him for supporting the "Fusion Ticket" and for endorsing Democrat John McEnery. Because of the pending Impeachment Trial in the Louisiana Senate, Lieutenant Governor Pinckney Pinchback entered the Governor's Office and assumed that power. By the way, probably because the charge was not prosecutable, the Senate never tried Warmoth — the Customhouse Faction of the Republican Party had made their point and put their man in the Governor's office. William Kellogg would soon replace Pinchback, completing the coup, which had been sustained by Federal authorities, defeating the "Fusion Ticket" with Federal bayonets. Committees in the Federal House and Senate would investigate the actions of Judge Edward Durell, find fraud, and recommend that the Fusion Ticket be put in power or a new election be held. However, the Federal House and Senate would do neither. "The Kellogg Government [would remain] in power." [R205;195-197]

Horace Greeley died on November 29, at the age of 61 years, a few weeks after the death of his wife. He had suffered much misfortune since helping, in 1867, to pay the $100,000 bail for Jeff Davis. Subscriptions to his New York *Tribune* — for decades the most influential newspaper in the United States — had steadily declined and he had gradually lost control over its editorial policy. His venture into politics had failed — losing his 1869 race for New York State Comptroller — and getting pitifully little support for the recent Liberal Republican Party crusade, which he had wholeheartedly supported. He had been among those defrauded by Philip Arnold in the "Diamond Hoax of 1872" swindle. The final blow put him down — just before his death he lost control of his newspaper to Whitehall Reid, editor of the New York *Herald*. Death followed a few weeks after entering Dr. George Choate's sanitarium, where he was seeking help for mental illness — or, perhaps, just some peace and quiet.

Charles Sumner was back in his Senate seat when the session opened in early December. But this time he was not considered a member of the Republican Party. He was a member of the weak Liberal Republican Party, and no more. Yet, Sumner's desertion of the Republican Party was rather being ignored by the public the Liberal Republican Party's former Presidential candidate, Horace Greeley, had gone mad and had died the previous week. Anyway, voters in Massachusetts seemed much more interested in following Henry Wilson, who would soon assume the office of Vice President. On the other hand, Republican leaders in the Senate — Conkling, Morton, Carpenter, and Logan — had no intention of inviting Sumner back into the Republican Party. On the second day of the session they informed him that the Caucus of Republican Senators would be limited to men "who supported the Platform and candidates agreed upon by the Republican National Convention held at Philadelphia." All supporters of the Liberal Republican Party, who had convened in Cincinnati, were thereby firmly excluded. In a meek attempt to save face, Sumner advised the Republican leadership that his physician had ordered him to decline membership on any Senate Committees. That way, the scattering of newspapermen who supported Sumner could allege that Sumner he had — himself — requested that he not be assigned to any Committees.

But Sumner did not allow any physician to suppress his eagerness to advance legislative proposals from the floor of the Senate. He immediately requested that time be scheduled for future submission of his new African American bill. He announced that he would be resubmitting his bill to require that payments to holders of Federal bonds be paid in gold and silver coin, instead of paper money — to end "the derangement of trade, the lawlessness of speculation, the check to honest business, the high scale of prices, private losses, the bankruptcy of great houses, and general anxiety." He again denounced the Internal Revenue Service and its "army of tax collectors who swarmed over the land." He complained that "taxes have been too numerous, too various in character, and assessed in [too many] different ways." But the greatest excitement would be created by his bill to prohibit veteran soldiers from displaying battlefield names on their regimental flags.

> Military parades were very popular in the States north of Maryland, Kentucky and Missouri. And these parades were often integrated into Republican Party campaign rallies. Furthermore it was customary to sew the names of battlefields onto the regimental flags which individual Federal veterans units displayed while parading. So Sumner would be unsuccessful at striking battlefield names from regimental flags. The Massachusetts House would pass a resolution of censure "strongly condemning" the proposal, which they would call "an insult to the [Federal] soldiery of the nation," that deserved "the unqualified condemnation of the people of [Massachusetts]." And the Federal House would concur, and send to the Senate a bill which forbid the removal of battlefield names from Federal regimental flags because "the national unity cannot fail to be strengthened by the remembrance of the services of those who fought the battles of the [Federal Army] in the late [conquest of the Confederacy]." [R73;563-565]

Meanwhile in Washington City, on December 11, Lucius Lamar proved victorious in getting his political disabilities removed, clearing the way for him to seek acceptance of his election credentials in the Federal House a year later, in December 1873, to represent Mississippi's House District 1. Biographer Edward Mayes would later tell the story:

> "In December [Lucius Lamar] repaired to Washington [City] in order to press his application for relief. His petition, along with the memorial prepared by [Mississippi] Governor R. C. Powers, was introduced in the House by [Representative Henry] Dawes, of Massachusetts, on the 5th, and was at once referred to the Judiciary Committee. On the 9th [Representative John] Bingham, of Ohio, for the Committee, reported a bill, and advised the House that it was unanimously recommended. He called special attention to the fact that the petition was favorably indorsed 'by most of the [Federal] officials in the State.' Thereupon the bill was passed, under a suspension of the rules, by a vote of 111 to 13.

> "On the next day its passage was reported to the Senate, and on the 11th that body referred it to the Select Committee on the Removal of Political Disabilities. On the same day [Senator George] Vickers, of Maryland, for the Committee, reported it as unanimously approved, stating that a large number of Republicans had certified that the election at which [Lucius] Lamar was chosen was orderly and fair, and that there could be no objection to the removal of his disabilities. The bill was thereupon passed by unanimous consent."

Ulysses Grant signed the Lamar Bill on December 17, thereby closing forever "the Confederate record of Lucius Lamar." We recognize that the gerrymandering of District 1 by Republicans in the Mississippi Legislature — aimed at making the other 5 districts "safe" for Republicans — rather forced Republicans in the Federal House and Senate to make no objection to the Democrat consequently elected. In 12 months, in early December 1873, Lucius Lamar would take his seat in the Federal House.

But Lamar's victory came with a price — almost immediately after the removal of his political disabilities, he became gravely ill and unable to return to Mississippi. Biographer Edward Mayes would tell the story:

> "The anxieties and excitement caused by [the effort in Washington] came very near costing [Lamar] his life. The infirmity to which he was subject seemed usually, when it visited him at all,

to come immediately after the relaxation of some great nervous tension. The bill for his relief had no sooner passed than he was seized with a vertigo in its severest form. He was taken over to Baltimore, where, at the home of Dr. A. T. Bledsoe, his old chief at the University [of Mississippi], he was most tenderly and carefully nursed through his illness. For several days it looked as if the end had come, but his strong constitution finally prevailed, and health slowly returned. A few days later he was able to return [to Mississippi], although on crutches and very weak."

During the next 11 months Lamar would focus on recovering his health and on better understanding the political minds of northern States Republican politicians. He contemplated tactics for positively influencing those northern States minds in the Federal House — despite his past record as a former State Secessionist and Confederate leader. And, to a lesser extent, he would remain engaged in Mississippi politics. [R205;175-176, R206;110]

Likewise, Charles Sumner was suffering from the pressure and disappointments from frequent rebukes, which were weighing heavily upon his fragile health. Biographer David Donald would explain the situation as of only about two weeks into the session:

"Though he had gained strength during his trip abroad, he still suffered from spasms of the bladder, probably caused by prostatitis, which obliged him to get out of bed 20 or 30 times each night to urinate, and he continued to have attacks of angina pectoris, which came upon him unexpectedly. Only a few days after the opening of [the Senate] and the introduction of his battle-flags resolutions, he went out at night to hear a lecture by the British scientist, John Tyndall, and afterward, walking two blocks to catch the streetcar, had a violent seizure. Though looking quite feeble, he forced himself to go to the Senate the next day and continued to attend until December 19, when the attacks occurred so frequently and the pain became so great that he was obliged to absent himself for the remainder of the session." [R73;566-567]

The Year of 1873

1Q73

Meanwhile in Louisiana, on January 14, the two contending Republican Factions established two separate State Governments, both headquartered at New Orleans — one properly elected, the other taking power via a military coup. The Customhouse Faction — backed by Ulysses Grant and brother-in-law James Casey, in charge of the Federal Customhouse for the Port of New Orleans, and recently empowered by its December coup — launched its new government, led by its so-called Governor, William Kellogg. Nearby, the Fusion Ticket Faction, a combination of State Republicans and Democrats, having won the most votes during the past November election, according to the most reliable vote counts, established its new government, led by the elected Governor, Democrat John McEnery. Not long afterward, the Grant Administration would force the dismissal of the legitimate McEnery Government, including arrests of members of the Fusion Ticket Legislature, who would be "marched out of their hall between files of soldiers and taken to the guardhouse." This military intervention would allow the coup victors — the Customhouse Faction and its so-called Governor, William Kellogg — to pass "stringent laws for the collection of taxes, more than $2,000,000 of which [would be] alleged to be in arrears, in which provision [would be] made for calling out the militia to aid the tax gatherers. As might be expected, considering the circumstances of the coup, there would be riots and bloodshed. To avoid further calamity, Governor McEnery would, for the time being, give up his claim to the office and the Federal troops would be withdrawn. [R205;201]

Meanwhile in South Carolina, the third group of Kuklux trials began in the winter session of the Federal Court in Columbia. You will recall the first group of Kuklux trials had taken place in Columbia one year previously and the second group had taken place in Charleston in the spring. The same pattern of legal procedures continued for the second Columbia trials.

1.   Robert Moore of York was tried for conspiracy to interfere with voting rights and for participating in the murder of Tom Roundtree. He was acquitted of the murder charge, found guilty of the conspiracy charge and sentenced to 5 years in prison and fined $100.

2. John Craig and other men from Laurens were charged with conspiracy to interfere with voting rights, but the Jury could not reach a verdict. None of the men were tried again.

As in the other Court sessions, several of the accused forfeited their right to a trial by pleading guilty. In this manner 8 men accepted sentences, ranging from 2 to 5 years in prison and fines ranging from $100 to $500. [R201;214-215]

While these trials were taking place in Columbia and Charleston, several cases were being advanced to the Federal Supreme Court in hopes of finding the Federal Enforcement Acts in violation of the Federal Constitution. Former Attorney Generals Reverdy Johnson of Maryland and Henry Stanbery of Ohio were leaders in these appeals. They pressed for a decision on behalf of Dr. Edward Avery of York only to have the appeal dismissed. Then, they pressed for a decision on behalf of T. Jefferson Greer, but the Court was equally divided on the question, thereby giving no opinion. Finally, "the case of Elijah Ross Sepaugh was duly argued," but before a decision was reached the Federal Prosecutor withdrew, resulting in dismissal by the Supreme Court.

You will recall that Republican leaders released Jeff Davis after two years in prison because they feared the Supreme Court would find State Secession to have been legal, thereby putting in question all of the political power Federals had gained by the military conquest of the Confederacy. Republican leaders had a similar problem with the legality of the package of Federal Enforcement Acts (also called Kuklux Acts). Would they dare face a deliberation in the Federal Supreme Court over the Kuklux Act? No. Again, Republican leaders would withdraw from the courts rather than risk confronting the legality of widespread arrests and imprisonments without benefit of the writ of *habeas corpus* — most of them former Confederates, essentially all of them Democrats. Historian John Reynold would explain how the Federal Kuklux Act was allowed to die and how President Ulysses Grant arranged to pardon all men who had not yet completed their prison terms.

> "Thus it came about that every effort to have the judgment of the Supreme Court upon the constitutionality of the Enforcement Act and the Kuklux Act came to naught.

> "In the summer of 1873 President Grant [would declare] a purpose to pardon all convicted Kuklux whose neighbors and fellow citizens might ask for clemency for them. Applications were made accordingly, and one by one the parties involved were set free. Except in the cases where the term of imprisonment was one year or less, none of them served out his term."

But, you should not be surprised to learn that well connected Republicans in South Carolina made good money by arresting men (typically former Confederates and Democrat voters) and gathering "evidence" to prosecute them for violating the Enforcement Act and the Kuklux Act. At about the same time that the constitutionality of those acts became highly questionable, the South Carolina Government appropriated $35,000 to pay "rewards of $200 for each person arrested, with proof to convict." Of this "reward" money, Federal cavalry leader Major Lewis Merrill managed to scoop up $15,700 and his helper got $5,000; two U. S. Commissioners got a total of $8,200, and a U. S. Marshall got $1,200. Many Democrats questioned the legality of State reward money going to Federal leaders who were already receiving Federal Government pay for performing their job. Of course, the Republican newspaper in Columbia needed its money, too. It printed daily stenographic reports from the trials in that city, charging taxpayers $45,788 for work that was, firstly, not necessary, and secondly, could had been accomplished by competitive bid for about $10,000. [R201;215-217]

The South Carolina Legislature adjourned on February 26 after 76 days in session, including Sundays and Christmas. At the opening of the session Governor Franklin Moses had submitted a financial statement giving total State deficiencies not funded as $1,266,395, made up of: printing ($325,000), schools ($300,000: the entire appropriation), bills payable ($230,000), pay certificates ($20,000) and "other purposes" ($391,395). As you might expect, Moses was fully acquainted with fraud and "stealing" taxpayer money. The Republican Faction that had "bolted" from the regular party in August and nominated Tomlinson for Governor had acted over concerns of vast corruption within the regular Republican Party, seeing the regular Party nominee Moses as a ring-leader. Accordingly, during the campaign, "particular stress was laid upon the issuance by Moses of fraudulent pay certificates — the amount being stated at $1,200,000."

Legislative expenses of the session totaled $817,017, itemized as follows:

Printing	$450,000.
Pay to Representatives and Senators	$103,600.
Legislative accounts and claims passed	$72,803.
Pay to 176 clerks	$50,857.
Wines, liquors, cigars, groceries, etc.	$50,412.
Stationary	$30,876.
Furniture	$17,286.
Laborers	$5,680.
Thirty two Messengers	$4,075.
Eight Sergeants-at-arms	$3,900.
Newspapers	$3,649.
Other	$23,879.

Notable legislation follows:

The property tax rate was set at 12 mils for State revenue and from 3 to 6 mils for county revenue.

There had been a poll tax of one dollar required of each voter, but not enforced by the past Republican government. That changed, in theory, as the Legislature passed an act requiring enforcement of the tax, which sounded tough enough, but would it be enforced against African American men (Republicans)? Historian John Reynold would describe the enforcement penalty:

"An act to enforce the collection of the poll tax imposed a penalty of one dollar for non-payment, and upon failure then to pay, the delinquent was required to labor on some public road for 3 days."

A Normal School was authorized to operate on the grounds of the University of South Carolina, located in Columbia. By this time the buildings were almost empty because the University had rapidly declined since the Republican Party had taken over the State Government. European American professors and students had left as Republicans had moved to admit African American students, almost all of them not capable of doing college level work. So the Republican solution was 1), to create on the campus a Normal School, which, although open to both races, would attract only African American students and be essentially a grammar school, and 2), to recast the University so it would attract African American students and operate at the academic level of a high school.

A sum of $250,000 was appropriated to pay bills submitted by the Republican Printing Company for work allegedly performed in 1870-71 and 1871-72.

A resolution passed which instructed South Carolina's 5 Representatives to the Federal House "to use their influence against the withdrawal of [Federal] troops from this State and to represent to the [Federal President] that the withdrawal of the same would be at the present time detrimental to the permanent establishment and maintenance of law and order in this State." [R201;230-238]

March 1873 Through February 1877 — Political Reconstruction During the Second Ulysses Grant Administration

It is now time to review a summary of the 1872 Federal elections in the summarized format that has begun each four-year segment of this study. After this review, the narrative history will resume.

The Republican Party re-nominated Ulysses Grant for a second term without significant opposition. DeGregorio would provide a brief account of the re-nomination:

> "Grant's re-nomination was assured as Republicans convened in Philadelphia in June 1872. Vice President Colfax was denied re-nomination, largely for his part in the Crédit Mobilier scandal. Senator Henry Wilson of Massachusetts was nominated in his place. The Republican platform denounced racial and religious discrimination, applauded women's "admission to wider spheres of influence," and advocated the abolition of the franking privilege, a continued hard-money policy, and expanded foreign trade and shipbuilding."

The Democratic Party was in such disarray in 1872 they could not agree on a candidate to put up against President Grant, despite the vulnerability of the scandal-ridden man. Those scandals had prompted a Faction of Republicans to bolt the Party and offer their own anti-administration candidate — Horace Greeley, editor-owner of the New York *Tribune*. Believing Greeley to be their only realistic chance of defeating Grant, Democrats, at their National Convention, simply endorse the Greeley ticket. DeGregorio would summarize the offshoot Liberal Republican Party, Greeley's career and the Democratic Party situation.

> "Born in Amherst, New Hampshire, Greeley was raised amid poverty and had little formal education, although he was a brilliant child, able to read at age three. He was apprenticed to a printer in his youth and thus learned the rudiments of journalism. Moving to New York City, he founded the *New Yorker* in 1834 and 7 years later the New York *Tribune*, destined to become under his guidance among the most influential dailies of the nineteenth century. In its pages Greeley editorially championed the rights of workingmen, promoted a protective [tax on imports], opposed [African American bonding], denounced the Mexican War, and criticized big business. He also encouraged development of the frontier, summarizing his philosophy in a famous bit of advice — "Go west, young man, and grow up with the country." He helped establish the Republican Party in 1854. As [southern States seceded], Greeley at first advocated letting [them go in peace]. But with [Lincoln's Proclamation to Subjugate Democrat States and Invade the Confederacy, Greeley] urged vigorous prosecution of the [military campaign] and pressed for [making bonded African Americans independent]. After the war he offered limited support [for the Republican Party's programs to politically reconstruct the conquered States] but also pleaded for amnesty for [Secessionists] and was among those to sign a bail bond for the release of former Confederate President Jefferson Davis. Greeley supported Grant in 1868 but, disappointed in his performance, joined Liberal Republicans in seeking to deny his reelection. At a convention of this anti-Grant faction held in Cincinnati in May 1872, Greeley vied for the nomination with Charles Francis Adams of Massachusetts, the son of President John Quincy Adams. The two exchanged the lead on the first several ballots; Greeley was nominated on the sixth tally. B. Gratz Brown of Missouri was nominated for Vice President. The Liberal Republican Platform denounced the corruption of the Grant Administration and called for reform of the civil service, universal amnesty for former [Secessionists] restoration of home rule in the southern States, a one-term presidency, and resumption of specie payments. Democrats were in such disarray that they offered no candidate. Instead, at their Convention in Baltimore in July 1872, Delegates endorsed the Greeley-Brown ticket as their only chance to defeat Grant — this despite Greeley's long-standing antipathy to Democratic principles. Within weeks after his defeat by Grant, Greeley died in Pleasantville, New York."

In the vast majority of the conquered region, (regular) State Republican Party Machines retained firm political control, empowered by the votes of African American men. DeGregorio describes the campaign:

" 'Never in American history have two more unfit men been offered to the country for the highest office,' wrote Eugene H. Roseboom of this contest in his history of presidential elections. Grant remained aloof, allowing subordinates to explain away the scandals that had rocked the Administration. Greeley opened his campaign in August with a speech in Portland, Maine, and carried the fight for clean, honest government across the country. Despite Greeley's [very influential support of Exclusionism and Abolitionism during the 1850's, the southern States European American who were men allowed to vote] reluctantly rallied to him rather than face four more years of [Republican Political Reconstruction] under Grant, whereas [African American men] remained loyal to the President and the [Republican Political Machines]. Business interests and veterans supported Grant; the major nonpartisan newspapers endorsed Greeley. In the end, Grant's prestige as a war hero and the belief that he personally had not been involved in the scandals carried the day for [regular] Republicans."

Grant won the election with 56 percent of the popular vote; Greeley received the remaining 44 percent. Grant won 81 percent of the electoral vote. Greeley died before the Electoral College met, so his votes were given as follows: Hendricks of Illinois, 12%; Brown of Missouri, 5%; others, 2%. Grant carried 29 States; from north to south they were: Maine, New Hampshire, Vermont, Massachusetts, Rhode Island, Connecticut, New York, New Jersey, Pennsylvania, Ohio, Indiana, Michigan, Illinois, Wisconsin, Minnesota, Iowa, Nebraska, Kansas, Nevada, Oregon, California, Delaware, West Virginia, Virginia, North Carolina, South Carolina, Alabama, Florida, and Mississippi. Greeley won electoral votes in 6 States as follows: Maryland, Kentucky, Missouri, Tennessee, Georgia and Texas.

The Republican Party retained its huge majority in the Senate and substantially increased its firm majority in the House. Republicans held 67 percent of the Senate seats versus 26 percent for Democrats and 6 percent for non-aligned Senators. Republicans held 65 percent of the House seats versus 31 percent for Democrats and 5 percent for non-aligned Representatives. The mid-term elections produced huge Democratic gains — an event that foreshadowed the beginning of the end of Republican Political Reconstruction. The Republican Senate majority was reduced to 59 percent; Democrats held 38 percent and non-aligned held 3 percent. The House changed to Democratic control as Democrat seats expanded to 58 percent, Republican seats shrank to 32 percent and non-aligned held the balance of 5 percent.

Hamilton Fish of, New York, remained as Secretary of State. William Richardson, of Massachusetts, replaced George Boutwell at Secretary of the Treasury. Forced to resign soon thereafter over a scandal, Richardson was replaced by Benjamin Bristow, of Kentucky. When a "Whisky Ring" scandal exposed by Bristow threatened Grant's private secretary, Bristow was fired and replaced by Lot Morrill, of Maine. William Belknap, of Iowa, continued at Secretary of War, but resigned in 1876 as the Senate prepared to impeach him for allegedly accepting bribes from traders at Native American trading posts. Grant then appointed Alphonso Taft, of Ohio, to the War job, but three months later moved him to Attorney General and appointed James Cameron, of Pennsylvania, who finished out the term. Cameron's father, Simon, you will recall as a leading Pennsylvania politician in the 1850's and Abe Lincoln's first Secretary of War — prior to Edwin Stanton. George Williams, of Oregon, continued as Attorney General, but he fell from grace when his involvement in Oregon election fraud surfaced. Grant then selected Edwards Pierrepont, of New York, to be Attorney General, but he resigned a year later to become Minister to Great Britain. As previously mentioned, Alfonso Taft, of Ohio, then transferred to Attorney General. George Robeson, of New Jersey, continued as Secretary of the Navy. John Creswell, of Maryland, continued as Postmaster General, but resigned early in the term. Grant turned to Virginia and appointed James Marshall to replace Creswell, but Marshall only lasted a month or so. Next Grant appointed Marshall Jewell, of Connecticut, who held the job until 1876. After Jewell left, James Tyner, of Indiana, finished the term. Columbus Delano, of Ohio, continued at Secretary of the Interior, but resigned in 1875. Grant appointed Zachariah Chandler, of Michigan to finish the term.

Colorado was granted statehood in 1876.

Having concluded the summary of the 1872 Federal elections and the organization of the Second Ulysses Grant Administration, the narrative history resumes.

Narrative History Resumes, March 1873.

Charles Sumner dutifully arrived at his Senate seat at the opening of the new session on March 4. He had been absent since the week before Christmas, complaining of grave health problems. Now, if Sumner had been permitted to caucus with the majority Republican Party, and been assigned to important Committees, perhaps chairing one of them, then his grave health might not have kept him away. But that was not the case. He was an outcast, a victim of the times — neither Republican nor Democrat. He belonged instead to the declining third-party movement known as the Liberal Republican Party.

Seeking comfort, Sumner had turned again to the quack physician, Charles Brown-Sequard, to whom he had first submitted his care in 1856 while in Paris. Back then, Brown-Sequard diagnosed that Sumner was suffering complications from the caning that had been administered by Preston Brooks a few months previously. During the intervening years Brown-Sequard had moved his practice from France to New York City, but even that was not convenient to Washington City, so for day-to-day help, Sumner had used Joseph Johnson, a young physician in town. Both physicians agreed on the same diagnosis: "both his angina and his bladder trouble were consequences of the injuries Preston Brooks had inflicted upon him in 1856." Later autopsy evidence would prove that the correct diagnosis would have been: restricted blood flow from a severely blocked left coronary artery, which denied sufficient blood flow to the heart muscles. Of course receipt of a caning about the head and shoulders does not cause a man's arteries to ossify. But the miss-diagnosis seemed to assure Sumner that his suffering was but another chapter in his epic martyrdom on behalf of heroic and noble political causes. And the miss-diagnosis helped newspapermen in Massachusetts explain to voters why they had a moral obligation to support Sumner and elect him to another term in the Senate.

The two physicians ordered Sumner to get lots of rest and to take lots of medicines. Brown-Sequard first tried bromides; then he tried atropine and finally hyoscyamine. To counter the pain during an angina attack, he ordered hypodermic injections of morphine to which a solution of salts of atropine and strychnine were added. Sumner complained, "I take medicines enough to cure a family — poison by phial, poison by pill, poison by powder and poison by injection." And the local physician, Johnson, stopped by nightly to inject morphine to make Sumner sleep through the night. "But this is not the sleep of which poets write," Sumner complained, for "the next day I naturally suffer in strength."

When the Massachusetts Legislature convened in early January, a group of Sumner supporters lobbied Legislators to rescind the past censure against Sumner's failed Federal bill to strike battlefield names from Federal regimental flags. Many prominent Sumner supporters endorsed the appeal: poets, including John Whittier, Wadsworth Longfellow and Oliver Holmes; industrialists, including Amos Lawrence; educators, including Charles Eliot; lawyers, including George Hillard; politicians, including Governor William Washburn, himself. But some prominent veteran activists in the past Abolition and Exclusion Movements testified against rescinding the censure, including William Garrison and Julia Howe. But Sumner's most powerful enemy was Ben "Beast" Butler. Legislators loyal to "The Beast" teamed with those otherwise opposed to rescinding the censure. And that coalition voted as a block to elect George Boutwell to the Senate seat that Henry Wilson had just vacated to become Vice President. So Sumner would see Boutwell leave his Treasury Secretary job and become the other Senator from Massachusetts. After the Boutwell vote, the Legislature voted to defeat the bill that would have rescinded its past censure of Sumner for seeking to strike battlefield names from Federal regimental flags. [R73;567-571]

(2Q73)

On May 10, Charles Sumner quietly and agreeably divorced his estranged wife, Alice. She had left him 6 years earlier — back in June of 1867 — after only 8 months of marriage. You will recall the story:

> Alice was the widow of a Federal soldier who was killed in the Invasion of the Confederacy. She was independently wealthy, for both her first husband's parents and her parents were well-to-do, socially prominent Bostonians. Sadly, the normal happiness expected for newlyweds lasted only a few weeks. Then the marriage began deteriorating. With her daughter by her first marriage, Alice first lived in Boston and spent the summer vacationing in the Berkshires; then they moved to Paris.

Divorce lawyers for both parties were in agreement, and the court hearing only consumed a mere 15 minutes. The divorce was granted on the grounds that Alice had deserted Charles, and that accusation was certainly truthful enough. Alice's father, Samuel Hooper, whose Washington City house was next to Charles' house, was also in agreement, and the two men would continue to be good friends. Apparently, Alice, although still a young woman, had no immediate plans to remarry. [R73;571-572]

Meanwhile, the Carolina Insurance Company was near bankruptcy when Jeff Davis traveled to New York City during July in search of a company-saving loan. He needed at least $150,000 to forestall bankruptcy. Although he was surely anxious to save the company, Jeff was desperate to sustain the viability of the insurance policies for which numerous clients had been faithfully paying their premiums. But, Davis' task was exceedingly difficult, because a financial depression gripped The States. The economic depression was also destroying the Republican Party's political domination over the country, both north and south, giving new life to the Democratic Party. Biographer Hudson Strode would describe the scope of the financial panic, known as "The Great Depression" until the 1930's:

> "The time could hardly have been more inauspicious for securing a sizable loan. The year 1873 was marked in the [The] States by financial panic, which had begun the year before. Commercial failures followed one upon another with enormous liabilities. As industries closed down, hundreds of thousands of laborers were thrown out of work, and bread lines formed in the northern cities. When shaky banks collapsed, sound ones were ruined by 'runs' of frightened depositors. Stock quotations dropped alarmingly. The strained and unnatural situation between the Federal [Government] and the southern [States] people served as a discouragement to normal enterprise. Investigation of private frauds and official corruption shook the public confidence."

Varina and Winnie had gone to vacation with friends in Drummondsville, Canada, and Maggie and Jeff, Jr. were "paying guests of the Preston Johnston's in Lexington, Virginia," thereby freeing Jeff to devote full attention to business. Davis thought his best chance for a company-saving loan was at Jay Cooke and Company, "a powerful and respected firm of financiers" in New York City. There, he "laid frankly before bankers and insurance men the figures of his company," for he had never resorted to deception in pursuit of a goal. But Jay Cooke and Company was in financial difficulty itself. Cooke officials did not know it at the time, but in only two months the New York Stock Exchange would stop operations for 10 days and Jay Cooke and Company would go out of business. Cooke officials refused to grant the loan under any discussed collateral method. [R19;382]

(3Q73)

Jeff would write Varina in disappointment from his New York City hotel on July 12:

> "Dear Wife,
>
> "Yours of the 9th has just arrived and finds me preparing to leave. I have had a vexatious time here and all to no purpose. The great number of deaths [in the former Confederate States] during the last year has alarmed the Insurance men. They fear the rate will continue, and rightly conclude that if it does, the [insurance] business [in our region] must be ruinous in the end. I have done every thing except ask for money as a personal favor; that I have been urged to do, and have, as you will anticipate, refused to consider. It is a sad hour and however unjustly must be seriously damaging to my future prospects for business.
>
> "I go hence to Baltimore, will be there one or two days, may go to Richmond, Virginia, but expect in any event to be in Memphis in say 10 days and shall hope to hear from you there. Kiss dear Winnie for her Father. Remember me affectionately to Mary [Ahern]. God grant you may all soon be well and comfortable. . . ."

Jeff Davis had a hopeful meeting with the Piedmont and Arlington Company in Baltimore. He actually left town expecting that Arlington's officers would acquire the Carolina Insurance Company. But, stopping over in Louisville as he traveled home to Memphis, Davis receive a telegram from Wade Hampton, President of Carolina's Virginia branch, informing him that the deal with Piedmont and Arlington had fallen through.

After attending church on July 27, Jeff wrote to Varina from Memphis to explain how the whole burden of the Carolina Insurance Company was pressing down on him personally:

"Those who organized the Carolina [Insurance Company] and involved it in all the difficulties which not oppress it, are so insensible of their responsibility and so happy in shifting the burden to my shoulders, that so far from having their aid to effect such a loan as you suggest, they cannot be induced promptly to pay their own notes. It was that which drove me East to seek relief. Perhaps it would have been justifiable to quit a crew that was scuttling the ship, but I thought only of my obligation to the owners, and felt like the seaman who last leaves the wreck.

"I hope to save the policy holders, and then my conscience will be easy though my pockets be empty." [R19;383-384, R30;363]

Meanwhile, in Oxford, Mississippi, Lucius Lamar — preparing for taking his seat in the Federal House in early Demember — was spending some time reading and corresponding to improve his understanding of the attitudes of northern States Republican politicians and to devise means of dealing with such men in a positive manner. Biographer Edward Mayes would describe this effort:

"During all of the year of 1873 [Lamar] was pondering most carefully and anxiously over his future in [the Federal House]. How could he best help onward the cause to which he had consecrated himself: the perfect reconciliation of the [northern States] and the [southern States]? That was the overwhelming problem. He corresponded on the subject with several of the leading conservative statesmen [in the northern States] — M. C. Kerr, of Indiana, and others — and the import of his letters was this: knowing the [northern States political] mind as you know it, what would you do if you were in my place? He received many valuable suggestions; the principal value of which, however, consisted in their confirmation of his own conceptions, rather than in marking out of any new lines of thought or policy." [R205;176]

Meanwhile, Charles Sumner returned to Boston in August — arriving as a rather feeble man who exercised a mere remnant of the political power of years past — his frailty evoking an intensified sympathy that was reminiscent of the days following the caning administered by Preston Brooks. Political friends, figuring they would not have Charles Sumner around much longer, rallied a bit to him. So he purposely sought out his bedrock political supporters in an attempt to rebuild a power structure upon their foundations. Support still existed among intellectual idealists; veteran Abolitionists and Exclusionists; certain religious cults such as Transcendentalists, and Harvard men. Biographer David Donald would determine that support for Sumner was also on the rise because of increasing disgust over discovery of more scandalous corruption among leaders in the Grant Administration, and because of fears that, should Ben "Beast" Butler gain greater power in Massachusetts, he would damage the Massachusetts State Government through similar scandalous corruption. [R73;573]

Meanwhile, from about August 6 through 12, Jeff Davis was in Richmond. His primary purpose for coming to Richmond was to work with Wade Hampton in search of means to save the Carolina Insurance Company, but Hampton was delayed due to his wife's illness. So Davis accepted an invitation to come to Montgomery White Sulphur Springs and speak to the Virginia Historical Association, the invitation having been extended by Association President Jubal Early. This was only the second public speaking engagement Davis had accepted within the former Confederate States since completion of the Federal conquest — the previous speech, as you recall, having been the eulogy at Robert Lee's funeral almost three years earlier. Up to this point, Davis had been careful to avoid any pubic statement that might give newspapermen in the northern States a reason to accuse him of criticizing the victorious Federals, for he understood the eagerness of northern States politicians who sought to use him as a whipping boy to further their ambitions. Even the slightest critical comment could be used by such men to inflame voter anger toward the conquered States, even though the conquest had been consummated 8 years previously. But the November elections had signaled a changed in public mood. So Davis felt it was now time to speak out among friends at the Virginia Historical Association.

Jeff Davis denounced before the Virginia Historical Association the Republican program for Political Reconstruction in the conquered States, telling those in attendance that the States of the Confederacy had been "cheated rather than conquered." Davis said that he personally believed that, if Confederates had realized how, as conquered people, their State governments would have been subjugated under Republican Political Machines, they would have fought on as guerrillas rather than surrender. People in the northern States were cheated by the Republicans as well, Davis asserted, explaining that they were rallied to war by Abe Lincoln's promise that the only military objective was to force the Confederate States back under the Federal Government where they would be permitted to retain their historic constitutions, laws, customs and institutions. Had the people of the northern States known the true intent of the Republican's Invasion of the Confederacy, Davis said, many would have refused to participate in the critical first months of the invasion. At one point Davis used these words:

> "If it had been anticipated that it was the purpose of [the Federals in] Washington to destroy the regular State Governments, [make Republican voters of the African American men], and subject the [European American] people to their rule, did any sane man doubt that the Confederate Government and its armies in the field would have been more thoroughly sustained than they were?"

At another point Jeff Davis told the Historical Association that he had never seen a southern [State] woman who was [remade in the Republican image]. Hudson Strode would report that Davis went on to urge children of the former Confederate States to "cherish the principles of freedom and State Rights, for which their fathers and forefathers had fought," and that "no [denial of voting rights], hardship, persecution, or malignant report could diminish one jot his love of liberty."

There would be a "howl raised in the North" over Jeff Davis' remarks at the Virginia Historical Association meeting. And some newspapermen in the former Confederate States would join in criticizing Davis for giving those in the North their excuse to "howl." But Historical Association President Jubal Early would fight back in a September 5 letter in the Chester *Reporter* where he would blast critical southern States newspapermen with words similar to the following:

> "In our judgment such stuff as [your newspaper reporting] has done the [southern States] 10,000 times more damage than all the speeches Jeff Davis ever made. It shows to our conquerors that we don't respect ourselves. . . . They would crush out of our souls the love we feel for the causes for which we fought, because in that sentiment they recognized an unrelenting enemy to the warfare they are waging on civil liberty itself."

Few would ever explain in so few words how far-reaching would be the power wielded by the victor's demand that they, and they alone, would be allowed to write the history of what they called the "Civil War."

Jeff Davis was back in Richmond — conferring with Wade Hampton on what could be done to salvage the Carolina Insurance Company — when a telegram arrived from Memphis announcing that the Carolina had been sold. Apparently, while Davis had been away seeking life-saving financial aid, the Carolina Board of Directors had struck a deal with a local insurance company which was in no better financial condition than was Carolina. The buyer was Southern Life of Memphis. It appears that the Carolina board just wanted to dump their company to avoid personally overseeing a bankruptcy action. Wade Hampton could not believe the telegram was true. He called it "a trick." But Davis was less doubtful. He called it "a blunder." Jeff would learn upon his return to Memphis a few days later, that all but one Director had voted to sell. It is rather obvious that company Directors had chosen to sell while Davis was out of town, so as to avoid the ordeal of outvoting him in a face-to-face meeting. Jeff wrote Varina, who was vacationing with the girls in Canada: "The evil genius of the Carolina took possession and destroyed all for which my trip was made." A few days later in another letter to Varina, Jeff wrote:

> "The seed sown when I was in New York had germinated and there was assurance that I could soon get $150,000 of new stock taken on the condition of taking a charter in Maryland and removing the parent office from Memphis to Baltimore. Thus the debts of the Carolina would have been paid at once. . . ."

Davis had no signed deal with New York financiers, but he was telling Varina that he had received indications that a deal could have been struck if the Board had just given him a little more time. But Jeff knew there was nothing he could do to reverse events. Instead of criticizing the Directors "before the public in the language of censure," upon his return to Memphis, Davis tendered his resignation as President. The resignation was accepted and his salary was stopped immediately. He then directed his energy toward raising the $5,650 he still owed on his personal holding of Carolina Insurance Company stock, which was valued at $15,000. But Davis would soon learn that his iron company stocks were "under a cloud" and other shareholders were selling at heavy losses. Upon the final liquidation of the Carolina Insurance Company some months into the future, Davis' investment of $15,000 would be a total loss. Of this time in the Davis family, Hudson Strode would conclude: "Now four years older than when he had sailed back from England in 1869 to take the insurance position, Jefferson Davis would have to make a fresh start in the business world." [R19;384-395, R199;201, R200;128-129]

Meanwhile on September 10 in Masschusetts, members of the State Historical Society voted to accept Charles Sumner into the organization. This seems on little import, but apparently, up to this time, the Society had repeatedly "blackballed" Sumner. Sumner's election to membership was a sign that the veteran Boston families of Beacon Hill were turning around to embrace him. That same day, Society President Robert Winthrop invited Sumner to dinner. And it is noteworthy that Sumner's last invitation to dine with the Winthrop's had been extended 30 years previously.

Sumner enjoyed time with Wadsworth Longfellow at the seashore. And, as usual, he took time to visit Ralph Emerson, the Transcendentalist Cult leader. Veteran Boston families of Beacon Hill had ostracized Emerson for a substantial number of years, but that, too, had passed, and those powerful families were again embracing Emerson. But Emerson and Sumner had always been on friendly terms. Emerson would always be Sumner's guest whenever he came to Washington City. In fact, it had been Emerson who had sponsored Sumner for membership in Boston's Saturday Club — that "exclusive Boston group devoted to the discussion of ideas and letters." You should note that the Saturday Club, and the Francis Bird Political Machine, which also met of Saturday's, were different organizations.

Sumner spent most of his time, while in Massachusetts, editing and proofreading the many volumes of his *Works*. The books were slowly being published. John Owen helped with literary revisions and George Nichols helped with "meticulous" proofreading. And the effort was costing Sumner some significant money. He was paying Nichols $1,500 per year, and he was paying Owen according to the time he spent. And Sumner had numerous bills to pay for medications and physician visits. Then there was the need to pay off the loan he had taken out to fund the previous year's expensive vacation and buying trip in Europe. Paying bills was made even more difficult by the economic depression had settled upon the nation during 1873.

In great need of money to pay off debts, Charles Sumner decided to sign up with James Redpath's company for a lecture tour, hoping to make some sorely needed money. Recognized as the "best lecture agent in the country," Redpath promised Sumner many full houses if he had the stamina to handle the travel and speaking. Sumner explained to a friend: "Only in the lecture field can I make anything. I know no senatorial way. This is my excuse." Surprisingly, Sumner's quack physician, Charles Brown-Sequard, gave his permission, although many friends thought Sumner too feeble to undertake such a strenuous effort. Wadsworth Longfellow exclaimed, "What folly!" But his friend Edward Pierce, arranged for his brother, Henry Pierce, a wealthy man and a Representative in the Federal House, to issue Sumner a personal loan to permit him to pay his bills without striding forth to lecture. Sumner knew his limitations, for he readily accepted the loan, and withdrew his offer to lecture for Redpath. "Mr. Redpath," he wrote, "this is the saddest day of my life."

But Charles Sumner had also to worry about threats to his political career from Ben "Beast" Butler. Butler wanted to be elected Governor of Massachusetts in two years and afterward elected to Sumner's Senate seat. Ulysses Grant was backing the "Beast." Treasury Secretary William Richardson was backing the "Beast." And the new Massachusetts Senator, George Boutwell was backing the "Beast." Biographer David Donald would write:

> "During the fall of 1873, driving himself to the point of exhaustion, Sumner put on a magnificent demonstration of vitality. He seemed omnipresent as he turned up for the monthly dinners of the Saturday Club, attended the meetings of the Radical Club, where Boston intellectuals discussed such topics as the character of Portia in 'Merchant of Venice,' or introduced an obscure English writer Edward Jenkins, to the Boston Lyceum. . . . [Ben "Beast" Butler] was now so powerful that Sumner did not dare come out in open opposition to him, as he and [Henry] Wilson had done in 1871."

So, instead of denouncing Ben "Beast" Butler, Sumner was undertaking a campaign to impress the Republican and third-party candidates for the Legislature, for it would be they who would actually vote to re-elect him, or someone else, to his Senate seat. He spoke before a farmer's club. He addressed the Commercial Club of Boston, where he endeavored to "charm" bankers and merchants by allowing them to witness that he had interests beyond his various African American bills. He spoke before the Banks Club and the Massachusetts Club. He "engaged in a cautious flirtation" with labor groups despite their enthusiasm for "The Beast." Sumner even announced his support for mandating an 8-hour work-day. But Sumner shunned any attempt to win political friends among advocates of outlawing alcoholic beverages, for "The Beast" seemed to have that Faction in his hip pocket. Sumner suddenly showered some attention on advocates for giving the right to vote to women. Sumner handed activist Susan Anthony some of his African American speeches and said "put 'sex' where I have 'race' or "African American," and you have the best and strongest arguments I can make for woman." And he assured her that nowhere in the Federal Constitution were States prohibited from allowing women to vote. Sumner won this poltical tug. Perhaps "The Beast" overplayed his hand. Perhaps the country-wide economic depression soured voters on such a close alley of Ulysses Grant. Perhaps Sumner's little campaign efforts were helpful in defeating "The Beast" as well. In any event, he failed to [either get the nomination, or win the general election]. [R73;573-579,581]

(4Q73)

Jeff Davis had suffered the loss of his favorite sister, Lucinda Stamps earlier in 1873. He had written Varina, lamenting, "the last link that bound me to happy childhood is broken." In early November, he was again saddened upon hearing that Mary Lee had just died. Jeff wrote her son Custis:

> "The grief you feel is intensely shared by me, for your mother was to me the object of highest admiration and most respectful regard. A bitter experience has taught me how vain are the words of consolation in such sorrow as yours, but you have the comfort of knowing that the loss is ours, the gain is hers."

Meanwhile in Mississippi, the race for Governor was decided. Adelbert Ames defeated James Alcorn. Lucius Lamar, Federal Representative-elect, had favored Alcorn as the "lesser of the two evils," and had won for him Oxford and surrounding Lafayette County, but Ames won by a wide margin. Both Ames and Alcorn had been Federal Senators for a time, each enjoying being elected to that high office through skillful political manipulation, Alcorn having taken the seat previously occupied by Hiram Revels, the famous African American. One faction of the Mississippi Republican Party had supported Ames, the other Alcorn, and the political animosity between the two had been substantial, even carrying over to the floor of the Federal Senate, where Ames, in one example, had complained that James Alcorn, "my colleague, is not connected with my State by any of the ties that make up the reality of the representative. He is not a citizen of Mississippi. He has never contributed a dollar to her taxes. He is not identified with her to the extent of even a technical residence."

At the Mississippi Republican State Convention, Adelbert Ames had won the nomination for Governor over Alcorn — prompting Alcorn and his supporters to immediately bolt the Party and nominate an "independent" slate of State candidates, with James Alcorn at the top. Seeing little hope for a Democrat nominee, the Democratic State Convention had declared it was "inexpedient" to present a ticket to voters, freeing Democrats to back Alcorn as the "lesser of two evils." African Americans were effectively organized to vote for the straight Republican Party ticket, giving victory to Ames as Governor; A. K. Davis, an African American, as Lieutenant Governor; Thomas Cordoza, an African American, as Superintendent of Education, and James Hill, also an African American, as Secretary of State; European Americans were elected to the other 3 offices. This had been the year that the Mississippi Republican Party had honored demands from African Americans that men of their race share in high office. The vote was 69,870 for Ames versus 50,490 for Alcorn. Corruption would mark the offices of Davis and Cordoza, but Hill would prove to be "a competent officer" and, in 1876, escape the wave of Impeachment charges leveled at others.

Governor Adelbert Ames would be inaugurated on January 22, 1874 and the Mississippi Legislature, overwhelmingly Republican, would also convened at that time. The State House would consist of 77 Republicans, 36 Democrats and several independents. Of these, 55 were African Americans and 15 Republicans who had come into the State following its conquest and entered into politics. The State Senate would consist of 25 Republicans and 12 Democrats. Of these 9 would be African Americans and 9 would be men who had come into the State following its conquest and entered into politics. The House would elect Issac Shadd, an African American, as Speaker. [R205;176-178]

Meanwhile on November 24, the South Carolina Legislature wrapped up an "extra session" that had begun on October 21 at the call of Governor Franklin Moses. On opening day Moses had explained that pending State bankruptcy had required that the Legislature convene 5 weeks ahead of the normal schedule. He warned that, "certain bond-creditors of the State, holding or representing bonds of several classes, having in the last resort appealed to the Supreme Court," did obtain a judgment that the bonds were valid, but in that ruling had directed the Comptroller-General to levy a tax to pay the past and current interest due on the bonds, setting a deadline of "on or before the 15th day of November next." The Court's decision covered 5 classes of bonds amounting in the aggregate to $3,549,000. Moses reported that the total debt of the State had risen to $15,027,503 and total floating debt of the State had risen to $5,306,398. The sum of these two forms of State debt "was thus declared to be $20,333,901 — an increase of about $14,000,000 in the 6 years of so-called Republican rule." Moses reported that the bond trading market was discounting South Carolina bonds by 15 cents to 40 cents on the dollar. The Legislature had then proceeded to deal with impending State Government bankruptcy.

Of course, political friends had to be rewarded during this 5-week emergency session. The Republican Printing Company was given $125,000 for some extra work, plus $50,000 for printing related to the 5-week session. Also the South Carolina Bank and Trust Company was given $125,000. This so-called bank was "a private bank run by one Hardy Solomon, a European American man who seemed wholly devoid of character and whose business as a broker was chiefly the cashing of State paper held by officials of high or low degree, by members of the Legislature, and by different fellows who, calling themselves "attachés," received money for ficticious services."

Regarding action on the huge debt of $20,333,901, the Legislature, passed what would be called the "Consolidation Act," which:

1. Repudiated $5,965,000 of debt that was classified as "Conversion bonds."

2. Repudiated half of the remaining bond debt, by declaring that it was only worth 50 cents on the dollar and would be treated as such.

3. Stipulated that interest on debt not repudiated in total or in part would be paid from an additional annual property tax levy "of 2 mils — the enactment of the levy to be endorsed on each bond and to form a part of the contract thus made between the State and the bondholder." This scheme was apparently an attempt to remove debt liability from the heads of the Legislators and place it upon the heads of the taxpayers.

The special session of the Mississippi Legislature ended on November 24 and the regular session began the following day.

A few days later, on December 1, Lucius Lamar was on hand in Washington City and promptly took his seat in the Federal House, representing District 1, Mississippi. He would be assigned to the Committee on Elections. [R201;238-240, R205;178]

Charles Sumner was also in his Senate seat on opening day. But he continued to be an outsider, without any Committee assignments, for Republicans refused to invite him back into their Party. Again Sumner came forth will a stack of proposed legislation to be scheduled for attention. His drafts of bills included an Amendment to the Federal Constitution restricting Federal Presidents to one 6-year term, a bill requiring that Federal bond holders be paid in gold and silver coin, and a bill to mix European American and African American students in the same class-rooms in the public schools in and around Washington City. But his most passionately advocated bill would be the African American bill he would again submit. This version would "erase the last legal distinctions between [European Americans] and [African Americans] and would thus complete the work of [Political Reconstruction of the conquered States].

But Sumner would get no-where with his latest proposed African American Bill. Senators would vote to submit it to the Judiciary Committee, where Sumner had no significant influence. Hardly anyone in the Senate thought favorably of the bill. Even Senators elected by Republican Political Machines in the former Confederate States had no enthusiasm for it. Of that response, Sumner complained: "I regret much to see how little pluck there is among [African American Senators]. "They are considering how to surrender on the [African American Bill], through fear of [Ulysses Grant]!" [R73;579-580]

Meanwhile in Mississippi, Jeff Davis, and the other executors of Joseph's estate, met with Ben and Isaiah Montgomery during December, to learn that the brothers had again been unable to turn a profit from farming the two Davis farms they had purchased from Joseph in a seller-finance transaction — unable to pay any of the soon-to-be-due 1873 interest payment of $18,000. But Jeff and the other executors, to avoid foreclosure proceedings, agreed to reduce the 1873 interest obligation to $15,000 and postponed the due date until October, 1874. So, it would be at least late in 1874 before Jeff and Varina could hope for any revenue from the estate's mortgage on the two farms formerly held by Jeff and brother Joseph. [R19;388]

Meanwhile, Ulysses Grant nominated Caleb Cushing of Masschusetts to the Chief Justice job, made vacant by the death of Salmon Chase, 65. A summation of Chase's life is inserted below:

> Over the past 32 years, since 1841, Salmon Chase had been a major Liberty Party political leader, then a major Free Soil Democrat political leader and then a major Republican political leader — Federal Senator from Ohio (1849-1855); Governor of Ohio (1856-1860), Treasury Secretary in the Lincoln Administration (1861-1864), and Chief Justice of the Supreme Court (1864-1873). He had championed Abolitionism and Exclusionism prior to the launch of the Republican Party, enabling him to ride those issues to political power.

Strangely, Charles Sumner had some difficulty deciding to vote for Cushing, in spite of the fact that Cushing was also of Massachusetts, a favorite dinner companion and a close collaborator on his "Claims on England" efforts. And Cushing had worked with Sumner in codifying the Federal statutes. Yet Sumner must had been troubled by recalling that Cushing had, long ago, been a Democrat, been Attorney General in the Franklin Pierce Administration, and been a close friend to Jefferson Davis. Many others must have shared Sumner's opposition to Cushing, for he did not win confirmation in the Senate. It seems that opposition to Cushing firmed after evidence was uncovered that, in the formative days of the Confederacy, before Abe Lincoln announced the Federal Invasion campaign, Cushing had recommended a friend for a job in the Confederate Government. That was the kiss of death. Grant immediately withdrew Cushing's name. Grant's next choice for Chief Justice was Morrison Waite, like the former Chief Justice, also of Ohio. Sumner was opposed to Waite, but was unable to rally opposition. But, rather than vote against Waite, Sumner merely abstained. Yet, Waite was confirmed, would work the job for 14 years, would write more than 1,000 opinions, and would view issues mostly as a "strict constructionist." [R73;581]

Before leaving the year 1873, it is appropriate to report on Lucius Lamar's first month in the Federal House. Biographer Edward Mayes would later describe Lamar's early impressions:

> "[Lamar] found that sectional animosity was strong and bitter; that the purposes and aspirations of the [southern States] people were grossly misrepresented from many powerful quarters, and were generally most sadly misunderstood; that, based upon such misrepresentations and misunderstandings, measures had been, and constantly were, introduced, which to him and his people appeared most hostile and deadly to their happiness, their prosperity, and their liberty."

Lucius Lamar and Alexander Stephens — the former Vice President of the Confederate States and, like Lamar, recently elected to the Federal House from Georgia — visited Ulysses Grant at the President's Residence shortly before Christmas for a visit, which Lamar afterward described in a letter to Judge Thomas Wharton at Jackson, Mississippi. Dated December 25, it said in part:

> "Well, I have seen [Ulysses] Grant once. I went with Stephens. We were carried into a reception room, and were told that the President would be in in a few moments. Very soon another person came in, whom I took to be one of the upper servants. He said: 'Good morning, Mr. Stephens.' Mr. Stephens, to my utter astonishment, replied: 'Good morning, Mr. President. Allow me to introduce Col. Lamar, member of Congress from Mississippi.' I had seen his pictures, and had heard A. G. Brown describe him, but I was taken by surprise. He is, at first sight, the most ordinary man I ever saw in prominent position.

"I judge him to be a man of rather a narrow range of ideas, but of clear perception within the range of his mental vision [and] close observation, and accustomed to forming very decided opinions about men and things. He does not look at you when he converses. There is nothing furitive in his manner. He simply looks straight by you. Once he turned and looked at me very steadily and sharply all over, and then turned his eyes from me and began to talk very freely.

"I take him to be the most ambitious man that we have ever had [in that office]. His schemes are startling. With the machinery of the Civil Rights bill transferring to the Federal Courts jurisdiction, civil and criminal, over the protection of persons, property, and liberty, in every State, against injuries committed on account of race; with control of telegraph lines and railroads, which he is seeking to get; and with all the emissaries, spies, employees, and tools that the patronage gives him, there will be no limit to the despotic power which he is ever ready to use relentlessly and fearlessly for his own purposes; which purposes are the most arbitrary that have ever yet been cherished by a Federal Executive." [R205;178-180]

The Year of 1874

(1Q74)

On January 22, in Jackson, Adelbert Ames, Republican, was inaugurated as Mississippi's new Governor. He then proceeded to address the State Legislature, controlled overwhelmingly by Republicans. The Senate was presided over by Lieutenant Governor Alexander Davis and the Speaker of the House was Isaac Shadd, an African American who would prove to be far less competent and honest than his predecessor, John Lynch, an honorable man previously mentioned. Ames advocated substantial cuts in State spending, recognizing that, by this time, Mississippi had descended into a very difficult financial mess — although taxes had risen from 1 mil in 1869 to 14 mils in 1874, State spending was exceeding receipts by 20 percent and State financial paper was selling at 60 to 80 cents on the dollar. Although this difficulty was not as bad as in South Carolina, financial sanity was sorely needed, and Ames recommended that spending be reduced 25 percent and not allowed to exceed revenues. He provided details, by department, itemizing areas of spending that ought to be trimmed. But there was little evidence that Legislators were taking that advice very seriously. Nor were Legislators apt to take seriously recommendations of a Taxpayers Convention, which would be held shortly, and which would "call attention to the alleged abuses of the State Government, its wastefulness and extravagance," and compare it to the situation prior to State secession. [R204;294-297]

Meanwhile, on January 25, Jeff Davis boarded a riverboat for New Orleans. After a few days in the city he planned to take the S. S. *Alabama* to Liverpool, England for a stay of several months. Jeff's doctors had advised him that, after the stress of the Carolina Insurance Company failure and with the continuing stress of Republican political domination of the conquered States, Jeff needed the sea voyage and the time away from home to strengthen his health. Furthermore, Jeff again hoped to make business contacts that would lead to a new job. Varina had been urging her husband to make the voyage, and feared that he might back out at the last minute. To ensure against that, she surprised Jeff by arriving in New Orleans the day before the ship was to leave. There, she gave him a pair of woolen slippers she had knitted, and saw him safely off at the dock the next day. [R19;390-391]

Meanwhile, Charles Sumner's abject political weakness became more evident when, on February 16, Ulysses Grant nominated William Simmons to be collector of Federal import taxes at Boston Harbor. Simmons was a political supporter of Ben "Beast" Butler, and everyone realized that Simmons' confirmation would advance "The Beast's" political domination over the Massachusetts Republican Party. The Port Collector's office provided enormous opportunities for handing out political jobs and engaging in bribery, graft and corruption. A few days later, the Senate voted 27 to 11 to confirm Simmons. Biographer David Donald would write: "Jubilantly ["The Beast"] announced that he was now the dominant force in Massachusetts politics and 'that nobody will be re-elected who opposes him and [William] Simmons.' " But attacks of angina were surely even more a factor in Sumner's loss of political power. Of the injections of morphine he was frequently receiving, Sumner would report that the hypodermic needle "works upon me like magic." Donald would add: "Too ill to make more than an infrequent appearance in the Senate, [Sumner] now had to admit that he was an invalid and spent nearly all his time quietly at home." Few missed having Sumner around in the Senate. He was neither Republican nor Democrat and had no Committee assignments. Furthermore, his interest in Federal

Senate legislation was limited to his African American bill. His only other political concern dealt with getting the Massachusetts State Legislature to rescind its past censure of him over his failed effort to prohibit sewing battlefield names on Federal regimental flags. Of the latter interest he finally won a small victory — in February his political friends managed to get up enough votes to rescind the past censure. David Donald would write:

> "On February 11, the Massachusetts Senate voted overwhelmingly to repeal, and two days later the House did so as well. During the discussion one Legislator voiced a concern that many of his colleagues had left unsaid: he urged 'that the censure should be removed while [Charles] Sumner is still with us.' " [R73;583-584]

Meanwhile in Columbia, South Carolina, a second Taxpayers' Convention began on February 17. It would last 4 days. Very well attended, Delegates came from all but 2 counties. The Honorable William Porter of Charleston served as President of the Convention, which passed the following resolutions:

> "Resolved. That in this State taxation has reached the last point of endurance, and that the taxpayers cannot continue to bear the excessive burdens imposed upon them."

> "Resolved. That the Executive Committee be empowered to prepare a system of organization of Tax Unions throughout the State, with authority to take all necessary steps for carrying the same into effect."

> "Resolved. That, [because] a large proportion of property holders and tax-payers of the State are practically debarred from representation in the General Assembly, [the] adoption of the cumulative system of voting" is advocated since it "would tend to secure a fair representation of the minority." We therefore appoint a Committee of Five to "ask the General Assembly to give an early and earnest consideration to [a system of cumulative voting], with the view of applying this system in the conduct of the State election next fall."

> "Resolved. That a Committee of Fifteen be appointed by the Chair to proceed to Washington [City] and present to the [Federal President and the Federal House and Senate, the resolutions of this Convention]."

The Convention failed in its attempted to force Francis Cardozo, the State Treasurer, to provide copies of vouchers for which he paid the Republican Printing Company $331,000 during 1873. Cardozo simply replied: "I have no right to permit any one to inspect my vouchers except those who are legally authorized to do so."

The Committee of Fifteen, proceeded to Washington City and submitted the Taxpayers' Convention's Memorial to the Federal House and Senate. In part, the Memorial stated:

> South Carolinians suffer greatly because "those owning the property have no voice in [State and Local] governments, and those imposing the taxes [have] no share in the burden thereof. The taxes have advanced yearly, until in many cases they consume more than one-half of the income from the property taxed. The annual expenses of the [State] Government have advanced from $400,000 before the [War Between the States] to $2,500,000 at the present time. The following comparisons of leading items of expenditures will best exhibit the change:

	1865-66	1873
Salaries	$76,481	$230,797
Public printing	17,447	331,946
Legislative expenses	51,337	291,339
Public asylums	25,897	128,432
Contingent fund	6,093	75,034
Sundries	83,413	298,668
Subtotal	$260,669	$1,356,217
Deficiencies	0	$540,328
Total	**$260,669**	**$1,896,545"**

These facts exhibit the unprecedented spectacle of a State in which the Government is arrayed against property. It has been openly avowed by prominent members of the Legislature that the taxes should be increased to a point which will compel the sale of the great body of the land and take it away from the former owners. . . . [As a direct result of] default in payment of taxes for the year 1872 alone 268,523 acres of land were forfeited to the State. . . . Lands are unavailable as security; mortgages on default of payment cannot sell; wages have declined; the cost of living is made greater by the addition of the taxes to the price of commodities; the poor are made poorer and rendered every day more incapable of purchasing lands and more hopeless of rising above the condition of mere laborers. . . . The public debt had in 6 years been raised from $5,000,000 to $16,000,000, and that without advancing any public work and without adding one dollar to the public property or to the payment of the public debt. . . . The clerks of the Legislature, in their personal capacity, made contracts with themselves as private persons for the public printing. . . . In the Executive Department all these evils culminate. . . . To detect and punish these crimes is impossible; the Governor controls the avenues of justice."

The Committee of Fifteen would meet with President Ulysses Grant on March 30. [R201;245-253]

Meanwhile Massachusetts Governor William Washburn had arranged for J. B. Smith, a friend of Sumner's who was of partial African ancestry, to personally deliver the State Legislature's two resolutions rescinding its past censure of Sumner. Accordingly, Smith arrived in Washington City on March 7. After handing the papers to Sumner, Smith observed: "As he read them, he turned his head and wept as I never saw man weep before." Sumner dried his eyes and told Smith: "I knew Massachusetts would do me justice."

The next day Sumner suffered severe angina attacks, probably made more intense because of the excitement over the rescinding resolutions, and over another public matter. It seems that newspapers were reporting the details of the divorce settlement between Charles and Alice. Biographer David Donald would write: "Late at night on March 8 [Sumner] suffered an acute spasm of angina and was in excruciating pain for hours. He continued to suffer the next day until a massive injection of morphine allowed him to sleep."

Two days later, on March 10, Sumner, with great physical effort, went to the Senate Chamber to be present when George Boutwell ceremoniously presented the two rescinding resolutions, for he wanted very much to be present to witness the event. Afterward, Sumner seemed excited about his vindication and mixed socially with Senators in the chamber. But after a while he turned to Orris Ferry of Connecticut and said "Ferry, I have a toothache in my heart. I think I shall go home." But Sumner began to feel better by the time servants had brought the carriage and horses belonging to his neighbor, Samuel Hooper. So Sumner turned to Henry Pierce and Benjamin Perley Poore and invited them to come over later for dinner. That evening Pierce and Poore observed that Sumner seemed unusually agitated over news that Samuel Howe "was organizing a public dinner in Boston for [Buenaventura] Báez," who no longer held power in the politically turbulent Dominican Republic. Sumner kept returning the subject of conversation to Báez, as he repeatedly expressed his fear that Ulysses Grant would resurrect his campaign to annex the Dominican Republic under the Federal Government, perhaps to establish a land to which African Americans could be deported, or otherwise encouraged to move to. It was the African American issues surrounding the Dominican Republic question that so stirred Sumner's passions. Realizing the overexcited Sumner needed to get rest, Pierce and Perley left earlier than normal — about 9 that evening. But Sumner did not go to bed, as his dinner guests had hoped. Instead he went into his study to work on his diary and perhaps his *Works* publication. While in the study, Sumner wrote: "Something very different from a dinner should be [Buenaventura Báez's] lot. There are many bad men in the world, but he is among the worst."

It was about 11 that night when servants heard a loud bang come from the study. They rushed in and discovered that Sumner had fallen to the floor, and was in great pain. Servants called Sumner's physician, Joseph Johnson. Johnson injected morphine, then a bit later a second injection. Sumner slept fitfully under the influence of the morphine, but fearing he might die of over-sedation, Johnson awoke him every two hours to administer stimulants. Sumner's heart was in the final stages of failure. He was semi-conscious during the morning. A few friends stopped by. When lucid he would complain, "I am so tired." He told his secretary, "I should not regret this if my book were finished." He told Rockwood Hoar, "You must take care of the African American bill, — my bill, the [African American] bill, don't let it fail." An hour later he told Frederick Douglass, "Don't let the bill fail."

Sumner asked for more morphine at 2 that afternoon, but Johnson explained his body could not stand it. Shortly afterward Sumner told Hoar, "tell Emerson how much I love and revere him." Hoar reassured the dying man: "[Emerson] said of you once, that he never knew so white a soul."

It was about 2:30 when the end came. Sumner "was seized by a violent spasm, followed by vomiting. Suddenly throwing himself back on the bed and gasping for air, he died." The day was Wednesday, March 11, 1874. He was 63 years old. [R73;584-587]

An elaborate funeral for Charles Sumner began on Friday, March 13 at 9 in the morning, for Republican majorities in both the Federal House and the Federal Senate voted to temporarily adjourn to devote that day entirely to a state funeral for the deceased champion of Abolitionism, Exclusionism and Republican idealism. Sumner's emotional and theoretical demagoguery, so influential in the northeastern States, had been a major boost to the Republican Party across all the northern States, and both the Party's history, and the man who had helped so much to make that history, needed to be celebrated. "It was the first time in [America] that a [Federal] Senator's memory had been so honored." The public filed by the coffin until noon, viewing the body. Then at 12:30 p. m. the coffin was brought into the Senate Chamber where Ulysses Grant, his Cabinet, the Supreme Court Justices, members of the diplomatic corps, Federal Senators and Federal Representatives were in attendance, while 5,000 others crowded the halls or stood outside. Sumner's Senate seat was draped in black fabric. There, in the Chamber that had witnessed his profound yet mysterious influence, Republican leaders conducted a formal state ceremony and eulogy.

Then the coffin was put on a special funeral train bound for Boston. The train halted in New York for the night. The next morning, Saturday, the train proceeded on to Boston. Crowds gathered at every railroad station from Springfield, Massachusetts to the outskirts of Boston to see the black funeral train speed past, and church bells rang as the train passed through. And bells in Christain churches tolled even though the deceased Sumner was not a Christian. A huge crowd met the train at the Boston station and followed the casket as it was transported to Doric Hall in the Massachusetts State House building. Acting as the Federal Senate's President pro tempore, Henry Anthony turned Sumner's body over to the Governor of the State of Massachusetts with these words:

> "We are commanded . . . to render back to you your illustrious dead. . . . With reverent hands we bring to you his mortal part that it may be committed to the soil of the renowned [State] which gave him birth. Take it; it is yours. The part which we do not return to you is not wholly yours to receive, nor altogether ours to give. It belongs to the country, to mankind, to [the independence of African Americans], to civilization, to humanity."

> Realizing that Sumner had not been a Christian, Anthony had craftily omitted any notion that the "part which we do not return to you" in any way belonged to Almighty God.

The next day, Sunday, the coffin, now sealed, lay in state in Doric Hall attended by African American veterans of the conquest of the Confederacy. A sign, admonishing, "Don't Let the [African American] Bill Fail," lay upon the coffin. During Sunday and the early hours of Monday, 40,000 people filed past the closed coffin, three abreast. All business shut down on Monday for the funeral, and thousands of out-of-towners joined Bostonians in filling the streets. Organizers had decided to conduct a funeral service at King's Chapel, the Episcopal Church to which Sumner's mother had belonged, for Sumner had never joined a church himself. Burial was planned at Mount Auburn Cemetery, which was located about 5 miles beyond the King's Chapel. So, Monday morning, through an immense crowd of onlookers, the funeral procession transported the casket from Doric Hall to King's Chapel. Pallbearers included Wadsworth Longfellow, Ralph Emerson, John Whittier, Robert Winthrop, Charles Adams, and 5 former Massachusetts Governors. After the pallbearers bore the casket into the church, ministers performed the standard Episcopal service for the dead. Then the casket was brought back outside and the funeral procession resumed the trip to the cemetery. Vice President Henry Wilson, who had worked for many years alongside Sumner as Massachusetts' other Federal Senator, was at the head of the procession. Lined up behind Wilson were the Massachusetts Representatives to the Federal House, the Massachusetts Governor, the Boston Mayor and the Harvard College President. At the very rear of the procession marched about 2,000 African Americans who were members of African American fraternal groups.

The procession moved slowly because the massive crowds had created an immense traffic jam. For example, it was stalled for 45 minutes in front of Alice's house. Alice had chosen to not attend her former husband's. After all, the marriage had been good no more than two months, if that. Within 6 months she had packed and was gone for good — off to Paris to live for many years. Now back home in Boston, she had just completed the divorce court process a few weeks previously. Peaking "through tightly drawn blinds," Alice looked down upon the stalled funeral procession of her former husband, reflecting on their brief life together and the scene before her eyes. After a bit she said:

"That is just like Charles; he never did show tact."

Newspapers were giving extensive coverage of the funeral, many publishing extensive reviews of Sumner's life. On Wednesday, March 18 Carl Schurz would deliver an elaborate eulogy in Boston's Music Hall. Enthusiastic eulogists would extolled grandly. Timothy Howe would call Sumner, "the greatest of our Senators and of our Citizens alike." The editor of The Springfield *Republican* would moan, "The noblest head in [Federal Government] has fallen, and the most accomplished and illustrious of our [politicians] is no more." Hoping to top that, a Massachusetts Legislator would proclaim: "Not only has [the Federal Government] lost her greatest and best [politician], but the world has lost its ablest and most devoted friend." Eleven weeks later, on June 9, the Massachusetts State Government would host a eulogy on the late Charles Sumner, at which time John Whittier would read a, "funeral ode on Sumner," and George Curtis would deliver "a commemorative oration." Before 12 months would pass, publishers would print at least four books containing eulogies and tributes to Sumner.

Allow me to present a brief analysis of the man, his private and political life:

What had Charles Sumner accomplished that merited such stupendous praise? Biographer David Donald would ponder the question. He would observe that: "No one tried to explain Sumner's fame in terms of legislation which he had pushed through" the Senate. Although contemporaries viewed Sumner as the greatest champion of Federal legislation designed to benefit African Americans, Donald would observe that Sumner had not been the author of any of the three Constitutional Amendments that had been submitted to the States by the House and Senate. In fact, in each case, he had opposed the final language that the Senate eventually approved. Upon what was the praise based? Donald's answer would be: "A large number of the eulogists concluded that Sumner's fame rested upon the special role he had so long played in [America's] public life, that of the idealist in politics."

But how had a mere idealist gotten elected to the Federal Senate and continually won reelection? David Donald would give a lot of the credit to Boston's Francis Bird Political Machine. The Bird Machine had recognized that a brilliant and gifted demagogue was essential to maintaining political power in a State whose voter demography had been as ethnically turbulent and rapidly changing as it was in Massachusetts during Sumner's adult life. During those years, more and more voters had been downtrodden emigrant factory workers. The Bird Machine had discovered that Sumner could persuade them to vote against Massachusetts Democratic candidates through his passionate and idealist denunciations of Democrats in the southern States. He was capable of black-balling well-meaning Massachusetts Democrats by branding them as no better that the hated southern States Democrats. Bird had known that these emigrant factory workers would naturally vote against the Whig Party if Whig politicians revealed their true, but hidden, goals for Massachusetts legislation. Bird therefore had resolved that Whig politicians needed an idealistic diversion with which to fool voters into voting for Whig candidates for political jobs within the State. He had resolved to put forward persuasive demagogues. When Abolitionists had suggested that their agenda be that diversion, it had attracted some intellectual adherents, but after that success, this overly-idealistic movement had stalled. So it was necessary to transform the Abolition political movement into the Exclusion political movement to truly develop a powerful and effective diversion. Bird had discovered that he could exercise considerable control over Massachusetts State politics by advocating a Federal program to confine African Americans (legally only those bonded, but in practice all) to the southern States, a policy of Exclusionism. And the Exclusionist Movement had given birth to "Bleeding Kansas" and the Republican Party. And Charles Sumner had been Exclusionism's most celebrated spokesman, most celebrated martyr and most celebdrated idealist.

Yet, Charles Sumner had been rejected by the Republican Party during the last year of his life, for he had lost his Party affiliation when he joined the Liberal Republican Party in a futile attempt to defeat Ulysses Grant. He had destroyed himself in his fervent effort to destroy those about him with whom he disagreed. He knew no way to compromise, no way to see any merit in opposing ideas. To be his friend, one had to agree with almost everything he said. Alice had him figured:

"That is just like Charles; he never did show tact."

Several years earlier, Julia Ward Howe had been so upset with Sumner upon hearing him remark that he had "long since, ceased to take any interest in individuals," that she had felt compelled to rebuke him. "You have made great progress. God has not yet gone so far — at least according to the last accounts." And back when they were both young and of courting age, Julia (to become the poet behind the horrific Battle Hymn of the Republic) had understood why Charles Sumner would never have a successful marriage. He had "no heart," she admonished. To that complaint Charles had countered:

"I have a heart — it is not my fault if all its throbbings have been in vain."

Julia was right. Sumner had copious idealistic notions of how the world should be, but on a personal basis, Sumner had "no heart." By my observation:

"He had been an incomplete man." [R73;4-10]

At this point in our narrative history — where so much of the story is told through the lives of major political leaders — only one man remains. Stephen Douglas is gone. Abe Lincoln is gone. Thad Stevens is gone. So is Charles Sumner. Only Jeff Davis remains — my hero among the lot and I hope yours, too. As we continue with "Political Reconstruction and the Struggle for Healing," you will follow the lives of three others needed to complete the story. I expect you will also come to see these men as heros. Of course, I am speaking of Wade Hampton, Lucius Lamar and Grover Cleveland.

Meanwhile, on March 17, three weeks after the conclusion of the South Carolina Taxpayers' Convention, the regular session of the Legislature concluded its session. The following noteworthy actions should be reported:

The past year's deficit remained huge, with total tax collections at $1,719,728, compared to obligations of $2,260,056, plus unpaid outstanding interest.

Property taxes were fixed at 12 mils for the State, which, if all were paid, would generate $2,654,347. Because property had been reappraised to higher values, the new obligation exceeded the previous tax burden, which had been $2,512,215 based on a 15 mil rate.

The Legislature revised the boundaries of the 5 Federal House Districts, gerrymandering the lines to ensure that African Americans were in the majority in each.

An Act to Regulate the Public Printing required that printing be contracted to the lowest "responsible" bidder. Would that stop the graft in printing work?

Historian John Reynold would report an interesting story arising from this session: "A joint resolution to appoint a Committee to assist in the prosecution of Niles G. Parker, late Treasurer of the State, for his conduct in connection with the over-issue of Conversion bonds, was duly passed, and it was formally ratified in the Senate chamber. Between that chamber and the Governor's office the paper was 'lost,' and thus it never became effective." Parker would never be punished for his crimes. [R201;240-245]

On or shortly after November 30, the Committee of Fifteen from the South Carolina Taxpayers' Convention met with President Ulysses Grant. Grant was well prepared to rebut the appeal by the Committee's leader, William Porter of Charleston, for he had been well schooled by an earlier meeting with Senator John Patterson, of South Carolina. After listening to Porter's speech, Grant replied:

"Gentlemen: After listening to your remarks, I do not see that there is anything that can be done either by the Executive or by the Legislative branch of the [Federal] Government to better the condition of things which you have described. **The State of South Carolina has a complete sovereign existence**, and must make its own laws. If its citizens are suffering from those laws it is a matter very much to be deplored. Where the fault lies may be a question worth looking into. Whether a part of the cause is not due to yourselves — whether it is not owing to the extreme views which you have held — whether your action has not consolidated the non-taxpaying portion of the community against you — are questions which I leave to your own consideration. Allow me to say, however, that I always feel great sympathy with any people who are badly governed and overtaxed, as is the case in Louisiana, and seems to also be the condition of South Carolina."

The Federal President's reply to the South Carolinians requires commentary:

Perhaps you are as amazed as I am that Ulysses Grant, of all people, alleged, "**The State of South Carolina has a complete sovereign existence**." How does that square with the Republican Party's denial of the right of State Secession and its dispatching of Federal warships to Charleston harbor to incite an artillery exchange? How does that square with the Republican Party's military invasion campaign — a horrific and bloody War between the States, War between Republicans and Democrats? How does that square with the imprisonment of Jeff Davis on a charge of Treason? What about Grant's commander, William Sherman, whose 60,000 Federals swept through South Carolina and burned the capital, Columbia? How did a war against civilians square with the notion that "**The State of South Carolina has a complete sovereign existence**"? It does not square. A formerly sovereign State like South Carolina — together with 12 other formerly sovereigns — had created the Federal Government; so any of those 13 ought to have been able to reverse that creation process and secede from the Federal Government, leaving the others to remain or leave as they wished. The Federal Constitution expressly forbid making war against any State. Sorry for belaboring this point, but I was just as amazed by Grant's dialog as you probably were.

Returning to Grant's reply to the Committee of Fifteen — the President further claimed to be greatly offended by a speech that had been delivered by Martin Gary of Edgefield during the Taxpayers' Convention. (We should suspect that, before the Committee arrived, John Patterson had showed Grant a report on Gary's speech.) Anyway, Grant claimed that Gary's speech "contained a viler and more villainous slander than I have ever experienced before, even among my bitterest enemies in the [northern States]."

So, the Committee of Fifteen received no help from the Federal Executive. It presented a Memorial to the Federal House and to the Federal Senate. Both likewise claimed the issues presented in the Memorial were beyond their jurisdiction. The only encouragement came from a minority report from members of the House Committee on the Judiciary, a Committee controlled by Democrats. A minority of the Democrats on this Committee reported, "In view of the whole case, we cannot hesitate to recommend the appointment of a [Joint House and Senate Investigating Committee]." [R201;263-265]

(2Q74)

On April 27 the Federal Senate devoted the day to presenting tributes to the late Charles Sumner. Senators speaking would include Republicans George Boutwell of Massachusetts, John Sherman of Ohio, Justin Morrill of Vermont and Henry Anthony of Rhode Island as well as Democrat Allen Thurman of Ohio. The following day, Representative Rockwood Hoar, Republican of Massachusetts, rose and moved for corresponding presentations of eulogies in the Federal House:

"Resolved, That as an additional mark of respect to the memory of Charles Sumner, long a Senator from Masschusettts, and in symphathy with the action of the Senate, business be now suspended in this House to allow fitting tributes to be paid to his public and private virtues."

Representative Rockwood Hoar began the occasion by delivering "an address of a lofty and appreciative strain."

As previously arranged with the concurrence of the leadership of the Republican-controlled House, Representative Lucius Lamar, of Mississippi, rose to second the motion and deliver a substantial eulogy, which he had carefully prepared in advance. Why Lamar — a recent addition to the Federal House, a Democrat, a former Confederate leader and a politician from Mississippi, where Jeff Davis — a former Federal Senator and Confederate President — had risen to political power? Why Lamar, who had never spoken with Sumner, revealing that fact in his own words: "It was my misfortune, perhaps my fault, personally never to have known this eminent philanthropist and statesman."? Was Lamar overly influenced by Sumner's lukewarm support of the Liberal Republican-Democrat political coalition that had attempted to defeat Ulysses Grant's reelection? Biographer Edward Mayes — Lamar's son-in-law, and greatly impressed by what he perceived to have been a turning point in political relations between the two sections of the country — would later explain his thoughts in a most complementary account:

> "The Massachusetts Delegation in the House [had] invited [Representative] Lamar to second the usual resolutions in that body and to deliver a memorial address. Here was an opportunity to make his appeal for 'peace between the sections,' and he seized upon it. He seized upon it all the more gladly because his heart was full of kindly feeling toward Mr. Sumner, very much softened toward the great scholar and statesman who, at the other extreme [politically, among the States], had felt the same generous impulses with himself, and had undertaken the same great labor of pacification. It was one of those golden and rare occasions when the most exalted feeling runs hand in hand with the subtlest worldly wisdom."

In fact, biographer Mayes believed this eulogy was "the turning point of Lamar's political career:

> "The turning point of Mr. Lamar's political career was the Sumner eulogy. Indeed, that great speech is believed by his admirers and friends to have been the deathblow to sectional animosity, and by consequence the turning point of our post bellum national history. Through it, and through his subsequent labors in pursuance of the spirit which it evidenced and of the policy it inaugurated, many claim for him the enviable position of the most practically patriotic, the strongest, and the most useful man of our [Federal Government] since the [American] Civil War."

Lucius Lamar had several advantages in making the most of this opportunity. First, as previously mentioned, throughout most of 1873, he had studied the mind of northern States political leaders, corresponded on the subject, and envisioned ways he might reduce sectional hatreds — to contribute positively in "The Struggle for Healing." Second, he was well versed in law and academics, the intellectual equal to Sumner and his most "learned" admirers. Third, his experience in Washington City had been in the deceased's last several months of life — a time when Sumner had been an outcast in the Republican Party, punished for supporting the Liberal Republican-Democrat effort to defeat Grant's reelection and in some ways also attempting to contribute positively in the country's "Struggle for Healing," in spite of the fact that his last dying words, addressed to Rockwood Hoar, had been: "Take care of my Civil Rights Bill." Biographer Edward Mayes, biased by a loving attitude toward his father-in-law, surely overstated the impact of this occasion on American history. But the impact cannot be discounted. It was meaningful.

Was the choice of Lamar for the second eulogy speech a setup, a trap — a scheme intended to further aggravate northern States passions against the southern States people? The audience represented "the most distinguished and intellectual men in the nation. The galleries were crowded with visitors, amongst whom were numbered members of brilliant diplomatic corps from all over the enlightened world. The House [floor] was thronged: on the one side friends, full of misgivings; on the other, opponents, cold, curious, critical. The speaker was a 'fire eater' of the long ago. The odor of 'rebellion' hung about" the designee. Of this concern, biographer Edward Mayes would write:

> "That a Mississippi Representative . . . should pronounce a eulogy upon [Charles Sumner] was naturally regarded as a curious spectacle of questionable taste. Perhaps no one expected aught but a purely perfunctory performance, an unwilling tribute to a dead foe exacted by the good breeding of civilization.

> "But the generosity of the [nature of the southern States people], its chivalric passion which concedes so much to honesty of purpose and to high-hearted devotion to sincere conviction, had not been taken into account; and Mr. Lamar, who so thoroughly embodied the loftiest [of such] sentiment, amazed the doubters."

Lamar's eulogy to the late Charles Sumner, slightly condensed, follows:

> "Mr. Speaker: In rising to second the resolutions just offered, I desire to add a few remarks which have occurred to me as appropriate to the occasion. I believe that they express a sentiment which pervades the hearts of all the people whose representatives are here assembled. Strange as, in

looking back upon the past, the assertion may seem, impossible as it would have been 10 years ago to make it, it is not the less true that today Mississippi regrets the death of Charles Sumner, and sincerely unites in paying honors to his memory. Not because of the splendor of his intellect, though in him was extinguished one of the brightest of the lights which have illustrated the councils of the [Federal] Government for nearly a quarter of a century; not because of the high culture, the elegant scholarship, and the varied learning which revealed themselves so clearly in all his public efforts as to justify the application to him of Johnson's felicitous expression, "He touched nothing which he did not adorn;" not this, though these are qualities by no means, it is to be feared, so common in public places as to make their disappearance, in even a single instance, a matter of indifference; but because of those peculiar and strongly marked moral traits of his character which gave the coloring to the whole tenor of his singularly dramatic public career; traits which made him for a long period to a large portion of his countrymen the object of as deep and passionate a hostility as to another he was one of enthusiastic admiration, and which are not the less the cause that now unites all these parties, ever so widely differing, in a common sorrow today over his lifeless remains."

"As [Lamar] proceeded with the address, it was evident that something unusual was going on. The House became hushed and reverent. The faces of the members and the vast auditory were turned, rapt and attentive upon the speaker."

"It is of these high moral questions which I wish to speak; for these have been the traits which in after years, as I have considered the successive acts and utterances of this remarkable man, fastened most strongly my attention, and impressed themselves most forcible upon my imagination, my sensibilities, my heart. I leave to others to speak of his intellectual superiority, of those rare gifts with which nature had so lavishly endowed him, and of the power to use them which he had acquired by education. I say nothing of his vast and varied stores of historical knowledge, or of the wide extent of his reading in the elegant literature of ancient and modern times, or of his wonderful power or retaining what he had read, or of his readiness in drawing upon these fertile resources to illustrate his own arguments. I say nothing of his eloquence as an orator, of his skill as a logician, or of his powers of fascination in the unrestrained freedom of the social circle, which, last, it was my misfortune not to have experienced.

"These, indeed, were the qualities which gave him eminence not only in our country, but throughout the world; and which have made the name of Charles Sumner an integral part of our nation's glory. They were the qualities which gave to those moral traits of which I have spoken the power to impress themselves upon the history of the age and of civilization itself; and without which those traits, however intensely developed, would have exerted no influence beyond the personal circle immediately surrounding their possessor. More eloquent tongues than mine will do them justice.

"Let me [now] speak of the characteristics which brought the illustrious Senator who has just passed away into direct and bitter antagonism for years with my own State and her sister [southern States].

"Charles Sumner was born with an instinctive love of freedom, and was educated from his earliest infancy to the belief that freedom is the natural and indefeasible right of every intelligent being having the outward form of man. . . . Thus were combined in him the characteristics which have in all ages given to religion her martyrs, and to patriotism her self-sacrificing heroes. To a man thoroughly permeated and imbued with such a creed, and animated and constantly actuated by such a spirit of devotion, to behold a human being or a race of human beings restrained of their natural right to liberty, for no crime by him or them committed, was to feel all the belligerent instincts of his nature roused to combat. The fact was to him a wrong which no logic could justify. It mattered not how humble in the scale of rational existence the subject of this restraint might be, how dark his skin, or how dense his ignorance. Behind all that lay, for him, the great principle that liberty is the birthright of all humanity, and that every individual of every race who has a soul to save is entitled to the freedom which may enable him to work out his salvation.

"It mattered not that the slave might be contented with his lot; that his actual condition might be immeasureably more desirable than that from which it had transplanted him; that it gave him physical comfort, mental and moral elevation, and religious culture not possessed by his race in any other condition; that his bonds had not been place upon his hands by the living generation; that the mixed social system of which he formed an element had been regarded by the fathers of the Republic, and by the ablest statesmen who had risen up after them, as too complicated to be broken up without danger to society itself, or even to civilization; or, finally that the actual state of things had been recognized and explicitly sanctioned by the very organic law of the Republic. . . .

"[Yet] in this fiery zeal, and this earnest warfare against the wrong, as he viewed it, there entered no enduring personal antimosity toward the men whose lot it was to be born to the system which he denounced. [Furthermore], it has been the kindness of the sympathy, which in these later years [of his life] he has displayed toward the impoverished and suffering people of the southern States, that has unveiled to me the generous and tender heart which beat beneath the bosom of the zealot, and has forced me to yield him the tribute of my respect — I might even say of my admiration. . . .

"He always insisted that the most ample protection and the largest safeguards should be thrown around the liberties of the newly enfranchised African race . . . [and he] opposed to the last any and every scheme which should fail to provide the surest guarantees for the personal freedom and political rights of the race which he had undertaken to protect. Whether his measures to secure this result showed him to be a practical statesman or a theoretical enthusiast, is a question on which any decision we may pronounce today must await the inevitable revision of posterity. The spirit of magnanimity, therefore, which breathes in his utterances and manifests itsef in all his acts affecting the [southern States people] during the last two years of his life, was as evidently honest as it was grateful to the feelings of those toward whom it was displayed.

By this time, many on the floor and in the galleries were seen to be sobbing, wiping away tears, tears of memories of loved ones lost in the Invasion of the Confederacy, of sons among the 360,000 Federals who had died in the military campaign, including Abe Lincoln himself. Could there have been another way to deal with State Secession? "The Speaker, James Blaine of Maine, sat motionless, his face turned away, with tears stealing down his cheeks." Others were being similarly moved. Lamar continued:

"[Digressing briefly to the issue of regimental flags, let me say], it was certainly a gracious act toward the [southern States] — though unhappily it jarred upon the sensibilities of the people at the [northern States], and estranged from him the great body of his political friends — to propose to erase from the banners of the [Federal] Army the mementos of the bloody internecine struggle, which might be regarded as assailing the pride or wounding the sensibilities of the [southern States] people. That proposal will never be forgotten by that people so long as the name of Charles Sumner lives in the memory of man. But, while it touched the [hearts of the southern States people], and elicited [their] profound gratitude, [they] would not have asked of the [northern States] such an act of self-renunciation. Conscious that they themselves were animated by devotion to constitutional liberty, and that the brightest pages of history are replete with evidences of the depth and sincerity of that devotion, they cannot but cherish the recollections of sacrifices endured, the battles fought, and the victories won in defense of their hapless cause. . . .

"Let us hope that future generations, when they remember the deeds of heroism and devotion done on both sides, will speak not of [northern States] prowess and [southern States] courage, but of the heroism, fortitude, and courage of Americans in a war of ideas; a war in which each section signalized its consecration to the principles, as each understood them, of American liberty and of the [Federal] Constitution received from their fathers. . . ."

Moving toward his close, passionately seeking victory in America's "Struggle for Healing," Lamar continued:

"Charles Sumner, in [later] life, believed that all occasion for strife and distrust between the [northern States people] and the [southern States people] had passed away, and that there no longer remained any cause for continued estrangement between these two sections of our common country. Are there not many of us who believe the same thing? Is not that the common sentiment — or if it is not, ought it not to be — of the great mass of our people, north and south? Bound to each other by a common [Federal Constitution], destined to live together under a common

[Federal] Government, forming unitedly but a single member of the great family of nations, shall we not now at last endeavor to grow toward each other once more in heart, as we are already indissolubly linked to each other in fortunes?

"The [southern States people] — prostrate, exhausted, drained of [their] lifeblood, as well as of [their] material resources, yet still honorable and true — [accept] the bitter award of the bloody arbitrament without reservation, resolutely determined to abide the result with chivalrous fidelity. Yet, as if struck dumb by the magnitude of [their] reverses, [they still] suffer on in silence.

"The [northern States people], exultant in [their] triumph, and elated by success, still [cherish], as we are assured, a heart full of magnanimous emotions toward her disarmed and discomfited [former] antagonist; and yet, as if mastered by some mysterious spell, silencing [their] better impulses, [their] words and acts are the words and acts of suspicion and distrust.

"Would that the spirit of the illustrious dead whom we lament today could speak from the grave to both parties to this deplorable discord in tones which should reach each and every heart throughout this broad territory:

"My countrymen! Know one another, and you will love one another."

Biographer Edward Mayes would describe the scene at the conclusion of Lamar's eulogy:

"On both sides of the House members wept. The scarred veterans of a hundred fields, and the callous actors in a hundred debates, Democrats and Republicans alike, melted into tears. Said one spectator afterwards: 'those who listened sometimes forgot to respect Sumner in respecting Lamar.' When he closed all seemed to hold their breath, as if to prolong a spell; and then a spontaneous burst of applause broke out from all the floor and all the galleries, coming up heartily and warmly, especially from the Republican side. Such a thing as Democrats and Republicans uniting in a hearty and sympathetic applause of the same speech had never been heard of before; and the Speaker, gavel in hand, did not attempt to check it. "My God!, exclaimed Lyman Tremaine, of New York, rushing up to Mr. Kelly, of Pennsylvania, with tears in his eyes; 'what a speech! And how it will ring through the country!' "

And it did "ring through the country." Lamar's eulogy of the late Charles Sumner would be "printed in [almost] every newspaper in America." It would be printed at many places around the world, even into some school textbooks. Praise was most profound from Massachusetts newspapers, including the Boston *Daily Advertiser*, The Boston *Transcript*, The Boston *Herald*, The Boston *Globe* and The Springfield *Republican*. Praise around the country was evident in reports by The New York *Commercial Advertiser*, The Philadelphia *Press*, The Petersburg (Virginia) *Index and Appeal*, The Savannah *Advertiser-Republican*, The Richmond *Enquirer*, The Louisville *Courier-Journal*, The Cincinnati *Commercial*, The Memphis *Appeal*, The New Orleans *Times*, The Jackson *Clarion*, and on and on throughout the States. Of course, some newspapers were critical; but time would soon reveal that their criticisms would melt away.

In the Afterward section of this history, you will learn that Lucius Lamar would be nominated to and confirmed for the Federal Supreme Court. Most Republican Senators would, without success, oppose the appointment. A Republican voting to confirm would be Willliam Stewart of Nevada, who would explain that vote with the following words:

"When a member of the Senate in the year 1874, my attention, with that of many other Senators, was attracted to Mr. Lamar by his eulogy on Charles Sumner, which thrilled both Houses of Congress and the country with admiration for its eloquence, its exalted sentiments, and its appeals for the restoration of that lofty and enlarged patriotism which embraces both sections of the country. Those who were most enthusiastic in praise of that speech were then the most ardent of Republicans, and I distinctly call to mind a tribute paid by George Hoar, then member of the House of Representatives and now Senator from Massachusetts. I have it before me in the *North American Review* for January and February, 1878, Volume 126. It is a follows:

"The eloquent words of Mr. Lamar, of Mississippi, so touched the hearts of the people of the [northern States] that [those words] may fairly be said to have been of themselves an important influence in mitigating the estrangements of a generation."

Reinforcing that opinion would be commentary in the *Illustrated American*, commenting on the life and influence of Lucius Lamar following his death. Of the eulogy to the late Lamar, it said:

"The House listened entranced. The country read with awe and admiration a tribute so earnest, so graceful, so truthful, so imbued with fraternal appreciation, so tinctured with loftly sentiment that, insensibly, the soul of the man lost seemed to be found in the man that perpetuated his memory. The heart of the land went out to Lamar. The 'bloody shirt' became a byword and scorn. The warriors of peace that had traded upon the agonies of war were discredited, and discredited forever. Lamar had closed the gaping chasm of civil war.

"Never in the history of civil convulsions was the single voice of honor so potent; never was the magnanimous impulse of manhood so generously accepted, so universally understood. From the hour of the Sumner eulogy until the hour of his death, Lamar meant to the [southern States] the voice that had stilled faction, restored constitutional right; to the [northern States] the intellect that had penetrated the darkness of [doubt among its people]. This surely was a great role to play: to bring distrusting, self-destroying millions together; to make the mulctuary covenant of the Appomattox apple tree the broad charter of a reunited people. Lamar's single speech did that, for, though the powers of partisan darkness held sway a little longer, the heart of the [northern States people] had been too deeply touched; and in 1874 the miscreant regime of carpetbag anarchy in the [southern States] began to topple, and fell with a crash in 1876.

"It is therefore, as the inspired pacificator, that Lamar will stand out unique, almost incomprehensible, to other times than those that knew the incredible baseness of the policies that followed the [conquest of the Confederacy]."

I have presented, in extraordinary detail, Lucius Lamar's eulogy on Charles Sumner, partly because it is through the lives of both men that much of the *Bloodstains* history is told, and partly because there is evidence that this time in 1874 represented the beginning of the end of the Republican Party's control over political life in the former Confederate States, signaling that so-called "home rule" would soon be achieved. It is likely that the high praise of Lamar's eulogy, as reported herein, is substantially overstated, but to discount the event as trivial would be just as wrong. Let us agree that Lamar's eulogy on the late Charles Sumner represented the beginning of the end of Republican domination over the conquered Confederate States through their Political Machines, empowered by the votes of African American men. [R205;181-194]

Meanwhile, Jeff Davis returned to Memphis in late May. His three months away in Europe had been invigorating and helpful to his health, but had not produced any employment invitations. Jeff had certainly made himself available, but he had not pressed friends and acquaintances to find him a business position. He had not formally applied for any jobs. In an April letter to Varina, Jeff had explained, that "the dignity conferred upon me does not permit me, as another might, to ask employment by personal application." And he added, "Dear old wife, I hear you say — we can fast, we can toil in secret, but we cannot crawl in public." And all too often Jeff had sensed that a friend truly wanted to find him a position in his company, but had avoided pursuit of the matter over "a dread of displeasing the [people of the northern States]." [R19;391-394]

Meanwhile in Mississippi, Governor Adelbert Ames, being of a northern State himself, decided to take a vacation in a northern State, leaving the Governor's office to the Lieutenant Governor, Alexander Davis, an African American who was determined to make the most of this opportunity to intervene on behalf of other African Americans. Davis promptly discharged the employees about the capitol and appointed his friends — he dismissed the Governor's private secretary — and he appointed his friends as Chancellors for several Judicial Districts, ignoring the plans of Governor Ames. Furthermore, to help African Americans evade legal trouble, he issued 23 pardons, commutations, and remissions of forfeiture between June 15 and July 25, and another batch of 34 when Ames would again be absent for a month in the autumm. In one of these situations, he took a bribe of $800 for pardoning a criminal convicted of murder. Ames would essentially reverse the appointments upon both returns from vacations, but the pardons, commutations and remissions would stick. Since most lawyers in Mississippi were Democrats, Ames turned to men who had come down from the northern States for many of his appointments. However, as historian James Garner would conclude, many of the men appointed by Ames to the judiciary were incompetent, so neither Ames or Davis were benefiting

Mississippi. Garner would further surmise that, upon analyzing cases brought to the State Supreme Court, its Justices were reasonably competent. Circuit Judges would not be up for appointment until 6-year terms expired in 1876. [R204;297-305]

Meanwhile, in Washington City, the Federal House and Senate adjourned. Lucius Lamar had completed his first year as the Democratic Representative from Mississippi District 1. Of this event, the *Hernando* (Mississippi) *Press* said:

> "The first session of the 43rd Congress has closed. To Mississippians it is chiefly remarkable as being the first Congress in which they have been represented since 1861. Certainly, we have reason to be proud of this, our first Representative in 13 years" — Lucius Lamar.

Certainly Lamar had made a big impact with his eulogy on the late Charles Sumner. And he had worked hard as a member of the House Committee on Elections, advising a family member, "No man has worked harder than I have this session. My work has been unobtrusive, but faithful." Of particular note had been a speech concerning evaluation of a special election in Louisiana for a seat in the Federal House, pitting the credentials of Republican Pinckney Pinchback, of very slight African ancestry, and former Lieutentant Governor (mentioned previously with regard to the 1872 coup), versus George Sheridan. Who was George Sheridan?

> Born in Massachusetts and moving to Chicago in 1858 with his parents at the age of 18, George Sheridan was an officer in the Federal Army. After the conquest of the Confederacy Sheridan took up residence in New Orleans where he headed up the Louisiana State Militia during the administration of Governor Henry Warmoth. He was elected to the Federal House in 1872. At this point in the history, he had been the apparent loser in a 1874 special election in which he was forced to run against another Republican, Pinckney Pinchback, but the election returns were in dispute. At this time in our history, those competing returns are being examined by the Elections Committee of the Federal House.

Based on his Elections Committee work, Lamar had engaged in floor debate on this credentials contest, with a focus on "Misrule in the Southern States" — explaining to the House the then-current attitude of southern States people toward the past contentious political issues of State Secession and African American bonding. In part Lamar had said:

> "Sir, the [southern States] people believe that [military] conquest has shifted the [Federal Government's authority] from the basis of compact and consent to that of force. They fully recognize the fact that every claim to the right of [State Secession] is extinguished and eliminated from the American system, and no longer constitutes a part of the apparatus of the American Government. They believe that the institution of [African American bonding], with all its incidents and affinities, is dead, extinguished, sunk into a sea that gives not up the dead. They cherish no aspirations nor schemes for its resuscitation. With their opinions on the rightfulness of [African American bonding] unchanged by the events of war, yet as an enlightened people accepting what is inevitable, they would not, if they could, again identify their destiny as a people with an institution that stands antagonized so utterly by all the sentiments and living forces of modern civilization. In a word they regard the new Amendments to the [Federal] Constitution, which secure to the [African] race [independence and freedom], citizenship, and suffrage, to be not less sacred and inviolable than the original charter as it came from the hands of the fathers. They owe allegiance to the latter; they have pledged their parole of honor to keep the former, and it's the parole of honor of a soldier race."

This speech, at the time, had been considered the most helpful explanation of the political situation. The Boston *Advertixer*, a Republican paper, had commented: "Mr. Lamar, of Mississippi, made in the House, Monday, another of those stirring and eloquent speeches which are sure to strike a sympathetic chord in the hearts of all generous people." The *New York Tribune* had commented: "Mr. Lamar, of Mississippi, again distinguished himself today as an able and eloquent representative of the [southern States], and a real statesman, by delivering a prepared speech on the present political condition of [that section]." The Jackson (Mississippi) *Clarion* commented: "It was a most triumphant vindication of a wronged people, executed in a style so knightly as to disarm opposition and compel attention and respect." [R205;197-199]

Meanwhile in Mississippi, during the summer of 1874, the Republican Political Machine's excessive doting upon African American figureheads showed signs of inciting the race war that Republicans had unsuccessfully sought during the days of the Invasion campaign. Some Machine leaders had organized into military groups a sizable number of African American men who lived in Madison Parish, Louisiana, which lay just across the Mississippi River from Warren county and its principle city of Vicksburg. They had let it be known that those military groups might "march on Vicksburg" and attack the European Americans living there. Then, on July 9, the Warren county Clerk of Chancery, a boastful African American named Davenport, made a speech which was reprinted in the Vicksburg newspapers. Davenport announced that marriages between African American men and European American women would soon be commonplace, for "the [European American] women might now see that the [African American] was the coming man." He added that, if he were not married, he could get the daughter of one of the best Vicksburg European American families. If necessary, he "would buckle on a brace of pistols and meet the woman's father or brothers who would dare interfere with his affairs." Such boasting of social upheaval and such threat of racial violence prompted nomination in Warren county of a "Taxpayer's" ticket of European American men, including Richard O'Leary, their candidate for Mayor. Many African American men living on the now-sold Davis farms would plan to support the Taxpayer's ticket. In an attempt to circumvent defeat, Machine Republicans would cite rumors of racial violence and appeal to Ulysses Grant to send in Federal troops to achieve the unspoken objective of assuring their candidates won the election, but Grant would refuse. There would be no significant racial violence, and the Taxpayer's ticket would win. Biographer Hudson Strode would write, "This election in Vicksburg [and Warren county] with a split [African American] vote marked a turning point in the political affairs of Mississippi, though not the end of trouble." [R19;394-395, R204;310]

Meanwhile, on September 14 in New Orleans, a Mass Meeting of citizens assembled on Canal Street. Their object was to force the abdication of Governor William Kellogg and Lieutenant Governor Ceasar Antoine, an African American native of New Orleans, who, along with those controlling the State Legislature, had seized State power in the previously mentioned coup of December 1872, which had been organized by the Customshouse Faction of the Louisiana Republican Party, led by Ulysses Grant's brother-in-law James Casey, who was the Collector of Federal import and export taxes at the Port of New Orleans, and the Federal Marshall, Stephen Packard, with help from Judge Edward Durell. Participants in this Mass Meeting were dead serious because many had been denied the right to vote in the upcoming November election in a fraudulent attempt to sustain the incumbents in office for another 2 years. According to the account of historian Edward Mayes:

> "[The mass meeting] adopted resolutions reciting that [Governor] Kellogg and his Lieutenant Governor, although defeated in [the elections of November] 1872, had seized the Executive chair by fraud and violence; that, in order to control the result of the approaching [November 1874] election, Kellogg had, under an act passed by his Legislature for that purpose, secured to himself and his partisans the power of denying registration to *bona fide* citizens, whose applications for *mandamus* to compel registration were refused — the law, indeed, punishing the courts themselves if they dared to entertain such appeals; that Kellogg was a mere usurper, whose government was arbitrary, unjust and oppressive, and could only maintain itself by Federal intervention; that the election laws under which the coming election was being conducted were designed to perpetuate his usurpation, by depriving the people of their right to vote. These resolutions concluded by demanding Kellogg's immediate abdication. A Committee of Five was then appointed to wait upon him with this demand."

The demand was submitted. Kellogg refused to abdicate. Matters quickly became serious. A call to arms was advocated.

Now, you will recall that the legitimate winner of the November 1872 State election had been Democrat John McEnery, candidate for Governor, and David Penn, candidate for Lieutenant Governor. Well, on this day of September 14, McEnery was out of the State, but Penn was in New Orleans. Penn decided to lead in the call to arms. He issued a Proclamation, calling upon the militia of the State, 'without regard to color or previous condition, to arm and assemble under the respective officers, for the purpose of driving the usurpers from power'. "

A large number of armed men responded to the call to arms, forming the militia called up by Penn. Their number was estimated at between 700 and 1,500. The New Orleans Police Department, under James Longstreet, rushed in armed men and some artillery to disarm the militia. A large scale battle ensued. Historian Mayes would continue:

> "The police were defeated, with a loss of 14 killed and about 30 wounded; the militia losing 12 killed and 13 wounded, some of the latter mortally. Next morning the police laid down their arms, and the capitol, with all of the State property and records, was taken possession of by the militia for Lieutenant Governor Penn; the [African Americans] in the streets, many of them, cheering the victors."

Lieutenant Governor Penn, having just now taken the office to which he had been elected back in November 1872, immediately informed Ulysses Grant of the events and asked that he "withhold any aid or protection from our enemies, and the enemies of republican rights and of the peace and liberty of the people."

Grant refused, issuing the following day a Proclamation "commanding 'the turbulent and disorderly persons' to disperse and retire peacefully to their respective homes within 5 days, and to submit themselves thereafter to the laws and constituted authorities of the State" — in other words to obediently submit to the rule of the Customshouse Faction, which had seized power in the December 1872 coup.

The participants in the New Orleans mass meeting of September 14 relented, Lieutenant Governor David Penn retired, and the Customshouse Faction resumed power. Perhaps there were bigger fish to fry. The key to liberty was in Democrats gaining control of the Federal House, then the Federal Senate, then the Office of Federal President. If the citizens of New Orleans could just endure a little more abuse at the hands of the Customshouse Faction of the Louisiana Republican Party, the brother-in-law and the President — denying, by their own peaceful conduct, the inflammatory stories northern States newspapermen sought — better days hopefully lay around the corner. Almost all of the Representatives in the Federal House (Mississippi being an exception) and one-third of the Federal Senators would be standing for election in 6 weeks. (It seems that the Mississippi Legislature had voted to shift the time for electing Representatives to the Federal House from the even years to the odd years, starting in 1875. This meant that Lucius Lamar did not have to stand for election in 1874.) [R205;201-203]

Meanwhile, in late September, Jeff Davis received the trunk of valuable papers and personal items that Federal agents had seized in Florida while he was imprisoned at Fortress Monroe. Federal War Department men, after taking for themselves 5 boxes of cigars and the double-barreled pistol that Jeff had used as a young Lieutenant "fresh out of West Point," returned the trunk with some personal items and the following documents:

> "ledgers and portfolios, bank passbooks and canceled checks, scores of telegrams, and carefully marked packets of family letters. One envelope contained locks of hair, photographs, and a letter of Andrew Jackson, dated May 2, 1831. One package contained letters of condolence on the death of their little boy Joe. There were letters from Ben Montgomery before and during the war about plantation affairs." [R19;397]

Also, Jeff and Varina were thrilled to receive the family picture album that George Jones had recovered in Iowa. It was a dear family treasure because the album contained pictures of the Davis' dead children and other relatives. D. C. Moore was the Federal soldier who had stolen the album from Varina's trunk after the Davis' had been captured in Georgia. Jeff had learned of the album's whereabouts through Moore's advertisement to sell the thing for $45. So, Jeff had mailed his friend, George Jones a letter asking that he purchase the album on his behalf. But Jones had not bothered to pay Moore any money. Instead Jones had "taken his attorney as constable with a writ to Moore's house in the country and simply repossessed it" as stolen property. However, Davis would never recover the box of special papers that had been seized in Hinds County and sent by William Sherman to Washington. Davis believed papers in that box would help him recover title to Brierfield Farm. But, according to public records, that box would never be found in the Archives of the Federal War Department. [R19;396-398]

The November 3 elections throughout the States brought great news for Democrats across the land. In addition to substantially trimming the Republican majority in the Federal Senate, the Democratic Party won a "landslide" victory among candidates for the Federal House, giving it an "overwhelming majority" in the next House to convene in March, 1875. The House in 1874 had originally consisted of 194 Republicans, 92 Democrats and 14 others. The House in March 1875 would consist of only 109 Republicans, a majority of 169 Democrats and 14 others. This constituted a huge loss of 85 Republican seats. After that date further Republican political Reconstruction legislation — designed to sustain the State Party Machines in the former Confederacy — would be unattainable. "A wave of jubilation swept over" the Southern States. But the sitting Congress still had a short session, to convene in early December, with which Republicans could secure their final acts of political subjugation. It would be best to guard against that. No one knew more clearly of that danger than did Representative Lucius Lamar of Mississippi District 1, a member of the House Elections Committee. [R205;203]

Historian James Rhodes would describe the passions that had led to the massive Republican defeat:

"The political revolution from 1872 to 1874 was due to the failure of the southern [States] policy of the Republican Party, to the Credit Mobilier and Sanborn contract scandals, to corrupt and inefficient administration in many departments . . . [Grant's] backsliding in the cause of Civil Service Reform [and] by the failure of the Republican Party to grapple successfully with the . . . [severe economic] depression following the financial Panic of 1873 [resulting in] many men consequently out of employment."

Yes, Rhodes correctly defined how Republican behavior led to their defeat, but there is another side of the story — how Democrat behavior led to their victory. In the former Confederate States, the European American population was successful in their adopted policy of passive and patient resistance to Republican subjugation, suffering as they must to avoid, 1), giving Ulysses Grant excuses to expand Federal military intervention and 2), denying northern States Republican newspapermen stories useful to the Party's election campaigns in the northern States. Therefore, in summation, Democratic victory was the result of 1), the economic depression, 2), Republican failures and 3), the policy of passive resistance adopted by the conquered Confederates.

The same day, in Louisiana, the Customshouse Faction of the Republican Party was again defeated at the poles, but again the results were fraudulently altered to deny the victors the offices to which they had been elected. Historian Edward Mayes would explain:

"In [Louisiana] the oppression of the people had gone beyond endurance. The public funds had been wasted and embezzled. Public debts had been piled up until the values of property were destroyed by excessive taxation. The November elections resulted again in a Conservative victory by a majority of about 6,000 votes, many [African Americans] voting that ticket. The [Customshouse Faction], however, still had the Returning Board. By throwing out the votes of some parishes altogether, by cutting off some of the vote in these, and by adding to the vote of those — all under pretext of intimidation of voters, this Board reversed the popular verdict, and announced a [Customshouse Faction] victory as to the State Treasurer (the only State officer voted for) and a majority in the Legislature." [R205;205]

At the same time South Carolina voters cast ballots for State and local offices and for Representatives in the Federal House. The reign of the Republican Party continued, but cracks appeared in the armor that protected their domination. For example, the new Legislature, in joint ballot, would consist of 76 European Americans versus 73 African Americans, so the former racial minority would soon have a razor thin majority. In the State House, Republicans would outnumber Conservatives by 92 versus 33; in the Senate by 26 versus 7. "Conservative" was the new name, for the opposition had recast itself as "Conservatives" instead of "Democrats." Thanks to the power of gerrymandering, all 5 members of the Federal House would be Republicans, 2 of them African Americans. "Regular Republican" Daniel Henry Chamberlain won the race for Governor by a vote of 80,403 versus 68,818 for opponent Judge Green, candidate of Republicans who called themselves, "Independent Republicans." The Conservatives had chosen to endorse Green in instead of fielding a third candidate for Governor. Daniel Henry Chamberlain was generally called D. H. Chamberlain.

This was a peaceful election as historian John Reynold would explain:

"There [had been] but few disturbances — these in every instance growing out of guarrels between persons of the two Factions of the Republican Party. There were Federal troops stationed in many towns, but there was no occasion for them to leave their quarters." Of course, as the election season began, Republican leaders had indicated no intention of recognizing the peaceful intent of the European Americans of South Carolina. Senator John J. Patterson (Honest John Patterson) began the propaganda campaign in Washington City with this press release to northern newspapers:

> "Senator Patterson, of South Carolina, arrived here today, with accounts of fresh outrages, and depicts with great earnestness the Terrorism that exists in his State [against] the [African Americans] and the [European American] Republicans. He says he has never seen such a condition of affairs in the State before; that murders and murderous outrages are of almost daily occurrence, and he fears an armed outbreak is inevitable. He says that the ones who led in the Kuklux outrages are organizing and drilling rifle clubs all over the State, and that no Republican is admitted. He says that the leader of the organization, whoever he is, can call into the field 25,000 drilled men fully armed and equipped. The Senator said he had a militia composed mostly of [African Americans], but if they were called out they would be attacked and a war of races would ensue. The Senator said the only hope for South Carolina is in the Federal army . . . ."

President Ulysses Grant [had] acted accordingly, directing Federal Army commanders in South Carolina "for such a disposition of troops as would meet the situation as it had been presented to the Executive." On September 25, Governor Franklin Moses [had] "officially telegraphed to President Grant that a reign of terror existed in Edgefield County." This so-called "reign of terror" had been observed when [African American men] "to the number of 300, all armed, had gathered near Reese's Store, under the command of Ned Tennant, a captain of militia." A "committee" of European American men [had gone] to "parley" with Tennant, with success, defusing the situation and eventually resulting in Tennant's militia delivering up their guns to Federal officers.

Yes, history shows us that the election of 1874 had been peaceful in South Carolina, in spite of Republican efforts to stir up trouble.

The political tug in South Carolina was focused on debating what constituted good government. A State Tax Union Meeting had convened in Columbia on September 10 to debate issues and agree on relevant resolutions. One resolution rebutted President Grant's September 2 declaration, in which he had said: "The recent atrocities in Alabama, Louisiana and South Carolina show a disregard for law, civil rights and personal protection that ought not to be tolerated in any civilized government." The Meeting resolved:

> "We have failed to ascertain a single case in the State of an injury, outrage or wrong committed during the present year by a [European American] man upon [an African American] in the slightest degree attributable to the race, color or previous condition of servitude of the [African American], or upon any Republican on account of his political opinions.

> "There have been too many instances of outrages committed upon [European Americans] by [African Americans] because the sufferers were [European American]; but these are not within the scope of the matter submitted to us.

> "There have been instances, of late, of flagrant breaches of the peace, but these have been between [African Americans], or caused by armed bands of [African Americans] assembling on Sunday and on other days and threatening violence to [European Americans]; or by [African Americans] endeavoring to resist arrest of those of their [race]. These cases are also outside of the matter submitted to us.

> "We deem it, however, not irrelevant to report that a conflict of races has only been avoided by the uniform forbearance of the [European Americans]. . . ."

The South Carolina Republican Party had met in Convention in Columbia on September 8, where it had nominated D. H. Chamberlain with 73 votes — 33 votes more than given to Judge John Green of Sumter. In a generous speech, Chamberlain "pledged himself and the Republican Party of South Carolina to retrenchment, reform and good government." The Convention also "passed a resolution of thanks to Senator Patterson for his 'efforts in behalf of peace,' and to President Grant and the Department of Justice for the prompt response to Honest John's request for troops."

Of conflict within the Republican Party, historian John Reynold would write:

> "The conservative people of South Carolina were almost unanimously opposed to Chamberlain — regarding him as partly responsible . . . for the misgovernment and the corruption under which the State has suffered for 6 years. . . . Many Republicans of both races felt that Chamberlain was unworthy and that his nomination was the work of men who had brought the Party to disgrace."

In response to that discontent, a large faction within the Republican Party had gathered in Convention on October 2 in Charleston and nominated Judge John Green of Sumter for Governor and Martin Delany, a physician living in Charleston, for Lieutenant Governor. Calling themselves the "Independent Republican Party of South Carolina," the Convention resolved:

> "Resolved: That, while maintaining the integrity of the Republican Party of South Carolina, we cordially invite the whole people of the State to support the nominees of this Convention as the only means of preserving their common interests — especially requesting that the Conservatives, having persistently declared that their desire was only for good government without regard to partisan politics, now attest the sincerity of their declarations by marching with us, shoulder to shoulder, for the triumphant election of [John] Green and [Martin] Delany and with the certain redemption of the State from the corrupt 'rings' which have disgraced the Republican Party and trampled upon the interests of the Republicans and Conservatives alike."

A brief biography of the candidate for Lieutenant Governor, Martin Delany, is appropriate:

> Born in western Virginia in 1812, Delany was a very capable African American of nearly pure African ancestry, who, although not a college graduate, was experienced in many impressive ways — formerly a newspaper editor in Pittsburg, a practicing physician in Canada (Harvard Medical School), an explorer in Africa, a tourist in Europe and a Federal Army surgeon (Major). Associated with the Newly Independent African Amercian Men's Bureau, and practicing medicine in Charleston, Delany was, in the words of historian John Reynold, "a man of unusual intelligence and a very good speaker."

The Conservatives of South Carolina had gathered in Convention on October 8 to nominate candidates for State offices. The Convention had been called by James Chesnut, as authorized by the earlier State Tax Union gathering. This was not the South Carolina Democratic Party, which had decided to not field candidates for State offices. But it did represent the interests of Democrates. The Convention endorsed Independent Republican Party candidates John Green and Martin Delany.

To summarize, as mentioned earlier, D. H. Delaney won for regular Republicans by a vote of 80,403 to 68,818, and the Party won firm control of the State House and State Senate and won all 5 races for the Federal House. [R201;272-285]

Meanwhile, the Federal House and Senate convened in early December for the final short session, which would conclude in late February, 1875. Republicans knew that Democrats would control the Federal House in March, meaning that further partisan legislation designed to subjugated the southern States under Republican Machine rule would have to be passed in the next few weeks or not at all. To Democrats, the watchwords were "delay, delay, delay." Any bill delayed past February would die. Two key bills were to be pursued by Republicans: a "Civil Rights Bill" and a "Force Bill." Therefore, Republicans desperately needed racial conflict to rally their supporters.

Meanwhile on Monday, December 7, just inside the city limits of Vicksburg, fighting erupted between European Americans and African Americans, which left many African Americans dead. The number of killed African Americans is uncertain. An Investigating Committee from Congress would report 29; historian Edward Mayes would report only 15, and another historian would report 59. Logic suggests that the actual number killed was above 15 and not more than 29. In any event the deaths were numerous. Only 2 European Americans were killed. The cause of this fighting is best understood if we first recap the political and economic situation in Mississippi during the whole year of 1874, all under the leadership of Republican Adelbert Ames, Governor. [R204;333-334, 205;235]

As mentioned earlier, the Mississippi State Tax levy in 1874 was 14 mils on the dollar of property valuation, having risen from 1 mil prior to State secession — in itself a burden that could not be sustained. But the added burden of exhorbitant county taxes made the problem disasterous. State law limited the sum of State and county taxes at no more than 25 mils, meaning the various 1874 county taxes should have been capped at 11 mils, maximum. But in the 34 counties controlled by Republicans, the added county tax averaged 13.5 mils, 18 county levies exceeding the lawful 11-mil cap. In the 39 counties controlled by Democrats, it was not much less, averaging 12.5 mils, 16 county levies exceeding the lawful 11-mil cap. Two examples are noteworthy — in Republican Warren County, which contained farms formerly owned by Joseph and Jeff Davis, the county tax was 14 mils, but to that was added 21.5 mils for residents of county-seat Vicksburg, making the total burden for them a levy of 49.5 mils, or essentially 5 percent of assessed value. In Lucius Lamar's Lafayette County, the levy was 10 mils. The highest tax rate was Colfax County (now Clay County) at 23.3 mils, followed by 18.5 mils in Grenada County and Tallahatchee County, all Republican controlled. The lowest tax rate was in De Soto County (5.3 mils) and Tate County (7 mils), both Republican-controlled, and in Pontotoc (6.2 mils) Pearl and Jasper (7.5 mils) and Yallobusha (8 mils), the latter being Democrat-controlled. All of the remaining county levies exceeded 8.4 mils.

Considering the widespread depression in land prices and the poor income from crops, the 2.5 to 5 percent taxation of property led to "wholesale confiscation of property. The [newspapers] . . . contained whole pages of delinquent tax lists. In some communities, the tax payers decided that it was better to allow their property to be confiscated, and take the chances of being able to redeem it in after years. Over 6,000,000 acres of land — one-fifth of the area of the State — were forfeited during this period, on account of the inability of owners to pay the taxes." State Auditor W. H. Gibbs would later testify before a Federal House Investigating Committee:

Question: "Can you inform us what proportion of the lands of Mississippi have been forfeited to the State for taxes?"

Answer: "About one-fifth."

Question: "You are correct in the statement that it is one-fifth?"

Answer: "Yes. The entire area is about 30,000,000 acres. There are owned by the State and the Levy Boards about 6,000,000 acres."

This vast land of 6,000,000 acres exceeded by 2,000 square miles the States of Connecticut, Rhode Island, and Delaware combined. For example, the lists in 1875 of lands advertised for sale, in Hinds County alone, covered two full pages of the Jackson *Pilot*."

Of the disparity between political power over government, versus financial support of government, historian James Garner would later surmise:

In 1874, out of 140,000 voters, 75,000 were on the delinquent tax list. Warren County (including Vicksburg) had 5,000 [African American] voters, and 4,686 delinquents. Hinds, with nearly 6,000 voters, had 4,972 delinquents. . . . The Majority of the delinquents were, of course, [African American] voters. A comparatively small proportion of them owned real estate at this time. There were many counties in which [the African American population] did not pay $1,000 in taxes, yet they held the majority of the offices and administered the governments." [R204;305-314]

Now, let us focus on Warren County and the seat of Vicksburg, population 11,000, with African Americans in the majority. Since the onset of Republican rule, most of the city and county offices had been held by African Americans. Historian James Garner would describe the situation in Warren County and Vicksburg during early 1874:

"The Senators and Representatives in the State Legislature were all [African Americans], the Sheriff could not write a simple return, and he was believed to be dishonest; the Chancery Clerk was corrupt beyond doubt, and not intelligent enough to enter a plain continuance on the records; the Circuit Clerk and every member of the Board of Supervisors except one were [African Americans], and scarcely one of them could read or write; and 4 of the 8 Councilmen of Vicksburg were [African Americans]. In fact, there were only 3 [European American] officers in the County. The [African Americans] . . . had declared that the [European Americans] should not hold any of the offices. The [European Americans] complained that they paid 99 percent of the taxes of the County, all of which were assessed, collected, and disbursed by [African American] officials."

"The County and City debts, which in 1869 ammounted to $13,000, had increased until the City debt alone aggregated $1,400,000. Large sums of money had been squandered by the City Government in grants to railroad companies and in public improvements. [Early in the year, European Americans in Vicksburg had] organized a Tax-payer's League, the chief purpose of which was to carry the municipal election in the fall."

The Tax-payer League, forming a local "People's Party," had nominated qualified candidates for the offices in Vicksburg, including Richard O'Leary for Mayor. The "People's Party" drew substantial support from European Amerian Republicans and from "40 or 50 [African American] voters who had a substantial interest in the welfare of the City." The campaign had been intense, including parades and intimidation, but, in the end, except for two School Trustees, the "People's Party" had been victorious on the day of the election, August 4, when "the largest vote ever recorded in the City was polled."

With the Vicksburg City Government under the control of taxpayers and advocates of good government, activists turned their campaign toward reforming the Warren County Government, especially the replacement of Sheriff Peter Crosby, an African American, who, by virtue of his office was also the collector of State and County taxes, which totaled $160,000. This obligation required that he post bond to ensure the safekeeping of the collected taxes, but Crosby's bond was, under the most liberal assessment, not worth half that amount. Activists demanded that Crosby strengthen his bond or resign the office of Sheriff. Crosby refused to do either. Furthermore, the Chancery Clerk, George Davenport, also an African American, had forged "a large amount of County Warrants," which were circulating, a criminal offense. On December 2, a "Tax-payer's Convention" of Warren County citizens demanded the resignation of the Sheriff and Chancery Clerk. Davenport resigned and departed for another State, but Crosby refused. The response:

"His refusal was reported to the Convention, whereupon that body, 500 strong, proceeded to the Courthouse, repeated the request, and forcibly secured his resignation."

Barred from the Sheriff's office, Crosby left for Jackson to obtain Governor Adelbert Ames' help in getting the office back. Meanwhile, the Convention named a former Federal soldier to be acting Sheriff until another could be elected. In Jackson, Ames told Crosby to gather a posse and take back the office himself. Crosby returned to organize the African Americans into a posse. On, Sunday, December 6, Crosby's appeal was announced in all the African American churches "by ministers who impressed upon their congregations the duty of arming and marching to Crosby's aid." The target was the Warren County Courthouse in Vicksburg. The time for action was on the morning of the following day, Monday.

Meanwhile, from Jackson, Governor Adelbert Ames had issued a Proclamation accusing European Americans in Warren County and Vicksburg of depriving African Americans of their civil and political rights, and commanding the European Americans to disperse immediately. At the same time he ordered an African American militia company to cooperate with Crosby in regaining his office of Sheriff of Warren County. But "there were two [European American] militia companies in Vicksburg [commanded] by European American men" who had been officers in the Federal Army (a colonel and a brigadier general). Governor Adelbert Ames refused to communicate with these two militia commanders and instructed the commander of the African American militia company to take no orders from either European American militia company commander.

This set the stage for what would be called "The Vicksburg Riots." The conflict would be race against race, and Governor Adelbert Ames seemed to be eagerly anticipating the result. Concerned, the European Americans of Vicksburg, who, expecting trouble, stationed lookouts who were active all night long as Sunday transitioned to Monday. Historian James Garner would tell the story:

"Not long after day break, a "watchman announced that a large body of [African Americans] was approaching the city. The streets were soon filled with excited men, and weeping women and children. At 8:00 [Mayor Richard O'Leary] published and circulated a manifesto declaring that [Governor Adelbert Ames'] Proclamation was false, warned all armed bodies to disperse at once, and commanded all good citizens to hold themselves in readiness to report at any call for the purpose of enforcing his orders. At 12:00, [the Mayor] issued another Proclamation closing the saloons, and advising the people to be 'quiet and discreet, but firm.' The city was then placed under martial law, and supreme command delegated to [a former Confederate] officer. With a force of 100 men, he moved out to meet the approaching [African American] host. The two leaders had a conference, and the [African Americans] agreed to withdraw. As they proceeded to do so, they were fired into, as they claim, with the result that 7 were killed. While this was going on, another battle was taking place at the Pemberton monument. In the several conflicts which ensued, 2 [European Americans] and 29 [African Americans] were killed. Thirty (30) prisoners were taken, but were soon released.

"The testimony as to who began the firing [would be] conflicting. The [European Americans would] claim that the [African Americans] fired upon them first. [During the subsequent investigation], all the [European Americans], Republicans as well as Democrats, were found [to have been on the same side] in the conflict. A [former Federal] Army officer [would testify] that 100 [former Federal] soldiers [had taken] part in the fight — a more conspicuous part than taken by the [former Confederates]."

Ten (10) days after the armed fight in Vicksburg, the Mississippi Legislature would convene at the request of Governor Adelbert Ames, who had "recommended that the Legislature make provision for suppressing the 'insurrection' in Warren County, and for suppressing similar outbreaks likely to occur elsewhere." The Legislature would comply, "adopting a Joint Resolution calling upon [Ulysses Grant] for [Federal] troops." A quick election would be held in Warren County to select a replacement for Sheriff Crosby. African Americans would boycott the election, that allowing A. J. Flannagan to easily win and take over the duties of the Sheriff's office.

But, Federal troops would be on the way. On January 5, Philip Sheridan, a senior Federal Army commander of whom you are familiar, announced that he had taken command over the Federal Military District comprised of Mississippi, Louisiana and Arkansas, and further announced that Federal troops "would be sent to Vicksburg the following day." On Monday, January 18, a squad of Federal Army soldiers "entered the Sheriff's Office, ejected Sheriff Flannagan and put Peter Crosby back into the office.

Of this political affair, historian James Garner would write that Peter Crosby's "influence over the [African Americans in Warren County] was absolute — they being "fooled into marching upon the city in a mole-like way" — they being "fired into and dispersed as any mob would have been, Crosby, in the meantime, having deserted them." An Investigating Committee would arrived from the Federal House and Senate, made up of men from Illinois, Michigan, Wisconsin, Pennsylvania and Maryland, and interview 115 people. The majority report would blame the fight on European Americans, but admit that "much misgovernment existed in the affairs of [Warren] County." [R204;305-337]

The Year of 1875

(1Q75)

Meanwhile in New Orleans, the Customshouse Faction of the Louisiana Republican Party seemed to be in the majority as the Legislature convene in the Statehouse at noon on January 4. But the majority was slim and schemes were afoot. Yet, 1,800 Federal troops surrounded the building on orders by Governor William Kellogg, of the Customshouse Faction. Historian Edward Mayes would describe the scene whereby Democrats, being denied their seats, were maneuvered into the chamber:

"The Legislature assembled without any disturbance. The Clerk of the late House, William Vigers, called the body to order. He called the roll of members furnished by the [Customshouse Faction-controlled] Returning Board. One hundred and two members answered to their names, of whom 52 were Republicans [of the Customshouse Faction] and 50 were Conservatives. While the result was being announced one of the Conservative members nominated for Temporary Speaker Louis Wiltz, [a Democrat and native of New Orleans]. The Clerk declared the motion out of order; but the mover put the motion himself, and announced that it was carried.

"Mr. Wiltz took possession of the Chair, and amid much confusion a Clerk and Sergeant-at-Arms were nominated, voted for, and declared elected. A resolution was then offered to seat 5 gentlemen, [who had been elected to the House but denied by the Returning Board]. The resolution was put to the House, declared carried, and the 5 members were sworn in. The House then proceeded to organize. Seventy-one members were present; 57 voted — a legal quorum — and Mr. Wiltz, receiving 55 votes, was declared elected." Business of the House continued. "The Committee on Elections then reported, and on its report 8 other claimants of seats were received and sworn in as members."

Most of the Republicans had already left the hall, taking with them the Returning Board's fraudulent list, to seek military support from Federal troops, which was quickly given to them. Historian Edward Mayes would describe the intervention by Federal troops:

"Thereupon, at 3 o'clock in the afternoon, [Regis DeTrobriand, a high-ranking Federal officer and] in full uniform, with his sword by his side, accompanied by two members of his staff and by [Republican Clerk William] Vigers, entered the hall where the Legislature was in session, and exhibited to Speaker [Louis] Wiltz a communication from [William] Kellogg as Governor, requesting that he should 'immediately clear the hall and Statehouse of all persons not returned as legal members of the House of Representatives by the Returning Board of the State.' The 5 members first seated, as above described, were those intended. They declined to go out. A file of [Federal] soldiers was then brought into action. They entered the hall with fixed bayonets, seized the 5 members, and, against their protests, ejected them from their seats and the hall by force. When that had been done, the Conserevative members left in a body with solemn protest. The soldiery kept possession of the hall; and then, under their protection, the Republican members organized the Legislature to suit themselves, [the Customshouse Faction retaining control]."

You will recall that the first Republican military-enforced coup had occurred in December 1872. The second such coup was now completed in January 1875. Later, at 9 pm the same day, Philip Sheridan, the Federal commander — known to history for his notoriuos 1864 "scorched earth" strategy, resulting in the destruction of almost everything of value in the Valley of Virginia — assumed control over the Federal Military District made up of Louisiana, Mississippi and Arkansas. Perhaps planning to resume his militant style, he advised Washington, "that a spirit of defiance to all lawful authority was rife in [Louisiana]; that lawlessness and murder were so regarded as to give impunity to all who chose to indulge in either; and that the civil government appeared powerless to punish, or even to arrest. On the next morning he sent to the Secretary of War the following notorious dispatch:

"I think that the Terrorism now existing in Louisiana, Mississippi, and Arkansas could be entirely removed, and confidence and fair dealing established, by the arrest and trial of the ringleaders of the armed [European American] leagues. If [the Federal House and Senate] would pass a bill declaring them banditti, they could be tried by a military commission. The ringleaders of this banditti, who murdered men here on the 14th of last September, and also more recently in Vicksburg, Mississippi, should in justice to law and order, and the peace and prosperity of this southern part of the country, be punished. It is possible that if the President would issue a Proclamation declaring them banditti, no further action need be taken except that which would devolve upon me."

But the attitudes of many in the northern States, toward people of the southern States, had moderated, and the years of corruption and abuses by the Grant Administration had created widespread revulsion. Sheridan was out of step with the changing times. Historian Edward Mayes would report: "Mass meetings were held in Cincinatti, New York, and other northern [States] cities, denouncing the action of the Administration and the dispatches of Sheridan. Several days later a "monster meeting" would be held at Cooper Institute, where prominent Republicans (including William Cullen Bryant, William Everts and Charles Dana) denounced the maltreatment of Louisiana. The editor of the *Cincinnati Commercial* warned, "If it is made a Party test to sustain Sheridan's Louisiana literature, there is an end of the Republican Party." [R205;206-213]

Meanwhile, on January 5 in Mississippi — being inspired by the actions of Warren County taxpayers — opponents of Republican misrule finally made a bold stand:

"A State Convention of taxpayers assembled in Jackson, to take some united action on the [vileness of Republican Political Reconstruction]. . . . Members included such leading citizens as ex-

Governors B. G. Humphreys and Charles Clark, ex-Senator A. G. Brown, ex-Representative Reuben Davis, a couple of Generals, and [Lucius Lamar]. A memorial of grievances was prepared and copies sent both to [Adelbert] Ames and to [Ulysses] Grant. It portrayed the desperate situation in Mississippi and expressed indignation at the exorbitant taxation — an unbearable burden laid upon a people of agriculturists, 'whose crops were in all degrees of failure,' oftentimes after the crops were ready to harvest, some [Republican Political Machine] agitator or [African American] preacher would appear, stir the laborers to discontent and cause them to move away, leaving the crops to spoil in the fields. The memorial emphasized the needless and corrupt waste of county and State funds by an alien [puppet] government. [However], despite all the protests, Governor Ames still had power to enforce his will. On January 15, he would reinstate Peter Crosby as Sheriff, and in February he would arrange for the notorious George Davenport to resume his old office as Clerk of Chancery. [Lamar wrote a friend that] Spies and secret detectives swarm through the country, dogging the footsteps of our best citizens, following up with arrests, arbitrary searches, indefinite and unexplained imprisonments, trials before vindictive and partisan juries for the purposes of insuring convictions. . . [because] the Administration of [Ulysses] Grant had never ceased to treat the [people of the conquered States] with contemptuous distrust, severity, and vengeance." [R19;399-400]

Meanwhile, as February drew to a close in Washington City and recently elected Democrats loomed in the wings to soon take solid control of the Federal House, much tension surrounded the fight over passage of the Republican's "Civil Rights Bill" and their "Force Bill." The Republican Party's "Civil Rights Bill" and "Force Bill" were the two key partisan actions designed to retain Republican rule in the Reconstructed former Confederate States. The Party expected to pass the "Civil Rights Bill" rather easily, but the "Force Bill" was proving to be much more difficult to put into law. There were problems in the House and in the Senate. Fortunately for Democrats, House speaker James Blaine, although a Republican leader, was rather opposed to the "Force Bill," perhaps thinking a supportive attitude might hurt his dream of someday being elected President.

Lucius Lamar was among the House Democrats who were working to retard progress on the "Force Bill," hoping a vote could be delayed beyond the end of the month, when the term of the present Congress would expire. Lamar and Blaine were on good terms — the marvelous eulogy on the late Charles Sumner having encouraged that friendship. Biographer Edward Mayes would describe the political drama as Democrats tried to delay action on the "Force Bill:"

"[On February 24] the 'Force Bill' was called up [in the House] for consideration. Only 7 more working days remained to the Republicans before the adjournment of Congress would be forced by the lapse of time. To the opponents of the Bill, delay meant everything. It was their only refuge. If only time could be consumed until it should be too late for the Bill, when passed by the House, to be also considered and passed by the Senate, then it could be defeated; otherwise not. Therefore, they began to filibuster."

The filibuster lasted through the 24th and through 4:10 pm on the 25th, at which time the House, worn out, adjourned until 11:00 am on the 26th. During the night of the 25th Lucius Lamar managed to go over and visit with Speaker Blaine at his residence. The two men talked about the "Force Bill," both wishing to see it killed by the passage of time. Blaine suggested to Lamar a further delaying tactic to use the following day. When the minutes of the previous session were being read, he advised, Democrats should demand a reading of all the votes, name by name, 40 votes having been recorded — a process that would consume several hours. With the Speaker's help, the Democrats used this tactic effectively, creating further delay. When the "Force Bill" was finally passed by the House at midnight on February 28, insufficient time was left for Senate consideration and voting, and the Bill never became law.

But the "Civil Rights Bill" did become law, signed by President Grant on March 1. You will recall that this bill, first introduced in 1872, had been the great passion of the late Charles Sumner, and that advocating its passage had occupied the last words of the dying man. Historian James Murphy would explain:

"The battered remains of Sumner's Civil Rights bill became law. The Civil Rights Act of 1875 marked the end of an era. Advocates of [special protections for African Americans] would not achieve another victory in [that century], and ultimately even this last accomplishment would be declared unconstitutional by the Federal Supreme Court."

A footnote on the relationship between Blaine and Lamar is appropriate. The words of Lamar biographer Edward Mayes:

"For his friendly service in this matter, Mr. Lamar ever entertained the greatest gratitude to Mr. Blaine. He spoke of it frequently; and in the heated Presidential campaign of 1884 (Republican James Blaine versus Democrat Grover Cleveland), when Mr. Blaine was subjected to much severe criticism and abuse, in his public speeches Mr. Lamar refused to make any personal assaults upon him, saying that he never forgot what he had done for the [southern States] in 1875."

Again, we see how Lucius Lamar's skills in cultivating positive relations between political leaders of the two sections of the country yielded benefits to the southern States people. [R205;213-215, R206;131]

Meanwhile, on March 26 in Columbia, the South Carolina Legislature completed the session which had begun on November 24 — a session in which Governor D. H. Chamberlain had been closely involved. Concerned over how government corruption had splintered the Republican Party — in the northern States as well as in South Carolina — Chamberlain had championed legislative reforms aimed at curbing corruption and reigning in spending. His success in that endeavor was significant and earned praise, as historian John Reynold would describe:

"The course of Governor Chamberlain in his relations to the Legislature, just adjourned, was heartily commended by numbers of the Conservative papers in South Carolina and by leading journals, without regard to politics, in other parts of the country. These papers united in the declaration that the Governor had sought to perform every promise and redeem every pledge that he had made in his campaign speeches, his inaugural and his messages. From the [European Americans] of South Carolina, whose sentiments the State press undoubtedly expressed, there was the assurance that the Governor's efforts towards the restoration of good government and honest administration would always command the hearty and active support of those people.

"The Governor was the recipient of several invitations indicating the impressions he had made among the real citizenship," within the State and without, including — "the law school of Yale College, at centennial celebrations of the battle of Lexington and the Mecklenburg Declaration of Independence."

Republicans had dominated the State House 91 to 33, and the State Senate 26 to 7, but in joint session African Americans were slightly in the minority by 3 seats. However, an African American from Aiken, Robert Elliott, had been elected Speaker of the House. Of Elliot, historian John Reynold would write:

"Elliot had been a conspicuous figure in South Carolina politics. . . . He was the first Chairman of the House Committee on Railroads, and in that capacity was believed to have received large bribes from John Patterson . . . . Elliott received one bribe of more than $10,000 and, according to common report at the time, considerable sums beside. He was generally considered utterly corrupt . . . . As a product of [the Republican reign] in South Carolina Robert Elliot must be classed among the very lowest and the very worst. [Elliott's campaign for Speaker] was said to have cost over $5,000"

Outgoing Governor Franklin Moses had declined to send the usual message to the Legislature upon its November 24 convening. Instead D. H. Chamberlain, inaugurated on December 1, personally delivered a passionate address, in which he advocated:

"The paramount duty before us may be stated to be the practice and enforcement of economy and honesty in the administration of the Government. Fortunately our evils are chiefly evils of administration. Our State Constitution commands the undivided approval of our people. The body of our statute law is believed to be, in general, just and wise. The present demand is for a faithful application and enforcement of the existing Constitution and laws; in a word, good administration.

Among specific requests were these three: "shortening the session to a term not exceeding 30 days;" contracting State printing work based on competitive bids, and ensuring that "the existing scheme of public education be carefully fostered, liberally supported and generally improved."

To his credit, Governor Chamberlain had killed by vetoes several significant legislative bills that violated his promises for "good administration." Notable legislation that had passed and won his signature is summarized below:

"The 'civil rights' act was amended so as to prohibit parties keeping an inn, restraurant or other place of accommodation or refreshment from discriminating between persons on account of race, color or previous condition — such discrimination punishable by fine and imprisonment."

Pay for members of the General Assembly was limited to $600 per regular session plus 20 cents per mile traveled.

An act, nicknamed the "Bonanza" bill, provided for payment of past monetary claims against the State Government, when proven, to be paid on the basis of 50 cents on the dollar, limited to a total State payout of $250,000, to be funded by a one-half of one mil tax to be collected in 1875, 1876, 1877 and 1878.

With only minor exceptions, the tax levy for the year beginning November 1, 1874 was confirmed at 10.25 mils for the State, plus 3 mils for each county, with extra levies in several counties ranging from 1 to 3 mils.

Appropriations totaled over $1,250,000. Noteworthy spending categories included:

Interest of State debt (estimated):	$203,000.
Education, including the University and School Commissioners:	$425,450.
Judicial Department and Penitentiary:	$101,900.
Executive Department:	$38,200.
Printing by Republican Printing Company (the only bidder):	$50,000.
Lunatic Asylum:	$75,000.

During the session Governor Chamberlain had urged an improvement of the Trial Justice System, as he was understandably concerned that, holding office in South Carolina, "there were quite 200 trial justices who could neither read or write the English language." Seeking to break with past Republican practice, he had admonished Senators: "My determination is not to consent to the appointment of any man as trial Justice whom I do not upon my conscience believe to be honest and capable." As a consequence Chamberlain had made several appointments from among the Conservatives, some being accepted and some being rejected by the Senate.

Two important votes in joint assembly had elevated qualified men to be judges in the circuit courts. Jacob Reed of Anderson, a former Democrat candidate for the Federal House and a former Confederate officer, won election to the first circuit, based on qualifications and his past support of Chamberlain for Governor over Independent Republican candidate Judge John Green. Coincidently, Green had died soon after the election, creating a vacancy in the 3rd Circuit, which was filled by the election of Archibald Shaw. Of Judge Shaw, historian John Reynold would write:

"He was a man of good mind, excellent judgment and studious habits. His course on the bench — ended by his death in 1878 — was throughout creditable to him, satisfactory to all parties and honorable to the profession whose highest principles had been illustrated in the career of this capable lawyer and upright judge. He never affiliated with the Republican Party." [R201;286-300]

(2Q75)

On June 14, 1875, Texas Governor Richard Coke mailed a letter to Jeff Davis, formally offering him the Presidency of the Texas Agricultural and Mechanical College (called Texas A & M today). Texans had become enthusiastic about making the offer back in May, for it was then that Davis had agreed to travel to Texas to attend an Agricultural Fair at Houston. That had been a pleasant experience and had afforded him the opportunity to see Texas and talk with Texans. The Houston *Chronicle* had reported that, "the enthusiasm which the presence of [Jeff] Davis has inspired among those in attendance upon our Fair must be very grateful to him, and double so when it is considered that he is now only a private citizen, wrecked in fortune and stripped of power." And the newspaper added that Davis "has received the warmest tokens of admiration from our people." Of the trip, Jeff had written home to Varina:

> "The people here in Houston have been more than kind and in general wish to make it my interest to remain with them. Some propose the Presidency of the Agricultural Mechanical College, which is immediate; others the Presidency of a Railroad to the Pacific, which is prospective. But I have declined the first, and nobody has power to offer the second. The route from Austin to Dallas passes by Bryan, the site of the College, and gives an opportunity to see it."

The formal offer included an annual salary of $4,000 and "a residence, properly furnished, and as much land as he desired for gardens." Coke expressed great confidence that Davis would succeed at building up the college, and assured him that the people of Texas "would never cease to love and honor" him. But Jeff would not accept right away. Varina was strongly against the move to Texas, and Jeff truly worried about the difficulty she would face adjusting to the hot weather and remoteness of Bryan. [R19;401-404]

Several Mississippians were writing to encourage Jeff to remain in his home State and a good job prospect arose which he could work from there. Some men in Vicksburg and New Orleans, who had succeeded in salvaging considerable capital in spite of the confiscatory taxation of the past 10 years, were planning to launch a British company they had named the "Mississippi Valley Association." Hudson Strode would explain the business concept and Jeff Davis' initial excitement about the idea:

> "Its purposes were to induce European immigration into [the State of] Mississippi by grants of virgin lands and to collect from British capitalists 1,500,000 pounds to build merchant ships to develop direct trade connections between the Mississippi River region and both England and South America. The scheme was as yet somewhat nebulous, but Davis was asked to head the movement on his side of the ocean. A dream of empire still underlay the surface of Davis' thoughts, and he envisioned the reestablishment of New Orleans as a queen among seaports and foresaw a bright future for the whole Mississippi Delta."

(3Q75)

On July 14, Davis declined the offer of the Presidency of the Texas Agricultural and Mechanical College. Three weeks later he would write the London members of the Mississippi Valley Association accepting their offer that he head up their interests in The States, should they make "the needful arrangements for compensation." [R19;404]

Meanwhile, during July in South Carolina, two corrupt leaders of State Republican rule were falling from grace. It was announced during that month that Hardy Solomon's so-called bank, the "South Carolina Bank and Trust Company, had suspended payment and ceased to do business." Of course Solomon did not lose his money, having withdrawn $75,000, more than half of that during the previous 5 months. The State lost its entire deposit with Solomon, totalling $205,753.79. In other action, former State Treasurer Niles Parker was hauled into court during July as defendant in civil cases brought by the State of South Carolina. One case sought to recover losses of $250,000 in fraudulent bond payments. Another involved $28,100 "arising from the sales of property of the State." A third sought recovery of $25,000 in fraudulent dealings with Hardy Solomon. There was also a "criminal charge of breach of trust and larceny of the bond coupons," involving $75,000. Parker would never be forced to reimburse the State or serve time in prison because, he "soon fled the State, and no further action was taken against him." All the State received was some Parker property worth about $15,000." [R201;305-310]

Meanwhile on August 3, the Mississippi Democratic State Convention met in Jackson, for, in November, voters were scheduled to elect Representatives to the Federal House, the State Treasurer, the State Legislature and all county and local officials. The office of the existing Governor, Adelbert Ames, would continue another year. Historian James Garner would explain that an assertive attitude prevailed:

> "The Democrats resolved to make a supreme effort to carry the election. For the first time since 1868, they were strongly united, and with some hope of success, although a Republican majority of 30,000 was to be overcome."

This was a new attitude. They had made no effort to nominate a ticket in 1869. By 1873 they had essentially disbanded. This year, 1875, would be different. Why? Historian Jame Garner would explain:

> "They were now encouraged by the schism in the Republican Party, having reason to believe that they would secure the support of many of the [European American] Republicans and [African Americans] who were identified with the State. The result of the recent election in the [northern States], by which the [Federal House] had become [solidly] Democratic, also gave them hope."

Lucius Lamar was prominent as a speaker and leader and passionately encouraged the European American people of Mississippi to rally to "a bugle call to action" and, in biographer Hudson Strode's words, strive to "throw off the oppressive yoke that was destroying them." [R204;372-375]

Meanwhile in early September, Jeff Davis boarded the "Memphis and Ohio" for St. Louis. He was likely enthusiastic about the trip and his renewed role as a nation-builder. He no longer had power of political or military office, but he nevertheless believed people would listen as he appealed to them to come together and better their lives by building a more cooperative economy. As the new spokesman for the Mississippi Valley Association, Davis was undertaking a speaking tour of several Missouri agricultural fairs to promote expanded trade among the States served by the Mississippi River. Jeff was accompanied by a reporter from the Memphis *Appeal* and by his son Jeff, Jr. who had arranged to delay, by a few weeks, his arrival at the Virginia Military Institute to began his college work.

Davis had been giving more thought to a serious effort at writing his history of the Confederacy. So he had continued gathering material and corresponding with sources and those offering to help. One such collaborator, W. T. Walthall, had written that he was especially eager to help with an intensified effort. In response, Jeff had replied:

> "Like yourself I have argued against the idea of leaving history to posterity. While admitting that the future historian may alone be able to write without bias and therefore to make a history in the higher sense of the word, surely unless contemporaries furnish the material posterity cannot judge of events and describe their causes."

As the steamboat plied up the Mississippi River, Davis discovered he was accompanied by a surprise visitor — James Redpath. Redpath had actually traveled to Memphis to persuade Davis to undertake a public speaking tour of States in the northeast, but finding Davis about to board the train, had decided to go along for the ride so they could talk in that manner. Redpath, although more recently known for his work as a lecture manager, had a famous past in writing in the mid-1850's newspaper propaganda to benefit the Exclusion Movement and the emerging Republican Party. He had been especially effective in dispatching propaganda stories out of Bleeding Kansas. During the Invasion of the Confederacy, he had worked as a field correspondent for the New York *Tribune*. After the conquest was completed, he had worked as the Superintendent of Education for the remade State of South Carolina. In that capacity, Redpath had overseen the establishment of Republican-sponsored schools for African Americans. Perhaps Davis would have taken more seriously Redpath's offer to arrange a series of lectures in the northeastern States, if he had been more confident that agitators would refrain from harassment. And he had good reason to worry about protestors. He had received a speaking invitation from the Fair Committee at Columbus, Indiana, only to witness a few weeks later that invitation being withdrawn because of the "violent storm of opposition" that was raised around Columbus immediately after plans for his attendance were announced. The Winnebago County Agriculture Society of Rockford, Illinois had issued a similar invitation, complete with a promise of "a grand ovation of 40,000 hearers, and a compensation of $500." But that invitation too had been withdrawn after protestors surfaced. Traveling to Missouri to speak in public was a rather large step for Jeff Davis. Perhaps some years later, he would be received in the Republican States further north. So, Davis felt he had to decline James Redpath's offer to arrange a lecture series in the northeastern States. However, biographer Hudson Strode would write that, "in the talk on the train, the men took a liking to each other." And surprisingly, that liking for each other would grow into a useful cooperative effort in future years. I encourage readers to pay special attention to this paragraph, for Redpath would be of great help to Davis in future years.

Davis' speech at the De Soto, Missouri Fair on September 8 would be covered extensively by the New York *Times*, with much of the speech reported verbatim. The newspaper probably wanted to alert its readers about an emerging movement to redirect the shipment of goods produced for export in the upper Mississippi Valley States and the Ohio Valley States. During the first days of its creation, the Confederate Government had encouraged the Federal States to continue to ship their exports overseas through the seaport of New Orleans, even though that meant shipping via a foreign country. And the Confederate Government had pledged to keep port fees and taxes to a minimum to ensure that exporters in the Federal States remained comfortable with all aspects of the import and export services provided by the New Orleans port. But after Abe Lincoln had pronounced his Invasion of the Confederacy and a blockade of her seaports, producers in the Mississippi Valley and Ohio Valley States had been forced to ship their exports by railroad across the mountains, or by barge through the Great Lakes and connecting canals, to New York City, or similar northeastern coast seaports. But, even though redirecting current shipments to New Orleans by riverboat would have been obviously much less expensive and beneficial to the people who were better served by the great rivers, commercial businesses in New York State and the New England States stood opposed. Once again they prepared to oppose a movement which benefited others but threatened to reduce their commercial and political influence across the Federal States. Although their States were geographically in the far northeast corner of the country, they wanted to remain the center of its commercial activity. It was an old political battle. The same political battle had been fought over Texas statehood, over taking Mexican lands, and over helping Cuba win independence. That old political battle had delayed, by around 10 years, construction of a railroad to the Pacific coast because they had opposed the low-cost route through Texas to southern California. Continuing to fight that old political battle, many of them had helped destroy the national Democratic Party by bankrolling the Exclusion and Abolition movements, including their activities in Bleeding Kansas. And that old battle had given rise to the sectional Republican Party. The same battle — transformed into a military invasion, complete with 620,000 dead warriors — had been fought to subjugate the Confederacy. As victors, they had secured continued dominance by putting Republican Political Machines in control of governments within the conquered States. More recent evidence of the old political battle surfaced over buying Alaska, and it festered beneath the political surface with talk of invading Canada and putting her provinces under the Federal Government. So I must assume the New York *Times* had printed 7 columns of extracts from Jeff Davis' speech at De Soto, Missouri to alert regional commercial leaders of a potential new threat to their continued economic dominance.

Biographer Hudson Strode would write: "While there was nothing political in any of the Missouri speeches, New York was concerned because Davis was advocating direct trade between the Mississippi River towns and Europe and South America, thus, by-passing New York and avoiding transshipment. Freight rates by boat, Davis said, were only one-third as expensive as by railroad." Therefore, Davis urged the people of southern and northern Mississippi valley States to unite in promoting commercial activity that would benefit all. At another point, Davis endorsed improved schools that would serve all residents, and he "advocated the establishment in the Mississippi Valley of at least one great University." Then Davis — unable to speak of "our country" because Republicans refused to give him citizenship — closed his address:

> "Let me express the heartfelt wish that all your days may be days of happiness, that all your paths may be those of peace, that your future may be equal to that grand development of which I believe *your country* capable. And though I, with many years upon my head and trials which have multiplied the drain upon my life, cannot hope to see [that] consummated, I shall die praying for you, men, women and children, every good of which you are worthy."

Davis would travel on to the fair at Fulton, Missouri where he would address a crowd of 10,000. Then he would speak before 15,000 at the fair at Kansas City. On September 18 he and son Jeff, Jr. would depart Missouri for Denver, Colorado to inspect a mine high up in the Rocky mountains. [R19;405-408]

Meanwhile, in Mississippi, political campaigning was intense. Democrats were united and persistent. Republicans were, in some counties divided into two factions, and the leadership of Governor Adelbert Ames was accepted by some Republicans and opposed by others, damaging his ability to control events or successfully call in Federal troops. Historian James Garner would generally describe the August-September-October campaign season:

"The campaign was one of unprecedented vigor and enthusiasm. The [European Americans] left their fields, shops, and stores to take part in the canvass, and for 3 months little else seems to have been done. Every man was pressed into service. 'Mississippi demands,' said the Macon *Beacon*, 'that every man shall do his duty in the campaign.'

"The Republicans were almost equally active and determined. They devoted themselves to organizing and drilling the [African American men], who were enrolled in clubs, usually one in each community; weekly meetings were held, generally in out-of-the-way places and at night, at which the [African American men] were harangued by [European American] leaders, who carefully instructed them how to register, how to approach the polls, and how to vote. . . . [Speakers advised them to] never follow their former [owners] in politics, but to watch them and be sure to take a different course. [Speakers warned] Democratic success meant the re-inslavement of the [African] race . . . [and] the disestablishment of the public school system [for African American children] . . ."

"Upon the advice of the [Democrat] State Committee, the [European Americans] organized themselves into clubs, generally of a semi-military character, had parades, barbecues, mammoth torchlight processions with banners and transparencies, fired anvils and even used cannons in their demonstrations. Many of their organizations were furnished with military equipments, for which purpose extensive importations of arms were made, almost every town receiving a consignment. Individuals were investing in personal arms, including approximately 10,000 modern Springfield rifles. The Jackson *Clarion* explained that "it was not unusual for gentlemen of means to purchase improved firearms." Monster open-air meetings were held in almost every neighborhood of the State. The Chairman of the Executive Committee was overwhelmed with requests for speakers. Orators of national repute were brought from other States to aid in arousing the people to a sense of the importance of the contest. The New York *Tribune* said the only campaign in the country that had any life in it was the one in Mississippi; that the Democrats were holding immense mass meetings throughout the State, and a notable feature of these gatherings was the attendance of large numbers of [African Americans]." [R204;372-375]

Considering the intensity of the campaigning and the effort by Republicans to encourage racial hatred, it is not surprising that the political tension pervading the State occasionally turned violent in a few communities. The first notable incident had occurred in Vicksburg during a celebration on the Fourth of July, which "resulted in the breaking up of the meeting and the death of several [African Americans]." On September 1 violence had erupted at a Republican political rally in Yazoo City, resulting in the death of 1 European American and 3 African Americans. Three days later, on September 4 violence had erupted at Clinton, in Hinds County," this being "the most noteworthy of the riots of 1875" of which more will be said shortly. Later, on October 9, violence would erupt at Friars Point in Coahoma County a conflict between Republican political factions that would result in the death of 2 European Americans and 6 African Americans.

What had sparked the "riot" at the little seminary town of Clinton on September 4? The occasion was a Republican campaign barbecue attended by between 1,200 and 1,500 African Americans and about 100 European American men. The Republican leadership had agreed to let a Democrat speaker first address the crowd, which he did without difficulty. But as soon as the Republican speaker mounted the stage, "a tremendous firing commenced, and the [African Americans] began to run. How the disturbance started is a question upon which the testimony would be conflicting. The Republicans would charge that it was brought about by 4 or 5 drunken [European American] men. The Democrats, on the other hand, wouls claim that it was begun by the [African Americans]." Irregardless of how it had begun, "in the fight that ensued, several [African American men] and 3 [European American] men were killed, two of the latter being young men, who, it was alleged, were pursued across the field, overtaken, and horribly murdered and mutilated." Historian James Garner would further explain:

"During the days following the riot, a sort of reign of terror existed in the community. [African American men] suspected of being implicated in the killing of the [European American] men at Clinton were killed, the number being variously estimated at from 20 to 30. Many [African Americans], in fear, abandoned their homes and crops and fled. . . ."

You have observed that, in response to previous political violence during campaign seasons, Republican Governors throughout most of the former Confederate States had consistently telegraphed Ulysses Grant requesting more Federal troops, the unspoken reason for that need being to restrain the Democrats. This, Governor Adelbert Ames did on September 8, alleging that "domestic violence in its most aggravated form prevails in various parts of the State beyond the power of the authorities to suppress." But had Governor Ames done all in his power to suppress the violence? Not according to the Chairman of the Mississippi Democratic Party, who advised Attorney General Edwards Pierrepont in Washington City, in a September 9 telegraph: "the employment of [Federal] troops would but increase the distrust of the people in the good faith of the present State Government." On September 10 Pierrepont telegraphed Ames seeking details on the nature of the emergency, but Ames did not reply. The following day the Mississippi Democratic Chairman telegraphed Pierrepont a second time, advising that offers of help by the men of Mississippi were being made to the Governor's office, but being refused, and that peace would prevail unless violence was encouraged by State authorities.

Now, Ulysses Grant was approaching the end of his second term as Federal President. His political standing had badly deteriorated — abuse of political patronage had bred much corruption and the Democratic Party now controlled the Federal House. He had no intention of seeking a third term in office. Informed people across the northern States, including politicians in Washington, understood that State and local governments in Mississippi were corrupt and ugly and that political oppression of its European American population was insufferable. For what purpose should Grant send more Federal troops once again? There was no reason. Should not the Governor first convene the Mississippi Legislature and ask it for any additional State funding or authority he needed? Grant thought so. Accordingly, Attorney General Pierrepont wrote a long letter to Governor Ames, which said, in part:

> Often quoting from a dispatch from Grant, who was absent from Washington, Pierrepont wrote that the public was tired of the annual campaign-season outbreaks of violence in the former Confederate States, and that most Americans were ready to condemn any interference by Federal troops before the Governor of the affected State had exhausted his own resources. Pierrepont closed with this quote from Grant's dispatch:
>
> > "We [do not] see why you do not call the [Mississippi] Legislature together and obtain from them whatever powers and money you may need. I suggest that you take all lawful means and all needed measures to preserved the peace by the forces in your own State, and let the country see that the citizens of Mississippi, who are largely favorable to good order, and are largely Republicans, have the courage and the manhood to fight for their rights and to destroy the bloody ruffians who murder the innocent and unoffending [African American] men."

Actually, Governor Adelbert Ames already had the "lawful means" to address the emergency. The Mississippi Legislature had passed a bill, known as the "Gatling Gun Act," in the spring of the year, which had "authorized the Governor to organize 2 regiments of 10 companies each, and to purchase 4 or more Gatling guns, and to organize a corps of select officers and men from the infantry to send with the guns. Money had been appropriated — $60,000 total, $5,000 of it for the purchase of arms. But Governor Ames had not moved to implement the "Gatling Gun Act" — until now, mid September.

So it was at this point that Governor Ames moved to implement the "Gatling Gun Act," to put the State on what Democrats called "a war footing." Under Ames' leadership, orders were issued for 1,000 Springfield breech-loading rifles, 1,500 haversacks and 5,000 military rations of salted pork and bacon. Contacting the Commander over Federal Troops in Louisiana, Mississippi and Arkansas, Ames requested that "a company of troops be sent to Yazoo, and some to Jackson, as the latter would be the chief seat of war, if war we have." Of these war-like preparations, Historian James Garner would write:

> "These preparations 'alarmed' the [European Americans], who asserted that the purpose of the Governor was to provoke a conflict between the races such as would induce the sending of [Federal] troops, which, together with the [African American] militia, would enable the Governor to control the approaching election in the interest of the Republican Party."

The leader of the Mississippi militia was a notorious European American from a northern State and his 5 militia regimental commanders would be Republicans, 3 of them African American men. Many lesser commanders would be African American. Ames' reliance on African Americans in his Mississippi militia would further infuriate the European Americans of the State. [R204;375-383]

(4Q75)

The situation in Mississippi took a dramatic turn for the better upon the arrival on October 5 of C. K. Chase of New York. Chase was "an accredited agent of the [Federal] Department of Justice, having been commissioned by Attorney General Edwards Pierrepont to investigate the condition of affairs, and report to [Ulysses Grant] if, in his opinion, the necessity for [Federal] troops existed, and if possible to quiet the political excitement which was now at a fever heat." Perhaps to keep an eye on the Federal agent, Ames invited him to stay at the Governor's Residence and extended cordial hospitality. But Chase did not come alone — he had arranged for "a number of detectives from New York and Washington [City]," to come to different sections of Mississippi to "keep him informed of the condition of affairs." Chase also maintained close contact with J. Z. George, Chairman of the Mississippi Democratic Party, seeking his account of reported incidents of political violence.

Soon after the arrival of C. K. Chase and his team of detectives, a call was made in newspapers for concerned citizens — understood to mean Democrats — to gather at a formal Meeting in Jackson's Angelo Hall to address the political unrest and the involvement of Ames' armed militia, which was daily expanding. The Meeting, in progress by October 15, was well attended and believed by Republicans to be a platform for demanding that the militia be disarmed and disbanded. The Meeting designated a Committee of about 13, headed by Democrat Chairman J. Z. George, to leave Angelo Hall and call on Adelbert Ames at the Governor's Residence, which was agreed to. At the Governor's Residence, with Chase also in attendance it is presumed, the Democrats asked the Governor to disarm and disband the militia. Meanwhile Democrats in Angelo Hall waited for news. The news would be excellent. Historian James Garner would describe the Governor's response:

> ". . . in view of the assurances from the citizens that they desired peace and good order and a fair election, and that they would by example and precept do all in their power to maintain peace and secure a fair election, he was willing to meet their views as far as he could, and with this end in view he would promise to disband the militia; that not more companies should be organized; and that their guns should be deposited in certain depots and there guarded by [Federal] troops to be detailed for that purpose, or by men selected by himself and [Democrat Chairman George.]"

> "The result of the interview was then reported to the Meeting [at Angelo Hall], the agreement was ratified, and a Committee of 20 citizens was appointed to return to the [Governor's Residence] and express the thanks of the Meeting for what the Governor had done. There can be little doubt that this arrangement prevented bloodshed. Much credit for [what would be known as the 'Peace Treaty'] was due to C. K. Chase, the Special Agent of the Department of Justice."

> "On the following day, October 16, Governor Adelbert Ames wrote Attorney General Edwards Pierrepont, saying, "Through the timely intervention of [Agent] C. K. Chase, a bloody revolution has been averted." A reply from Pierrepont would be written on October 23, which, in part, said, ". . . I have to say that the course you have taken meets the approval of the President and the Cabinet, and that they are each and all much gratified that your judicious course in making this settlement and producing peace without bloodshed proves that you have acted wisely. . . ." But should violence erupt, Pierrepont promised, the Federal Department of Justice "will always be ready to aid you in any lawful way to preserve order and to give the right to every citizen to vote as he pleases." [R204;386-389]

Meanwhile, in Kentucky, during a stopover at Manitou Springs, Jeff Davis had accepted a just-received invitation to speak at a State agricultural fair and visit his birthplace at nearby Fairview. Biographer Hudson Strode would tell the story:

> "On October 9 there was a mighty demonstration at the fairgrounds when Jefferson Davis appeared and made a brief speech. Kentuckians gave him an ovation even beyond that of the Texans. He wrote Varina:

"The reception here has surpassed anything I could have expected. Many say, 'I wish your wife had come' and that you might have witnessed an enthusiasm and cordiality — a wild burst of affection — exceeding anything I ever had before. I do sadly regret your absence.

"Women who have lost and suffered and bearded men who have served in battle, melt into tears and vainly try to express their love.

"With love to each and all of our household, I am ever devotedly,

"Your Husband"

Of the visit to to Fairview, Hudson Strode would continue:

"It was the first visit to his birthplace since he had left it at the age of two. When he went to see the log house of his babyhood, a very old woman, who had been a teen-age hired girl in the Davis family, showed him the very corner where stood the bed in which he was born, and she pointed out the exact location of his crib. It was a moving and exhilarating experience, and Davis returned to Memphis in good spirits. . . ." [R19;403, R30;418]

Great news! Mississippi Democrats won an overwhelming victory at the polls on November 3. The Party "carried the State by a majority of over 30,000" as they elected the State Treasurer (the only Executive office up for election), a majority of the Mississippi House and a majority of the Mississippi Senate. The Legislature would convene on January 4, 1876. Of the 116 members of the House, 97 would be conservatives (all but 2 of them claiming to be Democrats and one of them being an African American) and 19 would be Republicans (16 of them being African Americans). Of the 37 members of the Senate, 26 would be conservatives (all claiming to be Democrats) and 11 would be Republicans (5 of whom would be African Americans). Of course, the administration of Republican Governor Adelbert Ames would remain in power except for the incoming State Treasurer, William Hemmingway.

Local elections in Mississippi went heavily Democratic as well — 62 of the 74 counties in Mississippi would soon to be controlled primarily by Democratic officials. Republicans received almost no votes in some counties (as examples: only 4 votes in Kemper County; only 12 in Tishomingo County and only 7 in Yazoo County in spite of its African American majority of 2,000).

Mississippi Democrats won big victories in the races for the Federal House:

- In District 1, Democrat Lucius Lamar faced no opposition.

- In District 2, Mr. Walls, a Republican also supported by the Democratic Party, defeated the Republican supported by Governor Adelbert Ames' Faction.

- In District 3, Democrat Hernando Money defeated his Republican opponent, Mr. Powers.

- In District 4, Democrat Otho Singleton defeated his Republican opponent.

- In District 5, Democrat Charles Hooker defeated his Republican opponent.

- In District 6, Republican John Lynch barely outvoted his Democrat opponent by a 231 vote margin.

So, Democrats would be sending 4 of Mississippi's 6-man Delegation to the Federal House, and expect friendly relations with one of the other 2, Republican, Mr. Walls. Only 1 Representative would be from Governor Ames' Republican Faction, what little would be left of it.

Historian James Garner would write: "This election ended the rule" in Mississippi of adventurous politicians from the northern States, called 'carpet baggers,' whose political power had been sustained by Republicans in the Federal Government and enabled by Federal troops and the votes of the African American Loyal Leagues" Political Machine. And this election "marks the beginning of a new era in the history of the State. It possessed many of the elements of a real revolution." But, unlike the American Revolution, which started with 13 British colonies declaring independence as 13 sovereign States and ended with the bloody defeat of the British military — Mississippi had just experienced a relatively bloodless revolution. The tax-paying population of Mississippi had suffered far more political oppression than had the tax-paying colonists, yet the more oppressed population achieved its revolution more swiftly and without military conflict. How could that have been? Looking back from our perspective today, do we see evidence that the 1875 political revolution in Mississippi exhibited similarities to the "passive resistance" revolution led my Mahathma Gandi in India 80 to 90 years later?

Suggestive answers to that proposed question follow:

"Indimidation was successfully practiced by the [European Americans], but, in most cases, it was resorted to before election day." Rivalries among Republican factions had weakened the Loyal Leagues Political Machine. Kuklux intimidation techniques had seriously "spooked" the superstitious African Americans.

"Unchecked power corrupts!" Republicans, in total control over the political and social fabric of Mississippi, had rapidly grown corrupt and had split into Factions. The Factions expended political capital fighting among themselves. Historian James Garner would conclude that, "a more important reason for the overthrow of the Republicans was the schism in their own ranks." Historian James Garner would conclude, "There is little doubt that some [African Americans], who had accumulated property, and who were naturally opposed to the heavy taxes levied by the State Government, preferred to see a change in administration." A prominent European American Republican leader would later report: "The naked truth is, less than a baker's dozen of the prominent Republican leaders who had a substantial interest in the welfare of the State were supporters of Governor Ames in the election of 1875." Concerning the rank and file, "Fights were almost as common occurrences between the different wings of the Republican Party as between the Democrats and Republicans."

Mississippi employers, primarily employers of farm laborers, had taken a page from the political playbooks of northern States Republican parties — President Ulysses Grant being its most noted practicioner — which called for using political patronage to exert political control over voters. If the Republican Party, in control of the governments of the northern States and of the Federal Government, could reward and punish voters by handing out political patronage jobs only to their Republican supporters, could not Mississippi cotton farmers reward and punish their employees by offering employment only to Democrat supporters, or at least choosing not to employ Republican supporters? Mississippi employers thought the answer was "yes" and many African Americans had decided to "follow the money." The editor of the Jackson *Clarion* would say he saw 500 African Americans in a Democratic procession in Raymond, and a similar sight in Jackson. Another trusted observer noted a change in the attitudes of African Americans, who were observed in attendance by the hundreds to hear Democratic speakers.

Hiram Revels, the noted Mississippi African American leader and former Republican member of the Federal Senate, wrote Ulysses Grant, 3 days after the election, explaining in detail why the Mississippi Republican Party had been so thoroughly crushed. Exerpts from the letter follow:

"[Since the beginning of Republican rule in Mississippi], the masses of my people have been, as it were, enslaved in mind by unprincipled adventurers, who, caring nothing for country, were willing to stoop to anything no matter how infamous, to secure power to themselves, and perpetuate it. . . . [But] as [my people] grow older in freedom do they in wisdom. A great portion of them have learned that they were being used as mere tools, and, as in the late election, not being able to correct existing evils among themselves, they determined, by casting their ballots against these unprincipled adventurers, to overthrow them. . . . My people [had] been told by these schemers, when men [were being] placed on the ticket who were notoriously corrupt and dishonest, that they must vote for them; that the salvation of the Party depended on it; that the man who scratched a ticket was not a Republican. This is only one of the many means these unprincipled demagogues have devised to perpetuate the intellectual bondage of my people. To defeat this policy, at the late election men, irrespective of race, color, or party affiliation, united, and voted together against men known to be incompetent and dishonest."

"The great mass of [Mississippi European Americans] have abandoned their hostility to the [Federal] Government and Republican principles [concerning race relations] and today accept as a fact that all men are born free and equal, and I believe are ready to guarantee to my people every right and privilege guaranteed to an Amerian citizen."

Hiram Revels' apparent expectation that Mississippians "are ready to guarantee to my people every right and privilege guaranteed to an American citizen," would prove in time to be too optimistic. The Republican-inflicted damage to political relations over the previous 10 years had been too great and much time would be needed for healing. African American men would give in to pressures to forgo their obligation to vote — although a majority of the population they would not stand up against pressures to become a minority at the polls. Yet, overall, the playing field in 1876 and beyond would be much more nearly level, and intelligent and honest hard work would allow men of good character to succeed within the limits of individual ability and to raise happy and loving families. Many years later, a noted African American leader from Georgia would only ask that men be judged by the "strength of their character," not by the "color of their skin." And "strength of character" had won the day in Mississippi on November 3, 1875. [R204;389-401]

Meanwhile, happiness over Democratic victories and the "good spririts" Jeff brought home from his visit to his Fairview, Kentucky birthplace were soon dampened with grief over news that Varina's youngest brother, Jeffy D. Howell, had lost his life while commanding the old passenger ship, *Pacific*, on the run between Seattle and San Francisco. Jeff and Varina had mostly reared Jeffy through childhood, and Jeff had loved him as if he were a son. Jeff and Varina felt the loss grievously. After having previously lost three sons they had to endure the loss of dear Jeffy D. Biographer Hudson Strode would describe the tragic accident:

> "On November 4, shortly after clearing the harbor of Seattle in a fog, the *Pacific* was run into by a sailing vessel and both ships were wrecked. [Jeffy] Howell got his 300 passengers and the crew into lifeboats and rafts. Then he stripped to his underwear for swimming and stayed with his ship until she sank. He managed to reach a small raft, with an old lady who had insisted on clinging to him. Finally, after four nights and three days of exposure, cold, sleeplessness, and hunger, his strength gave out and he was swept into the sea. When his body was washed ashore, a gold ring was taken from his finger and sent to the grief-stricken Varina." [R19;403]

On November, Jeff went down to the Gulf Coast to see the beach-front lots that Varina had selected, 18 years previously, in 1857, while Jeff had been a member of the United States Senate. During her 1857 visit, Varina had immediately fallen in love with that stretch of the Gulf Coast and those beach-front lots, and she had persuaded Jeff to permit her to arrange to purchase the lots for their future retirement home. Jeff had never seen the lots, and had no burning need to see them in at this point in his life because he was financially unable to retire and even less capable of financing the construction of a retirement home. But he had been in Montgomery, Alabama on business, and had found it convenient to detour over to see the lots, which were near a little coastal village called Mississippi City. Jeff hoped to visit Sarah Dorsey while at the coast. Sarah and Samuel Dorsey had long been dear friends of Jeff and Varina, but Samuel had passed away some years previously and left Sarah widowed. The Dorsey beach-house, which they had named "Beauvoir," was about midway between Mississippi City and Biloxi. Biloxi lay about 10 miles along the coast to the east and Handsboro lay about 10 miles along the coast to the west. After his inspection trip, a very pleased Jeff wrote Varina:

> "I left Montgomery on Monday morning and came to [this coastal village, which they call Mississippi City,] during the night of the same day. In the early morning I got up and the moaning of the winds among the pines and the rolling waves of the Gulf on the beach gave to me a sense of rest and peace which made me wish to lay me down and be at home until this trial is past.

> "After breakfast I rode [in a rented buggy] down the coast to the lots you long ago selected for our home and found the fence so entirely gone and the bushes so thick that I could but doubt whether the work we paid for had ever been done.

> "I then went on to [Sarah] Dorsey's [beach-house], but she had left for their [farm] last Saturday. [Her beach-house, Beauvoir,] is a fine place, large and beautiful house, and many orange trees yet full of fruit.

> "I then went to Handsboro [about 1.2 miles in from the beach]. The heaviness of the sand had worn down the horses so much that I had to put off 'till the morrow to go out to the Bayou Bernard[, which ran from west to east about 1.5 miles in from the beach], and see what kind of a sheep walk the children and I could make there.

"I have gone to the Turkey Creek bridge, [which crossed that creek near where it flowed into the Bayou Bernard, about three miles north-north-east of Mississippi City,] traveled up the Bayou [Bernard] until the water ceased to be salty and wound through the pine forest over to the Pass Christian road [which led to that coastal town about 10 miles west of Mississippi City], and thence back to the [Mississippi City] Hotel of Col. Nixon, who has made kind inquiries for you.

"Everything is to me like an *ignis fatuus*, save that my pursuit does not bring me to a relieving precipice.

"For the time and forever affectionately,

"Your Husband." [R30,421-422]

Biographer Hudson Strode would write that Jeff, "standing alone on the cultivated space of land between [Sarah Dorsey's house] and the beach in the shadow of spreading live oaks, fell in love with Beauvoir on that day, November 18, 1875, not dreaming that he would spend the last dozen years of his life there and die in legal possession" of the place. [R19;409-410]

Meanwhile, the Federal House and Senate convened on December 6 in an historic session — historic in that the Democratic Party was in control of the Federal House for the first time since long before 7 States had seceded. Not since early 1855 had the Democratic Party enjoyed firm control of the House. The drought had lasted a span of 20 years. Furthermore, this month of December 1875 marked the first time Democrats had control of any of the 3 seats of Federal Power (President, Senate, House) since those 7 States had seceded. For the people of the southern States and for Americans everywhere who had cherished the principles of a strictly limited Federal Government and fundamental State Sovereignty, as embedded in the Federal Constitution, it had been a long and torturous 20 years. Lucius Lamar was present in his seat, recognized as a leader among the few Democrats from the former Confederate States still struggling to overcome oppressive Republican rule. In fact, on the Saturday prior to opening day, Lamar had been elected to be Permanent Chairman of the Democratic Caucus. His address to his fellow Democratic Representatives, designed to inspire and give direction, is worthy of presentation here in a condensed form:

Lamar's opening: "Gentlemen: In calling me to this position of responsibility and distinction you have conferred an honor which I appreciate most highly, and for which I thank you most cordially. . . . The people of this country, by overwhelming majorities of States and of majorities in States, have placed the Democratic Party, after a long period of exclusion from power, in possession of the most important department of the Federal Government.

Regarding abuse of political patronage: "The members of the House of Representatives have no patronage whatever beyond appointment of a military or naval cadet . . . [but we are] the only department of the Federal Government directly responsible to the people of the country, and receiving its powers directly from their hands. . . . [Because] the civil service of this country has not been directed from consideration of public good, but from those of Party profit, and for corrupt, selfish, and unpatriotic designs, . . . the people demand at our hands a sweeping and thorough reform."

Regarding Federal revenue, debt and economy in government: "There is also an imperative demand that a vigilant examination be made into the administration of the public revenue. . . . [We must bring] down the expenses of the [Federal] Government to the needs only of economical administration [and] perfect and adopt such a system of taxation as will bring in the required revenue with the fewest restrictions upon commerce and with the least burden to the people. . . . [Furthermore, we need to address] the evils of an irredeemable currency . . . [and] see that the national debt is paid in full."

Regarding limited Federal powers: "The grandest aspiration of the Democratic Party is, and its crowning glory will be, to restore the [Federal] Constitution to its pristine strength and authority, and to make it the protector of every section and of every State . . . and of every human being of every race, color, and condition in the land."

Regarding *The Struggle for Healing*: "Apprehension and distrust of one part of the nation that [southern States people] would be an element of disturbance . . . has mainly disappeared, and this is evidenced by your election. In its stead has grown a more fraternal feeling, which regards us of the southern States as fellow-citizens of the same great nation. . . . [We all] want a [Federal] Government that we can love and revere, and serve from the motive of reverence and love. . . . Let me say here that no government, no nation, can prosper without this vital fire."

Regarding Lamar's instruction to his compatriots: "Gentlemen, we are here as Democrats, members of a political party which has a long, a glorious history. Let us, in our duties this winter, recall and revive those principles, the faithful maintenance of which by the fathers of our country secured it, for so long a period, the confidence and support of the people. Let us seek to renew the prosperity, to advance the greatness and glory, of our country. . . . [Let us exhibit] statesmanship, patriotism, and strength of purpose. . . . [Let us address existing government] corruption and maladministration, . . . clearing away these corruptions. If we are wise, we shall so rule ourselves and so serve our country as to retain the confidence of these voters. Reforms are urgently needed. Let us wisely make them."

Lamar's close: "A renewed prosperity is everywhere earnestly desired. Let us, by removing unjust discriminations, by imposing a rigid economy [in government], by restoring a sound currency, by securing the equal rights of all States and all people, make the Democratic Party the author of a new prosperity. So we may begin for our party a new and glorious career, in which its history shall be once more, as formerly, the story of [America's] greatest grandeur, and of the people's universal happiness and contentment."

At the close there was great applause and widespread newspaper coverage praised the speech. Two examples: The New York *World* said, "Mr. Lamar did his work nobly, and his words will arouse a cordial and responsive echo in every Democratic heart from Maine to Texas, from New York to California." The Richmond *Enquirer* said, "We have read nothing in a long time emanating from any public man more full of pith and meaning, or more pointed and forcible, than this brief speech, which will stir the country like a bugle blast, and inspire the Democracy with new hope, while it reanimates them with a determination to persevere in their noble effort to restore the [Federal] Government to a sound constitutional basis." [R205;265-269]

The Year of 1876

(1Q76)

On New Year's Day, 1876, Jeff gave his daughter Margaret in marriage to a young bank cashier named Addison Hayes. The marriage ceremony was held at St. Lazarus Episcopal Church in Memphis. Lazarus was from a prominent North Carolina family, but at this point his future financial success was uncertain. Jeff perhaps harbored a father's natural concern over how fitting his daughter's new husband would prove to be. But that concern would eventually give way to contentment, for Lazarus would have a successful career and be a fine husband and father. Margaret and Addison would eventually move to Colorado. Two girls and a boy would be born before Jeff would die, and he would greatly enjoy playing with them when they came to visit. The boy, Addison Jefferson Hayes, would eventually legally change his name to Addison Jefferson Hayes-Davis in tribute to his grandfather. And Margaret would be notably attentive to her mother during old age. [R19;410,502]

Three days later, on January 4, the Mississippi House and Senate, now controlled by Democrats, convened in Jackson. That same day Governor Adelbert Ames addressed a joint session, delivering the customary "Annual Message." But there was nothing customary about what Ames said. He declared that the Mississippi House and Senate, which he was addressing, were illegal bodies, and that "the late election had been carried by fraud and violence." Accommodation was not possible. Two days later the House approved a resolution appointing a Committee to investigate the conduct of the Governor and "report to the House whether there were good reasons for his Impeachment." The Committee would go to work in earnest, working 3 to 5 hours per day for 38 days, taking testimony from 45 witnesses, and filling 5 volumes of documentation.

On January 6 the Mississippi Democratic-Conservative Caucus met to decide on its candidate for the Federal Senate. The Caucus chose Lucius Lamar "with great enthusiasm, and without a single dissenting voice." Lamar was dutifully elected and would relocate to the other side of the Capitol and take his seat in the Federal Senate on March 4, 1877. [R204;408-409, R205;272]

Meanwhile, on January 9, James Blaine rose in the Federal Senate and demanded that Jeff Davis be excluded from the Universal Amnesty Bill because, so Blaine alleged, he was "the author, knowingly, deliberately, guiltily, and willfully of the gigantic murders and crimes of [the Confederate prisoner-of-war camp near Andersonville, Georgia], in comparison with which I here before God, measuring my words, knowing their full extent and import, declare that neither the deeds of the Duke of Alva in the Low Countries, nor the massacre of St. Bartholomew, nor the thumb screws and engines of torture of the Spanish Inquisition, begin to compare in atrocity." Blaine further alleged that Jeff Davis had deliberately sent [R. B.] Winder to [that Confederate prisoner-of-war camp] "to construct that den of horrors." Yet, Blaine continued, Jeff Davis could have stopped the alleged torture that took place in those alleged Confederate torture chambers "by a wink of his eye, by a wave of his hand, by a nod of his head." Then Blaine shouted in fever pitch that he stood forever "against crowning with the honors of full American citizenship the man who organized that [program of] murder." Now James Blaine was not just another Senator, or a man who had lost his senses. He was actually a more practical-minded man than Charles Sumner. But James Blaine would lie and swear before God Almighty without regard to the truth. Oh, he figured everyone would assume he was exaggerating, more or less. But like demagogues who had preceded him and like those to follow, James Blaine figured that, if a fellow tells a lie that is so enormous as to be even unbelievable, then many folks will assume that there had been a little truth buried somewhere in that lie. Where there is smoke there must be a little bit of fire, many would suspect. The bigger the lie the better! And why was James Blaine so vindictive toward powerless Jefferson Davis? Because he was seeking the Republican nomination for Federal President, and he figured rank and file Republicans would love him for it.

An infuriated Benjamin Hill of Georgia rose up and denounced Blaine's vindictive display of demagoguery. In the words of Hudson Strode:

> "Listening in shocked amazement to Blaine's outrageous display of demagoguery, Senator Benjamin Hill of Georgia got control of his emotions sufficiently to rise on the floor to answer Blaine with withering contempt. He pointed out that when [Henry] Wirz was offered life and liberty upon the one condition that he would implicate [Jeff Davis] in the crime of which [Wirz] stood accused, [he] had gallantly replied, 'I would not become a traitor against [Jeff] Davis or anybody else, even to save my life.' Hill quoted Wirz's confession to Father Boyle just before [the Federals hung him]: 'I do not know anything about Jefferson Davis.' 'What Wirz would not do to save his life,' proclaimed Hill with devastating effect, '[James] Blaine would do to secure a political office'."

On January 10, Senator Samuel Cox of New York likewise denounced Blaine's vindictive display of demagoguery. In part Cox said:

> "Ten years after the [conquest of the Confederacy], the [most militant] Republicans still proposed the bad rule of force and the bravado of brigadiers to coerce States and upturn established institutions. Though it often babbled of concord and made festive speeches about fraternal feeling it returned to the low instincts of Party advantage and discordant legislation.

> "Poison, not oil, was poured into the [conquered people's] unhealed wounds of war. . . . Undisciplined ravage and reprisals of fraud were followed by rancor and unrest. The friends of the [most militant Republicans] actually talked [confiscation and deportation], but the better angels of our nature fled aghast from the spectacle.

> "When a great scholar wrote to the conquering Charlemagne how to treat the subjugated Huns, his advice was: First, send gentle-mannered men among them. Second, do not require the tithe. Better lose the tithe than prejudice the people. Treat mortals with kindness. One sacred stream flows for us all.

> "But when the Federal Congress sent its decrees to the [conquered States] and the emissaries of discord to execute them, it was a question which was the worse curse, the agents of the [Republican Governments] or the fraudulent taxes! . . . No forgiveness to the enemy, no measures of moderation.

> "Then came the juggling pretenses of amnesty; now and then, for treachery and Party service, individual disabilities were removed. During this decade of wrong, outraging every lesson of

history and every tenet of political philosophy, every code of humane law and every attribute of divine justice, most of the leading men of the stricken [former Confederate States] remained disabled."

Samuel Cox of New York State was not yet through, for he continued to blast away at Blaine's display of preposterous demagoguery. He accused Blaine of "partisan services and base treachery to recruit his failing ranks" in the Republican Party. He called Blaine's motion to exclude Jeff Davis from the Universal Amnesty Bill an "invidious exception that marred the general harmony which was about to pervade the land." He blamed Blaine for seeking to kill the bill "to keep alive the very embers of despair." Then he closed with acid contempt: "The gentleman from Maine is known to be a candidate for the Presidency, but that is no reason why he should be a mean man."

After Jeff Davis learned of the Senate fight over the Universal Amnesty Bill, he wrote Representative Proctor Knott, Democrat of Kentucky, Chairman of the House Committee on Amnesty, urging that the bill be passed whether he was excluded or included:

> "I express my regret that any of my compatriots should suffer by identification with me. . . . Further, it may be proper to state that I have no claim to pardon, not having in any way repented, or changed the convictions on which my political course was founded, as well before, as during, and since the [Federals invaded the Confederacy]"

Writing back, Proctor Knott assured Jeff Davis that his attitude was "perfectly consistent with the genuine dignity and manliness, illustrated by your whole career, public and private. . . . If you knew me personally, it would perhaps be unnecessary for me to assure you that such an exhibition of a chivalrous self-abnegation on your part has increased if possible my admiration of your character." Then Knott offered the following political analysis:

> "Of course every intelligent mind in the [northern States] understands perfectly well that the objection to embracing you in the provisions of the bill was merely to pander to the meanest passions of the rabble and to furnish materials for the miserable scoundrelly demagogues in ensuing campaigns for the Presidency."

The Universal Amnesty Bill was finally passed, and it did exclude one man, and one man only. That man was Jefferson Davis. James Blaine had so aroused hatred toward Jeff Davis that too may Republicans were too scared to oppose him on it. So Jeff Davis would forevermore be a man without a country. Blaine had won the political battle, but not the political war. Surprisingly, Lucius Lamar would find a way to sustain a dialog with the man. But Blaine's swearing, before Almighty God, all those lies about Jeff Davis had embarrassed too many Republicans. For considerable time Republicans would defeat his efforts to gain their nomination for Federal President — that is until 1884. However, in that year Blaine would lose to Democrat Grover Cleveland, ending 24 years of firm Republican Party control of the office of Federal President. [R19;411-414]

Meanwhile, in Jackson, Mississippi, Impeachment was progressing against Republican officials in charge of the State Government. Governor Adelbert Ames was not the only target. All elected Republicans in the Ames Administration were targets. A clean sweep was needed. On February 14 Articles of Impeachment were approved against Alexander K. Davis, an African American holding the office of Lieutenant Governor. Much evidence of misconduct had been uncovered by the House Committee that had been investigating Governor Adelbert Ames since January 7, and some of it applied to Davis' conduct. Ten African American Representatives were among the large majority approving Impeachment proceedings against Davis. Two days later, on February 16, similar Articles of Impeachment were approved against Thomas. W. Cordoza, also an African American, holding the office of Superintendent of Education. Cordoza's resignation would be accepted allowing him to evade a Senate trial, but Democrats insisted of carrying through with a Senate trial of the Lieutenant Governor, to ensure that, once Ames was convicted, there would be no way for a Republican Lieutenant Governor to assume the office of Governor.

The Senate trial of Governor Adelbert Ames was called on March 16 and began on March 28. Ames "employed able legal counsel" including Roger Pryor of New York City. But on the same day, Ames submitted an offer to resign if the charges were dismissed. The bargain was struck. By a vote of 78 to

10 the House directed the Managers to dismiss the Articles of Impeachment. By a vote of 26 to 3 the Senate dismissed the charges. The following day, March 29, Ames issued the following letter:

"Executive Office, Jackson, Mississippi, March 29, 1876

"To the People of the State of Mississippi:

"I hereby respectfully resign my office of Governor of Mississippi.

(Signed) Adelbert Ames.

John Stone, who had led the Democratic Party's successful 1875 campaign, assumed the office of Acting Governor of Mississippi. Historian James Garner would write: "Shortly after tendering his resignation, Governor Ames, left the State, and has resided in [a northern State] ever since." [R204;401-407, R206;160]

The Mississippi Democratic Party would keep its promise to African Americans with regard to improvements in the education system begun in 1870 by the Republicans under Superintendent Henry Pease. Historian James Garner would explain:

"When the [Republicans] surrendered the [Mississippi] Government to the [Democratic Party] in 1876, the public school system which they had fathered had become firmly established, its efficiency increased, and its administration made somewhat less expensive than at first. There does not seem to have been any disposition upon the part of the Democrats to abolish it or impair its efficiency. On the other hand, they kept their promise to the [African Americans], made provisions for continuing the system, and guaranteed an annual 5 months' term instead of 4, as formerly. Moreover, the cost of maintaining the schools was very largely reduced, and the administration decentralized and democratized, thereby removing what had been a strong obstacle to peace and good order."

For example, the school system would become less dependent on migrant European American teachers from the northern States as many positions gravitated to Mississippians of both races, resulting in a more reasonable pay scale. The average monthly teacher salary — $60 in 1870-71, reducing to $55 in 1875-76 — would be $40 in 1876-77 and down further the following year to $29.

Republicans had also established two State African American normal schools, one at Holly Springs and one at Tougaloo, which were liberally supported by the Legislature. And they furthermore had established an African American State University, it being located at Rodney and initially led by former Federal Senator Hiram Revels. But the University had experienced a crisis in 1874 when Governor Adelbert Ames had replaced Revels with a political favorite. Historian James Garner would describe the resulting chaos before this crisis eventually passed:

"The students revolted at the removal of Revels, and about 60 of them withdrew. The President was unable to maintain discipline, the University was declared to be in 'rebellion,' and a Joint Committee of the [Mississippi] Legislature was appointed to investigate its condition."

The Democratic Party would continue the operation of these schools of higher learning, giving the State a growing pool of educated African Americans, most notably African American school teachers who would fill jobs at African American schoolhouses and become respected leaders in their communities.

Lieutenant Governor Alexander K. Davis would attempt to resign, but the Senate would proceed with the trial, which would end on March 13 with an overwhelming non-partisan conviction vote of 32 versus 4. The editor of a Republican newspaper in Jackson would concur: "It must be admitted by fair-minded and unprejudiced Republicans that the verdict rendered was, under the circumstances, just and proper." [R204;366-371]

(2Q76)

Meanwhile on April 14 in Columbia, the South Carolina Legislature concluded its 1875-76 winter session, which had begun on November 23, 1975. Historian John Reynold, having lived through the era and later written definitively of its history, would conclude, "The administration of Governor Chamberlain may be said to have ended with the close of the Legislative session of 1875-76." A few pages later, you will learn that the Democratic Party would win the fall election of 1876, signaling the end of Republican rule in South Carolina. So, a few paragraphs are now appropriate to report on this closing chapter of governance under Republican rule.

During his term to date, Governor D. H. Chamberlain had made commendable progress in reducing the corruption of the State Government, and, in his address to Legislators at the opening of the session on November 23, 1875, had praised them for improvements already enacted and urged them to enact many more economies. He reported that collections of taxes had been outstanding over the past fiscal year, only $12,519 of the $1,555,202 tax levy remaining uncollected. He thanked the Legislature for reducing "Legislative expenses and contingent funds," and asked for more frugality in the session just opening.

However, the Legislature paid little attention to Chamberlain's recommendation that it reduce appropriations for the coming fiscal year to about $670,000, instead appropriating a total of $909,200, distributed as follows:

Schools ($250,000) and School Commissioners ($32,200):	$282,200.
Interest on debt, estimated:	$200,000.
Lunatic Asylum, Orphan Asylum and Institute for Deaf and Dumb and Blind:	$82,500.
University, Agricultural College and Normal School:	$68,400.
Executive Department:	$57,500.
Judicial Department:	$57,300.
Printing:	$50,000.
Penitentiary:	$42,000.
Auditors:	$40,000.
Remainder:	$29,300.

Prior to this Legislative session, Governor Chamberlain had vetoed a property tax levy of 13 mils to finance Government operations during the coming fiscal year, recommending instead a sharply reduced levy of 8-1/2 mils. The Legislature settled between those numbers, enacting a levy of 11 mils to be paid to the State Treasury. Additional levies on property were authorized for the various counties, ranging from 2 to 5 mils, to be paid to the county treasuries. Two additional taxes were levied on property for the purpose of paying off State Government debt. One, to be known as the "Big Bonanza," was an annual levy of 1 mil, assessed for the three years beginning November 1, 1875. This was intended to raise about $500,000, to pay off debt at par. The other, to be known as the "Little Bonanza," was an annual levy of 1/2 mil, to pay off about $500,000 in debt at 50 cents on the dollar. All of these levies added up to between 14-1/2 and 17-1/2 mils, a substantial burden on many who were struggling to hold on to their farms.

Several other notable events, as would be recorded by historian John Reynold, had occurred during the course of the legislative session:

> The House impeached Judge Montgomery Moses, of the Seventh Circuit Court, on a charge of "high crimes and misdemeanors." The Senate tried the case and found Moses guilty as charged. Governor Chamberlain then proceeded to appoint L. C. Northrop, of Charleston, to fill the vacancy. Reynold would find Northrop to have been "a man of small abilities and little legal knowledge."

> Considerable controversy surrounded the heated election, in joint session, to two State judgeships, one sought by W. J. Whipper (an African American and member of the House, who had migrated from a northern State) and the other sought by Franklin J. Moses (the notorious former Governor of which much has been told on previous pages). The voting was highly racial: Whipper won on the votes of 74 African Americans and 9 European Americans (83 of 142 cast) and Moses won on a similar racial vote of 64 and 6 (70 of 139 cast). In Reynold's words:

>> "The election of Whipper and Moses caused widespread indignation and disgust. Governor Chamberlain declared it 'a horrible disaster — a disaster equally great to the State and to the Republican Party — a calamity infinitely greater than any which has yet fallen on this State or upon any of the South.' He further said: 'Neither Whipper nor Moses has any qualities which approach to a qualification of judicial positions. The reputation of Moses is covered deep with charges, which are believed by all who are familiar with the facts, of corruption, bribery and the utter prostitution of all his official powers to the worst possible purposes'."

Chamberlain refused to sign commissions for Whipple and Moses, denying them the lucrative judicial jobs for which they aspired, and intensifying the schism within the South Carolina Republican Party — a schism between politicians intent of sustaining and protecting fraudulent government (Whipple/Moses Faction) and politicians advocating reform and more honest government (Chamberlain Faction).

Regarding the condition at this time of the public schools and colleges, historian John Reynold would conclude:

"The school system was still grossly inefficient. There was yet due to teachers over $185,000 for services already rendered, whilst the number of fraudulent pay certificates issued by irresponsible school boards was unknown. The University was still a mixed school for [European Americans and African Americans], upon which large sums were annually spent in paying professors for giving college education which in the cases of a majority of the students was pretense only. The Agricultural College was still suffering from the fraudulent diversion of the bonds given by [the Federal Government] for its support."

Since the beginning of Republican rule over South Carolina, commencing in 1868, I have presented many financial numbers to describe the magnitude and persistence of the graft, corruption and suffering of the property owners of the State, as well as revealing the, sadly, minimal effort being made to improve the economic life of the African American population. I will now wrap up this account with a few words from historian John Reynold:

"After the Legislative session concluded in April 1876, "the domination of the [African American] continued — disguised though it was as the rule of the Republican Party. Confidence in that Party as organized and influenced had been totally destroyed — this by the manifest disinclination of the majority in the Legislature to reduce expenses and their evident purpose to set their schemes above the rights of the minority [European American population]. The election of Whipper and Moses was but the outburst of a feeling that really controlled every Republican member of that body.

"The [European] race in South Carolina, their property, their liberties, their opportunities in life, lay at the mercy of an ignorant majority [race] under the leadership of corrupt men." [R201;314-336]

Three weeks later, on May 4, the South Carolina Democratic Party met in Convention in Columbia to lay strategy for the upcoming fall State elections. All counties were represented except for Lancaster and Marlboro. J. B. Kershaw was elected President of the Convention and a State Executive Committee was named. The more aggressive Delegates favored nominating a full "Straightout" ticket, "from Governor to coroner," to compete in the upcoming election, whereas the more cautious Delegates favored supporting Republican Governor D. H. Chamberlain for re-election in order to concentrate on winning control of a majority of the seats in the State Legislature. Advocates of the "Straightout" strategy won, adopting an enabling resolution by a vote of 70 to 42. It was further resolved that the State Executive Committee, "whenever in their judgment it may be deemed proper, to call a Convention of the Democratic Party to nominate State officers and announce a Platform of principles." [R201;340-344]

Meanwhile, on May 24, Jeff, Varina and their 11-year-old daughter Winnie boarded the S. S. *Memphis* for Liverpool, England. He needed to travel to London to confer with the Executive Committee of the Mississippi Valley Association. The British members of the Association had a big job to accomplish: they had to raise capital to build merchant vessels to dramatically increase the overseas shipping capacity in and out of the port of New Orleans. It would be Jeff's job to encourage producers of export goods to choose New Orleans over New York, but that would come to naught if the new merchant ships were not constructed. Jeff had been formally elected President of the American branch of the Mississippi Valley Association at the Association's February meeting in New Orleans, and his salary and expense account was now satisfactory. The salary was pegged at $6,000 per year and the travel expense allowance was "liberal." Vicksburg members of the Association had already advanced $1,000 to cover travel expenses. Jeff anticipated he would be doing a lot of traveling as he promoted increased import-export commerce through the seaport at New Orleans. [R19;415]

Jeff was surely grateful for the advance of his expense allowance, because the Montgomery's were still pleading an inability to pay any interest on their 1867 purchase of his and Joseph's farmland along the

Mississippi River. In a March 22 letter to Varina, Jeff had reported that Ben Montgomery's eldest son, Thornton, had delivered the bad news, which they had become sadly accustomed to receiving every year:

> ". . . The Montgomery's have again failed to pay the [bank] drafts, which were taken [by us] in settlement [of the pledged past-due interest] last winter. Thornton came to see me yesterday and said they had given Hamer & Mitchell [Company] mules and supplies to cover what was due to them, but that he could not get money for us, and that their Commission Merchant here would not accept their [bank] drafts, but that he would go to Vicksburg and try to get the [commission] house there to accept drafts payable in September, [1876].

> "When what would be satisfactory cannot be had it only remains to take the best which is attainable. The low price of cotton is the excuse and no doubt partially accounts for the failure [to make enough money to pay our interest debt]." [R19;416, R30;426]

(3Q76)

As the 1876 elections approached, the Republican Party was clearly in great need of all the fraudulent vote manipulation it could arrange, when considering the multitude of scandals being laid at the feet of the Grant Administration, one of them being the "Whisky Ring" conspiracy. John McDonald, supervisor of the Internal Revenue Office at St. Louis, was the chief manipulator of the scheme whereby Whisky distillers conspired to keep for themselves much of the whisky tax due the Federal Government — a scandal that had reached all the way to Grant's private secretary. Furthermore, a House investigation of suspected bribery had nabbed William Belknap, Grant's Secretary of War. The House had impeached Belknap, but the accused had resigned before the Senate could try his case. In another embarrassment, Robert Schenck, Grant's Minister to Great Britain, had become embroiled over the "Emma Mine Scandal." Grant's efforts to protect Schenck had prompted the New York *Tribune* to claim, "Grant always stands by a friend in trouble, though it involves the [Federal] Government in disgrace." And perhaps the worst political difficulty was tied to the series of railroad scandals, which had ensnared presidential hopeful James Blaine. These scandals had weakened the popularity of the Republican Party in the northern States and had helped to justify "home rule" for the former Confederate States, a position the Democratic Party endorsed.

As previously reported, there had been a dramatic reversal in the political makeup of the Federal House. During the past 1873-1875 term, Republicans had controlled 65 percent of the seats, but in the current 1875-1877 term, Democrats were controlling 59 percent of the seats. So, from the powerful position of the Federal House, the Democratic Party was tearing down the Republican Political Machines in the former Confederate States. Restrictions on voting by European Americans were being overturned and interference by Federal troops was being withheld. Consequently, the Democratic Party was gaining new life in the southern States, and most governments in the region were being remade to serve all of the people of their respective States. By the time of the 1876 Fall elections, Republican Political Machines would hold firm control over only 3 of the 11 former Confederate States — South Carolina, Florida and Louisiana. Sadly, Republican Political Machines in these three remaining States would steal the election for Republican Rutherford Hayes, the Governor of Ohio, who would be the apparent loser to Democrat Samuel Tilden, the Governor of New York State. Both candidates had been nominated at their respective National Conventions during June. Of particular interest to us are the campaigns in South Carolina and Mississippi. [R19;420]

In South Carolina on July 4, a racial incident occurred in Hamburg, which would soon result in tragic bloodshed. It seems that two European American men, traveling down the main road in a buggy, were stopped by a company of African American militiamen who intentionally blocked the road and, before the buggy was finally allowed to pass through, "the [African Americans] cursed and vilified them in the grossest manner and beat their drums around the horse's head." The father of one of the men filed a complaint seeking a warrant for the arrest of the militiamen and their leader (an African American known as Doc Adams) "for obstructing a highway." The arrest was made and a trial was scheduled, which drew considerable attention, since this kind of behavior had been persistent and the local European Americans were earnest about curbing it. Matthew Butler, lawyer for the prosecution, attempted to defuse the anger by asking Doc Adams to apologize. Adams refused. Then Butler sought to defuse the anger by persuading Adams and his militiamen to deliver up their guns to be returned to officials in Columbia. Apparently Adams refused this proposal as well. Alarmed, a sizable contingency of concerned European Americans arrived from nearby Augusta. Seeing the anger on the faces of the growing number of European Americans, Adams and his militiamen retreated to their "fortified . . . drill room in a brick building, defied the European Americans, raised a yell and fired from the windows — to which those outside responded with a volley. The first man killed was European American "McKie Meriwether, a worthy young citizen of Edgefield," shot through the head. So, what should have been nothing more than deplorable insulting behavior, a refusal to apologize and a defiant attitude toward legal process, had escalated into gunfire and murder. The anger was later described as "the culmination of the system of insulting and outraging [the European Americans], which the [African Americans] had adopted [in the town] for several years." Historian John Reynold would describe the sad history of how the European Americans then took their revenge:

> "In the meantime, a small cannon had been brought from Augusta, and from it 4 or 5 charges of canister [were] successfully fired on the building occupied by the [militiamen]. . . . As [they] were escaping from the building they were fired on and one of their number was killed. The rest were captured and later 5 of these — regarded as the ringleaders in bringing on the difficulty — were singly shot to death by their infuriated captors."

Matthew Butler, deploring the excessive retaliation, said, "Many things were done on this terrible night which cannot be justified, but the [African Americans] 'sowed the wind and reaped the whirlwind'." Governor D. H. Chamberlain, seeing an opportunity to exploit the tragedy for political benefit, called the incident, " 'the Hamburg massacre,' denouncing it as an act of 'atrocity and barbarism,' evidencing a 'murderous and inhuman spirit' and presenting a 'darker picture of human cruelty than the slaughter of Custer and his soldiers'." But, apparently more concerned about the Fall elections than about justice, the Chamberlain Administration would not back up that rhetoric and prosecute anyone for the killing of the African Americans. On the other hand, as you would expect, Chamberlain used the incident to appeal to President Ulysses Grant for more Federal troops to maintain peace, and Grant readily agreed that Federal troops would be provided to him as needed. (Chamberlain wanted these troops to help maintain Republican domination during the upcoming elections.) [R201;344-347]

By the way, on August 1, Colorado was granted Statehood. It would support the Republican Party.

Meanwhile, on August 15 in Columbia, Delegates to the South Carolina Democratic Party Convention assembled "to announce a platform of principles, nominate State officers and electors for President and Vice-President, and to consider such other business as may be brought before it." This would be an historic gathering that would dramatically change the course of political history in South Carolina. The first order of business was to elect the President of the Convention. Two men were advanced, one favoring nominating a full slate immediately, the other seeking to delay action until after the Republican State Convention. Advocates of immediate action carried the floor by a vote of 80 to 66. "The announcement of the result was received with cheers from the floor of the hall. It appeared that South Carolina Democrats were energized and ready to take on the Republican Party "straightout." But further debate followed, for Delegates were not yet united in their purpose — the "Straightouts" sought to proceed with nominations, but a sizable contingent cautioned, "It is inexpedient at this time to make a nomination for State officers or to adopt a Platform. . . ." The Delegates then cleared the hall of everyone who was not a Delegate and began debate in secrecy.

The Platform, as submitted by the drafting committee, was "unanimously adopted," signaling a sense of unity. A summation follows: "The Democratic Party of South Carolina, in Convention assembled, announces the following as its Platform of Principles:

> "We declare our acceptance, in perfect good faith, of the Thirteenth, Fourteenth and Fifteenth Amendments to the Federal Constitution. Accepting and standing upon them, we turn from the settled and final past to the great living and momentous issues of the present and the future.

> "We adopt the Platform of Principles announced by the National Democratic Party recently assembled at St. Louis and [our support of candidates Samuel Tilden and Thomas Hendricks] . . . .

> ". . . We demand a genuine and thorough reform in the State of South Carolina, and call upon all its citizens, irrespective of race, color or previous condition, to rally with us to its redemption, for it is

evident that substantial and lasting reform is impossible within the ranks of the Republican Party of this State.

"We charge that Party with arraying race against race, creating disturbances and fomenting difficulties; with prostituting the elective franchise, tampering with the ballot box and holding unfair and fraudulent elections; with having accumulated an enormous debt, mismanaged finances and injured the credit of the State; with levying exorbitant taxes and squandering them when collected . . .

"We charge its legislation as demoralizing, partisan and disgraceful, and the venality and corruption which have characterized every branch of the Government, executive, legislative and judicial, have no parallel in the history of nations. . . . And to crown its disgraceful rule it has attempted to elevate to the bench two most corrupt and degraded men. . . .

". . . It is our firm conviction that all the people of the State, of both races, desire peace and prosperity. We, therefore, call upon our fellow citizens, irrespective of race or past Party affiliation, to join with us in restoring the good name of our State, and in elevating it to a place of dignity and character among the commonwealths of this great country.

"We discountenance all disturbances of the peace of the State, and denounce all instigators and promoters thereof; and earnestly call upon all of our fellow citizens, irrespective of Party lines, to exercise forbearance and cultivate good will . . . . We desire a fair, peaceful election, appealing to the reason, and not the passions, of the people . . . and a fair count. . . .

"Our object is reform, retrenchment and relief, that by honestly and economy we may reduce the taxes and lighten the burdens of the people, giving at the same time absolute security and protection to the rights and property of all.

"Upon this paramount issue we cordially invite the cooperation of every Democrat and every Republican who is earnest and willing, in this crisis of our State, to unite with us in this great work."

The secret debate concluded with agreement, by a vote of 82 to 65, "That this Convention do now proceed to nominate candidates for Governor and other State officers." At that point, it was obvious that the South Carolina Democratic Party was energized and eager to take on the Republicans "straightout."

Matthew Butler, a former Confederate General, nominated Wade Hampton for Governor. Robert Aldrich seconded the nomination. Hampton then addressed the Delegates regarding his availability and — thinking about his prominent war record as commander over the Confederate cavalry — his genuine concerns that "Hampton" at the head of the State ticket might, at the national level, harm the Democratic Party's campaign for Federal President. Hampton's complete remarks follow:

"Mr. President and Gentlemen: I need not tell you that the words of kindly allusion to myself which I have heard spoken have deeply touched my heart. But I desire to say a few words in personal explanation. I have all along refrained from expressing my opinion in one way or another, except when called upon to do so as a Delegate. I have not tried to influence this Convention in word or deed. I came here only to pour oil on the troubled waters, if necessary, and to promote unity and harmony if I could.

"In the card I published in the Columbia *Register* the other day I expressed my opinions fully and earnestly. When the war was raging I was asked to come here and allow my name to be used as a candidate for Governor, but I preferred to stay where I thought I could do the most good for my State and my country; and since the war I have never offered one word of advice unless it was asked of me. I felt that my day was past, and that in returning to my native State I was like him who said: 'An old man whose heart is broken is come to lay his weary bones among you. Give me a little earth for charity'."

"I have claimed nothing from South Carolina but a grave in yonder churchyard. But I have always said that if I could ever serve her by word or deed, her men had only to call me and I would devote all my time, my energy and my life to her service.

"I will now be perfectly unreserved with you on another point. Men whose patriotism is beyond question, and in whose wisdom I have great confidence, think that my nomination would injure the Democratic Party of the United States. If it were left with me to decide between that Party and the interest of South Carolina, I would not hesitate in my choice. But I believe the success of the Democratic Party of the United States will bring success to South Carolina, and that if [Samuel] Tilden is elected we can call South Carolina our own. Now, I do not wish to embarrass the gentlemen of the Convention, nor to jeopardize the general Democratic Party. I would, indeed, gladly decline the nomination. Besides this, there are men in South Carolina who think I possess a disqualification of which I cannot divest myself, and would not if I could. I mean what they call my war record. That is the record of 50,000 South Carolina soldiers, and if I am to forfeit that, and say that I am ashamed to have been one of them, all the offices in the world might perish before I would accept them.

"These are grave topics, gentlemen, and I implore you to look over the whole field and not let any kindness for me lead you astray. I will now retire, so that you may discuss them freely. If you decide to nominate some other as true and as sincere as I, and I know there are thousands of them, I will devote myself to secure his election. Come weal or come woe, I am with you to the last."

Wade Hampton withdrew from the hall. John Bratton, also a Confederate commander, was nominated, but rose to decline in favor of Hampton. Former Democratic Governor John Manning was then nominated, but he likewise rose to decline in favor of Hampton. The Convention then, unanimously and by acclamation, nominated Wade Hampton for Governor.

The Convention proceeded to nominate candidates for the remaining State offices:

For Lieutenant Governor — W. D. Simpson, of Laurens.
For Secretary of State — R. M. Sims, of York.
For Attorney-General — James Conner, of Charleston.
For Superintendent of Education — Hugh Thompson, of Richland.
For Comptroller-General — Johnson Hagood, of Barnwell.
For Treasurer — S. L. Leaphart, of Richland.
For Adjutant-General — E. W. Moise, of Sumter.

The Convention proceeded to nominate candidates for the Federal House:

For the First District — J. S. Richardson.
For the Second District — Michael P. O'Connor
For the Third District — D. Wyatt Aiken.
For the Fourth District — John H. Evins.
For the Fifth District — G. D. Tillman.

Nominations complete, Wade Hampton was invited to come into the hall and address the Convention. The complete text of his address is given below:

"Mr. President and Gentlemen of the Convention — In accepting the honorable post to which you have called me, that of our standard-bearer in the great struggle for reform which you have begun, I do so with the most grateful appreciation of your kindness and the most profound sense of the high duties, the grave responsibilities, pertaining to the position. In the better days of our country, when the surest passports to official station were found in the ability, the honesty and the integrity of her public servants, the most distinguished sons of South Carolina looked upon the chief magistracy of the State as the goal of their highest ambition and the best reward of their public services. If men of whom Carolina is justly proud held in such deserved estimation the distinction of being thought worthy by their fellow citizens of the highest office in the gift of the State in the days of her prosperity and peace, how much more highly should I esteem the honor you have done me by calling me unanimously to lead you in this hour of gloom and peril.

"You are struggling for the highest stake for which a people ever contended, for you are striving to bring back to your prostrate State the inestimable blessings which can only follow orderly and regulated liberty under free and good government. We believe that these blessings can only be secured by a complete change in the administration of our public affairs, National and State, and believing this, our sympathies and our interests lead us naturally and inevitably into alliance with that great Party upon whose banners are inscribed the watchwords of Democracy — 'Reform, good government, hard money and home rule.'

"You have endorsed and ratified the Platform of the Democratic Party adopted in St. Louis, and planting yourselves firmly on that, you look forward hopefully and confidently to a victory in which you will not only share, but to which you will have contributed. The Platform which you have adopted here is so catholic in its spirit, so strong in its foundations, so broad in its construction that every man in South Carolina who honestly desires reform can find room to stand upon it. With such a Platform, where our citizens of all parties and all races can stand assured of equal rights and full protection, you can surely bring back to our distracted State the great blessings of good government.

"For myself, should I be elevated to the high position for which you have nominated me, my sole effort shall be to restore our State Government to decency, to honesty, to economy and to integrity. I shall be the Governor of the whole people, knowing no Party, making no vindictive discriminations, holding the scales of justice with firm and impartial hand, seeing, as far as in me lies, that the laws are enforced in justice tempered with mercy, protecting all classes alike, and devoting every effort to the restoration of prosperity and the reestablishment of honest government.

"Thanking you, gentlemen, for the honor you have conferred upon me, and invoking the blessing of God on your praiseworthy effort to redeem our State, I here pledge myself to work with you in that sacred cause with all the zeal, all the energy, all the ability and all the constancy of which I am capable."

The historic 1876 South Carolina Democratic Party Convention adjourned on the afternoon of August 17. [R201;347-355]

South Carolina Democrats quickly went to work to win the election. The women set down and sewed red shirts for the men, for the red shirt was to be the uniform for Democrats of both races in all meetings, parades and rallies. Democratic clubs recruited members of both races, seeking out all willing African American men and guaranteeing their protection from harm from vindictive Republicans, helping them establish Democratic Clubs officered by African American men, and assuring them protection and special prominence at gatherings. Historian John Reynold would explain:

"Proper steps were taken for the enrollment of [African American] voters into Democratic clubs officered by [African American] men — the assurance being given in the plainest language that any attempt by Republicans, [of either race], to intimidate, injure or oppress any [African American] because he should join a Democratic club or should declare his purpose to vote for Hampton would lead to bloodshed in which the intimidators would surely be the sufferers. The [African American] Democrats, whenever they appeared in a procession or at a meeting, wore the Democratic uniform — the red shirt — and sometimes a single [African American] was detailed to appear in public in that garb, the purpose being to impress the fact that [an African American] man could thus show himself to others of his race and yet go unharmed. . . .

"For the prevention of trouble nothing could be expected of the State Government or any of its agents. . . . The Republican leaders in South Carolina — from D. H. Chamberlain down — apparently desired bloodshed. . . . [Therefore], every Democratic club constituted an organization available in case of trouble. The men were sufficiently provided with arms, and especial care was taken that, in the event of any disturbance, the members — especially in thinly settled neighborhoods — should be properly notified. There were also some military organizations among the [European Americans] — rifle clubs and saber clubs."

The South Carolina Republican Party Convention opened in Columbia on September 13. A long and detailed platform was adopted, endorsing the National Party Platform and candidates Hayes and Wheeler; praising Ulysses Grant; declaring "our abhorrence and repudiation of all forms of violence, intimidation or fraud in the conduct of elections;" pledging to enact 8 new Amendments to the State Constitution; pledging to pass 7 named pieces of legislation; pledging help with fencing farmland to contain cattle; pledging to ask the Federal Government to pardon South Carolinians who in the past had evaded Federal taxes — but there was more. The Platform then tore into the State and National

Democratic parties with a vengeance, accusing them both, in lengthy detail, of all imaginable past, present and future horrors:

"We charge the Democratic Party with perversion of all truth and history; with opposition to all the interests of the masses; with fostering class preferences and discriminations; with a denial of rights to those who do not accept their political dogmas; with constant and persistent antagonism to the principles of justice and humanity; with a resistance to the manifest will of the people and the spirit of the age; with a determination to make [African American bonding] national and liberty sectional; with a purpose to rend the [former Federation of States] in twain to perpetuate human bondage; with plunging the [States] into a fratricidal war; with deluging the land in blood and filling it with sorrow and distress; with burdening the people with a debt that makes a higher taxation necessary and continuous; with opposition to [reconstructing the political structure of the governments] of the States they had violently forced into a Confederacy; with resistance to the passage and ratification of the Amendments to the [Federal] Constitution, made necessary by the results of the [War between the States], which clothed the humblest in the nation with citizenship and placed in his hands the power of protecting it; with a purpose to reopen sectional prejudices and animosities, to make 'the war a failure,' '[Political] Reconstruction void,' and the Amendments to the Constitution nullities; with deception, misrepresentation, extravagance in the conduct of government, dishonesty in the disbursement of the pubic funds, and an abuse of the public confidence; with fraud in the management of elections; with intimidation of Electors; with atrocities during political campaigns unheard of in civilized communities; with assassinations and murders of those whose only offending was a steadfast adherence to the principles of the Republican Party; with threatenings of violence and death against those who advocate the perpetuity of the Republican Party; with armed preparation and hostile intent in the [Southern States], intending by such formidable array to frighten or force Republicans into a support of their Party and partisans, or to remain away from the polls; with dissembling to the [Northern States], by assurances of an acceptance of the results of the war, a desire for reconciliation and brotherly relations, when they are only thirsting for the opportunity to secure what they have lost by the ascendancy of the National Democratic Party to power, and thus inflict upon the nation further evils and embarrassments; with nominating National and State officers known for their antagonism to all the Republican Party has accomplished."

Delegates at the Republican State Convention then proceeded to nominate candidates for State offices. On the first ballot Governor D. H. Chamberlain was nominated for re-election, receiving 88 votes versus 35 for others. Others were then nominated as follows:

For Lieutenant-Governor — R. H. Gleaves.
For Attorney-General — R. B. Elliot.
For Treasurer — Francis Cardozo.
For Secretary of State — H. E. Hayne.
For Comptroller-General — T. C. Dunn.
For Adjutant-General — James Kennedy.
For Superintendent of Education — John R. Tolbert.

Historian John Reynold would describe the situation in the first weeks following the two conventions, with particular attention to the lasting influence of the legislative fight between Republican factions, which had resulted in electing Whipper and Moses to State judgeships, followed by Chamberlain's vetoes:

"There was much dissatisfaction among a large class of Republicans of both races, these claiming that the State [Republican] ticket as a whole was unworthy, that Elliott's nomination [for Attorney-General] was especially disgraceful, and that Governor Chamberlain had surrendered to the worst men in his Party — the very men who had promoted the election of Whipper and Moses, who had opposed his reforms and who had denounced him in most violent language. . . . It was generally felt that Governor Chamberlain had surrendered to the very men who had perpetrated the wrongs against which the taxpayers had long protested — who were indeed notoriously corrupt — whose bad character, in each instance, was actually known to him. . . .

"Immediately upon the adjournment of the Republican Convention, Judge Thompson H. Cooke, of the Eighth Circuit, declared for Hampton, and offered his services to the Democratic Committee. A few days afterwards Judge Mackey made a like declaration. Both of these converts did active and effective work for the Hampton ticket.

"There were numerous defections among the [European American] Republicans and some of the best [African American] men in every county joined in the Democratic movement. The number of [African American] men in the clubs grew apace — this notwithstanding the persecution visited upon them by others of their race. [African American] Democrats were pursued, insulted, beaten, wounded, threatened with death, expelled from church and subjected to numerous indignities and annoyances, and would have suffered much more but for the constant watchfulness of the [European Americans]."

Campaigning began in early September and by mid-month was in earnest across the State. The level of public enthusiasm for Hampton and the Democratic ticket was huge and earnest everywhere, but much more muted in counties where African Americans outnumbered European Americans by large majorities. [R201;362-374]

Meanwhile in Europe, Jeff Davis was traveling some on business while also seeking out a boarding school for daughter Winnie. But Varina remained in London, for she was still suffering from a long bout of illness that, according to the diagnosis of attending doctors, was caused by excessive nervousness and despair. Varina had apparently worried herself sick over the combination of political strife and Jeff's business difficulties. In fact Varina had spent much of their stay in London lying in bed. It was under those conditions that they had carried through with plans to enroll 11-year-old Winnie in the Misses Friedlander's School for Girls in Carlsruhe, Germany. Jeff said goodbye to Winnie in September as he saw her and a Memphis friend, Pinnie Meredith, off at the London station. Jeff had arranged for an adult friend to escort Winnie and Pinnie to Carlsruhe because he thought it best to stay close to Varina, for she seemed so ill at the time. Pinnie Meredith was also enrolled in the school. The school was a favorite of European royalty. The school was largely sponsored by the daughter of Kaiser Wilhelm I of Prussia, and was located near his palace. Biographer Hudson Strode would explain:

"It was often the custom of well-to-do Americans in the last half of the nineteenth century to give their teen-age daughters a season or two of European education. Several girls of prominent families [in the former Confederate States] attended the Carlsruhe school . . . and Emily Mason in Paris approved of it. . . . [Jeff and Varina] hoped that some special blessing would come from Winnie's education in an exclusive Continental school. [Jeff] was certain that Winnie had the capabilities of profiting by the regime of the German establishment. She was remarkably bright and imaginative, and, except for her inability to spell correctly or punctuate, quite advanced for her years. Although shy, she was somewhat full of herself and desirous of attention. [Jeff] thought it well for his little girl to get away from her mother, who was inclined to smother her with constant solicitude for her health. But he felt a pang at the thought of a long separation." [R19;417]

Jeff would leave Varina for a few days in late October to visit Winnie to be sure that she had adjusted to boarding school life and that the headmistress, Miss Friedlander, would be satisfied with her progress and ability to succeed at the required school work. Jeff would write Varina from Carlsruhe:

"The children are both well and heavier than when they left us. Miss Friedlander insisted upon giving me a room in her house and thus I spent the evening in the midst of the pupils. The girls are very genteel and show to each other the most affectionate consideration. . . . Winnie has come to give me a morning kiss and says give my love to Mother and tell her I will write to her tomorrow, . . . Miss Friedlander has a high and just appreciation of [Winnie] and is not at all disposed to give her up. So you may consider the matter settled and I will tell you all about it when we meet." [R30;436]

Meanwhile, intense political campaigning continued in South Carolina. Historian John Reynold would continue telling the amazing the story:

"The Democratic canvass opened at Anderson on September 2, and a meeting was held in every county — the final 'rally' being at Columbia on November 4. Every meeting was attended by all the [European American] men of the county, except the very few that it was thought necessary to leave at home — these, in many of the counties, patrolling the roads to look out for any misconduct of the [African Americans] and visiting the houses to let the women and children know of their movements.

"The Democratic clubs (every man in a red shirt) came to the county seat in military order, each commanded by its president. The column was formed by marshals or aides under the orders of the county chairman and he commanded the procession — riding with his staff at the head of the column as it escorted the canvassers to the place of speaking. The red shirt procession was a feature of every campaign meeting — the number of mounted men in [red shirts] varying, according to the [European American] population of the county, from 500 to 5,000. . . . A thousand men on horseback, riding in easy order, every man yelling as long as his throat could stand the effort — the marshals meantime riding up and down the column, carrying orders or 'closing up' the men — the route to the speaking ground lined with men . . . women and children, waving flags or hats or handkerchiefs to the riders and doing their part to increase the volume of lusty yells and defiant hurrahs — such a body of men might well be taken for one double their number in fact.

"On arriving at the speaking ground (usually a grove on the outskirts) the ranks were opened, and [Wade] Hampton, escorted by committeemen and others in red shirts, walked to the stand. Usually he was greeted with the songs of young women, who strewed his path with flowers. Music was an invariable feature. The mounted men formed a semi-circle in front, except that a place near the stand was reserved for the [African American] voters — who were always urged to attend. . . . The presence of the good women and their hearty interest in the campaign helped to show that it was not a mere effort to get office or to oust officeholders, but a movement of the people against unworthy men in control of the State. . . .

"[Wade] Hampton spoke in every county, and there were speeches by the other nominees and by gentlemen detailed for this service in different parts of the State. [Although there] was little reference to national politics . . . [European American men] were exhorted to work unceasingly for the election of the [complete] Democratic ticket, and . . . to see [to it] that no [African American] man should ever suffer because of his joining a Democratic club or for otherwise showing his purpose to vote the Hampton ticket.

"Besides the campaign meetings at the county seats, there was a canvass of every county by the Democratic nominees for the Legislature and for the different county offices. Impromptu meeting were also held on the [larger farms], these addressed by citizens who were not candidates at all. . . . Individual work among the [African Americans] was unceasing. Whatever the occasion, whenever a [European American] man had a chance to talk to [an African American] there was an effort to win a vote for Hampton. Little attention was paid to the so-called leaders among the [African Americans] — except to let them understand that they must not trouble [African American] Democrats, that they must not stir up strife, and that in case of disturbance they must expect to suffer. [European American] Republicans, both rare and unobtrusive, were not regarded as of any particular consequence. . . . Every means was taken to maintain the peace. Coolness, forbearance, prudence, were incessantly urged upon the [European Americans].

"A distinct feature of the campaign was the plan to 'divide time' at [African American] meetings whenever these were known to be contemplated."

Toward the goal to "divide time," Democrat leaders intentionally arrived at outdoors Republican rallies where Governor Chamberlain was to speak and where much, if not most, of the audience consisted of African American voters. This effort produced dramatic debate at four Republican rallies: Edgefield, Newberry, Abbeville and Midway. At Edgefield, for example, there were "several hundred mounted Democrats present. There, after Chamberlain spoke, Democrat leaders Matthew Butler and Judge Mackey, in turn, mounted the platform and addressed the gathering, where each "denounced the Governor in plainest language, and held him up to the [African Americans] as unworthy of all things." Other Democrats did similar service for the Party at Newberry, Abbeville and Midway. For obvious reasons, Republicans refused to agree to Democratic efforts to formalize the concept of "divided time" and engage in official debates. So Democrats speaking at Republican gatherings was always an impromptu affair. That aggressive campaign tactic reduced Republican eagerness to hold rallies and, regarding those held, reduced their effectiveness in energizing the Republican base. Violence never occurred at these "divided time" political gatherings according to historian John Reynold, who would write — "There was neither bloodshed nor any breach of the peace at any of these joint meetings." Republican campaigners did not reciprocate by seeking to "divide time" at Democrat rallies. [R201;355-361]

(4Q76)

Although the campaign in South Carolina was generally a peaceful contest between strong political wills, there were incidents of violence and death prior to Election Day. However, on Election Day there would be no violent incidents — that would be a peaceful day. Mention has been made of European American Democrats parading in red shirts on horseback and patrolling their counties — to ensure, as best they could, that African Americans did not initiate violent conflict — and of their Democratic clubs and rifle and saber clubs. The words of historian John Reynold are useful in describing the corresponding militant behavior of African American Republicans:

> "There was constant danger of disturbance. It was evident that many of the [African Americans were armed — armed with guns furnished by the State. The number thus supplied was reported to be 40,000, but it was certainly not so large. The arms had been distributed secretly. In some sections of the lower counties, where [African Americans] largely outnumbered [European Americans], the conduct of the [African American] soldiers and of [African American] mobs carrying guns was well calculated to cause race conflicts. They paraded the roads, they went about in squads, they made a display of their guns, they threatened [European Americans] with violence and swore vengeance upon any [African American] who should vote the Democratic ticket.... All the self-control that the [European Americans] could exercise, all their resolution to follow their leaders' advice to keep the peace at all hazards, was needed to prevent bloodshed. The arming of the [African Americans] and their hostile demonstrations served to swell the enrollment and improve the equipment of the [European American] rifle clubs.

> "Despite the determination of the [European Americans] to keep the peace and to strike in self-defense only, there were serious disturbances — each resulting in the loss of life."

There were deaths at the "Charleston Riot" on September 6, the "Ellenton Riot" on September 15, the "Cainhoy Massacre" on October 16 and at Edgefield on October 17. Violent threats against Democrats of both races came close to bloodshed at Mount Pleasant, at Beaufort and again at Charleston. Some details follow:

> At Charleston, on September 6, during a meeting of one of the city's [African American] Democratic clubs, two African Americans "were prominent in their advocacy of the Hampton ticket." A mob of African American Republicans "planned to break up the meeting, but were prevented by the presence of a number of [European American] men. When the meeting closed, the [European American] men, fearing trouble, formed a hollow square and placed the two [African Americans] within." An African American Republican, armed with a club, struck the first blow and a fight with fists, clubs and pistols ensued. "The [European American] men persistently defended the two [African American] Democrats until these were carried to a place of safety." Policemen strove to break up the fight. "In this affair, one [European American] man, J. M. Buckner, was mortally shot and died the day following, and 7 were wounded — two severely. Five [African American] men — 3 of them being of the police force — were wounded, but not seriously." It seems rather amazing that the loss on life was not greater. The two African American Democrats were not among the injured.

> At Ellenton, beginning on September 15 and lasting 3 days, riotous racial conflict resulted in 17 killed and 10 wounded — among European Americans, 2 killed and 8 wounded, and among African Americans, 15 killed and 2 wounded. The trouble began when two African Americans broke into a home "with burglarious intent" and there encountered the mother and son of the house, the father being away at the time. The burglars severely beat the mother and beat the boy, then fled when the mother confronted them with her husband's rifle, which they did not realize was then not loaded. One of the burglars was soon arrested and positively identified by the mother. That

burglar named his accomplice, Fred Pope, and a warrant was issued by an African American justice for Pope's arrest. A legally-authorized posse, proceeding down the road to find Pope and arrest him, in due course arrived at Rouse's Bridge and there found Pope with many armed African Americans in a defiant stance. There was a parley and both sides agreed to disperse. During the course of that and the next day, African Americans instigated violence, staging ambushes, setting fires to buildings and tearing up a railroad track, causing a train to wreck. When attacked, the European Americans fought back in hard pursuit, resulting in the greater death toll among the African Americans. Historian John Reynold would describe the concluding scene:

> "The [European Americans] were preparing to charge the [African Americans] in the swamp, when a company of [Federal] infantry (sent on the demand of Governor Chamberlain) appeared on the scene. It was agreed that [both races] disperse. The [European Americans] retired first, and the [African Americans] promptly followed their example."

The "Cainhoy Massacre" occurred on October 16 near the village of Cainhoy, about 10 miles northeast of Charleston, where a political meeting was in progress, in which both Democrats and Republicans were speaking. Both sides had agreed that no guns would be brought to the joint meeting, but many African American participants had hidden many guns a short distance away to have them at the ready. Very soon after an African American Republican leader "began speaking, a company of [African Americans] marched out of the swamp with their weapons and opened fire upon the [European Americans], who were unarmed." Gunfire from the African Americans killed 6 European Americans and wounded 16, some of them severely. Only one African American was killed, that occurring after the African Americans had begun shooting. Soon afterward Governor Chamberlain arranged for a company of Federal troops to go to the area around Cainhoy, and those soldiers remained there until after the election.

On October 17 there was gunfire following a Democratic campaign meeting at Edgefield. "A party of 6 [European American] men were riding along the main road, about a mile and a half from town, when two of them were fired upon by a party of [African American] militia in ambush. One of them — John Gilmore — was instantly killed and the other badly wounded." Later, as the coroner was riding toward the place where Gilmore was killed, "he was shot from ambush — one ball shattering his leg and wounding his horse. There was intense excitement and there were threats of retaliation upon the [African American] militia, but the counsels of prudent leaders prevented further trouble." I have no evidence that the guilty party was ever apprehended.

On the night of October 23, at Mount Pleasant, a village across the Cooper River from Charleston, "a mob of several [African Americans], armed with guns, behaved in a manner to cause fears for the lives of the inhabitants." But the European Americans managed to gather into a single house and "the [European American] men of the place, aided by some of the [African American] Democrats, kept guard around the building during the entire night. The threat subsided the next day.

At both Charleston and Beaufort, African American Democrats were harassed and attempts to instigate armed conflict were not uncommon. At one point, "a club of [African American] Democrats, mounted, were assailed with brickbats, and a number of them were badly hurt." As a general rule, deaths were "prevented only by the coolness and forbearance of the [European Americans]."

On October 7, only three weeks after the South Carolina Republican Party State Convention, Governor Chamberlain, had issued a Proclamation commanding certain European Americans to disperse. Greatly alarmed over the Hampton campaign's superb organization, enthusiasm and determination to prevail, Chamberlain was firing the first salvo in what would be an escalating program to impose Federal and State military control — his objective being not peace, but Republican victory. The Proclamation said:

> "Whereas, it has been made known to me by written and sworn evidence that there exist such unlawful obstructions, combinations and assemblages of persons in the counties of Aiken and Barnwell that it has become impracticable, in my judgment as Governor of the State, to enforce, by the usual course of judicial proceedings, the laws of the State within said counties, by reason whereof it has become necessary, in my judgment as Governor, to call forth and employ the

military force of the State to enforce the faithful execution of the law; and whereas, it has been made known to me as Governor that certain organizations and combinations of men exist in all the counties of the State, commonly known as 'rifle clubs;' and whereas, such organizations and combinations of men are illegal and strictly forbidden by the laws of this State; and whereas, such organizations and combinations of men are engaged in promoting illegal objects and in committing open acts of lawlessness and violence:

> Now, therefore, I, Daniel H. Chamberlain, Governor of said State, do issue this my proclamation . . . commanding . . . said unlawful combinations and assemblages of persons in the counties of Aiken and Barnwell to disperse . . . [and commanding] said organizations or combinations of men commonly known as 'rifle clubs' . . . forthwith to disband and cease to exist in any place and under any circumstances in the State."

Later on the same day, the Democratic State Executive Committee issued the following rebuttal to Chamberlain's accusative Proclamation:

> "The charges preferred by Governor Chamberlain against the citizens of the State are false and libelous as his threatened usurpation of power is tyrannical and unwarranted; and his extraordinary Proclamation can be explained only upon the assumption that Governor Chamberlain, with a similar disregard of law and fact, is determined to resort to the most extreme measures to prevent the otherwise certain defeat of himself and his corrupt Party.

> "There have been disturbances in Aiken County, non-political in their character. They have long since ceased . . . The disturbances in Barnwell were Republican in their origin, beginning in the resistance, by an armed band of [African Americans] of the arrest of a robber for whom a warrant had been duly issued. This band tore up a railroad, wrecked the train, fired upon and wounded the sheriff of the county . . . .

> "[European American men] throughout the State have volunteered their services to the Governor to maintain the law, and he has refused them . . . solely to furnish a pretext for the introduction of Federal troops to be placed under the control of irresponsible and unscrupulous officials, to overawe the people and control the election. . . . Its sole object is to irritate and provoke collisions which may be the excuse for an appeal to [the Federal Government] to garrison the State.

> "We shall counsel our people to preserve the peace, observe the laws and calmly await the day of their deliverance from this wanton despotism."

The Democrat rebuttal was quickly confirmed by telegrams from four Justices (Moses, Willard, Mackey and Cooke) declaring that no lawlessness existed beyond what could be handled through ordinary legal proceedings. The sheriffs of Aiken and Barnwell counties declared that they were in full control and needed no help.

Two days after the October 7 Proclamation and Democrat answer, Governor Chamberlain published an address to the people of the United States claiming that, "the lawlessness, terrorism and violence" in South Carolina, referred to two days earlier, in actuality "far exceeded in extent and atrocity any statements yet made public" and, therefore:

> "I pledge myself to the [people of the United States] to prove a condition of affairs in this State, produced by the Democratic Party, more disgraceful than any statement yet made by me, and I shall not stay my hand until punishment overtakes its guilty authors. My only offense is too great caution in obtaining evidence, and too great delay in exercising my utmost powers to protect [the citizens of South Carolina]."

Like clockwork, Ulysses Grant, issued his Proclamation on October 17, ordering Federal troops to enforce martial law in parts of South Carolina:

> "Whereas, It has been satisfactorily shown to me that insurrection and domestic violence exist in several counties of the State of South Carolina . . .

> "Whereas, The Legislature of said State is not now in session . . .

"Whereas, It is required that whenever it may be necessary, in the judgment of the President, to use the military force . . .

"Now, therefore, I, Ulysses S. Grant, President of the United States, do hereby make Proclamation and command all persons engaged in said unlawful and insurrectionary proceedings to disperse and retire peaceably to their respective abodes within three days from this date, and hereafter abandon said combinations and submit themselves to the laws and the constituted authorities of said State."

On that same day, William T. Sherman, commanding the indicated Federal troops, was ordered thusly:

"Sir: In view of the existing condition of affairs in South Carolina . . . you will immediately order all the available force in the Military Division of the Atlantic to report to General Ruger, commanding at Columbia, South Carolina, and instruct that officer to station his troops in such localities that they may be most speedily and effectually used, in case of resistance to the authority of the United States. . ."

South Carolina Democrat leaders fully realized that Republican imposition of martial law was a trap aimed at breaking the discipline among their State's European American population — a few acts of political violence was all that Republicans needed to gain control over the election. Just a few. Could the Democrat leadership of the State keep peace in the face of the many anticipated provocations? Democrats were united in attempting to achieve just that. And their savvy leader, Wade Hampton, was determined to do all he could to inspire a total attitude of compliance to martial law. Cool heads could be victorious. Passive resistance was acceptable, but active, overt resistance would play into Republican hands. Hampton sent telegrams to leadership in Barnwell and Aiken — "Urge our people to submit peaceably to martial law. I will see and consult with them." And to M. C. Butler — "Use your influence to keep our people in Aiken from resisting marital law."

The South Carolina Democratic Executive Committee published the following address to the people of the State on October 18 — formalizing the protest against the Republican Party's attempt to win the election by inciting racial violence (bottom up) to be stamped out by military means (top down) — yet firmly guiding European Americans to resist only peacefully and passively, all the while focusing on winning the election at the ballot box. Portions of the publication follow:

"To the people of the State of South Carolina who desire honest government, without regard to political party or race:

"His Excellency, the President of the United States, did, on the 17th day of this month, issue a Proclamation whereby he commanded "all persons engaged in unlawful and insurrectionary proceedings to disperse and retire peaceably . . .

"This Proclamation is based upon the statements made by Daniel H. Chamberlain, the Governor of this State; which statements are aimed exclusively against his political opponents and are proven to be untrue by the testimony of every Judge in the State . . .

"We say this much for our vindication: Never has a people suffered more by dishonor of office and dishonesty of officers. . . . Our State is but a petty portion of the [country], but we call upon our sister States of the North to remember that the experiment now being made for 'the domination of our elections by the bayonet and by soldiers as the irresistible instruments of a revolutionary local despotism,' if successful, will become the precedent before which the whole fabric of American liberty will fall, and will be applied to other States just as soon as Party exigencies require it. . . .

"We bow in perfect submission to the Proclamation of his Excellency the President, and exhort our fellow citizens whom we represent in the present canvass to yield full and entire obedience to every command of the said Proclamation. . . . [Yet we must affirm our innocence of the charges brought against us.]

"We are not engaged in 'unlawful and insurrectionary proceedings.' We cannot 'disperse' because we are not gathered together. We cannot 'retire peaceably to our abode,' because we are in our homes at peace, disturbed alone by the political agitations created by the Governor and his minions. But we resignedly — and cheerfully in the performance of our duty — suspend the exercise of our individual and private rights in order to prevent evil to the whole people.

"Relying upon the universal sense of right, and appealing to the Almighty to sustain us, we exhort our people to the continuance of submissions to the authorities of the Government, feeling sure that time and patience will work our deliverance."

Federal troops entered South Carolina in large numbers, "the whole force concentrated there being estimated at 5,000 men. Before the day of election, [there would be] a company or more at almost every county seat in the State.

Of this overt Republican provocation, historian John Reynold would surmise:

"There was no resistance — and none was ever thought of. The rifle clubs all disbanded — at least they ceased their drills, parades and other appearances in public. . . . The action of the President and the Governor served but to strengthen the determination of the [European Americans] to carry the State. It served also to bring over the doubtful and some in actual affiliation with the Republican Party. It is safe to say that not more than 1,000 [European Americans] voted for Chamberlain.

"The Federal officials were called into requisition. In Aiken and Barnwell [counties] there were upwards of 200 arrests — the parties being charged with violations of the Enforcement Act . . . There were some arrests in Edgefield, Pickens and Marion — the offense of the accused consisting in 'dividing time' at Republican meetings. The parties promptly gave bail. A few only of those arrested [would ever be] tried and these — citizens of Aiken County — [would not be] convicted. The jury [would fail] to agree."

"As the election approached, the activity of the Democrats increased — so that for some little time before the day fixed by law the [European Americans] of South Carolina did practically nothing but work for Hampton and his ticket. Stores were actually closed, farms were left almost to take care of themselves, and everybody went to work for the redemption of the State. 'Hurrah for Hampton' went out all over South Carolina, and in that slogan there was a ring of resolution that [foretold the end of African American] rule in this commonwealth."

Finally, on November 7, South Carolinians went to their respective polling places and cast their votes. The day "passed off without bloodshed and without serious beaches of the peace. Historian John Reynold would describe the event:

"The election machinery was practically in the control of the Republicans — two of the three managers at each polling-place being of their Party. At each poll there were two Federal supervisors — one from each political Party. At many county seats and at some other points there were [Federal] troops, but as their officers strictly obeyed the orders given them not to act except to preserve the peace there was not occasion for any of them to leave camp . . . for none of them was seen elsewhere.

"The [European American] Democrats worked with great activity during the entire day — their energies directed to having all their [African American] recruits vote without molestation from any source and to making votes among [men of that race] who had hitherto persisted in calling themselves Republicans. Efforts among the [African American] men were centered on the State and county tickets. Many [of that race] voted for Hayes and Hampton — this accounting for the fact that, whilst Hampton won, the Republicans got in their electoral ticket. In some of the lower counties [closer to the coast, African American] Democrats were subjected to threats and even assaults, and in Charleston County there were numerous act of intimidation and fraud."

The election returns were compiled slowly, with the apparent lead in the [races for Governor and President] switching several time. Two days after the election, on the 9th, Hampton was ahead by 2,974 votes. Ten days after the election, on the 17th, he was ahead by a much slimmer margin, 1,323, representing 50.4 percent of the votes cast.

Help from African American voters made possible Hampton's election. Historian John Reynold would analyze the election returns by county, comparing the majorities for Hampton or Chamberlain to their respective 1875 State census racial populations. African Americans were in the majority in 23 of the State's 32 counties. But 9 of those 23 counties gave Hampton vote majorities totaling 8,682. The 9

African-American-majority counties [for Hampton] were Abbeville, Aiken, Barnwell, Edgefield, Lancaster, Laurens, Marlboro, Union and York.

Of the other State offices, the results indicated that "Democrats elected the Secretary of State, the Attorney General and the Comptroller General, whilst the Republicans elected the Treasurer, the Superintendent of Education and the Adjutant-General."

Results indicated split control of the Legislature, the House to consist of 64 Democrats and 60 Republicans, the Senate to consist of 15 Democrats and 18 Republicans, giving Democrats a majority of 1 on joint ballot (important in electing a Federal Senator). The Senate was almost impossible to win for the Democrats because only half of the Senate seats had been up for election.

Regarding races for seats in the Federal House, Democrats managed to win 2 of the State's 5 — DemocratsWyatt Aiken and John Evins each winning by 58 to 42 percent majorities.

However, Governor Chamberlain was not about to give up without a more protracted fight. He expected help from the Republican partisans who controlled the election returns certification process throughout the State:

> South Carolina Republicans controlled the local, three-man Boards of Canvassers in each county and the Board of State Canvassers in Columbia. Governor Chamberlain had appointed all three men on each local board, giving Republicans undue influence there. The Board of State Canvassers was made up of "H. E. Hayne, Secretary of State; Francis Cardozo, Treasurer; T. C. Dunn, Comptroller-General; William Stone, Attorney-General; and H. W. Purvis, Adjutant and Inspector General" — all of them "active partisans for Governor Chamberlain, and three of them, Hayne, Cardozo and Dunn, constituting a majority of the board, were candidates for reelection."

Furthermore, for several more months, Chamberlain still had access to help from President Grant and aimed to take full advantage of that as well. Of such defiant schemes, historian John Reynold would write:

> "The Republican managers, including Governor Chamberlain, denied that the Democrats had won, and vehemently declared that there had been monstrous frauds and general intimidation."

Anticipating a continuing fight to secure the offices won at the polls, Hampton encouraged restraint in celebration and charitable feelings among all:

> "To the People of the State:

> "In offering to our people my heartfelt congratulations and gratitude for the grand victory they have won, I venture to beg them to prove themselves worthy of it by a continued observance of good order and a rigid preservation of peace. Let us show that we seek only the restoration of good government, the return of prosperity and the establishment of harmony to the whole people of the State.

> "In the hour of our victory we should be magnanimous, and we should strive to forget the animosities of the contest by recalling the grand results of our success. Proscribing none for difference of opinion, regarding none as enemies, save such as are inimical to law and order, let us all unite in the patriotic work of redeeming the State. By such conduct we can not only bring about good feeling among all classes, but can most surely reap the best fruits of victory." [R201;361-397]

Meanwhile, in the race for Governor of Louisiana, Democrat Francis Nicholls appeared to have won more votes than Republican Stephen Packard. You will recall that Packard, as Federal Marshal of New Orleans, had been a powerful leader among the Customhouse Faction of the Louisiana Republican Party — especially during the 1872 election — then being aligned with Ulysses Grant's brother-in-law, James Casey, Federal Collector of the New Orleans Port. Who was the Democrat, Francis Nicholls?

> Born in Louisiana in 1834, Francis Nichols received his primary schooling in New Orleans. He then attended the United States Military Academy at West Point, graduating in 1855. He fought the Seminoles in Florida for a while, but may have found that distasteful, for he resigned his commission after a year, returning home. He studied law in his home State and began a career as a

lawyer, practicing in Napoleonville. He joined the Confederate Army early in 1861 and fought at First Manassas and in the Shenandoah Valley, there receiving a wound that forced the amputation of his left arm. Nevertheless he advanced in rank to command a brigade of Louisiana infantry. Remaining in the defense of Virginia, Nichols was again wounded in May 1863 at the Battle of Chancellorsville, losing his left foot. At this point, being too disabled to continue in command, he returned west to direct the Volunteer and Conscript Bureau until the final defeat of the Confederacy. He then returned to Louisiana and resumed the practice of law. At this time in our history he had apparently won the election for Louisiana Governor.

But the Louisiana Republican Party and its candidate for Governor, Stephen Packard, would not concede defeat — in spite of a vote count that showed his opponent had outdistanced him by 8,000 votes. The Republican-controlled State Returning Board would examine the vote, allege irregularities and throw out votes here and there until they would be able to calculate that their man, Packard, was the winner. Both Packard and Nichols would be inaugurated and establish parallel and competing Louisiana State Governments. This conflict would remain until March of the following year, 1877.

Leaving South Carolina and Louisiana for a moment and looking across the remaining States, unofficial election results showed that, in the voting for Federal President, Democrat Samuel Tilden had won — receiving about 250,000 more popular votes and a comfortable majority of the electoral votes. But the results were close enough to be reversed by political manipulation in three former Confederate States. Horace Greeley's New York *Tribune* was so confident that New Yorker Samuel Tilden had won the election that it ran a huge headline: "Tilden Elected." But the New York *Times*, which had been transformed into a Republican newspaper, urged Rutherford Hayes and Republican Party leaders to refrain from conceding quite yet. Undoubtedly, the editors at the *Times* had performed some quick calculations and discovered that Republicans could order their officials in three former Confederate States to destroy enough Tilden ballots and stuff in enough fraudulent Hayes ballots to reverse the outcome of the election and exclude Tilden from the White House. It would take all the votes of those three States. That was a lot of fraudulent vote fixing, but Republican Political Machines still controlled the election process in South Carolina, Florida and Louisiana. Those three corrupt Republican Governments could steal the election for Hayes. [R19;420-421]

Meanwhile in Europe in mid-November, Jeff and Varina Davis decided to live apart for a while — she to stay behind to complete her recovery from illness in London and be closer to daughter Winnie's German school, and he to return to the lower Mississippi Valley to attend to urgent business demands. Accordingly, Jeff boarded the S. S. *Adriatic* in mid-November to return to New Orleans. He needed to be in Vicksburg on December 1 to meet with lawyers about foreclosure and ownership of his and Joseph's farmland along the Mississippi River. The Montgomery's were still making no progress in paying past-due mortgage payments on the farmland. Furthermore, Jeff needed to report bad news to members of the American branch of the Mississippi Valley Association. [R19;416]

Meanwhile in South Carolina, Republican leaders had contested the Democrat election majorities in Edgefield, Laurens and Barnwell counties — the majority of the population in each county being African American — and the State Democratic leadership had immediately involved the State Supreme Court in adjudicating the canvassing of the election returns. On November 14 the State Supreme Court heard arguments over the nature of the powers held by the Board of State Canvassers — to what extent were those powers administrative and to what extent were they judicial. Soon afterward, the Court ruled that the Board must show cause why they should not be limited to exercising only administrative powers, lest they be ruled in contempt of court. The order was served upon the Board and it resolved to obey it, but in fact proceeded to exercise unlawful judicial powers.

On November 21 the South Carolina Board of State Canvassers filed with the Court, "a certified statement of the persons who at the general election on the 7th had received the greatest number of votes for the offices for which they were respectively candidates, according to the statements of the boards of county canvassers, at the same time informing the Court that there were clerical errors in regard to T. C. Dunn and J. R. Tolbert, and that there were contests and protests from the counties of Barnwell, Edgefield and Laurens, on account of alleged irregularities, frauds and intimidation in said counties." The next day, "the Court commanded the Board of Canvassers forthwith to declare duly elected as Senators and Representatives the persons who, according to the Board's certified statement to the

Court, had received the greatest number of votes, and to deliver immediately a certified statement and declaration thereof to the Secretary of State" to be made official and to be published in newspapers. During that same day, the Board was in secret secession, changing the vote results and scheming to defy the Court order to show cause why it should exercise judicial powers. Historian John Reynold would describe what the Board did:

> "The Board on November 22 assembled, without the knowledge of any of the parties interested, corrected the alleged clerical errors in favor of Dunn and Tolbert, thereby reversing the certified aggregation of votes which they had submitted to the Court, and further failed to certify as elected the persons who in Edgefield and Laurens had received the greatest number of votes for seats in the General Assembly. . . . The Board next proceeded to declare elected all the Republican candidates for State offices (except Governor and Lieutenant-Governor) and then between the hours of 12, noon, and 1, afternoon, adjourned *sine die*."

The Supreme Court found the Board in contempt of court, fined each member $1,500, and ordered the Sheriff to place all 5 men in the Richland County jail, "to remain until the further order of the court," which was done.

Wade Hampton immediately thereafter issued a message "To the People of South Carolina:"

> "The Board of State Canvassers have by their unprecedented action today shown not only their contempt and defiance of the Supreme Court of the State, but their utter disregard of their own office and integrity. While the grave questions determining the results of the recent election were pending before the Supreme Court, composed of three judges belonging to the Republican Party, and in direct violation of the orders of this tribunal, the Board have issued Certificates of Election to the Republican Presidential Electors, and to Republican State officers, and have refused to give Certificates to Democratic members of the Legislature, shown by the returns of this same Board to have been elected in the counties of Edgefield and Laurens.

> "This high-handed outrage is well calculated to arouse the indignation of our long-suffering people, but I assure them that this daring and revolutionary act of the Board can have no force whatever. I appeal to you, therefore, in the fullest confidence that the appeal will not be unheeded, that you will maintain, even under these provocations, your character of an orderly and law-abiding people. During the late exciting political canvass you have studiously avoided even the semblance of a purpose to disturb the pubic peace or to transgress the law.

> "Your cause, and it is the cause of constitutional government in this country, has been carried to the highest court in the State, and we are willing to abide by its decision, feeling assured that this tribunal will see that the laws shall be enforced and justice succeed."

But Republicans appealed to Judge Hugh Bond in the Federal Circuit Court, which began its session in Columbia on November 27. "On the opening of the Federal Court, Hayne and others, constituting the Board of State Canvassers, petitioned Judge Bond for a *writ of habeas corpus*, commanding the Richland Sheriff to bring the prisoners before him on that day," to inquire of the cause of their detention and so forth. The Sheriff turned the 5 men over to the U. S. Marshall and arguments were heard by Judge Bond, much of the debate concerning State versus Federal jurisdiction over enforcement of State constitutional law. At the conclusion of arguments, Judge Bond discharged the prisoners from custody, ruling that, "it is competent for a Federal court to issue the *writ of habeas corpus*, in favor of prisoners for contempt by a State court, where the acts of alleged contempt were committed in the performance of duties created by the Constitution and laws of the United States, and the petitioners were acting under the protection of the laws and the courts of the United States," Although this did not totally resolve issues over who was, in fact, elected in disputed races, it did, as a practical matter, represent the end of legal attempts to define the legitimate election winners. [R201;397-407]

The political struggle now moved from the courts to the South Carolina Legislature, which opened on November 28. There, Republicans aimed to receive Legislative power from the Federal Troops requested by Governor Chamberlain on the 26th, immediately authorized by President Ulysses Grant and immediately communicated by J. D. Cameron, Secretary of War, to General Thomas H. Ruger, or Col. H. M. Black, responsible for Federal troops in Columbia:

"The following has been received from the President:

"Sir — D. H. Chamberlain is now Governor of the State of South Carolina beyond any controversy, and remains so until a new Governor shall be duly and legally inaugurated under the Constitution. The [Federal] Government has been called upon to aid with the military and naval forces of the United States to maintain republican government in the State against resistance too formidable to be overcome by the State authorities. You are directed, therefore, to sustain Governor Chamberlain in his authority against domestic violence until otherwise directed."

"U. S. Grant."

Cameron further instructed Ruger and Black: "In obeying these instructions you will advise with the Governor, and dispose of your troops in such a manner as may be deemed best in order to carry out the spirit of the above order of the President."

Accordingly, "On the demand of Governor Chamberlain, General Ruger, at midnight before the day for the meeting of the Legislature, placed a company of [Federal] infantry in the State House. Most of these troops were stationed on the upper floor, about midway between the door of the Senate chamber and that of the Hall of the House. A sentinel was posted at each of the doors opening into the first floor of the building — north, east, south, west."

Shortly before noon, the stage was set for the confrontation at the doorway into the Hall of the House on the second floor of the State Capitol building. Federal soldiers, armed with loaded rifles with bayonets fixed, guarded the doorway and protected John Dennis, who had been appointed by Governor Chamberlain to admit all elected Representatives except for Democrats from Edgefield and Laurens counties, whose presence would have given control of the House to the Democratic Party. The Republican Representatives promptly arrived as a group and gained entrance to the Hall.

"The Republican members-elect, numbering 59, assembled in the Hall and proceeded to organize themselves as the House of Representatives. They elected E. W. M. Mackey [as] Speaker" and other Republicans to the other offices."

Shortly afterward, "The Democratic members-elect, numbering 64, proceeded in a body to the Hall of the House, the Edgefield Delegation in front and the Laurens men coming next. When the head of the column reached the door, the Edgefield members demanded admittance, at the same time presenting the certified copy (made by the Clerk of the Supreme Court) of the State Canvassers' report of the vote in that county for members of the House, showing that the bearers had each received a majority of the votes cast. Dennis, supported on each side by [a Federal infantryman], refused to recognize these certificates as lawful credentials and forbade the holders to enter. Thereupon the Democratic members retired, leaving one of their number to observe for a time the doings of the Mackey body. Shortly after this [Wade] Hampton and A. C. Haskell approached the House door and demanded to be admitted as spectators" and were refused. Then the Federal troops "were marched to the Hall door, made to open ranks and face inward . . . with loaded rifles and bayonets fixed . . . . The troops had thus taken actual possession of the Hall of the House."

A leader of the barred Democrat Representatives, before they retired, made a formal protest of their maltreatment, in part alleging, "We, a majority of the House of Representatives elect, protest against the refusal to admit us to the Hall of Representatives. We protest against the military power of the United States barring [our] passage . . . . [Yet] it is our purpose to offer no resistance to this armed intervention, but to make our solemn appeal to the American people without distinction of Party. . . . "

Outside, "an immense crowd had assembled in front of the State House," giving rise to urgent concerns that those men might storm the building. Wade Hampton took immediate action, appearing on the front steps and addressing the angry crowd:

"My friends: I am truly doing what I have done earnestly during this whole exciting contest, pouring oil on the troubled waters. It is of the greatest importance to us all, as citizens of South Carolina, that peace should be preserved. I appeal to you all, [of both races], as Carolinians, to use every effort to keep down violence or turbulence. One act of violence may precipitate bloodshed and desolation. I implore you, then, to preserve the peace. I beg all of my friends to disperse, to leave the grounds of the State House, and I advise all the [African Americans] to do the same. Keep perfectly quiet, leave the streets, and do nothing to provoke a riot. We trust to the law and the Constitution, and we have perfect faith in the justness of our cause."

Historian John Reynold would report that, in response, "the crowd promptly and quietly dispersed."

Meanwhile, the Democratic Representatives-elect, as a body, walked to Carolina Hall, located diagonally in the rear of the Richland County Courthouse, and there organized and elected William H. Wallace as Speaker. Defections from the Republican House — which I will be calling the "Mackey House" — began immediately, although slowly. J. W. Westberry of Sumter and W. H. Reedish of Orangeburg, both African American, deserted Mackey and were "duly sworn in" to the Democratic House. Two days later two European Americans deserted Mackey and would be likewise sworn in. After this the struggle would become rather comical:

> "In the [Republican-controlled] House of which Mackey claimed to be Speaker, resolutions [would soon be] adopted which purported to unseat the Democratic members elected from Abbeville, Aiken and Barnwell and seat the Republican claimants. These latter [would be] duly sworn in — including an [African American] personating Silas Cave, of Barnwell. A few days later Cave [would] himself [turn] up, and he too [would be] solemnly sworn in."

While these shenanigans transpired in the Hall of the South Carolina House, a similar tug had been going on in the Senate Chambers. The only difference was in the numbers — since only half of the Senate seats had been up for election, Republicans had retained a legitimate majority. Nevertheless, Republicans had refused to allow the Democrat Senators from Edgefield and Laurens counties to be seated. This was likewise protested. In the Senate, the contest was over which House of Representatives body constituted the body with which the Senate was to coordinate legislative activity — the Mackey House or the Wallace House.

Arriving early on November 30, the Democrat Representatives surprised the door-keepers at the Hall of the State House and swarmed in authorities or troops realized what was happening. They were already in seats and conducting business before the Republican Representatives arrived according to their appointed starting time. This set the stage for a struggle within the Hall of the House, on the second floor of the Capitol building. "Mackey ascended the stand and demanded that Speaker Wallace should vacate his chair. The latter refused and made a brief statement of his claims as the presiding officer of the lawful House." Sergeants-at-arms of both bodies advanced and the danger of bloodshed seemed eminent. At this point, Thomas H. Ruger, commander of the Federal troops in Columbia, began to backpeddle and recant his enforcement of Republican exclusion of targeted Democrats. He sent a dispatch to Washington City, addressed to William T. Sherman or the Secretary of War, dated December 1, stating that he and his men had "carefully abstained from interference with the organization of the [South Carolina] House from the first. . . ." A Committee was appointed to negotiate issues and violence was avoided on December 1, 2 and 3 as both bodies remained in the Hall day and night to avoid either being locked out. Violence was being avoided, but perhaps only because Republicans were cooking up a plot to bring up from Charleston about 100 rough-and-tough African American men, collectively known as the "Hunkidori Club" and get them into the Hall of the House with secret orders to physically throw out the Representatives from Edgefield and Laurens counties. Historian John Reynold would describe the "Hunkidori Club" plot:

> "The plan, as arranged by Governor Chamberlain, was to appoint these [African American] roughs to be Sergeants-at-Arms of the House, each wearing a badge which should be concealed till the time should come to consummate the bloody scheme. Members of the Mackey body were to retire and their places to be filled by the roughs — the badges of the latter still concealed — and others of these were to be admitted to the floor of the House. When arrangements should be completed the roughs were to expose their badges and Mackey was to demand the retirement of the Edgefield and Laurens members. Refusal to retire was to be met by force, and resistance was to be overcome by the immediate intervention of the Federal troops waiting just outside the Hall."

But the plot became known to Democrats and an alarm was sent out across the State "requesting the presence in Columbia of armed [European American] men" in large numbers. And they quickly came. "By Monday morning quite 2,000 had come to Columbia, and there were additions by every [arriving] train — so that by Monday night the number assembled had reached 5,000. They were all well armed and were in most instances organized by counties into companies, each commanded by a head officer." It was decided that, in response to any forceful action taken to violently remove Democrat Representatives should that occur, the first Republican deaths would be Mackey and Chamberlain.

But cooler heads prevailed, and, on the morning of December 4, the Wallace House voluntarily left the Hall of the Representatives and resumed its legislative obligations at Carolina Hall, recognizing that the State Constitution only required that it do its work in Columbia, any building in the city being equally acceptable. Men of the "Hunkidori Club" were sent back to Charleston.

At this point the State Supreme Court became again involved:

"Proceedings were taken in the Supreme Court to have that tribunal decide which of the two bodies, each claiming to be the House of Representatives, was the lawful House. The specific object of the proceedings, brought against H. E. Hayne, as Secretary of State, and E. W. M. Mackey, [as so-called Speaker], was to compel the delivery to Speaker Wallace of the returns of the vote for Governor and Lieutenant Governor — this in order that the lawful House and the Senate might ascertain and declare the result of the election for those two offices."

"On December 6, after full argument, the Supreme Court decided that 'William H. Wallace is the legal speaker of the lawfully-constituted House of Representatives of the State of South Carolina, and, as such officer, was and is entitled to the possession of the returns of the election for Governor and Lieutenant Governor'."

But it seemed that D. H. Chamberlain was one step ahead of the State Supreme Court. The previous day, December 5, the Republican members of the Senate (except for Mr. Cochran of Anderson) repaired to the Hall of the House, where they and the Mackey body, [acting in joint session,] went through the form of aggregating and declaring the vote for Governor and Lieutenant Governor. The votes of Edgefield and Laurens [counties] having been thrown out, the results were declared as Chamberlain, 86,216, and Hampton, 83,071 — Chamberlain the winner. The following day, December 7, the Republican Senators (except Cochran of Anderson) "joined the Mackey body for the purpose of inaugurating Daniel H. Chamberlain as Governor." Chamberlain immediately delivered his acceptance address, which began in a civil manner:

"Gentlemen of the Senate and House of Representatives:

"I accept the office to which by the voice of a majority of the people of this State I have a second time been called . . . ."

But his address quickly digressed into a long-winded and defiant tirade against his political enemies.

He "was then 'sworn in' by the Probate Judge of Richland County."

That night Wade Hampton delivered an address in which he again counseled peaceful behavior, but revealed a backbone that was becoming stridently tested. Believing that a Military Governor, appointed by the Federal President, would be preferable to Chamberlain and his shenanigans, "it was in this speech that Wade Hampton said:

'The people have elected me Governor, and, by the Eternal God, I will be Governor or we shall have a Military Governor'."

During these weeks, news of the political struggle in South Carolina had been widely reported and, in early December, two Investigating Committees, one from the Federal House and another from the Federal Senate, had come to the State to investigate the votes, the court actions and the allegations. And this attention from outside the State was working to discredit Chamberlain and his supporters and to vindicate Hampton and the Democrats. The tide was turning. The Federal troops no longer backed Chamberlain's schemes. And, in obedience to the State Supreme Court order, the Secretary of State gave Democrats the certified election returns. Historian John Reynold would describe the situation:

"In the House of Representatives on December 10 a concurrent resolution was adopted and sent to the Senate, fixing December 14 as the day for tabulating the returns of the vote for Governor and Lieutenant Governor, declaring the election, and inaugurating the two officers-elect."

On that day, upon a certified statement of the Secretary of State, made up of the returns of the Commissioners of Election in the several counties (including Edgefield and Laurens) the vote for Governor and Lieutenant Governor was ascertained and declared as follows:

Wade Hampton, Democrat	92,261
D. H. Chamberlain, Republican	91,127
William D. Simpson, Democrat	91,689
R. Howell Gleaves, Republican	91,150

Inauguration ceremonies were to be conducted outdoors, on a wooden platform, in front of Carolina Hall, to accommodate the huge crowd expected. "The platform was beautifully decorated with wreaths and garlands of flowers and evergreens, among which was plainly seen the [United States flag] as well as the State flag. As [Wade] Hampton came upon the platform he was received with a volume of cheers that indicated both the extent and the enthusiasm of the welcome." The "crowd filled the lot in front of the building and extended down neighboring streets. People watched from windows and roof tops. . . . The Columbia Flying Artillery fired their guns, having renamed their battery the 'Hampton Saluting Club'." Then the crowd became silent as Hampton began to speak:

"It is with feelings of profoundest solicitude that I assume the arduous duties and grave responsibilities of the high position to which the people of South Carolina have called me. It is amid events unprecedented in this republic that I take the chair as Chief Magistrate of this State. After years of misrule, corruption and anarchy, brought upon us by venal and unprincipled political adventurers, the honest people of the State, without regard to Party or race, with one voice demanded reform and with one purpose devoted themselves earnestly and solemnly to this end. . . ."

Following introductory remarks, Hampton presented a detailed account of the struggles of the campaign, of the unconstitutional imposition of Federal troops across the State and even into the Hall of the House of Representatives and of the other efforts to deny Democrats the victories they had won at the ballot box. This sad saga, he argued, represented a threat to American's liberties in every State, not just South Carolina. And he admonished that maintaining a strong bulwark against such threats is every man's duty. Specifically, he submitted:

"Our duty, the duty of every patriot, is to demand a strict construction of the [Federal] Constitution and a rigid adherence to its provisions. We can only thus preserve our liberties and government."

Advancing toward a close of his address before the exuberant crowd, Hampton turned to the promises made during the campaign and how he intended to keep them — all of them.

"A great task is before the Conservative Party of this State. They entered on this contest with a Platform so broad, so strong, so liberal, that every honest citizen could stand upon it. They recognized and accepted the Amendments of the [Federal] Constitution in good faith; they pledged themselves to work reform and to establish good government; they promised to keep up an efficient system of public education; and they declared solemnly that all citizens of South Carolina, of both races and of both parties, should be regarded as equals in the eye of the law; all to be protected in the enjoyment of every political right now possessed by them.

"To the faithful observance of these pledges we stand committed, and I, as the representative of the Conservative Party, hold myself bound by every dictate of honor and of good faith to use every effort to have these pledges redeemed fully and honestly. It is due not only to ourselves but to the [African Americans] of the State that wide, just and liberal measures should prevail in our Legislation. We owe much of our late success to these [African American] voters who were brave enough to rise above the prejudice of race and honest enough to throw off the shackles of Party in their determination to save the State. To those who, misled by their fears, their ignorance, or by evil counseling, turned a deaf ear to our appeals, we should not be vindictive but magnanimous. Let us show to all of them that the true interests of both races can best be secured by cultivating peace and promoting prosperity among all classes of our fellow citizens. I rely confidently on the support of the members of the [State House and State Senate] in my efforts to attain these laudable ends, and I trust that all branches of [our State] Government will unite cordially in this patriotic work. If so united, and working with resolute will and earnest determination, we may hope soon to see the dawn of a brighter day for our State.

"God in His infinite mercy grant that it may come speedily, and may He shower the richest blessings of peace and happiness on our whole people."

Judge Thomas Mackey administered the oath of office, followed by cheers and another report from the "Hampton Saluting Club." William Simpson was next sworn in as Lieutenant Governor. At that point the celebration erupted with greater enthusiasm:

"As Governor Hampton was about to retire he was taken by four young men, placed in a chair and by them borne to his hotel — the people following in a rush and cheering as they went. The cry 'Hurrah for Hampton' was stronger and more significant than ever."

But D. H. Chamberlain steadfastly refused to step down. South Carolina would be going through many weeks of a "Dual Government," a tug for control that would take too many pages in this history if described in detail. So for a while, only the highlights will be presented. [R201;397-430, R199;256]

Meanwhile, Jeff Davis, being focused on politics and commerce in Mississippi and Louisiana and on efforts to retain his farms, was perhaps not as aware of the astounding events taking place in South Carolina as he might otherwise have been. During late November and early December he had been busy with business issues and deliberations about what he ought to do with the rest of his life. He had arrived in Memphis in late November and had been happy to see his married daughter, Margaret and his college-age son Jeff, Jr. Both had "found their father looking better than they had seen him since the [retreat from besieged Richmond]." Meeting with lawyers in Vicksburg, Jeff had learned, once again, that the Montgomery's claimed they had not made enough money in 1876 to enable them to pay even a little on the past-due Mississippi farmland mortgage. So again, Jeff had no expectations for income from that mortgage, prompting further talk of foreclosure proceedings directed at reclaiming the Davis farms. On the evening of December 9, from New Orleans, Jeff would write Varina, in London, concerning their financial problems. Two men mentioned in the letter need to be introduced — Dr. J. H. D. Bowmar was "a close family friend in Vicksburg" who had been helping Jeff by observing progress or lack thereof at the two Davis Bend farms — Robert Boyle, of Memphis, was a past official at Carolina Insurance Company "to whom Jeff had turned over money to lend at safe interest," who would soon be forced into bankruptcy.

"Mr. Bowmar had mismanaged affairs [concerning our farms] at Davis Bend so as to postpone, it may be to lose, a part of what was due [to us from] there. After a while we shall get something, now little if anything. Robert Boyle will pay just as much as we can force out of him, no more, and nothing can be obtained at present. Now having told you the worst, I have to add 'be not dismayed, we will get through,' provided you get well and return in cheerfulness."

Earlier in that same day, Jeff Davis had reported to the Board of the Mississippi Valley Society of New Orleans on his earlier efforts in London to move forward with expanded trade in and out of the Port of New Orleans. Jeff had been compelled to deliver bad news. He related the Board's disappointment in the same evening letter previously mentioned:

"I came to New Orleans to report to the Board of the Mississippi Valley Society and have just returned from a meeting. They listened to my statement and were disappointed rather than indignant at the tergiversation which I had to relate."

"The tergiversation" was the British Board's avoidance of decisions or firm action by **roundabout ways**. The British had been unable to arrange financing, and only offered a little hope for later financing through some new "Trust and Loan Company." But Davis had confessed to the New Orleans Board that he was very pessimistic over ever receiving that financing. In fact, Jeff Davis was ordering his life on the assumption that the Mississippi Valley Society was a dying organization.

In this same evening letter to Varina, Jeff also expressed great concern over Republican ballot stuffing in Louisiana, aimed at stealing the election for Rutherford Hayes, as he wrote of the frantic ballot fraud that was taking place all around him:

"The excitement over the fraud in counting the vote in Louisiana is intense here, but they have become accustomed to injustice and will suffer long."

Perhaps that "injustice" and "long-suffering" was also propelling Jeff Davis to trim his financial requirements and find a quiet place to complete his life's work — a quiet place to write the true and factual history of the Confederate States of America. He told Varina as much near the end of his December 9 letter from New Orleans:

"I do not know how long will be my stay here and have nothing definite in view unless the Trust and Loan Company be organized, except to join W. L. Walthall at Mobile and push forward the 'Memoirs'."

The "Memoirs'." Yes, the history of the Confederacy — *The Rise and Fall of the Confederate Government*." [R19;419, R30;439, R149;597]

Now preserving the true and factual history of the Confederate Government was Davis' most important mission. He understood that and Varina did as well. Yet, it would be an uphill battle, because the Republican Party was intent on destroying Confederate truth and facts in every way possible. And the Republican Party still held immense power. But Jeff realized his work had to be done. And Hudson Strode, historian and Davis biographer, would certainly appreciate those efforts at preserving the true and factual history, for without factual resource materials historians of his time, and or our time as well, would be reduced to far too much guess-work. Of the decision to begin on the history, Strode would write:

"Davis had really reached the end of his row. He would start work on his book. [W. L.] Walthall was ready and eagerly waiting. Appletons, the New York publishers, were prepared to pay advances for Walthall's assistance. But where was Davis to find the quiet place in which to write?"

Jeff Davis inspected his beach-front lots near Mississippi City again on December 10, and he hired a man to clear out some of the underbrush. He thought about building a small cottage on the property where he could write, but made no immediate moves to talk with a builder. This time Sarah Dorsey was at her beach-house, *Beauvoir*, about 5 miles to the east, so Jeff visited her. As he looked for a place to write, he was surely feeling drawn to this coastal Mississippi beach. He returned to Sarah Dorsey's beach-house in mid-December for a more extended visit. At that point Sarah invited him to consider writing his book at her "east pavilion-cottage," which was situated very near her main beach house. The cottage was a square, hip-roofed building with a pillared porch on all four sides and one large room in the middle. Sarah suggested that she could have the back porch of the cottage enclosed to make a small bedroom and a dressing room. She also offered to have the wall of the main room lined with bookshelves. Furthermore, she offered to have her servants provide meals and laundry service. Sarah was most eager that Jeff accept her offer to write his book at *Beauvoir* and Jeff was delighted over the invitation. But he insisted that Sarah charge him room and board and asked if she could find a spot for Robert Brown, an African American who had long served him and wanted to leave Memphis and join him at the beach. Sarah agreed that would be fine. She suggested $50 per month for both men. Then Sarah offered, for a certain number of hours each day, to help with the tedious job of copying documents and marked-up edits in longhand script. Jeff was to receive amanuensis services to boot!

Jeff had known Sarah since she was a child, for she had been a girlhood friend of Varina and had often visited Joseph's farm, Hurricane. Her father had been a wealthy farmer. The main family farm was in Louisiana, but he also had farms in Mississippi and Arkansas. He had maintained a house in Natchez, and it was there that Sarah and Varina had played together as girls. Sarah had gone to England for her final schooling, and had made friends among prominent British families during those years. She had married Samuel Dorsey who had been working on one of the family farms as a supervisor until his death a few months earlier. Samuel was from a respected Maryland family, and had done a splendid job of managing the farms after the death of Sarah's father. Sarah had strongly supported the Confederacy and had "stoutly upheld the Confederate cause in London drawing rooms" during an extended stay in 1871. She corresponded with numerous prominent people, including people in Britain and in India. Furthermore, she had written four books which had been published under the pen name of Filia. With the recent death of her husband, Sarah had decided to simplify her life by settling down at the beach, and by inviting a cousin, Mrs. Cochran, to live there with her. Mrs. Cochran was also an old friend of Jeff and Varina. And Jeff loved Sarah's beach house and the surrounding grounds, as biographer Hudson Strode would describe:

"When Davis arrived at *Beauvoir* as a guest in mid-December he was again struck by its pervading peace. The immediate grounds were extensive, shaded by magnolias, cedars, and live oaks draped in pale gray moss. The sea stretched before the house and a large orange grove lay behind it. Beyond were pine woods traversed by a clear brook, its banks a tangle of bay, wild azalea, sweet olive, and yellow jasmine. Then came 6 acres of scuppernong vineyards and beyond those the Louisville and Nashville Railroad cut through the property. Across the tracks stretched a virgin forest of long-leaf pine, which belonged to the 600 acre [property]." [R19;419-422]

Meanwhile in Washington City, for the past 2 weeks the political crisis had escalated because Democrats, for good reasons, continued to earnestly believe that Republicans had been and continued to be conspiring to steal the election for President by manipulating the vote counts in Florida, Louisiana and South Carolina, as well as to win a small technical question involving gaining one Elector in Oregon. If only one of these vote counts could be awarded to the Democrat — even the one vote in Oregon — then Tilden would be elected. Of this political fight biographer Edward Mayes would write:

"With such an array of chances in favor of the Democrats it was natural that they should be much elated, and that the Republicans should be greatly alarmed and aroused to strenuous efforts to save their imperiled power. Early in November, an eager and passionate discussion of the situation [had begun], which increased in bitterness as the weeks passed by. Party was arrayed against Party, and again the division was dangerously sectional. The Republicans denounced the Democratic majorities in [Florida, Louisiana and South Carolina] as the criminal results of fraud and intimidation. The Democrats, on the other hand, denounced the returns made [by Republican officials] from those States as a fraudulent reversal of the popular vote, made by corrupt conspiracies and sustained by an illegal and oppressive use of the bayonet in the interest of Faction."

A detailed review of the vote count tallies of Florida, Louisiana, South Carolina and Oregon is appropriate, because if the votes were accepted as being for Democrat Tilden in any of these situations, or more likely, if the vote of any of the four States was thrown out, Republican Hayes would be defeated and Tilden inaugurated. The account below is quoted from biographer Edward Mayes:

Florida, 4 votes: "The [Republican-controlled] "Returning Board," against a small popular majority, declared Republican Electors chosen and those Electors voted for Hayes and Wheeler; but at the same time the Democratic Electors voted for Tilden and Hendricks. The [Republican] Governor had duly forwarded the Republican votes under a proper certificate. At the same election [in November], however, State officers had been chosen [by Florida voters], and as a result thereof a Democratic Governor and Legislature came into office. Thereupon, in January a statute was passed requiring a new canvass of the popular vote, and that canvas resulted in a declaration of the election of the Democratic Electors. The new Democratic Governor then forwarded a proper certificate that the vote of Florida had been cast for Tilden and Hendricks."

Louisiana, 8 votes: "There were also conflicting certificates: one in favor of Hayes and Wheeler from [Republican] W. P. Kellogg, claiming to be Governor, and acting as such; the other from [Democrat John] McEnery, also claiming to be Governor of the State, in favor of Tilden and Hendricks."

South Carolina, 7 votes: "The [Republican] Governor, [D H Chamberlain], certified Hayes and Wheeler votes, while certain persons claiming to have been duly chosen as Presidential Electors certified their own votes in favor of Tilden and Hendricks, and also certified the facts upon which they claimed that the withholding from them by the Governor and the Secretary of State of the customary and regular certificates was wrongful and illegal."

Oregon, 3 votes: "From Oregon also appeared two conflicting certificates: one by the Governor certifying 3 Hayes and Wheeler votes and one by the Governor certifying two Hayes and Wheeler votes and one for Tilden and Hendricks; the point at issue being, in its essence, that one of the electors chosen by the Republican majority was disqualified to hold the office, wherefore it devolved upon his Democratic competitor."

Summation: "The decision of any one of these 4 contentions in favor of the Democrats" — involving 20 votes of the total of 369 — "would have [elected] Tilden, while the Republicans needed to prevail in all in order to [elect] Hayes." [R205;291]

Lucius Lamar was immediately thrown into the thick of the political fray because he held a leadership position in the Federal House. Biographer James Murphy would describe the political conflict as the Federal House and Senate gathered to open respective sessions in early December:

"Lamar traveled into the crisis atmosphere which hung over Washington in December. Party spirit bred tension and divided the capital into political war camps. Republicans adamantly maintained that the electoral vote in [Florida, Louisiana and South Carolina] belonged to Hayes. Democrats were just as convinced that Tilden had been elected and that the Republicans would unjustly refuse to honor the popular mandate.

"Democratic Party solidarity broke down under the pressure and gave way to bitter division. The northern [States] wing generally opposed compromise, and some of its members threatened armed resistance as a last alternative to defeat. The southern [States] wing, chastened by defeat in war, counseled a more moderate course. . . . Many men, including Lamar, thought the danger of civil conflict to be real, and this conviction [would weigh] heavily upon [Representatives and Senators] during the [upcoming] days of decision."

The Federal Constitution gave the House and Senate the authority to pass judgment on the election of Electors to the Electoral College, which meant that Congress was responsible for deciding disputed vote tallies. The Constitution defined that responsibility with the following words:

"The President of the Senate shall, in the presence of the Senate and House of Representatives, open all the Certificates, and the vote shall then be counted."

Simple enough; but what about disputes between two versions of the count from a State such as Florida? What body was to rule when two competing Certificates were presented? The Senate was expected to favor the Republican Electors and the House was expected to favor the Democrat Electors, except where individuals would buck the respective Party lines and seek to find the truth of the issue — unlikely to occur often. If the Senate and House would fail to agree on a Certificate from a State, the validity of the election would suffer grave damage and threaten the authority of the Federal Government. As you learned from *Bloodstains*, Volume 2, *The Demagogues*, The Federal Invasion of the Confederacy had essentially been a war between Republicans, who controlled the northern States and Democrats, who controlled the southern States, consisting of Delaware, Maryland, Kentucky, Missouri and all States to the south out to Texas. Memory of the horrible destruction of that political war moved most Democrats from the Southern States to seek a political compromise without force of arms. But many Democrats from the northern States, having suffered far less from the past war, were insistent on proving that the Republican vote manipulations in Florida, South Carolina and Louisiana were fraudulent, thereby giving the victory to Tilden. Although appearing the weaker Faction on the surface, Democrats from the southern States were seeking a prize of great value, a concession from the next Administration — whether led by Hayes or Tilden — to remove Federal Troops from their region, stop supporting corrupt Republican State Governments in their region and accept unmolested Home Rule. If Hayes would agree to demands by southern States for unmolested Home Rule, Democrats from those States, including Lucius Lamar and Wade Hampton, were willing to allow the Republican Party to hold the office of Federal President for 4 more years. Negotiations on the part of political leaders from the southern States involved such strategy.

Lucius Lamar was Chairman of the Democratic Party Caucus in the Federal House, which deliberated in early December on the course to be taken. Logically, Lamar's opinions on the issue were sought. In an interview on December, 10 he said he believed the Federal Constitution provided a path for resolving the political conflict. If the Senate and House refused to agree on selecting among competing vote certificates, then both should "immediately proceed in their respective duties — [the House] to elect the President and the [Senate] to elect the Vice President. Let the Constitution be maintained inviolate, and there need be no disorganizing collisions and no necessity for resorting to force." Lamar was referring to the following language in the Federal Constitution:

". . . If no person have a majority, then from the 5 highest on the list, the said House shall in like manner choose the President. But in choosing the President, the votes shall be taken by States, the representation from each State having one vote; a quorum for this purpose shall consist of a member or members from two thirds of the States, and a majority of all the States shall be necessary to a choice. In every case, after the President, the person having the greatest number of votes of the Electors shall be the Vice President. But, if there should remain two or more who have equal votes, the Senate shall choose from them by ballot the Vice President."

So, we see that at this time in American history, the above procedure would have equalized the Electoral power of small population States and large population States.

On December 11 a Joint House-Senate Committee on Electoral College Issues was formed in Congress. The Joint Committee elected Lucius Lamar as Chairman. Concerning this responsibility, biographer James Murphy would write, "From this vantage point [Lamar] saw that the impasse would not be resolved through any such simplistic application of established law as he had suggested." No progress was immediately made and Christmas recess began on December 19. [R206;164-166, R205;290-293]

Meanwhile in South Carolina, the Hampton Administration was pressing to take the reigns of government. On December 15 Lieutenant Governor W. D. Simpson notified the State Senate by letter, "I respectfully announce to you that as Lieutenant Governor I am present in the city of Columbia and am prepared to discharge the duties of . . . President of the Senate;" said letter being, upon receipt, intentionally buried in the Senate Judiciary Committee. On December 18 Governor Wade Hampton notified the "Executive Chamber" by letter, "Sir: As Governor of South Carolina, chosen by the people thereof, I have qualified in accordance with the Constitution, and I hereby call upon you as my predecessor in office to deliver up to me the great seal of the State, together with the possession of the State House, the public records, and all other matters and things appertaining to said office." D. H. Chamberlain quickly replied by letter, "I do not recognize in you any right to make the foregoing demand, and I hereby refuse compliance therewith." So Republicans, in control of the Governor's office and the State Senate, refused to turn power over to Hampton and Simpson. But Democrats controlled the State House and, on December 20, proceeded to join with the Democratic Senators and, voting as a joint body, did elect Democrat Matthew Butler to the Federal Senate by a vote of 64 out of a total of 79.

With regard to raising money to finance the Democrat-controlled Government of South Carolina, a workable plan quickly emerged, taking advantage of the overwhelming support from the citizens who actually paid the taxes. "The House of Representatives authorized Governor Hampton to call upon the taxpayers to contribute each a sum not exceeding one-fourth of the tax last paid — the amount so contributed to be deducted from the contributor's tax as fixed by the levy to be made by the Legislature when the Senate should recognize the authority of the lawful House and the lawful Governor." Splendid idea! Hampton reduced the contribution to 10 percent and the money rolled in. What about money to pay for government printing? The Presbyterian Publishing House in Columbia offered to print everything needed on credit.

In response, Republicans engaged in a futile attempt to persist as a political body of significance, although they were without money to pay for their actions. The Republican House, hoping to destroy Hampton and others with huge fines and imprisonment, combined with the Senate to pass "a bill to prevent and punish any person or persons for setting up, or attempting to set up, or maintaining a government of the State in opposition to the legitimate and lawful government of the State," imposing fines of up to $100,000 and imprisonment up to 40 years. Striving to elect a Federal Senator by so-called "joint ballot," and encouraged by promises of $20,000 in bribe money, Republican Senators and Representatives "elected" David T. Corbin to that Federal office. All of it was a sordid affair, what might be expected as the final act of corrupt rule by the Republican Party in South Carolina. The Republican (Mackey) House adjourned *sine die* on December 22, the same day as did the lawful Senate and the lawful House. [R201;430-435]

Meanwhile in Washington City, Lucius Lamar and Thomas Bayard of the Federal Senate paid a visit on Samuel Tilden in hopes of gaining an understanding of the candidate's intentions to assert his right to be named the winner of the election for President. Would Tilden actively engage in securing the office to which he had been apparently elected or would he quietly sit back and let others deal with the controversy over the vote count in Florida, South Carolina and Louisiana? Of this meeting, biographer James Murphy would write:

> "The meeting did nothing to resolve the dilemma. Tilden presented no plan of action and gave no indication of his intentions. Lamar must have returned deeply shaken in his hope for a peaceful Democratic inauguration. Without leadership from the Party's candidate, a catastrophic debacle was likely. In light of Tilden's earlier rejection of . . . advice to meet with Hayes, this interview offered anything but reassurance." [R206;166-167]

From South Carolina, Wade Hampton sent letters dated December 23 to both Hayes and Tilden, the apparent intent of both being to signal that Democrats in South Carolina were focused on securing political control over State and local government, leaving to authorities at the Federal level the question of whether South Carolina's vote for President should be credited to Hayes or Tilden. In other words, support our victory securing home rule, and we will cooperate with a Hayes Administration, even if empowered by fraudulent manipulation of the vote count in South Carolina. The copy sent to Hayes said, in part:

> "To His Excellency, R. B. Hayes, Governor of Ohio:

> "My Dear Sir — I have the honor to enclose a copy of my inaugural as the duly elected Governor of South Carolina. . . . [Furthermore,] I deem it proper to declare that profound peace prevails throughout the State, that the course of judicial proceedings is obstructed by no combination of citizens thereof, and that the laws for the protection of the inhabitants in all their rights of person, property and citizenship are being enforced in our courts. . . . The people of this State . . . have such faith in the justice of their cause that they propose to leave its vindication to the proper legal tribunals, appealing at the same time to the patriotism and public sentiment of the whole country. . . . [Regarding the contest for Federal President,] it is their firm and deliberate purpose to condemn any solution of the existing political problem that involves the exhibition of armed force, or that moves through any other channel than the prescribed forms of the [Federal] Constitution, or the peaceful agencies of law.

> "Trusting that a solution may be had which, while maintaining the peace of the country, shall do no violence to the constitutional safeguards of popular rights, and will tend still further to unite the people of all the States in an earnest effort to preserve the peace and sustain the laws and the Constitution, I am, very respectfully, your obedient servant,

> > "Wade Hampton,
> > "Governor of South Carolina.

> "P. S. — As the settlement of the vexed political questions which now agitate the public mind must ultimately depend upon yourself or upon your distinguished competitor for the Presidency, I have addressed a letter similar to this to his Excellency, Governor Tilden." [R201;444-445]

Meanwhile in New Orleans, Jeff Davis spent Christmas Eve alone in a hotel. Varina and Winnie were in Europe. Son Jeff may not have made the effort during the Christmas break to return home from his college in Virginia. Maggie was married. So, as 1876 was drawing to a close, Jeff, father and husband, was in New Orleans alone pondering his future. Jeff had rather resigned himself that his nation-building days were over and that he should take up nation-teaching instead. He had sought to put national interests before sectional interests throughout his long military and political career. For example, as a much younger man, Davis had sought the national interest when dealing with:

1. National expansion westward;
2. Political harmony among the States;
3. Encouraging everyone to believe that the Federal Constitution meant what it said;
4. Expanding railroads westward in the most cost-effective way;
5. Strengthening the Federal military without regard to sectional jealousies, and,
6. Preserving the national character of the Democratic Party.

When his State had seceded, Jeff Davis had resigned from the Federal Senate. When elected President of the Confederacy, he had again dedicated himself to nation-building — this time at the highest level of leadership. More recently, Davis had even ventured into a new phase of nation-building when he had begun working for improved commercial ties between the Port of New Orleans and the States of the Mississippi Valley and the Ohio Valley. But that last effort had died before it even got a good start.

So what was Jeff Davis to do? If he could not be engaged in nation-building, then he would move on to nation-teaching. Jeff Davis had come to that point in his life when he understood that his greatest contribution to his fellow man would be to preserve a "truthful" history of the political and military events surrounding the formation of the Confederacy, the Federal Invasion and eventual conquest and the subjugation of her States by the Republican-led Federal Government. Even though victors normally win the right to tell the history of their times, many former Confederates were determined that the victors would hold a monopoly over the discourse — they would write the history, too. And chief among those "truthful" history writers would be the Confederacy's President, Jefferson Davis. This new mission was on Jeff's mind as he wrote to Varina on Christmas Eve. He was obviously reluctant to tell Varina by overseas mail about his decision to accept Sarah Dorsey's offer to set up his book-writing effort in the cottage in her side yard. So he only hinted at a beach house as he wrote of asking a niece to find a small beach cottage he might rent. Jeff knew that Varina, who he often called Winnie to show affection, was still suffering from emotional insecurity and he did not want to give her any reason to become jealous or imagine family problems that did not exist.

"This evening of the anniversary when families are wont to be united, ours are scattered far and wide. It is sad to me to realize that an ocean rolls between me and my dear Winnie. God grant that our sacrifice may be blessed by the restoration of your health. Addison and Maggie and Jeff have all written to urge me to be with them on Christmas, but I could not consistently leave here until something more definite is reached [with regard to the fate of the Mississippi Valley Association].

"I went last Monday to see our niece, Nannie Smith, at Biloxi. I [had earlier] invested ten dollars in the hire of a [African American] to clear up our lot, [but recently] postponed any further effort, though often pressed to build a house. Weary of wandering and anxious to get books and papers together for the work always in contemplation, I was tempted to get a small house on the beach, but had before my eyes the fear of your not liking it and so was silent. If Nannie Smith would get a house in a quiet place I might take a room by the year. . . .

"Two Congressional Committees are here inquiring into the election in Louisiana and the Hotel was thronged by a mongrel multitude, so, when I returned from the sea shore, I came to Mary Stamps. . . I will not weary you with details of our political 'muddle' as it is commonly called, but will give you my hopeful opinion — that we shall have a peaceful solution and that [Samuel] Tilden will be the next President. The scenes through which we are passing would be ridiculous if less tragical, and may well induce those who doubt the capacity of man for self government, to say, 'I told you so'." [R30;440-441]

The Year of 1877

(1Q77)

By January 1877 Mississippi Democrats had been in control of State and local governments for the duration of 1876, sufficient time to establish a record, which we should now take time to examine. We start with the overall pattern of State spending before State secession; then look at the years following the conquest of the Confederacy, ending with the first year of Home Rule. A table of annual State expenditures for each year gives a good understanding:

Year	Controlling Party	State Annual Expenditure	State Tax Rate, Mils
1860	Democrat	$663,536	1.0
1865	Democrat	$1,410,250	1.0
1866	Democrat	$1,860,809	1.0
1867	Democrat	$625,818	1.0
1868	Democrat	$525,679	1.0
1869	Democrat	$463,220	1.0
1870	Republican	$1,061,250	5.0
1871	Republican	$1,729,046	4.0

1872	Republican	$1,596,829	8.5
1873	Republican	$1,450,633	12.5
1874	Republican	$1,319,282	14.0
1875	Republican	$1,430,102	9.5
1876	Democrat	$518,709	6.5

Note that, in the two years following the conquest (1865 and 1866), Democrats had authorized spending far in excess of the levels customary prior to secession, as illustrated by comparison to the 1860 expenditure. In those two years attempts had been made to recover from the destructions of war and comply with Federal demands. This increased spending by Democrats had not been met with a higher property tax rate, in recognition of the then dire economic situation on Mississippi farms. The property tax rate was held at the pre-war level of 1 mil — 0.1 cents per dollar of valuation. But, after those two years, Democrats had, for the 3 subsequent years (1867, 1868 and 1869), dramatically reduced spending — down to pre-war levels. But, when Republicans took control of the State Government and most county and local governments, spending for 1870 and beyond leaped back up and property tax rates soared. Instead of the 1 mil rate prior to 1870, State property tax rates rose as high as 14 mils (1874). County and town spending and property tax rates likewise soared. On the other hand, when Democrats won back control in the elections of 1875, taxes and spending performance (1876) was dramatically improved over the prior Republican record. State spending plummeted to pre-war levels and the property tax rate was cut to 6.5 mils — 0.65 cents per dollar of valuation. County and town spending and property tax rates were likewise reduced. [R204;320-324]

Meanwhile, on January 18 in Washington City, the political fight over the vote count for Federal President — of which Lucius Lamar was intimately involved from his position of leadership — rose to a climax. The House Electoral Committee and the Senate Electoral Committee, "after many consultations," agreed to a plan to transfer the authority of accepting and rejecting vote count Certificates to an "Electoral Commission," which was in itself a Committee. The proposal allowed individual Representatives and Senators to escape the public exposure that casting individual votes on specific Certificates would entail. They could all "hide" behind the decisions of the "Electoral Commission." Politically, this ability to avoid exposure must have been attractive. On this day of January 18, the House and Senate Electoral Committees submitted separate bills to the House and Senate, respectively, which, if passed, delegated power to an "Electoral Commission," composed of 15 members: 5 Senators to be chosen by the Senate, expected to be 3 Republican partisans and 2 Democrat partisans; 5 Representatives to be chosen by the House, expected to be 3 Democrat partisans and 2 Republican partisans; 4 Justices of the Supreme Court from named judicial districts (first, third, eighth and ninth), designed to ensure sectional balance, giving 2 Republican Justices and 2 Democrat Justices — plus one more member, a fifth Justice to be elected by the other 4. The "Electoral Commission" would be given the following power:

> "[All] conflicting Certificates of electoral votes, as they should be reached in the regular process of counting, should be referred to the Commission 'which shall proceed to consider the same with the same powers, if any, now possessed by the [House and Senate] acting separately or together, and, by a majority of votes, decide whether any and what votes from such State are the votes provided for by the [Federal Constitution], and how many and what persons were duly appointed Electors in such State, and may therein take into view such petitions, depositions, and other papers, if any, as shall, by the [Federal] Constitution and now existing law, be competent and pertinent in such consideration; . . . and the counting of the votes shall proceed in conformity therewith, unless . . . the [House and Senate] shall separately concur in ordering otherwise. . . .'"

Clearly, delegating the decision on accepting or rejecting vote count Certificates to the "Electoral Commission" freed the Representatives and Senators from the political liability associated with choosing sides. The bill establishing the Electoral Commission passed both the House and Senate easily, the process being completed on January 29. Lamar favored the bill and argued for it in opposition to a few noted Republicans, such as John Sherman of Ohio in the Senate and James Garfield, also of Ohio, in the House.

Lucius Lamar and other Democrats were hopeful that Justice David Davis of Illinois would be selected as the fifth member of the Electoral Commission, for he would be fair to the Democrat Party. In fact

Davis was the only Justice available who was considered a Democrat. However — and this action would be critical — the Illinois Legislature elected Davis to the Federal Senate just as the Electoral Commission bill was progressing through the Federal House and Senate. Surprise: David Davis decided to duck the responsibility of participating in the Electoral Commission, choosing instead to immediately resign from the Supreme Court to take his seat in the Senate. Illinois Democrats had badly miscalculated, for they should have simply postponed for a few weeks the votes to elect their next Senator. If Davis had been selected as the fifth Justice on the Commission, Tilden might have been declared the winner of the election. With David Davis unavailable, the four Justices elected Justice Joseph Bradley, a former New Jersey lawyer and a Republican, but considered the least partisan of those available (by the way, Bradley had purchased the grand Washington home built in 1857 by Stephen Douglas, of whom much is written in *Bloodstains*, and he and his family were living there at this time). Bradley, clearly a Republican, doomed the Democrats to be a minority of 7 to the Republican's 8. Only one of the 15 members of the Electoral Commission was from a former Confederate State, that person being Representative Eppa Hunton of Virginia. [R205;293-299]

The House and Senate began examining the vote count Certificates in late January, taking the States in alphabetical order. On February 1 they submitted their first conflicting Certificates to the Electoral Commission, those two being from Florida. You will recall that the Florida story went like this:

> "The [Republican-controlled] "Returning Board," against a small popular majority, declared Republican Electors chosen, and those Electors voted for Hayes and Wheeler; but at the same time the Democratic Electors voted for Tilden and Hendricks. The [Republican] Governor had duly forwarded the Republican votes under a proper Certificate. At the same election [in November], however, State officers had been chosen [by Florida voters], and as a result thereof a Democratic Governor and Legislature came into office. Thereupon, in January, a statute was passed requiring a new canvass of the popular vote, and that canvas resulted in a declaration of the election of the Democratic Electors. The new Democratic Governor then forwarded a proper certificate that the vote of Florida had been cast for Tilden and Hendricks."

The Electoral Commission met in the Supreme Court building, Justice Nathan Clifford of Maine, considered a Democrat, presiding. Lawyers for Hayes and lawyers for Tilden presented arguments before the Commission. Lawyers for Tilden argued that the Commission should investigate the actions of the Florida Returning Board and the Governor and reverse or throw out the votes if appropriate. Lawyers for Hayes argued that the Commission should refrain from investigating the Florida Returning Board's activity and merely accept the Hayes vote because the Governor had certified it. Would the Electoral Commission investigate the Florida vote? No. After due deliberation, on February 9, the Electoral Commission, by a party line vote, retained the Florida vote because the Governor had certified it and declared the total for Hayes and Wheeler.

On February 16, in a similar Party line vote, the Commission gave the votes of Louisiana to Hayes and Wheeler. Likewise, on February 23, the single Oregon vote in question was awarded to Hayes and Wheeler. Then, on February 27, the votes of South Carolina were awarded to Hayes and Wheeler. In the end the Hayes and Wheeler Republican ticket was elected by one vote, 185 to 184. Tilden had carried the popular vote by 4,288,546 versus 4,034,311, exceeding the Republican vote by 6.3 percent.

Among the northern States, Tilden received the electoral votes of New York (35), Connecticut (6), New Jersey (9) and Indiana (15), the remainder going to Hayes. Among the southern States Tilden received the undisputed electoral votes of Delaware (3), Maryland (8), West Virginia (5), Virginia (11), Kentucky (12), Missouri (15), North Carolina (10), Tennessee (12), Arkansas (8), Georgia (11), Alabama (10), Mississippi (8), and Texas (8). The far west States went for Hayes: Colorado (3), Oregon (3), Nevada (3) and California (6). If we reverse the 19 votes from Returning Boards in Florida, South Carolina and Louisiana, because they were probably fraudulently declared for Hayes, we find that the Democratic Party received a solid vote total of 140 from the southern States, all the way up to Delaware. This Democrat vote was augmented by 65 votes from 4 northern States giving Tilden a total vote of 205 out of 369, or 56 percent. The southern States, including those that had failed to secede in 1861, were at this time clearly the bedrock of the Democrat Party, and would be for generations to come. Republican candidate James Garfield would lose Florida, South Carolina and

Louisiana in the 1880 election, reinforcing our assumption that Hayes, in reality, had lost those States in 1876.

Of this result biographer Edward Mayes would write:

"The Commission had decided in every instance on strict Party lines, 8 Republicans voting steadily against 7 Democrats. Despite the discussions about the possibility of such a course, there had still been a strong expectation otherwise; and that it should indeed prove so was a grievous disappointment to the country. The proud office of the President was felt to be degraded by the rendition of an unjust judgment and the sense of patriotism suffered. That men so able and good should apparently be susceptible to such influences staggered faith in human virtue. It was not so much the decision as the method of it."

In 1878 Lucius Lamar would explain this pivotal moment in American political history with the following words:

"I believe that the most dangerous event in our history, not excepting the War of Secession, was the contest over the result of the Presidential election of 1876. The war of Secession must have ended either as it did, in the restoration of the [seceded States under the Federal Government], or else in the [survival] of two republics, based on different systems, but equally represented by strong and civilized governments. But if this last contest had reached no legal and peaceful solution, if it had resulted in the establishment of the principle that a Presidential election may be determined by force alone, there would have been an end to constitutional government on this continent. We should have been degraded to the condition of Mexico and the South American republics, and could have looked forward to a future only of revolutions and counter revolutions, savage outbreaks, bloody retaliations, and despotic suppressions."

"The most dangerous feature of the contest was its sectional character. Mr. Tilden's majority came mainly from the [southern States], having carried every Southern State, three of which were put in dispute by the cheating, fraudulent action of Returning Boards and the false Certificates of State Governors. Mr. Hayes had a decided popular majority in the northern States, a majority accustomed to look upon any active assertion of southern [States] ideas in national politics with strong distrust and apprehension. In all of those States there was only one Democratic legislature. The Republicans were in possession of all the Governmental bureaus and of the powers exercised through them, as well as of the Presidency and its overshadowing power. The [Federal] Constitution had provided no method of solution of this controversy, and the need of a quick solution was imperious. Unfortunately, the two Houses of Congress were divided politically. The Republican Senate demanded the installation of Hayes, on the Certificates based on the returns of the Returning Boards, as the only lawful criterion of election. The Democratic House asserted its right to go behind those returns and investigate the truth. . . .

"[Without a peaceful solution] the Republicans would undoubtedly have inaugurated Mr. Hayes. The Republican Chief Justice would have sworn in him, not Mr. Tilden. The Republican Senate would have recognized Mr. Hayes, would have confirmed all of his Cabinet and other appointments and would have refused to entertain any nominations sent in by Mr. Tilden. The Republican bureaus would have been delivered over to Mr. Hayes' nominees, and would have been closed to those of Mr. Tilden. President Grant, with the entire military force of the United States at his command, would have supported Mr. Hayes with arms, and the Tilden Government would have melted away like that of McEnery in Louisiana, or else it would have meant civil war.

"But, worst still, Mr. Tilden would have been forced to rely upon a solid and armed [Southern States] against what would have been shown to be a solid [northern States], aroused to resist the rule of a President set up by what was called 'the Confederate House.' The Democratic [people of the northern States were] prepared for no such issue, and would not have gone into it. Whatever were their wishes and intentions, no Democratic [statesman of a northern State] could have withstood the outbreak of popular sentiment whenever the [southern States], just admitted for the first time to [their] full equality [under the Federal Government], and that upon probation, and under a suspicion and a misgiving, should again [be accused of plunging] the nation into the horrors of a civil war." [R205;293-301]

Rutherford Hayes was sworn in on March 3, a Saturday, and he delivered his inaugural address on Monday, March 5. Portions of his address follow:

" . . . The permanent pacification of the country upon such principles and by such measures as will secure the complete protection of all its citizens in the free enjoyment of all their constitutional rights is now the one subject in our public affairs which all thoughtful and patriotic citizens regard as of supreme importance.

"Many of the calamitous efforts of the tremendous revolution which has passed over the southern States still remain. The immeasurable benefits which will surely follow, sooner or later, the hearty and generous acceptance of the legitimate results of that revolution have not yet been realized. Difficult and embarrassing questions meet us at the threshold of this subject. The people of those States are still impoverished, and the inestimable blessing of wise, honest, and peaceful local self-government is not fully enjoyed. Whatever difference of opinion may exist as to the cause of this condition of things, the fact is clear that in the progress of events the time has come when such government is the imperative necessity required by all the varied interests, public and private, of those States. But it must not be forgotten that only a local government which recognizes and maintains inviolate the rights of all is a true self-government.

"With respect to the two distinct races whose peculiar relations to each other have brought upon us the deplorable complications and perplexities which exist in those States, it must be a government which guards the interests of both races carefully and equally. It must be a government which submits loyally and heartily to the [Federal] Constitution and the laws — the laws of the nation and the laws of the States themselves — accepting and obeying faithfully the whole [Federal] Constitution as it is.

". . . The question we have to consider for the immediate welfare of [the people of] those [southern States] is the question of government or no government; of social order and all the peaceful industries and the happiness that belongs to it, or a return to barbarism. It is a question in which every citizen of the nation is deeply interested, and with respect to which we ought not to be, in a partisan sense, either Republicans or Democrats, but fellow-citizens and fellowmen, to whom the interests of a common country and a common humanity are dear. . . .

"The evils which afflict the southern States can only be removed or remedied by the united and harmonious efforts of both races, actuated by motives of mutual sympathy and regard; and while in duty bound and fully determined to protect the rights of all by every constitutional means at the disposal of my Administration, I am sincerely anxious to use every legitimate influence in favor of honest and efficient local self-government as the true resource of those States for the promotion of the contentment and prosperity of their citizens. In the effort I shall make to accomplish this purpose, I ask the cordial cooperation of all who cherish an interest in the welfare of the country, trusting that Party ties and the prejudice of race will be freely surrendered in behalf of the great purpose to be accomplished.

"In the important work of restoring the [southern States] it is not the political situation alone that merits attention. The material development of that section of the country has been arrested by the social and political revolution through which it has passed, and now needs and deserves the considerate care of the [Federal] Government within the just limits prescribed by the [Federal] Constitution and wise public economy.

"But at the basis of all prosperity, for that as well as for every other part of the country, lies the improvement of the intellectual and moral condition of the people. Universal suffrage should rest upon universal education. To this end, liberal and permanent provision should be made for the support of free schools by the State governments, and, if need be, supplemented by legitimate aid from national authority.

"Let me assure my countrymen of the southern States that it is my earnest desire to regard and promote their truest interest — the interests of the [European American] and of the [African American] people both and equally — and to put forth my best efforts in behalf of a civil policy which will forever wipe out in our political affairs the [distinction between the two races] and the distinction between [northern States people and southern States people], to the end that we may have not merely a united [northern States population] or a united [southern States population], but a united country."

What is meant by the perceived threat of a potential "return to barbarism" is unclear, but it must have satisfied the emotional prejudices of the Republican faithful. That comment aside, it was with these final words that Rutherford Hayes concluded his historic public disclosure of the long-sought promise to permit home rule in the southern States, thereby signaling an end to the Republican program — empowered by Political Machines — for Reconstructing the State and local governments of the conquered States. This accomplished, he proceeded to the subject of reform in the procedures regulating Federal civil service political appointments, referred to as "civil service reform." Civil service reform had become a major political issue for Democrats in the northern States, for Democrats had suffered for 16 years under the escalating corruption among Republicans appointed in the Lincoln, Johnson and Grant administrations, becoming most severe during the Grant Administration. Hayes continued:

"I ask the attention of the public to the paramount necessity of reform in our civil service — a reform not merely as to certain abuses and practices of so-called official patronage which have come to have the sanction of usage in the several Departments of our Government, but a change in the system of appointment itself; a reform that shall be thorough, radical, and complete; a return to the principles and practices of the founders of the [Federal] Government. They neither expected nor desired from public officers any partisan service. They meant that public officers should owe their whole service to the Government and to the people. They meant that the officer should be secure in his tenure as long as his personal character remained untarnished and the performance of his duties satisfactory. They held that appointments to office were not to be made nor expected merely as rewards for partisan services, nor merely on the nomination of members of [the Federal House and Senate], as being entitled in any respect to the control of such appointments. . . .

"The President of the United States of necessity owes his election to office to the suffrage and zealous labors of a political Party, the members of which cherish with ardor and regard as of essential importance the principles of their Party organization; but he should strive to be always mindful of the fact that he serves his Party best who serves the country best."

The events of the past four months — the Federal election of November 1876 — the post-election political crisis created by fraudulent vote counting by Republican State officials in Florida, South Carolina and Louisiana — the political maneuvering over those fraudulent vote counts in the Federal House and Senate — struggles over threats of renewed war between the political parties — culminating in the historic and successful negotiations to secure home rule for the southern States in exchange for allowing the fraudulent votes to stand. These historic four months constitute a ringing climax in America's "Struggle for Healing."

One more climax is yet to come — the election of Grover Cleveland as Federal President — the first Democrat to be elected to that office since 1856.

Before moving to the overview of the Rutherford Hayes Administration, it is appropriate to complete describing an event concerning Wade Hampton and another concerning Jeff Davis.

Returning to events in South Carolina, "Governor Hampton's authority was soon recognized, respected and obeyed by the circuit judges and the county officials. Hampton was running the Executive office in rooms above a store in Columbia with the help of Johnston Hagood, acting as Comptroller-General, a private secretary and a clerk. On March 1 Hagood would report that revenue of $119,432 had been received and $37,795 had been dispersed to cover salaries and expenses. But Republicans were not yet defeated. They retained a glimmer of hope — if only some newsworthy violence could be incited. Toward that goal, Ulysses Grant, by Proclamation, on February 20, directed Federal troops in South Carolina to prohibit any parades by rifle clubs in honor of George Washington's birthday. Parades, planned in Columbia and Charleston, were dutifully canceled, as "to this Proclamation there was obedience prompt and uncomplaining." Democrats in South Carolina had learned how to defuse, with passive resistance, Republican attempts to incite violence — a dramatic change in political strategy from their militant April 1861 response to Abe Lincoln's "relief" scheme, clearly designed to incite Confederates to fire the coveted "first shot" in Charleston Harbor. [R201;435-441]

Meanwhile, by February, Jeff Davis was comfortably settled into the cottage at Sarah Dorsey's beach house, *Beauvoir*. Workmen had finished revising the layout of the cottage so that Jeff could work and sleep there. Furthermore, Sarah Dorsey had found a place for William Walthall to live on nearby property. Walthall would be working full-time helping edit Davis' history and would be an intermediary with the publisher in New York. Davis was delighted that Walthall had succeeded in recovering the official Confederate letters and documents which Jeff had left with Mrs. Leovy in South Carolina with instructions to hide them from the Federals until they were called for. Many vital materials had been gathered into the cottage, and the three-person team — Jeff Davis, William Walthall and Sarah Dorsey — was busy at work writing the history of the Confederate Government. Of those early weeks of organizing records and writing Hudson Strode would report:

"At long last Jefferson Davis had found a haven. Often, after the revival of sad memories by the writing, he could lie awake at night and find balm in the murmur of the sea rolling up the beach. And in the afternoons, tired from the concentration on composition, he would stroll in the forest, where he found the sighing of the wind in the pines soothing. Sometimes he would take a detour down a path to a fern-bordered spring and sit in meditation." [R19;423-425]

March 1877 Through February 1881 – The Struggle for Healing During the Rutherford Hayes Administration

It is now time to review a summary of the 1876 Federal elections in the summarized format that has begun each four-year segment of this study. After this review, the narrative history will resume.

Rutherford Hayes was of Scotch and English ancestry. His great-great-great-grandfather had emigrated from Scotland in 1680 and settled in Connecticut. His two grandfathers and three of his great-grandfathers fought in the American Revolution. His father, also named Rutherford Hayes, was a Vermont merchant and farmer. He moved to Delaware, Ohio in 1817 and there prospered as a merchant, but suddenly died of a fever shortly before the future President's birth in 1822 at the family's Ohio home. The baby's mother, Sophia Birchard Hayes was a native of Vermont. After her husband's death she remained a widow, supporting her family by renting out the family farm for a share of the crop. She lived to see Rutherford's election to Congress. Rutherford had one sister to live to maturity.

Never knowing his father, Rutherford was raised in town by his mother and her brother, Sardis Birchard, a bachelor who lived nearby. Rutherford learned elementary reading, writing and arithmetic in a school in town. Then, at age 14, he attended the Norwalk Academy. At 15, he left Ohio to prepare for college at a school in Middletown, Connecticut. Then, at 16, he returned to Ohio to attend Kenyon College. He graduated as class valedictorian in 1842. Rutherford then studied under a law firm in Columbus, Ohio for 10 months and finally entered Harvard Law School in 1843 to polish his education. At Harvard he experienced the attitudes of major Massachusetts intellectuals such as Joseph Story, Simon Greenleaf and Jared Sparks. Graduating in 1845, Hayes returned to Ohio and obtained his law license.

Hayes first practiced law in what is now Fremont, Ohio. Joining the Whig Party, he campaigned locally for Zachary Taylor in the 1848 election. He moved to Cincinnati soon thereafter and worked as a lawyer in that city throughout his career. He remained with Whig Party, supporting Winfield Scott for President in 1852. That same year Hayes married Lucy Webb of Cincinnati. Well educated and a graduate of Wesleyan Women's College, Lucy was the daughter of a Cincinnati physician and was descended from 7 veterans of the American Revolution. Lucy was an avid Abolitionist and Exclusionist and encouraged her new husband to embrace the new Republican Party. Hayes apparently agreed with his new wife and supported John Fremont for President in 1856.

Hayes worked his first political job at age 36 when the Cincinnati City Council appointed him to be City Solicitor because the incumbent had died in office. Hayes won the post on the thirteenth City Council ballot, defeating Caleb Smith, Abe Lincoln's future Secretary of the Interior. Hayes won election to the post at the next local election, but was defeated on his attempt at reelection in 1859. Hayes supported Abe Lincoln for President in 1860.

By 1860 Rutherford and Lucy Hayes had three children who would live to maturity. Sardis Hayes became a Harvard-educated lawyer. James, who graduated from Cornell, would work at the White House with his father and then pursue a distinguished military career. Rutherford Platt, who also graduated from Cornell, would spend his life promoting libraries and the development of Asheville, North Carolina.

In June 1861 Hayes volunteered for the Army in response to Lincoln's call for troops to invade the Confederacy. During a four-year military career stretching to June 1865, Hayes saw considerable fighting and was wounded several times, once seriously. He began his career with the politically-appointed rank of Major, but by March 1865 he had earned the rank of Brigadier General of Volunteers.

In 1865 Hayes, running as a Republican, won election to the Federal House for the District that included Cincinnati. In the House he joined the Republican Faction that sought more harsh treatment of the conquered States. He voted to Impeach President Andrew Johnson. As Chairman of the Joint Library Committee he pushed through a bill to expand the Library of Congress.

Hayes left the House to run for Governor of Ohio, defeating Democrat Allen Thurman in 1867 and, for a second term, defeating Democrat George Pendleton in 1869. Hayes supported Grant for President in 1868. Honoring the precedent of a two-term limit for Ohio governors, Hayes declined nomination to a third term. Hayes vigorously supported Grant as an Ohio delegate to the 1872 Republican National Convention. In an 1872 bid to return to Congress, Hayes was defeated by Henry Banning, who ran on both the Democratic Party and the Liberal Republican Party tickets. Still eager for political office, Hayes sought to win another election for Governor of Ohio. He won again, defeating incumbent Democrat William Allen and holding the job during the 1876-1877 term.

Hayes was somewhat of a long-shot candidate for the 1876 Republican nomination for President, even though the Convention was held in his home town. He squeaked out a 6-vote margin to win the nomination. DeGregorio would summarize the Republican National Convention:

"As Republicans convened in Cincinnati in June 1876, the clear front-runner for the nomination was James Blaine of Maine, first dubbed the Plumed Knight by Robert Ingersoll in a stirring nominating speech at this Convention. Blaine came within 27 votes of the nomination. Through the first 4 ballots, Hayes trailed Blaine, Oliver Morton of Indiana, Benjamin Bristow of Kentucky, and Roscoe Conkling of New York. On the 5th tally Hayes surged to third place and on the next vote overtook second place, though he still lagged far behind Blaine, 308-113. But a stop-Blaine movement rallied to Hayes, putting him over the top on the 7th with 384 votes, a scant 6 votes more than was needed, to 351 for Blaine. Representative William Wheeler of New York was nominated for Vice President. The Republican Platform promised 'permanent pacification' of the [conquered States], continued sound-money policy, and civil service reform; opposed Federal aid to Catholic or other sectarian schools and land grants to railroads or other corporations; called for a Congressional investigation of the effects of Oriental immigration 'upon the moral and material interest of the country;' and vowed to eradicate polygamy, 'that relic of barbarism,' in Utah."

The Democratic Party nominated Governor Samuel Tilden of New York as its candidate for President. Tilden, a New York lawyer, had been an early supporter of the Exclusionist faction of the New York Democratic Party, which had looked to Martin Van Buren for leadership. DeGregorio would summarize Tilden's rise in New York politics and the 1876 Democratic National Convention:

"Born at New Lebanon, New York, the son of a Democratic Party worker, Tilden from his youth was active in Party affairs, supporting the [Andrew] Jackson and [Martin] Van Buren Administrations. Admitted to the bar in 1841, he quickly prospered as an able corporate attorney. He early [supported Abolitionism and Exclusionism], joining the Barnburners, the [Exclusionist] faction of the New York Democrats. As Chairman of the New York Democratic Committee in 1866-1874, he brought down the notorious Tweed Ring and encouraged the election of reform Democrats. His campaign against corruption earned him the [office of Governor], 1874-1876, and a national reputation as a champion of reform. At the Democratic National Convention in St. Louis, the first held west of the Mississippi, in June 1876, Tilden organizers dominated the proceedings from the start. He was nominated on the second ballot with 535 votes, to 60 for Thomas Hendricks of Indiana, 59 for Winfield Hancock of Pennsylvania, and 54 for William Allen of Ohio. Hendricks was nominated for Vice President. The Democratic Platform pledged to replace the corruption of the Grant Administration with honest, efficient government and to end 'the rapacity of carpetbag tyrannies' in the [conquered States],' called for treaty protection for naturalized [American] citizens visiting their homeland, restrictions on Oriental immigration, and tariff reform; and opposed land grants to railroads."

The 1876 election campaign focused on charges of corruption in the Grant Administration and rebuttals. Republicans worked to discredit Democrats and the Party of the defeated Confederacy. A few former Confederate States remained in various stages of military occupation and Republican voter domination. DeGregorio would summarize the 1876 campaign:

"Each candidate drew support from reformers. Carl Schurz stumped for Hayes; Charles Francis Adams and James Russell Lowell endorsed Tilden. Tilden supporters lambasted Republicans for the corruption of the Grant Administration, and Hayes backers waved the 'bloody shirt,' labeling Democrats the Party of [southern States Secession]. Although Republicans were still the dominant Party nationwide, the backlash against the Grant scandals, Tilden's sterling record against the Tweed Ring in New York [City], and the resurgence of [European American home rule] in the [southern States] encouraged Democrats.

"[Democrats] made one tactical blunder, which as it turned out, cost them the election: The Democratically controlled House promoted the admission of Colorado to the Union in 1876, believing that it was a safe State for Tilden. Instead, the new State voted for Hayes, giving him three electoral votes, without which [Hayes would have surely lost].

"Soon after the election, Hayes conceded to a reporter that he thought he had lost to Tilden. Although Tilden won the popular vote and was [substantially] ahead in electoral votes, the returns of three states — South Carolina, Louisiana, and Florida, all controlled by Republicans — were in confusion. One electoral vote in Oregon also was under challenge. Not counting the disputed electoral votes, Tilden led 184-166, just 1 vote shy of a majority. To win, Hayes needed every vote in dispute. Hayes appeared to be ahead in South Carolina, but Tilden led in Florida and Louisiana until Republican officials there ruled numbers of Democratic ballots invalid. . . .

You have already read in detail the saga of the Electoral Commission and how the Republican Party stole the 1876 election for Hayes. Tilden had 51 percent of the popular vote to 48 percent for Hayes. Voters gave Democrat Tilden an electoral vote majority of at least 53 percent, but Republican fraud reduced that number to 49.86 percent. Properly awarding that one vote in Oregon, all of Louisiana and all of Florida to Tilden, the Democratic candidate won 19 states. From north to south they were: Connecticut, New York, New Jersey, Indiana, Delaware, West Virginia, Maryland, Kentucky, Missouri, Virginia, North Carolina, Tennessee, Arkansas, Georgia, Alabama, Mississippi, Louisiana, Florida, and Texas. On the same basis, Republican Hayes won 18 states: Maine, New Hampshire, Vermont, Massachusetts, Rhode Island, Pennsylvania, Ohio, Illinois, Michigan, Minnesota, Wisconsin, Iowa, Nebraska, Kansas, Oregon, Colorado, Nevada and California. It is not possible to determine which candidate received the most valid votes in South Carolina.

The Democratic Party retained control of the Federal House and achieved big gains toward winning the Senate. Republicans were left with a slim 51 percent margin for control of the Senate, down from their comfortable 59 percent margin. Two years earlier, Democrats had achieved huge gains in the House to take control for the first time since James Buchanan's first two years as President. In 1876 Democrats lost ground, but held on to control of the House with a workable 52 percent margin, down from their much more comfortable margin of 58 percent. At midterm Democrats controlled the Senate by a margin of 55 percent and the controlled the House by a margin of 51 percent versus 44 percent for Republicans and 5 percent for non-aligned Representatives. Presidential imposter Hayes would have to deal with the opposition Party in the House throughout his term.

Hayes appointed William Evarts, of New York Secretary of State. He appointed John Sherman, of Ohio, Secretary of the Treasury. He appointed George McCrary, of Iowa, Secretary of War. When McCrary resigned in 1879 to take a seat in the Senate, Hayes appointed Alexander Ramsey, of Minnesota. He appointed Charles Devens, of Massachusetts, Attorney General. He appointed Richard Thompson, of Virginia, Secretary of the Navy. Hayes fired Thompson in 1880 for accepting the chairmanship of the American Advisory Committee of the Panama Canal Company of France and replaced him with Nathan Goff, of West Virginia. Hayes appointed David Key, a Tennessee Democrat, Postmaster General. When Key resigned to accept a Federal judgeship, Hayes turned to Horace Maynard, also of Tennessee. Hayes appointed Carl Schurz, of Missouri, Secretary of the Interior.

So, Hayes fulfilled his promise to include men from the southern States in his Cabinet, going with Thompson of Virginia for the Navy job and Key of Tennessee for the Postmaster job.

Fulfilling another promise Hayes would soon withdraw the last occupation army forces from the conquered States, formally ending Republican Political Reconstruction.

To record the Republican 1876 electoral theft for posterity, the Democratic Party 1880 Platform would proclaim, "The great fraud on 1876-77, by which, upon a false count of the Electoral votes of two States, the candidate defeated at the polls was declared to be President, and for the first time in American history, the will of the people was set aside under a threat of military violence, struck a deadly blow at our system of representative government." [R2;279-292]

The narrative history resumes, March 1877

On March 6 Lucius Lamar was sworn in as Senator from Mississippi. There was only one dissenting vote, his political reputation being firmly understood. His illustrious career in the Federal House was concluded and his career in the Federal Senate would be determined by future events. But, at first, his visits in the Senate would be rare as he would be recuperating from illness. Lamar would be assigned to the Committee on Railroads and the Committee on Education and Labor. He would be pleased with the Railroad Committee assignment, where he hoped to be influential in advocating expansion of sorely needed railroads in the southern States, especially a railroad to the west through Texas. His experience at the University of Mississippi would be helpful when the Senate considered legislation concerning education. [R205;318, R206;189]

Meanwhile, on the Gulf Coast, Jeff Davis was surely pleased with progress toward home rule for his former Confederate States. By this time, writing the history of the Confederacy was well underway. He explained the work and the beach house surroundings in a letter to his 12-year-old daughter Winnie:

"I received your two welcome letters. In the absence of the pleasure of looking at your dear little face and reading in your eyes the expression of your tender love, the greatest consolation is to have frequent letters from you. . .

"Your Brother Jeff is with me, he reads some French and some medicine, occasionally writes for me, and seems quite contented here. I dictate daily for 3 or 4 hours, for a book of reminiscences of my public career. [Sarah] Dorsey acts sometimes as my amanuensis and [William] Walthall assists in compiling and hunting up authorities. . .

"My cottage is a square building; the roof is composed of four triangles meeting in the center. Originally it had one room and galleries all around it, but one of the galleries has been closed so as to make a chamber and dressing room. So that now the original room with shelves is my library and office. Robert [Brown] is with me and sleeps in the dressing room.

"The grounds are extensive and shaded by live oaks, magnolias, cedars, etc. The sea is immediately in front, and an extensive orange orchard is near. Beyond that is one of those clear brooks, common to the pine woods, its banks lined with a tangle wood of sweet bay, wild olive and vines. Then comes a vineyard, then a railroad, and then stretching far, far away a forest of stately long-leaved pine. By night I hear the murmur of the sea, rolling on to the beach; by day a short walk brings one to where the winds sigh through the pines, a sad yet soothing sound. I send in the letter three of the wood flowers — azalea, yellow jasmine, and a variety of wild olive.

"Give my cordial love to dear Pinnie [Meredith] and my respectful regard to the Misses Friedlander."

A month later Jeff would mail Winnie orange blossoms with the comment: "I send enclosed an orange bloom. The orange grove here is quite extensive and the flowers perfume the air for some distance from the trees." [R30;451-452]

By mid-March a political movement was underway among Senate Republicans to establish a Federal "Commission" to go to southern States and "investigate" political activity, especially in South Carolina and Louisiana. This movement greatly troubled Democrats, who were eager to see Rutherford Hayes issue orders to remove Federal troops from those two remaining States, as promised in his Inaugural Address a few days previously. In this atmosphere of great concern, Lucius Lamar, impaired by his bout with illness, set down and wrote a hearth-felt, yet demanding letter, to Rutherford Hayes. Lamar intended to employ all of the substantial political capital he had earned in past encounters. This letter appears to have had a major impact on Hayes, possibly halting the Republican effort to establish their "Commission." In any event, the letter was quickly followed by Hayes' invitation to parley with Wade Hampton and D. H. Chamberlain, separately, at the President's residence. First, we read Lamar's letter to Grant, dated March 22:

"Mr. President: A severe illness has alone prevented my calling upon you before this, and my regret at my disability has been intensified to positive distress by the news that you had decided to send a Commission to Louisiana.

"I respectfully ask you to read what I am about to say with a candid allowance for that difference of opinion which, in public affairs, must exist between men of equally patriotic and disinterested purposes.

"The position toward your Administration which has been taken by southern [States] Senators, *in solido*, rests upon the foundation of your Inaugural Address, vis.: that you would not consent to sustain, by unconstitutional interposition of the Federal forces, State governments which had no support in the character, the intelligence, and the material interests of the States which they misruled. We felt that this resolution, promptly and firmly carried into effect, gave the [southern States] that for which [their people] had most earnestly contended. Believing this, we were willing to suppress the disappointment at the loss of a political victory which seemed so near and so precious, and to mark our sense of the justice and wisdom of such a course by giving you that cordial support which extreme partisans in your own political following seemed unwilling to give. But the support, to be honorable to us and useful to you, must have a sure foundation.

"When you made the declaration in your Inaugural there were but two States to which your language could apply, and the universal sense of the country made the immediate application. It was understood that you meant to withdraw the troops from South Carolina and Louisiana; to say, as your predecessor, Mr. Van Buren, had said in a not dissimilar case, that the differences between the local authorities of a State were not subjects for the armed intervention of the Federal Government.

"All that was required was an order to withdraw the troops from those States where they were a positive interference with the popular will, and in which the condition produced by their presence was a daily violation of your own sense of constitutional right, and threatened still further and more mischievous complication. Upon that subject we thought you had made up your mind; and indeed, Mr. President, you told me that you had.

"I cannot conceal from you the extreme concern which I feel lest your present decision be considered as implying a doubt as to the possibility of your action. In reality it is so considered. The facts are all before you. Without undertaking to extenuate or exaggerate, nothing is more certain today than the fact that the Packard and Chamberlain governments do not have the support of the character, intelligence or property of Louisiana and South Carolina, and that they exist in these States only so long as they are supported by you. If they were the best governments in the world, as they are confessedly the worst, this would be sufficient, upon the principles of your Inaugural. No Commission can alter the truth; no Commission can make it clearer. You know, and they know, that, if the troops are withdrawn, these governments will not exist a month.

"More than that, the country recognized the fact and the justice of the spirit in which you proposed to deal with it. Had your order been issued the day upon which your Cabinet was confirmed, not one man in the Republic would have been surprised; and nothing but the delay so far has encouraged, in some quarters, the hope that possibly the policy of the Inaugural will be abandoned. But every day's delay does make that a possibility. Men who dared not oppose what your constitutional duty so plainly prescribed and the people so universally demanded are beginning to hope that you can refuse the one and avoid the other.

"I know that deliberate action is wise; but in many cases prompt action is the best considered, because its wisdom consists in its promptness. I know that you desire, and properly desire, to carry the American people with you, step by step; but they were with you when you started in this course, and they are not faltering now.

"No sir; your declaration of what you would do prevented a fearful crisis at the [southern States], but the tension is too severe. If you would achieve what you have begun, you must do as you said that you would do.

"This Commission is a declaration of doubt on your part. Mr. President, there can be no doubt. If this case is again to be argued, we [southern States] Senators cannot be found in alliance with those who maintain any other ground. [Southern States] Senators will not hear in silence the slanderous denunciations heretofore uttered on the floor of the Senate. We cannot join in any palliation of the enormous iniquity of those State governments. We cannot willingly acquiesce in the delay which is to be prolonged at the expense of so much suffering and in the face of so much danger.

"As for the opposition to your policy by some of your own household, it will be opposed to the end; nothing will reconcile them to the abandonment of the grasp which Party has upon those afflicted States. By others it will be opposed so long as you allow it to be a subject of discussion; but their opposition will vanish before the simple words, 'I will.'

"The American people understand this question today perfectly. These governments cannot last. They will not be maintained. Military domination you can establish down there, but carpetbag governments you cannot uphold without a tremendous army in each State. Withdraw the troops at once, and your act will be recognized with gratitude, because it will secure the peaceful and quiet dissolution of those pretended governments. But allow this action to be the subject of prolonged and angry discussion, let the [southern States] people feel that it is doubtful whether their courageous patience will win them justice, and you will not secure those governments; they will go as certainly as at your bidding, but they will go amid the wrath of an indignant and outraged people, and leave you as a legacy questions far more dangerous in their settlement.

"I wish I could make you realize how hopefully I relied on the honesty of your purpose, the patriotism of your intention; but this dilatory policy means certain failure and fearful exasperations. Believe me when I say, as sincerely and anxiously as man ever spoke, that it is due to yourself, to your own Party, to the country (may I not say to us of the [southern States]?), to adopt in this matter a policy as prompt as it is positive.

"For myself, I have, as perhaps you know, gone great lengths in the policy of conciliation. I would go even further to secure peace to my troubled land.

"I regarded you as one who was about to introduce an era destined to be illustrious as one of peace, prosperity, and nationality. But today I hardly dare to look that hope steadfastly in the face, lest it be shown to be an unreality; and you must permit me to enter my solemn and sorrowful protest against your policy of delay.

"I have written this in sickness. I trust that in what I have said I have shown the respect I entertain for you personally, and officially the just appreciation I have of the grave responsibility you bear." [R205;307-309]

In spite of Rutherford Hayes' promises in his Inaugural to removed Federal troops from South Carolina, D. H. Chamberlain refused to turn over to Wade Hampton the official office of the Governor of South Carolina. The day after Lucius Lamar's letter to Hayes, March 23, Hayes and his Cabinet were engaged in deliberation over whether or not to sustain Chamberlain. We can assume that Lamar's letter was influential because the Hayes Administration promptly invited both Chamberlain and Hampton to come to Washington City and separately discuss the issue with the President. The invitation by Hayes' secretary said, in part:

"It will give the President great pleasure to confer with you in person, if you shall find it convenient to visit Washington and shall concur with him in thinking such a conference the readiest and best mode of placing your views as to the political situation in your State before him. . . . It is the earnest desire of the President to be able to put an end as speedily as possible to all appearance of intervention of [Federal] military authority in the political derangements with affect the government and afflict the people of South Carolina."

D. H. Chamberlain left immediately for Washington City, intent on getting there first. He met with Hayes on March 27, there asserting that he was, in fact, the legal Governor and that Federal troops had to remain at the State House to enforce that so-called fact. Wade Hampton — accompanied by Federal Senator Matthew Butler, State Attorney General James Conner and a large delegation of business leaders — left late that day or early the following day, explaining to the crowd gathered at the Columbia railway station to see them off: "I go to Washington simply to state before the President the fact that the people of South Carolina have elected me Governor of that State. . . . I am going there to demand our rights — nothing more — and, so help me God, to take nothing less." The party arrived in Washington City at 3:00 a. m. on March 29 and took rooms in the Willard Hotel. Little time for rest was allowed, as

Hampton and Conner — accompanied by Federal Senator John Gordon of Georgia — were urged to meet with Hayes and his Cabinet that morning and remain to lunch with the President and the First Lady. After lunch Hayes invited Hampton to accompany him on a carriage ride where the two could talk in private. It seems the men enjoyed each others company. A reporter for the New York *Tribune* wrote, "Wade Hampton's presence in Washington excites more attention than that of any other public man since President Hayes came." On March 30 and 31 notes were exchanged and positions were clarified.

Meanwhile, on March 29 in Mississippi, Adelbert Ames gave up his claim to be the Governor of the State and resigned, allowing a peaceful transition of power to Democrat Governor John Stone. [R199;263-265, R201;452-457, R205;314]

(2Q77)

On the following day, Sunday, April 1, Wade Hampton, was again invited to the President's residence. He left this meeting with Rutherford Hayes with the understanding that all questions were resolved in his favor. He reported by telegraph to Lieutenant Governor Simpson: "Everything satisfactorily and honorably settled. I expect our people to preserve absolute peace and quiet. My word is pledged for this. I rely on them." Meanwhile, D. H. Chamberlain had followed up his March 27 meeting with Hayes by sending a long and argumentative letter, which was read to Hayes' Cabinet on April 2. The Cabinet was not impressed. It decided to instruct the Federal military to remove troops from the State House in Columbia on April 10. The South Carolina Democrats had won!

Three days later, on April 5, Wade Hampton and most or all of his party boarded a train for Columbia.

Of the return trip, biographer Walter Cisco would write:

> "The journey became a continuous ovation. A special train met him in Charlotte, where he was sent on his way by an enthusiastic crowd and a military escort. One reporter said, 'The locomotive and entire train were covered with wreaths and flowers. The car reserved for the Governor was carpeted especially and upholstered with flowers, growing flowers in every window. Over in South Carolina the country people had built great arches spanning the track over which the train was to run. At Rock Hill, Chester, Winnsboro were arches, profusions of flowers, cheering crowds, bands, rockets.' The flower-laden train rolled to a stop in Columbia at 4:30 on the afternoon of Saturday, April 7. The crowd that met Hampton at the station was 'enormous and enormously happy.' Rifle clubs stood in formation. The band of the 18th [Federal] Infantry Regiment played. The State was wild with joy. Hampton's message was simple. 'Forget we are Democrats or Republicans, [European Americans or African Americans], and remember only that we are all South Carolinians'."

On April 10, as commanded by President Hayes, the 20 Federal troops holding the State House marched out by way of the south door into the fresh air of a Carolina spring." The constables, including Hunkidories from Charleston it is presumed, "were nowhere to be seen. The capitol was almost empty." At noon the next day, April 11, a day without a crowd or demonstration, Wade Hampton Manning, personal secretary of Wade Hampton, "walked to the State House and [D. H.] Chamberlain's secretary handed him the keys." That afternoon Hampton telegraphed Senator Gordon in Washington: "Perfect peace prevails. The troops have been withdrawn, and Chamberlain surrenders South Carolina. Thank you."

> Peace did prevail, but the State House was a stinking mess. It appears that toilet facilities were totally inadequate for the troops and the "constables." Two days later the *News and Courier* reported: "A squad of convicts from the Penitentiary was busily engaged today in the very necessary labor of scouring the floors of the rooms which had been thoroughly defiled by Chamberlain's special constables during their occupancy. This Herculean task will have to be performed throughout the entire building."

By May 1 all the lawfully elected men would be in possession of their offices throughout South Carolina. Departed would be R. H. Gleaves, the Republican candidate for Lieutenant Governor, who had been illegally acting as President of the State Senate. Except for action against Edmund Mackey and the other Republican Representatives from Charleston County, Democrats would act with generosity toward the Republicans who had occupied the State House under the protection of Federal Troops. On the other hand, action against Edmund Mackey and the Representatives from Charleston County would be severe.

Wade Hampton convened a Special Session of the South Carolina Legislature on April 24. The first order of business was to reconcile the Certificates of Election for Republicans who had revolted and participated in the illegal Mackey House and to address disputed Certificates concerning a few State Senate seats. Biographer Robert Ackerman would tell the story:

> Representative James Orr, Jr., son of former Governor James Orr, Sr., chaired the Committee named to decide on the merits of applicants. Of the 55 members of the Mackey House that sought acceptance, the Committee "decided to recommend that some . . . be accepted and some [be] rejected, according to the merits of their claims. Some were allowed to recant, confess their mistakes, and be seated as legal representatives. Those about to be forgiven came and stood before the Speaker's stand 'like a parcel of disgraced school boys about to be lectured.' Two of the Mackey House were denied the opportunity to recant. Two resigned. One refused to take the oath. In one case the vacated seat went to the Democrat who had the next highest number of votes in the [prior fall] election. In the other case the House directed new elections. . . . The House decided, because of fraud, to reject the entire Delegation elected from [Charleston County on the previous November] and to order new elections."

Democrats would call a new Charleston County Convention and nominate 14 European Americans and 3 African Americans as their slate of candidates. They would win "a complete victory" in the special June 16 election. By summer there would be only 37 Republicans in the 124-seat House.

In the State Senate, under the leadership of Lt. Governor William Simpson, Democrats would be awarded the 4 seats representing the counties where Republicans had previously challenged the election returns of the prior November. This reduced Republican membership in the Senate to only 15 of the 33 seats (two Republicans would eventually resign and be replaced by Democrats, dropping the number to 13). Therefore, by summer the Democratic Party would be in full control of the South Carolina Legislature.

Associate Justice Amiel Willard would be elected Chief Justice of the State Supreme Court. Willard, an Associate Justice since 1968 and formerly a New York lawyer, had come to South Carolina as commander of a Federal African American regiment, stayed on and had evolved into a competent and respected judge. [R199;265-267, R201;460-462]

Meanwhile in Louisiana, Federal Troops were withdrawn on April 24 and Republican Stephen Packard, having pretended to be Governor, left without troop support, retired from the field, and the administration of Democrat Governor Francis Nicholls, already perceived in many ways to be the legitimate leader and in command of considerable portions of the State, took uncontested control of the Louisiana State Government.

Meanwhile on the Gulf Coast, Jeff Davis, in early June, took a break from writing his history of the Confederacy, and departed from the beach-house cottage for Memphis. He was eager to see his first grandchild and to visit the new parents: his daughter Maggie and his son-in-law Addison Hayes. On June 9, the day before Jeff's arrival, Maggie had written her mother, Varina, still in England:

> "My baby was thin when he was born and every one discouraged me about him. I felt so very helpless and miserable. I longed so to nurse him and tried so hard, and I think I would have had enough if I had not been so much disheartened. Now my milk is nearly gone and I have to use condensed milk. It agrees with him splendidly and he weighs more. Now [that] I have nursed him into a pretty fat little baby every one admires him. He is named Jefferson Davis and called Jeffie D."

Jeff happily wrote Varina the next day: "Our Grand Son is a bright and beautiful child. Is getting plump as a partridge." Although Jeff wished that Varina was in Memphis sharing the joy of seeing their first grandchild, he seemed to accept his frail wife's decision to remain in England during their daughter Winnie's summer vacation from her boarding school in Carlsruhe, Germany. Of that Jeff wrote, "Though it is a bitter disappointment to my hopes, for you to remain abroad this summer, it's what my judgment told me you should do. To return to this malarial region before white frost has fallen, would be surely hazardous to you."

Jeff, Jr. had been living with his father at the beach-house cottage and helping, where he could with the writing work. Officials at the Virginia Military Institute, where he had attended college as a freshman, had recommended that, because of poor grades, he be withdrawn from further study. Jeff, Jr. and his father were close. Jeff, Jr. had written Varina a tender and loving letter from the beach-house cottage about four weeks earlier:

> "Father is well, interested in the task of writing his book. He is looking better than I ever saw him although very anxious about our darling Mother. . . . The other day I longed for you to be behind the door when my father was talking about you — he told me that you were a woman worthy the worship of any son. I felt just like picking him up and kissing him." [R30;455-456]

(3Q77)

Tragically, Jeff and Varina's infant grandson died soon after Jeff returned to the beach-house cottage to resume work on his history. A few days afterward, Sarah Dorsey invited the grieving parents, Maggie and Addison Hayes to come down to the beach and spend some vacation time near Jeff. Sarah made rooms available in her beach-house, because there was not room for them in the tiny cottage where Jeff and Robert Brown slept. The time at the beach was helpful to both Maggie and Addison. It appears that Maggie was planning to stay all summer, but Addison planned to return to his job after spending his vacation time. Jeff wrote Varina on July 15:

> "Jeff, Jr. returned, and, as I had proposed, Maggie and Addison came with him. Maggie was both mentally and physically in need of a change of scene and air. She has rallied in spirits and is much improved in bodily health. I will keep her with me if I can until cool weather, and if she will not stay here so long shall insist on her going to the mountains. [Sarah] Dorsey at first wished to regard Maggie as a guest, but agreed to keep us all for $100 per month, which she said was equal to half of her current expenses.

> "Maggie reads, Addison fishes; they both bathe and drive, and seem to be quite satisfied. Indeed Maggie thinks you would like the sea coast if you would try it now. . ."

In that same letter, Jeff notified Varina that, "I wrung out of the Montgomery's a payment of $2,500 and shall try to anticipate the shipment of the next crop, so as to get something more in the fall." It seems that Jeff, as one of the executors of his brother, Joseph's estate, had managed to get some of the money that the Montgomery's owed on the mortgage. This is the first reported payment after so many years of failure to pay any interest on the farmland that Joseph had sold to the Montgomery's while Jeff was imprisoned at Fortress Monroe. [R30;458]

(4Q77)

Toward the end of October, Jeff and Jeff, Jr. took time off from the writing work to rush up to Memphis to see Varina, Maggie and Addison. Yes, to see Varina. She had returned to The States and was with Maggie and Addison in Memphis. Varina had written Jeff in a September 9th letter that, as soon as she had seen Winnie off to another school-year at Carlsruhe, she planned to return to The States on the *Spain*. Jeff had learned from other sources that the *Spain* was scheduled to leave Liverpool on October 10 and arrive in New York City on or about October 20. Very much looking forward to being together with Varina again, Jeff had hoped to receive definite word of her actual departure via a transatlantic cable telegram. With such assurances, Jeff had considered traveling to New York to accompany Varina on a visit with Maggie in Memphis, afterward continuing together to the beach-house cottage. And Varina was aware of Sarah Dorsey's sincere invitation to come live at the beach-house and help with the writing of the Confederate history. But Jeff was also very aware of Varina's firm determination to avoid contact with her girl-hood and life-long friend, Sarah Dorsey. Persuading Varina to come to the beach-house was going to be most difficult, but Jeff and Jeff, Jr. were determined to make every effort to win her over. In the already mentioned September 9 letter, Varina had written:

> "I am sorry not to have written [Sarah] Dorsey — but I do not think I could satisfy you and her if I did and therefore am silent. I do not desire ever to see her [beach]-house — and cannot say so and therefore have been silent. Nothing on earth would pain me like living in that kind of community

in her house. I am grateful for her kindness to you and my children, but do not desire to be under any more obligation to her." [R30;462]

On October 28, while Jeff was in Memphis reuniting with Varina and attempting to change her mind about joining him at the beach, Nathan Forrest was brought into the city from his Mississippi River farm in a pitiful dying condition. Forrest was once a robust and highly successful Confederate cavalry commander, but a long bout with diabetes had shrunk his emaciated body to a weight of only 100 pounds. The coincidence of Jeff being in Memphis at the time permitted him to spend some precious last hours with his good friend. Biographer Hudson Strode would write:

> "[Jeff] Davis sat by his bedside and held his hand. Besides their love for the Confederacy, Davis and Forrest had in common the belief that railroads might be the key to [prosperity in the former Confederate States]. Though Davis had never got to be head of a railroad as he had hoped, Forrest had been President of the Selma, Marion and Memphis line, which his fierce energy and shrewdness had created and promoted; but in the end he had met with failure. On the evening of the 29th, Forrest died. He was buried from the Court Street Cumberland Presbyterian Church, which he had joined less than two years before. Jefferson Davis was one of his pallbearers." [R19;430]

After spending 10 days with Varina, Jeff returned alone to the beach-house cottage. As feared, he had failed to persuade Varina to join him. Varina planned to spend many months with Maggie and Addison, at least as long as they would have her. Jeff, Jr. had decided to stay in Memphis. He wanted to spend time with his mother, and Addison had helped by getting Jeff, Jr. a job at the bank where he worked. [R19;430]

Meanwhile in Washington City, a Special Session of Congress convened on October 15, prior to the Regular Session, which always opened in early December. Lucius Lamar was present at the Senate, but still recovering from illness. Yet, he was ready for business. His first speaking appearance on the Senate floor would occur on November 30 where he would advocate that Matthew Butler be seated as the rightful Senator from South Carolina. In this speech, Lamar presented "a fine argument on the relations of the State Legislatures and their members to the election" of Federal Senators under the Federal Constitution and Federal laws. Learned legal arguments of this nature were among Lamar's strongest assets.

Meanwhile in Mississippi, the Republican Party essentially disbanded — ceased to exist. It did not offer candidates in the 1877 election contests. One reason for this collapse was the adroit handling of patronage by Lucius Lamar and other wise leaders. The State's second Senator was Blanche Bruce, a Republican and an African American, one of the few Mississippi Republicans with political influence:

> Born in Virginia to Pettis Perkinson, a European American farmer and his bonded servant, Polly Bruce, Blanche Bruce had enjoyed a secure childhood as a member of Perkinson's family. When old enough seek a career, his father had given him his independence and apprenticed him for training. He had worked in the printing trade and attended Oberlin College in Ohio for two years. Bruce had not fight during the Invasion of the Confederacy, instead moving to Missouri and forming an African American school. After the conquest of Mississippi, Bruce had acquired land in the Delta region and become a reasonably wealthy land owner and farmer. He had entered into Mississippi politics as a Republican and risen to be elected to the Federal Senate in February 1874. He would hold the Senate job for a full 6 year term, the first African American to do so.

Lamar invited Bruce to his Washington residence and conferred with him on patronage and other matters concerning Mississippi. Lamar made sure that Bruce was involved in awarding patronage jobs, such a post office jobs, to capable African Americans. In exchange Bruce agreed that Mississippi politicians who had come from the northern States and other "mischievous" European American men be removed from office in Mississippi — allowing the few Mississippi African Americans capable of competent government office work to find positions. Mississippi had evolved into a one-party State. [R205;321-322]

Meanwhile, on the Gulf Coast, former Confederate leaders would often come to visit Jeff Davis at the beach-house and Sarah Dorsey always encouraged such activity. She enjoyed the thrill of participating in the important historical discussions which were so important to the completeness of the emerging history of the Confederacy. Biographer Hudson Strode would write: "She would put them up for the night or for days, and she enjoyed being hostess at these historical conferences." Strode would further write of Jubal Early's visit during the Christmas season:

> "[Sarah] Dorsey approached [Jubal Early] on the subject of [Jeff] Davis' financial condition. During his first year's residence with her, [Sarah] Dorsey had become aware of his near-destitution. She had discovered that he had been living on the principal of a small sum he had managed to invest through his nephew-in-law, [Federal Representative] Charles Brodhead of Pennsylvania. She began the conversation with Early on the veranda, and then she asked him to walk with her on the beach, where they could not possibly be overheard. She told him that she felt that she would not live long and that it was her intention to leave her estate to [Jeff] Davis, but that it must be kept absolutely secret, for he would not permit anything of the kind if it came to his knowledge. From experience, she had learned that any income from [farms], especially those subject to floods, was uncertain at best." [R19;431-432]

The Year of 1878

(1Q78)

Although Varina refused to come to the beach to help Jeff with the writing, she did help from Memphis by editing some sections and by adding insight into others. Since her teenage years, Varina had been unusually interested in politics had always been more eager to engage in political, literary or business conversation with men than to engage in girl-talk with women. In a letter dated February 4, she had submitted a thorough analysis of the behavior and motives of the three Confederate representatives at the January, 1865 Hampton Roads Peace Conference — R. M. T. Hunter, John Campbell and Alexander Stephens. Varina's analysis had focused on Hunter's behavior and motives, because he had, during the intervening years, accused Jeff Davis of preventing a peace agreement with the Federals merely over the terminology: "our common country." The Lincoln Administration had insisted on this terminology, because it had steadfastly pretended that the Confederate States of American did not exist. In fact the Johnson Administration continued that policy and refused bringing closure to the Federal conquest of the Confederacy through any document other than surrender agreements with individual Confederate military commanders. At one point in her long and detailed letter on the matter, Varina wrote:

> "I remember that there was a debate over the expression 'two countries' and that you settled it by the argument that if there were not two countries, then you had no authority in the matter. . . . It was to surrender our claim to any consideration at once, to use the words 'our common country.' . . . You remember that these words, 'our common country,' were believed by everyone then to be a suggestion of Seward's in order necessarily to defeat the objects of the [Peace] Conference." [R30;468-469]

In his reply a few days latter, Jeff expressed his appreciation for her in-depth analysis: "Your review of Hunter is very forcible and reminds of something I had forgotten." Biographer Hudson Strode would write that Jeff "tried to draw [Varina] into the writing by appealing to her for help. He really needed her assistance on numerous points. Like himself, she was blessed with an extraordinary memory, and she would always answer clearly to the best of her ability. She even confessed to a 'grateful sense of being permitted to help'." [R30;471, R19-432-433]

Meanwhile, the Federal Senate passed the Bland-Allison Silver Act on February 15, Lucius Lamar voting no. Rutherford Hayes vetoed the bill but the House and Senate voted to override the veto. The Act carried the names of its primary sponsors: Democrat Representative Richard Bland of Missouri and Republican Senator William Allison of Iowa. Lamar's "no" vote was no surprise, considering his January 12 speech on the floor of the Senate explaining why the bill should be defeated. This Silver Act directed the Federal Mint to purchase $2,000,000 to $4,000,000 worth of silver per month at market prices and to coin it into silver dollars. The Senate vote culminated a long political battle between advocates of maintaining the gold standard for the dollar at $20.67 per ounce (each dollar being worth 1.50 grams of gold) and advocates of allowing the dollar to be revalued to a silver standard at a ratio of 16 ounces of silver to 1 ounce of gold, making silver worth $1.29 per ounce. Advocates of basing the dollar on silver, as several European countries had done, were called "Silverites." Silverites were

Inflationists. Realizing that gold had become more than 16 times dearer than silver, debtors liked the idea of using silver-based dollars to pay off loans established on the basis of gold-based dollars. Debt holders, including the wealthy financiers in the northeastern States, especially New York and Massachusetts, wanted loans given in gold-based dollars to, likewise, be paid back in gold-based dollars. Since the supply of silver exceeded the demand for it because of new western mine discoveries, silver miners and mine owners in the west, such as Colorado and Nevada, were Silverites. They looked forward to making millions of dollars selling silver bars to the Federal Government for silver coins and silver bullion. Lamar had voted "no" in spite of the fact that the Mississippi Legislature had approved a resolution calling for their Senator to vote in the affirmative — a decidedly bold and stubborn act of defiance. Most of Lamar's constituents in Mississippi had been attracted to the idea of silver-based inflation, believing it would stimulate the area's depressed economy, improving prices for farm land and farm products and easing the difficulties in paying off mortgages and tax obligations. Lamar's support of a gold-based monetary policy strengthened his ties with powerful Republican financial and commercial men in the northeastern States, reinforcing the good feelings initiated during his famous 1873 speech upon the floor of the Federal House in which he had eulogized the late Charles Sumner. [R205;323-348, R206;191-196]

(2Q78)

Meanwhile in South Carolina, April 1878 represented the end of the first 12 months of rule by Democrats and the Wade Hampton Administration — the first year of the new era that followed 8 years of corrupt Republican rule — so a presentation of major Democratic Party achievements is appropriate.

Once in control of the Legislature, South Carolina Democrats turned to rectifying perceived problems in the Judicial branch.

Attorney General James Conner brought suit against 6 of the 8 Circuit Judges, claiming their original elections were unconstitutional because each had been selected by voice vote, not by ballot. In January 1878 the State Supreme Court agreed with Conner and ordered their removal. The Legislature would vote to replace them with 4 Democrats and 2 Republicans.

Turning to the State Supreme Court, legislators voted to Impeach Associate Justice Jonathan Jasper Wright "for inappropriate behavior, and recommended he resign to avoid disgrace," even though Wade Hampton reportedly had found no fault in Wright, who held the historical distinction of being the first African American Justice to ever sit on a State Supreme Court anywhere in the United States. Born in Pennsylvania, educated in New York and admitted to the Pennsylvania Bar in August 1865 (the first African American accepted by that State's lawyers), Wright had come to South Carolina 8 months later to help Oliver Howard, Chief of the Newly Independent African American Men's Bureau, with issues involving African Americans. He had been appointed Associate Justice in 1870. In response to the Impeachment vote, Wright chose to resign and take a teaching position at Claflin College, located in Orangeburg. Claflin had been established in 1869 by Methodists for the purpose of educating African Americans. Today the school is known as Claflin University.

But there was no effective campaign to purge the State Supreme Court of Republicans, except for replacing the late Chief Justice, Franklin Moses, Sr., who died in March 1877. Franklin, Sr., a Justice in the State Supreme Court since 1868 was the father of Franklin Moses, Jr., who, you will recall, had been Republican Speaker of the House and Republican Governor. Both father and son were native South Carolinians. The Moses family was Jewish. Wade Hampton favored naming Republican Amiel J. Willard to the top post of Chief Justice, and the State Legislature elected him to that office, all but one Democrat concurring. Willard, a well established New York lawyer prior to State Secession, had joined the Federal Army and commanded African American troops in South Carolina. Republicans had elected him to the State Supreme Court in July 1868, and his performance during the subsequent 8 years had not greatly displeased Democrats. Of Willard's selection the Charleston *News and Courier* would say:

"Liberality in union is announced and affirmed as the governing idea of the Democratic Party in South Carolina. In other words the principles and policy advocated by Governor Hampton during the canvas and after the [1876] election have carried the day. The Democratic Party opposes thieves but not all [officials of northern States] birth."

With Democrats in full control, the State quickly witnessed major changes in the administration of the South Carolina State Government, even during these first 12-months. The Legislature "established a Joint Committee to investigate the misdeeds of [Republican] rule of the last 8 years. The likelihood that many former Republican officeholders would be charged with crimes presented the possibility of a compromise, which could be face-saving for both Democrats and Republicans." There were investigations of rioting and voter intimidation during the 1876 election period as well. But, the general mood was to minimize prosecutions and build feelings of cooperation.

Wade Hampton appointed over 116 African Americans to office during his term as Governor, "mostly at the county or municipal level." Former Governor Robert Scott observed that, during these first 12 months in office, Hampton had "already appointed more [African Americans] to office than were appointed during the first two years that I was Governor."

A major concern was administration and funding of the State's segregated public schools, which had suffered mismanagement and corruption during Republican rule. Hampton insisted of continuing the Republican policy of segregating schools by race. But he also insisted on equivalent per-pupil funding of each system in spite of the fact that European American taxes funded both systems almost entirely. In the summer a property special tax of 2 mils was approved for added support of public schools. By the 1879-1880 school year, funding would be $351,395, approximating the highest funding level during Republican rule and being much more effectively spent with little corruption. The allocation of this funding calculated to $2.75 per European American student and $2.51 per African American student, very near parity in spite of the fact that the African American student population was the larger of the two. "By the end of 1878 South Carolina would have more schools and more teachers than the year before." However, the funding gap would steadily grow in future years, to the detriment of African American schools. Democrats closed the State supported University of South Carolina in Columbia, which Republicans had integrated but which was in practice an African American school. Soon afterward the Legislature reopened the University as a segregated institution for European American students and made plans for a corresponding college for the State's African Americans.

Regarding paying off the huge State debt that Republican misrule had accumulated, Hampton said he favored a policy of honoring all such debt that could be deemed to be legitimate, for he "was unalterable opposed to mass repudiation" of that debt. The State property tax rate was set at 7 mils, lower than the range of 10 to 12 mils levied by the Republican Legislature in the last 5 years of its rule. The tax rate would have been lower but for the heavy burden of paying off the large debt. In April of the previous year, when Democrats had taken control of the State Government, that debt had stood at $5,600,000. The interest due immediately amounted to $270,000, about equal to planned spending for education. Hampton recommended that the Legislature establish a Joint Committee to study the origins of the debt and determine which portion was legitimate and which portion was fraudulent and available for renunciation without dishonor. The Joint Committee reported on its findings in February 1878, recommending that two-thirds of the debt, a whopping $3,600,000, should be repudiated. Hampton refused to consider such a massive repudiation. Biographer Ron Andrew would explain:

> "Hampton was able to marshal enough support to defeat the [Legislature's] adoption of this report, and State leaders continued throughout the remainder of the year to work out a compromise. The State [would not resolve] the issue until 1879, after Hampton would leave left the Governor's office. In the end, the State [would repudiate] $1,100,000 of its debt and [honor] the other $4,500,000."

South Carolina's Representatives in the 1877-1878 Federal House consisted of three Republicans (Joseph Rainey, Richard Cain and Robert Smalls) and two Democrats (Wyatt Aiken and John Evins). Democrats would replace Rainey, Cain and Smalls two years later, at the 1878 elections. Rainey was an African American from Charleston. Cain was an African American from the northern States. Smalls was an African American also mostly of Charleston.

John Patterson was one of South Carolina's Federal Senators when Hampton took the reins as Governor. Because Hampton considered Patterson to have been "the most notorious thief" of the

Republican's 8-year rule, he insisted that criminal prosecution of Patterson was to be pursued despite the general feelings of forgiveness and amnesty that anchored his plans for peaceful political transition to Democratic rule. While Patterson was still in the Federal Senate, the Hampton Administration charged him with "bribery, fraud and conspiracy." Patterson offered to resign from the Senate if the charges were dropped, but Hampton firmly refused. He would retain his seat in the Federal Senate until 1879, at which time he would be replaced by Governor Wade Hampton. The other Senator from South Carolina was Matthew Butler, Democrat.

The Hampton Administration also attempted to prosecute Howard Kimpton, who had been South Carolina's financial agent in New York during the Franklin Moses, Jr. Administration. There was evidence that Kimpton had personally pocketed over $700,000 in commissions on bond sales — but, "no one could even begin to estimate" what he took from fraudulent "over-sale of bond issues, receipt of interest of monies guaranteed by him, or his profits from participation in the two railroad frauds that made dozens rich." However, South Carolina would never succeed in apprehending Kimpton or having him extradited from Massachusetts of any other northern State.

On May 19 the Legislature ratified an Amendment to the State Constitution which required each county to levy a 2 mil property tax and a $1.00 capitation tax to provide money for public schools. The Amendment ensured that no man could be denied his vote at the polls because of failure to pay the $1.00 capitation tax, but history would show that failure to pay the $1.00 tax would eventually be used to restrict voting.

Meanwhile, on May 20, Jeff Davis received a telegram from his lawyer, W. B. Pittman: "Your case again decided in your favor. Former decree of [Mississippi] Supreme Court stands." Thus ended the court battle that Jeff had reluctantly decided to fight to obtain title to his Mississippi River farm, Brierfield. Foreclosing on the mortgage, which his brother, Joseph had given to the Montgomery's to finance their purchase of both Jeff's farm and Joseph's farm had been rather straightforward. The Mississippi State Government was no longer in the hands of the Republican Political Machine, so there was no bias against the Davis family during foreclosure proceedings. The Montgomery's had failed to pay any significant portion of the past due interest. Furthermore, there had been no payment toward the principle, which had been due in full two years previously, in 1876. So, foreclosure was straightforward, and may have been finalized earlier, or as part of the court's final decree. The issue in the lawsuit had not been foreclosure; it had been a dispute among members of the Davis family over who owned Brierfield farm. A review of this family story is appropriate:

In 1835, Joseph had offered to give Jeff 1,800 acres of his 6,900 acres of his land holdings along the Mississippi River. Joseph had made the offer because he had wanted his brother to live near him, and he had known that his brother wanted to leave the army, settle down and marry Sarah Knox Taylor. The 1,800 acres had never been cultivated, so Jeff was obviously looking at some hard work clearing the land and putting it to productive use. And Joseph had also offered to lend Jeff enough money to purchase several bonded African Americans to perform most of the work. But — and this is important — Joseph had apparently never pledged to deed the land over to Jeff at any specific date. Yet, he had assured Jeff that the land would become his legally when the proper time came. It seems that Joseph had not wanted to give the land to Jeff during the bachelor years that had followed Sarah Knox's tragic death, for Jeff had no heirs then. Like many farmers, who viewed land as the family's crucial asset to be passed down through the generations, Joseph had wanted to be sure that the land remained in the Davis family in the event of Jeff's untimely death. Then, after Jeff married Varina, Joseph had probably been concerned that — especially since Varina was so much younger than Jeff — if he was then given title to the land, it might pass into the hands of Varina's family. And there are strong indications that Joseph was dead set against that outcome. Anyway, Joseph must have figured that there was ample time to deal with transferring the land later. Perhaps, as Jeff rose to great prominence as a national leader, Joseph had perhaps begun to think Jeff might not ever return to farming. Then chaos had descended. Mississippi had seceded, Jeff had assumed leadership in Montgomery, Abe Lincoln had Proclaimed his Federal Invasion, and Jeff had moved on to Richmond. At that point Joseph had wisely retained legal title to reduce the likelihood that the Federals might confiscate Jeff's farm.

Joseph must have become exceedingly alarmed over the likelihood of vast Federal land confiscation after the November, 1866 Federal elections, for, a few weeks later, he had dispatched Mary Stamps to Fortress Monroe to seek Jeff's permission to sell his farm to the Montgomery's, complete with an enabling $300,000, 10-year, Davis-financed mortgage. Joseph had figured he could protect the land from Federal confiscation if it was sold to African Americans, and that, as holder of a 10-year mortgage, he and Jeff stood a good chance of either getting their money or getting the land back. Joseph, who died on September 18, 1870, had received no interest payments from the Montgomery's during his lifetime. Yet he had never made any attempt to foreclose on the mortgage, for he had forever feared confiscation by the Federals, and the Republican Political Machine still controlled Mississippi State and local governments at the time of his death.

At this point, the muddled issue of who owned Brierfield farm surfaced, for Joseph's will did not specifically declare the 1,800 acre Brierfield section to be Jeff's farmland. The will simply bequeathed $20,000 to each of Jeff's four children. But the estate had no cash, so no money could be paid unless the estate foreclosed on the farms and sold them to raise cash. It seems that Joseph had feared that — even after his death — he had to keep the ownership of Brierfield muddled to keep it from being confiscated by the Federals. But the primary heirs, Joseph's two grandchildren, who Jeff dearly loved, had insisted that they should inherit the entire dual-farm mortgage — and thereby the right to foreclose on both farms. For three years, Jeff had pondered giving those dearly loved family members foreclosure rights to his farm. But, he loved Brierfield farm and frankly needed the money it could earn. So, in late 1873, Jeff had hired a lawyer and filed a civil lawsuit seeking ownership to the rights to foreclose on Brierfield farm. Primary defendants were Joseph's granddaughter, Lise Mitchell Hamer, and his grandson, Joe Mitchell. The lawsuit went all the way to the Mississippi Supreme Court and through an appeal for a review before it was concluded. The Court confirmed Jeff's ownership of Brierfield farm and furthermore, that Jeff's children were entitled to the $80,000 in notes that Joseph had bequeathed to them. Since the estate still had no cash to pay the $80,000, it was agreed to survey the two farms and move some acreage from Hurricane farm to Brierfield farm to satisfy the $80,000 obligation. Biographer Hudson Strode would write:

> "It was Mary Stamp's testimony that had swayed the Judges; particularly the fact that Joseph Davis had asked her to see his brother in prison to secure his permission to let him sell Brierfield [farm] to the Montgomery's. Almost everyone in Mississippi believed the decision just. And even the [unfriendly] Chicago *Tribune* declared: 'The courts were compelled to decide in favor of Jefferson Davis, because the law was plainly on his side.' [Jeff] Davis could not be over-elated at his victory, however, for so much bitterness had been stirred up. His once beloved Lise had turned caustic against him. Four years of worry and [lawyers fees] had led up to the final verdict." [R19;434]

The big winner had been the adept late Joseph Davis! He had succeeded in evading Thad Stevens and Federal land confiscation. All 6,900 acres still belonged to the Davis families. [R19;298-299,320,326-327,341,368,371,387-388,398,400-401,410-411,415,427-428,434]

Meanwhile, on May 28 Lucius Lamar delivered a speech on the floor of the Senate advocating Federal financial support for the Texas & Pacific Railroad Company toward its goal of laying track from central Texas to San Diego, California. Lamar had been a member of the House Committee on Railroads and had likewise been assigned to the Senate Committee on Railroads, continuing to exercise that expertise. Two railroad expansions were being considered. One was a plan for the Southern Pacific to build eastward from Fort Yuma, Arizona into Texas and from there to points eastward. The other was for the Texas & Pacific to complete building across Texas and continue westward to a junction with the Southern Pacific, thereby connecting to San Diego. The Texas & Pacific construction project, still within Texas, was behind schedule and Federal financial help was needed. But, more urgently needed was a boost to the southern States economy that a financially healthy Texas & Pacific line would provide. However advocates for Federal financial help for the Texas & Pacific would fail in their efforts. A year later, in 1879, Jay Gould would acquire an interest in the Texas & Pacific, allowing it to build westward to a junction two years later with the Southern Pacific at Sierra Blanca, Texas, thereby completing a direct railroad across Texas to the Pacific port at San Diego. [R205;350-351, R206;198]

After the Federal Senate adjourned in June, Lucius Lamar returned to Mississippi, fully recognizing that he would be facing voters, politicians and newspapermen who were mad about his opposition to the Bland-Allison Silver Act, which had become law in spite of Republican Rutherford Hayes' veto. After some well-earned rest he had expected to launch a tour to explain his monetary policy throughout Mississippi. But a very bad Yellow Fever epidemic struck the lower Mississippi valley, beginning in New Orleans and moving north, somehow skipping over the Lamar home town of Oxford, but reaching Tennessee and strickening Jeff and Varina's only remaining son, Jeff, Jr., who was working at a job in a Memphis bank. The epidemic did not subside until December. By that time Grenada alone had reported over 1,000 cases of "Yellow Jack" and the death toll had reached 350. People had deserted towns and move out into the countryside attempting to find "better air."

Down at the coast, ever since Jeff moved into the beach-house cottage, Sarah Dorsey had been trying various approaches to lure her life-long friend, Varina to join her husband. It was sometime in July, during the height of the summer vacation season, that Sarah presented another lure. She invited a large number of the more prominent vacationers and residents of the Gulf Coast region to a party in honor of Varina. She prepared a room for Varina and made sure that she was fully aware of the big party. Would she leave Memphis and come to the party? Well, Varina had already been weakening in her resolve to stay away from Sarah's beach house. In late March or early April, she had moved out of Margaret and Addison Hayes' house to a nearby boarding house. It appears that Margaret and Addison were growing tired of mother and mother-in-law severely overstaying her welcome. After, three months of living in the boarding house, Varina was apparently ready to give in and join Jeff at the beach house cottage. She arrived with her trunk the very morning of the party. A reporter, covering the party for the New Orleans *Times Democrat*, wrote that Varina "reigned with queenly dignity." But the reporter and the guests had not seen Varina's terrible outburst a few hours before the party had begun. As biographer Hudson Strode explains it:

> "None of the company dreamed that, just before the guests arrived, Varina had lashed out at Sarah Dorsey in an uncontrolled fit of temper and rushed off to the woods, where the agitated hostess sought her out and appeased her. Such storms were generally as quickly over with Varina as a summer squall on the Gulf. Though she had left the whole household shattered by her outburst, she appeared in the drawing room serene and scintillating."

Sarah Dorsey continued to appease Varina and help her adjust to living at her beach house in the midst of Jeff's writing effort. She stopped helping Jeff with the writing so that Varina could be the sole woman helping with that. Sarah must have done a magnificent job with the very talented, but temperamental Varina, for after a few weeks at the beach house, Varina would write Emily Mason in Paris:

> "We may be, I suppose, considered settled here for a long time to come, as [Jeff] has his material [located here] for his work. We board with [Sarah] Dorsey and there is no one else in the house. She has a charming temper and makes us very comfortable, and thus she secures companionship when otherwise she would be alone. I am very fond of her, but do not like the climate."

And a cheerful September 19th letter from Jeff, Jr. in Memphis to his father further demonstrated Varina's excellent adjustment to living at Sarah Dorsey's beach house. Jeff, Jr. wrote, "I am delighted to know that my darling mother has at last found something that she likes about the Sea Coast. I felt sure she would like it after a while."

But the Jeff and Varina were extremely worried that their children might succumb to the Yellow Fever epidemic. A letter from Jeff to Bishop William Green at Sewanee, Tennessee gives a sense of that worry:

> "We are surrounded here by the dread scourge, which has this season desolated our land. Our children near Memphis are in like conditions; but a merciful Providence has thus far spared them. We ask your prayers for further safety."

But young Jeff, Jr. would be stricken with Yellow Fever shortly afterward.

Fear of Yellow Fever, but most importantly public quarantine rules, prevented Lucius Lamar from touring the State to explain his views on monetary policy and explain his refusal to abide by the instructions of the Mississippi Legislature demanding that he vote against the Silver Bill. Lamar was also unable to canvas his State on behalf of Democrats running for the Federal House.

Yellow Fever was striking the Davis family — on October 11 Jeff and Varina received a terrifying telegram from Addison Hayes in Memphis, reporting that Jeff, Jr. had been stricken with the disease. The Yellow Fever epidemic that had "swept up the Delta from New Orleans to beyond Memphis" was unusually virulent — deadly. Memphis had been under "strict quarantine." Jeff had written daughter Maggie two weeks earlier, warning, "We have it now in Mississippi City, in Biloxi, and one case near Handsboro. He added that, as far as practicable, "we avoid intercourse with persons coming from infected places. . . . As for myself," Jeff assured, "I have passed unharmed through so many epidemics, that I think I am more than usually exempt." Jeff told Maggie that his greatest concern was for her, Addison and Jeff, Jr. He did not have Yellow Fever, but was too unwell at the time to risk a trip to Memphis, for he might become a patient instead of a nurse. Varina wanted to go to Memphis to help, but Jeff feared she would arrive sick as well because, "it was impossible to go otherwise than through New Orleans, and by that route it was necessary to remain in the City some 20 hours and then to pass through many infected places." Jeff's writing assistant, William Walthall, volunteered to go to Memphis to look after Jeff, Jr., and that proposal seemed to make the most sense, because Walthall had previously gained "a large experience in the Yellow Fever." Jeff explained in a letter to Addison that we "consented to accept the kind offer of William Walthall to go instead of either of us, and take charge of our son. I did and do feel some confidence that I could, as I have done in former times, pass through the contagion unscathed and you can realize how much I desire to be with my child, but reason compels me to admit that Walthall can do more for him than I could. May God shield him and our other two children is my constant prayer." And Walthall did succeed in getting to Memphis and in passing through the quarantine barriers. Jeff, Jr. rallied on October 15th and Maggie wired hopefully that the crisis had passed. But Jeff, Jr. suffered a violent relapse the following day. That evening Walthall telegraphed parents Jeff and Varina, reporting, "He died quietly and peacefully at five this afternoon. Burial tomorrow at ten." [R19;435-436, R30;487-489, R30;493]

Biographer Hudson Strode would write: "Jefferson Davis, anguished by the loss of his fourth son, wandered hither and thither about the mansion grounds and through the forest all the next day in search of ease for his grief." The next day Jeff wrote Addison, the son-in-law who would become his "son:"

"Dear Addison,

". . . The last of my sons has left me; I am crushed under such heavy and repeated blows. I presume not God to scorn, but the many and humble prayers offered before my boy was taken from me, are hushed in the despair of my bereavement. . .

"I thank you from the bottom of my heart for your unfailing efforts to save my boy to me. My own [Maggie] is your further charge.

"Your Mother is prostrate under a complication of painful disease, among which neuralgia is chief. She was far from well when we received the first news of our boy's attack; she has grown worse from that time, and now is quite helpless in bed. We are endeavoring to keep her quiet and to obtain for her sleep, the absolutely needed remedy for nerves and brain. . .

"If my good friend [William] Walthall is yet with you, do tell him if words can convey it, how grateful I am to him.

"With tenderest love to my darling daughter, and to my son Addison, I am,

"Jefferson Davis"

As Jeff had reported to Addison, Varina was sick in bed with "brain fever" and there was fear that she would die as well. Fortunately, Sarah Dorsey "gave herself over to constant and tender nursing," and for two weeks "she did not leave the sickroom except for short intervals." Under such loving care, Varina recovered.

But, what was Jeff Davis to do? Four sons buried. None left to carry on the Davis family tradition of leadership in private enterprise, in military service or in government service — local, State or Federal. This was perhaps a time when Jeff Davis recommitted himself to serve the 260,000 Confederates who had died in the defense of State Secession and the survival of the Confederate States of America. Those men were to become his 260,000 sons. The cause for which they had fought was to be explained and justified in his writing of the history of Confederacy. Those men were to be his "sons," and he intended to serve them and bestow honor upon the cause for which they had fought and upon their bravery.

Meanwhile early the following month voting across the States, northern, southern and western, showed that Democrats would control, by a small majority, the Federal House. And Democrats would control more State Legislatures, providing more Democrats for the Federal Senate. In the Senate, instead of being a minority of 36 Democrats to 39 Republicans and 1 other, Democrats would be enjoying a strong majority of 42 Democrats to 33 Republicans and 1 other. So in 1879, Democrats would control the Federal House and the Federal Senate, while Republicans would control only the office of President.

Looking at the voting results for South Carolina, we find that Wade Hampton and State Democrats won overwhelming victories in the Tuesday, November 6 elections. Running unopposed, Hampton received 119,550 votes to only 213 opposed. Only 3 Republicans were elected to the State House and only 5 Republicans would return to the State Senate. There would be 6 African American Democrats in the new Legislature. Of the 5 South Carolinians in the Federal House, all of them would be Democrats.

However, on the following day, tragedy would befall the victor in the race for Governor, while on a deer hunt with companions in the Wateree Swamp, east of Columbia. Biographer Walter Cisco would tell the story:

> Wade Hampton "spent Wednesday night east of Columbia at the home of a friend. The next morning he set out alone into the moss-hung wilderness, expecting to meet up with other members of the party. He was riding a borrowed animal, described as 'a young, half-broken mule.' Hearing the baying of hounds, Hampton followed, pushing deeper into the woods. Even at 60 Hampton remained an expert rider, described by a friend as 'an iron man physically.'

> "At four o'clock on that November afternoon, he had still not caught up with the other hunters. Hampton spotted a deer, raised his rifle, took aim, and fired. Preparing to dismount, he leaned forward as he threw the reins over a tree limb. Without warning the mule bolted. Hampton had but a moment to react. Rather than remain in the saddle to be pummeled by overhanging branches, he jumped, landing full force on his right foot. The pain was intense. He had broken both bones in his lower leg and the tibia, the large bone, was protruding through the flesh. Blood was flowing from the injury caused by this compound fracture. Hampton lay on the forest floor in desperate need of help.

> "He still had his rifle and a hunting horn and began to use them to signal. A high wind dissipated the sounds. The far-away hunting party finally heard shots, but it was the frequency of the reports that caught the attention of [Thomas Taylor who sent an African American] servant to investigate. At about sundown, two hours after the accident, Hampton was found lying on his back with his head resting against the base of a tree.

> "The rescuers immediately sent for a wagon equipped with a spring suspension and laid a mattress in the bed. They had to cut a crude road through the woods, allowing enough clearance for the vehicle. While they waited with the governor, and before darkness descended, someone noticed that Hampton had taken careful aim at a target — and hit the mark every time.

> "The 16-mile journey back to Hampton's home took half the night. Bumping along a dirt road, badly injured, must have brought to mind that agonizing retreat from Gettysburg 15 years earlier. Dr. Benjamin Taylor met his old friend at Hampton's home and there dressed the wound. A newspaperman reported:

>> "It was found that the small bone of the right leg was broken about 6 inches above the ankle, that the larger bone had been completely severed just about its terminus at the ankle joint, and that the upper end of the lower section had swerved from its place, and penetrating the

surrounding flesh protruded into plain view. The protrusion of the bone had cause considerable loss of blood."

"Early on the morning of Friday, November 8, . . . Hampton was anesthetized with chloroform as [Dr. Taylor and two other physicians] put the ankle back into position, a procedure that required considerable force and was complicated by the fractures. Hampton slept through the day."

At first the doctors believed that Hampton's leg would heal, that amputation would not be needed. However, that was not to be. The wound was severe and, in those days — with antibiotics not yet discovered — a severe compound facture like Hampton had suffered was often followed by infections that would lead to amputations. [R199;281-284]

Meanwhile on the Gulf Coast, Jeff Davis felt he was ready by November 27 to write a detailed letter to Winnie, who was still at Misses Friedlander's boarding school in Germany:

"What is unusual in [Yellow Fever,] Jeff, Jr. retained his faculties to the last. In Christian faith he received the comforts of our church, and peacefully his spirit passed from those who loved him here, but may we not hope to a love better worth than ours. I write in the cottage where he and I worked together before he went to take a place in the bank at Memphis; around me are many objects associated with him and dear, very dear, for his sake. I have bowed to the blows, but in vain have sought for consolation. So many considerations, not selfish, plead for his longer stay on earth that I only shut my eyes, to what it is not permitted me to see, and stifling the outward flow, let my wounds bleed inwardly." [R30;493]

To add a bit of cheerfulness to the otherwise sad letter, Jeff told Winnie how much everyone at the beach house enjoyed the pictures of her that had been received in a previous letter. He said that Sarah Dorsey "greatly admired the one in standing posture and wished she had one. . . . [and that Robert Brown] says he cannot tell you how much he loves you, but hopes you know it." [R30;492-493]

Meanwhile in South Carolina, it was clear by early December that Wade Hampton's leg was not healing well. There was talk of electing him to the Federal Senate, to occupy the seat soon to be vacated by the notorious, historically corrupt John Patterson, Republican. In the Federal Senate Hampton would have a less demanding job, easier on his injury; and, on that national stage, he would be an excellent spokesman for, not just South Carolina, but all of the former Confederate States. Furthermore, Lieutenant Governor William Simpson was capable and in political agreement with Hampton's philosophy — he would be expected to execute Hampton's agenda of peaceful racial accommodation and sound financial management. On December 10, at noon, State Representative Samuel McGowan of Abbeville rose in the South Carolina House to address the Chair:

"Mr. Speaker, I have the honor to nominate for the great office of Senator from South Carolina one whose past history marks with certainty his future course; one who is in the truest sense, the embodiment of the brave, just, conservative Democracy of the State."

The motion was seconded and a letter from Hampton was read which advised that, concerning the wishes of the Legislature, he left his future "entirely to their judgment;" whether as Governor or as Senator, "I will with equal cheerfulness accord with their desire." A vote was taken: all but two in the State House voted to send Hampton to the Federal Senate and all in the State Senate concurred.

Meanwhile, while the votes were being taken, surgeons were amputating Wade Hampton's lower right leg. It had not healed and there seemed to be no alternative. Those voting that day, especially those who had also survived the Federal Invasion of the Confederacy, were remembering lost fathers, sons and brothers, and remembering the many veteran amputees who struggled to move about their homeland in the southern States. Tearful eyes punctuated the casting of the votes.

The amputation would be a medical success and Wade Hampton would be fitted with an artificial leg fabricated from cork-wood. In future years this robust outdoorsman would be found more often fishing a trout stream and less often on the hunt for wild game. He was 60 years old. [R199;284-285]

So, in March or soon afterward, Wade Hampton would be joining Lucius Lamar in the Federal Senate. Meanwhile, Lamar was at work in the Senate when, on December 12 in Mississippi — with reference to Lamar's February vote in the Senate against the Bland-Allison Silver Act, contrary to instructions from the Mississippi Legislature — the editor of the Jackson *Clarion* wrote Jeff Davis at Beauvoir asking his opinion on a Federal Senator's responsibility to vote in accordance with directions by his State Legislature. Considering Davis' reluctance to engage in debate over the politics of the day, it is surprising that an answer was forthcoming. His answer to the question about a Federal Senator's obligation to obey instructions from his State Legislature is presented below in part. The letter was dated December 14, from Beauvoir. After a fitting acknowledgement that he was a mere bystander with no political responsibilities, Davis entered into the meat of the issue. These two brief paragraphs suffice to explain his thoughts.

"The two houses of Congress represent — the one, the people; the other, the States themselves. If the people of a Congressional District were to assemble in mass and instruct their Representative upon any particular question, who will gainsay their right to do so, or his duty to obey?

"In the compact of the Union it was provided that the Representatives of the States, their Senators, should be chosen by their respective Legislatures. Those Legislatures do, in that connection, express the voice of the State; and the Senator who accepts his election by the Legislature as such expression of the will of the State would seem to be estopped from contending at any future time that the Legislature was not the proper channel through which the State should speak to him."

The editor of the *Clarion* would wait until January 15 to print Davis' letter in his newspaper. Many other newspapers would reprint the letter, putting considerable pressure on Senator Lamar to never, ever again disobey the Mississippi Legislature when, on rare occasions, it submitted specific instruction on policy. Actually, the Davis letter did not hurt Lamar politically, for, to people in the northern States, being at odds with the former Confederate President was a plus, and the statue and influence that Lamar was gaining on the national stage was giving Mississippians more reason to return him to Washington. [R205;362-364]

The Year of 1879

(1Q79)

During February, Varina left the beach house to spend time in Memphis with Maggie and Addison. It was her first return visit since Sarah Dorsey had — using the lure of a party in her honor — enticed Varina to leave Memphis and come to the beach to join her husband. Sarah must have been thinking of putting the beach house in Jeff's name for some time and thought it best to arrange the sell while Varina was out of town. You will recall that, 14 months previously, Sarah had spoken to Jubal Early about leaving her complete estate to Jeff, if he outlived her. At some point afterward it had occurred to Sarah that she should go ahead and put the beach house in Jeff's name though a simple sales transaction. So, one day in February, Sarah offered to sell the beach house and its surrounding 600 acres to Jeff for an agreed price of $5,500. Sarah offered to accept payment in three equal installments of $1,833.33 each, and Jeff sealed the deal by paying down the first installment. Sarah's timing for proposing the sell was not entirely sparked by Varina's temporary absence. She had been unwell, and the physician she had consulted in New Orleans had determined that she was suffering from cancer. But she had told none of her friends of her disease. Since Jeff had not been needing Sarah's help with the writing work, she was thinking she might leave the coast and spend most of her remaining time at one of her Louisiana farms. [R19;439-440]

Meanwhile during February, a tug of war began between the Federal House, controlled by the Democratic Party, and Rutherford Hayes with regard to Democrat desires to repeal most if not all of the Enforcement Acts of 1870 and 1871. The Democrat strategy to effect the repeals was to attach amendments to key appropriation bills, including the Army Appropriation Bill and the bill funding Congress, the Executive Department and the Judicial Department. During February the Federal House passed both funding bills with amendments attached which greatly reduced the ability of the Federal Government to police elections. But the Republican-controlled Federal Senate refused to agree, so neither funding bill was submitted to Rutherford Hayes for his signature. The outgoing 45th Congress would finish its term without providing the crucial funding. Consequently, Hayes issued a proclamation on March 5 calling the incoming 46th Congress — which would now include Senator Wade Hampton — into Special Session, beginning March 18, for the purpose of submitting bills to his desk to fund the Army and to fund Congress, the Executive Department and the Judicial Department.

But Hayes' hand would be weaker next time, for Democrats would control the Senate as well as the House in the 46th Congress.

Meanwhile Lucius Lamar — as a member of the Senate Select Committee on Epidemic Diseases — and fellow Democrats sought Federal help in fighting Yellow Fever, which had killed 20,000 people earlier in the year in the horrific epidemic along the lower Mississippi River and Gulf Coast. They were successful on March 3, establishing by law a Federal National Board of Health. Some detail on this subject is appropriate:

On June 2, the new Federal National Board of Health would be granted "wide quarantine powers." Established, through the political support of Democrats, including Lucius Lamar, for a 4-year period, until June 2, 1883, the enabling law stated that a new law would be needed to extend the Board. It was authorized to enforce medical quarantines both inland and along coastal regions, having controlling authority over State boards and State quarantine officials. The new health organization was intended to focus on inland public health, augmenting the efforts of the seaport-oriented Marine Hospital Service, and the numerous State public health departments, such as the Board of Health of the State of Louisiana, not replacing any of them. However, the Federal Board of Health was to hold quarantine power over State boards when attempting to check the spread of infectious diseases, such as malaria and yellow fever, since their spread could rapidly jump across State boundaries. Local disease agents, such as polluted drinking water, were more readily fully addressed by the State boards of health.

Prior to this time, Federal efforts toward public health were pursued through the United States Marine Hospital Service, which was charged with the medical care of seamen and the operation of its hospitals in American seaports. The Chief of the Marine Hospital Service was John Woodworth, Surgeon General of the Service from 1871 until his death two weeks after the creation of the National Board of Health. Upon completing his medical training at the Chicago Medical College in 1862, Woodworth had joined the Federal Army as a Surgeon, moving with Federals across Tennessee, Georgia and South Carolina, including with forces under the command of William Sherman. But the Marine Hospital Service was not just going to vanish or be absorbed into the new National Board of Health, and soon, on April 3, John Hamilton of Illinois would be named Supervising Surgeon General over that organization.

It is important to realize that it would not be until 1881 that mosquitoes would first be suspected as the carrier of yellow fever, that first suggestion being by Dr. Carlos Finlay of Cuba, and not until the 1890s that this method of infection was conclusively proven. The disease had originated in central Africa, and then spread to South America and the Gulf region. The disease agent is a virus, only treatable by vaccines which would not be developed until the 1930's. Enforced quarantine — restricting commerce and travel by people through police action — would be the only weapon during epidemics until the world learned in the late 1890's that mosquito nets and wetlands mosquito control were effective weapons, these also fighting the spread of malaria.

Allowing a few Federal officials to order quarantines of commerce and travel was considered a violation of State rights, so political maneuvering was not surprising, especially since the carrier of the disease was unknown (eventually it would be proven that person A could not give the disease to person B unless a mosquito bit A, then B). The most important struggle over State versus Federal authority over public health would be centered in New Orleans, a major seaport where sailors, travelers and cargo arrived from the Caribbean, the Gulf, and Central and South America. Fortunately, a repeat of the 1878 yellow fever epidemic would not occur over the following 5 year period. Politicians would become forgetful and susceptible to attempts to bring public health back under military control. Consequently, United States Marine Hospital Service leader John Hamilton, an effective political manipulator, would be successful in persuading the Federal House and Senate to forgo passing a bill to continue the National Board of Health past the June 2, 1883 limit of its authorization. Consequently, the responsibilities given to the new National Board of Health would be returned to the Marine Hospital Service four years later, in 1883. History shows that "the defenders of the National Board of Health were good sanitarians but poor politicians." [*American Journal of Public Health*, August, 1943, 925-930.]

With the Democrats scheduled to take control of the Federal Senate on March 18, notable Republicans resorted to waving the bloody shirt in hopes of disrupting progress on Democrat legislation and gaining northern States votes in the upcoming 1880 elections. In this vein, during early March, George Hoar of Massachusetts argued before the Federal Senate that Jeff Davis must be denied the benefits being granted to other veterans of the Mexican War in the Pension Bill being debated at that time. Hoar complained that Davis was unfit for any Federal pension because of his subsequent participation in Mississippi's secession and his leadership of the Confederate Government. Hoar alleged that Davis was no better than the notorious Revolutionary War traitor, Benedict Arnold of Connecticut and Massachusetts or the traitor Aaron Burr of New York. When Hoar finished, Lucius Lamar rose to defend Jeff Davis' name. Although Lamar's words were extemporaneous, his language was so compelling and meaningful, that many people today consider it the most meaningful description of the man:

> "*Mr. President*: It is with extreme reluctance that I rise to say a word upon this subject. I must confess my surprise and regret that the Senator from Massachusetts should have wantonly, without provocation, flung this insult" —

The Presiding Officer quickly interrupted, proclaiming that Lamar was out of order. Lamar protested and demanded a decision by the Senators present with regard to his being "out of order." A vote was called, for or against the Chair's ruling. The Presiding Officer announced the decision:

> "The judgment of the Chair is reversed, and the Senate decides that the words uttered by the Senator from Mississippi are in order, and the Senator from Mississippi will proceed."

Lamar continued, freely delivering his well-conceived remarks without notes or preparatory thought.

> "The only difference between myself and Jefferson Davis is that his exalted character, his preeminent talents, his well-established reputation as a statesman, as a patriot, and as a soldier, enabled him to take the lead in the cause to which I consecrated myself and to which every fiber of my heart responded. There was no distinction between insult to him and southern [States] people, except that he was their chosen leader, and they his enthusiastic followers; and there has been no difference since.

> "Jefferson Davis, since the [War Between the States], has never counseled insurrection against the authority of this government. Not one word has he uttered inconsistent with the greatness and glory of this American Republic. The Senator from Massachusetts can point to no utterance of Jefferson Davis which bids the people of the [southern States] to cherish animosities and hostilities to this Union, nor does he cherish them himself.

> "The Senator — it pains me to say it — not only introduced this amendment [to exclude Jefferson Davis from the benefits envisioned for all other veterans], but he coupled that honored name with treason; for, sir, he is honored among the [southern States] people. He did only what they sought to do; he was simply chosen to lead them in a cause which we all cherished; and his name will continue to be honored for his participation in that great movement which inspired an entire people, the people who were animated by motives as sacred and noble as ever inspired the breast of a Hampden or a Washington. I say this as a Union man today. The people of the [southern States] drank their inspiration from the fountain of devotion to liberty and to constitutional government. We believed that we were fighting for it, and the Senator cannot put his finger upon one distinction between the people of the [southern States] and the man whom the Senator has today selected for dishonor as the representative of the [southern States people].

> "Now, sir, I do not wish to make any remarks here that will engender any excitement or discussion; but I say that the Senator from Massachusetts connected that name with treason. We all know that the results of [the War Between the States] have attached to the people of the [southern States] the technical crime of rebellion, and we submit to it; but that was not the sense in which the gentleman used that term as applied to Mr. Davis. He intended to affix (I will not say that he intended, but the inevitable effect of it was to affix) upon this aged man, this man broken in fortune, suffering from bereavement, an epithet of odium, an imputation of moral turpitude.

"Sir, it required no courage to do that; it required no magnanimity to do it; it required no courtesy. It only required hate, bitter, malignant, sectional feeling, and a sense of personal impunity. The gentleman, I believe, takes rank among Christian statesmen. He might have learned a better lesson even from the pages of mythology. When Prometheus was bound to the rock it was not an eagle, it was a vulture, that buried his beak in the tortured vitals of the victim.

"I send to the desk a letter written by Mr. Davis upon this subject to Mr. Singleton, a gentleman who represents one of the districts of Mississippi in the other House; and, with the expression of my opinion that the Senator from Massachusetts does not represent Massachusetts in the step that he has taken and the sentiments that he has uttered this day, I shall take my seat."

The Secretary thusly read the letter from Davis for all in the Senate chamber to hear.

"Dear Sir: I am quite unwilling that personal objections to me by members of Congress should defeat the proposed measure to grant pensions to the veterans of the War Against Mexico. I therefore request and authorize you, should the fate of the bill depend upon excluding me from its benefits, in my behalf, to ask my friends and the friends of the measure, silently, to allow a provision for my exclusion from the benefits of the bill to be inserted in it. . . ."

Senator James Blaine then jumped into the fray, siding with Hoar and agitating the "bloody shirt." Lucius Lamar countered with further defense of the lost cause of the Confederate States. But in the end the amendment excluding Jefferson Davis was adopted. Of course Lamar's defense was about the principal of the issue, not about giving his friend Jeff Davis a shot at a little pension money. This sectional feud — for the most part incited by Republican Senators Hoar and Blaine and defended by Democrat Senator Lamar — was widely described in a Washington newsletter, and widely circulated by newspapers, giving readers fresh insight into the passions that — 18 years, almost a generation earlier — had moved southern States people to vote for State secession and to follow Jeff Davis, their elected leader. As a reader of *Bloodstains*, you are well aware of Jeff Davis' acts of heroism and splendid military leadership during the War Against Mexico — heroism recognized all across the United States — heroism most noteworthy in the battle of Buena Vista, where, under the overall command of Zachary Taylor, both he and Robert E. Lee earned worthy recognition. Through the considerable detail provided herein concerning this March 1879 Senate fight, you are gaining a better sense of the passions and justifications that lingered, even when State Secession had faded 18 years into history.

On March 15 Jeff Davis penned a thank-you note and mailed it to his friend Lucius Lamar:

"My Dear Sir: Please accept my thanks for your defense of me against the petty malignity of Hoar, Blaine, and others. I am truly thankful for the kindness of the other Senators who spoke in my behalf; but it was needful, for my entire satisfaction, that Mississippi's Senator should be heard in my vindication." [R205;365-371, R19;440]

March 18, 1879 represented a major milestone in returning the United States to a healthy two-party Federal Government. For the first time since 1853, a span of 26 years, both the Federal House and the Federal Senate were under the control of the Democratic Party. In the House, Democrats held 149 seats versus 130 for Republicans and 14 by men of other party affiliations. In the Senate Democrats held 42 seats versus 33 for Republicans and 1 by a man of another party. Democrat control of both the House and the Senate was a spectacular event in American history. It would last only two years and not be repeated until the second administration of Grover Cleveland in 1893, long after the close of the history covered by *Bloodstains*. This would be followed by 20 years of Republican control until the first years of the Woodrow Wilson Administration, beginning in 1913, an unusual era of Democratic Party domination that would last for 6 years, continuing through the horrors of World War I.

When the Session opened on March 18 Lucius Lamar advanced in his Committee assignments. He succeeded Republican Blanche Bruce as Chairman of the Mississippi River Committee and became a member of the Judiciary Committee and the Railroad Committee. Later in the session he would fill a vacancy in the Education and Labor Committee. "In addition to these standing committees, he again served on the Select Committee on Epidemic Diseases." Wade Hampton was still regaining his strength from the leg amputation due to a nasty infection, not arriving at the Senate until April 16.

The political tug over repealing the 1870-71 Enforcement Acts — the last of the three also called the "Kuklux Act" — was now well underway. So, this is a good time to review, in a concise manner, the substance of the three Enforcement Acts, which had been passed in 1870 and 1871, at the height of Republican dominance in the conquered Confederate States, with its attendant, rabid corruption. Democrats advocated repealing the three Enforcement Acts of 1870-71, which, taken together, authorized the Federal Army to police voter registration and voting at the polls during local, State and Federal elections. Republicans wanted to continue Federal Army involvement in these election matters as a means of boosting Republican votes in the former Confederate States. The three Enforcement Acts are summarized below:

- The First Enforcement Act (May 31, 1870) — this Federal statute, consisting of 23 detailed sections of legal requirements regulating voter registration and procedures at polling places, criminalized voter intimidation, threats (such as loss of employment) and bribery (vote buying) aimed at reducing or influencing the votes of African American men. Concerning enforcement, it authorized policing by Federal Marshals and, when specially authorized by the President, also by the Federal military (and State militia under Federal command), including authorization to suspend the writ of *habeas corpus*. It placed judicial enforcement, criminal trials and sentencing in the hands of Federal district attorneys and Federal Courts, even in State and local elections.

- The Second Enforcement Act (February 28, 1871) — this Federal statute amended the First Enforcement Act, adding 19 detailed sections of law further regulating voter registration and procedures at polling places, underscoring the dominant role of Federal Marshals and Federal Courts in regulating elections, even when as few as 2 citizens in a town of 20,000 applied for Federal law enforcement.

- The Third Enforcement Act (April 30, 1871) — also called the "Kuklux Act," this Federal statute, consisting of 7 detailed sections of law, made it a Federal crime for "two or more persons" to "go in disguise upon the public highway or upon the premises of another for the purpose, either directly or indirectly, of depriving any person or any class of persons of the equal protection of the laws . . . ." Enforcement was by Federal Marshals and prosecution was to be in Federal Courts. Conviction carried a penalty of $500 to $5,000 and/or 6 months to 6 years in prison. The Federal President was authorized to enforce the Act with State Militia and Federal troops. The Federal President was authorized to, when he believed it necessary, suspend the writ of *habeas corpus*. In every trial of a person charged with violating the Act, no European American could serve on the jury if he had given aid to or supported the former Confederate Government.

On April 15, shortly before the first vote on repealing the 1870-71 Enforcement Acts, Wade Hampton arrived at the Federal Senate, feeling well enough to take the seat to which he had been elected. His recovery from the amputation had taken longer than had been expected. He had not felt like taking a buggy ride until January 15, 5 weeks after the surgery. Eventually doctors concluded that the end of the bone had died, requiring a supplemental surgery. Hampton had resigned as Governor and handed the reins to William Simpson on February 26. The Senate had convened on March 18, South Carolina only being represented by Matthew Butler. Butler understood — he had lost a leg in the Battle of Brandy Station. South Carolina was about to be represented in the Federal Senate by two amputees!

When Hampton arrived at the Senate chamber, Henry Dawes of Massachusetts was addressing the chamber. Matthew Butler kindly interrupted Dawes to announce that Senator-elect Wade Hampton "was present and prepared to claim his seat:"

> "Hampton and Butler advanced to the desk of Vice President William Wheeler, where Hampton took the oath of office. It was remarked that South Carolina had only half the legs of sister States, but "as much brains as any."

A few days later Hampton would be assigned to three Committees: Military Affairs, Mines and Mining, and Transportation Routes to the Seaboard. We can be sure that Senator Lucius Lamar warmly greeted his former Confederate compatriot. We will find that of these two, Senator Hampton and Senator Lamar, it will be Lamar who makes the greater mark in national politics. Yet Hampton will be a notable and effective spokesman when championing the interests of the former Confederate States. [R199;289]

Soon after Wade Hampton took his seat in the Federal Senate, it passed an Army Appropriations Bill that included an amendment which repealed portions of the 1870-71 Enforcement Acts, including the section that permitted the President to send in Federal soldiers to police polling places and to assign Federal Marshals to enforce election laws. Rutherford Hayes promptly vetoed the bill, leaving the army not yet funded.

Meanwhile, on the Mississippi coast, upon Varina's return to the beach house, Jeff explained how Sarah had sold them the place and how he had sealed the deal promptly. He further explained that Sarah had left to live at another place she owned. Perhaps, even then, Jeff did not know that Sarah was very ill with cancer. Apparently Varina accepted Jeff's decision to purchase the beach house, for "she settled down to the inevitable and took an absorbed interest in his book. . . . Varina carried on a tremendous correspondence in the search for facts and corroborations of this and that." Materials arrived every day. Notable contributors included W. L. Trenholm, Jubal Early, James Seddon and Judah Benjamin. Josiah Gorgas sent a masterful accounting of the history of the Confederate Ordnance Department which Jeff was able to include in his book just about as it was received. [R19;441]

Meanwhile, political maneuvers continued in Washington City over repeal of the Enforcement Acts. Unable to override Rutherford Hayes' veto of the Army Appropriations Bill, in May the House and Senate sent another version of the Army Appropriations bill to Rutherford Hayes for his signature. Like the previous bill, this bill rescinded that portion of the 1870-71 Enforcement Acts which allowed the Federal President to send the Federal Army to police elections unless they were requested by the States "where such force was to be used." Hayes promptly vetoed this bill, too.

The Army Appropriations Bill was again on the Senate floor. As part of that debate, on June 5, Wade Hampton delivered a notable one-hour speech in the Federal Senate during debate over a new version of the bill, this one including an amendment repealing the ban on former Confederates serving on juries. Hampton presented the following appeal to fellow Senators from the northern States:

Senator Thomas Bayard, a sponsor of the bill being debated, introduced Hampton:

> "Mr. President, I understood yesterday from the honorable Senator from South Carolina [Mr. Hampton] that he desired to address the Senate upon the subject-matter of this bill, and therefore, I yield to him for the purpose of expressing his views upon it, and after he has concluded, I will give my reasons why this bill should become a law."

Wade Hampton then began:

> "Mr. President, I beg to acknowledge my obligations to the Senator from Delaware [Mr. Bayard] for the courtesy which enables me to submit a few remarks to the Senate; and in taking up this bill which he has laid before the Senate, I do not proposed to discuss it specially; I rather prefer to make general remarks upon the subjects which have been under discussion during this session."

After 15 minutes of general remarks, Hampton launched into his argument that the Army be funded for the honorable purposes for which it existed, but that it no longer be available as a political enforcer for the benefit of the Federal President and his political Party:

> "In no event can I consent to aid in disbanding the Army or to impairing its efficiency. It is the Army of the [southern States] as well as of the [northern States]; it is the Army of the whole country. . . . In the late civil [military] contest, on many a bloody field, I tested its valor, and no word nor act nor act of mine shall depreciate its value or lessen it usefulness. But, because I so regard it, no act of mine shall tend to degrade its rank and file into a police squad nor convert its officers into detectives. I will not so legislate that — against its own honorable instincts and traditions — it shall be the instrument of tyranny in the hands of a factious Party or of an Executive who might be so unscrupulous as to use it unlawfully. . . .

> "If the democratic doctrine that Federal troops cannot lawfully be used at the polls, or cannot interfere in State matters unless specially requested to do so by the constituted authorities of a State be a heresy, we have the strongest Republican authority to sustain that heresy."

Then Hampton cited with quotes, the acts where senior Republican Federal and State officials had denounced the interference of Federal troops at polls in the northern States. He quoted Pennsylvania Governor John Geary, Republican, in his protest over using Federal troops at an election in Philadelphia. He quoted Republican Carl Schurz, of which you have read much, in his protest over using Federal troops in Louisiana. He quoted noted Republican William Evarts of New York (whose Federal political career included Senator, Secretary of State and Attorney General) who insisted:

"When men vote, and when their chosen officers meet, and when without violence and without demonstration of insurrection they undertake to conduct the affairs of their political government, no soldiers can interfere."

Then Hampton declared, "I am sustained by the language of the [Federal] Supreme Court, where Justice Nelson, in delivering the opinion of the court, wrote:

"The General Government and the States, although both exist within the same territorial limits, are separate and distinct sovereignties, acting separately and independently of each other within their respective spheres."

Hampton argued that, since the creation of the Federal Government, Congress has been fully capable of dealing with fraudulent elections, by its power to deny a seat to a person whose claim to that seat was determined to be the consequence of a fraudulent election process. Specifically, he said:

"Congress can punish with disfranchisement any community which would force into these Halls an improperly elected member; and that is a safer, a surer, a more constitutional safeguard than the exercise of any doubtful or unlawful [military] power by the Federal Government."

From this point to his close, Hampton transitioned into his general defense of the loyalty of the people of the former Confederate States and their political representatives. Hampton's years in the Federal Senate would not be marked by many important speeches or leadership actions. So, let us use this event of June 5, 1879 as a characterization of the nature of the man, the Senator and the advocate of honorable and trusting accord between the people of the southern States and their brethren in the other States. In a large measure, he was and would be a positive advocate of that lofty goal and, along with Lucius Lamar and other advocates, successful in winning the "Struggle for Healing."

Concerning the insinuation that the southern States are "not true to the Union" Hampton said:

"We are tauntingly told that proof of [the charge that the southern States are not true to the Union] is found in the presence on this floor of 22 members who served in the Confederate Army, and the [southern States people are] reproached, nay, denounced, for sending such men to represent [them] here. Sir, the answer to this charge is simple.

"Nearly every man in the [southern States] who could bear arms was in her armies and she can scarcely be reproached with justice for trusting and honoring in peace the men who risked their fortunes and their lives for her in war. And when the fact is cited that, while the [southern States send] so many of her old soldiers to represent [them] in this august assembly, the [northern States send] but 4, I submit that the reproach, if reproach rests anywhere, belongs rather to the [northern States] than to the [southern States]. I feel that I but speak the sentiments of every man here who was in the Confederate service when I express my deep regret that there are not in this Chamber more of the men who met us in battle, for if opposed to us politically they would, if true soldiers and gentlemen, treat us with the respect that brave men never fail to accord to each other. And, sir, had these great opposing armies, which for 4 years confronted each other in a death grapple, been left to make and enforce the terms of peace, not only would the country have been spared much of the suffering and the humiliation it has experienced, but it would have enjoyed a peace honorable alike to conquerors and conquered. We should long ere this have seen a union re-established on the basis of fraternal reconciliation and a whole people bound together by the indissoluble bonds of mutual respect, common interests, and a common destiny. Such, at least, is the firm conviction of every true soldier in the [southern States] and all [their] sons were soldiers. Nor is this conviction wanting among the brave soldiers of the [northern States], for I have heard it expressed by them time and again. . . .

"We [Senators of the southern States] are here because we do represent the popular majority, the character, the intelligence, and the property of the States which have sent us. We are here because left to themselves the instincts of the recently enfranchised [African American] voters have taught them that their interests are identical with ours. We are here because, belonging to your own race, trained in the same political experience as your own, taught by years of rule how to govern, we could not be subordinated — and the people of the country did not wish us to be subordinated, to such a mass of ignorant voters as you had rashly and suddenly created. We are here, we trust, for the good of the whole country. What we were you knew when you insisted that we should still be part and parcel of this Union.

"For the past you cannot expect us to apologize; to do so would be to sacrifice our own self-respect and to forfeit the respect of all honorable men. In the heat of conflict we struck hard blows, and doubtless we spoke hard words. But does remembering or repeating them now bring us any nearer to the peace and harmony for which the whole country so ardently longs? The men who served in the opposing armies are now the strongest advocates of a true reconciliation. We learned in a common school how to respect our enemies; we learned that personal courage and honor and truth were better guarantees of patriotism than constitutional learning or eloquent speech; we learned at least that in spite of differences, even unto death, there was a common country which we could better serve in friendship than in hatred, and were our antagonists of the late war here today, in the contests on this floor as in fiercer battles of yore, whoever might be the victor, we should be assured of a fair field and an honest surrender."

At this point the applause from the galleries prompted the presiding officer to admonish, "The Chair gives notice that if further applause occurs in the galleries he will order them to be cleared." Hampton continued:

". . . We ask you to strike from the statute-book legislation which was as much the instrument of war, the expression of distrust, as were armies and navies and military districts. We say, if you bring us back as States, treat us as States. We ask you to remove the disability which forbids a citizen to serve on a jury when it does not forbid him to serve on the bench. We ask you to leave the ballot box free, as it has been through nearly the whole of our political existence. . . . Surely in the face of the recent decision of the [Federal] Supreme Court in regard to the juror's oath, in face of the legislation of nearly a century in reference to military interference at the polls, you cannot charge us with revolution or treason in making these requests. . . .

"In the great contest in which we failed we lost much. We lost power and wealth and precious lives. But when the people of the United States declare that the right of self-government is extinguished in the States; that the prerogative of a free vote, which is the distinguishing glory of American citizenship, can be exercised only under the supervision of a Federal marshal or the protection of a Federal soldier; that the duties of Governors and Legislatures to maintain the dignity and to preserve the peace of sovereign States has been transferred to the [Federal] President; and when it has become revolution and treason to ask the people to consider these things, then will the memory of our poor losses be forgotten in the overwhelming calamities which would follow the loss of American freedom. . . .

"Mr. President, patriotic men of all parties, north and south, can join heart and hand in the effort to perpetuate on this continent constitutional liberty as established by our fathers. In this noble work we of the [southern States] will not prove laggards. We wish to promote the best interests of the whole country; we wish to restore harmony and good-will; we hope to see permanent peace and widespread prosperity among all classes of our people; we desire to see the painful memories of the late unhappy war buried in our own hearts, not rising to the lips in bitter words which can only provoke sectional animosity; and we propose, in spite of misapprehension, misrepresentation, and denunciation, to stand firmly by the Constitution in its integrity, to maintain the Union in perpetuity, trusting, hoping, praying that to our children, if not to us, it may be given too see the States of this mighty Republic bound together, not alone by the ties of material interest, but by the cords of true fraternity, ruled by a great, a happy, a free people crowned with all the blessings and with all the glories which God in His infinite mercy can bestow."

The floor returned to Senator Thomas Bayard, who proceeded to give his reasons why the bill ought to become law. [Congressional Record, Senate, First Session, June 5, pages 1778-1781]

Who were the 22 Confederate veterans Wade Hampton claimed to be sitting in the Federal Senate during June 1879? In my research of the question, I have identified 18 military veterans and two members of the Confederate Senate. Perhaps others can reconcile the claim of 22. Here are the names and the highest ranks attained during the era of the Confederacy, according to my investigation. I found none outside of the southern States and none in Delaware or Maryland:

Alabama	John T. Morgan (D), Brigadier General, Calvary. George S. Houston (D), did not serve in the war.
Arkansas	Augustus H. Garland (D), Confederate House and Senate. James D. Walker, Colonel, Arkansas Infantry, POW for 2 years.
Florida	Charles W. Jones (D), did not serve in the war. Call Wilkinson (D), Adjutant General.
Georgia	Benjamin H. Hill (D), Confederate Senate. John B. Gordon (D), Major General.
Kentucky	James B. Beck (D), did not serve in the war. John S. Williams (D), Brigadier General.
Louisiana	William P. Kellogg (R), did not serve in the war. Benjamin F. Jonas (D), Major.
Mississippi	Blanche K. Bruce (R), did not serve in the war. Lucius Lamar (D), Colonel.
Missouri	Francis M. Cockrell (D), Brigadier General. George G. Vest (D), Confederate Senate.
North Carolina	Matt W. Ransom (D), Brigadier General. Zebulon B. Vance (D), Colonel and Governor of Confederate North Carolina.
South Carolina	Calbraith Butler (D), Major General. Wade Hampton (D), Lieutenant General.
Tennessee	James E. Bailey (D), Colonel. Isham G. Harris (D), Governor of Confederate Tennessee and Army Staff Officer.
Texas	Samuel B. Maxey (D), Major General. Richard Coke (D), Captain.
Virginia	John W. Johnston (D) Abington, Virginia local government official. Robert E. Withers (D), Colonel.

By the way, my great great grandfather, Moses White was a private under Matt W. Ransom, who is listed above as a Senator from North Carolina.

On June 18, while Army appropriations remain deadlocked, Lucius Lamar, Chairman of the Senate Mississippi River Committee, succeed in winning passage of an Act to establish a Mississippi River Commission. Unlike typical Federal railroad bills, most of them having been sectionally competitive and divisive, this River bill was a cooperative effort in support of both the northern States and the southern States. Lamar had obtained a unanimous consent to bring the bill forward through the crowded Senate docket and had secured a solid favorable vote. The new Commission would oversee the River from its headwaters in Minnesota to the Gulf of Mexico, making surveys and planning for improvements in the river channel, protecting the banks, improving navigation, preventing destructive flooding and promoting commerce. Among the men assigned to lead the Commission would be James Eads of Missouri, who had built the advanced and powerful river gunboats, which in 1862 and 1863 had played a major role in the Federal conquest of the Cumberland River down to Nashville, the Tennessee River down to Pittsburg Landing and the Mississippi River down to New Orleans [R206;206]

Meanwhile, the third attempt at passing an Army Appropriations Bill had been delayed by an unmerciful filibuster by Republican Senators, led by Roscoe Conklin of New York State and James Blaine of Maine. Finally, on June 20, a bill was passed which did not specifically prohibit soldiers from policing elections, but containing the provision that "no money appropriated should be paid for the subsistence, equipment, transportation, or compensation of any portion of the Army of the United States 'to be used as a police force to keep the peace at the polls at any election held within any State'." This bill Hayes signed into law, finally obtaining money to fund the Army. But Democrats passed a companion bill at the same time that was aimed directly at the policing issue, which prohibited assigning soldiers to missions to police elections. This passed the House and the Senate, but was vetoed by Hayes on June 23. So, through filibustering and extended special sessions of Congress, Republicans had retained the slight possibility that Federal troops might some day again police elections, but popular objections to such action was firmly impressed upon the public mind. As mentioned in detail earlier, Wade Hampton had been helpful in presenting the Democratic argument. But Lucius Lamar did not get involved in fighting the Republican filibuster. As a matter of fact he would leave the Senate after voting for the Army Appropriations Bill and be back in Mississippi on June 24. The Federal Senate would adjourn on July 1. Republican manipulation of elections via Federal troops, as had occurred after the conquest of the Confederacy, was not likely to be repeated in the future. But, the tug of war between Republican Rutherford Hayes and Democrats in control of the Federal House and Senate would never be resolved to either's satisfaction. [R206;206, R205;377-393, R200;240-241, R208;448-449, R209;482-483]

(3Q79)

Meanwhile in New Orleans, Sarah Dorsey's cancer had been very aggressive, for she died on July 4, just four and a half months after she had sold her beach house to Jeff Davis. Jeff was at her bedside in New Orleans when she passed away. Jeff had been present when she had taken Holy Communion, and had written down her deathbed bequests of favorite pieces to go to various nieces, cousins, friends and servants. Sarah explained to Jeff that she had given her brothers money and property in the past, only to see them squander her gifts, so she intentionally wanted to omit them in her will. As death had neared, and she had lost her ability to speak, she had asked Jeff to repeat the Beatitudes to her, and "at the end of each verse she had gently nodded her head."

A few hours after Sarah passed away, Jeff wrote William Walthall, asking him to compose obituary notices for the local papers along the coast area where they lived. And Jeff added this comment:

"You know more than most others how self-sacrificing she was, how noble in sentiment, how grand in intellect, but you cannot know how deeply grateful I am for her years of unvarying kindness and service. And therefore cannot realize how sorrowfully I feel her loss."

Jeff accompanied the body up the Mississippi to Natchez and attended the service when her remains were buried beside her husband in the family cemetery plot. Then he returned to New Orleans, and may have been present when Sarah Dorsey's lawyer opened and read her will. As she had told him at her deathbed, she left nothing to her brothers, and they were surely disappointed, for they most expected a large inheritance since their sister left no living children. As might be expected, Sarah's will forgave the money Jeff still owned on the beach house, so that he would own it free and clear. But to everyone's surprise, the will bequeathed to Jeff her three Louisiana farms and everything she owned. Everything! The will said:

"I owe no obligation of any sort whatever to any relative of my own. I have [already] done all I could for them. . . .

"I therefore give and bequeath all my property, real, personal, and mixed, wherever located and situated, wholly and entirely, without hindrance or qualification, to my most honored and esteemed friend, Jefferson Davis, ex-President of the Confederate States, for his own sole use and benefit, in fee simple forever; and I hereby constitute him my sole heir, executive, and administrator. If Jefferson Davis should not survive me, I give all that I have bequeathed him to his youngest daughter, Varina. I do not intend to share in the ingratitude of my country towards the man who is in my eyes the highest and noblest in existence." [R19;443]

After leaving Washington City, Lucius Lamar did not remain in Mississippi long. An outbreak of Yellow Fever was reported in Memphis, indicating a return of the horrible 1878 epidemic. Furthermore a growth in his nose was causing considerable pain and needed to be removed. An eastern surgeon was preferred. These too issues prompted Lamar and his family to relocate to Virginia for much of the remainder of the summer. Renewed growth followed the first surgery, "causing his head and eyes to ache;" but the second "arrested the trouble." The growth would be deemed to have been benign. The Yellow Fever outbreak would prove to me milder that before, and Lamar would return to Mississippi in mid-September to aid the Democratic political campaign, speaking "at different points in the State," the first address being delivered at Oxford on September 29, followed by Coffeeville, Jackson, Vicksburg, Meridian, Columbus and other places. [R205;397-408]

(4Q79)

Lucius Lamar's mother, Sarah Bird Lamar, died suddenly of heart disease at Macon, Georgia on October 31. She had been born in Milledgeville, Georgia, and was to be interred there beside her first husband, Lucius' father, Lucius, Sr. She had been widowed with 5 children at age 32, and had remarried 17 years later, in 1851. Her second husband, Hiram Troutman, lived near Macon and she had moved to his home following the marriage. Both she and Hiram had suffered near blindness from cataracts, but successful surgery had rectified the problem, easing the burdens of her later years. [R205;411]

Returning to Jeff Davis, we find that, like many landowners in Louisiana, Sarah Dorsey had owed considerable money, and, as Executor of her estate, Jeff had to settle those accounts. The most important gift, was the beach house, Beauvoir, for, even today, it is still maintained as a museum and a memorial to the former President. In a letter to a friend, Jeff assessed the net value of the bequest:

> "There has been a vast exaggeration as to the value of the estate, which to a great extent consists of wild and unsaleable land, to pay the taxes on which has been so great a [burden] that much of that kind of property has been forfeited. The gross income of all her property is say about $2,500 and I shall be glad if in the next two years this suffices to liquidate the claims against the estate.

> "As to this place, her former residence [at the beach], it never was the source of income and it will require a great improvement in the current expenses of maintaining it as a residence. The depreciation of property in the neighborhood has been great for many years." [R30;496]

Meanwhile on December 22, Wade Hampton lost his beloved son Wade Hampton, IV to malaria. Wade, IV had been managing the Hampton farms in Mississippi and had become stricken by the disease "during an unusually warm autumn." He had married during the summer. There were no children. He was 38 years old. The father's remaining children were sons Alfred and McDuffie and daughters Daisy and Sally. Of course, he had several grandchildren. Yet, the loss of Wade, IV struck him hard. Three months later he would write, in despair, "Life seems closed to me, and I have nothing but duty to live for." Yet he would persevere. [R208;445]

The Year of 1880

(1Q80)

Suffering from illness in late November, Lucius Lamar had not left Mississippi for Washington City as he normally would have. Communications with Senate colleagues indicated that no crucial votes were pending. But perhaps most importantly, Lamar wanted to lobby the State Legislature over its selection of the next Federal Senator to replace Republican Blanche Bruce, whose term would expire in March 1881. Lamar favored his old political friend Edward Walthall, but two others, including James George, had important support. Furthermore, Walthall, being from northern Mississippi, provided no geographic balance. Apparently passionate in his advocacy of Walthall, Lamar went to Jackson in January and stayed for several days, earnestly advocating for his friend. A three-way contest in the Democratic Party caucus would rage for over a week, but the excitement of the contest caused Lamar to suffer an attack of paralysis the evening following the first balloting. "For a moment he seemed dangerously ill. A doctor applied leeches to his head, a respected treatment during the nineteenth century, but his condition remained serious." Meanwhile, several days later, on the 49th ballot, the caucus finally chose James George, who was the Chief Justice of the Mississippi Supreme Court, greatly disappointing Lamar. With the aid of crutches, he returned to Oxford to regain his health. This illness was described as "another of his apoplectic attacks, quite severe this time, followed by partial paralysis, from which he recovered but slowly." In modern medical terms, he had probably suffered from a small brain bleed, probably triggered by excessive excitement, nervous tension and elevated blood pressure. With time, the brain would recover. By February 10th, Lamar was back in Washington City, not well, but able to get around on crutches. A letter home dated February 17 said:

". . . I took my seat in the Senate yesterday, and received many cordial hand pressures. Conkling was not among those who welcomed me. He stood aloof and eyed me gloomily. . . . My own health is good. I am easily fatigued, and writing makes my head swim. My arm is heavy and weak; but I have thrown aside my crutches, and walk with a stick." [R205;411-414, R206;214-216]

(2Q80)

Jeff and Varina had worked together diligently on the history of the Confederacy since she had joined him at the beach house in July, 1878. By late April, 1880, the first of the two volumes was ready for delivery to the publisher's editors. Their progress is preserved in a letter which Varina wrote to Winnie on April 25:

"We are about as usual now. Your Father is as well, though of course not so vigorous, as any man of 30. I have tried everything with him, and think I have now settled on a plan to keep him well. The weary recital of the weary [Defense of the Confederacy], to be compiled into a splendid but heartbreaking record of cherished hopes now blasted, brave warriors bleeding and dying, and noble men living, yet dead, in that they are hopeless — this tremendous record is being given to the world, and the while as he writes the graves give up their dead, and they stalk before us all gory and downcast, but for all that a gallant, proud army, ready if they could again put on their fleshy shield to do battle for their rights.

"The first volume of the book is to be delivered in a few days — 1st of May.

"God bless you my child — more at length tomorrow or next day.

"With devoted love,

"Your Mother." [R30;500]

By mid-June the Federal Senate was again moving toward the end of its session as the upcoming election for Federal President heightened political maneuvering. Desperately, Republicans, a minority in the Senate, had attempted to win enough votes from northern States Democrats to pass a bill authorizing Federal troops to police polling places during elections. The bill failed, with Lamar and other Democrats voting against it as a block.

There was another debate that month of a sectional nature: a debate about concerns over the migration of African Americans from former Confederate States, northward into the northern States. Some in the northern States applauded the migration, anticipating the arrival of farm laborers trained in their craft. In fact an organization called the National Emigration Society was assisting migrants in their journey north. Some in the southern States expressed grave concerns, anticipating a shortage of affordable farm laborers. At one point a group of Mississippi Democrats, confronting the captain and crew of a Mississippi River steamboat, persuaded them to leave 1,500 African Americans stranded on the river bank. Northern States Republicans, who were suspected of liking the idea of new Republican voters coming to their State while attempting to deflect political backlash over the social disruption it was causing, charged that African Americans were being persecuted in their homelands and being driven out. That sort of explanation supported a renewed waving of the "bloody shirt" and agitation for Federal troops at southern States polls on Election Day. The Senate established a Special Investigating Committee to look into this pattern of migration, headed by Democrat Daniel Voorhees of Indiana, and focused on African Americans arriving in his State. Voorhees was a long-time Democrat who had opposed the Federal Invasion of the Confederacy. A majority Democrat report and a minority Republican report followed. The Democrat report found that maltreatment was not a factor and that Republicans had encouraged the African Americans to migrate. The Republican report charged that the migration was an "exodus" prompted by maltreatment of African Americans in southern States.

Lucius Lamar would make a notable speech during this debate. But before viewing his comments, we ought to explore the migration patterns of African Americans from the days prior to State Secession to the present time, with a focus on 1860 through 1890. Does history give evidence of "outrages" in the former Confederate States which support the demagoguery being dispensed by the Republican Senators?

I have selected 13 States for a study of the northern States, including Kansas, due to its history as the territory called, "Bleeding Kansas," and including Oregon, due to its history of excluding African Americans from living within its boundaries by force of the Oregon State Constitution (Oregon Exclusionism would be official State law until removed from its State Constitution in 1927).

The data in the table presented below supports the observations which follow:

State	1860	1870	1880	1890	1930	1960	2010
Selected Northern States							
Massachusetts	9,602	13,947	18,697	22,144	53,365	111,842	434,398
Connecticut	8,627	9,668	11,547	12,300	29,354	107,447	362,296
New York	49,005	52,081	65,104	70,092	626,143	1,417,311	3,073,800
New Jersey	25,318	30,658	38,853	47,638	208,828	514,875	1,204,826
Pennsylvania	56,949	65,294	85.535	107,596	431,257	852,750	1,377,689
Ohio	56,949	63,213	79,900	87,113	309,304	786,097	1,407,681
Indiana	11,428	24,560	39,228	45,215	111,982	269,275	591,397
Illinois (Exclusionism)	7,628	28,762	46,368	57,028	328,972	1,037,470	1,866,414
Michigan	6,799	11,849	15,100	15,223	169,453	717,581	1,400,362
Wisconsin	1,171	2,113	2,702	2,444	10,739	74,546	359,148
Kansas (Bleeding)	625	17,108	43,107	49,710	66,344	91,445	167,864
Oregon (Exclusionism)	128	346	487	1,186	2,234	18,133	69,206
California	4,086	4,272	6,018	11,322	122,044	883,861	2,299,072
Tot. 13 N. States	238,315	323,871	452,646	529,011	2,470,019	6,882,633	14,614,153
Percent Gain		36	40	17	367	179	112
Percent Gain per Decade		36	40	17	47	41	18
State	**1860**	**1870**	**1880**	**1890**	**1930**	**1960**	**2010**
Middle States and DC							
Delaware	21,627	22,794	26,442	28,386	32,602	60,688	191,814
Dist. Columbia							305,125
Maryland	171,131	175,391	210,230	215,657	276,379	518,410	1,700,298
Kentucky	236,167	222,210	271,451	268,071	226,040	215,949	337,520
Missouri	118,503	118,071	145,350	150,184	223,840	390,853	693,391
Tot. 4 M States+DC	547,428	538,466	653,473	662,298	758,861	1,185,900	3,228,148
Percent Gain		-2	21	1	15	56	172
Percent Gain per Decade		-2	21	1	3	16	22
State	**1860**	**1870**	**1880**	**1890**	**1930**	**1960**	**2010**
Former Confederate States							
Va. and W. Va.	548,907	530,821	657,502	668,128	795,058	905,636	1,614,523
North Carolina	361,522	391,650	531,277	561,018	918,647	1,114,907	2,048,628
Tennessee	283,019	322,331	403,151	430,678	477,646	586,876	1,057,315
Arkansas	111,259	122,169	210,666	309,117	478,463	388,787	449,895
South Carolina	412,320	415,814	604,332	688,934	793,681	829,291	1,290,684
Georgia	465,598	545,142	725,133	858,815	1,071,125	1,122,596	2,950,435
Alabama	437,770	475,510	600,103	678,489	944,834	980,271	1,251,311

Mississippi	437,404	444,201	650,291	742,559	1,009,718	915,843	1,098,385
Florida	62,677	91,689	126,690	166,180	431,828	880,186	2,999,862
Louisiana	350,373	364,210	483,655	559,193	776,326	1,039,207	1,452,396
Texas	182,921	253,475	393,384	488,171	854,964	1,187,125	2,979,598
Tot. 11 C. States	3,653,770	3,957,012	5,386,184	6,151,282	8,552,290	9,950,725	19,193,032
Percent Gain		8	36	14	39	16	93
Percent Gain per Decade		8	36	14	9	5	14

Combination of 28 Selected States Plus D. C.

Tot. 28 States+DC	4,439,513	4,819,349	6,492,303	7,342,591	11,781,170	18,019,258	37,035,333
Percent Gain		9	35	13	60	53	106
Percent Gain per Decade		9	35	13	13	15	15.5

The observations:

- In spite of the Federal invasion of the Confederacy and the suffering imposed on the Confederate people, including episodes of starvation, impaired health and disease, between 1860 and 1870 the African American population grew by 9 percent over all 28 States, 8 percent in the Confederate States and 36 percent in the northern States, while dropping slightly, by 2 percent, in the middle States. This encourages the belief that African Americans coped rather well with the difficulties hurled at them, exhibiting good cooperative and survival skills.

- The enormous 35 percent growth in the African American population across the 28 selected States during the 1870-1880 decade is evidence of a rebound in having children and enjoying better diet and health. African American population growth was only slightly higher in the northern States (40 percent) than in the former Confederate States (36 percent). Migration northward from the middle States is evident in that section's loss of 2 percent in African American population. Unusual northward migration out of the former Confederate States is refuted by the census data.

- The 1880 census data gives no indication that people in the former Confederate States were encouraging mass migration northward by threats or any other method. The gain in Senator Daniel Voorhees State of Indiana was only from 24,560 to 39,228, a gain of 60 percent, but far below the gain in formerly "Bleeding Kansas," which was from 17,108 to 43,107, a gain of 152 percent. So why was Democrat Voorhees agitating in the northern States against the arriving African Americans? This was politics. Voters could be easily convinced that Republicans wanted African Americans to migrate northward to swell the Republican vote in their respective States, so agitating the issue could swing European Americans to the Democratic Party.

- By 1880 the 452,646 African Americans living in the selected 13 northern States exceeded the 1860 population by 90 percent, a major growth in only 20 years. The irony of this societal transformation is remarkable. It was only 25 years earlier, in 1855, that the Republican Party had risen from nothing to domination of northern States politics, a process requiring only 5 years, a process fueled by political agitation over "Bleeding Kansas" and Exclusionism. Republican Exclusionists had advocated a political fence along the boundary with the middle States to prevent African Americans from migrating north. Republican Abolitionists had encouraged northern States African Americans to migrate northward into Canada. Republican Deportationists had foreseen mass migration (deportation) beyond the boundaries of the United States and had been encouraging a vastly expanded deportation program. A northern States policy of Exclusionism — coupled with preservation of laws permitting African American bonding in the southern States, and coupled with the absence of charitable people buying bonded African Americans and making them independent — had been predicted to result in a future northern States society nearly devoid of African Americans and, taken to its extreme, the eventual "extinction" of African Americans throughout the United States (a racial cleansing that Republican Abe Lincoln had said might take 100 years). By what logic had Demagogues projected that African Americans would become "extinct?" A convincing argument based on facts had always been purposefully avoided, thereby leaving people to wonder on their own — if owners in the southern States were breeding African Americans, like, say, cattle, as some were led to believe, then the breeding would decline as fewer would be needed on the farms and, perhaps, the foreseen decline would be aided by a deportation program to send them to Africa or Central America or "back" to Africa.

- Moving past 1880 and into the future of our historical time-line, we see that the 1890 census would show that the African American population growth across the 28 selected States would returned to normal, at 13 percent for the decade. The 17 percent gain in the northern States would apparently result from the only 1 percent gain in the middle States, since the former Confederate States would sustain a normal 14 percent African American population growth.

- Three other census records are presented here to reveal how the African American population grew in the selected 28 States plus the District of Columbia, providing a perspective from the point of view of today's readers of *Bloodstains*. The data would show that there would be considerable northward migration after the development of the automobile, bus and diesel locomotives, and during the economic growth following World War I, so the 1930 census is presented. There would be considerable northward and westward migration after the economic growth following World War II, so the 1960 census is presented. Finally, to bring us up to date, the recent 2010 census is presented. Since these snapshots cover spans of 30 or 40 years each, the growth rate is calculated as percent growth for each span and, to make rates comparable for each column, also as percent growth per decade.

- The 1930 census would show a huge migration taking place out of the middle States (growth of only 3 percent per decade) and a substantial migration out of the former Confederate States (growth of only 9 percent per decade) and into the northern States, where growth was huge, at 47 percent per decade. More African Americans would be living in New York State than in Tennessee, Arkansas or Florida. Migration would continue out of the middle States, where growth would be a paltry 3 percent per decade. In spite of the loss from migration northward, the population in the former Confederate States would remain healthy, growing at 9 percent per decade. Within the former Confederate States, there would be considerable migration to North Carolina (manufacturing), Florida (fruits and vegetables) and Texas (ranching and cotton).

- The 1960 census would show the huge migration into the northern and western States continuing, the population growing there by 41 percent per decade. California would see the most remarkable growth (irrigated crops), holding a population by 1960 that would exceed that of 4 of the former 11 Confederate States. New York and New Jersey would see huge growth as well, its combined population of almost 2 million exceeding that of Tennessee, Arkansas and South Carolina combined. African Americans would be drawn to northern Illinois and southern Michigan, creating a combined population in those two northern States that would likewise be moving toward 2 million. Migration out of the former Confederate States would be evident by its slow African American growth of 5 percent per decade. By 1960, of the 28 selected States, only 55 percent of African Americans would be living in the former 11 Confederate States. Within those States, considerable growth would be evident in Florida (fruits and vegetables) and a slight loss in population would occur in Arkansas and Mississippi.

- Finally, looking at the recent 2010 census, we observe that, of the 28 selected States plus the District of Columbia, only 52 percent of African Americans would be living in the former Confederate States, a slight reduction from the 55 percent shown for 1960, thereby revealing that migration out of the former Confederate States was arrested. This would be explained by sluggish economic growth in the northern States (Pennsylvania); rapid economic growth and construction in the former Confederate States (North Carolina, Georgia, Florida and Texas); more generous Federal and State welfare programs, including support for single mothers with children (the "Great Society" Federal programs), and growth in African American employment in the Federal Government (northern Virginia). Of the two Pacific States, California would experience huge growth, moving from 883,861 to 2,299,072, a population exceeding every former Confederate State except for Georgia, Florida and Texas. On the other hand, growth in Oregon would remain sluggish, a result of the fact that the Oregon State Constitution had prohibited any new African American residents prior to 1927. New York would be home to more African Americans than any of the 28 States, holding a population in excess of 3 million, slightly exceeding Georgia, Florida or Texas.

- Data is not shown for the decline in marriages within the African American population and the rise of children born out of wedlock, which would be dramatic between 1930 and 2010. The overall population gain of 15.0 percent per decade from 1930 to 1960 and the 15.5 percent gain per decade from 1960 to 2010 would give evidence of the impact of supportive Federal and State welfare programs for single mothers, most especially the "Great Society" programs launched during the Lyndon Johnson Administration.

This population study now behind us, we return to the June 1880 debate on the floor of the Senate concerning the African American migration and which political Party was to be blamed. Following the "bloody shirt" denunciation of the southern States people by James Blaine of Maine and William Windom of Minnesota, who was chosen to speak for the minority members of the Special Committee, Lucius Lamar rose to deliver his defense of southern States society. In part he said:

"The truth is, all these statements, so far as they represent the condition of things at the [southern States], are unjust and deceiving. The [southern States are] no such country as is represented. I do not deny that there has been violence there. I deplore it; I condemn it. Respecting these cases of violence, you will find, when you get down to the bottom facts, that they are generally precipitated by unscrupulous political Demagogues and tricksters, who inflame the prejudices and passions of the races for their own political purposes. But these cases of violence no longer occur to any appreciable extent.

"The great trouble has been that the investigating committees, which have been sent to the [southern States in years past] and have brought hither their reports, went with purposes hostile to the character of that people. Accordingly, their entire social and political system has been uncovered to hostile eyes. Every evil, every faith, has been searched out as with a microscope, and dragged pitilessly into view; [but] all that is good has been utterly ignored. Sir, no society on earth can undergo such a process of investigation as that to which [the people of the southern States have] been subjected without becoming a spectacle of shame.

"Sir, you may distort the most perfect specimen of human beauty, by searching only for the blemishes and defects and looking at those through a magnifying and refracting glass, into a hideous deformity.

"Sir, the enemies of the [southern States] have pursued this course. Every act of violence, every murder, every uprising of an angry mob, which has neither the head to think nor the heart to feel; every instance, every incident, which can bring reproach upon a community, has been hunted out and magnified and multiplied and grouped together and presented to the world as the portrait of the [southern States].

"The just and equitable operation of equal laws; the administration of justice; the Constitution, safe in the affections of the people; the colleges, academies, and schools; the busy hum of industry; the plenty that reward the toil of the laborer; the worship that ascends to Heaven from thousands of Christian churches; the flame of domestic love, ever burning and every pure upon the altars of happy homes — have been steadily ignored and concealed.

"And, sir, I say today, with all the emphasis of truth, that if, in the history of the last 10 years, the coming of peace has been delayed; if in that time the good have been disheartened and the base encouraged; if the two races have not moved forward with the progress which was expected toward a common prosperity, it is because the Senators and public men who wielded the powers of this great [Federal] Government, and had the confidence of the mighty constituencies behind them, have not risen to the level of their duty and opportunity to bring, as they could have done, rest and quiet and love and universal patriotism over this troubled land."

Leaving this population study and the June 1880 Senate debate, we move forward to the Democratic National Convention, held in Cincinnati, in the Cincinnati Music Hall, on June 22 through 24. Democrats were enthusiastic, many believing Thomas Bayard of Delaware was the strongest candidate, best able to unify the Party. But Bayard was considered to be of the southern States culture, and politicians feared that would put him at a disadvantage in the crucial northern States, such as New York, Pennsylvania, Ohio and Indiana. Delegates were excited, with good reason, anticipating they had a great chance to elect the next Federal President. The southern States appeared to be solidly Democratic but elsewhere the contest would be difficult. So the objective was to win enough northern and western States to add to the southern States and, thereby, build a majority. An example of the enthusiasm was seen in the roar sparked by the entrance upon the floor of South Carolinians Hampton and Butler — a newspaperman from Charleston reported, "When Wade Hampton, preceded by Senator [Calbraith] Butler, came across the floor on his crutches the applause was vociferous, and cries of 'Hampton, Hampton,' echoed through the air."

Nominations began on June 23. Delaware nominated Thomas Bayard, the favorite of the southern States. When Pennsylvania's turn came, it nominated General Winfield Hancock of the Federal Army, having been its senior Major General since 1872. Hancock had been born in Pennsylvania, graduated from West Point in 1844 and experienced a long and successful military career. He had played major roles in the War against Mexico, the Seminole Nation, the invasion of the Confederacy, oversight of occupied Louisiana and Texas, followed by campaigns against Native Americans in the western territories. Hancock's nomination created a roar of enthusiasm, especially from the galleries. When it came South Carolina's turn to nominate, Wade Hampton told the Convention his State had no other nominee to advance. Biographer Walter Cisco would continue the story:

> "Cheering Delegates shouted for [Hampton] to come to the platform, and there [he] made a short speech. He thought it a 'happy omen' that both South Carolina and Massachusetts supported Bayard. 'The [southern States] asks for no place, no power, no patronage, no office,' insisted Hampton. He had confidence in Hancock, but preferred Bayard only 'because we believe him to be the strongest candidate'."

The first ballot tally was extremely close, with Hancock at 171, Bayard at 163.5, Samuel Tilden at 38 and 16 other nominees receiving the remainder. Democratic Party rules required a two-thirds majority to nominate. The next day, voting continued. During the second ballot, vote switching became rampant and Hancock won the nomination. In the cheering that followed the selection of Hancock, speakers advanced to the platform to pledge support and encourage enthusiastic campaigning. Among them was Wade Hampton. A Charleston newspaperman reported:

> "In response to loud calls, Wade Hampton advanced to the platform and said, in behalf of the solid South, which was once arrayed against the gallant soldier, he pledged to him its solid vote."

Hampton later consoled Thomas Bayard in a letter, saying that he regretted that, on the first ballot, Delegates from the southern States had intentionally cast a portion of their votes for others "until it could be ascertained what your [northern States] strength was." In hindsight, Hampton called the tactic "a great mistake. It led to the accidental position Hancock obtained and then the galleries nominated him." But Hampton said he believed that Bayard's strength at the Convention did succeed in defeating the supporters of Samuel Tilden and "for this, at least, I am delighted." [R199;292-293]

On the way from Washington City to Mississippi, Lucius Lamar had stopped in Cincinnati to attend the Democratic Convention. Although not a Delegate, he, like Hampton and others from the southern States, had supported Senator Thomas Bayard of Delaware for the office of President. Although Lamar had wished for Bayard's selection, he probably knew that was nothing but wishful thinking.

(3Q80)

Lucius Lamar campaigned in Mississippi for Winfield Hancock for President. His health was improved but at times he still suffered from unsteadiness, what he called "vertigo." Furthermore his wife Virginia was seriously sick, the preliminary diagnosis being "consumption," presumably what we call "tuberculosis" today. Notwithstanding Virginia's illness, Lamar pushed himself to campaign vigorously for the Democratic Party candidates, including speeches in mid-September at Lafayette Springs. Although the diagnosis of "consumption" was confirmed by the end of the month, Lamar pressed on, speaking at Holly Springs on October 4 and later in the month, while stopping at towns along the Mobile and Ohio Railroad, speaking at "West Point, Macon, Meridian and other places."

(4Q80)

Democrat Winfield Hancock lost to James Garfield by an Electoral vote of 214 versus 155, the popular vote margin being much less (4,453,295 versus 4,414,082). And Democrats in the northern States suffered broad losses in other races — a great disappointment to Democrats throughout the nation. Not only did they lose the opportunity to win the office of President, they lost their past 6-years control over the Federal House, and their past 2-years control over the Federal Senate was reduced to a virtual tie, Democrat Senators and Republican Senators holding an equal number of seats. On March 4, 1881, Lamar would witness the start of a protracted political fight over which Party would control the Senate. [R205;420-422]

Prior to traveling to Washington City, Lucius Lamar escorted his wife to his her sister's house in New Orleans where she could spend the winter months. Virginia's health seemed to be improving and she felt the warmer climate of New Orleans would suit her better than that of Washington.

The Year of 1881

(1Q81)

The Federal Senate would begin a Special Session on March 4, in accordance with a Proclamation of newly inaugurated President, James Garfield. Wade Hampton would be in his seat. Lucius Lamar would remain in Washington while his wife, suffering from tuberculosis, stayed with her sister in New Orleans. Our history takes a brief break for a presentation of an overview of the election of Garfield and the organization of the Garfield Administration.

March 1881 Through February 1885 – The Struggle for Healing During the Garfield and Arthur Administrations

It is now time to review a summary of the 1880 Federal elections in the summarized format that has begun each four-year segment of this study. After this review, the narrative history will resume.

James Garfield was of English and French Huguenot ancestry. His great-great-great-great-great-grandfather, Edward Garfield had emigrated from England to Massachusetts in 1630. His grandfather had moved west to New York and his father, Abram Garfield had moved further west to Ohio. In 1820 Abram married Eliza Ballou, who had been born in New Hampshire and raised in New York and Ohio. The couple settled in a log cabin near Cleveland, Ohio where Abram worked at farming and as a construction supervisor on the Ohio and Erie Canal. James was born in 1831. Sadly, Abram died when the baby was only 18 months old.

Little James was raised amid poverty by his mother who received some help from his Uncle. A bright lad, Garfield excelled in elementary school. At age 17, while working as a carpenter to pay expenses, Garfield attended an academy at Chester, Ohio. Then he attended a school at the Eclectic Institute in Hiram, Ohio for three more years, where he taught and performed odd jobs to offset expenses. In 1854, at age 23, the young man entered Williams College in Massachusetts where, as the oldest member of his class, Garfield excelled in debate and leadership. He graduated, with honors in 1856. Attracted to politics and the new sectional Republican Party, Garfield supported John Fremont for President in 1856. After graduation, Garfield returned to Hiram and taught at the Eclectic Institute. He was promoted to President of the institute in 1857. Studying law on the side, Garfield obtained a license to practice law in 1860 — the year Abe Lincoln was elected President.

James Garfield married Lucretia Rudolph of Hiram in 1858. Lucretia was the daughter of Zebulon Rudolph, a local farmer and co-founder of the school where James worked. Well educated, Lucretia had been a school teacher prior to their marriage.

Garfield joined the fusion of Exclusionist politicians in the 1858 Ohio State elections and ran for the State Senate. He was elected. An ardent Exclusionist and eager to promote the sectional Republican Party by demonizing the southern States, Garfield praised John Brown, whose martyrdom he predicted, "Shall be the dawn of a better day." By 1860 Garfield had joined the Republican Party, and that year he campaigned for Abe Lincoln for President. He welcomed the fight at Fort Sumter as all the excuse Republicans needed to invade the Confederacy.

Eager to participate in the invasion, Garfield quickly arranged for appointment as a lieutenant in the Federal army in August 1861. Fighting in neutral Kentucky in January, 1862, he won promotion to brigadier general. He helped lead the invasion into Tennessee and fought in the bloody battle at Pittsburg Landing in April 1862. In early summer, Garfield returned home to convalesce from illness and to run for the Federal House, believing that defeating northern States Democrats in the 1862 mid-term elections was more important than defeating Confederates on the battlefield. After defeating his Democratic opponent, with about 70 percent of the vote, Garfield traveled to east Tennessee to join General Rosecrans as Chief of Staff. After a short stay, he resigned from the army and traveled to Washington to attend the opening session of Congress in December 1863.

Garfield aligned with the more Militant Faction of the Republican Party. As a member of the House Military Affairs Committee, he sponsored the Military Draft Bill and taunted the Lincoln Administration for advancing invasion forces too slowly. In the 1864 elections Garfield joined the Republican Faction that sought to dump Lincoln for a more militant man, such as Ohio Senator Salmon Chase. When Lincoln succeeded in holding onto the nomination, Garfield reluctantly supported his re-election, but refused to actively campaign on his behalf. As the defeat of the Confederacy loomed, Garfield sided with those Republicans who sought the harshest treatment of the conquered States. He supported movements to confiscate the farms and homes of all Confederates and to execute or exile Confederate leaders. Garfield voted to impeach President Johnson.

Garfield supported Ulysses Grant for President in 1868 and 1872. During Grant's two administrations Garfield held leading House financial positions including Chairman of the Banking and Currency Committee, Chairman of the Appropriations Committee, and member of the Ways and Means

Committee. He advocated hard money policies. He sought nebulous middle ground in disputes over import tax rates. "I am for a protection which leads to ultimate free trade. I am for that free trade which can be achieved only through protection." He opposed federally funded welfare projects to help folks in need during the depression of the 1870's. Garfield supported Rutherford Hayes for President in 1876. As one of the 15 members of the Electoral Commission, he voted to steal the office of President from the winner of the election, Democrat Samuel Tilden, and give it to the loser, Republican Rutherford Hayes.

The 1880 Republican Convention bogged down in a tug of war between the Faction supporting the nomination again of former President Ulysses Grant and the anti-Grant forces, who rallied to James Blaine of Maine and John Sherman of Ohio. President Rutherford Hayes had declined to accept renomination. Ex-president Grant still had plenty of friends in spite of 8 years of scandals and questions of competence. Garfield, leader of the Ohio Delegation, had impressed many Delegates with his nomination speech for Sherman. DeGregorio would tell how, after many, many ballots, the Convention finally leaped to Garfield on the 36th ballot and closed the deal on the 37th:

"Incumbent President Rutherford Hayes kept his pledge to retire at the end of one term. As Republicans convened in Chicago in June 1880, the clear front-runner for the nomination was former President Ulysses Grant, seeking an unprecedented third term. Anti-Grant forces coalesced around James Blaine of Maine and John Sherman of Ohio. Grant was the candidate of the Stalwarts, or conservative Republicans. Sherman and Blaine divided the support of the Half Breeds, the moderate Faction of the Party. Garfield was head of the Ohio Delegation, Chairman of the Rules Committee, and leader of the Sherman forces. As Rules Committee Chairman, Garfield was instrumental in getting the Convention to reject the unit rule, a victory for the anti-Grant forces, for without it the former President had little chance to attain a majority. Roscoe Conkling of New York nominated Grant in a bombastic address that rocked the Convention. Garfield followed the nominating speech for Sherman, by contrast a low-key, yet equally moving, address that convinced some Delegates that Garfield would make an ideal compromise candidate. The Convention deadlocked through 33 ballots, with Grant in the lead with just over 300 votes, more than 70 votes shy of the nomination, followed by Blaine, whose vote ranged form 270 to 285, and Sherman, hovering around 100. Garfield, meanwhile, had been receiving 1 or 2 scattered courtesy votes. But as the Convention dragged on, he came under increasing pressure to break with Sherman and declare his own candidacy. This he refused to do. Then, on the 34th ballot, Wisconsin suddenly cast 16 votes for Garfield, who promptly reaffirmed his loyalty to Sherman. On the next tally Garfield received 50 votes, and on the 36th ballot the Blaine and Sherman forces rallied to his banner. The final vote was Garfield, 399; Grant, 306; Blaine, 42; Elihu Washburne of Illinois, 5; and Sherman, 3. To observers, Garfield seemed genuinely stunned by it all. To placate the Stalwarts, Chester Arthur of New York was nominated for Vice President. The Republican Platform largely reiterated the Platform of 1876."

You will recall that the 1876 Platform had "promised 'permanent pacification' of the [conquered States], continued sound-money policy, and civil service reform; opposed Federal aid to Catholic or other sectarian schools and land grants to railroads or other corporations; called for a congressional investigation of the effects of Oriental immigration 'upon the moral and material interest of the country;' and vowed to eradicate polygamy, 'that relic of barbarism,' in Utah."

Democrats seemed to settle rather easily on running Winfield Hancock, a career military man from Pennsylvania. Winfield Hancock was born in Pennsylvania. His father was a lawyer. He graduated from West Point in 1844 and served in the Mexican War and the Seminole War but made his reputation during the Civil War. He was among the invasion forces in Virginia, fighting to reach Richmond from the east, fighting at Antietam and retreating to Gettysburg, Pennsylvania to defend that area from a Confederate counterattack. He was seriously wounded at Gettysburg, but recovered to return to Virginia and participate in the conquest of Richmond. After the conquest of the Confederacy, Major General Hancock was assigned briefly to Native American Territory in Kansas. Shortly thereafter he was assigned the job of Military Governor of the conquered States of Louisiana and Texas. In that post he attempted to restore civilian control under less harsh measures than desired by Republicans in Washington. He returned to the eastern military section in 1872. DeGregorio would describe the Democratic Convention:

"As early as 1868 Hancock was being mentioned as a presidential contender. At the Democratic Convention in Cincinnati in June 1880, Hancock emerged the leading candidate after Samuel Tilden of New York withdrew his name from consideration. On the first ballot Hancock led with 171 votes to 153 1/2 for Thomas Bayard of Delaware, 81 for Henry Payne of Ohio, 68 1/2 for Allen Thurman of Ohio, and the rest scattered. On the next tally, Tilden supporters pushed Samuel Randall of Pennsylvania to second place with 128 1/2 votes, but Hancock held such a commanding lead with 320 votes that masses of Delegates bolted to him before the second ballot was recorded, giving him 705 votes and the nomination. William English of Indiana was nominated for Vice President. The Democratic Platform condemned centralization of power in Washington, promised hard money and a tariff for revenue only, called for civil service reform, opposed monopolies, encouraged the labor movement, and called for 'No more Chinese immigration'."

Republican Garfield won the election in a very close race. DeGregorio would describe the campaign:

"In this lackluster campaign, the candidates differed little on the issues. Only the [import tax percentage] question divided them. Republicans supported a high [tax on imports]; Democrats favored one 'for revenue only.' The [tax on imports] became a source of embarrassment to Democrats when Hancock, asked by a reporter for his position on the issue, dismissed it as 'a local question.' The gaffe only reinforced his image as a career military officer with little grounding in politics or affairs of state. Garfield, by contrast, could point to his long service in the House. His record proved a mixed blessing, however, as Democrats lambasted him for his part in the Credit Mobilier scandal. Incumbent President Rutherford Hayes wholeheartedly endorsed Garfield but warned him to keep a low profile during the campaign. This Garfield did, calmly receiving delegations of supporters at his home in Mentor, Ohio, while leaving the politicking to others. To win, Garfield needed the [pro-patronage Faction] and the pro-Grant [Faction] led by New York Party boss Roscoe Conkling. For some time Conkling refused to lift a finger for the nominee. But in a meeting with Conkling subordinates in New York, Garfield reportedly agreed to consult with them on patronage for the State, something President Hayes had refused to do. The meeting, later dubbed the Treaty of Fifth Avenue, brought about Conkling's active support. Hancock, working from a solid base of support in the South, sought to woo northern [States] reformers by pledging genuine civil service reform. The business community, fearful of Hancock's [stand against high import taxes], contributed heavily to the Garfield campaign. Labor, too, was wary of Hancock, because as a military officer he had helped break a railroad strike."

Republican candidate Garfield won the popular vote by a whisker: 48.3 percent versus 48.2 percent for Democrat Hancock. Garfield won 58 percent of the electoral vote. Except for New Jersey, Garfield captured all northern States with a victory sweep that stretched from New England to Oregon, winning 19 States. From north to south, Garfield won Maine, New Hampshire, Vermont, Massachusetts, Connecticut, Rhode Island, New York, Pennsylvania, Ohio, Indiana, Illinois, Michigan, Wisconsin, Minnesota, Iowa, Nebraska, Kansas, Oregon, and Colorado. Hancock captured all States of the conquered Confederacy and those States that had bordered the Confederacy, plus Nevada and California, winning 19 States. From north to south, Hancock's States were New Jersey, Delaware, Maryland, West Virginia, Kentucky, Missouri, Nevada, California, Virginia, North Carolina, Tennessee, Arkansas, South Carolina, Georgia, Alabama, Mississippi, Louisiana, Texas, and Florida.

The Democratic Party suffered much worse in Congress. The majority they had enjoyed in the House for the previous 6 years was lost. The majority they had just gained in the Senate two years previously was reduced to a tie with the resurgent Republican Party — Senate Republicans were tied with Senate Democrats, each holding 49.3 percent of the seats. The balance — just one seat — was held by a non-aligned Senator. Republicans held a razor-thin, 50.2 percent of the House seats. Democrats held 46.1 percent and non-aligned Representatives held 3.7 percent. The mid-term elections changed the Senate little, but produced a sweeping victory for the Democratic Party in the House. The second half of the Garfield/Arthur Administration dealt with a Senate made up of 50 percent Republican seats, 47.3 percent Democrat seats and 2.6 percent non-aligned seats and dealt with a House made up of 61 percent Democrat seats, 36 percent Republican seats and 3 percent non-aligned seats.

Garfield appointed James Blaine of Maine to be Secretary of State. This outraged New York Party boss Roscoe Conkling who had expected to get the job. He appointed William Windom of Minnesota to be

Secretary of the Treasury. This also upset Conkling who had been pushing one of his men. Seeking to rally Republican Factions with memories of the glory-days of the conquest of the Confederacy, Garfield appointed Abe Lincoln's son Robert to be Secretary of War. Garfield appointed Wayne MacVeagh of Pennsylvania to be Attorney General. He appointed William Hunt of Louisiana — his token southern States man — to be Secretary of the Navy. Thomas James of New York was named Postmaster General. Samuel Kirkwood of Iowa was appointed to be Secretary of the Interior.

A major patronage appointment fight took place between the President and New York Party boss Roscoe Conkling over who would get the important post of Collector of the Port of New York. Garfield succeeded in winning support in the Senate for his man, William Robertson. Conkling's failure to persuade Senators to defeat Robertson's confirmation broke his grip on a large Faction within the Republican Party. Fraudulent awards of rural mail contracts — so called Star Routes — produced a scandal that Garfield immediately directed his new Postmaster General to investigate. Second Assistant Postmaster General Thomas Brady of Arkansas and others were eventually implicated in the scheme, which prosecutors estimated costs taxpayers $4 million. Convictions were not obtained, but the scandal added pressure for civil service reform. Another action added pressure for civil service reform. That was the assassination of President Garfield by a Republican political worker who had been denied a political appointment — a fellow from New Jersey named Charles Guiteau. A member of the Republican pro-patronage Faction, Guiteau's bullets achieved his personal objective of putting a pro-patronage Republican in the office of President.

Guiteau had been stalking Garfield for three weeks before he caught him in range at Washington's railroad station, as his target strolled arm in arm with Secretary of State Blaine. Shot in the back by two bullets, the President would have recovered with modern medicine, but infection set in and he died on September 19, 1881 — two and a half months later — from infections resulting from unsterile medical procedures. Guiteau was immediately captured by police in attendance at the railroad station and seemed to enjoy the publicity he received during his captivity and trial. He was found guilty and hanged about a year after he shot Garfield. By the way, shortly before he shot Garfield, Guiteau had written, "The President's tragic death was a sad necessity, but it will unite the Republican Party and save the Republic. . . . His death was a political necessity."

Vice President Chester Arthur was sworn in as President on September 19, 1881, at his home in New York City, by a New York State Supreme Court Justice a few hours after Garfield passed away.

Chester Arthur was of Scotch-Irish and English heritage. His father, the Reverend William Arthur, was born and educated in Ireland before immigrating to Quebec, Canada as a young man. In 1821 William married Malvina Stone, a native of Vermont who had moved to Quebec. The couple came to the United States in 1828 where William preached at Baptist churches in Vermont and New York. A staunch Abolitionist, William was a co-founder of the New York Antislavery Society. The fifth of eight children to live to maturity, Chester was born in 1829 at the parsonage in Vermont. Although political opponents later charged he had been born in Canada and was therefore not a citizen, no proof of that accusation ever surfaced. Although the couple strove to instill religious convictions in Chester, he never joined a church or submitted to baptism.

Moving from church to church, young Chester grew up in 7 towns in Vermont and New York. He learned the fundamentals of reading, writing and arithmetic from his father. He then attended an academy in what is now Greenwich, New York. At age 15 he enrolled at the Lyceum in Schenectady. As a student, he supported Henry Clay for President. In 1845 he entered Union College in Schenectady, pursued a classical education, and graduated in the top third of his class in 1848. After graduation, he combined teaching school, in Vermont and New York, with studying law. He supported Whig candidate Winfield Scott for President in 1852. Chester received his New York State license to practice law in 1854. Chester's first job as a licensed lawyer was at a New York City law firm of Culver, Parker and Arthur. In 1855 he won a lawsuit against a Brooklyn streetcar company which had forced an African American from a "European American only" streetcar. This court decision led to elimination of separate seating restrictions in New York City public transportation. Perhaps inspired by New England Exclusionists to become involved in "Bleeding Kansas," Arthur resigned from his law partnership in 1856 and teamed up with fellow lawyer Henry Gardiner and relocated to Kansas Territory. Realism may have set in rather quickly, for Arthur only spent three months in Kansas before returning to New York City. In 1860 Arthur campaigned vigorously for Republican candidate John Fremont for President. Arthur joined the New York State militia in February 1858 as a brigade judge advocate. In 1860 he supported Lincoln for President. Shortly before Lincoln assumed office, Arthur was appointed engineer in chief of the New York State militia with rank of brigadier general. Shortly after Lincoln took power, Arthur was promoted to acting assistant quartermaster general, headquartered in New York City. In February 1863 Arthur became inspector general and in July quartermaster general. New York Republican Governor Edwin Morgan said of Arthur, "He was my chief reliance in the duties of equipping and transporting troops and munitions of war." Leaving the military in December 1862, Arthur missed the extremely bloody years of 1863, 1864 and early 1865. It appears that he never faced combat. Arthur joined the New York State pro-patronage Faction of the Republican Party which was led by Roscoe Conkling. He supported Lincoln for reelection in 1864. He became Chairman of the State Republican Executive Committee in 1868. He campaigned for Grant for President in 1868, a great friend of pro-patronage Republicans. He won appointment to a high paying ($10,000 per year) job as chief lawyer for the New York City Tax Commission in 1869 and 1870.

Arthur followed the New York City Tax Commission job with an even more lucrative job in 1871, when President Grant named him Collector of the Port of New York, where about 75 percent of the country's Federal import tax was collected at the Customhouse. Arthur would remain in that high-paying job until 1878. He obviously supported Grant's reelection in 1872. A loyal leader in the pro-patronage Faction, Arthur supported Conkling for the 1876 Republican presidential nomination and pressured Customhouse employees into contributing big money to the Republican coffers. When it became obvious that Conkling could not win the balloting for the nomination, Arthur participated in the New York Delegation's switch to Rutherford Hayes in order to stop James Blaine. Arthur campaigned for Hayes for President and again pressured his Customhouse employees to contribute money to the 1876 Republican coffers. Trouble arrived when newly-elected President Hayes decided to clean up the corrupt patronage machine that had just helped to elect him. His civil service reform agenda included Arthur's import tax collection empire at New York City. The Jay Commission, created in 1877 to investigate alleged corruption in the New York Customhouse, called Arthur in for questioning as its first witness. In spite of Arthur's attempts to convince the Commission otherwise, its report condemned the Customhouse for giving jobs to political hacks without regard for merit, and requiring employees to kick back part of their salary to the Republican Party. President Hayes offered a face-saving out to Arthur when he offered him a job in the U. S. embassy in Paris. But Arthur refused the Paris job. On July 11, 1878, Hayes fired him and put Edwin Merritt in charge of the New York Customhouse. Arthur returned to working as a New York City lawyer. Although he had made a fortune by government appointments, Arthur had not yet faced the voters in quest of an elective office.

Arthur went to the 1880 Republican Convention as a leader in the pro-patronage Faction led by Roscoe Conkling and a supporter of ex-President Grant's return from retirement. Through a Grant presidency, pro-patronage Republicans hoped to hold fast to their lucrative patronage machinery. The pro-patronage Republican Faction remained a powerful force in the Republican Party in spite of its defeat at the Convention. Successful nominee James Garfield extended an olive branch to the Conkling Faction by inviting Levi Morton to accept the nomination for Vice President. However, Morton declined the offer. Undaunted, Garfield turned to another prominent Conkling man. Surprisingly, he turned to scandal-tarnished Chester Arthur who seemed to be ready to defy Conkling's directive to his people that they must decline any offer to be nominated for Vice President. When Conkling pressured Arthur to decline, Arthur reportedly retorted, "The office of the Vice President is a greater honor than I ever dreamed of attaining." Consequently, Republican James Garfield had one of Roscoe Conkling's men on his ticket — the same fellow that outgoing Republican President Rutherford Hayes had fired because of big-time corruption. Arthur's nomination was easily accepted by 70 percent of the Convention Delegates on the first ballot.

The Senate was tied politically when it convened in March, 1881, so the first task for the new Vice President was to cast the tie-breaking vote that permitted the Republican Party to win the power to organize the Senate and appoint Committee chairmen. When President James Garfield moved against the Roscoe Conkling Faction by nominating his own man to take Arthur's old lucrative job of Collector of the Port of New York, Arthur turned on his President. Perhaps unappreciative of Garfield's generous offer of the office of Vice President, Arthur attempted to help the Conkling pro-patronage forces defeat, in the Senate confirmation vote, his President's nominee. As reported earlier, President Garfield nevertheless won enough votes to defeat the Conkling pro-patronage forces and put his man at the head of the New York Customshouse. That defeat represented the end of Conkling's political power. The New York State Legislature refused to reelect him to the Senate. But a Conkling man would get the last word, for, as you know, Charles Guiteau of near-by New Jersey drilled two bullets into President Garfield's back on July 2, 1881. Chester Arthur and Roscoe Conkling heard the news shortly afterward as together they stepped off a steamer in New York City. Rumors abounded that Chester Arthur, Roscoe Conkling or some other big-name pro-patronage Republican had hired Guiteau to assassinate the President and elevate super-pro-patronage politician Chester Arthur to the office, but no conspiracy was ever proven.

The assassination of President Garfield and the elevation of Chester Arthur produced a massive upheaval in the President's Cabinet. Garfield's appointees generally wanted no part of an Arthur Administration, and perhaps Arthur wanted to be rid of some of these men. Only Abe Lincoln's son was sufficiently indifferent to not care and too sacred to be fired. Secretary of State James Blaine of Maine stayed on only until December 1881. Then Arthur replaced Blaine with Frederick Frelinghuysen of New Jersey. Secretary of the Treasury William Windom of Minnesota stayed on only until November 1881. Then Arthur replaced Windom with pro-patronage Republican Charles Folger of New York. Ironically it was Folger who instituted the civil service system in the Treasury Department. Folger died in office and was replaced by Walter Gresham of Indiana, who Arthur transferred from Postmaster General. Folger's death was not considered suspicious, but after a few weeks, Gresham resigned to take a job on the U. S. Circuit Court. Hugh McCulloch of Indiana, who had headed Treasury during the Lincoln-Johnson Administration, returned to finish the last year as Secretary of the Treasury. Abe Lincoln's son Robert remained as Secretary of War. Because of his name, his job was probably too sacred to tamper with. Attorney General Wayne MacVeagh stayed on only until he resigned in October 1881. Unable to convince him to stay on, Arthur replaced MacVeagh with Benjamin Brewster of Pennsylvania. The Administration's token, southern States Democrat, Secretary of the Navy William Hunt of Louisiana, stayed on until 1882, when he resigned to become Minister to Russia. Arthur appointed William Chandler of New Hampshire to replace Hunt. Postmaster General Thomas James of New York resigned in December despite Arthur's request that he remain. Timothy Howe of Wisconsin replaced James, but died in office in 1883. His death was not considered suspicious. Arthur then appointed Walter Gresham to the Postmaster job, but Gresham was transferred to Treasury in 1884. Frank Hatton of Iowa was promoted from first assistant postmaster to finish the term. Most of the Cabinet members appointed by Arthur were pro-patronage Republicans.

Democratic Senator George H. Pendleton of Ohio sponsored a bill to establish a Civil Service system for Federal Government employees, thereby destroying the traditional political spoils system. Support for the bill was assured in the Democrat-controlled House. It also passed in the Senate. And, President Arthur — suddenly transformed into a civil service politician — signed it. The patronage system, which had bloated politics with greedy men and smothered would-be statesmen, was finally dead. DeGregorio would describe the Pendleton Act of 1883:

> "This bill created the modern civil service system. Reformers had been calling for an end to the spoils system for more than a decade, but not until President Garfield was gunned down by a disappointed office seeker did national sentiment prod Congress to action. President Arthur, himself a product and long practitioner of the spoils system, angered his old friends and delighted his former critics in signing the measure and enforcing it in good faith. The measure, sponsored by Democratic Senator George H. Pendleton of Ohio, created a bipartisan three-man Civil Service Commission to oversee the system. Arthur made clear his commitment by appointing three men long identified with civil service reform, notably its Chairman, Dorman Eaton, a leader of the reform movement in New York and author of the Pendleton Act. The new law provided for open, competitive exams for applicants for government jobs classified under civil service, banned the practice of exacting political contributions from civil servants or otherwise pressing them into partisan service, excluded alcoholics from the civil service, and curbed nepotism."

Displaying a remarkably modern attitude about his job, Arthur once replied, "I may be President of the United States, but my private life is nobody's damn business." [R2;293-316]

Having concluded the summation of the 1880 Federal elections and the organization of the James Garfield Administration and the Chester Arthur Administration, the narrative history resumes.

The Narrative History Resumes, March 1881.

On March 4 the Federal Senate began a called Special Session for the purpose of approving Cabinet appointments and addressing any foreign treaty issues needing its attention. But of primary importance to most Senators was the issue of which Party was to control the Senate. Of the 76 seats, 37 were held by Democrats, 37 by Republicans, 1 by David Davis of Illinois (formerly a noted Republican with an illustrious career, but now an Independent) and 1 by William Mahone of Virginia (a former high-ranking Confederate officer, railroad executive and, politically, a Readjuster). The key to organizing the Senate was in winning the votes of Davis and Mahone. Win one and the Vice President would tip control to the Republicans; win both and the Democrats would win control.

Readers of *Bloodstains* will recall, from Volumes 1 and 2, that David Davis, as Judge, had presided over the Illinois Eighth Circuit Court, from 1848 to 1862, covering many of the years that Abe Lincoln had practiced law in that State. You will also recall that David Davis had exerted substantial influence in favor of Abe Lincoln at the 1860 Republican Northern States Convention in Chicago, thereafter managing the Lincoln campaign for President. You will also recall from Volume 3, that Abe Lincoln had appointed David Davis to the Federal Supreme Court in October 1862, taking the seat of Justice John Archibald Campbell, whose resignation on April 30, 1861 was noted. (Campbell had returned to his home in Alabama, in protest over Lincoln's disregard of the constitutional authority of the Supreme Court and his unilateral April 15 proclamation calling for military subjugation of Democrat-controlled States — Delaware, Maryland, Kentucky and Missouri — and military conquest of what was to become 11 seceded States.) David Davis' career on the Supreme Court had been noteworthy as well. He had written the majority opinion in the very important 1866 case, *Ex Parte Milligan*, which declared that trial of a civilian by a military tribunal violated the Federal Constitution — this being a landmark decision ensuring American freedom from abuse by arbitrary military power. Although a Republican in the early days of the Party, during the first Ulysses Grant Administration, David Davis had supported the Liberal Republican Movement and had evolved into, officially, a non-aligned Independent in politics. Furthermore, Justice David Davis had played a major role during Republican efforts to steal the 1876 election for Rutherford Hayes. You will recall that Republicans had rigged the vote counts in Florida, Louisiana and perhaps South Carolina in an attempt to prevent the election of Democrat Samuel Tilden, and that an Electoral Commission had been named to adjudicate the contest. Well, David Davis, being an Independent, had been expected to be the deciding vote on that Commission, providing a majority vote for Democrat Tilden. Believing Davis wanted to leave the Court and join the Senate, and believing facilitating that move would win his support for an honest examination of the vote count for President in Florida, Louisiana and South Carolina, Democrats in the Illinois Legislature had elected him to the Federal Senate, expecting his resignation from the Supreme Court would occur after the Electoral Commission completed its examination. It was a trap. It did not happen. Apparently, Davis had wanted to avoid responsibility for ruling on the rigged votes for Hayes. To duck responsibility, he had resigned the Supreme Court on March 4, 1877 and taken his seat in the Senate. The Justice taking his place on the Commission had been a loyal Republican, so the vote went by Party lines, without an examination of the vote count, thereby denying the office of President to the man who had been elected to it, Samuel Tilden, Democrat Governor of New York. With regard to the organization of the Senate in March 1881, Democrats could count on the vote of David Davis. That gave them 38 votes. They still needed the vote of Virginia Readjuster, William Mahone.

So, what about William Mahone of Virginia? How would he vote? About what issue had Virginia's Readjusters been so passionate?

The Readjuster Faction of the Virginia Democratic Party was unique to that State. When the Federal Army had enforced a political division of Virginia, pulling off the western counties to make a new State, it rather freed the people in the western Virginia counties from obligations to pay the debt of the Virginia State Government, a sizable burden following the Federal conquest, by 1880 figured to be $45,000,000. How to pay off this debt, whether or not to repudiate all or part of it, was the issue debated in Virginia between "Funders" and "Readjusters," both sides being outgrowths of the Virginia Democratic Party. Virginia's Funders, the majority within the Party, wanted to split the debt, whereby their State would accept the obligation to pay $30,000,000 and West Virginia would be responsible for paying the remaining $15,000,000. That did not reduce the debt sufficiently for the other Virginia Faction — they wanted further debt adjustment — they wanted to repudiate the accumulated interest on the $30,000,000 split as well, thereby cutting it to an obligation of only $20,000,000. These men, a minority within the Party were called the "Readjuster" faction. To be competitive in Virginia State elections, Readjusters had arranged a political fusion with Republicans and Greenbackers, had held a separate State Convention and fielded Fusion candidates for the Virginia House and Senate. They had been so successful that enough Readjusters had been elected to organize the Virginia House and elect William Mahone to the Federal Senate, even without the votes of Republicans or Greenbackers. So Malone did not have to feel politically indebted to the Republicans, but he could be persuaded.

Which way would Mahone vote? Could Republicans lure away a former high-ranking Confederate officer? Perhaps his more recent experiences could be exploited, connected to his career climb from eminent railroad engineer to President of several Virginia railroads that would grow into the Norfolk and Western system, one of today's major railroad companies. We know that, upon entering the Senate in 1881, Mahone needed friends among immensely wealthy Republican financial men, for his Virginia railroads had greatly suffered in the financial panic of 1873 and had been taken over by Scottish bondholders, who were presently looking for a financial escape route. Wonderful news — before the year 1881 would be over, the Scottish bondholders would be paid when financial men in America's northern States would buy their Virginia railroads, supporting the old adage: money talks.

Republican Senators believed their struggle to win Readjuster Mahone's vote was more than a fight to organize the Senate — it was also a key battle in what they perceived to be a political war being waged to break apart the Democratic Party's solid grip on the southern States — Virginia being that war's first battlefield. Applying promises of Senate offices to Mahone's Virginia friends, Chairmanship of the Senate Agriculture Committee, control over Virginia patronage appointments, and other perks, Republicans persuaded Mahone to side with them. On March 14, Democrats, unaware of the backroom deal, called for a vote and were shocked to see William Mahone, a former high-ranking Confederate military officer, abandon them as he voted with the Republicans. Now the Vice President could control the vote to organize. But several Republican Senators were absent, and Democrats would not easily give up. They insisted on continuing to control the Senate as long as possible. Except for political speechmaking, the Special Session was stalemated, and weeks of inaction grew into a month.

Senator James Cameron of Pennsylvania, son of Simon Cameron, Abe Lincoln's Secretary of War prior to Edwin Stanton, said as much in remarks delivered on March 21, when he submitted:

"All that we ask is that [Virginians] shall stand with [we Republicans] in favor of securing to each lawful [Virginia] voter the right to cast one free and un-intimidated ballot, and to have it honestly counted. We know, and our opponents know, that if Virginia takes her stand upon that Platform the solid [political allegiance of the southern States] is a thing of the past; and this is the true meaning of the present struggle [to organize the Federal Senate]."

(2Q81)

On April 1 Lucius Lamar rose to deliver a substantial speech, encouraging fellow Senators to set aside attempts to influence Virginia voters and proceed with the business for which they had been called into Special Session. His comments regarding allegiance in the southern States to the Democratic Party are noteworthy. He began:

"An entire month, saving two or three days, has elapsed since the commencement of this session. . . . We were called here [on March 4] for the purpose of adjusting our relations with foreign nations and confirming appointments nominated by [President James Garfield]. This, and this alone, is the business for which this body was convened . . . yet, sir, though that long time has elapsed, this body has scarcely entered upon this discharge of the business which it was called specially to consider."

Lamar's address was to a great extent in answer to the complaints by Republican Senators that, acting in collusion as the "Solid South," Democrats had prevented, and continued to prevent, the Republican

Party from being politically competitive in that section of the country. Some of his remarks on that subject follow:

"What harm had, 'the solid South' done to the prosperity and glory of this country? It is but a short time since it became 'solid' by the cessation of the reign of force and bayonets. Take her history from that time as connected with [our Federal Government], and show me where she has deducted anything from your national security or abstracted a single iota from your national prosperity. She came here through her Representatives, first as a part of the minority, and soon afterwards as a part of the majority in both branches of Congress. She came at a time when your commerce was languishing, your agriculture prostrate; when mercantile insolvencies and bankruptcies were rushing like a simoon across this nation; when your currency was depreciated; when the balance of trade was against you; and when, according to the statistics of your journals, 3,000,000 tramps were wandering aimless and homeless through the length and breadth of your land. The 'solid South' has been here from that time to this; and during the entire period of the presence of her Representatives in this Chamber and in the other House the world has held its breath in silent astonishment at the progress that you, the country, have made in all that adorns and fortifies and ennobles a nation. Your commerce has revived; your agriculture is prosperous; your manufactories are operating to the full extent of their capacity, the demand for their products far exceeding their abilities to supply them; your currency is the best in the world; the balance of trade is in your favor; and all along this line of progress we find, according to the recent census, that the [southern States] in every element of prosperity [are] not far behind the foremost States of the North and the West. . .

"[Turning to past political corruption, as in the Ulysses Grant Administration, I remind you that] the 'solid South' was not here [in the Federal House and Senate] when that shame [of corruption among Federal officials] fell upon the nation; and it seems to me, sir, that when men [today], with this record fresh in their memories, clamor about the dangers and the vices of the 'solid South,' their cheeks would mantle with shame. . . . [Furthermore], I have heard that suspicion haunts the footsteps of the trusted companions of [President James Garfield]. [But] one thing is certain, sir, and that is that since the 'solid South' has been here, [in these Chambers], no such corruption has reveled in the high places of this government. I do not say that it was her influence which has eliminated it; but I do say that contemporaneously and simultaneously with her presence here it took its flight, and I claim that she has been no obstacle to the restoration of purity in the administration of your public affairs. . . .

"[In many ways the 'solid South' is not solid, for] there is greater diversity of sentiment among them upon every subject of national interest than there is in the representation of any other section of the country. . . . There is one point, and only one, upon which they are 'solid,' on which they will remain 'solid;' and neither Federal bayonets nor Federal honors will dissolve that solidity. They are 'solid' in defense of and for the protection of their own civilization, their own society, their own religion, against the rule of the incompetent, the servile, the ignorant, and the vicious. . . .

"Mr. President, I am too much exhausted to detain the Senate longer. I have said nothing today that was intended to stir up any feeling of animosity between individuals or sections. I belong to that class of public men who were Secessionists. Every throb of my heart was for the disunion of these States. If that deducts from the force of the statements that I have made today, it is due to candor and to you to admit it. I confess that I believed in the right of [State] secession and that I believed in the propriety of its exercise. I will say further that it was a cherished conception of my mind: that of two great free Republics on this continent, each pursuing its own destiny and the destiny of its people and their happiness according to its own will. . . .

"But, sir, that conception is gone; it is sunk forever out of sight. Another one has come in its place; and, by the way, it is my first love. The elements of it were planted in my heart by my father, they were taught by my mother, and they were nourished and developed by my own subsequent reflection. May I tell you what it is, sir? It stands before me now, simple in its majesty and sublime in its beauty. It is that of one grand, mighty, indivisible Republic upon this continent, throwing its loving arms around all sections, omnipotent for protection, powerless for oppression, cursing none, blessing all!"

Eventually, a bargain would be struck between Democrats and Republicans in the Senate for, sort-of, joint control. Eventually, the body would get down to business and complete the work for which Senators had been called, finally adjourning the Special Session on May 20. [R205;422-430,739-748]

Meanwhile on the Gulf Coast, with Varina's help with correspondence, analysis, and taking down dictation, Jeff was approaching the end of the research and writing of the second volume of his history, *The Rise and Fall of the Confederate Government*. The publisher, Appleton's of New York City, had dispatched W. T. Tenney down to the beach house to speed the work and help with the editing. Biographer Hudson Strode would write: "with his objectivity and literary perception," Tenney "was to prove efficient in the finishing stages of the bulky manuscript. He was, as well, a pleasant house guest." During the push to complete the book, Varina and Jeff would sometimes work through the night. That was the situation at 4 o'clock one late April morning as Varina completed taking down the following dictation:

> "My first object in this work was to prove, by historical authority, that each of the States, as sovereign parties to the compact [creating the Federal Government], had the reserved power to secede from it whenever it should be found not to answer the ends for which it was established. If this has been done, it follows that the [invasion and its defense] was, on the part of the [Federal] Government, one of aggression and usurpation, and, on the part of the [Confederacy], was for the defense of an inherent, unalienable right.

> "My next purpose was to show, by the gallantry and devotion of the Southern people, in their unequal struggle, how thorough was their conviction of the justice of their cause; that, by their humanity to the wounded and captives, they proved themselves the worthy descendants of chivalric sires, and fit to be free; and that, in every case, as when our army invaded Pennsylvania, by their respect for private rights, their morality and observance of the laws of civilized war, they are entitled to the confidence and regard of mankind.

> "The want of space has compelled me to omit a notice of many noble deeds, both of heroic men and women. The roll of honor, merely, would fill more than the pages allotted to this work. To others, who can say *cuncta quorum vidi*, I must leave the pleasant task of paying the tribute due to their associate patriots.

> "In asserting the right of [State] secession, it has not been my wish to incite to its exercise. I recognize the fact that the [invasion and its defense] showed [secession] to be impracticable, but this did not prove it to be wrong; now that it may not be again attempted, and that the [Federal Government] may promote the general welfare, it is needful that the truth, the whole truth, should be known, so that crimination and recrimination may forever cease, and then, on the basis of fraternity and faithful regard for the rights of the States, there may be written on the arch of [our Federation of States], *Esto perpetua*." [R33;645]

Varina later wrote that, after Jeff had finish the above dictation, she "looked up after a momentary silence to remind him that he had forgotten to continue, and he smilingly said, 'I think I am done.' And so was finished his life's work for his countrymen." [R13;830]

In June, *The Rise and Fall of the Confederate Government* was published by Appleton of New York City. The two thick volumes were mostly sold by subscription in various bindings which carried widely different price tags. Additionally, Jeff Davis had arranged in Canada for publication of a Canadian edition at Longmans. Varina would write: "the expense of an assistant, and the price of the book, which placed it beyond the reach of poor Confederates, as well as the fact that an inadequate compensation to [Jeff] had been agreed upon by his agent with the [Appleton publishers], prevented the book from being pecuniarily remunerative to him; but [Jeff] said he had not undertaken it as a matter of profit, and therefore must be satisfied if the end was gained of setting the righteous motives of the [Confederacy] before the world." Jeff Davis' history was "welcomed and praised" by most people in the former Confederate States and Maryland, Kentucky and Missouri. And the book received "some high commendations from English periodicals." However, commentators in the northern States, seeing how effectively the book undermined their self-glorifying historical fabrications, sought to minimize exposure by mostly ignoring the book's publication. Of the reaction to Davis' book, biographer Hudson Strode would write:

"The [northern States] Newspapers on the whole ignored *The Rise and Fall*. Only brief mentions were made in even professedly Democratic organs. A few magazines reviewed the work grudgingly. The *Nation* resented Davis' emphasis that [African American bonding] had been injected into the contest as a political rather than a moral question, that the Emancipation Proclamation had been a war measure, as [Abe] Lincoln [had] freely admitted. And it disliked Davis' holding to the fact that the issue had been between centralization [under an all-powerful Federal Government] and [decentralization under a limited Federal Government, the concept of] State Rights."

But many years after first publication, Burgess Montgomery would like what he was reading in the book, according to a letter he would send to Varina. Burgess was a nephew of the late Ben Montgomery, the talented African American to whom Joseph Davis had self-financed the sale of Brierfield farm, in a successful attempt to avoid its confiscation by the Federals. Burgess, who would be working in a Federal Government clerical job in Washington City, would have finished reading the first volume of *The Rise and Fall* at the time he would write Varina in 1895. In that letter Montgomery would write: "I have just finished reading the first volume, commencing with the second volume, and judging from what I have read thus far, I am satisfied to say, there is not, to my mind, a book or volume in existence containing a more truthful, succinct, and impartial, account of the casualties of the late [military conflict] and its subsequent events."

The great history completed, in August, Jeff and Varina left for France and England to vacation, to fetch daughter Winnie and to bring her back to The States. [R19;449-451, R30;519]

(3Q81)

Meanwhile in Mississippi, Lucius Lamar began an intense canvass of the State in support of Democrats running for State and local offices. Furthermore, Lamar was working to improve his standing with the people of Mississippi. His campaign swing began on September 5 at DeKalb, where, according to a newspaper report, he "was greeted with rounds of applause, which only ceased when he ascended the stand." He spoke of "the aims and principles involved in the recent coalition of the [Mississippi Greenback and Republican parties]. . . . His speech was almost exclusively directed to the discussion of the vital issues involved in the State election, and touched scarcely at all on national politics." From there he progressed to Canton, then to Yazoo City, then to Kosciusko, Brandon, Quitman, Waynesboro, Scranton, Handsboro, Pascagoula, and, on September 30, Raymond.

Because a Special Session of Congress was called for early October, Lamar took leave of his campaigning on September 30 to return to Washington City. By the time the Special Session ended on October 29, Lamar was back in Mississippi, speaking at Hillsboro and Forest, then Brookhaven, Hazlehurst, Natchez, Fayette, Port Gibson, and finally, on November 7, at Holly Springs. The following day, November 8, voters went to the polls fully ready to keep Democrats in office in their State and local governments. Of his canvass of voters, biographer Edward Mayes would write:

"Before this powerful and brilliant canvass what opposition to Mr. Lamar's reelection existed in the State melted away like November frost before the rising sun. His positions were so high, so unselfish, and so patriotic; his arguments were so clear and strong; his illustrations and anecdotes so graphic and scintillating; his personality so magnetic, and the sweep of his passion so dynamic, that none could stand before him."

When the new Mississippi Legislature would meet in January 1882, no candidate for the Federal Senate other than Lucius Lamar would be considered. He would be elected for another 6-year term by the unanimous votes of both the Mississippi House and the Mississippi Senate. [R205;433-448]

(4Q81)

Meanwhile in December, Jeff and Varina returned from Europe with daughter Winnie, now 17 years old. Both parents had enjoyed seeing friends and vacationing in France and England. Jeff was surely excited about seeing Winnie, for it had been almost 5 years since he had kissed his daughter goodbye in Carlsruhe, Germany. Although Varina had been with Winnie rather often during the first few years, she was obviously excited as well. Both parents perhaps had some regrets about sending Winnie, as a 12-year-old girl to Germany for so long; and many years later, Winnie would, in an article for the *Ladies*

Home Journal, write critically about parents educating pre-college-age girls abroad. But the Davis family decision could not be recast, and Winnie, had obviously benefited in many ways from the experience. [R19;449-451]

The Year of 1882 (Start of Grover Cleveland Story)

(1Q82)

It is now time to turn our attention to Buffalo, New York and begin following the career of a principled lawyer by the name of Grover Cleveland, a Democrat, age 44. On January 1, 1882 Cleveland begin work as the Mayor of Buffalo, having won the office in a remarkable landslide municipal election. How had this come about?

Apparently "a Ring composed of members of both political parties were in control of the Board of Aldermen of Buffalo, and their works of corruption were a scandal to honest men. Leading members of both parties, determined upon reform, therefore consulted together." The Aldermen had remained corrupt whether the Mayor was a Republican (as in 1880-81) or a Democrat (as in 1878-79), for no Mayor in recent times had challenged the Ring. The reform movement intensified when the Republican Party, at their City Convention on October 19, 1881, nominated, for Mayor and other offices, noted Corruptionists. An important Republican Faction then bolted and told Democrats that they would back their candidate for Mayor if they would nominate a good one. Thus encouraged, Democratic leaders sought a reform candidate pledged to rid the city of the Corruptionists. Grover Cleveland looked to be the man. His performance as Sheriff had exhibited the drive and backbone they were seeking. At first Cleveland refused to allow the reformers to put his name in nomination, preferring to continue with his successful law career in the Buffalo firm of Cleveland and Bissell. But the reformers persisted, and eventually Cleveland relented and allowed his name to be put forward to head the Democrat ticket. Actually, there was one name on the proposed ticket to whom Cleveland objected, that of John Sheehan. Fortunately, Sheehan agreed to retire, paving the way for the ticket to be advanced. At the Buffalo Democratic Convention on October 25, "Cleveland was nominated by acclamation, and the Independents, who had formed a temporary political organization of their own, at once endorsed him."

In his speech accepting the Democratic Party nomination he had addressed the Party faithful with the following assurances, saying in part:

"I accept the nomination tendered to me. I believe much can be done to relieve our citizens from our present load of taxation, and that a more rigid scrutiny of all public expenditures will result in a great saving to the community. I also believe that some extravagance in our city government may be corrected without injury to the public service. There is, or there should be, no reason why the affairs of our city should not be managed with the same care and the same economy as private interests; and when we consider that pubic officials are the trustees of the people and hold their places and exercise their powers for the benefit of the people, there should be no higher inducement to a faithful and honest discharge of public duty."

As the energetic political campaign had approached Election Day Cleveland was enjoying widespread support, not just from Democrats, but from Republicans as well. The final vote had been a landslide — Cleveland outvoting the Republican candidate 15,120 to 11,528, even though Republicans running for State offices won a substantial majority in Buffalo voting. Democrats had also won the post of City Attorney, City Controller and City Treasurer, giving Cleveland a firm hand in future confrontations with the Alderman ring.

At his inauguration as Mayor of Buffalo, Grover Cleveland addressed those in attendance with the following message, saying in part:

"We hold the money of the people in our hands to be used for their purposes and to further their interests as members of the municipality, and it is quite apparent that, when any part of the funds which the taxpayers have thus entrusted to us are diverted to other purposes, or when, by design or neglect, we allow a greater sum to be applied to any municipal purpose than is necessary, we have, to that extent, violated our duty. There surely is no difference in his duties and obligations, whether a person is entrusted with the money of one man or many."

At this point I will step back in time and present a brief biography of Democrat Grover Cleveland to enable you to understand the background of this remarkable man. Why remarkable? Because, a few pages forward in *Bloodstains*, he will be advancing from Mayor of Buffalo, to Governor of New York State, to President of the United States — all in the short span of 4 years.

The biography:

Grover Cleveland was born on March 18, 1837, in Caldwell, New Jersey, a small community near Newark, the fifth child of the Reverend Richard Cleveland and his wife Ann Neal Cleveland. The baby was named for Stephen Grover, who had preceded his father as pastor of Caldwell's First Presbyterian Church. A brief biography of the parents, up to this point, is appropriate:

Richard, born in 1804 at Norwich, Connecticut, received an excellent education at Yale College, "where he took high honors as of the class of 1824." Then he relocated to Baltimore, Maryland where he taught school and continued his study for the ministry. While in Baltimore he had met Ann Neal and apparently fell in love with her. During the winter of 1827-1828 he took courses at Princeton Theological Seminary. On September 10, 1829, Richard and Ann were married. Six weeks later, on October 15, Richard Cleveland "was ordained and installed minister of the Congregational Church in Windham, Connecticut."

Little is known about Ann Neal, but that she was of Irish and French descent and her father, Abner Neal, was a "rather wealthy bookseller and publisher of law books" in Baltimore. He had "been driven from Ireland for political activities." Her mother, Barbara Real or Reel, was "a German Quakeress from Germantown, Pennsylvania." So Ann's heritage was neither of the northern States nor of the southern States culture, but a blend of those persuasions, and she had grown up among the southern culture. On the other hand Richard was of the northern culture, of the northeastern States. Children followed as Richard moved about from church to church as is customary of ministers. For Ann, moving from Baltimore to Connecticut was a bit difficult but she bore it lovingly. Biographer Robert McElroy would explain:

"When Ann left her father's house, her [independent African American] maid, who had cared for her from infancy, begged to be allowed to accompany her. Thus attended, and rejoicing in many bright articles of personal adornment, she entered the [Connecticut] manse only to find that [African American] maids were regarded as unnecessary luxuries, and objectionable, as savoring of [African American bonding]. She soon understood also that jewelry was unbecoming a minister's wife. So the faithful servant was cheerfully returned to her [Maryland] home, the treasured little ornaments were laid aside without a sigh, and the bright heart of Ann Neal Cleveland beat under costumes suitable to the wife of a village minister of [Connecticut]. But the young couple were poor only in goods. They had education, culture, congeniality, and spiritual wealth — resources sufficient to encourage hope of a happy future."

However, the young couple left the northern States culture of Connecticut 4 years later, in 1833, as, now with two children, a boy and a girl, Richard was transferred to a Presbyterian church in Portsmouth, Virginia, allowing Ann to experience life again in the southern States culture. There, another baby girl blessed the growing family. But the Virginia assignment lasted only 2 years, until October 1834. From Virginia, Richard was transferred to Caldwell, New Jersey, where he took the post of pastor of the First Presbyterian Church. A baby girl was born weeks later. Then, after two years, the boy of whom we are most interested was born: Grover.

When Grover was 4 years old his father was transferred west to a Presbyterian church in Fayetteville, New York, located "only a mile from the Erie Canal and 8 miles from Syracuse," then a thriving trading center, arriving in 1841. "Located in a rich grain-growing region," Fayetteville had a "tannery, a pearl-barley mill and a lime factory." All of upper and western New York State was then "rapidly filling with settlers." The remaining children were born there. Grover had two older sisters, Anna and Mary and two older brothers, William Neal and Richard Cecil. The younger siblings were Margaret Louise, Lewis Frederick, Susan and Rose.

There was a "good academy" in the village, which benefited Grover's older siblings, especially the oldest boy, William. Grover began his education in "the little red frame district schoolhouse. Then at age 11 he entered the "academy, a substantial stone edifice just across the road." The family remained in Fayetteville until Grover was 14 years old. Biographer Robert McElroy would describe what it was like for a boy growing toward the teenage years in Reverend Cleveland's family:

"The commands of the Bible, the memorizing of the Westminster Catechism, the strictest observance of Sunday as the [Presbyterians] understood it, were the elements upon which the character of Grover Cleveland were built. Father, mother and 9 children were all supported by the minister's salary, which seldom exceeded $600 a year. Under such conditions, simple, cultivated, religious, Grover Cleveland passed the most formative years of his life. With the help of the academy and of his intelligent and well-trained father, he acquired a reasonable proficiency in Latin and mathematics, and an interest in religious questions which [would last] throughout his life . . . .

"Such was the atmosphere in which Grover Cleveland passed his childhood. It inevitably tended to produce a keen sense of personal responsibility, to make trustworthy character, for its ethical basis was absolute. It taught that there is a right which is eternally right, and a wrong which must remain forever wrong."

But the strict family life that had molded the character of teenaged Cleveland was to soon crash upon the rocks. Father Richard's health begin to fail — feeding 11 people on his meager church salary was nearly impossible and better educations for the children could be found elsewhere. So Reverend Cleveland accepted a job late in 1850, at $1,000 per year, as District Secretary of the American Home Missionary Society in Clinton, New York, "the great foster-mother of struggling new churches both West and East." Located about 30 miles due east of Fayetteville, Clinton was the home of Hamilton College, where brother William had already begun his college training, for he was destined to also become a minister. Grover attended the town academy for a few months upon the family's arrival. Apparently he "studied doggedly but without brilliancy." So it was decided that schooling would have to wait. Furthermore, the family needed money. Grover soon returned to Fayetteville to clerk at a local general store, operated by John McVicar. He clerked for two years earning $50 the first year and $100 the second, with board and lodging provided. He returned to Clinton in the spring of 1852, at about the time that older brother William completed his education at Hamilton College. At this time Grover anticipated his turn at finishing preparatory work, followed by entering Hamilton College.

But that was not to be, for his father, in more desperately failing health, suffering from gastric ulcer, had to leave his job in Clinton and take a "rural pastorate" at the hamlet of Holland Patent, located on the Black River 12 miles north of Utica. He was installed on September 14 in "a ceremony of great dignity, with no fewer than 7 other ministers taking part in the exercises." He preached again the following Sunday. "Then he was prostrated by his disease, and gradually sank." The relaxed life style was not beneficial — acute peritonitis developed, he died soon afterward and was buried in the cemetery of the Presbyterian Church he had just begun to serve. Biographer Allan Nevins would write: "The funeral was held . . . in the presence of many ministers — for Richard Cleveland's work had made him known and beloved throughout that section of the State."

Ann Neal Cleveland, widowed with 4 children younger than 16-year-old Grover, remained in Holland Patent. Members of the church offered assistance, but "the family was too proud to accept help from its neighbors." However, Ann did accept the offer to let the family remain in the parsonage rent-free, a benefit that would persist many years. Grover sought work to help support the family.

The first opportunity for work came from his oldest brother, William, who had graduated from Hamilton College in 1851. William took a job as a teacher and caretaker at the New York Institute for the Blind, a State-supported facility, and asked Grover to come and work there as well. So Grover went and resided in New York City for a year, until the fall of 1854, "living and working in the Institution." William and Grover were in charge of about 60 blind boys, day and night, awake and asleep, and taught various classes to the student body, consisting of about 120 blind boys and girls ranging in ages from 8 to 25. Grover taught the younger children. The job was confining, giving little opportunity to interact with the city's citizens and cultural attractions. Biographer Allan Nevins would conclude: "The cold halls, strict hours, poor meals, and atmosphere of human affliction made it a depressing place, and Cleveland found it particularly dreary." Grover, age 17, returned to Holland Patent after one year of service.

Grover was 18 years old when he decided to leave the family home in Holland Patent, with $25 borrowed from a benefactor, and strike out for the west, following in the footsteps of thousands of similar young men of great ambition but slight resources. His goal was Cleveland, Ohio (perhaps the name attracted him). But he stopped along the way to visit his uncle, Lewis Allen, husband of the late Richard Cleveland's sister and a well-to-do Shorthorn cattle breeder, whose home was at Black Rock, on the Niagara River, on the outskirts of Buffalo. Uncle Lewis persuaded Grover to stay in the area and give Buffalo a try. For starters he paid his nephew $60 to help finish the Shorthorn herd book, which he was going to publish for the benefit of America's stockmen. Far more important were the introductions to important people of Buffalo, allowing young Grover to network to great benefit. Although Grover had no college training he wanted to be a lawyer. In those days, even in western New York State, a smart man could privately study law, pass the bar exam and form a law practice without college training. This was more true the further west a man traveled, a good example being Illinois and Abe Lincoln. Accordingly, Uncle Allen arranged a law clerkship for Grover at the Buffalo law office of Rogers, Bowen and Rogers, all three partners being strong Democrats specializing in civil law. Since none of the three partners had ever graduated from college, Grover would be with men who knew how to advance without benefit of college connections. Biographer Allan Nevins would tell that, on Grover's first day in the office, the senior partner, Henry Rogers, "threw a copy of Blackstone down on Cleveland's desk with a bang, announcing grimly, 'That's where they all begin'." Biographer Robert McElroy would elaborate.

> Mr. Rogers "had a simple theory of education: 'If a boy has brains he will find out for himself without any telling.' Grover Cleveland was accordingly given a table, a shelf of law books, and permission to study law, in so far as that occupation did not interfere with his clerical duties."

Many years later Grover would tell the story himself, assuming the third person in his narrative (the "young man" is himself):

> "I know a young man who, when quite young, determined to acquire a college education and enter the legal profession, [but] the door to a college education was inexorably closed against him. [So,] he at once set his heart on studying law without collegiate training. When it soon appeared that even this must be postponed, he quite cheerfully set about finding any kind of honest work. After an unsuccessful quest for employment near home, he started for the West. He had adversity in abundance. After securing a temporary job, he was handed Blackstone's Commentaries and turned loose to browse in the library of a law office. When, on the first day of his study, all the partners and clerks forgot he was in a corner of the library and locked him in during the dinner hour, he merely said to himself, 'Some day I will be better remembered'."

Events would prove that Buffalo was an ideal place for Grover Cleveland to settle and build a career. Buffalo was "where the waters of Lake Erie began their race down the Niagara River into Lake Ontario" and where the Erie Canal terminated. "It was a Western city with a New England core," easily "the largest on the Great Lakes." Buffalo "was the northern gateway to the West" with a population measured at 42,000 in 1850, to become 81,000 in 1860. It held more population than Pittsburg and almost as much as Cincinnati. But it was not particularly peaceful. Biographer Allan Nevins would explain:

> "Buffalo was one of the roughest and most dangerous [cities] in America. It was sown with saloons. Along the waterfront were solid rows of dives of the worst order — barrel houses, dens selling Monongahela whiskey at 4 cents a glass, brothels and gambling joints. . . . Prostitutes numbered [in the] hundreds. . . . With bad water and gutters carrying sewage, with little care and less knowledge regarding epidemics, disease ran riot. Typhoid, smallpox and typhus often slew by wholesale."

The population was a combination of people from the northeastern States and people from Germany, the Germans coming in greater numbers more recently:

> "During the 1840's came a steady inflow of Germans, refugees from oppression and poverty. They were a hardworking [ethnic group] who somehow amassed capital as rapidly as they learned the language. Soon almost half the stores seemed to be German. The Germans established iron-foundries, flour mills, tanneries, and breweries; they furnished the bakers, grocers, expert mechanics, and cabinet-makers. Their contribution to cultural life lay in music, fine handicrafts, and an appreciation of the uses of leisure which many [people of the northeastern States] lacked."

The time would soon arrive when railroads would continue, unbroken, past Buffalo to Cleveland, Chicago and points west, but the Erie Canal would continue to carry the heavy bulk materials, such as iron ore and coal. There were growing iron works, brass foundries and machine shops. The most noteworthy resident had been Millard Fillmore.

The partners in the law firm were Henry Rogers, 55 when Grover first arrived, Dennis Bowen, 35 and Sherman Rogers, 25. The firm "cultivated a civil rather than criminal practice, and preferred a few clients of large interests — banks, manufacturers, shippers, and merchants. One of their principal accounts was with Wells Fargo, and another with Pratt & Company, iron-masters." Grover took leave from the firm on occasion to work on updated editions of his uncle's Shorthorn herdbook, from the second through the fifth editions. Uncle Lewis would write in the fifth edition, dated 1861, about "the kindness, industry, and ability of my young friend and kinsman, Grover Cleveland, Esq." When in Buffalo, which was most of the time, Grover lodged at the Southern Hotel, where would be found "cattle-drovers and farmers, a rough, shrewd, talkative set of men." Weekends often found him at his aunt and uncle's home.

As with most newspapermen and lawyers of that era, politics was an important aspect of Grover's life. Beginning in 1856, the year John Fremont ran unsuccessfully for President as a Republican, Grover was aligned with the Democratic Party — even though Uncle Lewis Allen had been a Whig before becoming a Republican in 1855, when he had presided over the first Erie County Republican Party Convention. No, Grover did not follow his uncle's lead, choosing instead to align with the lawyers in the firm where he worked, the friends he had made among "the hotel-lobby and the bar-room set," and the local politicians who held power. Democrat Israel Hatch was elected to the Federal House during 1856, but would be defeated by a Republican in the midterm elections of 1858. But in Buffalo, Democrats more firmly ran the city, and, as the saying goes, "all politics is local." Democrat Eli Cook had been Mayor in 1853-55; Democrat Frederick Stevens was the current Mayor, 1855-1858, and he would be succeeded by a third Democrat, Timothy Lockwood, in 1858. Furthermore, Dennis Bowen, of the law firm, was a Democrat Alderman and both of the Rogers were "firmly Democratic." Biographer Allan Nevins would observe, "The elder Rogers had been a lifelong follower of [Andrew] Jackson, and was proud to recall that [James] Polk had appointed him Collector of the Port of Buffalo." Of Grover Cleveland choosing the Democratic Party, biographer Robert McElroy would write: "[The Democratic Party] seemed to him to represent greater solidarity and conservatism. He was repelled by the [John] Fremont candidacy [of 1856], which struck him as 'having a good deal of fuss and feathers about it'."

After three and a half years of self study and observation in the law firm of Rogers, Bowen and Rogers, Grover Cleveland stood for examination and, in May 1859, the Supreme Court admitted him to the bar of the State of New York. Although the State allowed him to form his own law practice, he decided to remain in the firm of Rogers, Bowen and Rogers as managing clerk. Considering the heightened political sectionalism of 1859, including the terrorist attack at Harpers' Ferry, Virginia by John Brown's gang, this was a time to move cautiously and conservatively in pursuit of career advancement, and Cleveland was probably acting in that self-interest.

Furthermore, since 1856, there had been overwhelming defeats for Democrats all across the northern States. Republicans, members of a sectional Party which intentionally excluded the southern States, had gained much power in the northern States in the mid-term elections of 1858, creating panic among northern States Democrats. The 1859 State and local elections continued the destruction. In full panic, northern States Democrats at the 1860 Democratic Party National

Convention, desperate to cling to what remained of their local political influence, and with no prospects for national victory, forced a split into two Democrat Factions. Each Faction offered its candidate for President, with little hope of national victory, but with desperate hope of local and State victory. A fourth Party arose and offered a candidate for President as well. In the four-way race, by winning all the northern States electoral votes, Republicans, won the office of President. Recognizing that Republicans were intent on subjugating the southern States under a Federal Government that would not be properly constrained by the Federal Constitution, States had begun to secede in December 1860. South Carolina was first, basically repealing, by legal votes of the people, the process by which it and 12 others had created the Federal Government, each independently placing itself under it. Six more States followed and the 7 joined together under a new, and clearly limited, federal government, called the Confederate States of America. By the spring of 1861 Republicans controlled most Legislatures and all Governors' offices in the northern States — empowering the Republican Party with control over the State Militia of every northern State. Democrats controlled all the southern States, including the States of Delaware, Maryland, Kentucky and Missouri.

Did Grover Cleveland and his Democrat friends, including the lawyers at Rogers, Bowen and Rogers, favor letting the seceded States go in peace while initiating discussion of relations between the two countries, or did they favor an armed invasion to force those States back under the Federal Government? No clear answer to that question exists, that I have found. It all happened so quickly. Once State Militia swept into Maryland, and the subjugation of Kentucky and Missouri was underway, speaking out against the Republican military campaign was difficult and many who tried to do so found themselves imprisoned. So, during February and March of 1861 it was hard for a Democrat to be open about his opinions, and by June, the issue was no longer germane, the die had been cast. So Grover obediently continued his work as managing clerk of Rogers, Bowen and Rogers. The younger Rogers "gravitated into the Republican ranks, but the other two [lawyers] remained Democrats, as did Cleveland.

Grover Cleveland became more involved in Democrat politics during the campaign of 1862, the second year of the Republican Invasion Campaign. At the October 1862 Democratic Buffalo City Convention he was nominated for Supervisor of the Second Ward and, in November, elected by 509 votes to that post. The Second Ward "contained many Germans, with whom Cleveland was popular." At this same election Democrat Cyrenius Torrance won the office of District Attorney by a vote of 12,000 to 9,300. Furthermore, there were clear signs that Democrats were staging a comeback at this time, it being also the 1862 mid-term national elections. Support was waning for the Republican's military invasion campaign — the horrible death toll coming home to roost. Democrat Horatio Seymour won the race for Governor of New York State, the largest of the States, with a victory margin of over 10,000 votes. A. P. Laning, a Buffalo lawyer who would later become Cleveland's law partner, had been Chairman of the Platform Committee at the Democratic Party New York State Convention. The Democrat Platform, although not calling for withdrawal of Federal troops, urged a negotiated settlement with the seceded States, denounced the illegal and arbitrary arrest of civilians, and demanded full freedom of the press and of speech. The Federal House seat for the district that included Buffalo was won by Elbridge Spaulding, Republican, former Whig and long-ago Buffalo Mayor (1847).

Shortly after the 1862 election, Democrat Cyrenius Torrance chose Cleveland, 25, to be Assistant District Attorney. Cleveland accepted the offer even though it only paid $500 a year, compared to the $1,000 annual earnings he had been getting at Rogers, Bowen and Rogers. The lower earnings would cut into what he could send home to his mother and sisters at Holland Patent, but he figured the experience might become a launch pad into a political career, which appealed to him, especially considering the upsurge in Democratic strength in Buffalo and across the State. Perhaps he also figured the new job would keep him out of the fighting. A younger brother, Lewis Frederick Cleveland, had enlisted at the outset of the fighting, in May 1861 (he would be a soldier for two years and leave without injury). Another younger brother, Richard Cecil Cleveland, had enlisted in July 1861 (he would be a soldier for three years and also leave without injury). The Cleveland family had contributed enough, one might reason.

Newly elected District Attorney Cyrenius Torrance was "an elderly lawyer" who would become mostly "ill and infirm." Therefore, the hard work fell to his assistant, Grover Cleveland. Biographer Allan Nevins would describe Cleveland's job as Assistant District Attorney for Erie County, New York:

> "Grover labored constantly in the dingy prosecutor's office in the old courthouse of Erie County. Since Torrance was ill and infirm, most of the hard work fell upon his assistant. It was excellent legal training and it gave Cleveland a clear insight, which he needed and [would use] later as Mayor, into the seamy side of local government. The District Attorney is above everything else the investigating officer of the community. It is his business not only to prosecute common malefactors, but to keep an eye on the administration of the city and county to detect malfeasance and corruption. . . . Torrance did not distinguish himself in public investigation, but Cleveland nevertheless learned a good deal. . . . In short, he and not Torrance was the real district attorney."

Grover Cleveland's name was among those drawn in July 1863, on the first day of selecting Federal Army draftees in Buffalo, this draft being authorized by the Conscription Act of March 3, 1863. He quickly arranged to pay a substitute $150 to take his place. The volunteer substitute was George Brinske or Benninsky, who had come to the United States in 1851, and since 1856 had been a sailor on the Great Lakes. George would be lucky — he would never be "in any important battle as a combatant."

During the political campaign season of 1864 the defeat of the Confederacy seemed not far away even though Confederates at Richmond and Petersburg were holding off Federals in Virginia and Federals occupying Atlanta seemed to be reluctant to strike out on a destructive war against civilians. Abe Lincoln was running for a second term as President and Representatives in the Federal House were standing for election, as were one-third of those in the Senate. This was a difficult time for Democrats in Buffalo. For example, Grover Cleveland lost his bid to be re-elected to Supervisor of the Second Ward.

During the political campaign of 1865 the District Attorney's office held by Cyrenius Torrance was up for election and he was obviously too ill to run again. So Democrats nominated Grover Cleveland as their candidate for District Attorney. The Democratic newspaper in Buffalo supported Cleveland with praise, such as:

> Cleveland is a man "whose close application, gentlemanly deportment and conceded ability have given him a standing at the bar which has seldom been gained by one of his years. . . . [He] has discharged his duties with an ability and fidelity which have secured the commendation of men of all parties. He is a young man, who, by his unaided exertions, had gained a high position at the bar, and whose character is above reproach. He will be supported by hundreds of Republicans on these grounds."

But his was not to be. During the four years of the invasion campaign, deaths among Federals in the Army and Navy had totaled 360,000 men, and Republicans pinned those deaths on Democrats. A Democrat victory, even in local elections was hard to achieve. Although Cleveland won 7 of the 13 wards in Buffalo, he lost votes in the outlying county region. Republican Lyman Bass won the office of District Attorney.

However, during his three years in the DA's office, Cleveland had gained considerable statue among Buffalo lawyers and, consequently, became, at age 28, a partner in the law office of former State Treasurer Isaac Vanderpoel. Four years later, in 1869, Vanderpoel would resign and the firm would be known as Laning, Cleveland and Folsom. During these years Cleveland "disliked criminal cases, and would never accept a retainer from a man whom he knew to be crooked; he liked to prepare civil cases in his office, and then let" other lawyers in the firm present arguments in court. "He preferred an equitable [negotiated] adjustment to a showy victory on technical points of law." Yet, although successful in his career, Grover was not yet a married man. It appears that romance was being postponed by his unusually strong focus on career advancement.

Grover Cleveland's career took an unusual turn in the fall of 1870, the year of the first mid-term elections of the Ulysses Grant Administration. That year Democrats persuaded Cleveland to run for the office of Sheriff of Erie County. What was it like being Sheriff of rough and tumble Buffalo? Biographer Allan Nevins would figure it this way:

> First, about Buffalo — "In 1873 the city [would have] 673 saloons for a population of less than 150,000 [and] few cities of Buffalo's size had so many groggeries and disorderly houses, or witnessed so many assaults, robberies, and murders. . . . He [would be] one of the chief law officers of a county that, with its large population of canal-hands, sailors, roustabouts, vagabonds, and other riff-raff, was full of rowdyism and crime. . . . Gambling houses operated 7 days in the week, saloons and brothels were always open, and under the name of sacred concerts, Sunday performances of the vilest kind were permitted, at which the audiences were composed of loafers, thieves and prostitutes."

> Second, about Cleveland — Grover was a man who exhibited two characters. One character resembled "a hard-working young lawyer, spending incredibly long hours at his desk and seeming to those, who knew him but slightly, to be growing into a stiff, heavy, and stern man." The other character resembled "a roistering blade, who knew the inside of dozens of saloons, led the chorus in lusty drinking songs, and prided himself on feats of conviviality which sometimes, as he [would] put it later, caused him to 'lose a day'. . . On hot summer evenings he was fond of the German beer-gardens, with their sawdust, music, pretty girls, and jovial banter. . . . This dual character of the man accounts in part for his curious" acceptance of the challenge to seek the Erie County Sheriff's office.

> In conclusion: although the office of Sheriff was usually awarded to "a political hack . . . it was [Cleveland's] association with the saloon and livery-stable set that made him willing to consider such an office." He would certainly know his way around such crowds and not be intimidated.

Grover Cleveland won the election, by 303 votes and took office on January 1, 1871. Biographer Robert McElroy would describe the excitement:

> "At once [Cleveland] became the hope, and soon the despair, of the hungry pack of Democratic politicians bent on gain. For years they had watched the Republicans fatten on the spoils which went with this office. Their day had come at last. A Democrat was Sheriff of Erie County."

But a wholesale change of jobs was not to be. Cleveland reappointed the second in command in the office, W. L. G. Smith, "a Democratic attorney and a man of exceptional ability." He also reappointed the Jailer, and 8 Deputy Sheriffs under him. Others, including turnkeys, janitors and clerks would remain at their jobs. Buffalo was a dangerous city and Cleveland knew that better than most. Therefore, one would suppose, he wanted experienced and proven men under him.

Perhaps the most noteworthy aspect of Cleveland's administration of the Sheriff's office was his well publicized attack on wasteful spending of the public money that was entrusted to it. He diligently sought the lowest bidder in selecting suppliers, regardless of Party. Even the firewood to heat the county jail received his attention as he personally measured the size of the stacks and, when finding them short, forced the vendor to make up the shortfall. Perhaps refusal to help his Democrat friends with jobs and contracts dampened their enthusiasm for supporting him for re-election.

Family tragedy struck the Cleveland's in 1872. Grover's youngest brother, Lewis F. Cleveland (known as Fred), had acquired a lease on a summer resort, the Royal Victoria Hotel, in Nassau in the Bahamas Islands, and brother Richard C. Cleveland (known as Cecil) planned to help with running the place. But, while the two brothers sailed from New York to Nassau on the steamer *Missouri*, they drowned when the ship caught fire and burned at sea 25 miles off of Great Abaco, a Bahamas island, with the loss of approximately 80 other passengers. Fred, the younger of these brothers, had been the most successful, becoming owner of the Fairfield House Hotel in Connecticut. The estates, which Grover administered, would go to sister, Louise, "who had accepted the burden of staying with and caring for their mother."

Grover would only be a one-term Sheriff. A Republican, John Weber, would win the election of 1873. He would praise Cleveland after taking the office, stating that he had "administered with great efficiency."

For the next 8 years, 1874 through 1881, Grover Cleveland worked in Buffalo law firms that featured his name: first Bass, Cleveland and Bissell, then Cleveland and Bissell. Among the firm's clients were "the Standard Oil Company, the Merchants' and Traders' Bank, the Buffalo, Rochester & Pittsburg Railroad, and the Lehigh Valley Railroad." Cleveland had opportunities to expand his horizons beyond Buffalo, but declined — for example he refused an 1881 offer to be the attorney for the New York Central Railroad with an annual salary of $15,000, choosing instead to keep at his present practice, which earned him approximately $10,000 each year. Biographer Allan Nevis would explain:

> "He told his friends that having saved about $75,000, he did not need the money, and that acceptance would restrict his personal freedom in the choice of his work and the control of his time more than he could endure."

One would suppose that, without wife and children and responsibilities to send money to Holland Patent, Cleveland simply did not place a high value on a high income if it meant lots of out-of-town travel and high-pressure work.

It was during these years that Grover Cleveland decided that he should accept the responsibility for having fathered a child with Maria Halpin, at the time of the birth a 33-year-old widow (he would have been 36 years old). In 1874 she had given birth to a boy, whom she had named Oscar Folsom Cleveland. It is believed that she had taken several lovers and identification of the true father was uncertain. But Grover accepted the responsibility and gave her financial support.

Reflecting on Cleveland's career in Buffalo from the perspective of 1881, a lifelong friend and admirer, John Milburn, would write:

> "He was an outstanding lawyer at the Buffalo bar, but with a distinctly local reputation and acquaintance. . . . He was a prominent citizen, deeply respected for his independence, force of character, and inbred integrity. He was genial and companionable . . . . He did his work with extraordinary thoroughness. That thoroughness was a specific characteristic. He gave his best to everything he did. . . . His physical endurance was extraordinary, beyond anything I have ever known. He would subject himself to enormous strains of work and I never heard him complain of fatigue. . . . His commanding qualities were those of judgment, earnestness, and moral force, lightened by a keen sense of humor. . . . He was recognized on all sides as a power in the community, which would be more and more visible as some emergency arose, bringing it into full play."

The brief biography being now up to date, I shall summarize:

- This was the boy, Grover Cleveland, raised in upstate New York — the son of a Presbyterian minister, who had been raised and trained in Connecticut, and his Maryland-born wife — a marriage that had joined together, as man and wife, the northern States culture (Connecticut) and the southern States culture (Maryland).

- This was the man, Grover Cleveland — who had persevered under economic hardship to become a successful lawyer without benefit of a college education.

- This was the political leader, Grover Cleveland — who would soon become one of America's greatest Presidents — not unlike President Harry Truman, also a Democrat — both Cleveland and Truman being incorruptible — both always accountable for their actions — both rising to the supreme leadership of our nation — both without benefit of college — yet neither appreciated by today's historians as they ought to be. [R81;2-23, R211;21-39, R212;8-84]

We now resume our continuing history. Grover Cleveland has been Mayor of Buffalo for 4 months. Wade Hampton is at his seat in the Federal Senate. It is late April or Early May, 1882.

During late April and early May, in the Federal Senate, Wade Hampton was involved in notable confrontation over a bill which had advanced to floor debate, from the Committee on Military Affairs, of which he was a member (furthermore, Hampton had been chosen to present the bill to the floor for debate). This bill, if passed, would repeal the 1866 law forbidding former Confederates from holding positions as officers in the Federal Army. Some Republicans, still struggling to wave the "bloody shirt," argued that legal discrimination against former Confederates should remain on the statute books — in the words of Vermont Senator George Edmunds, that discriminatory law should remain as an "everlasting monument" to the military triumph of the "right side" in the Federal conquest of the State Secessionists. Edmunds argued, in part:

> For example, if this bill were to be made law, it would allow the President "to appoint Mr. Jefferson Davis . . . to be a brigadier-general and commander-in-chief . . . in the Army of the United States." . . . I think . . . it is better to preserve some everlasting monument that there was a right side and a wrong side to [the combatants]. And I think inasmuch as the [Federal Government] turned out to be on the right side . . . it is well to teach all future generations that the moment the struggle was over we did not forget that there was any distinction in the right and the wrong of that contest. . . . I think it better that this perpetual statute-book should hold some unextinguished memorial that we knew the difference between one side and the other."

Senators from the former Confederate States took obvious offense over the "Bloody Shirt" allegation that the Federal conquest of 11 seceded States was a military conquest of "right" over "wrong." Senator Samuel Maxey, of Texas, replied:

> "The war has been over for 17 years, and a man who served in the Confederate Army or in the civil employment of the Confederacy in any capacity whatever, or in the [Confederate] Navy is declared by this [1866] statute to have committed the unpardonable sin: 'Stand by thyself, come not near me; for I am holier than thou.' I do not like that sort of sentiment. I do not believe in it. . . . It is putting the brand of Cain upon every man who ever served in the Confederate Army or Navy or civil service. He can be a Senator, he can be a Representative, he can sit in Cabinet council, [but you argue he cannot be even a lowly non-commissioned officer in the Federal Army].
>
> "If this discrimination is to be kept up to the end of time, no man who served in the civil employment of the Confederacy, as the honorable Senator from Arkansas on my left did, or who served in the [Confederate Army], as a good many of us [in this Senate] did, or in the Confederate Navy, can hold the most humble position in [today's United States] Army. If that is to be the sentiment . . . then let us know it, let us understand it, be fair about it, be candid about it, and let us understand where our people stand in regard to this matter."

Wade Hampton also engaged in this debate:

> "I think [the statute] should be repealed, because now, while some young men who were in the Confederate Army can enlist, and many have enlisted in the United States Army, they are precluded by the statute from any mode of acquiring promotion, though they have been the most gallant soldiers in the service. . . . I regretted very much hearing the remarks of [Senator Edmunds] of Vermont. . . . I was sorry to hear him say that he wanted a class of his fellow-citizens to stand as a monument forever of our unhappy war. Nor do I agree with him in assuming to myself what he has attempted to do — pronounce emphatically who was 'right' and who was 'wrong.' My convictions were as sincere as his, and I hope as honest; but I will recall to him an instance that happened during the war and commend it to his consideration:
>
> > "There was an old gentleman who had two sons, one in the Federal and one in the Confederate service. In the providence of God they were both brought home to him dead at one time. He buried them side by side, and the only epitaph he put on their tombs was: 'God alone knows who was right.' . . . ."
>
> "No great question or right [has ever been] settled in the world, and none will ever be settled as long as the world lasts, by the sword."

George Vest of Missouri then added his comments to the spirited discussion:

" . . . I served in the military and civil service of the late Confederacy . . . [and I] believe, sir, that the people of the United States, the great body of them, are anxious to obliterate every mark and monument of the late War between the States or between the [Federal] Government and certain States. . . . Recent events have shown, if they show anything, that the great body of the people of this country, north, south, east and west, desire, above all things, material advancement and material prosperity without going back to the obsolete ideas of sectional hate and sectional strife. . . . Your flag, our flag, waves in triumph . . . from one end of the Union to the other [and] not one man, woman or child disputes the national supremacy. Your taxes are collected; your national name is respected. . . . Will any Senator on the other side of this Chamber tell me that this [1866] statute . . . is necessary for any purpose except to voice and express the hate that ought to have died with the [military] success of the national Government?" [R199;290]

Meanwhile, from Mid-April to Mid-May, Jeff and Varina were in Vicksburg and Brierfield farm, along the swollen Mississippi River, to see what they could do to cope with flood damage and to help the tenant farmers who lived there and earned their living working the fields. The tenant farmers had just suffered terrible damage from spring flooding, a problem that was occurring more and more often as northern States forests were cut and prairie grasslands were plowed to turn the upper Mississippi drainage basin into farm fields. Beginning with the couple's trip to Europe the previous year, son-in-law Addison Hayes, commuting from Memphis, had been acting as business manager for the farm, including the required bookkeeping, so that task no longer burdened Jeff. Jeff had written Addison on April 20 from Vicksburg: "I propose to go to the Brierfield [farm] tomorrow on the 'Headlight' and fear there will be little land to be seen. . . . The anomalous action of the river puts it out of my power to form any opinion of the future, but I hope we may yet make a partial crop of cotton."

On another trip a little later, with the floodwaters further receded, Varina accompanied Jeff to Brierfield. She wanted to personally assess the flood damage and help figure out what they could do to help the tenants, many of whom had once worked the farm as bonded African Americans. Upon the couple's arrival, led by Burgess Montgomery, a "little brass band" greeted Jeff and Varina — complete with new uniforms that Jeff had purchased after a previous visit. Many years later Montgomery would explain:

"[I had written Jeff Davis] on behalf of the Band, asking his kind assistance in procuring uniform suits for the latter, in reference to which, I am proud to say, he promptly responded, as was usual for him in all matters or requests pertaining to the promotion and advancement of his [African American] friends. . . and in a very short time the [newly-uniformed] Band was called together to receive their true friends, the Honorable Jefferson Davis and Mrs. Varina Davis. . . and, [whenever] you and [Jeff Davis] were on a visit to [Brierfield farm], it was always for me, a great pleasure to call the Band out for a serenade in honor of your distinguished and welcome presence in our midst."

Jeff and Varina did what they could to help the tenants, and according to Burgess Montgomery, their efforts were appreciated. Montgomery would write Jeff Davis that he would be forever grateful for their contributions "to the needs of the many that were rendered destitute by the floods, who would otherwise have undergone severe hardship and suffering were it not for the generous and immediate aid extended them by [Jeff] Davis." About this time Varina's brother, Becket Howell, arrived at Brierfield farm to handle the day-to-day supervisory tasks that Addison Hayes was unable perform from Memphis. Although the floodwaters still covered some low-lying fields and still covered some low spots in the farm roads, Becket, having just arrived, wrote Jeff the following optimistic report on May 25:

"I arrived here all safe on Monday and found every thing moving along. All the teams are at work breaking up land and planting just as fast as they can. The water is going down and I think if we don't have mishaps, we will make a very fair crop. We have nearly all of the [unflooded] land planted and a good deal of cotton up and chopped out."

Sadly, Becket Howell, at Brierfield in October, would suffer an illness and die. [R19;458-459, R30; 518-520]

Meanwhile on July 19, Grover Cleveland's mother, Ann Neal Cleveland, died at her home at Holland Patent, in central New York State. By the way, the youngest brother of the family, the late Lewis F. Cleveland, known as Fred, had, many years earlier, purchased from the Presbyterian Church the home where Mrs. Cleveland had been living since the death of her husband. Consequently, the siblings agreed that it should go to sister Louise, who had been at the home for many years, caring for the mother. All 7 of the surviving children were present for the funeral, even Anna Cleveland Hastings, wife of a missionary, "who happened to be back from Ceylon" at the time. As is so often the case with family funerals, the occasion, although sad, gave the siblings a chance to be together and share life experiences. Mayor Grover Cleveland's stories should have been the most exciting subjects for family discussion, but, according to biographer Allan Nevins, "To none of the family did [Grover] breathe a hint that he might be a candidate for Governor" of New York State. Nevertheless, he was personally advancing his political opportunity, although quietly, taking care to not become engaged in any deal-making. His political strength lay in his record of honesty in government and personal character. That needed to remain untarnished.

But some men were already publicly advancing the name of Mayor Grover Cleveland of Buffalo. The day before Mrs. Cleveland's passing, the Buffalo *Courier* had advocated Cleveland as a strong candidate for the Democratic nomination for the Governor's office. Biographer Allan Nevins would find that, "within a few weeks, the Cleveland 'boom' was well underway in western New York State." But the voting power of the State was located in the east, especially in the metropolitan region centered on New York City, consisting of Manhattan, Brooklyn, Queens, The Bronx and Staten Island, which would not be consolidated as The City of Greater New York until 1898, a region powered politically by machine politics and the votes of recent immigrants, especially the recent Irish immigrants. How could a recently-elected Mayor from western New York State, not known in the east, without state-wide experience, compete with the eastern power block and Tammany Hall? There was little time to build a campaign surge — the Democratic State Convention was scheduled to open in Syracuse on September 21, two months into the future.

Before relating the political events of those two months, from latter July to latter September, time should be devoted to understanding New York State politics. We should begin with the metropolis centered on New York City (Manhattan Island). A Democratic Party political machine, called Tammany, had controlled city government, more often than not, since 1830. A description of Tammany's history is appropriate:

> This political machine, generally referred to as "Tammany Hall," but also as "Tammany," begin in New York City in 1786 as a branch of the Society of St. Tammany, the founding chapter having originated 14 years earlier, in Philadelphia in 1772. It was named for Tamanend, the Native American chief of one of the clans, or tribes, that made up the Lenni-Lenape Nation, which occupied the Delaware Valley at the time Philadelphia was established. Tamanend had cooperated with colonists and William Penn in peaceful joint occupation of the region, reportedly assuring colonists — think colonists, not Native Americans — that they could "live in peace as long as the waters run in the rivers and creeks and as long as the stars and moon endure." By the way, there is a statute to Chief Tamanend in Philadelphia which repeats the Native American's promise. Similar branches of the Society of St. Tammany sprung up in many places in the colonies, and persisted for a while after they became States, as far west as the Ohio River Valley and as far south as Savannah, Georgia. But none evolved into a powerful political machine except for the Society's branch on Manhattan Island, eventually headquartered in a fine, three-story stone building on East 14th Street, complete with a white marble statue of Tamanend prominently positioned across the front edge of the roof within a sheltering stone arch. The people who controlled the Manhattan Democracy operated from that building and their political machine was known by the name of the building, "Tammany Hall."

By honoring Chief Tammany, those colonists who had arrived early to North America as well as their native-born children believed they were likewise honored over and above Europeans who had more recently arrived. Along that vein of thinking, the Society attracted the older settlers and their children and tended to exclude the more recent immigrants. The organization in some ways resembled a genealogical society, a precursor to the Sons or the Daughters of the American Revolution. The primary event of the various chapters was their May First celebrations of Native

American identity. Philadelphia held its "Annual Tammany Festival." The Manhattan chapter did as well, calling its Hall a "wigwam" and its chief leader the "Grand Sachem," and holding its first "Tammany Festival" in 1787. Perhaps, in the middle 1800's, a recently-arrived Irishman — craving acceptance as a "red-blooded American hoping soon to be a bona fide citizen" — was impressed by Tammany's political organizers as they sought votes in exchange for acceptance, help in navigating new surroundings and a little prestige.

By summer 1882, Mayor Grover Cleveland had received notable attention in western New York State — and a little as far away as the eastern portion — for his vetoes of some of Buffalo's graft-tainted activity, but most notably for his veto in June of a 5-year Buffalo street-cleaning contract:

> On June 19, the Aldermen composing the City Council selected George Talbot for cleaning "the paved streets and alleys of the city during the next 5 years" — at a contract price of $422,500. The Aldermen had approved the contract by a vote of 15 to 11. But 5 other bids for the same work were much lower, the best bid being Thomas Maytham's at $313,500. Suspecting graft and kickbacks to greedy politicians, Cleveland was incensed. He vetoed the $422,500 contract because — as he explained in rather rough-talking language — "I regard it as the culmination of a most bare-faced, impudent, and shameless scheme to betray the interests of the people, and to worse than squander the public money." Shamed, the Aldermen reversed their votes, choosing the best bidder by a vote of 23 to 2. And that outfit would, over 5 years, clean Buffalo's streets to "general satisfaction."

Other efforts by Cleveland were yielding success and bringing him recognition during the summer, even though his victories were also being won over the objections of obstinate Buffalo Aldermen:

> Mayor Cleveland achieved better economy on "repair and refurnishing of the schools," more critical staff analysis of the merits of various contractor bid proposals, and getting a full day's work out of city employees, who, unfortunately, had become accustomed to leaving work an hour early. "At the same time, [Cleveland] was vetoing a multitude of petty bits of graft which the Aldermen, or rather a corrupt combination of 15 Aldermen and certain contractors, with singular pertinacity, were trying to thrust past him."

But the biggest municipal problem that Cleveland set out to tackle, and quickly so, with all the might he could muster, was that of a dangerous sewage problem where the Hamburg Canal (a section of the Erie Canal traversing the city) collected sewage which stagnated therein and threatened the health and lives of the citizens:

> In Cleveland's Inaugural Address, by which he began his Administration, he had warned that the "number of deaths in the previous calendar year approximated 4,000, of which 1,378, or more than a third, were from epidemic diseases, typhoid being the most prominent. He declared that the abatement of the Hamburg Canal nuisance could no longer be postponed." Because much of the land of the city sloped naturally down to the canal, sewage drained into it and stagnated there. The solution seemed to be a parallel new sewer line above the canal, which would collect the sewage before it reached the canal, and cause collected sewage to flow northward into the Niagara River, where the huge and rapidly flowing Great Lakes water outflow would greatly dilute the sewage, facilitate its treatment and carry it away from the city. This problem had stymied the city sanitation department and its city engineer for a decade, resulting in no action and a project estimate of $1,568,000, which had proven very difficult to fund. Cleveland wanted engineering experts, from wherever they could be found in the country, to come and study Buffalo's problem — then design a solution that would technically work, be affordable and be accomplished in a reasonable and expedited time frame. The city staff and the Aldermen resisted mightily (outside experts would prevent them from personally making money on the project). Cleveland would hear nothing of it. "With a crushing message" on March 26 he insisted on bringing in experts. Cleveland proposed to the New York Legislature a bill to create a Sewer Commission, which would have the authority to oversee project design and construction. There was a political fight, but the Legislature passed the bill in June. After a fight over appointment of men to the Commission, Cleveland's 5 nominees were accepted. The project would be a success:

The Commission "conferred with the best sanitary engineers of the country, and on their advice adopted a plan that met all requirements at an estimated cost of only $764,370." Finally, arrangements were made for municipal bonds to fund the project.

Also, several community water wells in the city were found to be health hazards — the city chemist, upon checking water quality, found that 13 community wells were "vile, and disgustingly contaminated with filth." Over some resistance by Aldermen, Cleveland made sure that these contaminated wells were shut down and that arrangements were made to pipe clean city water to people who had been using them.

At an ideal time, centered on June, recognition of Cleveland's success with improving conditions in Buffalo became known to Legislators in Albany (Sanitary Commission bill) and, through newspaper reports, to political leaders across the State (street cleaning contract). He earned the moniker, "the veto mayor." His activities, his reforms and gains in governmental efficiency were creating some excitement for Cleveland as a candidate for Governor.

Two other Democrats were being prominently mentioned as candidates for Governor:

Roswell Flower of Watertown, New York, a "debonair young leader, who, while he had made a dashing record as a financier in Watertown and New York City, and had served capably in [the Federal House], was principally qualified in the eyes of the politicians by his wealth, which promised large and careless campaign disbursements."

Henry Slocum of Brooklyn, who, as you will recall, had been one of the two major military leaders under William Sherman, who had commanded the huge Federal Army that, following the 1864 elections in the northern States, inflicted upon the citizenry of Georgia a 60-mile-wide swath of destruction, expanding eastwardly all the way to Savannah. By the way, the people of the future metropolis of New York would remember the name "General Slocum" with images of horror:

On June 15, 1904, the excursion ferry, "General Slocum," would leave the East River pier on Manhattan's Third Street, with 1,358 passengers and 23 crewmen, bound for a picnic on Long Island. The steamboat had been chartered by "a tightly knit German community" that was looking forward to their annual picnic outing. Many women and children were on board. But, shortly after casting off, a fire broke out in the bow of the ship, which spread amazingly rapidly toward the stern. The captain managed to run the ship aground, but not quickly enough. Of the 1,358 passengers, 1,021 died. Seems that bad luck accompanied the name, "General Slocum." But that was in the future. In 1884, Slocum was considered a viable candidate for Governor.

How had New York Democrats been choosing their nominee? For decades, Party leaders normally managed to pull the strings and give the nomination to men they favored. Leaders in Albany and leaders in the metropolitan New York City region were considered "the real arbiter of Party destiny:"

Daniel Manning of Albany, Chairman of the New York State Democratic Committee, and editor of the Albany *Argus* newspaper, directed "the immense influence of the Tilden organization. He supported Slocum and was hostile toward Flower over past grievances.

Of course there were the Democrat machines of the metropolitan New York City region. At this time there were three Democrat organizations that controlled various Factions of Democrat votes in the region and its 72 votes at the State Convention:

In New York City, **Tammany Hall** Democrats, awarded 24 Delegates and able to control many thousands of votes, especially of recent Irish immigrants, were led by "Boss" John Kelly. Kelly was playing his cards close to his chest, hoping to figure prominently in last minute deal making and vote trading. He planned to divide the votes of his New York City Delegation among various candidates until a likely winner emerged. Then he planned to trade votes to make the most of the opportunity.

The County Democracy, a new "reform organization" in the region, awarded 38 Delegates, disliked Slocum but did not come out for a candidate. This group, founded in April 1881, was led primarily by three reformers:

- Abram Hewitt — Representative in the Federal House, former Tilden campaign manager, a wealthy ironmaster and son-in-law of Peter Cooper. Of the three, Hewitt was by far the most powerful.

- William Whitney — a brilliant, handsome and very wealthy corporate lawyer.

- Hubert Thompson — a promising and likable young man.

The County Democracy had already scored a major success over Tammany Hall. By October 1881, it had claimed 26,500 enrolled members. In November its candidates had "swept local elections — choosing 4 of the 7 State Senators, 12 of the 24 Members of the State Assembly and 12 of the 22 City Aldermen.

Irving Hall, another group in the region, awarded 10 Delegates and not aligned with Tammy Hall, were of lesser power.

Nearby, **Brooklyn Democrats**, under Boss McLaughlin were backing Slocum. The western section of the State could be counted for Cleveland, that being his political base.

The New York Democratic State Convention met in Syracuse on September 21, 1882. The first round of votes for the nomination for Governor were counted as 98 for Slocum, 97 for Flower and 66 for Cleveland, with approximately 121 spread out among other candidates (the Tammany Hall Delegates were parceled out among most of the field, with Cleveland receiving 6). From Albany, Daniel Manning, the State Chairman and newspaper editor, as expected, had given all of the votes under his control to Slocum. The County Democracy had given its 38 votes to a fourth candidate, Allan Campbell. The second ballot count was 123 for Slocum, 123 for Flower and 71 for Cleveland. Then the third roll call began. Of this critical point, biographer Allan Nevins would write, "The danger now was of a sudden break to Slocum, for Manning's influence was tremendous, and if the County Democracy turned to the Brooklyn general, he would be within reach of a majority." But, Abram Hewitt moved the County Democracy's 38 votes to Cleveland, moving him toward the lead. Tammany Hall still split its 24 votes among several candidates, seeming not to recognize that momentum was shifting to Cleveland supporters. Then Delegates originally favoring Flower, including those representing Albany and Rensselaer, started casting votes instead for Cleveland, putting the Mayor from Buffalo into a commanding lead. A beaten "Boss John Kelly" belatedly switched the votes of Tammany Hall to Cleveland as the casting came to a close. The final vote was Cleveland 211, Slocum, 156 and Flower 15. The Convention nominated David Hill, of Elmira, for Lieutenant Governor. Hill, 39, a former Speaker of the General Assembly, was Mayor of Elmira and, like Cleveland, a bachelor. Of Cleveland's clean-cut victory, biographer Allan Nevins would write:

"Thus Cleveland won his nomination without incurring any political debts of importance. He was bound neither to Manning [of Albany] nor to Tammany [of New York City]; his sole obligation was to his friends in western New York State and to the County Democracy. Buffalo celebrated his nomination with cannon and bunting."

Not long afterward, Grover Cleveland sat down and penned a letter David Hill, in part saying:

"Accept my hearty congratulations on your nomination. Now let us go to work and show the people of the State what two bachelor mayors can do."

New York State Democrats had good reason to be optimistic about prospects for victory, because the State Republican Party was in shambles, badly split into factions. Biographer Allan Nevis would explain:

On the day of his nomination, Grover Cleveland's election seemed "assured; for the Republican split had forged the final link in the chain of circumstances which was to make him Governor by an unequalled majority. For years the Republicans had sown the wind, and now they were reaping the whirlwind. They had permitted the Party to be torn by a protracted feud between the Stalwarts, or followers of [Ulysses] Grant and Roscoe Conklin, and the Half-Breeds, or followers of James Blaine and James Garfield, and the inevitable disaster had followed.

Republican Governor Alonzo Cornell's "firm and honest administration had been one of the best in the history of [New York State], but Roscoe Conkling and President Chester Arthur had marked him for a cruel humiliation."

How had this happened?

In 1881, New York State's two Federal Senators, Roscoe Conkling and Thomas Platt, both Republicans, had become so furious with President James Garfield over which Republicans were to receive patronage that they both resigned their seats, expecting the New York Legislature to re-elect them both, right away. Surprise! Governor Alonzo Cornell did not champion either man's re-election and the Legislature was not all that enthusiastic either. Neither man was re-elected. Chester Arthur and Conklin were furious, especially at the lack of support from Governor Cornell. Conkling took a job as attorney for Jay Gould — the notoriously powerful New York financial manipulator, whom you will recall, had been tight with the Tweed Ring of Tammany Hall, had caused great panic when cornering the nation's gold market, had then turned to taking control of various railroads, starting with the Erie Railroad, then the Union Pacific and the Missouri Pacific, at one time controlling 15 percent of the country's railroad track. He even gained controlling interest in the Western Union telegraph company. So, how did Conklin's legal work for Gould make trouble for Governor Cornell? Well, being Gould's attorney, Conklin was furious with Cornell over his veto of legislation that would have been favorable to the Gould companies. So, that is why Roscoe Conkling and Chester Arthur had marked Governor Alonzo Cornell for cruel humiliation, a feud that had torn the New York Republican Party into opposing Factions.

At the New York Republican Convention, the feud described above blocked the nomination of Governor Alonzo Cornell for a second term. Charles Folger was nominated instead. Folger had been a lawyer, State Senator, Chief Judge of the New York Court of Appeals, and was presently Secretary of the Treasury in the Chester Arthur Administration, a job he would retain during and after defeat. So Secretary Folger was President Arthur's man and Arthur and Conklin wanted Cornell out of the Governor's office and their man in. Many objected to disgracing Cornell, even appealing to Folger to refuse the nomination. Henry Ward Beecher said, "When Cornell went out, Avarice and Revenge kissed each other." *Harper's Weekly* figured, the nomination of Folger "was procured by the combined power of fraud and patronage, and to support it would be to acquiesce in them as legitimate forces in a convention." Folger refused to step down, dooming the Republican campaign to defeat. Furthermore, because the Republican feud had grown out of in-fighting over patronage, demonstrating clearly its corrupting nature, the feud served to boost the candidacy of Democrat Grover Cleveland, who was becoming widely known as a man of principle who fought corruption in government to best serve the people. Two years from this point, during the campaign for President, many admirers of Cleveland would shout, "We love him for the enemies he has made." And Cleveland would that day pledge to voters:

"Public Office is a Public Trust." [R211;84-105]

(4Q82)

The New York State campaign was a 6-weeks affair in which Republican Charles Floger went around the State making speeches while Grover Cleveland remained in Buffalo leaving the campaigning to Democrat leaders, such as State Party Chairman and influential newspaperman Daniel Manning, who managed the overall effort from Albany, and Grover's law partner, Wilson Bissell, who handled more personal matters from Buffalo. Folger tried to stir up excitement. Biographer Allan Nevins would condense Folger's speech-making into this capsule:

"Folger went about the State raising the alarmist cry that a Democratic victory would unsettle industry and cause a shrinkage of stock values. 'Do the business interests of the country dread a return of the Democratic Party to power?' he demanded. "Will the election of Cleveland increase this dread? These are questions for hesitating Republicans to ponder'." [R211;105]

The result was a landslide for Democrats! Grover Cleveland, a Buffalo lawyer and the city's Mayor, who had not personally campaigned, received 535,318 votes. Charles Folger, the Secretary of the

Treasury and recognized as a widely experienced political leader at both State and Federal levels, who had personally campaigned, received 342,464 votes. The Democrat majority was an amazing 192,854 votes.

Biographer Allan Nevins would describe the vote-counting scene in Buffalo:

"A 6:00 pm a Mutual Union [telegraph line] was run into [Grover Cleveland's] office and a [telegraph] operator began rattling off returns. Bissell, Sicard, and 'Charley' McCune were at hand, and others came and went; among them Sherman Rogers, who had been active in his behalf as an independent Republican. The Mayor read the returns as they came in, making comments with characteristic composure. At midnight it was plain that he had been chosen by a landslide vote, and after general handshaking he went to the rooms of the Democratic Club, where he was presented with a 'handsome' chair, its arms and backs made of the horns of Texas steers, and the evening ended in a celebration." [R211;105-106]

Meanwhile Lucius Lamar left Mississippi in late November for the opening of the Federal Senate, being present on the first day, December 1. He had left Mississippi in better spirits, believing that his wife Virginia's health seemed improved. By February he would be intensely involved in the debate over new taxes on imports. [R205;449]

Very near the end of the year Grover Cleveland resigned the office of Mayor of Buffalo, turning the office over to capable hands. Then, on the last day of the year, he and Wilson Bissell boarded the train to Albany and walked from the Albany railroad station to the Executive residence without fanfare and without being recognized. You see, Cleveland, unlike his rival for the office, had traveled the State very little in recent years. Few would have recognized him, and none happen to have done so. Outgoing Governor Alonzo Cornell had vacated the residence, allowing Cleveland to move right in.

(1Q83)

On New Years Day, Grover Cleveland met outgoing Governor Alonzo Cornell inside the Senate Chamber to briefly talk and await the noon-time hour. Then both men walked out of the Chamber and into the bright cold winter air and together mounted the speaker's rostrum to address the gathered crowd and take part in the Inaugural ceremony. Cornell — speaking first and "reading from his prepared manuscript" — generously "extended his wishes for a successful [Cleveland Administration]." Cleveland then rose to deliver the address which he and Wilson Bissell had carefully crafted, but doing so without referring to notes, thereby imparting a strong sense of being in command of the situation. One prominent observer noted that, "as [Cleveland] took the oath of office, he seemed fairly to radiate physical energy." Biographer Paul Jeffers would write, "They found [Cleveland's speech] ringing and clear, and many marveled that he spoke without a script or notes." Apt humility was projected as the speaker admitted that he was untried in the office he was assuming: "You have assembled today to witness the retirement of an officer, tried and trusted, from the highest place in the State, and the assumption of its duties by one yet to be tried." This complement to the outgoing Republican Governor was rather sincere, for many observers had come to believe that, among former New York Governors, Cornell ranked among the best. Biographer Alyn Brodsky would describe Cleveland's Inaugural address as "a laundry list of promises" to the people of New York State:

- Management of the State Government would be with "honesty, economy and the application of sound business principles."

- Reforms would be instituted in the "State Militia, the Insurance Department, the Banking Department and the New York City Harbormaster's system."

- Reforms would be instituted as well in the "system of taxation."

- Patronage appointments would go to "qualified men familiar with the routine and responsibility of the offices" to which they would be assigned, meaning political appointments would be far fewer in number.

Immediately after the noon-day Inaugural on that historic New Year's Day, Governor Cleveland walked to the Executive residence and opened the doors to anyone who wanted to see him and talk with him. Although a drastic departure from precedence, this welcoming style of governance would become a feature of the Cleveland Administration. One of his first decisions was to make Daniel Lamont his political amanuensis. A reporter for the *Albany Argus* newspaper and one of Samuel Tilden's protégés, Lamont had been recommended to Cleveland by Daniel Manning, who, as you know, was the publisher of the newspaper and Chairman of the New York State Democratic Party. At the time 31 years old, Lamont had already gained considerable political experience as Clerk of the New York Assembly and as Chief Clerk of the New York Department of State. Of this, biographer Alyn Brodsky would write: "The 31-year-old Lamont and 45-year-old Cleveland formed an immediate mutual admiration society that would end only with Lamont's death 20 years later," for Lamont would continue serving Cleveland in Washington City. In other words, "Lamont functioned as faithful friend, candid critic, and closest confidant, in addition to acting as Cleveland's buffer with the press" when he would become President in 1885.

As Cleveland began his job as Governor, he was blessed to have a New York State General Assembly that was controlled by Democrats for the first time in many years — the Senate consisting of 18 Democrats versus 14 Republicans and the House consisting of 84 Democrats versus 42 Republicans, both solid majorities, so it would appear. However, "for years a bipartisan alliance had existed in the Senate between the Tammany Democrats and the machine Republicans, and Cleveland was aware that at any moment the upper chamber might be ruthlessly swung against him." Biographer Allan Nevins continues the story with this analysis of the political situation facing Cleveland during the first months of his Administration:

> "The Governor knew, like everyone else who mingled with politicians and read the newspapers, that [metropolitan] New York politics were both corrupt and merciless. [Compared to Tweed's reign], the forces of graft were more numerous, protean, and expert. Most of the corruption was arranged for directly with the members and on the spot, for fully a third of the Legislature had its price, and the price was known. . . . Lobbyists would sometime invade the floor of the Assembly and draw venal men into the halls with no concealment of their purpose.

> "Half the legislation that was introduced concealed some job or steal, and intelligent members like [Republican leader Theodore] Roosevelt spent much of their time in trying to ascertain the hidden wickedness in measures that looked innocent. . . . Dishonest tactics on the part of big business by no means constituted the principal menace. For every bill corruptly introduced in behalf of corporations, ten 'strike' bills were introduced in an effort to blackmail them. They would progress to a certain point, and then payment would be made to stop them. . . . Upright men were shadowed by detectives trying to pin some scandal on them, and woe betide the legislator who, in that wide-open city, was caught."

Cleveland realized that John Kelly and his Tammany Democratic machine was the main threat. Biographer Allan Nevins would describe Kelly:

> "The determined Irish leader had dared to throw down the gage of battle before [former Governor Samuel] Tilden himself, and for all the need of Party harmony in 1884, he was not likely to hesitate to attack Cleveland. Nearing the end of his long career, the 61 year old boss was now almost as powerful as ever. By a long series of services, he had endeared himself to the Irish voters of New York City. . . . [For example], when the Native-born American [political] movement [had] reared its head in New York, he distinguished himself as its opponent, won the warm friendship of Archbishop Hughes, and was rewarded by the Irish and Germans with a seat in Congress, which he held for 2 terms in the stormy years just before the [War Between the States]. From that hour his influence grew steadily. . . . He had become a rich man [but] no one quite knew how. . . . After Tweed fell he [had] persuaded [Samuel] Tilden and Charles O'Conor to confirm him as the leader of a 'new' and better Tammany. . . . Meanwhile, Kelly had confirmed his hold upon the Irish Catholics by his marriage in 1876 to a niece of Cardinal McCloskey, the American head of the [Catholic] Church."

By the way, in *Bloodstains*, Volume 2, *The Demagogues*, you learned much about the "Native American political movement" of the 1850's. You remember that its members were derisively called "No Nothings," and that, attempting to impart some meaning to the organization's name, I had called that organization the "Secret Order," and that the "Order" would later rise above its original secrecy to become the "American Party." A review is appropriate of this "Native-born American political movement" to freshen your memory of the political turmoil that had stirred the northern States electorate during the 1850's, the era of the Demagogues. I quote from Volume 2:

> "The Secret Order was a secret political movement that had been founded around 1850 by Charles Allen of New York City. The organization, which called itself the 'Order of the Star Spangled Banner,' committed its members to reduce the political power of immigrants and politicians who 'pandered to them.' But this organization had been quite feeble, having only acquired 43 members by 1852. But agitation against immigrant and Catholic influence had expanded the membership to as much as 50,000 men by May 1854. Growth had been amazingly rapid thereafter, spreading to other northern States like wildfire. By the end of October membership would be estimated at over 1,000,000 men. Membership would grow further to its peak in 1855. . . . This many politically minded men, from diverse backgrounds, operating in unison from within a secret order, were surely capable of deciding numerous elections in several northern States.

> "The Secret Order was a revolt against the dramatic rise in immigration from 1845 to 1854. During this span of 10 years 2,900,000 immigrants had arrived in The States. This amounted to 14.5 percent of the 1845 population."

The Secret Order had been very powerful in the northern States when the Republican Party was founded in that region in 1854 and 1855. Then, impressed by the passions being generated by "Bleeding Kansas" propaganda, many members of the Secret Order had set aside immigrant agitation and gone over to the new Republican Party — and the rest is history. Since Irish and German immigrants, mostly Catholic, were targeted by the Secret Order, John Kelly had earnestly opposed its agenda and had been successful in encouraging immigrants to seek protection under Tammany and the Democratic Party. [R211;107-114, R214;52-54]

Meanwhile during February, the Federal Senate was engaged in a heated debate over Republican efforts to raise the schedule of taxes on imports, especially on classes of products that were close to being undersold by imports, or on classes where politically influential domestic producers were eager to raise the prices on their products. Republicans had only a few days remaining before they were to lose the political advantage in the Federal House and they were desperate to use that advantage to increase taxes on imports wherever possible. Let us recap the situation as of February, 1883:

> As you know, the "Stalwart" Faction of the Republican Party had lost the 1880 nomination for President to James Garfield, of Ohio, but had won the nomination of its man, New Yorker Chester Arthur, for Vice President. With Arthur now in control of the Executive branch, as a result of Garfield's death at the hand of Charles Guiteau, of New Jersey, who had been enraged at being rejected for a diplomatic post, Republicans seemed to have the political power to press for higher tax rates on imports, but time was running out. Arthur knew the score, for he had been Collector of the Port of New York from 1871 to 1878, having been appointed by Ulysses Grant, and he had been and continued to be closely aligned with "Stalwart" leader Roscoe Conkling of New York. A Republican Party political activist since 1856, Arthur had been well trained in the importance of political patronage and service to commercial and manufacturing leaders in the northeastern States. Since Republicans in the House had lost badly in the elections held three months previously, the Party was desperate to increase taxes on favored items before it would lose the advantage in early March. On the other hand, the situation in the Federal Senate would remain very competitive during the upcoming transition, for the new Senate would be 38 Republicans, 36 Democrats and 2 other men.

The debate had nothing to do with raising more revenue for the Federal Government, for Federal revenue exceeded Federal spending and history had shown that more often than not lower import taxes resulted in higher revenues, due to the increased tonnage of imports commensurate with the lower rates. Readers of *Bloodstains* will recall that, since its founding, the Democratic Party had traditionally advocated import tax rates that were only sufficient for Federal revenue needs, whereas protectionist tax rates had been traditionally sought by Whigs and by parties that replaced Whigs, the last being the Republican Party, organized in 1856. Readers of *Bloodstains* will also recall that the sectional fight that gave rise to the Republican Party in the northern States was as much about "low tax rates approaching free trade" versus "high tax rates for protection" as it was about allowing bonded African Americans to migrate into the National Territories. Furthermore, in January 1883, the taxes on imports were already far higher than needed for Federal revenue needs and constituted artificial price supports, reducing the purchasing power and standard of living of most citizens, especially families who earned their living by agriculture. The debate was intense. Then, on February 7, it became Lucius Lamar's turn to argue against "protection for protection's sake." Since the political fight over high import taxes for protection was a major theme in the "History of the Politics that Produced the American Civil War," and since we are only two years from the close of *Bloodstain's* presentation of this story, considerable time will be devoted to understanding Lamar's speech — especially since you are about to recognize that his was an excellent history lesson. Lamar begins:

"Mr. President: I have taken no part in the debate on this bill, but have listened to it with great attention, and have noted the votes on the various amendments which have been proposed to the measure under consideration. The progress of the discussion and the votes together show that it is impossible to effect any large reduction or any material reduction of the taxes and at the same time retain the system of 'protection for protection's sake.' One or the other must be given up. . . .

"The Senator from Maine, in an able speech at the last session [alleged]: 'If there was no public debt, no interest to pay, no pension list, no army and no navy to support, I should still oppose free trade and its twin sister, tariff for revenue, and be in favor of protective duties.' . . . Well, sir, we have been living for 23 years — 18 of them years of peace, under a tariff for protection, whose duties are universally admitted to be too high with respect to revenue or to taxes. . . .

"The Senator from Vermont says that [the bill before us] is based upon the report of the Tariff Commission. I propose to call attention to that report. The testimony taken by the Commission fills two large volumes of 2,600 pages. These pages certainly present a most remarkable — I may say imposing — exhibit of the condition of American manufactures and of the genius and capacity of our people for those mechanic arts and scientific appliances which have done so much for the elevation and civilization of the human race."

Then Lamar presented the present situation based on data in the Tariff Commission Report:

Concerning pig iron, he said: "Makers of pig iron are more fearful of the foreign manufacturer of the same produce than the makers of any other manufactured product in the country. Makers of domestic pig iron complain, 'we see our markets constantly filled with foreign brands of pig iron, our furnaces idle."

Concerning wool, he said: "There is testimony that 'We have 42,000,000 sheep, while Australia has 72,000,000. . . . Labor must be higher here, because it must be intelligent. Land is higher and growing higher. Climate anywhere requires shelter and some feeding. . . . Sheep husbandry cannot be imperiled without great lost to the country. It supplies cheap, wholesome meat, which is one of the heavy items of expense in every family. All meat food is lower in price because of mutton in every market; but for sheep, fresh meat would be impossible in thousands of families. An industry so general, that feeds and clothes our people as no other nation is clothed, that reclaims waste lands and enriches all soil, is an industry that should receive full protection [through] tariff legislation."

On the other hand, other animals raised for meat (chickens, hogs, cattle) were not to be protected by protective taxes on imports. Neither was fiber grown for clothing, such as cotton. Why? Because sheep were primarily raised in States controlled by the Republican Party and cotton was grown primarily in States controlled by the Democratic Party.

From the Tariff Report, Lamar pulled data and testimony on other products where producers pleaded for high taxes on imports. Then he embarked upon a lesson on the history of American protective taxes on imports, beginning with Colonial times, basing his remarks on James Bishop's "*History of American Manufactures*," which presented comprehensive data on production, imports and tariffs from 1608 to 1860. Lamar first addressed the Colonial period:

"Sir, there have been long periods of time in the history of this country when protective tariffs were not in operation. Did our manufactures cease to exist during those periods? I have before me Bishop's '*History of American Manufactures*,' from the earliest time down to 1860. No one can read this history — although written by a Protectionist — without becoming convinced that American manufactures are the natural growth of this country, and have demonstrated their capacity to exist and grow and thrive under any kind of tariff, high or low, protective *per se*, or for revenue only. Sir, long before the era of protective tariffs, long before we had a national tariff of any kind — indeed, from the earliest Colonial period down to the Revolutionary War — manufactures existed and flourished and attained a vigorous life and an ample development [even while] exposed to foreign competition, unaided by the legislation of the mother country, and in defiance of its hostile and prohibitory enactments."

Concerning the southern Colonies and beginning in 1608, Lamar quoted an historian's description of glass being made 275 years earlier, in 1608, in Virginia Colony: " 'The glass house stood in the woods about a mile from Jamestown and although very unpretending in its dimensions and appointments, it was doubtless the first manufactory ever erected in this country'." Lamar further noted an early Virginia salt work and an early iron works. Then he explained what happened to those enterprises: "The candid historian is, however, compelled to state that these manufacturing enterprises were not destined to a long existence in Virginia. They had to succumb to competition, not from competition of foreign pauper labor, Mr. President, but to a competition then, as now, more formidable than pauper labor — to wit, the superior attractions of agriculture. The cultivation of tobacco became profitable, and all the artisans quit their work and devoted themselves to its culture."

Concerning the northern Colonies and beginning in 1623, Lamar, again quoting Bishop, told the Senators: "With a sterile soil and a rugged climate, they early betook themselves to manufacturing and commercial enterprises . . . . Shipbuilding commenced within 3 years after the [1620] landing of the Plymouth Colony, [drawing on] the almost inexhaustible wealth of the American forests. . . . Glass manufactures [were established] in Massachusetts, New Jersey, Pennsylvania and New York, [but suffered from the] tendency of labor to desert the factory for the field. Even servants, imported from Europe for different trades, so soon as their indentures expired, quit their occupations and obtained a small piece of land. [Yet] the progress of the manufacture of glass during that period was remarkable. . . . As early as 1645, regular [iron] works were established at various points. . . . [These early enterprises led to establishment of] furnaces, foundries, rolling mills, bloomeries, forge hammers, nail works, wire mills [and the fabrication of] bells, firearms, sheet iron for tinware, wire . . . shovels, swords, scythes, metal buttons, cannon balls . . . axes . . . saws . . . cutlery and other finished products."

Concerning exports from the Colonies, Lamar presented tables of exports of bar iron and pig iron, from 1750 to 1776, illustrating that, "there were substantial exports, particularly to Scotland." Reading from Bishop, he explained, "The Colonies in 1770 were exporting a large amount of lumber, embracing boards, plank, scantling; timber for masts, spars and buildings; staves, heads, headings, hoops, poles, frames of houses, etc. The growth of these industries was so rapid that they excited the jealously and apprehension of English manufacturers." The British Government was permitting the export to the homeland of many raw materials, such as lumber, pig and bar iron, tobacco and raw wool and cotton, but prohibiting vertical expansion into manufactured finished goods, most especially goods made from iron. To inhibit vertical integration, Parliament enacted prohibitions such as:

> "From and after the 24th day of June, 1750, no mill or other engine for slitting or rolling iron, or any plating forge to work with a tilt hammer, or any furnace for making steel shall be erected, or, after such erection, continued in any of His Majesty's Colonies of America."

And at the same time, by acts of Parliament in 1650, 1651, 1661 and 1669, London required that all exports from the American Colonies be shipped directly to England, even including cotton and raw wool and woolen fabrics and clothing. London prohibited Colonists from seeking better markets elsewhere. Yet, Lamar was able to tell fellow Senators that, during this time, "the Colonies grew and prospered, not only unaided by the legislation of the mother country, but in spite, as I said before, of her unfriendly and prohibitory enactments."

Next, Lamar turned to the history of exports following the Declaration of Independence and the subsequent war in Defense of Independence:

Concerning the Revolutionary War, he told fellow Senators: "During the Revolutionary War the growth of manufactures was greatly stimulated." But a business depression followed the peace, in which "all industries shared . . . [even though there were] no greater importations immediately after the peace than there [had been] for some years before the war."

In the subsequent 23-year era, 1789 to 1812, up to James Madison's first term, the tax on imports averaged approximately 10 percent. Powerful business interests, had pleaded for "protective tariffs" on imports, but failed in 1789 to win approval of the high tax rates sought, having to settle on a tax table ranging from only 5 to 15 percent, considered a "tariff for revenue" only. Of this beginning, Lamar advised fellow Senators that the tariff of 1789 "furnishes a precedent, though certainly the duties were for revenue purposes, and at the lowest rates which have ever existed in this country." Fabrics were taxed at 7 percent, produces of iron at 7.5 percent. Taxes on imports rose slightly over the 13-year span, but not to levels considered "protective." Lamar cites statistics showing exceptional growth in manufacturing without benefit of "protective tariff" rates. He concluded, "There was a large surplus in the [Federal] Treasury after paying a large amount of public debt. It was a period of steady growth and prosperity."

Of the subsequent wartime era, 1812-1816, Lamar explained: this "was a period of war and of war duties, and manufacturers enjoyed that kind of development and prosperity which war engenders. . . . [There was] great inflation of the currency growing out of the enormous issues of paper money . . . ."

We now enter a time of a major advance in technology, the era of the steam engine, which was enabling round-trip river transportation on the Mississippi and Ohio Rivers, the major steam pioneer in America being the Pittsburg Steam Engine Company, established in 1811, which manufactured Scotsman James Watt's designs and subsequent improvements. In the study of the political history of taxes on imports and political restrictions on trade, it is important to keep in mind how advances in technology influenced political adjustments, because agricultural, scientific and industrial advances had a far greater influence on politics and government policy than the political struggles between parties and factions within parties.

Of the subsequent 8-year era, 1816 to 1824 — beginning in the second James Madison Administration and continuing through most of the two James Monroe Administrations — with an average tariff of approximately 20 percent, Lamar submitted: "the tariff of 1816 was the inauguration of the protective system" of high tariffs on imports. Quoting from Benson Lossing's "History of American Arts and Manufacture," Lamar advised, prior to 1816, "there had been 25 acts in which tariffs had been established, all for revenue. [But] in the spring of that year the first of a series of tariffs for the protection of American manufactures was established, under the sanction of President James Madison. It was the progenitor of all the subsequent protective tariffs." But, Lamar explained, manufacturers demanded yet higher protective rates, resulting in the tariff of 1818, which listed rates "much higher than [would be experienced in the tariff of] 1861;" followed by the tariff of 1819, listing rates "still higher;" followed by the tariff of 1819, for "protection begets protection;" followed by the tariff of 1824, "which [Horace] Greeley styled, 'the tariff of unqualified protection'."

In the 9-year era of 1824 to 1833 — from the last year of the second James Monroe Administration, through the John Quincy Adams Administration and through the first Andrew Jackson Administration — taxes on imports averaged approximately 35 percent. This was a period of rising and high taxes on imports, designed to support artificially high prices on domestic manufacturers goods, culminating in the Tariff of 1828, with tax rates as high as 45 percent, referred to as the "Tariff of Abominations." You will recall the "Tariff of Abominations" as being proposed by President John Quincy Adams, of Massachusetts, and voted into law by a supportive House and Senate. Yet, in spite of the consequential elevated price supports derived from Adams' higher tax rates, manufacturing failed to prosper, as evidenced by Lamar's quotation from James Bishop:

"An unusual degree of distress prevailed at this time among the manufacturers of [the northeastern States], particularly in the cotton [fabric] branch, producing numerous failures and great depreciation of the value of stocks. The cause was by some ascribed to the disappearance of specie, and by others to overspeculation, which had tempted great numbers into manufacturing with insufficient capital and, consequently, overproduction."

Lamar reported that, although imports "steadily decreased, . . . exports of American manufacturers declined steadily to the close." But it was Lamar's quote from John Calhoun that better explained how rising tariff rates hurt people engaged in American agriculture:

> "Desolation spread itself over the entire staple region; its commercial cities were desolated. Charleston parted with her last ship, and grass grew in her once busy streets. The political condition of the country presented a prospect not less dreary; a deep and growing conflict between the two great sections agitated the whole country, and a vast revenue beyond its most extravagant wants gave the [Federal Government] boundless patronage and power which were rapidly changing the character of the Government and spreading corruption far and wide through every condition of society."

Although the Tariff of 1832 reduced rates slightly from the 1828 rate sheet, Lamar concluded: "Sir, if manufacturers could not prosper during that period, their case would indeed be a hopeless one."

The subsequent era, 1833 to 1843, was a period of reduced taxes on imports, made possible by Democrat Presidents Andrew Jackson and Martin Van Buren and House and Senate sessions which were predominantly Democrat-controlled. In this era the tariff rate schedule declined toward 20 percent maximums: The Tariff of 1833 was called the "Compromise Tariff," for it greatly trimmed the 1832 rate schedule in response to the protests of the South Carolina Legislature. Because many import items were not taxed, the average import tax was low, being 13 percent in 1840. Of this 1833-1847 era of low taxation, Lamar reminded fellow Senators of its remarkable success:

> "Under the Compromise Tariff the tonnage at once began to increase until at the close of the period it had nearly doubled itself. The exports of domestic products also increased under the Compromise Tariff; and, though checked by the financial embarrassments of 1836 and 1837, yet in 9 years the exports of American manufacturers greatly increased, such was the effect of low duties in enlarging the market for our manufactured products, and infusing into our manufacturing industries the vigor to compete in foreign markets; and the same was true of our agricultural interests. Under this system of progressive reduction [in rates] new factories were springing up over the country, and older ones [were] undergoing large extensions. . . . Notwithstanding the depressions consequent upon the financial panic of 1837, manufacturing industry . . . had become vigorous, expanded, and capable of entering on equal terms the field of universal competition."

We move next to the 4 year era of 1843 to 1847. Reflecting the change in political power in Washington City, with Whig William Henry Harrison as President and the Whig Party in control of the House and Senate, the tariff rate schedule increased to an average of almost 40 percent. This resulted from the Tariff of 1842, called the "Black Tariff." It again remarkably raised the schedule of tax rates, sending them upward toward 40 percent, some items much higher. Iron manufacturers, of both raw and finished products, were rewarded with taxes on imported competition which computed to almost 65 percent of the import prices, with some items, such as nails and hoop iron for barrels exceeding 100 percent. Furthermore the percentage of import items on the duty list was increased from 50 percent of items to over 85 percent of items. So, this 1843-1847 era, in which Whigs replaced Democrats in the seats of power, the country suffered a dramatic escalation of punitive taxation, prompting a dramatic inflation in the domestic retail prices of most products, hitting hardest upon the vast majority of Americans, who still made their living off agriculture. Because the volume of highly taxed imports fell dramatically, the average duty was not as high as one would expect, averaging 24 percent in 1845. Of these few years of punitive tariffs, Lucius Lamar told fellow Senators:

> "In 1840 there was a great political revolution which swept the Democracy out of power and brought the Whigs in. Contrary to the expectation of the people . . . [the Tariff law of 1832] was repealed and the tariff of 1842 was enacted, for which the Whig Party was hurled out of power in the subsequent elections; and the Tariff of 1842 was repealed as soon as the Democracy could get the opportunity. [Since the Whig's tariff was in operation only] 3 years and 11 months,] to attribute to it the impulse and revival of industries in this country, which [had begun many years] before the tariff was enacted and [would continue for many years] after it was repealed, through a long period of unexampled prosperity, is simply to make an assertion which needs no reply."

We are now entering upon the time when railroads became a major factor in American history. The first major line was in South Carolina, the 136 mile Charleston to Hamburg railroad, which had begun operation in 1833, then the longest railroad on earth. By 1850 total track mileage in America was: 2,507 miles in the northeastern States, 3,202 in the middleeastern States, 2,036 in the southern States and 1,276 in what is now called the midwestern States. In 1852 of the Baltimore and Ohio line would be completed to the Ohio River.

During the era from 1847 to 1860 the schedule of tariff rates was greatly cut. James Polk of Tennessee had led the Democrats to power in the elections of 1844. Under the subsequent guidance of Treasury Secretary Robert Walker, as you will recall, a schedule of greatly reduced tax rates on imports was enacted, this being the Walker Tariff of 1846. This schedule of low tariffs would last through the Zachary Taylor/Millard Fillmore Whig Administrations, since Democrats were in control of both the House and the Senate, and through the subsequent Administrations of Democrats Franklin Pierce and James Buchanan, Democrats also then in control of the House and Senate. So 1847 to 1860 was a long, 14-year era of low import tax rates. During this era, tariff income was double or triple that of previous eras, providing 80 to 95 percent of total Federal receipts — essentially funding the Federal Government by itself. Customs revenue represented 15 to 23 percent of the total value of imports. The tax schedule listed tariffs of 25 percent or less. Because, Federal revenues were exceeding spending in mid-decade, Democrats further reduced the tariff schedule in 1857 to around 21 percent on taxed items, about 17 percent overall. Even at these low tax rates, revenue remained unchanged (1855 collections were $53,000,000; 1860 collections were $53,200,000).

Lucius Lamar next described to fellow Senators the truthful history of this 1847-1860 era, which his opponents in the Senate criticized as being a "period of free trade and adversity."

"Sir, [to the contrary,] it was a period of revenue tariffs with the incidental protection that such tariffs afford. I remember well, sir, the circumstances under which that tariff was enacted. I recollect the predictions of evil . . . made by the opponents . . . of that measure. I remember well the prophecies of what would be its ruinous effects; they predicted that American manufactures would expire under its baleful operations, and that our country would become little more than a commercial dependency of England. . . .

"I remember also the promises of good which its friends made in its behalf. I am almost tempted to read to the Senate a portion of the great report of Robert Walker, in which he depicts the future grandeur and glory of the country [resulting from] the revenue tariff proposed by him. Sir, time has passed; which [advocacy] was right? Did that tariff entail ruin and destruction upon manufacturing industries? On the other hand, did it not accomplish that which its friends and advocates promised it would achieve?"

Lamar then turned to a recognized historian, J. Randolph Tucker, for the answer to the question just posed:

"Speaking of the immense extension of domestic manufactures in the decade from 1840 to 1850, [historian Randolph Tucker] says: 'The astounding fact was revealed that the capital invested in manufacturing, not counting any establishment that produced under $500 a year, exceeded $550,000,000, and that the annual product had reached $1,019,000,000. Vast as this production [was for the 1840-1850 decade], we find 10 years later, [in the 1850-1860 decade], an increase [in annual product] of more than 86 percent [beyond that]'."

Lamar then concluded his presentation on the era: "Sir, from 1850 to 1860 the wealth of this country increased, an estimated, 126 percent [and] the capital in manufactures increased by 90 percent, the [annual] product by 86 percent and the profits on capital [by] 47 percent."

Finally, Lamar arrived at the taxation era from 1861 to 1881. This era began with the notorious Morrill Tariff of early 1861, enacted immediately after the secession of 7 States and the withdrawal of its Democrats from the House and Senate. With southern States Democrats leaving due to secession and northern States Democrats leaving due to defeats at the polls, Republicans were free to raise taxes on imports to very high levels, and did so with alacrity, effective early April: to an average of 36 percent on dutiable items, equating to 26 percent overall. Rates were thereafter steadily increased, rising by 1865 to 48 percent on dutiable items, equating to 38 percent overall. This pattern of high tariffs was in effect at the time that Lucius Lamar was speaking before the Senate, and it was his object to argue for drastically cutting those tariff rates. In part, he said:

"It is this period [of 1861 to present], sir, which the Senator says is a 'period of protection and prosperity'." But protection is not the cause of the prosperity — "through revenue duties, through the [low taxation] periods of so-called free trade, through periods of depression, through periods of every kind, manufacturers have continued to grow at a pace corresponding with the wants of the country, and have taken no step backward under any circumstances, and have been overwhelmed by no adverse fortunes. . . . This grand and rapid development . . . was not [due to] our restriction on foreign trade, but [due to the] absolute freedom of commerce between the States which our [Federal] Constitution has established. Nowhere on earth has commerce been so unrestricted, upon such a scale, and through such vast sections, divided by great mountains and rivers, and abounding in all varieties of soil, climate, productions, and conditions."

[So, Senators from the northern States, why do you allege that] your manufactures under this protective system are depressed [and] tottering on the verge of universal bankruptcy? It cannot be, as in 1837 and in 1817 and 1857, be attributed to financial crises; for never was our currency in a better condition that it is at this time, [our only concern being future inflation due to] the overvaluation of our silver. . . . In [the financial crisis of] 1873 there was the same sort of distress [in manufacturing] that exists at this time, [caused by] the sudden contraction of the currency following an enormous inflation, a time when high taxes on imports] could not shelter protected industries from the devastation. . . .

"In 1868 . . . what was the condition of [northern States] manufacturing industries? [At that time Justin] Morrill, of Vermont, [complained before this body that] 'there is not [a woolen textile] establishment [or woolgrower] that is not losing money [and similar distress plagues] the cotton interest, [and] the whole circle of manufacturers are in no better circumstances. . . . [Concerning distress among farmers raising hogs in western States] such as Ohio, Illinois or Iowa . . . they have been feeding out grain to [pigs] which, unfed, would have brought more than all their pork.' [And, similarly, Representative William Kelley of Pennsylvania, speaking before the Federal House, complained that], 'the loom and the spindle, no longer able to yield a profit to their proprietors, stand idle; the fires are extinguished in forge and furnace; and the rolling mill does not send forth its hum of cheerful and profitable industry . . . and [in December 1867] the glass factories of Pittsburg [employing 1,800 workers, were] closed.'

"Sir, these are not the accusations of an enemy to the protective system; they are the reluctant admissions and confessions which inexorable fact extorts. Behold, sir, the fruits of the protective system! Depression, poverty, impoverishment, and ruin in 1868; in 1873, impotent to stem the tide of financial ruin that swept far and wide the wrecks of capital and labor; and in 1883, [our present year], the entire fabric of manufacturing capital and labor resting upon the narrow and uncertain basis of [Federal] Government taxation!"

Concerning the alleged need for protective tariffs to defend against lower wages paid in Europe or elsewhere, Lamar argued, "It is England, sir, that pays the highest wages for labor of any in the civilized world, our own, perhaps, excepted, . . . far above those of France or Germany or Belgium or Russia, yet the products of the higher waged labor of English manufactures vie with us on our own soil. [Concerning agriculture, we observe that] in the markets of England, France and Germany our cotton and cereals and meats meet in successful competition the low waged labor of Russia, of India, of Egypt, and even the slave labor of Brazil. . . . The two highest wage-paying nations of the world — England with her manufactures and America with her staples — are the ones whose products undersell all others. . . . [We find the answer in Henry Fawcett's 'Manual of Political Economy' . . . where on page 170 he says:

" 'The cost of labor is determined by comparing the wages the laborer receives with the amount of wealth which is produced by his labor. If, therefore, labor is rendered more efficient, the cost of labor is manifestly diminished'."

"Thus, India, where the cotton spinner gets only 20 pence a week, is flooded by the cotton [fabrics] of England, where the spinner receives 20 shillings. . . .

"It is not high wages in the United States which hinders the successful competition of American manufactures with the products of England. . . . If further proof were required, these two large volumes [of economic statistics] given us by the Tariff Commission are full of irresistible evidence that the whole effect of all past protection, for 1861 to 1883, has been to make the manufacturers more clamorous for protection than ever and more afraid of foreign competition than ever [while facilitating] increased cost of production. . . [The Tariff Commission heard testimony illustrating this economic fact:]

" 'Unfortunately, protection begets protection. The cloth is protected because the wool is protected; again, it is the protected because the dyestuffs are protected; once more, it is protected because oil and chemicals are protected; then, there is a cry that machinery is protected; in short all and everything used to manufacture woolen goods is protected'."

From this point on, Lamar transitioned to his close:

"Mr. President, there is one competition which our manufacturing industry has to encounter that is more powerful in limiting its growth than perhaps any other cause. It is found in the inviting and bounteous fields of American agriculture. [Even the very high wages paid by manufacturers] are often insufficient to keep a man in workshop, mill, coal pit, or glass foundry, when within his reach is a home of his own on his own land, where in his double capacity of proprietor and laborer he and his family can enjoy the entire fruits of his own labor. . . . The avowed object of the protective system is to counteract this superior attractiveness of [our] agriculture industry and to divert capital and labor from it into manufactures. . . . [Yet,] it is impossible for any combination of capital and labor to resist a popular movement animated by a strong sentiment of moral right and justice.

"I, sir, have seen something of this in my own experience. I saw a great institution, which was more firmly entrenched in statutes and organic law than the manufacturers are in this tariff law, become an object of popular uprising. I was among those, sir, who shared in the attempt to resist it; and I saw that institution go down — with all its vast capital, with all the political privileges which it conferred, with all the constitutional rights by which it was guaranteed — go down beneath the irreversible fiat of the American people. Sir, I warn the manufacturers of this country. The handwriting is upon the wall of this protective system, and I trust that they will have the intelligence to comprehend its import."

The debates and voting in the House and Senate resulted in the Tariff Act of 1883, called the Mongrel Tariff, signed into law on March 3. It only moderated the protective system of tariffs to a small degree, leaving strong protective barriers to foreign competition. [R205;748-773]

This history of Federal taxes on imports will be continued up to the present time near the close of *Bloodstains* to give you an up-to-date understanding of the role of the politics of import-export tax policy on the lives and welfare of the American people.

(2Q83)

May 4 was to be the final day of the session of the New York General Assembly. Even at this point, the struggle persisted between Governor Grover Cleveland, advocate of civil service reform, and most of the Assembly's Senators and Representatives, advocates of continued political patronage awards. The most contentious office not yet confirmed had been Cleveland's April 27th nomination of William Murtha for New York Immigration Commissioner. Murtha was an aid to Hugh McLaughlin, political boss over the Brooklyn Democracy, which meant that Murtha was not a Tammany Hall man. But Murtha was noted for his charitable work and Cleveland had been impressed during a personal interview. Cleveland liked Murtha, his perceived ability and record, and figured he would honestly and efficiently administer the office to which he was being nominated. But John Kelly, political boss over Tammany, was earnestly opposed. So he had instructed his men in the State Senate to sit on the bill, hoping to negotiate replacement of Murtha with his man. Control over immigration was very important to Kelly because Tammany was primarily empowered by the votes of Irish immigrants. Its influence over newly arrived immigrants, their future rise to citizenship and their future allegiance to the Tammany political machine was crucial. Furthermore, the Immigration Commissioner controlled approximately "200 subordinate offices." Yet, on the morning of the final day, May 4, Murtha's appointment was still not addressed and Cleveland had not bent to negotiate an alternate, infuriating

Kelly. So, what did Cleveland do? He dumped more coal onto the fire: he sent to the Senate the last of his appointments — and not one job was offered to Tammany. The nominees included quarantine commissioners, port-wardens and harbor-masters. One Tammany operative, in astonishment, complained, "Out of all the 300 places that would have come into Democratic hands through these nominations, Tammany was not guaranteed so much as a night watchman at Castle Garden." The standoff stood. Tammany Democrats and Republicans joined in "holding up the entire list of nominations." Meanwhile, Cleveland, in an office below the Senate Chamber, exclaimed to his private secretary, Daniel Lamont, "Give me a sheet of paper. I'll tell the people what a set of damned rascals they have upstairs!" And the Governor proceeded to pen a scathing denunciation of the fighting among the "spoilsmen" then taking place on the Senate floor above his office — politicians fighting for control of the spoils gained through political patronage. The letter was sufficiently long to tell the story, key aspects of it being related here using the words of biographer Allan Nevins:

> Cleveland "recalled the extravagance, the corruption, the disgraceful dissensions, and the swindling that had marked the work of the existing officers. Murtha, he declared, was a man of acknowledged honesty and experience, whose benevolence would insure a kindly administration." In his concluding remarks Cleveland wrote, 'The refusal to confirm the appointee is not based upon any allegation of unfitness, nor has such a thing been suggested. It concededly and openly, as I understand the situation, has its rise in an overweening greed for patronage which may attach to the place, and which will not be promised in advance, and in questionable partisanship'."

This letter was for public consumption through the newspapers of the State, and the Senators on the floor above knew it. Unable to conceive of a useful reply, the Senators did nothing. They simply closed the session for 1883 that May 4 evening, adjourning *sine die*. The appointive offices would be vacant. Cleveland's standing with voters was not damaged by the unresolved stand-off, but John Kelly and Tammany Hall would consider him enemy number one. Yet, even more so, many voters came to "love" their Governor "for the enemies he has made." What of the unfilled jobs — the immigration commissioner, quarantine commissioners, port-wardens and harbor-masters. The city would manage without the first two classes of jobs and apparently the latter two would be found to be unnecessary, for the shippers and merchants would get along fine without them as "the City Department of Docks competently took over their duties."

But, that day, before the Senate adjourned, one important bill was passed with few dissenting votes. Representative Theodore Roosevelt, a young and rising Republican, just as passionate about civil service reform as was the Governor, had introduced a "Civil Service" bill "in answer to the demand of public opinion." The bill established an administrative office controlled by three Commissioners, which Cleveland would ensure to be held by qualified men.

Overall, the Assembly enacted several important bills, which Cleveland signed, including reapportionment of New York State into Congressional Districts and removing unnecessary rules requiring local governments to apply to the Assembly for permission to take on projects for which approval served no useful purpose. But the primary positive accomplishment was the substantial reduction in political patronage and its attendant corruption. [R211;114-124]

(3Q83)

During most of August, Grover Cleveland was fishing. He had earned it over the previous 7 months and the pressures of his job were finally at a low ebb, for the month was considered a time for vacations. According to biographer Allan Nevins, he had lived simply and labored long hours at his job in Albany:

> "[Former Governors Samuel] Tilden and [Alonzo] Cornell had numerous servants in Albany and entertained lavishly, but Cleveland lived simply. One of his sisters, usually [Mary Cleveland] Hoyt, acted as housekeeper, and he brought William Sinclair from his Buffalo club to look after details. . . . Most of the Governor's time, indeed, was spent in his office. He rose at seven, breakfasted at eight, and walked to the Capitol before nine. At half-past twelve he walked back for lunch, returning in an hour; at five dropped his pen, and after chatting for an hour with friends, walked home for dinner. [Samuel] Tilden, with his French chef borrowed from [New York City's] Delmonico's, had made dining an art, but Cleveland's table was plain. . . . In the evening he

usually returned to his office to labor again with Lamont from half-past eight to well after eleven, finally pushing away his paper with his stock witticism: 'Well, I guess we'll quit and call it half a day'."

Again using the words of biographer Allan Nevins, a portrait of the August fishing vacation follows:

On his first Adirondacks trip, "accompanied by the Rev. A. H. Corliss, Dr. Claude Wilson, and J. K. Brown, [the party] drove to Studor's Hotel at White Lake Corners, then crossed to Camp Corliss on the Woodhull Reservoir, where [Wilson] Bissell joined him, and after a week went on to the Fulton Chain of lakes, a route which combined good fishing with easy communications to Albany. The letters he sent back to Lamont were full of high spirits. Late in August he enclosed to his secretary a note which accused the party of stealing bait. 'I think,' ran his comment, 'that this is pretty mean treatment to begin with, and I suspect that this is a pretty rough country. At this rate I am liable to be accused of rape before I get back.' He added that, 'I went to church three times yesterday, and had big audiences on all occasions.' A few days later he was writing: "I am in disgrace, with myself at least, just at present. I had a beautiful shot at a deer Saturday and missed him. We are now preparing to start again for my last chance'." [R211;127-130]

(4Q83)

Tammany Hall and its leader John Kelly, insistent on pressing its factious fight with Democrats beyond the New York City metropolitan region, so disrupted what harmony could have remained within the Party, that, in the November elections, Republicans won control of the State House, the State Senate and the office of Secretary of State. By refusing Kelly's demand for control over political patronage, Cleveland had lost the political alliance that could have sustained Democrats in the elections. Like previous Democrat Governors of the State, Horatio Seymour and Samuel Tilden, Cleveland's attitude toward Tammany Hall was "an attitude of instinctive and uncompromising hostility. Biographer Allan Nevins would elaborate:

"When up-State Democrats thought of Tammany they thought of the draft riots, the Tweed Ring, the political Gangsterism of an ignorant, venal Irish element that was deeply repugnant to their own [English culture]. Since they neither understood Tammany nor wanted to understand it, they had no tolerance for it. At a later date [Theodore] Roosevelt, who possessed the advantage of being born in New York City, [would show] a certain respect for the boss-system, for he realized that it was a symptom of definite social conditions, and that even Tammany performed some useful functions; but to Cleveland it was a pernicious growth. . . . Tammany was interfering with his honest work and was threatening him, and he brusquely thrust Tammany aside. . . . [Yet] his breach with Tammany [would catch] the public imagination as nothing else could."

Yes, despite Cleveland's "you-be-damnedness" attitude, the breach would eventually elevate the Governor to President of the United States, for voters would come to love him "for the enemies he had made." [R211;125-126]

The Year of 1884

(1Q84)

The Republican-controlled New York State Assembly convened on January 1, putting Governor Grover Cleveland in the position of sharing power with the opposition Party. Biographer Allan Nevins would describe the essence of this time:

"If the outstanding feature of the first legislative session had been Cleveland's clash with Tammany, that of the second was his working partnership with Theodore Roosevelt. It was a happy conjunction of stars which brought together the two greatest men New York [State] had produced since [John] Jay and [Alexander] Hamilton. In 1882, then 23 and fresh from Harvard, Roosevelt had entered the [State House] from the 21st district of New York."

Roosevelt was reelected the next year and worked for reform during the 1883 session. Again reelected, "he entered the 1884 session an influential figure, and at the opening of the session achieved a key position. The Republican Speaker, Titus Sheard, appointed him Chairman of the Committee on Cities, with authority to bring in measures for their better government; and with characteristic zeal Roosevelt began drafting a broad set of reforms." Many of Roosevelt's reform measures were passed by the House and Senate, and Cleveland, defying the outcrying of Tammany and other city machine Democrats, would sign the bills and publicize that he "was willing to go much further on this same path." [R211;138-142]

Meanwhile in Mississippi, men were looking forward with hope that the year 1884 would be the year that the Democratic Party would finally win control of the office of Federal President. Democrats had won the 1880 election for President with their candidate Samuel Tilden, but had agreed to forego contesting Republican theft of the election in exchange for withdrawal of Federal troops. Now, Democrats controlled all of the southern States and had every reason to expect that Republicans would be unable to steal elections there again. Thusly emboldened, there was widespread enthusiasm by March for recognizing the State's most famous leader, Jefferson Davis, in some politically-significant way. At first Jeff had expressed his reluctance to be drawn into such prominent public life, but he eventually relented and agreed to participate in the event that was scheduled for March, 10. Davis was 75 years old and the conquest of Confederate Mississippi had occurred almost 19 years previously. Both houses of the Mississippi Legislature gathered at the Capitol to receive Davis and hear him speak. The galleries and the windows were full of spectators. As Governor Robert Lowry escorted Davis to the front, "cheer after cheer went up, handkerchiefs waved, and [Davis] knew that he was appreciated by his own people." Lieutenant Governor G. D. Shands introduced Davis as "the embodied history of the [Southern States]." Biographer Hudson Strode would write that Davis' speech was "dignified, thoughtful, positive, [and] winning;" and "his voice still held its stirring quality." Jeff spoke of a bright future for his beloved State and her people, but he did not limit his speech to matters of which Republican politicians would be indifferent. After a while he spoke of the Confederacy and the cause for which Confederates had defended their nation:

> "It has been said that I should apply to the [Federal Government] for a pardon, but repentance must precede the right of pardon, and I have not repented. Remembering, as I must, all which has been suffered, all which has been lost, disappointed hopes and crushed aspirations, yet I deliberately say, if it were to do over again, I would again do just as I did in 1861.

> "No one is an arbiter of his own fate. . . Our people have accepted the decree. It therefore behooves them, as they may, to promote the general welfare of [our country], to show to the world that hereafter, as heretofore, the patriotism of our people is not measured by lines of latitude and longitude, but is as broad as the obligations they have assumed and embraces the whole of our ocean-bound domain.

> "I will now, Senators and Representatives, and ladies and gentlemen, bid you an affectionate, and, it may be, a last farewell." [R19;69-470]

Jeff Davis would forever remain firmly dedicated to the political concept of State Sovereignty, which had been, unquestionably, a fundamental principle of the Founding Fathers. He would always believe that the strongest form of government a nation could possibly devise would be a group of democratic Sovereign States bound together under a strictly limited Federal Government. The Founding Fathers had been right and nothing during the intervening decades had changed that conclusion: not advancements in industry, transportation, communication and education; not growth in population and territory, not increased ethnic and religious diversity. This, Jeff Davis would always hold to be a self-evident truth.

Meanwhile in late March, the Federal Senate began debate over a Federal Aid to Education bill sponsored by Republican Henry Blair of New Hampshire. Similar bills had been proposed in the past, both in the House and the Senate, but none had passed both in the same session. Blair's Senate bill would have divided among the States $15,000,000 in Federal money to be used to improve instruction in "reading, writing, arithmetic and geography" in public grammar schools. The allocation formula was aimed at benefiting illiterate students, meaning that the former Confederate States, with their large populations of illiterate African American children would receive about two-thirds of the money being granted.

Although the bill would take Federal taxes, mostly collected in the more wealthy northern States, and redistribute most of the money to the less wealthy former Confederate States, not all Senators from the benefiting States were in favor of the bill, citing concerns about Federal interference with local affairs, especially concerns about political activism aimed at weakening the Democratic Party in the southern States. However, neither Wade Hampton or Lucius Lamar allowed "State Rights" concerns to turn them away from supporting the bill. They both favored it and encouraged its passage in speeches they presented on the Senate floor.

Wade Hampton presented his arguments on March 27 and Lucius Lamar presented his arguments on March 28, beginning with a firm endorsement:

" . . . I have watched [proposals for Federal aid to education] from the time it was first introduced in the House, many years ago, down to the present time, when it has taken its present shape as presented by [Senator Henry Blair] of New Hampshire. I have watched it with deep interest and intense solicitude. In my opinion, it is the first step, and the most important step, that this Government has ever taken, in the direction of the solution of what is called the race problem; and I believe that it will tell more powerfully and decisively upon the future destinies of the [African American] race than any measure or ordinance that has yet been adopted in reference to it — [even] more decisively than the [Thirteenth, Fourteenth and Fifteenth amendments to the Federal Constitution]."

To put perspective on the unique educational problems in some southern States farming communities, Lamar gave this example:

"The culture of the cotton crop, especially in the lower portions of the Gulf States, requires nearly all the months of the year. They begin in the early part of the year, sometimes in December of the preceding year, to bed up the land; the field work goes on until in July, when we have a short vacation through August into September; [this allowing] the children to go in larger numbers to the schools until about the middle of September, when cotton picking commences, and continues until Christmas and often later. But if our [school] terms were prolonged, as they would be if we had the means of employing the teachers, there would be all through the year children sent to those schools for short periods, where they are now excluded by the shortness of our present period."

Among supporters of Federal aid to education were northern-States men who were insisting on placing Federal agents in control of spending the money, because, in their view, school administrators and teachers in the former Confederate States were incompetent to do the job and racially biased toward diverting most of the money to the European American students if given the chance. Lamar submitted that such organizational concerns were unfounded. In his first example Lamar quoted from testimony given by J. H. Smart, who had been for many years Indiana's Superintendent of Public Education, and who had traveled the southern States and studied their schools. Smart's testimony was, in part:

". . . Throughout the length and breadth of the southern States, without one exception, the [African American] people are given the same advantages that the [European American] people are given. . . . And I believe from what I saw that we are able to trust [their school administrators] with whatever [monetary] means we can appropriate, and I speak after some investigation and after deliberations."

In his second example, Lamar cited the testimony of Dr. Mayo of Massachusetts, who was widely recognized as a valid authority. Dr. Mayo's testimony was, in part:

"I have no hesitation in announcing to you, gentlemen, my conviction that never with 10 years in the history of the world has an effort so great, so persistent, and so absolutely heroic been made by any people for the education of the children as by the leading class of the people in our southern States. . . . A better class of people, more earnest, more determined to improve, more self-denying, working on wages painfully and sometimes pitifully inadequate, cannot be found in any Christian land than the majority of the public school teachers in the [southern States]. The State superintendents of education and many of the city and county supervisors are the same sort of people as our leading educators of the [northern States]. . . . And now the traveler through the [southern States] finds himself everywhere in the presence of an educational revival as marked as in [the northeastern States] in the days of Horace Mann; and the blessedness of this revival is that it is bringing together the children and youth, their teachers, the younger parents, and the more thoughtful people of the [northern and southern States], as no movement in the political, the ecclesiastical, or even the industrial sphere of national life, can possibly succeed in doing."

Lamar closed by explaining how education was key to elevating African Americans to successful lives as independent, self-reliant people:

"In my opinion, this bill is a decided step toward the solution of the problem of race. The problem of race in a large part is the problem of illiteracy. Most of the evils, most of the difficulties which have grown up out of that problem, have arisen from a condition of ignorance, prejudice, and superstition. . . . A people who remain ignorant and superstitious and debased cannot be made free by all the constitutional guarantees and statutes with which you surround them. You may force power upon them and subject others to their rule, but the great attribute of self-government — and that real liberty which comes from it — you cannot confer on them while they remain ignorant and in bondage to their own passions and to their own prejudices and superstitions. . . . [Liberty] is a boon that cannot be conferred upon men [because], to be permanently possessed and enjoyed, it must be earned."

Lamar, drawing upon his practical experiences and academic background in Georgia and Mississippi, thoroughly understood that educating young African Americans was "a task of colossal magnitude," a challenge of "great difficulty," because "a dense mass of ignorance has to be penetrated."

"I am not an optimist as to the rapid progress of the [African American] people in education. However earnest they may be, there will be great difficulty, even with the aid of the Federal Government in establishing effective schools for all. We are yet but in the incipience of this great work, hardly gone further than establishing the educational machinery on the ground. A task of colossal magnitude is before us, and a dense mass of ignorance has to be penetrated. . . . But the great idea of popular education . . . will inspire, both to guard and guide, the vast host in its slow, hesitating, but onward, advance to knowledge and true freedom." [R205;774-779]

(2Q84)

The Republican National Convention opened in Chicago on June 3. Many Delegates had arrived with the intention of punishing their incumbent President, Chester Arthur, because of his reluctant acceptance of legislation that promised to depoliticize most Federal Government jobs. Without those thousands upon thousands of jobs to hand out to Party workers, Republican politicians feared they might lose their majority status. Arthur had to go. Party discipline demanded it. The dump-Arthur Delegates were strongly attracted to James Blaine of Maine, who had been an original founder of their Party and a recognized leader from its inception. Blaine enjoyed strong support from Delegates who wished to continue to favor big-business interests and to hand out Federal jobs as rewards for Party faithfulness.

James Blaine was nominated by William West of Ohio. West wove the standard Republican hate propaganda into his nominating speech, calling again for old-school Republican politics:

"Four and twenty years of the grandest history in the annals of recorded time have distinguished the ascendancy of the Republican Party. Skies have lowered, and reverses have threatened. Our [Federal] flag is still there, waving above the [White House]; not a stain on its folds, not a cloud on its glory. To it are stretched the imploring hands of ten million [Northern States Democrats, who are even today willing to be subservient to Democrat politicians who now hold power in the former Confederate States]; while, above, from the portals of light, is looking down the spirit of [Abe Lincoln,] the immortal martyr who first bore [the Federal flag] to victory [in our conquest of the Confederacy], bidding us hail and Godspeed. In six campaigns [for the Federal presidency] has that symbol of [the Conquest of the Confederacy], of [making bonded African Americans independent], of humanity, and of progress, been borne in triumph." [R18;74-76]

Although William Curtis and Carl Schurz led a significant opposition faction that wanted to depoliticize almost all Federal jobs, their candidate, George Edmunds, and their reform movement, would fail to carry the Convention. On the first ballot Blaine received almost 4 times as many votes as Edmunds. On the fourth ballot, Blaine was nominated. Arthur had been dumped and Blaine had been nominated. Too many Republican politicians wanted to continue the old politics based on political patronage. They proposed to again base the Party's campaign theme on convincing voters in the northern States to reject Democratic Party candidates on their ballots, not because they might not be good legislators, but because they were friends of so-called "evil" politicians from the far-away former Confederate States. Republican leaders would again demagogue the myth that a vote for the Democratic candidate was an act of treason. But many Republicans were not enthusiastic about Blaine, about minimizing political patronage or about continuing to demonize people of the southern States for political gain in the northern States. Many Republicans sought civility and harmony among all of the country's citizens. These threatened to revolt, to withdraw from supportive campaigning.

The outcome of the Republican National Convention worked to boost enthusiasm for nominating Grover Cleveland as the Democrat's candidate, for his reform advocacy would draw support from the defeated Edmunds supporters within the Republican ranks. Biographer Allan Nevins would observe that "the nomination [of Blaine] was the signal for revolt [within Republican ranks], which took the most experienced observers by surprise, for in volume and intensity it surpassed the hopes of the Democrats and the fears of the Republicans." For example, Grover Cleveland, perhaps believing too much that Theodore Roosevelt represented the Republican future, had assured friends just prior to the Republican Convention: "Oh, neither Blaine nor Arthur will be nominated. I have observed that in time of crisis the moral sense of the Republican Party comes uppermost. The crisis is here. The Republican situation demands the nomination of Edmunds, and Edmunds will be nominated." But Cleveland was wrong! Blaine was of the old school and many reform-minded Republicans disliked his scandalous former railroad business deals, his reliance on "waving the bloody shirt" and the "spoils system." Opportunities for the Democratic nominee for President looked good, but there was one major problem for Grover Cleveland — Democrats had to carry populous New York State to win in the Electoral College and victory in New York State was difficult without the support of John Kelly and Tammany Hall.

But who would Democrats turn to if not Governor Grover Cleveland? Former New York Governor Samuel Tilden — winner of the 1880 election, which had been stolen — was 70 years old, in "frail health" and had "suffered a paralytic stroke which left him unable to speak above a whisper or walk except with tottering gait." He declined to be considered. There were several "favorite sons," such as Indiana's Thomas Hendricks, who had been Tilden's 1880 running mate. But most Democrat Delegates believed the race for the nomination was between:

- Thomas Bayard of Delaware, sympathetic toward the southern States culture and a long-time favorite of southern States Democrats, had a substantial block of supporters, but his association with southern States friends was too strong, making it difficult to defend him against "bloody shirt" demagoguery.

- Allen Thurman of Ohio "was growing infirm, while his views on money were distrusted" by many.

- Ben Butler of Massachusetts (The Beast) — who was hated by southern States Democrats like the plague, as readers of *Bloodstains* are all too aware — had, in May, won the nomination of two little third Party outfits, one called the "Greenback Party," the other called the "Anti-Monopoly Party." With these nominations in his pocket, he was brazenly going about seeking to influence Democrat Delegates, especially Tammany Hall men, to also nominate him at their Convention.

- Grover Cleveland had the support of much of New York State, including the Tilden-Manning machine under Daniel Manning of Albany, the County Democracy under Abram Hewitt and William Whitney, Irving Hall's organization, most western New York State Democrats encouraged by Cleveland's political friends in Buffalo, and Democrats in Counties including Ulster, St. Lawrence, Clinton and Essex. Furthermore, Edgar Apgar, "brilliant and resourceful as ever, toured the whole State," encouraging Delegates to go for Cleveland.

Opposition to Cleveland focused on arguments that he was too inexperienced and that, because "he was opposed by Tammany Hall, the trade unions and the Catholic hierarchy," victory in New York State was doubtful, thereby assuring a Democratic Party defeat. Charles Dana of the New York *Sun*, attacked

Cleveland as would "a lifelong enemy," on occasion accusing him of "a plodding mind, limited knowledge, and narrow capacities."

New York State Democrats convened at Saratoga on June 18 to elect 72 Delegates to the National Convention, representing 12 percent of the 601 votes needed to nominate by the National Party's two-thirds rule. Daniel Manning of Albany maintained firm control. The Platform Committee insisted on "the election of a President whose character and public reputation shall give to the whole people assurance of an honest, impartial, and efficient administration of the laws, without suspicion of personal ends or private interests." By way of appeasement, Tammany Hall was given half of the Delegates from New York County. Most importantly, the Convention adopted the unit rule, meaning that every one of the New York State 72 votes would likely be cast for Governor Cleveland. Others outside the Democratic Party were lining up behind Cleveland as well. "A distinguished committee of Republican bolters met in New York City and adopted resolutions condemning James Blaine and calling on the Democrats to make a nomination which they could support," a request that a Cleveland candidacy was sure to satisfy. "A conference of Independents in Boston a few days earlier, on June 13, had taken the same step. *Harper's Weekly* on July 5 "came out flatly for Cleveland." And although southern States Delegates were expected to vote almost to the man for Thomas Bayard on the first ballot, they appeared to be agreeable to switch to Cleveland if the Convention was seen moving in that direction. [R211;145-150, R81;72-77]

(3Q84)

At Chicago, campaigning was underway by Friday, July 4, four days before the Tuesday opening of the Democratic National Convention. The arm-twisters were already in place when train-loads of Delegates began arriving that Friday. Tammany Hall agent Thomas Grady was "on the scene, laboring energetically to influence [local newspapers] against Cleveland, and filling the saloons and lobbies with his whispering campaign. While he accused Cleveland of being anti-Catholic and anti-Irish, up-State allies of Tammany disseminated reports that Cleveland was a dissolute drunkard." But Cleveland supporters were arriving in force.

"At dawn on Sunday, July 6, the County Democracy arrived with 3 brass bands, their Cleveland banners gleaming silver and gold under the first rays of sunlight. Later in the day came two long trains, 25 cars in each, bearing Kelly, Croker, and 700 Tammany braves, all wearing tall white hats. Another long special train drew in with the Democrats of Irving Hall and Hill's followers of the southern tier. Manning was early on the ground, taking charge of the Palmer House headquarters — 3 immense parlors, with a life-size portrait of Cleveland over the entrance. When the Alabama Delegation under "Fighting Joe" Wheeler arrived, Cleveland seemed to gain strength, and when the South Carolina Delegation under Wade Hampton arrived, Cleveland gained more. Yet there was stubborn resistance to Cleveland in some northern States Delegations, and these were coalescing around Ben "Beast" Butler of Massachusetts.

Campaigning and promise swapping was everywhere on Monday, July 7. That morning the New York State Delegation of 72 men met to cast their votes for their first ballot choices. John Kelly and his Tammany Hall force had worked over the State's Delegates intensely and the vote was agonizing close. On this first test vote, by a majority of 37 to 35, the New York State Delegation selected Governor Cleveland. Of that slim, but crucial majority of two, a Delegate would later remark, "by what small chances do we live in history." A bit later, "the Brooklyn Delegation announced that it stood by Cleveland," giving him 45 assured Delegates from New York State's allotment of 72. The unit rule should give him the remainder.

Biographer Allan Nevins would write, "By the opening day, Tuesday, July 8, it was clear that the Convention was to be nothing more than a savage fight of two Party marplots, [Ben Beast] Butler and [John] Kelly, against [Grover] Cleveland. [Yet] the result could hardly be in doubt." Early on, John Kelly pressed Delegates to vote for or against allowing a Delegation to abide by a unit rule. Cleveland Delegates favored permitting a Delegation to have a unit rule and others opposed it. This was an important vote. Allowance for a unit rule was upheld by a vote of 463 versus 322, a strong indication of Cleveland strength. Consequently, New York State would vote as a block of 72 under the careful management of Daniel Manning.

The second day, Wednesday, July 9, nominating speeches were delivered. The atmosphere was festive and congenial. "The bands played selections from the new operas *Patience* and *Iolanthe*; [northern States Delegates] cheered Dixie, and [southern States Delegates], Yankee Doodle." Near the top of the alphabet, Delaware began by nominating Senator Thomas Bayard.

Wade Hampton was at the Convention, a Delegate from South Carolina. Of course, he supported his friend, Thomas Bayard. Yet he recognized that Bayard was from a southern-culture State (Delaware) and that there was scant likelihood of a man from a southern-culture State receiving the nomination. At one point he told the Convention, "We [men of the southern States] should be the last people in the world to attempt to strike him down because of his fidelity to us in our days of trouble and to the Constitution. If he is unacceptable to the [northern States] we can't help it." [R199;295]

Indiana was recognized and Thomas Hendricks nominated Joseph McDonald. Allen Thurman was nominated. John Carlisle was nominated. None of these nominations were met with notable enthusiasm, but when Daniel Lockwood of Buffalo "rose to nominate Grover Cleveland, the Convention awoke to a sense of excitement." In part, Lockwood told the Convention:

> "A little more than three years ago, I had the honor at the city of Buffalo to present the name of this same gentleman for the office of Mayor of that city. It was presented then for the same reason, and from the same causes, that we present it now. It was because the government of that city had become corrupt, had become debauched, and political integrity sat not in high places. The people looked for a man who would represent honest government, and without any hesitation they named Grover Cleveland.

> "The result of that election and of his holding that office was that in less than 9 months the State of New York found herself in a position to want just such a candidate and for just such a purpose. At the State Convention of 1882 his name was placed in nomination for the office of Governor of the State of New York. The same people, the same class of people, knew that that meant honest government, it meant pure government, it meant Democratic government, and it was ratified; and, gentlemen, now, after 18 months of service there, the Democracy of the State of New York come to you and ask you to go to the country, to go to the Independent and Democratic voters of the country, to go to the young men of the country, the new blood of the country, and present the name of Grover Cleveland as your standard bearer."

There were other speeches and other nominations, including Allan Thurman of Ohio. And Tammany Hall machine men schemed to stop the stampede toward Cleveland, but it was Governor Edward Bragg of Wisconsin, a former Federal high-ranking army officer, who, in a seconding speech, best explained why young Democrats so loved Grover Cleveland:

> "They love him, gentlemen, and they respect him, not only for himself, for his character, for his integrity and judgment and iron will, but they love him most of all for the enemies he had made."

Amid the shouts of approval throughout the hall, an infuriated and beaten John Kelly "lunged at the platform," screaming, "In behalf of his enemies, I accept your statement." Men in the galleries, among them veterans of the War Between the States, encouraged the verbal battle, shouting, "A little more grape, Captain Bragg."

Biographer Allan Nevins would explain:

> "The fact was that the Convention was sick of Tammany; sick of its greed, its jealous spirit, its squabbles, its predictions of defeat. It was always kicking and bolting; it had opposed [Samuel] Tilden and [Winfield] Hancock . . .; it was responsible for nothing but mischief."

Finally, the nominating speeches were done. The Convention turned to its evaluation of the Party Platform. The Platform was read and rather quickly adopted. But Ben "Beast" Butler felt compelled to deliver his minority report, forcing Delegates to remain for a while past midnight.

On the morning of July 11, the first votes for President were cast. A two-thirds majority was needed, amounting to 547 votes. On the first vote, Cleveland secured what looked to be an insurmountable lead: 392 for Grover Cleveland; 170 for Thomas Bayard of Delaware (southern States votes that were easily switchable to Cleveland); 88 for Allan Thurman of Ohio; 78 for Samuel Randall of Pennsylvania (votes that Cleveland supporters had a good shot at winning over); 56 for McDonald; 27 for Carlisle, and 9 for others (Ben Beast Butler was out as a Republican candidate, but remained on two third-Party tickets). At this point Delegates retired for the day.

During the night Daniel Manning held a meeting with Samuel Randall, pledging that he could control the patronage in Pennsylvania if he would persuade his supporters to switch to Cleveland. The bargain was made. Pennsylvania would switch from Randall to Cleveland.

When the Convention opened the following morning, July 12, Illinois switched 10 votes to Cleveland, Missouri switched 15 to Cleveland. Then State after State, led by North Carolina, clamored to switch votes to Cleveland. As Delegation after Delegation began switching to Cleveland, it became apparent that he was swiftly headed toward nomination. The enthusiastic hall rocked with the chant: "We love him for the enemies he has made."

The final tally was 683 for Cleveland; 81-1/2 for Bayard; 45-1/2 for Hendricks, and 10 for others. Governor Grover Cleveland of New York State was the Democratic Party nominee for the office of Federal President.

Delegates then proceeded to nominate their candidate for Vice President. They selected Thomas Hendricks of Indiana. This would be a fortunate decision. Biographer Allan Nevins would surmise, Hendricks' nomination was a "shrewd move, for his strength [would prove to be] the decisive factor that fall in carrying Indiana," essential to victory.

Meanwhile in Albany, Grover Cleveland was at his post during Chicago's Democratic National Convention. Over the several days he had kept pace of events by telephone and telegraph, but had avoided excessive distractions. At the time his nomination was secured, he, John Farnsworth and Daniel Lamont were working over government papers in the Governor's office:

"At about 1:45 pm [John] Farnsworth heard against the westerly wind what he thought was a cannon shot. A second later there was an unmistakable roar from a brass piece which the Young Men's Democratic Club had placed at the foot of State Street. Farnsworth leaped to his feet, remarking, 'They are firing a salute, Governor, for your nomination.' 'That's what it means,' said Lamont. 'Do you think so? Well, anyhow we'll finish up this work,' and they resumed."

"In a couple of minutes the telephone rang, Lamont answered and a voice said: 'Tell the Governor he has been nominated on the second ballot.' Lamont announced the news. Cleveland replied, " 'Is that so, Dan?,' said the Governor, as his face brightened up for the first time. 'By Jove, that is something, isn't it?' After an exchange of congratulations Cleveland remarked, 'Lamont, I wish you would telephone that to the [Executive residence]. Sister will want to hear it'."

By the end of the day, approximated 1,500 telegrams would be received. The excitement for Cleveland was tremendous.

That evening Democrats in Albany celebrated their Governor's nomination for President with lights and a 5,000-citizen parade. And Grover Cleveland launched his campaign for the office then and there with a straightforward, easily understood speech defining why they must work hard for his election.

"Fellow-Citizens: . . . The American people are about to exercise, in it highest sense, their power of right and sovereignty. They are to call in review before them their public servants and the representatives of political Parties, and demand of them an account of their stewardship.

"Parties may be so long in power, and may become so arrogant and careless of the interests of the people, as to grow heedless of their responsibility to their masters. But the time comes, as certainly as death, when the people weigh them in balance.

"The issues to be adjudicated by the nation's great assize are made up and are about to be submitted. We believe that the people are not receiving at the hands of the Party which for nearly 24 years had directed the affairs of the nation, the full benefits to which they are entitled, of a pure, just and economical rule; and we believe that the ascendancy of genuine Democratic principles will insure a better government, and greater happiness and prosperity to all the people.

"To reach the sober thought of the nation, and to dislodge an enemy entrenched behind spoils and patronage involve a struggle, which, if we underestimate, we invite defeat. I am profoundly impressed with the responsibility of the part assigned to me in this contest. My heart, I know, is in the cause, and I pledge you that no effort of mine shall be wanting to secure the victory which I believe to be within the achievement of the Democratic hosts.

"Let us, then, enter upon the campaign now fairly opened, each one appreciating well the part he has to perform, ready, with solid front, to do battle for better government, confidently, courageously, always honorably, and with a firm reliance upon the intelligence and patriotism of the American people."

Part of every campaign in those days was the publication of major campaign literature. Toward that goal a well-known newspaperman, William Hudson, an enthusiastic Cleveland supporter, interviewed the candidate extensively and researched his speeches and accomplishments. Hudson had covered the Democratic National Convention in Chicago and was just back in New York State reflecting on how he could best headline before his readers Grover Cleveland's vision for better government. Hudson observed that Cleveland had said, in accepting the Democratic Party's nomination for Mayor of Buffalo: "Public officials are the trustee's of the people, and hold their places and exercise their powers for the benefit of the people." And as Buffalo's Mayor, he had said: "We are the Trustees and agents of our fellow citizens, holding their funds in sacred trust." Later, in accepting the Democratic Party nomination for Governor, Cleveland had said: "Public officers are the servants and agents of the people, to execute laws which the people have made and within the limits of a Constitution which they have established. Hudson observed that Cleveland had often referred to "trustee" and "public official." Suddenly, as in a flash, Hudson had his slogan:

"Public office is a Public Trust."

"Where the deuce did I say that?," Cleveland asked.

"You've said it a dozen times publicly, but not in those few words," Hudson replied.

"That's so," Cleveland affirmed. "That's what I believe. That's what I've said a little better because more fully."

"But this has the merit of brevity," Hudson explained, "and that is what is required here. The question is, Will you stand for this form?"

"Oh, yes," Cleveland assured. "That's what I believe. I'll stand for it and make it my own."

And, shortly thereafter newspapers across the nation were announcing the presidential campaign theme for Grover Cleveland and the Democratic Party:

"Public office is a Public Trust." [R81;76-88]

The weak economy in the northern States was a significant factor for the 1884 elections, but it was improving as the fall months arrived. Biographer Allan Nevins would explain:

"The business depression of 1884, which began to lift in the autumn, assisted the Democratic campaign far less than [supporters] had hoped. . . . Before the campaign opened, the shocking failure of Grant & Ward, sinking the aged [Ulysses Grant] into utter poverty, had created a national sensation. This occurred in May, and ruined many trusting investors. Other disastrous failures of the year included the Northern Pacific Railroad and the North River Construction Company. Stocks sank to a low level, there were many defaults, and unemployment increased. Inevitably this bred discontent with the Party in power, especially in New York State.

"[In spite of the weak economy] some business interests . . . feared the unsettling effects of a change, [so] Republicans made adroit use of [Ben "Beast"] Butler's candidacy [on two third-party tickets] to draw workingmen's votes away from Cleveland. The old Labor-Greenback movement had been powerful in the [northeastern States] in 1878, and there seemed a possibility of its revival. The Democrats, in their fear of the Greenback ticket, early sent Samuel Randall to Butler in an effort to get him to withdraw, but in vain, for he had already obtained a direct [financial] subsidy from [important Republican leaders and money sources]."

At the outset, Ben "Beast" Butler enjoyed the support of John Kelly and Tammany Hall, but this remarkable alignment soon dissolved. Yet Butler and the Greenbacks threatened to be spoilers.

Prohibitionists represented the other outlying third-Party movement. This Party was led by John St. John, a former two-term Governor of the State of Kansas, which, as you know, had been awarded statehood in 1861 following the horrific terrorism of "Bleeding Kansas" Territory — the primary basis of the political demagoguery that had given rise to the Republican Party. St. John had lost to Democrat George Glick in 1882, in a bid for a third term as Governor, mistakenly expecting to be re-elected by the avid support of a powerful Kansas Prohibition Movement. Democrat Glick had won the race by simply opposing Prohibition of alcoholic beverages. In spite of that defeat two years previously, St John was continuing to fight for Prohibition, enlarging the Movement to all States. Considering the history of Kansas Territory, it is not unreasonable to believe many people of the northern States culture who lived in Kansas were prone to political activism and believed they resided on a higher moral plane from which they were justified in overseeing the lesser folk from other regions. Perhaps, their former passion for Exclusionism, now long completed, was transformed into a new passion for Prohibitionism.

But the most important group outside of the two mainstream Parties, was the movement that spoke for most Independents, because a powerful unofficial third-Party element emerged, made up of Independents, which had leaders and speakers and campaign slogans. This unofficial Independent Party did not nominate a candidate for President — for the most part it adopted Grover Cleveland as its candidate. These campaigners were called the "Mugwumps." Biographer Allan Nevins would explain:

> "The Independents or Mugwumps, so called by a name first taken out of Eliot's Indian Bible in 1872, and now revived by Dana's [New York] *Sun*, became virtually a new Party — from 1884 to 1897 a Cleveland Party. They were able to decide at least one national election, and their faith was to be a leavening force in politics for a long generation."

Why did this political movement rise up at this time? Nevins understood it this way:

> "The hour was ripe for precisely such a movement. The health of a nation requires, from time to time, a far-reaching moral movement to awaken men from old lethargies and fix their eyes upon some new city in the heavens. Ever since the [Conquest of the Confederacy] the [Federal] Government had in great part been subject to the selfish materialism of the worst wing of the Republican Party. The Congressional oligarchy which had humiliated Andrew Johnson and crushed the [conquered Confederate States]; the placemen and Corruptionists who had molded [Ulysses] Grant to their desires; the favored groups which had obtained land-grants, subsidies, pensions, and tariffs; the quarrelsome gangs of Stalwarts and Half-Breeds who had kept the Hayes and Garfield-Arthur Administrations in turmoil — all these had aroused an increasing irritation. Men were in revolt against the entire system of government by special favor of which [Republican candidate James] Blaine was simply the emblem."

The list of prominent men who "bolted" the Republican Party and joined the Mugwumps is impressive, indicative of a sea-change in attitudes, a sense of moral cleansing. A partial list of prominent names — many of them Massachusetts men, many going back to the founding of the Republican Party — included Carl Schurz, Henry Ward Beecher, Charles Francis Adams, Jr., Benjamin H. Bristow, George Haven Putnam, Edward Atkinson, Moorfield Storey, Leverett Saltonstall, William Everett, James Freeman Clark, John C. Dodge, Richard H. Dana, Josiah Quincy, Winslow Warren, T. W. Higginson, Frederick J. Stimson, James Russell Lowell, Charles Eliot Norton, Theodore Lyman, Francis W. Bird, George Fred Williams and Harvard President Charles Eliot and most of his faculty.

The bolters included many prominent newspapermen. Biographer Allan Nevins would observe:

> "Still more ominously for the Republicans, newspapers all over the [northeastern States] halted, veered uncertainly, and then swung to the Democratic Party. In New York City new colors were hoisted by the *Times*, *Herald* and *Evening Post*, and by *Harper's Weekly*, the *Nation* and *Puck*. A squadron of influential journals elsewhere in the State joined them. In [States east of New York] there was an equally impressive list, including the Springfield *Republican*, the Boston *Transcript* and the Boston *Herald*. All these journals began printing long lists of former Republicans who refused to tolerate Blaine's nomination."

Besides suffering the loss of the bolters, the Republican Party was confronted with a stark campaign strategy dilemma — how could they develop an argument against Governor Grover Cleveland? Historian Robert McElroy would conclude, "A careful survey of [Grover] Cleveland's political career soon convinced the Republican campaign leaders that nothing could be gained by turning public attention in that direction. His record was above criticism. . . . He had, in the most literal sense, administered public office as a pubic trust, and even their ingenuity could not make a case against him. What about "waving the bloody shirt?" McElroy would observe, "Sectional hostilities, which had begun to fade by reason of lapse of time and wise methods of conciliation, were eagerly revived. But a new generation had come upon the scene, which could not be greatly moved by the 'waving of the bloody shirt'." Republican campaigners strove to make import taxation an issue, hoping industrialists and manufacturing labor would become fearful of lower prices and idled capacity if Democrats reduced the tax rate on imports. But the Platform had pledged Democrats "to revise the tariff in a spirit of fairness to all interests" taking care to reduce taxes so as "not to injure any domestic industries, but rather to promote their healthy growth." Voters seemed satisfied with that concept.

Actually, the Republican Platform and the Democrat Platform were almost identical. Both promised civil service reform and the stated tariff policies differed little — both pledging cautious reductions in the tax rate coupled with promises to protect businesses and workers. So Democrat campaign strategy focused on Blaine's long and storied record in public life, complete with scandals which were magnified as much as might be believed. This was orchestrated primarily by Pue Gorman of Maryland, who led the Executive Committee, Daniel Manning of Albany and William Whitney of the County Democracy in New York City:

> The "Mulligan letters," evidence of Blaine's involvement in scandals involving shady railroad deals, were used to discredit the Republican's character. In this effort the sleuthing of New York City Independents was most helpful. Newspaper articles and pamphlets trumpeted the story.

On the other hand, Republican campaign strategy focused on personal attacks on Grover Cleveland's character:

> Cleveland was lambasted for not joining the Federal Army, notwithstanding the fact that two of his brothers had done so, freeing Grover to make some money to support the mother and sisters. The substitute Grover had hired to serve in his place in the Federal Army was falsely characterized as a convict.

> Cleveland was attacked for having had a child with a Buffalo woman "whose illegitimate son was later placed in an orphan asylum." Cleveland, a bachelor, was especially vulnerable to this line of attack, and Republican newspapers ran with it like wildfire. This put the Cleveland campaign on the defensive, but his supporters rallied to the cause and stridently countered with the truth. As you learned earlier in this volume of *Bloodstains*, the event took place in Buffalo (1874-1876), the mother was Maria Halpin, a widow who knew several men intimately, and she had named the child Oscar Folsom Cleveland and charged Grover with its paternity. (Perhaps her husband had been killed during the Federal Invasion of the Confederacy; I do not know. That military conflict had wrecked the lives of so many families of her generation.) Grover, unsure of the child's father, agreed to pay support. Normally, an event of this nature would not merit much space in *Bloodstains*, but the sensation did influence the campaign and historians since have made much of it when telling the story of President Grover Cleveland, finding it handy at supporting the commonplace policy of glorifying Abe Lincoln while belittling Grover Cleveland. If you were to poll Americans today who admitted knowing at least one story about Grover Cleveland, the campaign attack mantra, "Ma, Ma, Where's My Pa." would top the list. The following account of Maria and her child, in the words of biographer Allan Nevins, will be sufficient:

>> "Maria Halpin was [at the time of the incident] a young widow of Pennsylvania family who, leaving two children behind her, came to Buffalo from Jersey City about 1871, and found employment first as a collar-maker and then in the drygoods store of Flint & Kent, where she was soon placed at the head of the cloak department. She was tall, pretty, pleasing in manner, and spoke French. She attended the fashionable St. John's Episcopal Church and made numerous friends. For a time she accepted the attentions of several men, including Cleveland, who was a year her elder — she was 36 in 1874. When a son was born to her on September 14

of that year, whom she named Oscar Folsom Cleveland, she charged Cleveland with its paternity."

"While nursing the child, the mother, then living at 11 East Genesse Street, began drinking heavily and neglecting it. In these circumstances Cleveland turned to a much older friend who had been County Judge while he was Sheriff, Roswell Burrows, and placed the entire matter in his hands. Burrows, after investigation, and without Cleveland's immediate knowledge, had the woman taken to the Providence Asylum, an institution for mentally deranged persons managed by the Sisters of Charity. Mrs. Halpin was persuaded to remain here for a short time, while legal steps were taken through the Overseer of the Poor to commit the boy to the Protestant Orphan Asylum on Main Street (March 9, 1876), at the usual board rate of $5 a week, which Cleveland was to pay through Judge Burrows. At the same time, Cleveland gave Mrs. Halpin the means of establishing a business of her own in Niagara Falls. But growing lonely for the child and finding that by surrendering him she had lost her claim on the supposed father, she immediately returned to recover her son. When this failed, she took the desperate step, on April 28, 1878, of kidnapping him. Judge Burrows intervened again, and in July there was a final commitment of the boy to the orphanage, from which later he was adopted by one of the best families in western New York [State], in time, [in the 1900's], becoming a distinguished professional man. He thus disappeared from Cleveland's life."

Of course, the campaign was to be much more than "Ma, Ma, where's my Pa." Deals needed to be made with Tammany. But Cleveland refused to strike any bargaining deals with John Kelly and Tammany Hall. So, Thomas Hendricks, Grover's running mate, took on the task, and pacified Kelly with some deals on political patronage. In exchange Tammany Hall dropped endorsement of Ben "Beast" Butler and gave the Cleveland-Hendricks ticket "grudging support."

The Republican campaign worked diligently to get out the Federal veteran's vote, using the officials in the Federal Pensions Bureau as field campaign workers, under the direction of Bureau Chief W. W. Dudley, all salaries and expenses paid by the taxpayers. "Unquestionably thousands of veterans who might have voted for Cleveland were persuaded that the continuance of the pension system depended upon Republican success." This was part of the larger Republican effort, well described by John Carlisle of Kentucky in a speech he would make in 1888:

"It was said that the election of a Democratic President would be immediately followed by the prostration of our manufacturing industries, the derangement of our finances, the debasement of our currency, and the destruction of the public credit; and that even the civil and political rights of the people would not be secure. According to these partisan prophets, the Supreme Court of the United States was to be reorganized and the Constitutional Amendments annulled; the [Federal] soldiers and sailors were to be deprived of the pensions and bounties heretofore granted to them, and all the terms and agreements [that had been secured while remaking the political structure of conquered Confederate States] were to be entirely disregarded."

Such serious charges, fabrications one would argue, were not the only persuasive factors in the campaign. There was an event in New York City, late in the campaign, that should have been minor, but which became pivotal — likely to become the reason that Blaine would lose New York State and therefore, the election. This took place in the morning of October 29.

An advertisement had invited clergymen to meet with Blaine at the Fifth Avenue Hotel for conversation. Prominent clergy ignored the event but a good number of minor clergy did come, the most prominent being S. Burchard, pastor of the Murray Hill Presbyterian Church. He was apparently the spokesman for the group. A supporter of the Blaine campaign, he addressed the candidate and lambasted Cleveland and the Democrats as the Party of "Rum, Romanism, and Rebellion." A catchy alliterative phrase if I do say so myself. Blaine thought nothing of the remark and neither did the newspapermen who were covering the gathering. "But the ever-alert managers of the Democratic headquarters had taken the precaution of shadowing Blaine with a shorthand reporter."

Back at Democrat Headquarters, Oscar Straus read the insulting remark and decided to broadcast it across the country in every newspaper that was willing to pick it up — a great "get out the vote" stimulus, with Election Day near at hand. Biographer Allan Nevins would write:

"Within a few hours the principal cities were being placarded with the insulting alliteration. When Blaine passed through New Haven the next day, he was greeted with a shower of Rum-Romanism-Rebellion handbills. The effect was profound. Blaine's managers were relying heavily upon his strength with the Irish Catholics, and a hurricane had burst upon the fields white for the harvest."

But that was not the only problem for Blaine that day. In the evening, well-healed New York [City] supporters wined and dined with the candidate at a "prosperity dinner" held at posh Delmonico's. Biographer Allan Nevins would tell this story:

"At seven o'clock long lines of carriages were leaving their occupants at the doors. At half-past seven Blaine, amid handclapping, entered the ballroom where the covers had been laid. He was escorted to the post of honor by William Evarts and Cyrus Field, and took his seat as the room resounded with three cheers proposed by A. R. Whitney. The decorations were elaborate — smilax, roses, and costly orchids, expensive confectioneries, and in front of the principal guest a magnificent bed of hothouse flowers lettered J. G. B. Among the guests were Jay Gould, the best-hated man in America; Russell Sage, famous for his griping hand; John Roach, a wealthy government contractor; Henry Clews, Levi Morton, D. O. Mills, Charles Tiffany, Cornelius Bliss, Whitelaw Reid, and Lloyd Aspinwall.

"Evarts presided and made a harmless speech. In his response Blaine seemed to talk of nothing but money. The next day the New York *World* filled half its front page with Walt McDougall's cartoon of 'The Royal Feast of Belshazzar Blaine and the Money Kings,' and the comments of many newspapers were scathing. At a time when [newspapers were] filled with news of factories closing down, when three-fifths of the iron furnaces were banked, and when business of all kinds was at a low ebb, with multitudes out of work, Blaine had appeared at a banquet offered by wealth and privilege, and had made a speech which was one long glorification of plutocracy. At a stroke he had lost the votes of thousands of workingmen."

Election Day was Tuesday, November 4. The weather in upstate New York was rather raw, discouraging the less determined and less hardy of the voting men — not a good omen for Democrats. Grover voted in Buffalo and then returned to Albany.

You will recall that Democrats had won the election for President in 1876 under the candidacy of former New York Governor Samuel Tilden — only to have it stolen from them by Republican vote rigging in Florida and Louisiana and perhaps South Carolina as well. Now, in 1884, total Democrat victory in all of the 11 former Confederate States seemed assured, because Republicans, having lost power in South Carolina, Florida and Louisiana in 1877, had no way to rig votes there. In 1880 South Carolina had voted for the Democratic candidate for President by a 66 to 34 percent margin; in Florida the margin had been 54 to 46 percent, in Louisiana, 62 to 37 percent. Among the 8 other States of the former Confederacy, Tilden had won by an average margin of 26 percent, and in 1880 the average Democrat margin in all 11 States had been 22 percent. These 11 States were certain to deliver 103 Electoral College votes to Cleveland.

The 5 States immediately north of the Confederate States were also certain to vote Democrat in 1884. These States — Delaware, Maryland, West Virginia, Kentucky and Missouri — had supported Democrat Samuel Tilden by margins that averaged 16 percent and had supported the Democrat candidate for President in 1880 by margins that averaged 10 percent. These 5 States would deliver 46 Electoral College votes to Cleveland.

So, with Republicans shut out of the southern culture, the only potential source of Electoral College votes for candidate James Blaine was within the northern Culture. In 1876, Democrat Samuel Tilden had won Connecticut, New York, New Jersey and Indiana. Those 4 States of the northern culture, combined with the 16 States of the southern culture, had given Tilden the victory, only to have it stolen by Republican vote rigging as mentioned above. In 1880, the Democrat candidate for President had won New Jersey and Nevada, and by only a margin of a mere 144 votes, had also won California. But these 3 States had far too few Electoral College votes to, when combined with the southern culture vote, to win for the Democrats. Republicans had won the vote in the northern-culture States by margins that averaged 10 percentage points in 1876 and averaged 12 percentage points in 1880. Many of those States were overwhelmingly Republican, for the margins of a group, consisting of Maine, Massachusetts, Rhode Island, Vermont, Minnesota, Iowa, Nebraska and Kansas, had averaged 24 percentage points in 1876. Those 8 States were beyond reach for Democrats. The hopeful States for them were New York (a must win), Connecticut, New Jersey, Indiana, Nevada and California. Also in play, but not likely for Democrats, were the States of New Hampshire, Pennsylvania, Ohio, Illinois and Oregon. In 1876, Democrats had lost those 5 States by an average margin of only 3 percentage points. The hopeful States had 76 Electoral College votes and when the certain southern culture vote was added on, the victory margin would be 56 percent. The other 5 States considered in play gave opportunities for other victory combinations. But, by any combination, if New York was lost, the Republicans were sure to win.

When the votes were counted, results showed that all 16 States of the southern culture had voted to elect Grover Cleveland — the 5 north of the former Confederacy (Delaware, Maryland, West Virginia, Kentucky and Missouri) yielding victory margins that averaged 9 percentage points and the 11 within the former Confederacy yielding victory margins that averaged 20 percentage points. Only Virginia and West Virginia gave Blaine a threatening vote (Cleveland won Virginia 51 to 49 percent and West Virginia 51 to 48 percent). Of the 5 States of the northern culture that were in play but not likely for Democrats (New Hampshire, Pennsylvania, Ohio, Illinois and Oregon), Republican James Blaine won them all, the average of the margins being 5 percentage points. Of the Democrat's hopeful northern culture States (New York, Connecticut, New Jersey, Indiana, Nevada and California), returns showed a 50 to 48 percent victory in Indiana, thanks to the candidate for Vice President, a 49 to 47 percent victory in New Jersey, and a 49 to 48 percent victory in Connecticut, with crucial New York State being too close to call. Out west, Nevada and California were not even close, the former going Republican by 44 to 56 percent and the later by 45 to 52 percent. The outcome of the contest depended on the decision by New York State voters. All eyes were on that contest, and "in the minds of all [of] Cleveland's friends was the fear of a repetition" of Republican vote stealing, this time in New York State. They all too well remembered the theft of the election of 1876, by which former New York Governor Samuel Tilden, Democrat, had been denied the Presidency he had rightfully won. To fend off such thievery, telegrams under the name of Chairman Daniel Manning sped throughout the night from Albany to Democrat leaders in all sections of the State:

> "The only hope of our opponents is in a fraudulent count in the country districts. Call to your assistance today vigilant and courageous friends, and see that every vote cast is honestly counted. Telegraph me your estimate, and let me hear from you from time to time until actual figures are known."

While the telegrams began their work, as Tuesday night shifted to Wednesday morning, Grover Cleveland bid their dispatchers good night and went off to bed.

During the day of Wednesday, "a few counties in [the State] remained to be heard from" but Cleveland looked to be ahead by the slightest of margins. Ominously, the Associated Press reported Blaine the likely winner. Democrats worried that Western Union, the telegraph company, was "delaying and falsifying the returns." These concerns were not imagined: later the Chief of the Bureau of Elections, Republican leader John O'Brien, "would be accused of accepting, two days before the election, checks for $50,000 each from Jay Gould and the Union League Club to be used in buying blocks of Democratic votes" thereby diverting them to Blaine. And biographer Allan Nevins would tell of the large crowds that gathered in New York City during the day to watch news of the returns:

> "In New York City on Wednesday the multitudes in front of the bulletin boards cheered madly for Cleveland. As night fell the concourse swelled to immense proportions, and a mass of men and boys marched down Broadway to the Western Union building on Dey Street, threatening violence, while another crowd moved up Fifth Avenue toward Gould's house, singing, 'We'll hang Jay Gould to a sour apple tree'."

On Thursday the outcome was still in doubt, although most observers felt Cleveland would win. Yet some newspapers predicted it for Blaine.

On Friday the New York *Tribune* still claimed a Blaine victory, but before the day was over the New York *Sun* and the Albany *Journal*, newspapers that had backed Blaine, "conceded Cleveland's election."

Finally, on Saturday, November 8, well before dawn, at 1:20 a. m., the Associated Press announced that a Cleveland victory was certain. Not long afterward Blaine conceded. Upon learning of Blaine's concession, Cleveland, mindful of how Samuel Tilden had not fought back when his election had been stolen from him 8 years earlier, told friends:

> "I am glad of it. I am glad they yield peaceably. If they had not, I should have felt it my duty to take my seat anyhow."

And history is rather confident that he would have. But this action, this potential reaction to a standoff that might have escalated into another cascade of State secession, another conflict of arms, would not be necessary. The Republican Party conceded and the Democratic Party gained control of the President's office.

The vote in New York State was Grover Cleveland, 563,048; James Blaine, 562,001; John St. John, 24,999, and Ben Butler, 16,955. The margin of Cleveland over Blaine was 1,047 votes, one of the closest elections in American history. The vote in the Electoral College would be Cleveland, 219 and Blaine, 182.

Former Kansas Governor, John St. John, and his movement to Prohibit alcoholic beverages, coupled with the outcry over Democrats being characterized very late in the campaign as supporters of "Rum, Romanism and Rebellion," had drawn 24,999 New York State votes away from the major-parties contest, most of those voters being normally inclined to side with the Democracy. On the other hand, Ben "Beast" Butler, carrying the banner for two small groups, the Anti-Monopoly Party and the Greenback Party, had drawn 16,955 votes away from the major-parties contest, most of those voters being normally inclined to side with the Republican Party. Biographer Allan Nevins would conclude that the damage done to Blaine by the Prohibition Party was considerably worse that the damage done to Cleveland by supporters of Ben Butler, the notorious "Beast" of formerly occupied New Orleans. This pattern — the Prohibition Party hurting the Republican Party more than Butler's group hurt Cleveland — is also seen in the returns from Connecticut, New Jersey and Indiana, where Cleveland won, but by small margins. [R211;156-188, R81;72-99]

Meanwhile, on that Saturday in Oxford, Mississippi, Lucius Lamar, relaxing in bed at his son-in-law's house, was rather taking it easy after the grueling campaign, for he had worked hard on behalf of Democrats, including Grover Cleveland. He lay there in sadness, "disheartened" by what he had presumed to be another defeat at the Federal level, for delayed election return news seemed to always result in Republican victories. But then, he heard a noise, of which his biographer and son-in-law Edward Mayes would tell:

> "A young man from the village came hallooing and leaping, waving a telegram for [Lucius Lamar]. It was from John Gordon, a former Confederate commander. The message said, "Thank God! Cleveland is elected. Turn the rascals out!" Lamar was disbelieving — delayed election returns had always signaled defeat. "I don't believe it! Gordon is too impulsive; he is deceiving himself." But, before long, confirmation of the glorious news arrived at the house. Soon the full impact of the meaning of the event gained control over his mind. He announced, "It is a terrible responsibility!" Mayes then observed his father-in-law fall "into a long and deep reverie, one of those phases in which those who knew him rightly knew that he was engaged in earnest thought. The overwhelming flood of 28 years' duration had rolled away; the Democratic Party, which had ruled the destinies of the country for 60 years of its existence and then had been overturned in a ruin apparently hopeless and irremediable, had been restored to power. . . . He took no part in the merrymaking, for the spell of the future was upon him." [R205;460]

Demonstrations of joy were evident in many places in much of the country. Of these, biographer Paul Jeffers would say:

> "Demonstrations also erupted in the streets of Buffalo, Albany and cities across the nation, particularly in the [southern States]. In Atlanta a session of the Legislature was brought to a halt by

5,000 exultant Georgians delivering 'a message from the American people.' Cannons thundered and hymns were sung across the former Confederacy to salute the ending of a quarter century of punishing retribution for the [War Between the States] under Republican Presidents."

The news was also joyously received at the Hampton home in Columbia and at Beauvoir on the Mississippi Gulf coast. Celebrating privately, undoubtedly grateful that at, the age of 76 years, he had lived to see the day finally come, Jeff Davis wisely kept a low profile, correctly understanding that his participation in public celebration would harm the Democracy. But Governor Hampton joined the celebratory crowd of fellow Democrats on the State House grounds in Columbia on Thursday, November 14, and spoke — assuring the African Americans present that "they would find the Democratic Party was their best friend." Hampton had been campaigning for the Democratic ticket across the State, speaking to crowds in Anderson, Abbeville, Aiken, Lancaster, Charleston, Beaufort and Eastover. At Anderson he had assured African American voters that "the national Democrats would protect their rights. . . . On occasion he was greeted by bands of red-shirted riders, reminiscent of the campaign of 1876." Then, Republicans had fraudulently rigged the vote totals in Florida and Louisiana, to deny Tilden the office of President, which he had earned. Not this time! Hampton was looking forward to returning to the Federal Senate if the South Carolina Legislature would vote to re-elect him in December. [R200;254, R199;296]

The Year of 1885

(1Q85)

On February 5 Wade Hampton wrote Grover Cleveland, encouraging him to include men from the southern States, including the former Confederate States, in his Cabinet, for "such action on your part will go far to unite the whole country." Hampton had been re-elected on December 9 to serve another 6-year term in the Federal Senate and he looked forward to interacting as a Senator with the upcoming Cleveland Administration. [R199;296, R200;254]

But Republicans, such a John Sherman of Ohio, remained intent on perpetuating sectional animosity. During January John Sherman denounced Jeff Davis as a traitor and slandered his name upon the floor of the Federal Senate in a most malicious way — a continuation of the political campaign to demonize Democrats by "waving the bloody shirt," a tactic that had failed to defeat Grover Cleveland's bid for President. William Sherman had alleged before an autumn, 1884 gathering of Federal army veterans that Jeff Davis had been a "conspirator" whose 'war' object had been "to get a fulcrum from which to operate against the [northern] States and to make [the people of the northern States bonded European Americans]. By such twisting of the truth, William Sherman had been recasting the "Federal Invasion of the Confederacy" into the "Federal Defense against the Confederate Conspiracy." The "intent to bond northern workers," to enslave them, had not been a new Republican allegation. In the late 1850's the more fantastic Republican demagogues, as they had been building the Republican Party, had occasionally alleged that Democratic politicians in the southern States harbored macabre plans to seize the Federal Government, subjugate the northern States and make bonded European Americans of the workers in those States. Of course, there had never been any evidence to support such fantastic lies, but that lie was useful in gaining votes by scaring the ebee-geebies out of enough naive people to make them vote against the Democrats in their State. And New England textile mill owners had delighted in scaring overworked and underpaid employees with alleged threats of their being enslaved by those southern devils. Then, as mentioned at the start of this paragraph, William Sherman's brother, Senator John Sherman, had come to the General's defense by blasting Davis on the Senate floor and calling him a "traitor." Davis answered John and William Sherman in a public letter, dated January 30, where he said:

> "The epithet of 'traitor,' which [John] Sherman in [Senate] debate applied to myself, is his mode of retaliation for my denunciation of his brother. I have been compelled to prove [William] Sherman to be a falsifier and a slanderer in order to protect my character against his willful and unscrupulous mendacity.

> "As **the Republican Party renounced the issue of treason when it abandoned my trial in 1867**, not at my instance, but in face of my defiance, its leaders of the present day but stultify themselves in the cry of traitor which they raise at the mention of my name. . . .

"[William Sherman] stands pilloried before the public and all future history as an imbecile scold, or an infamous slanderer — as either, he is harmless." [R13;831-847, R19;473]

In spite of occasional public fights such as the one with the Sherman brothers, Jeff and Varina were enjoying retirement at the beach house on the Mississippi coast. Biographer Hudson Strode would write:

"Never a devotee of early rising, [Jeff Davis] customarily rose at nine, read his mail, and answered some of it. Often he rode about his [land]; though he was approaching 80 he still enjoyed being in the saddle. In the evenings he would read poetry or history or enjoy a lively game of euchre; at which he was expert. He liked the salt water bathing and never tired of the sound of the sea." [R19;475]

Grover Cleveland was sworn into office on March 4. He would name a Cabinet of the men he thought best qualified for those jobs:

For Secretary of State, he was selecting Thomas Bayard, of Delaware, age 56.

Born in 1828 in Wilmington to a wealthy Delaware family, Thomas was the son of James Bayard, Jr., who would become a Federal Senator (Democrat Party, 1851-1864), and was a grandson of James Bayard, Sr., a former Federal Senator of that State (Federalist Party, 1805-1813). The baby's mother was Anne Francis Bayard. He had practiced law in Delaware with his father; then in Philadelphia with a friend, then returning in 1858 to his father's practice in Wilmington. A Peace Democrat, he and his father opposed the Federal Invasion of the Confederacy, but, recognizing the futility of Delaware secession, stood in opposition to such a movement. Thomas was elected to replace his father in the Federal Senate in 1868, serving there until resigning to take the post of Secretary of State. He had been a favorite nominee of southern States Delegates at the Democrat National Conventions of 1876, 1880 and, as you have already read, 1884.

For Treasury Secretary, he was selecting Daniel Manning, of his own State, New York, age 53.

Daniel Manning was born in 1831 in Albany, New York, to a modest family. At age 11 he dropped out of school and began work at the Albany *Atlas*, a local newspaper, which would merge into the Albany *Argus*. By age 34 he had risen to editor and by 1873, at age 42, to owner. A close friend of Samuel Tilden, he was Chairman of the New York State Democratic Party from 1881 to 1885 and a key supporter of Grover Cleveland during his campaigns for Governor and for President. He would resign from the newspaper prior to moving into Cleveland's Cabinet.

For Postmaster General, he was selecting William Vilas, of Wisconsin, age 44.

William Vilas was born in Vermont in 1840. His father, Levi Vilas, moved the family to Madison, Wisconsin in 1851. He graduated from the University of Wisconsin in Madison in 1858 and the law school at the University of Albany, New York in 1860. Not long afterward be became an officer in the Federal Army. After the conquest of the Confederacy he returned to Madison where he practiced law and worked as a Professor of Law at the University of Wisconsin (1868 to 1885). Active in politics but not holding office, Vilas presided over the 1884 Democratic National Convention. He would leave the University to serve in Cleveland's Cabinet.

For Secretary of War, he was selecting William Endicott of Massachusetts, age 58.

William Endicott was born in 1826 in Salem, Massachusetts to William and Mary Putnam Endicott. A direct descendant of Massachusetts Governor John Endicott, he was of a prominent Massachusetts family. He graduated from Harvard University and then Harvard Law School, beginning the practice of law in 1850. He married Ellen Peabody, granddaughter of Joseph Peabody who had become one of America's wealthiest men by his death in 1844. A Whig, then a Democrat by 1856, Endicott did not participate in the Federal invasion of the Confederacy. He was a Justice in the Massachusetts Supreme Court (1873 to 1882). A Democrat in Republican Massachusetts, Endicott failed to win a race for the Federal House

(1879) and a race for Governor (1884). He would leave his law practice to serve in Cleveland's Cabinet.

For Secretary of Navy, he was selecting William Whitney, also of New York, age 43.

Born in Massachusetts in 1841, William Whitney was the son of James Whitney, of a prominent industrial family, and Laurinda Collins, a descendant of Plymouth Governor William Bradford. His older brother, Henry Whitney, would become very prosperous (Metropolitan Steamship Company, Dominion Coal Company, Dominion Iron and Steel Company). William graduated from Yale University in 1863 and Harvard Law School in 1864. He did not join in the Federal invasion of the Confederacy. After Harvard he relocated to New York City where he began the practice of law. In 1869 he married Flora Payne of Ohio, daughter of Henry Payne, a lawyer and Democrat politician of that State. In New York City politics he was actively aligned with the County Democracy and opposed to Tammany Hall. He would leave his law practice to serve in Cleveland's Cabinet.

For Secretary of Interior, he was selecting Lucius Lamar of Mississippi, age 59.

Born in 1825 near Eatonton, Georgia, Lucius Lamar was the grandson of John Lamar, a Georgia farmer, and was the son of Lucius Lamar, Sr. and wife Sarah Bird, daughter of a Georgia physician. Grandfather John Lamar's other son was Mirabeau Lamar, the second President of the Republic of Texas. Lucius graduated from Georgia's Emory College and married Virginia Longstreet of Georgia, daughter of Emory's President, Rev. August Longstreet, formerly a lawyer, a judge and a Methodist minister. Lucius entered law in Georgia and became a judge. When Rev. Longstreet left Emory to become President of Mississippi University in Oxford, Lucius followed, taught at the school and practiced law, thereafter calling the State his home. Elected to the Mississippi Convention in 1860, he was a leader in advocating State Secession. He enlisted in the Confederate Army and participated in the defense of Richmond, but recurring illness limited his abilities. His brother Jefferson Lamar died in battle while leading a charge. Following the defeat of the Confederacy, Lamar returned to Mississippi and practiced law. He was the first Democrat to be elected to the Federal House from Reconstructed Mississippi, taking his seat in 1873. He was elected to the Federal Senate in 1877 remaining there until called to join Grover Cleveland's Cabinet.

For Attorney General, he was selecting Augustus Garland, of Arkansas, age 52.

Augustus Garland was born in 1832 in Covington, Tennessee to Rufus and Barbara Hill Garland. The family moved to Lost Prairie, Arkansas while Augustus was a baby but his father died soon after. His mother married Thomas Hubbard when Augustus was 4 years old. He attended college in Kentucky and studied law in Arkansas, joining his step-father for a while in the practice. He married Sarah Sanders in 1853 and relocated to Little Rock in 1856, becoming a prominent attorney. He supported the Constitutional Union Party in 1860, voting as an Elector for nominees John Bell and Edward Everett. He advocated against State Secession until Abe Lincoln attempted to call for Arkansas militia to invade the Confederacy. He represented Arkansas in the Confederate Congress until the defeat of the Confederacy. During Republican control of Arkansas, he petitioned the Federal Supreme Court to overturn the political disbarment of former Confederate officials, winning his case in a 5-4 decision (1866, *Ex parte Garland*), thereby opening the way for former Confederate officials to return to positions in the Federal judiciary. He was elected Governor of Arkansas (late 1874 to early 1877) and then to the Federal Senate, remaining there until called to Cleveland's Cabinet.

For the country's farmers, he would initiate a new Federal Department.

In 1885 Grover Cleveland would name Norman Colman of Missouri to the position of Commissioner of Agriculture. Coleman would oversee Federal support of the nation's agriculture industry — the very industry that the Republican Party had subordinated to manufacturing and commercial interests through high import taxation and political sectionalism. Coleman would encourage the creation of a Federal Department of Agriculture, and be named its first Secretary, but too late in Cleveland's term for Senate confirmation of the appointment.

On March 4 Grover Cleveland took the oath of office using the Bible given him as a child by his mother. In the words of biographer Allan Nevins, the Inaugural Address was "delivered in vibrant tones," impressing those listening to be a "fine" effort. But the most surprising aspect of that "fine" effort was the fact that Cleveland refused to use a manuscript, moving one noted listener to remark, "God, what a magnificent gambler!" The address was delivered from the heart, striking at the heart of the government corruption attendant to political patronage. No more honorable, honest and determined man had ever, or would ever, hold the office of President of the United States. The full text of the address, as recorded by a shorthand reporter, follows:

President Grover Cleveland's First Inaugural Address

Wednesday, March 4, 1885

In the presence of this vast assemblage of my countrymen, I am about to supplement and seal by the oath which I shall take the manifestation of the will of a great and free people. In the exercise of their power and right of self-government they have committed to one of their fellow-citizens a supreme and sacred trust, and he here consecrates himself to their service.

This impressive ceremony adds little to the solemn sense of responsibility with which I contemplate the duty I owe to all the people of the land. Nothing can relieve me from anxiety lest by any act of mine their interests may suffer, and nothing is needed to strengthen my resolution to engage every faculty and effort in the promotion of their welfare.

Amid the din of Party strife the people's choice was made, but its attendant circumstances have demonstrated anew the strength and safety of a government by the people. In each succeeding year it more clearly appears that our democratic principle needs no apology, and that in its fearless and faithful application is to be found the surest guaranty of good government.

But the best results, in the operation of a government wherein every citizen has a share, largely depend upon a proper limitation of purely partisan zeal and effort and a correct appreciation of the time when the heat of the partisan should be merged in the patriotism of the citizen.

Today the Executive branch of the Government is transferred to new keeping. But this is still the Government of all the people, and it should be none the less an object of their affectionate solicitude. At this hour the animosities of political strife, the bitterness of partisan defeat, and the exultation of partisan triumph should be supplanted by an ungrudging acquiescence in the popular will and a sober, conscientious concern for the general weal. Moreover, if from this hour we cheerfully and honestly abandon all sectional prejudice and distrust, and determine, with manly confidence in one another, to work out harmoniously the achievements of our national destiny, we shall deserve to realize all the benefits which our happy form of government can bestow.

On this auspicious occasion we may well renew the pledge of our devotion to the [Federal] Constitution, which, launched by the founders of the Republic and consecrated by their prayers and patriotic devotion, has for almost a century borne the hopes and the aspirations of a great people through prosperity and peace and through the shock of foreign conflicts and the perils of domestic strife and vicissitudes.

By the Father of his Country, our Constitution was commended for adoption as "the result of a spirit of amity and mutual concession." In that same spirit it should be administered, in order to promote the lasting welfare of the country and to secure the full measure of its priceless benefits to us and to those who will succeed to the blessings of our national life. The large variety of diverse and competing interests subject to Federal control, persistently seeking the recognition of their claims, need give us no fear that "the greatest good to the greatest number" will fail to be accomplished if in the halls of national legislation that spirit of amity and mutual concession shall prevail in which the Constitution had its birth. If this involves the surrender or postponement of private interests and the abandonment of local advantages, compensation will be found in the assurance that the common interest is subserved and the general welfare advanced.

In the discharge of my official duty I shall endeavor to be guided by a just and unstrained construction of the Constitution, a careful observance of the distinction between the powers granted to the Federal Government and those reserved to the States or to the people, and by a cautious appreciation of those functions which by the Constitution and laws have been especially assigned to the Executive branch of the Government.

But he who takes the oath today to preserve, protect, and defend the Constitution of the United States only assumes the solemn obligation which every patriotic citizen — on the farm, in the workshop, in the busy marts of trade, and everywhere — should share with him. The Constitution which prescribes his oath, my countrymen, is yours; the Government you have chosen him to administer for a time is yours; the suffrage which executes the will of freemen is yours; the laws and the entire scheme of our civil rule, from the town meeting to the State capitals and the national capital, is yours. Your every voter, as surely as your Chief Magistrate, under the same high sanction, though in a different sphere, exercises a public trust. Nor is this all. Every citizen owes to the country a vigilant watch and close scrutiny of its public servants and a fair and reasonable estimate of their fidelity and usefulness. Thus is the people's will impressed upon the whole framework of our civil polity — municipal, State, and Federal; and this is the price of our liberty and the inspiration of our faith in the Republic.

It is the duty of those serving the people in public place to closely limit public expenditures to the actual needs of the Government, economically administered, because this bounds the right of the Government to exact tribute from the earnings of labor or the property of the citizen, and because public extravagance begets extravagance among the people. We should never be ashamed of the simplicity and prudential economies which are best suited to the operation of a republican form of government and most compatible with the mission of the American people. Those who are selected for a limited time to manage public affairs are still of the people, and may do much by their example to encourage, consistently with the dignity of their official functions, that plain way of life which among their fellow-citizens aids integrity and promotes thrift and prosperity.

The genius of our institutions, the needs of our people in their home life, and the attention which is demanded for the settlement and development of the resources of our vast territory dictate the scrupulous avoidance of any departure from that foreign policy commended by the history, the traditions, and the prosperity of our Republic. It is the policy of independence, favored by our position and defended by our known love of justice and by our power. It is the policy of peace suitable to our interests. It is the policy of neutrality, rejecting any share in foreign broils and ambitions upon other continents and repelling their intrusion here. It is the policy of Monroe and of Washington and Jefferson — "Peace, commerce, and honest friendship with all nations; entangling alliance with none."

A due regard for the interests and prosperity of all the people demands that our finances shall be established upon such a sound and sensible basis as shall secure the safety and confidence of business interests and make the wage of labor sure and steady, and that our system of revenue shall be so adjusted as to relieve the people of unnecessary taxation, having a due regard to the interests of capital invested and workingmen employed in American industries, and preventing the accumulation of a surplus in the Treasury to tempt extravagance and waste. Care for the property of the nation and for the needs of future settlers requires that the public domain should be protected from purloining schemes and unlawful occupation.

The conscience of the people demands that the [Native Americans] within our boundaries shall be fairly and honestly treated as wards of the Government and their education and civilization promoted with a view to their ultimate citizenship, and that polygamy in the Territories, destructive of the family relation and offensive to the moral sense of the civilized world, shall be repressed.

The laws should be rigidly enforced which prohibit the immigration of a servile class to compete with American labor, with no intention of acquiring citizenship, and bringing with them and retaining habits and customs repugnant to our civilization.

The people demand reform in the administration of the Government and the application of business principles to public affairs. As a means to this end, civil-service reform should be in good faith enforced. Our citizens have the right to protection from the incompetency of public employees who hold their places solely as the reward of partisan service, and from the corrupting influence of those who promise and the vicious methods of those who expect such rewards; and those who worthily seek public employment have the right to insist that merit and competency shall be recognized instead of Party subserviency or the surrender of honest political belief.

In the administration of a government pledged to do equal and exact justice to all men, there should be no pretext for anxiety touching the protection of [African Americans] in their rights, or their security in the enjoyment of their privileges under the Constitution and its amendments. All discussion as to their fitness for the place accorded to them as American citizens is idle and unprofitable, except as it suggests the necessity for their improvement. The fact that they are citizens entitles them to all the rights due to that relation and charges them with all its duties, obligations, and responsibilities.

These topics and the constant and ever-varying wants of an active and enterprising population may well receive the attention and the patriotic endeavor of all who make and execute the Federal law. Our duties are practical and call for industrious application, an intelligent perception of the claims of public office, and, above all, a firm determination, by united action, to secure to all the people of the land the full benefits of the best form of government ever vouchsafed to man. And let us not trust to human effort alone, but humbly acknowledging the power and goodness of Almighty God, who presides over the destiny of nations, and who has at all times been revealed in our country's history, let us invoke His aid and His blessings upon our labors.

Biographer Allan Nevins would close his reporting of this historic day with these words:

"That evening, while [John Philip] Sousa's Marine Band played for the Inaugural Ball, the doors of the White House closed upon a President who felt hardly the respite of an hour from the demands of the office-seekers. Every friend had his pleas." [R211;189-198, R81;100-111]

Close

As President, Grover Cleveland would fight many battles from the fortress of the White House before he would successfully deliver his promised era of a Federal Government closely limited by a just and unstrained construction of the Constitution, which is economically administered, with proper limitations upon purely partisan zeal and without sectional prejudice and distrust. Even before his arrival in Washington, he would realize, "Henceforth I must have no friends," and accordingly, he would consistently turn down appeals to give Federal jobs to the patronage-starved Democratic Party faithful. He would persevere against a Republican-controlled Senate which would attempt to block his personnel moves by invoking the same "Tenure of Office Act" that Republicans had set up to entrap Andrew Johnson and bring about his Impeachment Trial. But Grover Cleveland would doggedly push toward his goals and almost all Federal employment would eventually become depoliticized and a Federal Civil Service System would become firmly established.

Four years later, Republicans would join forces with the Faction of Democratic politicians who were unhappy over not getting Federal jobs, and that combination would derail Grover Cleveland's bid for a second term. But Cleveland would not remain on the sidelines for long. Four years after defeat, he would again be nominated by the Democratic Party and be returned by thankful voters to another four years in the White House, the only non-incumbent to ever be reelected President.

Riding upon Grover Cleveland's determined shoulders, the Republican Party's politics of demagoguery, deception and corrupt administration would fall victim to the Democratic Party's politics of truth, honesty and economical administration, communicated so effectively through a simple slogan:

"Public Office is a Public Trust."

As if we were on the scene, we have now "lived" through a vast narrative history in search of the answer to the question those bloodstains on the floor of that Tennessee farmhouse cried out to a boy of ten: "Someday, you must tell us 'Why?'." And to understand "Why?" it has been necessary to undertake a long journey through history — a journey now complete.

- Together we have journeyed through the saga of *The Nation Builders* — there witnessing the creation of sovereign States out to the Pacific and a Federal government clearly limited by a Federal Constitution, that representing, perhaps, mankind's greatest achievement in the history of the world —

- Together we have jouneyed through the trials of *The Demagogues* — witnessing their campaign to destroy that greatest achievement of mankind, mistakenly believed to have been secure in a clearly limited Federal Constitution —

- Together we have journeyed through the horror of *The Bleeding* — mourning quietly as we advanced from page to page and buried our ancestor's loved ones —

- Together we have journeyed through *Political Reconstruction and the Struggle for Healing* — maddened by the viciousness and corruption endured — taking pride in the patient resolve of a conquered people —

- And together we have finally arrived at March 4, 1885, where a fitting close to our history resides.

We readers know that the Constitutional principle of State Sovereignty, which the Confederacy had striven to uphold, at such great cost, would forever be a "Lost Cause." We readers know that the victorious Federal Government would continue to grow to greater and greater size and power as it would find new ways to regulate, to tax, to spend, to redistribute wealth and to constrain State rights and personal liberty. But the horribly destructive forces of Political Sectionalism, Fratricidal War and Military Rule would never again rise up to lay waste the American people. So I expect you concur with my conclusion, on balance, that Grover Cleveland's 1884 election and subsequent arrival at the White House should conclude this story of that dreadful era questioned by the *Bloodstains* on the floors of that Tennessee farmhouse, which had cried out to that boy of ten, now an old man, simply pleading, "Someday you must tell us 'Why?'." We have "lived" through our history up to the year 1885 and, at this time, we leave those pages to the future in the belief that the sickness has past, and that:

The nation was healed.

The Afterward

Before closing this book, it is necessary to briefly conclude the biographies of the living — the four men and the one woman with whom we "lived" as we journeyed through our history. We start with Wade Hampton, move on to Lucius Lamar, then to Grover Cleveland and finally wrap up with Jeff and Varina Davis. From this point forward, the stories are told in the past tense, as normally encountered in biographies and histories.

Wade Hampton — The Remainder of His Life

Wade Hampton's activities in the Federal Senate need little mention from this point onward, allowing us to focus on more meaningful events.

Hampton lost his daughter Sally Hampton Haskell to illness on April 7, 1886. At age 41, she left her husband John Haskell with the responsibility for raising the four children. Three days earlier Hampton had written Grover Cleveland concerning his recent appointment to represent the Senate in the annual examination of cadets at West Point, explaining in part: "I have been detained here by the desperate and I fear hopeless illness of my eldest daughter." Two months later, on June 8, he would lose his brother Christopher, age 64. Christopher had been managing the Mississippi farms. Two months after that, Charleston suffered the worst earthquake to ever strike the eastern United States. The quake of August 31, 1886 killed 92 people and destroyed much of the city. Hampton appealed to Grover Cleveland to visit the South Carolina coast and offer encouragement, writing, "Coming on your own accord, to visit your fellow citizens who have suffered so greatly, would gratify them more than if you came on a formal invitation." But Grover never found the time.

In November 1886 Hampton became entangled in brush while hunting on family farmland in Mississippi and accidentally discharged his gun into his horse, which fell upon him. He managed to squirm free and walk 5 miles for help, recovering after a few days of bed rest. At age 68, Hampton was still tough.

In February 1887 Hampton supported a Senate bill that instructed the Federal Treasury to reimburse African Americans for financial losses resulting from Freedman's Bank swindles during the late 1860's and the 1870's. In support of the bill, Hampton told the Senate, "I want to see those people paid who were . . . so faithful during the whole war to our women and children, and who have been deceived; and if it is a gratuity from the United States Government, I for one shall vote for it with infinite pleasure." A small percentage of those targeted for help would be men and women who had belonged to Hampton prior to being made independent. He cared for them and they were generally respectful of him.

During Hampton's latter days in the Senate, he told his friend Senator George Vest, of Missouri, about a personal war-time incident worthy of mention:

> Hampton had come across a Federal soldier bathing in a creek and proceeded to capture him. The prisoner pleaded that he was only a commissary clerk, not a fighting man, and was on a brief furlough so he could visit his sweetheart. Touched, Hampton told the prisoner he could go on his way. But when the prisoner proceeded to gather up his uniform clothing along the creek bank, Hampton told him to leave them behind, for good clothing was sorely needed in the Confederate ranks. Understanding, the necked soldier started walking away. But Hampton, apparently enjoying the humor in the event, quickly told the man to return and dress. At this point in the story, Hampton told Vest, "He was profuse in his thanks, and said he would name his first boy after me." Advancing the story to the present time, Hampton continued, "Last evening, when I started up on the elevator at my hotel, a well dressed young fellow spoke to me and inquired if I was not Senator Wade Hampton." I said that I was. Then the young fellow asked Hampton if he remembered the story of the capture and release of the necked prisoner. I said that I did. Then the fellow replied, "Well, that prisoner was my father, and my first name is Wade Hampton. Good evening, sir." In the words of biographer, Walter Cisco, "The stranger [then] stepped from the elevator and disappeared, leaving Hampton speechless."

As the years passed by, European Americans became more concerned about the ability of the vast majority of African Americans to participate intelligently in government, whether at the county, State or national levels — or even as no more than informed and trustworthy voters. These discussions fell under the topic of "The Race Problem." Hampton participated as did many in the political sphere, irregardless of their section. An example of his observations can be seen in an article he wrote for the July 1890 issue of *The Arena*. Based on his observations at the time, Hampton wrote that "the masterful, the conquering, and the unconquerable Caucasians" would never be ruled by a race of people out of Africa. As evidence, he submitted: "If any proof is necessary to show that the [African] is incapable of self-government, one need only turn to the history of Liberia, San Domingo, and Haiti, to have all his doubts dispelled." He believed that unrestricted voting rights for African American men, as forced on the States by Republican political leaders during the late 1860's, had proven to be a "calamity." He added:

> "In [the Republican's] senseless advocacy of universal suffrage, they have not only thrown wide open the doors leading to American citizenship, admitting thus the Anarchist, the Communist, the Nihilist, and all the other scum of European nations, but they have injected into our body politic millions of ignorant, uneducated [African Americans], who have no more comprehension of our system of government than their African forefathers had."

Hampton saw benefits in encouraging African Americans to migrant out of the southern States to the north and to the west, to everywhere reduce their voting power to distinct minorities, thereby minimizing the impact of their political influence:

> "Scatter [them] over the land . . . to the fertile fields of the [western States] or to [the northeastern States], the home of [their] special friends, [so as to] lift a great burden from the [southern States], where [their] presence is a menace to our institutions. . . . [Let those sections] have the benefit of their presence, or learn by actual experience how baleful an influence they exercise. . . . This continent belongs to those who conquered the wilderness, who have taught to the world how a people can govern themselves, and who want no foreign element — people of African descent or recent arrivals from Europe or Asia — to debase their civilization."

In time, dispersal of the African American population would take place. Forty years later, the 1930 census would show, for the first time since 1820, that, in Mississippi, European Americans outnumbered African Americans.

Votes in the South Carolina General Assembly, concluded on December, 11, 1890, forced Wade Hampton to prepare to leave the Federal Senate at the conclusion of his present term, for he had not been reelected. The replacement would be John Irby, of the Benjamin Tillman Faction of the South Carolina Democratic Party. South Carolina's political complexion was undergoing dramatic changes. In November elections, the Tillman Faction had been dramatically victorious over the Traditional Democrat Faction. In the Governor's race, Tillman had crushed his opponent by a vote of 59,159 to 14,828, and Tillman Faction men were now dominating the State House and Senate. The vote ousting Hampton was Irby 102 and Hampton 42. For a short while Hampton worried over how to meet his family's financial obligations. He concluded his January 16, 1891 farewell speech on the Senate floor with the following words:

> "During the time I have had the honor to represent my State in this body not one word of recrimination, nor one calculated to keep alive sectional animosity, has escaped my lips. The thunders of war had scarcely ceased to reverberate when I, in opposition to the feelings and apprehensions of many of my fellow citizens, urged them, not only to deal justly with [African Americans], but to accord to them all the rights which would necessarily follow their [men being given the right to vote]. From that day to the present I have steadily and constantly advocated the same policy, not because it was politic, but because it was right."

The Charleston *News and Courier* praised Hampton's record in the Federal Senate, submitting that "the country will miss the counsel of one of the wisest and most conservative statesmen of his generation."

But Wade Hampton's retirement from government lasted only 2 years. On March 21, 1893 the Federal Senate unanimously approved Grover Cleveland's appointment of Hampton to the office of Railroad Commissioner. Joseph Johnston, the former high ranking Confederate commander, had held that post from 1885 until his death in March 1891. Cleveland's November 1892 election to a second term as Federal President had given Democrats another chance to award the Railroad job to a southern States man. Cleveland chose Hampton and the soon-to-be-75-year-old appointee was looking forward to a new career riding, inspecting and overseeing Federal interests in the nation's railroad network, particularly the network that had been made possible by Federal land grants.

On May 16, 1893, seated comfortably in a private railroad car provided by the Union Pacific, Wade Hampton, staff and guests set out from Washington Station on the Baltimore and Ohio Railroad for points west. His job, created by the Thurman Act of 1878, was to inspect and report annually on the status of those western railroads which were indebted to the Federal Government as a result of past "Federal loans and generous land grants." The first annual report to Interior Secretary Hoke Smith was due on November 1. Hampton had a lot to see — a lot of track, equipment and financial records to inspect — a lot of railroad men to talk with and evaluate. The outstanding debt of concern exceeded $115,000,000. But it would not be all work. There would be grand sites to see, fish to catch and dear family with which to spend time. Fortunately his staff included a secretary and a railroad engineer who would be preparing a "meticulously detailed inspection" and analysis of the condition of the 5 railroads involved in transcontinental traffic. He would enjoy time with 32-year-old daughter Daisy and 27-year-old granddaughter Ann Hampton Haskell, neither married, each of whom had invited a lady friend from Virginia to join in the adventure.

Traveling day and night, the party headed west to Chicago, taking time to visit the World's Columbian Exhibition. Then they continued west, crossed the Mississippi River and continued to Omaha. Upon leaving Omaha on the Union Pacific line, still in their private car, the party only traveled during the day to permit inspections. Their route took them through Denver and Cheyenne to Salt Lake City. There they visited the Mormon Temple and Tabernacle while observing that, "some of these Mormon houses have a front door for each wife . . . where the wives all live in the same house." Before leaving Salt Lake, Hampton, his secretary and a railroad superintendent set off on a fishing trip in Idaho, leaving the girls for a time to enjoy Salt Lake City. Unfortunately, "fishing in Billinger Creek and Malad River proved unproductive."

The party transferred to the Central Pacific Railroad, headed west to Nevada and climbed over the Sierra Mountains down into Sacramento and on to Oakland. They took the ferry to San Francisco, where they lodged in the "very large and magnificent" Palace Hotel, staying a few days to enjoy the city. From there, they traveled south along the coast to Los Angeles, then north again through the Central Valley to again enter Sacramento. Then it was further north to Portland, where they stayed a few days, then further north to Tacoma, Washington.

On June 24, the private car was coupled to the Cannon Ball Express, heading east across the Cascades, passing through Spokane, Idaho and into Montana, where they took a break for a 2-day to visit of the geysers at Yellowstone, which included a little fishing, "leaving the ladies to look around."

> "We rode two miles up the river and hitched our horses and started in. We fished until nearly 8 o'clock, and between us caught a dozen fine 2-pound trout . . . . [Hampton was much elated] and only stopped when we could not see any longer."

Then it was eastward through the Badlands, across the Missouri River, through Bismarck and into Minneapolis on July 1. They arrived back at Washington Station on July 8, having completed an 8-week, 10,200-mile journey through 18 States. Hampton would report that the Union Pacific and Central Pacific properties were "in excellent physical condition." Biographer Walter Cisco would provide details of Hampton's first annual report:

> In this first report to Interior Secretary Hoke Smith, Hampton "blamed the failure of the [1878] Thurman Act on shortcomings in the law itself," which had not foreseen the competitive struggles resulting from the subsequent capacity expansion to 5 transcontinental railroads. "'The completion and opening of these roads to traffic revolutionized the condition which [had] prevailed' a generation earlier. [Believing that] foreclosure was a poor solution to the problem, . . . Hampton recommended that the President be allowed to appoint a Commission 'with full power to settle the indebtedness.' If Congress would not agree to that, he suggested that they place all of the Pacific railroads under the Thurman Act, and make them pay 50 percent of net earnings, instead of the 25 percent as then required. 'The companies named are abundantly able to do this,' [Hampton advised]."

Four years later, Wade Hampton submitted his final annual report, dated November 1, 1897, and resigned a week later. At the age of 79 years, retirement must have looked attractive. Grover Cleveland's term as President had concluded earlier in the year and Republican William McKinley was now in office. A forthcoming Republican appointee needed time to inspect the railroads.

Wade Hampton returned to South Carolina to fill the role of honored hero of the "Lost Cause" and the post-war struggles against Republican subjugation. He would continue to speak to gatherings of Confederate veterans and members of the Sons of Confederate Veterans organization, which was being established as a follow-through of the father's organization. At a SCV meeting he charged the son's:

> "It will be the task of your organization and kindred ones . . . to preserve the honor and to preserve from detraction the memory of those who sacrificed everything. . . . [Do not believe allegations that], because of the failure of our cause there was no truth or justice in it. Any human undertaking, however just it may be, may fail, but the everlasting principle of right and justice can never be blotted out. A great truth, like the God-head whence it emanates, is eternal, and it will live 'till the last syllable of recorded time.' . . .

> "[For myself, I] feel some pride in the result of that memorable political contest of 1876 — in my judgment the most memorable ever waged on this continent, for home rule, for personal liberty and State Rights, for it was my good fortune to bear the standard, placed by our people in my hands, to victory, and whatever Fate may have in store for me, nothing can ever deprive me of the honest pride I feel that I contributed, in part, to the glorious victory won then by the people of my State."

But Hampton had more trials yet to endure. On May 2, 1899, at 3 AM, he awoke to find his house was on fire. He and Daisy escaped and nearby African Americans helped save some furniture. But "all his papers, books, and most of his possessions were lost. The humble brick abode had consisted of four rooms, plus a wood-framed addition. If it had been closer to the Hampton family's main house, Southern Cross, Federal troops would have noticed it in 1865 and also burned it down during their campaign to destroy Columbia. He wrote a friend, "I have saved some clothes, my gun and fishing tackle. . . . We are in an outhouse, quite comfortable. If I had only saved my tent, I would be all right." Yet, Hampton persevered. He traveled to Charleston a few days later to join with Stephen D. Lee, Joseph Wheeler and others in the 1899 National Reunion of Confederate veterans, where former Confederate soldiers gave him "one of the grandest ovations of his life."

Friends and comrades would purchase a building lot in Columbia at the corner of Barnwell and Senate Streets and construct a modest home for their aged hero, just a "few blocks from Hampton's church and near to neighbors and friends. . . . The sight of the old man sitting on the porch of his new home became a familiar sight to Columbians."

In 1901 a crowd of admiring veterans came to the house to cheer on their old leader. From the front porch, Hampton offered a few words, in part saying:

> "I want you to try to teach to your children and to your children's children that ours was not a lost cause. I want you to tell them that we were fighting for the right. . . . The greatest honor that I felt during the war was once when I came upon a poor private who was dying. I stopped beside him and he said: 'I am happy to die fighting and I am proud to die fighting under you.' I pray God to bless you."

On the other hand, Hampton had personally dispatched many an enemy. Biographer Walter Cisco would give a count:

> "Once a cavalry veteran asked Hampton how many Yankees he had personally dispatched in hand-to-hand combat during the war. The old man remembered 11 — '2 with my sword and 9 with my pistol.'

> " 'How about the 2 at Trevilian Station?', [the veteran] replied, trying to jog the General's memory.

> "Oh, well, I did not count them, they were running."

Wade Hampton, 84, passed away at home on April 11, 1902, a victim of valvular heart disease. Realizing for 10 days that their father was dying, the family had been gathering. "Sisters Kate and

Caroline, daughter Daisy and sons McDuffie and Alfred were among those there." Prior to passing he had asked for a simple funeral, a favorite hymn, "Lead, Kindly Light," and a blessing:

"All my people, black and white — God bless them all."

Governor Miles McSweeney declared April 13 a day of mourning. Special trains brought mourners, including many veterans, from all over the State. Newspapers estimated 20,000 were present. A horse-drawn hearse, driven by a former Hampton bonded African American, conveyed the body to Trinity Church, where room for 1,200 was found, the rest remaining outdoors. In the words of biographer Robert Ackerman, "The funeral itself represented the end of an era." [R199;295;324, R200;255;272]

We now move to the final, triumphant days in the life of Lucius Lamar.

Lucius Lamar — The Remainder of His Life

All of Grover Cleveland's nominations to his Cabinet were approved unanimously on March 6, 1885, only 2 days after the Inaugural, in spite of the fact that Republicans held a solid 43 to 34 majority in the Federal Senate. Lucius Lamar began immediately to assume the office of Secretary of the Interior. The other members of the Cleveland Cabinet were Thomas Bayard of Delaware, Secretary of State; Daniel Manning of New York, Secretary of the Treasury; Augustus Garland of Arkansas, Attorney-General; William Edicott of Massachusetts, Secretary of War; William Vilas of Wisconsin, Postmaster-General, and William Whitney of New York, Secretary of the Navy. Because this was peacetime, free of important difficulties with foreign nations, the posts of State, War and Navy were of minor importance during this first Cleveland Administration. Because of a pledge for civil service reform, the Federal Postal Service had become far less important for political patronage, thereby reducing the importance of Whitney's post. The monetary situation was rather stable, reducing the importance of Manning's Treasury. That meant that the two most important Cabinet posts were the offices of the Attorney General, held by Arkansan Garland, and Interior, held by Mississippian Lamar. Internal legal issues were important during the transition to Democratic control and the final integration of the former Confederate States into the national fabric, and oversight of those issues was Arkansan Garland's job. But even that job was less important than was the one assigned to Mississippian Lucius Lamar — Interior:

- Under Lamar would be administration of vast Alaska (gold would be discovered later) and all of the National Territories situated between Canada and Mexico, which would later become the States of North Dakota, South Dakota, Montana, Washington, Idaho, Wyoming, Utah and Oklahoma, the latter 8 collectively containing a land mass exceeding 1,000,000 square miles, equivalent to the total area of the 29 smallest States among the 40 then part of the Federal Union, those 29 ranging from miniscule Rhode Island to sizable Florida.

  Much of the land under the control of the Interior Department in 1885 was held by railroad corporations which had taken the land as Federal gifts meant to compensate them for the large investment expenditure of railroad construction, but corporations had not yet earned the rights to much of that claimed land because of failures to meet construction performance deadlines — a performance failure that had been rather ignored by previous Republican administrations for political reasons. Much land was also claimed by individuals and corporations through fraudulent, illegal applications, again a problem that had been rather ignored by previous Republican administrations. Finally, considerable land claims held by private citizens were of questionable validity. Secretary Lamar and his staff set out immediately to rectify this Republican largess and return lands to the public domain in every case where return was proper and fitting. By the time of the Department's third annual report, dated November 1, 1887, Interior had "restored" the following land acreage to the public domain:

Land taken back from railroad corporations, acres	30,281,000
Land taken back due to fraud, illegality, etc., acres	14,239,000
Land taken back from inappropriate private land claims	576,000
Total land restored to the public domain, acres	45,096,000

  By the way, this amount of restored land, over 45,000,000 acres, approximated the combined size of the States of Ohio and Indiana. Furthermore, as of October 1887, the Interior

Department was contesting ownership of 9,499,000 acres through investigations and court proceedings. Clearly, Lucius Lamar recognized that public land represented the greatest wealth collectively belonging to the people of the United States and that it should be preserved to the public benefit through its honest, lawful administration. You will recall that this issue had long divided Republicans and Democrats. From 1854 onward, Republicans had been persistently agitating for high import taxes to "protect domestic industry," financing the Federal Government on the backs of domestic consumers, while practically giving away western land to whoever wanted to live there. On the other hand, you will also recall that Democrats sought to dramatically cut taxes on imports, thereby lowering prices paid by consumers everywhere, while charging more reasonable prices at public land sales to balance Federal revenue needs. In other words, Republicans traditionally were often agreeable to almost give land away for political purposes while Democrats wanted a fair market price for this most valuable of national resources.

- Under Lamar would be administration of the nation's small, remaining 260,000 Native American population and their reservations, including many disputes over education, land ownership (individual versus tribal), fencing and grazing rights. Expressing concerns over their welfare and potential extinction, he wrote, "The principal difficulties to be overcome were the strong tendency of the [Native American] toward wildness, cruelty and idleness; and the persistent invasion of the reservations by great syndicates of cattle raisers under the cover of leases from the tribes." In what would become Oklahoma, so-called 'Sooners' threatened to invade and settle the land in defiance of Federal law, which had long reserved it for exclusive Native American use. This conflict Lamar was forced to deal with:

You will recall that Oklahoma, which in the Choctaw language means "Red People," had been set aside in the 1830's for the Five Civilized Tribal Nations — Choctaw, Creek, Seminole, Chickasaw and Cherokee. With the promise that Oklahoma would forever be their homelands, these Native Americans had been removed from southern States east of the Mississippi River during the 1830's, some migrating there voluntarily and many forcibly. In subsequent decades Federals had also moved northern and western tribes into Oklahoma, creating a mixture of the established Five Civilized Tribal Nations — which had established towns and were practicing agriculture — and the many newly arriving migratory hunter-gather tribes, in total numbering about 62 tribes within the boundaries of the United States. During the War Between the States, most Native Americans of the Five Civilized Tribal Nations had sided with the Confederacy and many had fought for it, recognizing that their Confederate neighbors would be more willing to protect Native land rights than the aggressive, double-dealing Federals. You will recall that the last Confederate to surrender had been General Stan Watie of the Cherokee Nation, who had surrendered his army on June 23, 1865.

Sponsored by the Federal Senate, and passed in that body just before the Republican 43-34 majority would drop to a small, 39-37 majority, the General Allotment Act of 1887, was signed on February 8, 1887, during Lamar's last year overseeing Interior matters. Also called the Dawes Act, this legislation began the process of taking (basically seizing) Oklahoma land reserved by Treaty for Native American nations and opening it up for European American settlement. The sponsor of the Act was Senator Henry Dawes, Republican of Massachusetts and Chairman of the Senate Committee on [Native American] Affairs. You may recall that Dawes had succeeded Charles Sumner in 1875. He would hold that seat until 1893. The act called for a survey of Native American tribal lands, particularly in Oklahoma, for the purpose of opening over half of it to settlement by European Americans, and distributing much of the remaining tribal land as small parcels to be owned by individual Native Americans. Sadly, over a period of several decades, Dawes' land redistribution program would deprive Native Americans and their respective nations of about 90,000,000 acres of land that had been given to them through various treaties and about 90,000 Native Americans would become homeless. The 1887 act initially excluded the Five Civilized Tribal Nations from its reach, but under Dawes subsequent activism, they, too, would eventually become victims of the Federal land grab — a large section of Cherokee land would be taken from the Cherokee Nation in 1893.

Except for initial survey planning, Lucius Lamar would not oversee the Department of Interior during implementation of the Dawes Act of 1887. In his November 1, 1887 annual report, in the section covering Native American relations, Lamar recommended that only a portion of each reservation be sub-divided for individual ownership because, "we must lead the Indians into holding lands in severalty by ripening their right of occupancy under their communal system into a fee simple by a gradual process. . . . Those who urge the speedy breaking up of tribal relations, the obliteration of the reservation system, and the localization of individuals upon separate allotments of land as a general policy, overlook the important fact that the Indian race is not a homogeneous race. It consists of numerous widely separated tribes, speaking separate languages, and varying greatly in customs, habits and conditions, from the enlightened Commonwealth of Five [Civilized] Nations to the wild, fierce, roving bands who eke out by plunder the scanty subsistence that they derive from the chase and government rations. . . . Each must be managed as its peculiar circumstances and conditions require."

- Under Lamar was also the new Federal Bureau of Labor, which had been established in 1884 and placed under the Interior Department. The Bureau's scope of activities was expanding from mainly conducting studies of labor issues, to investigation of management-labor disputes and on toward arbitrating such disputes.

- Lamar was also involved in setting up the new Interstate Commerce Commission, established in early 1887, recommending that it be authorized to report directly to President Cleveland. The ICC was created in an attempt to exercise greater control over railroads, including rate regulation and curbing fee discrimination.

On January 5, 1887 Lucius Lamar married Henrietta [Dean] Holt of Macon, Georgia, the widow of William Holt, a former Confederate military officer and former President of the Southwestern Railroad Company. She was the daughter of James Dean, a farmer "of wealth, a politician of importance, and a citizen of public spirit." Lamar's son-in-law and biographer Edward Mayes would describe his wife's step-mother:

"As a young lady, Miss Hennie Dean was admired for her attractions of person and mind, not only in her native city of Macon, but also throughout the State of Georgia, and beyond. She married [William] Holt when quite young. At the time of her second marriage she retained much of her youthful beauty. She was fair, with a figure somewhat inclining to [plumpness], but not too stout; with a fine presence, and an abundance of the silken, silvery hair which is sometimes very lovely, and was so in her case. Of mild and retiring, although self-possessed, manners, loving the domesticities and disliking all forms of display and publicity, a devout member of the Church, a devoted mother, a tender, thoughtful, and helpful wife, having many precious early memories in common with her [second] husband, she was to Mr. Lamar in his old age a great grace and a great consolation."

Grover Cleveland appointed Lucius Lamar to the Federal Supreme Court on December 6, 1887. On January 18, 1888, he was sworn is as a new Associate Justice to assume the seat last occupied by William Woods, of Ohio, who had died on May 14, 1887. Woods, a Yale graduate, Ohio lawyer and politician, had joined the Federal Army in 1862 and, by 1864, had risen to command a full division of William Sherman's troops during their devastation of a 60-mile swath of Georgia from Atlanta to Savannah. Woods had remained in the southern States, begun farming cotton and received appointments to increasingly important judicial jobs, culminating, in an 1869 appointment by Ulysses Grant to the Federal Supreme Court. So, the contrast in political philosophy could not have been stronger between Woods — a former senior Federal military officer over America's most horrific military campaign against a civilian population — and Lamar — a former Confederate military officer and defender of the nation's heritage, which stipulated that Federal power be sharply limited by strict construction of the Federal Constitution. History suggests that Lamar's appointment by Grover Cleveland on December 6 had represented the final hurdle in bringing former Confederates into the mainstream of Federal political influence. Although election of a former Confederate to the office of Federal President would have been a more important validation of success in the struggle for healing, that would never occur. No former Confederate would ever be elected Federal President — therefore, elevation of Lamar to the Federal Supreme Court, was the greatest evidence that northern-States

"Bloody Shirt" political demagoguery had at last been buried. But would the Federal Senate confirm Lamar? That had been far from assured in December.

Biographer James Murphy would describe the Senate's confirmation fight:

> "On January 7, 1888, [Lamar] gave [Grover] Cleveland his resignation with the explanation that he feared to embarrass the Administration if he should remain in the [Cabinet]. Three days later the [Republican-led Senate] Judiciary Committee reported an adverse recommendation. The full Senate vote did not at first look much more promising. Membership at that time included 37 Democrats, 38 Republicans and one Independent. Before the Senate went into executive session, however, it became apparent that Party lines might not hold. Then when final action came on January 16, Republicans William Stewart of Nevada and Leland Stanford of California crossed over; H. H. Riddleberger, the Independent from Virginia, also voted with the Democrats. The [small] breach in Republican discipline gave Lamar a 32 to 28 victory."

Feelings favoring sectional reconciliation were much stronger in the States west of the former Confederacy than in the States to the north. Men living in the far west at the time of State secession had participated very little in the subsequent fighting. Afterward, many former Confederates had migrated to the far west. Furthermore, passions for limited government power — a noticeable ingrained regional characteristic — were more strongly held in that growing region. Finally, both Senator Stewart and Senator Stanford, both living in California during the War Between the States, had avoided being drawn into the conflict. It had not been their fight.

For insight into Senator Stewart's opinion of extinguishing the flames of sectional hatred once and for all, we turn to a letter he had written to a California constituent on January 7, the day Lamar stepped down from the post of Secretary of the Interior:

> "The public press has so framed the issue that the rejection of Mr. Lamar will be construed both in the North and the South as a declaration that his participation in the [War Between the States] disqualifies him and all others occupying the same position for a place on the Supreme Bench. It is unreasonable to expect that the people of 11 States of the Union shall, during all the present generation, be excluded from participation in the judicial determinations of the highest court of the United States."

Lucius Lamar would be involved in 890 Supreme Court decisions during the 4 years of his service as Associate Justice. He would author 94 decisions, a typical number for an Associate. Except for cases involving State Rights, where Lamar generally sided with limiting Federal Power, he tended to vote with the majority, only authoring 3 dissenting opinions. Justices found Lamar's broad experience outside of the practice of law to be a helpful resource during discussions of cases under consideration. That admiration would be evident in the comments of one of his colleagues, revealed in an 1891 publication:

> "Fully, Mr. Cleveland made no mistake in appointing [Justice Lamar]. Whatever doubts existed as to his fitness for the Supreme Bench, growing out of his long political and parliamentary career and absence from the active practice of his profession, have wholly disappeared. This will be conceded by all who have read his opinions. He has sound judgment, a calm temperament, and a strong sense of justice. He possesses the judicial faculty in a very high degree. He takes broad, comprehensive views of legal and constitutional questions, and states his conclusions with unusual clearness and force, and in language most aptly chosen to express the precise idea of his mind. His brethren are greatly attached to him."

Lucius Lamar passed away peacefully on January 23, 1893 at the home of W. H. Virgin, a son-in-law of his wife's, in Vineville, a suburb of Macon, Georgia. He was 67 years old. He and wife Henrietta had left Washington in December, intending to visit Georgia (her home in Macon, his father's grave and places of his younger days), then proceeding to the Mississippi coast, where he had hoped to regain his strength, and then return to Washington for the upcoming session of the Federal Supreme Court. His son-in-law and biographer Edward Mayes would report, "For the last 31 years of his life [Mr. Lamar] was more or less seriously troubled with organic weaknesses. He was never free of this embarrassment after his attack of vertigo in Virginia, shortly subsequent to the Battle of Williamsburg." Mayes wrote that serious attacks were quite debilitating and "less dangerous cases . . . were frequent. However, the gravity of those attacks diminished as Mr. Lamar grew older. That of 1890 was the last of the graver sort."

Early in the day, accompanied by his wife's cousin, Lucius had taken the electric street car to Macon, to visit a friend and had returned in renewed spirits, eating a hearty supper. But afterward he had "complained of suffocation" when lying down and was helped to a chair near the fire. "In this position his life passed out without a struggle, and so quietly and peacefully that those about him did not know the exact moment at which the soul took its flight."

Biographer James Murphy would conclude that, although Lamar had on occasion suffered from lung hemorrhaging, he had not responded to the normal treatment of the day for patients suffering from tuberculosis, thereby giving greater weight to doctors' suspicions of a "gradual deterioration of the arteries and kidneys over a period of years."

In Washington, Secretary of the Interior John Noble, of Missouri, issued the following directive, dated January 24, 1893:

> "It becomes my painful duty to announce the death on yesterday, at Vineville, Macon, Georgia, of Lucius Quintus C. Lamar, Secretary of the Interior from March 6, 1885, to January 10, 1888, when he resigned to take the place as Associate Justice of the Supreme Court of the United States. It belongs to others with whom he served in Congress, on the Bench, and in other relations in private and official life, to speak of his merits there. It is with pleasure that testimony is here borne to his valuable labors in this Department, which were faithfully performed with that clearness of apprehension, sense of justice, and goodness of heart for which he was distinguished. In token of appreciation of his services and respect for his memory, the Department will be draped in mourning for 20 days on and from this date, the flag carried at half-mast, and the Department closed on the day of his funeral."

The body "lay in state" at the home of his wife's son-in-law, W. H. Virgin, in Vineville, where visitors and relatives were received. Services at Mulberry Street Church followed, complete with many musical interludes. Dr. Chandler, President of Emory College, delivered an extensive and meaningful eulogy. This was followed by another eulogy by Bishop Fitzgerald. From there a procession accompanied the body to Riverside Cemetery. The Macon *Telegraph* reported that the funeral and burial, a 6-hour observance, "was without doubt one of the notable events in the history of this city. . . . It was perhaps the largest funeral ever seen in Macon." The report included the following revelation:

> "Justice Lamar had for many years carried in his inside vest pocket a small copy of the Constitution of the United States. Next to his Bible, it was the book that he loved best, and he referred to it often. Those who knew him well also knew of this little book. In life he was never without it, and yesterday the little book was buried with him. Held in his right hand, it lies close to the heart that loved its teachings and upheld its rights at all times."

In Washington City, on March 18, the Bar of the Supreme Court held a remembrance of the late Justice in which William Vilas of Wisconsin — a friend of Lamar's and Postmaster General in the first Cleveland Administration — presented a eulogy in which he said, in part:

> "It was given to him to see, with a clearness which few besides him shared, the true relations between his conquered people and the triumphant [northern States] . . . . Thus, in Lamar, to a degree unsurpassed, was displayed the magnanimity of the conquered which can nobly inspire and receive that other magnanimity which the conqueror may nobly show. It was he who could be tolerated, while yet the passions of civil war were still uncooled, to defend in Congress from reproach which he deemed unjust — even Jefferson Davis himself — because it was he also who could, in the same body, reach to a just comprehension of the greatness of Charles Sumner, and dare to do his memory noble honor, reckless of the frowns of embittered critics behind him.

> "And so it is that to none more upon his side is to be ascribed the achievement of that concord which has at last come to bless our land with such beneficence that he is now recognized its enemy who will touch the chord of remembrance for a single discordant tone to mar the harmony of our common love for our common country."

A subsequent eulogy, written by his close personal and political friend, Edward Walthall, now a Federal Senator representing Mississippi, said, in part:

"The late Justice Lamar must be ranked among the most noticeable figures of the generation in which he lived . . . . He was the strongest man that I ever knew. He was strong in the power of concentrated thought and of accurate, vigorous and graceful expression; strong in force of will and continuity of purpose and of effort; but strongest in searching for the essential truth, of every question with which he had to deal, and in standing by it fearlessly when he found it."

Chief Justice Melville Fuller of Maine added the following eulogy to complete the observance:

"Although he was not spared to give many years to its labors, Mr. Justice Lamar was long enough upon this Bench to exhibit, on a comparatively new field, his undoubted intellectual power, and to demonstrate the possession of marked judicial qualities. The remarkable career which preceded his appointment, crowded with varied incident and filled with distinguished service in public station . . . well prepared him for the consideration of those grave public questions that so often press for solution before this tribunal. Experience in affairs had made him sage; and the wisdom thus acquired was aided by that 'desire to seek, patience to doubt, fondness to meditate, slowness to assert, readiness to reconsider' . . . . Such was indeed his nature; and leadership came to him, not merely by reason of his courage, his eloquence, his statesmanlike views, and general ability, but largely, perhaps chiefly, because of his simplicity and singlemindedness, his integrity of thought as well as honesty in action, and that unobtrusive and unselfish devotion to duty which give entrance to the kingdom that 'cometh without observation'."

In October 1894, Lucius Lamar's remains were removed from Macon and brought to Oxford, Mississippi, where, on the 26th, they were laid beside those of his first wife and mother of his children. The Memphis *Commercial-Appeal* reported the event:

"There was laid to rest today in the beautiful St. Peter's Cemetery, among a solid bank of flowers, all that was mortal of the late Justice L. Q. C. Lamar, the [southern States'] greatest orator and statesman. The funeral services were in the Methodist Church, and were conducted by Rev. J. E. Thomas. The procession to the cemetery was then formed on Depot Street, and was fully a mile long, over 2,000 people taking part, and some of the most distinguished men in the State being present.

"All business houses and residences were draped, and all the schools (including the University) suspended and formed a large part of the procession, showing that the memory of this great man is ever near to the hearts of the people of Oxford, who knew and loved him best."

Edward Mayes, Lamar's son-in-law, closed his definitive biography with the following words — of which no one can improve:

"In the world's history, as it is commonly written and commonly read, it is natural and inevitable that the figures which most attract attention and dazzle the imagination should be those which form the centers of events more or less dramatic — great soldiers, whose genius and valor decide the fate of empires on stricken fields; great explorers, whose enterprise gives new realms to civilization; great inventors, whose arts revolutionize the social life of mankind; great physicians, whose discoveries go far to dull the scythe of death. It is not with them, or such as they are, that Mr. Lamar's place must be found.

"But there is another, and even a more valuable historic field; one which is, in effect, the spirit, as distinguished from the body, of all history. It is the story of the great undercurrents of the mighty moral movements which create nations, and profoundly modify their destinies for weal or woe, and lead them on to increasing glory or to ruin. In this domain is Mr. Lamar's place. It must be remembered of him that, with other noble and true men, he greatly contributed to the restoration of hope and vital force to the stricken half of a great people, torn and disheartened by civil strife; and that, perhaps more than any other, at the peril of his personal reputation and fortunes, he rose on stepping-stones of his dead self to better things, and inspired his people with his own high resolve to cast away resentful sectionalism and to enter into a broader and more wholesome life with the renewed spirit of a nation." [R205;471-592]

And as a reader of *Bloodstains, Political Reconstruction and the Struggle for Healing*, you now recognize that the three most important events testifying that "Healing" had been accomplished were:

1. Wade Hampton's peaceful return of South Carolina's State Government to home rule,
2. Democrat Grover Cleveland's election as Federal President, and
3. Lucius Lamar's appointment to Secretary of Interior and then to the Federal Supreme Court.

We now move to the close of Grover Cleveland's career and life.

Grover Cleveland — The Remainder of His Life

Since Grover Cleveland was a bachelor, his sister Rose Hoyt served as hostess at White House functions until he married. That historic event took place at the White House on the evening of June 2, 1886, President Cleveland, 49, marrying Frances Folsom, 21. Frances was the daughter of Oscar Folsom of Buffalo, who had been a law partner of Grover's during younger days and a close friend. In fact Grover had visited and admired the new baby girl shortly after the birth. After Oscar was killed in a tragic buggy accident when Frances was 11 years old, Grover had stepped in to act as an advisor to the widow and daughter. They had remained friends after Grover became Governor and relocated to Albany, being invited as special guests to the Executive residence to be on hand when William Vilas and the Notification Committee arrived to formally ask Cleveland to accept the Democratic Party's nomination for President. For a fortnight in April 1885, mother and daughter had been guests at the White House. In June Frances had graduated from Wells College in Aurora, New York. Cleveland had proposed in August, but the engagement was kept a secret until just before the wedding.

In 1886 Grover Cleveland purchased for $21,500 a country house on 27 acres of land, located almost 2 miles from Georgetown and a little over 3 miles from the White House. He considered it an investment and a convenient escape from the summer heat and political intensity within his official residence.

Beginning on September 30, 1887, Grover and Frances Cleveland set out on a three-week tour of the upper Mississippi Valley and several southern States. Visits were first made to Chicago, and as far west as St. Paul and Omaha. Descending the Mississippi River, they visited St. Louis. Of special note was the stop at Nashville, Tennessee, where the Cleveland's engaged Democrats who were exuding renewed hope. Historian Allan Nevins would explain:

> "The climax of the trip was his visit to the [southern States]. At Nashville he called on the widow of President Polk, and Mrs. Cleveland and Mrs. Polk compared notes on White House life. Near that city, he spent Sunday at one of the most famous of [southern States] farms, Belle Meade, owned by Judge Howell E. Jackson, a former Senator. Great crowds at every station cheered him as he passed southward by way of Chattanooga to Atlanta, where he was to visit the Piedmont Exposition. In Montgomery, Senators Pugh and Morgan welcomed Cleveland to the old Confederate Capital. Then, with stops at Tecumseh and Asheville, the special train, laden with mementos, lumbered northward, reaching Washington [City] on October 22."

I was touched by the visit to Belle Meade because, in 1947, my father would build our modest home on the edge of what was once that large farm. (During the construction Dad, Mother, my brother and I lived with my grandfather in Murfreesboro, the site of the "Bloodstains.") Grover was touched by a sign he glimpsed as the train entered Chattanooga — "Our Grover; he has filled the bloody chasm."

The former Confederate States were experiencing renewed economic vitality as former Confederates were viewed as remarkably patriotic. Steel mills were rapidly expanding in Birmingham and manufacturing was growing in Atlanta. Cottonseeds, recently discovered to be of value, were being crushed for their oil content, 600,000 tons taking that route in 1885. In the 5-year period of 1882 to 1886, the wealth of the region was estimated to have grown by 40 percent. And northern industrialists and philanthropists were sending money south, including Cornelius Vanderbilt who enabled the University bearing his name in Nashville (I graduated from Vanderbilt with a degree in chemical engineering in 1860).

But feelings of sectional strife still surfaced on occasion, encouraged by political ambitions, and advocates of increased pensions for Federal soldiers, even for the dependent parents of Federal soldiers. The Dependent Pensions Bill passed the House and then the Senate in early 1887, only to be vetoed by Cleveland, noting that he could not believe proud Federal Army veterans wanted to squander an honorable pension system on "an indiscriminate body of charity-seekers." The veto was upheld. This was followed by a squabble over returning captured regimental flags to Confederate veterans groups. A large collection of deteriorating flags stored in the War Department basement and attic had long been withheld from distribution to Confederate groups, but freely sent to Federal groups upon request. All flags needed to be removed and more carefully stored, so most folks figured. Cleveland's June 1887 executive order to freely send flags to both veterans groups, which he viewed as contributing to sectional healing, was met by an uproar in the northern States.

This fuss was followed by controversy over Cleveland's nomination of Lucius Lamar to the Federal Supreme Court in December. Clearly, Republicans already were in campaign mode, working to defeat a Cleveland second term in the upcoming fall 1888 elections. Cleveland biographer Allan Nevins would write of Lamar and this historic event:

> "Cleveland's nomination of Lamar to the Supreme Court at the close of 1887 brought forth a new spasm of the old [Confederate hatred]. The fine old Mississippi sage was so admirably suited for the place that it was difficult to find fault with him. Yet [John] Ingalls [of Kansas], a [Massachusetts lawyer who had moved to Bleeding Kansas Territory and there fanned the flames of bloody Political Sectionalism], declared that [Lamar] represented all that was bad in the past, dangerous in the present, and menacing in the future of the country. Others, including [John] Sherman [of Ohio] and [George] Edmunds [of Vermont], announced that they would do everything in their power to prevent confirmation. The Judiciary Committee delayed action until the Party vote could be worked up to the point of rejection, and then made an adverse report. Fortunately, several [western States] Republicans refused to stand with the [northeastern States] on the issue, and with the aide of [William] Steward of Nevada and Leland Stanford of California, Lamar was confirmed by the narrow margin of 32 to 28. . . . The vote was thus a notable victory for sectional tolerance; and now that one of [their] old soldiers was on the Supreme Bench, the [people of the former Confederate States] had further reason to think of the [Federal Government as their] own."

Grover Cleveland was defeated by Benjamin Harrison of Indiana in the 1888 election for President. Harrison was a lawyer and politician who had joined the Republican Party at the outset, supported Abe Lincoln and joined in the Federal Invasion of the Confederacy, rising to command a regiment of infantry. He had represented Indiana in the Federal Senate from 1881 until 1887, failing reelection since Democrats then controlled the State legislature. The vote for President was, across the country, uniformly sectional — Democrats again winning all former Confederate States, plus Delaware, Maryland, West Virginia, Kentucky and Missouri, while capturing only New Jersey and Connecticut from the northern and western States sections. The race was only close in Indiana (49.0 v 48.7 percent) and New York (49.3 v 48.2 percent). Cleveland lost the electoral vote 233 to 168, but won the popular vote 49 percent to 48 percent — a margin of 100,000 votes.

Upon leaving the, White House Grover and Frances Cleveland went to New York City, staying a short time at the Victoria Hotel, then staying at "a dignified four-story residence of red brick and brownstone," on Madison Avenue, complete with furnishings and "handsome oak paneling." Late in 1892 they moved to a New York City house next door to one of Grover's friends. Grover agreed to work in a New York City law firm — Bangs, Stetson, Tracy and MacVeagh — not as a partner but as "counsel," occasionally writing briefs while strictly preferring to abstain from court appearances in favor of reviewing legal disputes, offering advice and even arbitrating or negotiating settlements based on the basic tenants of law, trying to be fair to both parties. A nice bonus was Cleveland's free access to the law library and secretary staff.

Frances Cleveland gave birth to daughter Ruth in the Madison Avenue house on October 3, 1891. In a letter to a friend shortly afterward, Grover happily described the baby as "a little strong, healthy girl."

But the best days for Grover and Frances were the weeks spent at a summer retreat they purchased in Massachusetts in the Cape Cod section of the State on the south side of Buzzards Bay near Borne (viewed on a map the site is directly south of Boston). Located on the water with great views, this summer retreat was a large clapboard two-story residence with porches on the sides, secluded from the public road on several acres of land and ideally designed for the summer season. Grover was attracted to the region by the good fishing, both salt-water fishing in Buzzards Bay and its inlets, and freshwater trout fishing in the ponds, prevalent to the south of the house. Friends of the Cleveland's, the Richard

Gilder's, had a summer home in the area and had recommended it. The Cleveland's named their summer home "Gray Gables," a name inspired by its appearance and the gray clapboard siding. (The home cannot be visited; it was consumed in a fire years after the Cleveland's sold it). Biographer Allan Nevins would write:

"It is probable that Cleveland spent the happiest days of his life at Gray Gables. He went to Buzzards Bay each summer with the eagerness of a city-jaded boy escaping to the woods."

When Delegates to the 1892 Democratic Party National Convention gathered in Chicago to nominate their candidate for President, Grover Cleveland was chosen on the first ballot (June 22, 1892), receiving a vote of 617-1/2, which exceeded the 607 vote minimum required to nominate. Delegates nominated Adlai Stevenson of Illinois for Vice President.

Born into the southern culture in Kentucky in 1835, Stevenson had, at age 16, moved with his family to Bloomington, in central Illinois, returned to Kentucky to complete his college education, then went back to Illinois to take over his father's sawmill business. He had begun the practice of law in 1857, at age 23, and as a young man had supported the Democratic Party and Stephen Douglas. The selection of Stevenson for Vice President balanced the Democrat ticket geographically, to a slight degree sectionally, and also with regard to monetary policy (Cleveland defended "hard money" and Stevenson advocated "soft money"). You may remember the name, "Adlai Stevenson," from your youthful days as I do — his grandson of the same name was the Democrat candidate for President in 1852 and 1856, in both campaigns losing to Dwight Eisenhower.

Two weeks earlier, the Republican Convention had nominated President Benjamin Harrison of Indiana for a second term. Of the 1892 campaign, biographer Allan Nevins would write:

"The campaign of 1892 was the cleanest, quietest, and most creditable in the memory of the post-war generation. Not merely was there almost no abuse of either nominee, and almost no waving of the "bloody shirt;" there was an unprecedented calmness in facing the issues. Many speakers on both sides frankly confessed that the opposing candidate would fill the presidency with credit."

Yet the campaign season did have to weather social conflict, including a bloody labor war at a Carnegie steel works near Pittsburg, pitting 270 heavily armed Pinkerton guards against striking workers and a mob of 5,000 supporters of the Amalgamated Association of Iron and Steel Workers. There, 10 were killed and 60 wounded. The union argued that the high import taxes on steel billets was making Carnegie and his investors rich, while little of the largess was going to higher wages at the mill. This was fuel for fierce debates over who benefited from high import taxes, industrialists or labor. This was followed by a strike by coal miners in eastern Tennessee. Then came a strike by switchmen at the important Buffalo rail yards, involving a crackdown by several thousand New York militia. Democrats, having no chance of defeating Republicans, in their strongholds of Colorado, Idaho, Kansas, North Dakota and Wyoming, simply endorsed the candidate of the Populist Party, James Weaver of Iowa, who was making a very strong third Party campaign. Cleveland's only notable campaign speech was the one in New York's Madison Square Garden, where he addressed 20,000 people, accepting the nomination by the Democratic Party. Most of the summer was spent quietly with Frances at Gray Gables. But a heavy workload of correspondence greatly limited his time on the water fishing.

Grover Cleveland won all the electoral votes from the States of the southern culture plus New Jersey, Connecticut, New York, a few in Ohio, Indiana, Illinois, Wisconsin, a few in Michigan, a few in North Dakota, and most of California. Populist Party candidate James Weaver won all of Kansas, Colorado, Idaho, and Nevada and a portion of the Electoral votes in Oregon and North Dakota. Where did all of these new States come from? This had all happened in 1889 and 1890:

During the Benjamin Harrison Administration the nation had grown by 6 new States — North Dakota (1889), South Dakota (1889), Montana (1889), Washington (1889), Idaho (1890) and Wyoming (1890) — giving Republicans and Populists a boost of 12 new seats in the Federal Senate and greatly diminishing the influence of southern States Senators. This represented an explosion in Federal Senators, even exceeding the 10 seats added after the election of Abe Lincoln — Kansas (1861), West Virginia (1863), Nevada (1864), Nebraska (1867) and Colorado (1876). Prior to that Minnesota (1858) and Oregon (1859) had been added by the Republican House and Senate during the contentious James Buchanan Administration. As you will recall, when the people of the Nation of Texas had been invited to forgo nationhood and become a State under the Federal Government, they had been promised, by a Treaty between the two nations, to be given 8 addition Senate seats when population growth called for it — to expand their government into five States: East Texas, South Texas, North Texas, West Texas and Central Texas. This promise to the people of Texas would never be fulfilled.

The electoral vote was 277 for Cleveland, 145 for Republican Harrison and 22 for Populist Weaver. The popular vote was 46.1 percent for Cleveland, 43.0 percent for Harrison, 8.5 percent for Weaver and 2.4 percent for other candidates.

Grover Cleveland's Cabinet consisted of Walter Gresham of Indiana as Secretary of State; John Carlisle of Kentucky as Secretary of the Treasury; Daniel Lamont of New York, formerly Cleveland's private secretary, as Secretary of War; Richard Olney of Boston, Massachusetts as Attorney General; Hilary Herbert of Alabama as Secretary of the Navy; Wilson Bissell of New York as Postmaster General; Hoke Smith of Georgia as Secretary of the Interior, and Sterling Morton of Nebraska as Secretary of Agriculture, the new Cabinet office that had been created with support from Lucius Lamar during the last months of Cleveland's first term.

During Cleveland's second term he would appoint two men to the Federal Supreme Court: Edward White of Alabama and Rufus Peckham of New York. White would be named Chief Justice by Democrat President William Howard Taft in 1910, becoming the first Chief Justice from a southern State since the time of Roger Taney of Maryland, a span of 46 years. You will recall that, upon Taney's death in 1864, President Abe Lincoln had appointed Salmon Chase of Ohio, thus losing for the southern culture its influence with the Chief Justice. You will also recall that Taney had been appointed Chief Justice by Tennessean Andrew Jackson in 1835, replacing John Marshall of Virginia, who had held the post since being selected by the first President John Adams in 1801.

A bloodless but despicable political coup in Hawaii occupied Grover Cleveland as soon as he was inaugurated — a coup by scheming Americans, which had been hatched on an accelerated pace to be completed before Republican Harrison left office — to make it difficult for incoming Democrat President Cleveland to rescue the victims of the scheme:

In early January, 1893, descendants of missionaries from Congregational Churches in Massachusetts and neighboring States (formerly Puritan Separatists) had joined forces with wealthy Americans who had arrived latter, together totaling less than 2,000 strong, had taken over much of the Hawaiian land and had created a large sugar empire, using laborers from among the 40,000 Hawaiians of pure and mixed blood, the 30,000 Chinese and Japanese immigrants and the 9,000 Portuguese immigrants. These powerful Americans, small in number but well organized, clever and well connected to United States officials, had overthrown the Hawaiian Government, led by Queen Liliuokalani, and seized control of Honolulu on Oahu, the largest and most useful island in the chain. The American Minister, John Stevens, in cahoots with the coup instigators, had authorized on January 14 the landing of United States Marines from ships in Pearl Harbor to intimidate opponents of the coup. Two weeks later, on February 1, Minister Stevens had proclaimed that Hawaii was an "American Protectorate" and ordered that the American flag be flown over the Government building in Honolulu. Back in Washington City, President Harrison's Secretary of State, John Foster of Indiana, "disallowed the Protectorate," but his order was ignored. Americans representing the revolutionaries arrived in San Francisco on January 28 and Washington City on February 3, and quickly negotiated a so-called treaty of annexation between themselves (representing the islands of Hawaii) and Foster (representing the United States), which reduced the independent nation of Hawaii to an occupied American territory. Foster sped this so-called "treaty" to the Federal Senate on February 15, urging that it be ratified before Cleveland had a chance to interfere. Supporters of speedy annexation were seen to chant:

> ". . . . Liliuokalani
> Give us your little brown hannie!"

Grover Cleveland was not amused. On March 9 he had the so-called treaty of annexation withdrawn from Senate consideration and began an investigation to determine if there was anything he could do at that late hour to reverse the coup and restore Hawaii to the Hawaiian people. He found that, following a special 1875 treaty allowing Hawaiian sugar to be imported duty-free, unlike sugar from the Caribbean, the island economy had been transformed — "American speculators were attracted, great corporations were formed, thousands of Chinese and Japanese were imported, and the character of the industry was radically changed. The acreage planted to sugar soon doubled, and most of it passed into the hands of stock companies, capitalized and managed abroad." But their advantage over foreign producers had vanished in 1890 with the passage of the McKinley Act, which allowed duty-free imports of sugar from other regions, including the nearby Caribbean Islands where sugar cane abounded. Corporate leaders and investors had retaliated by launching the coup a little over one year later.

When Cleveland asked Sanford Dole, the so-called President of Hawaii, to voluntarily withdraw and allow power to return to the Queen, Dole refused. Debates in Washington City about taking forceful action to restore the Queen ensued. Most in the Federal House and Senate, many supportive of imperialistic expansion, were against forceful action in Honolulu, and, technically, they needed to be involved since contemplated action resembled an act of war. Cleveland eventually recognized that he was trapped, unable to rescue the Hawaiian people from the aggression of the descendants of the missionaries whose religious creed had been handed down from their ancestors, the Puritan Separatists. Who was Sanford Dole?

His father Daniel Dole had come to Hawaii from Maine as a Congregational missionary and gained the trust of the Hawaiian leaders. Sanford had been born to Daniel's wife, Emily Ballard Dole, in Honolulu, in 1844, and trained in law in Massachusetts. Upon returning to Hawaii, he had become a confidant of Hawaiian leaders and politically ingrained. His cousin James Dole would come to Hawaii in 1899 and found the Hawaiian Pineapple Company, later to be called the Dole Food Company.

As Cleveland's second term neared its close, the Democratic Party was undergoing an historic transformation. William Jennings Bryan gained control of Democratic Party politics. Cleveland was no longer viewed as the Party's leader. Bryan was. The Populist Movement Bryan championed split the Democratic Party into two Factions. The Gold-Democrat Faction, being conservative in philosophy and insisting on maintaining a sound dollar pegged to gold, was supported by most industrial and commercial men, mostly in the eastern States. Cleveland identified with these men. The Regular Democrat Faction, being progressive, imperialistic and liberal in philosophy and insisting on taking the dollar off the gold standard in favor of a new silver standard, thereby enabling inflation, was led by Bryan, who championed the common man, agitated emotional issues and exploited class envy. This Faction swept up the majority of Democrat voters. Bryan would run for President in 1896, 1900 and 1908, never winning, but exerting a powerful influence on America's advancing political evolution toward expanded, imperialistic, progressive and controlling government. A devout Presbyterian, he was born and raised in central Illinois and became an Illinois lawyer. Then, in 1887, at age 27, he moved to Lincoln Nebraska, where he engaged in the practice of law and political activism. Although Grover Cleveland and William Jennings Bryan were both Democrats, they were poles apart in their respective philosophy concerning the proper role of the Federal Government in American society.

In a landslide victory for Republicans, William McKinley defeated Democrat-Populist William Jennings Bryan in the fall 1896 election for President. Actually, Grover Cleveland was not terribly disappointed over the Republican victory — he felt more in agreement with McKinley's views of the Federal Government's proper role than with Bryan's. The evening before the Inauguration, Cleveland and McKinley dined together at the White House. The next morning they rode together to the Capitol and stood side by side during the swearing in of the new President. Biographer Allan Nevins would describe the parting:

Cleveland "warned McKinley of the danger of a war with Spain; but the subject on which he spoke to him with special earnestness was the preservation of a sound currency. The day might come again, he said in effect, when gold Democrats and gold Republicans would have to stand together against the Silverites, and he hoped that McKinley would do nothing to make such a union difficult."

Frances Cleveland and the children had already departed Washington City for Princeton, New Jersey, where the family had purchased a house with the intention of making that college town their permanent residence. But Grover was eager to first go fishing. March would bring warmer weather to the North Carolina coast, so he boarded a lighthouse tender and headed south with friends to fish and shoot ducks and game in the sound west of Cape Hatteras. Soon after the inaugural parade, he boarded the tender, took a seat and confided to his friends, "I have had a long talk with McKinley. He is an honest, sincere, and serious man. I feel that he is going to do his best to give the country a good Administration. He impressed me as a man who will have the best interests of the country at stake."

Princeton, New Jersey would suit the Cleveland's admirably. The State often voted Democratic. The college was a conservative Presbyterian institution with which Cleveland felt comfortable. His late father, a Presbyterian minister, would have liked it, too. "The pretty village retained an air of isolation, for it lay off the main railroad line." Andrew West, Professor of Classics, had encouraged the Cleveland's to choose Princeton, and they named the house they purchased "Westland" in his honor. It was "a large colonial mansion of severely simple aspect, built of stone and covered with stucco, and surrounded by spacious grounds." The family would summer at Gray Gables on Buzzards Bay in Massachusetts. To facilitate Grover's passion for hunting and fishing, he purchased "a rocky little farm about 3 miles from Princeton as a convenient stopping-place when out for a day's hunting; for he liked to shoot rabbits and quail across the snowy fields, and sometimes he fished on Millstone River. At age 59, he considered himself, for the most part, a retired man. Estimates had it that his assets in cash and property totaled between $300,000 and $350,000 — money saved from his law practice, his salary as President and the sale of his country house and land located near Washington City, which, you will recall, he had purchased for $21,000 in 1886.

Cleveland would never write a political history or an autobiography, but he would write many articles for popular magazines, including the *Saturday Evening Post, Collier's*, the *Atlantic*, the *Ladies' Home Journal* and others. He wrote 3 essays which were combined into a book titled, "*Presidential Problems*," which discussed 3 contentious issues he had dealt with as President, for which he was paid. His only contribution toward teaching Princeton students was a few lectures he presented under the series titled, "*Henry Stafford Little Lectureship on Public Affairs*." Although not on the faculty, Cleveland had access to an office at Princeton and used the library. He accepted the honorary degree of "Doctor of Laws" in June 1897. Thereafter, he participated in the annual June commencement exercises.

Summers found the Cleveland's at Gray Gables on Buzzards Bay. There "he went trout fishing with Joe Jefferson or [Richard] Olney. Repeated winter trips, usually before Christmas, were made to General Porter Alexander's estate in South Carolina to hunt ducks. He more than once visited Jefferson and other friends in Florida." Cruising excursions on E. C. Benedict's yacht, *Oneida*, were not infrequent, including trips to Maine, to South Carolina and once to Bermuda.

In 1900 the Democratic Party National Convention again selected Populist William Jennings Bryan as its candidate for President. Republicans nominated Theodore Roosevelt for a second term. Cleveland strongly opposed Bryan and the 1900 Democrat platform, which supported valuing the dollar in silver on the basis on 16 ounces of silver per ounce of gold. Roosevelt won the election, receiving 56 percent of the popular vote and 71 percent of the Electoral vote. Cleveland was distraught and saw no hope for a national victory by the Democratic Party, unless the southern States took the lead in reforming Democrat policies. In a letter to Hoke Smith, on January 20, 1901, Cleveland expressed the belief that Democrats could never win a national election advocating Bryan's 1886 and 1890 Populist agenda:

"Of one thing I feel absolutely certain: none of the States lost to the ticket called Democratic last November will ever be regained upon the 1886 and 1890 platforms. The redemption or continued failure of the Democratic Party is in the hands of its [southern States] wing. And my belief is that the young [southern States] Democrats who have a future before them, and who must have cast upon them the welfare of their section and the promotion of Democracy as an element in that welfare as well as in the safety of the country, must work out this salvation."

The Democratic Party political tide had turned back southward. In 1884 the tide had flowed north to sweep Democrat New York Governor Grover Cleveland into the White House and given southern States political leaders a long-denied voice in the Federal Executive, plus the appointment of Lucius Lamar to the Federal Supreme Court — enabling southern States Democrats to finally be engaged at the national level. Although the Republican Party had staged a comeback in 1888, it lost to a resurging Cleveland in 1892. But by 1896 the northern States Democracy had been disastrously splintered by William Jennings Bryan's Populist demagoguery, opening the door for an 1896 landslide Republican victory by William McKinley and by Theodore Roosevelt in 1900. The northern States Democracy was in disarray and only its bedrock base in the southern States seemed to retain belief in the founders' principals of a limited and conservative Federal Government — the core conservative political views Cleveland had forever embraced. The tide had turned south. In Cleveland's view only the southern States could restore the Democracy to political health.

In 1901 Grover Cleveland became a trustee of Princeton University. He would remain a trustee until his death. This involved him with his friend Andrew West, who was named in 1901 to head a new graduate school and with Woodrow Wilson, who became President of Princeton in 1902. In time, West and Wilson would lock horns on how the graduate program ought to be run and where new buildings ought to be built. Cleveland found himself siding with West and opposing Wilson. These controversies concerned Cleveland and caused him to be distrustful of Wilson.

Grover and Frances suffered greatly when their oldest child, Ruth, age 12, died of diphtheria on January 7, 1904. Could they ever enjoy summers at Gray Gables without Ruth? Furthermore, Grover had been concerned that a proposed Cape Cod Canal would disrupt the serenity in the upper end of Buzzards Bay where the house was situated. So, for the summer following Ruth's death, the Cleveland's leased out Gray Gables and vacationed in the hills of New Hampshire. In that region they found a new summer home, near Tamworth, Lake Ossipee and Lake Winnipesaukee where they liked "the mountain air and varied scenery." Inspired by the great views of Mt. Chocorua and Mt. Passonconway, the Cleveland's named their new summer home "Intermont."

Democrats nominated Alton Parker of New York as their candidate for President in 1904. He was up against incumbent Republican Theodore Roosevelt. Democrats at the Convention would have nominated Grover Cleveland had he been younger and in good health, for, after 8 years of rejection, they had returned to embrace much of his political views, they had returned from the extremes of William Jennings Bryan's Populist agenda. Cleveland was admired. However, Parker "proved a weak candidate" and Roosevelt was reelected, carrying every State beyond the boundaries of the southern States.

Of Grover Cleveland's last years, biographer Allan Nevins would write, "Cleveland's last years were as bright and serene as his failing health permitted. He had everything to make him happy — young children, a devoted wife, work to do, boon friends, public honors — and he appreciated them. . . . As old political resentments were forgotten he had become a national figure, esteemed and praised by all. His 70th birthday in 1907 was the occasion for an informal national celebration. . . . [but Cleveland] went south on a gunning trip to escape any spontaneous observation."

His health rapidly declined. By April 1908, "he was in the grip of gastro-intestinal disease complicated by ailments of the heart and kidneys." He celebrated his 71st birthday with his family trying to recuperate at Lakewood. He became worse and was secretly transported back to his home at Princeton "stretched on a mattress in a private automobile." He died on June 24, 1908. A private funeral was held at his home in Princeton, only a select number being invited. Attendees included "President Theodore Roosevelt, Chief Justice Melville Fuller, 6 members of Cleveland's Cabinets; and intimate friends." The Presbyterian service was limited to "some simple passages of scripture." Newspapers were "unrestrained" in printing their eulogies. Of course, flags were at half mast. He was buried at the Princeton Cemetery. [R211;73-76,213,304,312-339,426-427,439-459,487-509,552-588,716-766]

Grover Cleveland had lived through an amazing 71 years in American history, including — America's greatest imperialistic act: its War Against Mexico, which yielded its great western expansion — Bleeding Kansas and the political demagoguery that gave rise to the Republican Party, State Secession and that Party's Invasion of the Confederacy, which killed 360,000 Federals — The Political Reconstruction in the conquered States that subjugated State Rights and enabled contagious political corruption, fueled by sectional hatreds and excessive political patronage — Cleveland's own magnificent success at restoring the New York State Government and the Federal Government to foundations of honesty, economy, common sense efficiency and limited exercise of powers — Cleveland's own magnificent success at returning the southern States to a position of influence in the Federal Executive and the Federal Supreme Court — and finally, the splintering of the Democratic Party by William Jennings Bryan, fatally crippling the conservative foundation of the nation's oldest political organization.

Most of America's advances during his life were not created by political leaders, but by scientists and industrial pioneers, and many students of history overlook this most important factor. Prior to his birth, the big industrial advance had been the steam engine and travel upstream by steam-powered boats. The other great advances had taken place after his birth. Among those were the upgraded iron called steel, the telegraph, the telephone, the electric generator, the electric motor, the beginnings of electric power distribution, the extraction of petroleum and its refining into fuels and lubricants, the internal combustion engine and all the machines it could drive, including the automobile, farm tractors, harvesters and electric generators. Although he lived to see great technological advances, particularly the internal combustion engine and the first automobiles, he would not live to witness the invention of the airplane and see how man's technological advances, in the hands of evil political imperialists, would ignite a war far more destructive than the one Abe Lincoln launched: the Great War we now call World War I. His children would see that war, and see Woodrow Wilson advance his Progressive political agenda, even see Franklin Roosevelt advance Progressivism farther, even see earth's great military rematch, World War II.

Like so many people of the southern States culture — including Robert E. Lee, Jefferson Davis, Wade Hampton, and Lucius Lamar, to name a few, of which much has been written herein — Grover Cleveland "valued character above everything else; and his career shows why that valuation is a just one. . . . Intellectually, his chief characteristic was his powerful common sense; his mind was always vigorous, deliberate, and logical."

I am writing this in 2011 and 2012, a time when character is so lacking in American political leaders, so seldom sought or admired, and so sorely needed. What would Grover think of — An unsustainable Federal debt of more than $16,000,000,000,000 — An intentionally inflationary monetary system where, instead of 35 paper dollars, it takes 1,700 paper dollars to buy one ounce of gold, where instead of 16 to 1, the gold-to-silver ratio is 50 to 1 — A bankrupt national retirement program called Social Security — State Rights so minimal that the Federal Government controls anything and everything it wants to control, including the education of our children — In a reversal of the Imperialism Cleveland detested, instead of annexing so-called third world nations, Federal leaders give money to their governments, encouraging further corruption — A lawless, unenforced national border and a Federal refusal to identify illegal aliens or deport them — A corrupt judicial system that enables attorneys to gain wealth and exert political influence far in excess of their value to our society — Excessive Federal expansion and enforcement of so-called environmental laws, which is destroying America's ability to compete in a global economy and endangering our energy independence and national security — Excessive Federal involvement in personal medical care, subjugating the free market and threatening national bankruptcy — A regressive scale of income tax deductions and progressive scale of income tax percentages, together designed to allow nearly half of American voters to escape paying any Federal income taxes at all, and making a mockery of the democratic ideal that all citizens be treated equally before the law — Political demagoguery that exploits class envy, empowered by voters excused from paying Federal income taxes, while making the most successful Americans work like slaves for almost half of the year to pay off the taxes demanded of them — A welfare system that facilitates an unproductive work ethic — Dysfunctional, illogical, unprovable and scientifically corrupt policies to promote "diversity" with regard to race, ethnicity and other so-called groupings of individuals, all in the name of "political correctness."

Makes a person yearn for the reincarnation of one of America's greatest Presidents, Governor Grover Cleveland of New York State.

There was much I could have written about Grover Cleveland's 8 years as President. Those were important years in our nation's history. But those years are beyond the scope of *Bloodstains*. For that history, I refer interested readers to *Grover Cleveland, A Study in Courage*, by Allan Nevins, published in 1932 by Dodd, Mead & Company of New York.

Before moving on to the final days of Jeff and Varina Davis, let us take a few minutes to reflect on relevant political commentary that is helpful in relating the political history presented in *Bloodstains* to the succeeding political history up to today, the year 2012.

Relevant Political Commentary

At about the time that Grover Cleveland was elected Governor of New York State, in 1883, major advances in technology were upon the horizon. The incandescent electric light bulb, invented by Thomas Edison in 1878, had experienced first practical commercialization by 1882. Nikola Tesla, a Serbian-American, would invent the first practicable AC motor in 1888 and with it the polyphase electric power transmission system, using transformers to enable high voltage transmission over long distances. His inventions would be commercialized by George Westinghouse, who had formed Westinghouse Electric Company two years earlier. This would make possible modern alternating current electric generation plants powered by coal-fired steam turbines or water turbines. At the same time as Tesla's advancements, two types of internal combustion engines were being developed: by 1886 German Karl Benz had advanced the design of the spark-ignition engine and, in 1893, German Rudolph Diesel invented the compression ignition engine. But wide-spread economic use of the internal combustion engine would have to await cheap and plentiful diesel fuel, gasoline and lubricants, all derived from petroleum. This began for America in 1901 with the Spindletop Hill discovery in Texas and construction of the Texas Oil Company refinery at Port Arthur, Texas. Spindletop, producing 17,400,000 barrels of crude in 1902 alone, would give birth to the Texas Oil Company (later Texaco), the Gulf Oil Company (later Chevron) and the Humble Oil Company (later Exxon-Mobile). This in turn would give birth to affordable trucks and automobiles, and to more efficient farm tractors, railroad locomotives, river boats and marine vessels. Mass production of automobiles and trucks, based on the principal of interchangeable parts, would begin in Michigan in 1908 and rapidly advance by 1913 to permit efficient manufacture of the Ford Model T, freeing the everyday man from dependence on draft animals for transportation and mobility. Using a light-weight gasoline engine they personally built, Orville and Wilbur Wright would demonstrate the first human flight in an airplane on the North Carolina coast in late 1903 and the following year would be making test flights in Ohio. They would form the Wright Company in 1910 and build airplanes for commercial and military use. Others would greatly improve on the Wright's designs and the airplane would become a significant weapon of war in World War I.

Federal taxes on imports would continue in political flux. The Tariff Act of 1890, called the McKinley Tariff, would dramatically reverse the 1883 Mongrel Tariff's trend toward lower-rates, thereby raising protective rates to almost 50 percent. The Tariff Act of 1894, called the Wilson-Gorman Tariff, would reduce rates for some items, but retain protectionist policies, disappointing President Grover Cleveland and Democrats who had campaigned on greatly reduced taxes on imports. The modest reductions in the 1894 schedule would be reversed by increases decreed in the Tariff Act of 1897, called the Dingley Tariff. A fight among Republicans over the 1909 Payne-Aldrich Tariff, resulting in little overall change is tax rates, would cause the Party to split into the Old Guard Faction (Republican Party) led by President Taft and a new Progressive Faction led by Theodore Roosevelt (Bull Moose Party). That Republican split over tariff taxation, by dividing the Republican vote, would allow the Democratic Party to come to power in 1913, led by Democrat Woodrow Wilson, who would be reelected in 1916. Democrats would control the Federal House and Senate until the political tides of World War I would return both to Republican control in 1919. This era of Democratic Party dominance (1913 to 1918) would finally put an end to 100 years of Federal tariff schedules designed to protect American industry with heavy taxes on imports, while allowing domestic manufacturers to raise prices and forego improvements in their processes, machinery and work methods. The eras of Whig and Republican high import taxation would be over.

> Democrat control from 1913 through 1918 would permit passage of the Underwood Tariff of 1913, named for Representative Oscar Underwood of Alabama. This would forever terminate the Whig and Republican programs of high "protective" taxes on imports, reducing the rate schedule to values resembling those set by the Walker Tariff of 1857, during the Administration of Democrat James Buchanan, prior to State secession. The duty on woolens would drop from 56 percent to 18.5 percent and would go to zero on steel rails, raw wood, iron ore, agricultural implements and many foodstuffs.

At this time, taxes on the income of corporations and wealthy individuals would begin replacing tariff revenues, having become a legal method of taxation with passage in 1913 of an enabling Amendment to the Federal Constitution. By 1917, income taxes would exceed taxes on imports in providing Federal revenue. Tariff revenue, as a percentage of the value of all imports would fall steadily from 1920 onward: ranging between 19 and 13 percent during the years 1920 to 1940; between 7 and 5 percent during the years 1948 to 1970, between 4 to 3 percent for 1980 to 1995, and between 2 to 1 percent forward to the present day — overall an insignificant and miniscule degree of "protection." On the other hand, tax revenue on corporate and individual income and on payrolls (Social Security and Medicare) would rise exponentially to, today, become 77 times more than revenue derived from taxes on imports. So today, trade between the nations of the world is almost as tax-free and open as it has always been within our American States.

There are three concepts we need to understand, resulting from this watershed year of 1913:

- By the Federal Government relying on taxes on imports for almost all of its revenue, as it had prior to 1913, it had been, 1), helping wealthy owners of manufacturing enterprises and their friends in banking and commerce to become rich while paying little in Federal taxes, and, 2), burdening everyday Americans, notably farmers, with the cost of paying artificially high prices on manufactured goods, essentially a flat tax on them. Surprisingly for a democratic republic, the wealthy privileged group could cast only a small percentage of the votes on Election Day, yet they had long been successful in getting government to do their bidding.

- On the other hand, by the Federal Government relying little on taxes on imports and mostly on taxes on the income of corporations and wealthy individuals, as it began to do after 1913, it was, 1), forcing wealthy owners of manufacturing enterprises to be more efficient and to pay high taxes in support of Federal revenue demands, and, 2), allowing individuals who were not wealthy, such as small-scale farmers, tradesmen, laborers and unwed mothers, to avoid paying very much at all in Federal taxes. So the small, once-privileged group of the wealthy was no longer privileged. There's would become a struggle to avoid being taxed beyond an ability to endure.

- As I write this, the day seems not far off into the future when a controlling majority of voters will be able and willing to elect Federal Representatives and Senators with a mission to raise the progressive Federal income tax schedule so high that a socialistic redistribution of wealth will prevail all across the land — crushing incentives to work hard, to start and expand enterprises and to propel the economy forward — thereby beginning a slow but steady descent into a lasting economic depression, a quagmire, a cult of envy and sameness, all in the name of equality — by that I mean a societal equality of mediocrity.

My political commentary now complete, we now move to the final days of Jeff and Varina Davis and their children.

Jeff and Varina Davis — The Remainder of Their Lives

Jeff Davis survived many of his top Confederate leaders. Since Robert Lee's death at age 63, in 1870, several other younger members of the top Confederate leadership had not lived to celebrate the Inauguration of the first Democratic President since before the Federal Invasion. John Breckinridge had died in 1875; Braxton Bragg in 1876; Raphael Semmes in 1877; brother-in-law Dick Taylor and John Hood in 1879; and Alexander Stephens in 1883. Joe Johnston and Pierre Beauregard were alive, and remained hopeful that their rather frequent criticisms of Jeff Davis and his past leadership would somehow enhance their reputations. James Longstreet was alive, but would be forever an embarrassment to former Confederates because of his past willingness to turn his back on them and work with Republican Political Machines during the years of Political Reconstruction. Yet 6 other top former Confederate leaders had lived to celebrate Grover Cleveland's election, and all of these were true friends and supporters of Jeff Davis. They were Jubal Early, Dabney Maury, Stephen Lee, Fitzhugh Lee, Wade Hampton and John Gordon.

On April 27, 1886, Jeff Davis and Winnie boarded a special railroad car at the beach house, Beauvoir, and headed off to Montgomery, Alabama. Jeff had accepted an invitation to participate in the dedication of Montgomery's new Soldiers' Monument. Varina and Maggie had to cancel their plans to bring the three grandchildren and accompany Jeff and Winnie when they discovered that the baby, Addison Jefferson, had just come down with scarlet fever. Reporter Frank Burr of the New York *World*, wrote that, "half a carload of floral offerings were showered upon [Davis] during his [rail] trip and thousands of other tokens of love." The arriving train was greeted by a huge crowd, cannon fire and "the old familiar" Confederate Yell. John Gordon barely managed to escort Davis through the crowd to an awaiting carriage drawn by four white horses. Burr would write:

> "The boom of artillery grew louder and the crash of small arms and fireworks mingled strongly with the cheers of the half-wild populace as the procession moved. Added to the flash of colored fires from the curbstones was the constant discharge of Roman candles, rockets and bombs. The flames of the variously colored lights and lanterns which lined the streets and the lighted windows and brilliant electric sparks helped to make a perfect archway of fires more than a half a mile long."

The crowd pressed in on Jeff Davis as many hoped to be close enough to touch him. A band playing "Dixie" led the procession. Disbanded Montgomery Confederate army units, dressed in their uniforms, marched before and after the carriage. Jeff was greeted by a large crowd, including many women, upon his arrival at the Exchange Hotel. The huge crowd was described as "a sea of faces." Jeff and Winnie spent the night in room 101 — the very same room Jeff had occupied on his first night in Montgomery — the night before he was Inaugurated as President of the Confederacy, back in February of 1861 — the night before William Yancey would proclaim, "The hour and the man have met."

On the second day, Davis was honored in a ceremony on the steps of the Alabama State Capitol building. The huge crowd was far larger than the one that had attended his Inauguration in 1861. Although his main speech would be at the monument dedication the following day Jeff, made a few brief remarks before John Gordon began his eulogy of the former President. Through those remarks Davis assured the crowd that their fight had been "the only kind of which Christianity approved — a holy war of defense." Then he added this tribute to the youngest Confederate soldiers:

> "Well do I remember seeing your gentle boys so small, to use a farmer's phrase, that they might have been called seedcorn, moving on with eager step and fearless brow to the carnival of death. I looked upon them when their knapsacks and muskets seemed heavier than the boys, and my eyes filled with tears. Many of them found nameless graves. But they live in memory and their spirits stand out, the grand reserve of that column which is marching on with unfaltering steps toward the goal of constitutional liberty."

On the third day, Davis dedicated the Soldiers' Monument as the cornerstone was being laid. This monument, he declared, will commemorate "the deeds of Alabama's sons who died that you and your descendants should have the inheritance your fathers in the War of Independence left you." Contrasting those two wars, Davis admonished, "The War between the States was not revolution, as sovereigns never rebel." But Davis devoted much of his speech to encouraging Alabamians "to promote the welfare and happiness of their common country." In his report that night to the New York *World*, Frank Burr would write:

> "How this old man, who is fast nearing his 80 years, has stood the exactions of the past two days is a mystery to everyone. He has been moving about a great deal, and has met hundreds of people and shaken them by the hand. Yet he seems well and in the best of spirits. This welcome has evidently given him a new lease on life."

The next morning, April 30, Jeff and Winnie left Montgomery for rebuilt Atlanta and another celebration of the former Confederacy. Davis was frequently cheered by large crowds along the route, invariably bearing spring flowers. Often "standing knee-deep in flowers" at the rear of the train during brief stops, Davis delivered brief two-minute greetings to those gathered about. At Auburn the cadets gave Davis a 21 gun salute. A crowd of 40,000 lined Peachtree Street — including 6,000 flower-tossing public school children — as Davis rode along for half a mile to Mrs. Benjamin Hill's house, where he would be spending the night. By the next day, incoming trains brought in 50,000 more celebrants, and the Atlanta *Constitution* declared that, "at no period in her previous history" had the city "had within her borders such a host."

The next day, Jeff Davis was the guest of honor at the huge outdoor celebration staged at Atlanta's monument to Confederate commander Benjamin Hill. The crowd numbered 50,000 Confederate veterans and many more as well. During his introductory greeting, Henry Grady looked at Jeff Davis and declared: "Never King inhabited more splendid palace than the millions of brave hearts in which your dear name and fame are forever enshrined." Davis then delivered a brief eulogy of Benjamin Hill, closing with an appeal for an enhanced spirit of national cooperation, for "ours is a day of peace." While the crowd cheered Davis' closing remarks, Henry Grady led Winnie forward and presented her to the crowd as the "Daughter of the Confederacy." With that, "Hats flew into the air and the cheering was like thunder."

A bit later during the ceremony at the Benjamin Hill Monument, a man came unexpectedly riding up on horseback and stopped before the stage. It was James Longstreet. Longstreet had not been invited to the ceremony, for former Confederates had despised the way he had embraced Republicans after defeat. Perhaps Longstreet had come to make amends. How would Davis react to this uninvited arrival?

> "Longstreet dismounted and slowly approached. Davis rose and went forward. Then in an impulsive gesture he held out his arms. The men embraced. The eyes of Lee's Old War Horse were wet. Some men in the crowd thought of the return of the Prodigal Son as Longstreet was offered a seat on the stage."

There were many critical newspaper reports and editorials in northern States newspapers about the Montgomery and Atlanta celebrations, but some were refreshingly understanding. An example of the later would be found in the Massachusetts Springfield *Republican*, which commended the Confederates for their "unswerving purpose, bravery and resolution" as they fought for their cause. Continuing, the editor would write:

> "And when the end came it was the defeat of men devoted to what was in their estimation a patriotic purpose. . . . Now they gather to commemorate the lost cause, with no desire to recall it, only to recognize it for what it was to them, to assert it to the world and go about their affairs again.

> "That is the way we read the honors to Jefferson Davis. . . . How could we respect the [defeated Confederate] people if they did not believe in the thing they undertook to do . . . if they did not honor their leaders and their soldiers, nor exalt their services and their sacrifices? They do well to cherish the sentiment that hallows their story."

Jeff and Winnie left Atlanta in a special railroad car bound for Savannah. They stayed in Savannah for four days as guests of the Comers, whose house faced the square. On May 6, Davis delivered a speech honoring the centennial of the Chatham Artillery of Revolutionary War fame. And shortly thereafter he delivered a speech honoring Nathanael Greene, who, as second-in-command to George Washington, had so ably led patriots in the newly independent southern States, formerly Colonies, in their successful fight to wear down British loyalist forces and trap them 50 miles north of the North Carolina border for the final victory. Greene, who was from Rhode Island, had fought alongside Washington in the northern Colonies for several years, and there had earned Washington's utmost respect, so he was not a native of a southern Colony. Perhaps it was that cooperative effort of southern Colony patriots fighting under the able leadership of a northern Colony commander that would urge Jeff Davis to use such strong language in defense of the cause of State Sovereignty — the political principle for which the Confederacy had been formed — the political principle whose resurrection Davis yet still advocated:

> "In 1776 the Colonies acquired State Sovereignty. They revolted from the mother country in a desperate struggle that was the cause for which they fought. Is it a lost cause now? Never! . . . The independence of these States, the Constitution, liberty, State Sovereignty, which they won in 1776, and which Nathanael Green, son of Rhode Island, helped to win for Georgia, can never die!"

Biographer Hudson Strode would write:

> "When he had finished, there was a mighty surge in the crowd, and the stage was filled with shouting veterans eager to grasp [Davis'] hand. [He] was in grave danger of being crushed, as the men, wild with enthusiasm, shoved and pushed to touch him. After some exciting confusion, a lane was at length cleared and [Davis] was escorted through the applauding crowd to his carriage."

Later at an evening banquet, Davis assured northern States newspapermen that he had no intention of inciting violence: "There are some who take it for granted that when I allude to State Sovereignty I want to bring on another war. I am too old to fight again, and God knows I do not want you to have the necessity of fighting again." And some newspapermen in the northern States seemed satisfied with Davis' intentions. Editors of the Lowell, Massachusetts *Sun* would write:

"Jefferson Davis suddenly emerges from his long retirement, journeys among his people and everywhere receives the most overwhelming manifestation of heartfelt affection, devotion, and reverence.

"Such homage is significant, startling. And it is useless to attempt to deny, disguise, or evade the conclusion that there must be something great and noble and true in him and in the cause to evoke this homage."

Jeff Davis and Winnie returned from Savannah to the beach house and some much-needed rest. Appreciative letters greeted him, among them a letter from a New York lawyer, Gideon Tucker, who had once been Secretary of State for New York. Tucker had written:

"As one of those who through the long and dreadful [Invasion], always opposed Coercion and deplored bloodshed, who believed that the cause of representative government was cruelly damnified by the people of my section, I cannot refrain from congratulating you at this moment upon the consistency and dignity of your course.

"I trust your life may yet be prolonged sufficiently to see some returning reason come to the people of the [northern States], and lead them to consider what a spectacle they presented to the world from 1861 to 1865, when, under the name of [making African Americans independent], they fought for dominion."

Another letter arrived from Davis' friend, William Green, Chancellor of the University of the South:

"I was with you in spirit during your late 'ovation' in Alabama and Georgia; and no heart among those vast crowds sent up warmer thanksgiving to God, at seeing such just and long-due honors paid to you, insufficient as they were to repay you for what you have suffered for them. It is good to see how truly you are loved by all our people."

In October, 1886, Jeff Davis again journeyed away from the beach house to participate in a special ceremony. This time he traveled to Fairview, Kentucky to the dedication of Bethel Baptist Church. Construction of the Church building had just been completed. It was on the land where Davis had been born. Admiring Kentuckians had donated money to purchase the land in 1885 and to build the church in Davis' honor. In fact the benefactors had deeded the land to Jeff, who in turn had deeded it to the Bethel Baptist Association. Jeff's father Samuel had been a Baptist. Jeff insisted that the dedication be a rather quiet affair and that his travel schedule be unannounced. Biographer Hudson Strode would write:

"Davis listened to eulogistic speeches and the ritual of dedication. When it was all over, the demand for him to speak was so insistent that he finally rose and spoke briefly of his faith in a God who favored no special denomination — "I am not a Baptist." He mentioned President Holley of Transylvania, a Northern Unitarian, who had taught him when he was a college lad of a kind of universal love without prejudice. He spoke of the Kentucky pioneers, who, like his father, lived 'in a day before the dawn of sectional strifes.' In their beautiful, pristine surroundings, he said, it was no wonder that the early Kentuckians had learned that God was love."

During the summer of 1887 Jeff Davis helped Isaiah Montgomery and other African Americans establish an African American communal-style community to be called Mound Bayou. Isaiah Montgomery was the African American who, as a lad, had rowed Davis out into the Mississippi to catch the riverboat to begin the trip to Montgomery to be sworn in as President of the Confederacy. Mound Bayou was to be a community populated only by people of African descent. It would be located midway between Memphis and Vicksburg on a tract of land owned by the L N O & T railroad. The railroad wanted to encourage settlement in a "wilderness of deltaland along its right of way" and Montgomery and his friends wanted to establish a community "free from the restraints and prejudices of the civilization they had known." Montgomery envisioned an agricultural community where he hoped "to train and educate the youth that they may be well qualified to take up farm work and bring to it a higher development, instead of being drawn away by the peculiar attractions of town and city life." Montgomery asked for Davis' help, which he gladly provided through a letter encouraging the railroad executives to cooperate with the project. A deal was struck and the Mound Bayou community was established. Isaiah Montgomery would be the first mayor. Over the following years the Mound Bayou community would become a resounding success. Biographer Hudson Strode would write of this community in which only African Americans were permitted to live:

> "On April 12, 1902, [Isaiah] Montgomery [would write Varina] Davis that the land holdings of the Mound Bayou Corporation had increased to 20,000 acres, 'with many improvements in the way of business establishments and cottages, with schools and churches fairly represented.' The first child born in Mound Bayou, B. A. Green, became a Harvard graduate and served 7 consecutive years as mayor.

> "In 1960 the town's population was 1,354, all [African Americans], and in the entire community dwelt some 8,000 [African Americans]. The citizens are highly respected by the neighboring [European American] people in the county and throughout the State as loyal Americans. The original jail was demolished years ago, 'as there was not need of it'."

During the summer of 1888, James Redpath, at the time Managing Editor of the *North American Review*, began an extensive writing and publication collaboration with Jeff Davis, including spending approximately 3 months on-site at Beauvoir, where Jeff, Varina and James engaged together in cooperative writing and editing work. You will recall James Redpath as the impressionable 25-year-old newspaperman who had so fervently produced Exclusionist propaganda (what most called anti-slavery propaganda) during the days of Bleeding Kansas — persuasively but deceptively alleging that southern States settlers were responsible for the Terrorism that was almost always inflicted, instead, by Terrorists from the northern States, such as Massachusetts. Apparently, in the years since then, there had been a political transformation in the mind of the Scottish-born Redpath, as he had witnessed the war that he had helped to ignite, and as he had witnessed the political corruption that had followed the fighting. Perhaps, in middle life, Redpath was attracted by a common ancestry with many southern States people. Perhaps his changed attitudes were his way of apologizing for past journalistic dishonesty. In any event, Redpath had grown to admire Jeff Davis more and more as the years had progressed, beginning in 1875 when he had arranged to meet Davis and had come away very impressed. Therefore, now, as he settled in at Beauvoir during the summer of 1888, Redpath "became quite attached to the old statesman, and he enjoyed the slow-paced life on the Gulf Coast, as well as the interesting visitors who came to Beauvoir." During several visits in 1888, he convinced Davis to write three magazine articles, for which payment would be given:

- A 35-page magazine article to be titled "Andersonville and other War Prisons,"
- A 12-page magazine article to be titled, "Robert E. Lee," and
- A 15-page magazine article to be titled, "The Doctrine of State Rights."

Redpath would also convince Davis to write a substantial history book:

> A not-so-short, 505-page history to be titled, "*A Short History of the Confederate States of America.*"

Davis would immediately began writing the first of the three magazine articles — the one about the true situation surrounding the huge Confederate prisoner-of-war camp that had been established near Andersonville, Georgia. You will recall that, while Davis was imprisoned at Fortress Monroe, Edwin Stanton and the Andrew Johnson Administration had convicted and executed Henry Wirz, the camp's commander, on falsified war-crimes accusations. Well, Redpath wanted an article from Davis that would explain the truth of the stalled cartel prisoner exchange negotiations and of the conditions at Andersonville and other camps, both north and south. Davis would complete the article on December 10, 1888, but publication at the *Review* would stall. *Belford's Magazine* would eventually publish the story. Why *Belford's Magazine* instead of the *North American Review*? It seems that the management of the *Review* would think the prison article too critical of the Lincoln Administration. But Redpath would not be deterred. He would resign from the *Review* and join with Robert Belford and his magazine and his book-publishing company, also in New York. *Belford's Magazine* would publish "Andersonville and Other War Prisons," serializing it as two parts — part one in the January 1890 issue and part two in the February issue (you may go to the internet to download the articles).

Redpath would preface Davis' *Belford's Magazine* article with the following testimony:

"Before I had been with [Jeff] Davis three days, every preconceived idea of him utterly and forever disappeared. Nobody doubted [Jeff] Davis' intellectual capacity, but it was not his mental power that most impressed me. It was his goodness, first of all, and then his intellectual integrity. I never saw an old man whose face bore more emphatic evidences of a gently, refined, and benignant character. He seemed to me the ideal embodiment of 'sweetness and light'."

The article about Robert E. Lee would be published in the January 1890 issue of *North American Review*, pages 56 through 67. It would be a brief biography with emphasis on personal interactions between Lee and Davis during the Defense of the Confederacy. Davis closed the article with the following tribute:

"Descended from a long line of illustrious warriors and statesmen, Robert Edward Lee added new glory to the name he bore, and, whether measured by a martial or an intellectual standard, will compare favorably with those whose reputation it devolved upon him to sustain and emulate."

The article titled, "The Doctrine of State Rights," would be published in the *North American Review* the following month, February 1890, pages 205 through 220. It would be a learned and thorough essay on the subject, complete with a powerful defense of the principle of State Sovereignty upon which the Federal Government had been formed. As Davis neared his close, he presented the essence of the argument:

"It had, so far as I know, in all the earlier periods of our history been uniformly held that allegiance was primarily due to the State of which the individual was a citizen, and that allegiance in the United States resulted from the fact that the State to which each individual belonged was by compact a member of the Union.

"When [7 of the] southern States had, in the required mode of expressing their sovereign will — that is, by Convention of the people of the state — resumed the grants made by them as parties to the Federal compact, they, following the precedent of 1787, formed a new union styled the Confederate States of America.

"The wish of all, and the general expectation, was that the separation should be peaceable. For this purpose, one of the first acts of the Confederate Government was to send Commissioners to the United States Government to adjust all questions which would naturally arise in a dissolution of partnership. Our overtures were rejected, as I feared they would be, for the question was ever ringing in my ears, "If we let the [southern States] go where will we get a revenue?" With continued assurances of peaceful intention, the Federal Government made ready for war."

Belford's Magazine would publish a condensed variation on the State Rights theme in May 1890, titled, "Historical Vindication of Secession," also written by Jeff Davis. (You may go to the internet to download these three articles.)

James Redpath left the beach house later in 1888 but would return in 1889 to assist Jeff and Varina in writing the *"Short History of the Confederate States."* Belford Company would publish the 505-page history book in 1890. (A reprint of that book is available through Sprinkle Publications.)

Jeff Davis began the introduction to his comprehensive Confederate history as follows:

"The vindication of the Southern States for their Ordinances of Secession in 1861 involves two considerations, namely: their rightful power to withdraw from the Union into which they had entered by voluntary compact; and the causes that justified the exercise of that power.

"In treating this question in its two-fold aspect, the legal and the moral, it is not intended to vex the weary ear by adducing time-worn arguments; but, believing the case to be one which must be adjusted finally by historical facts, the candid reader is asked, without favor or prejudice, to make a decision [based] on the unquestionable record."

The first 42 pages of this history dealt with political struggles prior to Secession, including the north-south boundary agreed to in the 1820 Missouri Compromise, 1850 decision to exclude bonded African Americans from the Pacific States (California statehood), "Bleeding Kansas" and the Terrorist raid by the gang led by John Brown. The next 30 pages dealt with State Secession and attempts to peacefully separate. Pages 72 through 481 covered Confederate efforts to defend the new nation. The final 24 pages covered surrender, capture and the onset of Reconstruction. Near the end of his history Davis devoted a few sentences to his personal imprisonment at Fortress Monroe:

"Bitter tears have been shed by the gentle, and stern reproaches have been made by the magnanimous, on account of the needless torture to which I was subjected, and the heavy fetters riveted upon me, while in a stone casement and surrounded by a strong guard; but all these were less excruciating than the mental agony my captives were able to inflict. It was long before I was permitted to hear from my wife and children, and this, and things like this, was the power which education added to savage cruelty. But I do not propose now and here to enter upon the story of my imprisonment . . . ."

Redpath's admiration of Jeff Davis would be evident in his "own little work," titled, *Neither Traitor nor Rebel*, where, in part, he would submit that Davis was:

"A statesman with clean hands and pure heart, who served his people faithfully from budding manhood to hoary age, without thought of self, with unbending integrity and to the best of his great ability."

Unfortunately, James Redpath's literary collaboration with Jeff and Varina Davis would be cut short by his tragic accidental death on February 10, 1891 — on that day, in New York City, he would be run over by a horse-drawn trolley and killed. Redpath would be 57 years old. I find no record of an accusation that the driver intentionally murdered Redpath in that New York City street because of his friendship with Jeff Davis, but one can speculate, I suppose.

During September 1888, a young man, Fred Wilkinson, came to the Davis beach house to ask for Winnie's hand in marriage. Fred was the son of a Syracuse, New York family that had once been rather wealthy, but Fred's father had "lost most of the family fortune just before his death." However, a spacious and grand house in Syracuse remained with Fred and his two sisters. Fred would assure Jeff that he was a State Rights Democrat, and that he had nothing to do with the Federal Invasion of the Confederacy. Nevertheless, Syracuse was in the far north, and Jeff and Varina were both reluctant to give consent. On the other hand, man to man, Jeff took a liking to Fred, and that would be in his favor. In fact, a few months later, Winnie would tell neighbors that her father had given his consent.

Winnie had met Fred Wilkinson during a visit with the Pulitzer family in New York during September 1888. Joseph Pulitzer, a Hungarian immigrant and a Jewish man, was editor of the New York *World*, and would become renowned for the Pulitzer Prize awards for excellence in journalism. Joseph's wife, Kate, was a Virginian. The Pulitzers had become fond of Winnie when she had stayed with them for a while the previous year. Joseph Pulitzer was a State Rights Democrat who "had come to admire [Jeff] Davis in his prison days." And he was developing an admiration for Varina's writing skills, as demonstrated in her letters.

While inspecting his Mississippi River farm, Brierfield, in November 1889, Jeff Davis became deathly ill. Varina had remained behind at the beach house because "some members of [Jeff's] family were visiting us." She received a telegram from a Davis Brierfield employee on the 11th warning of Jeff's grave illness, and was already en route by train to New Orleans where she planned to take a riverboat up to Brierfield. With unsteady hand, Jeff wrote Varina on the 12th: "If I can get to the landing I will go down [to New Orleans] on the [Leathers] riverboat." He had been too sick to do much inspecting, but he summarized what he saw in one sentence: "Nothing is as it should be, and I am not able even to look at the place."

Jeff was saddened by having poured so much money into protective dikes which had proved powerless to prevent Mississippi spring floods from sweeping away his precious topsoil. Gradually, the river was winning. It had already cut across the neck of Davis Bend peninsula and converted it into an island, accessible only by boat. Unfortunately, passenger riverboats were scheduled to pass Davis Island only at night. Eventually riverboats plying the Mississippi would head straight across what was once Davis farmland through a short-cut pathway to their destination.

On the night of the 13th Jeff, now only "half-conscious," was driven "through the rain" to the riverboat landing to catch the senior Leathers riverboat. Before departing, he autographed an album for the plantation manager's niece, Alice Desmaris, with the following greeting: "May all your paths be peaceful and pleasant, charged with the best fruit, the doing good to others." That night, as Jeff traveled downstream on the senior Leathers' riverboat, Varina was traveling upstream on a riverboat captained by Leathers' son. When the boats approached each other that night, young Leathers determined that Jeff Davis was aboard his father's riverboat, and maneuvered to permit Varina to transfer. Varina would write, "He was asleep when I met him, but waked very soon and seemed better for meeting me." Two physicians consulted at Bayou Sara diagnosed, "acute bronchitis complicated with grave malarial trouble." Varina took Jeff to a friend's home in New Orleans, the home of C. S. Fenner. Under the care of New Orleans doctors, Jeff made "a brave struggle to overcome the unseen forces to which he at last suddenly succumbed."

The Davis' older daughter Margaret was with her husband and four little children in Colorado. Winnie was in France vacationing with the Pulitzer family. At the suggestion that his daughters be summoned to his bedside, Jeff replied: "Let our darlings be happy while they can. I may get well." But, in spite of the best medical care available and Varina's nursing, Jeff would not get well this time. During his suffering he told Varina, "I have much to do, but if it is God's will, I must submit." Later he told her, "I want to tell you I am not afraid to die." As the fight to live turned hopeless he spoke his last words, "Pray excuse me, I cannot take it." Jefferson Finis Davis passed away with Varina at his bedside on December 8, 1889.

Exhausted, Varina turned to her relative Edgar Farrar and to C. E. Fenner, and asked them to send out notices and make funeral arrangements. Burial, for a while at least, would be near New Orleans at the tomb of the Confederate Army of Northern Virginia at Metairie. The funeral would be at noon, December 11. After and appropriate time with the immediate family, the body would lie in state in the City Hall. Flags throughout the former Confederate States would be lowered to half-mast, and many public buildings would be hung in black.

For a while the body was with the immediate family at the Fenner home. Mary Stamps spent some precious minutes alone with the body of "the man she had idolized and who had found with her a spiritual rapport such as he had perhaps never known with any other human being." The only non-family member permitted into the drawing room, where the body lay, was Milo Cooper, an aged African American who had known Jeff since both were boys. Hudson Strode would write: "As he beheld the still face he remembered as a youth, the old [African American] broke into heavy weeping. Then he dropped to his unsteady knees and prayed for those left behind."

The public viewed the body beginning at 10 a.m. on December 11. A double line passed by all day. Of one noteworthy visitor, Hudson Strode would write, "Because of his unsteady feet," George Jones, of Iowa, "was escorted by an ex-Confederate soldier to the dais. For a long time he gazed in silence at the calm face of the man to whom he had been devoted for more than 6 decades. Then he bent over the casket as if to kiss the brow, while tears dropped on the glass." George Jones had been Jeff's true friend since teenage days at Transylvania College. He had been a Federal Senator from Iowa for many years and had been a commander in the Federal Army. But always, Jeff and George had been true friends.

A bit later, a group of African Americans from Davis Bend passed by the casket. Among the group was William Sanford. While "gazing on his old friend," Sanford wept "unashamedly." As Sanford was leaving the room, a newspaperman from a northern State asked him how he felt toward Jeff Davis, the man to which he had once been bonded. Sanford would wipe his eyes and reply: "That I loved him this shows, and I can say that every [African American] man he ever owned loved him." For three days, the line of mourners filed by — a population of between 50,000 and 100,000 people. "In viewing the body of Jefferson Davis women found consolation for hurts they had cherished for a quarter century: for husbands, fathers, sons, brothers killed; for homes burned; [farms] lost; for all the humiliations and criminal stupidity of [the Republican Reconstruction of the governments of the conquered States]." Trains arriving from three directions brought in mourners and, since all hotels and boarding houses filled the first night, over 1,000 private homes offered rooms for rent. Some delegations simply chartered sleeping railroad cars.

Many admirers who were unable to journey to New Orleans sent telegrams and letters to Varina. Among them was a letter from 13 African Americans from Brierfield farm which said in part, "We, the old servants and tenants of our beloved [past owner], Honorable Jefferson Davis, have cause to mingle our tears over his death, who was always so kind and thoughtful of our peace and happiness." Thornton

Montgomery sent a letter in which he said, "I appreciate your great loss, and my heart goes out to you in this hour of your deepest affliction." Thornton was the African American who Jeff had helped educated. He had written from Christine, North Dakota, where had become "a man of means."

At noon on December 11, eight former Confederate soldiers hoisted the casket upon their shoulders and bore it to the outdoor catafalque. A silk Confederate flag that belonged to Jeff and Varina covered the coffin, and atop the flag laid a fresh sheaf of wheat, symbolizing the Confederate Army of Virginia, and the sword Jeff had worn at Buena Vista during the War with Mexico. A vast "multitude" jammed Lafayette Square to observe the funeral ceremony while Varina, family, relatives and a few close friends watched from seats set up in the Mayor's parlor. Biographer Hudson Strode would write:

> "As the coffin appeared on the portico, a clock struck the hour of noon, cannon boomed, and the great bell in the near-by First Presbyterian Church began to toll. It was a signal for all the bells of New Orleans to sound the call to mourning. Simultaneously, in cities and towns from northern Virginia to San Antonio, Texas, minute guns were fired and bells tolled; and no one anywhere had to ask, "For whom does the bell toll?"

Ebenezer Thompson, the Rector of the Church of the Redeemer, the Davis' little church in Biloxi, Mississippi, began the Episcopal burial service with the words: "I am the resurrection and the life." A boy choir sang *Through the Valley of the Shadow of Death*." Digressing from the Episcopal liturgy for a moment, Bishop J. N. Galleher of Louisiana added, "Through every day of his illustrious life he was an incorruptible and impassioned defender of the liberties of men. . . He suffered many and grievous wrongs, suffered most for the sake of others." Father Darius Hubert, who had been a Catholic chaplain of the Confederate Army, delivered the closing prayer:

> "O God, loving and compassionate Father, in the name of my heart-broken comrades, I beseech Thee to behold us in our bereavement, from whom Thou hast taken one who was to us a chief, a leader, and a noble and constant exemplar."

Then 8 former Confederate artillerymen hoisted the casket upon their shoulders and carried it to an elaborate waiting caisson, which included a canopy of black drapery ornamented with silver fringe and supported by 6 vertical bronze cannon barrels. Six black horses with silver-trimmed harness drew the caisson, each with a former Confederate soldier walking beside with hand on bridle. The caisson began moving as the first of 7 bands began to play. Varina, daughter Margaret Hayes and Jeff's nephew Joseph Davis followed the procession in the first of 8 family carriages, while Robert Brown rode on top, beside the driver. "Thousands of marching Confederate veterans from all over the nation were followed by 30 aged men who had fought in the Mexican War." As the procession approached the cemetery, it passed the "black-draped equestrian statue of Albert Sidney Johnston. Half a mile beyond was the tomb of the [Confederate] Army of Northern Virginia, a great green mound rising in parterres, ornamented with flowering shrubs, and crowned by a statue of Stonewall Jackson atop a fifty-foot column." Arriving at the tomb, Varina, escorted by J. U. Payne, and Margaret Hayes, escorted by nephew Joseph Davis, stepped down from their carriage and approached the tomb, with Robert Brown following close behind.

Bishop Thompson of Mississippi then began the Episcopal graveside service. A choir chanted the anthem: "*I Heard a Voice from Heaven Saying Unto Me, Write: Blessed are the Dead Who Die in the Lord. For they Rest from their Labors*." Then a bugler played "taps." Then Bishop Galleher consigned the body to the dust: "In the name of God, Amen." But Bishop Galleher added his personal epithet:

> "We here consign the body of Jefferson Davis, a servant of his State and country and a soldier in their armies; sometime member of Congress, Senator from Mississippi, and Secretary of War of the United States; the first and only President of the Confederate States of America; born in Kentucky on the third of June, 1808, died in Louisiana on the sixth of December, 1889, and buried here by the reverent hands of his people."

Hudson Strode would write:

> "The December sun was sinking behind a bank of cumulus clouds edged with flaming gold as the soldiers once more raised the casket to their shoulders. They marched around the base of the monument to the open doorway leading into the chamber of the dead and descended the stairs.

When [Varina] Davis and her escort started down the steps, three volleys from a Louisiana battery rent the air. The soldier's funeral was over."

The Republican Administration of Benjamin Harrison ignored Jeff Davis' passing. No flags flew at half mast for that past Secretary of War. Of course not! James Blaine, Secretary of State for Harrison, had been at the forefront of Republican efforts to prevent Jeff Davis from even getting back his citizenship. How could such men consider affording Davis the honor always before granted to past War Department heads? And a few prominent northern newspapers used Davis' funeral as another opportunity to discredit his memory. But a survey by biographer Hudson Strode would reveal that, "The majority of leading northern [States] papers, in fact, were not only fair, but admiring in their comments." The Davis' friend, Joseph Pulitzer, would write in his paper, the New York *World*:

"The death of Jefferson Davis ends a most remarkable chapter of history. . . . He was the chosen chieftain of the new Republic which strove to establish itself, and whose adherents battled for its existence with a heroism the memory of which is everywhere cherished as one that does honor to the American character and name. . . . He sacrificed all for the cause he cherished, and he alone of all the [people of the former Confederate States] has borne the cross of martyrdom.

"He was a man of commanding ability, spotless integrity, and controlling conscience. . . . He was proud, sensitive, and honorable in all his dealings and in every relation of life. . . . A great soul has passed."

And the New York *Times* would present a sentiment that closely paralleled the typical northern viewpoint: the people of the northern States should respect the people of the former Confederate States for showing respect to their defeated military men. And on the occasion of Jeff Davis' funeral, this typical northern attitude would be briefly extended to include respect for those showing respect for their defeated political leaders. In part, the *Times* said:

"The [people of the former Confederate States love] his memory as [they] should love it and as the people of every patriotic country should and ever will respect it. Were the people of the [former Confederate States] to forget him, or fail to honor the man who endured so patiently for their sake, they in turn should deserve none of respect or place in the minds of men who have manhood."

After a period of grieving, Varina realized that she had before her at the beach house the start of a biography that Jeff had begun at the urging of James Redpath. And Redpath remained faithful, coming to the beach house during the summer of 1890 to work side-by-side with the inspired and determined Varina. Others, including John Dimitry of New Orleans, helped, but Varina was the engine pulling the train. Of her long hours, biographer Ishbel Ross would write:

"All though the summer . . . Varina was working with some degree of desperation on her *Memoir*. She had to revise it 3 times for purposes of condensation. . . . Varina not only exhausted herself but she wore out her collaborators. Both Redpath and Dimitry found her exacting and fanatically industrious at her task. As he was about to leave Beauvoir, Redpath wrote to Dimitry that he had not had a 10-minute recess to himself, as 'Mrs. Davis has been at work herself and kept me at work, from morning to night. . . . In fact, she works longer than, I fear, is good for her and certainly longer than I like. But she is so nervous and anxious about the book that of the two evils she has probably chosen the least.' She had revised her collaborators' work sentence by sentence and 'in most cases verified or modified or simplified [the drafts Dimitry and Redpath had worked up at New Orleans]. By the end of August, Redpath was 'tired of the lonely drudgery,' and Winnie walked into the study one day to find her mother in a dead faint from exhaustion."

Perhaps the most revealing characterization of her husband is given in the following, carefully-constructed sentence from page 923 of Volume 2 of her *Memoir*:

"Forty-three years of intimate companionship, from the beginning of his political career until the end, left me with the profoundest respect for his unswerving mental and moral integrity, his staunch adherence to principle, his self-immolating devotion to duty, his calm, invincible courage, his wide sympathy with mankind, and his unfeigned reverence for his Creator."

Late in the fall of 1890 Varina left the beach house for New York City, perhaps leaving to see her *Memoir* through publication at Belford Company. Sadly, as mentioned earlier, only a few weeks later, on February 10, 1891, James Redpath would be killed — run over by a horse-drawn trolley. And Varina suffered heart problems and be ill throughout the winter, the hard work at the beach house having taken a severe toll on her body. But Varina's *Memoir* was, nevertheless, published that Spring. Although Varina's book is a very important historical record of her husband and the Confederate States of America, a bankruptcy of Belford Company soon followed the publication and far fewer copies would be sold than expected. (You can purchase reprints today from publishers, such as The Nautical & Aviation Publishing Company of America.)

With the help of the Pulitzer's, Varina settled into rooms in New York to pursue her passion for writing. Winnie came to New York City that winter to stay with Varina but she would be too sick to be of much help. Fortunately, Varina's other daughter, Margaret Hayes, came from her Colorado home to spend the summer at Narragansett Pier, Rhode Island, taking Winnie and Varina with her, and it was only then that Varina's health improved. From this point forward, Varina and Winnie would be able to make a living writing and editing for Joe Pulitzer's Sunday edition of the New York *World* — both retained at $1,500 per year, with writing assignments arriving periodically. A favorite of mine was Varina's article "Christmas at the White House of the Confederacy." Winnie would write two novels, which would be published: *The Veiled Doctor* and *A Romance of Summer Seas*. Son-in-law Addison Hayes and his wife Margaret would be ever ready to help with finances when needed.

In late May 1893, Jeff Davis' remains were removed from the temporary Confederate military tomb near New Orleans and there lie in state before being transported, by special train to Richmond for permanent burial. Daughters Margaret Hayes and Winnie traveled with the funeral train, but poor health forced Varina to await the arrival in Richmond:

> "After a formal lying in state in Confederate Memorial Hall, New Orleans, a special train moved slowly on its way to Virginia, making stops along the way. Crowds assembled to watch the final journey of the Confederate chief, and bonfires blazed through the night. Children gathered at the stations to offer bouquets of magnolia and yellow jessamine to the guards. They strewed flowers along the track at Beauvoir, where a great storm came up suddenly and the dust of Mississippi blew across the train. Wreaths hung on the little frame station, and friends climbed into the family car to greet Winnie and Margaret. It rained in Montgomery where the Confederate flag that had floated over Fort Sumter hung with a Buena Vista flag on the Capitol. Minute guns were fired, and 10,000 visited the bier of Jefferson Davis. At Danville the crowd gathered at the station sang, 'Nearer, My God, to Thee.' Church bells tolled throughout the [southern States]. Varina joined her daughters in Richmond. . . .

> "[Varina rode with Jubal Early] under the burning sun in the long procession to Hollywood Cemetery. Jefferson Davis was laid to rest on an oval-shaped plateau slanted toward the James River. . . . [As the graveside ceremony neared its close, complete with military salutes,] Varina, who had stayed in her carriage under the trees, now moved forward. She watched the slowly sinking coffin and her self-control deserted her. Her body trembled and she bowed her head. A group of veterans, watching her, cried like children. The few surviving generals at the graveside stood with bared heads, silvered now. A bugle sounded as Varina drove away, a drooping figure heavily shrouded."

But her mind was still vibrant, as the editor of the New York *Sunday World* would explain to readers in the following editorial:

> "While her health is poor, her mind and her person are worthy of the great position she had held and still holds. She is one of the rare human beings who retain in age the brightness and strength of mind that usually pertain only to middle life. Apart from the respect which is hers from her high place beside her husband in Confederate history, she is in all worthy of love and admiration on her own account. . . . Her appearance and manners have all the dignity and grace of a queen. . . . With all the domestic virtues of Queen Victoria, she has a mind of masculine strength and culture. Her conversation shows learning and appreciation without any pretense. She has read and traveled and has studied human nature under all conditions. The long years of distinguished Governmental position of her husband gave her opportunities which she used as few persons do use them."

The body of Jefferson Davis was near the tombs of Presidents James Madison and John Tyler. The Davis plot would eventually be the resting place for Varina, their 6 children, Addison Hayes, and several grandchildren.

In the summer of 1896 Varina and Winnie returned to Richmond as guests of honor at that year's Reunion of Confederate Veterans, when the cornerstone of the Jefferson Davis monument was laid. There was a "great parade" and Stephen D. Lee delivered the oration. Varina and Winnie were serenaded as they looked out from the balcony of the Jefferson Hotel, invoking poignant memories of the early days of the Confederate capital in Richmond. A reception for Winnie and Robert Lee's daughter Mildred was held at the Masonic Temple. The White House of the Confederacy was again opened to the public and operated by the Confederate Memorial Literary Society. Varina held a "reception in the familiar rooms, receiving old friends and their sons and daughters."

As the years progressed, Varina and Winnie enjoyed summers at Narragansett Pier, Rhode Island, often seeing "something of the Pulitzers." But Winnie would never recover a vibrant health. She embarked on a trip to Egypt, Italy and France during the spring of 1898, in hopes it would revive her spirits, but to no avail. She remained ill.

On June 3, 1898, Wade Hampton wrote Varina Davis a loving message to honor her husband's 90th birthday, had he still been living. Recalling a long-ago letter received from Varina upon the death of wife Mary, Wade wrote from Washington City:

"My dear friend,

". . . More than 10 years ago you wrote to me, to comfort me when one of the greatest sorrows of my life had come upon me, and though your letter touched my heart deeply, I had not the courage to reply to it. But your kindness then has never been forgotten and I have often thought of you and of your dear husband.

"Every manifestation and respect that he has received has gratified me greatly as showing how dear he still is to those for whom he labored and suffered. This is his birthday, and while he would regard it as an empty compliment to wish him 'many happy returns,' when he has found like all of us that no happiness is to be looked for here, he will be pleased to know how many heartfelt prayers go up to him on this day. None are more sincere than mine, for I have shared in his sufferings, and I have loved him sincerely.

"I am tied down here, having no interest in public life, and only remaining in it because my people insist on my doing so. But the life is harder than when I lived in camp!

"I hope to here from you again and with the most affectionate greeting to you and yours, I am,

"Sincerely your friend,

"Wade Hampton."

Sadly, Winnie died on September 18, 1898 at the age of 33 years, from an ailment described as "malarial gastritis." She was honored by a full military funeral in Richmond as the body was laid to rest in the Davis plot at Hollywood Cemetery. The romance between Winnie Davis and Fred Wilkinson, of Syracuse, had never consummated in marriage. The romance had never rebounded from the setback created by loss to fire of the fine and spacious Wilkinson family home in Syracuse. Considering the loss of the family home and Fred's modest income during the early years of their romance, Varina must have thought Fred incapable of properly providing for her daughter. But perhaps the greater difficulty in moving toward marriage had been Winnie's recurring heath problems. Winnie "was the fifth of Varina's children to die, but now she had grandchildren to comfort her," including Jefferson Hayes-Davis, who had changed his name from "Hayes" to "Hayes-Davis" to honor his grandfather. With Jefferson and his sister Lucy Hayes staying with Varina in New York City for Christmas 1898, she would write, "I am not alone. . . . I love my grandchildren dearly."

During 1899 Varina and daughter Margaret went to the family beach house and decided on how to distribute the family relics among museums, friends and family. "The ultimate distribution of most of the Davis treasures was to the Confederate Museum in Richmond, the White House of the Confederacy in Montgomery, Confederate Memorial Hall in New Orleans, and Beauvoir itself." By this time Varina was 73 years old and rather feeble. Fortunately Margaret was able to visit New York City for long stretches to help care for her mother:

"Margaret was a handsome, clever, and capable woman whose marriage had been a happy one. Her children and her grandchildren had been trained to pay honor to Varina, when they were in the east, or were on their way to Europe." Margaret would explain her devotion to Varina with the following words: "I spent more than half the months of the year with her of late years, and nursed her and cared for her with untiring devotion. She and I had long and intimate conversations on all the subjects nearest to her heart. . . ."

In late 1902 Varina sold, for a token $10,000 price, the beach house, and the land in its vicinity, to a Veterans Association for its project of constructing apartments for Confederate soldiers and their wives and widows. But she arranged to have the beach house itself — Beauvoir — and its nearby surroundings preserved as a permanent shrine to her husband's memory. I encourage anyone who finds themselves near Biloxi or Gulfport, Mississippi to take time to visit Beauvoir, which remains an inspiring tribute to the Davis family and the memory of the Confederacy. In 1905 Varina sold the "extra acres" beyond (across the railroad tracks I suppose) for $5,000. By the way, Winnie had refused in 1893 an offer by a hotel developer to sell Beauvoir and the surrounding land for $90,000.

Varina caught a cold in New York City in late September 1906. The illness digressed into pneumonia. She was still "conscious when Margaret and her family arrived from Colorado on October 11." Death occurred on October 16. In addition to family and friends, Kate Pulitzer was at her bedside. "A small service" was "held in the hotel apartment" prior to moving the body toward Richmond, where a military funeral was anticipated. "A committee arrived from Richmond to accompany the funeral party south . . . and the train drew slowly into Richmond on the morning of October 19. . . . It rained and stormed "as she was buried in Hollywood Cemetery and [as] a mass of brightly colored autumn leaves swirled over the sodden ground around her grave."

Margaret selected inscriptions for the tomb stones commemorating her parents.

Jointly, for her parents:

"Whom God hath joined together let no man put asunder. Lord Keep their memories Green."

For her mother, alone:

"Beloved and faithful wife of Jefferson Davis and devoted mother of his children.
'Her children raise up and call her blessed; her husband also, and he praiseth her.'
'She stretcheth out her hand to the poor; yes she reacheth forth her hands to the needy.'
'Give her of the fruit of her hands and let her own works praise her in the gates'."

Biographer Ishbel Ross would conclude:

"Varina's turbulent life was over at last and she rested at peace on the quiet hillside. The White House of the Confederacy was within walking distance. The wooded hills, the meandering James, the church spires of Richmond, were all within easy range. She had rounded her 80th year and had outlived her battle-scarred generation. She had developed strength and worldly wisdom and had figured more significantly in the history of the Confederacy than was recognized at the time. She had experienced such moments of crisis as come to few women in a lifetime, and had shared in counsels that involved the fate of a nation."

In 1909, twenty years after Jeff Davis' passing, 6,000 admirers gathered at Fairview, Kentucky to dedicate the Jefferson Davis Memorial Park and its 351-foot obelisk that rises high above the rolling Kentucky hills. The park and monument is beside the Bethel Baptist Church, which had been built earlier in Davis' honor and dedicated in his presence at an October 1886 ceremony. The obelisk, which resembles the Washington Monument in the Washington City, contains an elevator which takes visitors to the top for a splendid view of the surrounding Kentucky farmland. When newly built, the Davis Monument at Fairview, Kentucky would be the second tallest monument in the Western Hemisphere — second only to the Washington Monument. The monument, which was recently beautifully restored, is recommended today for the agenda of any history enthusiast who finds himself of herself in the vicinity of Nashville, Tennessee or Bowling Green or Hopkinsville, Kentucky. [R19;473-530, R90;345-420, R13;918-939]

This concludes the narrative, styled — *Bloodstains, An Epic History of the Politics that Produced the American Civil War.*

A Word of Appreciation

I want to thank you for reading the four volumes of *Bloodstains*, for completing this major journey from ancient times to 1885; for joining with me in covering a vast time, a huge continent, three great races of mankind, and ugly politics, and more ugly politics; for accompanying me as we both have wrestled with the propaganda laid down by clever political partisans, suffered a horrible war and the struggle that followed, sorted fact from fiction, sifted for the truth, probed into the hearts of powerful men long dead — and for acquiring the deep understanding only obtainable through such a wrestle. I thank you for accompanying me as together we have lived through those turbulent and amazing times.

You now fully understand how truthful knowledge can be the engine of success, while misconception is so often the bondsman of the brain. As you have read these past pages, you have quite likely cast aside old misconceptions and found new understanding. You now understand "why" without me having ever told you so. You understand "why" because you have "lived" those times with uncanny perception, and thereby you truly understand "what", "who", "where", "when" and "how." You understand them so clearly and so deeply that you now know "why." In your heart you know "why." In your bones you know "why." A thousand times you know "why." You know "why" because you have "lived" those times with all-seeing eyes and all-hearing ears, and through that knowledge you have unleashed God's gift of wisdom. You know the truth, and the truth has set you free — free of misconception and confusion; free of the sense of "guilt" that is expected of a European American descended from people of the southern States culture, should you be one — or, should you be an African American, free of a sense of "rage" against the southern States culture.

The people this history reveals were predominantly the Nation Builders. If you are descended from the Nation Builders you should be proud of that heritage. As you have learned, the Nation Builders were primarily of the southern States culture, of European descent, of African descent or of both, who, prior to the 1850's, had settled from Virginia and Maryland westward across the Ohio Valley to Missouri and from the Carolinas westward across the southern States out to Texas. Early in American history, mostly during Colonial times, they had come from Europe and from Africa. From Europe many had forsaken the security of their homeland, crossed the Atlantic and bravely pioneered from the seaboard westward, leading the effort to tame the land, establish new farms and raise large families — rapidly filling the land with descendants and building prosperous new States. From Africa many had bravely endured capture and enslavement by their African neighbors, endured frightful ocean voyages to North America in sailing ships, many operated by men who lived in or near Massachusetts, and endured and learned from the hard work demanded of an underclass — also rapidly filling the land with descendants. Together, descendents from Europe and descendants from Africa had learned from one another, evolving a southern States culture that, for the most part, had held together during four years of horrific war.

In the long view, this biracial pioneering effort was a process — I view it as God's process — by which the African and the European were brought together, to grow up together, side-by-side, for generation after generation, and to become greater, wiser, more successful and more compassionate than either race could have been without such close association with the other. I am proud to be of this southern States culture. And I am proud to be an American. Today, we descendants of the southern States culture have no desire to leave for our ancestral homeland in Europe or Africa. We have built this nation and we intend to raise our children here, imparting in them the brotherhood I feel existing between everyone of the southern States culture, encompassing both those descended from Europeans and those descended from Africans.

You now understand the "American Civil War," also called the "War Between the States," also called the "Federal Invasion of the Confederacy." And you now understand the era that followed, called the Political "Reconstruction" of the conquered State governments.

These conflicts can quite meaningfully be described as the military and political war "Against the Democratic Party." Throughout these campaigns the Republican Party publicly downplayed its political ambitions while censuring the press and imprisoning dissenters, striving mightily to portray its military campaign as a war between geographic sections — North against South — or a War of insurrection — Union against Rebel — but we know it to have been a war between political parties —

Republicans against Democrats. The Republican program called, "Reconstruction," continued the conflict as a political fight. The more you think in those terms — Republicans versus Democrats — the more clearly you will understand the true history.

The Republican Party had come to power agitating against the people of the southern States culture — agitating against both those of European descent and those of African descent — agitating for Exclusion of those of African descent from the National Territories and all future States and hinting strongly of future Deportation. In 1860 the Republican Party did not exist where the southern States culture predominated. Those people were Democrats or former Whigs. There, Republicans were as rare as hen's teeth.

As we know, political agitation and demagoguery of this sort did not die out after the conquest of the Confederacy. It just took different forms — targeted to divide different bonds of brotherhood to agitate for political effect. Yes, political agitation persists, seeking to divide us, one way or the other, even to this day — one example being the attempt to break the natural bonds of brotherhood that persists between the southern State culture's European descendants and its African descendants. I can only advise you to resist such political agitation, fight it by telling the truthful history, and encourage a redoubling of efforts to strengthen bonds of brotherhood among us all.

On the wall of the study where I write, hangs a long and bloodstained board from the floor of the upstairs room in Granddad's house, which, you will remember, a Federal surgeon had used for many amputations during the Battle of Murfreesboro, Tennessee. As I write this line I am looking at that bloodstained board, recalling how those bloodstains had called out to me as a child, crying out: "Someday you must tell us why?" I have done so, and now you can do so as well.

By reading Volume 4, *Political Reconstruction and The Struggle for Healing*, you now understand the politics that followed the war — how the Republican Party remade the society and political order of the southern States and then withdrew — how Confederates, both African Americans and European Americans, struggled to rise again from their devastated land — how Democrats struggled against Republicans to return local, State and Federal governments back to the people, back to a two-party democratic political system.

This is the concluding volume in my four-part *Epic History of the Politics that Produced the American Civil War*. Thank you for joining me in "living" this final era. If you have missed reading any of the foregoing volumes, I recommend that you now complete your journey through history by going back in time and doing so.

You are invited to visit my website: www.civilwarcauses.com and to seek copies of my books on www.amazon.com, either as print books or as e-books.

Goodbye.

References to all Four Volumes of *Bloodstains*

R1 *Basic History of the United States*, Charles A & Mary R. Beard (William Beard update), Doubleday, 1944, 1960.

R2 *The Complete Book of U. S. Presidents*, William A. DeGregorio, Wing, 1984, 1989, 1991, and 1993.

R3 *The Coming of the Civil War*, Avery Craven, U. of Chicago Press, 1942, 1957, paperback.

R4 *Reconstruction: The Ending of the Civil War*, Avery Craven, Holt, Rinehart and Winston, New York, 1969.

R5 *An Historian and the Civil War*, Avery Craven, U. of Chicago Press, 1964.

R6 *Lincoln*, David Herbert Donald, Simon & Schuster, 1995.

R7 *Stones River — Bloody Winter in Tennessee*, James L. McDonough, The U. of Tenn. Press, 1980.

R8 *Herndon's Life of Lincoln*, With Introduction by Henry Steele Commager, Da Capo Press, 1983.

R9 *Civil War in the Making, 1815-1860*, Avery Craven, Louisiana State U. Press, 1980, paperback.

R10 *Stephen A. Douglas*, Robert W. Johannsen, Oxford U. Press, 1973.

R11 *Jefferson Davis, the Man and His Hour*, William C. Davis, Harper Collins, 1991.

R12 *Jefferson Davis, Ex-President of the Confederate States of America, A Memoir by his wife Varina Davis, Volume I*, Reprint by The Nautical & Aviation Publishing Company of America, Baltimore MD, originally published 1890 by Belford Co., New York.

R13 *Jefferson Davis, Ex-President of the Confederate States of America, A Memoir by his wife Varina Davis, Volume II*, Reprint by The Nautical & Aviation Publishing Company of America, Baltimore MD, originally published 1890 by Belford Co., New York.

R14 *Lincoln's Herndon, a Biography*, David Herbert Donald, Da Capo Press, 1948 (paperback reprint).

R15 *Abraham Lincoln — His Speeches and Writings*, Edited by Ray P. Basler, Da Capo Press, An unabridged republication of the 1846 edition, paperback.

R16 *Family Encyclopedia of American History*, The Reader's Digest, 1975.

R17 *Jefferson Davis, American Patriot, 1808-1861*, Hudson Strode, Harcourt Brace and Co., New York, 1955.

R18 *Jefferson Davis, Confederate President*, Hudson Strode, Harcourt Brace and Co., New York, 1959.

R19 *Jefferson Davis, Tragic Hero, 1864-1889, The Last Twenty-five Years*, Hudson Strode, Harcourt Brace and Co., New York, 1964.

R20 *Bleeding Kansas*, Alice Nichols, Oxford U. Press, 1954.

R21 *Uncle Tom's Cabin, or Life Among the Lowly*, Harriet Beecher Stowe, 1851-1852, paperback reprint by Signet.

R22 *Life of Black Hawk*, Black Hawk, Edited by Milo Milton Quaife, (reprint of original publication by Russell, Odiome & Metcalf, Boston, 1834), 1994.

R23 *Cherokee Tragedy, The Ridge Family and the Decimation of a People*, Thurman Wilkins, Second Edition, Revised, U. of Oklahoma Press, Norman, OK, 1970, 1986.

R24 *Trail of Tears, The Rise and Fall of the Cherokee Nation*, John Ehle, Anchor, New York, 1988.

R25 *The Cherokees, A Population History*, Russell Thornton, U. of Nebraska Press, Lincoln, NE, (first printing 1942), 1990.

R26   *Democracy in America, Alexis de Tocqueville*, Translated by George Lawrence 1848, Edited by J. P. Mayer, Harper Perennial, 1988, paperback.

R27   *The Federalist, a Commentary on the Constitution of the United States*, Alexander Hamilton, John Jay and James Madison, reprint by The Modern Library, New York.

R28   *John C. Calhoun and the Price of Union*, John Niven, Louisiana State U. Press, Baton Rouge, LA, 1988, paperback.

R29   *The President's Wife, Mary Todd Lincoln*, Ishbel Ross, G. P. Putnam's Sons, New York, 1973.

R30   *Jefferson Davis: Private Letters, 1823-1889*, Hudson Strode, Da Capo Press, New York, (original by Harcourt, Brace & World, 1966), 1995, paperback.

R31   *Abraham Lincoln: His Speeches and Writings*, Roy P. Basler, (originally published in 1946 by World Publishing Co., Cleveland), Da Capo Press, 1990.

R32   *The Rise and Fall of the Confederate Government*, Jefferson Davis, Volume I, (Originally published in 1881), Da Capo Press, 1990.

R33   *The Rise and Fall of the Confederate Government*, Jefferson Davis, Volume II, (Originally published in 1881), Da Capo Press, 1990.

R34   *Atlas of the North American Indian*, Carl Waldman, Facts On File, New York, 1985.

R35   *The Politicos 1865-1896*, Matthew Josephson, Harcourt, Brace and Co., New York, first edition, 1938.

R36   *The Chronological History of the Negro in America*, Peter M. Bergman, Harper & Row, New York, 1969.

R37   *The Glorious Cause, The American Revolution, 1763-1789*, Robert Middlekauff, Oxford U. Press, New York, 1982, paperback.

R38   *Harriet Beecher Stowe*, Noel B. Gerson, Praeger Publishers, New York, 1976.

R39   *History of England*, W. E. Lunt, Third Edition, Harper & Brothers, New York, 1946.

R40   *The Bell Curve, Intelligence and Class Structure in American Life*, Richard J. Herrnstein and Charles Murray, The Free Press, New York, 1994.

R41   *The Southeastern Indians*, Charles Hudson, The U. of Tennessee Press, 1976, paperback reprint, 1994.

R42   *Henry Ward Beecher, An American Portrait*, The Press of the Readers Club, New York (originally published 1927 by George H. Doran Company), 1942.

R43   *The Life of Andrew Jackson*, Marquis James, (Complete in one Volume; Part One: The Border Captain, copyright 1933; and Part two: Portrait of a President, copyright 1933) The Bobbs-Merrill Company, Indianapolis, 1938.

R44   *The Man Who Killed Lincoln*, Philip van Doren Stern, The Literary Guild of America, Inc., New York, 1939.

R45   *Life and Times of Frederick Douglass*, Frederick Douglass, (Originally published in 1892, reprint by Collier Books, London, 1962, paperback.

R46   *The Civil and Political History of the State of Tennessee*, John Haywood, (Originally published 1823), Publishing House of the Methodist Episcopal Church, South, Nashville, 1891.

R50   *The Book of Morman*, Joseph Smith, The Church of Jesus Christ of Latter-day Saints, Salt Lake City, Utah, (First published 1830), 1920.

R51   *Reconstruction, Political and Economic, 1865-1877*, William A. Dunning, Harper Torchbooks, New York (Originally published as Volume 22 in The American Nation series in 1907), 1962.

R52   *The Causes of the American Civil War*, Edited by Edwin C. Rozwenc, D. C. Heath and Company, Lexington MA, 1961.

R53   *The New Century History of the United States*, Edward Eggleston, American Book Company, New York, 1904, 1907, 1919, 1923.

R54   *Incident at Harper's Ferry*, Edward Stone, Prentice-Hall, Inc., Englewood Cliffs, NJ, 1956.

R55   *Ghosts of the Confederacy, Defeat, the Lost Cause, and the Emergence of the New South, 1865 to 1913*, Gaines M. Foster, Oxford U. Press, New York, 1987.

R56   *The Shadow of a Dream, Economic Life and Death in the South Carolina Low Country*, 1670-1920, Peter A. Coclanis, Oxford U. Press, New York, 1989.

R57   *Nashville, Personality of a City*, Alfred Leland Crabb, 1960, The Bobbs-Merrill Co., 1st ed., 1960.

R58   *History of Nashville Tennessee*, Publishing House of the Methodist Episcopal Church, South, Nashville, TN, 1890, Facsimile reproduction of the original 1890 edition.

R59   *The Civil War in Middle Tennessee*, Ed Huddleston, (Originally published in The Nashville Banner in four parts), The Pantheon Press, Nashville, TN 1965.

R60   *Nashville, The Faces of Two Centuries*, 1780-1980, John Egerton and Nashville Magazine, PlusMedia Incorporated, 1979.

R61   *Profiles in Courage*, John F. Kennedy, Harper & Row, New York, (Originally published 1955), 1956 paperback.

R62   *History of Providence Presbyterian Church*, Louise Barber Matthews, Brooks Litho, Charlotte, NC, 1967.

R63   *Life of Thurlow Weed, Including His Autobiography and A Memoir, Embellished with Portraits and Other Illustrations*, Volume 1 of a two-volume set, Harriet Weed, Houghton, Miffin and Company, New York, 1883.

R64   *The Tragic Era, The Revolution after Lincoln*, Claude G. Bowers, Blue Ribbon Books, New York, 1929.

R65   *John C. Calhoun, American Portrait*, Margaret L. Coit, Houghton Mifflin Company, Boston, Sentry Edition, 1961, paperback.

R66   *Redcoats and Rebels, The American Revolution through British Eyes*, Christopher Hibbert, 1990, Avon Books paperback edition, 1991.

R67   *The History of Scotland*, Peter and Fiona Somerset Fry, 1982, Barnes & Noble edition, 1995.

R68   *Charles Sumner and the Coming of the Civil War*, David Donald, Alfred A. Knopf, New York, 1960, 1st edition.

R69   *The Story of the Democratic Party*, Henry Minor, The Macmillan Co., New York, 1928, 1st edition.

R70   *Franklin Pierce, Young Hickory of the Granite Hills*, Roy Franklin Nichols, University of Pennsylvania Press, 1931, (2nd edition, 1958).

R71   *Reconstruction, America's Unfinished Revolution, 1863-1877*, Eric Foner, Harper & Row, N. Y., 1988, (paperback reprint, 1989).

R72   *Free Soil, Free Labor, Free Men, the Ideology of the Republican Party before the Civil War*, Eric Foner, new introduction by the author, Oxford U. Press, 1970, 1995 new edition, paperback.

R73   *Charles Sumner*, David Herbert Donald, two books combined in one paperback reprint with new introduction by the author, comprised of *Charles Sumner and the Coming of the Civil War* (first pub. 1960), and Charles Sumner and the *Rights of Man* (first pub. 1970), Da Capo Press, 1996.

R74   *The Secret Six, John Brown and the Abolitionist Movement*, Otto Scott, Copyright 1979, Uncommon Books, Third printing, 1993, paperback.

R75   *Edmund Ruffin, Southerner: A Study in Secession*, Avery Craven, copyright 1932, 1991 printing by Louisiana U. Press, paperback.

R76   *John Brown, The Making of a Martyr*, Robert Penn Warren, J. S. Sanders & Co., Nashville, Copyright 1929, paperback reprint, 1993.

R77   *Duel between The First Ironclads*, William C. Davis, Doubleday (Barnes & Noble printing), 1975.

R78   *The Civil War Day by Day - An Almanac 1861-1865*, E. B. Long with Barbara Long, 1971, Da Capo paperback, 1971.

R79   *Abraham Lincoln, The Prairie Years and The War Years*, one-volume Edition, Copyright 1929, 1925, Harvest Book paperback reprint, 1982.

R80   *Nativism and Slavery, The Northern Know Nothings and the Politics of the 1850s*, Tyler Anbinder, Oxford U. Press, 1992, 1994 paperback edition.

R81   *Grover Cleveland, The Man and the Statesman*, Vol. 1, Robert McElroy, Harper & Brothers, 1923.

R82   *Grover Cleveland, The Man and the Statesman*, Vol. 2, Robert McElroy, Harper & Brothers, 1923.

R83   *The Origins of the Republican Party, 1852-1856*, William E. Gienapp, Oxford University Press, 1987.

R84   *The Anti-Federalist Papers and the Constitutional Convention Debates*, Edited by Ralph Ketcham, Mentor paperback, 1986.

R85   *Black Confederates and Afro-Yankees in Civil War Virginia*, Ervin L. Jordan, Jr., University Press of Virginia paperback, 1995.

R86   *Thaddeus Stevens, Scourge of the South*, Fawn M. Brodie, W. W. Norton Co., 1959, first edition.

R87   *The Know-Nothing Party in Massachusetts, The Rise and Fall of a People's Movement*, John R. Mulkern, Northeastern U., Boston, 1990.

R88   *The Making of the African Diaspora in the Americas 1441-1900*, Vincent Bakpetu Thompson, Longman Group, 1987, paperback, 1988.

R89   *Yankees and God, A History of New England Culture and the Four Phases of Puritanism fro the Seventeenth to the Twentieth Century*, Chard Powers Smith, George J. McLeod, 1954.

R90   *First Lady of the South, The Life of Mrs. Jefferson Davis*, Ishbel Ross, Harper & Brothers, 1958.

R91   *Southern History of the War*, Edward A. Pollard, first published in 1866, reprint with two volumes in one by The Fairfax Press.

R92   *The Evolution of Man and Society*, C. D. Darlington, Simon and Schuster, 1969.

R93   *John Sherman's Recollections of Forty Years in the House, Senate and Cabinet*, Autobiography by John Sherman, The Werner Co., 1895.

R94   A *Diary from Dixie*, Mary Boykin Chesnut, 1823-1886, 1949, 1980 paperback reprint, Harvard U. Press.

R95   *The Book of Man, The Human Genome Project and the Quest to Discover our Genetic Heritage*, Walter Bodmer and Robin McKie, Oxford U. Press, 1994, 1997 paperback.

R96   Old *Thad Stevens, A Story of Ambition*, Richard N. Current, 1942, Greenwood Press reprint, 1980.

R97   A *Review of The Political Conflict in America . . . Comprising also a Resume of the Career of Thaddeus Stevens . . .* Alexander Harris, 1876, 1970 reprint by Negro Universities Press.

R98   *Thaddeus Stevens*, Vol. 31 in *American Statesmen Series*, reprint by Houghton, Mifflin and Co., 1899.

R99   *The Nat Turner Slave Insurrection*, F. Roy Johnson, Johnson Publishing Co., 1966.

R100   *Destruction and Reconstruction*, Richard Taylor, 1879, reprint by Blaisdell Publishing Co.

R101   *Kansas, A History of the Jayhawk State*, William Frank Zornow, 1957, U. of Oklahoma Press.

R102   *Thaddeus Stevens, A Being Darkly Wise and Rudely Great*, Ralph Korngold, 1955, first edition, Harcourt, Brace and Co.

R103   *Richard Taylor, Soldier Prince of Dixie*, T. Michael Parrish, 1992, The U. of North Carolina Press, first edition.

R104   *Jefferson Davis' Mexican War Regiment*, Joseph E. Chance, 1991, U. Press of Mississippi, 1st ed.

R105   *Jackson versus Biddle, The Struggle over the Second Bank of the United States, Selected readings selected by Amherst College*, with introduction by George Rogers Taylor, D. C. Heath and Co., 1949.

R106   *The Era of Reconstruction*, 1865-1877, Kenneth M. Stampp, Alfred A. Knopf, 1965, first edition.

R107   *Salmon Portland Chase*, Volume 32 of the *American Statesmen* series, Albert Bushnell Hart, Houghton, Mifflin and Co., Standard Library Edition, 1899.

R108   *Portrait of an Abolitionist, A Biography of George Luther Stearns*, 1809-1867, Charles E. Heller, Greenwood Press, 1996.

R109   *William Preston Johnston, A Transitional Figure of the Confederacy*, Arthur Marvin Shaw, Louisiana State U. Press, Baton Rouge, LA, 1943.

R110   *Horace Greeley, Printer, Editor, Crusader*, Henry Luther Stoddard, G. P. Putnam's Sons, New York, 1946.

R111   *The Life and Public Services of Hon. Henry Wilson*, Thomas Russell and Elias Nason, B. B. Russell, Boston, MA, 1872.

R112   *Life of Henry Clay,* in *American Statesman Series*, Carl Schurz, Volume II, Edinburg, 1887.

R113   *Daniel Webster, The Expounder of the Constitution*, Everett Pepperrell Wheeler, G. P. Putnam's Sons, New York, 1905.

R114   *The Randolphs, The Story of a Virginia Family*, H. J. Eckenrode, The Bobbs-Merrill Co., New York, 1946.

R115   *Parties and Slavery*, volume 18 of *The American Nation: A History* series, Theodore Clarke Smith, Harper & Brothers, New York, 1906.

R116   *Causes of the Civil War*, volume 19 of *The American Nation: A History* series, French Esnor Chadwick, Harper & Brothers, New York, 1906.

R117   *A History of the American People,* Volume I: The Creation of a New Occidental Power, 1500-1850, Nathaniel Wright Stephenson, Charles Scribner's Sons, New York, 1934.

R118   *The Growth of American Nationality, 1492 - 1865*, Fred W. Wellborn, The Macmillan Co., New York, 1943.

R119   *The Growth of the United States*, Ralph Volney Harlow, Henry Holt and Co., 1925, revised 1934 edition.

R120   *The Roots of American Civilization, A History of American Colonial Life*, Curtis P. Nettels, F. S. Crofts & Co., 1938, second printing, 1939.

R121   *The United States, Experiment in Democracy*, Avery Craven and Walter Johnson, Ginn and Co., Boston and others, 1947.

R122   [Alabama Claims] *The Case of The United States to be laid before the Tribunal of Arbitration to be convened at Geneva under the provisions of the Treaty between The United States of America and Her Majesty The Queen of Great Britain, concluded at Washington, May 3, 1871*, Submitted by Hamilton Fish, Secretary of State, February 13, 1872, U. S. Government Printing Office, Washington, 1872, second edition (not the Geneva edition).

R123   *A History of Trade Unionism in the United States*, Selig Perlman, The Macmillan Co., New York, 1922.

R124   *The Civil War and Reconstruction*, J. G. Randall, D. C. Heath and Co., Boston, 1937.

R125   *The Founding of New England*, James Truslow Adams, Little, Brown, and Co., Boston, 1933.

R126   *The Lower South in American History*, William G. Brown, The Macmillan Co., New York, 1903.

R127   *Benjamin Franklin Wade: Radical Republican from Ohio*, H. L. Trefouse, Twayne Publishers, New York, 1963.

R128   *The General's Wife, The Life of Mrs. Ulysses S. Grant*, Ishbel Ross, Dodd, Mead & Company, New York, 1959.

R129   *African Exodus, The Origins of Modern Humanity*, Christopher Stringer and Robin McKie, Henry Holt and Co., New York, 1996.

R130   *Humans at the End of the Ice Age, The Archaeology of the Pleistocene-Holocene Transition*, Straus, Lawrence Guy, et al, editors, Plenum Press, New York, 1996.

R131   *The Liberator, William Lloyd Garrison, a Biography*, John L. Thomas, Little Brown and Co., Boston, 1963, first edition.

R132   *The Robber Barons*, Matthew Josephson, 1934, Harvest Book reprint, 1962.

R133   *Noah's Flood, The New Scientific Discoveries about the Event that Changed History*, William Ryan and Walter Pitman, Simon & Schuster, New York, 1998.

R134   *No Better Place to Die, The Battle of Stones River*, Peter Cozzens, U. of Illinois Press, 1990, paperback edition, 1991.

R135   *Eyewitnesses at the Battle of Stones River*, David R. Logston, self-published, 1989.

R136   *Southern by the Grace of God*, Michael Andrew Grissom, Pelican Publishing Co, Gretna, LA, 1997.

R137   *A Comparative Study of the Reading Achievements of [European American] and [African American] Children*, Larry Jordan Willis, PhD Thesis, George Peabody College for Teachers, Nashville, TN, 1939.

R137   *Diary of a Tar Heel Confederate Soldier*, Louis Leon, Stone Publishing Company, 1913, Reprint by Major Egbert A. Ross Camp 1423 SCV, Charlotte, NC.

R138   *The Constitution of the United States of America*, Washington, D. C.

R139   *In Congress, July 4, 1776. A Declaration by the Representatives of the United States of America, in General Congress Assembled*, Washington, D. C.

R140   *Coastal New England, Its Life and Past*, William F. Robinson, The Wellfleet Press, 1989.

R141   *Jefferson Davis: Unconquerable Heart*, Felicity Allen, U. of Missouri Press, Columbia and London, 1999.

R142   *Arms and Equipment of the Civil War*, Jack Coggins, Broadfoot Publishing Co., Wilmington, NC, 1990 reprint, paperback.

R143   *Jefferson Davis in South Carolina*, Sam Thomas, Palmetto Conservation Foundation, 1998.

R144   *High Crimes & Misdemeanors, The Impeachment and Trial of Andrew Johnson*, Gene Smith, William Morrow and Company, Inc., New York, 1977.

R145   *A History of the English-Speaking Peoples, Volume 1, The Birth of Britain*, Winston S. Churchill, 1956, reprint by Dodd, Mead & Company, New York, 1966.

R146   *A History of the English-Speaking Peoples, Volume 2, The New World*, Winston S. Churchill, 1956, reprint by Dodd, Mead & Company, New York, 1966.

R147   *A History of the English-Speaking Peoples, Volume 3, The Age of Revolution*, Winston S. Churchill, 1956, reprint by Dodd, Mead & Company, New York, 1966.

R148   *A History of the English-Speaking Peoples, Volume 4, The Great Democracies*, Winston S. Churchill, 1956, reprint by Dodd, Mead & Company, New York, 1966.

R149   *Jefferson Davis, American*, William J. Cooper, Jr., Alfred A. Knopf, New York, 2000.

R150   *The Raven, A Biography of Sam Houston*, Marquis James, U. of Texas Press, Austin, paperback reprint from 1929 first edition, 1999 (Winner of Pulitzer Prize).

R151   *Lee, An abridgment in one volume of the four-volume R. E. Lee*, Douglas Southall Freeman (1961), abridged by Richard Harwell, Touchtone, New York, 1997, paperback.

R152   *A New History of Texas*, Anna J. Hardwicke Pennybacker, Tyler Texas, 1888.

R153   *The Tercentenary History of Canada*, Frank Basil Tracy, Volume 1, P. F. Collier & Son, New York and Toronto, 1908.

R154   *The Tercentenary History of Canada*, Frank Basil Tracy, Volume 2, P. F. Collier & Son, New York and Toronto, 1908.

R155   *The Tercentenary History of Canada*, Frank Basil Tracy, Volume 3, P. F. Collier & Son, New York and Toronto, 1908.

R156   A compilation of Abe Lincoln parentage studies, including: Barton, William E., *The Life of Abraham Lincoln*, 1925; Cathey, James H., *The Genesis of Lincoln*, 1899; Coggins, J. C., *Abraham Lincoln, North Carolinian with Proof*, 1927; Hertz, Emanuel, *The Hidden Lincoln* (From the Letters and Papers of William H. Herndon), 1938; Thomas, Benjamin P., *Portrait For Posterity*, 1947; Warren, Louis A., *Lincoln's Parentage and Childhood*, 1926; and on the internet at www.inlow.org and elsewhere.

R157   *The American Conscience, The Drama of the Lincoln-Douglas Debates*, Saul Sigelschiffer, Horizon Press, New York, 1973.

R158   *Early American History (1492-1789), Political, Social, Economic*, Jennings B. Sanders, Prentice-Hall, New York, 1938.

R159   *George Mason, Constitutionalist*, Helen Hill, Peter Smith, Gloucester, Massachusetts, 1966.

R160   The Congressional Globe, Washington, D. C. in accordance with the date noted.

R161   The Real Lincoln, A New Look at Abraham Lincoln, His Agenda, and an Unnecessary War, Thomas J. DiLorenzo, Prima Publishing, Roseville, California, 2002.

R162   Root, Elihu, Ainsworth, Fred C. and Kirley, Joseph W., *The War of the Rebellion: A Compilation of the Official Records of the Union and Confederate Armies*, Washington Government Printing Office, 128 volumes, 1880-1901.

R163   Evans, Clement A.. Editor, *Confederate Military History, A Library of Confederate States History*, written by Distinguished Men of the South, 12 Volumes, Confederated Publishing Company, Atlanta, 1899.

R164   Richardson, James D., *A Compilation of the Messages and Papers of the Confederacy including the Diplomatic Correspondence*, 1861-1865, 2 volumes, United States Publishing Company, Nashville, 1906.

R165   Rowland, Dunbar, *Jefferson Davis, Constitutionalist, His Letters, Papers and Speeches, Mississippi Department of Archives and History*, 10 volumes, Jackson, Mississippi, 1923.

R166   Southern Historical Society Papers, 1876 through 2,000, Richmond, Virginia.

R167   Miller, Marion Mills, Editor, *Life and Works of Abraham Lincoln, 9 volumes*, The Current Literature Publishing Company, New York, 1907.

R168   Keckley, Elizabeth, *Behind the Scenes, or, Thirty Years a [Bonded Person], and Four Years in the White House*, G. W. Carleton and Company, New York, 1868.

R169   Snead, Thomas Lowndes, *The Fight for Missouri, From the Election of Lincoln to the Death of Lyon*, Charles Scribner's Sons, New York, 1886.

R170   Smith, Edward Conrad, *The Borderland in the Civil War*, The MacMillan Company, New York, 1927.

R171   Parrish, William E., *Turbulent Partnership, Missouri and the Union, 1861-1865*, U. of Missouri Press, 1963.

R172   Phillips, Christopher, *Damned Yankee, The Life of General Nathaniel Lyon*, U. of Missouri Press, 1990.

R173   Parrish, William E., *Frank Blair, Lincoln's Conservative*, U. of Missouri Press, 1998.

R174   Shalhope, Robert E., *Sterling Price, Portrait of a Southerner*, U. of Missouri Press, 1971.

R175   Melish, Joanne Pope, *Disowning Slavery, Gradual Emancipation and Race in New England, 1780-1860*, Cornell U. Press, 1998.

R176   Poulson, Barry W., Economic History of the United States, Macmillan Publishing Co., 1981.

R177   Burnham,Philip, *So Far from Dixie: Confederates in Yankee Prisons*, Taylor Trade Publishing, 2003.

R178   Potter, David M., *The Impending Crisis, 1848-1861*, Harper Perennial, paperback, 1976.

R179   Brown, Kent Masterson, *The Civil War in Kentucky, Battle for the Blewgrass State*, Savas Publishing Co., 2000.

R180   Coulter, E. Merton, The Civil War and Readjustment in Kentucky, U. of North Carolina Press, 1926, 1966 reprint by Peter Smith.

R181   Toomey, Daniel C., The Civil War in Maryland, Toomey Press, 1983 (2004).

R182   Denton, Lawrence M., *A Southern Star for Maryland*, Publishing Concepts, 1995.

R183   Talbert, Bart Rhett, *Maryland: The South's First Casualty*, Rockbridge Publishing Co., 1995.

R184   Macfarlane, Kate, *The Polarization of Civil War Era Baltimore*, United States Naval Academy, Annapolis, 2002.

550

R185   Hesseltine, William B., *Civil War Prisons, A Study in War Psychology*, Ohio State U. Press, 1930, republished in 1964 by Frederick Ungar Publishing Co., New York.

R186   Hesseltine, William B., Editor, *Civil War Prisons*, (a compilation of 7 magazine articles), Kent State U. Press, 1962.

R187   Horigan, Michael, *Elmira, Death Camp of the North*, Stackpole Books, 2002.

R188   Washington, Booker T., *Up From Slavery*, first published in 1901, reprint by Dover Publioations, N. Y., 1995.

R189   Richburg, Keith B., *Out of America, A Black Man Confronts Africa*, BasicBooks, 1997.

R190   Levy, George, *To Die in Chicago, Confederate Prisoners at Camp Douglas 1862-65*, Pelican Publishing Co., Gretna, LA, 1999.

R191   Futch, Ovid L., *History of Andersonville Prison*, University Press of Florida, 1968, Paperback reprint, 1999.

R192   Stevenson, Alexander F., *The Battle of Stone's River near Murfreesboro, Tennessee, December 30, 1862 to January 3,1863*, first published in 1884, The Scholar's Bookshelf, Cranbury, NJ, Paperback, 2004.

R193   Catton, Bruce, *The Coming Fury*, Doubleday & Co., Garden City, NY, 1961.

R194   Howe, Julia Ward, *Reminiscences 1819-1899*, 1899, Reprinted in 1969 by Negro University Press, New York.

R195   Kennon, Donald R. and Rogers, Rebecca M., *The Committee on Ways and Means, A Bicentennial History, 1789-1989*, U. S. Government Printing Office, 1989.

R196   The writer's folder containing documents collected while following Jeff Davis' route of retreat from Charlotte, North Carolina to Washington, Georgia.

R197   Wellman, Manly Wade, *Giant in Gray, A biography of Wade Hampton of South Carolina*, 1949, Reprint by Morningside Bookshop, 1980.

R198   Longacre, Edward G., *Gentleman and Soldier, A Biography of Wade Hampton III*, Rutledge Hill Press, Nashville, Tennessee, 2003.

R199   Cisco, Walter Brian, *Wade Hampton, Confederate Warrior, Conservative Statesman*, Brassey's Inc., Washington, D. C., 2004.

R200   Ackerman, Robert K., *Wade Hampton III*, The University of South Carolina Press, Columbia, S. C., 2007.

R201   Reynold John Schreiner, *Reconstruction in South Carolina, 1865-1877*, The State Publishing Company, Columbia, S. C., 2005, recent paperback photocopy "Rare Reprint" by "Kessinger Publishing."

R202   Fleming, Walter L., *Documentary History of Reconstruction: Political, Military, Social, Religious, Educational & Industrial, 1865 to the Present Time, Volume 2*, The Arthur H. Clark Company, 1907, Cleveland, Ohio, recent paperback photocopy "Rare Reprint" by "Kessinger Publishing."

R203   Craven, Avery, *Reconstruction: The Ending of the Civil War*, Holt, Rinehart and Winston, Inc., New York, 1969, paperback.

R204   Garner, James Wilford, *Reconstruction in Mississippi*, The MacMillan Company, 1902, recent paperback photocopy "Rare Reprint."

R205   Mayes, Edward, *Lucius Q. C. Lamar: His Life, Times, and Speeches, 1825-1893*, Publishing House of the Methodist Episcopal Church, South, Nashville, Tennessee, 1896.

R206   Murphy, James B., *L. Q. C. Lamar, Pragmatic Patriot*, Louisiana State University Press, Baton Rouge, 1973.

R207   Fleming, Walter L., *Documentary History of Reconstruction: Political, Military, Social, Religious, Educational & Industrial, 1865 to the Present Time, Volume 1*, The Arthur H. Clark Company, 1907, Cleveland, Ohio, recent hardback photocopy by The Arthur H. Clark Co., Cleveland, OH, 1906.

R208   Andrew, Rod, Jr., *Wade Hampton, Confederate Warrior to Southern Redeemer*, UNC Press, 2008.

R209   *Hymn and Tune Book of the Methodist Episcopal Church South*, Nashville, TN, 1898.

R210   Watkins, James L., *Production and Price of Cotton for One Hundred Years*, U. S. Dept. of Agriculture, Washington: Government Printing Office, 1895.

R211   Nevins, Allan, *Grover Cleveland, a Study in Courage*, Dodd, Mead & Company, New York, 1932.

R212   Dorsheimer, William and Hensel, W. U., *Lives and Public Services of Hon. Grover Cleveland and Hon. Thomas A. Hendricks*, Phillips & Burrows, Deposit, N. Y., 1884.

R213   Jeffers, H. Paul, *An Honest President, The Life and Presidencies of Grover Cleveland*, William Morrow, New York, NY, 2000.

R214   Brodsky, Alyn, *Grover Cleveland, A Study in Character*, St. Martin's Press, New York, NY, 2000.

R215   Thomas, Harrison Cook, *The Return of the Democratic Party to Power in 1884*, Columbia University Press, NY, 1919, reprinted by AMS Press, NY, 1969.

R216   Eckenrode, Hamilton James, *The Political History of Virginia During the Reconstruction*, Johns Hopkins University Studies, Series XXII, Nos. 6-7-8, The Johns Hopkins Press, 1904.

R217   Goldfield, David, *America Aflame, How the Civil War Created a Nation*, Bloomsberry Press, NY, 2011.

Index to Volume 4

Y

www.ingramcontent.com/pod-product-compliance
Lightning Source LLC
Chambersburg PA
CBHW080526090426
42733CB00015B/2496